THE HEATH INTRODUCTION TO LITERATURE

THE HEATH INTRODUCTION TO
Literature

Alice S. Landy
Lesley College

D. C. Heath and Company
Lexington, Massachusetts • Toronto

Acknowledgments

Amiri Baraka (LeRoi Jones). "W.W" from *Black Magic Poetry 1961–1967*. Copyright © 1967 by LeRoi Jones. Reprinted with permission of the Ronald Hobbs Literary Agency 1979.

W. H. Auden. "The Unknown Citizen." Copyright 1940 and renewed 1968 by W. H. Auden. Reprinted from *Collected Shorter Poems, 1927–1957,* by W. H. Auden, by permission of Random House, Inc.

James Baldwin. "Sonny's Blues" excerpted from *Going to Meet the Man* by James Baldwin. Copyright © 1957 by James Baldwin. Originally published in *Partisan Review*. Reprinted by permission of The Dial Press.

John Barth. "Lost In the Funhouse." Copyright © 1967 by The Atlantic Monthly Company, from the book *Lost in the Funhouse* by John Barth. Reprinted by permission of Doubleday & Company, Inc.

Donald Barthelme. "The Balloon" from *Unspeakable Practices, Unnatural Acts* by Donald Barthelme. Copyright © 1966, 1968 by Donald Barthelme. This selection appeared originally in *The New Yorker*. Reprinted with the permission of Farrar, Straus & Giroux, Inc.

Jorge Luis Borges. "The South." Reprinted by permission of Grove Press, Inc. Copyright © 1962 by Grove Press, Inc. Translated from the Spanish copyright © 1956 by Emece Editores, S. A., Buenos Aires.

Gwendolyn Brooks. "We Real Cool," "The Bean Eaters" from *The World of Gwendolyn Brooks* (1971) by Gwendolyn Brooks. Copyright © 1959 by Gwendolyn Brooks Blakely. Reprinted by permission of Harper & Row, Publishers, Inc.

Albert Camus. "The Guest" from *Exile and the Kingdom* by Albert Camus, translated by Justin O'Brien. Copyright © 1957, 1958 by Alfred A. Knopf, Inc. Reprinted by permission of Alfred A. Knopf, Inc.

Countee Cullen. "For a Lady I Know" from *On These I Stand* by Countee Cullen. Copyright 1925 by Harper & Row, Publishers, Inc.; renewed, 1953 by Ida M. Cullen. Reprinted by permission of Harper & Row, Publishers, Inc.

E. E. Cummings. "All in green went my love riding," "in Just-Spring," "the Cambridge ladies who live in furnished souls." Selections are reprinted from *Tulips & Chimneys* by E. E. Cummings, edited by George James Firmage, with the permission of Liveright Publishing Corporation. Copyright 1923, 1925 and renewed 1951, 1953 by E. E. Cummings. Copyright © 1973, 1976 by Nancy T. Andrews. Copyright © 1973, 1976 by George James Firmage.

Emily Dickinson. "There's a Certain Slant of Light," "Tell All the Truth but Tell It Slant," "The Poets Light but Lamps." Reprinted by permission of the publishers and the Trustees of Amherst College from *The Poems of Emily Dickinson,* edited by Thomas H. Johnson, Cambridge, Mass.: The Belknap Press of Harvard University Press. Copyright © 1951, 1955 by the President and Fellows of Harvard College.

T. S. Eliot. "The Love Song of J. Alfred Prufrock," "Journey of the Magi" from *Collected Poems 1909–1962* by T. S. Eliot, copyright 1936, by Harcourt Brace Jovanovich, Inc.; copyright © 1963, 1964 by T. S. Eliot. Reprinted by permission of the publisher and Faber and Faber Ltd.

William Faulkner. "A Rose for Emily." Copyright 1930 and renewed 1958 by William Faulkner. Reprinted from *Collected Stories of William Faulkner* by William Faulkner, by permission of Random House, Inc.

Lawrence Ferlinghetti. "The pennycandy store beyond the El" from *A Coney Island of the Mind,* © 1958 by Lawrence Ferlinghetti. Reprinted by permission of New Directions.

Robert Frost. "The Road Not Taken," "Design" from *The Poetry of Robert Frost*

Alfred A. Knopf, Inc. and renewed 1952 by John Crowe Ransom. Reprinted from *Selected Poems,* Third Edition, Revised and Enlarged, by John Crowe Ransom, by permission of Alfred A. Knopf, Inc.

Henry Reed. "Naming of Parts," "Unarmed Combat," from *A Map of Verona.* Reprinted by permission of Jonathan Cape Ltd.

Adrienne Rich. "Aunt Jennifer's Tigers" is reprinted from *Poems, Selected and New, 1950–1974,* by Adrienne Rich, by permission of W. W. Norton & Company, Inc. Copyright © 1975, 1973, 1971, 1969, 1966 by W. W. Norton & Company, Inc. Copyright © 1951 by Adrienne Rich.

Theodore Roethke. "My Papa's Waltz," copyright 1942 by Hearst Magazines, Inc., and "I Knew A Woman," copyright 1954 by Theodore Roethke, both from *The Collected Poems of Theodore Roethke.* Reprinted by permission of Doubleday & Company, Inc.

Carl Sandburg. "Cool Tombs" from *Cornhuskers* by Carl Sandburg, copyright 1918 by Holt, Rinehart and Winston, Inc., copyright 1944 by Carl Sandburg. "Fog" from *Chicago Poems* by Carl Sandburg, copyright 1916 by Holt, Rinehart and Winston, Inc., copyright 1944 by Carl Sandburg. Both selections reprinted by permission of Harcourt Brace Jovanovich, Inc.

"The Second Shepherd's Play" from *A Treasury of the Theatre,* John Gassner, editor. Copyright © 1935, 1940, 1950, 1951, 1963, by Simon and Schuster, Inc. Reprinted by permission of Simon & Schuster, a Division of Gulf & Western Corporation.

Anne Sexton. "Her Kind" from *To Bedlam and Part Way Back,* by Anne Sexton. Copyright © 1960 by Anne Sexton. Reprinted by permission of Houghton Mifflin Company.

William Shakespeare. *Hamlet,* edited by Willard Farnham, in "The Pelican Shakespeare." General Editor: Alfred Harbage (rev. ed.; New York: Penguin Books, 1970). Copyright © Penguin Books Inc., 1957, 1970. Reprinted by permission of Penguin Books.

Bernard Shaw. *Major Barbara.* Copyright 1907, 1913, 1930, 1941, Bernard Shaw. Copyright © 1957, The Public Trustee as Executor of the Estate of Bernard Shaw. Copyright © 1971, The Trustees of the British Museum, The Governors and Guardians of the National Gallery of Ireland and The Royal Academy of Dramatic Art. Reprinted by permission of Dodd, Mead & Company, Inc. and The Society of Authors on behalf of the Bernard Shaw Estate.

Sophocles. *Oedipus Rex:* An English version by Dudley Fitts and Robert Fitzgerald. Copyright 1949 by Harcourt Brace Jovanovich, Inc.; renewed 1977 by Cornelia Fitts and Robert Fitzgerald. Reprinted by permission of the publisher. CAUTION: All rights, including professional, amateur, motion picture, recitation, lecturing, public reading, radio broadcasting, and television are strictly reserved. Inquiries on all rights should be addressed to Harcourt Brace Jovanovich, Inc., 757 Third Avenue, New York, N.Y. 10017.

John Steinbeck. "The Chrysanthemums" from *The Long Valley* by John Steinbeck. Copyright 1937, © 1965 by John Steinbeck. Reprinted by permission of Viking Penguin Inc.

Wallace Stevens. "The World as Meditation." Copyright 1952 by Wallace Stevens. Reprinted from *Collected Poems of Wallace Stevens* by Wallace Stevens, by permission of Alfred A. Knopf, Inc.

Dylan Thomas. "Fern Hill," "Do Not Go Gentle Into That Good Night," "In My Craft or Sullen Art" from *The Poems of Dylan Thomas.* Copyright 1946 by New Directions Publishing Corporation. Copyright 1952 by Dylan Thomas. Reprinted by permission of New Directions and The Trustees for the Copyrights of the late Dylan Thomas.

Richard Wilbur. "Love Calls Us to the Things of This World" from *Things of This World,* © 1956 by Richard Wilbur, and "Place Pigalle" from *The Beautiful Changes,* © 1947, 1975 by Richard Wilbur. Reprinted by permission of Harcourt Brace Jovanovich, Inc.

Richard Wright. "Bright and Morning Star" in *Uncle Tom's Children* by Richard Wright. Copyright 1938 by Richard Wright; renewed, 1966 by Ellen Wright.

William Butler Yeats. "An Irish Airman Foresees His Death" from *Collected Poems* by William Butler Yeats, copyright 1919 by Macmillan Publishing Co., Inc., renewed 1947 by Bertha Georgie Yeats. "The Folly of Being Comforted from *Collected Poems* by William Butler Yeats, copyright 1903 (New York: Macmillan, 1956). "Sailing to Byzantium" from *Collected Poems* by William Butler Yeats, copyright 1928 by Macmillan Publishing Co., Inc., renewed 1956 by Georgie Yeats. Reprinted by permission of Macmillan Publishing Co., Inc., and Michael and Anne Yeats and Macmillan London Limited.

PREFACE

In designing and writing *The Heath Introduction to Literature,* we have begun from the groundwork laid by previous Heath Introductions to Fiction, Drama, and Poetry—books that themselves drew on the help and expertise of scores of teachers of English and the humanities. This text differs from those earlier ones in bringing together all three genres within one volume; in ordering its material in thematic rather than chronological fashion; and in providing new introductions and study questions that make the book not just an anthology, but a unified teaching plan.

The book is divided into four parts. The first part supplies a general introduction to the study of literature. Its opening chapter, on reading literature, introduces the student to the basic components of literature—plot, character, and theme—and to basic critical concepts such as unity and inevitability. This chapter also introduces the philosophy of the text: that literature is a dialogue between writer and reader, an art form whose subject is a vision of humanity and the universe. The second chapter, on writing about literature, reiterates these fundamentals and shows how they underlie the skills and techniques of writing about literature. While the first chapter is philosophical in bent, the second is practical. Work plans, diagrams, and lists of questions make the idea of writing concrete and comprehensible, and provide "how-to's" for the assignments in the rest of the book.

Although these introductory chapters precede the structured parts on fiction, drama, and poetry, they need not be read first. The instructor who wishes to begin with short stories or poems can elicit spontaneous student responses, unguided by study questions. The questions raised in the introductory chapters can then be applied to works everyone has recently read, and the focus of the course will be clearly defined as being the reading *of* (rather than *about*) literature.

The first genre to be studied is fiction. Its presentation is organized around modes of narration and narrative techniques. The interplay of listener and narrator is thus highlighted, and the basic framework of the text is kept simple. Within this framework, other concepts appear as a natural outgrowth of the subject under discussion and easily become a part of the student's critical vocabulary. The presentation provides a variety of critical concepts within a firmly structured framework—a more satisfying organization than the "grasshopper" approach in which each chapter, or each story, heralds a new topic and leaves students and instructors alike negotiating the jumps between topics as best they can.

After fiction comes drama. We chose to place drama after fiction for the following reasons:

- The period of time covered by a drama is usually slightly shorter than the period covered by a piece of fiction; the time span covered by a poem is usually briefer still. Thus, drama can be seen as a halfway point between the relaxed time frames of fiction and the tighter ones of poetry.
- Drama tends to sustain a slightly higher emotional pitch than does fiction, and poetry is pitched to an even greater level of intensity.
- Drama provides a natural extension for discussions of plot, character, and thought (begun while studying fiction). Plot is all but absent from most poetry.
- Both drama and fiction are multi-voiced; poetry is usually single-voiced.
- Drama makes use of both prose and poetry and may therefore be seen as bridging the gap between the other two genres.
- The book's treatment of drama and fiction lays a firm foundation for the study of poetry. The essential notions of voice, character, and persona have been established. Discussions can build on them for a closer study of word choice, rhythms, and imagery.

The movement of the text, then, is from *fiction,* in which narrator and characters share the stage, with the narrator often judging the other characters, to *drama,* in which the characters usually hold the stage alone and the reader must judge between them, to *poetry,* in which most typically a single character speaks a moment's drama, appealing to the reader with words and cadence alike, often in the most direct manner.

Within each section there are plentiful study aids: introductory essays, study questions, suggestions for essays and for further thinking. Objective and subjective responses both have their place as answers to these questions; the emphasis is on knowing which is which and on achieving a judicious balance between the two. In general, questions near the beginning of a section will offer more guidance than those that come later, thus tacitly encouraging students to greater independence as their skills and familiarity with literature grow. Some sets of questions are constructed so that they form an example of how to organize an essay; others concentrate on showing how to follow a theme through a play, story, or poem; still others encourage students to look at a work from as many angles as possible.

In short, we feel that a good textbook, like the literature it contains, must offer variety within unity, and we have done our best to achieve that goal. Our thanks to the many friends who helped us: especially to Paul Fideler of Lesley College, for his insights into critical philosophy and his willing and patient comments on the manuscript; and to William E. Tanner, Texas Woman's University, for his wise suggestions on content and structure. Finally, we thank you, the users of this book, who bring to it your own love of literature and skills in teaching. May you enjoy using it, and may it serve you well.

ALICE LANDY
H. HOLTON JOHNSON

CONTENTS

ON LITERATURE   1

  1 **The Bases of Literature**   3

  2 **Writing About Literature**   9

FICTION   15

Fiction as Narrative   17

  1 **The Art of Narration: Giving Meaning to Action**   17
    I. L. PERETZ • *If Not Higher*   18
    SHIRLEY JACKSON • *The Lottery*   23

  2 **The Omniscient Narrator**   34
    NATHANIEL HAWTHORNE • *Young Goodman Brown* 35
    ALBERT CAMUS • *The Guest*   47
    STEPHEN CRANE • *The Open Boat*   60

  3 **The First-Person Narrator**   81
    HERMAN MELVILLE • *Bartleby the Scrivener*   84
    CHARLOTTE PERKINS GILMAN • *The Yellow Wall-Paper*   116
    JOSEPH CONRAD • *Youth*   131

Character Study and Social Comment   157

  4 **Looking Inward and Outward**   157
    WILLIAM FAULKNER • *A Rose for Emily*   160

JAMES BALDWIN • *Sonny's Blues*   169
TILLIE OLSEN • *Help Her to Believe*   197
JOYCE CAROL OATES • *How I Contemplated the World from
         the Detroit House of Correction and
         Began My Life Over Again*   204

AN ANTHOLOGY OF SHORT STORIES

AN ANTHOLOGY OF SHORT STORIES   219

EDGAR ALLAN POE • *The Fall of the House of Usher*   221
JAMES JOYCE • *Counterparts*   237
FRANZ KAFKA • *The Bucket-Rider*   246
D. H. LAWRENCE • *The Rocking-Horse Winner*   248
ERNEST HEMINGWAY • *The Snows of Kilimanjaro*   261
JOHN STEINBECK • *The Chrysanthemums*   281
RICHARD WRIGHT • *Bright and Morning Star*   291
DORIS LESSING • *How I Finally Lost My Heart*   320
FLANNERY O'CONNOR • *A Good Man Is Hard to Find*   330
JORGE LUIS BORGES • *The South*   344
JOHN BARTH • *Lost in the Funhouse*   350
DONALD BARTHELME • *The Balloon*   370

DRAMA

DRAMA   375

1   **Reading Drama**   377

2   **Origins of English Drama**   383
SOPHOCLES • *Oedipus Rex*   389
(Translated by DUDLEY FITTS and ROBERT FITZGERALD)
ANONYMOUS • *The Second Shepherds' Play*   433
(A modernized version by JOHN GASSNER)

3   ***Hamlet* and Elizabethan Tragedy**   459
WILLIAM SHAKESPEARE • *Hamlet*   463

4   **Modern Drama**   583
BERNARD SHAW • *Preface to Major Barbara*   586
BERNARD SHAW • *Major Barbara*   614
ARTHUR MILLER • *Death of a Salesman*   694

POETRY

POETRY   779

1   **Reading Poetry**   781
ANONYMOUS • *Get Up and Bar the Door*   784

ANONYMOUS • *Lord Randal*   785
ANONYMOUS • *The Cherry-Tree Carol*   786

Elements of Poetry   788

2 **Repetition and Rhythm**   788
ANONYMOUS • *Back and Side Go Bare*   789
THOMAS HARDY • *The Ruined Maid*   790
ANONYMOUS • *All Night by the Rose*   791
WILLIAM BLAKE • *The Lamb*   792
WILLIAM BLAKE • *The Tyger*   792
E. E. CUMMINGS • *All in green went my love riding*   793

3 **Compression and Verse Forms**   796
COUNTEE CULLEN • *For a Lady I Know*   798
GWENDOLYN BROOKS • *We Real Cool*   798
EZRA POUND • *In a Station of the Metro*   799
DENISE LEVERTOV • *Six Variations (part iii)*   800
H. D. (HILDA DOOLITTLE) • *Heat*   800
EZRA POUND • *L'Art, 1910*   800
EMILY DICKINSON • *There's a Certain Slant of Light*   801
EMILY DICKINSON • *Tell All the Truth but Tell It Slant*   801

4 **Word Choice: Meanings and Suggestions**   803
EMILY DICKINSON • *The Bustle in a House*   804
WILLIAM WORDSWORTH • *She Dwelt Among the Untrodden Ways*   806
ROBERT HERRICK • *Upon Julia's Clothes*   806
A. E. HOUSMAN • *With Rue My Heart Is Laden*   806
CARL SANDBURG • *Cool Tombs*   807
EZRA POUND • *These Fought in Any Case*   808
E. E. CUMMINGS • *in Just-   spring*   809

The Speaker in the Poem   811

5 **The Speaker's Voice**   811
THEODORE ROETHKE • *My Papa's Waltz*   813
THEODORE ROETHKE • *I Knew a Woman*   813
ANONYMOUS • *Western Wind*   814
SIR JOHN SUCKLING • *The Constant Lover*   815
SIR THOMAS WYATT • *They Flee from Me*   815
THOMAS HARDY • *The Man He Killed*   816
WILLIAM BUTLER YEATS • *An Irish Airman Foresees His Death*   817

6   The Speaker's Vision   819

DANTE GABRIEL ROSSETTI • *The Woodspurge*   820
D. H. LAWRENCE • *Piano*   821
SIR PHILIP SIDNEY • *Sonnet 31*   822
JOHN KEATS • *When I Have Fears*   822
GERARD MANLEY HOPKINS • *Spring and Fall*   823
RALPH WALDO EMERSON • *Hamatreya*   824

7   Beyond the Speaker: The Double Vision of Irony   827

ADRIENNE RICH • *Aunt Jennifer's Tigers*   828
GEORGE MEREDITH • *Sonnet 17*   829
A. E. HOUSMAN • *When I Was One-and-Twenty*   829
WILLIAM BUTLER YEATS • *The Folly of Being Comforted*   830
PERCY BYSSHE SHELLEY • *Ozymandias*   830
W. H. AUDEN • *The Unknown Citizen*   831
HENRY REED • *Naming of Parts*   832

Imagery   834

8   Similes, Metaphors, and Personification   834

WALT WHITMAN • *The Dalliance of the Eagles*   835
ALFRED, LORD TENNYSON • *The Eagle*   835
LANGSTON HUGHES • *Harlem*   838
JOHN KEATS • *On First Looking into Chapman's Homer*   839
CARL SANDBURG • *Fog*   840
BEN JONSON • *A Pindaric Ode*   841
DENISE LEVERTOV • *Losing Track*   841
WILLIAM WORDSWORTH • *Composed upon Westminster Bridge,*
                                    September 3, 1802   842
SYLVIA PLATH • *Morning Song*   842
RICHARD WILBUR • *Love Calls Us to the Things of This World* 843

9   Symbol and Allegory   845

GEORGE HERBERT • *Love (III)*   847
WILLIAM BLAKE • *The Sick Rose*   847
RALPH WALDO EMERSON • *Days*   848
ROBERT FROST • *The Road Not Taken*   848
ALLEN GINSBERG • *In back of the real*   849
JOHN KEATS • *Ode on a Grecian Urn*   849

10   Conceits and Allusions   852

JOHN DONNE • *Hymn to God My God, in My Sickness*   853

HENRY REED • *Unarmed Combat*   854
ANONYMOUS • *Sumer Is Icumen In*   856
EZRA POUND • *Ancient Music*   857
EDMUND SPENSER • *Sonnet 15*   857
WILLIAM SHAKESPEARE • *Sonnet 18*   858
JOHN DONNE • *The Sun Rising*   859
SIR PHILIP SIDNEY • *Leave Me, O Love*   860
ANDREW MARVELL • *To His Coy Mistress*   860
ROBERT GRAVES • *Down, Wanton, Down!*   862

11   Patterns of Imagery   863
PERCY BYSSHE SHELLEY • *Ode to the West Wind*   864
JOHN KEATS • *Ode to a Nightingale*   866
MATTHEW ARNOLD • *Dover Beach*   869
WILLIAM BUTLER YEATS • *Sailing to Byzantium*   870
DYLAN THOMAS • *Fern Hill*   871

Sound   873

12   Meter and Its Variations   873
ANONYMOUS (*modern version by Ezra Pound*) • *The Seafarer*   878
GERARD MANLEY HOPKINS • *Pied Beauty*   880
ALFRED, LORD TENNYSON • *The Splendor Falls on Castle Walls* 881
GEORGE HERBERT • *The Collar*   882

13   Rhyme Schemes and Verse Forms   884
DYLAN THOMAS • *Do Not Go Gentle into That Good Night*   886
WILLIAM SHAKESPEARE • *Sonnet 116*   887
JOHN DONNE • *Sonnet 10*   888
JOHN MILTON • *On His Blindness*   888
GERARD MANLEY HOPKINS • *(Carrion Comfort)*   889
LOUIS MACNEICE • *Sunday Morning*   889
ROBERT FROST • *Design*   890
WILLIAM WORDSWORTH • *Ode: Intimations of Immortality*   891

AN ANTHOLOGY OF POEMS   897

Country and City Scenes   899
CHRISTOPHER MARLOWE • *The Passionate Shepherd to His Love* 899
SIR WALTER RALEGH • *The Nymph's Reply to the Shepherd*   900
ROBERT BROWNING • *Home-Thoughts, from Abroad*   900

WILLIAM BLAKE • *London*   901
T. S. ELIOT • *The Love Song of J. Alfred Prufrock*   902
RICHARD WILBUR • *Place Pigalle*   905
ROBERT LOWELL • *For the Union Dead*   906
LAWRENCE FERLINGHETTI • *The pennycandy store beyond the El*   908
ALLEN GINSBERG • *A Supermarket in California*   909
AMIRI BARAKA (LEROI JONES) • *W. W.*   910

Portraits   911

WILLIAM COWPER • *The Castaway*   911
ALFRED, LORD TENNYSON • *Ulysses*   913
ROBERT BROWNING • *The Bishop Orders His Tomb at
                           Saint Praxed's Church*   914
WALLACE STEVENS • *The World as Meditation*   918
T. S. ELIOT • *Journey of the Magi*   919
E. E. CUMMINGS • *the Cambridge ladies who live in furnished souls*   920
JOHN CROWE RANSOM • *Bells for John Whiteside's Daughter*   920
GWENDOLYN BROOKS • *The Bean Eaters*   921
ANNE SEXTON • *Her Kind*   922

Poets on Poetry   923

ROBERT HERRICK • *The Argument of His Book*   923
WILLIAM SHAKESPEARE • *Sonnet 55*   923
EMILY DICKINSON • *The Poets Light but Lamps*   924
WALT WHITMAN • *Out of the Cradle Endlessly Rocking*   924
JAMES WELDON JOHNSON • *O Black and Unknown Bards*   930
A. E. HOUSMAN • *"Terence, This Is Stupid Stuff . . ."*   931
ROBINSON JEFFERS • *Love the Wild Swan*   933
ROBINSON JEFFERS • *Cassandra*   933
DYLAN THOMAS • *In My Craft or Sullen Art*   934
MARIANNE MOORE • *Poetry*   934
ARCHIBALD MACLEISH • *Ars Poetica*   936

Index of Terms   937
Index of Authors and Titles   943
Index of First Lines   947

THE HEATH INTRODUCTION TO LITERATURE

ON LITERATURE

1 The Bases of Literature

Literature has its roots in one of the most basic human desires—the desire for pleasure. Its writers find one source of pleasure in mastering the difficult demands of their craft. If they do well, they then reap a second delight from witnessing the pleasure their work gives to others. Readers, meanwhile, derive pleasure from literature's power to imitate life. A truly good book can speak of imaginary people so vividly that they seem more alive than people we meet on the street and can make us care about its characters as if they were close friends.

We are always curious about each other, and usually curious about ourselves as well. Why do we behave as we do? What are the causes of our actions? Literature is far from having all the answers. But it does offer hints, suggestions, and flashes of insight. Moreover, it offers them in such a way as to refresh and encourage our own thinking, and so leads us to insights of our own. Readers have many standards for judging writers. But one enduring standard is the writers' power to interpret us, as humans, to ourselves. The greater the writers' knowledge of people seems to be, the more openly they share their knowledge with us, the higher we rate them. We speak with disdain of shallow or insincere writers; we demand truth and sincerity even in the most fantastic fiction.

Literature, then, exists because it pleases us. And it pleases us by imitating life—or, more precisely, by displaying its writers' visions of life as it is or as the writers think it should be. But how does it contrive its imitation? Its only medium is words; and we know how hard it is to make words say what we want them to say. How do writers handle their words to get such powerful effects from them? What guidelines help them make the million-and-one choices that result in a play, a poem, or a story?

The first necessities for any work of literature—and therefore the first things that writers must consider—are **plot** and **character.** These may occur to a writer in either order. That is, a writer may first imagine some characters, and then decide what actions they are to perform; or a writer may envision some action, and then decide on the people who must perform it. Every work of literature, however, must have both action and characters. It cannot please us, or hold our interest, otherwise.

It may seem that poetry is an exception to this rule. While stories and plays tend to present fully developed plots with sequences of actions with discernible beginnings, middles, and ends, poems more often plunge us into the middle of an event, and may tell us neither what came before the event nor what comes after it. Here, for instance, is a poem with no physical action at all. Yet it shows us one person, at least, and gives us some insight into his actions and feelings.

GEORGE GORDON, LORD BYRON (1788–1824)

So We'll Go No More A-Roving

So we'll go no more a-roving
   So late into the night,
Though the heart be still as loving,
   And the moon be still as bright.

5 For the sword outwears its sheath,
   And the soul wears out the breast,
And the heart must pause to breathe,
   And Love itelf have rest.

Though the night was made for loving,
10 And the day returns too soon,
   Yet we'll go no more a-roving
   By the light of the moon.

We know several things about the speaker of this poem. We know that he has enjoyed "roving," and that he still thinks warmly of it, since he declares that "the night was made for loving, / And the day returns too soon." We know that he feels weary, like a sheath worn out by the motions of the sword within it. We hear him declare that his roving days are done. But we also hear him speak of pausing and resting, verbs that imply an eventual return to action. And so we begin to wonder: is he really finished with love, as he says he is? The action of the poem might thus be described as the act of the lover forswearing love. Its interest arises from our recognition of the complex emotions the renunciation reveals. It is the action, and the emotion, of a moment; but it is none the less real—and none the less action—for its momentary nature.

For now, however, let us return to the more thoroughly developed plots of drama and fiction. These, too, must find some balance between action and emotion, some method of telling us both what the characters do and how they feel. A given story may emphasize action or feeling; that choice, like so many others, is up to its writer. But it must contain some of both. We have no interest in unfeeling characters, or in characters who do nothing.

In addition to a plot and to characters who act and feel, a work of literature must have **unity** and **coherence.** It must make us believe that its characters really would have committed the actions it says they commit, and that the actions could really have taken place. At its best, the movement of a play, a poem, or a story must make us feel that the tale could have reached no other end, and that it could have reached it in no other way. When this happens, the story's ending seems inevitable. Its characters and its actions have convinced us wholly. A sense of inevitability is thus another hallmark of a fine work of literature. Works so marked tend to be moving and powerful.

The **language** of a work of literature is also important. Words have so many undercurrents of meaning that the change of one word may change our image of a scene or a character. Consider, for instance, the difference between *a thin, tense man; a thin, nervous man;* and *a thin, harried man*—or the difference between *a plump woman, a well-rounded woman,* and *an overweight woman.* A writer's language must be chosen with care. It should carry overtones that enrich our sense of the story, thus adding to the pleasure we get from the tale. And it must avoid all false tones, for those would diminish our pleasure. Again, we demand at least that the words fit the actions and characters of which they tell. And again, we shall find that the best seem almost inevitable. Reading them, we cannot imagine the author having used any other words.

When we read, we don't want to be aware of these choices of words and acts and characters. We don't want to hear the author muttering behind the scenes: "I need this word, not that one. This character must say this; that description must carry this message." Rather, we want to be able to concentrate on the story itself, accepting everything within it as valid and necessary parts of its world. When we discuss and analyze works of literature, however, we do become aware of the choices the writers made in constructing them. We note who the characters are and how they relate to each other. We observe how the action begins, how it ends, and how it is carried from beginning to ending. We study the ways in which the language characterizes people and events and consider the broader or deeper meanings it suggests.

These questions, we may note, are **questions of fact.** Their answers can be found, decided, and agreed upon. We can count the characters in *Hamlet,* and we will learn that Hamlet is a prince of Denmark, that Gertrude is his mother and Claudius his stepfather, and that the ghost who appears from time to time is the ghost of Hamlet's murdered father. Similarly, we learn that eight people are killed during the course of the play (one by stabbing, one by drowning, two by beheading, one by poison, and three by some combination of sword wounds and poison) and that virtually none of the major characters is still alive when the play ends. There is no question about any of these happenings and no reason to argue about them.

Questions of fact, however, are only a beginning in thinking about a work of literature. They tell us certain choices a writer has made, but they rarely tell us why the writer has made those particular choices. To learn that, we must go on to **questions of interpretation,** questions that deal with the artistic vision underlying the work and thus with such issues as theme, pattern, message, and meaning.

Message and **meaning** are not universal to literature. They belong to one school of literature, the **didactic.** When writers or critics demand that a story carry a message to its readers, that it "mean something" to them, they are saying that literature should teach us something and that it should appeal to our sense of moral values. At its simplest, this approach ends in pat morals: "Always tell the truth; stop beating up on your fellow humans." On a more sophisticated level, however, didacticism becomes what the critic Matthew Arnold called "high seriousness" and produces literature that deals with such complex questions as the value of human life and the sources of human ideals and aspirations.

Not all literature is didactic. Some writers believe that literature does not need to make a moral statement. For these writers, a work of literature is important for its own sake, not for any message it might carry. As one modern poet put it, "A poem should not mean, but be."[1] In works like these, the concept of message does not apply; to impose it upon them is to falsify the intent of the writer.

The questions of **theme** and **pattern,** however, concern all literature. Within any work of literature that strikes us as unified and complete we will find some sort of pattern into which its parts fit or through which they are perceived. Didactic tales, for example, present acts and people in terms of a moral order. Hence the tales tend to be built around patterns

---

[1] Archibald MacLeish, "Ars Poetica," p. 936.

of good and evil, temptation and response. In contrast, a Romantic poem describing a summer day might have sensory impressions of light and shade, coolness and warmth, as its unifying vision.

There may be many patterns—patterns of action, characterization, language, or metaphor—within a single work. Sometimes each will work separately; sometimes several will be intertwined to bear on a single theme. Sometimes, too, several themes will be interwoven within one work to create a complexity of vision that no single theme could contain. But always there will be that sense of a single ordered vision embracing and unifying all the patterns or themes.

Sometimes the main theme of a work is announced by its author. Joseph Conrad, for instance, wrote a story that tells of a twenty-year-old man's first voyage to the East. He titled the story "Youth." He had its hero tell the tale himself, looking back on his voyage from the age of forty-two, and had him interrupt his story from time to time with exclamations such as, "O youth! The strength of it, the faith of it, the imagination of it!"[2] By doing so, Conrad made it perfectly clear that the hero's vision of what youth was and what his own youth had meant to him would be the main theme of his story. More often, however, deciding what themes are being worked out is our affair; and here interpretation becomes most individual and most varied.

We all read the same words when we read a story. We observe the same characters acting out the same deeds and passions. But we each interpret them a little differently because of our individual views of life, our interests, and our experience. When we try to explain how the story works, therefore, or decide what themes are being emphasized, we read some of our own perceptions into the story.

If we realize that we are interpreting, all is well. Then we can say, "This is how it seems to me." We can look for patterns of language or imagery and details of action or characterization to support our view. We can listen to others who have other views and evaluate the support they bring for their arguments; and, in the end, we can probably come to a pretty fair idea of what the story does have to offer and how it is able to offer it.

On the other hand, if we do not recognize the extent to which we are active interpreters of what we read, we may have trouble when we try to deal with such subjective issues as theme or message. For then we may make the error of saying, "I see this. Therefore the author intended it that way and I have found the only correct interpretation this story can possibly have." Since very few works of literature will not admit some variance of interpretation, definitive statements such as this are wrong more often than not. It is true that there are limits to the range of

---

[2] p. 137.

interpretations we can apply to a work of literature if we are to read it honestly on its own terms. Within those limits, however, we must be willing to acknowledge various ways of looking at it.

We must also be willing to allow our perceptions to change. It often happens that what we notice the first time we read a story is not what seems most important to us later on. Nor would it make sense to talk or write about a poem or a story if our perception of it could not be enriched by the discussion. Too, we must be willing to use our full judgment, to read the story carefully and attentively. We must be sure we are trying to discover what it really does say rather than simply assuming that it says what we want it to say. Once we have done this, however, we should be able to feel comfortable with our judgments and our responses. Above all, we must not undervalue ourselves. We are the people for whom these stories, plays, and poems are written. If we cannot trust ourselves, we will have a hard time trusting them.

2 Writing About Literature

Literature allows writers to share their ideas and visions with their readers. Their work is not complete until someone has read it and responded to it.

As readers, we too have something to say. At the very least, we have opinions about the work itself, but we also may have other ideas to express. Perhaps we are moved to compare this story with others, or perhaps it has given us some new ideas that we want to explore further. Sometimes we share our ideas directly with others in face-to-face discussions. At other times, we become writers in order to communicate our thoughts and opinions.

The first part of writing about literature, therefore, is thinking about it. This step is perhaps the most vital part of the process, for we need to know not only what we think but why we think as we do. Which of our thoughts come from the work itself? Which have been inspired by it? Which come from our predispositions and preconceptions about literature?

We enjoy stories for many reasons. Some are intrinsic to the story itself: language artfully used, characters we believe in and care about, actions that carry significant messages for us or give us new insight into ourselves and our society. (Whether the story provides that insight by answering questions for us or by urging us into asking our own questions does not matter here. What does matter is that the impetus for question or answer comes from within the story itself.) Other causes of enjoyment are external, coming not from the artistry of the story, but from the fact that the story fits our current notions of what a story should be like, or calls forth some pleasant personal memories. In short, the external factors in our response to a story come from things we already think or feel. Intrinsic factors come from the writer's craftsmanship and art.*

When we read for pleasure alone, we need not care where our pleasure comes from. Any appeal a story may have will be welcome. When we study literature, however, we want to concentrate on the intrinsic qualities of the works we read, for they can teach us most about the craft and the workings of literature. It is a story's intrinsic qualities, therefore, and our response to them, that we want to write about when we write about literature.

When we rule out external responses to literature, and say that we are only going to talk and write about its intrinsic qualities, we are not denying the individuality of our responses. In fact, only when we escape from our prejudices and preconceptions about literature can we respond most freely to the stories we read. Even when we write most directly of the story itself and the art which created it, our writing will contain an emotional component as well as an intellectual one. Emotion and intellect together answer such questions as, "Does the hero's death seem inevitable?" and "How has it been made to seem so?"

All analysis ends in judgment. All questions of, "How is this done?" begin or end with, "Is it a success?" It would be useless to ask, "How has the writer characterized his heroine?" if we could not also ask, "Has he made me care what happens to her?" Literature appeals to mind and emotions alike; our response, therefore, must be both analytic and emotional, objective and subjective. Concentrating on those things that are intrinsic to the story does not deny the subjective component of our response. Rather, it frees us for more truly personal reactions, subjective and objective alike, even while it helps us recognize how and why we are responding.

Before we begin to write about a story, therefore, we should ask ourselves some version of the following questions:

1. Which aspects of the story had the greatest impact on me?
2. What did they seem to be saying? How did they say it? (or, What did they make me think that seemed new to me? How did they make me think it?)

---

* What is true for stories is true for plays and poems as well. For the rest of this chapter, therefore, I shall use the word "stories" to stand for all types of literature, rather than repeating the more awkward phrases "stories, plays, and poems" and "works of literature."

3. How did other aspects of the story support or contribute to my response?
4. How did these particular aspects of the story help create the story's total effect?

We start, that is, with our response to the story; we move from there to an analysis of the art which creates the response; and then we return to the overall impression or effect.

When we write, we follow the same pattern of response, analysis, and final judgment. Unless we have unlimited time and paper, however, we will not be able to write down all that we have thought about the story. Choices must be made: What shall I include? What shall I emphasize? To make those choices, we must consider not only the story and our response to it, but the purpose of our paper and the audience for which we are writing it.

Let's look at two extreme examples. Let's imagine, first, that we keep a journal or diary and that we want to record in it the fact that we read and enjoyed a story. In this case, our main interest would be our own reaction to the story; our writing, therefore, would concentrate on our subjective response. We would mention only those incidents or characters that impressed us most strongly; and we could write in whatever style we pleased, for we would be our only audience.

At the other extreme, suppose we were writing a paper for a scholarly journal. In this case, we would write in an objective, balanced style, presenting carefully worked out analyses of each aspect of the story that related to our topic. We would define our terms carefully and provide adequate illustrations to support our thesis. In fact, we would be writing almost like a debater, trying to make our points as clear, convincing, and firmly based on factual evidence as possible.

Somewhere between these extremes lie most writing assignments. Two we might look at are book reviews and English papers. Let's consider what these types of writing most often say. Then let's look at how they can go about saying it.

Book reviews tend to be frankly subjective, focusing on "What I liked and why I liked it." (Or, alternatively, "Why you shouldn't waste time or money on this book.") By its very nature, a review commits the reviewer to making judgments: the book may be "one of the year's best," or "not up to this author's usual standards," or simply "a pleasant afternoon's reading." Too, the reviewer may try to judge what type of reader would enjoy the book most: "Readers with a taste for psychological studies will enjoy . . .", or "Mystery fans will welcome the appearance of. . . ."

A brief review may contain little more than these judgments. A more thorough one will usually provide some evidence to support them, by discussing some particularly outstanding character or episode or by quoting a few lines of description or dialogue as a sample of the writer's style. Readers of reviews are presumed to be asking themselves, "Is this a book I want to read?" Through judgments and illustrations supporting the judgments, reviews are designed to help readers answer that question.

A review, therefore, will generally begin in one of two ways. It will either start right out with its broadest judgment to show exactly where the reviewer stands, or it will start out with a "teaser," a quote or detail from the book that seems striking enough to catch the readers' attention and "tease" them into reading at least the review, if not the book itself.

Then will come the explanation, details, and analyses. What was it that made the experience of reading the book so enjoyable? Why is the teaser a good sample of what the book has to offer? Reviews may focus on one aspect of a book, such as its characters, or they may glance at many aspects in turn. But they must maintain a balance between the personal interest of the reviewers' subjective comments and the objective analyses with which they try to convince us that they are sound judges of books whose opinions should be respected. And they must bring their comments and analyses together again in a final summary, judgment, or call to action: "Rush right out and buy this book; you won't be disappointed."

Reviewers, then, consider their audience (potential readers of the book being reviewed) and their purpose (telling their readers that the book exists and helping them decide whether or not they want to read it). They offer their own judgments, support them with relevant evidence, and draw all together to a logical conclusion.

English papers demand many of the same techniques as reviews and are often written in similar formats. They vary in scope and purpose, however, more than reviews do. The assignments in this book provide a range of possible types of papers.

Many of the assignments are quite narrowly defined. Their purpose is to make you look closely at some particular technique of the writer's— the role of the narrator in a story, for example, or the way a theme is carried through a tale. In this case your writing, too, must be tightly focused, your style almost wholly objective. Your first sentence will probably state your basic theme; and every sentence that follows, down to your final summation, will bear directly on that theme. The particular points you discuss, and the order in which you present them, may be suggested by the questions or instructions of the assignment itself. The evidence with which you support your answers will come from within the story. But the finished product will be very much your own: a tight, coherent piece of writing built on your own handling of the material given to you by the story.

Other assignments are broader, or ask that you define your own subject. (For example, "What do you think is the major theme of this story? How would you support your view?") Now your own judgments must be more boldly expressed. You must decide which aspects of the story should be

FIGURE ONE

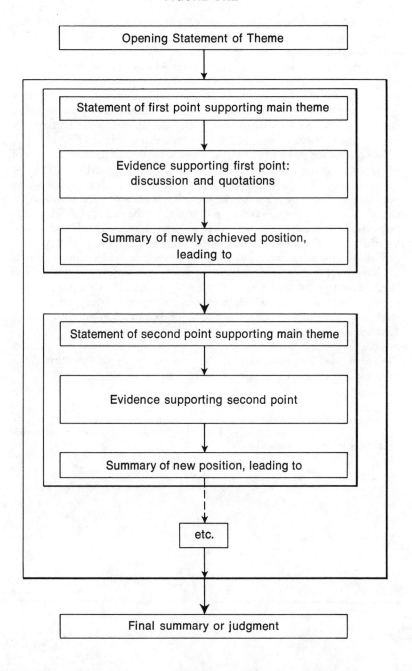

emphasized and which are irrelevant to the question at hand. Your responsibility is not only to provide evidence to support a theory you were told to discuss, but first to set up your theory and then to support it.*

Again, you will want a tightly focused paper, making full use of detailed evidence. But your opening, conclusion, and whatever general statements control your central discussion will be somewhat broader in their implications than those of the earlier assignment, and they will represent your own judgments as to what is most important to the story and to your essay. This essay, too, will follow the general format of initial response → analysis → final summary. But the analysis will be fuller and more complex than is necessary with a more narrowly defined paper.

As you can see in Figure One, the general pattern of statement → proof → summary is useful for each point within the analysis, just as it is for the essay as a whole. We use each new statement to remind ourselves and our readers just where we are in our argument, and each summary to establish our new position before proceeding to the next point. This step-by-step construction, together with a careful focusing of each point toward our main theme, will create a unified, tightly argued paper.

The act of writing about literature, by forcing us to look closely at what we have read and to analyze both the work and our own responses, can thus be seen as the final step in the act of reading. Now we are not only enjoying the words by which someone else speaks to us, we also are stretching our own minds to the task of communicating with others. Reading and writing, we take an active role and thus reassert ourselves as active, thinking, feeling beings. The opportunity to make that reassertion may well represent one of the deepest values of literature. It is certainly an opportunity well worth our taking.

---

* The study questions in chapter 6 will help bridge the gap between these two types of assignments by suggesting how one goes about choosing a theme and gathering evidence to support it.

FICTION

FICTION AS NARRATIVE

1 *The Art of Narration:*
Giving Meaning to Action

Fiction is the art of the storyteller. Not only are writers of fiction storytellers themselves, but within every story they create a new storyteller, the narrator of the tale. It is the narrator's voice we hear speaking as we read a novel or short story. The narrator introduces the tale to us, keeps us amused during its telling, and dismisses us at its end. The narrator describes scenes and characters, relates events, sets the tone of the tale and supplies whatever meanings or explanations the author sees fit to provide.

Reader and story are thus brought together by the narrator. For this reason, the study of fiction usually begins with a study of types of narrators and narrations. Let us begin by looking at a very brief story, a modern tale which, being strongly reminiscent of folk tales, suggests some of the oldest traditions of storytelling. Notice the simplicity of the action and the sharp contrasts drawn among the few characters. Listen to the voice of the storyteller as he builds his tale.

I. L. PERETZ (1851–1915)

If Not Higher

Early every Friday morning, at the time of the Penitential Prayers, the Rabbi of Nemirov would vanish.

He was nowhere to be seen—neither in the synagogue nor in the two Houses of Study nor at a *minyan*. And he was certainly not at home. His door stood open; whoever wished could go in and out; no one would steal from the rabbi. But not a living creature was within.

Where could the rabbi be? Where should he be? In heaven, no doubt. A rabbi has plenty of business to take care of just before the Days of Awe. Jews, God bless them, need livelihood, peace, health, and good matches. They want to be pious and good, but our sins are so great, and Satan of the thousand eyes watches the whole earth from one end to the other. What he sees he reports; he denounces, informs. Who can help us if not the rabbi!

That's what the people thought.

But once a Litvak came, and he laughed. You know the Litvaks. They think little of the Holy Books but stuff themselves with Talmud and law. So this Litvak points to a passage in the *Gemarah* —it sticks in your eyes—where it is written that even Moses, our Teacher, did not ascend to heaven during his lifetime but remained suspended two and a half feet below. Go argue with a Litvak!

So where can the rabbi be?

"That's not my business," said the Litvak, shrugging. Yet all the while—what a Litvak can do!—he is scheming to find out.

That same night, right after the evening prayers, the Litvak steals into the rabbi's room, slides under the rabbi's bed, and waits. He'll watch all night and discover where the rabbi vanishes and what he does during the Pentitential Prayers.

Someone else might have got drowsy and fallen asleep, but a Litvak is never at a loss; he recites a whole tractate of the Talmud by heart.

At dawn he hears the call to prayers.

The rabbi has already been awake for a long time. The Litvak has heard him groaning for a whole hour.

Whoever has heard the Rabbi of Nemirov groan knows how much

sorrow for all Israel, how much suffering, lies in each groan. A man's heart might break, hearing it. But a Litvak is made of iron; he listens and remains where he is. The rabbi, long life to him, lies on the bed, and the Litvak under the bed.

Then the Litvak hears the beds in the house begin to creak; he hears people jumping out of their beds, mumbling a few Jewish words, pouring water on their fingernails, banging doors. Everyone has left. It is again quiet and dark; a bit of light from the moon shines through the shutters.

(Afterward the Litvak admitted that when he found himself alone with the rabbi a great fear took hold of him. Goose pimples spread across his skin, and the roots of his earlocks pricked him like needles. A trifle: to be alone with the rabbi at the time of the Penitential Prayers! But a Litvak is stubborn. So he quivered like a fish in water and remained where he was.)

Finally the rabbi, long life to him, arises. First he does what befits a Jew. Then he goes to the clothes closet and takes out a bundle of peasant clothes: linen trousers, high boots, a coat, a big felt hat, and a long wide leather belt studded with brass nails. The rabbi gets dressed. From his coat pocket dangles the end of a heavy peasant rope.

The rabbi goes out, and the Litvak follows him.

On the way the rabbi stops in the kitchen, bends down, takes an ax from under the bed, puts it in his belt, and leaves the house. The Litvak trembles but continues to follow.

The hushed dread of the Days of Awe hangs over the dark streets. Every once in a while a cry rises from some *minyan* reciting the Penitential Prayers, or from a sickbed. The rabbi hugs the sides of the streets, keeping to the shade of the houses. He glides from house to house, and the Litvak after him. The Litvak hears the sound of his heartbeats mingling with the sound of the rabbi's heavy steps. But he keeps on going and follows the rabbi to the outskirts of the town.

A small wood stands behind the town.

The rabbi, long life to him, enters the wood. He takes thirty or forty steps and stops by a small tree. The Litvak, overcome with amazement, watches the rabbi take the ax out of his belt and strike the tree. He hears the tree creak and fall. The rabbi chops the tree into logs and the logs into sticks. Then he makes a bundle of the wood and ties it with the rope in his pocket. He puts the bundle of wood on his back, shoves the ax back into his belt, and returns to the town.

He stops at a back street beside a small broken-down shack and knocks at the window.

"Who is there?" asks a frightened voice. The Litvak recognizes it as the voice of a sick Jewish woman.

"I," answers the rabbi in the accent of a peasant.

"Who is I?"

Again the rabbi answers in Russian. "Vassil."

"Who is Vassil, and what do you want?"

"I have wood to sell, very cheap." And, not waiting for the woman's reply, he goes into the house.

The Litvak steals in after him. In the gray light of early morning he sees a poor room with broken, miserable furnishings. A sick woman, wrapped in rags, lies on the bed. She complains bitterly, "Buy? How can I buy? Where will a poor widow get money?"

"I'll lend it to you," answers the supposed Vassil. "It's only six cents."

"And how will I ever pay you back?" said the poor woman, groaning.

"Foolish one," says the rabbi reproachfully. "See, you are a poor sick Jew, and I am ready to trust you with a little wood. I am sure you'll pay. While you, you have such a great and mighty God and you don't trust him for six cents."

"And who will kindle the fire?" said the widow. "Have I the strength to get up? My son is at work."

"I'll kindle the fire," answers the rabbi.

As the rabbi put the wood into the oven he recited, in a groan, the first portion of the Penitential Prayers.

As he kindled the fire and the wood burned brightly, he recited, a bit more joyously, the second portion of the Penitential Prayers. When the fire was set he recited the third portion, and then he shut the stove.

The Litvak who saw all this became a disciple of the rabbi.

And ever after, when another disciple tells how the Rabbi of Nemirov ascends to heaven at the time of the Penitential Prayers, the Litvak does not laugh. He only adds quietly, "If not higher."

"Early every Friday morning . . . the Rabbi of Nemirov would vanish." The statement is blunt and surprising. Rabbis do not usually vanish. We read on, expecting some explanation for the rabbi's behavior. But we find only more mystery. First the narrator tells us where the rabbi isn't. Then he tells us where the townspeople think he is; then he introduces the Litvak who argues that the rabbi can't be there, either. "So where can the rabbi be?" By the time the Litvak sets out to discover the answer, we may be pardoned for being curious ourselves. The narrator has certainly done his best to catch our interest and make us curious.

We notice, meanwhile, that the narrator is not unbiased. Although he takes no direct part in the tale, he does identify himself somewhat with the townspeople, slipping from the statement that "*they* want to be pious and good" to the recognition that *"our* sins are so great. . . . Who can help us if not the rabbi!" He pulls back in the next sentence: "That's what the people thought"; but the identification remains in our minds.

That "our" and "us", in fact, might almost include us, the readers. Certainly the narrator treats us as people who share with him knowledge of rabbis and religious matters and Litvaks—especially Litvaks. "You know the Litvaks . . . . Go argue with a Litvak!" The Litvak has an important role in the story. In contrast to the townspeople, who are ready to spread and believe miraculous rumors, the Litvak is a sceptic. He is a well-read man, so studied in law and religious books that he can keep himself awake all night by reciting Biblical commentaries; but he is a sceptic, nonetheless. It is precisely because he is sceptical, however, that the Litvak becomes curious enough to find out the real answer to the mystery; and it is he who has the final word at the end of the tale.

The Litvak is almost a type or symbol of the person with more knowledge than faith. The narrator, in fact, insists on seeing him as a type—"a Litvak" rather than a man with a name. At the same time, his prejudice characterizes the narrator. We feel that he'd like to see the Litvak shown up, the rabbi and townsfolk triumphant; we feel he himself has a stake in the outcome of the tale.

As the tale continues, the suspense builds. The narrator helps it along by his talk of "groaning" and "hushed dread," his relation of how even the Litvak suffers "goose pimples" and "a great fear," how he "trembles" and quivers "like a fish in water."

Finally, the mystery is revealed. Now, for the first time, we hear voices other than the narrator's. We hear the rabbi (the only words we do hear from him) and the sick woman (the only characterization we have of her; and it's enough). We see what the Litvak sees, hear what he hears; and we are not told what to think about any of it. The narrator, who heretofore has been generous with his comments, is now letting actions and characters speak for themselves.

Even the conclusion is restrained. We learn that "the Litvak who saw all this became a disciple of the rabbi," and we learn his new attitude toward the tale that the rabbi ascends to heaven on Fridays. Note that this is the Litvak's attitude; it is he, not the narrator, who says "if not higher," and so makes the final judgment on the rabbi's actions. Note, too, that we are told nothing else of how the Litvak's life may have changed. What does becoming the rabbi's disciple mean for him? That we must figure out for ourselves.

The tale is rich in interpretive value. There is no need for the narrator to characterize the rabbi's actions; we can all supply our own view of their significance. Similarly, we can all tell what the Litvak means by his comment, "if not higher," though we might each phrase the meaning somewhat differently. At the start of the story, the Litvak was looking for something. At the end, he has found it, and we feel the value to him of the discovery. Yet even this is lightly handled, in keeping with the slightly humorous tone of the story. The narrator continues to focus on his one question, "Where does the rabbi go early Friday mornings?" It is the solution of that mystery, the resolution of that conflict between the Litvak and the townspeople, which he presents as the "quietly" triumphant ending of his story. Anything else we choose to read into it is our own affair.

"If Not Higher," then, is a tale (almost a "tall tale") told by a narrator who takes no direct part in the action, but who has some concern that the story come out well. His voice is a speaking voice, sometimes humorous, sometimes emphatic, sometimes exasperated. Clearly, this is a practiced speaker, a man who enjoys telling stories. We sense his enjoyment in every line of the tale.

In contrast, look at this next story. It too is told by a narrator who remains outside the action; it too is a tale that lends itself to symbolic interpretation. But notice the differences in tone and technique. What attitudes does this narrator convey? How far does she go in interpreting actions and characters for us?

SHIRLEY JACKSON (1919–1965)

The Lottery

The morning of June 27th was clear and sunny, with the fresh warmth of a full-summer day; the flowers were blossoming profusely and the grass was richly green. The people of the village began to gather in the square, between the post office and the bank, around ten o'clock; in some towns there were so many people that the lottery took two days and had to be started on June 26th, but in this village, where there were only about three hundred people, the whole lottery took less than two hours, so it could begin at ten o'clock in the morning and still be through in time to allow the villagers to get home for noon dinner.

The children assembled first, of course. School was recently over for the summer, and the feeling of liberty sat uneasily on most of them; they tended to gather together quietly for a while before they broke into boisterous play, and their talk was still of the classroom and the teacher, of books and reprimands. Bobby Martin had already stuffed his pockets full of stones, and the other boys soon followed his example, selecting the smoothest and roundest stones; Bobby and Harry Jones and Dickie Delacroix—the villagers pronounced this name "Dellacroy"—eventually made a great pile of stones in one corner of the square and guarded it against the raids of the other boys. The girls stood aside, talking among themselves, looking over their shoulders at the boys, and the very small children rolled in the dust or clung to the hands of their older brothers or sisters.

Soon the men began to gather, surveying their own children, speaking of planting and rain, tractors and taxes. They stood together, away from the pile of stones in the corner, and their jokes were quiet and they smiled rather than laughed. The women, wearing faded house dresses and sweaters, came shortly after their menfolk. They greeted one another and exchanged bits of gossip as they went to join their husbands. Soon the women, standing by their husbands, began to call to their children, and the children came reluctantly, having to be called four or five times. Bobby Martin ducked under his mother's grasping hand and ran, laughing, back to the pile of stones. His father spoke up sharply, and Bobby came quickly and took his place between his father and his oldest brother.

The lottery was conducted—as were the square dances, the teen-age club, the Halloween program—by Mr. Summers, who had time and energy to devote to civic activities. He was a round-faced, jovial man and he ran the coal business, and people were sorry for him, because he had no children and his wife was a scold. When he arrived in the square, carrying the black wooden box, there was a murmur of conversation among the villagers, and he waved and called, "Little late today, folks." The postmaster, Mr. Graves, followed him, carrying a three-legged stool, and the stool was put in the center of the square and Mr. Summers set the black box down on it. The villagers kept their distance, leaving a space between them-selves and the stool, and when Mr. Summers said, "Some of you fellows want to give me a hand?" there was a hesitation before two men, Mr. Martin and his oldest son, Baxter, came forward to hold the box steady on the stool while Mr. Summers stirred up the papers inside it.

The original paraphernalia for the lottery had been lost long ago, and the black box now resting on the stool had been put into use even before Old Man Warner, the oldest man in town, was born. Mr. Summers spoke frequently to the villagers about making a new box, but no one liked to upset even as much tradition as was represented by the black box. There was a story that the present box had been made with some pieces of the box that had preceded it, the one that had been constructed when the first people settled down to make a village here. Every year, after the lottery, Mr. Summers began talking again about a new box, but every year the subject was allowed to fade off without anything's being done. The black box grew shabbier each year; by now it was no longer completely black but splintered badly along one side to show the original wood color, and in some places faded or stained.

Mr. Martin and his oldest son, Baxter, held the black box securely on the stool until Mr. Summers had stirred the papers thoroughly with his hand. Because so much of the ritual had been forgotten or discarded, Mr. Summers had been successful in having slips of paper substituted for the chips of wood that had been used for generations. Chips of wood, Mr. Summers had argued, had been all very well when the village was tiny, but now that the population was more than three hundred and likely to keep on growing, it was necessary to use something that would fit more easily into the black box. The night before the lottery, Mr. Summers and Mr. Graves made up the slips of paper and put them in the box, and it was then taken to the safe of Mr. Summers' coal company and locked up until Mr. Summers was ready to take it to the square next morning. The rest of the year, the box was put away, sometimes one place, sometimes another; it had spent one year in Mr. Graves's barn and another year underfoot in the post office, and sometimes it was set on a shelf in the Martin grocery and left there.

There was a great deal of fussing to be done before Mr. Summers declared the lottery open. There were the lists to make up—of heads of families, heads of households in each family, members of each household in each family. There was the proper swearing-in of Mr. Summers by the postmaster, as the official of the lottery; at one time, some people remembered, there had been a recital of some sort, performed by the official of the lottery, a perfunctory, tuneless chant that had been rattled off duly each year; some people believed that the official of the lottery used to stand just so when he said or sang it, others believed that he was supposed to walk among the people, but years and years ago this part of the ritual had been allowed to lapse. There had been, also, a ritual salute, which the official of the lottery had had to use in addressing each person who came up to draw from the box, but this also had changed with time, until now it was felt necessary only for the official to speak to each person approaching. Mr. Summers was very good at all this; in his clean white shirt and blue jeans, with one hand resting carelessly on the black box. he seemed very proper and important as he talked interminably to Mr. Graves and the Martins.

Just as Mr. Summers finally left off talking and turned to the assembled villagers, Mrs. Hutchinson came hurriedly along the path to the square, her sweater thrown over her shoulders, and slid into place in the back of the crowd. "Clean forgot what day it was," she said to Mrs. Delacroix, who stood next to her, and they both laughed softly. "Thought my old man was out back stacking wood," Mrs. Hutchinson went on, "and then I looked out the window and the kids were gone, and then I remembered it was the twenty-seventh and came a-running." She dried her hands on her apron, and Mrs. Delacroix said, "You're in time, though. They're still talking away up there."

Mrs. Hutchinson craned her neck to see through the crowd and found her husband and children standing near the front. She tapped Mrs. Delacroix on the arm as a farewell and began to make her way through the crowd. The people separated good-humoredly to let her through; two or three people said, in voices just loud enough to be heard across the crowd, "Here comes your Missus, Hutchinson," and "Bill, she made it after all." Mrs. Hutchinson reached her husband, and Mr. Summers, who had been waiting, said cheerfully, "Thought we were going to have to get on without you, Tessie." Mrs. Hutchinson said, grinning, "Wouldn't have me leave m'dishes in the sink, now, would you, Joe?" and soft laughter ran through the crowd as the people stirred back into position after Mrs. Hutchinson's arrival.

"Well, now," Mr. Summers said soberly, "guess we better get started, get this over with, so's we can go back to work. Anybody ain't here?"

"Dunbar," several people said. "Dunbar, Dunbar."

Mr. Summers consulted his list. "Clyde Dunbar," he said. "That's right. He's broke his leg, hasn't he? Who's drawing for him?"

"Me, I guess," a woman said, and Mr. Summers turned to look at her. "Wife draws for her husband," Mrs. Summers said. "Don't you have a grown boy to do it for you, Janey?" Although Mr. Summers and everyone else in the village knew the answer perfectly well, it was the business of the official of the lottery to ask such questions formally. Mr. Summers waited with an expression of polite interest while Mrs. Dunbar answered.

"Horace's not but sixteen yet," Mrs. Dunbar said regretfully. "Guess I gotta fill in for the old man this year."

"Right," Mr. Summers said. He made a note on the list he was holding. Then he asked, "Watson boy drawing this year?"

A tall boy in the crowd raised his hand. "Here," he said. "I'm drawing for m'mother and me." He blinked his eyes nervously and ducked his head as several voices in the crowd said things like "Good fellow, Jack," and "Glad to see your mother's got a man to do it."

"Well," Mr. Summers said, "guess that's everyone. Old Man Warner make it?"

"Here," a voice said, and Mr. Summers nodded.

A sudden hush fell on the crowd as Mr. Summers cleared his throat and looked at the list. "All ready?" he called. "Now, I'll read the names—heads of families first—and the men come up and take a paper out of the box. Keep the paper folded in your hand without looking at it until everyone has had a turn. Everything clear?"

The people had done it so many times that they only half listened to the directions; most of them were quiet, wetting their lips, not looking around. Then Mr. Summers raised one hand high and said, "Adams." A man disengaged himself from the crowd and came forward. "Hi, Steve," Mr. Summers said, and Mr. Adams said, "Hi, Joe." They grinned at one another humorlessly and nervously. Then Mr. Adams reached into the black box and took out a folded paper. He held it firmly by one corner as he turned and went hastily back to his place in the crowd, where he stood a little apart from his family, not looking down at his hand.

"Allen," Mr. Summers said. "Anderson . . . Bentham."

"Seems like there's no time at all between lotteries any more," Mrs. Delacroix said to Mrs. Graves in the back row. "Seems like we got through with the last one only last week."

"Time sure goes fast," Mrs. Graves said.

"Clark . . . Delacroix."

"There goes my old man," Mrs. Delacroix said. She held her breath while her husband went forward.

"Dunbar," Mr. Summers said, and Mrs. Dunbar went steadily to the box while one of the women said, "Go on, Janey," and another said, "There she goes."

"We're next," Mrs. Graves said. She watched while Mr. Graves came around from the side of the box, greeted Mr. Summers gravely, and selected a slip of paper from the box. By now, all through the crowd there were men holding the small folded papers in their large hands, turning them over and over nervously. Mrs. Dunbar and her two sons stood together, Mrs. Dunbar holding the slip of paper.

"Harburt . . . Hutchinson."

"Get up there, Bill," Mrs. Hutchinson said, and the people near her laughed.

"Jones."

"They do say," Mr. Adams said to Old Man Warner, who stood next to him, "that over in the north village they're talking of giving up the lottery."

Old Man Warner snorted. "Pack of crazy fools," he said. "Listening to the young folks, nothing's good enough for *them*. Next thing you know, they'll be wanting to go back to living in caves, nobody work any more, live *that* way for a while. Used to be a saying about 'Lottery in June, corn be heavy soon.' First thing you know, we'd all be eating stewed chickweed and acorns. There's *always* been a lottery," he added petulantly. "Bad enough to see young Joe Summers up there joking with everybody."

"Some places have already quit lotteries," Mrs. Adams said.

"Nothing but trouble in *that*," Old Man Warner said stoutly. "Pack of young fools."

"Martin." And Bobby Martin watched his father go forward. "Overdyke . . . Percy."

"I wish they'd hurry," Mrs. Dunbar said to her older son. "I wish they'd hurry."

"They're almost through," her son said.

"You get ready to run tell Dad," Mrs. Dunbar said.

Mr. Summers called his own name and then stepped forward precisely and selected a slip from the box. Then he called, "Warner."

"Seventy-seventh year I been in the lottery," Old Man Warner said as he went through the crowd. "Seventy-seventh time."

"Watson." The tall boy came awkwardly through the crowd. Someone said, "Don't be nervous, Jack," and Mr. Summers said, "Take your time, son."

"Zanini."

After that, there was a long pause, a breathless pause, until Mr. Summers, holding his slip of paper in the air, said, "All right, fellows." For a minute, no one moved, and then all the slips of paper were opened. Suddenly, all the women began to speak at once, saying, "Who is it?" "Who's got it?" "Is it the Dunbars?" "Is it the Watsons?" Then the voices began to say, "It's Hutchinson. It's Bill," "Bill Hutchinson's got it."

"Go tell your father," Mrs. Dunbar said to her older son.

People began to look around to see the Hutchinsons. Bill Hutchinson was standing quiet, staring down at the paper in his hand. Suddenly, Tessie Hutchinson shouted to Mr. Summers, "You didn't give him time enough to take any paper he wanted. I saw you. It wasn't fair."

"Be a good sport, Tessie," Mrs. Delacroix called, and Mrs. Graves said, "All of us took the same chance."

"Shut up, Tessie," Bill Hutchinson said.

"Well, everyone," Mr. Summers said, "that was done pretty fast, and now we've got to be hurrying a little more to get done in time." He consulted his next list. "Bill," he said, "you draw for the Hutchinson family. You got any other households in the Hutchinsons?"

"There's Don and Eva," Mrs. Hutchinson yelled. "Make *them* take their chance!"

"Daughters draw with their husbands' families, Tessie," Mr. Summers said gently. "You know that as well as anyone else."

"It wasn't *fair*," Tessie said.

"I guess not, Joe," Bill Hutchinson said regretfully. "My daughter draws with her husband's family, that's only fair. And I've got no other family except the kids."

"Then, as far as drawing for families is concerned, it's you," Mr. Summers said in explanation, "and as far as drawing for households is concerned, that's you, too. Right?"

"Right," Bill Hutchinson said.

"How many kids, Bill?" Mr. Summers asked formally.

"Three," Bill Hutchinson said. "There's Bill, Jr., and Nancy, and little Dave. And Tessie and me."

"All right, then," Mr. Summers said. "Harry, you got their tickets back?"

Mr. Graves nodded and held up the slips of paper. "Put them in the box, then," Mr. Summers directed. "Take Bill's and put it in."

"I think we ought to start over," Mrs. Hutchinson said, as quietly as she could. "I tell you it wasn't *fair*. You didn't give him time enough to choose. *Every*body saw that."

Mr. Graves had selected the five slips and put them in the box, and he dropped all the papers but those onto the ground, where the breeze caught them and lifted them off.

"Listen, everybody," Mrs. Hutchinson was saying to the people around her.

"Ready, Bill?" Mr. Summers asked, and Bill Hutchinson, with one quick glance around at his wife and children, nodded.

"Remember," Mr. Summers said, "take the slips and keep them folded until each person has taken one. Harry, you help little Dave." Mr. Graves took the hand of the little boy, who came willingly with him up to the box. "Take a paper out of the box, Davy," Mr. Summers said. Davy put his hand into the box and laughed. "Take just *one* paper," Mr. Summers said. "Harry, you hold it for him." Mr. Graves took the child's hand and removed the folded paper from the tight fist and held it while little Dave stood next to him and looked up at him wonderingly.

"Nancy next," Mr. Summers said. Nancy was twelve, and her school friends breathed heavily as she went forward, switching her skirt, and took a slip daintily from the box. "Bill, Jr.," Mr. Summers said, and Billy, his face red and his feet over-large, nearly knocked the box over as he got a paper out. "Tessie," Mr. Summers said. She hesitated for a minute, looking around defiantly, and then set her lips and went up to the box. She snatched a paper out and held it behind her.

"Bill," Mr. Summers said, and Bill Hutchinson reached into the box and felt around, bringing his hand out at last with the slip of paper in it.

The crowd was quiet. A girl whispered, "I hope it's not Nancy," and the sound of the whisper reached the edges of the crowd.

"It's not the way it used to be," Old Man Warner said clearly. "People ain't the way they used to be."

"All right," Mr. Summers said. "Open the papers. Harry, you open little Dave's."

Mr. Graves opened the slip of paper and there was a general sigh through the crowd as he held it up and everyone could see that it was blank. Nancy and Bill, Jr., opened theirs at the same time, and both beamed and laughed, turning around to the crowd and holding their slips of paper above their heads.

"Tessie," Mr. Summers said. There was a pause, and then Mr. Summers looked at Bill Hutchinson, and Bill unfolded his paper and showed it. It was blank.

"It's Tessie," Mr. Summers said, and his voice was hushed. "Show us her paper, Bill."

Bill Hutchinson went over to his wife and forced the slip of paper out of her hand. It had a black spot on it, the black spot Mr. Summers had made the night before with the heavy pencil in the coal-company office. Bill Hutchinson held it up, and there was a stir in the crowd.

"All right, folks," Mr. Summers said. "Let's finish quickly."

Although the villagers had forgotten the ritual and lost the original black box, they still remembered to use stones. The pile of stones the boys had made earlier was ready; there were stones on the ground with the blowing scraps of paper that had come out of the box. Mrs. Delacroix selected a stone so large she had to pick it up with both hands and turned to Mrs. Dunbar. "Come on," she said. "Hurry up."

Mrs. Dunbar had small stones in both hands, and she said, gasping for breath, "I can't run at all. You'll have to go ahead and I'll catch up with you."

The children had stones already, and someone gave little Davy Hutchinson a few pebbles.

Tessie Hutchinson was in the center of a cleared space by now, and she held her hands out desperately as the villagers moved in on her. "It isn't fair," she said. A stone hit her on the side of the head.

Old Man Warner was saying, "Come on, come on, everyone." Steve Adams was in the front of the crowd of villagers, with Mrs. Graves beside him.

"It isn't fair, it isn't right," Mrs. Hutchinson screamed, and then they were upon her.

"If Not Higher" concentrates on action: the rabbi's mysterious Friday morning activities, the Litvak's detective work. Characterization is less important. The rabbi, the Litvak, and the sick woman are types rather than fully characterized individuals; and, except for the Litvak's conversion (about which we are told very little) they do not change or develop during the story.

"The Lottery," too, centers on action and mystery almost to the exclusion of individual characterization. Of all the townspeople, Old Man Warner alone stands out as a distinguishable figure. Even he is a type: the "Old Man," fiercely proud of his past, dismissing as "young fools" all those who would change things. The rest are simply members of a small farming community, so like each other that one description often serves for all. Thus, "the children came reluctantly, having to be called four or five times," and "the people . . . only half listened to the directions; most of them were quiet, wetting their lips, not looking around." These descriptions, moreover, center on observable facts: the number of times the children have to be called, the posture and nervous motions of the villagers. We were given some inside knowledge of the Litvak's sensations, being told that "a great fear took hold of him," that he "hears the sound of his heartbeats mingling with the sound of the rabbi's heavy steps." We are told almost nothing about the villagers' thoughts and emotions that any reporter at the scene of the lottery could not have told us.

The narrator can tell us facts about the lottery, however, which only a very well informed reporter could supply. She can inform us that "the original paraphernalia for the lottery had been lost long ago," that the current black box (which "had been put into use even before Old Man Warner, the oldest man in the town, was born") is still used because "no one liked to upset even as much tradition as was represented by the black box." She knows what parts of the ritual have been lost and what parts are imperfectly remembered; and from time to time, she doles out some bit of this information as background to the unfolding ritual.

Does the narrator also know why the lottery was originally instituted, or what this group of villagers, who have lost so much of its history, think it accomplishes? If she does, she doesn't tell us. The narrator of "If Not Higher" made a great mystery of the rabbi's whereabouts by insisting that they were a great mystery and by depicting all the townspeople as being in a state of wonder and suspense. The narrator of "The Lottery" creates suspense by describing in a calm, matter-of-fact way the matter-of-fact behavior of a group of undemonstrative people. The people are engaged in some poorly defined event that seems to represent a mildly exciting once-a-year break in their normal routine. Therefore, our suspense comes largely from the fact that we feel ourselves to be the only people who don't know what's going on. (Until Tessie Hutchinson first cries "It wasn't fair," for instance, we don't even know whether the "winner" of this lottery is lucky or unlucky.) And so we keep waiting for the explanation, which never comes.

We are given some clues as to what's going on; but the author slips them in so quietly that we may not realize that they are clues until we read the story a second time. The "pile of stones," for instance, is introduced as though it were merely part of the children's "boisterous play": "Bobby and Harry Jones and Dickie Delacroix . . . eventually made a great pile of stones in one corner of the square and guarded it against the raids of the other boys." Not until the very end of the story do we find out the significance of those stones: "Although the villagers had forgotten the ritual and lost the original black box, they still remembered to use stones." But we still are not told what meaning—if any—the townsfolk find in their use.

We are not even told directly that Tessie is killed. We have to fill in that fact for ourselves, an act of participation which for some readers adds a last gruesome twist to the end of the story. Tessie's protests have warned us that the lottery ends badly for the chosen one. But many readers still have trouble at first realizing just how badly it does end, especially since the narrator's calm, reportorial voice never changes its tone, reporting as objectively as ever the women's conversation and the fact that "someone gave little Davy Hutchinson a few pebbles." The almost casual acceptance by villagers and narrator alike of the stoning to death of a woman by her neighbors and family throws the full burden of reaction on us, while the "just plain folks" characterization of the villagers forces us to interpret the action in the broadest possible terms, asking not only, "Can these villagers really be doing this?" but also "Do people really act this way?"

All the unanswered questions rise at this point. Why are these people doing this thing? How do they justify it to themselves? All the action in "If Not Higher" was slightly unrealistic (one man hiding under a bed, another disguising himself), so the not-quite-realistic ending came as no shock. But the style of "The Lottery" has been unrelentingly realistic throughout, and its ending is a deliberate shock. All along we've been feeling, "Yes, a group of neighbors would behave as this group behaves. What a careful observer this writer is; what a fine eye for details of behavior she has." Now we want to say, "No; she's mistaken; they wouldn't do that." But the acceptance we've given the story so far, linked with our own knowledge of the ways people do behave toward each other, makes our rebellion all but impossible. We can dismiss the actual details; ritual stonings rarely occur in the twentieth century. But we cannot dismiss the symbolic import of the action, nor escape the grim vision of human nature that "The Lottery"'s action and narrator thrust upon us. Good humor and neighborliness are part of that vision; but what else is there? How would you personally interpret "The Lottery?"

QUESTIONS FOR FURTHER THOUGHT

When we study literature, we first look at each story as an entity in itself, existing on its own terms. We enter the world of the story and speak of its characters and narrator as though they were living people. Eventually, however, we begin to wonder about the writers of the stories. Why did they choose to create these characters, to have them perform these actions, to tell their tales from this particular point of view?

We can never know exactly what writers had in mind when they were writing their stories. The process of writing is too complex, with too much of it hidden even from the writers themselves, to allow any sure or simple answers to that question. But we should examine our own ideas on the subject—our sense of what the writers seem to consider important and what values or feelings of ours they seem to be invoking; for our impression of the writers' values and intentions plays an important part in our response to their work.

If we look back at "The Lottery" and "If Not Higher," for instance, we notice that these stories project nearly opposite views of their characters. To define the contrast, we can ask such questions as, "What things seem most important to the characters in each story? What mood are we in at the end of the story?" Judging from this opposition, we can then ask what aspects of human life each author seems to consider important. We can ask, "To what feelings of mine does each story appeal? To what values?" And we can then try to decide whether our sense of our own values and feelings, and of the authors', are as sharply opposed as our sense of the characters' values, or whether our sense of the authors' views and of the appeals which their tales make to us, do in fact share some common elements.

2 *The Omniscient Narrator*

"If Not Higher" and "The Lottery" are tales related by omniscient narrators. As the term implies, these narrators "know all" about the characters and events of which they tell. Somewhat distanced by their greater knowledge from action and actors alike, omniscient narrators project an air of authority over their material.

Their relation to the readers is a more variable matter. Peretz's narrator treats us familiarly, sharing occasional asides with us ("You know the Litvaks") or letting us into his characters' secrets. Jackson's narrator keeps us at the same distance that she keeps her material. (This type of narrator, who takes no sides, makes no interpretations, and lets us watch only the characters' public actions, rather than letting us into their private thoughts and feelings, is sometimes called an *objective narrator*, with the term *omniscient narrator* being reserved for those who do relate their characters' thoughts or interpret their actions for us.)

Here are two more stories told by omniscient narrators. Read them through and read the questions which follow them. Then read them again with the questions in mind, seeing how the narrators' voices help shape your view of the stories' action and characters.

NATHANIEL HAWTHORNE (1804–1864)

Young Goodman Brown

Young Goodman Brown came forth at sunset, into the street of Salem village, but put his head back, after crossing the threshold, to exchange a parting kiss with his young wife. And Faith, as the wife was aptly named, thrust her own pretty head into the street, letting the wind play with the pink ribbons of her cap, while she called to Goodman Brown.

"Dearest heart," whispered she, softly and rather sadly, when her lips were close to his ear, "prithee, put off your journey until sunrise, and sleep in your own bed to-night. A lone woman is troubled with such dreams and such thoughts, that she's afeard of herself, sometimes. Pray, tarry with me this night, dear husband, of all nights in the year!"

"My love and my Faith," replied young Goodman Brown, "of all nights in the year, this one night must I tarry away from thee. My journey, as thou callest it, forth and back again, must needs be done 'twixt now and sunrise. What, my sweet, pretty wife, dost thou doubt me already, and we but three months married!"

"Then God bless you!" said Faith with the pink ribbons, "and may you find all well, when you come back."

"Amen!" cried Goodman Brown. "Say thy prayers, dear Faith, and go to bed at dusk, and no harm will come to thee."

So they parted; and the young man pursued his way, until, being about to turn the corner by the meeting-house, he looked back and saw the head of Faith still peeping after him, with a melancholy air, in spite of her pink ribbons.

"Poor little Faith!" thought he, for his heart smote him. "What a wretch am I, to leave her on such an errand! She talks of dreams, too. Methought, as she spoke, there was trouble in her face, as if a dream had warned her what work is to be done to-night. But no, no! 't would kill her to think it. Well; she's a blessed angel on earth; and after this one night, I'll cling to her skirts and follow her to Heaven."

With this excellent resolve for the future, Goodman Brown felt himself justified in making more haste on his present evil purpose. He had taken a dreary road, darkened by all the gloomiest trees of the forest, which barely stood aside to let the narrow path creep through, and closed immediately behind. It was all as lonely as could be; and there is this peculiarity in such a solitude, that the traveller knows not who may be concealed by the innumerable trunks and the thick boughs overhead; so that, with lonely footsteps, he may yet be passing through an unseen multitude.

"There may be a devilish Indian behind every tree," said Goodman Brown to himself; and he glanced fearfully behind him, as he added, "What if the devil himself should be at my very elbow!"

His head being turned back, he passed a crook of the road, and looking forward again, beheld the figure of a man, in grave and decent attire, seated at the foot of an old tree. He arose at Goodman Brown's approach, and walked onward, side by side with him.

"You are late, Goodman Brown," said he. "The clock of the Old South was striking, as I came through Boston; and that is full fifteen minutes agone."

"Faith kept me back awhile," replied the young man, with a tremor in his voice, caused by the sudden appearance of his companion, though not wholly unexpected.

It was now deep dusk in the forest, and deepest in that part of it where these two were journeying. As nearly as could be discerned, the second traveller was about fifty years old, apparently in the same rank of life as Goodman Brown, and bearing a considerable resemblance to him, though perhaps more in expression than features. Still, they might have been taken for father and son. And yet, though the elder person was as simply clad as the younger, and as simple in manner too, he had an indescribable air of one who knew the world, and would not have felt abashed at the governor's dinner-table, or in King William's court, were it possible that his affairs should call him thither. But the only thing about him that could be fixed upon as remarkable, was his staff, which bore the likeness of a great black snake, so curiously wrought, that it might almost be seen to twist and wriggle itself like a living serpent. This, of course, must have been an ocular deception, assisted by the uncertain light.

"Come, Goodman Brown!" cried his fellow-traveller, "this is a dull pace for the beginning of a journey. Take my staff, if you are so soon weary."

"Friend," said the other, exchanging his slow pace for a full stop, "having kept covenant by meeting thee here, it is my purpose now to return whence I came. I have scruples, touching the matter thou wot'st of."

"Sayest thou so?" replied he of the serpent, smiling apart. "Let us walk on, nevertheless, reasoning as we go, and if I convince thee not, thou shalt turn back. We are but a little way in the forest, yet."

"Too far, too far!" exclaimed the goodman, unconsciously resuming his walk. "My father never went into the woods on such an errand, nor his father before him. We have been a race of honest men and good Christians, since the days of the martyrs. And shall I be the first of the name of Brown that ever took this path and kept—"

"Such company, thou wouldst say," observed the elder person, interrupting his pause. "Well said, Goodman Brown! I have been as well acquainted with your family as with ever a one among the Puritans; and that's no trifle to say. I helped your grandfather, the constable, when he lashed the Quaker woman so smartly through the streets of Salem. And it was I that brought your father a pitch-pine knot, kindled at my own hearth, to set fire to an Indian village, in King Philip's war. They were my good friends, both; and many a pleasant walk have we had along this path, and returned merrily after midnight. I would fain be friends with you, for their sake."

"If it be as thou sayest," replied Goodman Brown, "I marvel they never spoke of these matters. Or, verily, I marvel not, seeing that the least rumor of the sort would have driven them from New England. We are a people of prayer, and good works to boot, and abide no such wickedness."

"Wickedness or not," said the traveller with twisted staff, "I have a very general acquaintance here in New England. The deacons of many a church have drunk the communion wine with me; the selectmen, of divers towns, make me their chairman; and a majority of the Great and General Court are firm supporters of my interest. The governor and I, too—but these are state secrets."

"Can this be so!" cried Goodman Brown, with a stare of amazement at his undisturbed companion. "Howbeit, I have nothing to do with the governor and council; they have their own ways, and are no rule for a simple husbandman like me. But, were I to go on with thee, how should I meet the eye of that good old man, our minister, at Salem village? Oh, his voice would make me tremble, both Sabbath-day and lecture-day!"

Thus far, the elder traveller had listened with due gravity, but now burst into a fit of irrepressible mirth, shaking himself so violently, that his snakelike staff actually seemed to wriggle in sympathy.

"Ha! ha! ha!" shouted he, again and again; then composing himself, "Well, go on, Goodman Brown, go on; but, prithee, don't kill me with laughing!"

"Well, then, to end the matter at once," said Goodman Brown, considerably nettled, "there is my wife, Faith. It would break her dear little heart; and I'd rather break my own!"

"Nay, if that be the case," answered the other, "e'en go thy ways, Goodman Brown. I would not, for twenty old women like the one hobbling before us, that Faith should come to any harm."

As he spoke, he pointed his staff at a female figure on the path, in whom Goodman Brown recognized a very pious and exemplary dame, who had taught him his catechism in youth, and was still his moral and spiritual adviser, jointly with the minister and Deacon Gookin.

"A marvel, truly, that Goody Cloyse should be so far in the

wilderness, at nightfall!" said he. "But, with your leave, friend, I shall take a cut through the woods, until we have left this Christian woman behind. Being a stranger to you, she might ask whom I was consorting with, and whither I was going."

"Be it so," said his fellow-traveller. "Betake you to the woods, and let me keep the path."

Accordingly, the young man turned aside, but took care to watch his companion, who advanced softly along the road, until he had come within a staff's length of the old dame. She, meanwhile, was making the best of her way, with singular speed for so aged a woman, and mumbling some indistinct words, a prayer, doubtless, as she went. The traveller put forth his staff, and touched her withered neck with what seemed the serpent's tail.

"The devil!" screamed the pious old lady.

"Then Goody Cloyse knows her old friend?" observed the traveller, confronting her, and leaning on his writhing stick.

"Ah, forsooth, and is it your worship, indeed?" cried the good dame. "Yea, truly is it, and in the very image of my old gossip, Goodman Brown, the grandfather of the silly fellow that now is. But, would your worship believe it? my broomstick hath strangely disappeared, stolen, as I suspect, by that unhanged witch, Goody Cory, and that, too, when I was all anointed with the juice of smallage and cinque-foil and wolf's-bane—"

"Mingled with fine wheat and the fat of a new-born babe," said the shape of old Goodman Brown.

"Ah, your worship knows the recipe," cried the old lady, cackling aloud. "So, as I was saying, being all ready for the meeting, and no horse to ride on, I made up my mind to foot it; for they tell me there is a nice young man to be taken into communion to-night. But now your good worship will lend me your arm, and we shall be there in a twinkling."

"That can hardly be," answered her friend. "I may not spare you my arm, Goody Cloyse, but here is my staff, if you will."

So saying, he threw it down at her feet, where, perhaps, it assumed life, being one of the rods which its owner had formerly lent to the Egyptian Magi. Of this fact, however, Goodman Brown could not take cognizance. He had cast up his eyes in astonishment, and looking down again, beheld neither Goody Cloyse nor the serpentine staff, but his fellow-traveller alone, who waited for him as calmly as if nothing had happened.

"That old woman taught me my catechism!" said the young man; and there was a world of meaning in this simple comment.

They continued to walk onward, while the elder traveller exhorted his companion to make good speed and persevere in the path, discoursing so aptly, that his arguments seemed rather to spring up in the bosom of his auditor, than to be suggested by himself. As they went he plucked a branch of maple, to serve for a walking-stick, and began to strip it of the twigs and little boughs, which were wet with evening dew. The moment his fingers touched them, they became strangely withered and dried up, as with a week's sunshine. Thus the pair proceeded, at a good free pace, until suddenly, in a gloomy hollow of the road, Goodman Brown sat himself down on the stump of a tree, and refused to go any farther.

"Friend," said he, stubbornly, "my mind is made up. Not another step will I budge on this errand. What if a wretched old woman do choose to go to the devil, when I thought she was going to Heaven! Is that any reason why I should quit my dear Faith, and go after her?"

"You will think better of this by and by," said his acquaintance, composedly. "Sit here and rest yourself awhile; and when you feel like moving again, there is my staff to help you along."

Without more words, he threw his companion the maple stick, and was as speedily out of sight as if he had vanished into the deepening gloom. The young man sat a few moments by the roadside, applauding himself greatly, and thinking with how clear a conscience he should meet the minister, in his morning walk, nor shrink from the eye of good old Deacon Gookin. And what calm sleep would be his, that very night, which was to have been spent so wickedly, but purely and sweetly now, in the arms of Faith! Amidst these pleasant and praiseworthy meditations, Goodman Brown heard the tramp of horses along the road, and deemed it advisable to conceal himself within the verge of the forest, conscious of the guilty purpose that had brought him thither, though now so happily turned from it.

On came the hoof-tramps and the voices of the riders, two grave old voices, conversing soberly as they drew near. These mingled sounds appeared to pass along the road, within a few yards of the young man's hiding-place; but owing, doubtless, to the depth of the gloom, at that particular spot, neither the travellers nor their steeds were visible. Though their figures brushed the small boughs by the wayside, it could not be seen that they intercepted, even for a moment, the faint gleam from the strip of bright sky, athwart which they must have passed. Goodman Brown alternately crouched and stood on tiptoe, pulling aside the branches, and thrusting forth his head as far as he durst, without discerning so much as a shadow. It vexed him the more, because he could have sworn, were such a thing possible, that he recognized the voices of the minister and Deacon Gookin, jogging along quietly, as they were wont to do, when bound to some ordination or ecclesiastical council. While yet within hearing, one of the riders stopped to pluck a switch.

"Of the two, reverend Sir," said the voice like the deacon's, "I had rather miss an ordination dinner than to-night's meeting. They tell me that some of our community are to be here from Falmouth and beyond, and others from Connecticut and Rhode Island; besides several of the Indian powwows, who, after their fashion, know almost as much deviltry as the best of us. Moreover, there is a goodly young woman to be taken into communion."

"Mighty well, Deacon Gookin!" replied the solemn old tones of the minister. "Spur up, or we shall be late. Nothing can be done, you know, until I get on the ground."

The hoofs clattered again, and the voices, talking so strangely in the empty air, passed on through the forest, where no church had ever been gathered, nor solitary Christian prayed. Whither, then, could these holy men be journeying, so deep into the heathen wilderness? Young Goodman Brown caught hold of a tree, for support, being ready to sink down on the ground, faint and over-burthened with the heavy sickness of his heart. He looked up to the sky, doubting whether there really was a Heaven above him. Yet, there was the blue arch, and the stars brightening in it.

"With Heaven above, and Faith below, I will yet stand firm against the devil!" cried Goodman Brown.

While he still gazed upward, into the deep arch of the firmament, and had lifted his hands to pray, a cloud, though no wind was stirring, hurried across the zenith, and hid the brightening stars. The blue sky was still visible, except directly overhead, where this black mass of cloud was sweeping swiftly northward. Aloft in the air, as if from the depths of the cloud, came a confused and doubtful sound of voices. Once, the listener fancied that he could distinguish the accents of town's-people of his own, men and women, both pious and ungodly, many of whom he had met at the communion-table, and had seen others rioting at the tavern. The next moment, so indistinct were the sounds, he doubted whether he had heard aught but the murmur of the old forest, whispering without a wind. Then came a stronger swell of those familiar tones, heard daily in the sunshine, at Salem village, but never, until now, from a cloud at night. There was one voice, of a young woman, uttering lamentations, yet with an uncertain sorrow, and entreating for some favor, which, perhaps, it would grieve her to obtain. And all the unseen multitude, both saints and sinners, seemed to encourage her onward.

"Faith!" shouted Goodman Brown, in a voice of agony and desperation; and the echoes of the forest mocked him, crying—"Faith! Faith!" as if bewildered wretches were seeking her, all through the wilderness.

The cry of grief, rage, and terror was yet piercing the night, when the unhappy husband held his breath for a response. There was a scream, drowned immediately in a louder murmur of voices fading into far-off laughter, as the dark cloud swept away, leaving the clear and silent sky above Goodman Brown. But something fluttered lightly down· through the air, and caught on the branch of a tree. The young man seized it and beheld a pink ribbon.

"My Faith is gone!" cried he, after one stupefied moment. "There is no good on earth, and sin is but a name. Come, devil! for to thee is this world given."

And maddened with despair, so that he laughed loud and long, did Goodman Brown grasp his staff and set forth again, at such a rate, that he seemed to fly along the forest path, rather than to walk or run. The road grew wilder and drearier, and more faintly traced, and vanished at length, leaving him in the heart of the dark wilderness, still rushing onward, with the instinct that guides mortal man to evil. The whole forest was peopled with frightful sounds; the creaking of the trees, the howling of wild beasts, and the yell of Indians; while, sometimes, the wind tolled like a distant church bell, and sometimes gave a broad roar around the traveller, as if all Nature were laughing him to scorn. But he was himself the chief horror of the scene, and shrank not from its other horrors.

"Ha! ha! ha!" roared Goodman Brown, when the wind laughed at him. "Let us hear which will laugh loudest! Think not to frighten me with your deviltry! Come witch, come wizard, come Indian powwow, come devil himself! and here comes Goodman Brown. You may as well fear him as he fear you!"

In truth, all through the haunted forest, there could be nothing more frightful than the figure of Goodman Brown. On he flew, among the black pines, brandishing his staff with frenzied gestures, now giving vent to an inspiration of horrid blasphemy, and now shouting forth such laughter, as set all the echoes of the forest laughing like demons around him. The fiend in his own shape is less hideous, than when he rages in the breast of man. Thus sped the demoniac on his course, until, quivering among the trees, he saw a red light before him, as when the felled trunks and branches of a clearing have been set on fire, and throw up their lurid blaze against the sky, at the hour of midnight. He paused, in a lull of the tempest that had driven him onward, and heard the swell of what seemed a hymn, rolling solemnly from a distance, with the weight of many voices. He knew the tune. It was a familiar one in the choir of the village meeting-house. The verse died heavily away, and was lengthened by a chorus, not of human voices, but of all the sounds of the benighted wilderness, pealing in awful harmony together. Goodman Brown cried out; and his cry was lost to his own ear, by its unison with the cry of the desert.

In the interval of silence, he stole forward, until the light glared full upon his eyes. At one extremity of an open space, hemmed in by the dark wall of the forest, arose a rock, bearing some rude, natural resemblance either to an altar or a pulpit, and surrounded by four blazing pines, their tops aflame, their stems untouched, like candles at an evening meeting. The mass of foliage, that had overgrown the summit of the rock, was all on fire, blazing high into the night, and fitfully illuminating the whole field. Each pendent twig and leafy festoon was in a blaze. As the red light arose and fell, a numerous congregation alternately shone forth, then disappeared in shadow, and again grew, as it were, out of the darkness, peopling the heart of the solitary woods at once.

"A grave and dark-clad company!" quoth Goodman Brown.

In truth, they were such. Among them, quivering to-and-fro, between gloom and splendor, appeared faces that would be seen, next day, at the council-board of the province, and others which, Sabbath after Sabbath, looked devoutly heavenward, and benignantly over the crowded pews, from the holiest pulpits in the land. Some affirm that the lady of the governor was there. At least, there were high dames well known to her, and wives of honored husbands, and widows a great multitude, and ancient maidens, all of excellent repute, and fair young girls, who trembled lest their mothers should espy them. Either the sudden gleams of light, flashing over the obscure field, bedazzled Goodman Brown, or he recognized a score of the church members of Salem village, famous for their especial sanctity. Good old Deacon Gookin had arrived, and waited at the skirts of that venerable saint, his reverend pastor. But, irreverently consorting with these grave, reputable, and pious people, these elders of the church, these chaste dames and dewy virgins, there were men of dissolute lives and women of spotted fame, wretches given over to all mean and filthy vice, and suspected even of horrid crimes. It was strange to see, that the good shrank not from the wicked, nor were the sinners abashed by the saints. Scattered, also, among their pale-faced enemies, were the Indian priests, or powwows, who had often scared their native forest with more hideous incantations than any known to English witchcraft.

"But, where is Faith?" thought Goodman Brown; and, as hope came into his heart, he trembled.

Another verse of the hymn arose, a slow and mournful strain, such as the pious love, but joined to words which expressed all that our nature can conceive of sin, and darkly hinted at far more. Unfathomable to mere mortals is the lore of fiends. Verse after verse was sung, and still the chorus of the desert swelled between, like the deepest tone of a mighty organ. And, with the final peal of that dreadful anthem, there came a sound, as if the roaring wind, the rushing streams, the howling beasts, and every other voice of the unconverted wilderness were mingling and according with the voice of guilty man, in homage to the prince of all. The four blazing pines threw up a loftier flame, and obscurely discovered shapes and visages of horror on the smoke-wreaths, above the impious assembly. At the same moment, the fire on the rock shot redly forth, and formed a glowing arch above its base, where now appeared a figure. With reverence be it spoken, the apparition bore no slight similitude, both in garb and manner, to some grave divine of the New England churches.

"Bring forth the converts!" cried a voice, that echoed through the field and rolled into the forest.

At the word, Goodman Brown stepped forth from the shadow of the trees, and approached the congregation, with whom he felt a loathful brotherhood, by the sympathy of all that was wicked in his heart. He could have well-nigh sworn, that the shape of his own dead father beckoned him to advance, looking downward from a smoke-wreath, while a woman, with dim features of despair, threw out her hand to warn him back. Was it his mother? But he had no power to retreat one step, nor to resist, even in thought, when the minister and good old Deacon Gookin seized his arms, and led him to the blazing rock. Thither came also the slender form of a veiled female, led between Goody Cloyse, that pious teacher of the catechism, and Martha Carrier, who had received the devil's promise to be queen of hell. A rampant hag was she! And there stood the proselytes, beneath the canopy of fire.

"Welcome, my children," said the dark figure, "to the communion of your race! Ye have found, thus young, your nature and your destiny. My children, look behind you!"

They turned; and flashing forth, as it were, in a sheet of flame, the fiend-worshippers were seen; the smile of welcome gleamed darkly on every visage.

"There," resumed the sable form, "are all whom ye have reverenced from youth. Ye deemed them holier than yourselves, and shrank from your own sin, contrasting it with their lives of righteousness and prayerful aspirations heavenward. Yet, here are they all, in my worshipping assembly! This night it shall be granted you to know their secret deeds; how hoary-bearded elders of the church have whispered wanton words to the young maids of their households; how many a woman, eager for widow's weeds, has given her husband a drink at bedtime, and let him sleep his last sleep in her bosom; how beardless youths have made haste to inherit their father's wealth; and how fair damsels—blush not, sweet ones!—have dug little graves in the garden, and bidden me, the sole guest, to an infant's funeral. By the sympathy of your human hearts for sin, ye shall scent out all the places—whether in church, bed-chamber, street, field, or forest—where crime has been committed, and shall exult to behold the whole earth one stain of guilt, one mighty blood-spot. Far more than this! It shall be yours to penetrate, in every bosom, the deep mystery of sin, the fountain of all wicked arts, and which inexhaustibly supplies more evil impulses than human power—than my power, at its utmost!—can make manifest in deeds. And now, my children, look upon each other."

They did so; and, by the blaze of the hell-kindled torches, the wretched man beheld his Faith, and the wife her husband, trembling before that unhallowed altar.

"Lo! there ye stand, my children," said the figure, in a deep and solemn tone, almost sad, with its despairing awfulness, as if his once angelic nature could yet mourn for our miserable race. "Depending upon one another's hearts, ye had still hoped that virtue were not all a dream! Now are ye undeceived!—Evil is the nature of mankind. Evil must be your only happiness. Welcome, again, my children, to the communion of your race!"

"Welcome!" repeated the fiend-worshippers, in one cry of despair and triumph.

And there they stood, the only pair, as it seemed, who were yet hesitating on the verge of wickedness, in this dark world. A basin was hollowed, naturally, in the rock. Did it contain water, reddened by the lurid light? or was it blood? or, perchance, a liquid flame? Herein did the Shape of Evil dip his hand, and prepare to lay the mark of baptism upon their foreheads, that they might be partakers of the mystery of sin, more conscious of the secret guilt of others, both in deed and thought, than they could now be of their own. The husband cast one look at his pale wife, and Faith at him. What polluted wretches would the next glance show them to each other, shuddering alike at what they disclosed and what they saw!

"Faith! Faith!" cried the husband. "Look up to Heaven, and resist the Wicked One!"

Whether Faith obeyed, he knew not. Hardly had he spoken, when he found himself amid calm night and solitude, listening to a roar of the wind, which died heavily away through the forest. He staggered against the rock, and felt it chill and damp, while a hanging twig, that had been all on fire, besprinkled his cheek with the coldest dew.

The next morning, young Goodman Brown came slowly into the street of Salem village staring around him like a bewildered man. The good old minister was taking a walk along the grave-yard, to get an appetite for breakfast and meditate his sermon, and bestowed a blessing, as he passed, on Goodman Brown. He shrank from the venerable saint, as if to avoid an anathema. Old Deacon Gookin was at domestic worship, and the holy words of his prayer were heard through the open window. "What God doth the wizard pray to?" quoth Goodman Brown. Goody Cloyse, that excellent old Christian, stood in the early sunshine, at her own lattice, catechising a little girl, who had brought her a pint of morning's milk. Goodman Brown snatched away the child, as from the grasp of the fiend himself. Turning the corner by the meeting-house, he spied the head of Faith, with the pink ribbons, gazing anxiously forth, and bursting into such joy at sight of him that she skipt along the street, and almost kissed her husband before the whole village. But Goodman Brown looked sternly and sadly into her face, and passed on without a greeting.

Had Goodman Brown fallen asleep in the forest, and only dreamed a wild dream of a witch-meeting?

Be it so, if you will. But, alas! it was a dream of evil omen for young Goodman Brown. A stern, a sad, a darkly meditative, a distrustful, if not a desperate man did he become, from the night of that fearful dream. On the Sabbath day, when the congregation were singing a holy psalm, he could not listen, because an anthem of sin rushed loudly upon his ear, and drowned all the blessed strain. When the minister spoke from the pulpit, with power and fervid eloquence, and with his hand on the open Bible, of the sacred truths of our religion, and of saint-like lives and triumphant deaths, and of future bliss or misery unutterable, then did Goodman Brown turn pale, dreading lest the roof should thunder down upon the gray blasphemer and his hearers. Often, awaking suddenly at midnight, he shrank from the bosom of Faith, and at morning or eventide, when the family knelt down at prayer, he scowled, and muttered to himself, and gazed sternly at his wife, and turned away. And when he had lived long, and was borne to his grave, a hoary corpse, followed by Faith, an aged woman, and children and grandchildren, a goodly procession, besides neighbors not a few, they carved no hopeful verse upon his tombstone; for his dying hour was gloom.

QUESTIONS

1. Though the main action of "Young Goodman Brown" takes place in the woods outside Salem, the story begins and ends inside Salem village. What is gained by organizing the story in this way?

2. In the opening scene, we might particularly notice the introduction of Goodman Brown's wife, Faith. Why does the narrator say she is "aptly named"? How do Faith's talk of her "fears" and Brown's emphasis on the newness of their marriage set the stage for the story that follows?

3. How does the narrator's description of the forest and of Brown's thoughts (pp. 35–36) establish the atmosphere of the story? How would you describe the atmosphere thus created?

4. On pp. 36–40, what sort of argument is going on within Young Goodman Brown, or between him and his companion? What people does he encounter

during this time? What significance do these people have for him? What do you notice about the order in which he meets them?

5. On p. 41, the narrator remarks that "the fiend in his own shape is less hideous, than when he rages in the breast of man." Why does he place this comment at this point in the story? What development of action or characterization does it emphasize?

6. In the scene on pp. 43–44, with what is the fiend tempting Faith and Goodman Brown? What sort of faith is he trying to get them to renounce? With what would he replace it?

7. On p. 45, the narrator enters the story again to raise (and dismiss) the question of whether Brown's experience had been real or only a dream. Why should he raise the question if he does not intend to answer it? What is your reaction to the passage? (Had the notion that Brown's adventures might be a dream already entered your mind? If it had, what clues had put it there?)

8. Another way to read the story, already hinted at by the narrator in the opening scene, is as an **allegory,** a tale which has not only a literal but also a metaphorical meaning. The central figure in an allegory most often represents any or every person, while the action usually presents a struggle between good and evil forces anxious to save or damn the central character. Since the battleground for this struggle is the mind or soul of the disputed character, this type of allegory is called a **psychomachia,** or soul-battle. How would you interpret "Young Goodman Brown" as allegory? If it is a battle, who has won?

9. Is there one reading of the story—either as the tale of an actual happening, as a tale of a dream, or as an allegory—which seems most satisfactory to you? (If so, what reading is it, and why? If not, what is there in the story which keeps you from deciding?) How does the narrator seem to regard the story? How do his attempts to interpret it and the choice of interpretations he forces on you affect your response to the tale?

ALBERT CAMUS (1913–1960)

The Guest

The schoolmaster was watching the two men climb toward him. One was on horseback, the other on foot. They had not yet tackled the abrupt rise leading to the schoolhouse built on the hillside. They were toiling onward, making slow progress in the snow, among the stones, on the vast expanse of the high, deserted plateau. From time to time the horse stumbled. He could not be heard yet but the breath issuing from his nostrils could be seen. The schoolmaster calculated that it would take them a half hour to get onto the hill. It was cold; he went back into the school to get a sweater.

He crossed the empty, frigid classroom. On the blackboard the four rivers of France, drawn with four different colored chalks, had been flowing toward their estuaries for the past three days. Snow had suddenly fallen in mid-October after eight months of drought without the transition of rain, and the twenty pupils, more or less, who lived in the villages scattered over the plateau had stopped coming. With fair weather they would return. Daru now heated only the single room that was his lodging, adjoining the classroom. One of the windows faced, like the classroom windows, the south. On that side the school was a few kilometers from the point where the plateau began to slope toward the south. In clear weather the purple mass of the mountain range where the gap opened onto the desert could be seen.

Somewhat warmed, Daru returned to the window from which he had first noticed the two men. They were no longer visible. Hence they must have tackled the rise. The sky was not so dark, for the snow had stopped falling during the night. The morning had dawned with a dirty light which had scarcely become brighter as the ceiling of clouds lifted. At two in the afternoon it seemed as if the day were merely beginning. But still this was better than those three days when the thick snow was falling amidst unbroken darkness with little gusts of wind that rattled the double door of the classroom. Then Daru had spent long hours in his room, leaving it only to go to the shed and feed the chickens or get some coal. Fortunately the delivery truck from Tadjid, the nearest village to the north, had brought his supplies two days before the blizzard. It would return in forty-eight hours.

Besides, he had enough to resist a siege, for the little room was cluttered with bags of wheat that the administration had left as a supply to distribute to those of his pupils whose families had suffered from the drought. Actually they had all been victims because they were all poor. Every day Daru would distribute a ration to the children. They had missed it, he knew, during these bad days. Possibly one of the fathers or big brothers would come this afternoon and he could supply them with grain. It was just a matter of carrying them over to the next harvest. Now shiploads of wheat were arriving from France and the worst was over. But it would be hard to forget that poverty, that army of ragged ghosts wandering in the sunlight, the plateaus burned to a cinder month after month, the earth shriveled up little by little, literally scorched, every stone bursting into dust under one's foot. The sheep had died then by thousands, and even a few men, here and there, sometimes without anyone's knowing.

In contrast with such poverty, he who lived almost like a monk, in his remote schoolhouse, had felt like a lord with his whitewashed walls, his narrow couch, his unpainted shelves, his well, and his weekly provisioning with water and food. And suddenly this snow, without warning, without the foretaste of rain. This is the way the region was, cruel to live in, even without men, who didn't help matters either. But Daru had been born here. Everywhere else, he felt exiled.

He went out and stepped forward on the terrace in front of the schoolhouse. The two men were now halfway up the slope. He recognized the horseman to be Balducci, the old gendarme he had known for a long time. Balducci was holding at the end of a rope an Arab walking behind him with hands bound and head lowered. The gendarme waved a greeting to which Daru did not reply, lost as he was in contemplation of the Arab dressed in a faded blue *jellaba*, his feet in sandals but covered with socks of heavy raw wool, his head crowned with a narrow, short *chèche*. Balducci was holding back his horse in order not to hurt the Arab, and the group was advancing slowly.

Within earshot, Balducci shouted, "One hour to do the three kilometers from El Ameur!" Daru did not answer. Short and square in his thick sweater, he watched them climb. Not once had the Arab raised his head. "Hello," said Daru when they got up onto the terrace. "Come in and warm up." Balducci painfully got down from his horse without letting go of the rope. He smiled at the schoolmaster from under his bristling mustache. His little dark eyes, deep-set under a tanned forehead, and his mouth surrounded with wrinkles made him look attentive and studious. Daru took the bridle, led the horse to the shed, and came back to the two men who were now waiting for him in the school. He led them into his room. "I am going to heat up the classroom," he said. "We'll be more comfortable there."

When he entered the room again, Balducci was on the couch. He had undone the rope tying him to the Arab, who had squatted near the stove. His hands still bound, the *chèche* pushed back on his head, the Arab was looking toward the window. At first Daru noticed only his huge lips, fat, smooth, almost Negroid; yet his nose was straight, his eyes dark and full of fever. The *chèche* uncovered an obstinate forehead and, under the weathered skin now rather discolored by the cold, the whole face had a restless and rebellious look. "Go into the other room," said the schoolmaster, "and I'll make you some mint tea." "Thanks," Balducci said. "What a chore! How I long for retirement." And addressing his prisoner in Arabic, he said, "Come on, you." The Arab got up and, slowly, holding his bound wrists in front of him, went into the classroom.

With the tea, Daru brought a chair. But Balducci was already sitting in state at the nearest pupil's desk, and the Arab had squatted against the teacher's platform facing the stove, which stood between the desk and the window. When he held out the glass of tea to the prisoner, Daru hesitated at the sight of his bound hands. "He might perhaps be untied." "Sure," said Balducci. "That was for the trip." He started to get to his feet. But Daru, setting the glass on the floor, had knelt beside the Arab. Without saying anything, the Arab watched him with his feverish eyes. Once his hands were free, he rubbed his swollen wrists against each other, took the glass of tea and sucked up the burning liquid in swift little sips.

"Good," said Daru. "And where are you headed?"

Balducci withdrew his mustache from the tea. "Here, son."

"Odd pupils! And you're spending the night?"

"No. I'm going back to El Ameur. And you will deliver this fellow to Tinguit. He is expected at police headquarters."

Balducci was looking at Daru with a friendly little smile.

"What's this story?" asked the schoolmaster. "Are you pulling my leg?"

"No, son. Those are the orders."

"The orders? I'm not . . ." Daru hesitated, not wanting to hurt the old Corsican. "I mean, that's not my job."

"What! What's the meaning of that? In wartime people do all kinds of jobs."

"Then I'll wait for the declaration of war!"

Balducci nodded. "O.K. But the orders exist and they concern you too. Things are bubbling, it appears. There is talk of a forthcoming revolt. We are mobilized, in a way."

Daru still had his obstinate look.

"Listen, son," Balducci said. "I like you and you've got to understand. There's only a dozen of us at El Ameur to patrol the whole territory of a small department and I must be back in a hurry. He couldn't be kept there. His village was beginning to stir; they wanted to take him back. You must take him to Tinguit tomorrow before the day is over. Twenty kilometers shouldn't faze a husky fellow like you. After that, all will be over. You'll come back to your pupils and your comfortable life."

Behind the wall the horse could be heard snorting and pawing the earth. Daru was looking out the window. Decidedly the weather was clearing and the light was increasing over the snowy plateau. When all the snow was melted, the sun would take over again and once more would burn the fields of stone. For days still, the unchanging sky would shed its dry light on the solitary expanse where nothing had any connection with man.

"After all," he said, turning around toward Balducci, "what did he do?" And, before the gendarme had opened his mouth, he asked, "Does he speak French?"

"No, not a word. We had been looking for him for a month, but they were hiding him. He killed his cousin."

"Is he against us?"

"I don't think so. But you can never be sure."

"Why did he kill?"

"A family squabble, I think. One owed grain to the other, it seems. It's not at all clear. In short, he killed his cousin with a billhook. You know, like a sheep, *kreezk!*"

Balducci made the gesture of drawing a blade across his throat, and the Arab, his attention attracted, watched him with a sort of anxiety. Daru felt a sudden wrath against the man, against all men with their rotten spite, their tireless hates, their blood lust.

But the kettle was singing on the stove. He served Balducci more tea, hesitated, then served the Arab again, who drank avidly a second time. His raised arms made the *jellaba* fall open, and the schoolmaster saw his thin, muscular chest.

"Thanks, son," Balducci said. "And now I'm off."

He got up and went toward the Arab, taking a small rope from his pocket.

"What are you doing?" Daru asked dryly.

Balducci, disconcerted, showed him the rope.

"Don't bother."

The old gendarme hesitated. "It's up to you. Of course, you are armed?"

"I have my shotgun."

"Where?"

"In the trunk."

"You ought to have it near your bed."

"Why? I have nothing to fear."

"You're crazy, son. If there's an uprising, no one is safe; we're all in the same boat."

"I'll defend myself. I'll have time to see them coming."

Balducci began to laugh, then suddenly the mustache covered the white teeth. "You'll have time? O.K. That's just what I was saying. You always have been a little cracked. That's why I like you; my son was like that."

At the same time he took out his revolver and put it on the desk. "Keep it; I don't need two weapons from here to El Ameur."

The revolver shone against the black paint of the table. When the gendarme turned toward him, the schoolmaster caught his smell of leather and horseflesh.

"Listen, Balducci," Daru said suddenly, "all this disgusts me, beginning with your fellow here. But I won't hand him over. Fight, yes, if I have to. But not that."

The old gendarme stood in front of him and looked at him severely.

"You're being a fool," he said slowly. "I don't like it either. You don't get used to putting a rope on a man even after years of it, and you're even ashamed—yes, ashamed. But you can't let them have their way."

"I won't hand him over," Daru said again.

"It's an order, son, and I repeat it."

"That's right. Repeat to them what I've said to you: I won't hand him over."

Balducci made a visible effort to reflect. He looked at the Arab and at Daru. At last he decided.

"No, I won't tell them anything. If you want to drop us, go ahead; I'll not denounce you. I have an order to deliver the prisoner and I'm doing so. And now you'll just sign this paper for me."

"There's no need. I'll not deny that you left him with me."

"Don't be mean with me. I know you'll tell the truth. You're from around these parts and you are a man. But you must sign; that's the rule."

Daru opened his drawer, took out a little square bottle of purple ink, the red wooden penholder with the "sergeant-major" pen he used for models of handwriting, and signed. The gendarme carefully folded the paper and put it into his wallet. Then he moved toward the door.

"I'll see you off," Daru said.

"No," said Balducci. "There's no use being polite. You insulted me."

He looked at the Arab, motionless in the same spot, sniffed peevishly, and turned away toward the door. "Good-by, son," he said. The door slammed behind him. His footsteps were muffled by the snow. The horse stirred on the other side of the wall and several chickens fluttered in fright. A moment later Balducci reappeared outside the window leading the horse by the bridle. He walked toward the little rise without turning around and disappeared from sight with the horse following him.

Daru walked back toward the prisoner, who, without stirring, never took his eyes off him. "Wait," the schoolmaster said in Arabic and went toward the bedroom. As he was going through the door, he had a second thought, went to the desk, took the revolver, and stuck it in his pocket. Then, without looking back, he went into his room.

For some time he lay on his couch watching the sky gradually close over, listening to the silence. It was this silence that had seemed painful to him during the first days here, after the war. He had requested a post in the little town at the base of the foothills separating the upper plateaus from the desert. There rocky walls, green and black to the north, pink and lavender to the south, marked the frontier of eternal summer. He had been named to a post farther north, on the plateau itself. In the beginning, the solitude and the silence had been hard for him on these wastelands peopled only by stones. Occasionally, furrows suggested cultivation, but they had been dug to uncover a certain kind of stone good for building. The only plowing here was to harvest rocks. Elsewhere a thin layer of soil accumulated in the hollows would be scraped out to enrich paltry village gardens. This is the way it was: bare rock covered three quarters of the region. Towns sprang up, flourished, then disappeared; men came by, loved one another or fought bitterly, then died. No one in this desert, neither he nor his guest, mattered. And yet, outside this desert neither of them, Daru knew, could have really lived.

When he got up, no noise came from the classroom. He was amazed at the unmixed joy he derived from the mere thought that the Arab might have fled and that he would be alone with no decision to make. But the prisoner was there. He had merely stretched out between the stove and the desk and he was staring at the ceiling. In that position, his thick lips were particularly notice-able, giving him a pouting look. "Come," said Daru. The Arab got up and followed him. In the bedroom the schoolmaster pointed to a chair near the table under the window. The Arab sat down without ceasing to watch Daru.

"Are you hungry?"

"Yes," the prisoner said.

Daru set the table for two. He took flour and oil, shaped a cake in a frying pan, and lighted the little stove that functioned on bottled gas. While the cake was cooking, he went out to the shed to get cheese, eggs, dates, and condensed milk. When the cake was done he set it on the window sill to cool, heated some condensed milk diluted with water, and beat up the eggs into an omelette. In one of his motions he bumped into the revolver stuck in his right pocket. He set the bowl down, went into the classroom, and put the revolver in his desk drawer. When he came back to the room, night was falling. He put on the light and served the Arab. "Eat," he said. The Arab took a piece of the cake, lifted it eagerly to his mouth, and stopped short.

"And you?" he asked.

"After you. I'll eat too."

The thick lips opened slightly. The Arab hesitated, then bit into the cake determinedly.

The meal over, the Arab looked at the schoolmaster. "Are you the judge?"

"No, I'm simply keeping you until tomorrow."

"Why do you eat with me?"

"I'm hungry."

The Arab fell silent. Daru got up and went out. He brought back a camp cot from the shed and set it up between the table and the stove, at right angles to his own bed. From a large suitcase which, upright in a corner, served as a shelf for papers, he took two blankets and arranged them on the cot. Then he stopped, felt useless, and sat down on his bed. There was nothing more to do or to get ready. He had to look at this man. He looked at him therefore, trying to imagine his face bursting with rage. He couldn't do so. He could see nothing but the dark yet shining eyes and the animal mouth.

"Why did you kill him?" he asked in a voice whose hostile tone surprised him.

The Arab looked away. "He ran away. I ran after him."

He raised his eyes to Daru again and they were full of a sort of woeful interrogation. "Now what will they do to me?"

"Are you afraid?"

The Arab stiffened, turning his eyes away.

"Are you sorry?"

The Arab stared at him openmouthed. Obviously he did not understand. Daru's annoyance was growing. At the same time he felt awkward and self-conscious with his big body wedged between the two beds.

"Lie down there," he said impatiently. "That's your bed."

The Arab didn't move. He cried out, "Tell me!"

The schoolmaster looked at him.

"Is the gendarme coming back tomorrow?"

"I don't know."

"Are you coming with us?"

"I don't know. Why?"

The prisoner got up and stretched out on top of the blankets, his feet toward the window. The light from the electric bulb shone straight into his eyes and he closed them at once.

"Why?" Daru repeated, standing beside the bed.

The Arab opened his eyes under the blinding light and looked at him, trying not to blink. "Come with us," he said.

In the middle of the night, Daru was still not asleep. He had gone to bed after undressing completely; he generally slept naked. But when he suddenly realized that he had nothing on, he wondered. He felt vulnerable and the temptation came to him to put his clothes back on. Then he shrugged his shoulders; after all, he wasn't a child and, if it came to that, he could break his adversary in two. From his bed, he could observe him lying on his back, still motionless, his eyes closed under the harsh light. When Daru turned out the light, the darkness seemed to congeal all of a sudden. Little by little, the night came back to life in the window where the starless sky was stirring gently. The schoolmaster soon made out the body lying at his feet. The Arab was still motionless but his eyes seemed open. A faint wind was prowling about the schoolhouse. Perhaps it would drive away the clouds and the sun would reappear.

During the night the wind increased. The hens fluttered a little and then were silent. The Arab turned over on his side with his back to Daru, who thought he heard him moan. Then he listened for his guest's breathing, which had become heavier and more regular. He listened to that breathing so close to him and mused without being able to go to sleep. In the room where he had been sleeping alone for a year, this presence bothered him. But it bothered him also because it imposed on him a sort of brotherhood he refused to accept in the present circumstances; yet he was familiar with it. Men who share the same rooms, soldiers or prisoners, develop a strange alliance as if, having cast off their armor with their clothing, they fraternized every evening, over and above their differences, in the ancient community of dream and fatigue. But Daru shook himself; he didn't like such musings, and it was essential for him to sleep.

A little later, however, when the Arab stirred slightly, the schoolmaster was still not asleep. When the prisoner made a second move, he stiffened, on the alert. The Arab was lifting himself slowly on his arms with almost the motion of a sleepwalker. Seated upright in bed, he waited motionless without turning his head toward Daru, as if he were listening attentively. Daru did not stir; it had just occurred to him that the revolver was still in the drawer of his desk. It was better to act at once. Yet he continued to observe the prisoner, who, with the same slithery motion, put his feet on the ground, waited again, then stood up slowly. Daru was about to call out to him when the Arab began to walk, in a quite natural but extraordinarily silent way. He was heading toward the door at the end of the room that opened into the shed. He lifted the latch with precaution and went out, pushing the door behind him but without shutting it.

Daru had not stirred. "He is running away," he merely thought. "Good riddance!" Yet he listened attentively. The hens were not fluttering; the guest must be on the plateau. A faint sound of water reached him, and he didn't know what it was until the Arab again stood framed in the doorway, closed the door carefully, and came back to bed without a sound. Then Daru turned his back on him and fell asleep. Still later he seemed, from the depths of his sleep, to hear furtive steps around the schoolhouse. "I'm dreaming! I'm dreaming!" he repeated to himself. And he went on sleeping.

When he awoke, the sky was clear; the loose window let in a cold, pure air. The Arab was asleep, hunched up under the blankets now, his mouth open, utterly relaxed. But when Daru shook him he started dreadfully, staring at Daru with wild eyes as if he had never seen him and with such a frightened expression that the schoolmaster stepped back. "Don't be afraid. It is I. You must eat." The Arab nodded his head and said yes. Calm had returned to his face, but his expression was vacant and listless.

The coffee was ready. They drank it seated together on the cot as they munched their pieces of the cake. Then Daru led the Arab under the shed and showed him the faucet where he washed. He went back into the room, folded the blankets on the cot, made his own bed, and put the room in order. Then he went through the classroom and out onto the terrace. The sun was already rising in the blue sky; a soft, bright light enveloped the deserted plateau. On the ridge the snow was melting in spots. The stones were about to reappear. Crouched on the edge of the plateau, the schoolmaster looked at the deserted expanse. He thought of Balducci. He had hurt him, for he had sent him off as though he didn't want to be associated with him. He could still hear the gendarme's farewell and, without knowing why, he felt strangely empty and vulnerable.

At that moment, from the other side of the schoolhouse, the prisoner coughed. Daru listened to him almost despite himself and then, furious, threw a pebble that whistled through the air before sinking into the snow. That man's stupid crime revolted him, but to hand him over was contrary to honor; just thinking of it made him boil with humiliation. He simultaneously cursed his own people who had sent him this Arab and the Arab who had dared to kill and not managed to get away. Daru got up, walked in a circle on the terrace, waited motionless, and then went back into the schoolhouse.

The Arab, leaning over the cement floor of the shed, was washing his teeth with two fingers. Daru looked at him and said, "Come." He went back into the room ahead of the prisoner. He slipped a hunting jacket on over his sweater and put on walking shoes. Standing, he waited until the Arab had put on his *chèche* and sandals. They went into the classroom, and the schoolmaster pointed to the exit saying, "Go ahead." The fellow didn't budge. "I'm coming," said Daru. The Arab went out. Daru went back into the room and made a package with pieces of rusk, dates, and sugar in it. In the classroom, before going out, he hesitated a second in front of his desk, then crossed the threshold and locked the door. "That's the way," he said. He started toward the east, followed by the prisoner. But a short distance from the schoolhouse he thought he heard a slight sound behind him. He retraced his steps and examined the surroundings of the house; there was no one there. The Arab watched him without seeming to understand. "Come on," said Daru.

They walked for an hour and rested beside a sharp needle of limestone. The snow was melting faster and faster and the sun was drinking up the puddles just as quickly, rapidly cleaning the plateau, which gradually dried and vibrated like the air itself. When they resumed walking, the ground rang under their feet. From time to time a bird rent the space in front of them with a joyful cry. Daru felt a sort of rapture before the vast familiar expanse, now almost entirely yellow under its dome of blue sky. They walked an hour more, descending toward the south. They reached a sort of flattened elevation made up of crumbly rocks. From there on, the plateau sloped down—eastward toward a low plain on which could be made out a few spindly trees, and to the south toward outcroppings of rock that gave the landscape a chaotic look.

Daru surveyed the two directions. Not a man could be seen. He turned toward the Arab, who was looking at him blankly. Daru offered the package to him. "Take it," he said. "There are dates, bread, and sugar. You can hold out for two days. Here are a thousand francs too."

The Arab took the package and the money but kept his full hands at chest level as if he didn't know what to do with what was being given him.

"Now look," the schoolmaster said as he pointed in the direction of the east, "there's the way to Tinguit. You have a two-hour walk. At Tinguit are the administration and the police. They are expecting you."

The Arab looked toward the east, still holding the package and the money against his chest. Daru took his elbow and turned him rather roughly toward the south. At the foot of the elevation on which they stood could be seen a faint path. "That's the trail across the plateau. In a day's walk from here you'll find pasturelands and the first nomads. They'll take you in and shelter you according to their law."

The Arab had now turned toward Daru, and a sort of panic was visible in his expression. "Listen," he said.

Daru shook his head. "No, be quiet. Now I'm leaving you." He turned his back on him, took two long steps in the direction of the school, looked hesitantly at the motionless Arab, and started off again. For a few minutes he heard nothing but his own step resounding on the cold ground, and he did not turn his head. A moment later, however, he turned around. The Arab was still there on the edge of the hill, his arms hanging now, and he was looking at the schoolmaster. Daru felt something rise in his throat. But he swore with impatience, waved vaguely, and started off again. He had already gone a distance when he again stopped and looked. There was no longer anyone on the hill.

Daru hesitated. The sun was now rather high in the sky and beginning to beat down on his head. The schoolmaster retraced his steps, at first somewhat uncertainly, then with decision. When he reached the little hill, he was bathed in sweat. He climbed it as fast as he could and stopped, out of breath, on the top. The rock fields to the south stood out sharply against the blue sky, but on the plain to the east a steamy heat was rising. And in that slight haze, Daru, with heavy heart, made out the Arab walking slowly on the road to prison.

A little later, standing before the window of the classroom, the schoolmaster was watching the clear light bathing the whole surface of the plateau. Behind him on the blackboard, among the winding French rivers, sprawled the clumsily chalked up words he had just read: "You handed over our brother. You will pay for this." Daru looked at the sky, the plateau, and, beyond, the invisible lands stretching all the way to the sea. In this vast landscape he had loved so much, he was alone.

QUESTIONS

1. How does Camus' narrator introduce us to the setting and main character of his tale?
2. Note especially paragraph two on page 48. Why is it important that we are given this description of Daru's life and feelings now, before the action of the tale begins? How do Daru's feelings for the land affect your feelings for him?
3. How does Daru react to the approach of his visitors? to their arrival? to Balducci's revelation that the Arab is a murderer and that Daru is to deliver him to the police in the next village? Does Daru's refusal of Balducci's demand come as a surprise to you, or does it seem to fit what you've been learning about his character?
4. Notice, too, Balducci's reaction to Daru's refusal. What feelings toward the two men does it inspire in you? What bonds and conflicts between them does it suggest?
5. Re-read paragraph five on page 52 and the last paragraph on page 54. What do these passages contribute to your understanding of Daru and his actions?
6. What sort of interaction is taking place between Daru and the Arab in the scenes on pages 53–54 and 57? What does the Arab want from Daru? How is Daru responding?
7. Note the re-emphasis on Daru's love for the land at the end of the story. How have Daru's feelings about the land been used to characterize him throughout the story? What are they emphasizing now?
8. How does Daru's isolation now differ from the isolation which was just ending as the story began? To what extent do you feel this new isolation has been forced upon Daru? How much of it seems to be of his own making?

QUESTIONS FOR FURTHER THOUGHT

1. "Young Goodman Brown" and "The Guest" can both be considered tales in which the action centers upon the hero's refusal to make a commitment and his subsequent isolation and alienation from his fellow humans. How would you discuss this theme in the two stories? What aspects of action or characterization would you want to emphasize? What comparisons or contrasts would you want to make?
2. As we have already noted, the setting of each of these tales is endowed with symbolic value by its narrator. How would you plan an essay on the function of the setting in either or both of these tales, considering not only the meanings attached to the setting, but also the relation between setting, character, and action?

The next story, "The Open Boat," is based on a shipwreck actually suffered by its author, Stephen Crane. Yet Crane does not tell the tale in his own voice; rather, he tells it through an omniscient narrator. Read the story; then compose and answer your own set of questions to determine the narrator's tone of voice, his major concerns, and his attitudes towards the people and events he tells of. Finally, decide what Crane has gained by his choice of narrator.

STEPHEN CRANE (1871–1900)

The Open Boat

A Tale intended to be after the fact. Being the Experience of Four Men from the Sunk Steamer "Commodore"

I

None of them knew the color of the sky. Their eyes glanced level, and were fastened upon the waves that swept toward them. These waves were of the hue of slate, save for the tops, which were of foaming white, and all of the men knew the colors of the sea. The horizon narrowed and widened, and dipped and rose, and at all times its edge was jagged with waves that seemed thrust up in points like rocks.

Many a man ought to have a bath-tub larger than the boat which here rode upon the sea. These waves were most wrongfully and barbarously abrupt and tall, and each froth-top was a problem in small boat navigation.

The cook squatted in the bottom and looked with both eyes at the six inches of gunwale which separated him from the ocean. His sleeves were rolled over his fat forearms, and the two flaps of his unbuttoned vest dangled as he bent to bail out the boat. Often he said: "Gawd! That was a narrow clip." As he remarked it he invariably gazed eastward over the broken sea.

The oiler, steering with one of the two oars in the boat, sometimes raised himself suddenly to keep clear of water that swirled in over the stern. It was a thin little oar and it seemed often ready to snap.

The correspondent, pulling at the other oar, watched the waves and wondered why he was there.

The injured captain, lying in the bow, was at this time buried in that profound dejection and indifference which comes, temporarily at least, to even the bravest and most enduring when, willy nilly, the firm fails, the army loses, the ship goes down. The mind of the master of a vessel is rooted deep in the timbers of her, though he command for a day or a decade, and this captain had on him the stern impression of a scene in the grays of dawn of seven turned faces, and later a stump of a top-mast with a white ball on it that slashed to and fro at the waves, went low and lower, and down. Thereafter there was something strange in his voice. Although steady, it was deep with mourning, and of a quality beyond oration or tears.

"Keep 'er a little more south, Billie," said he.

" 'A little more south,' sir," said the oiler in the stern.

A seat in this boat was not unlike a seat upon a bucking broncho, and, by the same token, a broncho is not much smaller. The craft pranced and reared, and plunged like an animal. As each wave came, and she rose for it, she seemed like a horse making at a fence outrageously high. The manner of her scramble over these walls of water is a mystic thing, and, moreover, at the top of them were ordinarily these problems in white water, the foam racing down from the summit of each wave, requiring a new leap, and a leap from the air. Then, after scornfully bumping a crest, she would slide, and race, and splash down a long incline, and arrive bobbing and nodding in front of the next menace.

A singular disadvantage of the sea lies in the fact that after successfully surmounting one wave you discover that there is another behind it just as important and just as nervously anxious to do something effective in the way of swamping boats. In a ten-foot dingey one can get an idea of the resources of the sea in the line of waves that is not probable to the average experience which is never at sea in a dingey. As each slaty wall of water approached, it shut all else from the view of the men in the boat, and it was not difficult to imagine that this particular wave was the final outburst of the ocean, the last effort of the grim water. There was a terrible grace in the move of the waves, and they came in silence, save for the snarling of the crests.

In the wan light, the faces of the men must have been gray. Their eyes must have glinted in strange ways as they gazed steadily astern. Viewed from a balcony, the whole thing would doubtless have been weirdly picturesque. But the men in the boat had no time to see it, and if they had had leisure there were other things to occupy their minds. The sun swung steadily up the sky, and they knew it was broad day because the color of the sea changed from slate to emerald-green, streaked with amber lights, and the foam was like tumbling snow. The process of the breaking day was unknown to them. They were aware only of this effect upon the color of the waves that rolled toward them.

In disjointed sentences the cook and the correspondent argued as to the difference between a life-saving station and a house of refuge. The cook had said: "There's a house of refuge just north of the Mosquito Inlet Light, and as soon as they see us, they'll come off in their boat and pick us up."

"As soon as who see us?" said the correspondent.

"The crew," said the cook.

"Houses of refuge don't have crews," said the correspondent. "As I understand them, they are only places where clothes and grub are stored for the benefit of shipwrecked people. They don't carry crews."

"Oh, yes, they do," said the cook.

"No, they don't," said the correspondent.

"Well, we're not there yet, anyhow," said the oiler, in the stern.

"Well," said the cook, "perhaps it's not a house of refuge that I'm thinking of as being near Mosquito Inlet Light. Perhaps it's a life-saving station."

"We're not there yet," said the oiler, in the stern.

II

As the boat bounced from the top of each wave, the wind tore through the hair of the hatless men, and as the craft plopped her stern down again the spray slashed past them. The crest of each of these waves was a hill, from the top of which the men surveyed, for a moment, a broad tumultuous expanse, shining and wind-riven. It was probably splendid. It was probably glorious, this play of the free sea, wild with lights of emerald and white and amber.

"Bully good thing it's an on-shore wind," said the cook. "If not, where would we be? Wouldn't have a show."

"That's right," said the correspondent.

The busy oiler nodded his assent.

Then the captain, in the bow, chuckled in a way that expressed humor, contempt, tragedy, all in one. "Do you think we've got much of a show now, boys?" said he.

Whereupon the three were silent, save for a trifle of hemming and hawing. To express any particular optimism at this time they felt to be childish and stupid, but they all doubtless possessed this sense of the situation in their mind. A young man thinks doggedly at such times. On the other hand, the ethics of their condition was decidedly against any open suggestion of hopelessness. So they were silent.

"Oh, well," said the captain, soothing his children, "we'll get ashore all right."

But there was that in his tone which made them think, so the oiler quoth: "Yes! If this wind holds!"

The cook was bailing: "Yes! If we don't catch hell in the surf."

Canton flannel gulls flew near and far. Sometimes they sat down on the sea, near patches of brown seaweed that rolled over the waves with a movement like carpets on a line in a gale. The birds sat comfortably in groups, and they were envied by some in the dingey, for the wrath of the sea was no more to them than it was to a covey of prairie chickens a thousand miles inland. Often they came very close and stared at the men with black bead-like eyes. At these times they were uncanny and sinister in their unblinking scrutiny, and the men hooted angrily at them, telling them to be gone. One came, and evidently decided to alight on the top of the captain's head. The bird flew parallel to the boat and did not circle, but made short sidelong jumps in the air in chicken-fashion. His black eyes were wistfully fixed upon the captain's head. "Ugly brute," said the oiler to the bird. "You look as if you were made with a jack-knife." The cook and the correspondent swore darkly at the creature. The captain naturally wished to knock it away with the end of the heavy painter; but he did not dare do it, because anything resembling an emphatic gesture would have capsized this freighted boat, and so with his open hand, the captain gently and carefully waved the gull away. After it had been discouraged from the pursuit the captain breathed easier on account of his hair, and others breathed easier because the bird struck their minds at this time as being somehow gruesome and ominous.

In the meantime the oiler and the correspondent rowed. And also they rowed.

They sat together in the same seat, and each rowed an oar. Then the oiler took both oars; then the correspondent took both oars; then the oiler; then the correspondent. They rowed and they rowed. The very ticklish part of the business was when the time came for the reclining one in the stern to take his turn at the oars. By the very last star of truth, it is easier to steal eggs from under a hen than it was to change seats in the dingey. First the man in the stern slid his hand along the thwart and moved with care, as if he were of Sèvres. Then the man in the rowing seat slid his hand along the other thwart. It was all done with the most extraordinary care. As the two sidled past each other, the whole party kept watchful eyes on the coming wave, and the captain cried: "Look out now! Steady there!"

The brown mats of seaweed that appeared from time to time were like islands, bits of earth. They were travelling, apparently, neither one way nor the other. They were, to all intents, stationary. They informed the men in the boat that it was making progress slowly toward the land.

The captain, rearing cautiously in the bow, after the dingey soared on a great swell, said that he had seen the lighthouse at Mosquito Inlet. Presently the cook remarked that he had seen it. The correspondent was at the oars then, and for some reason he too wished to look at the lighthouse, but his back was toward the far shore and the waves were important, and for some time he could not seize an opportunity to turn his head. But at last there came a wave more gentle than the others, and when at the crest of it he swiftly scoured the western horizon.

"See it?" said the captain.

"No," said the correspondent slowly. "I didn't see anything."

"Look again," said the captain. He pointed. "It's exactly in that direction."

At the top of another wave, the correspondent did as he was bid, and this time his eyes chanced on a small still thing on the edge of the swaying horizon. It was precisely like the point of a pin. It took an anxious eye to find a lighthouse so tiny.

"Think we'll make it, captain?"

"If this wind holds and the boat don't swamp, we can't do much else," said the captain.

The little boat, lifted by each towering sea, and splashed viciously by the crests, made progress that in the absence of seaweed was not apparent to those in her. She seemed just a wee thing wallowing, miraculously top up, at the mercy of five oceans. Occasionally, a great spread of water, like white flames, swarmed into her.

"Bail her, cook," said the captain serenely.

"All right, captain," said the cheerful cook.

III

It would be difficult to describe the subtle brotherhood of men that was here established on the seas. No one said that it was so. No one mentioned it. But it dwelt in the boat, and each man felt it warm him. They were a captain, an oiler, a cook, and a correspondent, and they were friends, friends in a more curiously iron-bound degree than may be common. The hurt captain, lying against the water-jar in the bow, spoke always in a low voice and calmly, but he could never command a more ready and swiftly obedient crew than the motley three of the dingey. It was more than a mere recognition of what was best for the common safety. There was surely in it a quality that was personal and heartfelt. And after this devotion to the commander of the boat there was this comradeship that the correspondent, for instance, who had been taught to be cynical of men, knew even at the time was the best experience of his life. But no one said that it was so. No one mentioned it.

"I wish we had a sail," remarked the captain. "We might try my overcoat on the end of an oar and give you two boys a chance to rest." So the cook and the correspondent held the mast and spread wide the overcoat. The oiler steered, and the little boat made good way with her new rig. Sometimes the oiler had to scull sharply to keep a sea from breaking into the boat, but otherwise sailing was a success.

Meanwhile the lighthouse had been growing slowly larger. It had now almost assumed color, and appeared like a little gray shadow on the sky. The man at the oars could not be prevented from turning his head rather often to try for a glimpse of this little gray shadow.

At last, from the top of each wave the men in the tossing boat could see land. Even as the lighthouse was an upright shadow on the sky, this land seemed but a long black shadow on the sea. It certainly was thinner than paper. "We must be about opposite New Smyrna," said the cook, who had coasted this shore often in schooners. "Captain, by the way, I believe they abandoned that life-saving station there about a year ago."

"Did they?" said the captain.

The wind slowly died away. The cook and the correspondent were not now obliged to slave in order to hold high the oar. But the waves continued their old impetuous swooping at the dingey, and the little craft, no longer under way, struggled woundily over them. The oiler or the correspondent took the oars again.

Shipwrecks are apropos of nothing. If men could only train for them and have them occur when the men had reached pink condition, there would be less drowning at sea. Of the four in the dingey none had slept any time worth mentioning for two days and two nights previous to embarking in the dingey, and in the excitement of clambering about the deck of a foundering ship they had also forgotten to eat heartily.

For these reasons, and for others, neither the oiler nor the correspondent was fond of rowing at this time. The correspondent wondered ingenuously how in the name of all that was sane could there be people who thought it amusing to row a boat. It was not an amusement; it was a diabolical punishment, and even a genius of mental aberrations could never conclude that it was anything but a horror to the muscles and a crime against the back. He mentioned to the boat in general how the amusement of rowing struck him, and the weary-faced oiler smiled in full sympathy. Previously to the foundering, by the way, the oiler had worked double-watch in the engine-room of the ship.

"Take her easy, now, boys," said the captain. "Don't spend yourselves. If we have to run a surf you'll need all your strength, because we'll sure have to swim for it. Take your time."

Slowly the land arose from the sea. From a black line it became a line of black and a line of white, trees and sand. Finally, the captain said that he could make out a house on the shore. "That's the house of refuge, sure," said the cook. "They'll see us before long, and come out after us."

The distant lighthouse reared high. "The keeper ought to be able to make us out now, if he's looking through a glass," said the captain. "He'll notify the life-saving people."

"None of those other boats could have got ashore to give word of the wreck," said the oiler, in a low voice. "Else the life-boat would be out hunting us."

Slowly and beautifully the land loomed out of the sea. The wind came again. It had veered from the north-east to the south-east. Finally, a new sound struck the ears of the men in the boat. It was the low thunder of the surf on the shore. "We'll never be able to make the lighthouse now," said the captain. "Swing her head a little more north, Billie."

"'A little more north,' sir," said the oiler.

Whereupon the little boat turned her nose once more down the wind, and all but the oarsman watched the shore grow. Under the influence of this expansion doubt and direful apprehension was leaving the minds of the men. The management of the boat was still most absorbing, but it could not prevent a quiet cheerfulness. In an hour, perhaps, they would be ashore.

Their backbones had become thoroughly used to balancing in the boat, and they now rode this wild colt of a dingey like circus men. The correspondent thought that he had been drenched to the skin, but happening to feel in the top pocket of his coat, he found therein eight cigars. Four of them were soaked with sea-water; four were perfectly scatheless. After a search, somebody produced three dry matches, and thereupon the four waifs rode in their little boat, and with an assurance of an impending rescue shining in their eyes, puffed at the big cigars and judged well and ill of all men. Everybody took a drink of water.

IV

"Cook," remarked the captain, "there don't seem to be any signs of life about your house of refuge."

"No," replied the cook. "Funny they don't see us!"

A broad stretch of lowly coast lay before the eyes of the men. It was of low dunes topped with dark vegetation. The roar of the surf was plain, and sometimes they could see the white lip of a wave as it spun up the beach. A tiny house was blocked out black upon the sky. Southward, the slim lighthouse lifted its little gray length.

Tide, wind, and waves were swinging the dingey northward. "Funny they don't see us," said the men.

The surf's roar was here dulled, but its tone was, nevertheless, thunderous and mighty. As the boat swam over the great rollers, the men sat listening to this roar. "We'll swamp sure," said everybody.

It is fair to say here that there was not a life-saving station within twenty miles in either direction, but the men did not know this fact, and in consequence they made dark and opprobrious remarks concerning the eyesight of the nation's life-savers. Four scowling men sat in the dingey and surpassed records in the invention of epithets.

"Funny they don't see us."

The light-heartedness of a former time had completely faded. To their sharpened minds it was easy to conjure pictures of all kinds of incompetency and blindness and, indeed, cowardice. There was the shore of the populous land, and it was bitter and bitter to them that from it came no sign.

"Well," said the captain, ultimately, "I suppose we'll have to make a try for ourselves. If we stay out here too long, we'll none of us have strength left to swim after the boat swamps."

And so the oiler, who was at the oars, turned the boat straight for the shore. There was a sudden tightening of muscles. There was some thinking.

"If we don't all get ashore—" said the captain. "If we don't all get ashore, I suppose you fellows know where to send news of my finish?"

They then briefly exchanged some addresses and admonitions. As for the reflections of the men, there was a great deal of rage in them. Perchance they might be formulated thus: "If I am going to be drowned—if I am going to be drowned—if I am going to be drowned, why, in the name of the seven mad gods who rule the sea, was I allowed to come thus far and contemplate sand and trees? Was I brought here merely to have my nose dragged away as I was about to nibble the sacred cheese of life? It is preposterous. If this old ninny-woman, Fate, cannot do better than this, she should be deprived of the management of men's fortunes. She is an old hen who knows not her intention. If she has decided to drown me, why did she not do it in the beginning and save me all this trouble? The whole affair is absurd. . . . But no, she cannot mean to drown me. She dare not drown me. She cannot drown me. Not after all this work." Afterward the man might have had an impulse to shake his fist at the clouds: "Just you drown me, now, and then hear what I call you!"

The billows that came at this time were more formidable. They seemed always just about to break and roll over the little boat in a turmoil of foam. There was a preparatory and long growl in the speech of them. No mind unused to the sea would have concluded that the dingey could ascend these sheer heights in time. The shore was still afar. The oiler was a wily surfman. "Boys," he said swiftly, "she won't live three minutes more, and we're too far out to swim. Shall I take her to sea again, captain?"

"Yes! Go ahead!" said the captain.

This oiler, by a series of quick miracles, and fast and steady oarsmanship, turned the boat in the middle of the surf and took her safely to sea again.

There was a considerable silence as the boat bumped over the furrowed sea to deeper water. Then somebody in gloom spoke. "Well, anyhow, they must have seen us from the shore by now."

The gulls went in slanting flight up the wind toward the gray desolate east. A squall, marked by dingy clouds, and clouds brick-red, like smoke from a burning building, appeared from the south-east.

"What do you think of those life-saving people? Ain't they peaches?"

"Funny they haven't seen us."

"Maybe they think we're out here for sport! Maybe they think we're fishin'. Maybe they think we're damned fools."

It was a long afternoon. A changed tide tried to force them southward, but wind and wave said northward. Far ahead, where coastline, sea, and sky formed their mighty angle, there were little dots which seemed to indicate a city on the shore.

"St. Augustine?"

The captain shook his head. "Too near Mosquito Inlet."

And the oiler rowed, and then the correspondent rowed. Then the oiler rowed. It was a weary business. The human back can become the seat of more aches and pains than are registered in books for the composite anatomy of a regiment. It is a limited area, but it can become the theater of innumerable muscular conflicts, tangles, wrenches, knots, and other comforts.

"Did you ever like to row, Billie?" asked the correspondent.

"No," said the oiler. "Hang it!"

When one exchanged the rowing-seat for a place in the bottom of the boat, he suffered a bodily depression that caused him to be careless of everything save an obligation to wiggle one finger. There was cold sea-water swashing to and fro in the boat, and he lay in it. His head, pillowed on a thwart, was within an inch of the swirl of a wave crest, and sometimes a particularly obstreperous sea came inboard and drenched him once more. But these matters did not annoy him. It is almost certain that if the boat had capsized he would have tumbled comfortably out upon the ocean as if he felt sure that it was a great soft mattress.

"Look! There's a man on the shore!"

"Where?"

"There! See 'im? See 'im?"

"Yes, sure! He's walking along."

"Now he's stopped. Look! He's facing us!"

"He's waving at us!"

"So he is! By thunder!"

"Ah, now we're all right! Now we're all right! There'll be a boat out here for us in half an hour."

"He's going on. He's running. He's going up to that house there."

The remote beach seemed lower than the sea, and it required a searching glance to discern the little black figure. The captain saw a floating stick and they rowed to it. A bath-towel was by some weird chance in the boat, and tying this on the stick, the captain waved it. The oarsman did not dare turn his head, so he was obliged to ask questions.

"What's he doing now?"

"He's standing still again. He's looking. I think. . . . There he goes again. Toward the house. . . . Now he's stopped again."

"Is he waving at us?"

"No, not now! he was, though."

"Look! There comes another man!"

"He's running."

"Look at him go, would you."

"Why, he's on a bicycle. Now he's met the other man. They're both waving at us. Look!"

"There comes something up the beach."

"What the devil is that thing?"

"Why, it looks like a boat."

"Why, certainly it's a boat."

"No, it's on wheels."

"Yes, so it is. Well, that must be the life-boat. They drag them along shore on a wagon."

"That's the life-boat, sure."

"No, by—, it's—it's an omnibus."

"I tell you it's a life-boat."

"It is not! It's an omnibus. I can see it plain. See? One of these big hotel omnibuses."

"By thunder, you're right. It's an omnibus, sure as fate. What do you suppose they are doing with an omnibus? Maybe they are going around collecting the life-crew, hey?"

"That's it, likely. Look! There's a fellow waving a little black flag. He's standing on the steps of the omnibus. There come those other two fellows. Now they're all talking together. Look at the fellow with the flag. Maybe he ain't waving it."

"That ain't a flag, is it? That's his coat. Why, certainly, that's his coat."

"So it is. It's his coat. He's taken it off and is waving it around his head. But would you look at him swing it."

"Oh, say, there isn't any life-saving station there. That's just a winter resort hotel omnibus that has brought over some of the boarders to see us drown."

"What's that idiot with the coat mean? What's he signaling, anyhow?"

"It looks as if he were trying to tell us to go north. There must be a life-saving station up there."

"No! He thinks we're fishing. Just giving us a merry hand. See? Ah, there, Willie."

"Well, I wish I could make something out of those signals. What do you suppose he means?"

"He don't mean anything. He's just playing."

"Well, if he'd just signal us to try the surf again, or to go to sea and wait, or go north, or go south, or go to hell—there would be some reason in it. But look at him. He just stands there and keeps his coat revolving like a wheel. The ass!"

"There come more people."

"Now there's quite a mob. Look! Isn't that a boat."

"Where? Oh, I see where you mean. No, that's no boat."

"That fellow is still waving his coat."

"He must think we like to see him do that. Why don't he quit it? It don't mean anything."

"I don't know. I think he is trying to make us go north. It must be that there's a life-saving station there somewhere."

"Say, he ain't tired yet. Look at 'im wave."

"Wonder how long he can keep that up. He's been revolving his coat ever since he caught sight of us. He's an idiot. Why aren't they getting men to bring a boat out? A fishing boat—one of those big yawls—could come out here all right. Why don't he do something?"

"Oh, it's all right, now."

"They'll have a boat out here for us in less than no time, now that they've seen us."

A faint yellow tone came into the sky over the low land. The shadows on the sea slowly deepened. The wind bore coldness with it, and the men began to shiver.

"Holy smoke!" said one, allowing his voice to express his impious mood, "if we keep on monkeying out here! If we've got to flounder out here all night!"

"Oh, we'll never have to stay here all night! Don't you worry. They've seen us now, and it won't be long before they'll come chasing out after us."

The shore grew dusky. The man waving a coat blended gradually into this gloom, and it swallowed in the same manner the omnibus and the group of people. The spray, when it dashed uproariously over the side, made the voyagers shrink and swear like men who were being branded.

"I'd like to catch the chump who waved the coat. I feel like soaking him one, just for luck."

"Why? What did he do?"

"Oh, nothing, but then he seemed so damned cheerful."

In the meantime the oiler rowed, and then the correspondent rowed, and then the oiler rowed. Gray-faced and bowed forward, they mechanically, turn by turn, plied the leaden oars. The form of the lighthouse had vanished from the southern horizon, but finally a pale star appeared, just lifting from the sea. The streaked saffron in the west passed before the all-merging darkness, and the sea to the east was black. The land had vanished, and was expressed only by the low and drear thunder of the surf.

"If I am going to be drowned—if I am going to be drowned—if I am going to be drowned, why, in the name of the seven mad gods who rule the sea, was I allowed to come thus far and contemplate sand and trees? Was I brought here merely to have my nose dragged away as I was about to nibble the sacred cheese of life?"

The patient captain, drooped over the water-jar, was sometimes obliged to speak to the oarsman.

"Keep her head up! Keep her head up!"

" 'Keep her head up,' sir." The voices were weary and low.

This was surely a quiet evening. All save the oarsman lay heavily and listlessly in the boat's bottom. As for him, his eyes were just capable of noting the tall black waves that swept forward in a most sinister silence, save for an occasional subdued growl of a crest.

The cook's head was on a thwart, and he looked without interest at the water under his nose. He was deep in other scenes. Finally he spoke. "Billie," he murmured, dreamfully, "what kind of pie do you like best?"

V

"Pie," said the oiler and the correspondent, agitatedly. "Don't talk about those things, blast you!"

"Well," said the cook, "I was just thinking about ham sandwiches, and—"

A night on the sea in an open boat is a long night. As darkness settled finally, the shine of the light, lifting from the sea in the south, changed to full gold. On the northern horizon a new light appeared, a small bluish gleam on the edge of the waters. These two lights were the furniture of the world. Otherwise there was nothing but waves.

Two men huddled in the stern, and distances were so magnificent in the dingey that the rower was enabled to keep his feet partly warmed by thrusting them under his companions. Their legs indeed extended far under the rowing-seat until they touched the feet of the captain forward. Sometimes, despite the efforts of the tired oarsman, a wave came piling into the boat, an icy wave of the night, and the chilling water soaked them anew. They would twist their bodies for a moment and groan, and sleep the dead sleep once more, while the water in the boat gurgled about them as the craft rocked.

The plan of the oiler and the correspondent was for one to row until he lost the ability, and then arouse the other from his sea-water couch in the bottom of the boat.

The oiler plied the oars until his head drooped forward, and the overpowering sleep blinded him. And he rowed yet afterward. Then he touched a man in the bottom of the boat, and called his name. "Will you spell me for a little while?" he said, meekly.

"Sure, Billie," said the correspondent, awakening and dragging himself to a sitting position. They exchanged places carefully, and the oiler, cuddling down in the sea-water at the cook's side, seemed to go to sleep instantly.

The particular violence of the sea had ceased. The waves came without snarling. The obligation of the man at the oars was to keep the boat headed so that the tilt of the rollers would not capsize her, and to preserve her from filling when the crests rushed past. The black waves were silent and hard to be seen in the darkness. Often one was almost upon the boat before the oarsman was aware.

In a low voice the correspondent addressed the captain. He was not sure that the captain was awake, although this iron man seemed to be always awake. "Captain, shall I keep her making for that light north, sir?"

The same steady voice answered him. "Yes. Keep it about two points off the port bow."

The cook had tied a life-belt around himself in order to get even the warmth which this clumsy cork contrivance could donate, and he seemed almost stove-like when a rower, whose teeth invariably chattered wildly as soon as he ceased his labor, dropped down to sleep.

The correspondent, as he rowed, looked down at the two men sleeping underfoot. The cook's arm was around the oiler's shoulders, and, with their fragmentary clothing and haggard faces, they were the babes of the sea, a grotesque rendering of the old babes in the wood.

Later he must have grown stupid at his work, for suddenly there was a growling of water, and a crest came with a roar and a swash into the boat, and it was a wonder that it did not set the cook afloat in his life-belt. The cook continued to sleep, but the oiler sat up, blinking his eyes and shaking with the new cold.

"Oh, I'm awful sorry, Billie," said the correspondent, contritely.

"That's all right, old boy," said the oiler, and lay down again and was asleep.

Presently it seemed that even the captain dozed, and the correspondent thought that he was the one man afloat on all the oceans. The wind had a voice as it came over the waves, and it was sadder than the end.

There was a long, loud swishing astern of the boat, and a gleaming trail of phosphorescence, like blue flame, was furrowed on the black waters. It might have been made by a monstrous knife.

Then there came a stillness, while the correspondent breathed with the open mouth and looked at the sea.

Suddenly there was another swish and another long flash of bluish light, and this time it was alongside the boat, and might almost have been reached with an oar. The correspondent saw an enormous fin speed like a shadow through the water, hurling the crystalline spray and leaving the long glowing trail.

The correspondent looked over his shoulder at the captain. His face was hidden, and he seemed to be asleep. He looked at the babes of the sea. They certainly were asleep. So, being bereft of sympathy, he leaned a little way to one side and swore softly into the sea.

But the thing did not then leave the vicinity of the boat. Ahead or astern, on one side or the other, at intervals long or short, fled the long sparkling streak, and there was to be heard the whiroo of the dark fin. The speed and power of the thing was greatly to be admired. It cut the water like a gigantic and keen projectile.

The presence of this biding thing did not affect the man with the same horror that it would if he had been a picnicker. He simply looked at the sea dully and swore in an undertone.

Nevertheless, it is true that he did not wish to be alone. He wished one of his companions to awaken by chance and keep him company with it. But the captain hung motionless over the water-jar, and the oiler and the cook in the bottom of the boat were plunged in slumber.

VI

"If I am going to be drowned—if I am going to be drowned—if I am going to be drowned, why, in the name of the seven mad gods who rule the sea, was I allowed to come thus far and contemplate sand and trees?"

During this dismal night, it may be remarked that a man would conclude that it was really the intention of the seven mad gods to drown him, despite the abominable injustice of it. For it was certainly an abominable injustice to drown a man who had worked so hard, so hard. The man felt it would be a crime most unnatural. Other people had drowned at sea since galleys swarmed with painted sails, but still—

When it occurs to a man that nature does not regard him as important, and that she feels she would not maim the universe by disposing of him, he at first wishes to throw bricks at the temple, and he hates deeply the fact that there are no bricks and no temples. Any visible expression of nature would surely be pelleted with his jeers.

Then, if there be no tangible thing to hoot he feels, perhaps, the desire to confront a personification and indulge in pleas, bowed to one knee, and with hands supplicant, saying: "Yes, but I love myself."

A high cold star on a winter's night is the word he feels that she says to him. Thereafter he knows the pathos of his situation.

The men in the dingey had not discussed these matters, but each had, no doubt, reflected upon them in silence and according to his mind. There was seldom any expression upon their faces save the general one of complete weariness. Speech was devoted to the business of the boat.

To chime the notes of his emotion, a verse mysteriously entered the correspondent's head. He had even forgotten that he had forgotten this verse, but it suddenly was in his mind.

> "A soldier of the Legion lay dying in Algiers,
> There was lack of woman's nursing, there was dearth of woman's tears;
> But a comrade stood beside him, and he took that comrade's hand,
> And he said: 'I shall never see my own, my native land.' "

In his childhood, the correspondent had been made acquainted with the fact that a soldier of the Legion lay dying in Algiers, but he had never regarded the fact as important. Myriads of his schoolfellows had informed him of the soldier's plight, but the dinning had naturally ended by making him perfectly indifferent. He had never considered it his affair that a soldier of the Legion lay dying in Algiers, nor had it appeared to him as a matter for sorrow. It was less to him than the breaking of a pencil's point.

Now, however, it quaintly came to him as a human, living thing. It was no longer merely a picture of a few throes in the breast of a poet, meanwhile drinking tea and warming his feet at the grate; it was an actuality—stern, mournful, and fine.

The correspondent plainly saw the soldier. He lay on the sand with his feet out straight and still. While his pale left hand was upon his chest in an attempt to thwart the going of his life, the blood came between his fingers. In the far Algerian distance, a city of low square forms was set against a sky that was faint with the last sunset hues. The correspondent, plying the oars and dreaming of the slow and slower movements of the lips of the soldier, was moved by a profound and perfectly impersonal comprehension. He was sorry for the soldier of the Legion who lay dying in Algiers.

The thing which had followed the boat and waited had evidently grown bored at the delay. There was no longer to be heard the slash of the cut water, and there was no longer the flame of the long trail. The light in the north still glimmered, but it was apparently no nearer to the boat. Sometimes the boom of the surf rang in the correspondent's ears, and he turned the craft seaward then and rowed harder. Southward, someone had evidently built a watch-fire on the beach. It was too low and too far to be seen, but it made a shimmering, roseate reflection upon the bluff back of it, and this could be discerned from the boat. The wind came stronger, and sometimes a wave suddenly raged out like a mountain-cat, and there was to be seen the sheen and sparkle of a broken crest.

The captain, in the bow, moved on his water-jar and sat erect. "Pretty long night," he observed to the correspondent. He looked at the shore. "Those life-saving people take their time."

"Did you see that shark playing around?"

"Yes, I saw him. He was a big fellow, all right."

"Wish I had known you were awake."

Later the correspondent spoke into the bottom of the boat.

"Billie!" There was a slow and gradual disentanglement. "Billie, will you spell me?"

"Sure," said the oiler.

As soon as the correspondent touched the cold comfortable sea-water in the bottom of the boat, and had huddled close to the cook's life-belt he was deep in sleep, despite the fact that his teeth played all the popular airs. This sleep was so good to him that it was but a moment before he heard a voice call his name in a tone that demonstrated the last stages of exhaustion. "Will you spell me?"

"Sure, Billie."

The light in the north had mysteriously vanished, but the correspondent took his course from the wide-awake captain.

Later in the night they took the boat farther out to sea, and the captain directed the cook to take one oar at the stern and keep the boat facing the seas. He was to call out if he should hear the thunder of the surf. This plan enabled the oiler and the correspondent to get respite together. "We'll give those boys a chance to get into shape again," said the captain. They curled down and, after a few preliminary chatterings and trembles, slept once more the dead sleep. Neither knew they had bequeathed to the cook the company of another shark, or perhaps the same shark.

As the boat caroused on the waves, spray occasionally bumped over the side and gave them a fresh soaking, but this had no power to break their repose. The ominous slash of the wind and the water affected them as it would have affected mummies.

"Boys," said the cook, with the notes of every reluctance in his voice, "she's drifted in pretty close. I guess one of you had better take her to sea again." The correspondent, aroused, heard the crash of the toppled crests.

As he was rowing, the captain gave him some whiskey-and-water, and this steadied the chills out of him. "If I ever get ashore and anybody shows me even a photograph of an oar—"

At last there was a short conversation.
"Billie . . . Billie, will you spell me?"
"Sure," said the oiler.

VII

When the correspondent again opened his eyes, the sea and the sky were each of the gray hue of the dawning. Later, carmine and gold was painted upon the waters. The morning appeared finally, in its splendor, with a sky of pure blue, and the sunlight flamed on the tips of the waves.

On the distant dunes were set many little black cottages, and a tall white windmill reared above them. No man, nor dog, nor bicycle appeared on the beach. The cottages might have formed a deserted village.

The voyagers scanned the shore. A conference was held in the boat. "Well," said the captain, "if no help is coming, we might better try a run through the surf right away. If we stay out here much longer we will be too weak to do anything for ourselves at all." The others silently acquiesced in this reasoning. The boat was headed for the beach. The correspondent wondered if none ever ascended the tall wind-tower, and if then they never looked seaward. This tower was a giant, standing with its back to the plight of the ants. It represented in a degree, to the correspondent, the serenity of nature amid the struggles of the individual—nature in the wind, and nature in the vision of men. She did not seem cruel to him then, nor beneficent, nor treacherous, nor wise. But she was indifferent, flatly indifferent. It is, perhaps, plausible that a man in this situation, impressed with the unconcern of the universe, should see the innumerable flaws of his life, and have them taste wickedly in his mind and wish for another chance. A distinction between right and wrong seems absurdly clear to him, then, in this new ignorance of the grave-edge, and he understands that if he were given another opportunity he would mend his conduct and his words, and be better and brighter during an introduction or at a tea.

"Now, boys," said the captain, "she is going to swamp sure. All we can do is to work her in as far as possible, and then when she swamps, pile out and scramble for the beach. Keep cool now, and don't jump until she swamps sure."

The oiler took the oars. Over his shoulders he scanned the surf. "Captain," he said, "I think I'd better bring her about, and keep her head-on to the seas and back her in."

"All right, Billie," said the captain. "Back her in." The oiler swung the boat then and, seated in the stern, the cook and the correspondent were obliged to look over their shoulders to contemplate the lonely and indifferent shore.

The monstrous in-shore rollers heaved the boat high until the men were again enabled to see the white sheets of water scudding up the slanted beach. "We won't get in very close," said the captain. Each time a man could wrest his attention from the rollers, he turned his glance toward the shore, and in the expression of the eyes during this contemplation there was a singular quality. The correspondent, observing the others, knew that they were not afraid, but the full meaning of their glances was shrouded.

As for himself, he was too tired to grapple fundamentally with the fact. He tried to coerce his mind into thinking of it, but the mind was dominated at this time by the muscles, and the muscles said they did not care. It merely occurred to him that if he should drown it would be a shame.

There were no hurried words, no pallor, no plain agitation. The men simply looked at the shore. "Now, remember to get well clear of the boat when you jump," said the captain.

Seaward the crest of a roller suddenly fell with a thunderous crash, and the long white comber came roaring down upon the boat.

"Steady now," said the captain. The men were silent. They turned their eyes from the shore to the comber and waited. The boat slid up the incline, leaped at the furious top, bounced over it, and swung down the long back of the waves. Some water had been shipped and the cook bailed it out.

But the next crest crashed also. The tumbling, boiling flood of white water caught the boat and whirled it almost perpendicular. Water swarmed in from all sides. The correspondent had his hands on the gunwale at this time, and when the water entered at that place he swiftly withdrew his fingers, as if he objected to wetting them.

The little boat, drunken with this weight of water, reeled and snuggled deeper into the sea.

"Bail her out, cook! Bail her out," said the captain.

"All right, captain," said the cook.

"Now, boys, the next one will do for us, sure," said the oiler. "Mind to jump clear of the boat."

The third wave moved forward, huge, furious, implacable. It fairly swallowed the dingey, and almost simultaneously the men tumbled into the sea. A piece of life-belt had lain in the bottom of the boat, and as the correspondent went overboard he held this to his chest with his left hand.

The January water was icy, and he reflected immediately that it was colder than he had expected to find it off the coast of Florida.

This appeared to his dazed mind as a fact important enough to be noted at the time. The coldness of the water was sad; it was tragic. This fact was somehow so mixed and confused with his opinion of his own situation that it seemed almost a proper reason for tears. The water was cold.

When he came to the surface he was conscious of little but the noisy water. Afterward he saw his companions in the sea. The oiler was ahead in the race. He was swimming strongly and rapidly. Off to the correspondent's left, the cook's great white and corked back bulged out of the water, and in the rear the captain was hanging with his one good hand to the keel of the overturned dingey.

There is a certain immovable quality to a shore, and the correspondent wondered at it amid the confusion of the sea.

It seemed also very attractive, but the correspondent knew that it was a long journey, and he paddled leisurely. The piece of life-preserver lay under him, and sometimes he whirled down the incline of a wave as if he were on a hand-sled.

But finally he arrived at a place in the sea where travel was beset with difficulty. He did not pause swimming to inquire what manner of current had caught him, but there his progress ceased. The shore was set before him like a bit of scenery on a stage, and he looked at it and understood with his eyes each detail of it.

As the cook passed, much farther to the left, the captain was calling to him, "Turn over on your back, cook! Turn over on your back and use the oar."

"All right, sir." The cook turned on his back, and, paddling with an oar, went ahead as if he were a canoe.

Presently the boat also passed to the left of the correspondent with the captain clinging with one hand to the keel. He would have appeared like a man raising himself to look over a board fence, if it were not for the extraordinary gymnastics of the boat. The correspondent marvelled that the captain could still hold to it.

They passed on, nearer to shore—the oiler, the cook, the captain—and following them went the water-jar, bouncing gaily over the seas.

The correspondent remained in the grip of this strange new enemy—a current. The shore, with its white slope of sand and its green bluff, topped with little silent cottages, was spread like a picture before him. It was very near to him then, but he was impressed as one who in a gallery looks at a scene from Brittany or Algiers.

He thought: "I am going to drown? Can it be possible? Can it be possible? Can it be possible?" Perhaps an individual must consider his own death to be the final phenomenon of nature.

But later a wave perhaps whirled him out of this small deadly current, for he found suddenly that he could again make progress toward the shore. Later still, he was aware that the captain, clinging with one hand to the keel of the dingey, had his face turned away from the shore and toward him, and was calling his name. "Come to the boat! Come to the boat!"

In his struggle to reach the captain and the boat, he reflected that when one gets properly wearied, drowning must really be a comfortable arrangement, a cessation of hostilities accompanied by a large degree of relief, and he was glad of it, for the main thing in his mind for some moments had been horror of the temporary agony. He did not wish to be hurt.

Presently he saw a man running along the shore. He was undressing with most remarkable speed. Coat, trousers, shirt, everything flew magically off him.

"Come to the boat," called the captain.

"All right, captain." As the correspondent paddled, he saw the captain let himself down to bottom and leave the boat. Then the correspondent performed his one little marvel of the voyage. A large wave caught him and flung him with ease and supreme speed completely over the boat and far beyond it. It struck him even then as an event in gymnastics, and a true miracle of the sea. An overturned boat in the surf is not a plaything to a swimming man.

The correspondent arrived in water that reached only to his waist, but his condition did not enable him to stand for more than a moment. Each wave knocked him into a heap, and the under-tow pulled at him.

Then he saw the man who had been running and undressing, and undressing and running, come bounding into the water. He dragged ashore the cook, and then waded toward the captain, but the captain waved him away, and sent him to the correspondent. He was naked, naked as a tree in winter, but a halo was about his head, and he shone like a saint. He gave a strong pull, and a long drag, and a bully heave at the correspondent's hand. The correspondent, schooled in the minor formulae, said: "Thanks, old man." But suddenly the man cried: "What's that?" He pointed a swift finger. The correspondent said: "Go."

In the shallows, face downward, lay the oiler. His forehead touched sand that was periodically, between each wave, clear of the sea.

The correspondent did not know all that transpired afterward. When he achieved safe ground he fell, striking the sand with each particular part of his body. It was as if he had dropped from a roof, but the thud was grateful to him.

It seems that instantly the beach was populated with men, with blankets, clothes, and flasks, and women with coffee-pots and all the remedies sacred to their minds. The welcome of the land to the men from the sea was warm and generous, but a still and dripping shape was carried slowly up the beach, and the land's welcome for it could only be the different and sinister hospitality of the grave.

When it came night, the white waves paced to and fro in the moonlight, and the wind brought the sound of the great sea's voice to the men on shore, and they felt that they could then be interpreters.

The Structure of a Story

The ordering of incidents within a story may be spoken of as the **structure** of a story. Traditionally, a story's structure has been said to consist of four basic parts:

1. The **exposition.** The beginning of the story which introduces the reader to the tale's setting (time and place) and to some or all of its characters.
2. The **conflict.** Every story centers on a conflict of some sort: one person, or group of people, against another; people against nature; an individual against some rule or custom of society. Generally the conflict increases in tension or in complexity until it reaches a climax.
3. The **climax.** The point of greatest tension at which the turning-point or breaking-point is reached.
4. The **denouement** or **resolution.** The ending which brings the tale to a close, picking up the pieces of the action and reordering the lives left disordered by the conflict and its climax.

Of these four parts, only numbers two and three, the conflict and the climax, are essential. You don't have to begin with an exposition; your first sentence can show your characters already embroiled in their conflict. You don't have to end with a resolution; you can stop your tale short at its climactic moment, as Shirley Jackson does in "The Lottery." But you must have some sort of conflict in your action; and it must rise to some peak of intensity somewhere between the middle and end of your story.

To familiarize yourself with the notion of structure, analyze the structures of "Young Goodman Brown," "The Guest," and "The Open Boat." Do all four parts appear in each of these stories? What parts of each story would you assign to each section?

3
The First-Person Narrator

Omniscient narrators stand somewhat apart from their stories. Having no role in the action themselves, they can interpret its events and characters impartially. Thus, the narrator of "The Open Boat" speaks for all his tale's characters when he opens the story by declaring that "none of them knew the color of the sky" and closes it with, "they felt that they could then be interpreters." Even when an omniscient narrator shows us most of the story through one central character's eyes, as does the narrator of "Young Goodman Brown," he can still give us glimpses into minds and actions which that character cannot see, as when Hawthorne's narrator tells us that Brown's townsmen "carved no hopeful verse upon his tombstone." Moreover, he can still interpret the events he relates from his own point of view, even when his view of the matter conflicts with his central character's: "Had Goodman Brown fallen asleep in the forest . . . ?"

First-person narrators, on the other hand, are participants in their own stories. They are telling us of something that happened to them, and are telling their tale from their own point of view. They cannot see into the minds of the other characters; indeed, they may hardly understand their own actions. In contrast to the total knowledge of the omniscient narrator, the first-person narrator's powers of interpretation may be slight indeed.

As the narrator's knowledge shrinks, the readers' role expands. If we cannot trust the narrator as an omniscient, final authority, then our own wisdom and judgment must come into play. We must weigh the narrator's perceptions against our own and so create our own understanding of the actions and characters within the story.

Often, therefore, first-person narratives are rich in **irony,** with the narrators describing what they think they see and the readers interpreting the descriptions to discover what "really" happened. In these stories the relationship between reader and narrator is completely reversed. Now we are the wise ones, the ones with the fullest perception of what's going on. If we could only speak to these narrators, as they seem to be speaking to us, how much we could tell them!

In other stories, however, first-person narrators retain the full authority of the storyteller. Indeed, if the tales they tell are set far enough in their pasts, the narrators may view themselves as nearly omniscient. They know what they were thinking and feeling when the events took place, so they can take us into their major character's mind; they know how events turned out, so they feel that they can interpret the patterns within them. Moreover, they may feel that they have grown considerably wiser since the time of the actions they are relating and can therefore combine past feelings and present understanding to interpret events and emotions as no one else could.

In either case, and in less extreme cases as well, we often feel closer to first-person narrators than we feel either to omniscient narrators or to the characters they describe. The limitations of human knowledge and insight within which the first-person narrators work, the blend of attempted objectivity and personal involvement their voices convey, and their apparent openness in telling their own stories appeal to our sympathy and our sense of fellowship. In telling us, as they often do, of their dreams and desires, first-person narrators speak eloquently of human aspirations; in confessing (consciously or unconsciously) their shortcomings, they speak no less eloquently of human limitations.

In the stories that follow, we'll meet two types of first-person narrators. The narrator of "Bartleby the Scrivener" is a conscious storyteller, conscientious in telling his story as fully as he can, equally conscientious in admitting the limits of his knowledge. In fact, one of his themes is our limited ability to know and understand each other. The narrator of "The Yellow Wall-Paper," on the other hand, is not writing for an audience at all. Instead, she is writing a sort of diary for herself because writing is "a great relief to my mind." She writes things down as they occur, and thus has recorded each episode before the next one takes place. There is little room for hindsight in this sort of writing, little chance for the narrator to fit events into a pattern. We must provide the pattern ourselves, just as we must come to our understanding of the narrator, by observing how her feelings and perceptions change during the course of her narrative.

Both narrators engage us. The young wife in "The Yellow Wall-Paper," unconscious of our presence, speaks so openly to her "dead paper" of things she "would not say . . . to a living soul" that she seems to be speaking directly to us with the candor one reserves for one's closest friends. The lawyer who narrates the tale of Bartleby intends to present the scrivener to us as a man worth studying, but ends up presenting himself as well. Both narrators are easily as interesting as anyone else in the stories, although they remain unconscious of that fact. Intentionally or not, they are at the center of their stories.

HERMAN MELVILLE (1819–1891)

Bartleby the Scrivener

I am a rather elderly man. The nature of my avocations, for the last thirty years, has brought me into more than ordinary contact with what would seem an interesting and somewhat singular set of men, of whom, as yet, nothing, that I know of, has ever been written—I mean, the law-copyists, or scriveners. I have known very many of them, professionally and privately, and, if I pleased, could relate divers histories, at which good-natured gentlemen might smile, and sentimental souls might weep. But I waive the biographies of all other scriveners, for a few passages in the life of Bartleby, who was a scrivener, the strangest I ever saw, or heard of. While, of other law-copyists, I might write the complete life, of Bartleby nothing of that sort can be done. I believe that no materials exist, for a full and satisfactory biography of this man. It is an irreparable loss to literature. Bartleby was one of those beings of whom nothing is ascertainable, except from the original sources, and, in his case, those are very small. What my own astonished eyes saw of Bartleby, *that* is all I know of him, except, indeed, one vague report, which will appear in the sequel.

Ere introducing the scrivener, as he first appeared to me, it is fit I make some mention of myself, my *employés,* my business, my chambers, and general surroundings; because some such description is indispensable to an adequate understanding of the chief character about to be presented. Imprimis: I am a man who, from his youth upwards, has been filled with a profound conviction that the easiest

way of life is the best. Hence, though I belong to a profession proverbially energetic and nervous, even to turbulence, at times, yet nothing of that sort have I ever suffered to invade my peace. I am one of
those unambitious lawyers who never addresses a jury, or in any way
draws down public applause; but, in the cool tranquillity of a snug
retreat, do a snug business among rich men's bonds, and mortgages,
and title-deeds. All who know me, consider me an eminently *safe*
man. The late John Jacob Astor,[1] a personage little given to poetic
enthusiasm, had no hesitation in pronouncing my first grand point to
be prudence; my next, method. I do not speak it in vanity, but
simply record the fact, that I was not unemployed in my profession
by the late John Jacob Astor, a name which, I admit, I love to
repeat; for it hath a rounded and orbicular sound to it, and rings
like unto bullion. I will freely add, that I was not insensible to the
late John Jacob Astor's good opinion.

Some time prior to the period at which this little history begins, my
avocations had been largely increased. The good old office, now
extinct in the State of New York, of a Master in Chancery, had been
conferred upon me. It was not a very arduous office, but very pleasantly remunerative. I seldom lose my temper; much more seldom
indulge in dangerous indignation at wrongs and outrages; but, I
must be permitted to be rash here, and declare, that I consider the
sudden and violent abrogation of the office of Master in Chancery, by
the new Constitution, as a —— premature act; inasmuch as I had
counted upon a life-lease of the profits, whereas I only received those
of a few short years. But this is by the way.

My chambers were up stairs, at No. — Wall Street. At one end,
they looked upon the white wall of the interior of a spacious sky-light
shaft, penetrating the building from top to bottom.

This view might have been considered rather tame than otherwise,
deficient in what landscape painters call "life." But, if so, the view
from the other end of my chambers offered, at least, a contrast, if
nothing more. In that direction, my windows commanded an unob-
structed view of a lofty brick wall, black by age and everlasting
shade; which wall required no spy-glass to bring out its lurking
beauties, but, for the benefit of all near-sighted spectators, was
pushed up to within ten feet of my window panes. Owing to the great
height of the surrounding buildings, and my chambers being on the
second floor, the interval between this wall and mine not a little
resembled a huge square cistern.

At the period just preceding the advent of Bartleby, I had two
persons as copyists in my employment, and a promising lad as an

---

[1] *John Jacob Astor:* (1763–1848) an American fur trader and financier.

office-boy. First, Turkey; second, Nippers; third, Ginger Nut. These may seem names, the like of which are not usually found in the Directory. In truth, they were nicknames, mutually conferred upon each other by my three clerks, and were deemed expressive of their respective persons or characters. Turkey was a short, pursy Englishman, of about my own age—that is, somewhere not far from sixty. In the morning, one might say, his face was of a fine florid hue, but after twelve o'clock, meridian—his dinner hour—it blazed like a grate full of Christmas coals; and continued blazing—but, as it were, with a gradual wane—till six o'clock, P.M., or thereabouts; after which, I saw no more of the proprietor of the face, which, gaining its meridian with the sun, seemed to set with it, to rise, culminate, and decline the following day, with the like regularity and undiminished glory. There are many singular coincidences I have known in the course of my life, not the least among which was the fact, that, exactly when Turkey displayed his fullest beams from his red and radiant countenance, just then, too, at that critical moment, began the daily period when I considered his business capacities as seriously disturbed for the remainder of the twenty-four hours. Not that he was absolutely idle, or averse to business, then; far from it. The difficulty was, he was apt to be altogether too energetic. There was a strange, inflamed, flurried, flighty recklessness of activity about him. He would be incautious in dipping his pen into his inkstand. All his blots upon my documents were dropped there after twelve o'clock, meridian. Indeed, not only would he be reckless, and sadly given to making blots in the afternoon, but, some days, he went further, and was rather noisy. At such times, too, his face flamed with augmented blazonry, as if cannel coal had been heaped on anthracite. He made an unpleasant racket with his chair; spilled his sand-box; in mending his pens, impatiently split them all to pieces, and threw them on the floor in a sudden passion; stood up, and leaned over his table, boxing his papers about in a most indecorous manner, very sad to behold in an elderly man like him. Nevertheless, as he was in many ways a most valuable person to me, and all the time before twelve o'clock, meridian, was the quickest, steadiest creature, too, accomplishing a great deal of work in a style not easily to be matched—for these reasons, I was willing to overlook his eccentricities, though, indeed, occasionally, I remonstrated with him. I did this very gently, however, because, though the civilest, nay, the blandest and most reverential of men in the morning, yet, in the afternoon, he was disposed, upon provocation, to be slightly rash with his tongue—in fact, insolent. Now, valuing his morning services as I did, and resolved not to lose them—yet, at the same time, made uncomfortable by his inflamed ways after twelve o'clock—and being a man of peace, unwilling by my admonitions to call forth unseemly retorts from him, I took upon me, one Saturday noon (he was always worse on Saturdays) to hint to him, very kindly, that, perhaps, now that he was growing old, it might be well to abridge his labors; in short, he need not come to my chambers after twelve o'clock, but, dinner over, had best go home to his lodgings, and rest himself till tea-time. But no; he insisted upon his afternoon devotions. His countenance became intolerably fervid, as he oratorically assured me—gesticulating with a long ruler at the other end of the room—that if his services in the morning were useful, how indispensable, then, in the afternoon?

"With submission, sir," said Turkey, on this occasion, "I consider myself your right-hand man. In the morning I but marshal and deploy my columns; but in the afternoon I put myself at their head, and gallantly charge the foe, thus"—and he made a violent thrust with the ruler.

"But the blots, Turkey," intimated I.

"True; but, with submission, sir, behold these hairs! I am getting old. Surely, sir, a blot or two of a warm afternoon is not to be severely urged against gray hairs. Old age—even if it blot the page— is honorable. With submission, sir, we *both* are getting old."

This appeal to my fellow-feeling was hardly to be resisted. At all events, I saw that go he would not. So, I made up my mind to let him stay, resolving, nevertheless, to see to it that, during the afternoon, he had to do with my less important papers.

Nippers, the second on my list, was a whiskered, sallow, and, upon the whole, rather piratical-looking young man, of about five and twenty. I always deemed him the victim of two evil powers—ambition and indigestion. The ambition was evinced by a certain impatience of the duties of a mere copyist, an unwarrantable usurpation of strictly professional affairs, such as the original drawing up of legal documents. The indigestion seemed betokened in an occasional nervous testiness and grinning irritability, causing the teeth to audibly grind together over mistakes committed in copying; unnecessary maledictions, hissed, rather than spoken, in the heat of business; and especially by a continual discontent with the height of the table where he worked. Though of a very ingenious mechanical turn, Nippers could never get this table to suit him. He put chips under it, blocks of various sorts, bits of pasteboard, and at last went so far as to attempt an exquisite adjustment, by final pieces of folded blotting-paper. But no invention would answer. If, for the sake of easing his back, he brought the table lid at a sharp angle well up towards his chin, and wrote there like a man using the steep roof of a Dutch house for his desk, then he declared that it stopped the circulation in his arms. If now he lowered the table to his waistbands, and stooped over it in writing, then there was a sore aching in his back. In short, the truth of the matter was, Nippers knew not what he wanted. Or, if he wanted anything, it was to be rid of a scrivener's table altogether. Among the manifestations of his diseased ambition was a fondness he had for receiving visits from certain ambiguous-looking fellows in seedy coats, whom he called his clients. Indeed, I was aware that not only was he, at times, considerable of a ward-politician, but he occasionally did a little business at the Justices' courts, and was not unknown on the steps of the Tombs. I have good reason to believe, however, that one individual who called upon him at my chambers, and who, with a grand air, he insisted was his client, was no other than a dun, and the alleged title-deed, a bill. But, with all his failings, and the annoyances he caused me, Nippers, like his compatriot Turkey, was a very useful man to me; wrote a neat, swift hand; and, when he chose, was not deficient in a gentlemanly sort of deportment. Added to this, he always dressed in a gentlemanly sort of way; and so, incidentally, reflected credit upon my chambers. Whereas, with respect to Turkey, I had much ado to keep him from being a reproach to me. His clothes were apt to look oily, and smell of eating-houses. He wore his pantaloons very loose and baggy in summer. His coats were execrable; his hat not to be handled. But while the hat was a thing of indifference to me, inasmuch as his natural civility and deference, as a dependent Englishman, always led him to doff it the moment he entered the room, yet his coat was another matter. Concerning his coats, I reasoned with him; but with no effect. The truth was, I suppose, that a man with so small an income could not afford to sport such a lustrous face and a lustrous coat at one and the same time. As Nippers once observed, Turkey's money went chiefly for red ink. One winter day, I presented Turkey with a highly respectable-looking coat of my own—a padded gray coat, of a most comfortable warmth, and which buttoned straight up from the knee to the neck. I thought Turkey would appreciate the favor, and abate his rashness and obstreperousness of afternoons. But no; I verily believe that buttoning himself up in so downy and blanket-like a coat had a pernicious effect upon him—upon the same principle that too much oats are bad for horses. In fact, precisely as a rash, restive horse is said to feel his oats, so Turkey felt his coat. It made him insolent. He was a man whom prosperity harmed.

Though, concerning the self-indulgent habits of Turkey, I had my own private surmises, yet, touching Nippers, I was well persuaded that, whatever might be his faults in other respects, he was, at least, a temperate young man. But, indeed, nature herself seemed to have been his vintner, and, at his birth, charged him so thoroughly with an irritable, brandy-like disposition, that all subsequent potations were needless. When I consider how, amid the stillness of my chambers, Nippers would sometimes impatiently rise from his seat, and stooping over his table, spread his arms wide apart, seize the whole desk, and move it, and jerk it, with a grim, grinding motion on the floor, as if the table were a perverse voluntary agent, intent on thwarting and vexing him, I plainly perceive that, for Nippers, brandy-and-water were altogether superfluous.

It was fortunate for me that, owing to its peculiar cause—indigestion—the iritability and consequent nervousness of Nippers were mainly observable in the morning, while in the afternoon he was comparatively mild. So that, Turkey's paroxysms only coming on about twelve o'clock, I never had to do with their eccentricities at one time. Their fits relieved each other, like guards. When Nippers' was on, Turkey's was off; and *vice versa*. This was a good natural arrangement, under the circumstances.

Ginger Nut, the third on my list, was a lad, some twelve years old. His father was a car-man, ambitious of seeing his son on the bench instead of a cart, before he died. So he sent him to my office, as student at law, errand-boy, cleaner and sweeper, at the rate of one dollar a week. He had a little desk to himself, but he did not use it much. Upon inspection, the drawer exhibited a great array of the shells of various sorts of nuts. Indeed, to this quick-witted youth, the whole noble science of the law was contained in a nut-shell. Not the least among the employments of Ginger Nut, as well as one which he discharged with the most alacrity, was his duty as cake and apple purveyor for Turkey and Nippers. Copying law-papers being proverbially a dry, husky sort of business, my two scriveners were fain to moisten their mouths very often with Spitzenbergs, to be had at the numerous stalls nigh the Custom House and Post Office. Also, they sent Ginger Nut very frequently for that peculiar cake—small, flat, round, and very spicy—after which he had been named by them. Of a cold morning, when business was but dull, Turkey would gobble up scores of these cakes, as if they were mere wafers—indeed, they sell them at the rate of six or eight for a penny—the scrape of his pen blending with the crunching of the crisp particles in his mouth. Of all the fiery afternoon blunders and flurried rashnesses of Turkey, was his once moistening a ginger-cake between his lips, and clapping it on to a mortgage, for a seal. I came within an ace of dismissing him then. But he mollified me by making an oriental bow, and saying—

"With submission, sir, it was generous of me to find you in stationery on my own account."

Now my original business—that of a conveyancer and title hunter, and drawer-up of recondite documents of all sorts—was considerably increased by receiving the master's office. There was now great work for scriveners. Not only must I push the clerks already with me, but I must have additional help.

In answer to my advertisement, a motionless young man one morning stood upon my office threshold, the door being open, for it was summer. I can see that figure now—pallidly neat, pitiably respect-able, incurably forlorn! It was Bartleby.

After a few words touching his qualifications, I engaged him, glad to have among my corps of copyists a man of so singularly sedate an aspect, which I thought might operate beneficially upon the flighty temper of Turkey, and the fiery one of Nippers.

I should have stated before that ground glass folding-doors divided my premises into two parts, one of which was occupied by my scriveners, the other by myself. According to my humor, I threw open these doors, or closed them. I resolved to assign Bartleby a corner by the folding-doors, but on my side of them, so as to have this quiet man within easy call, in case any trifling thing was to be done. I placed his desk close up to a small side-window in that part of the room, a window which originally had afforded a lateral view of certain grimy backyards and bricks, but which, owing to subsequent erections, commanded at present no view at all, though it gave some light. Within three feet of the panes was a wall, and the light came down from far above, between two lofty buildings, as from a very small opening in a dome. Still further to a satisfactory arrangement, I procured a high green folding screen, which might entirely isolate Bartleby from my sight, though not remove him from my voice. And thus, in a manner, privacy and society were conjoined.

At first, Bartleby did an extraordinary quantity of writing. As if long famishing for something to copy, he seemed to gorge himself on my documents. There was no pause for digestion. He ran a day and night line, copying by sun-light and by candle-light. I should have been quite delighted with his application, had he been cheerfully industrious. But he wrote on silently, palely, mechanically.

It is, of course, an indispensable part of a scrivener's business to verify the accuracy of his copy, word by word. Where there are two or more scriveners in an office, they assist each other in this examina-tion, one reading from the copy, the other holding the original. It is a very dull, wearisome, and lethargic affair. I can readily imagine that, to some sanguine temperaments, it would be altogether intoler-able. For example, I cannot credit that the mettlesome poet, Byron, would have contentedly sat down with Bartleby to examine a law document of, say five hundred pages, closely written in a crimpy hand.

Now and then, in the haste of business, it had been my habit to assist in comparing some brief document myself, calling Turkey or Nippers for this purpose. One object I had, in placing Bartleby so handy to me behind the screen, was, to avail myself of his services on such trivial occasions. It was on the third day, I think, of his being with me, and before any necessity had arisen for having his own writing examined, that, being much hurried to complete a small affair I had in hand, I abruptly called to Bartleby. In my haste and natural expectancy of instant compliance, I sat with my head bent over the original on my desk, and my right hand sideways, and somewhat nervously extended with the copy, so that, immediately upon emerging from his retreat, Bartleby might snatch it and proceed to business without the least delay.

In this very attitude did I sit when I called to him, rapidly stating what it was I wanted him to do—namely, to examine a small paper with me. Imagine my surprise, nay, my consternation, when, without moving from his privacy, Bartleby, in a singularly mild, firm voice, replied, "I would prefer not to."

I sat awhile in perfect silence, rallying my stunned faculties. Immediately it occurred to me that my ears had deceived me, or Bartleby had entirely misunderstood my meaning. I repeated my request in the clearest tone I could assume; but in quite as clear a one came the previous reply, "I would prefer not to."

"Prefer not to," echoed I, rising in high excitement, and crossing the room with a stride. "What do you mean? Are you moon-struck? I want you to help me compare this sheet here—take it," and I thrust it towards him.

"I would prefer not to," said he.

I looked at him steadfastly. His face was leanly composed; his gray eye dimly calm. Not a wrinkle of agitation rippled him. Had there been the least uneasiness, anger, impatience or impertinence in his manner; in other words, had there been any thing ordinarily human about him, doubtless I should have violently dismissed him from the premises. But as it was, I should have as soon thought of turning my pale plaster-of-paris bust of Cicero out of doors. I stood gazing at him awhile, as he went on with his own writing, and then reseated myself at my desk. This is very strange, thought I. What had one best do? But my business hurried me. I concluded to forget the matter for the present, reserving it for my future leisure. So calling Nippers from the other room, the paper was speedily examined.

A few days after this, Bartleby concluded four lengthy documents, being quadruplicates of a week's testimony taken before me in my High Court of Chancery. It became necessary to examine them. It was an important suit, and great accuracy was imperative. Having all things arranged, I called Turkey, Nippers, and Ginger Nut, from the next room, meaning to place the four copies in the hands of my four clerks, while I should read from the original. Accordingly, Turkey, Nippers, and Ginger Nut had taken their seats in a row, each with his document in his hand, when I called to Bartleby to join this interesting group.

"Bartleby! quick, I am waiting."

I heard a slow scrape of his chair legs on the uncarpeted floor, and soon he appeared standing at the entrance of his hermitage.

"What is wanted?" said he, mildly.

"The copies, the copies," said I, hurriedly. "We are going to examine them. There"—and I held towards him the fourth quadruplicate.

"I would prefer not to," he said, and gently disappeared behind the screen.

For a few moments I was turned into a pillar of salt, standing at the head of my seated column of clerks. Recovering myself, I advanced towards the screen, and demanded the reason for such extraordinary conduct.

"*Why* do you refuse?"

"I would prefer not to."

With any other man I should have flown outright into a dreadful passion, scorned all further words, and thrust him ignominiously from my presence. But there was something about Bartleby that not only strangely disarmed me, but, in a wonderful manner, touched and disconcerted me. I began to reason with him.

"These are your own copies we are about to examine. It is labor saving to you, because one examination will answer for your four papers. It is common usage. Every copyist is bound to help examine his copy. Is it not so? Will you not speak? Answer!"

"I prefer not to," he replied in a flutelike tone. It seemed to me that, while I had been addressing him, he carefully revolved every statement that I made; fully comprehended the meaning; could not gainsay the irresistible conclusion; but, at the same time, some paramount consideration prevailed with him to reply as he did.

"You are decided, then, not to comply with my request—a request made according to common usage and common sense?"

He briefly gave me to understand, that on that point my judgment was sound. Yes: his decision was irreversible.

It is not seldom the case that, when a man is browbeaten in some unprecedented and violently unreasonable way, he begins to stagger in his own plainest faith. He begins, as it were, vaguely to surmise that, wonderful as it may be, all the justice and all the reason is on the other side. Accordingly, if any disinterested persons are present, he turns to them for some reinforcement of his own faltering mind.

"Turkey," said I, "what do you think of this? Am I not right?"

"With submission, sir," said Turkey, in his blandest tone, "I think that you are."

"Nippers," said I, "what do *you* think of it?"

"I think I should kick him out of the office."

(The reader, of nice perceptions, will here perceive that, it being morning, Turkey's answer is couched in polite and tranquil terms, but Nippers' replies in ill-tempered ones. Or, to repeat a previous sentence, Nippers' ugly mood was on duty, and Turkey's off.)

"Ginger Nut," said I, willing to enlist the smallest suffrage in my behalf, "what do *you* think of it?"

"I think, sir, he's a little *luny*," replied Ginger Nut, with a grin.

"You hear what they say," said I, turning towards the screen, "come forth and do your duty."

But he vouchsafed no reply. I pondered a moment in sore perplexity. But once more business hurried me. I determined again to postpone the consideration of this dilemma to my future leisure. With a little trouble we made out to examine the papers without Bartleby, though at every page or two Turkey deferentially dropped his opinion, that this proceeding was quite out of the common; while Nippers, twitching in his chair with a dyspeptic nervousness, ground out, between his set teeth, occasional hissing maledictions against the stubborn oaf behind the screen. And for his (Nippers') part, this was the first and the last time he would do another man's business without pay.

Meanwhile Bartleby sat in his hermitage, oblivious to everything but his own peculiar business there.

Some days passed, the scrivener being employed upon another lengthy work. His late remarkable conduct led me to regard his ways narrowly. I observed that he never went to dinner; indeed, that he never went anywhere. As yet I had never, of my personal knowledge, known him to be outside of my office. He was a perpetual sentry in the corner. At about eleven o'clock though, in the morning, I noticed that Ginger Nut would advance toward the opening in Bartleby's screen, as if silently beckoned thither by a gesture invisible to me where I sat. The boy would then leave the office, jingling a few pence, and reappear with a handful of ginger-nuts, which he delivered in the hermitage, receiving two of the cakes for his trouble.

He lives, then, on ginger-nuts, thought I; never eats a dinner, properly speaking; he must be a vegetarian, then; but no; he never eats even vegetables, he eats nothing but ginger-nuts. My mind then ran on in reveries concerning the probable effects upon the human constitution of living entirely on ginger-nuts. Ginger-nuts are so called, because they contain ginger as one of their peculiar constituents, and the final flavoring one. Now, what was ginger? A hot, spicy thing. Was Bartleby hot and spicy? Not at all. Ginger, then, had no effect upon Bartleby. Probably he preferred it should have none.

Nothing so aggravates an earnest person as a passive resistance. If the individual so resisted be of a not inhumane temper, and the resisting one perfectly harmless in his passivity, then, in the better moods of the former, he will endeavor charitably to construe to his imagination what proves impossible to be solved by his judgment. Even so, for the most part, I regarded Bartleby and his ways. Poor fellow! thought I, he means no mischief; it is plain he intends no insolence; his aspect sufficiently evinces that his eccentricities are involuntary. He is useful to me. I can get along with him. If I turn him away, the chances are he will fall in with some less-indulgent employer, and then he will be rudely treated, and perhaps driven forth miserably to starve. Yes. Here I can cheaply purchase a delicious self-approval. To befriend Bartleby; to humor him in his strange willfulness, will cost me little or nothing, while I lay up in my soul what will eventually prove a sweet morsel for my conscience. But this mood was not invariable with me. The passiveness of Bartleby sometimes irritated me. I felt strangely goaded on to encounter him in new opposition—to elicit some angry spark from him answerable to my own. But, indeed, I might as well have essayed to strike fire with my knuckles against a bit of Windsor soap. But one afternoon the evil impulse in me mastered me, and the following little scene ensued:

"Bartleby," said I, "when those papers are all copied, I will compare them with you."

"I would prefer not to."

"How? Surely you do not mean to persist in that mulish vagary?" No answer.

I threw open the folding-doors near by, and, turning upon Turkey and Nippers, exclaimed:

"Bartleby a second time says, he won't examine his papers. What do you think of it, Turkey?"

It was afternoon, be it remembered. Turkey sat glowing like a brass boiler; his bald head steaming; his hands reeling among his blotted papers.

"Think of it?" roared Turkey; ".I think I'll just step behind his screen, and black his eyes for him!"

So saying, Turkey rose to his feet and threw his arms into a pugilistic position. He was hurrying away to make good his promise, when I detained him, alarmed at the effect of incautiously rousing Turkey's combativeness after dinner.

"Sit down, Turkey," said I, "and hear what Nippers has to say. What do you think of it, Nippers? Would I not be justified in immediately dismissing Bartleby?"

"Excuse me, that is for you to decide, sir. I think his conduct quite unusual, and, indeed, unjust, as regards Turkey and myself. But it may only be a passing whim."

"Ah," exclaimed I, "you have strangely changed your mind, then—you speak very gently of him now."

"All beer," cried Turkey; "gentleness is effects of beer—Nippers and I dined together to-day. You see how gentle *I* am, sir. Shall I go and black his eyes?"

"You refer to Bartleby, I suppose. No, not to-day, Turkey," I replied; "pray, put up your fists."

I closed the doors, and again advanced towards Bartleby. I felt additional incentives tempting me to my fate. I burned to be rebelled against again. I remember that Bartleby never left the office.

"Bartleby," said I, "Ginger Nut is away; just step around to the Post Office, won't you? (it was but a three minutes' walk), and see if there is anything for me."

"I would prefer not to."

"You *will* not?"

"I *prefer* not."

I staggered to my desk, and sat there in a deep study. My blind inveteracy returned. Was there any other thing in which I could procure myself to be ignominiously repulsed by this lean, penniless wight?—my hired clerk? What added thing is there, prefectly reasonable, that he will be sure to refuse to do?

"Bartleby!"

No answer.

"Bartleby," in a louder tone.

No answer.

"Bartleby," I roared.

Like a very ghost, agreeably to the laws of magical invocation, at the third summons, he appeared at the entrance of his hermitage.

"Go to the next room, and tell Nippers to come to me."

"I prefer not to," he respectfully and slowly said, and mildly disappeared.

"Very good, Bartleby," said I, in a quiet sort of serenely-severe self-possessed tone, intimating the unalterable purpose of some terrible retribution very close at hand. But upon the whole, as it was drawing towards my dinner-hour, I thought it best to put on my hat and walk home for the day, suffering much from perplexity and distress of mind.

Shall I acknowledge it? The conclusion of this whole business was, that it soon became a fixed fact of my chambers, that a pale young scrivener, by the name of Bartleby, had a desk there; that he copied for me at the usual rate of four cents a folio (one hundred words); but he was permanently exempt from examining the work done by him, that duty being transferred to Turkey and Nippers, out of compliment, doubtless, to their superior acuteness; moreover, said Bartleby was never, on any account, to be dispatched on the most trivial errand of any sort; and that even if entreated to take upon him such a matter, it was generally understood that he would "prefer not to"—in other words, that he would refuse point-blank.

As days passed on, I became considerably reconciled to Bartleby. His steadiness, his freedom from all dissipation, his incessant industry (except when he chose to throw himself into a standing revery behind his screen), his great stillness, his unalterableness of demeanor under all circumstances, made him a valuable acquisition. One prime thing was this—*he was always there*—first in the morning, continually through the day, and the last at night. I had a singular confidence in his honesty. I felt my most precious papers perfectly safe in his hands. Sometimes, to be sure, I could not, for the very soul of me, avoid falling into sudden spasmodic passions with him. For it was exceeding difficult to bear in mind all the time those strange peculiarities, privileges, and unheard of exemptions, forming the tacit stipulations on Bartleby's part under which he remained in my office. Now and then, in the eagerness of dispatching pressing business, I would inadvertently summon Bartleby, in a short, rapid tone, to put his finger, say, on the incipient tie of a bit of red tape with which I was about compressing some papers. Of course, from behind the screen the usual answer, "I prefer not to," was sure to come; and then, how could a human creature, with the common infirmities of our nature, refrain from bitterly exclaiming upon such perverseness—such unreasonableness. However, every added repulse of this sort which I received only tended to lessen the probability of my repeating the inadvertence.

Here it must be said, that according to the custom of most legal gentlemen occupying chambers in densely-populated law buildings, there were several keys to my door. One was kept by a woman residing in the attic, which person weekly scrubbed and daily swept and dusted my apartments. Another was kept by Turkey for convenience sake. The third I sometimes carried in my own pocket. The fourth I knew not who had.

Now, one Sunday morning I happened to go to Trinity Church, to hear a celebrated preacher, and finding myself rather early on the ground I thought I would walk around to my chambers for a while. Luckily I had my key with me; but upon applying it to the lock, I found it resisted by something inserted from the inside. Quite surprised, I called out; when to my consternation a key was turned from within; and thrusting his lean visage at me, and holding the door ajar, the apparition of Bartleby appeared, in his shirt sleeves, and otherwise in a strangely tattered deshabille, saying quietly that he was sorry, but he was deeply engaged just then, and—preferred not admitting me at present. In a brief word or two, he moreover added, that perhaps I had better walk around the block two or three times, and by that time he would probably have concluded his affairs.

Now, the utterly unsurmised appearance of Bartleby, tenanting my law-chambers of a Sunday morning, with his cadaverously gentlemanly *nonchalance,* yet withal firm and self-possessed, had such a strange effect upon me, that incontinently I slunk away from my own door, and did as desired. But not without sundry twinges of impotent rebellion against the mild effrontery of this unaccountable scrivener. Indeed, it was his wonderful mildness chiefly, which not only disarmed me, but unmanned me as it were. For I consider that one, for the time, is somehow unmanned when he tranquilly permits his hired clerk to dictate to him, and order him away from his own premises. Furthermore, I was full of uneasiness as to what Bartleby could possibly be doing in my office in his shirt sleeves, and in an otherwise dismantled condition of a Sunday morning. Was anything amiss going on? Nay, that was out of the question. It was not to be thought of for a moment that Bartleby was an immoral person. But what could he be doing there?—copying? Nay again, whatever might be his eccentricities, Bartleby was an eminently decorous person. He would be the last man to sit down to his desk in any state approaching to nudity. Besides, it was Sunday; and there was something about Bartleby that forbade the supposition that he would by any secular occupation violate the proprieties of the day.

Nevertheless, my mind was not pacified; and full of a restless curiosity, at last I returned to the door. Without hindrance I inserted my key, opened it, and entered. Bartleby was not to be seen. I looked round anxiously, peeped behind his screen; but it was very plain that he was gone. Upon more closely examining the place, I surmised that for an indefinite period Bartleby must have ate, dressed, and slept in my office, and that, too, without plate, mirror, or bed. The cushioned seat of a rickety old sofa in one corner bore the faint impression of a lean, reclining form. Rolled away under his desk, I found a blanket; on a chair, a tin basin, with soap and a ragged towel; in a newspaper a few crumbs of ginger-nuts and a morsel of cheese. Yes, thought I, it is evident enough that Bartleby has been making his home here, keeping bachelor's hall all by himself. Immediately then the thought came sweeping across me, what miserable friendlessness and loneliness are here revealed! His poverty is great; but his solitude, how horrible! Think of it. Of a Sunday, Wall Street is deserted as Petra;[2] and every night of every day it is an emptiness. This building, too, which of week-days hums with industry and life, at nightfall echoes with sheer vacancy, and all through Sunday is forlorn. And here Bartleby makes his home; sole spectator of a solitude which he has seen all populous—a sort of innocent and transformed Marius brooding among the ruins of Carthage!

For the first time in my life a feeling of over-powering stinging

---

[2] *Petra:* ancient city in Syria.

melancholy seized me. Before, I had never experienced aught but a not unpleasing sadness. The bond of a common humanity now drew me irresistibly to gloom. A fraternal melancholy! For both I and Bartleby were sons of Adam. I remembered the bright silks and sparkling faces I had seen that day, in gala trim, swan-like sailing down the Mississippi of Broadway; and I contrasted them with the pallid copyist, and thought to myself, Ah, happiness courts the light, so we deem the world is gay; but misery hides aloof, so we deem that misery there is none. These sad fancyings—chimeras, doubtless, of a sick and silly brain—led on to other and more special thoughts, concerning the eccentricities of Bartleby. Presentiments of strange discoveries hovered round me. The scrivener's pale form appeared to me laid out, among uncaring strangers, in its shivering winding sheet.

Suddenly I was attracted by Bartleby's closed desk, the key in open sight left in the lock.

I mean no mischief, seek the gratification of no heartless curiosity, thought I; besides, the desk is mine, and its contents, too, so I will make bold to look within. Everything was methodically arranged, the papers smoothly placed. The pigeon holes were deep, and removing the files of documents, I groped into their recesses. Presently I felt something there, and dragged it out. It was an old bandanna hand-kerchief, heavy and knotted. I opened it, and saw it was a saving's bank.

I now recalled all the quiet mysteries which I had noted in the man. I remembered that he never spoke but to answer; that, though at intervals he had considerable time to himself, yet I had never seen him reading—no, not even a newspaper; that for long periods he would stand looking out, at his pale window behind the screen, upon the dead brick wall; I was quite sure he never visited any refectory or eating house; while his pale face clearly indicated that he never drank beer like Turkey, or tea and coffee even, like other men; that he never went anywhere in particular that I could learn; never went out for a walk, unless, indeed, that was the case at present; that he had declined telling who he was, or whence he came, or whether he had any relatives in the world; that though so thin and pale, he never complained of ill health. And more than all, I remembered a certain unconscious air of pallid—how shall I call it?—of pallid haughtiness, say, or rather an austere reserve about him, which had positively awed me into my tame compliance with his eccentricities, when I had feared to ask him to do the slightest incidental thing for me, even though I might know, from his long-continued motionless-ness, that behind his screen he must be standing in one of those dead-wall reveries of his.

Revolving all these things, and coupling them with the recently discovered fact, that he made my office his constant abiding place and home, and not forgetful of his morbid moodiness; revolving all these things, a prudential feeling began to steal over me. My first emotions had been those of pure melancholy and sincerest pity; but just in proportion as the forlornness of Bartleby grew and grew to my imagination, did that same melancholy merge into fear, that pity into repulsion. So true it is, and so terrible, too, that up to a certain point the thought or sight of misery enlists our best affections; but, in certain special cases, beyond that point it does not. They err who would assert that invariably this is owing to the inherent selfishness of the human heart. It rather proceeds from a certain hopelessness of remedying excessive and organic ill. To a sensitive being, pity is not seldom pain. And when at last it is perceived that such pity cannot lead to effectual succor, common sense bids the soul be rid of it. What I saw that morning persuaded me that the scrivener was the victim of inate and incurable disorder. I might give alms to his body; but his body did not pain him; it was his soul that suffered, and his soul I could not reach.

I did not accomplish the purpose of going to Trinity Church that morning. Somehow, the things I had seen disqualified me for the time from church-going. I walked homeward, thinking what I would do with Bartleby. Finally, I resolved upon this—I would put certain calm questions to him the next morning, touching his history, etc., and if he declined to answer them openly and unreservedly (and I supposed he would prefer not), then to give him a twenty dollar bill over and above whatever I might owe him, and tell him his services were no longer required; but that if in any other way I could assist him, I would be happy to do so, especially if he desired to return to his native place, wherever that might be, I would willingly help to defray the expenses. Moreover, if, after reaching home, he found himself at any time in want of aid, a letter from him would be sure of a reply.

The next morning came.

"Bartleby," said I, gently calling to him behind his screen.

No reply.

"Bartleby," said I, in a still gentler tone, "come here; I am not going to ask you to do anything you would prefer not to do—I simply wish to speak to you."

Upon this he noiselessly slid into view.

"Will you tell me, Bartleby, where you were born?"

"I would prefer not to."

"Will you tell me *anything* about yourself?"

"I would prefer not to."

"But what reasonable objection can you have to speak to me? I feel friendly towards you."

He did not look at me while I spoke, but kept his glance fixed upon my bust of Cicero, which, as I then sat, was directly behind me, some six inches above my head.

"What is your answer, Bartleby," said I, after waiting a considerable time for a reply, during which his countenance remained immovable, only there was the faintest conceivable tremor of the white attenuated mouth.

"At present I prefer to give no answer," he said, and retired into his hermitage.

It was rather weak in me I confess, but his manner, on this occasion, nettled me. Not only did there seem to lurk in it a certain calm disdain, but his perverseness seemed ungrateful, considering the undeniable good usage and indulgence he had received from me.

Again I sat ruminating what I should do. Mortified as I was at his behavior, and resolved as I had been to dismiss him when I entered my office, nevertheless I strangely felt something superstitious knocking at my heart, and forbidding me to carry out my purpose, and denouncing me for a villain if I dared to breathe one bitter word against this forlornest of mankind. At last, familiarly drawing my chair behind his screen, I sat down and said: "Bartleby, never mind, then, about revealing your history; but let me entreat you, as a friend, to comply as far as may be with the usages of this office. Say now, you will help to examine papers to-morrow or next day: in short, say now, that in a day or two you will begin to be a little reasonable:—say so, Bartleby."

"At present I would prefer not to be a little reasonable," was his mildly cadaverous reply.

Just then the folding-doors opened, and Nippers approached. He seemed suffering from an unusually bad night's rest, induced by severer indigestion than common. He overheard those final words of Bartleby.

"*Prefer not,* eh?" gritted Nippers—"I'd *prefer* him, if I were you, sir," addressing me—"I'd *prefer* him; I'd give him preferences, the stubborn mule! What is it, sir, pray, that he *prefers* not to do now?"

Bartleby moved not a limb.

"Mr. Nippers," said I, "I'd prefer that you would withdraw for the present."

Somehow, of late, I had got into the way of involuntarily using this word "prefer" upon all sorts of not exactly suitable occasions. And I trembled to think that my contact with the scrivener had already and seriously affected me in a mental way. And what further and deeper aberration might it not yet produce? This apprehension had not been without efficacy in determining me to summary measures.

As Nippers, looking very sour and sulky, was departing, Turkey blandly and deferentially approached.

"With submission, sir," said he, "yesterday I was thinking abut Bartleby here, and I think that if he would but prefer to take a quart of good ale every day, it would do much towards mending him, and enabling him to assist in examining his papers."

"So you have got the word, too," said I, slightly excited.

"With submission, what word, sir," asked Turkey, respectfully crowding himself into the contracted space behind the screen, and by so doing, making me jostle the scrivener. "What word, sir?"

"I would prefer to be left alone here," said Bartleby, as if offended at being mobbed in his privacy.

"*That's* the word, Turkey," said I—"*that's* it."

"Oh, *prefer?* oh yes—queer word. I never use it myself. But, sir, as I was saying, if he would but prefer—"

"Turkey," interrupted I, "you will please withdraw."

"Oh, certainly, sir, if you prefer that I should."

As he opened the folding-door to retire, Nippers at his desk caught a glimpse of me, and asked whether I would prefer to have a certain paper copied on blue paper or white. He did not in the least roguishly accent the word prefer. It was plain that it involuntarily rolled from his tongue. I thought to myself, surely I must get rid of a demented man, who already has in some degree turned the tongues, if not the heads of myself and clerks. But I thought it prudent not to break the dismission at once.

The next day I noticed that Bartleby did nothing but stand at his window in his dead-wall revery. Upon asking him why he did not write, he said that he had decided upon doing no more writing.

"Why, how now? what next?" exclaimed I, "do no more writing?"

"No more."

"And what is the reason?"

"Do you not see the reason for yourself," he indifferently replied.

I looked steadfastly at thim, and perceived that his eyes looked dull and glazed. Instantly it occurred to me, that his unexampled diligence in copying by his dim window for the first few weeks of his stay with me might have temporarily impaired his vision.

I was touched. I said something in condolence with him. I hinted that of course he did wisely in abstaining from writing for a while; and urged him to embrace that opportunity of taking wholesome exercise in the open air. This, however, he did not do. A few days after this, my other clerks being absent, and being in a great hurry to dispatch certain letters by the mail, I thought that, having nothing else earthly to do, Bartleby would surely be less inflexible than usual, and carry these letters to the post-office. But he blankly declined. So, much to my inconvenience, I went myself.

Still added days went by. Whether Bartleby's eyes improved or not, I could not say. To all appearance, I thought they did. But when I asked him if they did, he vouchsafed no answer. At all events, he would do no copying. At last, in reply to my urgings, he informed me that he had permanently given up copying.

"What!" exclaimed I; "suppose your eyes should get entirely well—better than ever before—would you not copy then?"

"I have given up copying," he answered, and slid aside.

He remained as ever, a fixture in my chamber. Nay—if that were possible—he became still more of a fixture than before. What was to be done? He would do nothing in the office; why should he stay there? In plain fact, he had now become a millstone to me, not only useless as a necklace, but afflictive to bear. Yet I was sorry for him. I speak less than truth when I say that, on his own account, he occasioned me uneasiness. If he would but have named a single relative or friend, I would instantly have written, and urged their taking the poor fellow away to some convenient retreat. But he seemed alone, absolutely alone in the universe. A bit of wreck in the mid Atlantic. At length, necessities connected with my business tyrannized over all other considerations. Decently as I could, I told Bartleby that in six days time he must unconditionally leave the office. I warned him to take measures, in the interval, for procuring some other abode. I offered to assist him in this endeavor, if he himself would but take the first step towards a removal. "And when you finally quit me, Bartleby," added I, "I shall see that you go not away entirely unprovided. Six days from this hour, remember."

At the expiration of that period, I peeped behind the screen, and lo! Bartleby was there.

I buttoned up my coat, balanced myself; advanced slowly towards him, touched his shoulder, and said, "The time has come; you must quit this place; I am sorry for you; here is money; but you must go."

"I would prefer not," he replied, with his back still towards me.

"You *must*."

He remained silent.

Now I had an unbounded confidence in this man's common honesty. He had frequently restored to me sixpences and shillings carelessly dropped upon the floor, for I am apt to be very reckless in such shirt-button affairs. The proceeding, then, which followed will not be deemed extraordinary.

"Bartleby," said I, "I owe you twelve dollars on account; here are thirty-two; the odd twenty are yours—Will you take it?" and I handed the bills towards him.

But he made no motion.

"I will leave them here, then," putting them under a weight on the table. Then taking my hat and cane and going to the door, I tranquilly turned and added—"After you have removed your things from these offices, Bartleby, you will of course lock the door—since every one is now gone for the day but you—and if you please, slip your key underneath the mat, so that I may have it in the morning. I shall not see you again; so good-by to you. If, hereafter, in your new place of abode, I can be of any service to you, do not fail to advise me by letter. Good-by, Bartleby, and fare you well."

But he answered not a word; like the last column of some ruined temple, he remained standing mute and solitary in the middle of the otherwise deserted room.

As I walked home in a pensive mood, my vanity got the better of my pity. I could not but highly plume myself on my masterly management in getting rid of Bartleby. Masterly I call it, and such it must appear to any dispassionate thinker. The beauty of my procedure seemed to consist in its perfect quietness. There was no vulgar bullying, no bravado of any sort, no choleric hectoring, and striding to and fro across the apartment, jerking out vehement commands for Bartleby to bundle himself off with his beggarly traps. Nothing of the kind. Without loudly bidding Bartleby depart—as an inferior genius might have done—I *assumed* the ground that depart he must; and upon that assumption built all I had to say. The more I thought over my procedure, the more I was charmed with it. Nevertheless, next morning, upon awakening, I had my doubts—I had somehow slept off the fumes of vanity. One of the coolest and wisest hours a man has, is just after he awakes in the morning. My procedure seemed as sagacious as ever—but only in theory. How it would prove in practice—there was the rub. It was truly a beautiful thought to have assumed Bartleby's departure; but, after all, that assumption was simply my own, and none of Bartleby's. The great point was, not whether I had assumed that he would quit me, but whether he would prefer so to do. He was more a man of preferences than assumptions.

After breakfast, I walked down town, arguing the probabilities *pro* and *con*. One moment I thought it would prove a miserable failure, and Bartleby would be found all alive at my office as usual; the next moment it seemed certain that I should find his chair empty. And so I kept veering about. At the corner of Broadway and Canal Street, I saw quite an excited group of people standing in earnest conversation.

"I'll take odds he doesn't," said a voice as I passed.

"Doesn't go?—done!" said I, "put up your money."

I was instinctively putting my hand in my pocket to produce my own, when I remembered that this was an election day. The words I had overheard bore no reference to Bartleby, but to the success or nonsuccess of some candidate for the mayoralty. In my intent frame of mind, I had, as it were, imagined that all Broadway shared in my excitement, and were debating the same question with me. I passed on, very thankful that the uproar of the street screened my momentary absent-mindedness.

As I had intended, I was earlier than usual at my office door. I stood listening for a moment. All was still. He must be gone. I tried the knob. The door was locked. Yes, my procedure had worked to a charm; he indeed must be vanished. Yet a certain melancholy mixed with this: I was almost sorry for my brilliant success. I was fumbling under the door mat for the key, which Bartleby was to have left there for me, when accidentally my knee knocked against a panel, producing a summoning sound, and in response a voice came to me from within—"Not yet; I am occupied."

It was Bartleby.

I was thunderstruck. For an instant I stood like the man who, pipe in mouth, was killed one cloudless afternoon long ago in Virginia, by summer lightning; at his own warm open window he was killed, and remained leaning out there upon the dreamy afternoon, till some one touched him, when he fell.

"Not gone!" I murmured at last. But again obeying that wondrous ascendancy which the inscrutable scrivener had over me, and from which ascendancy, for all my chafing, I could not completely escape, I slowly went down stairs and out into the street, and while walking round the block, considered what I should next do in this unheard-of perplexity. Turn the man out by an actual thrusting I could not; to drive him away by calling him hard names would not do; calling in the police was an unpleasant idea; and yet, permit him to enjoy his cadaverous triumph over me—this, too, I could not think of. What was to be done? or, if nothing could be done, was there anything further that I could *assume* in the matter? Yes, as before I had prospectively assumed that Bartleby would depart, so now I might retrospectively assume that departed he was. In the legitimate carrying out of this assumption, I might enter my office in a great hurry, and pretending not to see Bartleby at all, walk straight against him as if he were air. Such a proceeding would in a singular degree have the appearance of a home-thrust. It was hardly possible that Bartleby could withstand such an application of the doctrine of assumptions. But upon second thoughts the success of the plan seemed rather dubious. I resolved to argue the matter over with him again.

"Bartleby," said I, entering the office, with a quietly severe expression, "I am seriously displeased. I am pained, Bartleby. I had thought better of you. I had imagined you of such a gentlemanly organization, that in any delicate dilemma a slight hint would suffice—in short, an assumption. But it appears I am deceived. Why," I added, unaffectedly starting, "you have not even touched that money yet," pointing to it, just where I had left it the evening previous.

He answered nothing.

"Will you, or will you not, quit me?" I now demanded in a sudden passion, advancing close to him.

"I would prefer *not* to quit you," he replied, gently emphasizing the *not*.

"What earthly right have you to stay here? Do you pay any rent? Do you pay my taxes? Or is this property yours?"

He answered nothing.

"Are you ready to go on and write now? Are your eyes recovered? Could you copy a small paper for me this morning? or help examine a few lines? or step round to the post-office? In a word, will you do anything at all, to give a coloring to your refusal to depart the premises?"

He silently retired into his hermitage.

I was now in such a state of nervous resentment that I thought it but prudent to check myself at present from further demonstrations. Bartleby and I were alone. I remembered the tragedy of the unfortunate Adams and the still more unfortunate Colt in the solitary office of the latter; and how poor Colt, being dreadfully incensed by Adams, and imprudently permitting himself to get wildly excited, was at unawares hurried into his fatal act—an act which certainly no man could possibly deplore more than the actor himself. Often it had occurred to me in my ponderings upon the subject, that had that altercation taken place in the public street, or at a private residence, it would not have terminated as it did. It was the circumstance of being alone in a solitary office, up stairs, of a building entirely unhallowed by humanizing domestic associations—an uncarpeted office, doubtless, of a dusty, haggard sort of appearance—this it must have been, which greatly helped to enhance the irritable desperation of the hapless Colt.[3]

But when this old Adam of resentment rose in me and tempted me concerning Bartleby, I grappled him and threw him. How? Why, simply by recalling the divine injunction: "A new commandment give I unto you, that ye love one another." Yes, this it was that saved me. Aside from higher considerations, charity often operates as a vastly wise and prudent principle—a great safeguard to its possessor. Men have committed murder for jealousy's sake, and anger's sake, and hatred's sake, and selfishness' sake, and spiritual pride's sake; but no man, that ever I heard of, ever committed a diabolical murder for

---

[3] *Adams . . . Colt:* a widely publicized murder-case in which John C. Colt killed Samuel Adams, in New York City, in January, 1842.

sweet charity's sake. Mere self-interest, then, if no better motive can be enlisted, should, especially with high-tempered men, prompt all beings to charity and philanthropy. At any rate, upon the occasion in question, I strove to drown my exasperated feelings towards the scrivener by benevolently construing his conduct. Poor fellow, poor fellow! thought I, he don't mean anything; and besides, he has seen hard times, and ought to be indulged.

I endeavored, also, immediately to occupy myself, and at the same time to comfort my despondency. I tried to fancy, that in the course of the morning, at such time as might prove agreeable to him, Bartleby, of his own free accord, would emerge from his hermitage and take up some decided line of march in the direction of the door. But no. Half-past twelve o'clock came; Turkey began to glow in the face, overturn his inkstand, and become generally obstreperous; Nippers abated down into quietude and courtesy; Ginger Nut munched his noon apple; and Bartleby remained standing at his window in one of his profoundest dead-wall reveries. Will it be credited? Ought I to acknowledge it? That afternoon I left the office without saying one further word to him.

Some days now passed, during which, at leisure intervals I looked a little into "Edwards on the Will," and "Priestly on Necessity." Under the circumstances, those books induced a salutary feeling. Gradually I slid into the persuasion that these troubles of mine, touching the scrivener, had been all predestined from eternity, and Bartleby was billeted upon me for some mysterious purpose of an allwise Providence, which it was not for a mere mortal like me to fathom. Yes, Bartleby, stay there behind your screen, thought I; I shall persecute you no more; you are harmless and noiseless as any of these old chairs; in short, I never feel so private as when I know you are here. At last I see it, I feel it; I penetrate to the predestinated purpose of my life. I am content. Others may have loftier parts to enact; but my mission in this world, Bartleby, is to furnish you with office-room for such period as you may see fit to remain.

I believe that this wise and blessed frame of mind would have continued with me, had it not been for the unsolicited and un-charitable remarks obtruded upon me by my professional friends who visited the rooms. But thus it often is, that the constant friction of illiberal minds wears out at last the best resolves of the more generous. Though to be sure, when I reflected upon it, it was not strange that people entering my office should be struck by the peculiar aspect of the unaccountable Bartleby, and so be tempted to throw out some sinister observations concerning him. Sometimes an attorney, having business with me, and calling at my office, and finding no one but the scrivener there, would undertake to obtain some sort of precise information from him touching my whereabouts;

but without heeding his idle talk, Bartleby would remain standing immovable in the middle of the room. So after contemplating him in that position for a time, the attorney would depart, no wiser than he came.

Also, when a reference was going on, and the room full of lawyers and witnesses, and business driving fast, some deeply-occupied legal gentleman present, seeing Bartleby wholly unemployed, would request him to run round to his (the legal gentleman's) office and fetch some papers for him. Thereupon, Bartleby would tranquilly decline, and yet remain idle as before. Then the lawyer would give a great stare, and turn to me. And what could I say? At last I was made aware that all through the circle of my professional acquaintance, a whisper of wonder was running round, having reference to the strange creature I kept at my office. This worried me very much. And as the idea came upon me of his possibly turning out a long-lived man, and keep occupying my chambers, and denying my authority; and perplexing my visitors; and scandalizing my professional reputation; and casting a general gloom over the premises; keeping soul and body together to the last upon his savings (for doubtless he spent but half a dime a day), and in the end perhaps outlive me, and claim possession of my office by right of his perpetual occupancy: as all these dark anticipations crowded upon me more and more, and my friends continually intruded their relentless remarks upon the apparition in my room; a great change was wrought in me. I resolved to gather all my faculties together, and forever rid me of this intolerable incubus.

Ere revolving any complicated project, however, adapted to this end, I first simply suggested to Bartleby the propriety of his permanent departure. In a calm and serious tone, I commended the idea to his careful and mature consideration. But, having taken three days to meditate upon it, he apprised me, that his original determination remained the same; in short, that he still preferred to abide with me.

What shall I do? I now said to myself, buttoning up my coat to the last button. What shall I do? what ought I to do? what does conscience say I *should* do with this man, or, rather, ghost. Rid myself of him, I must; go, he shall. But how? You will not thrust him, the poor, pale, passive mortal—you will not thrust such a helpless creature out of your door? you will not dishonor yourself by such cruelty? No, I will not, I cannot do that. Rather would I let him live and die here, and then mason up his remains in the wall. What, then, will you do? For all your coaxing, he will not budge. Bribes he leaves under your own paper-weight on your table; in short, it is quite plain that he prefers to cling to you.

Then something severe, something unusual must be done. What! surely you will not have him collared by a constable, and commit his innocent pallor to the common jail? And upon what ground could you procure such a thing to be done?—a vagrant, is he? What! he a vagrant, a wanderer, who refuses to budge? It is because he will *not* be a vagrant, then, that you seek to count him *as* a vagrant. That is too absurd. No visible means of support: there I have him. Wrong again: for indubitably he *does* support himself, and that is the only unanswerable proof that any man can show of his possessing the means so to do. No more, then. Since he will not quit me, I must quit him. I will change my offices; I will move elsewhere, and give him fair notice, that if I find him on my new premises I will then proceed against him as a common trespasser.

Acting accordingly, next day I thus addressed him: "I find these chambers too far from the City Hall; the air is unwholesome. In a word, I propose to remove my offices next week, and shall no longer require your services. I tell you this now, in order that you may seek another place."

He made no reply, and nothing more was said.

On the appointed day I engaged carts and men, proceeded to my chambers, and, having but little furniture, everything was removed in a few hours. Throughout, the scrivener remained standing behind the screen, which I directed to be removed the last thing. It was withdrawn; and, being folded up like a huge folio, left him the motionless occupant of a naked room. I stood in the entry watching him a moment, while something from within me upbraided me.

I re-entered, with my hand in my pocket—and—and my heart in my mouth.

"Good-by, Bartleby; I am going—good-by, and God some way bless you; and take that," slipping something in his hand. But it dropped upon the floor, and then—strange to say—I tore myself from him whom I had so longed to be rid of.

Established in my new quarters, for a day or two I kept the door locked, and started at every footfall in the passages. When I returned to my rooms, after any little absence, I would pause at the threshold for an instant, and attentively listen, ere applying my key. But these fears were needless. Bartleby never came nigh me.

I thought all was going well, when a perturbed-looking stranger visited me, inquiring whether I was the person who had recently occupied rooms at No. — Wall Street.

Full of forebodings, I replied that I was.

"Then, sir," said the stranger, who proved a lawyer, "you are responsible for the man you left there. He refuses to do any copying; he refuses to do anything; he says he prefers not to; and he refuses to quit the premises."

"I am very sorry, sir," said I, with assumed tranquillity, but an inward tremor, "but, really, the man you allude to is nothing to me—he is no relation or apprentice of mine, that you should hold me responsible for him."

"In mercy's name, who is he?"

"I certainly cannot inform you. I know nothing about him. Formerly I employed him as a copyist; but he has done nothing for me now for some time past."

"I shall settle him, then—good morning, sir."

Several days passed, and I heard nothing more; and, though I often felt a charitable prompting to call at the place and see poor Bartleby, yet a certain squeamishness, of I know not what, withheld me.

All is over with him, by this time, thought I, at last, when, through another week, no further intelligence reached me. But, coming to my room the day after, I found several persons waiting at my door in a high state of nervous excitement.

"That's the man—here he comes," cried the foremost one, whom I recognized as the lawyer who had previously called upon me alone.

"You must take him away, sir, at once," cried a portly person among them, advancing upon me, and whom I knew to be the landlord of No. — Wall Street. "These gentlemen, my tenants, cannot stand it any longer; Mr. B——," pointing to the lawyer, "has turned him out of his room, and he now persists in haunting the building generally, sitting upon the banisters of the stairs by day, and sleeping in the entry by night. Everybody is concerned; clients are leaving the offices; some fears are entertained of a mob; something you must do, and that without delay."

Aghast at this torrent, I fell back before it, and would fain have locked myself in my new quarters. In vain I persisted that Bartleby was nothing to me—no more than to any one else. In vain—I was the last person known to have anything to do with him, and they held me to the terrible account. Fearful, then, of being exposed in the papers (as one person present obscurely threatened), I considered the matter, and, at length, said, that if the lawyer would give me a confidential interview with the scrivener, in his (the lawyer's) own room, I would, that afternoon, strive my best to rid them of the nuisance they complained of.

Going up stairs to my old haunt, there was Bartleby silently sitting upon the banister at the landing.

"What are you doing here, Bartleby?" said I.

"Sitting upon the banister," he mildly replied.

I motioned him into the lawyer's room, who then left us.

"Bartleby," said I, "are you aware that you are the cause of great tribulation to me, by persisting in occupying entry after being dismissed from the office?"

No answer.

"Now one of two things must take place. Either you must do something, or something must be done to you. Now what sort of business would you like to engage in? Would you like to re-engage in copying for some one?"

"No; I would prefer not to make any change."

"Would you like a clerkship in a dry-goods store?"

"There is too much confinement about that. No, I would not like a clerkship; but I am not particular."

"Too much confinement," I cried, "why you keep yourself confined all the time!"

"I would prefer not to take a clerkship," he rejoined, as if to settle that little item at once.

"How would a bar-tender's business suit you? There is no trying of the eye-sight in that."

"I would not like it at all; though, as I said before, I am not particular."

His unwonted wordiness inspirited me. I returned to the charge.

"Well, then, would you like to travel through the country collecting bills for the merchants? That would improve your health."

"No, I would prefer to be doing something else."

"How, then, would going as a companion to Europe, to entertain some·young gentleman with your conversation—how would that suit you?"

"Not at all. It does not strike me that there is anything definite about that. I like to be stationary. But I am not particular."

"Stationary you shall be, then," I cried, now losing all patience, and, for the first time in all my exasperating connection with him, fairly flying into a passion. "If you do not go away from these premises before night, I shall feel bound—indeed, I *am* bound—to—to—to quit the premises myself!" I rather absurdly concluded, knowing not with what possible threat to try to frighten his immobility into compliance. Despairing of all further efforts, I was precipitately leaving him, when a final thought occurred to me—one which had not been wholly unindulged before.

"Bartleby," said I, in the kindest tone I could assume under such exciting circumstances, "will you go home with me now—not to my office, but my dwelling—and remain there till we can conclude upon some convenient arrangement for you at our leisure? Come, let us start now, right away."

"No: at present I would prefer not to make any change at all."

I answered nothing; but, effectually dodging every one by the suddenness and rapidity of my flight, rushed from the building, ran up Wall Street towards Broadway, and, jumping into the first omnibus, was soon removed from pursuit. As soon as tranquillity returned, I distinctly perceived that I had now done all that I possibly could, both in respect to the demands of the landlord and his tenants, and with regard to my own desire and sense of duty, to benefit Bartleby, and shield him from rude persecution. I now strove to be entirely care-free and quiescent; and my conscience justified me in the attempt; though, indeed, it was not so successful as I could have wished. So fearful was I of being again hunted out by the incensed landlord and his exasperated tenants, that, surrendering my business to Nippers, for a few days, I drove about the upper part of the town and through the suburbs, in my rockaway; crossed over to Jersey City and Hoboken, and paid fugitive visits to Manhattanville and Astoria. In fact, I almost lived in my rockaway for the time.

When again I entered my office, lo, a note from the landlord lay upon the desk. I opened it with trembling hands. It informed me that the writer had sent to the police, and had Bartleby removed to the Tombs as a vagrant. Moreover, since I knew more about him than any one else, he wished me to appear at that place, and make a suitable statement of the facts. These tidings had a conflicting effect upon me. At first I was indignant; but, at last, almost approved. The landlord's energetic, summary disposition, had led him to adopt a procedure which I do not think I would have decided upon myself; and yet, as a last resort, under such peculiar circumstances, it seemed the only plan.

As I afterwards learned, the poor scrivener, when told that he must be conducted to the Tombs, offered not the slightest obstacle, but, in his pale, unmoving way, silently acquiesced.

Some of the compassionate and curious bystanders joined the party; and headed by one of the constables arm in arm with Bartleby, the silent procession filed its way through all the noise, and heat, and joy of the roaring thoroughfares at noon.

The same day I received the note, I went to the Tombs, or, to speak more properly, the Halls of Justice. Seeking the right officer, I stated the purpose of my call, and was informed that the individual I described was, indeed, within. I then assured the functionary that Bartleby was a perfectly honest man, and greatly to be compassionated, however unaccountably eccentric. I narrated all I knew, and closed by suggesting the idea of letting him remain in as indulgent confinement as possible, till something less harsh might be done— though, indeed, I hardly knew what. At all events, if nothing else could be decided upon, the almshouse must receive him. I then begged to have an interview.

Being under no disgraceful charge, and quite serene and harmless in all his ways, they had permitted him freely to wander about the prison, and, especially, in the inclosed grass-platted yards thereof. And so I found him there, standing all alone in the quietest of the yards, his face towards a high wall, while all around, from the narrow slits of the jail windows, I thought I saw peering out upon him the eyes of murderers and thieves.

"Bartleby!"

"I know you," he said without looking round—"and I want nothing to say to you."

"It was not I that brought you here, Bartleby," said I, keenly pained at his implied suspicion. "And to you, this should not be so vile a place. Nothing reproachful attaches to you by being here. And see, it is not so sad a place as one might think. Look, there is the sky, and here is the grass."

"I know where I am," he replied, but would say nothing more, and so I left him.

As I entered the corridor again, a broad meat-like man, in an apron, accosted me, and, jerking his thumb over his shoulder, said—"Is that your friend?"

"Yes."

"Does he want to starve? If he does, let him live on the prison fare, that's all."

"Who are you?" asked I, not knowing what to make of such an unofficially speaking person in such a place.

"I am the grub-man. Such gentlemen as have friends here, hire me to provide them with something good to eat."

"Is this so?" said I, turning to the turnkey.

He said it was.

"Well, then," said I, slipping some silver into the grub-man's hands (for so they called him), "I want you to give particular attention to my friend there; let him have the best dinner you can get. And you must be as polite to him as possible."

"Introduce me, will you?" said the grub-man, looking at me with an expression which seemed to say he was all impatience for an opportunity to give a specimen of his breeding.

Thinking it would prove of benefit to the scrivener, I acquiesced; and, asking the grub-man his name, went up with him to Bartleby.

"Bartleby, this is a friend; you will find him very useful to you."

"Your sarvant, sir, your sarvant," said the grub-man, making a low salutation behind his apron. "Hope you find it pleasant here, sir; nice grounds—cool apartments—hope you'll stay with us sometime— try to make it agreeable. What will you have for dinner to-day?"

"I prefer not to dine to-day," said Bartleby, turning away. "It would disagree with me; I am unused to dinners." So saying, he slowly moved to the other side of the inclosure, and took up a position fronting the dead-wall.

"How's this?" said the grub-man, addressing me with a stare of astonishment, "He's odd, ain't he?"

"I think he is a little deranged," said I, sadly.

"Deranged? deranged is it? Well, now, upon my word, I thought that friend of yourn was a gentleman forger; they are always pale and genteel-like, them forgers. I can't help pity 'em—can't help it, sir. Did you know Monroe Edwards?" he added, touchingly, and paused. Then, laying his hand piteously on my shoulder, sighed, "he died of consumption at Sing-Sing. So you weren't acquainted with Monroe?"

"No, I was never socially acquainted with any forgers. But I cannot stop longer. Look to my friend yonder. You will not lose by it. I will see you again."

Some few days after this, I again obtained admission to the Tombs, and went through the corridors in quest of Bartleby; but without finding him.

"I saw him coming from his cell not long ago," said a turnkey, "may be he's gone to loiter in the yards."

So I went in that direction.

"Are you looking for the silent man?" said another turnkey, passing me. "Yonder he lies—sleeping in the yard there. 'Tis not twenty minutes since I saw him lie down."

The yard was entirely quiet. It was not accessible to the common prisoners. The surrounding walls, of amazing thickness, kept off all sounds behind them. The Egyptian character of the masonry weighed upon me with its gloom. But a soft imprisoned turf grew under foot. The heart of the eternal pyramids, it seemed, wherein, by some strange magic, through the clefts, grass-seed, dropped by birds, had sprung.

Strangely huddled at the base of the wall, his knees drawn up, and lying on his side, his head touching the cold stones, I saw the wasted Bartleby. But nothing stirred. I paused; then went close up to him; stooped over, and saw that his dim eyes were open; otherwise he seemed profoundly sleeping. Something prompted me to touch him. I felt his hand, when a tingling shiver ran up my arm and down my spine to my feet.

The round face of the grub-man peered upon me now. "His dinner is ready. Won't he dine to-day, either? Or does he live without dining?"

"Lives without dining," said I, and closed the eyes.

"Eh!—He's asleep, ain't he?"

"With kings and counselors," murmured I.

✳

There would seem little need for proceeding further in this history. Imagination will readily supply the meagre recital of poor Bartleby's interment. But, ere parting with the reader, let me say, that if this little narrative has sufficiently interested him, to awaken curiosity as to who Bartleby was, and what manner of life he led prior to the present narrator's making his acquaintance, I can only reply, that in such curiosity I fully share, but am wholly unable to gratify it. Yet here I hardly know whether I should divulge one little item of rumor, which came to my ear a few months after the scrivener's decease. Upon what basis it rested, I could never ascertain; and hence, how true it is I cannot now tell. But, inasmuch as this vague report has not been without a certain suggestive interest to me, however sad, it may prove the same with some others; and so I will briefly mention it. The report was this: that Bartleby had been a subordinate clerk in the Dead Letter Office at Washington, from which he had been suddenly removed by a change in the administration. When I think over this rumor, hardly can I express the emotions which seize me. Dead letters! does it not sound like dead men? Conceive a man by nature and misfortune prone to a pallid hopelessness, can any business seem more fitted to heighten it than that of continually handling these dead letters, and assorting them for the flames? For by the cartload they are annually burned. Sometimes from out the folded paper the pale clerk takes a ring—the finger it was meant for, perhaps, moulders in the grave; a bank-note sent in swiftest charity—he whom it would relieve, nor eats nor hungers any more; pardon for those who died despairing; hope for those who died unhoping; good tidings for those who died stifled by unrelieved calamities. On errands of life, these letters speed to death.

Ah, Bartleby! Ah, humanity!

QUESTIONS

1. The narrator of "Bartleby the Scrivener" begins his narration with the word "I" and ends it with the word "humanity." We may wonder, therefore, if the events that form the conflict and climax of the story have altered the narrator's vision to allow his attention to shift from himself to others. If so, how did this happen? The following questions may help you develop your answer.

2. We note that the narrator begins his tale by introducing himself. Why does he do so? What does he reveal as his goals? What things does he seem to value most highly?

3. We might ask what tone of voice the narrator is using in this early part of the story. (Paragraph five may be especially helpful here.)

4. We then look at his introduction of his office and of his first staff member, Turkey. How does the lawyer/narrator act toward Turkey? What reasons does he give for acting as he does? Do his actions seem to match his reasons? What impression of the lawyer's character do we receive?

5. We then look at his introductions of Nipper and Ginger Nut, and end our study of the tale's introductory section by asking how the narrator's characterization of his three employees, and our impression of his interactions

with them, prepare the way for the introduction of Bartleby and for the narrator's response to him and to his behavior.

6. Having seen how the narrator prepares the way for the introduction of his main character, we now look at the first episodes involving that character (pp. 90–95) . How well does Bartleby fit into our picture of the office? What does this do for our sense of him and of his relationship with his employer?

7. We next ask, what is the turning-point of the story? How does it change the narrator's view of Bartleby? What emotions does it raise in him? What action does it prompt him to take? What are the results of that action?

8. We then examine the story's progress from this turning-point to Bartleby's death. We ask ourselves, what changes are taking place in the tone of the narrative? the actions? the characterizations? We examine our reactions to these changes and developments. Have we been prepared for them? Can we accept them, or do we find them out of character or hard to believe? How do we react to Bartleby's death? Has the death been made to seem inevitable? Does it seem appropriate that the narrator be the one to discover it? How do we feel now about the narrator's relation to Bartleby?

9. At this point, too, we might notice the use of walls to set scenes throughout the story. This will let us glance at the whole story once more, and will give us a good key for discussing some of the shifts in tone and atmosphere that occur as the story progresses. It will also let us sum up some of our impressions of Bartleby, since he is the character most closely associated with these walls. What is the effect on us of the combination of walls and Bartleby?

10. Similarly, we might look at mentions of money throughout the story. What character is most closely associated with them? What characterization do we draw from this association?

11. We must look at the after-note that ends the story, as well; asking what it adds to our sense of Bartleby, the narrator, and the story.

12. And then we must sum up our thoughts for ourselves. Has the narrator changed during the story? And, if he has, what do we make of the change?

13. Another way to approach the story would be to look at the effects of keeping Bartleby so sketchily characterized. We might ask how essential this pared-down characterization is to the story; how the narrator's sense of his own lack of knowledge about Bartleby affects him; and how it affects our feelings toward Bartleby, toward the narrator, and toward the relationship that develops between the two men. We might also ask whether the characterization given Bartleby suggests any symbolic values for Bartleby, the narrator, or their relationship; or whether you feel the story is better dealt with as a realistic tale.

CHARLOTTE PERKINS GILMAN (1860–1935)

The Yellow Wall-Paper

It is very seldom that mere ordinary people like John and myself secure ancestral halls for the summer.

A colonial mansion, a hereditary estate, I would say a haunted house, and reach the height of romantic felicity—but that would be asking too much of fate!

Still I will proudly declare that there is something queer about it.

Else, why should it be let so cheaply? And why have stood so long untenanted?

John laughs at me, of course, but one expects that in marriage.

John is practical in the extreme. He has no patience with faith, an intense horror of superstition, and he scoffs openly at any talk of things not to be felt and seen and put down in figures.

John is a physician, and *perhaps*— (I would not say it to a living soul, of course, but this is dead paper and a great relief to my mind) —*perhaps* that is one reason I do not get well faster.

You see he does not believe I am sick!

And what can one do?

If a physician of high standing, and one's own husband, assures friends and relatives that there is really nothing the matter with one but temporary nervous depression—a slight hysterical tendency—what is one to do?

My brother is also a physician, and also of high standing, and he says the same thing.

So I take phosphates or phospites—whichever it is, and tonics, and journeys, and air, and exercise, and am absolutely forbidden to "work" until I am well again.

Personally, I disagree with their ideas.

Personally, I believe that congenial work, with excitement and change, would do me good.

But what is one to do?

I did write for a while in spite of them; but it *does* exhaust me a good deal—having to be so sly about it, or else meet with heavy opposition.

I sometimes fancy that in my condition if I had less opposition and more society and stimulus—but John says the very worst thing I can do is to think about my condition, and I confess it always makes me feel bad.

So I will let it alone and talk about the house.

The most beautiful place! It is quite alone, standing well back from the road, quite three miles from the village. It makes me think of English places that you read about, for there are hedges and walls and gates that lock, and lots of separate little houses for the gardeners and people.

There is a *delicious* garden! I never saw such a garden—large and shady, full of box-bordered paths, and lined with long grape-covered arbors with seats under them.

There were greenhouses, too, but they are all broken now.

There was some legal trouble, I believe, something about the heirs and coheirs; anyhow, the place has been empty for years.

That spoils my ghostliness, I am afraid, but I don't care—there is something strange about the house—I can feel it.

I even said so to John one moonlight evening, but he said what I felt was a *draught,* and shut the window.

I get unreasonably angry with John sometimes. I'm sure I never used to be so sensitive. I think it is due to this nervous condition.

But John says if I feel so, I shall neglect proper self-control; so I take pains to control myself—before him, at least, and that makes me very tired.

I don't like our room a bit. I wanted one downstairs that opened on the piazza and had roses all over the window, and such pretty old-fashioned chintz hangings! but John would not hear of it.

He said there was only one window and not room for two beds, and no near room for him if he took another.

He is very careful and loving, and hardly lets me stir without special direction.

I have a schedule prescription for each hour in the day; he takes all care from me, and so I feel basely ungrateful not to value it more.

He said we came here solely on my account, that I was to have perfect rest and all the air I could get. "Your exercise depends on your strength, my dear," said he, "and your food somewhat on your appetite; but air you can absorb all the time." So we took the nursery at the top of the house.

It is a big, airy room, the whole floor nearly, with windows that look all ways, and air and sunshine galore. It was nursery first and then playroom and gymnasium, I should judge; for the windows are barred for little children, and there are rings and things in the walls.

The paint and paper look as if a boys' school had used it. It is stripped off—the paper—in great patches all around the head of my bed, about as far as I can reach, and in a great place on the other side of the room low down. I never saw a worse paper in my life.

One of those sprawling flamboyant patterns committing every artistic sin.

It is dull enough to confuse the eye in following, pronounced enough to constantly irritate and provoke study, and when you follow the lame uncertain curves for a little distance they suddenly commit suicide—plunge off at outrageous angles, destroy themselves in unheard of contradictions.

The color is repellent, almost revolting; a smouldering unclean yellow, strangely faded by the slow-turning sunlight.

It is a dull yet lurid orange in some places, a sickly sulphur tint in others.

No wonder the children hated it! I should hate it myself if I had to live in this room long.

There comes John, and I must put this away,—he hates to have me write a word.

We have been here two weeks, and I haven't felt like writing before, since that first day.

I am sitting by the window now, up in this atrocious nursery, and there is nothing to hinder my writing as much as I please, save lack of strength.

John is away all day, and even some nights when his cases are serious.

I am glad my case is not serious!

But these nervous troubles are dreadfully depressing.

John does not know how much I really suffer. He knows there is no *reason* to suffer, and that satisfies him.

Of course it is only nervousness. It does weigh on me so not to do my duty in any way!

I meant to be such a help to John, such a real rest and comfort, and here I am a comparative burden already!

Nobody would believe what an effort it is to do what little I am able,—to dress and entertain, and order things.

It is fortunate Mary is so good with the baby. Such a dear baby!

And yet I *cannot* be with him, it makes me so nervous.

I suppose John never was nervous in his life. He laughs at me so about this wall-paper!

At first he meant to repaper the room, but afterwards he said that I was letting it get the better of me, and that nothing was worse for a nervous patient than to give way to such fancies.

He said that after the wall-paper was changed it would be the heavy bedstead, and then the barred windows, and then that gate at the head of the stairs, and so on.

"You know the place is doing you good," he said, "and really, dear, I don't care to renovate the house just for a three months' rental."

"Then do let us go downstairs," I said, "there are such pretty rooms there."

Then he took me in his arms and called me a blessed little goose, and said he would go down to the cellar, if I wished, and have it whitewashed into the bargain.

But he is right enough about the beds and windows and things.

It is an airy and comfortable room as any one need wish, and, of course, I would not be so silly as to make him uncomfortable just for a whim.

I'm really getting quite fond of the big room, all but that horrid paper.

Out of one window I can see the garden, those mysterious deep-shaded arbors, the riotous old-fashioned flowers, and bushes and gnarly trees.

Out of another I get a lovely view of the bay and a little private wharf belonging to the estate. There is a beautiful shaded lane that runs down there from the house. I always fancy I see people walking in these numerous paths and arbors, but John has cautioned me not to give way to fancy in the least. He says that with my imaginative power and habit of story-making, a nervous weakness like mine is sure to lead to all manner of excited fancies, and that I ought to use my will and good sense to check the tendency. So I try.

I think sometimes that if I were only well enough to write a little it would relieve the press of ideas and rest me.

But I find I get pretty tired when I try.

It is so discouraging not to have any advice and companionship about my work. When I get really well, John says we will ask Cousin Henry and Julia down for a long visit; but he says he would as soon put fireworks in my pillow-case as to let me have those stimulating people about now.

I wish I could get well faster.

But I must not think about that. This paper looks to me as if it *knew* what a vicious influence it had!

There is a recurrent spot where the pattern lolls like a broken neck and two bulbous eyes stare at you upside down.

I get positively angry with the impertinence of it and the everlastingness. Up and down and sideways they crawl, and those absurd, unblinking eyes are everywhere. There is one place where two breadths didn't match, and the eyes go all up and down the line, one a little higher than the other.

I never saw so much expression in an inanimate thing before, and we all know how much expression they have! I used to lie awake as a child and get more entertainment and terror out of blank walls and plain furniture than most children could find in a toy-store.

I remember what a kindly wink the knobs of our big, old bureau used to have, and there was one chair that always seemed like a strong friend.

I used to feel that if any of the other things looked too fierce I could always hop into that chair and be safe.

The furniture in this room is no worse than inharmonious, however, for we had to bring it all from downstairs. I suppose when this was used as a playroom they had to take the nursery things out, and no wonder! I never saw such ravages as the children have made here.

The wall-paper, as I said before, is torn off in spots, and it sticketh closer than a brother—they must have had perseverance as well as hatred.

Then the floor is scratched and gouged and splintered, the plaster itself is dug out here and there, and this great heavy bed which is all we found in the room, looks as if it had been through the wars.

But I don't mind it a bit—only the paper.

There comes John's sister. Such a dear girl as she is, and so careful of me! I must not let her find me writing.

She is a perfect and enthusiastic housekeeper, and hopes for no better profession. I verily believe she thinks it is the writing which made me sick!

But I can write when she is out, and see her a long way off from these windows.

There is one that commands the road, a lovely shaded winding road, and one that just looks off over the country. A lovely country, too, full of great elms and velvet meadows.

This wall-paper has a kind of sub-pattern in a different shade, a particularly irritating one, for you can only see it in certain lights, and not clearly then.

But in the places where it isn't faded and where the sun is just so—I can see a strange, provoking, formless sort of figure, that seems to skulk about behind that silly and conspicuous front design.

There's sister on the stairs!

Well, the Fourth of July is over! The people are all gone and I am tired out. John thought it might do me good to see a little company, so we just had mother and Nellie and the children down for a week.

Of course I didn't do a thing. Jennie sees to everything now.

But it tired me all the same.

John says if I don't pick up faster he shall send me to Weir Mitchell in the fall.

But I don't want to go there at all. I had a friend who was in his hands once, and she says he is just like John and my brother, only more so!

Besides, it is such an undertaking to go so far.

I don't feel as if it was worth while to turn my hand over for anything, and I'm getting dreadfully fretful and querulous.

I cry at nothing, and cry most of the time.

Of course I don't when John is here, or anybody else, but when I am alone.

And I am alone a good deal just now. John is kept in town very often by serious cases, and Jennie is good and lets me alone when I want her to.

So I walk a little in the garden or down that lovely lane, sit on the porch under the roses, and lie down up here a good deal.

I'm getting really fond of the room in spite of the wall-paper. Perhaps *because* of the wall-paper.

It dwells in my mind so!

I lie here on this great immovable bed—it is nailed down, I believe—and follow that pattern about by the hour. It is as good as gymnastics, I assure you. I start, we'll say, at the bottom, down in the corner over there where it has not been touched, and I determine for the thousandth time that I *will* follow that pointless pattern to some sort of a conclusion.

I know a little of the principle of design, and I know this thing was not arranged on any laws of radiation, or alternation, or repetition, or symmetry, or anything else that I ever heard of.

It is repeated, of course, by the breadths, but not otherwise.

Looked at in one way each breadth stands alone, the bloated curves and flourishes—a kind of "debased Romanesque" with *delirium tremens*—go waddling up and down in isolated columns of fatuity.

But, on the other hand, they connect diagonally, and the sprawling outlines run off in great slanting waves of optic horror, like a lot of wallowing seaweeds in full chase.

The whole thing goes horizontally, too, at least it seems so, and I exhaust myself in trying to distinguish the order of its going in that direction.

They have used a horizontal breadth for a frieze, and that adds wonderfully to the confusion.

There is one end of the room where it is almost intact, and there, when the crosslights fade and the low sun shines directly upon it, I can almost fancy radiation after all,—the interminable grotesques seem to form around a common centre and rush off in headlong plunges of equal distraction.

It makes me tired to follow it. I will take a nap I guess.

I don't know why I should write this.

I don't want to.

I don't feel able.

And I know John would think it absurd. But I *must* say what I feel and think in some way—it is such a relief!

But the effort is getting to be greater than the relief.

Half the time now I am awfully lazy, and lie down ever so much.

John says I mustn't lose my strength, and has me take cod liver oil and lots of tonics and things, to say nothing of ale and wine and rare meat.

Dear John! He loves me very dearly, and hates to have me sick. I tried to have a real earnest reasonable talk with him the other day, and tell him how I wish he would let me go and make a visit to Cousin Henry and Julia.

But he said I wasn't able to go, nor able to stand it after I got there; and I did not make out a very good case for myself, for I was crying before I had finished.

It is getting to be a great effort for me to think straight. Just this nervous weakness I suppose.

And dear John gathered me up in his arms, and just carried me upstairs and laid me on the bed, and sat by me and read to me till it tired my head.

He said I was his darling and his comfort and all he had, and that I must take care of myself for his sake, and keep well.

He says no one but myself can help me out of it, that I must use my will and self-control and not let any silly fancies run away with me.

There's one comfort, the baby is well and happy, and does not have to occupy this nursery with the horrid wall-paper.

If we had not used it, that blessed child would have! What a fortunate escape! Why, I wouldn't have a child of mine, an impressionable little thing, live in such a room for worlds.

I never thought of it before, but it is lucky that John kept me here after all, I can stand it so much easier than a baby, you see.

Of course I never mention it to them any more—I am too wise,—but I keep watch of it all the same.

There are things in that paper that nobody knows but me, or ever will.

Behind that outside pattern the dim shapes get clearer every day.

It is always the same shape, only very numerous.

And it is like a woman stooping down and creeping about behind that pattern. I don't like it a bit. I wonder—I begin to think—I wish John would take me away from here!

It is so hard to talk with John about my case, because he is so wise, and because he loves me so.

But I tried it last night.

It was moonlight. The moon shines in all around just as the sun does.

I hate to see it sometimes, it creeps so slowly, and always comes in by one window or another.

John was asleep and I hated to waken him, so I kept still and watched the moonlight on that undulating wall-paper till I felt creepy.

The faint figure behind seemed to shake the pattern, just as if she wanted to get out.

I got up softly and went to feel and see if the paper *did* move, and when I came back John was awake.

"What is it, little girl?" he said. "Don't go walking about like that—you'll get cold."

I thought it was a good time to talk, so I told him that I really was not gaining here, and that I wished he would take me away.

"Why darling!" said he, "our lease will be up in three weeks, and I can't see how to leave before.

"The repairs are not done at home, and I cannot possibly leave town just now. Of course if you were in any danger, I could and would, but you really are better, dear, whether you can see it or not. I am a doctor, dear, and I know. You are gaining flesh and color, your appetite is better, I feel really much easier about you."

"I don't weigh a bit more," said I, "nor as much; and my appetite may be better in the evening when you are here, but it is worse in the morning when you are away!"

"Bless her little heart!" said he with a big hug, "she shall be as sick as she pleases! But now let's improve the shining hours by going to sleep, and talk about it in the morning!"

"And you won't go away?" I asked gloomily.

"Why, how can I, dear? It is only three weeks more and then we will take a nice little trip of a few days while Jennie is getting the house ready. Really dear you are better!"

"Better in body perhaps—" I began, and stopped short, for he sat up straight and looked at me with such a stern, reproachful look that I could not say another word.

"My darling," said he, "I beg of you, for my sake and for our child's sake, as well as for your own, that you will never for one instant let that idea enter your mind! There is nothing so dangerous, so fascinating, to a temperament like yours. It is a false and foolish fancy. Can you not trust me as a physician when I tell you so?"

So of course I said no more on that score, and we went to sleep before long. He thought I was asleep first, but I wasn't, and lay there for hours trying to decide whether that front pattern and the back pattern really did move together or separately.

On a pattern like this, by daylight, there is a lack of sequence, a defiance of law, that is a constant irritant to a normal mind.

The color is hideous enough, and unreliable enough, and infuriating enough, but the pattern is torturing.

You think you have mastered it, but just as you get well underway in following, it turns a back-somersault and there you are. It slaps you in the face, knocks you down, and tramples upon you. It is like a bad dream.

The outside pattern is a florid arabesque, reminding one of a fungus. If you can imagine a toadstool in joints, an interminable string of toadstools, budding and sprouting in endless convolutions—why, that is something like it.

That is, sometimes!

There is one marked peculiarity about this paper, a thing nobody seems to notice but myself, and that is that it changes as the light changes.

When the sun shoots in through the east window—I always watch for that first long, straight ray—it changes so quickly that I never can quite believe it.

That is why I watch it always.

By moonlight—the moon shines in all night when there is a moon—I wouldn't know it was the same paper.

At night in any kind of light, in twilight, candle light, lamplight, and worst of all by moonlight, it becomes bars! The outside pattern I mean, and the woman behind it is as plain as can be.

I didn't realize for a long time what the thing was that showed behind, that dim sub-pattern, but now I am quite sure it is a woman.

By daylight she is subdued, quiet. I fancy it is the pattern that keeps her so still. It is so puzzling. It keeps me quiet by the hour.

I lie down ever so much now. John says it is good for me, and to sleep all I can.

Indeed he started the habit by making me lie down for an hour after each meal.

It is a very bad habit I am convinced, for you see I don't sleep.

And that cultivates deceit, for I don't tell them I'm awake—O no!

The fact is I am getting a little afraid of John.

He seems very queer sometimes, and even Jennie has an inexplicable look.

It strikes me occasionally, just as a scientific hypothesis,—that perhaps it is the paper!

I have watched John when he did not know I was looking, and come into the room suddenly on the most innocent excuses, and I've caught him several times *looking at the paper!* And Jennie too. I caught Jennie with her hand on it once.

She didn't know I was in the room, and when I asked her in a quiet, a very quiet voice, with the most restrained manner possible, what she was doing with the paper—she turned around as if she had been caught stealing, and looked quite angry—asked me why I should frighten her so!

Then she said that the paper stained everything it touched, that she had found yellow smooches on all my clothes and John's, and she wished we would be more careful!

Did not that sound innocent? But I know she was studying that pattern, and I am determined that nobody shall find it out but myself!

Life is very much more exciting now than it used to be. You see I have something more to expect, to look forward to, to watch. I really do eat better, and am more quiet than I was.

John is so pleased to see me improve! He laughed a little the other day, and said I seemed to be flourishing in spite of my wall-paper.

I turned it off with a laugh. I had no intention of telling him it was *because* of the wall-paper—he would make fun of me. He might even want to take me away.

I don't want to leave now until I have found it out. There is a week more, and I think that will be enough.

I'm feeling ever so much better! I don't sleep much at night, for it is so interesting to watch developments; but I sleep a good deal in the daytime.

In the daytime it is tiresome and perplexing.

There are always new shoots on the fungus, and new shades of yellow all over it. I cannot keep count of them, though I have tried conscientiously.

It is the strangest yellow, that wall-paper! It makes me think of all the yellow things I ever saw—not beautiful ones like buttercups, but old foul, bad yellow things.

But there is something else about that paper—the smell! I noticed it the moment we came into the room, but with so much air and sun it was not bad. Now we have had a week of fog and rain, and whether the windows are open or not, the smell is here.

It creeps all over the house.

I find it hovering in the dining-room, skulking in the parlor, hiding in the hall, lying in wait for me on the stairs.

It gets into my hair.

Even when I go to ride, if I turn my head suddenly and surprise it—there is that smell!

Such a peculiar odor, too! I have spent hours in trying to analyze it, to find what it smelled like.

It is not bad—at first, and very gentle, but quite the subtlest, most enduring odor I ever met.

In this damp weather it is awful, I wake up in the night and find it hanging over me.

It used to disturb me at first. I thought seriously of burning the house—to reach the smell.

But now I am used to it. The only thing I can think of that it is like is the *color* of the paper! A yellow smell.

There is a very funny mark on this wall, low down, near the mopboard. A streak that runs round the room. It goes behind every piece of furniture, except the bed, a long, straight, even *smooch,* as if it had been rubbed over and over.

I wonder how it was done and who did it, and what they did it for. Round and round and round—round and round and round—it makes me dizzy!

I really have discovered something at last.

Through watching so much at night, when it changes so, I have finally found out.

The front pattern *does* move—and no wonder! The woman behind shakes it!

Sometimes I think there are a great many women behind, and sometimes only one, and she crawls around fast, and her crawling shakes it all over.

Then in the very bright spots she keeps still, and in the very shady spots she just takes hold of the bars and shakes them hard.

And she is all the time trying to climb through. But nobody could climb through that pattern—it strangles so; I think that is why it has so many heads.

They get through, and then the pattern strangles them off and turns them upside down, and makes their eyes white!

If those heads were covered or taken off it would not be half so bad.

I think that woman gets out in the daytime!

And I'll tell you why—privately—I've seen her!

I can see her out of every one of my windows!

It is the same woman, I know, for she is always creeping, and most women do not creep by daylight.

I see her on that long road under the trees, creeping along, and when a carriage comes she hides under the blackberry vines.

I don't blame her a bit. It must be very humiliating to be caught creeping by daylight!

I always lock the door when I creep by daylight. I can't do it at night, for I know John would suspect something at once.

And John is so queer now, that I don't want to irritate him. I wish he would take another room! Besides, I don't want anybody to get that woman out at night but myself.

I often wonder if I could see her out of all the windows at once.

But, turn as fast as I can, I can only see out of one at one time.

And though I always see her, she *may* be able to creep faster than I can turn!

I have watched her sometimes away off in the open country, creeping as fast as a cloud shadow in a high wind.

If only that top pattern could be gotten off from the under one! I mean to try it, little by little.

I have found out another funny thing, but I shan't tell it this time! It does not do to trust people too much.

There are only two more days to get this paper off, and I believe John is beginning to notice. I don't like the look in his eyes.

And I heard him ask Jennie a lot of professional questions about me. She had a very good report to give.

She said I slept a good deal in the daytime.

John knows I don't sleep very well at night, for all I'm so quiet!

He asked me all sorts of questions, too, and pretended to be very loving and kind.

As if I couldn't see through him!

Still, I don't wonder he acts so, sleeping under this paper for three months.

It only interests me, but I feel sure John and Jennie are secretly affected by it.

Hurrah! This is the last day, but it is enough. John to stay in town over night, and won't be out until this evening.

Jennie wanted to sleep with me—the sly thing! but I told her I should undoubtedly rest better for a night all alone.

That was clever, for really I wasn't alone a bit! As soon as it was moonlight and that poor thing began to crawl and shake the pattern, I got up and ran to help her.

I pulled and she shook, I shook and she pulled, and before morning we had peeled off yards of that paper.

A strip about as high as my head and half around the room.

And then when the sun came and that awful pattern began to laugh at me, I declared I would finish it to-day!

We go away to-morrow, and they are moving all my furniture down again to leave things as they were before.

Jennie looked at the wall in amazement, but I told her merrily that I did it out of pure spite at the vicious thing.

She laughed and said she wouldn't mind doing it herself, but I must not get tired.

How she betrayed herself that time!

But I am here, and no person touches this paper but me,—not *alive!*

She tried to get me out of the room—it was too patent! But I said it was so quiet and empty and clean now that I believed I would lie down again and sleep all I could; and not to wake me even for dinner—I would call when I woke.

So now she is gone, and the servants are gone, and the things are gone, and there is nothing left but that great bedstead nailed down, with the canvas mattress we found on it.

We shall sleep downstairs to-night, and take the boat home to-morrow.

I quite enjoy the room, now it is bare again.

How those children did tear about here!

This bedstead is fairly gnawed!

But I must get to work.

I have locked the door and thrown the key down into the front path.

I don't want to go out, and I don't want to have anybody come in, till John comes.

I want to astonish him.

I've got a rope up here that even Jennie did not find. If that woman does get out, and tries to get away, I can tie her!

But I forgot I could not reach far without anything to stand on!

This bed will *not* move!

I tried to lift and push it until I was lame, and then I got so angry I bit off a little piece at one corner—but it hurt my teeth.

Then I peeled off all the paper I could reach standing on the floor. It sticks horribly and the pattern just enjoys it! All those strangled heads and bulbous eyes and waddling fungus growths just shriek with derision!

I am getting angry enough to do something desperate. To jump out of the window would be admirable exercise, but the bars are too strong even to try.

Besides I wouldn't do it. Of course not. I know well enough that a step like that is improper and might be misconstrued.

I don't like to *look* out of the windows even—there are so many of those creeping women, and they creep so fast.

I wonder if they all come out of that wall-paper as I did?

But I am securely fastened now by my well-hidden rope—you don't get *me* out in the road there!

I suppose I shall have to get back behind the pattern when it comes night, and that is hard!

It is so pleasant to be out in this great room and creep around as I please!

I don't want to go outside. I won't, even if Jennie asks me to.

For outside you have to creep on the ground, and everything is green instead of yellow.

But here I can creep smoothly on the floor, and my shoulder just fits in that long smooch around the wall, so I cannot lose my way.

Why there's John at the door!

It is no use, young man, you can't open it!

How he does call and pound!

Now he's crying for an axe.

It would be a shame to break down that beautiful door!

"John dear!" said I in the gentlest voice, "the key is down by the front steps, under a plantain leaf!"

That silenced him for a few moments.

Then he said—very quietly indeed, "Open the door, my darling!"

"I can't," said I. "The key is down by the front door under a plantain leaf!"

And then I said it again, several times, very gently and slowly, and said it so often that he had to go and see, and he got it of course, and came in. He stopped short by the door.

"What is the matter?" he cried. "For God's sake, what are you doing!"

I kept on creeping just the same, but I looked at him over my shoulder.

"I've got out at last," said I, "in spite of you and Jennie. And I've pulled off most of the paper, so you can't put me back!"

Now why should that man have fainted? But he did, and right across my path by the wall, so that I had to creep over him every time!

QUESTIONS

1. Obviously, the yellow wallpaper is the central image in the story. One way to analyze the story, therefore, would be to trace the narrator's impressions of the wallpaper throughout the tale. We might ask how large a part the paper plays in her narration of each episode; how her description of the paper itself changes from scene to scene; how she describes the effect the paper has on her; and how those descriptions change. We might also ask how we respond to each change, each new description. How do we use the changing descriptions to interpret the narrator's state of mind? What feelings toward her do we have, and how do they change (or develop) as the story progresses?

2. For a brief paper, you might concentrate on the wallpaper as part of the tale's setting. Notice how the surroundings narrow for the narrator, from her de-

scription of the house and its grounds on the first day to her description of her path around the room on the final day. How has this narrowing been accomplished? What does it symbolize?

3. Another approach might be to ask why the wallpaper is in the narrator's room at all? What does her explanation of its presence tell you about her marriage—about her feelings about herself and her husband, and about his feelings about himself and her? How is this theme developed throughout the story? How does it end? (Make sure you take note of the tone of the story's final sentence!)

4. "The Yellow Wall-Paper" is certainly a tale that demands much participation from its readers. The narrator and her husband disagree about her needs and her health; and we feel ourselves called on to decide who is right. The wife also describes herself in solitude (particularly with reference to the wallpaper); and again we must decide how far to believe what she says, or how to reinterpret it. You might write a paper, therefore, discussing the narrative style of the tale, explaining where your sympathies lie at various points and describing the means by which the narrative shifts you from being a listener in the first scene (which is a fairly straightforward description) to being the only person who really understands what is going on in the final scene, the one who could answer the narrator's final question.

QUESTIONS FOR FURTHER THOUGHT

Unlike the central characters of "The Guest" and "Young Goodman Brown," who seem to have withdrawn from their fellow humans at least partly of their own volition, the narrators of "Bartleby the Scrivener" and "The Yellow Wall-Paper" want to communicate with other people, but are prevented from doing so. What would you say is blocking communication for them? Who or what is to be blamed for the miseries all four characters endure?

NARRATION IN LONGER TALES

Joseph Conrad's "Youth" is sometimes called a long story, sometimes a short novel. Whichever we call it, reading it gives us a chance to observe narration, characterization, and the handling of action and images on a broader scale than we've seen before. Moreover, "Youth" also contains a narrator who seems to delight in his role as a teller of tales; so it seems an appropriate story with which to close our section on narration.

JOSEPH CONRAD (1857–1924)

Youth

This could have occurred nowhere but in England, where men and sea interpenetrate, so to speak—the sea entering into the life of most men, and the men knowing something or everything about the sea, in the way of amusement, of travel, or of bread-winning.

We were sitting round a mahogany table that reflected the bottle, the claret glasses, and our faces as we leaned on our elbows. There was a director of companies, an accountant, a lawyer, Marlow, and myself. The director had been a *Conway* boy, the accountant had served four years at sea, the lawyer—a fine crusted Tory, High Churchman, the best of old fellows, the soul of honor—had been chief officer in the P. & O. service in the good old days when mail-boats were square-rigged at least on two masts, and used to come down the China Sea before a fair monsoon with stun'-sails set alow and aloft. We all began life in the merchant service. Between the five of us there was the strong bond of the sea, and also the fellowship of the craft, which no amount of enthusiasm for yachting, cruising, and so on can give, since one is only the amusement of life and the other is life itself.

Marlow (at least I think that is how he spelt his name) told the story, or rather the chronicle, of a voyage:

"Yes, I have seen a little of the Eastern seas; but what I remember best is my first voyage there. You fellows know there are those voyages that seem ordered for the illustration of life, that might stand for a symbol of existence. You fight, work, sweat, nearly kill yourself, sometimes do kill yourself, trying to accomplish something—and you can't. Not from any fault of yours. You simply can do nothing, neither great nor little—not a thing in the world—not even marry an old maid, or get a wretched 600-ton cargo of coal to its port of destination.

"It was altogether a memorable affair. It was my first voyage to the East, and my first voyage as second mate; it was also my skipper's first command. You'll admit it was time. He was sixty if a day; a little man, with a broad, not very straight back, with bowed shoulders and one leg more bandy than the other, he had that queer twisted-about appearance you see so often in men who work in the fields. He had a nutcracker face—chin and nose trying to come together over a sunken mouth—and it was framed in iron-gray fluffy hair, that looked like a chin strap of cotton-wool sprinkled with coal dust. And he had blue eyes in that old face of his, which were amazingly like a boy's, with that candid expression some quite common men preserve to the end of their days by a rare internal gift of simplicity of heart and rectitude of soul. What induced him to accept me was a wonder. I had come out of a crack Australian clipper, where I had been third officer, and he seemed to have a prejudice against crack clippers as aristocratic and high-toned. He said to me, 'You know, in this ship you will have to work.' I said I had to work in every ship I had ever been in. 'Ah, but this is different, and you gentlemen out of them big ships; . . . but there! I dare say you will do. Join tomorrow.'

"I joined tomorrow. It was twenty-two years ago; and I was just twenty. How time passes! It was one of the happiest days of my life. Fancy! Second mate for the first time—a really responsible officer! I wouldn't have thrown up my new billet for a fortune. The mate looked me over carefully. He was also an old chap, but of another stamp. He had a Roman nose, a snow-white, long beard, and his name was Mahon, but he insisted that it should be pronounced Mann. He was well connected; yet there was something wrong with his luck, and he had never got on.

"As to the captain, he had been for years in coasters, then in the Mediterranean, and last in the West Indian trade. He had never been round the Capes. He could just write a kind of sketchy hand, and didn't care for writing at all. Both were thorough good seamen of course, and between those two old chaps I felt like a small boy between two grandfathers.

"The ship also was old. Her name was the *Judea*. Queer name, isn't it? She belonged to a man Wilmer, Wilcox—some name like that; but he has been bankrupt and dead these twenty years or more, and his name don't matter. She had been laid up in Shadwell basin for ever so long. You can imagine her state. She was all rust, dust, grime—soot aloft, dirt on deck. To me it was like coming out of a palace into a ruined cottage. She was about 400 tons, had a primitive windlass, wooden latches on the doors, not a bit of brass about her, and a big square stern. There was on it, below her name in big letters, a lot of scroll work, with the gilt off, and some sort of a coat of arms, with the motto 'Do or Die' underneath. I remember it took my fancy immensely. There was a touch of romance in it, something that made me love the old thing—something that appealed to my youth!

"We left London in ballast—sand ballast—to load a cargo of coal in a northern port for Bankok. Bankok! I thrilled. I had been six years at sea, but had only seen Melbourne and Sydney, very good places, charming places in their way—but Bankok!

"We worked out of the Thames under canvas, with a North Sea pilot on board. His name was Jermyn, and he dodged all day long about the galley drying his handkerchief before the stove. Apparently he never slept. He was a dismal man, with a perpetual tear sparkling at the end of his nose, who either had been in trouble, or was in trouble, or expected to be in trouble—couldn't be happy unless something went wrong. He mistrusted my youth, my common sense, and my seamanship, and made a point of showing it in a hundred little ways. I dare say he was right. It seems to me I knew very little then, and I know not much more now; but I cherish a hate for that Jermyn to this day.

"We were a week working up as far as Yarmouth Roads, and then we got into a gale—the famous October gale of twenty-two years ago. It was wind, lightning, sleet, snow, and a terrific sea. We were flying light, and you may imagine how bad it was when I tell you we had smashed bulwarks and a flooded deck. On the second night she shifted her ballast into the lee bow, and by that time we had been blown off somewhere on the Dogger Bank. There was nothing for it but go below with shovels and try to right her, and there we were in that vast hold, gloomy like a cavern, the tallow dips stuck and flickering on the beams, the gale howling above, the ship tossing about like mad on her side; there we all were, Jermyn, the captain, everyone, hardly able to keep our feet, engaged on that gravedigger's work, and trying to toss shovelfuls of wet sand up to windward. At every tumble of the ship you could see vaguely in the dim light men falling down with a great flourish of shovels. One of the ship's boys (we had two), impressed by the weirdness of the scene, wept as if his heart would break. We could hear him blubbering somewhere in the shadows.

"On the third day the gale died out, and by-and-by a north-country tug picked us up. We took sixteen days in all to get from London to the Tyne! When we got into dock we had lost our turn for loading, and they hauled us off to a tier where we remained for a month. Mrs. Beard (the captain's name was Beard) came from Colchester to see the old man. She lived on board. The crew of runners had left, and there remained only the officers, one boy, and the steward, a mulatto who answered to the name of Abraham. Mrs. Beard was an old woman, with a face all wrinkled and ruddy like a winter apple, and the figure of a young girl. She caught sight of me once, sewing on a button, and insisted on having my shirts to repair. This was something different from the captains' wives I had known on board crack clippers. When I brought her the shirts, she said: 'And the socks? They want mending, I am sure, and John's—Captain Beard's— things are all in order now. I would be glad of something to do.' Bless the old woman. She overhauled my outfit for me, and meantime I read for the first time 'Sartor Resartus' and Burnaby's 'Ride to Khiva.' I didn't understand much of the first then; but I remember I preferred the soldier to the philosopher at the time; a preference which life has only confirmed. One was a man, and the other was either more—or less. However, they are both dead, and Mrs. Beard is dead, and youth, strength, genius, thoughts, achievements, simple hearts—all die . . . No matter.

"They loaded us at last. We shipped a crew. Eight able seamen and two boys. We hauled off one evening to the buoys at the dock-gates, ready to go out, and with a fair prospect of beginning the voyage next day. Mrs. Beard was to start for home by a late train. When the ship was fast we went to tea. We sat rather silent through the meal—Mahon, the old couple, and I. I finished first, and slipped away for a smoke, my cabin being in a deckhouse just against the poop. It was high water, blowing fresh with a drizzle; the double dock-gates were opened, and the steam colliers were going in and out in the darkness with their lights burning bright, a great plashing of propellers, rattling of winches, and a lot of hailing on the pier-heads. I watched the procession of headlights gliding high and of green lights gliding low in the night, when suddenly a red gleam flashed at me, vanished, came into view again, and remained. The fore-end of a steamer loomed up close. I shouted down the cabin, 'Come up, quick!' and then heard a startled voice saying afar in the dark, 'Stop her, sir.' A bell jingled. Another voice cried warningly, 'We are going right into that bark, sir.' The answer to this was a gruff 'All right,' and the next thing was a heavy crash as the steamer struck a glancing blow with the bluff of her bow about our fore-rigging. There was a moment of confusion, yelling, and running about. Steam roared. Then somebody was heard saying, 'All clear, sir.' . . . 'Are you all right?' asked the gruff voice. I had jumped forward to see the damage, and hailed back, 'I think so.' 'Easy astern,' said the gruff voice. A bell jingled. 'What steamer is that?' screamed Mahon. By that time she was no more to us than a bulky shadow maneuvering a little way off. They shouted at us some name—a woman's name, Miranda or Melissa—or some such thing. 'This means another month in this beastly hole,' said Mahon to me, as we peered with lamps about the splintered bulwarks and broken braces. 'But where's the captain?'

"We had not heard or seen anything of him all that time. We went aft to look. A doleful voice arose hailing somewhere in the middle of the dock, '*Judea* ahoy!' . . . How the devil did he get there? . . . 'Hallo!' we shouted. 'I am adrift in our boat without oars,' he cried. A belated waterman offered his services, and Mahon struck a bargain with him for half-a-crown to tow our skipper alongside; but it was Mrs. Beard that came up the ladder first. They had been floating about the dock in that mizzly cold rain for nearly an hour. I was never so surprised in my life.

"It appears that when he heard my shout 'Come up,' he understood at once what was the matter, caught up his wife, ran on deck, and across, and down into our boat, which was fast to the ladder. Not bad for a sixty-year-old. Just imagine that old fellow saving heroically in his arms that old woman—the woman of his life. He set her down on a thwart, and was ready to climb back on board when the painter came adrift somehow, and away they went together. Of course in the confusion we did not hear him shouting. He looked abashed. She said cheerfully, 'I suppose it does not matter my losing the train now?' 'No, Jenny—you go below and get warm,' he growled. Then to us: 'A sailor has no business with a wife—I say. There I was, out of the ship. Well, no harm done this time. Let's go and look at what that fool of a steamer smashed.'

"It wasn't much, but it delayed us three weeks. At the end of that time, the captain being engaged with his agents, I carried Mrs. Beard's bag to the railway station and put her all comfy into a third-class carriage. She lowered the window to say, 'You are a good young man. If you see John—Captain Beard—without his muffler at night, just remind him from me to keep his throat well wrapped up.' 'Certainly, Mrs. Beard,' I said. 'You are a good young man; I noticed how attentive you are to John—to Captain—' The train pulled out suddenly; I took my cap off to the old woman: I never saw her again . . . Pass the bottle.

"We went to sea next day. When we made that start for Bankok we had been already three months out of London. We had expected to be a fortnight or so—at the outside.

"It was January, and the weather was beautiful—the beautiful sunny winter weather that has more charm than in the summertime, because it is unexpected, and crisp, and you know it won't, it can't, last long. It's like a windfall, like a godsend, like an unexpected piece of luck.

"It lasted all down the North Sea, all down Channel; and it lasted till we were three hundred miles or so to the westward of the Lizards: then the wind went round to the sou'west and began to pipe up. In two days it blew a gale. The *Judea,* hove to, wallowed on the

Atlantic like an old candlebox. It blew day after day: it blew with spite, without interval, without mercy, without rest. The world was nothing but an immensity of great foaming waves rushing at us, under a sky low enough to touch with the hand and dirty like a smoked ceiling. In the stormy space surrounding us there was as much flying spray as air. Day after day and night after night there was nothing round the ship but the howl of the wind, the tumult of the sea, the noise of water pouring over her deck. There was no rest for her and no rest for us. She tossed, she pitched, she stood on her head, she sat on her tail, she rollled, she groaned, and we had to hold on while on deck and cling to our bunks when below, in a constant effort of body and worry of mind.

"One night Mahon spoke through the small window of my berth. It opened right into my very bed, and I was lying there sleepless, in my boots, feeling as though I had not slept for years, and could not if I tried. He said excitedly—

" 'You got the sounding-rod in here, Marlow? I can't get the pumps to suck. By God! it's no child's play.'

"I gave him the sounding-rod and lay down again, trying to think of various things—but I thought only of the pumps. When I came on deck they were still at it, and my watch relieved at the pumps. By the light of the lantern brought on deck to examine the sounding-rod I caught a glimpse of their weary, serious faces. We pumped all the four hours. We pumped all night, all day, all the week,—watch and watch. She was working herself loose, and leaked badly—not enough to drown us at once, but enough to kill us with the work at the pumps. And while we pumped the ship was going from us piecemeal: the bulwarks went, the stanchions were torn out, the ventilators smashed, the cabin door burst in. There was not a dry spot in the ship. She was being gutted bit by bit. The longboat changed, as if by magic, into matchwood where she stood in her gripes. I had lashed her myself, and was rather proud of my handiwork, which had withstood so long the malice of the sea. And we pumped. And there was no break in the weather. The sea was white like a sheet of foam, like a caldron of boiling milk; there was not a break in the clouds, no—not the size of a man's hand—no, not for so much as ten seconds. There was for us no sky, there were for us no stars, no sun, no universe—nothing but angry clouds and an infuriated sea. We pumped watch and watch, for dear life; and it seemed to last for months, for years, for all eternity, as though we had been dead and gone to a hell for sailors. We forgot the day of the week, the name of the month, what year it was, and whether we had ever been ashore. The sails blew away, she lay broadside on under a weather-cloth, the ocean poured over her, and we did not care. We turned those handles, and had the eyes of idiots. As soon as we had crawled on deck I used to take a round turn with a rope about the men, the pumps, and the mainmast, and we turned, we turned incessantly, with the water to our waists, to our necks, over our heads. It was all one. We had forgotten how it felt to be dry.

"And there was somewhere in me the thought: By Jove! this is the deuce of an adventure—something you read about; and it is my first voyage as second mate—and I am only twenty—and here I am lasting it out as well as any of these men, and keeping my chaps up to the mark. I was pleased. I would not have given up the experience for worlds. I had moments of exultation. Whenever the old dismantled craft pitched heavily with her counter high in the air, she seemed to me to throw up, like an appeal, like a defiance, like a cry to the clouds without mercy, the words written on her stern: '*Judea*, London. Do or Die.'

"O youth! The strength of it, the faith of it, the imagination of it! To me she was not an old rattletrap carting about the world a lot of coal for a freight—to me she was the endeavor, the test, the trial of life. I think of her with pleasure, with affection, with regret—as you would think of someone dead you have loved. I shall never forget her . . . Pass the bottle.

"One night when, tied to the mast, as I explained, we were pumping on, deafened with the wind, and without spirit enough in us to wish ourselves dead, a heavy sea crashed aboard and swept clean over us. As soon as I got my breath I shouted, as in duty bound, 'Keep on, boys!' when suddenly I felt something hard floating on deck strike the calf of my leg. I made a grab at it and missed. It was so dark we could not see each other's faces within a foot—you understand.

"After that thump the ship kept quiet for a while, and the thing, whatever it was, struck my leg again. This time I caught it—and it was a saucepan. At first, being stupid with fatigue and thinking of nothing but the pumps, I did not understand what I had in my hand. Suddenly it dawned upon me, and I shouted, 'Boys, the house on deck is gone. Leave this, and let's look for the cook.'

"There was a deckhouse forward, which contained the galley, the cook's berth, and the quarters of the crew. As we had expected for days to see it swept away, the hands had been ordered to sleep in the cabin—the only safe place in the ship. The steward, Abraham, however, persisted in clinging to his berth, stupidly, like a mule—from sheer fright I believe, like an animal that won't leave a stable falling in an earthquake. So we went to look for him. It was chancing death, since once out of our lashings we were as exposed as if on a raft. But we went. The house was shattered as if a shell had exploded inside. Most of it had gone overboard—stove, men's quarters, and their property, all was gone; but two posts, holding a portion of the bulkhead to which Abraham's bunk was attached, remained as if by a miracle. We groped in the ruins and came upon this, and there he was, sitting in his bunk, surrounded by foam and wreckage, jabbering cheerfully to himself. He was out of his mind; completely and for ever mad, with this sudden shock coming upon the fag-end of his endurance. We snatched him up, lugged him aft, and pitched him head-first down the cabin companion. You understand there was no time to carry him down with infinite precautions and wait to see how he got on. Those below would pick him up at the bottom of the stairs all right. We were in a hurry to go back to the pumps. That business could not wait. A bad leak is an inhuman thing.

"One would think that the sole purpose of that fiendish gale had been to make a lunatic of that poor devil of a mulatto. It eased before morning, and next day the sky cleared, and as the sea went down the leak took up. When it came to bending a fresh set of sails the crew demanded to put back—and really there was nothing else to do. Boats gone, decks swept clean, cabin gutted, men without a stitch but what they stood in, stores spoiled, ship strained. We put her head for home, and—would you believe it? The wind came east right in our teeth. It blew fresh, it blew continuously. We had to beat up every inch of the way, but she did not leak so badly, the water keeping comparatively smooth. Two hours' pumping in every four is no joke—but it kept her afloat as far as Falmouth.

"The good people there live on casualties of the sea, and no doubt were glad to see us. A hungry crowd of shipwrights sharpened their chisels at the sight of that carcass of a ship. And, by Jove! they had pretty pickings off us before they were done. I fancy the owner was already in a tight place. There were delays. Then it was decided to take part of the cargo out and calk her topsides. This was done, the repairs finished, cargo reshipped; a new crew came on board, and we went out—for Bankok. At the end of a week we were back again. The crew said they weren't going to Bankok—a hundred and fifty days' passage—in a something hooker that wanted pumping eight hours out of the twenty-four; and the nautical papers inserted again the little paragraph: '*Judea.* Bark. Tyne to Bankok; coals; put back to Falmouth leaky and with crew refusing duty.'

"There were more delays—more tinkering. The owner came down for a day, and said she was as right as a little fiddle. Poor old Captain Beard looked like the ghost of a Geordie skipper—through the worry and humiliation of it. Remember he was sixty, and it was his first command. Mahon said it was a foolish business, and would end badly. I loved the ship more than ever, and wanted awfully to get to Bankok. To Bankok! Magic name, blessed name. Mesopotamia wasn't a patch on it. Remember I was twenty, and it was my first second mate's billet, and the East was waiting for me.

"We went out and anchored in the outer roads with a fresh

crew—the third. She leaked worse than ever. It was as if those confounded shipwrights had actually made a hole in her. This time we did not even go outside. The crew simply refused to man the windlass.

"They towed us back to the inner harbor, and we became a fixture, a feature, an institution of the place. People pointed us out to visitors as 'That 'ere bark that's going to Bankok—has been here six months—put back three times.' On holidays the small boys pulling about in boats would hail, '*Judea,* ahoy!' and if a head showed above the rail shouted, 'Where you bound to?—Bankok?' and jeered. We were only three on board. The poor old skipper mooned in the cabin. Mahon undertook the cooking, and unexpectedly developed all a Frenchman's genius for preparing nice little messes. I looked languidly after the rigging. We became citizens of Falmouth. Every shopkeeper knew us. At the barber's or tobacconist's they asked familiarly, 'Do you think you will ever get to Bankok?' Meantime the owner, the underwriters, and the charterers squabbled amongst themselves in London, and our pay went on . . . Pass the bottle.

"It was horrid. Morally it was worse than pumping for life. It seemed as though we had been forgotten by the world, belonged to nobody, would get nowhere; it seeemed that, as if bewitched, we would have to live for ever and ever in that inner harbor, a derision and a byword to generations of longshore loafers and dishonest boatmen. I obtained three months' pay and a five days' leave, and made a rush for London. It took me a day to get there and pretty well another to come back—but three months' pay went all the same. I don't know what I did with it. I went to a music hall, I believe, lunched, dined, and supped in a swell place in Regent Street, and was back to time, with nothing but a complete set of Byron's works and a new railway rug to show for three months' work. The boatman who pulled me off to the ship said: 'Hallo! I thought you had left the old thing. *She* will never get to Bankok.' 'That's all *you* know about it,' I said scornfully—but I didn't like that prophecy at all.

"Suddenly a man, some kind of agent to somebody, appeared with full powers. He had grog blossoms all over his face, an indomitable energy, and was a jolly soul. We leaped into life again. A hulk came alongside, took our cargo, and then we went into dry dock to get our copper stripped. No wonder she leaked. The poor thing, strained beyond endurance by the gale, had, as if in disgust, spat out all the oakum of her lower seams. She was recalked, new coppered, and made as tight as a bottle. We went back to the hulk and reshipped our cargo.

"Then on a fine moonlight night, all the rats left the ship.

"We had been infested with them. They had destroyed our sails, consumed more stores than the crew, affably shared our beds and our dangers, and now, when the ship was made seaworthy, concluded to clear out. I called Mahon to enjoy the spectacle. Rat after rat appeared on our rail, took a last look over his shoulder, and leaped with a hollow thud into the empty hulk. We tried to count them, but soon lost the tale. Mahon said: 'Well, well! don't talk to me about the intelligence of rats. They ought to have left before, when we had that narrow squeak from foundering. There you have the proof how silly is the superstition about them. They leave a good ship for an old rotten hulk, where there is nothing to eat, too, the fools! . . . I don't believe they know what is safe or what is good for them, any more than you or I.'

"And after some more talk we agreed that the wisdom of rats had been grossly overrated, being in fact no greater than that of men.

"The story of the ship was known, by this, all up the Channel from Land's End to the Forelands, and we could get no crew on the south coast. They sent us one all complete from Liverpool, and we left once more—for Bankok.

"We had fair breezes, smooth water right into the tropics, and the old *Judea* lumbered along in the sunshine. When she went eight knots everything cracked aloft, and we tied our caps to our heads; but mostly she strolled on at the rate of three miles an hour. What could you expect? She was tired—that old ship. Her youth was where mine is—where yours is—you fellows who listen to this yarn; and what friend would throw your years and your weariness in your face? We didn't grumble at her. To us aft, at least, it seemed as though we had been born in her, reared in her, had lived in her for ages, had never known any other ship. I would just as soon have abused the old village church at home for not being a cathedral.

"And for me there was also my youth to make me patient. There was all the East before me, and all life, and the thought that I had been tried in that ship and had come out pretty well. And I thought of men of old who, centuries ago, went that road in ships that sailed no better, to the land of palms, and spices, and yellow sands, and of brown nations ruled by kings more cruel than Nero the Roman and more splendid than Solomon the Jew. The old bark lumbered on, heavy with her age and the burden of her cargo, while I lived the life of youth in ignorance and hope. She lumbered on through an interminable procession of days; and the fresh gilding flashed back at the setting sun, seemed to cry out over the darkening sea the words painted on her stern, '*Judea,* London. Do or Die.'

"Then we entered the Indian Ocean and steered northerly for Java Head. The winds were light. Weeks slipped by. She crawled on, do or die, and people at home began to think of posting us as overdue.

"One Saturday evening, I being off duty, the men asked me to give them an extra bucket of water or so—for washing clothes. As I did not wish to screw on the fresh-water pump so late, I went forward whistling, and with a key in my hand to unlock the forepeak scuttle, intending to serve the water out of a spare tank we kept there.

"The smell down below was as unexpected as it was frightful. One would have thought hundreds of paraffin lamps had been flaring and smoking in that hole for days. I was glad to get out. The man with me coughed and said, 'Funny smell, sir.' I answered negligently, 'It's good for the health, they say,' and walked aft.

"The first thing I did was to put my head down the square of the midship ventilator. As I lifted the lid a visible breath, something like a thin fog, a puff of faint haze, rose from the opening. The ascending air was hot, and had a heavy, sooty, paraffiny smell. I gave one sniff, and put down the lid gently. It was no use choking myself. The cargo was on fire.

"Next day she began to smoke in earnest. You see it was to be expected, for though the coal was of a safe kind, that cargo had been so handled, so broken up with handling, that it looked more like smithy coal than anything else. Then it had been wetted—more than once. It rained all the time we were taking it back from the hulk, and now with this long passage it got heated, and there was another case of spontaneous combustion.

"The captain called us into the cabin. He had a chart spread on the table, and looked unhappy. He said, 'The coast of West Australia is near, but I mean to proceed to our destination. It is the hurricane month too; but we will just keep her head for Bankok, and fight the fire. No more putting back anywhere, if we all get roasted. We will try first to stifle this 'ere damned combustion by want of air.'

"We tried. We battened down everything, and still she smoked. The smoke kept coming out through imperceptible crevices; it forced itself through bulkheads and covers; it oozed here and there and everywhere in slender threads, in an invisible film, in an incomprehensible manner. It made its way into the cabin, into the forecastle; it poisoned the sheltered places on the deck; it could be sniffed as high as the mainyard. It was clear that if the smoke came out the air came in. This was disheartening. This combustion refused to be stifled.

"We resolved to try water, and took the hatches off. Enormous volumes of smoke, whitish, yellowish, thick, greasy, misty, choking, ascended as high as the trucks. All hands cleared out aft. Then the poisonous cloud blew away, and we went back to work in a smoke that was no thicker now than that of an ordinary factory chimney.

"We rigged the force pump, got the hose along, and by-and-by it burst. Well, it was as old as the ship—a prehistoric hose, and past repair. Then we pumped with the feeble head-pump, drew water with buckets, and in this way managed in time to pour lots of Indian

Ocean into the main hatch. The bright stream flashed in sunshine, fell into a layer of white crawling smoke, and vanished on the black surface of coal. Steam ascended mingling with the smoke. We poured salt water as into a barrel without a bottom. It was our fate to pump in that ship, to pump out of her, to pump into her; and after keeping water out of her to save ourselves from being drowned, we frantically poured water into her to save ourselves from being burnt.

"And she crawled on, do or die, in the serene weather. The sky was a miracle of purity, a miracle of azure. The sea was polished, was blue, was pellucid, was sparkling like a precious stone, extending on all sides, all round to the horizon—as if the whole terrestrial globe had been one jewel, one colossal sapphire, a single gem fashioned into a planet. And on the luster of the great calm waters the *Judea* glided imperceptibly, enveloped in languid and unclean vapors, in a lazy cloud that drifted to leeward, light and slow: a pestiferous cloud defiling the splendor of sea and sky.

"All this time of course we saw no fire. The cargo smoldered at the bottom somewhere. Once Mahon, as we were working side by side, said to me with a queer smile: 'Now, if she only would spring a tidy leak—like that time when we first left the Channel—it would put a stopper on this fire. Wouldn't it?' I remarked irrelevantly, 'Do you remember the rats?'

"We fought the fire and sailed the ship too as carefully as though nothing had been the matter. The steward cooked and attended on us. Of the other twelve men, eight worked while four rested. Everyone took his turn, captain included. There was equality, and if not exactly fraternity, then a deal of good feeling. Sometimes a man, as he dashed a bucketful of water down the hatchway, would yell out, 'Hurrah for Bankok!' and the rest laughed. But generally we were taciturn and serious—and thirsty. Oh! how thirsty! And we had to be careful with the water. Strict allowance. The ship smoked, the sun blazed . . . Pass the bottle.

"We tried everything. We even made an attempt to dig down to the fire. No good, of course. No man could remain more than a minute below. Mahon, who went first, fainted there, and the man who went to fetch him out did likewise. We lugged them out on deck. Then I leaped down to show how easily it could be done. They had learned wisdom by that time, and contented themselves by fishing for me with a chain-hook tied to a broom handle, I believe. I did not offer to go and fetch up my shovel, which was left down below.

"Things began to look bad. We put the longboat into the water. The second boat was ready to swing out. We had also another, a fourteen-foot thing, on davits aft, where it was quite safe.

"Then behold, the smoke suddenly decreased. We redoubled our efforts to flood the bottom of the ship. In two days there was no smoke at all. Everybody was on the broad grin. This was on a Friday. On Saturday no work, but sailing the ship of course was done. The men washed their clothes and their faces for the first time in a fortnight, and had a special dinner given them. They spoke of spontaneous combustion with contempt, and implied *they* were the boys to put out combustions. Somehow we all felt as though we each had inherited a large fortune. But a beastly smell of burning hung about the ship. Captain Beard had hollow eyes and sunken cheeks. I had never noticed so much before how twisted and bowed he was. He and Mahon prowled soberly about hatches and ventilators, sniffing. It struck me suddenly poor Mahon was a very, very old chap. As to me, I was as pleased and proud as though I had helped to win a great naval battle. O! Youth!

"The night was fine. In the morning a homeward-bound ship passed us hull down—the first we had seen for months; but we were nearing the land at last, Java Head being about 190 miles off, and nearly due north.

"Next day it was my watch on deck from eight to twelve. At breakfast the captain observed, 'It's wonderful how that smell hangs about the cabin.' About ten, the mate being on the poop, I stepped down on the main deck for a moment. The carpenter's bench stood abaft the mainmast: I leaned against it sucking at my pipe, and the carpenter, a young chap, came to talk to me. He remarked, 'I think we have done very well, haven't we?' and then I perceived with annoyance the fool was trying to tilt the bench. I said curtly, 'Don't, Chips,' and immediately became aware of a queer sensation, of an absurd delusion—I seemed somehow to be in the air. I heard all round me like a pent-up breath released—as if a thousand giants simultaneously had said Phoo!—and felt a dull concussion which made my ribs ache suddenly. No doubt about it—I was in the air, and my body was describing a short parabola. But short as it was, I had the time to think several thoughts in, as far as I can remember, the following order: 'This can't be the carpenter—What is it?—Some accident—Submarine volcano?—Coals, gas!—By Jove! we are being blown up—Everybody's dead—I am falling into the afterhatch—I see fire in it.'

"The coal dust suspended in the air of the hold had glowed dull red at the moment of the explosion. In the twinkling of an eye, in an infinitesimal fraction of a second since the first tilt of the bench, I was sprawling full length on the cargo. I picked myself up and scrambled out. It was quick like a rebound. The deck was a wilderness of smashed timber, lying crosswise like trees in a wood after a hurricane; an immense curtain of soiled rags waved gently before me—it was the mainsail blown to strips. I thought, The masts will be toppling over directly; and to get out of the way bolted on all fours towards the poop-ladder. The first person I saw was Mahon, with eyes like saucers, his mouth open, and the long white hair standing straight on end round his head like a silver halo. He was just about to go down when the sight of the main deck stirring, heaving up, and changing into splinters before his eyes, petrified him on the top step. I stared at him in unbelief, and he stared at me with a queer kind of shocked curiosity. I did not know that I had no hair, no eyebrows, no eyelashes, that my young mustache was burnt off, that my face was black, one cheek laid open, my nose cut, and my chin bleeding. I had lost my cap, one of my slippers, and my shirt was torn to rags. Of all this I was not aware. I was amazed to see the ship still afloat, the poop-deck whole—and, most of all, to see anybody alive. Also the peace of the sky and the serenity of the sea were distinctly surprising. I suppose I expected to see them convulsed with horror . . . Pass the bottle.

"There was a voice hailing the ship from somewhere—in the air, in the sky—I couldn't tell. Presently I saw the captain—and he was mad. He asked me eagerly, 'Where's the cabin-table?' and to hear such a question was a frightful shock. I had just been blown up, you understand, and vibrated with that experience—I wasn't quite sure whether I was alive. Mahon began to stamp with both feet and yelled at him, 'Good God! don't you see the deck's blown out of her?' I found my voice, and stammered out as if conscious of some gross neglect of duty, 'I don't know where the cabin-table is.' It was like an absurd dream.

"Do you know what he wanted next? Well, he wanted to trim the yards. Very placidly, and as if lost in thought, he insisted on having the foreyard squared. 'I don't know if there's anybody alive,' said Mahon, almost tearfully. 'Surely,' he said, gently, 'there will be enough left to square the foreyard.'

"The old chap, it seems, was in his own berth, winding up the chronometers, when the shock sent him spinning. Immediately it occurred to him—as he said afterwards—that the ship had struck something, and he ran out into the cabin. There, he saw, the cabin-table had vanished somewhere. The deck being blown up, it had fallen down into the lazarette of course. Where we had our breakfast that morning he saw only a great hole in the floor. This appeared to him so awfully mysterious, and impressed him so immensely, that what he saw and heard after he got on deck were mere trifles in comparison. And, mark, he noticed directly the wheel deserted and his bark off her course—and his only thought was to get that miserable, stripped, undecked, smoldering shell of a ship back again with her head pointing at her port of destination. Bankok! That's what he was after. I tell you this quiet, bowed, bandy-legged, almost deformed little man was immense in the singleness of his idea and in his placid ignorance of our agitation. He motioned us forward with a commanding gesture, and went to take the wheel himself.

"Yes: that was the first thing we did—trim the yards of that wreck! No one was killed, or even disabled, but everyone was more or less hurt. You should have seen them! Some were in rags, with black faces, like coal-heavers, like sweeps, and had bullet heads that seemed closely cropped, but were in fact singed to the skin. Others, of the watch below, awakened by being shot out from their collapsing bunks, shivered incessantly, and kept on groaning even as we went about our work. But they all worked. That crew of Liverpool hard cases had in them the right stuff. It's my experience they always have. It is the sea that gives it—the vastness, the loneliness surrounding their dark stolid souls. Ah! Well! we stumbled, we crept, we fell, we barked our shins on the wreckage, we hauled. The masts stood, but we did not know how much they might be charred down below. It was nearly calm, but a long swell ran from the west and made her roll. They might go at any moment. We looked at them with apprehension. One could not foresee which way they would fall.

"Then we retreated aft and looked about us. The deck was a tangle of planks on edge, of planks on end, of splinters, of ruined woodwork. The masts rose from that chaos like big trees above a matted undergrowth. The interstices of that mass of wreckage were full of something whitish, sluggish, stirring—of something that was like a greasy fog. The smoke of the invisible fire was coming up again, was trailing, like a poisonous thick mist in some valley choked with dead wood. Already lazy wisps were beginning to curl upwards amongst the mass of splinters. Here and there a piece of timber, stuck upright, resembled a post. Half of a fife-rail had been shot through the foresail, and the sky made a patch of glorious blue in the ignobly soiled canvas. A portion of several boards holding together had fallen across the rail, and one end protruded overboard, like a gangway leading upon nothing, like a gangway leading over the deep sea, leading to death—as if inviting us to walk the plank at once and be done with our ridiculous troubles. And still the air, the sky—a ghost, something invisible was hailing the ship.

"Someone had the sense to look over, and there was the helmsman, who had impulsively jumped overboard, anxious to come back. He yelled and swam lustily like a merman, keeping up with the ship. We threw him a rope, and presently he stood amongst us streaming with water and very crestfallen. The captain had surrendered the wheel, and apart, elbow on rail and chin in hand, gazed at the sea wistfully. We asked ourselves, What next? I thought, Now, this is something like. This is great. I wonder what will happen. O youth!

"Suddenly Mahon sighted a steamer far astern. Captain Beard

said, 'We may do something with her yet.' We hoisted two flags, which said in the international language of the sea, 'On fire. Want immediate assistance.' The steamer grew bigger rapidly, and by-and-by spoke with two flags on her foremast, 'I am coming to your assistance.'

"In half an hour she was abreast, to windward, within hail, and rolling slightly, with her engines stopped. We lost our composure, and yelled all together with excitement, 'We've been blown up.' A man in a white helmet, on the bridge, cried, 'Yes! All right! all right! and he nodded his head, and smiled, and made soothing motions with his hand as though at a lot of frightened children. One of the boats dropped in the water, and walked towards us upon the sea with her long oars. Four Calashes pulled a swinging stroke. This was my first sight of Malay seamen. I've known them since, but what struck me then was their unconcern: they came alongside, and even the bowman standing up and holding to our main-chains with the boat-hook did not deign to lift his head for a glance. I thought people who had been blown up deserved more attention.

"A little man, dry like a chip and agile like a monkey, clambered up. It was the mate of the steamer. He gave one look, and cried, 'O boys—you had better quit.'

"We were silent. He talked apart with the captain for a time—seemed to argue with him. Then they went away together to the steamer.

"When our skipper came back we learned that the steamer was the *Sommerville,* Captain Nash, from West Australia to Singapore via Batavia with mails, and that the agreement was she should tow us to Anjer or Batavia, if possible, where we could extinguish the fire by scuttling, and then proceed on our voyage—to Bankok! The old man seemed excited. 'We will do it yet,' he said to Mahon, fiercely. He shook his fist at the sky. Nobody else said a word.

"At noon the steamer began to tow. She went ahead slim and high, and what was left of the *Judea* followed at the end of seventy fathom of tow-rope—followed her swiftly like a cloud of smoke with mastheads protruding above. We went aloft to furl the sails. We coughed on the yards, and were careful about the bunts. Do you see the lot of us there, putting a neat furl on the sails of that ship doomed to arrive nowhere? There was not a man who didn't think that at any moment the masts would topple over. From aloft we could not see the ship for smoke, and they worked carefully, passing the gaskets with even turns. 'Harbor furl—aloft there!' cried Mahon from below.

"You understand this? I don't think one of those chaps expected to get down in the usual way. When we did I heard them saying to each other, 'Well, I thought we would come down overboard, in a lump—

sticks and all—blame me if I didn't.' 'That's what I was thinking to myself,' would answer wearily another battered and bandaged scarecrow. And, mind, these were men without the drilled-in habit of obedience. To an onlooker they would be a lot of profane scallywags without a redeeming point. What made them do it—what made them obey me when I, thinking consciously how fine it was, made them drop the bunt of the foresail twice to try and do it better? What? They had no professional reputation—no examples, no praise. It wasn't a sense of duty; they all knew well enough how to shirk, and laze, and dodge—when they had a mind to it—and mostly they had. Was it the two pounds ten a month that sent them there? They didn't think their pay half good enough. No; it was something in them, something inborn and subtle and everlasting. I don't say positively that the crew of a French or German merchantman wouldn't have done it, but I doubt whether it would have been done in the same way. There was a completeness in it, something solid like a principle, and masterful like an instinct—a disclosure of something secret—of that hidden something, that gift, of good or evil that makes racial difference, that shapes the fate of nations.

"It was that night at ten that, for the first time since we had been fighting it, we saw the fire. The speed of the towing had fanned the smoldering destruction. A blue gleam appeared forward, shining below the wreck of the deck. It wavered in patches, it seemed to stir and creep like the light of a glowworm. I saw it first, and told Mahon. 'Then the game's up,' he said. 'We had better stop this towing, or she will burst out suddenly fore and aft before we can clear out.' We set up a yell; rang bells to attract their attention; they towed on. At last Mahon and I had to crawl forward and cut the rope with an ax. There was no time to cast off the lashings. Red tongues could be seen licking the wilderness of splinters under our feet as we made our way back to the poop.

"Of course they very soon found out in the steamer that the rope was gone. She gave a loud blast of her whistle, her lights were seen sweeping in a wide circle, she came up ranging close alongside, and stopped. We were all in a tight group on the poop looking at her. Every man had saved a little bundle or a bag. Suddenly a conical flame with a twisted top shot up forward and threw upon the black sea a circle of light, with the two vessels side by side and heaving gently in its center. Captain Beard had been sitting on the gratings still and mute for hours, but now he rose slowly and advanced in front of us, to the mizzen-shrouds. Captain Nash hailed: 'Come along! Look sharp. I have mail bags on board. I will take you and your boats to Singapore.'

" 'Thank you! No!' said our skipper. 'We must see the last of the ship.'

" 'I can't stand by any longer,' shouted the other. 'Mails—you know.'

" 'Ay! ay! We are all right.'

" 'Very well! I'll report you in Singapore . . . Good-by!' "

"He waved his hand. Our men dropped their bundles quietly. The steamer moved ahead, and passing out of the circle of light, vanished at once from our sight, dazzled by the fire which burned fiercely. And then I knew that I would see the East first as commander of a small boat. I thought it fine; and the fidelity to the old ship was fine. We should see the last of her. Oh the glamour of youth! Oh the fire of it, more dazzling than the flames of the burning ship, throwing a magic light on the wide earth, leaping audaciously to the sky, presently to be quenched by time, more cruel, more pitiless, more bitter than the sea—and like the flames of the burning ship surrounded by an impenetrable night.

"The old man warned us in his gentle and inflexible way that it was part of our duty to save for the underwriters as much as we could of the ship's gear. Accordingly we went to work aft, while she blazed forward to give us plenty of light. We lugged out a lot of rubbish. What didn't we save? An old barometer fixed with an absurd quantity of screws nearly cost me my life: a sudden rush of smoke came upon me, and I just got away in time. There were various stores, bolts of canvas, coils of rope; the poop looked like a marine bazaar, and the boats were lumbered to the gunwales. One would have thought the old man wanted to take as much as he could of his first command with him. He was very, very quiet, but off his balance evidently. Would you believe it? He wanted to take a length of old streamcable and a kedge-anchor with him in the longboat. We said, 'Ay, ay, sir,' deferentially, and on the quiet let the thing slip overboard. The heavy medicine chest went that way, two bags of green coffee, tins of paint—fancy, paint!—a whole lot of things. Then I was ordered with two hands into the boats to make a stowage and get them ready against the time it would be proper for us to leave the ship.

"We put everything straight, stepped the longboat's mast for our skipper, who was to take charge of her, and I was not sorry to sit down for a moment. My face felt raw, every limb ached as if broken, I was aware of all my ribs, and would have sworn to a twist in the backbone. The boats, fast astern, lay in a deep shadow, and all around I could see the circle of the sea lighted by the fire. A gigantic flame arose forward straight and clear. It flared fierce, with noises like the whir of wings, with rumbles as of thunder. There were cracks, detonations, and from the cone of flame the sparks flew upwards, as man is born to trouble, to leaky ships, and to ships that burn.

"What bothered me was that the ship, lying broadside to the swell and to such wind as there was—a mere breath—the boats would not keep astern where they were safe, but persisted, in a pig-headed way boats have, in getting under the counter and then swinging alongside. They were knocking about dangerously and coming near the flame, while the ship rolled on them, and, of course, there was always the danger of the masts going over the side at any moment. I and my two boat-keepers kept them off as best we could with oars and boat-hooks; but to be constantly at it became exasperating, since there was no reason why we should not leave at once. We could not see those on board, nor could we imagine what caused the delay. The boat-keepers were swearing feebly, and I had not only my share of the work, but also had to keep at it two men who showed a constant inclination to lay themselves down and let things slide.

"At last I hailed 'On deck there,' and someone looked over. 'We're ready here,' I said. The head disappeared, and very soon popped up again. 'The captain says, All right, sir, and to keep the boats well clear of the ship.'

"Half an hour passed. Suddenly there was a frightful racket, rattle, clanking of chain, hiss of water, and millions of sparks flew up into the shivering column of smoke that stood leaning slightly above the ship. The catheads had burned away, and the two red-hot anchors had gone to the bottom, tearing out after them two hundred fathom of red-hot chain. The ship trembled, the mass of flame swayed as if ready to collapse, and the fore top-gallant-mast fell. It darted down like an arrow of fire, shot under, and instantly leaping up within an oar's-length of the boats, floated quietly, very black on the luminous sea. I hailed the deck again. After some time a man in an unexpectedly cheerful but also muffled tone, as though he had been trying to speak with his mouth shut, informed me, 'Coming directly, sir,' and vanished. For a long time I heard nothing but the whir and roar of the fire. There were also whistling sounds. The boats jumped, tugged at the painters, ran at each other playfully, knocked their sides together, or, do what we would, swung in a bunch against the ship's side. I couldn't stand it any longer, and swarming up a rope, clambered aboard over the stern.

"It was as bright as day. Coming up like this, the sheet of fire facing me was a terrifying sight, and the heat seemed hardly bearable at first. On a settee cushion dragged out of the cabin, Captain Beard, with his legs drawn up and one arm under his head, slept with the light playing on him. Do you know what the rest were busy about? They were sitting on deck right aft, round an open case, eating bread and cheese and drinking bottled stout.

"On the background of flames twisting in fierce tongues above their heads they seemed at home like salamanders, and looked like a band of desperate pirates. The fire sparkled in the whites of their eyes, gleamed on patches of white skin seen through the torn shirts. Each had the marks as of a battle about him—bandaged heads, tied-up arms, a strip of dirty rag round a knee—and each man had a bottle between his legs and a chunk of cheese in his hand. Mahon got up. With his handsome and disreputable head, his hooked profile, his long white beard, and with an uncorked bottle in his hand, he resembled one of those reckless sea-robbers of old making merry amidst violence and disaster. 'The last meal on board,' he explained solemnly. 'We had nothing to eat all day, and it was no use leaving all this.' He flourished the bottle and indicated the sleeping skipper. 'He said he couldn't swallow anything, so I got him to lie down,' he went on; and as I stared, 'I don't know whether you are aware, young fellow, the man had no sleep to speak of for days—and there will be dam' little sleep in the boats.' 'There will be no boats by-and-by if you fool about much longer,' I said, indignantly. I walked up to the skipper and shook him by the shoulder. At last he opened his eyes, but did not move. 'Time to leave her, sir,' I said, quietly.

"He got up painfully, looked at the flames, at the sea sparkling round the ship, and black, black as ink farther away; he looked at the stars shining dim through a thin veil of smoke in a sky black, black as Erebus.

" 'Youngest first,' he said.

"And the ordinary seaman, wiping his mouth with the back of his hand, got up, clambered over the taffrail, and vanished. Others followed. One, on the point of going over, stopped short to drain his bottle, and with a great swing of his arm flung it at the fire. 'Take this!' he cried.

"The skipper lingered disconsolately, and we left him to commune alone for awhile with his first command. Then I went up again and brought him away at last. It was time. The ironwork on the poop was hot to the touch.

"Then the painter of the longboat was cut, and the three boats, tied together, drifted clear of the ship. It was just sixteen hours after the explosion when we abandoned her. Mahon had charge of the second boat, and I had the smallest—the 14-foot thing. The longboat would have taken the lot of us; but the skipper said we must save as much property as we could—for the underwriters—and so I got my first command. I had two men with me, a bag of biscuits, a few tins of meat, and a beaker of water. I was ordered to keep close to the longboat, that in case of bad weather we might be taken into her.

"And do you know what I thought? I thought I would part company as soon as I could. I wanted to have my first command all to myself. I wasn't going to sail in a squadron if there were a chance for independent cruising. I would make land by myself. I would beat the other boats. Youth! All youth! The silly, charming, beautiful youth.

"But we did not make a start at once. We must see the last of the ship. And so the boats drifted about that night, heaving and setting on the swell. The men dozed, waked, sighed, groaned. I looked at the burning ship.

"Between the darkness of earth and heaven she was burning fiercely upon a disc of purple sea shot by the blood-red play of gleams; upon a disc of water glittering and sinister. A high, clear flame, an immense and lonely flame, ascended from the ocean, and from its summit the black smoke poured continuously at the sky. She burned furiously, mournful and imposing like a funeral pile kindled in the night, surrounded by the sea, watched over by the stars. A magnificent death had come like a grace, like a gift, like a reward to that old ship at the end of her laborious days. The surrender of her weary ghost to the keeping of stars and sea was stirring like the sight of a glorious triumph. The masts fell just before daybreak, and for a moment there was a burst and turmoil of sparks that seemed to fill with flying fire the night patient and watchful, the vast night lying silent upon the sea. At daylight she was only a charred shell, floating still under a cloud of smoke and bearing a glowing mass of coal within.

"Then the oars were got out, and the boats forming in a line moved round her remains as if in procession—the longboat leading. As we pulled across her stern a slim dart of fire shot out viciously at us, and suddenly she went down, head first, in a great hiss of steam. The unconsumed stern was the last to sink; but the paint had gone, had cracked, had peeled off, and there were no letters, there was no word, no stubborn device that was like her soul, to flash at the rising sun her creed and her name.

"We made our way north. A breeze sprang up, and about noon all the boats came together for the last time. I had no mast or sail in mine, but I made a mast out of a spare oar and hoisted a boat-awning for a sail, with a boat-hook for a yard. She was certainly overmasted, but I had the satisfaction of knowing that with the wind aft I could beat the other two. I had to wait for them. Then we all had a look at the captain's chart, and, after a sociable meal of hard bread and water, got our last instructions. These were simple: steer north, and keep together as much as possible. 'Be careful with that jury rig, Marlow,' said the captain; and Mahon, as I sailed proudly past his boat, wrinkled his curved nose and hailed, 'You will sail that ship of yours under water if you don't look out, young fellow.' He was a malicious old man—and may the deep sea where he sleeps now rock him gently, rock him tenderly to the end of time!

"Before sunset a thick rain-squall passed over the two boats, which were far astern, and that was the last I saw of them for a time. Next day I sat steering my cockle-shell—my first command—with nothing but water and sky around me. I did sight in the afternoon the upper sails of a ship far away, but said nothing, and my men did not notice her. You see I was afraid she might be homeward bound, and I had no mind to turn back from the portals of the East. I was steering for Java—another blessed name—like Bankok, you know. I steered many days.

"I need not tell you what it is to be knocking about in an open boat. I remember nights and days of calm when we pulled, we pulled, and the boat seemed to stand still, as if bewitched within the circle of the sea horizon. I remember the heat, the deluge of rain-squalls that kept us bailing for dear life (but filled our water cask), and I remember sixteen hours on end with a mouth dry as a cinder and a steering-oar over the stern to keep my first command head on to a breaking sea. I did not know how good a man I was till then. I remember the drawn faces, the dejected figures of my two men, and I remember my youth and the feeling that will never come back any more—the feeling that I could last for ever, outlast the sea, the earth, and all men; the deceitful feeling that lures us on to joys, to perils, to love, to vain effort—to death; the triumphant conviction of strength, the heat of life in the handful of dust, the glow in the heart that with every year grows dim, grows cold, grows small, and expires—and expires, too soon, too soon—before life itself.

"And this is how I see the East. I have seen its secret places and have looked into its very soul; but now I see it always from a small boat, a high outline of mountains, blue and afar in the morning; like faint mist at noon; a jagged wall of purple at sunset. I have the feel of the oar in my hand, the vision of a scorching blue sea in my eyes. And I see a bay, a wide bay, smooth as glass and polished like ice, shimmering in the dark. A red light burns far off upon the gloom of the land, and the night is soft and warm. We drag at the oars with aching arms, and suddenly a puff of wind, a puff faint and tepid and laden with strange odors of blossoms, of aromatic wood, comes out of the still night—the first sigh of the East on my face. That I can never forget. It was impalpable and enslaving, like a charm, like a whis-pered promise of mysterious delight.

"We had been pulling this finishing spell for eleven hours. Two pulled, and he whose turn it was to rest sat at the tiller. We had made out the red light in that bay and steered for it, guessing it must mark some small coasting port. We passed two vessels, outlandish and high-sterned, sleeping at anchor, and, approaching the light, now very dim, ran the boat's nose against the end of a jutting wharf. We were blind with fatigue. My men dropped the oars and fell off the thwarts as if dead. I made fast to a pile. A current rippled softly. The scented obscurity of the shore was grouped into vast masses, a density of colossal clumps of vegetation, probably—mute and fantastic shapes. And at their foot the semicircle of a beach gleamed faintly, like an illusion. There was not a light, not a stir, not a sound. The mysterious East faced me, perfumed like a flower, silent like death, dark like a grave.

"And I sat weary beyond expression, exulting like a conqueror, sleepless and entranced as if before a profound, a fateful enigma.

"A splashing of oars, a measured dip reverberating on the level of water, intensified by the silence of the shore into loud claps, made me jump up. A boat, a European boat, was coming in. I invoked the name of the dead; I hailed: *Judea* ahoy! A thin shout answered.

"It was the captain. I had beaten the flagship by three hours, and I was glad to hear the old man's voice again, tremulous and tired. 'Is it you, Marlow?' 'Mind the end of that jetty, sir,' I cried.

"He approached cautiously, and brought up with the deep-sea lead-line which we had saved—for the underwriters. I eased my painter and fell alongside. He sat, a broken figure at the stern, wet with dew, his hands clasped in his lap. His men were asleep already. 'I had a terrible time of it,' he murmured. 'Mahon is behind—not very far.' We conversed in whispers, in low whispers, as if afraid to wake up the land. Guns, thunder, earthquakes would not have awakened the men just then.

"Looking around as we talked, I saw away at sea a bright light traveling in the night. 'There's a steamer passing the bay,' I said. She was not passing, she was entering, and she even came close and anchored. 'I wish,' said the old man, 'you would find out whether she is English. Perhaps they could give us a passage somewhere.' He seemed nervously anxious. So by dint of punching and kicking I started one of my men into a state of somnambulism, and giving him an oar, took another and pulled towards the lights of the steamer.

"There was a murmur of voices in her, metallic hollow clangs of the engine room, footsteps on the deck. Her ports shone, round like dilated eyes. Shapes moved about, and there was a shadowy man high up on the bridge. He heard my oars.

"And then, before I could open my lips, the East spoke to me, but it was in a Western voice. A torrent of words was poured into the enigmatical, the fateful silence; outlandish, angry words, mixed with words and even whole sentences of good English, less strange but even more surprising. The voice swore and cursed violently; it riddled the solemn peace of the bay by a volley of abuse. It began by calling me Pig, and from that went crescendo into unmentionable adjectives—in English. The man up there raged aloud in two languages, and with a sincerity in his fury that almost convinced me I had, in some way, sinned against the harmony of the universe. I could hardly see him, but began to think he would work himself into a fit.

"Suddenly he ceased, and I could hear him snorting and blowing like a porpoise. I said—

" 'What steamer is this, pray?'

" 'Eh? What's this? And who are you?'

" 'Castaway crew of an English bark burnt at sea. We came here tonight. I am the second mate. The captain is in the longboat, and wishes to know if you would give us a passage somewhere.'

" 'Oh, my goodness! I say . . . This is the *Celestial* from Singapore on her return trip. I'll arrange with your captain in the morning . . . and . . . I say . . . did you hear me just now?'

" 'I should think the whole bay heard you.'

" 'I thought you were a shore boat. Now, look here—this infernal lazy scoundrel of a caretaker has gone to sleep again—curse him. The light is out, and I nearly ran foul of the end of this damned jetty. This is the third time he plays me this trick. Now, I ask you, can anybody stand this kind of thing? It's enough to drive a man out of his mind. I'll report him . . . I'll get the Assistant Resident to give him the sack, by . . . See—there's no light. It's out, isn't it? I take you to witness the light's out. There should be a light, you know. A red light on the—'

" 'There was a light,' I said, mildly.

" 'But it's out, man! What's the use of talking like this? You can see for yourself it's out—don't you? If you had to take a valuable steamer along this God-forsaken coast you would want a light too. I'll kick him from end to end of his miserable wharf. You'll see if I don't. I will—'

" 'So I may tell my captain you'll take us?' I broke in.

" 'Yes, I'll take you. Good night,' he said, brusquely.

"I pulled back, made fast again to the jetty, and then went to sleep at last. I had faced the silence of the East. I had heard some of its languages. But when I opened my eyes again the silence was as complete as though it had never been broken. I was lying in a flood of light, and the sky had never looked so far, so high, before. I opened my eyes and lay without moving.

"And then I saw the men of the East—they were looking at me. The whole length of the jetty was full of people. I saw brown, bronze, yellow faces, the black eyes, the glitter, the color of an Eastern crowd. And all these beings stared without a murmur, without a sigh, without a movement. They stared down at the boats, at the sleeping men who at night had come to them from the sea. Nothing moved. The fronds of palms stood still against the sky. Not a branch stirred along the shore, and the brown roofs of hidden houses peeped through the green foliage, through the big leaves that hung shining and still like leaves forged of heavy metal. This was the East of the ancient navigators, so old, so mysterious, resplendent and somber, living and unchanged, full of danger and promise. And these were the men. I sat up suddenly. A wave of movement passed through the crowd from end to end, passed along the heads, swayed the bodies, ran along the jetty like a ripple on the water, like a breath of wind on a field—and all was still again. I see it now—the wide sweep of the bay, the glittering sands, the wealth of green infinite and varied, the sea blue like the sea of a dream, the crowd of attentive faces, the blaze of vivid color—the water reflecting it all, the curve of the shore, the jetty, the high-sterned outlandish craft floating still, and the three boats with tired men from the West sleeping unconscious of the land and the people and of the violence of sunshine. They slept thrown across the thwarts, curled on bottom-boards, in the careless attitudes of death. The head of the old skipper, leaning back in the stern of the longboat, had fallen on his breast, and he looked as though he would never wake. Farther out old Mahon's face was upturned to the sky, with the long white beard spread out on his breast, as though he had been shot where he sat at the tiller; and a man, all in a heap in the bow of the boat, slept with both arms embracing the stem-head and with his cheek laid on the gunwale. The East looked at them without a sound.

"I have known its fascinations since: I have seen the mysterious shores, the still water, the lands of brown nations, where a stealthy Nemesis lies in wait, pursues, overtakes so many of the conquering race, who are proud of their wisdom, of their knowledge, of their strength. But for me all the East is contained in that vision of my youth. It is all in that moment when I opened my young eyes on it. I came upon it from a tussle with the sea—and I was young—and I saw it looking at me. And this is all that is left of it! Only a moment; a moment of strength, of romance, of glamour—of youth! . . . A flick of sunshine upon a strange shore, the time to remember, the time for a sigh, and—good-by!—Night—Good-by . . . !"

He drank.

"Ah! The good old time—the good old time. Youth and the sea. Glamour and the sea! The good, strong sea, the salt, bitter sea, that could whisper to you and roar at you and knock your breath out of you."

He drank again.

"By all that's wonderful, it is the sea, I believe, the sea itself—or is it youth alone? Who can tell? But you here—you all had something out of life: money, love—whatever one gets on shore—and, tell me, wasn't that the best time, that time when we were young at sea; young and had nothing, on the sea that gives nothing, except hard knocks—and sometimes a chance to feel your strength—that only—that you all regret?"

And we all nodded at him: the man of finance, the man of accounts, the man of law, we all nodded at him over the polished table that like a still sheet of brown water reflected our faces, lined, wrinkled; our faces marked by toil, by deceptions, by success, by love; our weary eyes looking still, looking always, looking anxiously for something out of life, that while it is expected is already gone—has passed unseen, in a sigh, in a flash—together with the youth, with the strength, with the romance of illusions.

QUESTIONS

1. "Youth" is an example of a "frame story"—a story set within a second story. Thus, it contains two narrators, both of whom happen to speak in the first person. What are the advantages of this arrangement? What does it add to Conrad's treatment of the theme of youth?

2. Marlow begins his narration on what seems a sombre note, declaring that

> there are those voyages that seem ordered for the illustration of life, that might stand for a symbol of existence. You fight, work, sweat, nearly kill yourself, sometimes do kill yourself, trying to accomplish something—and you can't. Not from any fault of yours. You simply can do nothing . . . .

Yet he ends it with a paean in praise of youth as the best time of life—with the same voyage still serving as example. How does he get from one tone to the other? How does he keep the two outlooks balanced, without letting them contradict each other?

QUESTIONS FOR FURTHER THOUGHT

1. How would you compare the narrative style of "Youth" with that of "The Open Boat"? Which do you prefer? Why?

2. How would you compare the two stories as attempts to find some larger meaning in a tale of conflict between people and nature?

CHARACTER STUDY AND SOCIAL COMMENT

4 *Looking Inward and Outward*

Fiction is the most flexible of literary forms. A story can focus on two or three characters, as "If Not Higher," "The Guest," and "The Yellow Wall-Paper" do; or it may include an entire community in its cast of characters, as do "The Lottery" and "Young Goodman Brown." It may keep us distanced from its characters, as "The Lottery" does, or it may take us into their minds, as do "The Yellow Wall-Paper" and "Young Goodman Brown." In works that strive for immediate effect, as "The Yellow Wall-Paper" does, we may even seem to be watching the character's thoughts form, change, and re-form.

A story may focus exclusively on the events of a few hours, as "The Open Boat" does; it may suggest the years of history that lie behind the few hours it covers, as "The Lottery" does; or its action may cover the events of many years. Fiction writers may place their narrators inside the tale or outside it; they may choose to let all the tale's characters speak freely, or they may allow us to hear only the narrator's voice. They may restrict their narrators to reporting things heard or seen, or they may let them comment, interpret, or moralize freely. In choice of characters, action, and stance, the freedom that fiction gives its writers is immense.

Fiction also offers its writers the full range from realism to fantasy in which to place their stories. "The Open Boat," with its seemingly objective stance and its careful reporting of a common type of event, is an example of realism. "Young Goodman Brown," with its action poised between dream and waking and its use of supernatural characters, is an example of fantasy. Another example of fantasy is Edgar Allan Poe's "The Fall of the House of Usher," printed in the Anthology of Short Stories. This tale contains no supernatural characters, but its action and setting are even more fantastic and farther removed from everyday reality than those in Hawthorne's allegory. These styles, realism and fantasy, may be seen as the two ends of a scale, with other, less extreme styles falling between them. Where on the scale would you place "The Lottery"? "The Yellow Wall-Paper"? "If Not Higher"? "Bartleby the Scrivener"?

Finally, we may note that fiction is receptive to nearly every style of writing imaginable. The traditional style of the storyteller is marked by a clear exposition of events, a careful connection of one event with another, and a tendency to follow a straightforward time scheme from beginning to end. "If Not Higher" and "Bartleby the Scrivener" are both examples of this style of writing, as are such twentieth-century stories as "Counterparts" and "The Chrysanthemums," both of which appear in the anthology.

Straightforward exposition is also the style of folktales and fairy tales, of "once upon a time" and "there once lived a man." It is therefore considered to be the basic, traditional style of fiction. But it is far from being the only style. Even in the eighteenth and nineteenth centuries, fiction was being written in the less connected form of letters and diaries. "The Yellow Wall-Paper" is written in this way, though it differs from most examples of the style in using the journal format to suggest a growing insanity in its narrator. The twentieth century, however, is the century in which writers are most vigorously experimenting with new styles of writing. Notice, for example, the narrative techniques used in "Help Her to Believe" and "How I Contemplated the World from the Detroit House of Correction and Began My Life Over Again," both printed in this section, and "How I Finally Lost My Heart" and "Lost in the Funhouse," printed in the anthology. What's new or different about them? What have their authors achieved with the differences?

Fiction, then, is an art form of great flexibility. Largely because of this flexibility, works of fiction have the power to look in two directions at once. They can look into their characters, revealing their minds and feelings to us, exploring their personalities. And they can look out at the society to which the characters belong. Looking inward, they seem to ask, "What sort of people are these?" Looking outward, they seem to ask, "What has made them that way?"

Writers of fiction have long felt that their form's unique ability to deal with the common reality of everyday life made it an ideal vehicle for examining the interaction of individuals with their society. We find that concern reflected in nearly all forms of fiction, from old and traditional tales such as "Bartleby the Scrivener," to some of the most experimental contemporary works. Many Americans in the latter half of the twentieth century are deeply concerned with questions of society's influence and power over the individual and of the individual's own power to shape his or her own personality and future. Contemporary fiction reflects these concerns.

The four stories that follow are all works which engage our concern for some central character or characters, while forcing upon us some realization of or comment on the society in which these characters live. In these stories, as in others we have read, the physical settings often become metaphors for the social settings. The influence of society, and the characters' reactions to it, thus forms an important part of each tale.

As you read these stories, therefore, take note of their physical and social settings, and of how these settings are used to define the characters' actions and personalities. Take note, too—as always when dealing with fiction—of the narrators' voices. What tones of voice do you hear in these stories? What attitudes do they convey? How do the narrators blend their stories' dual focus on individual and society into a concern for the fulfillment or happiness of their central characters? What moods do they leave you in at the stories' ends? How do they get you there?

WILLIAM FAULKNER (1897–1962)

A Rose for Emily

I

When Miss Emily Grierson died, our whole town went to her funeral: the men through a sort of respectful affection for a fallen monument, the women mostly out of curiosity to see the inside of her house, which no one save an old man-servant—a combined gardener and cook—had seen in at least ten years.

It was a big, squarish frame house that had once been white, decorated with cupolas and spires, and scrolled balconies in the heavily lightsome style of the seventies, set on what had once been our most select street. But garages and cotton gins had encroached and obliterated even the august names of that neighborhood; only Miss Emily's house was left, lifting its stubborn and coquettish decay above the cotton wagons and the gasoline pumps—an eyesore among eyesores. And now Miss Emily had gone to join the representatives of those august names where they lay in the cedar-bemused cemetery among the ranked and anonymous graves of Union and Confederate soldiers who fell at the battle of Jefferson.

Alive, Miss Emily had been a tradition, a duty, and a care; a sort of hereditary obligation upon the town, dating from that day in 1894 when Colonel Sartoris, the mayor—he who fathered the edict that no Negro woman should appear on the street without an apron—remitted her taxes, the dispensation dating from the death of her father on into perpetuity. Not that Miss Emily would have accepted charity. Colonel Sartoris invented an involved tale to the effect that Miss Emily's father had loaned money to the town, which the town, as a matter of business, preferred this way of repaying. Only a man of Colonel Sartoris' generation and thought could have invented it, and only a woman could have believed it.

When the next generation, with its more modern ideas, became mayors and aldermen, this arrangement created some little dissatisfaction. On the first of the year they mailed her a tax notice. February came, and there was no reply. They wrote her a formal letter, asking her to call at the sheriff's office at her convenience. A week later the mayor wrote her himself, offering to call or to send his car for her, and received in reply a note on paper of an archaic shape, in a thin, flowing calligraphy in faded ink, to the effect that she no longer went out at all. The tax notice was also enclosed, without comment.

They called a special meeting of the Board of Aldermen. A deputation waited upon her, knocked at the door through which no visitor had passed since she ceased giving china-painting lessons eight or ten years earlier. They were admitted by the old Negro into a dim hall from which a stairway mounted into still more shadow. It smelled of dust and disuse—a close, dank smell. The Negro led them into the parlor. It was furnished in heavy, leather-covered furniture. When the Negro opened the blinds of one window, they could see that the leather was cracked; and when they sat down, a faint dust rose sluggishly about their thighs, spinning with slow motes in the single sun-ray. On a tarnished gilt easel before the fireplace stood a crayon portrait of Miss Emily's father.

They rose when she entered—a small, fat woman in black, with a thin gold chain descending to her waist and vanishing into her belt, leaning on an ebony cane with a tarnished gold head. Her skeleton was small and spare; perhaps that was why what would have been merely plumpness in another was obesity in her. She looked bloated, like a body long submerged in motionless water, and of that pallid hue. Her eyes, lost in the fatty ridges of her face, looked like two small pieces of coal pressed into a lump of dough as they moved from one face to another while the visitors stated their errand.

She did not ask them to sit. She just stood in the door and listened quietly until the spokesman came to a stumbling halt. Then they could hear the invisible watch ticking at the end of the gold chain.

Her voice was dry and cold. "I have no taxes in Jefferson. Colonel Sartoris explained it to me. Perhaps one of you can gain access to the city records and satisfy yourselves."

"But we have. We are the city authorities, Miss Emily. Didn't you get a notice from the sheriff, signed by him?"

"I received a paper, yes," Miss Emily said. "Perhaps he considers himself the sheriff . . . I have no taxes in Jefferson."

"But there is nothing on the books to show that, you see. We must go by the—"

"See Colonel Sartoris. I have no taxes in Jefferson."

"But Miss Emily—"

"See Colonel Sartoris." (Colonel Sartoris had been dead almost ten years.) "I have no taxes in Jefferson. Tobe!" The Negro appeared. "Show these gentlemen out."

II

So she vanquished them, horse and foot, just as she had vanquished their fathers thirty years before about the smell. That was two years after her father's death and a short time after her sweetheart—the one we believed would marry her—had deserted her. After her father's death she went out very little; after her sweetheart went away, people hardly saw her at all. A few of the ladies had the temerity to call, but were not received, and the only sign of life about the place was the Negro man—a young man then—going in and out with a market basket.

"Just as if a man—any man—could keep a kitchen properly," the ladies said; so they were not surprised when the smell developed. It was another link between the gross, teeming world and the high and mighty Griersons.

A neighbor, a woman, complained to the mayor, Judge Stevens, eighty years old.

"But what will you have me do about it, madam?" he said.

"Why, send her word to stop it," the woman said. "Isn't there a law?"

"I'm sure that won't be necessary," Judge Stevens said. "It's probably just a snake or a rat that nigger of hers killed in the yard. I'll speak to him about it."

The next day he received two more complaints, one from a man who came in diffident deprecation. "We really must do something about it, Judge. I'd be the last one in the world to bother Miss Emily, but we've got to do something." That night the Board of Aldermen met—three graybeards and one younger man, a member of the rising generation.

"It's simple enough," he said. "Send her word to have her place cleaned up. Give her a certain time do it in, and if she don't . . ."

"Dammit, sir," Judge Stevens said, "will you accuse a lady to her face of smelling bad?"

So the next night, after midnight, four men crossed Miss Emily's lawn and slunk about the house like burglars, sniffing along the base of the brickwork and at the cellar openings while one of them performed a regular sowing motion with his hand out of a sack slung from his shoulder. They broke open the cellar door and sprinkled lime there, and in all the outbuildings. As they recrossed the lawn, a window that had been dark was lighted and Miss Emily sat in it, the light behind her, and her upright torso motionless as that of an idol. They crept quietly across the lawn and into the shadow of the locusts that lined the street. After a week or two the smell went away.

That was when people had begun to feel really sorry for her. People in our town, remembering how old lady Wyatt, her great-aunt, had gone completely crazy at last, believed that the Griersons held themselves a little too high for what they really were. None of the young men were quite good enough for Miss Emily and such. We had long thought of them as a tableau, Miss Emily a slender figure in white in the background, her father a spraddled silhouette in the foregound, his back to her and clutching a horsewhip, the two of them framed by the backflung front door. When she got to be thirty and was still single, we were not pleased exactly, but vindicated; even with insanity in the family she wouldn't have turned down all of her chances if they had really materialized.

When her father died, it got about that the house was all that was left to her; and in a way, people were glad. At last they could pity Miss Emily. Being left alone, and a pauper, she had become humanized. Now she too would know the old thrill and the old despair of a penny more or less.

The day after his death all the ladies prepared to call at the house and offer condolence and aid, as is our custom. Miss Emily met them at the door, dressed as usual and with no trace of grief on her face. She told them that her father was not dead. She did that for three days, with the ministers calling on her, and the doctors, trying to persuade her to let them dispose of the body. Just as they were about to resort to law and force, she broke down, and they buried her father quickly.

We did not say she was crazy then. We believed she had to do that. We remembered all the young men her father had driven away, and we knew that with nothing left, she would have to cling to that which had robbed her, as people will.

III

She was sick for a long time. When we saw her again, her hair was cut short, making her look like a girl, with a vague resemblance to those angels in colored church windows—sort of tragic and serene.

The town had just let the contracts for paving the sidewalks, and in the summer after her father's death they began the work. The construction company came with niggers and mules and machinery, and a foreman named Homer Barron, a Yankee—a big, dark, ready man, with a big voice and eyes lighter than his face. The little boys would follow in groups to hear him cuss the niggers, and the niggers singing in time to the rise and fall of picks. Pretty soon he knew everybody in town. Whenever you heard a lot of laughing anywhere about the square, Homer Barron would be in the center of the group.

Presently we began to see him and Miss Emily on Sunday afternoons driving in the yellow-wheeled buggy and the matched team of bays from the livery stable.

At first we were glad that Miss Emily would have an interest, because the ladies all said, "Of course a Grierson would not think seriously of a Northerner, a day laborer." But there were still others, older people, who said that even grief could not cause a real lady to forget *noblesse oblige*—without calling it *noblesse oblige*. They just said, "Poor Emily. Her kinsfolk should come to her." She had some kin in Alabama; but years ago her father had fallen out with them over the estate of old Lady Wyatt, the crazy woman, and there was no communication between the two families. They had not even been represented at the funeral.

And as soon as the old people said, "Poor Emily," the whispering began. "Do you suppose it's really so?" they said to one another. "Of course it is. What else could . . ." This behind their hands; rustling of craned silk and satin behind jalousies closed upon the sun of Sunday afternoon as the thin, swift clop-clop-clop of the matched team passed: "Poor Emily."

She carried her head high enough—even when we believed that she was fallen. It was as if she demanded more than ever the recognition of her dignity as the last Grierson; as if it had wanted that touch of earthiness to reaffirm her imperviousness. Like when she bought the rat poison, the arsenic. That was over a year after they had begun to say "Poor Emily," and while the two female cousins were visiting her.

"I want some poison," she said to the druggist. She was over thirty then, still a slight woman, though thinner than usual, with cold, haughty black eyes in a face the flesh of which was strained across the temples and about the eye-sockets as you imagine a lighthouse-keeper's face ought to look. "I want some poison," she said.

"Yes, Miss Emily. What kind? For rats and such? I'd recom—"

"I want the best you have. I don't care what kind."

The druggist named several. "They'll kill anything up to an elephant. But what you want is—"

"Arsenic," Miss Emily said. "Is that a good one?"

"Is . . . arsenic? Yes, ma'am. But what you want—"

"I want arsenic."

The druggist looked down at her. She looked back at him, erect, her face like a strained flag. "Why, of course," the druggist said. "If that's what you want. But the law requires you to tell what you are going to use it for."

Miss Emily just stared at him, her head tilted back in order to look him eye for eye, until he looked away and went and got the arsenic and wrapped it up. The Negro delivery boy brought her the package; the druggist didn't come back. When she opened the package at home there was written on the box, under the skull and bones: "For rats."

IV

So the next day we all said, "She will kill herself"; and we said it would be the best thing. When she had first begun to be seen with Homer Barron, we had said, "She will marry him." Then we said, "She will persuade him yet," because Homer himself had remarked— he liked men, and it was known that he drank with the younger men in the Elks' Club—that he was not a marrying man. Later we said, "Poor Emily" behind the jalousies as they passed on Sunday afternoon in the glittering buggy, Miss Emily with her head high and Homer Barron with his hat cocked and cigar in his teeth, reins and whip in a yellow glove.

Then some of the ladies began to say that it was a disgrace to the town and a bad example to the young people. The men did not want to interfere, but at last the ladies forced the Baptist minister— Miss Emily's people were Episcopal—to call upon her. He would never divulge what happened during that interview, but he refused to go back again. The next Sunday they again drove about the streets, and the following day the minister's wife wrote to Miss Emily's relations in Alabama.

So she had blood-kin under her roof again and we sat back to watch developments. At first nothing happened. Then we were sure that they were to be married. We learned that Miss Emily had been to the jeweler's and ordered a man's toilet set in silver, with the letters H. B. on each piece. Two days later we learned that she had bought a complete outfit of men's clothing, including a nightshirt, and we said, "They are married." We were really glad. We were glad because the two female cousins were even more Grierson than Miss Emily had ever been.

So we were not surprised when Homer Barron—the streets had been finished some time since—was gone. We were a little disappointed that there was not a public blowing-off, but we believed that he had gone on to prepare for Miss Emily's coming, or to give her a chance to get rid of the cousins. (By that time it was a cabal, and we were all Miss Emily's allies to help circumvent the cousins.) Sure enough, after another week they departed. And, as we had expected all along, within three days Homer Barron was back in town. A neighbor saw the Negro man admit him at the kitchen door at dusk one evening.

And that was the last we saw of Homer Barron. And of Miss Emily for some time. The Negro man went in and out with the market basket, but the front door remained closed. Now and then we would see her at a window for a moment, as the men did that night when they sprinkled the lime, but for almost six months she did not appear on the streets. Then we knew that this was to be expected too; as if that quality of her father which had thwarted her woman's life so many times had been too virulent and too furious to die.

When we next saw Miss Emily, she had grown fat and her hair was turning gray. During the next few years it grew grayer and grayer until it attained an even pepper-and-salt iron-gray, when it ceased turning. Up to the day of her death at seventy-four it was still that vigorous iron-gray, like the hair of an active man.

From that time on her front door remained closed, save for a period of six or seven years, when she was about forty, during which she gave lessons in china-painting. She fitted up a studio in one of the downstairs rooms, where the daughters and granddaughters of Colonel Sartoris' contemporaries were sent to her with the same regularity and in the same spirit that they were sent to church on Sunday with a twenty-five-cent piece for the collection plate. Meanwhile her taxes had been remitted.

Then the newer generation became the backbone and the spirit of the town, and the painting pupils grew up and fell away and did not send their children to her with boxes of color and tedious brushes and pictures cut from the ladies' magazines. The front door closed upon the last one and remained closed for good. When the town got free postal delivery, Miss Emily alone refused to let them fasten the metal numbers above her door and attach a mailbox to it. She would not listen to them.

Daily, monthly, yearly we watched the Negro grow grayer and more stooped, going in and out with the market basket. Each December we sent her a tax notice, which would be returned by the post office a week later, unclaimed. Now and then we would see her in one of the downstairs windows—she had evidently shut up the top floor of the house—like the carven torso of an idol in a niche, looking or not looking at us, we could never tell which. Thus she passed from generation to generation—dear, inescapable, impervious, tranquil, and perverse.

And so she died. Fell ill in the house filled with dust and shadows, with only a doddering Negro man to wait on her. We did not even know she was sick; we had long since given up trying to get any information from the Negro. He talked to no one, probably not even to her, for his voice had grown harsh and rusty, as if from disuse.

She died in one of the downstairs rooms, in a heavy walnut bed with a curtain, her gray head propped on a pillow yellow and moldy with age and lack of sunlight.

V

The Negro met the first of the ladies at the front door and let them in, with their hushed, sibilant voices and their quick, curious glances, and then he disappeared. He walked right through the house and out the back and was not seen again.

The two female cousins came at once. They held the funeral on the second day, with the town coming to look at Miss Emily beneath a mass of bought flowers, with the crayon face of her father musing profoundly above the bier and the ladies sibilant and macabre; and the very old men—some in their brushed Confederate uniforms—on the porch and the lawn, talking of Miss Emily as if she had been a contemporary of theirs, believing that they had danced with her and courted her perhaps, confusing time with its mathematical progression, as the old do, to whom all the past is not a diminishing road but, instead, a huge meadow which no winter ever quite touches, divided from them now by the narrow bottle-neck of the most recent decade of years.

Already we knew that there was one room in that region above stairs which no one had seen in forty years, and which would have to be forced. They waited until Miss Emily was decently in the ground before they opened it.

The violence of breaking down the door seemed to fill this room with pervading dust. A thin, acrid pall of the tomb seemed to lie everywhere upon this room decked and furnished as for a bridal: upon the valance curtains of faded rose color, upon the rose-shaded lights, upon the dressing table, upon the delicate array of crystal and the man's toilet things backed with tarnished silver, silver so tarnished that the monogram was obscured. Among them lay a collar and tie, as if they had just been removed, which, lifted, left upon the surface a pale crescent in the dust. Upon a chair hung the suit, carefully folded; beneath it the two mute shoes and the discarded socks.

The man himself lay in the bed.

For a long while we just stood there, looking down at the profound and fleshless grin. The body had apparently once lain in the attitude of an embrace, but now the long sleep that outlasts love, that conquers even the grimace of love, had cuckolded him. What was left of him, rotted beneath what was left of the nightshirt, had become inextricable from the bed in which he lay; and upon him and upon the pillow beside him lay that even coating of the patient and biding dust.

Then we noticed that in the second pillow was the indentation of a head. One of us lifted something from it, and leaning forward, that faint and invisible dust dry and acrid in the nostrils, we saw a long strand of iron-gray hair.

QUESTIONS

1. Part of the effectiveness of "A Rose for Emily" comes from its surprise ending. How effective do you find the ending? Why?
2. How do the narrator and the townsfolk view the young Miss Emily? How does Miss Emily change with time? How does the town? How does the narrator's view of Miss Emily change? How does yours?

JAMES BALDWIN (1924–   )

Sonny's Blues

I read about it in the paper, in the subway, on my way to work. I read it, and I couldn't believe it, and I read it again. Then perhaps I just stared at it, at the newsprint spelling out his name, spelling out the story. I stared at it in the swinging lights of the subway car, and in the faces and bodies of the people, and in my own face, trapped in the darkness which roared outside.

It was not to be believed and I kept telling myself that as I walked from the subway station to the high school. And at the same time I couldn't doubt it. I was scared, scared for Sonny. He became real to me again. A great block of ice got settled in my belly and kept melting there slowly all day long, while I taught my classes algebra. It was a special kind of ice. It kept melting, sending trickles of ice water all up and down my veins, but it never got less. Sometimes it hardened and seemed to expand until I felt my guts were going to come spilling out or that I was going to choke or scream. This would always be at a moment when I was remembering some specific thing Sonny had once said or done.

When he was about as old as the boys in my classes his face had been bright and open, there was a lot of copper in it; and he'd had wonderfully direct brown eyes, and great gentleness and privacy. I wondered what he looked like now. He had been picked up, the evening before, in a raid on an apartment downtown, for peddling and using heroin.

I couldn't believe it: but what I mean by that is that I couldn't find any room for it anywhere inside me. I had kept it outside me for a long time. I hadn't wanted to know. I had had suspicions, but I didn't name them, I kept putting them away. I told myself that Sonny was wild, but he wasn't crazy. And he'd always been a good boy, he hadn't ever turned hard or evil or disrespectful, the way kids can, so quick, so quick, especially in Harlem. I didn't want to believe that I'd ever see my brother going down, coming to nothing, all that light in his face gone out, in the condition I'd already seen so many others. Yet it had happened and here I was, talking about algebra to a lot of boys who might, every one of them for all I knew, be popping off needles every time they went to the head. Maybe it did more for them than algebra could.

I was sure that the first time Sonny had ever had horse, he couldn't have been much older than these boys were now. These boys, now, were living as we'd been living then, they were growing up with a rush and their heads bumped abruptly against the low ceiling of their actual possibilities. They were filled with rage. All they really knew were two darknesses, the darkness of their lives, which was now closing in on them, and the darkness of the movies, which had blinded them to that other darkness, and in which they now, vindictively, dreamed, at once more together than they were at any other time, and more alone.

When the last bell rang, the last class ended, I let out my breath. It seemed I'd been holding it for all that time. My clothes were wet—I may have looked as though I'd been sitting in a steam bath, all dressed up, all afternoon. I sat alone in the classroom a long time. I listened to the boys outside, downstairs, shouting and cursing and laughing. Their laughter struck me for perhaps the first time. It was not the joyous laughter which—God knows why—one associates with children. It was mocking and insular, its intent was to denigrate. It was disenchanted, and in this, also, lay the authority of their curses. Perhaps I was listening to them because I was thinking about my brother and in them I heard my brother. And myself.

One boy was whistling a tune, at once very complicated and very simple, it seemed to be pouring out of him as though he were a bird, and it sounded very cool and moving through all that harsh, bright air, only just holding its own through all those other sounds.

I stood up and walked over to the window and looked down into the courtyard. It was the beginning of the spring and the sap was rising in the boys. A teacher passed through them every now and again, quickly, as though he or she couldn't wait to get out of that courtyard, to get those boys out of their sight and off their minds. I started collecting my stuff. I thought I'd better get home and talk to Isabel.

The courtyard was almost deserted by the time I got downstairs. I saw this boy standing in the shadow of a doorway, looking just like Sonny. I almost called his name. Then I saw that it wasn't Sonny, but somebody we used to know, a boy from around our block. He'd been Sonny's friend. He'd never been mine, having been too young for me, and, anyway, I'd never liked him. And now, even though he was a grown-up man, he still hung around that block, still spent hours on the street corner, was always high and raggy. I used to run into him from time to time and he'd often work around to asking me for a quarter or fifty cents. He always had some real good excuse, too, and I always gave it to him, I don't know why.

But now, abruptly, I hated him. I couldn't stand the way he looked at me, partly like a dog, partly like a cunning child. I wanted to ask him what the hell he was doing in the school courtyard.

He sort of shuffled over to me, and he said, "I see you got the papers. So you already know about it."

"You mean about Sonny? Yes, I already know about it. How come they didn't get you?"

He grinned. It made him repulsive and it also brought to mind what he'd looked like as a kid. "I wasn't there. I stay away from them people."

"Good for you." I offered him a cigarette and I watched him through the smoke. "You come all the way down here just to tell me about Sonny?"

"That's right." He was sort of shaking his head and his eyes looked strange, as though they were about to cross. The bright sun deadened his damp dark brown skin and it made his eyes look yellow and showed up the dirt in his conked hair. He smelled funky. I moved a little away from him and I said, "Well, thanks. But I already know about it and I got to get home."

"I'll walk you a little ways," he said. We started walking. There were a couple of kids still loitering in the courtyard and one of them said good night to me and looked strangely at the boy beside me.

"What're you going to do?" he asked me. "I mean, about Sonny?"

"Look. I haven't seen Sonny for over a year, I'm not sure I'm going to do anything. Anyway, what the hell can I do?"

"That's right," he said quickly, "ain't nothing you can do. Can't much help old Sonny no more, I guess."

It was what I was thinking and so it seemed to me he had no right to say it.

"I'm surprised at Sonny, though," he went on—he had a funny way of talking, he looked straight ahead as though he were talking to himself—"I thought Sonny was a smart boy, I thought he was too smart to get hung."

"I guess he thought so too," I said sharply, "and that's how he got hung. And how about you? You're pretty goddamn smart, I bet."

Then he looked directly at me, just for a minute. "I ain't smart," he said. "If I was smart, I'd have reached for a pistol a long time ago."

"Look. Don't tell *me* your sad story, if it was up to me, I'd give you one." Then I felt guilty—guilty, probably, for never having supposed that the poor bastard *had* a story of his own, much less a sad one, and I asked, quickly, "What's going to happen to him now?"

He didn't answer this. He was off by himself some place. "Funny thing," he said, and from his tone we might have been discussing the quickest way to get to Brooklyn, "when I saw the papers this morning, the first thing I asked myself was if I had anything to do with it. I felt sort of responsible."

I began to listen more carefully. The subway station was on the corner, just before us, and I stopped. He stopped, too. We were in front of a bar and he ducked slightly, peering in, but whoever he was looking for didn't seem to be there. The juke box was blasting away with something black and bouncy and I half watched the barmaid as she danced her way from the juke box to her place behind the bar. And I watched her face as she laughingly responded to something someone said to her, still keeping time to the music. When she smiled one saw the little girl, one sensed the doomed, still-struggling woman beneath the battered face of the semi-whore.

"I never *give* Sonny nothing," the boy said finally, "but a long time ago I come to school high and Sonny asked me how it felt." He paused, I couldn't bear to watch him, I watched the barmaid, and I listened to the music which seemed to be causing the pavement to shake. "I told him it felt great." The music stopped, the barmaid paused and watched the juke box until the music began again. "It did."

All this was carrying me some place I didn't want to go. I certainly didn't want to know how it felt. It filled everything, the people, the houses, the music, the dark, quicksilver barmaid, with menace; and this menace was their reality.

"What's going to happen to him now?" I asked again.

"They'll send him away some place and they'll try to cure him." He shook his head. "Maybe he'll even think he's kicked the habit. Then they'll let him loose"—he gestured, throwing his cigarette into the gutter. "That's all."

"What do you mean, that's *all*?"

But I knew what he meant.

"I *mean*, that's *all*." He turned his head and looked at me, pulling down the corners of his mouth. "Don't you know what I mean?" he asked softly.

"How the hell *would* I know what you mean?" I almost whispered it, I don't know why.

"That's right," he said to the air, "how would *he* know what I mean?" He turned toward me again, patient and calm, and yet I somehow felt him shaking, shaking as though he were going to fall apart. I felt that ice in my guts again, the dread I'd felt all afternoon; and again I watched the barmaid, moving about the bar, washing glasses, and singing. "Listen. They'll let him out and then it'll just start all over again. That's what I mean."

"You mean—they'll let him out. And then he'll just start working his way back in again. You mean he'll never kick the habit. Is that what you mean?"

"That's right," he said, cheerfully. *"You* see what I mean."

"Tell me," I said at last, "why does he want to die? He must want to die, he's killing himself, why does he want to die?"

He looked at me in surprise. He licked his lips. "He don't want to die. He wants to live. Don t nobody want to die, ever."

Then I wanted to ask him—too many things. He could not have answered, or if he had, I could not have borne the answers. I started walking. "Well, I guess it's none of my business."

"It's going to be rough on old Sonny," he said. We reached the subway station. "This is your station?" he asked. I nodded. I took one step down. "Damn!" he said, suddenly. I looked up at him. He grinned again. "Damn if I didn't leave all my money home. You ain't got a dollar on you, have you? Just for a couple of days, is all."

All at once something inside gave and threatened to come pouring out of me. I didn't hate him any more. I felt that in another moment I'd start crying like a child.

"Sure," I said. "Don't sweat." I looked in my wallet and didn't have a dollar, I only had a five. "Here," I said. "That hold you?"

He didn't look at it—he didn't want to look at it. A terrible, closed look came over his face, as though he were keeping the number on the bill a secret from him and me. "Thanks," he said, and now he was dying to see me go. "Don't worry about Sonny. Maybe I'll write him or something."

"Sure," I said. "You do that. So long."

"Be seeing you," he said. I went on down the steps.

And I didn't write Sonny or send him anything for a long time. When I finally did, it was just after my little girl died, he wrote me back a letter which made me feel like a bastard.

Here's what he said:

DEAR BROTHER,

You don't know how much I needed to hear from you. I wanted to write you many a time but I dug how much I must have hurt you and so I didn't write. But now I feel like a man who's been trying to climb up out of some deep, real deep and funky hole and just saw the sun up there, outside. I got to get outside.

I can't tell you much about how I got here. I mean I don't know how to tell you. I guess I was afraid of something or I was trying to escape from something and you know I have never been very strong in the head (smile). I'm glad Mama and Daddy are dead and can't see what's happened to their son and I swear if I'd known what I was doing I would never have hurt you so, you and a lot of other fine people who were nice to me and who believed in me.

I don't want you to think it had anything to do with me being a musician. It's more than that. Or maybe less than that. I can't get anything straight in my head down here and I try not to think about what's going to happen to me when I get outside again. Sometime I think I'm going to flip and *never* get outside and sometime I think I'll come straight back. I tell you one thing, though, I'd rather blow my brains out than go through this again. But that's what they all say, so they tell me. If I tell you when I'm coming to New York and if you could meet me, I sure would appreciate it. Give my love to Isabel and the kids and I was sorry to hear about little Gracie. I wish I could be like Mama and say the Lord's will be done, but I don't know it seems to me that trouble is the one thing that never does get stopped and I don't know what good it does to blame it on the Lord. But maybe it does some good if you believe it.

Your brother,

Sonny

Then I kept in constant touch with him and I sent him whatever I could and I went to meet him when he came back to New York. When I saw him many things I thought I had forgotten came flooding back to me. This was because I had begun, finally, to wonder about Sonny, about the life that Sonny lived inside. This life, whatever it was, had made him older and thinner and it had deepened the distant stillness in which he had always moved. He looked very unlike my baby brother. Yet, when he smiled, when we shook hands, the baby brother I'd never known looked out from the depths of his private life, like an animal waiting to be coaxed into the light.

"How you been keeping?" he asked me.

"All right. And you?"

"Just fine." He was smiling all over his face. "It's good to see you again."

"It's good to see you."

The seven years' difference in our ages lay between us like a chasm: I wondered if these years would ever operate between us as a bridge. I was remembering, and it made it hard to catch my breath, that I had been there when he was born; and I had heard the first words he had ever spoken. When he started to walk, he walked from our mother straight to me. I caught him just before he fell when he took the first steps he ever took in this world.

"How's Isabel?"

"Just fine. She's dying to see you."

"And the boys?"

"They're fine, too. They're anxious to see their uncle."

"Oh, come on. You know they don't remember me."

"Are you kidding? Of course they remember you."

He grinned again. We got into a taxi. We had a lot to say to each other, far too much to know how to begin.

As the taxi began to move, I asked, "You still want to go to India?"

He laughed. "You still remember that. Hell, no. This place is Indian enough for me."

"It used to belong to them," I said.

And he laughed again. "They damn sure knew what they were doing when they got rid of it."

Years ago, when he was around fourteen, he'd been all hipped on the idea of going to India. He read books about people sitting on rocks, naked, in all kinds of weather, but mostly bad, naturally, and walking barefoot through hot coals and arriving at wisdom. I used to say that it sounded to me as though they were getting away from wisdom as fast as they could. I think he sort of looked down on me for that.

"Do you mind," he asked, "if we have the driver drive alongside the park? On the west side—I haven't seen the city in so long."

"Of course not," I said. I was afraid that I might sound as though I were humoring him, but I hoped he wouldn't take it that way.

So we drove along, between the green of the park and the stony, lifeless elegance of hotels and apartment buildings, toward the vivid, killing streets of our childhood. These streets hadn't changed, though housing projects jutted up out of them now like rocks in the middle of a boiling sea. Most of the houses in which we had grown up had vanished, as had the stores from which we had stolen, the basements in which we had first tried sex, the rooftops from which we had hurled tin cans and bricks. But houses exactly like the houses of our past yet dominated the landscape, boys exactly like the boys we once had been found themselves smothering in these houses, came down into the streets for light and air and found themselves encircled by disaster. Some escaped the trap, most didn't. Those who got out always left something of themselves behind, as some animals amputate a leg and leave it in the trap. It might be said, perhaps, that I had escaped, after all, I was a school teacher; or that Sonny had, he hadn't lived in Harlem for years. Yet, as the cab moved uptown through streets which seemed, with a rush, to darken with dark people, and as I covertly studied Sonny's face, it came to me that what we both were seeking through our separate cab windows was that part of ourselves which had been left behind. It's always at the hour of trouble and confrontation that the missing member aches.

We hit 110th Street and started rolling up Lenox Avenue. And I'd known this avenue all my life, but it seemed to me again, as it had seemed on the day I'd first heard about Sonny's trouble, filled with a hidden menace which was its very breath of life.

"We almost there," said Sonny.

"Almost." We were both too nervous to say anything more.

We live in a housing project. It hasn't been up long. A few days after it was up it seemed uninhabitably new, now, of course, it's already run-down. It looks like a parody of the good, clean, faceless life—God knows the people who live in it do their best to make it a parody. The beat-looking grass lying around isn't enough to make their lives green, the hedges will never hold out the streets, and they know it. The big windows fool no one, they aren't big enough to make space out of no space. They don't bother with the windows, they watch the TV screen instead. The playground is most popular with the children who don't play at jacks, or skip rope, or roller skate, or swing, and they can be found in it after dark. We moved in partly because it's not too far from where I teach, and partly for the kids; but it's really just like the houses in which Sonny and I grew up. The same things happen, they'll have the same things to remember. The moment Sonny and I started into the house I had the feeling that I was simply bringing him back into the danger he had almost died trying to escape.

Sonny has never been talkative. So I don't know why I was sure he'd be dying to talk to me when supper was over the first night. Everything went fine, the oldest boy remembered him, and the youngest boy liked him, and Sonny had remembered to bring something for each of them; and Isabel, who is really much nicer than I am, more open and giving, had gone to a lot of trouble about dinner and was genuinely glad to see him. And she's always been able to tease Sonny in a way that I haven't. It was nice to see her face so vivid again and to hear her laugh and watch her make Sonny laugh. She wasn't, or, anyway, she didn't seem to be, at all uneasy or embarrassed. She chatted as though there were no subject which had to be avoided and she got Sonny past his first, faint stiffness. And thank God she was there, for I was filled with that icy dread again. Everything I did seemed awkward to me, and everything I said sounded freighted with hidden meaning. I was trying to remember everything I'd heard about dope addiction and I couldn't help watching Sonny for signs. I wasn't doing it out of malice. I was trying to find out something about my brother. I was dying to hear him tell me he was safe.

"Safe!" my father grunted, whenever Mama suggested trying to move to a neighborhood which might be safer for children. "Safe, hell! Ain't no place safe for kids, nor nobody."

He always went on like this, but he wasn't, ever, really as bad as he sounded, not even on weekends, when he got drunk. As a matter of fact, he was always on the lookout for "something a little better," but he died before he found it. He died suddenly, during a drunken weekend in the middle of the war, when Sonny was fifteen. He and Sonny hadn't ever got on too well. And this was partly because Sonny was the apple of his father's eye. It was because he loved Sonny so much and was frightened for him, that he was always fighting with him. It doesn't do any good to fight with Sonny. Sonny just moves back, inside himself, where he can't be reached. But the principal reason that they never hit it off is that they were so much alike. Daddy was big and rough and loud-talking, just the opposite of Sonny, but they both had—that same privacy.

Mama tried to tell me something about this, just after Daddy died. I was home on leave from the army.

This was the last time I ever saw my mother alive. Just the same, this picture gets all mixed up in my mind with pictures I had of her when she was younger. The way I always see her is the way she used to be on a Sunday afternoon, say, when the old folks were talking after the big Sunday dinner. I always see her wearing pale blue. She'd be sitting on the sofa. And my father would be sitting in the easy chair, not far from her. And the living room would be full of church folks and relatives. There they sit, in chairs all around the living room, and the night is creeping up outside, but nobody knows it yet. You can see the darkness growing against the window-panes and you hear the street noises every now and again, or maybe the jangling beat of a tambourine from one of the churches close by, but it's real quiet in the room. For a moment nobody's talking, but every face looks darkening, like the sky outside. And my mother rocks a little from the waist, and my father's eyes are closed. Everyone is looking at something a child can't see. For a minute they've forgotten the children. Maybe a kid is lying on the rug half asleep. Maybe somebody's got a kid on his lap and is absent-mindedly stroking the kid's head. Maybe there's a kid, quiet and big-eyed, curled up in a big chair in the corner. The silence, the darkness coming, and the darkness in the faces frightens the child obscurely. He hopes that the hand which strokes his forehead will never stop—will never die. He hopes that there will never come a time when the old folks won't be sitting around the living room, talking about where they've come from, and what they've seen, and what's happened to them and their kinfolk.

But something deep and watchful in the child knows that this is bound to end, is already ending. In a moment someone will get up and turn on the light. Then the old folks will remember the children and they won't talk any more that day. And when light fills the room, the child is filled with darkness. He knows that every time this happens he's moved just a little closer to that darkness outside. The darkness outside is what the old folks have been talking about. It's what they've come from. It's what they endure. The child knows that they won't talk any more because if he knows too much about what's happened to *them,* he'll know too much too soon, about what's going to happen to *him.*

The last time I talked to my mother, I remember I was restless. I wanted to get out and see Isabel. We weren't married then and we had a lot to straighten out between us.

There Mama sat, in black, by the window. She was humming an old church song, *Lord, you brought me from a long ways off.* Sonny was out somewhere. Mama kept watching the streets.

"I don't know," she said, "if I'll ever see you again, after you go off from here. But I hope you'll remember the things I tried to teach you."

"Don't talk like that," I said, and smiled. "You'll be here a long time yet."

She smiled, too, but she said nothing. She was quiet for a long time. And I said, "Mama, don't you worry about nothing. I'll be writing all the time, and you be getting the checks. . . ."

"I want to talk to you about your brother," she said, suddenly. "If anything happens to me he ain't going to have nobody to look out for him."

"Mama," I said, "ain't nothing going to happen to you *or* Sonny. Sonny's all right. He's a good boy and he's got good sense."

"It ain't a question of his being a good boy," Mama said, "nor of his having good sense. It ain't only the bad ones, nor yet the dumb ones that gets sucked under." She stopped, looking at me. "Your Daddy once had a brother," she said, and she smiled in a way that made me feel she was in pain. "You didn't never know that, did you?"

"No," I said, "I never knew that," and I watched her face.

"Oh, yes," she said, "your Daddy had a brother." She looked out of the window again. "I know you never saw your Daddy cry. But *I* did—many a time, through all these years."

I asked her, "What happened to his brother? How come nobody's ever talked about him?"

This was the first time I ever saw my mother look old.

"His brother got killed," she said, "when he was just a little younger than you are now. I knew him. He was a fine boy. He was maybe a little full of the devil, but he didn't mean nobody no harm."

Then she stopped and the room was silent, exactly as it had sometimes been on those Sunday afternoons. Mama kept looking out into the streets.

"He used to have a job in the mill," she said, "and, like all young folks, he just liked to perform on Saturday nights. Saturday nights, him and your father would drift around to different places, go to dances and things like that, or just sit around with people they knew, and your father's brother would sing, he had a fine voice, and play along with himself on his guitar. Well, this particular Saturday night, him and your father was coming home from some place, and they were both a little drunk and there was a moon that night, it was bright like day. Your father's brother was feeling kind of good, and he was whistling to himself, and he had his guitar slung over his shoulder. They was coming down a hill and beneath them was a road that turned off from the highway. Well, your father's brother, being always kind of frisky, decided to run down this hill, and he did, with that guitar banging and clanging behind him, and he ran across the road, and he was making water behind a tree. And your father was sort of amused at him and he was still coming down the hill, kind of slow. Then he heard a car motor and that same minute his brother stepped from behind the tree, into the road, in the moonlight. And he started to cross the road. And your father started to run down the hill, he says he don't know why. This car was full of white men. They was all drunk, and when they seen your father's brother they let out a great whoop and holler and they aimed the car straight at him. They was having fun, they just wanted to scare him, the way they do sometimes, you know. But they was drunk. And I guess the boy, being drunk, too, and scared, kind of lost his head. By the time he jumped it was too late. Your father says he heard his brother scream when the car rolled over him, and he heard the wood of that guitar when it give, and he heard them strings go flying, and he heard them white men shouting, and the car kept on a-going and it ain't stopped till this day. And, time your father got down the hill, his brother weren't nothing but blood and pulp."

Tears were gleaming on my mother's face. There wasn't anything I could say.

"He never mentioned it," she said, "because I never let him mention it before you children. Your Daddy was like a crazy man that night and for many a night thereafter. He says he never in his life seen anything as dark as that road after the lights of that car had gone away. Weren't nothing, weren't nobody on that road, just your Daddy and his brother and that busted guitar. Oh, yes. Your Daddy never did really get right again. Till the day he died he weren't sure but that every white man he saw was the man that killed his brother."

She stopped and took out her handkerchief and dried her eyes and looked at me.

"I ain't telling you all this," she said, "to make you scared or bitter or to make you hate nobody. I'm telling you this because you got a brother. And the world ain't changed."

I guess I didn't want to believe this. I guess she saw this in my face. She turned away from me, toward the window again, searching those streets.

"But I praise my Redeemer," she said at last, "that He called your Daddy home before me. I ain't saying it to throw no flowers at myself, but, I declare, it keeps me from feeling too cast down to know I helped your father get safely through this world. Your father always acted like he was the roughest, strongest man on earth. And everybody took him to be like that. But if he hadn't had *me* there—to see his tears!"

She was crying again. Still, I couldn't move. I said, "Lord, Lord, Mama, I didn't know it was like that."

"Oh, honey," she said, "there's a lot that you don't know. But you are going to find it out." She stood up from the window and came over to me. "You got to hold on to your brother," she said, "and don't let him fall, no matter what it looks like is happening to him and no matter how evil you gets with him. You going to be evil with him many a time. But don't you forget what I told you, you hear?"

"I won't forget," I said. "Don't you worry, I won't forget. I won't let nothing happen to Sonny."

My mother smiled as though she were amused at something she saw in my face. Then, "You may not be able to stop nothing from happening. But you got to let him know you's *there*."

Two days later I was married, and then I was gone. And I had a lot of things on my mind and I pretty well forgot my promise to Mama until I got shipped home on a special furlough for her funeral.

And, after the funeral, with just Sonny and me alone in the empty kitchen, I tried to find out something about him.

"What do you want to do?" I asked him.

"I'm going to be a musician," he said.

For he had graduated, in the time I had been away, from dancing to the juke box to finding out who was playing what, and what they were doing with it, and he had bought himself a set of drums.

"You mean, you want to be a drummer?" I somehow had the feeling that being a drummer might be all right for other people but not for my brother Sonny.

"I don't think," he said, looking at me very gravely, "that I'll ever be a good drummer. But I think I can play a piano."

I frowned. I'd never played the role of the older brother quite so seriously before, had scarcely ever, in fact, *asked* Sonny a damn thing. I sensed myself in the presence of something I didn't really know how to handle, didn't understand. So I made my frown a little deeper as I asked: "What kind of musician do you want to be?"

He grinned. "How many kinds do you think there are?"

"Be *serious*," I said.

He laughed, throwing his head back, and then looked at me. "I *am* serious."

"Well, then, for Christ's sake, stop kidding around and answer a serious question. I mean, do you want to be a concert pianist, you want to play classical music and all that, or—or what?" Long before I finished he was laughing again. "For Christ's *sake*, Sonny!"

He sobered, but with difficulty. "I'm sorry. But you sound so—*scared!*" and he was off again.

"Well, you may think it's funny now, baby, but it's not going to be so funny when you have to make your living at it, let me tell you *that*." I was furious because I knew he was laughing at me and I didn't know why.

"No," he said, very sober now, and afraid, perhaps, that he'd hurt me, "I don't want to be a classical pianist. That isn't what interests me. I mean"—he paused, looking hard at me, as though his eyes would help me to understand, and then gestured helplessly, as though perhaps his hand would help—"I mean, I'll have a lot of studying to do, and I'll have to study *everything*, but I mean, I want to play *with*—jazz musicians." He stopped. "I want to play jazz," he said.

Well, the word had never before sounded as heavy, as real, as it sounded that afternoon in Sonny's mouth. I just looked at him and I was probably frowning a real frown by this time. I simply couldn't see why on earth he'd want to spend his time hanging around night clubs, clowning around on bandstands, while people pushed each other around a dance floor. It seemed—beneath him, somehow. I had never thought about it before, had never been forced to, but I suppose I had always put jazz musicians in a class with what Daddy called "good-time people."

"Are you *serious?*"

"Hell, *yes*, I'm serious."

He looked more helpless than ever, and annoyed, and deeply hurt.

I suggested, helpfully: "You mean—like Louis Armstrong?"

His face closed as though I'd struck him. "No. I'm not talking about none of that old-time, down home crap."

"Well, look, Sonny, I'm sorry, don't get mad. I just don't altogether get it, that's all. Name somebody—you know, a jazz musician you admire."

"Bird."

"Who?"

"Bird! Charlie Parker! Don't they teach you nothing in the god-damn army?"

I lit a cigarette. I was surprised and then a little amused to discover that I was trembling. "I've been out of touch," I said, "You'll have to be patient with me. Now. Who's this Parker character?"

"He's just one of the greatest jazz musicians alive," said Sonny, sullenly, his hands in his pockets, his back to me. "Maybe *the* greatest," he added, bitterly, "that's probably why *you* never heard of him."

"All right," I said, "I'm ignorant. I'm sorry. I'll go out and buy all the cat's records right away, all right?"

"It don't," said Sonny, with dignity, "make any difference to me. I don't care what you listen to. Don't do me no favors."

I was beginning to realize that I'd never seen him so upset before. With another part of my mind I was thinking that this would probably turn out to be one of those things kids go through and that I shouldn't make it seem important by pushing it too hard. Still, I didn't think it would do any harm to ask: "Doesn't all this take a lot of time? Can you make a living at it?"

He turned back to me and half leaned, half sat, on the kitchen table. "Everything takes time," he said, "and—well, yes, sure, I can make a living at it. But what I don't seem to be able to make you understand is that it's the only thing I want to do."

"Well Sonny," I said, gently, "you know people can't always do exactly what they *want* to do—"

"*No*, I don't know that," said Sonny, surprising me. "I think people *ought* to do what they want to do, what else are they alive for?"

"You getting to be a big boy," I said desperately, "it's time you started thinking about your future."

"I'm thinking about my future," said Sonny, grimly. "I think about it all the time."

I gave up. I decided, if he didn't change his mind, that we could always talk about it later. "In the meantime," I said, "you got to finish school." We had already decided that he'd have to move in with Isabel and her folks. I knew this wasn't the ideal arrangement because Isabel's folks are inclined to be dicty and they hadn't especially wanted Isabel to marry me. But I didn't know what else to do. "And we have to get you fixed up at Isabel's."

There was a long silence. He moved from the kitchen table to the window. "That's a terrible idea. You know it yourself."

"Do you have a *better* idea?"

He just walked up and down the kitchen for a minute. He was as tall as I was. He had started to shave. I suddenly had the feeling that I didn't know him at all.

He stopped at the kitchen table and picked up my cigarettes. Looking at me with a kind of mocking, amused defiance, he put one between his lips. "You mind?"

"You smoking already?"

He lit the cigarette and nodded, watching me through the smoke. "I just wanted to see if I'd have the courage to smoke in front of you." He grinned and blew a great cloud of smoke to the ceiling. "It was easy." He looked at my face. "Come on, now. I bet you was smoking at my age, tell the truth."

I didn't say anything but the truth was on my face, and he laughed. But now there was something very strained in his laugh. "Sure. And I bet that ain't all you was doing."

He was frightening me a little. "Cut the crap," I said. "We already decided that you was going to go and live at Isabel's. Now what's got into you all of a sudden?"

"*You* decided it," he pointed out. "*I* didn't decide nothing." He stopped in front of me, leaning against the stove, arms loosely folded. "Look, brother. I don't want to stay in Harlem no more, I really don't." He was very earnest. He looked at me, then over toward the kitchen window. There was something in his eyes I'd never seen before, some thoughtfulness, some worry all his own. He rubbed the muscle of one arm. "It's time I was getting out of here."

"Where do you want to *go*, Sonny?"

"I want to join the army. Or the navy, I don't care. If I say I'm old enough they'll believe me."

Then I got mad. It was because I was so scared. "You must be crazy. You goddamn fool, what the hell do you want to go and join the *army* for?"

"I just told you. To get out of Harlem."

"Sonny, you haven't even finished *school*. And if you really want to be a musician, how do you expect to study if you're in the *army?*"

He looked at me, trapped, and in anguish. "There's ways. I might be able to work out some kind of deal. Anyway, I'll have the G.I. Bill when I come out."

"*If* you come out." We stared at each other. "Sonny, please. Be reasonable. I know the setup is far from perfect. But we got to do the best we can."

"I ain't learning nothing in school," he said. "Even when I go." He turned away from me and opened the window and threw his cigarette out into the narrow alley. I watched his back. "At least, I ain't learning nothing you'd want me to learn." He slammed the window so hard I thought the glass would fly out, and turned back to me. "And I'm sick of the stink of these garbage cans!"

"Sonny," I said, "I know how you feel. But if you don't finish school now, you're going to be sorry later that you didn't." I grabbed him by the shoulders. "And you only got another year. It ain't so bad. And I'll come back and I swear I'll help you do *whatever* you want to do. Just try to put up with it till I come back. Will you please do that? For me?"

He didn't answer and he wouldn't look at me.

"Sonny. You hear me?"

He pulled away. "I hear you. But you never hear anything *I* say."

I didn't know what to say to that. He looked out of the window and then back at me. "OK," he said, and sighed. "I'll try."

Then I said, trying to cheer him up a little, "They got a piano at Isabel's. You can practice on it."

And as a matter of fact, it did cheer him up for a minute. "That's right," he said to himself. "I forgot that." His face relaxed a little. But the worry, the thoughtfulness, played on it still, the way shadows play on a face which is staring into the fire.

But I thought I'd never hear the end of that piano. At first, Isabel would write me, saying how nice it was that Sonny was so serious about his music and how, as soon as he came in from school, or wherever he had been when he was supposed to be at school, he went straight to that piano and stayed there until suppertime. And, after supper, he went back to that piano and stayed there until everybody went to bed. He was at the piano all day Saturday and all day Sunday. Then he bought a record player and started playing records. He'd play one record over and over again, all day long sometimes, and he'd improvise along with it on the piano. Or he'd play one section of the record, one chord, one change, one progression, then he'd do it on the piano. Then back to the record. Then back to the piano.

Well, I really don't know how they stood it. Isabel finally confessed that it wasn't like living with a person at all, it was like living with sound. And the sound didn't make any sense to her, didn't make any sense to any of them—naturally. They began, in a way, to be afflicted by this presence that was living in their home. It was as though Sonny were some sort of god, or monster. He moved in an atmosphere which wasn't like theirs at all. They fed him and he ate, he washed himself, he walked in and out of their door; he certainly wasn't nasty or unpleasant or rude, Sonny isn't any of those things; but it was as though he were all wrapped up in some cloud, some fire, some vision all his own; and there wasn't any way to reach him.

At the same time, he wasn't really a man yet, he was still a child, and they had to watch out for him in all kinds of ways. They certainly couldn't throw him out. Neither did they dare to make a great scene about that piano because even they dimly sensed, as I sensed, from so many thousands of miles away, that Sonny was at that piano playing for his life.

But he hadn't been going to school. One day a letter came from the school board and Isabel's mother got it—there had, apparently, been other letters but Sonny had torn them up. This day, when Sonny came in, Isabel's mother showed him the letter and asked where he'd been spending his time. And she finally got it out of him that he'd been down in Greenwich Village, with musicians and other characters, in a white girl's apartment. And this scared her and she started to scream at him and what came up, once she began—though she denies it to this day—was what sacrifices they were making to give Sonny a decent home and how little he appreciated it.

Sonny didn't play the piano that day. By evening, Isabel's mother had calmed down but then there was the old man to deal with, and Isabel herself. Isabel says she did her best to be calm but she broke down and started crying. She says she just watched Sonny's face. She could tell, by watching him, what was happening with him. And what was happening was that they penetrated his cloud, they had reached him. Even if their fingers had been a thousand times more gentle than human fingers ever are, he could hardly help feeling that they had stripped him naked and were spitting on that nakedness. For he also had to see that his presence, that music, which was life or death to him, had been torture for them and that they had endured it, not at all for his sake, but only for mine. And Sonny couldn't take that. He can take it a little better today than he could then but he's still not very good at it and, frankly, I don't know anybody who is.

The silence of the next few days must have been louder than the sound of all the music ever played since time began. One morning, before she went to work, Isabel was in his room for something and she suddenly realized that all of his records were gone. And she knew for certain that he was gone. And he was. He went as far as the navy would carry him. He finally sent me a postcard from some place in Greece and that was the first I knew that Sonny was still alive. I didn't see him any more until we were both back in New York and the war had long been over.

He was a man by then, of course, but I wasn't willing to see it. He came by the house from time to time, but we fought almost every time we met. I didn't like the way he carried himself, loose and dreamlike all the time, and I didn't like his friends, and his music seemed to be merely an excuse for the life he led. It sounded just that weird and disordered.

Then we had a fight, a pretty awful fight, and I didn't see him for months. By and by I looked him up, where he was living, in a furnished room in the Village, and I tried to make it up. But there were lots of other people in the room and Sonny just lay on his bed, and he wouldn't come downstairs with me, and he treated these other people as though they were his family and I weren't. So I got mad and then he got mad, and then I told him that he might just as well be dead as live the way he was living. Then he stood up and he told me not to worry about him any more in life, that he *was* dead as far as I was concerned. Then he pushed me to the door and the other people looked on as though nothing were happening, and he slammed the door behind me. I stood in the hallway, staring at the door. I heard somebody laugh in the room and then the tears came to my eyes. I started down the steps, whistling to keep from crying, I kept whistling to myself, *You going to need me, baby, one of these cold, rainy days.*

I read about Sonny's trouble in the spring. Little Grace died in the fall. She was a beautiful little girl. But she only lived a little over two years. She died of polio and she suffered. She had a slight fever for a couple of days, but it didn't seem like anything and we just kept her in bed. And we would certainly have called the doctor, but the fever dropped, she seemed to be all right. So we thought it had just been a cold. Then, one day, she was up, playing, Isabel was in the kitchen fixing lunch for the two boys when they'd come in from school, and she heard Grace fall down in the living room. When you have a lot of children you don't always start running when one of them falls, unless they start screaming or something. And, this time, Grace was quiet. Yet, Isabel says that when she heard that *thump* and then that silence, something happened in her to make her afraid. And she ran to the living room and there was little Grace on the floor, all twisted up and the reason she hadn't screamed was that she couldn't get her breath. And when she did scream, it was the worst sound, Isabel says, that she'd ever heard in all her life, and she still hears it sometimes in her dreams. Isabel will sometimes wake me up with a low, moaning, strangled sound and I have to be quick to awaken her and hold her to me and where Isabel is weeping against me seems a mortal wound.

I think I may have written Sonny the very day that little Grace was buried. I was sitting in the living room in the dark, by myself, and I suddenly thought of Sonny. My trouble made his real.

One Saturday afternoon, when Sonny had been living with us, or, anyway, been in our house, for nearly two weeks, I found myself wandering aimlessly about the living room, drinking from a can of beer, and trying to work up the courage to search Sonny's room. He was out, he was usually out whenever I was home, and Isabel had taken the children to see their grandparents. Suddenly I was standing still in front of the living room window, watching Seventh Avenue. The idea of searching Sonny's room made me still. I scarcely dared to admit to myself what I'd be searching for. I didn't know what I'd do if I found it. Or if I didn't.

On the sidewalk across from me, near the entrance to a barbecue joint, some people were holding an old-fashioned revival meeting. The barbecue cook, wearing a dirty white apron, his conked hair reddish and metallic in the pale sun, and a cigarette between his lips, stood in the doorway, watching them. Kids and older people paused in their errands and stood there, along with some older men and a couple of very tough-looking women who watched everything that happened on the avenue, as though they owned it, or were maybe owned by it. Well, they were watching this, too. The revival was being carried on by three sisters in black, and a brother. All they had were their voices and their Bibles and a tambourine. The brother was testifying and while he testified two of the sisters stood together, seeming to say, Amen, and the third sister walked around with the tambourine outstretched and a couple of people dropped coins into it. Then the brother's testimony ended and the sister who had been taking up the collection dumped the coins into her palm and transferred them to the pocket of her long black robe. Then she raised both hands, striking the tambourine against the air, and then against one hand, and she started to sing. And the two other sisters and the brother joined in.

It was strange, suddenly, to watch, though I had been seeing these street meetings all my life. So, of course, had everybody else down there. Yet, they paused and watched and listened and I stood still at the window. "*Tis the old ship of Zion,*" they sang, and the sister with the tambourine kept a steady, jangling beat, "*It has rescued many a thousand!*" Not a soul under the sound of their voices was hearing this song for the first time, not one of them had been rescued. Nor had they seen much in the way of rescue work being done around them. Neither did they especially believe in the holiness of the three sisters and the brother, they knew too much about them, knew where they lived, and how. The woman with the tambourine, whose voice dominated the air, whose face was bright with joy, was divided by very little from the woman who stood watching her, a cigarette between her heavy, chapped lips, her hair a cuckoo's nest, her face scarred and swollen from many beatings, and her black eyes glittering like coal. Perhaps they both knew this, which was why, when, as rarely, they addressed each other, they addressed each other as Sister. As the singing filled the air the watching, listening faces underwent a change, the eyes focusing on something within; the music seemed to soothe a poison out of them; and time seemed, nearly, to fall away from the sullen, belligerent, battered faces, as though they were fleeing back to their first condition, while dreaming of their last. The barbecue cook half shook his head and smiled, and dropped his cigarette and disappeared into his joint. A man fumbled in his pockets for change and stood holding it in his hand impatiently, as though he had just remembered a pressing appointment further up the avenue. He looked furious. Then I saw Sonny, standing on the edge of the crowd. He was carrying a wide, flat notebook with a green cover, and it made him look, from where I was standing, almost like a schoolboy. The coppery sun brought out the copper in his skin, he was very faintly smiling, standing very still. Then the singing stopped, the tambourine turned into a collection plate again. The furious man dropped in his coins and vanished, so did a couple of the women, and Sonny dropped some change in the plate, looking directly at the woman with a little smile. He started across the avenue, toward the house. He has a slow, loping walk, something like the way Harlem hipsters walk, only he's imposed on this his own halfbeat. I had never really noticed it before.

I stayed at the window, both relieved and apprehensive. As Sonny disappeared from my sight, they began singing again. And they were still singing when his key turned in the lock.

"Hey," he said.

"Hey, yourself. You want some beer?"

"No. Well, maybe." But he came up to the window and stood beside me, looking out. "What a warm voice," he said.

They were singing *If I could only hear my mother pray again!*

"Yes," I said, "and she can sure beat that tambourine."

"But what a terrible song," he said, and laughed. He dropped his notebook on the sofa and disappeared into the kitchen. "Where's Isabel and the kids?"

"I think they went to see their grandparents. You hungry?"

"No." He came back into the living room with his can of beer. "You want to come some place with me tonight?"

I sensed, I don't know how, that I couldn't possibly say No. "Sure. Where?"

He sat down on the sofa and picked up his notebook and started leafing through it. "I'm going to sit in with some fellows in a joint in the Village."

"You mean, you're going to play, tonight?"

"That's right." He took a swallow of his beer and moved back to the window. He gave me a sidelong look. "If you can stand it."

"I'll try," I said.

He smiled to himself and we both watched as the meeting across the way broke up. The three sisters and the brother, heads bowed, were singing *God be with you till we meet again*. The faces around them were very quiet. Then the song ended. The small crowd dispersed. We watched the three women and the lone man walk slowly up the avenue.

"When she was singing before," said Sonny, abruptly, "her voice reminded me for a minute of what heroin feels like sometimes—when it's in your veins. It makes you feel sort of warm and cool at the same time. And distant. And—and sure." He sipped his beer, very deliberately not looking at me. I watched his face. "It makes you feel—in control. Sometimes you've got to have that feeling."

"Do you?" I sat down slowly in the easy chair.

"Sometimes." He went to the sofa and picked up his notebook again. "Some people do."

"In order," I asked, "to play?" And my voice was very ugly, full of contempt and anger.

"Well"—he looked at me with great, troubled eyes, as though, in fact, he hoped his eyes would tell me things he could never otherwise say—"they *think* so. And *if* they think so—!"

"And what do *you* think?" I asked.

He sat on the sofa and put his can of beer on the floor. "I don't know," he said, and I couldn't be sure if he were answering my question or pursuing his thoughts. His face didn't tell me. "It's not so much to *play*. It's to *stand* it, to be able to make it at all. On any level." He frowned and smiled: "In order to keep from shaking to pieces."

"But these friends of yours," I said, "they seem to shake themselves to pieces pretty goddamn fast."

"Maybe." He played with the notebook. And something told me that I should curb my tongue, that Sonny was doing his best to talk, that I should listen. "But of course you only know the ones that've gone to pieces. Some don't—or at least they haven't *yet* and that's just about all *any* of us can say." He paused. "And then there are some who just live, really, in hell, and they know it and they see what's happening and they go right on. I don't know." He sighed, dropped the notebook, folded his arms. "Some guys, you can tell from the way they play, they on something *all* the time. And you can see that, well, it makes something real for them. But of course," he picked up his beer from the floor and sipped it and put the can down again, "they *want* to, too, you've got to see that. Even some of them that say they don't—*some,* not all."

"And what about you?" I asked—I couldn't help it. "What about you? Do *you* want to?"

He stood up and walked to the window and remained silent for a long time. Then he sighed. "Me," he said. Then: "While I was downstairs before, on my way here, listening to that woman sing, it struck me all of a sudden how much suffering she must have had to go through—to sing like that. It's *repulsive* to think you have to suffer that much."

I said: "But there's no way not to suffer—is there, Sonny?"

"I believe not," he said, and smiled, "but that's never stopped anyone from trying." He looked at me. "Has it?" I realized, with this mocking look, that there stood between us, forever, beyond the power of time or forgiveness, the fact that I had held silence—so long!— when he had needed human speech to help him. He turned back to the window. "No, there's no way not to suffer. But you try all kinds of ways to keep from drowning in it, to keep on top of it, and to make it seem—well, like *you*. Like you did something, all right, and now you're suffering for it. You know?" I said nothing. "Well you know," he said, impatiently, "why *do* people suffer? Maybe it's better to do something to give it a reason, *any* reason."

"But we just agreed," I said, "that there's no way not to suffer. Isn't it better, then, just to—take it?"

"But nobody just takes it," Sonny cried, "that's what I'm telling you! *Everybody* tries not to. You're just hung up on the *way* some people try—it's not *your* way!"

The hair on my face began to itch, my face felt wet. "That's not true," I said, "that's not true. I don't give a damn what other people do, I don't even care how they suffer. I just care how *you* suffer." And he looked at me. "Please believe me," I said, "I don't want to see you—die—trying not to suffer."

"I won't," he said, flatly, "die trying not to suffer. At least, not any faster than anybody else."

"But there's no need," I said, trying to laugh, "is there? in killing yourself."

I wanted to say more, but I couldn't. I wanted to talk about will power and how life could be—well, beautiful. I wanted to say that it was all within; but was it? or, rather, wasn't that exactly the trouble? And I wanted to promise that I would never fail him again. But it would all have sounded—empty words and lies.

So I made the promise to myself and prayed that I would keep it.

"It's terrible sometimes, inside," he said, "that's what's the trouble. You walk these streets, black and funky and cold, and there's not really a living ass to talk to, and there's nothing shaking, and there's no way of getting it out—that storm inside. You can't talk it and you can't make love with it, and when you finally try to get with it and play it, you realize *nobody's* listening. So *you've* got to listen. You got to find a way to listen."

And then he walked away from the window and sat on the sofa again, as though all the wind had suddenly been knocked out of him. "Sometimes you'll do *anything* to play, even cut your mother's throat." He laughed and looked at me. "Or your brother's." Then he sobered. "Or your own." Then: "Don't worry. I'm all right now and I think I'll *be* all right. But I can't forget—where I've been. I don't mean just the physical place I've been, I mean where I've *been*. And *what* I've been."

"What have you been, Sonny?" I asked.

He smiled—but sat sideways on the sofa, his elbow resting on the back, his fingers playing with his mouth and chin, not looking at me. "I've been something I didn't recognize, didn't know I could be. Didn't know anybody could be." He stopped, looking inward, looking helplessly young, looking old. "I'm not talking about it now because I feel *guilty* or anything like that—maybe it would be better if I did, I don't know. Anyway, I can't really talk about it. Not to you, not to anybody," and now he turned and faced me. "Sometimes, you know, and it was actually when I was most *out* of the world, I felt that I was in it, and that I was *with* it, really, and I could play or I didn't really have to *play*, it just came out of me, it was there. And I don't know how I played, thinking about it now, but I know I did awful things, those times, sometimes, to people. Or it wasn't that I *did* anything to them—it was that they weren't real." He picked up the beer can; it was empty; he rolled it between his palms: "And other times—well, I needed a fix, I needed to find a place to lean, I needed to clear a space to *listen*—and I couldn't find it, and I—went crazy, I did terrible things to *me*, I was terrible *for* me." He began pressing the beer can between his hands, I watched the metal begin to give. It glittered, as he played with it, like a knife, and I was afraid he would cut himself, but I said nothing. "Oh well. I can never tell you. I was all by myself at the bottom of something, stinking and sweating and crying and shaking, and I smelled it, you know? *my* stink, and I thought I'd die if I couldn't get away from it and yet, all the same, I knew that everything I was doing was just locking me in with it. And I didn't know," he paused, still flattening the beer can, "I didn't know, I still *don't* know, something kept telling me that maybe it was good to smell your own stink, but I didn't think that *that* was what I'd been trying to do—and—who can stand it?" and he abruptly dropped the ruined beer can, looking at me with a small, still smile, and then rose, walking to the window as though it were the lodestone rock. I watched his face, he watched the avenue. "I couldn't tell you when Mama died—but the reason I wanted to leave Harlem so bad was to get away from drugs. And then, when I ran away, that's what I was running from—really. When I came back, nothing had changed, *I* hadn't changed, I was just—older." And he stopped, drumming with his fingers on the windowpane. The sun had vanished, soon darkness would fall. I watched his face. "It can come again," he said, almost as though speaking to himself. Then he turned to me. "It can come again," he repeated. "I just want you to know that."

"All right," I said, at last. "So it can come again. All right."

He smiled, but the smile was sorrowful. "I had to try to tell you," he said.

"Yes," I said. "I understand that."

"You're my brother," he said, looking straight at me, and not smiling at all.

"Yes," I repeated, "yes. I understand that."

He turned back to the window, looking out. "All that hatred down there," he said, "all that hatred and misery and love. It's a wonder it doesn't blow the avenue apart."

We went to the only night club on a short, dark street, downtown. We squeezed through the narrow, chattering, jam-packed bar to the entrance of the big room, where the bandstand was. And we stood there for a moment, for the lights were very dim in this room and we couldn't see. Then, "Hello, boy," said a voice and an enormous black man, much older than Sonny or myself, erupted out of all that atmospheric lighting and put an arm around Sonny's shoulder. "I been sitting right here," he said, "waiting for you."

He had a big voice, too, and heads in the darkness turned toward us.

Sonny grinned and pulled a little away, and said, "Creole, this is my brother. I told you about him."

Creole shook my hand. "I'm glad to meet you, son," he said, and it was clear that he was glad to meet me *there*, for Sonny's sake. And he smiled, "You got a real musician in *your* family," and he took his arm from Sonny's shoulder and slapped him, lightly, affectionately, with the back of his hand.

"Well. Now I've heard it all," said a voice behind us. This was another musician, and a friend of Sonny's, a coal-black, cheerful-looking man, built close to the ground. He immediately began confiding to me, at the top of his lungs, the most terrible things about Sonny, his teeth gleaming like a lighthouse and his laugh coming up out of him like the beginning of an earthquake. And it turned out that everyone at the bar knew Sonny, or almost everyone; some were musicians, working there, or nearby, or not working, some were simply hangers-on, and some were there to hear Sonny play. I was introduced to all of them and they were all very polite to me. Yet, it was clear that, for them, I was only Sonny's brother. Here, I was in Sonny's world. Or, rather: his kingdom. Here, it was not even a question that his veins bore royal blood.

They were going to play soon and Creole installed me, by myself, at a table in a dark corner. Then I watched them, Creole, and the little black man, and Sonny, and the others, while they horsed around, standing just below the bandstand. The light from the bandstand spilled just a little short of them and, watching them laughing and gesturing and moving about, I had the feeling that they, nevertheless, were being most careful not to step into that circle of light too suddenly: that if they moved into the light too suddenly, without thinking, they would perish in flame. Then, while I watched, one of them, the small, black man, moved into the light and crossed the bandstand and started fooling around with his drums. Then—being funny and being, also, extremely ceremonious—Creole took Sonny by the arm and led him to the piano. A woman's voice called Sonny's name and a few hands started clapping. And Sonny, also being funny and being ceremonious, and so touched, I think, that he could have cried, but neither hiding it nor showing it, riding it like a man, grinned, and put both hands to his heart and bowed from the waist.

Creole then went to the bass fiddle and a lean, very bright-skinned brown man jumped up on the bandstand and picked up his horn. So there they were, and the atmosphere on the bandstand and in the room began to change and tighten. Someone stepped up to the microphone and announced them. Then there were all kinds of murmurs. Some people at the bar shushed others. The waitress ran around, frantically getting in the last orders, guys and chicks got closer to each other, and the lights on the bandstand, on the quartet, turned to a kind of indigo. Then they all looked different there. Creole looked about him for the last time, as though he were making certain that all his chickens were in the coop, and then he—jumped and struck the fiddle. And there they were.

All I know about music is that not many people ever really hear it. And even then, on the rare occasions when something opens within, and the music enters, what we mainly hear, or hear corroborated, are personal private, vanishing evocations. But the man who creates the music is hearing something else, is dealing with the roar rising from the void and imposing order on it as it hits the air. What is evoked in him, then, is of another order, more terrible because it has no words, and triumphant, too, for that same reason. And his triumph, when he triumphs, is ours. I just watched Sonny's face. His face was troubled, he was working hard, but he wasn't with it. And I had the feeling that, in a way, everyone on the bandstand was waiting for him, both waiting for him and pushing him along. But as I began to watch Creole, I realized that it was Creole who held them all back. He had them on a short rein. Up there, keeping the beat with his whole body, wailing on the fiddle, with his eyes half closed, he was listening to everything, but he was listening to Sonny. He was having a dialogue with Sonny. He wanted Sonny to leave the shore line and strike out for the deep water. He was Sonny's witness that deep water and drowning were not the same thing—he had been there, and he knew. And he wanted Sonny to know. He was waiting for Sonny to do the things on the keys which would let Creole know that Sonny was in the water.

And, while Creole listened, Sonny moved, deep within, exactly like someone in torment. I had never before thought of how awful the relationship must be between the musician and his instrument. He has to fill it, this instrument, with the breath of life, his own. He has to make it do what he wants it to do. And a piano is just a piano. It's made out of so much wood and wires and little hammers and big ones, and ivory. While there's only so much you can do with it, the only way to find this out is to try and make it do everything.

And Sonny hadn't been near a piano for over a year. And he wasn't on much better terms with his life, not the life that stretched before him now. He and the piano stammered, started one way, got scared, stopped; started another way, panicked, marked time, started again; then seemed to have found a direction, panicked again, got stuck. And the face I saw on Sonny I'd never seen before. Everything had been burned out of it, and, at the same time, things usually hidden were being burned in, by the fire and fury of the battle which was occurring in him up there.

Yet, watching Creole's face as they neared the end of the first set, I had the feeling that something had happened, something I hadn't heard. Then they finished, there was scattered applause, and then, without an instant's warning, Creole started into something else, it was almost sardonic, it was *Am I Blue*. And, as though he commanded, Sonny began to play. Something began to happen. And Creole let out the reins. The dry, low, black man said something awful on the drums, Creole answered, and the drums talked back. Then the horn insisted, sweet and high, slightly detached perhaps, and Creole listened, commenting now and then, dry, and driving, beautiful and calm and old. Then they all came together again, and Sonny was part of the family again. I could tell this from his face. He seemed to have found, right there beneath his fingers, a damn brand-new piano. It seemed that he couldn't get over it. Then, for awhile, just being happy with Sonny, they seemed to be agreeing with him that brand-new pianos certainly were a gas.

Then Creole stepped forward to remind them that what they were playing was the blues. He hit something in all of them, he hit something in me, myself, and the music tightened and deepened, apprehension began to beat the air. Creole began to tell us what the blues were all about. They were not about anything very new. He and his boys up there were keeping it new, at the risk of ruin, destruction, madness, and death, in order to find new ways to make us listen. For, while the tale of how we suffer, and how we are delighted, and how we may triumph is never new, it always must be heard. There isn't any other tale to tell, it's the only light we've got in all this darkness.

And this tale, according to that face, that body, those strong hands on those strings, has another aspect in every country, and a new depth in every generation. Listen, Creole seemed to be saying, listen. Now these are Sonny's blues. He made the little black man on the drums know it, and the bright, brown man on the horn. Creole wasn't trying any longer to get Sonny in the water. He was wishing him Godspeed. Then he stepped back, very slowly, filling the air with the immense suggestion that Sonny speak for himself.

Then they all gathered around Sonny and Sonny played. Every now and again one of them seemed to say, Amen. Sonny's fingers filled the air with life, his life. But that life contained so many others. And Sonny went all the way back, he really began with the spare, flat statement of the opening phrase of the song. Then he began to make it his. It was very beautiful because it wasn't hurried and it was no longer a lament. I seemed to hear with what burning he had made it his, with what burning we had yet to make it ours, how we could cease lamenting. Freedom lurked around us and I understood, at last, that he could help us to be free if we would listen, that he would never be free until we did. Yet, there was no battle in his face now. I heard what he had gone through, and would continue to go through until he came to rest in earth. He had made it his: that long line, of which we knew only Mama and Daddy. And he was giving it back, as everything must be given back, so that, passing through death, it can live forever. I saw my mother's face again, and felt, for the first time, how the stones of the road she had walked on must have bruised her feet. I saw the moonlit road where my father's brother died. And it brought something else back to me, and carried me past it, I saw my little girl again and felt Isabel's tears again, and I felt my own tears begin to rise. And I was yet aware that this was only a moment, that the world waited outside, as hungry as a tiger, and that trouble stretched above us, longer than the sky.

Then it was over. Creole and Sonny let out their breath, both soaking wet, and grinning. There was a lot of applause and some of it was real. In the dark, the girl came by and I asked her to take drinks to the bandstand. There was a long pause, while they talked up there in the indigo light and after awhile I saw the girl put a Scotch and milk on top of the piano for Sonny. He didn't seem to notice it, but just before they started playing again, he sipped from it and looked toward me, and nodded. Then he put it back on top of the piano. For me, then, as they began to play again, it glowed and shook above my brother's head like the very cup of trembling.

QUESTIONS

1. Explore the use of music as a metaphor in "Sonny's Blues." How many types of music do you find in the story? What meanings does the narrator give them?

2. The narrator says that he and Sonny, riding through the streets of New York, "both were seeking through our separate cab windows . . . that part of ourselves which had been left behind. It's always at the hour of trouble and confrontation that the missing member aches." What has been amputated? What happens to the lost member during the course of the story?

3. "He wanted Sonny to leave the shore line and strike out for the deep water. He was Sonny's witness that deep water and drowning were not the same thing—he had been there, and he knew." Discuss this metaphor. Notice the word *witness*. It could come from legal terminology but in this story is has a different connotation. Discuss.

TILLIE OLSEN (1913–)

Help Her to Believe

I stand here ironing, and what you asked me moves tormented back and forth with the iron.

"I wish you would manage the time to come in and talk with me about your daughter. I'm sure you can help me understand her. She's a youngster who needs help and whom I'm deeply interested in helping."

"Who needs help." Even if I came, what good would it do? You think because I am her mother I have a key, or that in some way you could use me as a key? She has lived for nineteen years. There is all that life that has happened outside of me, beyond me.

And when is there time to remember, to sift, to weigh, to estimate, to total? I will start and there will be an interruption and I will have to gather it all together again. Or I will become engulfed with all I did or did not do, with what should have been and what cannot be helped.

She was a beautiful baby. The first and only one of our five that was beautiful at birth. You do not guess how new and uneasy her tenancy in her now-loveliness. You did not know her all those years she was thought homely, or see her poring over her baby pictures, making me tell her over and over how beautiful she had been—and would be, I would tell her—and was now, to the seeing eye. But the seeing eyes were few or nonexistent. Including mine.

I nursed her. They feel that's important nowadays. I nursed all the children, but with her, with all the fierce rigidity of first motherhood, I did like the books then said. Though her cries battered me to trembling and my breasts ached with swollenness, I waited till the clock decreed.

Why do I put that first? I do not even know if it matters, or if it explains anything.

She was a beautiful baby. She blew shining bubbles of sound. She loved motion, loved light, loved color and music and textures. She would lie on the floor in her blue overalls patting the surface so hard in ecstasy her hands and feet would blur. She was a miracle to me, but when she was eight months old I had to leave her daytimes with the woman downstairs to whom she was no miracle at all, for I worked or looked for work and for Emily's father, who "could no longer endure" (he wrote in his good-bye note) "sharing want with us."

I was nineteen. It was the pre-relief, pre-WPA world of the depression. I would start running as soon as I got off the streetcar, running

197

up the stairs, the place smelling sour, and awake or asleep to startle awake, when she saw me she would break into a clogged weeping that could not be comforted, a weeping I can hear yet.

After a while I found a job hashing at night so I could be with her days, and it was better. But it came to where I had to bring her to his family and leave her.

It took a long time to raise the money for her fare back. Then she got chicken pox and I had to wait longer. When she finally came, I hardly knew her, walking quick and nervous like her father, looking like her father, thin, and dressed in a shoddy red that yellowed her skin and glared at the pockmarks. All the baby loveliness gone.

She was two. Old enough for nursery school they said, and I did not know then what I know now—the fatigue of the long day, and the lacerations of group life in the nurseries that are only parking places for children.

Except that it would have made no difference if I had known. It was the only place there was. It was the only way we could be together, the only way I could hold a job.

And even without knowing, I knew. I knew the teacher that was evil because all these years it has curdled into my memory, the little boy hunched in the corner, her rasp, "why aren't you outside, because Alvin hits you? that's no reason, go out, scaredy." I knew Emily hated it even if she did not clutch and implore "don't go Mommy" like the other children, mornings.

She always had a reason why we should stay home. Momma, you look sick, Momma. I feel sick. Momma, the teachers aren't there today, they're sick. Momma, we can't go, there was a fire there last night. Momma, it's a holiday today, no school, they told me.

But never a direct protest, never rebellion. I think of our others in their three-, four-year-oldness—the explosions, the tempers, the denunciations, the demands—and I feel suddenly ill. I put the iron down. What in me demanded that goodness in her? And what was the cost, the cost to her of such goodness?

The old man living in the back once said in his gentle way: "You should smile at Emily more when you look at her." What *was* in my face when I looked at her? I loved her. There were all the acts of love.

It was only with the others I remembered what he said, and it was the face of joy, and not of care or tightness or worry I turned to them—too late for Emily. She does not smile easily, let alone almost always as her brothers and sisters do. Her face is closed and sombre, but when she wants, how fluid. You must have seen it in her pantomimes, you spoke of her rare gift for comedy on the stage that rouses a laughter out of the audience so dear they applaud and applaud and do not want to let her go.

Where does it come from, that comedy? There was none of it in her when she came back to me that second time, after I had had to send her away again. She had a new daddy now to learn to love, and I think perhaps it was a better time.

Except when we left her alone nights, telling ourselves she was old enough.

"Can't you go some other time, Mommy, like tomorrow?" she would ask. "Will it be just a little while you'll be gone? Do you promise?"

The time we came back, the front door open, the clock on the floor in the hall. She rigid awake. "It wasn't just a little while. I didn't cry. Three times I called you, just three times, and then I ran downstairs to open the door so you could come faster. The clock talked loud. I threw it away, it scared me what it talked."

She said the clock talked loud again that night I went to the hospital to have Susan. She was delirious with the fever that comes before red measles, but she was fully conscious all the week I was gone and the week after we were home when she could not come near the new baby or me.

She did not get well. She stayed skeleton thin, not wanting to eat, and night after night she had nightmares. She would call for me, and I would rouse from exhaustion to sleepily call back: "You're all right, darling, go to sleep, it's just a dream," and if she still called, in a sterner voice, "now go to sleep, Emily, there's nothing to hurt you." Twice, only twice, when I had to get up for Susan anyhow, I went in to sit with her.

Now when it is too late (as if she would let me hold and comfort her like I do the others) I get up and go to her at once at her moan or restless stirring. "Are you awake, Emily? Can I get you something?" And the answer is always the same: "No, I'm all right, go back to sleep, Mother."

They persuaded me at the clinic to send her away to a convalescent home in the country where "she can have the kind of food and care you can't manage for her, and you'll be free to concentrate on the new baby." They still send children to that place. I see pictures on the society page of sleek young women planning affairs to raise money for it, or dancing at the affairs, or decorating Easter eggs or filling Christmas stockings for the children.

They never have a picture of the children so I do not know if the girls still wear those gigantic red bows and the ravaged looks on the every other Sunday when parents can come to visit "unless otherwise notified"—as we were notified the first six weeks.

Oh it is a handsome place, green lawns and tall trees and fluted flower beds. High up on the balconies of each cottage the children stand, the girls in their red bows and white dresses, the boys in white suits and giant red ties. The parents stand below shrieking up to be heard and the children shriek down to be heard, and between them the invisible wall "Not To Be Contaminated by Parental Germs or Physical Affection."

There was a tiny girl who always stood hand in hand with Emily. Her parents never came. One visit she was gone. "They moved her to Rose College," Emily shouted in explanation. "They don't like you to love anybody here."

She wrote once a week, the labored writing of a seven-year-old. "I am fine. How is the baby. If I write my leter nicly I will have a star. Love." There never was a star. We wrote every other day, letters she could never hold or keep but only hear read—once. "We simply do not have room for chiidren to keep any personal possessions," they patiently explained when we pieced one Sunday's shrieking together to plead how much it would mean to Emily, who loved so to keep things, to be allowed to keep her letters and cards.

Each visit she looked frailer. "She isn't eating," they told us.

(They had runny eggs for breakfast or mush with lumps, Emily said later, I'd hold it in my mouth and not swallow. Nothing ever tasted good, just when they had chicken.)

It took us eight months to get her released home, and only the fact that she gained back so little of her seven lost pounds convinced the social worker.

I used to try to hold and love her after she came back, but her body would stay stiff, and after a while she'd push away. She ate little. Food sickened her, and I think much of life too. Oh she had physical lightness and brightness, twinkling by on skates, bouncing like a ball up and down up and down over the jump rope, skimming over the hill; but these were momentary.

She fretted about her appearance, thin and dark and foreign-looking at a time when every little girl was supposed to look or thought she should look a chubby blonde replica of Shirley Temple. The doorbell sometimes rang for her, but no one seemed to come and play in the house or be a best friend. Maybe because we moved so much.

There was a boy she loved painfully through two school semesters. Months later she told me how she had taken pennies from my purse to buy him candy. "Licorice was his favorite and I brought him some every day, but he still liked Jennifer better'n me. Why, Mommy?" The kind of question for which there is no answer.

School was a worry to her. She was not glib or quick in a world where glibness and quickness were easily confused with ability to learn. To her overworked and exasperated teachers she was an over-conscientious "slow learner" who kept trying to catch up and was absent entirely too often.

I let her be absent, though sometimes the illness was imaginary.

How different from my now-strictness about attendance with the others. I wasn't working. We had a new baby, I was home anyhow. Sometimes, after Susan grew old enough, I would keep her home from school, too, to have them all together.

Mostly Emily had asthma, and her breathing, harsh and labored, would fill the house with a curiously tranquil sound. I would bring the two old dresser mirrors and her boxes of collections to her bed. She would select beads and single earrings, bottle tops and shells, dried flowers and pebbles, old postcards and scraps, all sorts of oddments; then she and Susan would play Kingdom, setting up landscapes and furniture, peopling them with action.

Those were the only times of peaceful companionship between her and Susan. I have edged away from it, that poisonous feeling between them, that terrible balancing of hurts and needs I had to do between the two, and did so badly, those earlier years.

Oh there are conflicts between the others too, each one human, needing, demanding, hurting, taking—but only between Emily and Susan, no, Emily toward Susan that corroding resentment. It seems so obvious on the surface, yet it is not obvious. Susan, the second child, Susan, golden- and curly-haired and chubby, quick and articulate and assured, everything in appearance and manner Emily was not; Susan, not able to resist Emily's precious things, losing or sometimes clumsily breaking them; Susan telling jokes and riddles to company for applause while Emily sat silent (to say to me later: that was *my* riddle, Mother, I told it to Susan); Susan, who for all the five years' difference in age was just a year behind Emily in developing physically.

I am glad for that slow physical development that widened the difference between her and her contemporaries, though she suffered over it. She was too vulnerable for that terrible world of youthful competition, of preening and parading, of constant measuring of yourself against every other, of envy, "If I had that copper hair," "If I had that skin. . . ." She tormented herself enough about not looking like the others, there was enough of the unsureness, the having to be conscious of words before you speak, the constant caring—what are they thinking of me? without having it all magnified by the merciless physical drives.

Ronnie is calling. He is wet and I change him. It is rare there is such a cry now. That time of motherhood is almost behind me when the ear is not one's own but must always be racked and listening for the child cry, the child call. We sit for a while and I hold him, looking out over the city spread in charcoal with its soft aisles of light. "Shoogily," he breathes and curls closer. I carry him back to bed, asleep. *Shoogily.* A funny word, a family word, inherited from Emily, invented by her to say: *comfort.*

In this and other ways she leaves her seal, I say aloud. And startle at my saying it. What do I mean? What did I start to gather together, to try and make coherent? I was at the terrible, growing years. War years. I do not remember them well. I was working, there were four smaller ones now, there was not time for her. She had to help be a mother, and housekeeper, and shopper. She had to set her seal. Mornings of crisis and near hysteria trying to get lunches packed, hair combed, coats and shoes found, everyone to school or Child Care on time, the baby ready for transportation. And always the paper scribbled on by a smaller one, the book looked at by Susan then mislaid, the homework not done. Running out to that huge school where she was one, she was lost, she was a drop; suffering over the unpreparedness, stammering and unsure in her classes.

There was so little time left at night after the kids were bedded down. She would struggle over books, always eating (it was in those years she developed her enormous appetite that is legendary in our family) and I would be ironing, or preparing food for the next day, or writing V-mail to Bill, or tending the baby. Sometimes, to make me laugh, or out of her despair, she would imitate happenings or types at school.

I think I said once: "Why don't you do something like this in the school amateur show?" One morning she phoned me at work, hardly understandable through the weeping: "Mother, I did it. I won, I won; they gave me first prize; they clapped and clapped and wouldn't let me go."

Now suddenly she was Somebody, and as imprisoned in her difference as she had been in anonymity.

She began to be asked to perform at other high schools, even in colleges, then at city and statewide affairs. The first one we went to, I only recognized her that first moment when thin, shy, she almost drowned herself into the curtains. Then: Was this Emily? The control, the command, the convulsing and deadly clowning, the spell, then the roaring, stamping audience, unwilling to let this rare and precious laughter out of their lives.

Afterwards: You ought to do something about her with a gift like that—but without money or knowing how, what does one do? We have left it all to her, and the gift has as often eddied inside, clogged and clotted, as been used and growing.

She is coming. She runs up the stairs two at a time with her light graceful step, and I know she is happy tonight. Whatever it was that occasioned your call did not happen today.

"Aren't you ever going to finish the ironing, Mother? Whistler painted his mother in a rocker. I'd have to paint mine standing over an ironing board." This is one of her communicative nights and she tells me everything and nothing as she fixes herself a plate of food out of the icebox.

She is so lovely. Why did you want me to come in at all? Why were you concerned? She will find her way.

She starts up the stairs to bed. "Don't get me up with the rest in the morning." "But I thought you were having midterms." "Oh, those," she comes back in, kisses me, and says quite lightly, "in a couple of years when we'll all be atom-dead they won't matter a bit."

She has said it before. She *believes* it. But because I have been dredging the past, and all that compounds a human being is so heavy and meaningful in me, I cannot endure it tonight.

I will never total it all. I will never come in to say: She was a child seldom smiled at. Her father left me before she was a year old. I had to work her first six years when there was work, or I sent her home and to his relatives. There were years she had care she hated. She was dark and thin and foreign-looking in a world where the prestige went to blondeness and curly hair and dimples, she was slow where glibness was prized. She was a child of anxious, not proud, love. We were poor and could not afford for her the soil of easy growth. I was a young mother, I was a distracted mother. There were the other children pushing up, demanding. Her younger sister seemed all that she was not. There were years she did not want me to touch her. She kept too much in herself, her life was such she had to keep too much in herself. My wisdom came too late. She has much to her and probably nothing will come of it. She is a child of her age, of depression, of war, of fear.

Let her be. So all that is in her will not bloom—but in how many does it? There is still enough left to live by. Only help her to know—help make it so there is cause for her to know—that she is more than this dress on the ironing board, helpless before the iron.

JOYCE CAROL OATES (1938–)

How I Contemplated the World from the Detroit House of Correction and Began My Life Over Again

Notes for an essay for an English class at Baldwin Country Day School; poking around in debris; disgust and curiosity; a revelation of the meaning of life; a happy ending . . .

I Events

1. The girl (myself) is walking through Branden's, that excellent store. Suburb of a large famous city that is a symbol for large famous American cities. The event sneaks up on the girl, who believes she is herding it along with a small fixed smile, a girl of fifteen, innocently experienced. She dawdles in a certain style by a counter of costume jewelry. Rings, earrings, necklaces. Prices from $5 to $50, all within reach. All ugly. She eases over to the glove counter, where everything is ugly too. In her close-fitted coat with its black fur collar she contemplates the luxury of Branden's, which she has known for many years: its many mild pale lights, easy on the eye and the soul, its elaborate tinkly decorations, its women shoppers with their excellent shoes and coats and hairdos, all dawdling gracefully, in no hurry.

Who was ever in a hurry here?

2. The girl seated at home. A small library, paneled walls of oak. Someone is talking to me. An earnest, husky, female voice drives itself against my ears, nervous, frightened, groping around my heart, saying, "If you wanted gloves, why didn't you say so? Why didn't you ask for them?" That store, Branden's, is owned by Raymond Forrest who lives on Du Maurier Drive. We live on Sioux Drive. Raymond Forrest. A handsome man? An ugly man? A man of fifty or sixty, with gray hair, or a man of forty with earnest, courteous eyes, a good golf game; who is Raymond Forrest, this man who is my salvation? Father has been talking to him. Father is not his physician; Dr. Berg is his physician. Father and Dr. Berg refer patients to each other. There is a connection. Mother plays bridge with . . . On Mondays and

204

Wednesdays our maid Billie works at . . . The strings draw together in a cat's cradle, making a net to save you when you fall . . .

3. *Harriet Arnold's.* A small shop, better than Branden's. Mother in her black coat, I in my close-fitted blue coat. Shopping. Now look at this, isn't this cute, do you want this, why don't you want this, try this on, take this with you to the fitting room, take this also, what's wrong with you, what can I do for you, why are you so strange . . . ? "I wanted to steal but not to buy," I don't tell her. The girl droops along in her coat and gloves and leather boots, her eyes scan the horizon, which is pastel pink and decorated like Branden's, tasteful walls and modern ceilings with graceful glimmering lights.

4. Weeks later, the girl at a bus stop. Two o'clock in the afternoon, a Tuesday; obviously she has walked out of school.

5. The girl stepping down from a bus. Afternoon, weather changing to colder. Detroit. Pavement and closed-up stores; grillwork over the windows of a pawnshop. What is a pawnshop, exactly?

II *Characters*

1. The girl stands five feet five inches tall. An ordinary height. Baldwin Country Day School draws them up to that height. She dreams along the corridors and presses her face against the Thermoplex glass. No frost or steam can ever form on that glass. A smudge of grease from her forehead . . . could she be boiled down to grease? She wears her hair loose and long and straight in suburban teen-age style, 1968. Eyes smudged with pencil, dark brown. Brown hair. Vague green eyes. A pretty girl? An ugly girl? She sings to herself under her breath, idling in the corridor, thinking of her many secrets (the thirty dollars she once took from the purse of a friend's mother, just for fun, the basement window she smashed in her own house just for fun) and thinking of her brother who is at Susquehanna Boys' Academy, an excellent preparatory school in Maine, remembering him unclearly . . . he has long manic hair and a squeaking voice and he looks like one of the popular teen-age singers of 1968, one of those in a group, *The Certain Forces, The Way Out, The Maniacs Responsible.* The girl in her turn looks like one of those fieldsful of girls who listen to the boys' singing, dreaming and mooning restlessly, breaking into high sullen laughter, innocently experienced.

2. The mother. A Midwestern woman of Detroit and suburbs. Belongs to the Detroit Athletic Club. Also the Detroit Golf Club. Also the Bloomfield Hills Country Club. The Village Women's Club

at which lectures are given each winter on Genet and Sartre and James Baldwin, by the Director of the Adult Education Program at Wayne State University. . . . The Bloomfield Art Association. Also the Founders Society of the Detroit Institute of Arts. Also . . . Oh, she is in perpetual motion, this lady, hair like blown-up gold and finer than gold, hair and fingers and body of inestimable grace. Heavy weighs the gold on the back of her hairbrush and hand mirror. Heavy heavy the candlesticks in the dining room. Very heavy is the big car, a Lincoln, long and black, that on one cool autumn day split a squirrel's body in two unequal parts.

3. The father. Dr.   . He belongs to the same clubs as #2. A player of squash and golf; he has a golfer's umbrella of stripes. Candy stripes. In his mouth nothing turns to sugar, however; saliva works no miracles here. His doctoring is of the slightly sick. The sick are sent elsewhere (to Dr. Berg?), the deathly sick are sent back for more tests and their bills are sent to their homes, the unsick are sent to Dr. Coronet (Isabel, a lady), an excellent psychiatrist for unsick people who angrily believe they are sick and want to do something about it. If they demand a male psychiatrist, the unsick are sent by Dr.
(my father) to Dr. Lowenstein, a male psychiatrist, excellent and expensive, with a limited practice.

4. Clarita. She is twenty, twenty-five, she is thirty or more? Pretty, ugly, what? She is a woman lounging by the side of a road, in jeans and a sweater, hitchhiking, or she is slouched on a stool at a counter in some roadside diner. A hard line of jaw. Curious eyes. Amused eyes. Behind her eyes processions move, funeral pageants, cartoons. She says, "I never can figure out why girls like you bum around down here. What are you looking for anyway?" An odor of tobacco about her. Unwashed underclothes, or no underclothes, unwashed skin, gritty toes, hair long and falling into strands, not recently washed.

5. Simon. In this city the weather changes abruptly, so Simon's weather changes abruptly. He sleeps through the afternoon. He sleeps through the morning. Rising, he gropes around for something to get him going, for a cigarette or a pill to drive him out to the street, where the temperature is hovering around 35°. Why doesn't it drop? Why, why doesn't the cold clean air come down from Canada; will he have to go up into Canada to get it? will he have to leave the Country of his Birth and sink into Canada's frosty fields . . . ? Will the F.B.I. (which he dreams about constantly) chase him over the Canadian border on foot, hounded out in a blizzard of broken glass and horns . . . ?

"Once I was Huckleberry Finn," Simon says, "but now I am Roderick Usher." Beset by frenzies and fears, this man who makes my spine go cold, he takes green pills, yellow pills, pills of white and capsules of dark blue and green . . . he takes other things I may not mention, for what if Simon seeks me out and climbs into my girl's bedroom here in Bloomfield Hills and strangles me, what then . . . ? (As I write this I begin to shiver. Why do I shiver? I am now sixteen and sixteen is not an age for shivering.) It comes from Simon, who is always cold.

III *World Events*

Nothing.

IV *People & Circumstances Contributing to This Delinquency*

Nothing.

V *Sioux Drive*

George, Clyde G. 240 Sioux. A manufacturer's representative; children, a dog, a wife. Georgian with the usual columns. You think of the White House, then of Thomas Jefferson, then your mind goes blank on the white pillars and you think of nothing. Norris, Ralph W. 246 Sioux. Public relations. Colonial. Bay window, brick, stone, concrete, wood, green shutters, sidewalk, lantern, grass, trees, blacktop drive, two children, one of them my classmate Esther (Esther Norris) at Baldwin. Wife, cars. Ramsey, Michael D. 250 Sioux. Colonial. Big living room, thirty by twenty-five, fireplaces in living room, library, recreation room, paneled walls wet bar five bathrooms five bedrooms two lavatories central air conditioning automatic sprinkler automatic garage door three children one wife two cars a breakfast room a patio a larged fenced lot fourteen trees a front door with a brass knocker never knocked. Next is our house. Classic contemporary. Traditional modern. Attached garage, attached Florida room, attached patio, attached pool and cabana, attached roof. A front door mail slot through which pour *Time Magazine, Fortune, Life, Business Week,* the *Wall Street Journal,* the *New York Times,* the *New Yorker,* the *Saturday Review, M.D., Modern Medicine, Disease of the Month* . . . and also. . . . And in addition to all this, a quiet sealed letter from Baldwin saying: *Your daughter is not doing work compatible with her performance on the Stanford-Binet.* . . . And your son is not doing well, not well at all, very sad. Where is your son anyway? Once he stole trick-and-treat candy from

some six-year-old kids, he himself being a robust ten. The beginning.
Now your daughter steals. In the Village Pharmacy she made off
with, yes she did, don't deny it, she made off with a copy of *Pageant
Magazine* for no reason, she swiped a roll of Life Savers in a green
wrapper and was in no need of saving her life or even in need of
sucking candy; when she was no more than eight years old she stole,
don't blush, she stole a package of Tums only because it was out on
the counter and available, and the nice lady behind the counter
(now dead) said nothing. . . . Sioux Drive. Maples, oaks, elms.
Diseased elms cut down. Sioux Drive runs into Roosevelt Drive. Slow,
turning lanes, not streets, all drives and lanes and ways and passes. A
private police force. Quiet private police, in unmarked cars. Cruising
on Saturday evenings with paternal smiles for the residents who are
streaming in and out of houses, going to and from parties, a thousand parties, slightly staggering, the women in their furs alighting
from automobiles bought of Ford and General Motors and Chrysler,
very heavy automobiles. No foreign cars. Detroit. In 275 Sioux, down
the block in that magnificent French-Normandy mansion, lives
————————— himself, who has the C————— account itself, imagine
that! Look at where he lives and look at the enormous trees and
chimneys, imagine his many fireplaces, imagine his wife and children,
imagine his wife's hair, imagine her fingernails, imagine her bathtub
of smooth clean glowing pink, imagine their embraces, his trouser
pockets filled with odd coins and keys and dust and peanuts, imagine
their ecstasy on Sioux Drive, imagine their income tax returns,
imagine their little boy's pride in his experimental car, a scaled-down
C—————, as he roars around the neighborhood on the sidewalks
frightening dogs and Negro maids, oh imagine all these things,
imagine everything, let your mind roar out all over Sioux Drive and
Du Maurier Drive and Roosevelt Drive and Ticonderoga Pass and
Burning Bush Way and Lincolnshire Pass and Lois Lane.

When spring comes, its winds blow nothing to Sioux Drive, no
odors of hollyhocks or forsythia, nothing Sioux Drive doesn't already
possess, everything is planted and performing. The weather vanes,
had they weather vanes, don't have to turn with the wind, don't have
to contend with the weather. There is no weather.

VI *Detroit*

There is always weather in Detroit. Detroit's temperature is always
32°. Fast-falling temperatures. Slow-rising temperatures. Wind from
the north-northeast four to forty miles an hour, small-craft warnings,
partly cloudy today and Wednesday changing to partly sunny
through Thursday . . . small warnings of frost, soot warnings, traffic

warnings, hazardous lake conditions for small craft and swimmers, restless Negro gangs, restless cloud formations, restless temperatures aching to fall out the very bottom of the thermometer or shoot up over the top and boil everything over in red mercury.

Detroit's temperature is 32°. Fast-falling temperatures. Slow-rising temperatures. Wind from the north-northeast four to forty miles an hour. . . .

VII *Events*

1. The girl's heart is pounding. In her pocket is a pair of gloves! In a plastic bag! Airproof breathproof plastic bag, gloves selling for twenty-five dollars on Branden's counter! In her pocket! Shoplifted! . . . In her purse is a blue comb, not very clean. In her purse is a leather billfold (a birthday present from her grandmother in Philadelphia) with snapshots of the family in clean plastic windows, in the billfold are bills, she doesn't know how many bills. . . . In her purse is an ominous note from her friend Tykie *What's this about Joe H. and the kids hanging around at Louise's Sat. night? You heard anything?* . . . passed in French class. In her purse is a lot of dirty yellow Kleenex, her mother's heart would break to see such very dirty Kleenex, and at the bottom of her purse are brown hairpins and safety pins and a broken pencil and a ballpoint pen (blue) stolen from somewhere forgotten and a purse-size compact of Cover Girl Make-Up, Ivory Rose. . . . Her lipstick is Broken Heart, a corrupt pink; her fingers are trembling like crazy; her teeth are beginning to chatter; her insides are alive; her eyes glow in her head; she is saying to her mother's astonished face *I want to steal but not to buy.*

2. At Clarita's. Day or night? What room is this? A bed, a regular bed, and a mattress on the floor nearby. Wallpaper hanging in strips. Clarita says she tore it like that with her teeth. She was fighting a barbaric tribe that night, high from some pills; she was battling for her life with men wearing helmets of heavy iron and their faces no more than Christian crosses to breathe through, every one of those bastards looking like her lover Simon, who seems to breathe with great difficulty through the slits of mouth and nostrils in his face. Clarita has never heard of Sioux Drive. Raymond Forrest cuts no ice with her, nor does the C   account and its millions; Harvard Business School could be at the corner of Vernor and 12th Street for all she cares, and Vietnam might have sunk by now into the Dead Sea under its tons of debris, for all the amazement she could show . . . her face is overworked, overwrought, at the age of twenty

(thirty?) it is already exhausted but fanciful and ready for a laugh. Clarita says mournfully to me *Honey somebody is going to turn you out let me give you warning.* In a movie shown on late television Clarita is not a mess like this but a nurse, with short neat hair and a dedicated look, in love with her doctor and her doctor's patients and their diseases, enamored of needles and sponges and rubbing alcohol. . . . Or no: she is a private secretary. Robert Cummings is her boss. She helps him with fantastic plots, the canned audience laughs, no, the audience doesn't laugh because nothing is funny, instead her boss is Robert Taylor and they are not boss and secretary but husband and wife, she is threatened by a young starlet, she is grim, handsome, wifely, a good companion for a good man. . . . She is Claudette Colbert. Her sister too is Claudette Colbert. They are twins, identical. Her husband Charles Boyer is a very rich handsome man and her sister, Claudette Colbert, is plotting her death in order to take her place as the rich man's wife, no one will know because they are *twins.* . . . All these marvelous lives Clarita might have lived, but she fell out the bottom at the age of thirteen. At the age when I was packing my overnight case for a slumber party at Toni Deshield's she was tearing filthy sheets off a bed and scratching up a rash on her arms. . . . Thirteen is uncommonly young for a white girl in Detroit, Miss Brock of the Detroit House of Correction said in a sad newspaper interview for the *Detroit News;* fifteen and sixteen are more likely. Eleven, twelve, thirteen are not surprising in colored . . . they are more precocious. What can we do? Taxes are rising and the tax base is falling. The temperature rises slowly but falls rapidly. Everything is falling out the bottom, Woodward Avenue is filthy, Livernois Avenue is filthy! Scraps of paper flutter in the air like pigeons, dirt flies up and hits you right in the eye, oh Detroit is breaking up into dangerous bits of newspaper and dirt, watch out. . . .

Clarita's apartment is over a restaurant. Simon her lover emerges from the cracks at dark. Mrs. Olesko, a neighbor of Clarita's, an aged white wisp of a woman, doesn't complain but sniffs with contentment at Clarita's noisy life and doesn't tell the cops, hating cops, when the cops arrive. I should give more fake names, more blanks, instead of telling all these secrets. I myself am a secret; I am a minor.

3. My father reads a paper at a medical convention in Los Angeles. There he is, on the edge of the North American continent, when the unmarked detective put his hand so gently on my arm in the aisle of Branden's and said, "Miss, would you like to step over here for a minute?"

And where was he when Clarita put her hand on my arm, that wintry dark sulphurous aching day in Detroit, in the company of closed-down barber shops, closed-down diners, closed-down movie houses, homes, windows, basements, faces . . . she put her hand on my arm and said, "Honey, are you looking for somebody down here?"

And was he home worrying about me, gone for two weeks solid, when they carried me off . . . ? It took three of them to get me in the police cruiser, so they said, and they put more than their hands on my arm.

4. I work on this lesson. My English teacher is Mr. Forest, who is from Michigan State. Not handsome, Mr. Forest, and his name is plain, unlike Raymond Forrest's, but he is sweet and rodentlike, he has conferred with the principal and my parents, and everything is fixed . . . treat her as if nothing has happened, a new start, begin again, only sixteen years old, what a shame, how did it happen?— nothing happened, nothing could have happened, a slight physiological modification known only to a gynecologist or to Dr. Coronet. I work on my lesson. I sit in my pink room. I look around the room with my sad pink eyes. I sigh, I dawdle, I pause, I eat up time, I am limp and happy to be home, I am sixteen years old suddenly, my head hangs heavy as a pumpkin on my shoulders, and my hair has just been cut by Mr. Faye at the Crystal Salon and is said to be very becoming.

(Simon too put his hand on my arm and said, "Honey, you have got to come with me," and in his six-by-six room we got to know each other. Would I go back to Simon again? Would I lie down with him in all that filth and craziness? Over and over again.

a Clarita is being betrayed as in front of a Cunningham Drug Store she is nervously eying a colored man who may or may not have money, or a nervous white boy of twenty with sideburns and an Appalachian look, who may or may not have a knife hidden in his jacket pocket, or a husky red-faced man of friendly countenance who may or may not be a member of the Vice Squad out for an early twilight walk.)

I work on my lesson for Mr. Forest. I have filled up eleven pages. Words pour out of me and won't stop. I want to tell everything . . . what was the song Simon was always humming, and who was Simon's friend in a very new trench coat with an old high school graduation ring on his finger . . . ? Simon's bearded friend? When I was down too low for him, Simon kicked me out and gave me to him for three days, I think, on Fourteenth Street in Detroit, an airy room of cold cruel drafts with newspapers on the floor. . . . Do I really remember that or am I piecing it together from what they told me? Did they tell the truth? Did they know much of the truth?

VIII *Characters*

1. Wednesdays after school, at four; Saturday mornings at ten. Mother drives me to Dr. Coronet. Ferns in the office, plastic or real, they look the same. Dr. Coronet is queenly, an elegant nicotine-stained lady who would have studied with Freud had circumstances not prevented it, a bit of a Catholic, ready to offer you some mystery if your teeth will ache too much without it. Highly recommended by Father! Forty dollars an hour, Father's forty dollars! Progress! Looking up! Looking better! That new haircut is so becoming, says Dr. Coronet herself, showing how normal she is for a woman with an I.Q. of 180 and many advanced degrees.

2. Mother. A lady in a brown suede coat. Boots of shiny black material, black gloves, a black fur hat. She would be humiliated could she know that of all the people in the world it is my ex-lover Simon who walks most like her . . . self-conscious and unreal, listening to distant music, a little bowlegged with craftiness. . . .

3. Father. Tying a necktie. In a hurry. On my first evening home he put his hand on my arm and said, "Honey, we're going to forget all about this."

4. Simon. Outside, a plane is crossing the sky, in here we're in a hurry. Morning. It must be morning. The girl is half out of her mind, whimpering and vague; Simon her dear friend is wretched this morning . . . he is wretched with morning itself . . . he forces her to give him an injection with that needle she knows is filthy, she has a dread of needles and surgical instruments and the odor of things that are to be sent into the blood, thinking somehow of her father. . . . This is a bad morning, Simon says that his mind is being twisted out of shape, and so he submits to the needle that he usually scorns and bites his lip with his yellowish teeth, his face going very pale. *Ah baby!* he says in his soft mocking voice, which with all women is a mockery of love, *do it like this—Slowly—*And the girl, terrified, almost drops the precious needle but manages to turn it up to the light from the window . . . is it an extension of herself then? She can give him this gift then? *I wish you wouldn't do this to me,* she says, wise in her terror, because it seems to her that Simon's danger—in a few minutes he may be dead—is a way of pressing her

against him that is more powerful than any other embrace. She has to
work over his arm, the knotted corded veins of his arm, her forehead
wet with perspiration as she pushes and releases the needle, staring at
that mixture of liquid now stained with Simon's bright blood. . . .
When the drug hits him she can feel it herself, she feels that magic
that is more than any woman can give him, striking the back of his
head and making his face stretch as if with the impact of a terrible
sun. . . . She tries to embrace him but he pushes her aside and
stumbles to his feet. *Jesus Christ,* he says. . . .

5. Princess, a Negro girl of eighteen. What is her charge? She is
closed-mouthed about it, shrewd and silent, you know that no one
had to wrestle her to the sidewalk to get her in here; she came with
dignity. In the recreation room she sits reading *Nancy Drew and the
Jewel Box Mystery,* which inspires in her face tiny wrinkles of alarm
and interest: what a face! Light brown skin, heavy shaded eyes, heavy
eyelashes, a serious sinister dark brow, graceful fingers, graceful wrist-
bones, graceful legs, lips, tongue, a sugar-sweet voice, a leggy stride
more masculine than Simon's and my mother's, decked out in a dirty
white blouse and dirty white slacks; vaguely nautical is Princess'
style. . . . At breakfast she is in charge of clearing the table and
leans over me, saying, *Honey you sure you ate enough?*

6. The girl lies sleepless, wondering. Why here, why not there?
Why Bloomfield Hills and not jail? Why jail and not her pink
room? Why downtown Detroit and not Sioux Drive? What is the
difference? Is Simon all the difference? The girl's head is a parade of
wonders. She is nearly sixteen, her breath is marvelous with wonders,
not long ago she was coloring with crayons and now she is smearing
the landscape with paints that won't come off and won't come off her
fingers either. She says to the matron *I am not talking about anything,* not because everyone has warned her not to talk but because,
because she will not talk; because she won't say anything about
Simon, who is her secret. And she says to the matron, *I won't go
home,* up until that night in the lavatory when everything was
changed. . . . "No, I won't go home I want to stay here," she says,
listening to her own words with amazement, thinking that weeds
might climb everywhere over that marvelous $180,000 house and
dinosaurs might return to muddy the beige carpeting, but never
never will she reconcile four o'clock in the morning in Detroit with
eight o'clock breakfasts in Bloomfield Hills. . . . oh, she aches still
for Simon's hands and his caressing breath, though he gave her little
pleasure, he took everything from her (five-dollar bills, ten-dollar
bills, passed into her numb hands by men and taken out of her hands
by Simon) until she herself was passed into the hands of other men,

police, when Simon evidently got tired of her and her hysteria. . . .
No, I won't go home, I don't want to be bailed out. The girl thinks
as a *Stubborn and Wayward Child* (one of several charges lodged
against her), and the matron understands her crazy white-rimmed
eyes that are seeking out some new violence that will keep her in jail,
should someone threaten to let her out. Such children try to strangle
the matrons, the attendants, or one another . . . they want the locks
locked forever, the doors nailed shut . . . and this girl is no different
up until that night her mind is changed for her. . . .

IX *That Night*

Princess and Dolly, a little white girl of maybe fifteen, hardy
however as a sergeant and in the House of Correction for armed
robbery, corner her in the lavatory at the farthest sink and the other
girls look away and file out to bed, leaving her. God, how she is
beaten up! Why is she beaten up? Why do they pound her, why such
hatred? Princess vents all the hatred of a thousand silent Detroit
winters on her body, this girl whose body belongs to me, fiercely she
rides across the Midwestern plains on this girl's tender bruised body
. . . revenge on the oppressed minorities of America! revenge on
the slaughtered Indians! revenge on the female sex, on the male sex,
revenge on Bloomfield Hills, revenge revenge. . . .

X *Detroit*

In Detroit, weather weighs heavily upon everyone. The sky looms
large. The horizon shimmers in smoke. Downtown the buildings are
imprecise in the haze. Perpetual haze. Perpetual motion inside the
haze. Across the choppy river is the city of Windsor, in Canada. Part
of the continent has bunched up here and is bulging outward, at the
tip of Detroit; a cold hard rain is forever falling on the expressways.
. . . Shoppers shop grimly, their cars are not parked in safe places,
their windshields may be smashed and graceful ebony hands may
drag them out through their shatterproof smashed windshields, crying, *Revenge for the Indians!* Ah, they all fear leaving Hudson's and
being dragged to the very tip of the city and thrown off the parking
roof of Cobo Hall, that expensive tomb, into the river. . . .

XI *Characters We Are*
Forever Entwined With

1. Simon drew me into his tender rotting arms and breathed
gravity into me. Then I came to earth, weighed down. He said, *You
are such a little girl,* and he weighed me down with his delight. In

the palms of his hands were teeth marks from his previous life experiences. He was thirty-five, they said. Imagine Simon in this room, in my pink room: he is about six feet tall and stoops slightly, in a feline cautious way, always thinking, always on guard, with his scuffed light suede shoes and his clothes that are anyone's clothes, slightly rumpled ordinary clothes that ordinary men might wear to not-bad jobs. Simon has fair long hair, curly hair, spent languid curls that are like . . . exactly like the curls of wood shavings to the touch, I am trying to be exact . . . and he smells of unheated mornings and coffee and too many pills coating his tongue with a faint green-white scum. . . . Dear Simon, who would be panicked in this room and in this house (right now Billie is vacuuming next door in my parents' room; a vacuum cleaner's roar is a sign of all good things), Simon who is said to have come from a home not much different from this, years ago, fleeing all the carpeting and the polished banisters . . . Simon has a deathly face, only desperate people fall in love with it. His face is bony and cautious, the bones of his cheeks prominent as if with the rigidity of his ceaseless thinking, plotting, for he has to make money out of girls to whom money means nothing, they're so far gone they can hardly count it, and in a sense money means nothing to him either except as a way of keeping on with his life. *Each Day's Proud Struggle,* the title of a novel we could read at jail. . . . Each day he needs a certain amount of money. He devours it. It wasn't love he uncoiled in me with his hollowed-out eyes and his courteous smile, that remnant of a prosperous past, but a dark terror that needed to press itself flat against him, or against another man . . . but he was the first, he came over to me and took my arm, a claim. We struggled on the stairs and I said, *Let me loose, you're hurting my neck, my face,* it was such a surprise that my skin hurt where he rubbed it, and afterward we lay face to face and he breathed everything into me. In the end I think he turned me in.

2. Raymond Forrest. I just read this morning that Raymond Forrest's father, the chairman of the board at   , died of a heart attack on a plane bound for London. I would like to write Raymond Forrest a note of sympathy. I would like to thank him for not pressing charges against me one hundred years ago, saving me, being so generous . . . well, men like Raymond Forrest are generous men, not like Simon. I would like to write him a letter telling of my love, or of some other emotion that is positive and healthy. Not like Simon and his poetry, which he scrawled down when he was high and never changed a word . . . but when I try to think of something to say, it is Simon's language that comes back to me, caught in my head like a bad song, it is always Simon's language:

There is no reality only dreams
Your neck may get snapped when you wake
My love is drawn to some violent end
She keeps wanting to get away
My love is heading downward
And I am heading upward
She is going to crash on the sidewalk
And I am going to dissolve into the clouds

XII *Events*

1. Out of the hospital, bruised and saddened and converted, with Princess' grunts still tangled in my hair . . . and Father in his overcoat looking like a prince himself, come to carry me off. Up the expressway and out north to home. Jesus Christ, but the air is thinner and cleaner here. Monumental houses. Heartbreaking sidewalks, so clean.

2. Weeping in the living room. The ceiling is two stories high and two chandeliers hang from it. Weeping, weeping, though Billie the maid is *probably listening*. I will never leave home again. Never. Never leave home. Never leave this home again, never.

3. Sugar doughnuts for breakfast. The toaster is very shiny and my face is distorted in it. Is that my face?

4. The car is turning in the driveway. Father brings me home. Mother embraces me. Sunlight breaks in movieland patches on the roof of our traditional-contemporary home, which was designed for the famous automotive stylist whose identity, if I told you the name of the famous car he designed, you would all know, so I can't tell you because my teeth chatter at the thought of being sued . . . or having someone climb into my bedroom window with a rope to strangle me. . . . The car turns up the blacktop drive. The house opens to me like a doll's house, so lovely in the sunlight, the big living room beckons to me with its walls falling away in a delirium of joy at my return, Billie the maid is *no doubt* listening from the kitchen as I burst into tears and the hysteria Simon got so sick of. Convulsed in Father's arms, I say I will never leave again, never, why did I leave, where did I go, what happened, my mind is gone wrong, my body is one big bruise, my backbone was sucked dry, it wasn't the men who hurt me and Simon never hurt me but only those girls . . . my God, how they hurt me . . . I will never leave home again. . . . The car is perpetually turning up the drive and I am perpetually breaking down in the living room and we are perpetually taking the right exit from the expressway (Lahser Road) and the wall of the rest room is

perpetually banging against my head and perpetually are Simon's hands moving across my body and adding everything up and so too are Father's hands on my shaking bruised back, far from the surface of my skin on the surface of my good blue cashmere coat (dry-cleaned for my release) . . . . I weep for all the money here, for God in gold and beige carpeting, for the beauty of chandeliers and the miracle of a clean polished gleaming toaster and faucets that run both hot and cold water, and I tell them, *I will never leave home, this is my home, I love everything here, I am in love with everything here.* . . .

I am home.

QUESTIONS

1. In "Help Her to Believe" and "How I Comtemplated the World," an external demand sets the narrators thinking. What results does the thinking produce for each of them? Do the narrators seem to have gained anything? Is there any sense of peace or resolution at the stories' ends?
2. How do you react to the narrators' efforts to piece together their pasts? What do you foresee in their futures?

AN ANTHOLOGY OF
SHORT STORIES

EDGAR ALLAN POE (1809–1849)

The Fall of the House of Usher

Son coeur est un luth suspendu;
Sitôt qu'on le touche il résonne.

DE BÉRANGER

During the whole of a dull, dark, and soundless day in the autumn of the year, when the clouds hung oppressively low in the heavens, I had been passing alone, on horseback, through a singularly dreary tract of country; and at length found myself, as the shades of the evening drew on, within view of the melancholy House of Usher. I knew not how it was—but, with the first glimpse of the building, a sense of insufferable gloom pervaded my spirit. I say insufferable; for the feeling was unrelieved by any of that half-pleasurable, because poetic, sentiment with which the mind usually receives even the sternest natural images of the desolate or terrible. I looked upon the scene before me—upon the mere house, and the simple landscape features of the domain, upon the bleak walls, upon the vacant eye-like windows, upon a few rank sedges, and upon a few white trunks of decayed trees—with an utter depression of soul which I can compare to no earthly sensation more properly than to the after-dream of the reveler upon opium; the bitter lapse into everyday life, the hideous dropping off of the veil. There was an iciness, a sinking, a sickening of the heart, an unredeemed dreariness of thought which no goading of the imagination could torture into aught of the sublime. What was it—I paused to think—what was it that so un-nerved me in the contemplation of the House of Usher? It was a mystery all insoluble; nor could I grapple with the shadowy fancies that crowded upon me as I pondered. I was forced to fall back upon the unsatisfactory conclusion, that while, beyond doubt, there *are* combinations of very simple natural objects which have the power of

thus affecting us, still the analysis of this power lies among considerations beyond our depth. It was possible, I reflected, that a mere
different arrangement of the particulars of the scene, of the details of
the picture, would be sufficient to modify, or perhaps to annihilate,
its capacity for sorrowful impression; and, acting upon this idea, I
reined my horse to the precipitous brink of a black and lurid tarn
that lay in unruffled luster by the dwelling, and gazed down—but
with a shudder even more thrilling than before—upon the re-
modeled and inverted images of the gray sedge, and the ghastly tree
stems, and the vacant and eye-like windows.

Nevertheless, in this mansion of gloom I now proposed to myself a
sojourn of some weeks. Its proprietor, Roderick Usher, had been one
of my boon companions in boyhood; but many years had elapsed
since our last meeting. A letter, however, had lately reached me in a
distant part of the country—a letter from him—which in its wildly
importunate nature had admitted of no other than a personal reply.
The MS. gave evidence of nervous agitation. The writer spoke of
acute bodily illness, of a mental disorder which oppressed him, and
of an earnest desire to see me, as his best and indeed his only
personal friend, with a view of attempting, by the cheerfulness of my
society, some alleviation of his malady. It was the manner in which
all this, and much more, was said—it was the apparent *heart* that
went with his request—which allowed me no room for hesitation;
and I accordingly obeyed forthwith what I still considered a very
singular summons.

Although as boys we had been even intimate associates, yet I really
knew little of my friend. His reserve had been always excessive and
habitual. I was aware, however, that his very ancient family had been
noted, time out of mind, for a peculiar sensibility of temperament,
displaying itself, through long ages, in many works of exalted art,
and manifested of late in repeated deeds of munificent yet unobtru-
sive charity, as well as in a passionate devotion of the intricacies,
perhaps even more than to the orthodox and easily recognizable
beauties, of musical science. I had learned, too, the very remarkable
fact that the stem of the Usher race, all time-honored as it was, had
put forth at no period any enduring branch; in other words, that the
entire family lay in the direct line of descent, and had always, with
very trifling and very temporary variation, so lain. It was this
deficiency, I considered, while running over in thought the perfect
keeping of the character of the premises with the accredited character
of the people, and while speculating upon the possible influence
which the one, in the long lapse of centuries, might have exercised
upon the other—it was this deficiency, perhaps, of collateral issue,
and the consequent undeviating transmission from sire to son of the
patrimony with the name, which had, at length, so identified the two

as to merge the original title of the estate in the quaint and equivocal appellation of the "House of Usher"—an appellation which seemed to include, in the minds of the peasantry who used it, both the family and the family mansion.

I have said that the sole effect of my somewhat childish experiment, that of looking down within the tarn, had been to deepen the first singular impression. There can be no doubt that the consciousness of the rapid increase of my superstition—for why should I not so term it?—served mainly to accelerate the increase itself. Such, I have long known, is the paradoxical law of all sentiments having terror as a basis. And it might have been for this reason only, that, when I again uplifted my eyes to the house itself, from its image in the pool, there grew in my mind a strange fancy—a fancy so ridiculous, indeed, that I but mention it to show the vivid force of the sensations which oppressed me. I had so worked upon my imagination as really to believe that about the whole mansion and domain there hung an atmosphere peculiar to themselves and their immediate vicinity: an atmosphere which had no affinity with the air of heaven, but which had reeked up from the decayed trees, and the gray wall, and the silent tarn: a pestilent and mystic vapor, dull, sluggish, faintly discernible, and leaden-hued.

Shaking off from my spirit what *must* have been a dream, I scanned more narrowly the real aspect of the building. Its principal feature seemed to be that of an excessive antiquity. The discoloration of ages had been great. Minute fungi overspread the whole exterior, hanging in a fine tangled webwork from the eaves. Yet all this was apart from any extraordinary dilapidation. No portion of the masonry had fallen; and there appeared to be a wild inconsistency between its still perfect adaptation of parts and the crumbling condition of the individual stones. In this there was much that reminded me of the specious totality of old woodwork which has rotted for long years in some neglected vault, with no disturbance from the breath of the external air. Beyond this indication of excessive decay, however, the fabric gave little token of instability. Perhaps the eye of a scrutinizing observer might have discovered a barely perceptible fissure, which, extending from the roof of the building in front, made its way down the wall in a zigzag direction, until it became lost in the sullen waters of the tarn.

Noticing these things, I rode over a short causeway to the house. A servant in waiting took my horse, and I entered the Gothic archway of the hall. A valet, of stealthy step, thence conducted me, in silence, through many dark and intricate passages in my progress to the studio of his master. Much that I encountered on the way contributed, I know not how, to heighten the vague sentiments of which I have already spoken. While the objects around me—while the carvings of the ceilings, the somber tapestries of the walls, the ebon blackness of the floors, and the phantasmagoric armorial trophies which rattled as I strode, were but matters to which, or to such as which, I had been accustomed from my infancy—while I hesitated not to acknowledge how familiar was all this—I still wondered to find how unfamiliar were the fancies which ordinary images were stirring up. On one of the staircases, I met the physician of the family. His countenance, I thought, wore a mingled expression of low cunning and perplexity. He accosted me with trepidation and passed on. The valet now threw open a door and ushered me into the presence of his master.

The room in which I found myself was very large and lofty. The windows were long, narrow, and pointed, and at so vast a distance from the black oaken floor as to be altogether inaccessible from within. Feeble gleams of encrimsoned light made their way through the trellised panes, and served to render sufficiently distinct the more prominent objects around; the eye, however, struggled in vain to reach the remoter angles of the chamber, or the recesses of the vaulted and fretted ceiling. Dark draperies hung upon the walls. The general furniture was profuse, comfortless, antique, and tattered. Many books and musical instruments lay scattered about, but failed to give any vitality to the scene. I felt that I breathed an atmosphere of sorrow. An air of stern, deep, and irredeemable gloom hung over and pervaded all.

Upon my entrance, Usher arose from a sofa on which he had been lying at full length, and greeted me with a vivacious warmth which had much in it, I at first thought, of an overdone cordiality—of the constrained effort of the *ennuyé* man of the world. A glance, however, at his countenance, convinced me of his perfect sincerity. We sat down; and for some moments, while he spoke not, I gazed upon him with a feeling half of pity, half of awe. Surely man had never before so terribly altered in so brief a period as had Roderick Usher! It was with difficulty that I could bring myself to admit the identity of the wan being before me with the companion of my boyhood. Yet the character of his face had been at all times remarkable. A cadaverousness of complexion; an eye large, liquid, and luminous beyond comparison; lips somewhat thin and very pallid, but of a surpassingly beautiful curve; a nose of a delicate Hebrew model, but with a breadth of nostril unusual in similar formations; a finely molded chin, speaking, in its want of prominence, of a want of moral energy; hair of a more than weblike softness and tenuity; these features, with an inordinate expansion above the regions of the temple, made up altogether a countenance not easily to be forgotten. And now in the mere exaggeration of the prevailing character of these features, and of the expression they were wont to convey, lay so much of change that I doubted to whom I spoke. The now ghostly pallor of the skin, and the now miraculous luster of the eye, above all things startled and even awed me. The silken hair, too, had been suffered to grow all unheeded, and as, in its wild gossamer texture, it floated rather than fell about the face, I could not, even with effort, connect its arabesque expression with any idea of simple humanity.

In the manner of my friend I was at once struck with an incoherence, an inconsistency; and I soon found this to arise from a series of feeble and futile struggles to overcome an habitual trepidancy, an excessive nervous agitation. For something of this nature I had indeed been prepared, no less by his letter than by reminiscences of certain boyish traits, and by conclusions deduced from his peculiar physical conformation and temperament. His action was alternatively vivacious and sullen. His voice varied rapidly from a tremulous indecision (when the animal spirits seemed utterly in abeyance) to that species of energetic concision—that abrupt, weighty, unhurried, and hollow-sounding enunciation—that leaden, self-balanced and perfectly modulated guttural utterance—which may be observed in the lost drunkard, or the irreclaimable eater of opium, during the periods of his most intense excitement.

It was thus that he spoke of the object of my visit, of his earnest desire to see me, and of the solace he expected me to afford him. He entered, at some length, into what he conceived to be the nature of his malady. It was, he said, a constitutional and a family evil, and one for which he despaired to find a remedy—a mere nervous affection, he immediately added, which would undoubtedly soon pass off. It displayed itself in a host of unnatural sensations. Some of these, as he detailed them, interested and bewildered me: although, perhaps, the terms and the general manner of the narration had their weight. He suffered much from a morbid acuteness of the senses; the most insipid food was alone endurable; he could wear only garments of a certain texture; the odors of all flowers were oppressive; his eyes were tortured by even a faint light; and there were but peculiar sounds, and these from stringed instruments, which did not inspire him with horror.

To an anomalous species of terror I found him a bounden slave. "I shall perish," said he, "I *must* perish in this deplorable folly. Thus, thus, and not otherwise, shall I be lost. I dread the events of the future, not in themselves, but in their results. I shudder at the thought of any, even the most trivial, incident, which may operate upon this intolerable agitation of soul. I have, indeed, no abhorrence of danger, except in its absolute effect—in terror. In this unnerved—in this pitiable condition—I feel that the period will sooner or later arrive when I must abandon life and reason together, in some struggle with the grim phantasm, FEAR."

I learned moreover at intervals, and through broken and equivocal hints, another singular feature of his mental condition. He was enchained by certain superstitious impressions in regard to the dwelling which he tenanted, and whence, for many years, he had never ventured forth—in regard to an influence whose supposititious force was conveyed in terms too shadowy here to be restated—an influence which some peculiarities in the mere form and substance of his family mansion, had, by dint of long sufferance, he said, obtained over his spirit—an effect which the physique of the gray walls and turrets, and of the dim tarn into which they all looked down, had, at length, brought about upon the morale of his existence.

He admitted, however, although with hesitation, that much of the peculiar gloom which thus afflicted him could be traced to a more natural and far more palpable origin—to the severe and long-continued illness, indeed to the evidently approaching dissolution, of a tenderly beloved sister—his sole companion for long years, his last and only relative on earth. "Her decease," he said, with a bitterness which I can never forget, "would leave him (him the hopeless and the frail) the last of the ancient race of the Ushers." While he spoke, the lady Madeline (for so was she called) passed slowly through a remote portion of the apartment, and, without having noticed my presence, disappeared. I regarded her with an utter astonishment not unmingled with dread, and yet I found it impossible to account for such feelings. A sensation of stupor oppressed me, as my eyes followed her retreating steps. When a door, at length, closed upon her, my glance sought instinctively and eagerly the countenance of the brother, but he had buried his face in his hands, and I could only perceive that a far more than ordinary wanness had overspread the emaciated fingers through which trickled many passionate tears.

The disease of the lady Madeline had long baffled the skill of her physicians. A settled apathy, a gradual wasting away of the person, and frequent although transient affections of a partially cataleptical character, were the unusual diagnosis. Hitherto she had steadily borne up against the pressure of her malady, and had not betaken herself finally to bed; but, on the closing in of the evening of my arrival at the house, she succumbed (as her brother told me at night with inexpressible agitation) to the prostrating power of the destroyer; and I learned that the glimpse I had obtained of her person would thus probably be the last I should obtain—that the lady, at least while living, would be seen by me no more.

For several days ensuing, her name was unmentioned by either Usher or myself; and during this period I was busied in earnest endeavors to alleviate the melancholy of my friend. We painted and read together; or I listened, as if in a dream, to the wild improvisation of his speaking guitar. And thus, as a closer and still closer intimacy admitted me more unreservedly into the recesses of his spirit, the more bitterly did I perceive the futility of all attempt at cheering a mind from which darkness, as if an inherent positive quality, poured forth upon all objects of the moral and physical universe, in one unceasing radiation of gloom.

I shall ever bear about me a memory of the many solemn hours I thus spent alone with the master of the House of Usher. Yet I should fail in any attempt to convey an idea of the exact character of the studies, or of the occupations, in which he involved me, or led me the way. An excited and highly distempered ideality threw a sulphurous luster over all. His long improvised dirges will ring forever in my ears. Among other things, I hold painfully in mind a certain singular perversion and amplification of the wild air of the last waltz of Von Weber. From the paintings over which his elaborate fancy brooded, and which grew, touch by touch, into vagueness at which I shuddered the more thrillingly because I shuddered knowing not why;—from these paintings (vivid as their images now are before me) I would in vain endeavor to educe more than a small portion which should lie within the compass of merely written words. By the utter simplicity, by the nakedness of his designs, he arrested and overawed attention. If ever mortal painted an idea, that mortal was Roderick Usher. For me at least, in the circumstances then surrounding me, there arose, out of the pure abstractions which the hypochondriac contrived to throw upon his canvas, an intensity of intolerable awe, no shadow of which felt I ever yet in the contemplation of the certainly glowing yet too concrete reveries of Fuseli.

One of the phantasmagoric conceptions of my friend, partaking not so rigidly of the spirit of abstraction, may be shadowed forth, although feebly, in words. A small picture presented the interior of an immensely long and rectangular vault or tunnel, with low walls, smooth, white, and without interruption or device. Certain accessory points of the design served well to convey the idea that this excavation lay at an exceeding depth below the surface of the earth. No outlet was observed in any portion of its vast extent, and no torch or other artificial source of light was discernible; yet a flood of intense rays rolled throughout, and bathed the whole in a ghastly and inappropriate splendor.

I have just spoken of that morbid condition of the auditory nerve which rendered all music intolerable to the sufferer, with the exception of certain effects of stringed instruments. It was, perhaps, the narrow limits to which he thus confined himself upon the guitar, which gave birth, in great measure, to the fantastic character of his performances. But the fervid *facility* of his *impromptus* could not be so accounted for. They must have been, and were, in the notes, as well as in the words of his wild fantasias (for he not unfrequently accompanied himself with rhymed verbal improvisations), the result of that intense mental collectedness and concentration to which I have previously alluded as observable only in particular moments of the highest artificial excitement. The words of one of these rhapsodies I have easily remembered. I was, perhaps, the more forcibly impressed with it, as he gave it, because, in the under or mystic current of its meaning, I fancied that I perceived, and for the first time, a full consciousness, on the part of Usher, of the tottering of his lofty reason upon her throne. The verses, which were entitled "The Haunted Palace," ran very nearly, if not accurately, thus:

I

In the greenest of our valleys,
    By good angels tenanted,
Once a fair and stately palace—
    Radiant palace—reared its head.
In the monarch Thought's dominion,
    It stood there!
Never seraph spread a pinion
    Over fabric half so fair.

II

Banners yellow, glorious, golden,
    On its roof did float and flow,
(This—all this—was in the olden
    Time long ago)
And every gentle air that dallied,
    In that sweet day,
Along the ramparts plumed and pallid,
    A wingèd odor went away.

III

Wanderers in that happy valley
    Through two luminous windows saw
Spirits moving musically
    To a lute's well-tunèd law,
Round about a throne where, sitting,
    (Porphyrogene!)
In state his glory well befitting,
    The ruler of the realm was seen.

IV

And all with pearl and ruby glowing
    Was the fair palace door,
Through which came flowing, flowing, flowing,
    And sparkling evermore,
A troop of Echoes whose sweet duty
    Was but to sing,
In voices of surpassing beauty,
    The wit and wisdom of their king.

V

But evil things, in robes of sorrow,
　Assailed the monarch's high estate;
(Ah, let us mourn, for never morrow
　Shall dawn upon him, desolate!)
And round about his home the glory
　That blushed and bloomed
Is but a dim-remembered story
　Of the old time entombed.

VI

And travellers now within that valley
　Through the red-litten windows see
Vast forms that move fantastically
　To a discordant melody;
While, like a rapid ghastly river,
　Through the pale door,
A hideous throng rush out forever,
　And laugh—but smile no more.

I well remember that suggestions arising from this ballad led us into a train of thought, wherein there became manifest an opinion of Usher's which I mention not so much on account of its novelty (for other men have thought thus) as on account of the pertinacity with which he maintained it. This opinion, in its general form, was that of the sentience of all vegetable things. But in his disordered fancy the idea had assumed a more daring character, and trespassed, under certain conditions, upon the kingdom of inorganization. I lack words to express the full extent, or the earnest *abandon* of his persuasion. The belief, however, was connected (as I have previously hinted) with the gray stones of the home of his forefathers. The conditions of the sentience had been here, he imagined, fulfilled in the method of collocation of these stones—in the order of their arrangement, as well as in that of the many fungi which overspread them, and of the decayed trees which stood around—above all, in the long undisturbed endurance of this arrangement, and in its reduplication in the still waters of the tarn. Its evidence—the evidence of the sentience—was to be seen, he said (and I here started as he spoke), in the gradual yet certain condensation of an atmosphere of their own about the waters and the walls. The result was discoverable, he added, in that silent, yet importunate and terrible influence which for centuries had molded the destinies of his family, and which made *him* what I now saw him—what he was. Such opinions need no comment, and I will make none.

Our books—the books which, for years, had formed no small portion of the mental existence of the invalid—were, as might be supposed, in strict keeping with this character of phantasm. We pored together over such works as the Ververt and Chartreuse of

Gresset; the Belphegor of Machiavelli; the Heaven and Hell of Swedenborg; the Subterranean Voyage of Nicholas Klimm by Holberg; the Chiromancy of Robert Flud, of Jean D'Indaginé, and of De la Chambre; the Journey into the Blue Distance of Tieck; and the City of the Sun of Campanella. One favorite volume was a small octavo edition of the *Directorium Inquisitorium*, by the Dominican Eymeric de Gironne; and there were passages in Pomponius Mela, about the old African Satyrs and Ægipans, over which Usher would sit dreaming for hours. His chief delight, however, was found in the perusal of an exceedingly rare and curious book in quarto Gothic—the manual of a forgotten church—the *Vigiliæ Mortuorum Secundum Chorum Ecclesiæ Maguntinæ.*

I could not help thinking of the wild ritual of this work, and of its probable influence upon the hypochondriac, when one evening, having informed me abruptly that the lady Madeline was no more, he stated his intention of preserving her corpse for a fortnight (previously to its final interment) in one of the numerous vaults within the main walls of the building. The worldly reason, however, assigned for this singular proceeding was one which I did not feel at liberty to dispute. The brother had been led to his resolution (so he told me) by consideration of the unusual character of the malady of the deceased, of certain obtrusive and eager inquiries on the part of her medical men, and of the remote and exposed situation of the burial-ground of the family. I will not deny that when I called to mind the sinister countenance of the person whom I met upon the staircase, on the day of my arrival at the house, I had no desire to oppose what I regarded as at best but a harmless, and by no means an unnatural, precaution.

At the request of Usher, I personally aided him in the arrangements for the temporary entombment. The body having been encoffined, we two alone bore it to its rest. The vault in which we placed it (and which had been so long unopened that our torches, half smothered in its oppressive atmoshpere, gave us little opportunity for investigation) was small, damp, and entirely without means of admission for light; lying, at great depth, immediately beneath that portion of the building in which was my own sleeping apartment. It had been used, apparently, in remote feudal times, for the worst purposes of a donjon-keep, and in later days as a place of deposit for powder, or some other highly combustible substance, as a portion of its floor, and the whole interior of a long archway through which we reached it, were carefully sheathed with copper. The door, of massive iron, had been also similarly protected. Its immense weight caused an unusually sharp grating sound, as it moved upon its hinges.

Having deposited our mournful burden upon trestles within this region of horror, we partially turned aside the yet unscrewed lid of the coffin, and looked upon the face of the tenant. A striking similitude between the brother and sister now first arrested my attention; and Usher divining, perhaps, my thoughts, murmured out some few words from which I learned that the deceased and himself had been twins, and that sympathies of a scarcely intelligible nature had always existed between them. Our glances, however, rested not long upon the dead—for we could not regard her unawed. The disease which had thus entombed the lady in the maturity of youth, had left, as usual in all maladies of a strictly cataleptical character, the mockery of a faint blush upon the bosom and the face, and that suspiciously lingering smile upon the lip which is so terrible in death. We replaced and screwed down the lid, and, having secured the door of iron, made our way, with toil, into the scarcely less gloomy apartments of the upper portion of the house.

And now, some days of bitter grief having elapsed, an observable change came over the features of the mental disorder of my friend. His ordinary manner had vanished. His ordinary occupations were neglected or forgotten. He roamed from chamber to chamber with hurried, unequal, and objectless step. The pallor of his countenance had assumed, if possible, a more ghastly hue—but the luminousness of his eye had utterly gone out. The once occasional huskiness of his tone was heard no more; and a tremulous quaver, as if of extreme terror, habitually characterized his utterance. There were times, indeed, when I thought his unceasingly agitated mind was laboring with some oppressive secret, to divulge which he struggled for the necessary courage. At times, again, I was obliged to resolve all into the mere inexplicable vagaries of madness, for I beheld him gazing upon vacancy for long hours, in an attitude of the profoundest attention, as if listening to some imaginary sound. It was no wonder that his condition terrified—that it infected me. I felt creeping upon me, by slow yet certain degrees, the wild influences of his own fantastic yet impressive superstitions.

It was, especially, upon retiring to bed late in the night of the seventh or eighth day after the placing of the lady Madeline within the donjon, that I experienced the full power of such feelings. Sleep came not near my couch, while the hours waned and waned away. I struggled to reason off the nervousness which had dominion over me. I endeavored to believe that much, if not all, of what I felt was due to the bewildering influence of the gloomy furniture of the room—of the dark and tattered draperies which, tortured into motion by the breath of a rising tempest, swayed fitfully to and fro upon the walls, and rustled uneasily about the decorations of the bed. But my efforts were fruitless. An irrepressible tremor gradually pervaded my frame; and at length there sat upon my very heart an incubus of utterly causeless alarm. Shaking this off with a gasp and a struggle, I uplifted myself upon the pillows, and, peering earnestly within the intense darkness of the chamber, hearkened—I know not why, except that an instinctive spirit prompted me—to certain low and indefinite sounds which came, through the pauses of the storm, at long intervals, I knew not whence. Overpowered by an intense sentiment of horror, unaccountable yet unendurable, I threw on my clothes with haste (for I felt that I should sleep no more during the night) and endeavored to arouse myself from the pitiable condition into which I had fallen, by pacing rapidly to and fro through the apartment.

I had taken but few turns in this manner, when a light step on an adjoining staircase arrested my attention. I presently recognized it as that of Usher. In an instant afterward he rapped with a gentle touch at my door, and entered, bearing a lamp. His countenance was, as usual, cadaverously wan—but, moreover, there was a species of mad hilarity in his eyes—an evidently restrained *hysteria* in his whole demeanor. His air appalled me—but anything was preferable to the solitude which I had so long endured, and I even welcomed his presence as a relief.

"And you have not seen it?" he said abruptly, after having stared about him for some moments in silence—"you have not then seen it?—but, stay! you shall." Thus speaking, and having carefully shaded his lamp, he hurried to one of the casements, and threw it freely open to the storm.

The impetuous fury of the entering gust nearly lifted us from our feet. It was, indeed, a tempestuous yet sternly beautiful night, and one wildly singular in its terror and its beauty. A whirlwind had apparently collected its force in our vicinity; for there were frequent and violent alterations in the direction of the wind; and the exceeding density of the clouds (which hung so low as to press upon the turrets of the house) did not prevent our perceiving the lifelike velocity with which they flew careening from all points against each other, without passing away into the distance. I say that even their exceeding density did not prevent our perceiving this; yet we had no glimpse of the moon or stars, nor was there any flashing forth of the lightning. But the under surfaces of the huge masses of agitated vapor, as well as all terrestrial objects immediately around us, were glowing in the unnatural light of a faintly luminous and distinctly visible gaseous exhalation which hung about and enshrouded the mansion.

"You must not—you shall not behold this!" said I, shudderingly, to Usher, as I led him with a gentle violence from the window to a seat. "These appearances, which bewilder you, are merely electrical phenomena not uncommon—or it may be that they have their ghastly origin in the rank miasma of the tarn. Let us close this casement; the air is chilling and dangerous to your frame. Here is one of your favorite romances. I will read, and you shall listen;—and so we will pass away this terrible night together."

The antique volume which I had taken up was the *Mad Trist* of Sir Launcelot Canning; but I had called it a favorite of Usher's more in sad jest than in earnest; for, in truth, there is little in its uncouth and unimaginative prolixity which could have had interest for the lofty and spiritual ideality of my friend. It was, however, the only book immediately at hand; and I indulged a vague hope that the excitement which now agitated the hypochondriac might find relief (for the history of mental disorder is full of similar anomalies) even in the extremeness of the folly which I should read. Could I have judged, indeed, by the wild overstrained air of vivacity with which he hearkened, or apparently hearkened, to the words of the tale, I might well have congratulated myself upon the success of my design.

I had arrived at that well-known portion of the story where Ethelred, the hero of the Trist, having sought in vain for peaceable admission into the dwelling of the hermit, proceeds to make good an entrance by force. Here, it will be remembered, the words of the narrative run thus:

> "And Ethelred, who was by nature of a doughty heart, and who was now mighty withal, on account of the powerfulness of the wine which he had drunken, waited no longer to hold parley with the hermit, who, in sooth, was of an obstinate and maliceful turn, but, feeling the rain upon his shoulders, and fearing the rising of the tempest, uplifted his mace outright, and, with blows, made quickly room in the plankings of the door for his gauntleted hand; and now pulling therewith sturdily, he so cracked, and ripped, and tore all asunder, that the noise of the dry and hollow-sounding wood alarummed and reverberated throughout the forest."

At the termination of this sentence I started, and for a moment paused; for it appeared to me (although I at once concluded that my excited fancy had deceived me) —it appeared to me that from some very remote portion of the mansion there came, indistinctly, to my ears, what might have been, in its exact similarity of character, the echo (but a stifled and dull one certainly) of the very cracking and ripping sound which Sir Launcelot had so particularly described. It was, beyond doubt, the coincidence alone which had arrested my attention; for, amid the rattling of the sashes of the casements, and the ordinary commingled noises of the still increasing storm, the sound, in itself, had nothing, surely, which should have interested or disturbed me. I continued the story:

> "But the good champion Ethelred, now entering within the door, was sore enraged and amazed to perceive no signal of the maliceful hermit; but, in the stead thereof, a dragon of a scaly and prodigious demeanor,

and of a fiery tongue, which sate in guard before a palace of gold, with a floor of silver; and upon the wall there hung a shield of shining brass with this legend enwritten—
> Who entereth herein, a conqueror hath bin;
> Who slayeth the dragon, the shield he shall win
And Ethelred uplifted his mace, and struck upon the head of the dragon, which fell before him, and gave up his pesty breath, with a shriek so horrid and harsh, and withal so piercing, that Ethelred had fain to close his ears with his hands against the dreadful noise of it, the like whereof was never before heard."

Here again I paused abruptly, and now with a feeling of wild amazement; for there could be no doubt whatever that, in this instance, I did actually hear (although from what direction it proceeded I found it impossible to say) a low and apparently distant, but harsh, protracted, and most unusual screaming or grating sound —the exact counterpart of what my fancy had already conjured up for the dragon's unnatural shriek as described by the romancer.

Oppressed, as I certainly was, upon the occurrence of this second and most extraordinary coincidence, by a thousand conflicting sensations, in which wonder and extreme terror were predominant, I still retained sufficient presence of mind to avoid exciting, by any observation, the sensitive nervousness of my companion. I was by no means certain that he had noticed the sounds in question; although, assuredly, a strange alteration had during the last few minutes taken place in his demeanor. From a position fronting my own, he had gradually brought round his chair, so as to sit with his face to the door of the chamber; and thus I could but partially perceive his features, although I saw that his lips trembled as if he were murmuring inaudibly. His head had dropped upon his breast—yet I knew that he was not asleep, from the wide and rigid opening of the eye as I caught a glance of it in profile. The motion of his body, too, was at variance with this idea—for he rocked from side to side with a gentle yet constant and uniform sway. Having rapidly taken notice of all this, I resumed the narrative of Sir Launcelot, which thus proceeded:

> "And now, the champion having escaped from the terrible fury of the dragon, bethinking himself of the brazen shield, and of the breaking up of the enchantment which was upon it, removed the carcass from out of the way before him, and approached valorously over the silver pavement of the castle to where the shield was upon the wall; which in sooth tarried not for his full coming, but fell down at his feet upon the silver floor, with a mighty great and terrible ringing sound."

No sooner had these syllables passed my lips, than—as if a shield of brass had indeed, at the moment, fallen heavily upon a floor of silver—I became aware of a distinct, hollow, metallic and clangorous, yet apparently muffled reverberation. Completely unnerved, I leaped to my feet; but the measured rocking movement of Usher was undisturbed. I rushed to the chair in which he sat. His eyes were bent fixedly before him, and throughout his whole countenance there reigned a stony rigidity. But, as I placed my hand upon his shoulder, there came a strong shudder over his whole person; a sickly smile quivered about his lips; and I saw that he spoke in a low, hurried, and gibbering murmur, as if unconscious of my presence. Bending closely over him, I at length drank in the hideous import of his words.

"Not hear it?—yes, I hear it, and *have* heard it. Long—long—long—many minutes, many hours, many days, have I heard it—yet I dared not—oh, pity me, miserable wretch that I am!—I dared not—*I dared not speak! We have put her living in the tomb!* Said I not that my senses were acute? I *now* tell you that I heard her first feeble movements in the hollow coffin. I heard them—many, many days ago—yet I dared not—*I dared not speak!* And now—tonight—Ethelred—ha! ha!—the breaking of the hermit's door, and the death-cry of the dragon, and the clangor of the shield!—say, rather, the rending of her coffin, and the grating of the iron hinges of her prison, and her struggles within the coppered archway of the vault! Oh, whither shall I fly? Will she not be here anon? Is she not hurrying to upbraid me for my haste? Have I not heard her footsteps on the stair? Do I not distinguish that heavy and horrible beating of her heart? Madman!"—here he sprang furiously to his feet, and shrieked out his syllables, as if in the effort he were giving up his soul—*"Madman! I tell you that she now stands without the door!"*

As if in the superhuman energy of his utterance there had been found the potency of a spell, the huge antique panels to which the speaker pointed drew slowly back, upon the instant, their ponderous and ebony jaws. It was the work of the rushing gust—but then without the doors there *did* stand the lofty and enshrouded figure of the lady Madeline of Usher. There was blood upon her white robes, and the evidence of some bitter struggle upon every portion of her emaciated frame. For a moment she remained trembling and reeling to and fro upon the threshold—then, with a low moaning cry, fell heavily inward upon the person of her brother, and, in her violent and now final death-agonies, bore him to the floor a corpse, and a victim to the terrors he had anticipated.

From that chamber, and from that mansion, I fled aghast. The storm was still abroad in all its wrath as I found myself crossing the old causeway. Suddenly there shot along the path a wild light, and I turned to see whence a gleam so unusual could have issued; for the vast house and its shadows were alone behind me. The radiance was that of the full, setting, and blood-red moon, which now shone vividly through that once barely discernible fissure, of which I have before spoken as extending from the roof of the building, in a zigzag direction, to the base. While I gazed, this fissure rapidly widened— there came a fierce breath of the whirlwind—the entire orb of the satellite burst at once upon my sight—my brain reeled as I saw the mighty walls rushing asunder—there was a long tumultuous shouting sound like the voice of a thousand waters—and the deep and dank tarn at my feet closed sullenly and silently over the fragments of the House of Usher.

JAMES JOYCE (1882–1941)

Counterparts

The bell rang furiously and, when Miss Parker went to the tube, a furious voice called out in a piercing North of Ireland accent: "Send Farrington here!"

Miss Parker returned to her machine, saying to a man who was writing at a desk: "Mr. Alleyne wants you upstairs."

The man muttered *"Blast* him!" under his breath and pushed back his chair to stand up. When he stood up he was tall and of great bulk. He had a hanging face, dark wine-colored, with fair eyebrows and mustache: his eyes bulged forward slightly and the whites of them were dirty. He lifted up the counter and, passing by the clients, went out of the office with a heavy step.

He went heavily upstairs until he came to the second landing, where a door bore a brass plate with the inscription: MR. ALLEYNE. Here he halted, puffing with labor and vexation, and knocked. The shrill voice cried: "Come in!"

The man entered Mr. Alleyne's room. Simultaneously Mr. Alleyne, a little man wearing gold-rimmed glasses on a clean-shaven face, shot his head up over a pile of documents. The head itself was so pink and hairless it seemed like a large egg reposing on the papers. Mr. Alleyne did not lose a moment: "Farrington? What is the meaning of this? Why have I always to complain of you? May I ask you why you haven't made a copy of that contract between Bodley and Kirwan? I told you it must be ready by four o'clock."

"But Mr. Shelley said, sir—"

"Mr. Shelley said, sir . . . Kindly attend to what I say and not to what *Mr. Shelley says, sir.* You have always some excuse or another for shirking work. Let me tell you that if the contract is not copied before this evening I'll lay the matter before Mr. Crosbie. . . . Do you hear me now?"

"Yes, sir."

"Do you hear me now? . . . Ay, and another little matter! I might as well be talking to the wall as talking to you. Understand once for all that you get a half an hour for your lunch and not an hour and a half. How many courses do you want, I'd like to know. . . . Do you mind me now?"

"Yes, sir."

Mr. Alleyne bent his head again upon his pile of papers. The man stared fixedly at the polished skull which directed the affairs of Crosbie & Alleyne, gauging its fragility. A spasm of rage gripped his throat for a few moments and then passed, leaving after it a sharp sensation of thirst. The man recognized the sensation and felt that he must have a good night's drinking. The middle of the month was passed and, if he could get the copy done in time, Mr. Alleyne might give him an order on the cashier. He stood still, gazing fixedly at the head upon the pile of papers. Suddenly Mr. Alleyne began to upset all the papers, searching for something. Then, as if he had been unaware of the man's presence till that moment, he shot up his head again, saying: "Eh? Are you going to stand there all day? Upon my word, Farrington, you take things easy!"

"I was waiting to see—"

"Very good, you needn't wait to see. Go downstairs and do your work."

The man walked heavily toward the door, and as he went out of the room he heard Mr. Alleyne cry after him that if the contract was not copied by evening Mr. Crosbie would hear of the matter.

He returned to his desk in the lower office and counted the sheets which remained to be copied. He took up his pen and dipped it in the ink, but he continued to stare stupidly at the last words he had written: "In no case shall the said Bernard Bodley be" . . . The evening was falling, and in a few minutes they would be lighting the gas: then he could write. He felt that he must slake the thirst in his throat. He stood up from his desk and, lifting the counter as before, passed out of the office. As he was passing out the chief clerk looked at him inquiringly.

"It's all right, Mr. Shelley," said the man, pointing with his finger to indicate the objective of his journey.

The chief clerk glanced at the hatrack, but, seeing the row complete, offered no remark. As soon as he was on the landing the man pulled a shepherd's-plaid cap out of his pocket, put it on his head, and ran quickly down the rickety stairs. From the street door he walked on furtively on the inner side of the path toward the corner and all at once dived into a doorway. He was now safe in the dark snug of O'Neill's shop, and filling up the little window that looked into the bar with his inflamed face, the color of dark wine or dark meat, he called out: "Here, Pat, give us a G.P., like a good fellow."

The curate brought him a glass of plain porter. The man drank it at a gulp and asked for a caraway seed. He put his penny on the counter and, leaving the curate to grope for it in the gloom, retreated out of the snug as furtively as he had entered it.

Darkness, accompanied by a thick fog, was gaining upon the dusk of February, and the lamps in Eustace Street had been lit. The man went up by the houses until he reached the door of the office, wondering whether he could finish his copy in time. On the stairs a moist, pungent odor of perfumes saluted his nose: evidently Miss

Delacour had come while he was out in O'Neill's. He crammed his cap back again into his pocket and re-entered the office, assuming an air of absent-mindedness.

"Mr. Alleyne has been calling for you," said the chief clerk severely. "Where were you?"

The man glanced at the two clients who were standing at the counter as if to intimate that their presence prevented him from answering. As the clients were both male the chief clerk allowed himself a laugh.

"I know that game," he said. "Five times in one day is a little bit. . . . Well, you better look sharp and get a copy of our correspondence in the Delacour case for Mr. Alleyne."

This address in the presence of the public, his run upstairs, and the porter he had gulped down so hastily confused the man, and as he sat down at his desk to get what was required he realized how hopeless was the task of finishing his copy of the contract before half past five. The dark damp night was coming and he longed to spend it in the bars, drinking with his friends amid the glare of gas and the clatter of glasses. He got out the Delacour correspondence and passed out of the office. He hoped Mr. Alleyne would not discover that the last two letters were missing.

The moist, pungent perfume lay all the way up to Mr. Alleyne's room. Miss Delacour was a middle-aged woman of Jewish appearance. Mr. Alleyne was said to be sweet on her or on her money. She came to the office often and stayed a long time when she came. She was sitting beside his desk now in an aroma of perfumes, smoothing the handle of her umbrella and nodding the great black feather in her hat. Mr. Alleyne had swiveled his chair round to face her and thrown his right foot jauntily upon his left knee. The man put the correspondence on the desk and bowed respectfully, but neither Mr. Alleyne nor Miss Delacour took any notice of his bow. Mr. Alleyne tapped a finger on the correspondence and then flicked it toward him as if to say: "That's all right: you can go."

The man returned to the lower office and sat down again at his desk. He stared intently at the incomplete phrase: "In no case shall the said Bernard Bodley be" . . . and thought how strange it was that the last three words began with the same letter. The chief clerk began to hurry Miss Parker, saying she would never have the letters typed in time for post. The man listened to the clicking of the machine for a few minutes and then set to work to finish his copy. But his head was not clear, and his mind wandered away to the glare and rattle of the public house. It was a night for hot punches. He struggled on with his copy, but when the clock struck five he had still fourteen pages to write. Blast it! He couldn't finish it in time. He longed to execrate aloud, to bring his fist down on something violently. He was so enraged that he wrote "Bernard Bernard" instead of "Bernard Bodley" and had to begin again on a clean sheet.

He felt strong enough to clear out the whole office singlehanded. His body ached to do something, to rush out and revel in violence. All the indignities of his life enraged him. . . . Could he ask the cashier privately for an advance? No, the cashier was no good, no damn good: he wouldn't give an advance. . . . He knew where he would meet the boys: Leonard and O'Halloran and Nosey Flynn. The barometer of his emotional nature was set for a spell of riot.

His imagination had so abstracted him that his name was called twice before he answered. Mr. Alleyne and Miss Delacour were standing outside the counter, and all the clerks had turned round in anticipation of something. The man got up from his desk. Mr. Alleyne began a tirade of abuse, saying that two letters were missing. The man answered that he knew nothing about them, that he had made a faithful copy. The tirade continued: it was so bitter and violent that the man could hardly restrain his fist from descending upon the head of the manikin before him.

"I know nothing about any other two letters," he said stupidly.

"You—know—nothing. Of course you know nothing," said Mr. Alleyne. "Tell me," he added, glancing first for approval to the lady beside him, "do you take me for a fool? Do you think me an utter fool?"

The man glanced from the lady's face to the little egg-shaped head and back again, and almost before he was aware of it, his tongue had found a felicitous moment: "I don't think, sir," he said, "that that's a fair question to put to me."

There was a pause in the very breathing of the clerks. Everyone was astounded (the author of the witticism no less than his neighbors), and Miss Delacour, who was a stout, amiable person, began to smile broadly. Mr. Alleyne flushed to the hue of a wild rose, and his mouth twitched with a dwarf's passion. He shook his fist in the man's face till it seemed to vibrate like the knob of some electric machine: "You impertinent ruffian! You impertinent ruffian! I'll make short work of you! Wait till you see! You'll apologize to me for your impertinence or you'll quit the office instanter! You'll quit this, I'm telling you, or you'll apologize to me!"

He stood in a doorway opposite the office, watching to see if the cashier would come out alone. All the clerks passed out, and finally the cashier came out with the chief clerk. It was no use trying to say a word to him when he was with the chief clerk. The man felt that his position was bad enough. He had been obliged to offer an abject apology to Mr. Alleyne for his impertinence, but he knew what a hornet's nest the office would be for him. He could remember the way in which Mr. Alleyne had hounded little Peake out of the office in order to make room for his own nephew. He felt savage and thirsty and revengeful, annoyed with himself and with everyone else. Mr. Alleyne would never give him an hour's rest; his life would be a hell to him. He had made a proper fool of himself this time. Could he not keep his tongue in his cheek? But they had never pulled together from the first, he and Mr. Alleyne, ever since the day Mr. Alleyne had overheard him mimicking his North of Ireland accent to amuse Higgins and Miss Parker: that had been the beginning of it. He might have tried Higgins for the money, but sure, Higgins never had anything for himself. A man with two establishments to keep up, of course he couldn't. . . .

He felt his great body again aching for the comfort of the public house. The fog had begun to chill him, and he wondered could he touch Pat in O'Neill's. He could not touch him for more than a bob—and a bob was no use. Yet he must get money somewhere or other: he had spent his last penny for the G.P., and soon it would be too late for getting money anywhere. Suddenly, as he was fingering his watch chain, he thought of Terry Kelly's pawn office in Fleet Street. That was the dart! Why didn't he think of it sooner?

He went through the narrow alley of Temple Bar quickly, muttering to himself that they could all go to hell, because he was going to have a good night of it. The clerk in Terry Kelly's said a crown, but the consignor held out for six shillings; and in the end the six shillings was allowed him literally. He came out of the pawn office joyfully, making a little cylinder of the coins between his thumb and fingers. In Westmoreland Street the footpaths were crowded with young men and woman returning from business, and ragged urchins ran here and there yelling out the names of the evening editions. The man passed through the crowd, looking on the spectacle generally with proud satisfaction and staring masterfully at the office girls. His head was full of the noises of tram gongs and swishing trolleys, and his nose already sniffed the curling fumes of punch. As he walked on he preconsidered the terms in which he would narrate the incident to the boys:

"So I just looked at him—coolly, you know, and looked at her. Then I looked back at him again—taking my time, you know. 'I don't think that that's a fair question to put to me,' says I."

Nosey Flynn was sitting up in his usual corner of Davy Byrne's, and when he heard the story he stood Farrington a half one, saying it was as smart a thing as ever he heard. Farrington stood a drink in his turn. After a while O'Halloran and Paddy Leonard came in, and the story was repeated to them. O'Halloran stood tailors of malt, hot, all round, and told the story of the retort he had made to the chief clerk when he was in Callan's of Fownes's Street; but as the retort was after the manner of the liberal shepherds in the eclogues, he had to admit that it was not as clever as Farrington's retort. At this Farrington told the boys to polish off that and have another.

Just as they were naming their poisons who should come in but Higgins! Of course he had to join in with the others. The men asked him to give his version of it, and he did so with great vivacity; for the sight of five small hot whiskies was very exhilarating. Everyone roared laughing when he showed the way in which Mr. Alleyne shook his fist in Farrington's face. Then he imitated Farrington, saying, "And here was my nabs, as cool as you please," while Farrington looked at the company out of his heavy, dirty eyes, smiling and at times drawing forth stray drops of liquor from his mustache with the aid of his lower lip.

When that round was over there was a pause. O'Halloran had money, but neither of the other two seemed to have any; so the whole party left the shop somewhat regretfully. At the corner of Duke Street, Higgins and Nosey Flynn beveled off to the left, while the other three turned back toward the city. Rain was drizzling down on the cold streets, and when they reached the Ballast Office, Farrington suggested the Scotch House. The bar was full of men and loud with the noise of tongues and glasses. The three men pushed past the whining matchsellers at the door and formed a little party at the corner of the counter. They began to exchange stories. Leonard introduced them to a young fellow named Weathers who was performing at the Tivoli as an acrobat and knockabout *artiste*. Farrington stood a drink all round. Weathers said he would take a small Irish and Apollinaris. Farrington, who had definite notions of what was what, asked the boys would they have an Apollinaris too; but the boys told Tim to make theirs hot. The talk became theatrical. O'Halloran stood a round, and then Farrington stood another round, Weathers protesting that the hospitality was too Irish. He promised to get them in behind the scenes and introduce them to some nice girls. O'Halloran said that he and Leonard would go but that Farrington wouldn't go, because he was a married man; and Farrington's heavy, dirty eyes leered at the company in token that he understood he was being chaffed. Weathers made them all have just one little tincture at his expense and promised to meet them later on at Mulligan's in Poolbeg Street.

When the Scotch House closed they went round to Mulligan's. They went into the parlor at the back, and O'Halloran ordered small hot specials all around. They were all beginning to feel mellow. Farrington was just standing another round when Weathers came back. Much to Farrington's relief, he drank a glass of bitter this time. Funds were getting low, but they had enough to keep them going.

Presently two young women with big hats and a young man in a check suit came in and sat at a table close by. Weathers saluted them and told the company that they were out of the Tivoli. Farrington's eyes wandered at every moment in the direction of one of the young women. There was something striking in her appearance. An immense scarf of peacockblue muslin was wound round her hat and knotted in a great bow under her chin, and she wore bright yellow gloves, reaching to the elbow. Farrington gazed admiringly at the plump arm which she moved very often and with much grace, and when, after a little time, she answered his gaze, he admired still more her large dark brown eyes. The oblique, staring expression in them fascinated him. She glanced at him once or twice, and when the party was leaving the room, she brushed against his chair and said, "Oh, pardon!" in a London accent. He watched her leave the room in the hope that she would look back at him, but he was disappointed. He cursed his want of money and cursed all the rounds he had stood, particularly all the whiskies and Apollinaris which he had stood to Weathers. If there was one thing that he hated, it was a sponge. He was so angry that he lost count of the conversation of his friends.

When Paddy Leonard called him, he found that they were talking about feats of strength. Weathers was showing his biceps muscle to the company and boasting so much that the other two had called on Farrington to uphold the national honor. Farrington pulled up his sleeve accordingly and showed his biceps muscle to the company. The two arms were examined and compared, and finally it was agreed to have a trial of strength. The table was cleared, and the two men rested their elbows on it, clasping hands. When Paddy Leonard said "Go!" each was to try to bring down the other's hand on to the table. Farrington looked very serious and determined.

The trial began. After about thirty seconds Weathers brought his opponent's hand slowly down on to the table. Farrington's dark wine-colored face flushed darker still with anger and humiliation at having been defeated by such a stripling.

"You're not to put the weight of your body behind it. Play fair," he said.

"Who's not playing fair?" said the other.

"Come on again. The two best out of three."

The trial began again. The veins stood out on Farrington's forehead, and the pallor of Weathers' complexion changed to peony. Their hands and arms trembled under the stress. After a long struggle Weathers again brought his opponent's hand slowly on to the table. There was a murmur of applause from the spectators. The curate, who was standing beside the table, nodded his red head towards the victor and said with stupid familiarity: "Ah! that's the knack!"

"What the hell do you know about it?" said Farrington fiercely, turning on the man. "What do you put in your gab for?"

"Sh, sh!" said O'Halloran, observing the violent expression of Farrington's face. "Pony up, boys. We'll have just one little smahan more and then we'll be off."

A very sullen-faced man stood at the corner of O'Connell Bridge waiting for the little Sandymount tram to take him home. He was full of smoldering anger and revengefulness. He felt humiliated and discontented; he did not even feel drunk; and he had only twopence in his pocket. He cursed everything. He had done for himself in the office, pawned his watch, spent all his money; and he had not even got drunk. He began to feel thirsty again, and he longed to be back again in the hot, reeking public house. He had lost his reputation as a strong man, having been defeated twice by a mere boy. His heart swelled with fury, and when he thought of the woman in the big hat who had brushed against him and said "Pardon!" his fury nearly choked him.

His tram let him down at Shelbourne Road, and he steered his great body along in the shadow of the wall of the barracks. He loathed returning to his home. When he went in by the side door he found the kitchen empty and the kitchen fire nearly out. He bawled upstairs: "Ada! Ada!"

His wife was a little sharp-faced woman who bullied her husband when he was sober and was bullied by him when he was drunk. They had five children. A little boy came running down the stairs.

"Who is that?" said the man, peering through the darkness.

"Me, Pa."

"Who are you? Charlie?"

"No, Pa. Tom."

"Where's your mother?"

"She's out at the chapel."

"That's right. . . . Did she think of leaving any dinner for me?"

"Yes, Pa. I—"

"Light the lamp. What do you mean by having the place in darkness? Are the other children in bed?"

The man sat down heavily on one of the chairs while the little boy lit the lamp. He began to mimic his son's flat accent, saying half to himself: " 'At the chapel.' 'At the chapel,' if you please!" When the lamp was lit he banged his fist on the table and shouted: "What's for my dinner?"

"I'm going to . . . cook it, Pa," said the little boy.

The man jumped up furiously and pointed to the fire. "On that fire! You let the fire out! By God, I'll teach you to do that again!" He took a step to the door and seized the walking stick which was standing behind it. "I'll teach you to let the fire out!" he said, rolling up his sleeves in order to give his arm free play.

The little boy cried, "Oh, Pa!" and ran whimpering round the table, but the man followed him and caught him by the coat. The little boy looked about him wildly but, seeing no way of escape, fell upon his knees.

"Now, you'll let the fire out the next time!" said the man, striking at him vigorously with the stick. "Take that, you little whelp!"

The boy uttered a squeal of pain as the stick cut his thigh. He clasped his hands together in the air, and his voice shook with fright.

"Oh, Pa!" he cried. "Don't beat me, Pa! And I'll . . . I'll say a Hail Mary for you . . . I'll say a Hail Mary for you, Pa, if you don't beat me . . . I'll say a Hail Mary . . ."

FRANZ KAFKA (1883–1924)

The Bucket-Rider

Coal all spent; the bucket empty, the shovel useless; the stove breathing out cold; the room freezing; the leaves outside the window rigid, covered with rime; the sky a silver shield against anyone who looks for help from it. I must have coal; I cannot freeze to death; behind me is the pitiless stove, before me the pitiless sky, so I must ride out between them and on my journey seek aid from the coal-dealer. But he has already grown deaf to ordinary appeals; I must prove irrefutably to him that I have not a single grain of coal left, and that he means to me the very sun in the firmament. I must approach like a beggar who, with the death-rattle already in his throat, insists on dying on the doorstep, and to whom the grand people's cook accordingly decides to give the dregs of the coffee-pot; just so must the coal-dealer, filled with rage, but acknowledging the command, "Thou shalt not kill," fling a shovelful of coal into my bucket.

My mode of arrival must decide the matter; so I ride off on the bucket. Seated on the bucket, my hands on the handle, the simplest kind of bridle, I propel myself with difficulty down the stairs; but once down below my bucket ascends, superbly, superbly; camels humbly squatting on the ground do not rise with more dignity, shaking themselves under the sticks of their drivers. Through the hard frozen streets we go at a regular canter; often I am upraised as high as the first story of a house; never do I sink as low as the house doors. And at last I float at an extraordinary height above the vaulted cellar of the dealer, whom I see far below crouching over his table, where he is writing; he has opened the door to let out the excessive heat.

"Coal-dealer!" I cry in a voice burned hollow by the frost and muffled in the cloud made by my breath, "please, coal-dealer, give me a little coal. My bucket is so light that I can ride on it. Be kind. When I can I'll pay you."

The dealer puts his hand to his ear. "Do I hear rightly?" He throws the question over his shoulder to his wife. "Do I hear rightly? A customer."

"I hear nothing," says his wife, breathing in and out peacefully while she knits on, her back pleasantly warmed by the heat.

"Oh, yes, you must hear," I cry. "It's me; an old customer; faithful and true; only without means at the moment."

"Wife," says the dealer, "it's some one, it must be; my ears can't have deceived me so much as that; it must be an old, a very old customer, that can move me so deeply."

"What ails you, man?" says his wife, ceasing from her work for a moment and pressing her knitting to her bosom. "It's nobody, the street is empty, all our customers are provided for; we could close down the shop for several days and take a rest."

"But I'm sitting up here on the bucket," I cry, and unfeeling frozen tears dim my eyes, "please look up here, just once; you'll see me directly; I beg you, just a shovelful; and if you give me more it'll make me so happy that I won't know what to do. All the other customers are provided for. Oh, if I could only hear the coal clattering into the bucket!"

"I'm coming," says the coal-dealer, and on his short legs he makes to climb the steps of the cellar, but his wife is already beside him, holds him back by the arm and says: "You stay here; seeing you persist in your fancies I'll go myself. Think of the bad fit of coughing you had during the night. But for a piece of business, even if it's one you've only fancied in your head, you're prepared to forget your wife and child and sacrifice your lungs. I'll go."

"Then be sure to tell him all the kinds of coal we have in stock; I'll shout out the prices after you."

"Right," says his wife, climbing up to the street. Naturally she sees me at once. "Frau Coal-dealer," I cry, "my humblest greetings; just one shovelful of coal; here in my bucket; I'll carry it home myself. One shovelful of the worst you have. I'll pay you in full for it, of course, but not just now, not just now." What a knell-like sound the words "not just now" have, and how bewilderingly they mingle with the evening chimes that fall from the church steeple nearby!

"Well, what does he want?" shouts the dealer. "Nothing," his wife shouts back, "there's nothing here; I see nothing, I hear nothing; only six striking, and now we must shut up the shop. The cold is terrible; tomorrow we'll likely have lots to do again."

She sees nothing and hears nothing; but all the same she loosens her apron-strings and waves her apron to waft me away. She succeeds, unluckily. My bucket has all the virtues of a good steed except powers of resistance, which it has not; it is too light; a woman's apron can make it fly through the air.

"You bad woman!" I shout back, while she, turning into the shop, half-contemptuous, half-reassured, flourishes her fist in the air. "You bad woman! I begged you for a shovelful of the worst coal and you would not give me it." And with that I ascend into the regions of the ice mountains and am lost forever.

D. H. LAWRENCE (1885–1930)

The Rocking-Horse Winner

There was a woman who was beautiful, who started with all the advantages, yet she had no luck. She married for love, and the love turned to dust. She had bonny children, yet she felt they had been thrust upon her, and she could not love them. They looked at her coldly, as if they were finding fault with her. And hurriedly she felt she must cover up some fault in herself. Yet what it was that she must cover up she never knew. Nevertheless, when her children were present, she always felt the centre of her heart go hard. This troubled her, and in her manner she was all the more gentle and anxious for her children, as if she loved them very much. Only she herself knew that at the centre of her heart was a hard little place that could not feel love, no, not for anybody. Everybody else said of her: "She is such a good mother. She adores her children." Only she herself, and her children themselves, knew it was not so. They read it in each other's eyes.

There were a boy and two little girls. They lived in a pleasant house, with a garden, and they had discreet servants, and felt themselves superior to anyone in the neighbourhood.

Although they lived in style, they felt always an anxiety in the house. There was never enough money. The mother had a small income, and the father had a small income, but not nearly enough for the social position which they had to keep up. The father went into town to some office. But though he had good prospects, these prospects never materialized. There was always the grinding sense of the shortage of money, though the style was always kept up.

At last the mother said: "I will see if I can't make something." But she did not know where to begin. She racked her brains, and tried this thing and the other, but could not find anything successful. The failure made deep lines come into her face. Her children were growing up, they would have to go to school. There must be more money, there must be more money. The father, who was always very handsome and expensive in his tastes, seemed as if he never would be able to do anything worth doing. And the mother, who had a great belief in herself, did not succeed any better, and her tastes were just as expensive.

And so the house came to be haunted by the unspoken phrase: There must be more money! There must be more money! The children could hear it all the time, though nobody said it aloud. They heard it at Christmas, when the expensive and splendid toys filled the nursery. Behind the shining modern rocking horse, behind the smart doll's-house, a voice would start whispering: "There must be more money! There must be more money!" And the children would stop playing, to listen for a moment. They would look into each other's eyes, to see if they had all heard. And each one saw in the eyes of the other two that they too had heard. "There must be more money! There must be more money!"

It came whispering from the springs of the still-swaying rocking horse, and even the horse, bending his wooden, champing head, heard it. The big doll, sitting so pink and smirking in her new pram, could hear it quite plainly, and seemed to be smirking all the more self-consciously because of it. The foolish puppy, too, that took the place of the Teddy bear, he was looking so extraordinarily foolish for no other reason but that he heard the secret whisper all over the house: "There must be more money!"

Yet nobody ever said it aloud. The whisper was everywhere, and therefore no one spoke it. Just as no one ever says: "We are breathing!" in spite of the fact that breath is coming and going all the time.

"Mother," said the boy Paul one day, "why don't we keep a car of our own? Why do we always use uncle's, or else a taxi?"

"Because we're the poor members of the family," said the mother.

"But why are we, mother?"

"Well—I suppose," she said slowly and bitterly, "it's because your father has no luck."

The boy was silent for some time.

"Is luck money, mother?" he asked, rather timidly.

"No, Paul. Not quite. It's what causes you to have money."

"Oh!" said Paul vaguely. "I thought when Uncle Oscar said filthy lucker, it meant money."

"Filthy lucre does mean money," said the mother. "But it's lucre, not luck."

"Oh!" said the boy. "Then what is luck, mother?"

"It's what causes you to have money. If you're lucky you have money. That's why it's better to be born lucky than rich. If you're rich, you may lose your money. But if you're lucky, you will always get more money."

"Oh! Will you? And is father not lucky?"

"Very unlucky, I should say," she said bitterly.

The boy watched her with unsure eyes.

"Why?" he asked.

"I don't know. Nobody ever knows why one person is lucky and another unlucky."

"Don't they? Nobody at all? Does nobody know?"

"Perhaps God. But He never tells."

"He ought to, then. And aren't you lucky either, mother?"

"I can't be, if I married an unlucky husband."

"But by yourself, aren't you?"

"I used to think I was, before I married. Now I think I am very unlucky indeed."

"Why?"

"Well—never mind! Perhaps I'm not really," she said.

The child looked at her, to see if she meant it. But he saw, by the lines of her mouth, that she was only trying to hide something from him.

"Well, anyhow," he said stoutly, "I'm a lucky person."

"Why?" said his mother, with a sudden laugh.

He stared at her. He didn't even know why he had said it.

"God told me," he asserted, brazening it out.

"I hope He did, dear!" she said, again with a laugh, but rather bitter.

"He did, mother!"

"Excellent!" said the mother, using one of her husband's exclamations.

The boy saw she did not believe him; or, rather, that she paid no attention to his assertion. This angered him somewhat, and made him want to compel her attention.

He went off by himself, vaguely, in a childish way, seeking for the clue to "luck." Absorbed, taking no heed of other people, he went about with a sort of stealth, seeking inwardly for luck. He wanted luck, he wanted it, he wanted it. When the two girls were playing dolls in the nursery, he would sit on his big rocking horse, charging madly into space, with a frenzy that made the little girls peer at him uneasily. Wildly the horse careered, the waving dark hair of the boy tossed, his eyes had a strange glare in them. The little girls dared not speak to him.

When he had ridden to the end of his mad little journey, he climbed down and stood in front of his rocking horse, staring fixedly into its lowered face. Its red mouth was slightly open, its big eye was wide and glassy-bright.

"Now!" he would silently command the snorting steed. "Now, take me to where there is luck! Now take me!"

And he would slash the horse on the neck with the little whip he had asked Uncle Oscar for. He knew the horse could take him to where there was luck, if only he forced it. So he would mount again, and start on his furious ride, hoping at last to get there. He knew he could get there.

"You'll break your horse, Paul!" said the nurse.

"He's always riding like that! I wish he'd leave off!" said his elder sister Joan.

But he only glared down on them in silence. Nurse gave him up.

She could make nothing of him. Anyhow he was growing beyond her.

One day his mother and his Uncle Oscar came in when he was on one of his furious rides. He did not speak to them.

"Hallo, you young jockey! Riding a winner?" said his uncle.

"Aren't you growing too big for a rocking horse? You're not a very little boy any longer, you know," said his mother.

But Paul only gave a blue glare from his big, rather close-set eyes. He would speak to nobody when he was in full tilt. His mother watched him with an anxious expression on her face.

At last he suddenly stopped forcing his horse into the mechanical gallop, and slid down.

"Well, I got there!" he announced fiercely, his blue eyes still flaring, and his sturdy long legs straddling apart.

"Where did you get to?" asked his mother.

"Where I wanted to go," he flared back at her.

"That's right, son!" said Uncle Oscar. "Don't you stop till you get there. What's the horse's name?"

"He doesn't have a name," said the boy.

"Gets on without all right?" asked the uncle.

"Well, he has different names. He was called Sansovino last week."

"Sansovino, eh? Won the Ascot. How did you know his name?"

"He always talks about horse races with Bassett," said Joan.

The uncle was delighted to find that his small nephew was posted with all the racing news. Bassett, the young gardener, who had been wounded in the left foot in the war and had got his present job through Oscar Cresswell, whose batman he had been, was a perfect blade of the "turf." He lived in the racing events, and the small boy lived with him.

Oscar Cresswell got it all from Bassett.

"Master Paul comes and asks me, so I can't do more than tell him, sir," said Bassett, his face terribly serious, as if he were speaking of religious matters.

"And does he ever put anything on a horse he fancies?"

"Well—I don't want to give him away—he's a young sport, a fine sport, sir. Would you mind asking him yourself? He sort of takes a pleasure in it, and perhaps he'd feel I was giving him away, sir, if you don't mind."

Bassett was serious as a church.

The uncle went back to his nephew, and took him off for a ride in the car.

"Say, Paul, old man, do you ever put anything on a horse?" the uncle asked.

The boy watched the handsome man closely.

"Why, do you think I oughtn't to?" he parried.

"Not a bit of it! I thought perhaps you might give me a tip for the Lincoln."

The car sped on into the country, going down to Uncle Oscar's place in Hampshire.

"Honour bright?" said the nephew.

"Honour bright, son!" said the uncle.

"Well, then, Daffodil."

"Daffodil! I doubt it, sonny. What about Mirza?"

"I only know the winner," said the boy. "That's Daffodil."

"Daffodil, eh?"

There was a pause. Daffodil was an obscure horse comparatively.

"Uncle!"

"Yes, son?"

"You won't let it go any further, will you? I promised Bassett."

"Bassett be damned, old man! What's he got to do with it?"

"We're partners. We've been partners from the first. Uncle, he lent me my first five shillings, which I lost. I promised him, honour bright, it was only between me and him; only you gave me that ten-shilling note I started winning with, so I thought you were lucky. You won't let it go any further, will you?"

The boy gazed at his uncle from those big, hot, blue eyes, set rather close together. The uncle stirred and laughed uneasily.

"Right you are, son! I'll keep your tip private. Daffodil, eh? How much are you putting on him?"

"All except twenty pounds," said the boy. "I keep that in reserve."

The uncle thought it a good joke.

"You keep twenty pounds in reserve, do you, you young romancer? What are you betting, then?"

"I'm betting three hundred," said the boy gravely. "But it's between you and me, Uncle Oscar! Honour bright?"

The uncle burst into a roar of laughter.

"It's between you and me all right, you young Nat Gould," he said, laughing. "But where's your three hundred?"

"Bassett keeps it for me. We're partners."

"You are, are you! And what is Bassett putting on Daffodil?"

"He won't go quite as high as I do, I expect. Perhaps he'll go a hundred and fifty."

"What, pennies?" laughed the uncle.

"Pounds," said the child, with a surprised look at his uncle. "Bassett keeps a bigger reserve than I do."

Between wonder and amusement Uncle Oscar was silent. He pursued the matter no further, but he determined to take his nephew with him to the Lincoln races.

"Now, son," he said, "I'm putting twenty on Mirza, and I'll put five for you on any horse you fancy. What's your pick?"

"Daffodil, uncle."

"No, not the fiver on Daffodil!"

"I should if it was my own fiver," said the child.

"Good! Good! Right you are! A fiver for me and a fiver for you on Daffodil."

The child had never been to a race meeting before, and his eyes were blue fire. He pursed his mouth tight, and watched. A Frenchman just in front had put his money on Lancelot. Wild with excitement, he flayed his arms up and down, yelling "Lancelot! Lancelot!" in his French accent.

Daffodil came in first, Lancelot second, Mirza third. The child, flushed and with eyes blazing, was curiously serene. His uncle brought him four five-pound notes, four to one.

"What am I to do with these?" he cried, waving them before the boy's eyes.

"I suppose we'll talk to Bassett," said the boy. "I expect I have fifteen hundred now; and twenty in reserve; and this twenty."

His uncle studied him for some moments.

"Look here, son!" he said. "You're not serious about Bassett and that fifteen hundred, are you?"

"Yes, I am. But it's between you and me, uncle. Honour bright!"

"Honour bright all right, son! But I must talk to Bassett."

"If you'd like to be a partner, uncle, with Bassett and me, we could all be partners. Only, you'd have to promise, honour bright, uncle, not to let it go beyond us three. Bassett and I are lucky, and you must be lucky, because it was your ten shillings I started winning with . . ."

Uncle Oscar took both Bassett and Paul into Richmond Park for an afternoon, and there they talked.

"It's like this, you see, sir," Bassett said. "Master Paul would get me talking about racing events, spinning yarns, you know, sir. And he was always keen on knowing if I'd made or if I'd lost. It's about a year since, now, that I put five shillings on Blush of Dawn for him—and we lost. Then the luck turned, with that ten shillings he had from you, that we put on Singhalese. And since that time, it's been pretty steady, all things considering. What do you say, Master Paul?"

"We're all right when we're sure," said Paul. "It's when we're not quite sure that we go down."

"Oh, but we're careful then," said Bassett.

"But when are you sure?" smiled Uncle Oscar.

"It's Master Paul, sir," said Bassett, in a secret, religious voice. "It's as if he had it from heaven. Like Daffodil, now, for the Lincoln. That was as sure as eggs."

"Did you put anything on Daffodil?" asked Oscar Cresswell.

"Yes, sir, I made my bit."

"And my nephew?"

Bassett was obstinately silent, looking at Paul.

"I made twelve hundred, didn't I, Bassett? I told uncle I was putting three hundred on Daffodil."

"That's right," said Bassett, nodding.

"But where's the money?" asked the uncle.

"I keep it safe locked up, sir. Master Paul he can have it any minute he likes to ask for it."

"What, fifteen hundred pounds?"

"And twenty! and forty, that is, with the twenty he made on the course."

"It's amazing!" said the uncle.

"If Master Paul offers you to be partners, sir, I would, if I were you; if you'll excuse me," said Bassett.

Oscar Cresswell thought about it.

"I'll see the money," he said.

They drove home again, and sure enough, Bassett came round to the garden-house with fifteen hundred pounds in notes. The twenty pounds reserve was left with Joe Glee, in the Turf Commission deposit.

"You see, it's all right, uncle, when I'm sure! Then we go strong, for all we're worth. Don't we, Bassett?"

"We do that, Master Paul."

"And when are you sure?" said the uncle, laughing.

"Oh, well, sometimes I'm absolutely sure, like about Daffodil," said the boy; "and sometimes I have an idea; and sometimes I haven't even an idea, have I, Bassett? Then we're careful, because we mostly go down."

"You do, do you! And when you're sure, like about Daffodil, what makes you sure, sonny?"

"Oh, well, I don't know," said the boy uneasily. "I'm sure, you know, uncle; that's all."

"It's as if he had it from heaven, sir," Bassett reiterated.

"I should say so!" said the uncle.

But he became a partner. And when the Leger was coming on, Paul was "sure" about Lively Spark, which was a quite inconsiderable horse. The boy insisted on putting a thousand on the horse, Bassett went for five hundred, and Oscar Cresswell two hundred. Lively Spark came in first, and the betting had been ten to one against him. Paul had made ten thousand.

"You see," he said, "I was absolutely sure of him."

Even Oscar Cresswell had cleared two thousand.

"Look here, son," he said, "this sort of thing makes me nervous."

"It needn't, uncle! Perhaps I shan't be sure again for a long time."

"But what are you going to do with your money?" asked the uncle.

"Of course," said the boy, "I started it for mother. She said she had no luck, because father is unlucky, so I thought if I was lucky, it might stop whispering."

"What might stop whispering?"

"Our house. I hate our house for whispering."

"What does it whisper?"

"Why—why"—the boy fidgeted—"why, I don't know. But it's always short of money, you know, uncle."

"I know it, son, I know it."

"You know people send mother writs, don't you, uncle?"

"I'm afraid I do," said the uncle.

"And then the house whispers, like people laughing at you behind your back. It's awful, that is! I thought if I was lucky . . ."

"You might stop it," added the uncle.

The boy watched him with big blue eyes that had an uncanny cold fire in them, and he said never a word.

"Well, then!" said the uncle. "What are we doing?"

"I shouldn't like mother to know I was lucky," said the boy.

"Why not, son?"

"She'd stop me."

"I don't think she would."

"Oh!"—and the boy writhed in an odd way—"I don't want her to know, uncle."

"All right, son! We'll manage it without her knowing."

They managed it very easily. Paul, at the other's suggestion, handed over five thousand pounds to his uncle, who deposited it with the family lawyer, who was then to inform Paul's mother that a relative had put five thousand pounds into his hands, which sum was to be paid out a thousand pounds at a time, on the mother's birthday, for the next five years.

"So she'll have a birthday present of a thousand pounds for five successive years," said Uncle Oscar. "I hope it won't make it all the harder for her later."

Paul's mother had her birthday in November. The house had been "whispering" worse than ever lately, and, even in spite of his luck, Paul could not bear up against it. He was very anxious to see the effect of the birthday letter, telling his mother about the thousand pounds.

When there were no visitors, Paul now took his meals with his parents, as he was beyond the nursery control. His mother went into town nearly every day. She had discovered that she had an odd knack of sketching furs and dress materials, so she worked secretly in the studio of a friend who was the chief "artist" for the leading drapers. She drew the figures of ladies in furs and ladies in silk and sequins for the newspaper advertisements. This young woman artist earned several thousand pounds a year, but Paul's mother only made several hundreds, and she was again dissatisfied. She so wanted to be first in something, and she did not suceed, even in making sketches for drapery advertisements.

She was down to breakfast on the morning of her birthday. Paul watched her face as she read her letters. He knew the lawyer's letter. As his mother read it, her face hardened and became more expressionless. Then a cold, determined look came on her mouth. She hid the letter under the pile of others, and said not a word about it.

"Didn't you have anything nice in the post for your birthday, mother?" said Paul.

"Quite moderately nice," she said, her voice cold and absent.

She went away to town without saying more.

But in the afternoon Uncle Oscar appeared. He said Paul's mother had had a long interview with the lawyer, asking if the whole five thousand could be advanced at once, as she was in debt.

"What do you think, uncle?" said the boy.

"I leave it to you, son."

"Oh, let her have it, then! We can get some more with the other," said the boy.

"A bird in the hand is worth two in the bush, laddie!" said Uncle Oscar.

"But I'm sure to know for the Grand National; or the Lincolnshire; or else the Derby. I'm sure to know for one of them," said Paul.

So Uncle Oscar signed the agreement, and Paul's mother touched the whole five thousand. Then something very curious happened. The voices in the house suddenly went mad, like a chorus of frogs on a spring evening. There were certain new furnishings, and Paul had a tutor. He was really going to Eton, his father's school, in the following autumn. There were flowers in the winter, and a blossoming of the luxury Paul's mother had been used to. And yet the voices in the house, behind the sprays of mimosa and almond blossom, and from under the piles of iridescent cushions, simply trilled and screamed in a sort of ecstasy: "There must be more money! Oh-h-h, there must be more money. Oh, now, now-w! Now-w-w—there must be more money—more than ever! More than ever!"

It frightened Paul terribly. He studied away at his Latin and Greek with his tutors. But his intense hours were spent with Bassett. The Grand National had gone by: he had not "known," and had lost a hundred pounds. Summer was at hand. He was in agony for the Lincoln. But even for the Lincoln he didn't "know" and he lost fifty pounds. He became wild-eyed and strange, as if something were going to explode in him.

"Let it alone, son! Don't you bother about it!" urged Uncle Oscar. But it was as if the boy couldn't really hear what his uncle was saying.

"I've got to know for the Derby! I've got to know for the Derby!" the child reiterated, his big blue eyes blazing with a sort of madness.

His mother noticed how overwrought he was.

"You'd better go to the seaside. Wouldn't you like to go now to the seaside, instead of waiting? I think you'd better," she said, looking down at him anxiously, her heart curiously heavy because of him.

But the child lifted his uncanny blue eyes.

"I couldn't possibly go before the Derby, mother!" he said. "I couldn't possibly!"

"Why not?" she said, her voice becoming heavy when she was opposed. "Why not? You can still go from the seaside to see the Derby with your Uncle Oscar, if that's what you wish. No need for you to wait here. Besides, I think you care too much about these races. It's a bad sign. My family has been a gambling family, and you won't know till you grow up how much damage it has done. But it has done damage. I shall have to send Bassett away, and ask Uncle Oscar not to talk racing to you, unless you promise to be reasonable about it; go away to the seaside and forget it. You're all nerves!"

"I'll do what you like, mother, so long as you don't send me away till after the Derby," the boy said.

"Send you away from where? Just from this house?"

"Yes," he said, gazing at her.

"Why, you curious child, what makes you care about this house so much, suddenly? I never knew you loved it."

He gazed at her without speaking. He had a secret within a secret, something he had not divulged, even to Bassett or to his Uncle Oscar.

But his mother, after standing undecided and a little bit sullen for some moments, said:

"Very well, then! Don't go to the seaside till after the Derby, if you don't wish it. But promise me you won't let your nerves go to pieces. Promise you won't think so much about horse racing and events, as you call them!"

"Oh, no," said the boy casually. "I won't think much about them, mother. You needn't worry. I wouldn't worry, mother, if I were you."

"If you were me and I were you," said his mother, "I wonder what we should do!"

"But you know you needn't worry, mother, don't you?" the boy repeated.

"I should be awfully glad to know it," she said wearily.

"Oh, well, you can, you know. I mean, you ought to know you needn't worry," he insisted.

"Ought I? Then I'll see about it," she said.

Paul's secret of secrets was his wooden horse, that which had no name. Since he was emancipated from a nurse and a nursery-governess, he had had his rocking horse removed to his own bedroom at the top of the house.

"Surely, you're too big for a rocking horse!" his mother had remonstrated.

"Well, you see, mother, till I can have a real horse, I like to have some sort of animal about," had been his quaint answer.

"Do you feel he keeps you company?" she laughed.

"Oh, yes! He's very good, he always keeps me company, when I'm there," said Paul.

So the horse, rather shabby, stood in an arrested prance in the boy's bedroom.

The Derby was drawing near, and the boy grew more and more tense. He hardly heard what was spoken to him, he was very frail, and his eyes were really uncanny. His mother had sudden seizures of uneasiness about him. Sometimes, for half-an-hour, she would feel a sudden anxiety about him that was almost anguish. She wanted to rush to him at once, and know he was safe.

Two nights before the Derby, she was at a big party in town, when one of her rushes of anxiety about her boy, her first-born, gripped her heart till she could hardly speak. She fought with the feeling, might and main, for she believed in common sense. But it was too strong. She had to leave the dance and go downstairs to telephone to the country. The children's nursery-governess was terribly surprised and startled at being rung up in the night.

"Are the children all right, Miss Wilmot?"

"Oh, yes, they are quite all right."

"Master Paul? Is he all right?"

"He went to bed as right as a trivet. Shall I run up and look at him?"

"No," said Paul's mother reluctantly. "No! Don't trouble. It's all right. Don't sit up. We shall be home fairly soon." She did not want her son's privacy intruded upon.

"Very good," said the governess.

It was about one o'clock when Paul's mother and father drove up to their house. All was still. Paul's mother went to her room and slipped off her white fur coat. She had told her maid not to wait up for her. She heard her husband downstairs, mixing a whisky-and-soda.

And then, because of the strange anxiety at her heart, she stole upstairs to her son's room. Noiselessly she went along the upper corridor. Was there a faint noise? What was it?

She stood, with arrested muscles, outside his door, listening. There was a strange, heavy, and yet not loud noise. Her heart stood still. It was a soundless noise, yet rushing and powerful. Something huge, in violent, hushed motion. What was it? What in God's name was it? She ought to know. She felt that she knew the noise. She knew what it was.

Yet she could not place it. She couldn't say what it was. And on and on it went, like a madness.

Softly, frozen with anxiety and fear, she turned the door handle.

The room was dark. Yet in the space near the window, she heard and saw something plunging to and fro. She gazed in fear and amazement.

Then suddenly she switched on the light, and saw her son, in his green pyjamas, madly surging on the rocking horse. The blaze of light suddenly lit him up, as he urged the wooden horse, and lit her up, as she stood, blonde, in her dress of pale green and crystal, in the doorway.

"Paul!" she cried. "Whatever are you doing?"

"It's Malabar!" he screamed, in a powerful, strange voice. "It's Malabar."

His eyes blazed at her for one strange and senseless second, as he ceased urging his wooden horse. Then he fell with a crash to the ground, and she, all her tormented motherhood flooding upon her, rushed to gather him up.

But he was unconscious, and unconscious he remained, with some brain-fever. He talked and tossed, and his mother sat stonily by his side.

"Malabar! It's Malabar! Bassett, Bassett, I know it! It's Malabar!"

So the child cried, trying to get up and urge the rocking horse that gave him his inspiration.

"What does he mean by Malabar?" asked the heart-frozen mother.

"I don't know," said the father stonily.

"What does he mean by Malabar?" she asked her brother Oscar.

"It's one of the horses running for the Derby," was the answer.

And, in spite of himself, Oscar Cresswell spoke to Bassett, and himself put a thousand on Malabar: at fourteen to one.

The third day of the illness was critical: they were waiting for a change. The boy, with his rather long, curly hair, was tossing ceaselessly on the pillow. He neither slept nor regained consciousness, and his eyes were like blue stones. His mother sat, feeling her heart had gone, turned actually into a stone.

In the evening, Oscar Cresswell did not come, but Bassett sent a message, saying could he come up for one moment, just one moment? Paul's mother was very angry at the intrusion, but on second thought she agreed. The boy was the same. Perhaps Bassett might bring him to consciousness.

The gardener, a shortish fellow with a little brown moustache, and sharp little brown eyes, tiptoed into the room, touched his imaginary cap to Paul's mother, and stole to the bedside, staring with glittering, smallish eyes, at the tossing, dying child.

"Master Paul!" he whispered. "Master Paul! Malabar come in first all right, a clean win. I did as you told me. You've made over seventy thousand pounds, you have; you've got over eighty thousand. Malabar came in all right, Master Paul."

"Malabar! Malabar! Did I say Malabar, mother? Did I say Malabar? Do you think I'm lucky, mother? I knew Malabar, didn't I? Over eighty thousand pounds! I call that lucky, don't you, mother? Over eighty thousand pounds! I knew, didn't I know I knew? Malabar came in all right. If I ride my horse till I'm sure, then I tell you, Bassett, you can go as high as you like. Did you go for all you were worth, Bassett?"

"I went a thousand on it, Master Paul."

"I never told you, mother, that if I can ride my horse, and get there, then I'm absolutely sure—oh, absolutely! Mother, did I ever tell you? I'm lucky."

"No, you never did," said the mother.

But the boy died in the night.

And even as he lay dead, his mother heard her brother's voice saying to her: "My God, Hester, you're eighty-odd thousand to the good and a poor devil of a son to the bad. But, poor devil, poor devil, he's best gone out of a life where he rides his rocking horse to find a winner."

ERNEST HEMINGWAY (1899–1961)

The Snows of Kilimanjaro

Kilimanjaro is a snow covered mountain 19,710 feet high, and is said to be the highest mountain in Africa. Its western summit is called the Masai "Ngàje Ngài," the House of God. Close to the western summit there is the dried and frozen carcass of a leopard. No one has explained what the leopard was seeking at that altitude.

"The marvellous thing is that it's painless," he said. "That's how you know when it starts."

"Is it really?"

"Absolutely. I'm awfully sorry about the odor though. That must bother you."

"Don't! Please don't."

"Look at them," he said. "Now is it sight or is it scent that brings them like that?"

The cot the man lay on was in the wide shade of a mimosa tree and as he looked out past the shade onto the glare of the plain there were three of the big birds squatted obscenely, while in the sky a dozen more sailed, making quick-moving shadows as they passed.

"They've been there since the day the truck broke down," he said. "Today's the first time any have lit on the ground. I watched the way they sailed very carefully at first in case I ever wanted to use them in a story. That's funny now."

"I wish you wouldn't," she said.

"I'm only talking," he said. "It's much easier if I talk. But I don't want to bother you."

"You know it doesn't bother me," she said. "It's that I've gotten so very nervous not being able to do anything. I think we might make it as easy as we can until the plane comes."

"Or until the plane doesn't come."

"Please tell me what I can do. There must be something I can do."

"You can take the leg off and that might stop it, though I doubt it. Or you can shoot me. You're a good shot now. I taught you to shoot didn't I?"

"Please don't talk that way. Couldn't I read to you?"

"Read what?"

"Anything in the book bag that we haven't read."

"I can't listen to it," he said. "Talking is the easiest. We quarrel and that makes the time pass."

"I don't quarrel. I never want to quarrel. Let's not quarrel any more. No matter how nervous we get. Maybe they will be back with another truck today. Maybe the plane will come."

"I don't want to move," the man said. "There is no sense in moving now except to make it easier for you."

"That's cowardly."

"Can't you let a man die as comfortably as he can without calling him names? What's the use of slanging me?"

"You're not going to die."

"Don't be silly. I'm dying now. Ask those bastards." He looked over to where the huge, filthy birds sat, their naked heads sunk in the hunched feathers. A fourth planed down, to run quick-legged and then waddle slowly toward the others.

"They are around every camp. You never notice them. You can't die if you don't give up."

"Where did you read that? You're such a bloody fool."

"You might think about some one else."

"For Christ's sake," he said, "That's been my trade."

He lay then and was quiet for a while and looked across the heat shimmer of the plain to the edge of the bush. There were a few Tommies that showed minute and white against the yellow and, far off, he saw a herd of zebra, white against the green of the bush. This was a pleasant camp under big trees against a hill, with good water, and close by, a nearly dry water hole where sand grouse flighted in the mornings.

"Wouldn't you like me to read?" she asked. She was sitting on a canvas chair beside his cot. "There's a breeze coming up."

"No thanks."

"Maybe the truck will come."

"I don't give a damn about the truck."

"I do."

"You give a damn about so many things that I don't."

"Not so many, Harry."

"What about a drink?"

"It's supposed to be bad for you. It said in Black's to avoid all alcohol. You shouldn't drink."

"Molo!" he shouted.

"Yes Bwana."

"Bring whiskey-soda."

"Yes Bwana."

"You shouldn't," she said. "That's what I mean by giving up. It says it's bad for you. I know it's bad for you."

"No," he said. "It's good for me."

So now it was all over, he thought. So now he would never have a chance to finish it. So this was the way it ended in a bickering over a drink. Since the gangrene started in his right leg he had no pain and with the pain the horror had gone and all he felt now was a great tiredness and anger that this was the end of it. For this, that now was coming, he had very little curiosity. For years it had obsessed him; but now it meant nothing in itself. It was strange how easy being tired enough made it.

Now he would never write the things that he had saved to write until he knew enough to write them well. Well, he would not have to fail at trying to write them either. Maybe you could never write them, and that was why you put them off and delayed the starting. Well he would never know, now.

"I wish we'd never come," the woman said. She was looking at him holding the glass and biting her lip. "You never would have gotten anything like this in Paris. You always said you loved Paris. We could have stayed in Paris or gone anywhere. I'd have gone anywhere. I said I'd go anywhere you wanted. If you wanted to shoot we could have gone shooting in Hungary and been comfortable."

"Your bloody money," he said.

"That's not fair," she said. "It was always yours as much as mine. I left everything and I went wherever you wanted to go and I've done what you wanted to do. But I wish we'd never come here."

"You said you loved it."

"I did when you were all right. But now I hate it. I don't see why that had to happen to your leg. What have we done to have that happen to us?"

"I suppose what I did was to forget to put iodine on it when I first scratched it. Then I didn't pay any attention to it because I never infect. Then, later, when it got bad, it was probably using that weak carbolic solution when the other antiseptics ran out that paralyzed the minute blood vessels and started the gangrene." He looked at her, "What else?"

"I don't mean that."

"If we would have hired a good mechanic instead of a half baked kikuyu driver, he would have checked the oil and never burned out that bearing in the truck."

"I don't mean that."

"If you hadn't left your own people, your goddamned Old Westbury, Saratoga, Palm Beach people to take me on—"

"Why, I loved you. That's not fair. I love you now. I'll always love you. Don't you love me?"

"No," said the man. "I don't think so. I never have."

"Harry, what are you saying? You're out of your head."

"No. I haven't any head to go out of."

"Don't drink that," she said. "Darling, please don't drink that. We have to do everything we can."

"You do it," he said. "I'm tired."

Now in his mind he saw a railway station at Karagatch and he was standing with his pack and that was the headlight of the Simplon-Orient cutting the dark now and he was leaving Thrace then after the retreat. That was one of the things he had saved to write, with, in the morning at breakfast, looking out the window and seeing snow on the mountains in Bulgaria and Nansen's Secretary asking the old man if it were snow and the old man looking at it and saying, No, that's not snow. It's too early for snow. And the Secretary repeating to the other girls, No, you see. It's not snow and them all saying, It's not snow we were mistaken. But it was the snow all right and he sent them on into it when he evolved exchange of populations. And it was snow they tramped along in until they died that winter.

It was snow too that fell all Christmas week that year up in the Gauertal, that year they lived in the woodcutter's house with the big square porcelain stove that filled half the room, and they slept on mattresses filled with beech leaves, the time the deserter came with his feet bloody in the snow. He said the police were right behind him and they gave him woolen socks and held the gendarmes talking until the tracks had drifted over.

In Schrunz, on Christmas day, the snow was so bright it hurt your eyes when you looked out from the weinstube and saw every one coming home from church. That was where they walked up the sleigh-smoothed urine-yellowed road along the river with the steep pine hills, skis heavy on the shoulder, and where they ran that great run down the glacier above the Madlener-haus, the snow as smooth to see as cake frosting and as light as powder and he remembered the noiseless rush the speed made as you dropped down like a bird.

They were snow-bound a week in the Madlener-haus that time in the blizzard playing cards in the smoke by the lantern light and the stakes were higher all the time as Herr Lent lost more. Finally he lost it all. Everything, the skischule money and all the season's profit and then his capital. He could see him with his long nose, picking up the cards and then opening, "Sans Voir." There was always gambling then. When there was no snow you gambled and when there was too much you gambled. He thought of all the time in his life he had spent gambling.

But he had never written a line of that, nor of that cold, bright Christmas day with the mountains showing across the plain that Barker had flown across the lines to bomb the Austrian officers' leave train, machine-gunning them as they scattered and ran. He remem-

bered Barker afterwards coming into the mess and starting to tell about it. And how quiet it got and then somebody saying, "You bloody murderous bastard."

Those were the same Austrians they killed then that he skied with later. No not the same. Hans, that he skied with all that year, had been in the Kaiser-Jägers and when they went hunting hares together up the little valley above the saw-mill they had talked of the fighting on Pasubio and of the attack on Pertica and Asalone and he had never written a word of that. Nor of Monte Corno, nor the Siete Commum, nor of Arsiedo.

How many winters had he lived in the Voralberg and the Arlberg? It was four and then he remembered the man who had the fox to sell when they had walked into Bludenz, that time to buy presents, and the cherry-pit taste of good kirsch, the fast-slipping rush of running powder-snow on crust, singing "Hi! Ho! said Rolly!" as you ran down the last stretch to the steep drop, taking it straight, then running the orchard in three turns and out across the ditch and onto the icy road behind the inn. Knocking your bindings loose, kicking the skis free and leaning them up against the wooden wall of the inn, the lamplight coming from the window, where inside, in the smoky, new-wine smelling warmth, they were playing the accordion.

"Where did we stay in Paris?" he asked the woman who was sitting by him in a canvas chair, now, in Africa.

"At the Crillon. You know that."

"Why do I know that?"

"That's where we always stayed."

"No. Not always."

"There and at the Pavillion Henri-Quatre in St. Germain. You said you loved it there."

"Love is a dunghill," said Harry. "And I'm the cock that gets on it to crow."

"If you have to go away," she said, "is it absolutely necessary to kill off everything you leave behind? I mean do you have to take away everything? Do you have to kill your horse, and your wife and burn your saddle and your armour?"

"Yes," he said. "Your damned money was my armour. My Swift and my Armour."

"Don't."

"All right. I'll stop that. I don't want to hurt you."

"It's a little bit late now."

"All right then. I'll go on hurting you. It's more amusing. The only thing I ever really liked to do with you I can't do now."

"No, that's not true. You liked to do many things and everything you wanted to do I did."

"Oh, for Christ sake stop bragging, will you?"

He looked at her and saw her crying.

"Listen," he said. "Do you think that it is fun to do this? I don't know why I'm doing it. It's trying to kill to keep yourself alive, I imagine. I was all right when we started talking. I didn't mean to start this, and now I'm crazy as a coot and being as cruel to you as I can be. Don't pay any attention, darling, to what I say. I love you, really. You know I love you. I've never loved any one else the way I love you."

He slipped into the familiar lie he made his bread and butter by.

"You're sweet to me."

"You bitch," he said. "You rich bitch. That's poetry. I'm full of poetry now. Rot and poetry. Rotten poetry."

"Stop it. Harry, why do you have to turn into a devil now?"

"I don't like to leave anything," the man said. "I don't like to leave things behind."

✻

It was evening now and he had been asleep. The sun was gone behind the hill and there was a shadow all across the plain and the small animals were feeding close to camp; quick dropping heads and switching tails, he watched them keeping well out away from the bush now. The birds no longer waited on the ground. They were all perched heavily in a tree. There were many more of them. His personal boy was sitting by the bed.

"Memsahib's gone to shoot," the boy said. "Does Bwana want?"

"Nothing."

She had gone to kill a piece of meat and, knowing how he liked to watch the game, she had gone well away so she would not disturb this little pocket of the plain that he could see. She was always thoughtful, he thought. On anything she knew about, or had read, or that she had ever heard.

It was not her fault that when he went to her he was already over. How could a woman know that you meant nothing that you said; that you spoke only from habit and to be comfortable? After he no longer meant what he said, his lies were more successful with women than when he had told them the truth.

It was not so much that he lied as that there was no truth to tell. He had had his life and it was over and then he went on living it again with different people and more money, with the best of the same places, and some new ones.

You kept from thinking and it was all marvellous. You were equipped with good insides so that you did not go to pieces that way, the way most of them had, and you made an attitude that you cared nothing for the work you used to do, now that you could no longer do it. But, in yourself, you said that you would write about these people; about the very rich; that you were really not of them but a spy in their country; that you would leave it and write of it and for once it would be written by some one who knew what he was writing of. But he would never do it, because each day of not writing, of comfort, of being that which he despised, dulled his ability and softened his will to work so that, finally, he did no work at all. The people he knew now were all much more comfortable when he did not work. Africa was where he had been happiest in the good time of his life, so he had come out here to start again. They had made this safari with the minimum of comfort. There was no hardship; but there was no luxury and he had thought that he could get back into training that way. That in some way he could work the fat off his soul the way a fighter went into the mountains to work and train in order to burn it out of his body.

She had liked it. She said she loved it. She loved anything that was exciting, that involved a change of scene, where there were new people and where things were pleasant. And he had felt the illusion of returning strength of will to work. Now if this was how it ended, and he knew it was, he must not turn like some snake biting itself because its back was broken. It wasn't this woman's fault. If it had not been she it would have been another. If he lived by a lie he should try to die by it. He heard a shot beyond the hill.

She shot very well this good, this rich bitch, this kindly caretaker and destroyer of his talent. Nonsense. He had destroyed his talent himself. Why should he blame this woman because she kept him well? He had destroyed his talent by not using it, by betrayals of himself and what he believed in, by drinking so much that he blunted the edge of his perceptions, by laziness, by sloth, and by snobbery, by pride and by prejudice, by hook and by crook. What was this? A catalogue of old books? What was his talent anyway? It was a talent all right but instead of using it, he had traded on it. It was never what he had done, but always what he could do. And he had chosen to make his living with something else instead of a pen or a pencil. It was strange, too, wasn't it, that when he fell in love with another woman, that woman should always have more money than the last one? But when he no longer was in love, when he was only lying, as to this woman, now, who had the most money of all, who had all the money there was, who had had a husband and children, who had taken lovers and been dissatisfied with them, and who loved him dearly as a writer, as a man, as a companion and as a proud possession; it was strange that when he did not love her at all and was lying, that he should be able to give her more for her money than when he had really loved.

We must all be cut out for what we do, he thought. However you make your living is where your talent lies. He had sold vitality, in one form or another, all his life and when your affections are not too involved you give much better value for the money. He had found that out but he would never write that, now, either. No, he would not write that, although it was well worth writing.

Now she came in sight, walking across the open toward the camp. She was wearing jodphurs and carrying her rifle. The two boys had a Tommie slung and they were coming along behind her. She was still a good-looking woman, he thought, and she had a pleasant body. She had a great talent and appreciation for the bed, she was not pretty, but he liked her face, she read enormously, liked to ride and shoot and, certainly, she drank too much. Her husband had died when she was still a comparatively young woman and for a while she had devoted herself to her two just-grown children, who did not need her and were embarrassed at having her about, to her stable of horses, to books, and to bottles. She liked to read in the evening before dinner and she drank Scotch and soda while she read. By dinner she was fairly drunk and after a bottle of wine at dinner she was usually drunk enough to sleep.

That was before the lovers. After she had the lovers she did not drink so much because she did not have to be drunk to sleep. But the lovers bored her. She had been married to a man who had never bored her and these people bored her very much.

Then one of her two children was killed in a plane crash and after that was over she did not want the lovers, and drink being no anæsthetic she had to make another life. Suddenly, she had been acutely frightened of being alone. But she wanted some one that she respected with her.

It had begun very simply. She liked what he wrote and she had always envied the life he led. She thought he did exactly what he wanted to. The steps by which she had acquired him and the way in which she had finally fallen in love with him were all part of a regular progression in which she had built herself a new life and he had traded away what remained of his old life.

He had traded it for security, for comfort too, there was no denying that, and for what else? He did not know. She would have bought him anything he wanted. He knew that. She was a damned nice woman too. He would as soon be in bed with her as any one; rather with her, because she was richer, because she was very pleasant and appreciative and because she never made scenes. And now this life that she had built again was coming to a term because he had not used iodine two weeks ago when a thorn had scratched his knee as they moved forward trying to photograph a herd of waterbuck standing, their heads up, peering while their nostrils searched the air, their ears spread wide to hear the first noise that would send them rushing into the bush. They had bolted, too, before he got the picture.

Here she came now.

He turned his head on the cot to look toward her. "Hello," he said.

"I shot a Tommy ram," she told him. "He'll make you good broth and I'll have them mash some potatoes with the Klim. How do you feel?"

"Much better."

"Isn't that lovely? You know I thought perhaps you would. You were sleeping when I left."

"I had a good sleep. Did you walk far?"

"No. Just around behind the hill. I made quite a good shot on the Tommy."

"You shoot marvellously, you know."

"I love it. I've loved Africa. Really. If *you're* all right it's the most fun that I've ever had. You don't know the fun it's been to shoot with you. I've loved the country."

"I love it too."

"Darling, you don't know how marvellous it is to see you feeling better. I couldn't stand it when you felt that way. You won't talk to me like that again, will you? Promise me?"

"No," he said. "I don't remember what I said."

"You don't have to destroy me. Do you? I'm only a middle-aged woman who loves you and wants to do what you want to do. I've been destroyed two or three times already. You wouldn't want to destroy me again, would you?"

"I'd like to destroy you a few times in bed," he said.

"Yes. That's the good destruction. That's the way we're made to be destroyed. The plane will be here tomorrow."

"How do you know?"

"I'm sure. It's bound to come. The boys have the wood all ready and the grass to make the smudge. I went down and looked at it again today. There's plenty of room to land and we have the smudges ready at both ends."

"What makes you think it will come tomorrow?"

"I'm sure it will. It's overdue now. Then, in town, they will fix up your leg and then we will have some good destruction. Not that dreadful talking kind."

"Should we have a drink? The sun is down."

"Do you think you should?"

"I'm having one."

"We'll have one together. *Molo, letti dui whiskey-soda!*" she called.

"You'd better put on your mosquito boots," he told her.

"I'll wait till I bathe . . . ."

While it grew dark they drank and just before it was dark and there was no longer enough light to shoot, a hyena crossed the open on his way around the hill.

"That bastard crosses there every night," the man said. "Every night for two weeks."

"He's the one makes the noise at night. I don't mind it. They're a filthy animal though."

Drinking together, with no pain now except the discomfort of lying in the one position, the boys lighting a fire, its shadow jumping on the tents, he could feel the return of acquiescence in this life of pleasant surrender. She *was* very good to him. He had been cruel and unjust in the afternoon. She was a fine woman, marvellous really. And just then it occurred to him that he was going to die.

It came with a rush; not as a rush of water nor of wind; but of a sudden evil-smelling emptiness and the odd thing was that the hyena slipped lightly along the edge of it.

"What is it, Harry?" she asked him.

"Nothing," he said. "You had better move over to the other side. To windward."

"Did Molo change the dressing?"

"Yes. I'm just using the boric now."

"How do you feel?"

"A little wobbly."

"I'm going in to bathe," she said. "I'll be right out. I'll eat with you and then we'll put the cot in."

So, he said to himself, we did well to stop the quarrelling. He had never quarrelled much with this woman, while with the women that he loved he had quarrelled so much they had finally, always, with the corrosion of the quarrelling, killed what they had together. He had loved too much, demanded too much, and he wore it all out.

He thought about alone in Constantinople that time, having quarrelled in Paris before he had gone out. He had whored the whole time and then, when that was over, and he had failed to kill his loneliness, but only made it worse, he had written her, the first one, the one who left him, a letter telling her how he had never been able to kill it. . . . How when he thought he saw her outside the Regence *one time it made him go all faint and sick inside, and that he would follow a woman who looked like her in some way, along the Boulevard, afraid to see it was not she, afraid to lose the feeling it gave him. How every one he had slept with had only made him miss her more. How what she had done could never matter since he knew he could not cure himself of loving her. He wrote this letter at the*

Club, cold sober, and mailed it to New York asking her to write him at the office in Paris. That seemed safe. And that night missing her so much it made him feel hollow sick inside, he wandered up past Taxim's, picked a girl up and took her out to supper. He had gone to a place to dance with her afterward, she danced badly, and left her for a hot Armenian slut, that swung her belly against him so it almost scalded. He took her away from a British gunner subaltern after a row. The gunner asked him outside and they fought in the street on the cobbles in the dark. He'd hit him twice, hard, on the side of the jaw and when he didn't go down he knew he was in for a fight. The gunner hit him in the body, then beside his eye. He swung with his left again and landed and the gunner fell on him and grabbed his coat and tore the sleeve off and he clubbed him twice behind the ear and then smashed him with his right as he pushed him away. When the gunner went down his head hit first and he ran with the girl because they heard the M.P.'s coming. They got into a taxi and drove out to Rimmily Hissa along the Bosphorus, and around, and back in the cool night and went to bed and she felt as over-ripe as she looked but smooth, rose-petal, syrupy, smooth-bellied, big-breasted and needed no pillow under her buttocks, and he left her before she was awake looking blousy enough in the first daylight and turned up at the Pera Palace with a black eye, carrying his coat because one sleeve was missing.

That same night he left for Anatolia and he remembered, later on that trip, riding all day through fields of the poppies that they raised for opium and how strange it made you feel, finally, and all the distances seemed wrong, to where they had made the attack with the newly arrived Constantine officers, that did not know a god-damned thing, and the artillery had fired into the troops and the British observer had cried like a child.

That was the day he'd first seen dead men wearing white ballet skirts and upturned shoes with pompons on them. The Turks had come steadily and lumpily and he had seen the skirted men running and the officers shooting into them and running themselves and he and the British-observer had run too until his lungs ached and his mouth was full of the taste of pennies and they stopped behind some rocks and there were the Turks coming as lumpily as ever. Later he had seen the things that he could never think of and later still he had seen much worse. So when he got back to Paris that time he could not talk about it or stand to have it mentioned. And there in the café as he passed was that American poet with a pile of saucers in front of him and a stupid look on his potato face talking about the Dada movement with a Roumanian who said his name was Tristan Tzara, who always wore a monocle and had a headache, and, back at the apartment with his wife that now he loved again, the quarrel all

*over, the madness all over, glad to be home, the office sent his mail up
to the flat. So then the letter in answer to the one he'd written came
in on a platter one morning and when he saw the handwriting he
went cold all over and tried to slip the letter underneath another.
But his wife said, "Who is that letter from, dear?" and that was the
end of the beginning of that.*

*He remembered the good times with them all, and the quarrels.
They always picked the finest places to have the quarrels. And why
had they always quarrelled when he was feeling best? He had never
written any of that because, at first, he never wanted to hurt any one
and then it seemed as though there was enough to write without it.
But he had always thought that he would write it finally. There was
so much to write. He had seen the world change; not just the events;
although he had seen many of them and had watched the people, but
he had seen the subtler change and he could remember how the
people were at different times. He had been in it and he had watched
it and it was his duty to write of it; but now he never would.*

"How do you feel?" she said. She had come out from the tent now
after her bath.

"All right."

"Could you eat now?" He saw Molo behind her with the folding
table and the other boy with the dishes.

"I want to write," he said.

"You ought to take some broth to keep your strength up."

"I'm going to die tonight," he said. "I don't need my strength
up."

"Don't be melodramatic, Harry, please," she said.

"Why don't you use your nose? I'm rotted half way up my thigh
now. What the hell should I fool with broth for? Molo bring whiskey-
soda."

"Please take the broth," she said gently.

"All right."

The broth was too hot. He had to hold it in the cup until it cooled
enough to take it and then he just got it down without gagging.

"You're a fine woman," he said. "Don't pay any attention to
me."

She looked at him with her well-known, well-loved face from *Spur*
and *Town and Country,* only a little the worse for drink, only a little
the worse for bed, but *Town and Country* never showed those good
breasts and those useful thighs and those lightly small-of-back-caress-
ing hands, and as he looked and saw her well known pleasant smile,
he felt death come again. This time there was no rush. It was a puff,
as of a wind that makes a candle flicker and the flame go tall.

"They can bring my net out later and hang it from the tree and build the fire up. I'm not going in the tent tonight. It's not worth moving. It's a clear night. There won't be any rain." ·

So this was how you died, in whispers that you did not hear. Well, there would be no more quarrelling. He could promise that. The one experience that he had never had he was not going to spoil now. He probably would. You spoiled everything. But perhaps he wouldn't.

"You can't take dictation, can you?"

"I never learned," she told him.

"That's all right."

There wasn't time, of course, although it seemed as though it telescoped so that you might put it all into one paragraph if you could get it right.

There was a log house, chinked white with mortar, on a hill above the lake. There was a bell on a pole by the door to call the people in to meals. Behind the house were fields and behind the fields was the timber. A line of lombardy poplars ran from the house to the dock. Other poplars ran along the point. A road went up to the hills along the edge of the timber and along that road he picked blackberries. Then that log house was burned down and all the guns that had been on deer foot racks above the open fire place were burned and afterwards their barrels, with the lead melted in the magazines, and the stocks burned away, lay out on the heap of ashes that were used to make lye for the big iron soap kettles, and you asked Grandfather if you could have them to play with, and he said, no. You see they were his guns still and he never bought any others. Nor did he hunt any more. The house was rebuilt in the same place out of lumber now and painted white and from its porch you saw the poplars and the lake beyond; but there were never any more guns. The barrels of the guns that had hung on the deer feet on the wall of the log house lay out there on the heap of ashes and no one ever touched them.

In the Black Forest, after the war, we rented a trout stream and there were two ways to walk to it. One was down the valley from Triberg and around the valley road in the shade of the trees that bordered the white road, and then up a side road that went up through the hills past many small farms, with the big Schwarzwald houses, until that road crossed the stream. That was where our fishing began.

The other way was to climb steeply up to the edge of the woods and then go across the top of the hills through the pine woods, and then out to the edge of a meadow and down across this meadow to the bridge. There were birches along the stream and it was not big, but narrow, clear and fast, with pools where it had cut under the roots of the birches. At the Hotel in Triberg the proprietor had a fine season. It was very pleasant and we were all great friends. The next year came the inflation and the money he had made the year before was not enough to buy supplies to open the hotel and he hanged himself.

You could dictate that, but you could not dictate the Place Contrescarpe where the flower sellers dyed their flowers in the street and the dye ran over the paving where the autobus started and the old men and the women, always drunk on wine and bad marc; and the children with their noses running in the cold; the smell of dirty sweat and poverty and drunkenness at the Café des Amateurs and the whores at the Bal Musette they lived above. The Concierge who entertained the trooper of the Garde Republicaine in her loge, his horse-hair-plumed helmet on a chair. The locataire across the hall whose husband was a bicycle racer and her joy that morning at the Cremerie when she had opened L'Auto and seen where he placed third in Paris-Tours, his first big race. She had blushed and laughed and then gone upstairs crying with the yellow sporting paper in her hand. The husband of the woman who ran the Bal Musette drove a taxi and when he, Harry, had to take an early plane the husband knocked upon the door to wake him and they each drank a glass of white wine at the zinc of the bar before they started. He knew his neighbors in that quarter then because they all were poor.

Around that Place there were two kinds; the drunkards and the sportifs. The drunkards killed their poverty that way; the sportifs took it out in exercise. They were the descendants of the Communards and it was no struggle for them to know their politics. They knew who had shot their fathers, their relatives, their brothers, and their friends when the Versailles troops came in and took the town after the Commune and executed any one they could catch with calloused hands, or who wore a cap, or carried any other sign he was a working man. And in that poverty, and in that quarter across the street from a Boucherie Chevaline and a wine co-operative he had written the start of all he was to do. There never was another part of Paris that he loved like that, the sprawling trees, the old white plastered houses painted brown below, the long green of the autobus in that round square, the purple flower dye upon the paving, the sudden drop down the hill of the rue Cardinal Lemoine to the River, and the other way the narrow crowded world of the rue Mouffetard. The street that ran up toward the Pantheon and the other that he always took with the bicycle, the only asphalted street in all that quarter, smooth under the tires, with the high narrow houses and the cheap tall hotel where Paul Verlaine had died. There were only two rooms in the apartments where they lived and he had a room on the top floor of that hotel that cost him sixty francs a month where he

*did his writing, and from it he could see the roofs and chimney pots
and all the hills of Paris.*

*From the apartment you could only see the wood and coal man's
place. He sold wine too, bad wine. The golden horse's head outside
the Boucherie Chevaline where the carcasses hung yellow gold and
red in the open window, and the green painted co-operative where
they bought their wine; good wine and cheap. The rest was plaster
walls and the windows of the neighbors. The neighbors who, at
night, when some one lay drunk in the street, moaning and groaning
in that typical French ivresse that you were propaganded to believe
did not exist, would open their windows and then the murmur of
talk.*

*"Where is the policeman? When you don't want him the bugger is
always there. He's sleeping with some concierge. Get the* Agent." *Till
some one threw a bucket of water from a window and the moaning
stopped. "What's that? Water. Ah, that's intelligent." And the windows shutting. Marie, his femme de menage, protesting against the
eight-hour day saying, "If a husband works until six he gets only a
little drunk on the way home and does not waste too much. If he
works only until five he is drunk every night and one has no money.
It is the wife of the working man who suffers from this shortening of
hours."*

"Wouldn't you like some more broth?" the woman asked him
now.

"No, thank you very much. It is awfully good."

"Try just a little."

"I would like a whiskey-soda."

"It's not good for you."

"No. It's bad for me. Cole Porter wrote the words and the music.
This knowledge that you're going mad for me."

"You know I like you to drink."

"Oh yes. Only it's bad for me."

When she goes, he thought. I'll have all I want. Not all I want but
all there is. Ayee he was tired. Too tired. He was going to sleep a
little while. He lay still and death was not there. It must have gone
around another street. It went in pairs, on bicycles, and moved
absolutely silently on the pavements.

*No, he had never written about Paris. Not the Paris that he cared
about. But what about the rest that he had never written?*

*What about the ranch and the silvered gray of the sage brush, the
quick, clear water in the irrigation ditches, and the heavy green of
the alfalfa. The trail went up into the hills and the cattle in the*

summer were shy as deer. The bawling and the steady noise and slow moving mass raising a dust as you brought them down in the fall. And behind the mountains, the clear sharpness of the peak in the evening light and, riding down along the trail in the moonlight, bright across the valley. Now he remembered coming down through the timber in the dark holding the horse's tail when you could not see and all the stories that he meant to write.

About the half-wit chore boy who was left at the ranch that time and told not to let any one get any hay, and that old bastard from the Forks who had beaten the boy when he had worked for him stopping to get some feed. The boy refusing and the old man saying he would beat him again. The boy got the rifle from the kitchen and shot him when he tried to come into the barn and when they came back to the ranch he'd been dead a week, frozen in the corral, and the dogs had eaten part of him. But what was left you packed on a sled wrapped in a blanket and roped on and you got the boy to help you haul it, and the two of you took it out over the road on skis, and sixty miles down to town to turn the boy over. He having no idea that he would be arrested. Thinking he had done his duty and that you were his friend and he would be rewarded. He'd helped to haul the old man in so everybody could know how bad the old man had been and how he'd tried to steal some feed that didn't belong to him, and when the sheriff put the handcuffs on the boy he couldn't believe it. Then he'd started to cry. That was one story he had saved to write. He knew at least twenty good stories from out there and he had never written one. Why?

"You tell them why," he said.

"Why what, dear?"

"Why nothing."

She didn't drink so much, now, since she had him. But if he lived he would never write about her, he knew that now. Nor about any of them. The rich were dull and they drank too much, or they played too much backgammon. They were dull and they were repetitious. He remembered poor Julian and his romantic awe of them and how he had started a story once that began, "The very rich are different from you and me." And how some one had said to Julian, Yes, they have more money. But that was not humorous to Julian. He thought they were a special glamourous race and when he found they weren't it wrecked him just as much as any other thing that wrecked him.

He had been contemptuous of those who wrecked. You did not have to like it because you understood it. He could beat anything, he thought, because no thing could hurt him if he did not care.

All right. Now he would not care for death. One thing he had always dreaded was the pain. He could stand pain as well as any

man, until it went on too long, and wore him out, but here he had
something that had hurt frightfully and just when he had felt it
breaking him, the pain had stopped.

*He remembered long ago when Williamson, the bombing officer,
had been hit by a stick bomb some one in a German patrol had
thrown as he was coming in through the wire that night and, screaming, had begged every one to kill him. He was a fat man, very brave,
and a good officer, although addicted to fantastic shows. But that
night he was caught in the wire, with a flare lighting him up and his
bowels spilled out into the wire, so when they brought him in, alive,
they had to cut him loose. Shoot me, Harry. For Christ sake shoot me.
They had had an argument one time about our Lord never sending
you anything you could not bear and some one's theory had been
that meant that at a certain time the pain passed you out automatically. But he had always remembered Williamson, that night. Nothing passed out Williamson until he gave him all his morphine tablets
that he had always saved to use himself and then they did not work
right away.*

Still this now, that he had, was very easy; and if it was no worse as
it went on there was nothing to worry about. Except that he would
rather be in better company.

He thought a little about the company that he would like to
have.

No, he thought, when everything you do, you do too long, and do
too late, you can't expect to find the people still there. The people all
are gone. The party's over and you are with your hostess now.

I'm getting as bored with dying as with everything else, he
thought.

"It's a bore," he said out loud.

"What is, my dear?"

"Anything you do too bloody long."

He looked at her face between him and the fire. She was leaning
back in the chair and the firelight shone on her pleasantly lined face
and he could see that she was sleepy. He heard the hyena make a
noise just outside the range of the fire.

"I've been writing," he said. "But I got tired."

"Do you think you will be able to sleep?"

"Pretty sure. Why don't you turn in?"

"I like to sit here with you."

"Do you feel anything strange?" he asked her.

"No. Just a little sleepy."

"I do," he said.

He had just felt death come by again.

"You know the only thing I've never lost is curiosity," he said to her.

"You've never lost anything. You're the most complete man I've ever known."

"Christ," he said. "How little a woman knows. What is that? Your intuition?"

Because, just then, death had come and rested its head on the foot of the cot and he could smell its breath.

"Never believe any of that about a scythe and a skull," he told her. "It can be two bicycle policemen as easily, or be a bird. Or it can have a wide snout like a hyena."

It had moved up on him now, but it had no shape any more. It simply occupied space.

"Tell it to go away."

It did not go away but moved a little closer.

"You've got a hell of a breath," he told it. "You stinking bastard."

It moved up closer to him still and now he could not speak to it, and when it saw he could not speak it came a little closer, and now he tried to send it away without speaking, but it moved in on him so its weight was all upon his chest, and while it crouched there and he could not move, or speak, he heard the woman say, "Bwana is asleep now. Take the cot up very gently and carry it into the tent."

He could not speak to tell her to make it go away and it crouched now, heavier, so he could not breathe. And then, while they lifted the cot, suddenly it was all right and the weight went from his chest.

It was morning and had been morning for some time and he heard the plane. It showed very tiny and then made a wide circle and the boys ran out and lit the fires, using kerosene, and piled on grass so there were two big smudges at each end of the level place and the morning breeze blew them toward the camp and the plane circled twice more, low this time, and then glided down and levelled off and landed smoothly and, coming walking toward him, was old Compton in slacks, a tweed jacket and a brown felt hat.

"What's the matter, old cock?" Compton said.

"Bad leg," he told him. "Will you have some breakfast?"

"Thanks. I'll just have some tea. It's the Puss Moth you know. I won't be able to take the Memsahib. There's only room for one. Your lorry is on the way."

Helen had taken Compton aside and was speaking to him. Compton came back more cheery than ever.

"We'll get you right in," he said. "I'll be back for the Mem. Now I'm afraid I'll have to stop at Arusha to refuel. We'd better get going."

"What about the tea?"

"I don't really care about it you know."

The boys had picked up the cot and carried it around the green tents and down along the rock and out onto the plain and along past the smudges that were burning brightly now, the grass all consumed, and the wind fanning the fire, to the little plane. It was difficult getting him in, but once in he lay back in the leather seat, and the leg was stuck straight out to one side of the seat where Compton sat. Compton started the motor and got in. He waved to Helen and to the boys and, as the clatter moved into the old familiar roar, they swung around with Compie watching for wart-hog holes and roared, bumping, along the stretch between the fires and with the last bump rose and he saw them all standing below, waving, and the camp beside the hill, flattening now, and the plain spreading, clumps of trees, and the bush flattening, while the game trails ran now smoothly to the dry waterholes, and there was a new water that he had never known of. The zebra, small rounded backs now, and the wildebeeste, big-headed dots seeming to climb as they moved in long fingers across the plain, now scattering as the shadow came toward them, they were tiny now, and the movement had no gallop, and the plain as far as you could see, gray-yellow now and ahead old Compie's tweed back and the brown felt hat. Then they were over the first hills and the wildebeeste were trailing up them, and then they were over mountains with sudden depths of green-rising forest and the solid bamboo slopes, and then the heavy forest again, sculptured into peaks and hollows until they crossed, and hills sloped down and then another plain, hot now, and purple brown, bumpy with heat and Compie looking back to see how he was riding. Then there were other mountains dark ahead.

And then instead of going on to Arusha they turned left, he evidently figured that they had the gas, and looking down he saw a pink sifting cloud, moving over the ground, and in the air, like the first snow in a blizzard, that comes from nowhere, and he knew the locusts were coming up from the South. Then they began to climb and they were going to the East it seemed, and then it darkened and they were in a storm, the rain so thick it seemed like flying through a waterfall, and then they were out and Compie turned his head and grinned and pointed and there, ahead, all he could see, as wide as all the world, great, high, and unbelievably white in the sun, was the square top of Kilimanjaro. And then he knew that there was where he was going.

Just then the hyena stopped whimpering in the night and started to make a strange, human, almost crying sound. The woman heard it and stirred uneasily. She did not wake. In her dream she was at the house on Long Island and it was the night before her daughter's début. Somehow her father was there and he had been very rude. Then the noise the hyena made was so loud she woke and for a moment she did not know where she was and she was very afraid. Then she took the flashlight and shone it on the other cot that they had carried in after Harry had gone to sleep. She could see his bulk under the mosquito bar but somehow he had gotten his leg out and it hung down alongside the cot. The dressings had all come down and she could not look at it.

"Molo," she called, "Molo! Molo!"

Then she said, "Harry, Harry!" Then her voice rising, "Harry! Please, Oh Harry!"

There was no answer and she could not hear him breathing.

Outside the tent the hyena made the same strange noise that had awakened her. But she did not hear him for the beating of her heart.

JOHN STEINBECK (1902–1968)

The Chrysanthemums

The high grey-flannel fog of winter closed off the Salinas Valley from the sky and from all the rest of the world. On every side it sat like a lid on the mountains and made of the great valley a closed pot. On the broad, level land floor the gang plows bit deep and left the black earth shining like metal where the shares had cut. On the foothill ranches across the Salinas River, the yellow stubble fields seemed to be bathed in pale cold sunshine, but there was no sunshine in the valley now in December. The thick willow scrub along the river flamed with sharp and positive yellow leaves.

It was a time of quiet and of waiting. The air was cold and tender. A light wind blew up from the southwest so that the farmers were mildly hopeful of a good rain before long; but fog and rain do not go together.

Across the river, on Henry Allen's foothill ranch there was little work to be done, for the hay was cut and stored and the orchards were plowed up to receive the rain deeply when it should come. The cattle on the higher slopes were becoming shaggy and rough-coated.

Elisa Allen, working in her flower garden, looked down across the yard and saw Henry, her husband, talking to two men in business suits. The three of them stood by the tractor shed, each man with one foot on the side of the little Fordson. They smoked cigarettes and studied the machine as they talked.

Elisa watched them for a moment and then went back to her work. She was thirty-five. Her face was lean and strong and her eyes were as clear as water. Her figure looked blocked and heavy in her gardening costume, a man's black hat pulled low down over her eyes, clodhopper shoes, a figured print dress almost completely covered by a big corduroy apron with four big pockets to hold the snips, the trowel and scratcher, the seeds and the knife she worked with. She wore heavy leather gloves to protect her hands while she worked.

She was cutting down the old year's chrysanthemum stalks with a pair of short and powerful scissors. She looked down toward the men by the tractor shed now and then. Her face was eager and mature and handsome; even her work with the scissors was over-eager, over-powerful. The chrysanthemum stems seemed too small and easy for her energy.

She brushed a cloud of hair out of her eyes with the back of her glove, and left a smudge of earth on the cheek in doing it. Behind her stood the neat white farm house with red geraniums close-banked around it as high as the windows. It was a hard-swept looking little house, with hard-polished windows, and a clean mud-mat on the front steps.

Elisa cast another glance toward the tractor shed. The strangers were getting into their Ford coupe. She took off a glove and put her strong fingers down into the forest of new green chrysanthemum sprouts that were growing around the old roots. She spread the leaves and looked down among the close-growing stems. No aphids were there, no sowbugs or snails or cutworms. Her terrier fingers destroyed such pests before they could get started.

Elisa started at the sound of her husband's voice. He had come near quietly, and he leaned over the wire fence that protected her flower garden from cattle and dogs and chickens.

"At it again," he said. "You've got a strong new crop coming."

Elisa straightened her back and pulled on the gardening glove again. "Yes. They'll be strong this coming year." In her tone and on her face there was a little smugness.

"You've got a gift with things," Henry observed. "Some of those yellow chrysanthemums you had this year were ten inches across. I wish you'd work out in the orchard and raise some apples that big."

Her eyes sharpened. "Maybe I could do it, too. I've a gift with things, all right. My mother had it. She could stick anything in the ground and make it grow. She said it was having planters' hands that knew how to do it."

"Well, it sure works with flowers," he said.

"Henry, who were those men you were talking to?"

"Why, sure, that's what I came to tell you. They were from the Western Meat Company. I sold those thirty head of three-year-old steers. Got nearly my own price, too."

"Good," she said. "Good for you."

"And I thought," he continued, "I thought how it's Saturday afternoon, and we might go to Salinas for dinner at a restaurant, and then to a picture show—to celebrate, you see."

"Good," she repeated. "Oh, yes. That will be good."

Henry put on his joking tone. "There's fights tonight. How'd you like to go to the fights?"

"Oh, no," she said breathlessly. "No, I wouldn't like fights."

"Just fooling, Elisa. We'll go to a movie. Let's see. It's two now. I'm going to take Scotty and bring down those steers from the hill. It'll take us maybe two hours. We'll go in town about five and have dinner at the Cominos Hotel. Like that?"

"Of course I'll like it. It's good to eat away from home."

"All right, then. I'll go get up a couple of horses."

She said, "I'll have plenty of time to transplant some of these sets, I guess."

She heard her husband calling Scotty down by the barn. And a little later she saw the two men ride up the pale yellow hillside in search of the steers.

There was a little square sandy bed kept for rooting the chrysanthemums. With her trowel she turned the soil over and over, and smoothed it and patted it firm. Then she dug ten parallel trenches to receive the sets. Back at the chrysanthemum bed she pulled out the little crisp shoots, trimmed off the leaves of each one with her scissors and laid it on a small orderly pile.

A squeak of wheels and plod of hoofs came from the road. Elisa looked up. The country road ran along the dense bank of willows and cottonwoods that bordered the river, and up this road came a curious vehicle, curiously drawn. It was an old spring-wagon, with a round canvas top on it like the cover of a prairie schooner. It was drawn by an old bay horse and a little grey-and-white burro. A big stubble-bearded man sat between the cover flaps and drove the crawling team. Underneath the wagon, between the hind wheels, a lean and rangy mongrel dog walked sedately. Words were painted on the canvas in clumsy, crooked letters. "Pots, pans, knives, sisors, lawn mores. Fixed." Two rows of articles and the triumphantly definitive "Fixed" below. The black paint had run down in little sharp points beneath each letter.

Elisa, squatting on the ground, watched to see the crazy, loose-jointed wagon pass by. But it didn't pass. It turned into the farm road in front of her house, crooked old wheels skirling and squeaking. The rangy dog darted from between the wheels and ran ahead. Instantly the two ranch shepherds flew out at him. Then all three stopped, and with stiff and quivering tails, with taut straight legs, with ambassadorial dignity, they slowly circled, sniffing daintily. The caravan pulled up to Elisa's wire fence and stopped. Now the newcomer dog, feeling outnumbered, lowered his tail and retired under the wagon with raised hackles and bared teeth.

The man on the wagon seat called out. "That's a bad dog in a fight when he gets started."

Elisa laughed. "I see he is. How soon does he generally get started?"

The man caught up her laughter and echoed it heartily. "Sometimes not for weeks and weeks," he said. He climbed stiffly down, over the wheel. The horse and the donkey drooped like unwatered flowers.

Elisa saw that he was a very big man. Although his hair and beard were greying, he did not look old. His worn black suit was wrinkled and spotted with grease. The laughter had disappeared from his face and eyes the moment his laughing voice ceased. His eyes were dark and they were full of the brooding that gets in the eyes of team-sters and of sailors. The calloused hands he rested on the wire fence were cracked, and every crack was a black line. He took off his battered hat.

"I'm off my general road, ma'am," he said. "Does this dirt road cut over across the river to the Los Angeles highway?"

Elisa stood up and shoved the thick scissors in her apron pocket. "Well, yes, it does, but it winds around and then fords the river. I don't think your team could pull through the sand."

He replied with some asperity, "It might surprise you what them beasts can pull through."

"When they get started?" she asked.

He smiled for a second. "Yes. When they get started."

"Well," said Elisa, "I think you'll save time if you go back to the Salinas road and pick up the highway there."

He drew a big finger down the chicken wire and made it sing. "I ain't in any hurry, ma'am. I go from Seattle to San Diego and back every year. Takes all my time. About six months each way. I aim to follow nice weather."

Elisa took off her gloves and stuffed them in the apron pocket with the scissors. She touched the under edge of her man's hat, searching for fugitive hairs. "That sounds like a nice kind of a way to live," she said.

He leaned confidentially over the fence. "Maybe you noticed the writing on my wagon. I mend pots and sharpen knives and scissors. You got any of them things to do?"

"Oh, no," she said quickly. "Nothing like that." Her eyes hardened with resistance.

"Scissors is the worst thing," he explained. "Most people just ruin scissors trying to sharpen 'em, but I know how. I got a special tool. It's a little bobbit kind of thing, and patented. But it sure does the trick."

"No. My scissors are all sharp."

"All right, then. Take a pot," he continued earnestly, "a bent pot, or a pot with a hole. I can make it like new so you don't have to buy no new ones. That's a saving for you."

"No," she said shortly. "I tell you I have nothing like that for you to do."

His face fell to an exaggerated sadness. His voice took on a whining undertone. "I ain't had a thing to do today. Maybe I won't have no supper tonight. You see I'm off my regular road. I know folks on the highway clear from Seattle to San Diego. They save their things for me to sharpen up because they know I do it so good and save them money."

"I'm sorry," Elisa said irritably. "I haven't anything for you to do."

His eyes left her face and fell to searching the ground. They roamed about until they came to the chrysanthemum bed where she had been working. "What's them plants, ma'am?"

The irritation and resistance melted from Elisa's face. "Oh, those are chrysanthemums, giant whites and yellows. I raise them every year, bigger than anybody around here."

"Kind of a long-stemmed flower? Looks like a quick puff of colored smoke?" he asked.

"That's it. What a nice way to describe them."

"They smell kind of nasty till you get used to them," he said.

"It's a good bitter smell," she retorted, "not nasty at all."

He changed his tone quickly. "I like the smell myself."

"I had ten-inch blooms this year," she said.

The man leaned farther over the fence. "Look. I know a lady down the road a piece, has got the nicest garden you ever seen. Got nearly every kind of flower but no chrysanthemums. Last time I was mending a copper-bottom washtub for her (that's a hard job but I do it good), she said to me, 'If you ever run acrost some nice chrysanthemums I wish you'd try to get me a few seeds.' That's what she told me."

Elisa's eyes grew alert and eager. "She couldn't have known much about chrysanthemums. You can raise them from seed, but it's much easier to root the little sprouts you see there."

"Oh," he said. "I s'pose I can't take none to her, then."

"Why yes you can," Elisa cried. "I can put some in damp sand, and you can carry them right along with you. They'll take root in the pot if you keep them damp. And then she can transplant them."

"She'd sure like to have some, ma'am. You say they're nice ones?"

"Beautiful," she said. "Oh, beautiful." Her eyes shone. She tore off the battered hat and shook out her dark pretty hair. "I'll put them in a flower pot, and you can take them right with you. Come into the yard."

While the man came through the picket gate Elisa ran excitedly along the geranium-bordered path to the back of the house. And she returned carrying a big red flower pot. The gloves were forgotten now. She kneeled on the ground by the starting bed and dug up the sandy soil with her fingers and scooped it into the bright new flower pot. Then she picked up the little pile of shoots she had prepared. With her strong fingers she pressed them into the sand and tamped around them with her knuckles. The man stood over her. "I'll tell you what to do," she said. "You remember so you can tell the lady."

"Yes, I'll try to remember."

"Well, look. These will take root in about a month. Then she must set them out, about a foot apart in good rich earth like this, see?" She lifted a handful of dark soil for him to look at. "They'll grow fast and tall. Now remember this. In July tell her to cut them down, about eight inches from the ground."

"Before they bloom?" he asked.

"Yes, before they bloom." Her face was tight with eagerness. "They'll grow right up again. About the last of September the buds will start."

She stopped and seemed perplexed. "It's the budding that takes the most care," she said hesitantly. "I don't know how to tell you." She looked deep into his eyes, searchingly. Her mouth opened a little, and she seemed to be listening. "I'll try to tell you," she said. "Did you ever hear of planting hands?"

"Can't say I have, ma'am."

"Well, I can only tell you what it feels like. It's when you're picking off the buds you don't want. Everything goes right down into your fingertips. You watch your fingers work. They do it themselves. You can feel how it is. They pick and pick the buds. They never make a mistake. They're with the plant. Do you see? Your fingers and the plant. You can feel that, right up your arm. They know. They never make a mistake. You can feel it. When you're like that you can't do anything wrong. Do you see that? Can you understand that?"

She was kneeling on the ground looking up at him. Her breast swelled passionately.

The man's eyes narrowed. He looked away self-consciously. "Maybe I know," he said. "Sometimes in the night in the wagon there—"

Elisa's voice grew husky. She broke in on him. "I've never lived as you do, but I know what you mean. When the night is dark—why, the stars are sharp-pointed, and there's quiet. Why, you rise up and up! Every pointed star gets driven into your body. It's like that. Hot and sharp and—lovely."

Kneeling there, her hand went out toward his legs in the greasy black trousers. Her hesitant fingers almost touched the cloth. Then her hand dropped to the ground. She crouched low like a fawning dog.

He said, "It's nice, just like you say. Only when you don't have no dinner, it ain't."

She stood up then, very straight, and her face was ashamed. She held the flower pot out to him and placed it gently in his arms. "Here. Put it in your wagon, on the seat, where you can watch it. Maybe I can find something for you to do."

At the back of the house she dug in the can pile and found two old and battered aluminum saucepans. She carried them back and gave them to him. "Here, maybe you can fix these."

His manner changed. He became professional. "Good as new I can fix them." At the back of his wagon he set a little anvil, and out of an oily tool box dug a small machine hammer. Elisa came through the gate to watch him while he pounded out the dents in the kettles. His mouth grew sure and knowing. At a difficult part of the work he sucked his under-lip.

"You sleep right in the wagon?" Elisa asked.

"Right in the wagon, ma'am. Rain or shine I'm dry as a cow in there."

"It must be nice," she said. "It must be very nice. I wish women could do such things."

"It ain't the right kind of a life for a woman."

Her upper lip raised a little, showing her teeth. "How do you know? How can you tell?" she said.

"I don't know ma'am," he protested. "Of course I don't know. Now here's your kettles, done. You don't have to buy no new ones."

"How much?"

"Oh, fifty cents'll do. I keep my prices down and my work good. That's why I have all them satisfied customers up and down the highway."

Elisa brought him a fifty-cent piece from the house and dropped it in his hand. "You might be surprised to have a rival some time. I can sharpen scissors, too. And I can beat the dents out of little pots. I could show you what a woman might do."

He put his hammer back in the oily box and shoved the little anvil out of sight. "It would be a lonely life for a woman, ma'am, and a scarey life, too, with animals creeping under the wagon all night." He climbed over the single-tree, steadying himself with a hand on the burro's white rump. He settled himself in the seat, picked up the lines. "Thank you kindly, ma'am," he said. "I'll do like you told me; I'll go back and catch the Salinas road."

"Mind," she called, "if you're long in getting there, keep the sand damp."

"Sand, ma'am? . . . Sand? Oh, sure. You mean round the chrysanthemums. Sure I will." He clucked his tongue. The beasts leaned luxuriously into their collars. The mongrel dog took his place between the back wheels. The wagon turned and crawled out the entrance road and back the way it had come, along the river.

Elisa stood in front of her wire fence watching the slow progress of the caravan. Her shoulders were straight, her head thrown back, her eyes half-closed, so that the scene came vaguely into them. Her lips moved silently, forming the words "Good-bye—good-bye." Then she whispered, "That's a bright direction. There's a glowing there." The sound of her whisper startled her. She shook herself free and looked about to see whether anyone had been listening. Only the dogs had heard. They lifted their heads toward her from their sleeping in the dust, and then stretched out their chins and settled asleep again. Elisa turned and ran hurriedly into the house.

In the kitchen she reached behind the stove and felt the water tank. It was full of hot water from the noonday cooking. In the bathroom she tore off her soiled clothes and flung them into the corner. And then she scrubbed herself with a little block of pumice, legs and thighs, loins and chest and arms, until her skin was scratched and red. When she had dried herself she stood in front of a mirror in her bedroom and looked at her body. She tightened her stomach and threw out her chest. She turned and looked over her shoulder at her back.

After a while she began to dress, slowly. She put on her newest under-clothing and her nicest stockings and the dress which was the symbol of her prettiness. She worked carefully on her hair, pencilled her eyebrows and rouged her lips.

Before she was finished she heard the little thunder of hoofs and the shouts of Henry and his helper as they drove the red steers into the corral. She heard the gate bang shut and set herself for Henry's arrival.

His step sounded on the porch. He entered the house calling "Elisa, where are you?"

"In my room, dressing. I'm not ready. There's hot water for your bath. Hurry up. It's getting late."

When she heard him splashing in the tub, Elisa laid his dark suit on the bed, and shirt and socks and tie beside it. She stood his polished shoes on the floor beside the bed. Then she went to the porch and sat primly and stiffly down. She looked toward the river road where the willow-line was still yellow with frosted leaves so that under the high grey fog they seemed a thin band of sunshine. This was the only color in the grey afternoon. She sat unmoving for a long time. Her eyes blinked rarely.

Henry came banging out of the door, shoving his tie inside his vest as he came. Elisa stiffened and her face grew tight. Henry stopped short and looked at her. "Why—why, Elisa. You look so nice!"

"Nice? You think I look nice? What do you mean by 'nice?' "

Henry blundered on. "I don't know. I mean you look different, strong and happy."

"I am strong? Yes, strong. What do you mean 'strong?' "

He looked bewildered. "You're playing some kind of a game," he said helplessly. "It's a kind of a play. You look strong enough to break a calf over your knee, happy enough to eat it like watermelon."

For a second she lost her rigidity. "Henry! Don't talk like that. You didn't know what you said." She grew complete again. "I'm strong," she boasted. "I never knew before how strong."

Henry looked down toward the tractor shed, and when he brought his eyes back to her, they were his own again. "I'll get out the car. You can put on your coat while I'm starting."

Elisa went into the house. She heard him drive to the gate and idle down his motor, and then she took a long time to put on her hat. She pulled it here and pressed it there. When Henry turned the motor off she slipped into her coat and went out.

The little roadster bounced along on the dirt road by the river, raising the birds and driving the rabbits into the brush. Two cranes flapped heavily over the willow-line and dropped into the river-bed.

Far ahead on the road Elisa saw a dark speck. She knew.

She tried not to look as they passed it, but her eyes would not obey. She whispered to herself sadly. "He might have thrown them off the road. That wouldn't have been much trouble, not very much. But he kept the pot," she explained. "He had to keep the pot. That's why he couldn't get them off the road."

The roadster turned a bend and she saw the caravan ahead. She swung full around toward her husband so she could not see the little covered wagon and the mismatched team as the car passed them.

In a moment it was over. The thing was done. She did not look back. She said loudly, to be heard above the motor, "It will be good, tonight, a good dinner."

"Now you're changed again," Henry complained. He took one hand from the wheel and patted her knee. "I ought to take you in to dinner oftener. It would be good for both of us. We get so heavy out on the ranch."

"Henry," she asked, "could we have wine at dinner?"

"Sure we could. Say! That will be fine."

She was silent for a little while; then she said, "Henry, at those prize fights, do the men hurt each other very much?"

"Sometimes a little, not often. Why?"

"Well, I've read how they break noses, and blood runs down their chests. I've read how the fighting gloves get heavy and soggy with blood."

He looked around at her. "What's the matter, Elisa? I didn't know you read things like that." He brought the car to a stop, then turned to the right over the Salinas River bridge.

"Do any women ever go to the fights?" she asked.

"Oh, sure, some. What's the matter, Elisa? Do you want to go? I don't think you'd like it, but I'll take you if you really want to go."

She relaxed limply in the seat. "Oh, no. No. I don't want to go. I'm sure I don't." Her face was turned away from him. "It will be enough if we can have wine. It will be plenty." She turned up her coat collar so he could not see that she was crying weakly—like an old woman.

RICHARD WRIGHT (1906–1960)

Bright and Morning Star

I

She stood with her black face some six inches from the moist windowpane and wondered when on earth would it ever stop raining. It might keep up like this all week, she thought. She heard rain droning upon the roof and high up in the wet sky her eyes followed the silent rush of a bright shaft of yellow that swung from the airplane beacon in far off Memphis. Momently she could see it cutting through the rainy dark; it would hover a second like a gleaming sword above her head, then vanish. She sighed, troubling, Johnny-Boys been trampin in this slop all day wid no decent shoes on his feet. . . . Through the window she could see the rich black earth sprawling outside in the night. There was more rain than the clay could soak up; pools stood everywhere. She yawned and mumbled: "Rains good n bad. It kin make seeds bus up thu the ground, er it kin bog things down lika watah-soaked coffin." Her hands were folded loosely over her stomach and the hot air of the kitchen traced a filmy vein of sweat on her forehead. From the cook stove came the soft singing of burning wood and now and then a throaty bubble rose from a pot of simmering greens.

"Shucks, Johnny-Boy coulda let somebody else do all tha runnin in the rain. Theres others bettah fixed fer it than he is. But, naw! Johnny-Boy ain the one t trust nobody t do nothin. Hes gotta do it *all* hissef. . . ."

She glanced at a pile of damp clothes in a zinc tub. Waal, Ah bettah git t work. She turned, lifted a smoothing iron with a thick pad of cloth, touched a spit-wet finger to it with a quick, jerking motion: *smiiitz!* Yeah; its hot! Stooping, she took a blue work-shirt from the tub and shook it out. With a deft twist of her shoulders she caught the iron in her right hand; the fingers of her left hand took a piece of wax from a tin box and a frying sizzle came as she smeared the bottom. She was thinking of nothing now; her hands followed a life-long ritual of toil. Spreading a sleeve, she ran the hot iron to and fro until the wet cloth became stiff. She was deep in the midst of her work when a song rose up out of the far off days of her childhood and broke through half-parted lips:

Hes the Lily of the Valley, the Bright n Mawnin Star
Hes the Fairest of Ten Thousan t ma soul . . .

A gust of wind dashed rain against the window. Johnny-Boy
oughta c mon home n eat his suppah. Aw, Lawd! Itd be fine ef Sug
could eat wid us tonight! Itd be like ol times! Mabbe aftah all it
wont be long fo he comes back. Tha lettah Ah got from im last week
said *Don give up hope.* . . . Yeah; we gotta live in hope. Then both
of her sons, Sug and Johnny-Boy, would be back with her.

With an involuntary nervous gesture, she stopped and stood still,
listening. But the only sound was the lulling fall of rain. Shucks, ain
no usa me ackin this way, she thought. Ever time they gits ready to
hol them meetings Ah gits jumpity. Ah been a lil scared ever since
Sug went t jail. She heard the clock ticking and looked. Johnny-Boys
a *hour* late! He sho must be havin a time doin all tha trampin,
trampin thu the mud. . . . But her fear was a quiet one; it was more
like an intense brooding than a fear; it was a sort of hugging of hated
facts so closely that she could feel their grain, like letting cold water
run over her hand from a faucet on a winter morning.

She ironed again, faster now, as if she felt the more she engaged
her body in work the less she would think. But how could she forget
Johnny-Boy out there on those wet fields rounding up white and
black Communists for a meeting tomorrow? And that was just what
Sug had been doing when the sheriff had caught him, beat him, and
tried to make him tell who and where his comrades were. Po Sug!
They sho musta beat the boy somethin awful! But, thank Gawd, he
didnt talk! He ain no weaklin, Sug ain! Hes been lion-hearted all his
life long.

That had happened a year ago. And now each time those meetings
came around the old terror surged back. While shoving the iron a
cluster of toiling days returned; days of washing and ironing to feed
Johnny-Boy and Sug so they could do party work;. days of carrying a
hundred pounds of white folks' clothes upon her head across fields
sometimes wet and sometimes dry. But in those days a hundred
pounds was nothing to carry carefully balanced upon her head while
stepping by instinct over the corn and cotton rows. The only time it
had seemed heavy was when she had heard of Sug's arrest. She had
been coming home one morning with a bundle upon her head, her
hands swinging idly by her sides, walking slowly with her eyes in
front of her, when Bob, Johnny-Boy's pal, had called from across the
fields and had come and told her that the sheriff had got Sug. That
morning the bundle had become heavier than she could ever remember.

And with each passing week now, though she spoke of it to no one,
things were becoming heavier. The tubs of water and the smoothing

iron and the bundles of clothes were becoming harder to lift, with her back aching so; and her work was taking longer, all because Sug was gone and she didn't know just when Johnny-Boy would be taken too. To ease the ache of anxiety that was swelling her heart, she hummed, then sang softly:

> He walks wid me, He talks wid me
> He tells me Ahm His own. . . .

Guiltily, she stopped and smiled. Looks like Ah jus cant seem t fergit them ol songs, no mattah how hard Ah tries. . . . She had learned them when she was a little girl living and working on a farm. Every Monday morning from the corn and cotton fields the slow strains had floated from her mother's lips, lonely and haunting; and later, as the years had filled with gall, she had learned their deep meaning. Long hours of scrubbing floors for a few cents a day had taught her who Jesus was, what a great boon it was to cling to Him, to be like Him and suffer without a mumbling word. She had poured the yearning of her life into the songs, feeling buoyed with a faith beyond this world. The figure of the Man nailed in agony to the Cross, His burial in a cold grave, His transfigured Resurrection, His being breath and clay, God and Man—all had focused her feelings upon an imagery which had swept her life into a wondrous vision.

But as she had grown older, a cold white mountain, the white folks and their laws, had swum into her vision and shattered her songs and their spell of peace. To her that white mountain was temptation, something to lure her from her Lord, a part of the world God had made in order that she might endure it and come through all the stronger, just as Christ had risen with greater glory from the tomb. The days crowded with trouble had enhanced her faith and she had grown to love hardship with a bitter pride; she had obeyed the laws of the white folks with a soft smile of secret knowing.

After her mother had been snatched up to heaven in a chariot of fire, the years had brought her a rough workingman and two black babies, Sug and Johnny-Boy, all three of whom she had wrapped in the charm and magic of her vision. Then she was tested by no less than God; her man died, a trial which she bore with the strength shed by the grace of her vision; finally even the memory of her man faded into the vision itself, leaving her with two black boys growing tall, slowly into manhood.

Then one day grief had come to her heart when Johnny-Boy and Sug had walked forth demanding their lives. She had sought to fill their eyes with her vision, but they would have none of it. And she had wept when they began to boast of the strength shed by a new and terrible vision.

But she had loved them, even as she loved them now; bleeding, her heart had followed them. She could have done no less, being an old woman in a strange world. And day by day her sons had ripped from her startled eyes her old vision, and image by image had given her a new one, different, but great and strong enough to fling her into the light of another grace. The wrongs and sufferings of black men had taken the place of Him nailed to the Cross; the meager beginnings of the party had become another Resurrection; and the hate of those who would destroy her new faith had quickened in her a hunger to feel how deeply her new strength went.

"Lawd, Johnny-Boy," she would sometimes say, "Ah just wan them white folks t try t make me tell *who* is *in* the party n who *ain!* Ah jus wan em t try, Ahll show em somethin they never thought a black woman could have!"

But sometimes like tonight, while lost in the forgetfulness of work, the past and the present would become mixed in her; while toiling under a strange star for a new freedom the old songs would slip from her lips with their beguiling sweetness.

The iron was getting cold. She put more wood into the fire, stood again at the window and watched the yellow blade of light cut through the wet darkness. Johnny-Boy ain here yit . . . Then, before she was aware of it, she was still, listening for sounds. Under the drone of rain she heard the slosh of feet in mud. Tha ain Johnny-Boy. She knew his long, heavy footsteps in a million. She heard feet come on the porch. Some woman. . . . She heard bare knuckles knock three times, then once. Thas some of them comrades! She unbarred the door, cracked it a few inches, and flinched from the cold rush of damp wind.

"Whos tha?"

"Its me!"

"Who?"

"Me, Reva!"

She flung the door open.

"Lawd, chile, c mon in!"

She stepped to one side and a thin, blond-haired white girl ran through the door; as she slid the bolt she heard the girl gasping and shaking her wet clothes. Somethings wrong! Reva wouldna walked a mil t mah house in all this slop fer nothin! That gals stuck onto Johnny-Boy. Ah wondah ef anythin happened t im?

"Git on inter the kitchen, Reva, where its warm."

"Lawd, Ah sho is wet!"

"How yuh reckon yuhd be, in all tha rain?"

"Johnny-Boy ain here *yit?*" asked Reva.

"Naw! N ain no usa yuh worryin bout im. Jus yuh git them shoes off! Yuh wanna ketch yo deatha col?" She stood looking absently.

Yeah; its somethin about the party er Johnny-Boy thas gone wrong. Lawd, Ah wondah ef her pa knows how she feels bout Johnny-Boy? "Honey, yuh hadn't oughta come out in sloppy weather like this."

"Ah had t come, An Sue."

She led Reva to the kitchen.

"Git them shoes off n git close t the stove so yuhll git dry!"

"An Sue, Ah got somethin t tell yuh . . ."

The words made her hold her breath. Ah bet its somethin bout Johnny-Boy!

"Whut, honey?"

"The sheriff wuz by our house tonight. He come t see pa."

"Yeah?"

"He done got word from somewheres bout tha meetin tomorrow."

"Is it Johnny-Boy, Reva?"

"Aw, naw, An Sue! Ah ain hearda word bout im. Ain yuh seen im tonight?"

"He ain come home t eat yit."

"Where kin he be?"

"Lawd knows, chile."

"Somebodys gotta tell them comrades that meetins off," said Reva. "The sheriffs got men watchin our house. Ah had t slip out t git here widout em followin me."

"Reva?"

"Hunh?"

"Ahma ol woman n Ah wans yuh t tell me the truth."

"Whut, An Sue?"

"Yuh ain tryin t fool me, is yuh?"

"*Fool* yuh?"

"Bout Johnny-Boy?"

"Lawd, naw, An Sue!"

"Ef theres anythin wrong jus tell me, chile. Ah kin stan it."

She stood by the ironing board, her hands as usual folded loosely over her stomach, watching Reva pull off her water-clogged shoes. She was feeling that Johnny-Boy was already lost to her; she was feeling the pain that would come when she knew it for certain; and she was feeling that she would have to be brave and bear it. She was like a person caught in a swift current of water and knew where the water was sweeping her and did not want to go on but had to go on to the end.

"It ain nothin bout Johnny-Boy, An Sue," said Reva. "But we gotta do somethin er we'll all git inter trouble."

"How the sheriff know about tha meetin?"

"Thas whut pa wants t know."

"Somebody done turned Judas."

"Sho looks like it."

"Ah bet it wuz some of them new ones," she said.

"Its hard t tell," said Reva.

"Lissen, Reva, yuh oughta stay here n git dry, but yuh bettah git back n tell yo pa Johnny-Boy ain here n Ah don know when hes gonna show up. *Some*bodys gotta tell them comrades t stay erway from yo pas house."

She stood with her back to the window, looking at Reva's wide, blue eyes. Po critter! Gotta go back thu all tha slop! Though she felt sorry for Reva, not once did she think that it would not have to be done. Being a woman, Reva was not suspect; she would *have* to go. It was just as natural for Reva to go back through the cold rain as it was for her to iron night and day, or for Sug to be in jail. Right now, Johnny-Boy was out there on those dark fields trying to get home. Lawd, don let em git im tonight! In spite of herself her feelings became torn. She loved her son and, loving him, she loved what he was trying to do. Johnny-Boy was happiest when he was working for the party, and her love for him was for his happiness. She frowned, trying hard to fit something together in her feelings: for her to try to stop Johnny-Boy was to admit that all the toil of years meant nothing; and to let him go meant that sometime or other he would be caught, like Sug. In facing it this way she felt a little stunned, as though she had come suddenly upon a blank wall in the dark. But outside in the rain were people, white and black, whom she had known all her life. Those people depended upon Johnny-Boy, loved him and looked to him as a man and leader. Yeah; hes gotta keep on; he cant stop now. . . . She looked at Reva; she was crying and pulling her shoes back on with reluctant fingers.

"Whut yuh carryin on tha way fer, chile?"

"Yuh done los Sug, now yuh sendin Johnny-Boy . . . ."

"Ah got t, honey."

She was glad she could say that. Reva believed in black folks and not for anything in the world would she falter before her. In Reva's trust and acceptance of her she had found her first feelings of humanity; Reva's love was her refuge from shame and degradation. If in the early days of her life the white mountain had driven her back from the earth, then in her last days Reva's love was drawing her toward it, like the beacon that swung through the night outside. She heard Reva sobbing.

"Hush, honey!"

"Mah brothers in jail too! Ma cries ever day . . ."

"Ah know, honey."

She helped Reva with her coat; her fingers felt the scant flesh of the girl's shoulders. She don git ernuff t eat, she thought. She slipped her arms around Reva's waist and held her close for a moment.

"Now, yuh stop that cryin."

"A-a-ah c-c-cant hep it. . . ."

"Everythingll be awright; Johnny-Boyll be back."

"Yuh think so?"

"Sho, chile. Cos he will."

Neither of them spoke again until they stood in the doorway. Outside they could hear water washing through the ruts of the street.

"Be sho n send Johnny-Boy t tell the folks t stay erway from pas house," said Reva.

"Ahll tell im. Don yuh worry."

"Good-bye!"

"Good-bye!"

Leaning against the door jamb, she shook her head slowly and watched Reva vanish through the falling rain.

II

She was back at her board, ironing, when she heard feet sucking in the mud of the back yard; feet she knew from long years of listening were Johnny-Boy's. But tonight, with all the rain and fear, his coming was like a leaving, was almost more than she could bear. Tears welled to her eyes and she blinked them away. She felt that he was coming so that she could give him up; to see him now was to say good-bye. But it was a good-bye she knew she could never say; they were not that way toward each other. All day long they could sit in the same room and not speak; she was his mother and he was her son. Most of the time a nod or a grunt would carry all the meaning that she wanted to convey to him, or he to her. She did not even turn her head when she heard him come stomping into the kitchen. She heard him pull up a chair, sit, sigh, and draw off his muddy shoes; they fell to the floor with heavy thuds. Soon the kitchen was full of the scent of his drying socks and his burning pipe. Tha boys hongry! She paused and looked at him over her shoulder; he was puffing at his pipe with his head tilted back and his feet propped up on the edge of the stove; his eyelids drooped and his wet clothes steamed from the heat of the fire. Lawd, tha boy gits mo like his pa ever day he lives, she mused, her lips breaking in a slow, faint smile. Hols tha pipe in his mouth just like his pa usta hol his. Wondah how they woulda got erlong ef his pa hada lived? They oughta liked each other, they so mucha like. She wished there could have been other children besides Sug, so Johnny-Boy would not have to be so much alone. A man needs a woman by his side. . . . She thought of Reva; she liked Reva; the brightest glow her heart had ever known was when she had learned that Reva loved Johnny-Boy. But beyond Reva were cold white faces. Ef theys caught it means *death*. . . . She jerked around when she heard Johnny-Boy's pipe clatter to the floor. She saw him pick it up, smile sheepishly at her, and wag his head.

"Gawd, Ahm sleepy," he mumbled.

She got a pillow from her room and gave it to him.

"Here," she said.

"Hunh," he said, putting the pillow between his head and the back of the chair.

They were silent again. Yes, she would have to tell him to go back out into the cold rain and slop; maybe to get caught; maybe for the last time; she didn't know. But she would let him eat and get dry before telling him that the sheriff knew of the meeting to be held at Lem's tomorrow. And she would make him take a big dose of soda before he went out; soda always helped to stave off a cold. She looked at the clock. It was eleven. Theres time yit. Spreading a newspaper on the apron of the stove, she placed a heaping plate of greens upon it, a knife, a fork, a cup of coffee, a slab of cornbread, and a dish of peach cobbler.

"Yo suppahs ready," she said.

"Yeah," he said.

He did not move. She ironed again. Presently, she heard him eating. When she could no longer hear his knife tinkling against the edge of the plate, she knew he was through. It was almost twelve now. She would let him rest a little while longer before she told him. Till one er'clock, mabbe. Hes so tired. . . . She finished her ironing, put away the board, and stacked the clothes in her dresser drawer. She poured herself a cup of black coffee, drew up a chair, sat down and drank.

"Yuh almos dry," she said, not looking around.

"Yeah," he said, turning sharply to her.

The tone of voice in which she had spoken had let him know that more was coming. She drained her cup and waited a moment longer.

"Reva wuz here."

"Yeah?"

"She lef bout a hour ergo."

"Whut she say?"

"She said ol man Lem hada visit from the sheriff today."

"Bout the meetin?"

She saw him stare at the coals glowing red through the crevices of the stove and run his fingers nervously through his hair. She knew he was wondering how the sheriff had found out. In the silence he would ask a wordless question and in the silence she would answer wordlessly. Johnny-Boys too trustin, she thought. Hes trying t make the party big n hes takin in folks fastern he kin git t know em. You cant trust ever white man yuh meet. . . .

"Yuh know, Johnny-Boy, yuh been takin in a lotta them white folks lately . . ."

"Aw, ma!"

"But, Johnny-Boy . . ."

"Please, dont talk t me bout tha now, ma."

"Yuh ain t ol t lissen n learn, son," she said.

"Ah know whut yuh gonna say, ma. N yuh wrong. Yuh cant judge folks just by how yuh feel bout em n by how long yuh done knowed em. Ef we start that we wouldnt have *no*body in the party. When folks pledge they word t be with us, then we gotta take em in. Wes too weak to be choosy."

He rose abruptly, rammed his hands into his pockets, and stood facing the window; she looked at his back in a long silence. She knew his faith; it was deep. He had always said that black men could not fight the rich bosses alone; a man could not fight with every hand against him. But he believes so hard hes blind, she thought. At odd times they had had these arguments before; always she would be pitting her feelings against the hard necessity of his thinking, and always she would lose. She shook her head. Po Johnny-Boy; he don know . . .

"But ain nona our folks tol, Johnny-Boy," she said.

"How yuh know?" he asked. His voice came low and with a tinge of anger. He still faced the window and now and then the yellow blade of light flicked across the sharp outline of his black face.

"Cause Ah know em," she said.

"*Any*body mighta tol," he said.

"It wuznt nona *our* folks," she said again.

She saw his hand sweep in a swift arc of disgust.

"*Our* folks! Ma, who in Gawds name is *our* folks?"

"The folks we wuz born n raised wid, son. The folks we *know!*"

"We cant make the party grow tha way, ma."

"It mighta been Booker," she said.

"Yuh don know."

". . . er Blattberg . . ."

"Fer Chrissakes!"

". . . er any of the fo-five others whut joined las week."

"Ma, yuh jus don wan me t go out tonight," he said.

"Yo ol ma wans yuh t be careful, son."

"Ma, when yuh start doubtin folks in the party, then there ain no end."

"Son, Ah knows ever black man n woman in this parta the county," she said, standing too. "Ah watched em grow up; Ah even heped birth n nurse some of em; Ah knows em *all* from way back. There ain none of em that *coulda* tol! The folks Ah know jus don open they dos n ast death t walk in! Son, it wuz some of them *white* folks! Yuh just mark mah word n wait n see!"

"Why is it gotta be *white* folks?" he asked. "Ef they tol, then theys jus Judases, thas all."

"Son, look at whuts befo yuh."

He shook his head and sighed.

"Ma, Ah done tol yuh a hundred times. Ah cant see white n Ah cant see black," he said. "Ah sees rich men n Ah sees po men."

She picked up his dirty dishes and piled them in a pan. Out of the corners of her eyes she saw him sit and pull on his wet shoes. Hes goin! When she put the last dish away he was standing fully dressed, warming his hands over the stove. Jus a few mo minutes now n hell be gone, like Sug, mabbe. Her throat tightened. This black mans fight takes *ever*thin! Looks like Gawd put us in this world jus t beat us down!

"Keep this, ma," he said.

She saw a crumpled wad of money in his outstretched fingers.

"Naw, yuh keep it. Yuh might need it."

"It ain mine, ma. It berlongs t the party."

"But, Johnny-Boy, yuh might hafta go erway!"

"Ah kin make out."

"Don fergit yosef too much, son."

"Ef Ah don come back theyll need it."

He was looking at her face and she was looking at the money.

"Yuh keep tha," she said slowly. "Ahll give em the money."

"From where?"

"Ah got some."

"Where yuh git it from?"

She sighed.

"Ah been savin a dollah a week fer Sug ever since hes been in jail."

"Lawd, ma!"

She saw the look of puzzled love and wonder in his eyes. Clumsily, he put the money back into his pocket.

"Ahm gone," he said.

"Here; drink this glass of soda watah."

She watched him drink, then put the glass away.

"Waal," he said.

"Take the stuff outta yo pockets!"

She lifted the lid of the stove and he dumped all the papers from his pocket into the fire. She followed him to the door and made him turn around.

"Lawd, yuh tryin to maka revolution n yuh cant even keep yo coat buttoned." Her nimble fingers fastened his collar high around his throat. "There!"

He pulled the brim of his hat low over his eyes. She opened the door and with the suddenness of the cold gust of wind that struck her face, he was gone. She watched the black fields and the rain take him, her eyes burning. When the last faint footstep could no longer be heard, she closed the door, went to her bed, lay down, and pulled the cover over her while fully dressed. Her feelings coursed with the rhythm of the rain: Hes gone! Lawd, Ah *knows* hes gone! Her blood felt cold.

III

She was floating in a grey void somewhere between sleeping and dreaming and then suddenly she was wide awake, hearing and feeling in the same instant the thunder of the door crashing in and a cold wind filling the room. It was pitch black and she stared, resting on her elbows, her mouth open, not breathing, her ears full of the sound of tramping feet and booming voices. She knew at once: They lookin fer im! Then, filled with her will, she was on her feet, rigid, waiting, listening.

"The lamps burnin!"

"Yuh see her?"

"Naw!"

"Look in the kitchen!"

"Gee, this place smells like niggers!"

"Say, somebodys here er been here!"

"Yeah; theres fire in the stove!"

"Mabbe hes been here n gone?"

"Boy, look at these jars of jam!"

"Niggers make good jam!"

"Git some bread!"

"Heres some cornbread!"

"Say, lemme git some!"

"Take it easy! Theres plenty here!"

"Ahma take some of this stuff home!"

"Look, heres a pota greens!"

"N some hot cawffee!"

"Say, yuh guys! C mon! Cut it out! We didn't come here fer a feas!"

She walked slowly down the hall. They lookin fer im, but they ain got im yit! She stopped in the doorway, her gnarled, black hands as always folded over her stomach, but tight now, so tightly the veins bulged. The kitchen was crowded with white men in glistening raincoats. Though the lamp burned, their flashlights still glowed in red fists. Across her floor she saw the muddy tracks of their boots.

"Yuh white folks git outta mah house!"

There was a quick silence; every face turned toward her. She saw a sudden movement, but did not know what it meant until something hot and wet slammed her squarely in the face. She gasped, but did not move. Calmly, she wiped the warm, greasy liquor of greens from her eyes with her left hand. One of the white men had thrown a handful of greens out of the pot at her.

"How they taste, ol bitch?"

"Ah ast yuh t git outta mah house!"

She saw the sheriff detach himself from the crowd and walk toward her.

"Now, Anty . . ."

"White man, don yuh *Ant*y me!"

"Yuh ain got the right sperit!"

"Sperit hell! Yuh git these men outta mah house!"

"Yuh ack like yuh don like it!"

"Naw, Ah don like it, n yuh knows dam waal Ah don!"

"What yuh gonna do about it?"

"Ahm telling yuh t git outta mah house!"

"Gittin sassy?"

"Ef telling yuh t git outta mah house is sass, then Ahm sassy!"

Her words came in a tense whisper; but beyond, back of them, she was watching, thinking, judging the men.

"Listen, Anty," the sheriff's voice came soft and low. "Ahm here t hep yuh. How come yuh wanna ack this way?"

"Yuh ain never heped yo *own* sef since yuh been born," she flared. "How kin the likes of yuh hep me?"

One of the white men came forward and stood directly in front of her.

"Lissen, nigger woman, yuh talkin t *white* men!"

"Ah don care who Ahm talkin t!"

"Yuhll wish some day yuh did!"

"Not t the likes of yuh!"

"Yuh need somebody t teach yuh how t be a good nigger!"

"*Yuh* cant teach it t me!"

"Yuh gonna change yo tune."

"Not longs mah bloods warm!"

"Don git smart now!"

"Yuh git outta mah house!"

"Spose we don go?" the sheriff asked.

They were crowded around her. She had not moved since she had taken her place in the doorway. She was thinking only of Johnny-Boy as she stood there giving and taking words; and she knew that they, too, were thinking of Johnny-Boy. She knew they wanted him, and her heart was daring them to take him from her.

"Spose we don go?" the sheriff asked again.

"Twenty of yuh runnin over one ol woman! Now, ain yuh white men glad yuh so brave?"

The sheriff grabbed her arm.

"C mon, now! Yuh don did ernuff sass fer one night. Wheres tha nigger son of yos?"

"Don yuh wished yuh knowed?"

"Yuh wanna git slapped?"

"Ah ain never seen one of yo kind that wuznt too low fer . . ."

The sheriff slapped her straight across her face with his open palm. She fell back against a wall and sank to her knees.

"Is tha whut white men do t nigger women?"

She rose slowly and stood again, not even touching the place that ached from his blow, her hands folded over her stomach.

"Ah ain never seen one of yo kind tha wuznt too low fer . . ."

He slapped her again; she reeled backward several feet and fell on her side.

"Is tha whut we too low t do?"

She stood before him again, dry-eyed, as though she had not been struck. Her lips were numb and her chin was wet with blood.

"Aw, let her go! Its the nigger we wan!" said one.

"Wheres that nigger son of yos?" the sheriff asked.

"Find im," she said.

"By Gawd, ef we hafta find im well kill im!"

"He wont be the only nigger yuh ever killed," she said.

She was consumed with a bitter pride. There was nothing on this earth, she felt then, that they could not do to her but that she could take. She stood on a narrow plot of ground from which she would die before she was pushed. And then it was, while standing there feeling warm blood seeping down her throat, that she gave up Johnny-Boy, gave him up to the white folks. She gave him up because they had come tramping into her heart demanding him, thinking they could get him by beating her, thinking they could scare her into making her tell where he was. She gave him up because she wanted them to know that they could not get what they wanted by bluffing and killing.

"Wheres this meetin gonna be?" the sheriff asked.

"Don yuh wish yuh knowed?"

"Ain there gonna be a meetin?"

"How come yuh astin me?"

"There *is* gonna be a meetin," said the sheriff.

"Is it?"

"Ah gotta great mind t choke it outta yuh!"

"Yuh so smart," she said.

"We ain playing wid yuh!"

"Did Ah say yuh wuz?"

"Tha nigger son of yos is erroun here somewheres n Ah aim to find im," said the sheriff. "Ef yuh tell us where he is n ef he talks, mabbe hell git off easy. But ef we hafta find im, well kill im! Ef we hafta find im, then yuh git a sheet t put over im in the mawnin, see? Git yuh a sheet, cause hes gonna be dead!"

"He wont be the only nigger yuh ever killed," she said again.

The sheriff walked past her. The others followed. Yuh didnt git whut yuh wanted! she thought exultingly. N yuh ain gonna *never* git it! Hotly, something ached in her to make them feel the intensity of her pride and freedom; her heart groped to turn the bitter hours of her life into words of a kind that would make them feel that she had taken all they had done to her in stride and could still take more. Her faith surged so strongly in her she was all but blinded. She walked behind them to the door, knotting and twisting her fingers. She saw them step to the muddy ground. Each whirl of the yellow beacon revealed glimpses of slanting rain. Her lips moved, then she shouted:

"Yuh didnt git whut yuh wanted! N yuh ain gonna nevah git it!"

The sheriff stopped and turned; his voice came low and hard.

"Now, by Gawd, thas ernuff outta yuh!"

"Ah know when Ah done said ernuff!"

"Aw, naw, yuh don!" he said. "Yuh don know when yuh done said ernuff, but Ahma teach yuh ternight!"

He was up the steps and across the porch with one bound. She backed into the hall, her eyes full on his face.

"Tell me when yuh gonna stop talkin!" he said, swinging his fist.

The blow caught her high on the cheek; her eyes went blank; she fell flat on her face. She felt the hard heel of his wet shoes coming into her temple and stomach.

"Lemme hear yuh talk some mo!"

She wanted to, but could not; pain numbed and choked her. She lay still and somewhere out of the grey void of unconsciousness she heard someone say: *Aw fer chrissakes leave her erlone, its the nigger we wan.* . . .

IV

She never knew how long she had lain huddled in the dark hallway. Her first returning feeling was of a nameless fear crowding the inside of her, then a deep pain spreading from her temple downward over her body. Her ears were filled with the drone of rain and she shuddered from the cold wind blowing through the door. She opened her eyes and at first saw nothing. As if she were imagining it, she knew she was half lying and half sitting in a corner against a wall.

With difficulty she twisted her neck and what she saw made her hold her breath—a vast white blur was suspended directly above her. For a moment she could not tell if her fear was from the blur or if the blur was from her fear. Gradually the blur resolved itself into a huge white face that slowly filled her vision. She was stone still, conscious really of the effort to breathe, feeling somehow that she existed only by the mercy of that white face. She had seen it before; its fear had gripped her many times; it had for her the fear of all the white faces she had ever seen in her life. *Sue . . .* As from a great distance, she heard her name being called. She was regaining consciousness now, but the fear was coming with her. She looked into the face of a white man, wanting to scream out for him to go; yet accepting his presence because she felt she had to. Though some remote part of her mind was active, her limbs were powerless. It was as if an invisible knife had split her in two, leaving one half of her lying there helpless, while the other half shrank in dread from a forgotten but familiar enemy. *Sue its me Sue its me . . .* Then all at once the voice came clearly.

"Sue, its me! Its Booker!"

And she heard an answering voice speaking inside of her. Yeah, its Booker . . . The one whut jus joined . . . She roused herself, struggling for full consciousness; and as she did so she transferred to the person of Booker the nameless fear she felt. It seemed that Booker towered above her as a challenge to her right to exist upon the earth.

"Yuh awright?"

She did not answer; she started violently to her feet and fell.

"Sue, yuh hurt!"

"Yeah," she breathed.

"Where they hit yuh?"

"Its mah head," she whispered.

She was speaking even though she did not want to; the fear that had hold of her compelled her.

"They beat yuh?"

"Yeah."

"Them bastards! Them Gawddam bastards!"

She heard him saying it over and over; then she felt herself being lifted.

"Naw!" she gasped.

"Ahma take yuh t the kitchen!"

"Put me down!"

"But yuh cant stay here like this!"

She shrank in his arms and pushed her hands against his body; when she was in the kitchen she freed herself, sank into a chair, and held tightly to its back. She looked wonderingly at Booker. There was nothing about him that should frighten her so, but even that did not ease her tension. She saw him go to the water bucket, wet his handkerchief, wring it, and offer it to her. Distrustfully, she stared at the damp cloth.

"Here; put this on yo fohead . . ."

"Naw!"

"C mon; itll make yuh feel bettah!"

She hesitated in confusion. What right had she to be afraid when someone was acting as kindly as this toward her? Reluctantly, she leaned forward and pressed the damp cloth to her head. It helped. With each passing minute she was catching hold of herself, yet wondering why she felt as she did.

"Whut happened?"

"Ah don know."

"Yuh feel bettah?"

"Yeah."

"Who all wuz here?"

"Ah don know," she said again.

"Yo head still hurt?"

"Yeah."

"Gee, Ahm sorry."

"Ahm awright," she sighed and buried her face in her hands.

She felt him touch her shoulder.

"Sue, Ah got some bad news fer yuh . . ."

She knew; she stiffened and grew cold. It had happened; she stared dry-eyed, with compressed lips.

"Its mah Johnny-Boy," she said.

"Yeah; Ahm awful sorry t hafta tell yuh this way. But Ah thought yuh oughta know . . ."

Her tension eased and a vacant place opened up inside of her. A voice whispered, Jesus, hep me!

"W-w-where is he?"

"They got im out t Foleys Woods tryin t make him tell who the others is."

"He ain gonna tell," she said. "They jus as waal kill im, cause he ain gonna nevah tell."

"Ah hope he don," said Booker. "But he didnt have a chance t tell the others. They grabbed im jus as he got t the woods."

Then all the horror of it flashed upon her; she saw flung out over the rainy countryside an array of shacks where white and black comrades were sleeping; in the morning they would be rising and going to Lem's; then they would be caught. And that meant terror, prison, and death. The comrades would have to be told; she would have to tell them; she could not entrust Johnny-Boy's work to another, and especially not to Booker as long as she felt toward him as she did. Gripping the bottom of the chair with both hands, she tried to rise; the room blurred and she swayed. She found herself resting in Booker's arms.

"Lemme go!"

"Sue, yuh too weak t walk!"

"Ah gotta tell em!" she said.

"Set down, Sue! Yuh hurt! Yuh sick!"

When seated, she looked at him helplessly.

"Sue, lissen! Johnny-Boys caught. Ahm here. Yuh tell me who they is n Ahll tell em."

She stared at the floor and did not answer. Yes; she was too weak to go. There was no way for her to tramp all those miles through the rain tonight. But should she tell Booker? If only she had somebody like Reva to talk to! She did not want to decide alone; she must make no mistake about this. She felt Booker's fingers pressing on her arm and it was as though the white mountain was pushing her to the edge of a sheer height; she again exclaimed inwardly. Jesus, hep me! Booker's white face was at her side, waiting. Would she be doing right to tell him? Suppose she did not tell and then the comrades were caught? She could not ever forgive herself for doing a thing like that. But maybe she was wrong; maybe her fear was what Johnny-Boy had always called "jus foolishness." She remembered his saying, Ma, we cant make the party grow ef we start doubtin everbody. . . .

"Tell me who they is, Sue, n Ahll tell em. Ah jus joined n Ah don know who they is."

"Ah don know who they is," she said.

"Yuh *gotta* tell me who they is, Sue!"

"Ah tol yuh Ah don know!"

"Yuh *do* know! C mon! Set up n talk!"

"Naw!"

"Yuh wan em all t git *killed?*"

She shook her head and swallowed. Lawd, Ah don believe in this man!

"Lissen, Ahll call the names n yuh tell me which ones is in the party n which ones ain, see?"

"Naw!"

"Please, Sue!"

"Ah don know," she said.

"Sue, yuh ain doin right by em. Johnny-Boy wouldnt wan yuh t be this way. Hes out there holdin up his end. Les hol up ours . . ."

"Lawd, Ah don know . . ."

"Is yuh scared a me cause Ahm *white?* Johnny-Boy ain like tha. Don let all the work we done go fer nothin."

She gave up and bowed her head in her hands.

"Is it Johnson? Tell me, Sue?"

"Yeah," she whispered in horror; a mounting horror of feeling herself being undone.

"Is it Green?"

"Yeah."

"Murphy?"

"Lawd, Ah don know!"

"Yuh gotta tell me, Sue!"

"Mistah Booker, please leave me erlone . . ."

"Is it Murphy?"

She answered yes to the names of Johnny-Boy's comrades; she answered until he asked her no more. Then she thought, How he know the sheriffs men is watchin Lems house? She stood up and held onto her chair, feeling something sure and firm within her.

"How yuh know bout Lem?"

"Why . . . How Ah know?"

"Whut yuh doin here this tima night? How yuh know the sheriff got Johnny-Boy?"

"Sue, don yuh believe in me?"

She did not, but she could not answer. She stared at him until her lips hung open; she was searching deep within herself for certainty.

"You meet Reva?" she asked.

"Reva?"

"Yeah; Lems gal?"

"Oh, yeah. Sho, Ah met Reva."

"She tell yuh?"

She asked the question more of herself than of him; she longed to believe.

"Yeah," he said softly. "Ah reckon Ah oughta be goin t tell em now."

"Who?" she asked. "Tell *who?*"

The muscles of her body were stiff as she waited for his answer; she felt as though life depended upon it.

"The comrades," he said.

"Yeah," she sighed.

She did not know when he left; she was not looking or listening. She just suddenly saw the room empty and from her the thing that had made her fearful was gone.

V

For a space of time that seemed to her as long as she had been upon the earth, she sat huddled over the cold stove. One minute she would say to herself, They both gone now; Johnny-Boy n Sug . . . Mabbe Ahll never see em ergin. Then a surge of guilt would blot out her longing. "Lawd, Ah shouldna tol!" she mumbled. "But no man kin be so low-down as to do a thing like that . . ." Several times she had an impulse to try to tell the comrades herself; she was feeling a little better now. But what good would that do? She had told Booker the names. He jus couldnt be a Judas to po folks like us . . . He *couldnt!*

"An Sue!"

Thas Reva! Her heart leaped with an anxious gladness. She rose without answering and limped down the dark hallway. Through the open door, against the background of rain, she saw Reva's face lit now and then to whiteness by the whirling beams of the beacon. She was about to call, but a thought checked her. Jesus, hep me! Ah gotta tell her bout Johnny-Boy . . . Lawd, Ah cant!

"An Sue, yuh there?"

"C mon in, chile!"

She caught Reva and held her close for a moment without speaking.

"Lawd, Ahm sho glad yuh here," she said at last.

"Ah thought somethin had happened t yuh," said Reva, pulling away. "Ah saw the do open . . . Pa tol me to come back n stay wid yuh tonight . . ." Reva paused and started, "W-w-whuts the mattah?"

She was so full of having Reva with her that she did not understand what the question meant.

"Hunh?"

"Yo neck . . ."

"Aw, it ain nothin, chile. C mon in the kitchen."

"But theres blood on yo neck!"

"The sheriff wuz here . . ."

"Them fools! Whut they wanna bother yuh fer? Ah could kill em! So hep me Gawd, Ah could!"

"It ain nothin," she said.

She was wondering how to tell Reva about Johnny-Boy and Booker. Ahll wait a lil while longer, she thought. Now that Reva was here, her fear did not seem as awful as before.

"C mon, lemme fix yo head, An Sue. Yuh hurt."

They went to the kitchen. She sat silent while Reva dressed her scalp. She was feeling better now; in just a little while she would tell Reva. She felt the girl's finger pressing gently upon her head.

"Tha hurt?"

"A lil, chile."

"Yuh po thing."

"It ain nothin."

"Did Johnny-Boy come?"

She hesitated.

"Yeah."

"He done gone t tell the others?"

Reva's voice sounded so clear and confident that it mocked her. Lawd, Ah cant tell this chile . . .

"Yuh tol im, didnt yuh, An Sue?"

"Y-y-yeah . . ."

"Gee! Thas good! Ah tol pa he didnt hafta worry ef Johnny-Boy got the news. Mabbe thingsll come out awright."

"Ah hope . . ."

She could not go on; she had gone as far as she could. For the first time that night she began to cry.

"Hush, An Sue! Yuh awways been brave. Itll be awright!"

"Ain nothin awright, chile. The worls jus too much fer us, Ah reckon."

"Ef yuh cry that way itll make me cry."

She forced herself to stop. Naw; Ah cant carry on this way in fronta Reva . . . Right now she had a deep need for Reva to believe in her. She watched the girl get pine-knots from behind the stove, rekindle the fire, and put on the coffee pot.

"Yuh wan some cawffee?" Reva asked.

"Naw, honey."

"Aw, c mon, An Sue."

"Jusa lil, honey."

"Thas the way to be. Oh, say, Ah fergot," said Reva, measuring out spoonsful of coffee. "Pa tol me t tell yuh t watch out fer tha Booker man. Hes a stool."

She showed not one sign of outward movement or expression, but as the words fell from Reva's lips she went limp inside.

"Pa tol me soon as Ah got back home. He got word from town . . ."

She stopped listening. She felt as though she had been slapped to the extreme outer edge of life, into a cold darkness. She knew now what she had felt when she had looked up out of her fog of pain and had seen Booker. It was the image of all the white folks, and the fear that went with them, that she had seen and felt during her lifetime. And again, for the second time that night, something she had felt had come true. All she could say to herself was, Ah didnt like im! Gawd knows, Ah didnt! Ah tol Johnny-Boy it wuz some of them white folks . . .

"Here; drink yo cawffee . . ."

She took the cup; her fingers trembled, and the steaming liquid spilt onto her dress and leg.

"Ahm sorry, An Sue!"

Her leg was scalded, but the pain did not bother her.

"Its awright," she said.

"Wait; lemme put some lard on tha burn!"

"It don hurt."

"Yuh worried bout somethin."

"Naw, honey."

"Lemme fix yuh so mo cawffee."

"Ah don wan nothin now, Reva."

"Waal, buck up. Don be tha way . . . ."

They were silent. She heard Reva drinking. No; she would not tell Reva; Reva was all she had left. But she had to do something, some way, somehow. She was undone too much as it was; and to tell Reva about Booker or Johnny-Boy was more than she was equal to; it would be too coldly shameful. She wanted to be alone and fight this thing out with herself.

"Go t bed, honey. Yuh tired."

"Naw; Ahm awright, An Sue."

She heard the bottom of Reva's empty cup clank against the top of the stove. Ah *got* t make her go t bed! Yes; Booker would tell the names of the comrades to the sheriff. If she could only stop him some way! That was the answer, the point, the star that grew bright in the morning of new hope. Soon, maybe half an hour from now, Booker would reach Foleys Woods. Hes boun t go the long way, cause he don know no short cut, she thought. Ah could wade the creek n beat im there. . . . But what would she do after that?

"Reva, honey, go t bed. Ahm awright. Yuh need res."

"Ah ain sleepy, An Sue."

"Ah knows whuts bes fer yuh, chile. Yuh tired n wet."

"Ah wanna stay up wid yuh."

She forced a smile and said:

"Ah don think they gonna hurt Johnny-Boy . . . ."

"Fer *real*, An Sue?"

"Sho, honey."

"But Ah wanna wait up wid yuh."

"Thas mah job, honey. Thas whut a mas fer, t wait up fer her chullun."

"Good night, An Sue."

"Good night, honey."

She watched Reva pull up and leave the kitchen; presently she heard the shucks in the mattress whispering, and she knew that Reva had gone to bed. She was alone. Through the cracks of the stove she saw the fire dying to grey ashes; the room was growing cold again. The yellow beacon continued to flit past the window and the rain stiil drummed. Yes; she was alone; she had done this awful thing alone; she must find some way out, alone. Like touching a festering sore, she put her finger upon that moment when she had shouted her defiance to the sheriff, when she had shouted to feel her strength. She had lost Sug to save others; she had let Johnny-Boy go to save others; and

then in a moment of weakness that came from too much strength she
had lost all. If she had not shouted to the sheriff, she would have
been strong enough to have resisted Booker; she would have been
able to tell the comrades herself. Something tightened in her as she
remembered and understood the fit of fear she had felt on coming to
herself in the dark hallway. A part of her life she thought she had
done away with forever had had hold of her then. She had thought the
soft, warm past was over; she had thought that it did not mean much
when now she sang: *"Hes the Lily of the Valley, the Bright n
Mawnin Star"* . . . The days when she had sung that song were the
days when she had not hoped for anything on this earth, the days
when the cold mountain had driven her into the arms of Jesus. She
had thought that Sug and Johnny-Boy had taught her to forget Him,
to fix her hope upon the fight of black men for freedom. Through the
gradual years she had believed and worked with them, had felt
strength shed from the grace of their terrible vision. That grace had
been upon her when she had let the sheriff slap her down; it had been
upon her when she had risen time and again from the floor and faced
him. But she had trapped herself with her own hunger; to water the
long, dry thirst of her faith; her pride had made a bargain which her
flesh could not keep. Her having told the names of Johnny-Boy's
comrades was but an incident in a deeper horror. She stood up and
looked at the floor while call and counter-call, loyalty and counter-
loyalty struggled in her soul. Mired she was between two abandoned
worlds, living, but dying without the strength of the grace that either
gave. The clearer she felt it the fuller did something well up from the
depths of her for release; the more urgent did she feel the need to
fling into her black sky another star, another hope, one more terrible
vision to give her the strength to live and act. Softly and restlessly she
walked about the kitchen, feeling herself naked against the night, the
rain, the world; and shamed whenever the thought of Reva's love
crossed her mind. She lifted her empty hands and looked at her
writhing fingers, Lawd, whut kin Ah do now? She could still wade
the creek and get to Foleys Woods before Booker. And then what?
How could she manage to see Johnny-Boy or Booker? Again she
heard the sheriff's threatening voice: Git yuh a sheet, cause hes gonna
be dead! The sheet! Thas it, the *sheet!* Her whole being leaped with
will; the long years of her life bent toward a moment of focus, a
point. Ah kin go wid mah sheet! Ahll be doin whut he said! Lawd
Gawd in Heaven, Ahma go lika nigger woman wid mah windin sheet
t git mah dead son! But then what? She stood straight and smiled
grimly; she had in her heart the whole meaning of her life; her entire
personality was poised on the brink of a total act. Ah know! Ah
know! She thought of Johnny-Boy's gun in the dresser drawer. Ahll
hide the gun in the sheet n go aftah Johnny-Boys body. . . . She

tiptoed to her room, eased out the dresser drawer, and got a sheet. Reva was sleeping; the darkness was filled with her quiet breathing. She groped in the drawer and found the gun. She wound the gun in the sheet and held them both under her apron. Then she stole to the bedside and watched Reva. Lawd, hep her! But mabbe shes bettah off. This had t happen sometime . . . She n Johnny-Boy couldna been together in this here South . . . N Ah couldn't tell her about Booker. Itll come out awright n she wont nevah know. Reva's trust would never be shaken. She caught her breath as the shucks in the mattress rustled dryly; then all was quiet and she breathed easily again. She tiptoed to the door, down the hall, and stood on the porch. Above her the yellow beacon whirled through the rain. She went over muddy ground, mounted a slope, stopped and looked back at her house. The lamp glowed in her window, and the yellow beacon that swung every few seconds seemed to feed it with light. She turned and started across the fields, holding the gun and sheet tightly, thinking, **Po Reva** . . . Po critter . . . Shes fas ersleep . . .

VI

For the most part she walked with her eyes half shut, her lips tightly compressed, leaning her body against the wind and the driving rain, feeling the pistol in the sheet sagging cold and heavy in her fingers. Already she was getting wet; it seemed that her feet found every puddle of water that stood between the corn rows.

She came to the edge of the creek and paused, wondering at what point was it low. Taking the sheet from under her apron, she wrapped the gun in it so that her finger could be upon the trigger. Ahll cross here, she thought. At first she did not feel the water; her feet were already wet. But the water grew cold as it came up to her knees; she gasped when it reached her waist. Lawd, this creeks high! When she had passed the middle, she knew that she was out of danger. She came out of the water, climbed a grassy hill, walked on, turned a bend and saw the lights of autos gleaming ahead. Yeah; theys still there! She hurried with her head down. Wondah did Ah beat im here? Lawd, Ah *hope* so! A vivid image of Booker's white face hovered a moment before her eyes and a surging will rose up in her so hard and strong that it vanished. She was among the autos now. From nearby came the hoarse voices of the men.

"Hey, yuh!"

She stopped, nervously clutching the sheet. Two white men with shotguns came toward her.

"What in hell yuh doin out here?"

She did not answer.

"Didnt yuh hear somebody speak t yuh?"

"Ahm comin aftah mah son," she said humbly.

"Yo *son?*"

"Yessuh."

"What yo son doin out here?"

"The sheriffs got im."

"Holy Scott! Jim, its the niggers ma!"

"Whut yuh got there?" asked one.

"A sheet."

"A *sheet?*"

"Yessuh."

"Fer whut?"

"The sheriff tol me t bring a sheet t git his body."

"Waal, waal . . ."

"Now, ain tha somethin?"

The white men looked at each other.

"These niggers sho love one ernother," said one.

"N tha ain no lie," said the other.

"Take me t the sheriff," she begged.

"Yuh ain givin us *orders*, is yuh?"

"Nawsuh."

"Well take yuh when wes good n ready."

"Yessuh."

"So yuh wan his body?"

"Yessuh."

"Waal, he ain dead yit."

"They gonna kill im," she said.

"Ef he talks they wont."

"He ain gonna talk," she said.

"How yuh know?"

"Cause he ain."

"We got ways of makin niggers talk."

"Yuh ain got no way fer im."

"Yuh thinka lot of that black Red, don yuh?"

"Hes mah son."

"Why don yuh teach im some sense?"

"Hes mah son," she said again.

"Lissen, ol nigger woman, yuh stand there wid yo hair white. Yuh got bettah sense than t believe tha niggers kin make a revolution . . ."

"A black republic," said the other one, laughing.

"Take me t the sheriff," she begged.

"Yuh his ma," said one. "Yuh kin make im talk n tell whose in this thing wid im."

"He ain gonna talk," she said.

"Don yuh wan im t live?"

She did not answer.

"C mon, les take her t Bradley."

They grabbed her arms and she clutched hard at the sheet and gun; they led her toward the crowd in the woods. Her feelings were simple; Booker would not tell; she was there with the gun to see to that. The louder became the voices of the men the deeper became her feeling of wanting to right the mistake she had made; of wanting to fight her way back to solid ground. She would stall for time until Booker showed up. Oh, ef theyll only lemme git close t Johnny-Boy! As they led her near the crowd she saw white faces turning and looking at her and heard a rising clamor of voices.

"Whose tha?"

"A nigger woman!"

"Whut she doin out here?"

"This is his ma!" called one of the men.

"Whut she wans?"

"She brought a sheet t cover his body!"

"He ain dead yit!"

"They tryin t make im talk!"

"But he will be dead soon ef he don open up!"

"Say, look! The niggers ma brought a sheet t cover up his body!"

"Now, ain that sweet?"

"Mabbe she wans t hol a prayer meetin!"

"Did she git a preacher?"

"Say, go git Bradley!"

"O.K.!"

The crowd grew quiet. They looked at her curiously; she felt their cold eyes trying to detect some weakness in her. Humbly, she stood with the sheet covering the gun. She had already accepted all that they could do to her.

The sheriff came.

"So yuh brought yuh sheet, hunh?"

"Yessuh," she whispered.

"Looks like them slaps we gave yuh learned yuh some sense, didnt they?"

She did not answer.

"Yuh don need tha sheet. Yo son ain dead yit," he said, reaching toward her.

She backed away, her eyes wide.

"Naw!"

"Now, lissen, Anty!" he said. "There ain no use in yuh ackin a fool! Go in there n tell tha nigger son of yos t tell us whos in this wid im, see? Ah promise we wont kill im ef he talks. We'll let im git outta town."

"There ain nothin Ah kin tell im," she said.

"Yuh wan us t kill im?"

She did not answer. She saw someone lean toward the sheriff and whisper.

"Bring her erlong," the sheriff said.

They led her to a muddy clearing. The rain streamed down through the ghostly glare of the flashlights. As the men formed a semi-circle she saw Johnny-Boy lying in a trough of mud. He was tied with rope; he lay hunched and one side of his face rested in a pool of black water. His eyes were staring questioningly at her.

"Speak t im," said the sheriff.

If she could only tell him why she was here! But that was impossible; she was close to what she wanted and she stared straight before her with compressed lips.

"Say, nigger!" called the sheriff, kicking Johnny-Boy. "Heres yo ma!"

Johnny-Boy did not move or speak. The sheriff faced her again.

"Lissen, Anty," he said. "Yuh got mo say wid im than anybody. Tell im t talk n hava chance. Whut he wanna pertect the other niggers n white folks fer?"

She slid her finger about the trigger of the gun and looked stonily at the mud.

"Go t him," said the sheriff.

She did not move. Her heart was crying out to answer the amazed question in Johnny-Boy's eyes. But there was no way now.

"Waal, yuhre astin fer it. By Gawd, we gotta way to *make* yuh talk t im," he said, turning away. "Say, Tim, git one of them logs n turn that nigger upside-down n put his legs on it!"

A murmur of assent ran through the crowd. She bit her lips; she knew what that meant.

"Yuh wan yo nigger son crippled?" she heard the sheriff ask.

She did not answer. She saw them roll the log up; they lifted Johnny-Boy and laid him on his face and stomach, then they pulled his legs over the log. His kneecaps rested on the sheer top of the log's back and the toes of his shoes pointed groundward. So absorbed was she in watching that she felt that it was she who was being lifted and made ready for torture.

"Git a crowbar!" said the sheriff.

A tall, lank man got a crowbar from a nearby auto and stood over the log. His jaws worked slowly on a wad of tobacco.

"Now, its up t yuh, Anty," the sheriff said. "Tell the man whut t do!"

She looked into the rain. The sheriff turned.

"Mebbe she think wes playin. Ef she don say nothin, then break em at the kneecaps!"

"O.K., Sheriff!"

She stood waiting for Booker. Her legs felt weak; she wondered if she would be able to wait much longer. Over and over she said to herself, Ef he came now Ahd kill em both!

"She ain sayin nothin, Sheriff!"

"Waal, Gawddammit, let im have it!"

The crowbar came down and Johnny-Boy's body lunged in the mud and water. There was a scream. She swayed, holding tight to the gun and sheet.

"Hol im! Git the other leg!"

The crowbar fell again. There was another scream.

"Yuh break em?" asked the sheriff.

The tall man lifted Johnny-Boy's legs and let them drop limply again, dropping rearward from the kneecaps. Johnny-Boy's body lay still. His head had rolled to one side and she could not see his face.

"Jus lika broke sparrow wing," said the man, laughing softly.

Then Johnny-Boy's face turned to her; he screamed.

"Go way, ma! Go way!"

It was the first time she had heard his voice since she had come out to the woods; she all but lost control of herself. She started violently forward, but the sheriff's arm checked her.

"Aw, naw! Yuh had yo chance!" He turned to Johnny-Boy. "She kin go ef yuh talk."

"Mistah, he ain gonna talk," she said.

"Go way, ma!" said Johnny-Boy.

"Shoot im! Don make im suffah so," she begged.

"He'll either talk or he'll never hear yuh ergin," the sheriff said. "Theres other things we kin do t im."

She said nothing.

"Whut yuh come here fer, ma?" Johnny-Boy sobbed.

"Ahm gonna split his eardrums," the sheriff said. "Ef yuh got anythin to say t im yuh bettah say it *now!*"

She closed her eyes. She heard the sheriff's feet sucking in mud. Ah could save im! She opened her eyes; there were shouts of eagerness from the crowd as it pushed in closer.

"Bus em, Sheriff!"

"Fix im so he cant hear!"

"He knows how t do it, too!"

"He busted a Jew boy tha way once!"

She saw the sheriff stoop over Johnny-Boy, place his flat palm over one ear and strike his fist against it with all his might. He placed his palm over the other ear and struck again. Johnny-Boy moaned, his head rolling from side to side, his eyes showing white amazement in a world without sound.

"Yuh wouldnt talk t im when yuh had the chance," said the sheriff. "Try n talk now."

She felt warm tears on her cheeks. She longed to shoot Johnny-Boy and let him go. But if she did that they would take the gun from her, and Booker would tell who the others were. Lawd, help me! The men were talking loudly now, as though the main business was over. It seemed ages that she stood there watching Johnny-Boy roll and whimper in his world of silence.

"Say, Sheriff, heres somebody lookin fer yuh!"

"Who is it?"

"Ah don know!"

"Bring em in!"

She stiffened and looked around wildly, holding the gun tight. Is tha Booker? Then she held still, feeling that her excitement might betray her. Mabbe Ah kin shoot em both! Mabbe Ah kin shoot *twice!* The sheriff stood in front of her, waiting. The crowd parted and she saw Booker hurrying forward.

"Ah know em all, Sheriff!" he called.

He came full into the muddy clearing where Johnny-Boy lay.

"Yuh mean yuh got the names?"

"Sho! The ol nigger . . ."

She saw his lips hang open and silent when he saw her. She stepped forward and raised the sheet.

"Whut . . ."

She fired, once; then, without pausing, she turned, hearing them yell. She aimed at Johnny-Boy, but they had their arms around her, bearing her to the ground, clawing at the sheet in her hand. She glimpsed Booker lying sprawled in the mud, on his face, his hands stretched out before him; then a cluster of yelling men blotted him out. She lay without struggling, looking upward through the rain at the white faces above her. And she was suddenly at peace; they were not a white mountain now; they were not pushing her any longer to the edge of life. Its awright . . .

"She shot Booker!"

"She hada gun in the sheet!"

"She shot im right thu the head!"

"Whut she shoot im fer?"

"Kill the bitch!"

"Ah *thought* somethin wuz wrong bout her!"

"Ah wuz fer givin it t her from the firs!"

"Thas whut yuh git fer treatin a nigger nice!"

"Say, Bookers dead!"

She stopped looking into the white faces, stopped listening. She waited, giving up her life before they took it from her; she had done what she wanted. Ef only Johnny-Boy . . . She looked at him; he lay looking at her with tired eyes. Ef she could only tell im! But he lay already buried in a grave of silence.

"Whut yuh kill im fer, hunh?"

It was the sheriff's voice; she did not answer.

"Mabbe she wuz shootin at yuh, Sheriff?"

"Whut yuh kill im fer?"

She felt the sheriff's foot come into her side; she closed her eyes.

"Yuh black bitch!"

"Let her have it!"

"Yuh reckon she foun out bout Booker?"

"She mighta."

"Jesus Chris, whut yuh dummies *waitin* on!"

"Yeah; kill her!"

"Kill em *both!*"

"Let her know her nigger sons dead firs!"

She turned her head toward Johnny-Boy; he lay looking puzzled in a world beyond the reach of voices. At leas he cant hear, she thought.

"C'mon, let im have it!"

She listened to hear what Johnny-Boy could not. They came, two of them, one right behind the other; so close together that they sounded like one shot. She did not look at Johnny-Boy now; she looked at the white faces of the men, hard and wet in the glare of the flashlights.

"Yuh hear tha, nigger woman?"

"Did tha surprise im? Hes in hell now wonderin whut hit im!"

"C mon! Give it t her, Sheriff!"

"Lemme shoot her, Sheriff! It wuz mah pal she shot!"

"Awright, Pete! Thas fair ernuff!"

She gave up as much of her life as she could before they took it from her. But the sound of the shot and the streak of fire that tore its way through her chest forced her to live again, intensely. She had not moved, save for the slight jarring impact of the bullet. She felt the heat of her own blood warming her cold, wet back. She yearned suddenly to talk. "Yuh didnt git whut yuh wanted! N yuh ain gonna nevah git it! Yuh didnt kill me; Ah come here by mahsef . . ." She felt rain falling into her wide-open, dimming eyes and heard faint voices. Her lips moved soundlessly. *Yuh didnt git yuh didnt yuh didnt* . . . Focused and pointed she was, buried in the depths of her star, swallowed in its peace and strength; and not feeling her flesh growing cold, cold as the rain that fell from the invisible sky upon the doomed living and the dead that never dies.

DORIS LESSING (1919–   )

How I Finally Lost My Heart

It would be easy to say that I picked up a knife, slit open my side, took my heart out, and threw it away; but unfortunately it wasn't as easy as that. Not that I, like everybody else, had not often wanted to do it. No, it happened differently, and not as I expected.

It was just after I had had a lunch and a tea with two different men. My lunch partner I had lived with for (more or less) four and seven-twelfths years. When he left me for new pastures, I spent two years, or was it three, half dead, and my heart was a stone, impossible to carry about, considering all the other things weighing on one. Then I slowly, and with difficulty, got free, because my heart cherished a thousand adhesions to my first love—though from another point of view he could be legitimately described as either my second *real* love (my father being the first) or my third (my brother intervening).

As the folk song has it:

> I have loved but three men in my life,
> My father, my brother, and the man that took my life.

But if one were going to look at the thing from outside, without insight, he could be seen as (perhaps, I forget) the thirteenth, but to do that means disregarding the inner emotional truth. For we all know that those affairs or entanglements one has between *serious* loves, though they may number dozens and stretch over years, *don't really count.*

This way of looking at things creates a number of unhappy people, for it is well known that what doesn't really count for me might very well count for you. But there is no way of getting over this difficulty, for a *serious* love is the most important business in life, or nearly so. At any rate, most of us are engaged in looking for it. Even when we are in fact being very serious indeed with one person we still have an eighth of an eye cocked in case some stranger unexpectedly encountered might turn out to be even more serious. We are all entirely in agreement that we are in the right to taste, test, sip and sample a thousand people on our way to the *real* one. It is not too much to say that in our circles tasting and sampling is probably the second most important activity, the first being earning money. Or to put it another way, "If you are serious about this thing, you go on laying everybody that offers until something clicks and you're all set to go."

I have digressed from an earlier point: that I regarded this man I had lunch with (we will call him A) as my first love; and still do, despite the Freudians, who insist on seeing my father as A and possibly my brother as B, making my (real) first love C. And despite, also, those who might ask: What about your two husbands and all those affairs?

What about them? I did not *really* love them, the way I loved A.

I had lunch with him. Then, quite by chance, I had tea with B. When I say B, here, I mean my *second* serious love, not my brother, or the little boys I was in love with between the ages of five and fifteen, if we are going to take fifteen (arbitrarily) as the point of no return . . . which last phrase is in itself a pretty brave defiance of the secular arbiters.

In between A and B (my count) there were a good many affairs, or samples, but they didn't score. B and I *clicked,* we went off like a bomb, though not quite as simply as A and I had clicked, because my heart was bruised, sullen, and suspicious because of A's throwing me over. Also there were all those ligaments and adhesions binding me to A still to be loosened, one by one. However, for a time B and I got on like a house on fire, and then we came to grief. My heart was again a ton weight in my side.

> If this were a stone in my side, a stone,
> I could pluck it out and be free. . . .

Having lunch with A, then tea with B, two men who between them had consumed a decade of my previous years (I am not counting the test or trial affairs in between) and, it is fair to say, had balanced all the delight (plenty and intense) with misery (oh Lord, Lord) —moving from one to the other, in the course of an afternoon, conversing amiably about this and that, with meanwhile my heart giving no more than slight reminiscent tugs, the fish of memory at the end of a long slack line. . . .

To sum up, it was salutary.

Particularly as that evening I was expecting to meet C, or someone who might very well turn out to be C—though I don't want to give too much emphasis to C, the truth is I can hardly remember what he looked like, but one can't be expected to remember the unimportant ones one has sipped or tasted in between. But after all, he might have turned out to be C, we might have *clicked,* and I was in that state of mind (in which we all so often are) of thinking: He might turn out to be the one. (I use a woman's magazine phrase deliberately here, instead of saying, as I might. *Perhaps it will be serious.*)

So there I was (I want to get the details and atmosphere right) standing at a window looking into a street (Great Portland Street, as a matter of fact) and thinking that while I would not dream of regretting my affairs, or experiences, with A and B (it is better to have loved and lost than never to have loved at all), my anticipation of the heart because of spending an evening with a possible C had a certain unreality, because there was no doubt that both A and B had caused me unbelievable pain. Why, therefore, was I looking forward to C? I should rather be running away as fast as I could.

It suddenly occurred to me that I was looking at the whole phenomenon quite inaccurately. My (or perhaps I am permitted to say our?) way of looking at it is that one must search for an A, or a B, or a C or a D with a certain combination of desirable or sympathetic qualities so that one may click, or spontaneously combust: or to put it differently, one needs a person who, like a saucer of water, allows one to float off on him/her, like a transfer. But this wasn't so at all. Actually one carries with one a sort of burning spear stuck in one's side, that one waits for someone else to pull out; it is something painful, like a sore or a wound, that one cannot wait to share with someone else.

I saw myself quite plainly in a moment of truth: I was standing at a window (on the third floor) with A and B (to mention only the mountain peaks of my emotional experience) behind me, a rather attractive woman, if I may say so, with a mellowness that I would be the first to admit is the sad harbinger of age, but is attractive by definition, because it is a testament to the amount of sampling and sipping (I nearly wrote simpling and sapping) I have done in my time . . . there I stood, brushed, dressed, red-lipped, kohl-eyed, all waiting for an evening with a possible C. And at another window overlooking (I think I am right in saying) Margaret Street, stood C, brushed, washed, shaved, smiling: an attractive man (I think), and *he* was thinking: Perhaps she will turn out to be D (or A or 3 or ? or %, or whatever symbol he used). We stood, separated by space, certainly, in identical conditions of pleasant uncertainty and anticipation, and we both held our hearts in our hands, all pink and palpitating and ready for pleasure and pain, and we were about to throw these hearts in each other's face like snowballs, or cricket balls (How's that?) or, more accurately, like great bleeding wounds: "Take my wound." Because the last thing one ever thinks at such moments is that he (or she) will say: Take *my* wound, please remove the spear from *my* side. No, not at all, one simply expects to get rid of one's own.

I decided I must go to the telephone and say C!—You know that joke about the joke-makers who don't trouble to tell each other jokes, but simply say Joke 1, or Joke 2, and everyone roars with laughter, or snickers, or giggles appropriately. . . . Actually one could reverse the game by guessing whether it was Joke C (b) or Joke A (d) according to what sort of laughter a person made to match the silent thought. . . . Well, C (I imagined myself saying), the analogy is for our instruction: Let's take the whole thing as read or said. Let's not lick each other's sores; let's keep our hearts to ourselves. Because just consider it, C, how utterly absurd—here we stand at our respective windows with our palpitating hearts in our hands. . . .

At this moment, dear reader, I was forced simply to put down the telephone with an apology. For I felt the fingers of my left hand push outwards around something rather large, light, and slippery—hard to describe this sensation, really. My hand is not large, and my heart was in a state of inflation after having had lunch with A, tea with B, and then looking forward to C. . . . Anyway, my fingers were stretching out rather desperately to encompass an unknown, largish, lightish object, and I said: Excuse me a minute, to C, looked down, and there was my heart, in my hand.

I had to end the conversation there.

For one thing, to find that one has achieved something so often longed for, so easily, is upsetting. It's not as if I had been trying. To get something one wants simply by accident—no, there's no pleasure in it, no feeling of achievement. So to find myself heart-whole, or, more accurately, heart-less, or at any rate, rid of the damned thing, and at such an awkward moment, in the middle of an imaginary telephone call with a man who might possibly turn out to be C, well, it was irritating rather than not.

For another thing, a heart, raw and bleeding and fresh from one's side, is not the prettiest sight. I'm not going into that at all. I was appalled, and indeed embarrassed that *that* was what had been loving and beating away all those years, because if I'd had any idea at all—well, enough of that.

My problem was how to get rid of it.

Simple, you'll say, drop it into the waste bucket.

Well, let me tell you, that's what I tried to do. I took a good look at this object, nearly died with embarrassment, and walked over to the rubbish can, where I tried to let it roll off my fingers. It wouldn't. It was stuck. There was my heart, a large red pulsing bleeding repulsive object, stuck to my fingers. What was I going to do? I sat down, lit a cigarette (with one hand, holding the matchbox between my knees), held my hand with the heart stuck on it over the side of the chair so that it could drip into a bucket, and considered.

> If this were a stone in my hand, a stone,
> I could throw it over a tree. . . .

When I had finished the cigarette, I carefully unwrapped some tin foil, of the kind used to wrap food in when cooking, and I fitted a sort of cover around my heart. This was absolutely and urgently necessary. First, it was smarting badly. After all, it had spent some forty years protected by flesh and ribs and the air was too much for it. Secondly, I couldn't have any Tom, Dick and Harry walking in and looking at it. Thirdly, I could not look at it for too long myself, it filled me with shame. The tin foil was effective, and indeed rather striking. It is quite pliable and now it seemed as if there were a stylised heart balanced on my palm, like a globe, in glittering, silvery substance. I almost felt I needed a sceptre in the other hand to balance it. . . . But the thing was, there is no other word for it, in bad taste. I then wrapped a scarf around hand and tin-foiled heart, and felt safer. Now it was a question of pretending to have hurt my hand until I could think of a way of getting rid of my heart altogether, short of amputating my hand.

Meanwhile I telephoned (really, not in imagination) C, who now would never be C. I could feel my heart, which was stuck so close to my fingers that I could feel every beat or tremor, give a gulp of resigned grief at the idea of this beautiful experience now never to be. I told him some idiotic lie about having flu. Well, he was all stiff and indignant, but concealing it urbanely, as I would have done, making a joke but allowing a tiny barb of sarcasm to rankle in the last well-chosen phrase. Then I sat down again to think out my whole situation.

There I sat.

What was I going to do?

There I sat.

I am going to have to skip about four days here, vital enough in all conscience, because I simply cannot go heartbeat by heartbeat through my memories. A pity, since I suppose this is what this story is about; but in brief: I drew the curtains, I took the telephone off the hook, I turned on the lights, I took the scarf off the glittering shape, then the tin foil, then I examined the heart. There were two-fifths of a century's experiences to work through, and before I had even got through the first night, I was in a state hard to describe. . . .

> Or if I could pull the nerves from my skin
> A quick red net to drag through a sea for fish. . . .

By the end of the fourth day I was worn out. By no act of will, or intention, or desire, could I move that heart by a fraction—on the contrary, it was not only stuck to my fingers, like a sucked boiled sweet, but was actually growing to the flesh of my fingers and my palm.

I wrapped it up again in tin foil and scarf, and turned out the lights and pulled up the blinds and opened the curtains. It was about ten in the morning, an ordinary London day, neither hot nor cold nor clear nor clouded nor wet nor fine. And while the street is interesting, it is not exactly beautiful, so I wasn't looking at it so much as waiting for something to catch my attention while thinking of something else.

Suddenly I heard a tap-tap-tapping that got louder, sharp and clear, and I knew before I saw her that this was the sound of high heels on a pavement though it might just as well have been a hammer against stone. She walked fast opposite my window and her heels hit the pavement so hard that all the noises of the street seemed absorbed into that single tap-tap-clang-clang. As she reached the corner at Great Portland Street two London pigeons swooped diagonally from the sky very fast, as if they were bullets aimed to kill her; and then as they saw her they swooped up and off at an angle. Meanwhile she had turned the corner. All this has taken time to write down, but the thing happening took a couple of seconds: the woman's body hitting the pavement bang-bang through her heels then sharply turning the corner in a right angle; and the pigeons making another acute angle across hers and intersecting it in a fast swoop of displaced air. Nothing to all that, of course, nothing—she had gone off down the street, her heels tip-tapping, and the pigeons landed on my windowsill and began cooing. All gone, all vanished, the marvellous exact coordination of sound and movement, but it had happened, it had made me happy and exhilarated, I had no problems in this world, and I realized that the heart stuck to my fingers was quite loose. I couldn't get it off altogether, though I was tugging at it under the scarf and the tin foil, but almost.

I understood that sitting and analysing each movement or pulse or beat of my heart through forty years was a mistake. I was on the wrong track altogether: this was the way to attach my red, bitter, delighted heart to my flesh forever and ever. . . .

> Ha! So you think I'm done! You think. . . .
> Watch, I'll roll my heart in a mesh of rage
> And bounce it like a handball off
> Walls, faces, railings, umbrellas and pigeons' backs. . . .

No, all that was no good at all, it just made things worse. What I must do is to take myself by surprise, as it were, the way I was taken by surprise over the woman and the pigeons and the sharp sounds of heels and silk wings.

I put on my coat, held my lumpy scarfed arm across my chest, so that if anyone said: What have you done with your hand? I could say: I've banged my finger in the door. Then I walked down into the street.

It wasn't easy to go among so many people, when I was worried that they were thinking: What has that woman done to her hand? because that made it hard to forget myself. And all the time it tingled and throbbed against my fingers, reminding me.

Now I was out I didn't know what to do. Should I go and have lunch with someone? Or wander in the park? Or buy myself a dress? I decided to go to the Round Pond, and walk around it by myself. I was tired after four days and nights without sleep. I went down into the Underground at Oxford Circus. Midday. Crowds of people. I felt self-conscious, but of course need not have worried. I swear you could walk naked down the street in London and no one would even turn round.

So I went down the escalator and looked at the faces coming up past me on the other side, as I always do; and wondered, as I always do, how strange it is that those people and I should meet by chance in such a way, and how odd that we would never see each other again, or, if we did, we wouldn't know it. And I went on to the crowded platform and looked at the faces as I always do, and got into the train, which was very full, and found a seat. It wasn't as bad as at rush hour, but all the seats were filled. I leaned back and closed my eyes, deciding to sleep a little, being so tired. I was just beginning to doze off, when I heard a woman's voice muttering, or rather, declaiming:

"A gold cigarette case, well, that's a nice thing, isn't it, I must say, a gold case, yes. . . ."

There was something about this voice which made me open my eyes: on the other side of the compartment, about eight persons away, sat a youngish woman, wearing a cheap green cloth coat, gloveless hands, flat brown shoes, and lisle stockings. She must be rather poor—a woman dressed like this is a rare sight, these days. But it was her posture that struck me. She was sitting half twisted in her seat, so that her head was turned over her left shoulder, and she was looking straight at the stomach of an elderly man next to her. But it was clear she was not seeing it: her young staring eyes were sightless, she was looking inwards.

She was so clearly alone, in the crowded compartment, that it was not as embarrassing as it might have been. I looked around, and people were smiling, or exchanging glances, or winking, or ignoring her, according to their natures, but she was oblivious of us all.

She suddenly aroused herself, turned so that she sat straight in her seat, and directed her voice and her gaze to the opposite seat:

*"Well so that's what you think, you think that, you think that do
you, well, you think I'm just going to wait at home for you, but you
gave her a gold case and . . ."*

And with a clockwork movement of her whole thin person, she
turned her narrow pale-haired head sideways over her left shoulder,
and resumed her stiff empty stare at the man's stomach. He was
grinning uncomfortably. I leaned forward to look along the line of
people in the row of seats I sat in, and the man opposite her, a young
man, had exactly the same look of discomfort which he was determined to keep amused. So we all looked at her, the young, thin, pale
woman in her private drama of misery, who was so completely
unconscious of us that she spoke and thought out loud. And again,
without particular warning or reason, in between stops, so it wasn't
that she was disturbed from her dream by the train stopping at Bond
Street, and then jumping forward again, she twisted her body front-
ways, and addressed the seat opposite her (the young man had got
off, and a smart grey-curled matron had got in):

*"Well I know about it now, don't I, and if you come in all smiling
and pleased well then I know, don't I, you don't have to tell me, I
know, and I've said to her, I've said, I know he gave you a gold
cigarette case. . . ."*

At which point, with the same clockwork impulse, she stopped, or
was checked, or simply ran out, and turned herself half around to
stare at the stomach—the same stomach, for the middle-aged man was
still there. But we stopped at Marble Arch and he got out, giving the
compartment, rather than the people in it, a tolerant half-smile
which said: I am sure I can trust you to realize that this unfortunate
woman is stark staring mad. . . .

His seat remained empty. No people got in at Marble Arch, and
the two people standing waiting for seats did not want to sit by her
to receive her stare.

We all sat, looking gently in front of us, pretending to ourselves
and to each other that we didn't know the poor woman was mad and
that in fact we ought to be doing something about it. I even wondered what I should say: Madam, you're mad—shall I escort you to
your home? Or: Poor thing, don't go on like that, it doesn't do any
good, you know—just leave him, that'll bring him to his senses. . . .

And behold, after the interval that was regulated by her inner
mechanism had elapsed, she turned back and said to the smart
matron who received this statement of accusation with perfect self-
command:

"Yes, I know! Oh yes! And what about my shoes, what about them, a golden cigarette case is what she got, the filthy bitch, a golden case. . . ."

Stop. Twist. Stare. At the empty seat by her.

Extraordinary. Because it was a frozen misery, how shall I put it? A passionless passion—we were seeing unhappiness embodied, we were looking at the essence of some private tragedy—rather, Tragedy. There was no emotion in it. She was like an actress doing Accusation, or Betrayed Love, or Infidelity, when she has only just learned her lines and is not bothering to do more than get them right.

And whether she sat in her half-twisted position, her unblinking eyes staring at the greenish, furry, ugly covering of the train seat, or sat straight, directing her accusation to the smart woman opposite, there was a frightening immobility about her—yes, that was why she frightened us. For it was clear that she might very well (if the inner machine ran down) stay silent, forever, in either twisted or straight position, or at any point between them—yes, we could all imagine her, frozen perpetually in some arbitrary pose. It was as if we watched the shell of some woman going through certain predetermined motions.

For *she* was simply not there. *What* was there, who she was, it was impossible to tell, though it was easy to imagine her thin, gentle little face breaking into a smile in total forgetfulness of what she was enacting now. She did not know she was in a train between Marble Arch and Queensway, nor that she was publicly accusing her husband or lover, nor that we were looking at her.

And we, looking at her, felt an embarrassment and shame that was not on her account at all. . . .

Suddenly I felt, under the scarf and the tin foil, a lightening of my fingers, as my heart rolled loose.

I hastily took it off my palm, in case it decided to adhere there again, and I removed the scarf, leaving balanced on my knees a perfect stylised heart, like a silver heart on a Valentine card, though of course it was three-dimensional. This heart was not so much harmless, no that isn't the word, as artistic, but in very bad taste, as I said. I could see that the people in the train, now looking at me and the heart, and not at the poor madwoman, were pleased with it.

I got up, took the four or so paces to where she was, and laid the tin-foiled heart down on the seat so that it received her stare.

For a moment she did not react, then with a groan or a mutter of relieved and entirely theatrical grief, she leaned forward, picked up the glittering heart, and clutched it in her arms, hugging it and rocking it back and forth, even laying her cheek against it, while staring over its top at her husband as if to say: Look what I've got, I don't care about you and your cigarette case, I've got a silver heart.

I got up, since we were at Notting Hill Gate, and, followed by the pleased congratulatory nods and smiles of the people left behind, I went out onto the platform, up the escalators, into the street, and along to the park.

No heart. No heart at all. What bliss. What freedom. . . .

> Hear that sound? That's laughter, yes.
> That's me laughing, yes, that's me.

FLANNERY O'CONNOR (1925–1964)

A Good Man Is Hard to Find

The grandmother didn't want to go to Florida. She wanted to visit some of her connections in east Tennessee and she was seizing at every chance to change Bailey's mind. Bailey was the son she lived with, her only boy. He was sitting on the edge of his chair at the table, bent over the orange sports section of the *Journal.* "Now look here, Bailey," she said, "see here, read this," and she stood with one hand on her thin hip and the other rattling the newspaper at his bald head. "Here this fellow that calls himself The Misfit is aloose from the Federal Pen and headed toward Florida and you read here what it says he did to these people. Just you read it. I wouldn't take my children in any direction with a criminal like that aloose in it. I couldn't answer to my conscience if I did."

Bailey didn't look up from his reading so she wheeled around then and faced the children's mother, a young woman in slacks, whose face was as broad and innocent as a cabbage and was tied round with a green head-kerchief that had two points on the top like rabbit's ears. She was sitting on the sofa, feeding the baby his apricots out of a jar. "The children have been to Florida before," the old lady said. "You all ought to take them somewhere else for a change so they would see different parts of the world and be broad. They never have been to east Tennessee."

The children's mother didn't seem to hear her but the eight-year-old boy, John Wesley, a stocky child with glasses, said, "If you don't want to go to Florida, why dontcha stay at home?" He and the little girl, June Star, were reading the funny papers on the floor.

"She wouldn't stay at home to be queen for a day," June Star said without raising her yellow head.

"Yes and what would you do if this fellow, The Misfit, caught you?" the grandmother asked.

"I'd smack his face," John Wesley said.

"She wouldn't stay at home for a million bucks," June Star said. "Afraid she'd miss something. She has to go everywhere we go."

"All right, Miss," the grandmother said. "Just remember that the next time you want me to curl your hair."

June Star said her hair was naturally curly.

The next morning the grandmother was the first one in the car, ready to go. She had her big black valise that looked like the head of a hippopotamus in one corner, and underneath it she was hiding a basket with Pitty Sing, the cat, in it. She didn't intend for the cat to be left alone in the house for three days because he would miss her too much and she was afraid he might brush against one of the gas burners and accidentally asphyxiate himself. Her son, Bailey, didn't like to arrive at a motel with a cat.

She sat in the middle of the back seat with John Wesley and June Star on either side of her. Bailey and the children's mother and the baby sat in the front and they left Atlanta at eight forty-five with the mileage on the car at 55890. The grandmother wrote this down because she thought it would be interesting to say how many miles they had been when they got back. It took them twenty minutes to reach the outskirts of the city.

The old lady settled herself comfortably, removing her white cotton gloves and putting them up with her purse on the shelf in front of the back window. The children's mother still had on slacks and still had her head tied up in a green kerchief, but the grandmother had on a navy blue straw sailor hat with a bunch of white violets on the brim and a navy blue dress with a small white dot in the print. Her collar and cuffs were white organdy trimmed with lace and at her neckline she had pinned a purple spray of cloth violets containing a sachet. In case of an accident, anyone seeing her dead on the highway would know at once that she was a lady.

She said she thought it was going to be a good day for driving, neither too hot nor too cold, and she cautioned Bailey that the speed limit was fifty-five miles an hour and that the patrolmen hid themselves behind billboards and small clumps of trees and sped out after you before you had a chance to slow down. She pointed out interesting details of the scenery: Stone Mountain; the blue granite that in some places came up to both sides of the highway; the brilliant red clay banks slightly streaked with purple; and the various crops that made rows of green lace-work on the ground. The trees were full of silver-white sunlight and the meanest of them sparkled. The children were reading comic magazines and their mother had gone back to sleep.

"Let's go through Georgia fast so we won't have to look at it much," John Wesley said.

"If I were a little boy," said the grandmother, "I wouldn't talk about my native state that way. Tennessee has the mountains and Georgia has the hills."

"Tennessee is just a hillbilly dumping ground," John Wesley said, "and Georgia is a lousy state too."

"You said it," June Star said.

"In my time," said the grandmother, folding her thin veined fingers, "children were more respectful of their native states and their parents and everything else. People did right then. Oh look at the cute little pickaninny!" she said and pointed to a Negro child standing in the door of a shack. "Wouldn't that make a picture, now?" she asked and they all turned and looked at the little Negro out of the back window. He waved.

"He didn't have any britches on," June said.

"He probably didn't have any," the grandmother explained. "Little niggers in the country don't have things like we do. If I could paint, I'd paint that picture," she said.

The children exchanged comic books.

The grandmother offered to hold the baby and the children's mother passed him over the front seat to her. She set him on her knee and bounced him and told him about the things they were passing. She rolled her eyes and screwed up her mouth and stuck her leathery thin face into his smooth bland one. Occasionally he gave her a faraway smile. They passed a large cotton field with five or six graves fenced in the middle of it, like a small island. "Look at the graveyard!" the grandmother said, pointing it out. "That was the old family burying ground. That belonged to the plantation."

"Where's the plantation?" John Wesley asked.

"Gone With the Wind," said the grandmother. "Ha. Ha."

When the children finished all the comic books they had brought, they opened the lunch and ate it. The grandmother ate a peanut butter sandwich and an olive and would not let the children throw the box and the paper napkins out the window. When there was nothing else to do they played a game by choosing a cloud and making the other two guess what shape it suggested. John Wesley took one the shape of a cow and June Star guessed a cow and John Wesley said, no, an automobile, and June Star said he didn't play fair, and they began to slap each other over the grandmother.

The grandmother said she would tell them a story if they would keep quiet. When she told a story, she rolled her eyes and waved her head and was very dramatic. She said once when she was a maiden lady she had been courted by a Mr. Edgar Atkins Teagarden from Jasper, Georgia. She said he was a very good-looking man and a gentleman and that he brought her a watermelon every Saturday afternoon with his initials cut in it, E. A. T. Well, one Saturday, she said, Mr. Teagarden brought the watermelon and there was nobody at home and he left it on the front porch and returned in his buggy to Jasper, but she never got the watermelon, she said, because a nigger boy ate it when he saw the initials, E. A. T.! This story tickled John Wesley's funny bone and he giggled and giggled but June Star didn't think it was any good. She said she wouldn't marry a man that just brought her a watermelon on Saturday. The grandmother said she would have done well to marry Mr. Teagarden because he was a gentleman and had bought Coca-Cola stock when it first came out and that he had died only a few years ago, a very wealthy man.

They stopped at The Tower for barbecued sandwiches. The Tower was a part stucco and part wood filling station and dance hall set in a clearing outside of Timothy. A fat man named Red Sammy Butts ran it and there were signs stuck here and there on the building and for miles up and down the highway saying, TRY RED SAMMY'S FAMOUS BARBECUE. NONE LIKE FAMOUS RED SAMMY'S! RED SAM! THE FAT BOY WITH THE HAPPY LAUGH. A VETERAN! SAMMY'S YOUR MAN!

Red Sammy was lying on the bare ground outside The Tower with his head under a truck while a gray monkey about a foot high, chained to a small chinaberry tree, chattered nearby. The monkey sprang back into the tree and got on the highest limb as soon as he saw the children jump out of the car and run toward him.

Inside, The Tower was a long dark room with a counter at one end and tables at the other and dancing space in the middle. They all sat down at a broad table next to the nickelodeon and Red Sam's wife, a tall burnt-brown woman with hair and eyes lighter than her skin, came and took their order. The children's mother put a dime in the machine and played "The Tennessee Waltz," and the grandmother said that tune always made her want to dance. She asked Bailey if he would like to dance but he only glared at her. He didn't have a naturally sunny disposition like she did and trips made him nervous. The grandmother's brown eyes were very bright. She swayed her head from side to side and pretended she was dancing in her chair. June Star said play something she could tap to so the children's mother put in another dime and played a fast number and June Star stepped out onto the dance floor and did her tap routine.

"Ain't she cute?" Red Sam's wife said, leaning over the counter. "Would you like to come be my little girl?"

"No I certainly wouldn't," June Star said. "I wouldn't live in a broken-down place like this for a million bucks!" and she ran back to the table.

"Ain't she cute?" the woman repeated, stretching her mouth politely.

"Aren't you ashamed?" hissed the grandmother.

Red Sam came in and told his wife to quit lounging on the counter and hurry with these people's order. His khaki trousers reached just to his hip bones and his stomach hung over them like a sack of meal swaying under his shirt. He came over and sat down at a table nearby and let out a combination sigh and yodel. "You can't win," he said. "You can't win," and he wiped his sweating red face off with a gray handkerchief. "These days you don't know who to trust," he said. "Ain't that the truth?"

"People are certainly not nice like they used to be," said the grandmother.

"Two fellers come in here last week," Red Sammy said, "driving a Chrysler. It was a old beat-up car but it was a good one and these boys looked all right to me. Said they worked at the mill and you know I let them fellers charge the gas they bought? Now why did I do that?"

"Because you're a good man!" the grandmother said at once.

"Yes'm, I suppose so," Red Sam said as if he were struck with the answer.

His wife brought the orders, carrying the five plates all at once without a tray, two in each hand and one balanced on her arm. "It isn't a soul in this green world of God's that you can trust," she said. "And I don't count anybody out of that, not nobody," she repeated, looking at Red Sammy.

"Did you read about that criminal, The Misfit, that's escaped?" asked the grandmother.

"I wouldn't be a bit surprised if he didn't attact this place right here," said the woman. "If he hears about it being here, I wouldn't be none surprised to see him. If he hears it's two cent in the cash register, I wouldn't be a tall surprised if he . . ."

"That'll do," Red Sam said. "Go bring these people their Co'Colas," and the woman went off to get the rest of the order.

"A good man is hard to find," Red Sammy said. "Everything is getting terrible. I remember the day you could go off and leave your screen door unlatched. Not no more."

He and the grandmother discussed better times. The old lady said that in her opinion Europe was entirely to blame for the way things were now. She said the way Europe acted you would think we were made of money and Red Sam said it was no use talking about it, she was exactly right. The children ran outside into the white sunlight and looked at the monkey in the lacy chinaberry tree. He was busy catching fleas on himself and biting each one carefully between his teeth as if it were a delicacy.

They drove off again into the hot afternoon. The grandmother took cat naps and woke up every few minutes with her own snoring. Outside of Toombsboro she woke up and recalled an old plantation that she had visited in this neighborhood once when she was a young lady. She said the house had six white columns across the front and that there was an avenue of oaks leading up to it and two little wooden trellis arbors on either side in front where you sat down with your suitor after a stroll in the garden. She recalled exactly which road to turn off to get to it. She knew that Bailey would not be willing to lose any time looking at an old house, but the more she talked about it, the more she wanted to see it once again and find out if the little twin arbors were still standing. "There was a secret panel in this house," she said craftily, not telling the truth but wishing that she were, "and the story went that all the family silver was hidden in it when Sherman came through but it was never found . . ."

"Hey!" John Wesley said. "Let's go see it! We'll find it! We'll poke all the woodwork and find it! Who lives there? Where do you turn off at? Hey Pop, can't we turn off there?"

"We never have seen a house with a secret panel!" June Star shrieked. "Let's go to the house with the secret panel! Hey, Pop, can't we go see the house with the secret panel!"

"It's not far from here, I know," the grandmother said. "It wouldn't take over twenty minutes."

Bailey was looking straight ahead. His jaw was as rigid as a horseshoe. "No," he said.

The children began to yell and scream that they wanted to see the house with the secret panel. John Wesley kicked the back of the front seat and June Star hung over her mother's shoulder and whined desperately into her ear that they never had any fun even on their vacation, and that they could never do what THEY wanted to do. The baby began to scream and John Wesley kicked the back of the seat so hard that his father could feel the blows in his kidney.

"All right!" he shouted, and drew the car to a stop at the side of the road. "Will you all shut up? Will you all just shut up for one second? If you don't shut up, we won't go anywhere."

"It would be very educational for them," the grandmother murmured.

"All right," Bailey said, "but get this: this is the only time we're going to stop for anything like this. This is the one and only time."

"The dirt road that you have to turn down is about a mile back," the grandmother directed. "I marked it when we passed."

"A dirt road," Bailey groaned.

After they had turned around and were headed toward the dirt road, the grandmother recalled other points about the house, the beautiful glass over the front doorway and the candle-lamp in the hall. John Wesley said that the secret panel was probably in the fireplace.

"You can't go inside this house," Bailey said. "You don't know who lives there."

"While you all talk to the people in front, I'll run around behind and get in a window," John Wesley suggested.

"We'll all stay in the car," his mother said.

They turned onto the dirt road and the car raced roughly along in a swirl of pink dust. The grandmother recalled the times when there were no paved roads and thirty miles was a day's journey. The dirt road was hilly and there were sudden washes in it and sharp curves on dangerous embankments. All at once they would be on a hill, looking down over the blue tops of trees for miles around, then the next minute, they would be in a red depression with the dust-coated trees looking down on them.

"This place had better turn up in a minute," Bailey said, "or I'm going to turn around."

The road looked as if no one had traveled on it in months.

"It's not much farther," the grandmother said and just as she said it, a horrible thought came to her. The thought was so embarrassing that she turned red in the face and her eyes dilated and her feet jumped up, upsetting her valise in the corner. The instant the valise moved, the newspaper top she had over the basket under it rose with a snarl and Pitty Sing, the cat, sprang onto Bailey's shoulder.

The children were thrown to the floor and their mother, clutching the baby, was thrown out the door onto the ground, the old lady was thrown into the front seat. The car turned over once and landed right-side-up in a gulch on the side of the road. Bailey remained in the driver's seat with the cat—gray-striped with a broad white face and an orange nose—clinging to his neck like a caterpillar.

As soon as the children saw they could move their arms and legs, they scrambled out of the car, shouting. "We've had an ACCIDENT!" The grandmother was curled up under the dashboard, hoping she was injured so that Bailey's wrath would not come down on her all at once. The horrible thought she had had before the accident was that the house she had remembered so vividly was not in Georgia but in Tennessee.

Bailey removed the cat from his neck with both hands and flung it out the window against the side of a pine tree. Then he got out of the car and started looking for the children's mother. She was sitting against the side of the red gutted ditch, holding the screaming baby, but she only had a cut down her face and a broken shoulder. "We've had an ACCIDENT!" the children screamed in a frenzy of delight.

"But nobody's killed," June Star said with disappointment as the grandmother limped out of the car, her hat still pinned to her head but the broken front brim standing up at a jaunty angle and the violet spray hanging off the side. They all sat down in the ditch, except the children, to recover from the shock. They were all shaking.

"Maybe a car will come along," said the children's mother hoarsely.

"I believe I have injured an organ," said the grandmother, pressing her side, but no one answered her. Bailey's teeth were clattering. He had on a yellow sport shirt with bright blue parrots designed in it and his face was as yellow as the shirt. The grandmother decided that she would not mention that the house was in Tennessee.

The road was about ten feet above and they could see only the tops of the trees on the other side of it. Behind the ditch they were sitting in there were more woods, tall and dark and deep. In a few minutes they saw a car some distance away on top of a hill, coming slowly as if the occupants were watching them. The grandmother stood up and waved both arms dramatically to attract their attention. The car continued to come on slowly, disappeared around a bend and appeared again, moving even slower, on top of the hill they had gone over. It was a big black battered hearse-like automobile. There were three men in it.

It came to a stop just over them and for some minutes, the driver looked down with a steady expressionless gaze to where they were sitting, and didn't speak. Then he turned his head and muttered something to the other two and they got out. One was a fat boy in black trousers and a red sweat shirt with a silver stallion embossed on the front of it. He moved around on the right side of them and stood staring, his mouth partly open in a kind of loose grin. The other had on khaki pants and a blue striped coat and a gray hat pulled down very low, hiding most of his face. He came around slowly on the left side. Neither spoke.

The driver got out of the car and stood by the side of it, looking down at them. He was an older man than the other two. His hair was just beginning to gray and he wore silver-rimmed spectacles that gave him a scholarly look. He had a long creased face and didn't have on any shirt or undershirt. He had on blue jeans that were too tight for him and was holding a black hat and a gun. The two boys also had guns.

"We've had an ACCIDENT!" the children screamed.

The grandmother had the peculiar feeling that the bespectacled man was someone she knew. His face was as familiar to her as if she had known him all her life but she could not recall who he was. He moved away from the car and began to come down the embankment, placing his feet carefully so that he wouldn't slip. He had on tan and white shoes and no socks, and his ankles were red and thin. "Good afternoon," he said. "I see you all had you a little spill."

"We turned over twice!" said the grandmother.

"Oncet," he corrected. "We seen it happen. Try their car and see will it run, Hiram," he said quietly to the boy with the gray hat.

"What you got that gun for?" John Wesley asked. "Whatcha gonna do with that gun?"

"Lady," the man said to the children's mother, "would you mind calling them children to sit down by you? Children make me nervous. I want all you all to sit down right together there where you're at."

"What are you telling us what to do for?" June Star asked.

Behind them the line of woods gaped like a dark open mouth. "Come here," said their mother.

"Look here now," Bailey began suddenly, "we're in a predicament! We're in . . ."

The grandmother shrieked. She scrambled to her feet and stood staring. "You're The Misfit!" she said. "I recognized you at once."

"Yes'm," the man said, smiling slightly as if he were pleased in spite of himself to be known, "but it would have been better for all of you, lady, if you hadn't of reckernized me."

Bailey turned his head sharply and said something to his mother that shocked even the children. The old lady began to cry and The Misfit reddened.

"Lady," he said, "don't you get upset. Sometimes a man says things he don't mean. I don't reckon he meant to talk to you thataway."

"You wouldn't shoot a lady, would you?" the grandmother said and removed a clean handkerchief from her cuff and began to slap at her eyes with it.

The Misfit pointed the toe of his shoe into the ground and made a little hole and then covered it up again. "I would hate to have to," he said.

"Listen," the grandmother almost screamed, "I know you're a good man. You don't look a bit like you have common blood. I know you must come from nice people!"

"Yes mam," he said, "finest people in the world." When he smiled he showed a row of strong white teeth. "God never made a finer woman than my mother and my daddy's heart was pure gold," he said. The boy with the red sweat shirt had come around behind them and was standing with his gun at his hip. The Misfit squatted down on the ground. "Watch them children, Bobby Lee," he said. "You know they make me nervous." He looked at the six of them huddled together in front of him and he seemed to be embarrassed as if he couldn't think of anything to say. "Ain't a cloud in the sky," he remarked, looking up at it. "Don't see no sun but don't see no cloud neither."

"Yes, it's a beautiful day," said the grandmother. "Listen," she said, "you shouldn't call yourself The Misfit because I know you're a good man at heart. I can just look at you and tell."

"Hush!" Bailey yelled. "Hush! Everybody shut up and let me handle this!" He was squatting in the position of a runner about to sprint forward but he didn't move.

"I pre-chate that, lady," The Misfit said and drew a little circle in the ground with the butt of his gun.

"It'll take a half a hour to fix this here car," Hiram called, looking over the raised hood of it.

"Well, first you and Bobby Lee get him and that little boy to step over yonder with you," The Misfit said, pointing to Bailey and John Wesley. "The boys want to ask you something," he said to Bailey. "Would you mind stepping back in them woods there with them?"

"Listen," Bailey began, "we're in a terrible predicament. Nobody realizes what this is," and his voice cracked. His eyes were as blue and intense as the parrots in his shirt and he remained perfectly still.

The grandmother reached up to adjust her hat brim as if she were going to the woods with him but it came off in her hand. She stood staring at it and after a second she let it fall on the ground. Hiram pulled Bailey up by the arm as if he were assisting an old man. John Wesley caught hold of his father's hand and Bobby Lee followed. They went off toward the woods and just as they reached the dark edge, Bailey turned and supporting himself against a gray naked pine trunk, he shouted, "I'll be back in a minute, Mamma, wait on me!"

"Come back this instant!" his mother shrilled but they all disappeared into the woods.

"Bailey Boy!" the grandmother called in a tragic voice but she found she was looking at The Misfit squatting on the ground in front of her. "I just know you're a good man," she said desperately. "You're not a bit common!"

"Nome, I ain't a good man," The Misfit said after a second as if he had considered her statement carefully, "but I ain't the worst in the world neither. My daddy said I was different breed of dog from my brothers and sisters. 'You know,' Daddy said, 'it's some that can live their whole life out without asking about it and it's others has to know why it is, and this boy is one of the latters. He's going to be into everything!'" He put on his black hat and looked up suddenly and then away deep into the woods as if he were embarrassed again. "I'm sorry I don't have on a shirt before you ladies," he said, hunching his shoulders slightly. "We buried our clothes that we had on when we escaped and we're just making do until we can get better. We borrowed these from some folks we met," he explained.

"That's perfectly all right," the grandmother said. "Maybe Bailey has an extra shirt in his suitcase."

"I'll look and see terrectly," The Misfit said.

"Where are they taking him?" the children's mother screamed.

"Daddy was a card himself," the Misfit said. "You couldn't put anything over on him. He never got in trouble with the Authorities though. Just had the knack of handling them."

"You could be honest too if you'd only try," said the grandmother. "Think how wonderful it would be to settle down and live a comfortable life and not have to think about somebody chasing you all the time."

The Misfit kept scratching in the ground with the butt of his gun as if he were thinking about it. "Yes'm, somebody is always after you," he murmured.

The grandmother noticed how thin his shoulder blades were just behind his hat because she was standing up looking down on him. "Do you ever pray?" she asked.

He shook his head. All she saw was the black hat wiggle between his shoulder blades. "Nome," he said.

There was a pistol shot from the woods, followed closely by another. Then silence. The old lady's head jerked around. She could hear the wind move through the tree tops like a long satisfied insuck of breath. "Bailey Boy!" she called.

"I was a gospel singer for a while," The Misfit said. "I been most everything. Been in the arm service, both land and sea, at home and abroad, been twict married, been an undertaker, been with the railroads, plowed Mother Earth, been in a tornado, seen a man burnt alive oncet," and he looked up at the children's mother and the little girl who were sitting close together, their faces white and their eyes glassy; "I even seen a woman flogged," he said.

"Pray, pray," the grandmother began, "pray, pray . . ."

"I never was a bad boy that I remember of," The Misfit said in an almost dreamy voice, "but somewheres along the line I done something wrong and got sent to the penitentiary. I was buried alive," and he looked up and held her attention to him by a steady stare.

"That's when you should have started to pray," she said. "What did you do to get sent to the penitentiary that first time?"

"Turn to the right, it was a wall," The Misfit said, looking up again at the cloudless sky. "Turn to the left, it was a wall. Look up it was a ceiling, look down it was a floor. I forgot what I done, lady. I set there and set there, trying to remember what it was I done and I ain't recalled it to this day. Oncet in a while, I would think it was coming to me, but it never come."

"Maybe they put you in by mistake," the old lady said vaguely.

"Nome," he said. "It wasn't no mistake. They had the papers on me."

"You must have stolen something," she said.

The Misfit sneered slightly. "Nobody had nothing I wanted," he said. "It was a head-doctor at the penitentiary said what I had done was kill my daddy but I know that for a lie. My daddy died in nineteen ought nineteen of the epidemic flu and I never had a thing to do with it. He was buried in the Mount Hopewell Baptist church-yard and you can go there and see for yourself."

"If you would pray," the old lady said, "Jesus would help you."

"That's right," The Misfit said.

"Well then, why don't you pray?" she asked trembling with delight suddenly.

"I don't want no hep," he said. "I'm doing all right by myself."

Bobby Lee and Hiram came ambling back from the woods. Bobby Lee was dragging a yellow shirt with bright blue parrots in it.

"Throw me that shirt, Bobby Lee," The Misfit said. The shirt came flying at him and landed on his shoulder and he put it on. The grandmother couldn't name what the shirt reminded her of. "No, lady," The Misfit said while he was buttoning it up. "I found out the crime don't matter. You can do one thing or you can do another, kill a man or take a tire off his car, because sooner or later you're going to forget what it was you done and just be punished for it."

The children's mother had begun to make heaving noises as if she couldn't get her breath. "Lady," he asked, "would you and that little girl like to step off yonder with Bobby Lee and Hiram and join your husband?"

"Yes, thank you," the mother said faintly. Her left arm dangled helplessly and she was holding the baby, who had gone to sleep, in the other. "Hep that lady up, Hiram," The Misfit said as she struggled to climb out of the ditch, "and Bobby Lee, you hold onto that little girl's hand."

"I don't want to hold hands with him," June Star said. "He reminds me of a pig."

The fat boy blushed and laughed and caught her by the arm and pulled her off into the woods after Hiram and her mother.

Alone with The Misfit, the grandmother found that she had lost her voice. There was not a cloud in the sky nor any sun. There was nothing around her but woods. She wanted to tell him that he must pray. She opened and closed her mouth several times before anything came out. Finally she found herself saying, "Jesus, Jesus," meaning Jesus will help you, but the way she was saying it, it sounded as if she might be cursing.

"Yes'm," The Misfit said as if he agreed. "Jesus thown everything off balance. It was the same case with Him as with me except He hadn't committed any crime and they could prove I had committed one because they had the papers on me. Of course," he said, "they never shown me any papers. That's why I sign myself now. I said long ago, you get you a signature and sign everything you do and keep a copy of it. Then you'll know what you done and you can hold up the crime to the punishment and see do they match and in the end you'll have something to prove you ain't been treated right. I call myself The Misfit," he said, "because I can't make what all I done wrong fit what all I gone through in punishment."

There was a piercing scream from the woods, followed closely by a pistol report. "Does it seem right to you, lady, that one is punished a heap and another ain't punished at all?"

"Jesus!" the old lady cried. "You've got good blood! I know you wouldn't shoot a lady! I know you come from nice people! Pray! Jesus, you ought not to shoot a lady. I'll give you all the money I've got!"

"Lady," The Misfit said, looking beyond her far into the woods, "there never was a body that give the undertaker a tip."

There were two more pistol reports and the grandmother raised her head like a parched old turkey hen crying for water and called, "Bailey Boy, Bailey Boy!" as if her heart would break.

"Jesus was the only One that ever raised the dead," The Misfit continued, "and He shouldn't have done it. He thown everything off balance. If He did what He said, then it's nothing for you to do but thow away everything and follow Him, and if He didn't, then it's nothing for you to do but enjoy the few minutes you got left the best way you can—by killing somebody or burning down his house or doing some other meanness to him. No pleasure but meanness," he said and his voice had become almost a snarl.

"Maybe He didn't raise the dead," the old lady mumbled, not knowing what she was saying and feeling so dizzy that she sank down in the ditch with her legs twisted under her.

"I wasn't there so I can't say He didn't," The Misfit said. "I wisht I had of been there," he said, hitting the ground with his fist. "It ain't right I wasn't there because if I had of been there I would of known. Listen lady," he said in a high voice, "if I had of been there I would of known and I wouldn't be like I am now." His voice seemed about to crack and the grandmother's head cleared for an instant. She saw the man's face twisted close to her own as if he were going to cry and she murmured, "Why you're one of my babies. You're one of my own children!" She reached out and touched him on the shoulder. The Misfit sprang back as if a snake had bitten him and shot her three times through the chest. Then he put his gun down on the ground and took off his glasses and began to clean them.

Hiram and Bobby Lee returned from the woods and stood over the ditch, looking down at the grandmother who half sat and half lay in a puddle of blood with her legs crossed under her like a child's and her face smiling up at the cloudless sky.

Without his glasses, The Misfit's eyes were red-rimmed and pale and defenseless-looking. "Take her off and thow her where you thown the others," he said, picking up the cat that was rubbing itself against his leg.

"She was a talker, wasn't she?" Bobby Lee said, sliding down the ditch with a yodel.

"She would of been a good woman," The Misfit said, "if it had been somebody there to shoot her every minute of her life."

"Some fun!" Bobby Lee said.

"Shut up, Bobby Lee," The Misfit said. "It's no real pleasure in life."

JORGE LUIS BORGES (1899–   )

The South

The man who landed in Buenos Aires in 1871 bore the name of
Johannes Dahlmann and he was a minister in the Evangelical
Church. In 1939, one of his grandchildren, Juan Dahlmann, was
secretary of a municipal library on Calle Córdoba, and he considered
himself profoundly Argentinian. His maternal grandfather had been
that Francisco Flores, of the Second Line-Infantry Division, who had
died on the frontier of Buenos Aires, run through with a lance by
Indians from Catriel; in the discord inherent between his two lines of
descent, Juan Dahlmann (perhaps driven to it by his Germanic
blood) chose the line represented by his romantic ancestor, his
ancestor of the romantic death. An old sword, a leather frame containing the daguerreotype of a blank-faced man with a beard, the
dash and grace of certain music, the familiar strophes of *Martín
Fierro,* the passing years, boredom and solitude, all went to foster this
voluntary, but never ostentatious nationalism. At the cost of
numerous small privations, Dahlmann had managed to save the
empty shell of a ranch in the South which had belonged to the Flores
family; he continually recalled the image of the balsamic eucalyptus
trees and the great rose-colored house which had once been crimson.
His duties, perhaps even indolence, kept him in the city. Summer
after summer he contented himself with the abstract idea of possession and with the certitude that his ranch was waiting for him on a
precise site in the middle of the plain. Late in February, 1939,
something happened to him.

Blind to all fault, destiny can be ruthless at one's slightest distraction. Dahlmann had succeeded in acquiring, on that very afternoon,
an imperfect copy of Weil's edition of *The Thousand and One
Nights.* Avid to examine this find, he did not wait for the elevator
but hurried up the stairs. In the obscurity, something brushed by his
forehead: a bat, a bird? On the face of the woman who opened the
door to him he saw horror engraved, and the hand he wiped across
his face came away red with blood. The edge of a recently painted
door which someone had forgotten to close had caused this wound.
Dahlmann was able to fall asleep, but from the moment he awoke at
dawn the savor of all things was atrociously poignant. Fever wasted

him and the pictures in *The Thousand and One Nights* served to illustrate nightmares. Friends and relatives paid him visits and, with exaggerated smiles, assured him that they thought he looked fine. Dahlmann listened to them with a kind of feeble stupor and he marveled at their not knowing that he was in hell. A week, eight days passed, and they were like eight centuries. One afternoon, the usual doctor appeared, accompanied by a new doctor, and they carried him off to a sanitarium on the Calle Ecuador, for it was necessary to X-ray him. Dahlmann, in the hackney coach which bore them away, thought that he would, at last, be able to sleep in a room different from his own. He felt happy and communicative. When he arrived at his destination, they undressed him, shaved his head, bound him with metal fastenings to a stretcher; they shone bright lights on him until he was blind and dizzy, auscultated him, and a masked man stuck a needle into his arm. He awoke with a feeling of nausea, covered with a bandage, in a cell with something of a well about it; in the days and nights which followed the operation he came to realize that he had merely been, up until then, in a suburb of hell. Ice in his mouth did not leave the least trace of freshness. During these days Dahlmann hated himself in minute detail: he hated his identity, his bodily necessities, his humiliation, the beard which bristled upon his face. He stoically endured the curative measures, which were painful, but when the surgeon told him he had been on the point of death from septicemia, Dahlmann dissolved in tears of self-pity for his fate. Physical wretchedness and the incessant anticipation of horrible nights had not allowed him time to think of anything so abstract as death. On another day, the surgeon told him he was healing and that, very soon, he would be able to go to his ranch for convalescence. Incredibly enough, the promised day arrived.

Reality favors symmetries and slight anachronisms: Dahlmann had arrived at the sanitarium in a hackney coach and now a hackney coach was to take him to the Constitución station. The first fresh tang of autumn, after the summer's oppressiveness, seemed like a symbol in nature of his rescue and release from fever and death. The city, at seven in the morning, had not lost that air of an old house lent it by the night; the streets seemed like long vestibules, the plazas were like patios. Dahlmann recognized the city with joy on the edge of vertigo: a second before his eyes registered the phenomena themselves, he recalled the corners, the billboards, the modest variety of Buenos Aires. In the yellow light of the new day, all things returned to him.

Every Argentine knows that the South begins at the other side of Rivadavia. Dahlmann was in the habit of saying that this was no mere convention, that whoever crosses this street enters a more ancient and sterner world. From inside the carriage he sought out, among the new buildings, the iron grill window, the brass knocker, the arched door, the entrance way, the intimate patio.

At the railroad station he noted that he still had thirty minutes. He quickly recalled that in a café on the Calle Brazil (a few dozen feet from Yrigoyen's house) there was an enormous cat which allowed itself to be caressed as if it were a disdainful divinity. He entered the café. There was the cat, asleep. He ordered a cup of coffee, slowly stirred the sugar, sipped it (this pleasure had been denied him in the clinic), and thought, as he smoothed the cat's black coat, that this contact was an illusion and that the two beings, man and cat, were as good as separated by a glass, for man lives in time, in succession, while the magical animal lives in the present, in the eternity of the instant.

Along the next to the last platform the train lay waiting. Dahlmann walked through the coaches until he found one almost empty. He arranged his baggage in the network rack. When the train started off, he took down his valise and extracted, after some hesitation, the first volume of *The Thousand and One Nights*. To travel with this book, which was so much a part of the history of his ill-fortune, was a kind of affirmation that his ill-fortune had been annulled; it was a joyous and secret defiance of the frustrated forces of evil.

Along both sides of the train the city dissipated into suburbs; this sight, and then a view of the gardens and villas, delayed the beginning of his reading. The truth was that Dahlmann read very little. The magnetized mountain and the genie who swore to kill his benefactor are—who would deny it?—marvelous, but not so much more than the morning itself and the mere fact of being. The joy of life distracted him from paying attention to Scheherezade and her superfluous miracles. Dahlmann closed his book and allowed himself to live.

Lunch—the bouillon served in shining metal bowls, as in the remote summers of childhood—was one more peaceful and rewarding delight.

Tomorrow I'll wake up at the ranch, he thought, and it was as if he was two men at a time: the man who traveled through the autumn day and across the geography of the fatherland, and the other one, locked up in a sanitarium and subject to methodical servitude. He saw unplastered brick houses, long and angled, timelessly watching the trains go by; he saw horsemen along the dirt roads; he saw gullies and lagoons and ranches; he saw great luminous clouds that resembled marble; and all these things were accidental, casual, like dreams of the plain. He also thought he recognized trees and crop fields; but he would not have been able to name them, for his actual knowledge of the countryside was quite inferior to his nostalgic and literary knowledge.

From time to time he slept, and his dreams were animated by the impetus of the train. The intolerable white sun of high noon had already become the yellow sun which precedes nightfall, and it would not be long before it would turn red. The railroad car was now also different; it was not the same as the one which had quit the station siding at Constitución; the plain and the hours had transfigured it. Outside, the moving shadow of the railroad car stretched toward the horizon. The elemental earth was not perturbed either by settlements or other signs of humanity. The country was vast but at the same time intimate and, in some measure, secret. The limitless country sometimes contained only a solitary bull. The solitude was perfect, perhaps hostile, and it might have occurred to Dahlmann that he was traveling into the past and not merely south. He was distracted from these considerations by the railroad inspector who, on reading his ticket, advised him that the train would not let him off at the regular station but at another: an earlier stop, one scarcely known to Dahlmann. (The man added an explanation which Dahlmann did not attempt to understand, and which he hardly heard, for the mechanism of events did not concern him.)

The train laboriously ground to a halt, practically in the middle of the plain. The station lay on the other side of the tracks; it was not much more than a siding and a shed. There was no means of conveyance to be seen, but the station chief supposed that the traveler might secure a vehicle from a general store and inn to be found some ten or twelve blocks away.

Dahlmann accepted the walk as a small adventure. The sun had already disappeared from view, but a final splendor exalted the vivid and silent plain, before the night erased its color. Less to avoid fatigue than to draw out his enjoyment of these sights, Dahlmann walked slowly, breathing in the odor of clover with sumptuous joy.

The general store at one time had been painted a deep scarlet, but the years had tempered this violent color for its own good. Something in its poor architecture recalled a steel engraving, perhaps one from an old edition of *Paul et Virginie.* A number of horses were hitched up to the paling. Once inside, Dahlmann thought he recognized the shopkeeper. Then he realized that he had been deceived by the man's resemblance to one of the male nurses in the sanitarium. When the shopkeeper heard Dahlmann's request, he said he would have the shay made up. In order to add one more event to that day and to kill time, Dahlmann decided to eat at the general store.

Some country louts, to whom Dahlmann did not at first pay any attention, were eating and drinking at one of the tables. On the floor, and hanging on to the bar, squatted an old man, immobile as an object. His years had reduced and polished him as water does a stone or the generations of men do a sentence. He was dark, dried up, diminutive, and seemed outside time, situated in eternity. Dahlmann noted with satisfaction the kerchief, the thick poncho, the long *chiripá*, and the colt boots, and told himself, as he recalled futile discussions with people from the Northern counties or from the province of Entre Rios, that gauchos like this no longer existed outside the South.

Dahlmann sat down next to the window. The darkness began overcoming the plain, but the odor and sound of the earth penetrated the iron bars of the window. The shop owner brought him sardines, followed by some roast meat. Dahlmann washed the meal down with several glasses of red wine. Idling, he relished the tart savor of the wine, and let his gaze, now grown somewhat drowsy, wander over the shop. A kerosene lamp hung from a beam. There were three customers at the other table: two of them appeared to be farm workers; the third man, whose features hinted at Chinese blood, was drinking with his hat on. Of a sudden, Dahlmann felt something brush lightly against his face. Next to the heavy glass of turbid wine, upon one of the stripes in the table cloth, lay a spit ball of breadcrumb. That was all: but someone had thrown it there.

The men at the other table seemed totally cut off from him. Perplexed, Dahlmann decided that nothing had happened, and he opened the volume of *The Thousand and One Nights,* by way of suppressing reality. After a few moments another little ball landed on his table, and now the *peones* laughed outright. Dahlmann said to himself that he was not frightened, but he reasoned that it would be a major blunder if he, a convalescent, were to allow himself to be dragged by strangers into some chaotic quarrel. He determined to leave, and had already gotten to his feet when the owner came up and exhorted him in an alarmed voice:

"*Señor* Dahlmann, don't pay any attention to those lads; they're half high."

Dahlmann was not surprised to learn that the other man, now, knew his name. But he felt that these conciliatory words served only to aggravate the situation. Previous to this moment, the *peones'* provocation was directed against an unknown face, against no one in particular, almost against no one at all. Now it was an attack against him, against his name, and his neighbors knew it. Dahlmann pushed the owner aside, confronted the *peones*, and demanded to know what they wanted of him.

The tough with a Chinese look staggered heavily to his feet. Almost in Juan Dahlmann's face he shouted insults, as if he had been a long way off. His game was to exaggerate his drunkenness, and this extravagance constituted a ferocious mockery. Between curses and obscenities, he threw a long knife into the air, followed it with his eyes, caught and juggled it, and challenged Dahlmann to a knife fight. The owner objected in a tremulous voice, pointing out that Dahlmann was unarmed. At this point, something unforeseeable occurred.

From a corner of the room, the old ecstatic gaucho—in whom Dahlmann saw a summary and cipher of the South (his South) — threw him a naked dagger, which landed at his feet. It was as if the South had resolved that Dahlmann should accept the duel. Dahlmann bent over to pick up the dagger, and felt two things. The first, that this almost instinctive act bound him to fight. The second, that the weapon, in his torpid hand, was no defense at all, but would merely serve to justify his murder. He had once played with a poniard, like all men, but his idea of fencing and knife-play did not go further than the notion that all strokes should be directed upwards, with the cutting edge held inwards. *They would not have allowed such things to happen to me in the sanitarium,* he thought.

"Let's get on our way," said the other man.

They went out and if Dahlmann was without hope, he was also without fear. As he crossed the threshold, he felt that to die in a knife fight, under the open sky, and going forward to the attack, would have been a liberation, a joy, and a festive occasion, on the first night in the sanitarium, when they stuck him with the needle. He felt that if he had been able to choose, then, or to dream his death, this would have been the death he would have chosen or dreamt.

Firmly clutching his knife, which he perhaps would not know how to wield, Dahlmann went out into the plain.

JOHN BARTH (1930–)

Lost in the Funhouse

For whom is the funhouse fun? Perhaps for lovers. For Ambrose it is *a place of fear and confusion.* He has come to the seashore with his family for the holiday, *the occasion of their visit is Independence Day, the most important secular holiday of the United States of America.* A single straight underline is the manuscript mark for italic type, *which in turn* is the printed equivalent to oral emphasis of words and phrases as well as the customary type for titles of complete works, not to mention. Italics are also employed, in fiction stories especially, for "outside," intrusive, or artificial voices, such as radio announcements, the texts of telegrams and newspaper articles, et cetera. They should be used *sparingly.* If passages originally in roman type are italicized by someone repeating them, it's customary to acknowledge the fact. *Italics mine.*

Ambrose was "at that awkward age." His voice came out high-pitched as a child's if he let himself get carried away; to be on the safe side, therefore, he moved and spoke with *deliberate calm* and *adult gravity.* Talking soberly of unimportant or irrelevant matters and listening consciously to the sound of your own voice are useful habits for maintaining control in this difficult interval. *En route* to Ocean City he sat in the back seat of the family car with his brother Peter, age fifteen, and Magda G——, age fourteen, a pretty girl an exquisite young lady, who lived not far from them on B—— Street in the town of D——, Maryland. Initials, blanks, or both were often substituted for proper names in nineteenth-century fiction to enhance the illusion of reality. It is as if the author felt it necessary to delete the names for reasons of tact or legal liability. Interestingly, as with other aspects of realism, it is an *illusion* that is being enhanced, by purely artificial means. Is it likely, does it violate the principle of verisimilitude, that a thirteen-year-old boy could make such a sophisticated observation? A girl of fourteen is *the psychological coeval* of a boy of fifteen or sixteen; a thirteen-year-old boy, therefore, even one precocious in some other respects, might be three years *her emotional junior.*

Thrice a year—on Memorial, Independence, and Labor Days—the family visits Ocean City for the afternoon and evening. When Ambrose and Peter's father was their age, the excursion was made by train, as mentioned in the novel *The 42nd Parallel* by John Dos Passos. Many families from the same neighborhood used to travel together, with dependent relatives and often with Negro servants; schoolfuls of children swarmed through the railway cars; everyone shared everyone else's Maryland fried chicken, Virginia ham, deviled eggs, potato salad, beaten biscuits, iced tea. Nowadays (that is, in 19—, the year of our story) the journey is made by automobile—more comfortably and quickly though without the extra fun though without the *camaraderie* of a general excursion. It's all part of the deterioration of American life, their father declares; Uncle Karl supposes that when the boys take *their* families to Ocean City for the holidays they'll fly in Autogiros. Their mother, sitting in the middle of the front seat like Magda in the second, only with her arms on the seat-back behind the men's shoulders, wouldn't want the good old days back again, the steaming trains and stuffy long dresses; on the other hand she can do without Autogiros, too, if she has to become a grandmother to fly in them.

Description of physical appearance and mannerisms is one of several standard methods of characterization used by writers of fiction. It is also important to "keep the senses operating"; when a detail from one of the five senses, say visual, is "crossed" with a detail from another, say auditory, the reader's imagination is oriented to the scene, perhaps unconsciously. This procedure may be compared to the way surveyors and navigators determine their positions by two or more compass bearings, a process known as triangulation. The brown hair on Ambrose's mother's forearms gleamed in the sun like. Though right-handed, she took her left arm from the seat-back to press the dashboard cigar lighter for Uncle Karl. When the glass bead in its handle glowed red, the lighter was ready for use. The smell of Uncle Karl's cigar smoke reminded one of. The fragrance of the ocean came strong to the picnic ground where they always stopped for lunch, two miles inland from Ocean City. Having to pause for a full hour almost within sound of the breakers was difficult for Peter and Ambrose when they were younger; even at their present age it was not easy to keep their anticipation, *stimulated by the briny spume,* from turning into short temper. The Irish author James Joyce, in his unusual novel entitled *Ulysses,* now available in this country, uses the adjectives *snot-green* and *scrotum-tightening* to describe the sea. Visual, auditory, tactile, olfactory, gustatory. Peter and Ambrose's father, while steering their black 1936 LaSalle sedan with one hand, could with the other remove the first cigarette from a white pack of Lucky Strikes and, more remarkably, light it with a match forefingered from its book and thumbed against the flint paper without being detached. The matchbook cover merely advertised U. S. War Bonds and Stamps. A fine metaphor, simile, or other figure of speech, in addition to its obvious "first-order" relevance to the thing it describes, will be seen upon reflection to have a second order of significance: it may be drawn from the *milieu* of the action, for example, or be particularly appropriate to the sensibility of the narrator, even hinting to the reader things of which the narrator is unaware; or it may cast further and subtler lights upon the thing it describes, sometimes ironically qualifying the more evident sense of the comparison.

To say that Ambrose's and Peter's mother was *pretty* is to accomplish nothing; the reader may acknowledge the proposition, but his imagination is not engaged. Besides, Magda was also pretty, yet in an altogether different way. Although she lived on B—— Street she had very good manners and did better than average in school. Her figure was very well developed for her age. Her right hand lay casually on the plush upholstery of the seat, very near Ambrose's left leg, on which his own hand rested. The space between their legs, between her right and his left leg, was out of the line of sight of anyone sitting on the other side of Magda, as well as anyone glancing into the rearview mirror. Uncle Karl's face resembled Peter's—rather, vice versa. Both had dark hair and eyes, short husky statures, deep voices. Magda's left hand was probably in a similar position on her left side. The boys' father is difficult to describe; no particular feature of his appearance or manner stood out. He wore glasses and was principal of a T—— County grade school. Uncle Karl was a masonry contractor.

Although Peter must have known as well as Ambrose that the latter, because of his position in the car, would be the first to see the electrical towers of the power plant at V——, the halfway point of their trip, he leaned forward and slightly toward the center of the car and pretended to be looking for them through the flat pinewoods and tuckahoe creeks along the highway. For as long as the boys could remember, "looking for the Towers" had been a feature of the first half of their excursions to Ocean City, "looking for the standpipe" of the second. Though the game was childish, their mother preserved the tradition of rewarding the first to see the Towers with a candy-bar or piece of fruit. She insisted now that Magda play the game; the prize, she said, was "something hard to get nowadays." Ambrose decided not to join in; he sat far back in his seat. Magda, like Peter, leaned forward. Two sets of straps were discernible through the shoulders of her sun dress; the inside right one, a brassiere-strap, was fastened or shortened with a small safety pin. The right armpit of her dress, presumably the left as well, was damp with perspiration. The simple strategy for being first to espy the Towers, which Ambrose had understood by the age of four, was to sit on the right-hand side of the

car. Whoever sat there, however, had also to put up with the worst of
the sun, and so Ambrose, without mentioning the matter, chose
sometimes the one and sometimes the other. Not impossibly Peter
had never caught on to the trick, or thought that his brother hadn't
simply because Ambrose on occasion preferred shade to a Baby Ruth
or tangerine.

The shade-sun situation didn't apply to the front seat, owing to
the windshield; if anything the driver got more sun, since the person
on the passenger side not only was shaded below by the door and
dashboard but might swing down his sunvisor all the way too.

"Is that them?" Magda asked. Ambrose's mother teased the boys
for letting Magda win, insinuating that "somebody [had] a girl-
friend." Peter and Ambrose's father reached a long thin arm across
their mother to butt his cigarette in the dashboard ashtray, under the
lighter. The prize this time for seeing the Towers first was a banana.
Their mother bestowed it after chiding their father for wasting a half-
smoked cigarette when everything was so scarce. Magda, to take the
prize, moved her hand from so near Ambrose's that he could have
touched it as though accidentally. She offered to share the prize,
things like that were so hard to find; but everyone insisted it was hers
alone. Ambrose's mother sang an iambic trimeter couplet from a
popular song, femininely rhymed:

> "What's good is in the Army;
> What's left will never harm me."

Uncle Karl tapped his cigar ash out the ventilator window; some
particles were sucked by the slipstream back into the car through the
rear window on the passenger side. Magda demonstrated her ability
to hold a banana in one hand and peel it with her teeth. She still sat
forward; Ambrose pushed his glasses back onto the bridge of his nose
with his left hand, which he then negligently let fall to the seat
cushion immediately behind her. He even permitted the single hair,
gold, on the second joint of his thumb to brush the fabric of her skirt.
Should she have sat back at that instant, his hand would have been
caught under her.

Plush upholstery prickles uncomfortably through gabardine slacks
in the July sun. The function of the *beginning* of a story is to
introduce the principal characters, establish their initial relationships, set the scene for the main action, expose the background of the
situation if necessary, plant motifs and foreshadowings where appropriate, and initiate the first complication or whatever of the "rising
action." Actually, if one imagines a story called "The Funhouse," or
"Lost in the Funhouse," the details of the drive to Ocean City don't
seem especially relevant. The *beginning* should recount the events
between Ambrose's first sight of the funhouse early in the afternoon

and his entering it with Magda and Peter in the evening. The *middle* would narrate all relevant events from the time he goes in to the time he loses his way; middles have the double and contradictory function of delaying the climax while at the same time preparing the reader for it and fetching him to it. Then the *ending* would tell what Ambrose does while he's lost, how he finally finds his way out, and what everybody makes of the experience. So far there's been no real dialogue, very little sensory detail, and nothing in the way of a *theme*. And a long time has gone by already without anything happening; it makes a person wonder. We haven't even reached Ocean City yet: we will never get out of the funhouse.

The more closely an author identifies with the narrator, literally or metaphorically, the less advisable it is, as a rule, to use the first-person narrative viewpoint. Once three years previously the young people *aforementioned* played Niggers and Masters in the backyard; when it was Ambrose's turn to be Master and theirs to be Niggers Peter had to go serve his evening papers; Ambrose was afraid to punish Magda alone, but she led him to the whitewashed Torture Chamber between the woodshed and the privy in the Slaves Quarters; there she knelt sweating among bamboo rakes and dusty Mason jars, pleadingly embraced his knees, and while bees droned in the lattice as if on an ordinary summer afternoon, purchased clemency at a surprising price set by herself. Doubtless she remembered nothing of this event; Ambrose on the other hand seemed unable to forget the least detail of his life. He even recalled how, standing beside himself with awed impersonality in the reeky heat, he'd stared the while at an empty cigar box in which Uncle Karl kept stone-cutting chisels: beneath the words *El Producto,* a laureled, loose-toga'd lady regarded the sea from a marble bench; beside her, forgotten or not yet turned to, was a five-stringed lyre. Her shin reposed on the back of her right hand; her left depended negligently from the bencharm. The lower half of scene and lady was peeled away; the words EXAMINED BY —— were inked there into the wood. Nowadays cigar boxes are made of pasteboard. Ambrose wondered what Magda would have done, Ambrose wondered what Magda would do when she sat back on his hand as he resolved she should. Be angry. Make a teasing joke of it. Give no sign at all. For a long time she leaned forward, playing cowpoker with Peter against Uncle Karl and Mother and watching for the first sign of Ocean City. At nearly the same instant, picnic ground and Ocean City standpipe hove into view; an Amoco filling station on their side of the road cost Mother and Uncle Karl fifty cows and the game; Magda bounced back, clapping her right hand on Mother's right arm; Ambrose moved clear "in the nick of time."

At this rate our hero, at this rate our protagonist will remain in the funhouse forever. Narrative ordinarily consists of alternating dramatization and summarization. One symptom of nervous tension, paradoxically, is repeated and violent yawning; neither Peter nor Magda nor Uncle Karl nor Mother reacted in this manner. Although they were no longer small children, Peter and Ambrose were each given a dollar to spend on boardwalk amusements in addition to what money of their own they'd brought along. Magda too, though she protested she had ample spending money. The boys' mother made a little scene out of distributing the bills; she pretended that her sons and Magda were small children and cautioned them not to spend the sum too quickly or in one place. Magda promised with a merry laugh and, having both hands free, took the bill with her left. Peter laughed also and pledged in a falsetto to be a good boy. His imitation of a child was not clever. The boys' father was tall and thin, balding, fair-complexioned. Assertions of that sort are not effective; the reader may acknowledge the proposition, but. We should be much farther along than we are; something has gone wrong; not much of this preliminary rambling seems relevant. Yet everyone begins in the same place; how is it that most go along without difficulty but a few lose their way?

"Stay out from under the boardwalk," Uncle Karl growled from the side of his mouth. The boys' mother pushed his shoulder *in mock annoyance.* They were all standing before Fat May the Laughing Lady who advertised the funhouse. Larger than life, Fat May mechanically shook, rocked on her heels, slapped her thighs while recorded laughter—uproarious, female—came amplified from a hidden loudspeaker. It chuckled, wheezed, wept; tried in vain to catch its breath; tittered, groaned, exploded raucous and anew. You couldn't hear it without laughing yourself, no matter how you felt. Father came back from talking to a Coast-Guardsman on duty and reported that the surf was spoiled with crude oil from tankers recently torpedoed offshore. Lumps of it, difficult to remove, made tarry tidelines on the beach and stuck on swimmers. Many bathed in the surf nevertheless and came out speckled; others paid to use a municipal pool and only sunbathed on the beach. We would do the latter. We would do the latter. We would do the latter.

Under the boardwalk, matchbook covers, grainy other things. What is the story's theme? Ambrose is ill. He perspires in the dark passages; candied apples-on-a-stick, delicious-looking, disappointing to eat. Funhouses need men's and ladies' rooms at intervals. Others perhaps have also vomited in corners and corridors; may even have had bowel movements liable to be stepped in in the dark. The word *fuck* suggests suction and/or and/or flatulence. Mother and Father; grandmothers and grandfathers on both sides; great-grandmothers and great-grandfathers on four sides, et cetera. Count a generation as thirty years: in approximately the year when Lord Baltimore was granted charter to the province of Maryland by Charles I, five hundred twelve women—English, Welsh, Bavarian, Swiss—of every class and character, received into themselves the penises the intromittent organs of five hundred twelve men, ditto, in every circumstance and posture, to conceive the five hundred twelve ancestors of the two hundred fifty-six ancestors of the et cetera et cetera et cetera et cetera et cetera et cetera et cetera of the author, of the narrator, of this story, *Lost in the Funhouse.* In alleyways, ditches, canopy beds, pinewoods, bridal suites, ships' cabins, coach-and-fours, coaches-and-four, sultry toolsheds; on the cold sand under boardwalks, littered with *El Producto* cigar butts, treasured with Lucky Strike cigarette stubs, Coca-Cola caps, gritty turds, cardboard lollipop sticks, matchbook covers warning that A Slip of the Lip Can Sink a Ship. The shluppish whisper, continuous as seawash round the globe, tidelike falls and rises with the circuit of dawn and dusk.

Magda's teeth. She *was* left-handed. Perspiration. They've gone all the way, through, Magda and Peter, they've been waiting for hours with Mother and Uncle Karl while Father searches for his lost son; they draw french-fried potatoes from a paper cup and shake their heads. They've named the children they'll one day have and bring to Ocean City on holidays. Can spermatozoa properly be thought of as male animalcules when there are no female spermatozoa? They grope through hot, dark windings, past Love's Tunnel's fearsome obstacles. Some perhaps lose their way.

Peter suggested then and there that they do the funhouse; he had been through it before, so had Magda, Ambrose hadn't and suggested, his voice cracking on account of Fat May's laughter, that they swim first. All were chuckling, couldn't help it; Ambrose's father, Ambrose's and Peter's father came up grinning like a lunatic with two boxes of syrup-coated popcorn, one for Mother, one for Magda; the men were to help themselves. Ambrose walked on Magda's right; being by nature lefthanded, she carried the box in her left hand. Up front the situation was reversed.

"What are you limping for?" Magda inquired of Ambrose. He supposed in a husky tone that his foot had gone to sleep in the car. Her teeth flashed. "Pins and needles?" It was the honeysuckle on the lattice of the former privy that drew the bees. Imagine being stung there. How long is this going to take?

The adults decided to forgo the pool; but Uncle Karl insisted they change into swimsuits and do the beach. "He wants to watch the pretty girls," Peter teased, and ducked behind Magda from Uncle Karl's pretended wrath. "You've got all the pretty girls you need right here," Magda declared, and Mother said: "Now that's the gospel truth." Magda scolded Peter, who reached over her shoulder to sneak some popcorn. "Your brother and father aren't getting any." Uncle Karl wondered if they were going to have fireworks that night, what with the shortages. It wasn't the shortages, Mr. M—— replied; Ocean City had fireworks from prewar. But it was too risky on account of the enemy submarines, some people thought.

"Don't seem like Fourth of July without fireworks," said Uncle Karl. The inverted tag in dialogue writing is still considered permissible with proper names or epithets, but sounds old-fashioned with personal pronouns. "We'll have 'em again soon enough," predicted the boys' father. Their mother declared she could do without fireworks: they reminded her too much of the real thing. Their father said all the more reason to shoot off a few now and again. Uncle Karl asked *rhetorically* who needed reminding, just look at people's hair and skin.

"The oil, yes," said Mrs. M——.

Ambrose had a pain in his stomach and so didn't swim but enjoyed watching the others. He and his father burned red easily. Magda's figure was exceedingly well developed for her age. She too declined to swim, and got mad, and became angry when Peter attempted to drag her into the pool. She always swam, he insisted; what did she mean not swim? Why did a person come to Ocean City?

"Maybe I want to lay here with Ambrose," Magda teased.

Nobody likes a pedant.

"Aha," said Mother. Peter grabbed Magda by one ankle and ordered Ambrose to grab the other. She squealed and rolled over on the beach blanket. Ambrose pretended to help hold her back. Her tan was darker than even Mother's and Peter's. "Help out, Uncle Karl!" Peter cried. Uncle Karl went to seize the other ankle. Inside the top of her swimsuit, however, you could see the line where the sunburn ended and, when she hunched her shoulders and squealed again, one nipple's auburn edge. Mother made them behave themselves. "*You* should certainly know," she said to Uncle Karl. Archly. "That when a lady says she doesn't feel like swimming, a gentleman doesn't ask questions." Uncle Karl said excuse *him;* Mother winked at Magda; Ambrose blushed; stupid Peter kept saying "Phooey on *feel like!*" and tugging at Magda's ankle; then even he got the point, and cannonballed with a holler into the pool.

"I swear," Magda said, in mock *in feigned* exasperation.

The diving would make a suitable literary symbol. To go off the high board you had to wait in a line along the poolside and up the ladder. Fellows tickled girls and goosed one another and shouted to the ones at the top to hurry up, or razzed them for bellyfloppers. Once on the springboard some took a great while posing or clowning or deciding on a dive or getting up their nerve; others ran right off. Especially among the younger fellows the idea was to strike the funniest pose or do the craziest stunt as you fell, a thing that got harder to do as you kept on and kept on. But whether you hollered *Geronimo!* or *Sieg heil!*, held your nose or "rode a bicycle," pretended to be shot or did a perfect jackknife or changed your mind halfway down and ended up with nothing, it was over in two seconds, after all that wait. Spring, pose, splash. Spring, neat-o, splash. Spring, aw fooey, splash.

The grown-ups had gone on; •Ambrose wanted to converse with Magda; she was remarkably well developed for her age; it was said that that came from rubbing with a turkish towel, and there were other theories. Ambrose could think of nothing to say except how good a diver Peter was, who was showing off for her benefit. You could pretty well tell by looking at their bathing suits and arm muscles how far along the different fellows were. Ambrose was glad he hadn't gone in swimming, the cold water shrank you up so. Magda pretended to be uninterested in the diving; she probably weighed as much as he did. If you knew your way around in the funhouse like your own bedroom, you could wait until a girl came along and then slip away without ever getting caught, even if her boyfriend was right with her. She'd think *he* did it! It would be better to be the boyfriend, and act outraged, and tear the funhouse apart.

Not act; *be.*

"He's a master diver," Ambrose said. In feigned admiration. "You really have to slave away at it to get that good." What would it matter anyhow if he asked her right out whether she remembered, even teased her with it as Peter would have?

There's no point in going farther; this isn't getting anybody anywhere; they haven't even come to the funhouse yet. Ambrose is off the track, in some new or old part of the place that's not supposed to be used; he strayed into it by some one-in-a-million chance, like the time the roller-coaster car left the tracks in the nineteen-teens against all the laws of physics and sailed over the boardwalk in the dark. And they can't locate him because they don't know where to look. Even the designer and operator have forgotten this other part, that winds around on itself like a whelk shell. That winds around the right part like the snakes on Mercury's caduceus. Some people, perhaps, don't "hit their stride" until their twenties, when the growing-up business is over and women appreciate other things besides wisecracks and teasing and strutting. Peter didn't have one-tenth the imagination *he* had, not one-tenth. Peter did this naming-their-children thing as a joke, making up names like Aloysius and Murgatroyd, but Ambrose knew *exactly* how it would feel to be married and have children of your own, and be a loving husband and father, and go comfortably to work in the mornings and to bed with your wife at night, and wake up with her there. With a breeze coming through the sash and birds and mockingbirds singing in the Chinese-cigar trees. His eyes watered, there aren't enough ways to say that. He would be quite famous in his line of work. Whether Magda was his wife or not, one evening when he was wise-lined and gray at the temples he'd smile gravely, at a fashionable dinner party, and remind her of his youthful passion. The time they went with his family to Ocean City; the *erotic fantasies* he used to have about her. How long ago it seemed, and childish! Yet tender, too, *n'est-ce pas?* Would she have imagined that the world-famous whatever remembered how many strings were on the lyre on the bench beside the girl on the label of the cigar box he'd stared at in the toolshed at age ten while she, age eleven. Even then he had felt *wise beyond his years;* he'd stroked her hair and said in his deepest voice and correctest English, as to a dear child: "I shall never forget this moment."

But though he had breathed heavily, groaned as if ecstatic, what he'd really felt throughout was an odd detachment, as though someone else were Master. Strive as he might to be transported, he heard his mind take notes upon the scene: *This is what they call* passion. *I am experiencing it.* Many of the digger machines were out of order in the penny arcades and could not be repaired or replaced for the duration. Moreover the prizes, made now in USA, were less interesting than formerly, pasteboard items for the most part, and some of the machines wouldn't work on white pennies. The gypsy fortune-teller machine might have provided a foreshadowing of the climax of this story if Ambrose had operated it. It was even dilapidateder than most: the silver coating was worn off the brown metal handles, the glass windows around the dummy were cracked and taped, her kerchiefs and silks long-faded. If a man lived by himself, he could take a department-store mannequin with flexible joints and modify her in certain ways. *However:* by the time he was that old he'd have a real woman. There was a machine that stamped your name around a white-metal coin with a star in the middle: *A——*. His son would be the second, and when the lad reached thirteen or so he would put a strong arm around his shoulder and tell him calmly: "It is perfectly normal. We have all been through it. It will not last forever." Nobody knew how to be what they were right. He'd smoke a pipe, teach his son how to fish and softcrab, assure him he needn't worry about himself. Magda would certainly give, Magda would certainly yield a great deal of milk, although guilty of occasional solecisms. It don't taste so bad. Suppose the lights came on now!

The day wore on. You think you're yourself, but there are other persons in you. Ambrose gets hard when Ambrose doesn't want to, *and obversely.* Ambrose watches them disagree; Ambrose watches him watch. In the funhouse mirror-room you can't see yourself go on forever, because no matter how you stand, your head gets in the way.

Even if you had a glass periscope, the image of your eye would cover up the thing you really wanted to see. The police will come; there'll be a story in the papers. That must be where it happened. Unless he can find a surprise exit, an unofficial backdoor or escape hatch opening on an alley, say, and then stroll up to the family in front of the funhouse and ask where everybody's been; *he's* been out of the place for ages. That's just where it happened, in that last lighted room: Peter and Magda found the right exit; he found one that you weren't supposed to find and strayed off into the works somewhere. In a perfect funhouse you'd be able to go only one way, like the divers off the highboard; getting lost would be impossible; the doors and halls would work like minnow traps or the valves in veins.

On account of German U-boats, Ocean City was "browned out": streetlights were shaded on the seaward side; shop-windows and boardwalk amusement places were kept dim, not to silhouette tankers and Liberty-ships for torpedoing. In a short story about Ocean City, Maryland, during World War II, the author could make use of the image of sailors on leave in the penny arcades and shooting galleries, sighting through the crosshairs of toy machine guns at swastika'd subs, while out in the black Atlantic a U-boat skipper squints through his periscope at real ships outlined by the glow of penny arcades. After dinner the family strolled back to the amusement end of the boardwalk. The boys' father had burnt red as always and was masked with Noxzema, a minstrel in reverse. The grownups stood at the end of the boardwalk where the Hurricane of '33 had cut an inlet from the ocean to Assawoman Bay.

"Pronounced with a long *o*," Uncle Karl reminded Magda with a wink. His shirt sleeves were rolled up; Mother punched his brown biceps with the arrowed heart on it and said his mind was naughty. Fat May's laugh came suddenly from the funhouse, as if she'd just got the joke; the family laughed too at the coincidence. Ambrose went under the boardwalk to search for out-of-town matchbook covers with the aid of his pocket flashlight; he looked out from the edge of the North American continent and wondered how far their laughter carried over the water. Spies in rubber rafts; survivors in lifeboats. If the joke had been beyond his understanding, he could have said: "*The laughter was over his head.*" And let the reader see the serious wordplay on second reading.

He turned the flashlight on and then off at once even before the woman whooped. He sprang away, heart athud, dropping the light. What had the man grunted? Perspiration drenched and chilled him by the time he scrambled up to the family. "See anything?" his father asked. His voice wouldn't come; he shrugged and violently brushed sand from his pants legs.

"Let's ride the old flying horses!" Magda cried. I'll never be an author. It's been forever already, everybody's gone home, Ocean City's deserted, the ghost-crabs are tickling across the beach and down the littered cold streets. And the empty halls of clapboard hotels and abandoned funhouses. A tidal wave; an enemy air raid; a monster-crab swelling like an island from the sea. *The inhabitants fled in terror.* Magda clung to his trouser leg; he alone knew the maze's secret. "He gave his life that we might live," said Uncle Karl with a scowl of pain, as he. The fellow's hands had been tattooed; the woman's legs, the woman's fat white legs had. *An astonishing coincidence.* He yearned to tell Peter. He wanted to throw up for excitement. They hadn't even chased him. He wished he were dead.

One possible ending would be to have Ambrose come across another lost person in the dark. They'd match their wits together against the funhouse, struggle like Ulysses past obstacle after obstacle, help and encourage each other. Or a girl. By the time they found the exit they'd be closest friends, sweethearts if it were a girl; they'd know each other's inmost souls, be bound together *by the cement of shared adventure;* then they'd emerge into the light and it would turn out that his friend was a Negro. A blind girl. President Roosevelt's son. Ambrose's former archenemy.

Shortly after the mirror room he'd groped along a musty corridor, his heart already misgiving him at the absence of phosphorescent arrows and other signs. He'd found a crack of light—not a door, it turned out, but a seam between the plyboard wall panels—and squinting up to it, espied a small old man, *in appearance not unlike* the photographs at home of Ambrose's late grandfather, nodding upon a stool beneath a bare, speckled bulb. A crude panel of toggle- and knife-switches hung beside the open fuse box near his head; elsewhere in the little room were wooden levers and ropes belayed to boat cleats. At the time, Ambrose wasn't lost enough to rap or call; later he couldn't find that crack. Now it seemed to him that he'd possibly dozed off for a few minutes somewhere along the way; certainly he was exhausted from the afternoon's sunshine and the evening's problems; he couldn't be sure he hadn't dreamed part or all of the sight. Had an old black wall fan droned like bees and shimmied two flypaper streamers? Had the funhouse operator— gentle, somewhat sad and tired-appearing, in expression not unlike the photographs at home of Ambrose's late Uncle Konrad—murmured in his sleep? Is there really such a person as Ambrose, or is he a figment of the author's imagination? Was it Assawoman Bay or Sinepuxent? Are there other errors of fact in this fiction? Was there another sound besides the little slap slap of thigh on ham, like water sucking at the chine-boards of a skiff?

When you're lost, the smartest thing to do is stay put till you're found, hollering if necessary. But to holler guarantees humiliation as well as rescue; keeping silent permits some saving of face—you can act surprised at the fuss when your rescuers find you and swear you weren't lost, if they do. What's more you might find your own way yet, *however belatedly.*

"Don't tell me your foot's still asleep!" Magda exclaimed as the three young people walked from the inlet to the area set aside for ferris wheels, carrousels, and other carnival rides, they having decided in favor of the vast and ancient merry-go-round instead of the funhouse. What a sentence, everything was wrong from the outset. People don't know what to make of him, he doesn't know what to make of himself, he's only thirteen, *athletically and socially inept,* not astonishingly bright, but there are antennae; he has . . . some sort of receivers in his head; things speak to him, he understands more than he should, the world winks at him through its objects, grabs grinning at his coat. Everybody else is in on some secret he doesn't know; they've forgotten to tell him. Through simple *procrastination* his mother put off his baptism until this year. Everyone else had it done as a baby; he'd assumed the same of himself, as had his mother, so she claimed, until it was time for him to join Grace Methodist-Protestant and the oversight came out. He was mortified, but pitched sleepless through his private catechizing, intimidated by the ancient mysteries, a thirteen year old would never say that, resolved to experience conversion like St. Augustine. When the water touched his brow and Adam's sin left him, he contrived by a strain like defecation to bring tears into his eyes—but felt nothing. There was some simple, radical difference about him; he hoped it was genius, feared it was madness, devoted himself to amiability and inconspicuousness. Alone on the seawall near his house he was seized by the terrifying transports he'd thought to find in toolshed, in Communion-cup. The grass was alive! The town, the river, himself, were not imaginary; time roared in his ears like wind; the world was *going on!* This part ought to be dramatized. The Irish author James Joyce once wrote. Ambrose M—— is going to scream.

There is no *texture of rendered sensory detail,* for one thing. The faded distorting mirrors beside Fat May; the impossibility of choosing a mount when one had but a single ride on the great carrousel; the *vertigo attendant on his recognition* that Ocean City was worn out, the place of fathers and grandfathers, straw-boatered men and parasoled ladies survived by their amusements. Money spent, the three paused at Peter's insistence beside Fat May to watch the girls get their skirts blown up. The object was to tease Magda, who said: "I swear, Peter M——, you've got a one-track mind! Amby and me aren't *interested* in such things." In the tumbling-barrel, too, just inside the Devil's-mouth entrance to the funhouse, the girls were upended and their boyfriends and others could see up their dresses if they cared to. Which was the whole point, Ambrose realized. Of the entire funhouse! If you looked around, you noticed that almost all the people on the boardwalk were paired off into couples except the small children; in a way, that was the whole point of Ocean City! If you had X-ray eyes and could see everything going on at that instant under the boardwalk and in all the hotel rooms and cars and alley-ways, you'd realize that all that normally *showed,* like restaurants and dance halls and clothing and test-your-strength machines, was merely preparation and intermission. Fat May screamed.

Because he watched the goings-on from the corner of his eye, it was Ambrose who spied the half-dollar on the boardwalk near the tumbling-barrel. Losers weepers. The first time he'd heard some people moving through a corridor not far away, just after he'd lost sight of the crack of light, he'd decided not to call to them, for fear they'd guess he was scared and poke fun; it sounded like roughnecks; he'd hoped they'd come by and he could follow in the dark without their knowing. Another time he'd heard just one person, unless he imagined it, bumping along as if on the other side of the plywood; perhaps Peter coming back for him, or Father, or Magda lost too. Or the owner and operator of the funhouse. He'd called out once, as though merrily: "Anybody know where the heck we are?" But the query was too stiff, his voice cracked, when the sounds stopped he was terrified: maybe it was a queer who waited for fellows to get lost, or a longhaired filthy monster that lived in some cranny of the funhouse. He stood rigid for hours it seemed like, scarcely respiring. His future was shockingly clear, in outline. He tried holding his breath to the point of unconsciousness. There ought to be a button you could push to end your life absolutely without pain; disappear in a flick, like turning out a light. He would push it instantly! He despised Uncle Karl. But he despised his father too, for not being what he was supposed to be. Perhaps his father hated *his* father, and so on, and his son would hate him, and so on. Instantly!

Naturally he didn't have nerve enough to ask Magda to go through the funhouse with him. With incredible nerve and to everyone's surprise he invited Magda, quietly and politely, to go through the funhouse with him. "I warn you, I've never been through it before," he added, *laughing easily;* "but I reckon we can manage somehow. The important thing to remember, after all, is that it's meant to be a *fun*house; that is, a place of amusement. If people really got lost or injured or too badly frightened in it, the owner'd go out of business. There'd even be lawsuits. No character in a work of fiction can make a speech this long without interruption or acknowledgment from the other characters."

Mother teased Uncle Karl: "Three's a crowd, I always heard." But actually Ambrose was relieved that Peter now had a quarter too.

Nothing was what it looked like. Every instant, under the surface of the Atlantic Ocean, millions of living animals devoured one another. Pilots were falling in flames over Europe; women were being forcibly raped in the South Pacific. His father should have taken him aside and said: "There is a simple secret to getting through the funhouse, as simple as being first to see the Towers. Here it is. Peter does not know it; neither does your Uncle Karl. You and I are different. Not surprisingly, you've often wished you weren't. Don't think I haven't noticed how unhappy your childhood has been! But you'll understand, when I tell you, why it had to be kept secret until now. And you won't regret not being like your brother and your uncle. *On the contrary!"* If you knew all the stories behind all the people on the boardwalk, you'd see that *nothing* was what it looked like. Husbands and wives often hated each other; parents didn't necessarily love their children; et cetera. A child took things for granted because he had nothing to compare his life to and everybody acted as if things were as they should be. Therefore each saw himself as the hero of the story, when the truth might turn out to be that he's the villain, or the coward. And there wasn't one thing you could do about it!

Hunchbacks, fat ladies, fools—that no one chose what he was was unbearable. In the movies he'd meet a beautiful young girl in the funhouse; they'd have hairs-breadth escapes from real dangers; he'd do and say the right things; she also; in the end they'd be lovers; their dialogue lines would match up; he'd be perfectly at ease; she'd not only like him well enough, she'd think he was *marvelous;* she'd lie awake thinking about *him,* instead of vice versa—the way *his* face looked in different lights and how he stood and exactly what he'd said—and yet that would be only one small episode in his wonderful life, among many many others. Not a *turning point* at all. What had happened in the toolshed was nothing. He hated, he loathed his parents! One reason for not writing a lost-in-the-funhouse story is that either everybody's felt what Ambrose feels, in which case it goes without saying, or else no normal person feels such things, in which case Ambrose is a freak. "Is anything more tiresome, in fiction, than the problems of sensitive adolescents?" And it's all too long and rambling, as if the author. For all a person knows the first time through, the end could be just around any corner; perhaps, *not impossibly* it's been within reach any number of times. On the other hand he may be scarcely past the start, with everything yet to get through, an intolerable idea.

Fill in: His father's raised eyebrows when he announced his decision to do the funhouse with Magda. Ambrose understands now, but didn't then, that his father was wondering whether he knew what the funhouse was *for*—especially since he didn't object, as he should have, when Peter decided to come along too. The ticket-woman, witchlike, mortifying him when inadvertently he gave her his name-coin instead of the half-dollar, then unkindly calling Magda's attention to the birthmark on his temple: "Watch out for him, girlie, he's a marked man!" She wasn't even cruel, he understood, only vulgar and insensitive. Somewhere in the world there was a young woman with such splendid understanding that she'd see him entire, like a poem or story, and find his words so valuable after all that when he confessed his apprehensions she would explain why they were in fact the very things that made him precious to her . . . and to Western Civilization! There was no such girl, the simple truth being. Violent yawns as they approached the mouth. Whispered advice from an old-timer on a bench near the barrel: "Go crabwise and ye'll get an eyeful without upsetting!" Composure vanished at the first pitch: Peter hollered joyously, Magda tumbled, shrieked, clutched her skirt; Ambrose scrambled crabwise, tight-lipped with terror, was soon out, watched his dropped name-coin slide among the couples. Shame-faced he saw that to get through expeditiously was not the point; Peter feigned assistance in order to trip Magda up, shouted "I see Christmas!" when her legs went flying. The old man, his latest betrayer, cackled approval. A dim hall then of black-thread cobwebs and recorded gibber: he took Magda's elbow to steady her against revolving discs set in the slanted floor to throw your feet out from under, and explained to her in a calm, deep voice his theory that each phase of the funhouse was triggered either automatically, by a series of photoelectric devices, or else manually by operators stationed at peepholes. But he lost his voice thrice as the discs unbalanced him; Magda was anyhow squealing; but at one point she clutched him about the waist to keep from falling, and her right cheek pressed for a moment against his belt-buckle. Heroically he drew her up, it was his chance to clutch her close as if for support and say: "I love you." He even put an arm lightly about the small of her back before a sailor-and-girl pitched into them from behind, sorely treading his left big toe and knocking Magda asprawl with them. The sailor's girl was a string-haired hussy with a loud laugh and light blue drawers; Ambrose realized that he wouldn't have said "I love you" anyhow, and was smitten with self-contempt. How much better it would be to be that common sailor! A wiry little Seaman 3rd, the fellow squeezed a girl to each side and stumbled hilarious into the mirror room, closer to Magda in thirty seconds than Ambrose had got in thirteen years. She giggled at something the fellow said to Peter; she drew her hair from her eyes with a movement so womanly it struck Ambrose's heart; Peter's smacking her backside then seemed particularly coarse. But Magda made a pleased indignant face and cried, "All right for *you,* mister!" and pursued Peter into the maze without a backward glance. The sailor followed after, leisurely, drawing his girl against his hip; Ambrose understood not only that they were all so relieved to be rid of his burdensome company that they didn't even notice his absence, but that he himself shared their relief. Stepping from the treacherous passage at last into the mirror-maze, he saw once again, more clearly than ever, how readily he deceived himself into supposing he was a person. He even foresaw, wincing at his dreadful self-knowledge, that he would repeat the deception, at ever-rarer intervals, all his wretched life, so fearful were the alternatives. Fame, madness, suicide; perhaps all three. It's not believable that so young a boy could articulate that reflection, and in fiction the merely true must always yield to the plausible. Moreover, the symbolism is in places heavy-footed. Yet Ambrose M—— understood, as few adults do, that the famous loneliness of the great was no popular myth but a general truth—furthermore, that it was as much cause as effect.

All the preceding except the last few sentences is exposition that should've been done earlier or interspersed with the present action instead of lumped together. No reader would put up with so much with such *prolixity*. It's interesting that Ambrose's father, though presumably an intelligent man (as indicated by his role as grade-school principal), neither encouraged nor discouraged his sons at all in any way—as if he either didn't care about them or cared all right but didn't know how to act. If this fact should contribute to one of them's becoming a celebrated but wretchedly unhappy scientist, was it a good thing or not? He too might someday face the question; it would be useful to know whether it had tortured his father for years, for example, or never once crossed his mind.

In the maze two important things happened. First, our hero found a name-coin someone else had lost or discarded: *AMBROSE,* suggestive of the famous lightship and of his late grandfather's favorite dessert, which his mother used to prepare on special occasions out of coconut, oranges, grapes, and what else. Second, as he wondered at the endless replication of his image in the mirrors, second, as he *lost himself in the reflection* that the necessity for an observer makes perfect observation impossible, better make him eighteen at least, yet that would render other things unlikely, he heard Peter and Magda chuckling somewhere together in the maze. "Here!" "No, here!" they shouted to each other; Peter said, "Where's Amby?" Magda murmured. "Amb?" Peter called. In a pleased, friendly voice. He didn't reply. The truth was, his brother was a *happy-go-lucky youngster* who'd've been better off with a regular brother of his own, but who seldom complained of his lot and was generally cordial. Ambrose's throat ached; there aren't enough different ways to say that. He stood quietly while the two young people giggled and thumped through the glittering maze, hurrah'd their discovery of its exit, cried out in joyful alarm at what next beset them. Then he set his mouth and followed after, as he supposed, took a wrong turn, strayed into the pass *wherein he lingers yet.*

The action of conventional dramatic narrative may be represented by a diagram called Freitag's Triangle:

or more accurately by a variant of that diagram:

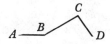

in which *AB* represents the exposition, *B* the introduction of conflict, *BC* the "rising action," complication, or development of the conflict, *C* the climax, or turn of the action, *CD* the dénouement, or resolution of the conflict. While there is no reason to regard this pattern as an absolute necessity, like many other conventions it became conventional because great numbers of people over many years learned by trial and error that it was effective; one ought not to forsake it, therefore, unless one wishes to forsake as well the effect of drama or has clear cause to feel that deliberate violation of the "normal" pattern can better can better effect that effect. This can't go on much longer; it can go on forever. He died telling stories to himself in the dark; years later, when that vast unsuspected area of the funhouse came to light, the first expedition found his skeleton in one of its labyrinthine corridors and mistook it for part of the entertainment. He died of starvation telling himself stories in the dark; but unbeknownst unbeknownst to him, an assistant operator of the funhouse, happening to overhear him, crouched just behind the plyboard partition and wrote down his every word. The operator's daughter, an exquisite young woman with a figure unusually well developed for her age, crouched just behind the partition and transcribed his every word. Though she had never laid eyes on him, she recognized that here was one of Western Culture's truly great imaginations, the eloquence of whose suffering would be an inspiration to unnumbered. And her heart was torn between her love for the misfortunate young man (yes, she loved him, though she had never laid though she knew him only—but how well!—through his words, and the deep, calm voice in which he spoke them) between her love et cetera and her womanly intuition that only in suffering and isolation could he give voice et cetera. Lone dark dying. Quietly she kissed the rough plyboard, and a tear fell upon the page. Where she had written in shorthand *Where she had written in shorthand* Where she had

written in shorthand *Where she* et cetera. A long time ago we should
have passed the apex of Freitag's Triangle and made brief work of
the *dénouement;* the plot doesn't rise by meaningful steps but winds
upon itself, digresses, retreats, hesitates, sighs, collapses, expires. The
climax of the story must be its protagonist's discovery of a way to get
through the funhouse. But he has found none, may have ceased to
search.

What relevance does the war have to the story? Should there be
fireworks outside or not?

Ambrose wandered, languished, dozed. Now and then he fell into
his habit of rehearsing to himself the unadventurous story of his life,
narrated from the third-person point of view, from his earliest
memory parenthesis of maple leaves stirring in the summer breath of
tidewater Maryland end of parenthesis to the present moment. Its
principal events, on this telling, would appear to have been *A, B, C,*
and *D.*

He imagined himself years hence, successful, married, at ease in the
world, the trials of his adolescence far behind him. He has come to
the seashore with his family for the holiday: how Ocean City has
changed! But at one seldom at one ill-frequented end of the boardwalk a few derelict amusements survive from times gone by: the great
carrousel from the turn of the century, with its monstrous griffins and
mechanical concert band; the roller coaster rumored since 1916 to
have been condemned; the mechanical shooting gallery in which only
the image of our enemies changed. His own son laughs with Fat May
and wants to know what a funhouse is; Ambrose hugs the sturdy lad
close and smiles around his pipestem at his wife.

The family's going home. Mother sits between Father and Uncle
Karl, who teases him good-naturedly who chuckles over the fact that
the comrade with whom he'd fought his way shoulder to shoulder
through the funhouse had turned out to be a blind Negro girl—to
their mutual discomfort, as they'd opened their souls. But such are
the walls of custom, which even. Whose arm is where? How must it
feel. He dreams of a funhouse vaster by far than any yet constructed;
but by then they may be out of fashion, like steamboats and excursion trains. Already quaint and seedy: the draperied ladies on the
frieze of the carrousel are his father's father's mooncheeked dreams; if
he thinks of it more he will vomit his apple-on-a-stick.

He wonders: will he become a regular person? Something has gone
wrong; his vaccination didn't take; at the Boy-Scout initiation camp-
fire he only pretended to be deeply moved, as he pretends to this
hour that it is not so bad after all in the funhouse, and that he has a
little limp. How long will it last? He envisions a truly astonishing
funhouse, incredibly complex yet utterly controlled from a great
central switchboard like the console of a pipe organ. Nobody had

enough imagination. He could design such a place himself, wiring and all, and he's only thirteen years old. He would be its operator: panel lights would show what was up in every cranny of its cunning of its multifarious vastness; a switch-flick would ease this fellow's way, complicate that's, to balance things out; if anyone seemed lost or frightened, all the operator had to do was.

He wishes he had never entered the funhouse. But he has. Then he wishes he were dead. But he's not. Therefore he will construct funhouses for others and be their secret operator—though he would rather be among the lovers for whom funhouses are designed.

DONALD BARTHELME (1931–   )

The Balloon

The balloon, beginning at a point on Fourteenth Street, the exact location of which I cannot reveal, expanded northward all one night, while people were sleeping, until it reached the Park. There, I stopped it; at dawn the northernmost edges lay over the Plaza; the free-hanging motion was frivolous and gentle. But experiencing a faint irritation at stopping, even to protect the trees, and seeing no reason the balloon should not be allowed to expand upward, over the parts of the city it was already covering, into the "air space" to be found there, I asked the engineers to see to it. This expansion took place throughout the morning, soft imperceptible sighing of gas through the valves. The balloon then covered forty-five blocks north-south and an irregular area east-west, as many as six crosstown blocks on either side of the Avenue in some places. That was the situation, then.

But it is wrong to speak of "situations," implying sets of circumstances leading to some resolution, some escape of tension; there were no situations, simply the balloon hanging there—muted heavy grays and browns for the most part, contrasting with walnut and soft yellows. A deliberate lack of finish, enhanced by skillful installation, gave the surface a rough, forgotten quality; sliding weights on the inside, carefully adjusted, anchored the great, vari-shaped mass at a number of points. Now we have had a flood of original ideas in all media, works of singular beauty as well as significant milestones in the history of inflation, but at that moment there was only *this balloon,* concrete particular, hanging there.

There were reactions. Some people found the balloon "interesting." As a response this seemed inadequate to the immensity of the balloon, the suddenness of its appearance over the city; on the other hand, in the absence of hysteria or other societally-induced anxiety, it must be judged a calm, "mature" one. There was a certain amount of initial argumentation about the "meaning" of the balloon; this subsided, because we have learned not to insist on meanings, and they are rarely even looked for now, except in cases involving the simplest, safest phenomena. It was agreed that since the meaning of the balloon could never be known absolutely, extended discussion was pointless, or at least less purposeful than the activities of those who, for example, hung green and blue paper lanterns from the warm gray underside, in certain streets, or seized the occasion to write messages on the surface, announcing their availability for the performance of unnatural acts, or the availability of acquaintances.

Daring children jumped, especially at those points where the balloon hovered close to a building, so that the gap between balloon and building was a matter of a few inches, or points where the balloon actually made contact, exerting an ever-so-slight pressure against the side of a building, so that balloon and building seemed a unity. The upper surface was so structured that a "landscape" was presented, small valleys as well as slight knolls, or mounds; once atop the balloon, a stroll was possible, or even a trip, from one place to another. There was pleasure in being able to run down an incline, then up the opposing slope, both gently graded, or in making a leap from one side to the other. Bouncing was possible, because of the pneumaticity of the surface, and even falling, if that was your wish. That all these varied motions, as well as others, were within one's possibilities, in experiencing the "up" side of the balloon, was extremely exciting for children, accustomed to the city's flat, hard skin. But the purpose of the balloon was not to amuse children.

Too, the number of people, children and adults, who took advantage of the opportunities described was not so large as it might have been: a certain timidity, lack of trust in the balloon, was seen. There was, furthermore, some hostility. Because we had hidden the pumps, which fed helium to the interior, and because the surface was so vast that the authorities could not determine the point of entry—that is, the point at which the gas was injected—a degree of frustration was evidenced by those city officers into whose province such manifestations normally fell. The apparent purposelessness of the balloon was vexing (as was the fact that it was "there" at all). Had we painted, in great letters, "LABORATORY TESTS PROVE" OR "18% MORE EFFECTIVE" on the sides of the balloon, this difficulty would have been circumvented. But I could not bear to do so. On the whole, these officers were remarkably tolerant, considering the dimensions of the anomaly, this tolerance being the result of, first, secret tests conducted by night that convinced them that little or nothing could be done in the way of removing or destroying the balloon, and, secondly, a public warmth that arose (not uncolored by touches of the aforementioned hostility) toward the balloon, from ordinary citizens.

As a single balloon must stand for a lifetime of thinking about balloons, so each citizen expressed, in the attitude he chose, a complex of attitudes. One man might consider that the balloon had to do with the notion *sullied,* as in the sentence *The big balloon sullied the otherwise clear and radiant Manhattan sky.* That is, the balloon was, in this man's view, an imposture, something inferior to the sky that had formerly been there, something interposed between the people and their "sky." But in fact it was January, the sky was dark and ugly; it was not a sky you could look up into, lying on your back in the street, with pleasure, unless pleasure, for you, proceeded from having been threatened, from having been misused. And the underside of the balloon was a pleasure to look up into, we had seen to that, muted grays and browns for the most part, contrasted with walnut and soft, forgotten yellows. And so, while this man was thinking *sullied,* still there was an admixture of pleasurable cognition in his thinking, struggling with the original perception.

Another man, on the other hand, might view the balloon as if it were part of a system of unanticipated rewards, as when one's employer walks in and says, "Here, Henry, take this package of money I have wrapped for you, because we have been doing so well in the business here, and I admire the way you bruise the tulips, without which bruising your department would not be a success, or at least not the success that it is." For this man the balloon might be a brilliantly heroic "muscle and pluck" experience, even if an experience poorly understood.

Another man might say, "Without the example of ———, it is doubtful that —— would exist today in its present form," and find many to agree with him, or to argue with him. Ideas of "bloat" and "float" were introduced, as well as concepts of dream and responsibility. Others engaged in remarkably detailed fantasies having to do with a wish either to lose themselves in the balloon, or to engorge it. The private character of these wishes, of their origins, deeply buried and unknown, was such that they were not much spoken of; yet there is evidence that they were widespread. It was also argued that what was important was what you felt when you stood under the balloon; some people claimed that they felt sheltered, warmed, as never before, while enemies of the balloon felt, or reported feeling, constrained, a "heavy" feeling.

Critical opinion was divided:

"monstrous pourings"

"harp"

XXXXXXX "certain contrasts with darker portions"

"inner joy"

"large, square corners"

"conservative eclecticism that has so far governed modern balloon design"

::::::: "abnormal vigor"

"warm, soft, lazy passages"

"Has unity been sacrificed for a sprawling quality?"

"Quelle catastrophe!"

"munching"

People began, in a curious way, to locate themselves in relation to aspects of the balloon: "I'll be at that place where it dips down into Forty-seventh Street almost to the sidewalk, near the Alamo Chile House," or, "Why don't we go stand on top, and take the air, and maybe walk about a bit, where it forms a tight, curving line with the façade of the Gallery of Modern Art—" Marginal intersections offered entrances within a given time duration, as well as "warm, soft, lazy passages" in which . . . But it is wrong to speak of "marginal intersections," each intersection was crucial, none could be ignored (as if, walking there, you might not find someone capable of turning your attention, in a flash, from old exercises to new exercises, risks and escalations). Each intersection was crucial, meeting of balloon and building, meeting of balloon and man, meeting of balloon and balloon.

It was suggested that what was admired about the balloon was finally this: that it was not limited, or defined. Sometimes a bulge, blister, or sub-section would carry all the way east to the river on its own initiative, in the manner of an army's movements on a map, as seen in a headquarters remote from the fighting. Then that part would be, as it were, thrown back again, or would withdraw into new dispositions; the next morning, that part would have made another sortie, or disappeared altogether. This ability of the balloon to shift its shape, to change, was very pleasing, especially to people whose lives were rather rigidly patterned, persons to whom change, although desired, was not available. The balloon, for the twenty-two days of its existence, offered the possibility, in its randomness, of mislocation of the self, in contradistinction to the grid of precise, rectangular pathways under our feet. The amount of specialized training currently needed, and the consequent desirability of long-term commitments, has been occasioned by the steadily growing importance of complex machinery, in virtually all kinds of operations; as this tendency increases, more and more people will turn, in bewildered inadequacy, to solutions for which the balloon may stand as a prototype, or "rough draft."

I met you under the balloon, on the occasion of your return from Norway; you asked if it was mine; I said it was. The balloon, I said, is a spontaneous autobiographical disclosure, having to do with the unease I felt at your absence, and with sexual deprivation, but now that your visit to Bergen has been terminated, it is no longer necessary or appropriate. Removal of the balloon was easy; trailer trucks carried away the depleted fabric, which is now stored in West Virginia, awaiting some other time of unhappiness, sometime, perhaps, when we are angry with one another.

DRAMA

1 Reading Drama

Analyzing Greek drama around 330 B.C., the philosopher Aristotle found each play to be composed of six parts: plot, character, thought, diction, spectacle, and music. Of these, he considered the plot—the putting together of diverse happenings to create a complete and unified action—to be the most important. Without plot, he says, there can be no play; for the chief purpose of drama is the acting-out of an action.

Characters come next in importance for Aristotle. Thought—by which he seems to mean not only the ideas expressed by the various speakers, but also their use of speech to sway the emotions of the audience—comes third. Diction, the choice of words, is fourth. Music and scenery, being pleasant and often impressive, but not essential, come last.

With the exception of music and spectacle, which apply only to plays in performance, Aristotle's categories are essentially the same categories we've been using in discussing fiction. The further we read in Aristotle, the more similarities we find: Aristotle warns would-be authors that their plots, to be complete, must have a natural beginning, middle, and end; that they must provide scope for their heroes to pass from happiness to unhappiness, or from unhappiness to happiness; and that they must be unified, containing nothing that could be taken away without leaving the drama incomplete.

He reminds writers that they are not historians, to ask what this or that man actually did; rather, they must deal in universal qualities, asking what this or that type of man would do in a given situation. Dramatists need not ask, "Has such a thing as this ever happened?" They need only wonder, "Will the audience believe that it could happen?" In fact, Aristotle declares, taking his argument to its farthest extreme, dramatists must write of what is probable even at the expense of what is possible. Given a choice between a possible but unlikely event and an impossible but seemingly probable one, the dramatist must choose the probable, believable event for his plot if he wishes the play to succeed.

In discussing characterization Aristotle reminds us that all characters must be people basically like ourselves, though some may be better and some worse. And again, he insists that consistency and probability are the two most important standards of judgment. The writer must make sure that the characters' actions are consistent with their natures, and that their natures remain consistent throughout the drama.

If we have not already discussed all of these ideas, at least we have no difficulty in applying them to the fiction we've read. To discuss consistency of character, for instance, we could look at any number of characters—at Daru in "The Guest," so consistently unable to link himself to his fellow humans; at the narrator of "Bartleby the Scrivener," with his deep and basically kindly desire for tranquility in human relations and his persistent and misplaced faith in money as a means of attaining that tranquility; or at the heroine of "The Yellow Wall-Paper," whose every step into madness is simply a more complete apprehension of fears and feelings already expressed. All are consistently drawn characters. Given their natures and situations created by their authors, they have no chance of escaping their fate.*

The basic elements of drama, then, are the same as those of fiction. It is the method of presentation that differs.

Fiction is the telling of tales. Its roots go back to the archetypal figure of the storyteller, rehearsing old legends and inventing new marvels for the listeners who surround him. The importance of voice in fiction, therefore, can hardly be overemphasized. One use of voice is evident in the many tales in which the narrative voice is that of the storyteller: tales such as those by Faulkner, Hemingway, Wright, and O'Connor. Another use can be seen in works such as those of Lessing and Barth, which begin in a storytelling voice and then move beyond that voice to more direct (if occasionally less coherent) appeals to the reader, asking the reader to join the narrator in considering what speech, writing, or storytelling implies.

A third use of voice is found in stories that discard the conscious narrative voice entirely, replacing it either with an inner "stream of conscious-

---

* This illustrates two other Aristotelian concepts as well. One is the movement from happiness to unhappiness: all three characters are happier when their tales begin than when they end. The second concept is that of inevitability, discussed on p. 5.

ness," as Olsen does in "Help Her to Believe," or with the fragmented set of impressions Oates uses in "How I Contemplated My Life." In both cases, the outer voice (the public voice) is being avoided in the hope that the inner, private voice will be the truer and more revealing voice, speaking with intense immediacy of tone and allowing us the fullest empathy with the speaker.

As fiction has become a more silent experience, writers seem to have attached increasing importance to the question of what voice would speak through their works. Listening to stories is still enjoyable. Any good story can be read aloud and be enjoyed the better for it. But our society seems to feel that listening to tales is a pleasure most proper for children and for those who cannot read to themselves. For most of us, therefore, fiction is something read silently and alone. It involves one book, one writer, one reader. We discuss stories in company, but we tend to read them in solitude.

Drama—in performance, at least—is wholly different. It is not written for one voice, but for many. It depends not on storytellers but on actors, men and women who impersonate their tale's characters not only in voice, but also in motion, gesture, and appearance, making them live for our eyes as well as our ears. Moreover, it is written for many viewers, for only in the midst of an audience can we appreciate fully the magic of drama. Laughing alone at a joke in print is enjoyable; being one laughing person among a hundred people can be hilarious.

Actors know this well. They know how fully they must bring their characters alive for their audience. They know, too, how dependent they are on the audience's response if they are to perform well. Many actors have declared that the best performances are those during which the emotions portrayed on stage are caught and sent back by the audience until audience and actors alike are caught up in the atmosphere they have created between them, and the illusion of the play becomes more real than the realities of the world outside. Similarly, many have said that acting in films, where no audience is present to reflect the emotional impact of the scene, is a more difficult and less enjoyable form of acting than acting on the stage. Playgoers and filmgoers, in their turn, agree that the experience of attending a live performance has an electric quality not to be found in viewing a film.

The fervor with which most of us discuss a really good play or film we've just seen, as opposed to the milder delight with which we discuss a really good book, testifies to the power of drama to move and delight us. A knowledge of the origins of drama, about which we shall speak in the next chapter, may help explain the intensity of our response. Within this course, however, we are readers rather than viewers of drama. And so the very power of drama in performance is likely to raise questions for us. "Here we are," we say, "with no stage, no actors—nothing but a playscript in front of us. What can we expect from this experience?"

Reading drama is certainly different from reading fiction. Drama gives us no narrator to describe scenes and characters, to comment on the significance of the action, to tie scenes together, or to provide a unifying viewpoint. Instead, drama gives us several characters, distinguished in the text only by their names, talking mostly to each other instead of to us, intent on their own affairs, entering and leaving the scene in bewildering succession.

If we were watching a play, we would recognize the characters by their appearance, mannerisms, and voices. Knowing the characters, we would then find it easy to follow the action. When we read a play, however, we must do without these visual clues. Or, rather, we must supply them for ourselves. We must use the text as the play's director would, judging from its words and from the actions they describe how the play would look and sound on stage.

Reading plays, in fact, gives our imagination free rein. How would I stage this scene? What sort of actor would I want for this role? What kind of stage setting would I use? Or, what kind of camera work would I use in a film? Which would be my long shots, which my close ups? What emotions will my filming be trying to capture?

Most of all, perhaps, you will think of the various characters as they are revealed in the text. What characteristics will each one exhibit? How will they carry themselves on stage? What tones of voice will they use in their speeches? How will they act toward each other?* The more clearly you can visualize the play's action and characters, the more readily the text will come alive for you.

Don't be afraid to experiment in your thinking. Actors, directors, and scene designers all allow themselves some freedom of interpretation when they put on a play. You can read for days about famous actors who have played Hamlet, each interpreting the role in his own way, emphasizing one aspect or another of the prince's complex personality. Why should not we, as readers, enjoy the same freedom to visualize the play, interpreting and fitting together its parts to develop our vision of its conflicts and its meanings?

The text of a play will supply us with plenty of help. Since drama does depend so largely on the art of the actor, dramatists must create characters who can carry the play by their speeches and actions. Everything the actors (and readers) need must be contained in the speeches and stage directions. Here are some of the things we can look for.

We can look for characters who, like first-person narrators in fiction, reveal in their speech information about their habits, personalities, and thinking—information they do not always know they are giving us. We can expect to be wiser than most of these characters because we have the

---

* A handy device for keeping track of a play's characters, in fact, is to "cast" the play for yourself with actors you'd enjoy watching in it. Then you can follow those actors through each scene, imagining how they would interpret the roles.

ability to stand apart from the action in which they participate, to see it fully or judge it objectively.

We can look for patterns in characterization. We can look for characters who support each other and characters who oppose each other. We can expect to see strong characters opposed to weak ones, inflexible characters opposed to reasonable ones, good characters opposed to evil ones.

There is always conflict in a play, just as there is in fiction; and the conflict is generally between people. Fiction writers such as Crane can deal with the conflict between people and nature. Dramatists, accustomed to thinking in terms of human actors and finding it difficult to bring an ocean on stage to act as antagonist, generally restrict themselves to conflicts among human beings.

The speeches of the actors, therefore, set down in the play's text, will describe the play's characters for us, develop the action and conflict of the play, and contain the play's themes. The conflict between the ideas expressed in speeches will often be basic to the conflict of the play. Thus, in *Oedipus Rex,* much of the play's conflict centers around the question of whether it is wise or foolish for Oedipus to seek the truth about Laios' murder. And in *Hamlet,* the conflict between Hamlet and Claudius over who shall rule Denmark becomes almost secondary to the mental conflicts between Hamlet and other characters (and within Hamlet himself) on the moral and practical issues arising from the political conflict.

Patterns of speech, characterization, and thought, then, are as important in drama as they are in fiction. Patterns of language and of imagery, too, are important. Some plays, such as *Death of a Salesman,* try to imitate everyday speech patterns in their language. Others shift those patterns somewhat. *The Second Shepherds' Play,* written, like most plays of its time, in rhymed verse, seeks a balance between natural-sounding speech and the emphatic qualities of rhyme. *Major Barbara,* while similarly keeping to some semblance of natural speech rhythms and vocabulary, permits its characters a greater fluency of speech and aptness of comic rejoinder than any ordinary conversation would show. Still other plays, such as *Hamlet* or *Oedipus Rex,* use the full power of poetry in their speeches. Dialogue in these plays can move in a few lines from the accents of everyday speech to those of extreme poetic passion, as the playwrights draw from the rhythms of poetry a capacity for dignity and grandeur and openness of expression that the limits of everyday speech deny them.

Patterns of imagery, too, can be used to great effect in these poetic plays. But imagery, as we have seen already in our work with fiction, is not restricted to poetry. Certainly, *Hamlet* is the richest in imagery of the five plays presented here. But all make some use of imagery, from the imagery of physical and mental blindness in *Oedipus Rex* to *Death of a Salesman*'s contrasted images of congested city and open country and its almost symbolic use of stockings as a visual image.

Reading drama, therefore, can offer an intensification of the pleasure provided by reading fiction. More richly patterned in action, language, and characterization than most short stories, allowing its readers more scope for interpretation and for the visual imagination, drama offers us a chance to be actors, director, and audience in one.

As a preliminary exercise to the study of drama, think back over the short stories you have read. Which ones could be easily turned into plays? Which ones not? In each case, what would be the major reasons behind your decision?

Then choose one story you think would make a good play, and decide what you'd have to do to make a play of it. What actors would your play need? How would you stage it? Would any rewriting be required? You might even try acting out a scene or so, to see what effect your dramatization would have on the story.

2 *Origins of English Drama*

English drama can be traced back to two origins, one in tenth-century England and one in ancient Greece. The two beginnings differed greatly in style and content, but did have one important thing in common: both formed parts of religious rituals.

Medieval Drama

Drama in medieval Europe seems to have begun as part of the Easter services. At some appropriate point during the Mass or the matins service, one or two men would unobtrusively position themselves near the altar or near some representation of a tomb. There, they would be approached by three other men, whose heads were covered to look like women and who moved slowly, as if seeking something. Singing in the Latin of the church service, the "angel" at the tomb would question the "women," "Whom seek you in the tomb, O followers of Christ?" The women would then sing the answer of the three Marys, "Jesus of Nazareth, who was crucified, O heavenly one." The angel then would sing again, "He is not here; he is risen, just as he foretold. Go, announce that he is risen from the tomb."

The dramatization might stop there, or it might continue with the showing of the empty tomb to the women, their song of joy, and the spreading of the good news to the disciples. In either case, the culmination of the drama would mark a return to the service itself with the singing of the Mass's *Ressurexi* ("I have risen") or the matins' final *Te deum, laudamus* ("We praise thee, Lord").

One medieval manuscript in particular emphasizes the closeness of the connection. It describes the singers of the *Te Deum* as rejoicing with the three women at Christ's triumph over death and commands that all the church bells be rung together as soon as the hymn of praise has begun. Drama and service thus celebrate the same event. The joy expressed by the women at the news of the resurrection is the same joy felt by the worshipers in the congregation.

Latin drama continued to develop within the church services. Manuscripts still survive, not only of Easter and Christmas plays but of plays dealing with prophets and saints as well. They show the plays growing longer and more elaborate than the early one just described, but they still emphasize the close ties between the plays and the services at which they are performed. Thus, one Christmas pageant of the shepherds calls for many boys dressed as angels to sit in the roof of the church and sing in loud voices the angels' song, "Glory to God." But it also directs that, at the end of the pageant, the shepherds must return into the choir, and there act as choir leaders for the Mass which follows.

By the fourteenth century, however, drama had also moved outside the church. There it was spoken almost wholly in the vernacular, though some bits of Latin, and a good deal of singing, remained. The plays were acted by laymen (including some professional actors) rather than by clerics, and they were developing modes of performance that might encompass up to three days of playing and involve most of the citizens of the towns where they were performed.

These were the Corpus Christi plays, also known as the "cycle plays" or the "mystery plays." Performed in celebration of Corpus Christi day, they comprised a series of pageants beginning with the creation of the world, proceeding through the history of the Old and New Testaments, and ending with the Last Judgment. Each pageant was performed on its own movable stage—its "pageant wagon." Mounted on four or six wheels, two stories high, the wagons provided facilities for some surprisingly complex stage effects and allowed each pageant to be presented several times at several different locations. One after another, the pageants would move through a town, usually stopping at three or four prearranged places to repeat their performances, so that everyone in town might see all of the twenty to fifty plays that made up the cycle.

The presentation of these cycles was undertaken by the towns themselves, with the town authorities ordering the performances. But the individual pageants were produced by the local trade and craft guilds. Ordinarily each guild would present one pageant, but sometimes several small guilds would team up to perform a single pageant or share the cost of a wagon that each could use. It is easy to imagine the competition this could produce, with each guild trying to outdo the next. But the plays were still religious in subject and import. They often spoke directly to the audience and always emphasized how the events they depicted pertained to each viewer's salvation.

Greek Drama

The other source of English drama was the drama of ancient Greece. We know less about the beginning of this drama, for it has left few records. We do know, however, that it began at festivals honoring Dionysus, a god who was supposed to have taught men to cultivate grapes and make wine. Song and dance were the means by which this god was worshipped. At early festivals, choruses of fifty men dressed in tattered garments with wine-smeared faces or disguised as Dionysus' mythical companions, the satyrs, sang hymns praising the god's deeds while they half-danced, half-mimed his exploits. Eventually one man stepped out of the chorus and engaged his fellows in dialogue. Later still, the soloist began impersonating the god, thus dramatizing the events of which he was singing.

Sometime during this process, the content of the songs also shifted. Some still pertained to Dionysus, but some dealt with other, human, heroes. Although worshippers were reportedly shocked at the first introduction of the new tales, asking, "What has this to do with Dionysus?", the novelty soon became the rule. By 530 B.C., these plays were being called tragedies and were competing in Athens for an annual prize.

In the next hundred years, tragedy reached what Aristotle considered its full form. A second and then a third actor was added. Episodes of dialogue among the actors, with the chorus occasionally joining in, became as important as the choric songs and dances with which they alternated. Painted backdrops, stage machinery, and special effects were introduced.

For all its developments, however, Greek drama remained a religious event. Plays were performed only at Dionysus' festivals; actors were considered his servants. Performances took place three times a year: twice at Athens, once at various rural festivals. The older of the Athenian festivals, the *Lenaea*, became the festival for comedy; but the *City Dionysia*, which drew visitors from all over Greece, was the festival for tragedy.

For this festival, three playwrights were chosen by Athenian authorities. Each was given a chorus and actors, who were paid and costumed by some rich citizen as a public service; each was allotted one day of the festival on which to perform. The performance would consist of three tragedies (sometimes on the same subject, sometimes not), folowed by a satyr play, an obscene or satiric parody of some legendary event. At the end of the three days of playing, a jury of ten citizens, chosen by lot, judged the plays and awarded the prizes.* Any Athenian was welcome to attend these plays, which were held in a natural ampitheatre that seated some 30,000 people. Since the theatre was reported to be crowded at every performance, we may assume that virtually everybody who could attend, did.

All in all, drama in ancient Athens seems to have been regarded almost as a public possession. Looked on with a mixture of religious devotion, civic pride, and open enjoyment, it maintained a great and general popularity that seems to have declined only with the decline of Athens itself. And still the plays remained influential, both in themselves and in the theory of drama that Aristotle's comments on them provided. First the Romans copied them. Then, some 1500 years later, Renaissance playwrights took ideas from both Greek and Roman drama. That development we will discuss in the next chapter.

Oedipus Rex and *The Second Shepherds' Play*

Let us look now at examples of Greek tragedy and medieval cycle plays. *Oedipus Rex* and *The Second Shepherds' Play* † are highly polished examples of their early forms. Song and poetic speech are important in both; both were meant for performance at religious festivals, and both performances would have been backed by a great deal of public enthusiasm and support. Beyond these similarities, however, we find substantial differences in the forms of the plays and in the attitudes they bring to their subjects.

Oedipus Rex is a tragedy. As such, it deals with a somewhat idealized, larger-than-life hero, a man caught in a dilemma between his ideals and his personal safety and fighting his way towards a terrifying knowledge. "Ah," cries the Shepherd in one climactic scene, "I am on the brink of dreadful speech." "And I of dreadful hearing," replies Oedipus. "Yet I must hear." This insistence on following through in a search, an action, the pursuit of an ideal, has always attracted readers, perhaps because we all know how difficult that sort of courage is to sustain. It is the one force that is constant in tragedy.

The sad or terrible ending, incidentally, is not essential to tragedy. Some Greek tragedies end happily, in a reconciliation of their opposed forces, new knowledge having created new peace. The essentials of tragedy are the the protagonist's own insistence on action or enlightenment and the ability of the play, however it ends, to arouse a sympathetic "fear and pity" (Aris-

---

* Sophocles, the author of *Oedipus Rex,* held the all-time record of eighteen first prizes, and is said never to have won less than second prize. Yet *Oedipus Rex* itself, which was praised by Aristotle and is still considered one of the finest of Greek tragedies, won only second prize when it was first produced.

† For some unknown reason, two Shepherds' Plays are included in the manuscript of the Wakefield cycle, where they are distinguished simply as *The First Shepherds' Play* and *The Second Shepherds' Play.*

totle's terms) in the audience as they watch the working-out of the hero's quest. These essentials *Oedipus Rex* clearly has.

The Second Shepherds' Play, on the other hand, deals primarily with comic characters. But we must say "primarily"; for the play as a whole will not fit into any of the classic forms of drama.

Greek drama segregated its forms carefully. Tragedy dealt with the noble, the heroic, the sacrificial. In performance, three tragedies would be followed by a satyr play, which turned heroic figures into tricksters or clowns and often mocked the very legends that had supplied the day's tragedies. Comedy had its own festival, in which it could deal with the more practical aspirations of everyday people—good food, warm beds, and peaceful households and cities. The heroes of comedy battle such unheroic opponents as thieves, con men, unreasonable parents, and crooked politicians. Often, they must resort to trickery to outwit these unsavory sorts, who may very well be tricksters themselves. A happy ending is guaranteed.

Medieval drama did not so carefully distinguish its forms. It had one central sacrificial subject: the death of Christ for the salvation of mankind. This sacrifice was always treated seriously; neither Christ nor Mary was ever burlesqued. But the world that Christ entered at his birth was the world of thin clothes and bad weather, of thieves and tricksters and con men, with the Devil himself, the arch-trickster, as Christ's opponent. It was, in short, the world of comedy. A drama which dealt with the history of man's fall and salvation would thus have to be both comic and tragic. There would be no way of separating the two.

Nor would medieval writers have wanted to separate them. Medieval art always seems to have preferred inclusiveness to exclusiveness. The great Gothic cathedrals themselves, with their profusion of sculpture and stained glass, would give their most prominent and most beautiful art to scenes of Christ, the Virgin, and the saints. But less prominent carvings would be likely to show small boys stealing apples, or people quarreling; while, in other places, comically or frighteningly grotesque demons would round out the portrayals.

A Corpus Christi cycle, therefore, would contain both serious and humorous elements. Some plays would be wholly serious; others would mix the serious with the comic. "The Sacrifice of Isaac," for instance, was always serious. The dilemma of the father, the emotions of the son as he realized what was happening, combined to produce plays which could virtually be described as tragedies with happy endings. "Noah's Flood," on the other hand, was usually given a comic treatment. (What would you do if your husband suddenly started building a giant boat in your front yard?) In some of the plays, Noah's wife thinks her husband has gone crazy. In others, she joins in the building until it is time to get on board, then rebels against leaving the world she knows and loves. In either case, a physical fight ensues before Noah can get her on board, and Noah's prophecies of doom are mixed with his complaints about marriage.

In any one cycle, the Nativity would be represented by several pageants. Usually, there would be the Nativity itself, then the play of the shepherds, then the pageant of the three kings. The first and third of these usually demanded a serious treatment. The second did not.

Shepherds are, by definition, common folk. In their poverty and low social standing, they bear many of the evils of this imperfect world. The shepherds' play, therefore, appealed to the medieval playwright as a vehicle for dramatizing the contrast between the beauty and heavenly nature of the Christ child and the harshness of the world into which he had been born. It always began on a comic note, with the shepherds bewailing their lot, and ended with their joy at having seen the Christ child.

The Second Shepherds' Play is thus not unique in its use of comedy to set off the miracle of the divine birth. It is unique in the skill with which comic and devotional elements parallel and comment on one another. The stage setting itself would express this symmetry. Imagine an open platform with two poor-looking houses at the rear, and you will have a rough idea of how the stage for *The Second Shepherds' Play* must have looked. One house will be the home of the thief Mak and his wife. The other will be the stable at Bethlehem. The area in front will be the fields where the shepherds watch, from which they will travel first to one house, then to the other. Both houses will be visible throughout the entire play, a quiet reminder of the contrasted trouble and joy they contain.

These, then, are the two "early" plays we will read. They are not in any sense primitive or imperfect. They show us, more clearly than many later plays, the essential elements of European drama. And they are representative of the types of drama that were the foundation of all later English and American drama.

SOPHOCLES (496–406 B.C.)

Oedipus Rex

Translated by Dudley Fitts and Robert Fitzgerald

C H A R A C T E R S

OEDIPUS, *King of Thebes, supposed son of Polybos and Meropê,*
  King and Queen of Corinth
IOKASTÊ, *wife of Oedipus and widow of the late King Laïos*
KREON, *brother of Iokastê, a prince of Thebes*
TEIRESIAS, *a blind seer who serves Apollo*
PRIEST
MESSENGER, *from Corinth*
SHEPHERD, *former servant of Laïos*
SECOND MESSENGER, *from the palace*
CHORUS OF THEBAN ELDERS
CHORAGOS, *leader of the Chorus*
ANTIGONE and ISMENE, *young daughters of Oedipus and*
  Iokastê. They appear in the Éxodos but do not speak.
SUPPLIANTS, GUARDS, SERVANTS

THE SCENE. *Before the palace of* OEDIPUS, *King of Thebes. A central door and two lateral doors open onto a platform which runs the length of the façade. On the platform, right and left, are altars; and three steps lead down into the* orchêstra *or chorus-ground. At the beginning of the action these steps are crowded by suppliants who have brought branches and chaplets of olive leaves and who sit in various attitudes of despair.* OEDIPUS *enters.*

PROLOGUE

OEDIPUS   My children, generations of the living
  In the line of Kadmos,[1] nursed at his ancient hearth:
  Why have you strewn yourselves before these altars
  In supplication, with your boughs and garlands?

---

[1] *Kadmos* founder of Thebes

The breath of incense rises from the city
With a sound of prayer and lamentation.
                                   Children,
I would not have you speak through messengers,
And therefore I have come myself to hear you—
I, Oedipus, who bear the famous name.
(*To a* PRIEST) You, there, since you are eldest in the company,
Speak for them all, tell me what preys upon you,
Whether you come in dread, or crave some blessing:
Tell me, and never doubt that I will help you
In every way I can; I should be heartless
Were I not moved to find you suppliant here.

PRIEST   Great Oedipus, O powerful king of Thebes!
You see how all the ages of our people
Cling to your altar steps: here are boys
Who can barely stand alone, and here are priests
By weight of age, as I am a priest of God,
And young men chosen from those yet unmarried;
As for the others, all that multitude,
They wait with olive chaplets in the squares,
At the two shrines of Pallas, and where Apollo
Speaks in the glowing embers.
                                   Your own eyes
Must tell you: Thebes is tossed on a murdering sea
And can not lift her head from the death surge.
A rust consumes the buds and fruits of the earth;
The herds are sick; children die unborn,
And labor is vain. The god of plague and pyre
Raids like detestable lightning through the city,
And all the house of Kadmos is laid waste,
All emptied, and all darkened: Death alone
Battens upon the misery of Thebes.

You are not one of the immortal gods, we know;
Yet we have come to you to make our prayer
As to the man surest in mortal ways
And wisest in the ways of God. You saved us
From the Sphinx, that flinty singer, and the tribute
We paid to her so long; yet you were never
Better informed than we, nor could we teach you:
A god's touch, it seems, enabled you to help us.

Therefore, O mighty power, we turn to you:
Find us our safety, find us a remedy,

Whether by counsel of the gods or of men.
A king of wisdom tested in the past
Can act in a time of troubles, and act well.
Noblest of men, restore
Life to your city! Think how all men call you
Liberator for your boldness long ago;
Ah, when your years of kingship are remembered,
Let them not say *We rose, but later fell*—
Keep the State from going down in the storm!
Once, years ago, with happy augury,
You brought us fortune; be the same again!
No man questions your power to rule the land:
But rule over men, not over a dead city!
Ships are only hulls, high walls are nothing,
When no life moves in the empty passageways.

OEDIPUS   Poor children! You may be sure I know
All that you longed for in your coming here.
I know that you are deathly sick; and yet,
Sick as you are, not one is as sick as I.
Each of you suffers in himself alone
His anguish, not another's; but my spirit
Groans for the city, for myself, for you.

I was not sleeping, you are not waking me.
No, I have been in tears for a long while
And in my restless thought walked many ways.
In all my search I found one remedy,
And I have adopted it: I have sent Kreon,
Son of Menoikeus, brother of the queen,
To Delphi, Apollo's place of revelation,
To learn there, if he can,
What act or pledge of mine may save the city.
I have counted the days, and now, this very day,
I am troubled, for he has overstayed his time.
What is he doing? He has been gone too long.
Yet whenever he comes back, I should do ill
Not to take any action the god orders.

PRIEST   It is a timely promise. At this instant
They tell me Kreon is here.

OEDIPUS   O Lord Apollo!
May his news be fair as his face is radiant!

PRIEST   Good news, I gather! he is crowned with bay,
The chaplet is thick with berries.

OEDIPUS   We shall soon know;
He is near enough to hear us now.

(*Enter* KREON.)

                                    O prince:
Brother: son of Menoikeus:
What answer do you bring us from the god?

KREON   A strong one. I can tell you, great afflictions
Will turn out well, if they are taken well.

OEDIPUS   What was the oracle? These vague words
Leave me still hanging between hope and fear.

KREON   Is it your pleasure to hear me with all these
Gathered around us? I am prepared to speak,
But should we not go in?

OEDIPUS   Speak to them all,
It is for them I suffer, more than for myself.

KREON   Then I will tell you what I heard at Delphi.
In plain words
The god commands us to expel from the land of Thebes
An old defilement we are sheltering.
It is a deathly thing, beyond cure;
We must not let it feed upon us longer.

OEDIPUS   What defilement? How shall we rid ourselves of it?

KREON   By exile or death, blood for blood. It was
Murder that brought the plague-wind on the city.

OEDIPUS   Murder of whom? Surely the god has named him?

KREON   My lord: Laïos once ruled this land,
Before you came to govern us.

OEDIPUS   I know;
I learned of him from others; I never saw him.

KREON   He was murdered; and Apollo commands us now
To take revenge upon whoever killed him.

OEDIPUS   Upon whom? Where are they? Where shall we find a clue
To solve that crime, after so many years?

KREON   Here in this land, he said. Search reveals
Things that escape an inattentive man.

OEDIPUS   Tell me: Was Laïos murdered in his house,
Or in the fields, or in some foreign country?

KREON   He said he planned to make a pilgrimage.
He did not come home again.

OEDIPUS   And was there no one,
No witness, no companion, to tell what happened?

KREON   They were all killed but one, and he got away

So frightened that he could remember one thing only.

OEDIPUS   What was the one thing? One may be the key
To everything, if we resolve to use it.

KREON   He said that a band of highwaymen attacked them,
Outnumbered them, and overwhelmed the king.

OEDIPUS   Strange, that a highwayman should be so daring—
Unless some faction here bribed him to do it.

KREON   We thought of that. But after Laïos' death
New troubles arose and we had no avenger.

OEDIPUS   What troubles could prevent your hunting down
the killers?

KREON   The riddling Sphinx's song
Made us deaf to all mysteries but her own.

OEDIPUS   Then once more I must bring what is dark to light.
It is most fitting that Apollo shows,
As you do, this compunction for the dead.
You shall see how I stand by you, as I should,
Avenging this country and the god as well,
And not as though it were for some distant friend,
But for my own sake, to be rid of evil.
Whoever killed King Laïos might—who knows?—
Lay violent hands even on me—and soon.
I act for the murdered king in my own interest.

Come, then, my children: leave the altar steps,
Lift up your olive boughs!
                                One of you go
And summon the people of Kadmos to gather here.
I will do all that I can; you may tell them that.

(*Exit a* PAGE.)

So, with the help of God,
We shall be saved—or else indeed we are lost.

PRIEST   Let us rise, children. It was for this we came,
And now the king has promised it.
Phoibos[1] has sent us an oracle; may he descend
Himself to save us and drive out the plague.

(*Exeunt* OEDIPUS *and* KREON *into the palace by the central door. The*
PRIEST *and the* SUPPLIANTS *disperse R and L. After a short pause the*
CHORUS *enters the* orchêstra.)

---

[1] *Phoibos* Apollo

PARODOS [1]

Strophe 1

CHORUS   What is God singing in his profound
 Delphi of gold and shadow?
 What oracle for Thebes, the sunwhipped city?
 Fear unjoints me, the roots of my heart tremble.
 Now I remember, O Healer, your power, and wonder:
 Will you send doom like a sudden cloud, or weave it
 Like nightfall of the past?
 Speak to me, tell me, O
 Child of golden Hope, immortal Voice.

Antistrophe 1

 Let me pray to Athenê, the immortal daughter of Zeus,
 And to Artemis her sister
 Who keeps her famous throne in the market ring,
 And to Apollo, archer from distant heaven—
 O gods, descend! Like three streams leap against
 The fires of our grief, the fires of darkness;
 Be swift to bring us rest!
 As in the old time from the brilliant house
 Of air you stepped to save us, come again!

Strophe 2

 Now our afflictions have no end,
 Now all our stricken host lies down
 And no man fights off death with his mind;
 The noble plowland bears no grain,
 And groaning mothers can not bear—
 See, how our lives like birds take wing,

---

[1] *Parados* the song or ode chanted by the chorus on their entry. It is accompanied by dancing and music played on a flute. The chorus, in this play, represents elders of the city of Thebes. They remain on stage (on a level lower than the principal actors) for the remainder of the play. The choral odes and dances serve to separate one scene from another (there was no curtain in Greek theatre) as well as to comment on the action, reinforce the emotion, and interpret the situation. The chorus also performs dance movements during certain portions of the scenes themselves. *Strophe* and *antistrophe* are terms denoting the movement and counter-movement of the chorus from one side of their playing area to the other. When the chorus participates in dialogue with the other characters, their lines are spoken by the Choragos, their leader.

Like sparks that fly when a fire soars,
To the shore of the god of evening.

Antistrophe 2

The plague burns on, it is pitiless,
Though pallid children laden with death
Lie unwept in the stony ways,
And old gray women by every path
Flock to the strand about the altars
There to strike their breasts and cry
Worship of Phoibos in wailing prayers:
Be kind, God's golden child!

Strophe 3

There are no swords in this attack by fire,
No shields, but we are ringed with cries.
Send the besieger plunging from our homes
Into the vast sea-room of the Atlantic
Or into the waves that foam eastward of Thrace—
For the day ravages what the night spares—
Destroy our enemy, lord of the thunder!
Let him be riven by lightning from heaven!

Antistrophe 3

Phoibos Apollo, stretch the sun's bowstring,
That golden cord, until it sing for us,
Flashing arrows in heaven!
                    Artemis, Huntress,
Race with flaring lights upon our mountains!
O scarlet god, O golden-banded brow,
O Theban Bacchos in a storm of Maenads,

(*Enter* OEDIPUS, *C.*)

Whirl upon Death, that all the Undying hate!
Come with blinding torches, come in joy!

SCENE I

OEDIPUS Is this your prayer? It may be answered. Come,
Listen to me, act as the crisis demands,
And you shall have relief from all these evils.

Until now I was a stranger to this tale,
As I had been a stranger to the crime.

Could I track down the murderer without a clue?
But now, friends,
As one who became a citizen after the murder,
I make this proclamation to all Thebans:
If any man knows by whose hand Laïos, son of Labdakos,
Met his death, I direct that man to tell me everything,
No matter what he fears for having so long withheld it.
Let it stand as promised that no further trouble
Will come to him, but he may leave the land in safety.

Moreover: If anyone knows the murderer to be foreign,
Let him not keep silent: he shall have his reward from me.
However, if he does conceal it; if any man
Fearing for his friend or for himself disobeys this edict,
Hear what I propose to do:

I solemnly forbid the people of this country,
Where power and throne are mine, ever to receive that man
Or speak to him, no matter who he is, or let him
Join in sacrifice, lustration, or in prayer.
I decree that he be driven from every house,
Being, as he is, corruption itself to us: the Delphic
Voice of Apollo has pronounced this revelation.
Thus I associate myself with the oracle
And take the side of the murdered king.

As for the criminal, I pray to God—
Whether it be a lurking thief, or one of a number—
I pray that that man's life be consumed in evil and wretchedness.
And as for me, this curse applies no less
If it should turn out that the culprit is my guest here,
Sharing my hearth.
                    You have heard the penalty.
I lay it on you now to attend to this
For my sake, for Apollo's, for the sick
Sterile city that heaven has abandoned.
Suppose the oracle had given you no command:
Should this defilement go uncleansed for ever?
You should have found the murderer: your king,
A noble king, had been destroyed!
                              Now I,
Having the power that he held before me,
Having his bed, begetting children there
Upon his wife, as he would have, had he lived—
Their son would have been my children's brother,

If Laïos had had luck in fatherhood!
(And now his bad fortune has struck him down)—
I say I take the son's part, just as though
I were his son, to press the fight for him
And see it won! I'll find the hand that brought
Death to Labdakos' and Polydoros' child,
Heir of Kadmos' and Agenor's line.[1]
And as for those who fail me,
May the gods deny them the fruit of the earth,
Fruit of the womb, and may they rot utterly!
Let them be wretched as we are wretched, and worse!

For you, for loyal Thebans, and for all
Who find my actions right, I pray the favor
Of justice, and of all the immortal gods.
CHORAGOS   Since I am under oath, my lord, I swear
I did not do the murder, I can not name
The murderer. Phoibos ordained the search;
Why did he not say who the culprit was?
OEDIPUS   An honest question. But no man in the world
Can make the gods do more than the gods will.
CHORAGOS   There is an alternative, I think—
OEDIPUS   Tell me.
Any or all, you must not fail to tell me.
CHORAGOS   A lord clairvoyant to the lord Apollo,
As we all know, is the skilled Teiresias.
One might learn much about this from him, Oedipus.
OEDIPUS   I am not wasting time:
Kreon spoke of this, and I have sent for him—
Twice, in fact; it is strange that he is not here.
CHORAGOS   The other matter—that old report—seems useless.
OEDIPUS   What was that? I am interested in all reports.
CHORAGOS   The king was said to have been killed by highwaymen.
OEDIPUS   I know. But we have no witnesses to that.
CHORAGOS   If the killer can feel a particle of dread,
Your curse will bring him out of hiding!
OEDIPUS   No.
The man who dared that act will fear no curse.

(*Enter the blind seer* TEIRESIAS, *led by a* PAGE.)

CHORAGOS   But there is one man who may detect the criminal.

---

[1] *Labdakos, Polydoros, Kadmos,* and *Agenor* father, grandfather, great-grand-
father, and great-great-grandfather of Laïos

This is Teiresias, this is the holy prophet
In whom, alone of all men, truth was born.

OEDIPUS   Teiresias: seer: student of mysteries,
Of all that's taught and all that no man tells,
Secrets of Heaven and secrets of the earth:
Blind though you are, you know the city lies
Sick with plague; and from this plague, my lord,
We find that you alone can guard or save us.

Possibly you did not hear the messengers?
Apollo, when we sent to him,
Sent us back word that this great pestilence
Would lift, but only if we established clearly
The identity of those who murdered Laïos.
They must be killed or exiled.
                              Can you use
Birdflight[1] or any art of divination
To purify yourself, and Thebes, and me
From this contagion? We are in your hands.
There is no fairer duty
Than that of helping others in distress.

TEIRESIAS   How dreadful knowledge of the truth can be
When there's no help in truth! I knew this well,
But did not act on it: else I should not have come.

OEDIPUS   What is troubling you? Why are your eyes so cold?

TEIRESIAS   Let me go home. Bear your own fate, and I'll
Bear mine. It is better so: trust what I say.

OEDIPUS   What you say is ungracious and unhelpful
To your native country. Do not refuse to speak.

TEIRESIAS   When it comes to speech, your own is neither temperate
Nor opportune. I wish to be more prudent.

OEDIPUS   In God's name, we all beg you—

TEIRESIAS   You are all ignorant.
No; I will never tell you what I know.
Now it is my misery; then, it would be yours.

OEDIPUS   What! You do know something, and will not tell us?
You would betray us all and wreck the State?

TEIRESIAS   I do not intend to torture myself, or you.
Why persist in asking? You will not persuade me.

OEDIPUS   What a wicked old man you are! You'd try a stone's
Patience! Out with it! Have you no feeling at all?

---

[1] *Birdflight* Prophets predicted the future or divined the unknown by observing the flight of birds.

TEIRESIAS   You call me unfeeling. If you could only see
   The nature of your own feelings . . .
OEDIPUS   Why,
   Who would not feel as I do? Who could endure
   Your arrogance toward the city?
TEIRESIAS   What does it matter?
   Whether I speak or not, it is bound to come.
OEDIPUS   Then, if "it" is bound to come, you are bound to tell me.
TEIRESIAS   No, I will not go on. Rage as you please.
OEDIPUS   Rage? Why not!
                        And I'll tell you what I think:
   You planned it, you had it done, you all but
   Killed him with your own hands: if you had eyes,
   I'd say the crime was yours, and yours alone.
TEIRESIAS   So? I charge you, then,
   Abide by the proclamation you have made:
   From this day forth
   Never speak again to these men or to me;
   You yourself are the pollution of this country.
OEDIPUS   You dare say that! Can you possibly think you have
   Some way of going free, after such insolence?
TEIRESIAS   I have gone free. It is the truth sustains me.
OEDIPUS   Who taught you shamelessness? It was not your craft.
TEIRESIAS   You did. You made me speak. I did not want to.
OEDIPUS   Speak what? Let me hear it again more clearly.
TEIRESIAS   Was it not clear before? Are you tempting me?
OEDIPUS   I did not understand it. Say it again.
TEIRESIAS   I say that you are the murderer whom you seek.
OEDIPUS   Now twice you have spat out infamy. You'll pay for it!
TEIRESIAS   Would you care for more? Do you wish to be
   really angry?
OEDIPUS   Say what you will. Whatever you say is worthless.
TEIRESIAS   I say you live in hideous shame with those
   Most dear to you. You can not see the evil.
OEDIPUS   Can you go on babbling like this for ever?
TEIRESIAS   I can, if there is power in truth.
OEDIPUS   There is:
   But not for you, not for you,
   You sightless, witless, senseless, mad old man!
TEIRESIAS   You are the madman. There is no one here
   Who will not curse you soon, as you curse me.
OEDIPUS   You child of total night! I would not touch you;
   Neither would any man who sees the sun.
TEIRESIAS   True: it is not from you my fate will come.

That lies within Apollo's competence,
As it is his concern.
OEDIPUS.   Tell me, who made
These fine discoveries? Kreon? or someone else?
TEIRESIAS   Kreon is no threat. You weave your own doom.
OEDIPUS   Wealth, power, craft of statesmanship!
Kingly position, everywhere admired!
What savage envy is stored up against these,
If Kreon, whom I trusted, Kreon my friend,
For this great office which the city once
Put in my hands unsought—if for this power
Kreon desires in secret to destroy me!

He has bought this decrepit fortune-teller, this
Collector of dirty pennies, this prophet fraud—
Why, he is no more clairvoyant than I am!
                                    Tell us:
Has your mystic mummery ever approached the truth?
When that hellcat the Sphinx was performing here,
What help were you to these people?
Her magic was not for the first man who came along:
It demanded a real exorcist. Your birds—
What good were they? or the gods, for the matter of that?
But I came by,
Oedipus, the simple man, who knows nothing—
I thought it out for myself, no birds helped me!
And this is the man you think you can destroy,
That you may be close to Kreon when he's king!
Well, you and your friend Kreon, it seems to me,
Will suffer most. If you were not an old man,
You would have paid already for your plot.
CHORAGOS   We can not see that his words or yours
Have been spoken except in anger, Oedipus,
And of anger we have no need. How to accomplish
The god's will best: that is what most concerns us.
TEIRESIAS   You are a king. But where argument's concerned
I am your man, as much a king as you.
I am not your servant, but Apollo's.
I have no need of Kreon or Kreon's name.

Listen to me. You mock my blindness, do you?
But I say that you, with both your eyes, are blind:
You can not see the wretchedness of your life,
Nor in whose house you live, no, nor with whom.
Who are your father and mother? Can you tell me?

You do not even know the blind wrongs
That you have done them, on earth and in the world below.
But the double lash of your parents' curse will whip you
Out of this land some day, with only night
Upon your precious eyes.
Your cries then—where will they not be heard?
What fastness of Kithairon[1] will not echo them?
And that bridal-descant of yours—you'll know it then,
The song they sang when you came here to Thebes
And found your misguided berthing.
All this, and more, that you can not guess at now,
Will bring you to yourself among your children.

Be angry, then. Curse Kreon. Curse my words.
I tell you, no man that walks upon the earth
Shall be rooted out more horribly than you.

OEDIPUS   Am I to bear this from him?—Damnation
Take you! Out of this place! Out of my sight!
TEIRESIAS   I would not have come at all if you had not asked me.
OEDIPUS   Could I have told that you'd talk nonsense, that
You'd come here to make a fool of yourself, and of me?
TEIRESIAS   A fool? Your parents thought me sane enough.
OEDIPUS   My parents again!—Wait: who were my parents?
TEIRESIAS   This day will give you a father, and break your heart.
OEDIPUS   Your infantile riddles! Your damned abracadabra!
TEIRESIAS   You were a great man once at solving riddles.
OEDIPUS   Mock me with that if you like; you will find it true.
TEIRESIAS   It was true enough. It brought about your ruin.
OEDIPUS   But if it saved this town?
TEIRESIAS *(to the* PAGE*)*   Boy, give me your hand.
OEDIPUS   Yes, boy; lead him away.

                            —While you are here
We can do nothing. Go; leave us in peace.
TEIRESIAS   I will go when I have said what I have to say.
How can you hurt me? And I tell you again:
The man you have been looking for all this time,
The damned man, the murderer of Laïos,
That man is in Thebes. To your mind he is foreign-born,
But it will soon be shown that he is a Theban,
A revelation that will fail to please.

                    A blind man,

---

[1] *Kithairon* the mountain where Oedipus was taken to be exposed as an
infant

Who has his eyes now; a penniless man, who is rich now;
And he will go tapping the strange earth with his staff.
To the children with whom he lives now he will be
Brother and father—the very same; to her
Who bore him, son and husband—the very same
Who came to his father's bed, wet with his father's blood.

Enough. Go think that over.
If later you find error in what I have said,
You may say that I have no skill in prophecy.

(*Exit* TEIRESIAS, *led by his* PAGE. OEDIPUS *goes into the palace.*)

ODE I

Strophe 1

CHORUS   The Delphic stone of prophecies
Remembers ancient regicide
And a still bloody hand.
That killer's hour of flight has come.
He must be stronger than riderless
Coursers of untiring wind,
For the son[1] of Zeus armed with his father's thunder
Leaps in lightning after him;
And the Furies hold his track, the sad Furies.

Antistrophe 1

Holy Parnassos'[2] peak of snow
Flashes and blinds that secret man,
That all shall hunt him down:
Though he may roam the forest shade
Like a bull gone wild from pasture
To rage through glooms of stone.
Doom comes down on him; flight will not avail him;
For the world's heart calls him desolate,
And the immortal voices follow, for ever follow.

Strophe 2

But now a wilder thing is heard
From the old man skilled at hearing Fate in the wing-beat
   of a bird.

---

[1] *son* Apollo
[2] *Parnassos* mountain sacred to Apollo

Bewildered as a blown bird, my soul hovers and can not find
Foothold in this debate, or any reason or rest of mind.
But no man ever brought—none can bring
Proof of strife between Thebes' royal house,
Labdakos' line, and the son of Polybos;
And never until now has any man brought word
Of Laïos' dark death staining Oedipus the King.

Antistrophe 2

Divine Zeus and Apollo hold
Perfect intelligence alone of all tales ever told;
And well though this diviner works, he works in his own night;
No man can judge that rough unknown or trust in second sight,
For wisdom changes hands among the wise.
Shall I believe my great lord criminal
At a raging word that a blind old man let fall?
I saw him, when the carrion woman[1] faced him of old,
Prove his heroic mind. These evil words are lies.

SCENE II

KREON   Men of Thebes:
I am told that heavy accusations
Have been brought against me by King Oedipus.

I am not the kind of man to bear this tamely.

If in these present difficulties
He holds me accountable for any harm to him
Through anything I have said or done—why, then,
I do not value life in this dishonor.
It is not as though this rumor touched upon
Some private indiscretion. The matter is grave.
The fact is that I am being called disloyal
To the State, to my fellow citizens, to my friends.
CHORAGOS   He may have spoken in anger, not from his mind.
KREON   But did you not hear him say I was the one
Who seduced the old prophet into lying?
CHORAGOS   The thing was said; I do not know how seriously.
KREON   But you were watching him! Were his eyes steady?
Did he look like a man in his right mind?
CHORAGOS   I do not know.

---

[1] *woman* the Sphinx

I can not judge the behavior of great men.
But here is the king himself.

(*Enter* OEDIPUS.)

OEDIPUS   So you dared come back.
Why? How brazen of you to come to my house,
You murderer!
                        Do you think I do not know
That you plotted to kill me, plotted to steal my throne?
Tell me, in God's name: am I coward, a fool,
That you should dream you could accomplish this?
A fool who could not see your slippery game?
A coward, not to fight back when I saw it?
You are the fool, Kreon, are you not? hoping
Without support or friends to get a throne?
Thrones may be won or bought: you could do neither.

KREON   Now listen to me. You have talked; let me talk, too.
You can not judge unless you know the facts.

OEDIPUS   You speak well: there is one fact; but I find it hard
To learn from the deadliest enemy I have.

KREON   That above all I must dispute with you.

OEDIPUS   That above all I will not hear you deny.

KREON   If you think there is anything good in being stubborn
Against all reason, then I say you are wrong.

OEDIPUS   If you think a man can sin against his own kind
And not be punished for it, I say you are mad.

KREON   I agree. But tell me: What have I done to you?

OEDIPUS   You advised me to send for that wizard, did you not?

KREON   I did. I should do it again.

OEDIPUS   Very well. Now tell me:
How long has it been since Laïos—

KREON   What of Laïos?

OEDIPUS   Since he vanished in that onset by the road?

KREON   It was long ago, a long time.

OEDIPUS   And this prophet,
Was he practicing here then?

KREON   He was; and with honor, as now.

OEDIPUS   Did he speak of me at that time?

KREON   He never did,
At least, not when I was present.

OEDIPUS   But . . . the enquiry?
I suppose you held one?

KREON   We did, but we learned nothing.

OEDIPUS   Why did the prophet not speak against me then?
KREON   I do not know; and I am the kind of man
Who holds his tongue when he has no facts to go on.
OEDIPUS   There's one fact that you know, and you could tell it.
KREON   What fact is that? If I know it, you shall have it.
OEDIPUS   If he were not involved with you, he could not say
That it was I who murdered Laïos.
KREON   If he says that, you are the one that knows it!—
But now it is my turn to question you.
OEDIPUS   Put your questions. I am no murderer.
KREON   First, then: You married my sister?
OEDIPUS   I married your sister.
KREON   And you rule the kingdom equally with her?
OEDIPUS   Everything that she wants she has from me.
KREON   And I am the third, equal to both of you?
OEDIPUS   That is why I call you a bad friend.
KREON   No. Reason it out, as I have done.
Think of this first: Would any sane man prefer
Power, with all a king's anxieties,
To that same power and the grace of sleep?
Certainly not I.
I have never longed for the king's power—only his rights.
Would any wise man differ from me in this?
As matters stand, I have my way in everything
With your consent, and no responsibilities.
If I were king, I should be a slave to policy.

How could I desire a scepter more
Than what is now mine—untroubled influence?
No, I have not gone mad; I need no honors,
Except those with the perquisites I have now.
I am welcome everywhere; every man salutes me,
And those who want your favor seek my ear,
Since I know how to manage what they ask.
Should I exchange this ease for that anxiety?
Besides, no sober mind is treasonable.
I hate anarchy
And never would deal with any man who likes it.
Test what I have said. Go to the priestess
At Delphi, ask if I quoted her correctly.
And as for this other thing: if I am found
Guilty of treason with Teiresias,
Then sentence me to death. You have my word

It is a sentence I should cast my vote for—
But not without evidence!
                              You do wrong
When you take good men for bad, bad men for good.
A true friend thrown aside—why, life itself
Is not more precious!
                              In time you will know this well:
For time, and time alone, will show the just man,
Though scoundrels are discovered in a day.

CHORAGOS   This is well said, and a prudent man would ponder it.
Judgments too quickly formed are dangerous.

OEDIPUS   But is he not quick in his duplicity?
And shall I not be quick to parry him?
Would you have me stand still, hold my peace, and let
This man win everything, through my inaction?

KREON   And you want—what is it, then? To banish me?

OEDIPUS   No, not exile. It is your death I want,
So that all the world may see what treason means.

KREON   You will persist, then? You will not believe me?

OEDIPUS   How can I believe you?

KREON   Then you are a fool.

OEDIPUS   To save myself?

KREON   In justice, think of me.

OEDIPUS   You are evil incarnate.

KREON   But suppose that you are wrong?

OEDIPUS   Still I must rule.

KREON   But not if you rule badly.

OEDIPUS   O city, city!

KREON   It is my city, too!

CHORAGOS   Now, my lords, be still. I see the queen,
Iokastê, coming from her palace chambers;
And it is time she came, for the sake of you both.
This dreadful quarrel can be resolved through her.

(*Enter* IOKASTÊ.)

IOKASTÊ   Poor foolish men, what wicked din is this?
With Thebes sick to death, is it not shameful
That you should rake some private quarrel up?
(*To* OEDIPUS) Come into the house.
                              —And you, Kreon, go now:
Let us have no more of this tumult over nothing.

KREON   Nothing? No, sister: what your husband plans for me
Is one of two great evils: exile or death.

OEDIPUS He is right.

Why, woman I have caught him squarely
Plotting against my life.

KREON   No! Let me die
Accurst if ever I have wished you harm!

IOKASTÊ Ah, believe it, Oedipus!
In the name of the gods, respect this oath of his
For my sake, for the sake of these people here!

Strophe 1

CHORAGOS Open your mind to her, my lord. Be ruled by her, I beg
you!

OEDIPUS What would you have me do?

CHORAGOS Respect Kreon's word. He has never spoken like a fool,
And now he has sworn an oath.

OEDIPUS You know what you ask?

CHORAGOS   I do.

OEDIPUS   Speak on, then.

CHORAGOS A friend so sworn should not be baited so,
In blind malice, and without final proof.

OEDIPUS You are aware, I hope, that what you say
Means death for me, or exile at the least.

Strophe 2

CHORAGOS No, I swear by Helios, first in Heaven!
May I die friendless and accurst,
The worst of deaths, if ever I meant that!
It is the withering fields
That hurt my sick heart:
Must we bear all these ills,
And now your bad blood as well?

OEDIPUS Then let him go. And let me die, if I must,
Or be driven by him in shame from the land of Thebes.
It is your unhappiness, and not his talk,
That touches me.

As for him—
Wherever he goes, hatred will follow him.

KREON Ugly in yielding, as you were ugly in rage!
Natures like yours chiefly torment themselves.

OEDIPUS Can you not go? Can you not leave me?

KREON   I can.
You do not know me; but the city knows me,
And in its eyes I am just, if not in yours.

(*Exit* KREON.)

Antistrophe 1

CHORAGOS   Lady Iokastê, did you not ask the King to go to
his chambers?
IOKASTÊ   First tell me what has happened.
CHORAGOS   There was suspicion without evidence; yet it rankled
As even false charges will.
IOKASTÊ   On both sides?
CHORAGOS   On both.
IOKASTÊ   But what was said?
CHORAGOS.   Oh let it rest, let it be done with!
Have we not suffered enough?
OEDIPUS   You see to what your decency has brought you:
You have made difficulties where my heart saw none.

Antistrophe 2

CHORAGOS   Oedipus, it is not once only I have told you—
You must know I should count myself unwise
To the point of madness, should I now forsake you—
                    You, under whose hand,
                          In the storm of another time,
                    Our dear land sailed out free.
                          But now stand fast at the helm!
IOKASTÊ   In God's name, Oedipus, inform your wife as well:
Why are you so set in this hard anger?
OEDIPUS   I will tell you, for none of these men deserves
My confidence as you do. It is Kreon's work,
His treachery, his plotting against me.
IOKASTÊ   Go on, if you can make this clear to me.
OEDIPUS   He charges me with the murder of Laïos.
IOKASTÊ   Has he some knowledge? Or does he speak from hearsay?
OEDIPUS   He would not commit himself to such a charge,
But he has brought in that damnable soothsayer
To tell his story.
IOKASTÊ   Set your mind at rest.
If it is a question of soothsayers, I tell you
That you will find no man whose craft gives knowledge
Of the unknowable.
                          Here is my proof:
An oracle was reported to Laïos once
(I will not say from Phoibos himself, but from
His appointed ministers, at any rate)

That his doom would be death at the hands of his own son—
His son, born of his flesh and of mine!

Now, you remember the story: Laïos was killed
By marauding strangers where three highways meet;
But his child had not been three days in this world
Before the king had pierced the baby's ankles
And left him to die on a lonely mountainside.

Thus, Apollo never caused that child
To kill his father, and it was not Laïos' fate
To die at the hands of his son, as he had feared.
This is what prophets and prophecies are worth!
Have no dread of them.

                    It is God himself
Who can show us what he wills, in his own way.

OEDIPUS   How strange a shadowy memory crossed my mind,
Just now while you were speaking; it chilled my heart.

IOKASTÊ   What do you mean? What memory do you speak of?

OEDIPUS   If I understand you, Laïos was killed
At a place where three roads meet.

IOKASTÊ   So it was said;
We have no later story.

OEDIPUS   Where did it happen?

IOKASTÊ   Phokis, it is called: at a place where the Theban Way
Divides into the roads toward Delphi and Daulia.

OEDIPUS   When?

IOKASTÊ   We had the news not long before you came
And proved the right to your succession here.

OEDIPUS   Ah, what net has God been weaving for me?

IOKASTÊ   Oedipus! Why does this trouble you?

OEDIPUS   Do not ask me yet.
First, tell me how Laïos looked, and tell me
How old he was.

IOKASTÊ   He was tall, his hair just touched
With white; his form was not unlike your own.

OEDIPUS   I think that I myself may be accurst
By my own ignorant edict.

IOKASTÊ   You speak strangely.
It makes me tremble to look at you, my king.

OEDIPUS   I am not sure that the blind man can not see.
But I should know better if you were to tell me—

IOKASTÊ   Anything—though I dread to hear you ask it.

OEDIPUS   Was the king lightly escorted, or did he ride
With a large company, as a ruler should?
IOKASTÊ   There were five men with him in all: one was a herald.
And a single chariot, which he was driving.
OEDIPUS   Alas, that makes it plain enough!

But who—
Who told you how it happened?
IOKASTÊ   A household servant,
The only one to escape.
OEDIPUS   And is he still
A servant of ours?
IOKASTÊ   No; for when he came back at last
And found you enthroned in the place of the dead king,
He came to me, touched my hand with his, and begged
That I would send him away to the frontier district
Where only the shepherds go—
As far away from the city as I could send him.
I granted his prayer; for although the man was a slave,
He had earned more than this favor at my hands.
OEDIPUS   Can he be called back quickly?
IOKASTÊ   Easily.
But why?
OEDIPUS   I have taken too much upon myself
Without enquiry; therefore I wish to consult him.
IOKASTÊ   Then he shall come.

But am I not one also
To whom you might confide these fears of yours?
OEDIPUS   That is your right; it will not be denied you,
Now least of all; for I have reached a pitch
Of wild foreboding. Is there anyone
To whom I should sooner speak?

Polybos of Corinth is my father.
My mother is a Dorian: Meropê.
I grew up chief among the men of Corinth
Until a strange thing happened—
Not worth my passion, it may be, but strange.
At a feast, a drunken man maundering in his cups
Cries out that I am not my father's son! [1]

---

[1] *not my father's son* Oedipus perhaps interprets this as an allegation that he is a bastard, the son of Meropê but not of Polybos. The implication, at any rate, is that he is not of royal birth, not the legitimate heir to the throne of Corinth.

I contained myself that night, though I felt anger
And a sinking heart. The next day I visited
My father and mother, and questioned them. They stormed,
Calling it all the slanderous rant of a fool;
And this relieved me. Yet the suspicion
Remained always aching in my mind;
I knew there was talk; I could not rest;
And finally, saying nothing to my parents,
I went to the shrine at Delphi.

The god dismissed my question without reply;
He spoke of other things.
                              Some were clear,
Full of wretchedness, dreadful, unbearable:
As, that I should lie with my own mother, breed
Children from whom all men would turn their eyes;
And that I should be my father's murderer.

I heard all this, and fled. And from that day
Corinth to me was only in the stars
Descending in that quarter of the sky,
As I wandered farther and farther on my way
To a land where I should never see the evil
Sung by the oracle. And I came to this country
Where, so you say, King Laïos was killed.

I will tell you all that happened there, my lady.

There were three highways
Coming together at a place I passed;
And there a herald came towards me, and a chariot
Drawn by horses, with a man such as you describe
Seated in it. The groom leading the horses
Forced me off the road at his lord's command;
But as this charioteer lurched over towards me
I struck him in my rage. The old man saw me
And brought his double goad down upon my head
As I came abreast.
                        He was paid back, and more!
Swinging my club in this right hand I knocked him
Out of his car, and he rolled on the ground.
                                    I killed him.

I killed them all.
Now if that stranger and Laïos were—kin,
Where is a man more miserable than I?
More hated by the gods? Citizen and alien alike

Must never shelter me or speak to me—
I must be shunned by all.
                              And I myself
Pronounced this malediction upon myself!

Think of it: I have touched you with these hands,
These hands that killed your husband. What defilement!

Am I all evil, then? It must be so,
Since I must flee from Thebes, yet never again
See my own countrymen, my own country,
For fear of joining my mother in marriage
And killing Polybos, my father.
                              Ah,
If I was created so, born to this fate,
Who could deny the savagery of God?

O holy majesty of heavenly powers!
May I never see that day! Never!
Rather let me vanish from the race of men
Than know the abomination destined me!

CHORAGOS   We too, my lord, have felt dismay at this.
    But there is hope: you have yet to hear the shepherd.

OEDIPUS   Indeed, I fear no other hope is left me.

IOKASTÊ   What do you hope from him when he comes?

OEDIPUS   This much:
    If his account of the murder tallies with yours,
    Then I am cleared.

IOKASTÊ   What was it that I said
    Of such importance?

OEDIPUS   Why, "marauders," you said,
    Killed the king, according to this man's story.
    If he maintains that still, if there were several,
    Clearly the guilt is not mine: I was alone.
    But if he says one man, singlehanded, did it,
    Then the evidence all points to me.

IOKASTÊ   You may be sure that he said there were several;
    And can he call back that story now? He can not.
    The whole city heard it as plainly as I.
    But suppose he alters some detail of it:
    He can not ever show that Laïos' death
    Fulfilled the oracle: for Apollo said
    My child was doomed to kill him; and my child—
    Poor baby!—it was my child that died first.

No. From now on, where oracles are concerned,
I would not waste a second thought on any.
OEDIPUS　You may be right.

But come: let someone go

For the shepherd at once. This matter must be settled.
IOKASTÊ　I will send for him.
I would not wish to cross you in anything,
And surely not in this.—Let us go in.

(Exeunt into the palace.)

ODE II

Strophe 1

CHORUS　Let me be reverent in the ways of right,
Lowly the paths I journey on;
Let all my words and actions keep
The laws of the pure universe
From highest Heaven handed down.
For Heaven is their bright nurse,
Those generations of the realms of light;
Ah, never of mortal kind were they begot,
Nor are they slaves of memory, lost in sleep:
Their Father is greater than Time, and ages not.

Antistrophe 1

The tyrant is a child of Pride
Who drinks from his great sickening cup
Recklessness and vanity,
Until from his high crest headlong
He plummets to the dust of hope.
That strong man is not strong.
But let no fair ambition be denied;
May God protect the wrestler for the State
In government, in comely policy,
Who will fear God, and on His ordinance wait.

Strophe 2

Haughtiness and the high hand of disdain
Tempt and outrage God's holy law;
And any mortal who dares hold
No immortal Power in awe
Will be caught up in a net of pain:

The price for which his levity is sold.
Let each man take due earnings, then,
And keep his hands from holy things,
And from blasphemy stand apart—
Else the crackling blast of heaven
Blows on his head, and on his desperate heart.
Though fools will honor impious men,
In their cities no tragic poet sings.

Antistrophe 2

Shall we lose faith in Delphi's obscurities,
We who have heard the world's core
Discredited, and the sacred wood
Of Zeus at Elis praised no more?
The deeds and the strange prophecies
Must make a pattern yet to be understood.
Zeus, if indeed you are lord of all,
Throned in light over night and day,
Mirror this in your endless mind:
Our masters call the oracle
Words on the wind, and the Delphic vision blind!
Their hearts no longer know Apollo,
And reverence for the gods has died away.

SCENE III

Enter IOKASTÊ.

IOKASTÊ   Princes of Thebes, it has occurred to me
To visit the altars of the gods, bearing
These branches as a suppliant, and this incense.
Our king is not himself: his noble soul
Is overwrought with fantasies of dread,
Else he would consider
The new prophecies in the light of the old.
He will listen to any voice that speaks disaster,
And my advice goes for nothing.

(*She approaches the altar, R.*)

                            To you, then, Apollo,
Lycéan lord, since you are nearest, I turn in prayer.
Receive these offerings, and grant us deliverance
From defilement. Our hearts are heavy with fear

When we see our leader distracted, as helpless sailors
Are terrified by the confusion of their helmsman.

(*Enter* MESSENGER.)

MESSENGER   Friends, no doubt you can direct me:
Where shall I find the house of Oedipus,
Or, better still, where is the king himself?
CHORAGOS   It is this very place, stranger; he is inside.
This is his wife and mother of his children.
MESSENGER   I wish her happiness in a happy house,
Blest in all the fulfillment of her marriage.
IOKASTÊ   I wish as much for you: your courtesy
Deserves a like good fortune. But now, tell me:
Why have you come? What have you to say to us?
MESSENGER   Good news, my lady, for your house and your husband.
IOKASTÊ   What news? Who sent you here?
MESSENGER   I am from Corinth.
The news I bring ought to mean joy for you,
Though it may be you will find some grief in it.
IOKASTÊ   What is it? How can it touch us in both ways?
MESSENGER   The word is that the people of the Isthmus
Intend to call Oedipus to be their king.
IOKASTÊ   But old King Polybos—is he not reigning still?
MESSENGER   No. Death holds him in his sepulchre.
IOKASTÊ   What are you saying? Polybos is dead?
MESSENGER   If I am not telling the truth, may I die myself.
IOKASTÊ (*to a* MAIDSERVANT)   Go in, go quickly; tell this to
your master.

O riddlers of God's will, where are you now!
This was the man whom Oedipus, long ago,
Feared so, fled so, in dread of destroying him—
But it was another fate by which he died.

(*Enter* OEDIPUS, *C.*)

OEDIPUS   Dearest Iokastê, why have you sent for me?
IOKASTÊ   Listen to what this man says, and then tell me
What has become of the solemn prophecies.
OEDIPUS   Who is this man? What is his news for me?
IOKASTÊ   He has come from Corinth to announce your
father's death!
OEDIPUS   Is it true, stranger? Tell me in your own words.
MESSENGER   I can not say it more clearly: the king is dead.

OEDIPUS   Was it by treason? Or by an attack of illness?

MESSENGER   A little thing brings old men to their rest.

OEDIPUS   It was sickness, then?

MESSENGER   Yes, and his many years.

OEDIPUS   Ah!

Why should a man respect the Pythian hearth,[1] or
Give heed to the birds that jangle above his head?
They prophesied that I should kill Polybos,
Kill my own father; but he is dead and buried,
And I am here—I never touched him, never,
Unless he died of grief for my departure,
And thus, in a sense, through me. No. Polybos
Has packed the oracles off with him underground.
They are empty words.

IOKASTÊ   Had I not told you so?

OEDIPUS   You had; it was my faint heart that betrayed me.

IOKASTÊ   From now on never think of those things again.

OEDIPUS   And yet—must I not fear my mother's bed?

IOKASTÊ   Why should anyone in this world be afraid,
Since Fate rules us and nothing can be foreseen?
A man should live only for the present day.

Have no more fear of sleeping with your mother:
How many men, in dreams, have lain with their mothers!
No reasonable man is troubled by such things.

OEDIPUS   That is true; only—
If only my mother were not still alive!
But she is alive. I can not help my dread.

IOKASTÊ   Yet this news of your father's death is wonderful.

OEDIPUS   Wonderful. But I fear the living woman.

MESSENGER   Tell me, who is this woman that you fear?

OEDIPUS   It is Meropê, man; the wife of King Polybos.

MESSENGER   Meropê? Why should you be afraid of her?

OEDIPUS   An oracle of the gods, a dreadful saying.

MESSENGER   Can you tell me about it or are you sworn to silence?

OEDIPUS   I can tell you, and I will.
Apollo said through his prophet that I was the man
Who should marry his own mother, shed his father's blood
With his own hands. And so, for all these years
I have kept clear of Corinth, and no harm has come—
Though it would have been sweet to see my parents again.

---

[1] *Pythian hearth* Delphi

MESSENGER   And is this the fear that drove you out of Corinth?

OEDIPUS   Would you have me kill my father?

MESSENGER   As for that
You must be reassured by the news I gave you.

OEDIPUS   If you could reassure me, I would reward you.

MESSENGER   I had that in mind, I will confess: I thought
I could count on you when you returned to Corinth.

OEDIPUS   No: I will never go near my parents again.

MESSENGER   Ah, son, you still do not know what you are doing—

OEDIPUS   What do you mean? In the name of God tell me!

MESSENGER   —if these are your reasons for not going home.

OEDIPUS   I tell you, I fear the oracle may come true. ·

MESSENGER   And guilt may come upon you through your parents?

OEDIPUS   That is the dread that is always in my heart.

MESSENGER   Can you not see that all your fears are groundless?

OEDIPUS   Groundless? Am I not my parents' son?

MESSENGER   Polybos was not your father.

OEDIPUS   Not my father?

MESSENGER   No more your father than the man speaking to you.

OEDIPUS   But you are nothing to me!

MESSENGER   Neither was he.

OEDIPUS   Then why did he call me son?

MESSENGER   I will tell you:
Long ago he had you from my hands, as a gift.

OEDIPUS   Then how could he love me so, if I was not his?

MESSENGER   He had no children, and his heart turned to you.

OEDIPUS   What of you? Did you buy me? Did you find me by
chance?

MESSENGER   I came upon you in the woody vales of Kithairon.

OEDIPUS   And what were you doing there?

MESSENGER   Tending my flocks.

OEDIPUS   A wandering shepherd?

MESSENGER   But your savior, son, that day.

OEDIPUS   From what did you save me?

MESSENGER   Your ankles should tell you that.

OEDIPUS   Ah, stranger, why do you speak of that childhood pain?

MESSENGER   I pulled the skewer that pinned your feet together.

OEDIPUS   I have had the mark as long as I can remember.

MESSENGER   That was why you were given the name you bear.

OEDIPUS   God! Was it my father or my mother who did it?
Tell me!

MESSENGER   I do not know. The man who gave you to me
Can tell you better than I.

OEDIPUS   It was not you that found me, but another?

MESSENGER   It was another shepherd gave you to me.

OEDIPUS   Who was he? Can you tell me who he was?

MESSENGER   I think he was said to be one of Laïos' people.

OEDIPUS   You mean the Laïos who was king here years ago?

MESSENGER   Yes; King Laïos; and the man was one of his
    herdsmen.

OEDIPUS   Is he still alive? Can I see him?

MESSENGER   These men here
    Know best about such things.

OEDIPUS   Does anyone here
    Know this shepherd that he is talking about?
    Have you seen him in the fields, or in the town?
    If you have, tell me. It is time things were made plain.

CHORAGOS   I think the man he means is that same shepherd
    You have already asked to see. Iokastê perhaps
    Could tell you something.

OEDIPUS   Do you know anything
    About him, Lady? Is he the man we have summoned?
    Is that the man this shepherd means?

IOKASTÊ   Why think of him?
    Forget this herdsman. Forget it all.
    This talk is a waste of time.

OEDIPUS   How can you say that,
    When the clues to my true birth are in my hands?

IOKASTÊ   For God's love, let us have no more questioning!
    Is your life nothing to you?
    My own is pain enough for me to bear.

OEDIPUS   You need not worry. Suppose my mother a slave,
    And born of slaves: no baseness can touch you.

IOKASTÊ   Listen to me, I beg you: do not do this thing!

OEDIPUS   I will not listen; the truth must be made known.

IOKASTÊ   Everything that I say is for your own good!

OEDIPUS   My own good
    Snaps my patience, then! I want none of it.

IOKASTÊ   You are fatally wrong! May you never learn who you are!

OEDIPUS   Go, one of you, and bring the shepherd here.
    Let us leave this woman to brag of her royal name.

IOKASTÊ   Ah, miserable!
    That is the only word I have for you now.
    That is the only word I can ever have.

   (*Exit into the palace.*)

CHORAGOS   Why has she left us, Oedipus? Why has she gone

In such a passion of sorrow? I fear this silence:
Something dreadful may come of it.
OEDIPUS   Let it come!
   However base my birth, I must know about it.
   The Queen, like a woman, is perhaps ashamed
   To think of my low origin. But I
   Am a child of Luck; I can not be dishonered.
   Luck is my mother; the passing months, my brothers,
   Have seen me rich and poor.
                   If this is so,
   How could I wish that I were someone else?
   How could I not be glad to know my birth?

ODE III

Strophe

CHORUS   If ever the coming time were known
   To my heart's pondering,
   Kithairon, now by Heaven I see the torches
   At the festival of the next full moon,
   And see the dance, and hear the choir sing
   A grace to your gentle shade:
   Mountain where Oedipus was found,
   O mountain guard of a noble race!
   May the god [1] who heals us lend his aid,
   And let that glory come to pass
   For our king's cradling-ground.

Antistrophe

   Of the nymphs that flower beyond the years,
   Who bore you,[2] royal child,
   To Pan of the hills or the timberline Apollo,
   Cold in delight where the upland clears,
   Or Hermês for whom Kyllenê's heights are piled?
   Or flushed as evening cloud,
   Great Dionysos, roamer of mountains,
   He—was it he who found you there,

---

[1] *god* Apollo

[2] *Who bore you* The chorus is suggesting that perhaps Oedipus is the son of one of the immortal nymphs and of a god—Pan, Apollo, Hermes, or Dionysos. The "sweet god-ravisher" (below) is the presumed mother.

And caught you up in his own proud
Arms from the sweet god-ravisher
Who laughed by the Muses' fountains?

SCENE IV

OEDIPUS   Sirs: though I do not know the man,
I think I see him coming, this shepherd we want:
He is old, like our friend here, and the men
Bringing him seem to be servants of my house.
But you can tell, if you have ever seen him.

(*Enter* SHEPHERD *escorted by* SERVANTS.)

CHORAGOS   I know him, he was Laïos' man. You can trust him.
OEDIPUS   Tell me first, you from Corinth: is this the shepherd
We were discussing?
MESSENGER   This is the very man.
OEDIPUS (*to* SHEPHERD)   Come here. No, look at me. You
must answer
Everything I ask.—You belonged to Laïos?
SHEPHERD   Yes: born his slave, brought up in his house.
OEDIPUS   Tell me: what kind of work did you do for him?
SHEPHERD   I was a shepherd of his, most of my life.
OEDIPUS   Where mainly did you go for pasturage?
SHEPHERD   Sometimes Kithairon, sometimes the hills near-by.
OEDIPUS   Do you remember ever seeing this man out there?
SHEPHERD   What would he be doing there? This man?
OEDIPUS   This man standing here. Have you ever seen him before?
SHEPHERD   No. At least, not to my recollection.
MESSENGER   And that is not strange, my lord. But I'll refresh
His memory: he must remember when we two
Spent three whole seasons together, March to September,
On Kithairon or thereabouts. He had two flocks;
I had one. Each autumn I'd drive mine home
And he would go back with his to Laïos' sheepfold.—
Is this not true, just as I have described it?
SHEPHERD   True, yes; but it was all so long ago.
MESSENGER   Well, then: do you remember, back in those days,
That you gave me a baby boy to bring up as my own?
SHEPHERD   What if I did? What are you trying to say?
MESSENGER   King Oedipus was once that little child.
SHEPHERD   Damn you, hold your tongue!
OEDIPUS   No more of that!
It is your tongue needs watching, not this man's.

SHEPHERD   My king, my master, what is it I have done wrong?

OEDIPUS   You have not answered his question about the boy.

SHEPHERD   He does not know . . . He is only making trouble . . .

OEDIPUS   Come, speak plainly, or it will go hard with you.

SHEPHERD   In God's name, do not torture an old man!

OEDIPUS   Come here, one of you; bind his arms behind him.

SHEPHERD   Unhappy king! What more do you wish to learn?

OEDIPUS   Did you give this man the child he speaks of?

SHEPHERD   I did.
   And I would to God I had died that very day.

OEDIPUS   You will die now unless you speak the truth.

SHEPHERD   Yet if I speak the truth, I am worse than dead.

OEDIPUS (*to* ATTENDANT)   He intends to draw it out, apparently—

SHEPHERD   No! I have told you already that I gave him the boy.

OEDIPUS   Where did you get him? From your house? From
     somewhere else?

SHEPHERD   Not from mine, no. A man gave him to me.

OEDIPUS   Is that man here? Whose house did he belong to?

SHEPHERD   For God's love, my king, do not ask me any more!

OEDIPUS   You are a dead man if I have to ask you again.

SHEPHERD   Then . . . Then the child was from the palace of Laïos.

OEDIPUS   A slave child? or a child of his own line?

SHEPHERD   Ah, I am on the brink of dreadful speech!

OEDIPUS   And I of dreadful hearing. Yet I must hear.

SHEPHERD   If you must be told, then . . .
                        They said it was Laïos' child;
   But it is your wife who can tell you about that.

OEDIPUS   My wife!—Did she give it to you?

SHEPHERD   My lord, she did.

OEDIPUS   Do you know why?

SHEPHERD   I was told to get rid of it.

OEDIPUS   Oh heartless mother!

SHEPHERD   But in dread of prophecies . . .

OEDIPUS   Tell me.

SHEPHERD   It was said that the boy would kill his own father.

OEDIPUS   Then why did you give him over to this old man?

SHEPHERD   I pitied the baby, my king,
   And I thought that this man would take him far away
   To his own country.
              He saved him—but for what a fate!
   For if you are what this man says you are,
   No man living is more wretched than Oedipus.

OEDIPUS   Ah God!
   It was true!

All the prophecies!
            —Now,
O Light, may I look on you for the last time!
I, Oedipus,
Oedipus, damned in his birth, in his marriage damned,
Damned in the blood he shed with his own hand!

(*He rushes into the palace.*)

ODE IV

Strophe 1

CHORUS   Alas for the seed of men.
    What measure shall I give these generations
    That breathe on the void and are void
    And exist and do not exist?
    Who bears more weight of joy
    Than mass of sunlight shifting in images,
    Or who shall make his thought stay on
    That down time drifts away?
    Your splendor is all fallen.
    O naked brow of wrath and tears,
    O change of Oedipus!
    I who saw your days call no man blest—
    Your great days like ghosts gone.

Antistrophe 1

    That mind was a strong bow.
    Deep, how deep you drew it then, hard archer,
    At a dim fearful range,
    And brought dear glory down!
    You overcame the stranger[1]—
    The virgin with her hooking lion claws—
    And though death sang, stood like a tower
    To make pale Thebes take heart.
    Fortress against our sorrow!
    True king, giver of laws,
    Majestic Oedipus!
    No prince in Thebes had ever such renown,
    No prince won such grace of power.

---

[1] *stranger* the Sphinx

Strophe 2

And now of all men ever known
Most pitiful is this man's story:
His fortunes are most changed, his state
Fallen to a low slave's
Ground under bitter fate.
O Oedipus, most royal one!
The great door[1] that expelled you to the light
Gave at night—ah, gave night to your glory:
As to the father, to the fathering son.
All understood too late.
How could that queen whom Laïos won,
The garden that he harrowed at his height,
Be silent when that act was done?

Antistrophe 2

But all eyes fail before time's eye,
All actions come to justice there.
Though never willed, though far down the deep past,
Your bed, your dread sirings,
Are brought to book at last.
Child by Laïos doomed to die,
Then doomed to lose that fortunate little death,
Would God you never took breath in this air
That with my wailing lips I take to cry:
For I weep the world's outcast.
I was blind, and now I can tell why:
Asleep, for you had given ease of breath
To Thebes, while the false years went by.

EXODOS [2]

Enter, from the palace, SECOND MESSENGER.

SECOND MESSENGER   Elders of Thebes, most honored in this land,
What horrors are yours to see and hear, what weight
Of sorrow to be endured, if, true to your birth,
You venerate the line of Labdakos!
I think neither Istros nor Phasis, those great rivers,
Could purify this place of all the evil

---

[1] *door* Iokastê's womb
[2] *Exodos* final scene

It shelters now, or soon must bring to light—
Evil not done unconsciously, but willed.

The greatest griefs are those we cause ourselves.
CHORAGOS   Surely, friend, we have grief enough already;
What new sorrow do you mean?
SECOND MESSENGER   The queen is dead.
CHORAGOS   O miserable queen! But at whose hand?
SECOND MESSENGER   Her own.
The full horror of what happened you can not know,
For you did not see it; but I, who did, will tell you
As clearly as I can how she met her death.

When she had left us,
In passionate silence, passing through the court,
She ran to her apartment in the house,
Her hair clutched by the fingers of both hands.
She closed the doors behind her; then, by that bed
Where long ago the fatal son was conceived—
That son who should bring about his father's death—
We heard her call upon Laïos, dead so many years,
And heard her wail for the double fruit of her marriage,
A husband by her husband, children by her child.

Exactly how she died I do not know:
For Oedipus burst in moaning and would not let us
Keep vigil to the end: it was by him
As he stormed about the room that our eyes were caught.
From one to another of us he went, begging a sword,
Hunting the wife who was not his wife, the mother
Whose womb had carried his own children and himself.
I do not know: it was none of us aided him,
But surely one of the gods was in control!
For with a dreadful cry
He hurled his weight, as though wrenched out of himself,
At the twin doors: the bolts gave, and he rushed in.
And there we saw her hanging, her body swaying
From the cruel cord she had noosed about her neck.
A great sob broke from him, heartbreaking to hear,
As he loosed the rope and lowered her to the ground.

I would blot out from my mind what happened next!
For the king ripped from her gown the golden brooches
That were her ornament, and raised them, and plunged
   them down

Straight into his own eyeballs, crying, "No more,
No more shall you look on the misery about me,
The horrors of my own doing! Too long you have known
The faces of those whom I should never have seen,
Too long been blind to those for whom I was searching!
From this hour, go in darkness!" And as he spoke,
He struck at his eyes—not once, but many times;
And the blood spattered his beard,
Bursting from his ruined sockets like red hail.

So from the unhappiness of two this evil has sprung,
A curse on the man and woman alike. The old
Happiness of the house of Labdakos
Was happiness enough: where is it today?
It is all wailing and ruin, disgrace, death—all
The misery of mankind that has a name—
And it is wholly and for ever theirs.

CHORAGOS   Is he in agony still? Is there no rest for him?
SECOND MESSENGER   He is calling for someone to open the
    doors wide
So that all the children of Kadmos may look upon
His father's murderer, his mother's—no,
I can not say it!
                    And then he will leave Thebes,
Self-exiled, in order that the curse
Which he himself pronounced may depart from the house.
He is weak, and there is none to lead him,
So terrible is his suffering.
                    But you will see:
Look, the doors are opening; in a moment
You will see a thing that would crush a heart of stone.

(*The central door is opened;* OEDIPUS, *blinded, is led in.*)

CHORAGOS   Dreadful indeed for men to see.
    Never have my own eyes
    Looked on a sight so full of fear.

Oedipus!
What madness came upon you, what daemon
Leaped on your life with heavier
Punishment than a mortal man can bear?
No: I can not even
Look at you, poor ruined one.
And I would speak, question, ponder,

If I were able. No.
You make me shudder.
OEDIPUS   God. God.
Is there a sorrow greater?
Where shall I find harbor in this world?
My voice is hurled far on a dark wind.
What has God done to me?
CHORAGOS   Too terrible to think of, or to see.

Strophe 1

OEDIPUS   O cloud of night,
Never to be turned away: night coming on,
I can not tell how: night like a shroud!
My fair winds brought me here.
                                    O God. Again
The pain of the spikes where I had sight,
The flooding pain
Of memory, never to be gouged out.
CHORAGOS   This is not strange.
You suffer it all twice over, remorse in pain,
Pain in remorse.

Antistrophe 1

OEDIPUS   Ah dear friend
Are you faithful even yet, you alone?
Are you still standing near me, will you stay here,
Patient, to care for the blind?
                                    The blind man!
Yet even blind I know who it is attends me,
By the voice's tone—
Though my new darkness hide the comforter.
CHORAGOS   Oh fearful act!
What god was it drove you to rake black
Night across your eyes?

Strophe 2

OEDIPUS   Apollo. Apollo. Dear
Children, the god was Apollo.
He brought my sick, sick fate upon me.
But the blinding hand was my own!
How could I bear to see
When all my sight was horror everywhere?
CHORAGOS   Everywhere; that is true.

OEDIPUS   And now what is left?
  Images? Love? A greeting even,
  Sweet to the senses? Is there anything?
  Ah, no, friends: lead me away.
  Lead me away from Thebes.
                    Lead the great wreck
  And hell of Oedipus, whom the gods hate.
CHORAGOS   Your misery, you are not blind to that.
  Would God you had never found it out!

Antistrophe 2

OEDIPUS   Death take the man who unbound
  My feet on that hillside
  And delivered me from death to life! What life?
  If only I had died,
  This weight of monstrous doom
  Could not have dragged me and my darlings down.
CHORAGOS   I would have wished the same.
OEDIPUS   Oh never to have come here
  With my father's blood upon me! Never
  To have been the man they call his mother's husband!
  Oh accurst! Oh child of evil,
  To have entered that wretched bed—
                    the selfsame one!
  More primal than sin itself, this fell to me.
CHORAGOS   I do not know what words to offer you.
  You were better dead than alive and blind.

OEDIPUS   Do not counsel me any more. This punishment
  That I have laid upon myself is just.
  If I had eyes,
  I do not know how I could bear the sight
  Of my father, when I came to the house of Death,
  Or my mother: for I have sinned against them both
  So vilely that I could not make my peace
  By strangling my own life.
                    Or do you think my children,
  Born as they were born, would be sweet to my eyes?
  Ah never, never! Nor this town with its high walls,
  Nor the holy images of the gods.
                    For I,
  Thrice miserable!—Oedipus, noblest of all the line
  Of Kadmos, have condemned myself to enjoy

These things no more, by my own malediction
Expelling that man whom the gods declared
To be a defilement in the house of Laïos.
After exposing the rankness of my own guilt,
How could I look men frankly in the eyes?
No, I swear it,
If I could have stifled my hearing at its source,
I would have done it and made all this body
A tight cell of misery, blank to light and sound:
So I should have been safe in my dark mind
Beyond external evil.
                              Ah Kithairon!
Why did you shelter me? When I was cast upon you,
Why did I not die? Then I should never
Have shown the world my execrable birth.

Ah Polybos! Corinth, city that I believed
The ancient seat of my ancestors: how fair
I seemed, your child! And all the while this evil
Was cancerous within me!
                              For I am sick
In my own being, sick in my origin.

O three roads, dark ravine, woodland and way
Where three roads met: you, drinking my father's blood,
My own blood, spilled by my own hand: can you remember
The unspeakable things I did there, and the things
I went on from there to do?
                              O marriage, marriage!
That act that engendered me, and again the act
Performed by the son in the same bed—
                              Ah, the net
Of incest, mingling fathers, brothers, sons,
With brides, wives, mothers: the last evil
That can be known by men: no tongue can say
How evil!
                    No. For the love of God, conceal me
Somewhere far from Thebes; or kill me; or hurl me
Into the sea, away from men's eyes for ever.

Come, lead me. You need not fear to touch me.
Of all men, I alone can bear this guilt.

(*Enter* KREON.)

CHORAGOS   Kreon is here now. As to what you ask,
   He may decide the course to take. He only
   Is left to protect the city in your place.
OEDIPUS   Alas, how can I speak to him? What right have I
   To beg his courtesy whom I have deeply wronged?
KREON   I have not come to mock you, Oedipus,
   Or to reproach you, either. (*To* ATTENDANTS)
                                    —You, standing there:
   If you have lost all respect for man's dignity,
   At least respect the flame of Lord Helios:
   Do not allow this pollution to show itself
   Openly here, an affront to the earth
   And Heaven's rain and the light of day. No, take him
   Into the house as quickly as you can.
   For it is proper
   That only the close kindred see his grief.
OEDIPUS   I pray you in God's name, since your courtesy
   Ignores my dark expectation, visiting
   With mercy this man of all men most execrable:
   Give me what I ask—for your good, not for mine.
KREON   And what is it that you turn to me begging for?
OEDIPUS   Drive me out of this country as quickly as may be
   To a place where no human voice can ever greet me.
KREON   I should have done that before now—only,
   God's will had not been wholly revealed to me.
OEDIPUS   But his command is plain: the parricide
   Must be destroyed. I am that evil man.
KREON   That is the sense of it, yes; but as things are,
   We had best discover clearly what is to be done.
OEDIPUS   You would learn more about a man like me?
KREON   You are ready now to listen to the god.
OEDIPUS   I will listen. But it is to you
   That I must turn for help. I beg you, hear me.

   The woman in there—
   Give her whatever funeral you think proper:
   She is your sister.
                —But let me go, Kreon!
   Let me purge my father's Thebes of the pollution
   Of my living here, and go out to the wild hills,
   To Kithairon, that has won such fame with me,
   The tomb my mother and father appointed for me,
   And let me die there, as they willed I should.

And yet I know
Death will not ever come to me through sickness
Or in any natural way: I have been preserved
For some unthinkable fate. But let that be.

As for my sons, you need not care for them.
They are men, they will find some way to live.
But my poor daughters, who have shared my table,
Who never before have been parted from their father—
Take care of them, Kreon; do this for me.

And will you let me touch them with my hands
A last time, and let us weep together?
Be kind, my lord,
Great prince, be kind!
                              Could I but touch them,
They would be mine again, as when I had my eyes.

(*Enter* ANTIGONE *and* ISMENE, *attended.*)

Ah, God!
Is it my dearest children I hear weeping?
Has Kreon pitied me and sent my daughters?
KREON   Yes, Oedipus: I knew that they were dear to you
In the old days, and know you must love them still.
OEDIPUS   May God bless you for this—and be a friendlier
Guardian to you than he has been to me!

Children, where are you?
Come quickly to my hands: they are your brother's—
Hands that have brought your father's once clear eyes
To this way of seeing—
                              Ah dearest ones,
I had neither sight nor knowledge then, your father
By the woman who was the source of his own life!
And I weep for you—having no strength to see you—,
I weep for you when I think of the bitterness
That men will visit upon you all your lives.
What homes, what festivals can you attend
Without being forced to depart again in tears?
And when you come to marriageable age,
Where is the man, my daughters, who would dare
Risk the bane that lies on all my children?
Is there any evil wanting? Your father killed
His father; sowed the womb of her who bore him;
Engendered you at the fount of his own existence!

That is what they will say of you.
Then, whom
Can you ever marry? There are no bridegrooms for you,
And your lives must wither away in sterile dreaming.

O Kreon, son of Menoikeus!
You are the only father my daughters have,
Since we, their parents, are both of us gone for ever.
They are your own blood: you will not let them
Fall into beggary and loneliness;
You will keep them from the miseries that are mine!
Take pity on them; see, they are only children,
Friendless except for you. Promise me this,
Great prince, and give me your hand in token of it.

(KREON *clasps his right hand.*)

Children:
I could say much, if you could understand me,
But as it is, I have only this prayer for you:
Live where you can, be as happy as you can—
Happier, please God, than God has made your father.

KREON　Enough. You have wept enough. Now go within.
OEDIPUS　I must; but it is hard.
KREON　　　　　　　　Time eases all things.
OEDIPUS　You know my mind, then?
KREON　　　　　　　　Say what you desire.
OEDIPUS　Send me from Thebes!
KREON　　　　　　　　God grant that I may!
OEDIPUS　But since God hates me . . .
KREON　　　　　　　　No, he will grant your wish.
OEDIPUS　You promise?
KREON　　　　　　I can not speak beyond my knowledge.
OEDIPUS　Then lead me in.
KREON　　　　　　Come now, and leave your children.
OEDIPUS　No! Do not take them from me!
KREON　　　　　　　　Think no longer
That you are in command here, but rather think
How, when you were, you served your own destruction.

(*Exeunt into the house all but the* CHORUS; *the* CHORAGOS *chants directly to the audience.*)

CHORAGOS　Men of Thebes: look upon Oedipus.

This is the king who solved the famous riddle
And towered up, most powerful of men.

No mortal eyes but looked on him with envy,
Yet in the end ruin swept over him.

Let every man in mankind's frailty
Consider his last day; and let none
Presume on his good fortune until he find
Life, at his death, a memory without pain.

QUESTIONS

According to Aristotle, tragedies such as *Oedipus Rex* succeed by arousing pity and fear in their audience—pity for the suffering the plays' heroes endure, fear that we might sometime face similar agonies. How does *Oedipus Rex* call forth these feelings? In thinking out your answer, you might want to consider:

1. What sort of person do you think Oedipus is? What are his strengths and weaknesses? How is he different from other characters in the play?
2. What sorts of tensions are built up (for Oedipus, for the other characters, and for the audience) by the gradual unfolding of the truth about Laïos' murder and Oedipus' history?
3. How does your knowledge of the story of Oedipus, and hence your knowledge of how the play will end, affect your reaction to such scenes as those with Tiresias and the shepherds?
4. How are the images of sight and blindness used throughout the play?

ANONYMOUS

The Second Shepherds' Play

A modernized version by John Gassner

CHARACTERS

FIRST SHEPHERD, *Coll*
SECOND SHEPHERD, *Gib*
THIRD SHEPHERD, *Daw*
MAK
MAK'S WIFE, *Gill*
AN ANGEL
THE VIRGIN MARY
THE INFANT CHRIST

One unchanged setting, consisting of two huts—one representing MAK'S *cottage and the other the manger or stable of the Nativity. The space between the two huts represents the moors or fields. The action occurs in Palestine, but only in name; actually the local color of the play is drawn from the countryside of Wakefield, England.*
The action is continuous; although scene divisions have been added to the original text, there is no need to drop curtains to indicate a lapse of time.

SCENE I

The moors.

1ST SHEPHERD   Lord, but these weathers are cold, and I am ill-
wrapped!
  Nearly numb of hand, so long have I napped;
  My legs, they fold; my fingers are chapped.
  It is not as I would, for I am all lapped
        In sorrow.
  In storms and tempest,
  Now in the east, now in the west,

Woe is him has never rest,
     Mid-day or morrow!

But we poor shepherds that walk on the moor,
In faith, we are near-hands out of the door.
No wonder, as it stands, if we be poor,
For the tilth of our lands lies as fallow as a floor,
     As ye ken.[1]
We are so lamed,
Overtaxed and blamed,[2]
We are made hand-tamed
     By these gentlery-men.

Thus they rob us of our rest, Our Lady them harry!
These men that are tied fast, their plough must tarry.
What men say is for the best, we find it contrary!
Thus are farming-men oppressed, in point to miscarry
     Alive:
Thus the lords hold us under,
Thus they bring us in blunder—
It were great wonder,
     If ever we should thrive.

Let man but get a painted sleeve or brooch nowadays,
Woe to one that grieves him or once gainsays;
No man dare reprove him that mastery has,
And yet may no man believe one word that he says—
     No letter!
He can make purveyance
With boast and braggance,
And all is through maintenance
     By men that are better.

There shall come a swain as proud as a po;[3]
And he must borrow my wain, my plow also
That I am full glad to grant before he go:
Thus live we in pain, anger, and woe,
     By night and day.
He must have if he wants it
Though I must do without it;
I were better off hanged
     Than once say him Nay!

---

1 *ken* know
2 *blamed* literally "crushed"
3 *po* peacock

It does me good as I walk thus by my own
Of this world for to talk in manner of moan.
To my sheep I will stalk and listen anon,
There abide on a ridge or sit on a stone
        Full soon.
For I think, pardie!
True men if they be,
We shall get more company
        Ere it be noon.

(*A* Second Shepherd *appears on the moor, without at first noticing the* First Shepherd, *so absorbed is he in his own thoughts*)

2ND SHEPHERD   *Benedicite*[1] and *Dominus!* what may this mean?
Why fares this world thus? Oft have we not seen:
Lord, these weathers are spiteful, and the winds are keen,
And the frosts so hideous they water my een:[2]
        No lie it be!
Now in dry, now in wet,
Now in snow, now in sleet,
When my shoes freeze to my feet,
        It is not at all easy.

But as far as I know, or yet as I go,
We poor wed men suffer much, we do;
We have sorrow then and then, it falls often so.
Poor Cappel, our hen, both to and fro
        She cackles,
But begin she to rock,
To groan or to cluck,
Woe is to him, our cock,
        For he is then in shackles!

These men that are wed have not all their will;
When they are set upon, they sigh full still.
God knows they are led full hard and full ill,
In bower or in bed they have their fill
        Beside.
My part have I found,
Know my lesson sound:
Woe is him that is bound,
        For he must abide.

---

[1] *Benedicite* he pronounces this, by contraction of the Latin for "Bless you," as "Bencité"
[2] *een* eyes

But now late in our lives—marvel to me!
That I think my heart breaks such wonder to see:
That, as destiny drives, it should so be
That some men will have two wives, and some have three
    In store.
To some is woe that have any,
But so far as I see, I tell ye,
Woe is him that has many,
      For he feels sore.

(*Addressing the audience*)

But young men awooing, by God that you bought,
Beware of a wedding and mind in your thought
"Had I known" is a thing that serves you nought.
So much still mourning has wedding home brought
    And grief,
With many a sharp shower;
For ye may catch in an hour
What shall savor full sour
    As long as you live.

For, as ever read I scripture, I have *her* I keep near:
As sharp as a thistle, as rough as a briar;
She is browed like a bristle with sour-looking cheer.
Had she once wet her whistle, she could sing full clear
    Her Pater-Noster.
She is as great as a whale,
She has a gallon of gall;
By Him that died for us all,
    I would I had run till I lost her!

(*By now he has been observed by the* FIRST SHEPHERD, *who rouses him from his meditations roughly*)

1ST SHEPHERD   God look over the row, you there, that deafly stand!
2ND SHEPHERD (*Startled*)   Yea, the devil in thy maw!
  —In tarrying, friend,
  Saw you Daw about?
1ST SHEPHERD   Yes, on fallow land
  I heard him blow. He comes here at hand
    Not far.
  Stand still!
2ND SHEPHERD   Why?
1ST SHEPHERD   For he comes on, hope I.

1ST SHEPHERD   He will din us both a lie
         Unless we beware.

(*A* THIRD SHEPHERD, *a boy called* DAW, *employed by the* FIRST SHEP-
HERD, *appears. The weather has put him out of humor*)

3RD SHEPHERD   Christ's cross me speed, and Saint Nicholas!
    Thereof had I need: it is worse than it was!
    Whoso could, take heed! and let the world pass;
    It is ever in dread and brittle as glass,
         And slides.
    This world fared never so,
    With marvels more and more,
    Now in weal, now in woe;
         And everything rides!

    Was never since Noah's flood such floods seen,
    Winds and rains so rude, and storms so keen;
    Some stammered, some stood in doubt, as I ween.
    Now God turn all to good! I say as I mean
         And ponder.
    These floods, so they drown
    Both fields and town
    And bear all down—
         That it is a wonder.

    We that walk in the nights our cattle to keep,
    We see sudden sights when other men sleep—

(*Noticing that he is being observed by the other* SHEPHERDS)

    But methinks my heart lightens, I see them peep.
    Yea, you tall fellows!—I think I'll give my sheep
         A turn.

(*He is about to turn away, but changes his mind*)

    But this is ill intent,
    For as I walk on this bent
    I may lightly repent
         And stub my toes.

(*Pretending to have just seen them*)

    Ah, sir, God you save, and you, master mine!

(*Coming up to them*)

    A drink fain would I have and somewhat to dine.

1ST SHEPHERD   Christ's curse, my knave, thou art a lazy swine!
2ND SHEPHERD   What, the boy pleases to rave? You'll wait on line
     When we have made it.
I'll drum on thy pate!
Though the knave comes late,
Yet is he in state
     To dine, if he had it.

3RD SHEPHERD (*Grumbling*)   Such servants as I, that sweats and
    swinks,[1]
Eats our bread dry, and that is ill, I thinks!
We are oft wet and weary when master-men winks,
Yet come full lately the dinners and the drinks.
     But neatly,
Both our dame and our sire,
When we have run in the mire,
They can nip us of our hire
     And pay us full lately.

But hear my oath: For the food that you serve, I say,
I shall do hereafter—work as you pay:
I shall work a little and a little play,
For yet my supper never on my stomach lay
     In the fields.
I won't complain, but a heap
With my staff I shall leap;
For a thing bought too cheap
     Nothing yields.

1ST SHEPHERD   Yea, thou wert a fool, lad, a-wooing to ride
With one that had but little for spending by his side.
2ND SHEPHERD   Peace, boy! And no more jangling I'll bide,
Or I shall make thee full sad, by heaven's King, beside,
     For thy gauds.[2]
Where are our sheep? Thy japes we scorn.
3RD SHEPHERD   Sir, this same day at morn
I left them in the corn
     When the bells rang Lauds.

They have pasture good, they cannot go wrong.
1ST SHEPHERD   That is right. By the rood, these nights are long!
Yet I would, ere we went, one gave us a song.

---

[1] *swinks* works; his speech is ungrammatical
[2] *gauds* tricks or jests

2ND SHEPHERD   So *I* thought as I stood—to cheer us along.

3RD SHEPHERD   I grant!

1ST SHEPHERD   Let me sing the tenory.

2ND SHEPHERD   And I the treble so high.

3RD SHEPHERD   Then the mean falls to me.
          Let's start the chant.

(*At this point,* MAK *appears, his cloak thrown over his tunic*)

MAK (*To himself*)   Lord, for Thy names seven, that made the moon
   and stars on high
   Well more than I reckon: Thy will, Lord, leaves me dry
   And lacking, so that of my wits I am shy:
   Now would God I were in heaven, for there no children cry
      So still.[1]

1ST SHEPHERD (*Looking around*)   Who is that pipes so poor?

MAK (*Still grumbling to himself*)   Would God knew how I endure:
   A man that walks on the moor
      Without his will.

(*The* SHEPHERDS *now recognize him as the thief they know.* MAK *is
startled, but pretends he does not know them*)

2ND SHEPHERD   Mak, where have you been? Tell us tidings.

3RD SHEPHERD   Is *he* come, then let each one take heed to his
   things.

(*He takes* MAK's *cloak from him and shakes it, to see whether* MAK
has stolen anything)

MAK (*Spluttering*)   What! I be a yeoman, I tell ye, of the king's.
   The self and same, sent from a great lording's
      And such.
   Fie on you! Go hence
   Out of my presence;
   I must have reverence—
      You grieve me much!

1ST SHEPHERD   Why make ye it so quaint, Mak? You do wrong.

2ND SHEPHERD   Mak, play ye the saint? For this do ye long?

3RD SHEPHERD   I know the knave can deceive, the devil him hang!

MAK   I shall make complaint and get ye many a thwang
      At a word
   When I tell my lord how ye do.

---

[1] *so still* so continuously

1st SHEPHERD (*Sarcastically*)   But, Mak, is that true
Come, that southern tooth[1] unscrew
    And set it in a turd.

2nd SHEPHERD   Mak, the devil in your eye, a stroke will I lend you.

(*He strikes him*)

3rd SHEPHERD   Mak, know ye not me? By God, I could beat ye too.

(*As he too is about to strike him,* MAK *draws back and pretends to have just recognized the* SHEPHERDS)

MAK   God, look—you all three? Methought—how do you do?
Ye are a fair company.
1st SHEPHERD   May we now recognize you?
2nd SHEPHERD   Blast your jest-dealing!
When a man so lately goes
What will good men suppose?
Ye have an ill name one knows
    For sheep-stealing.

MAK   And true as steel I am, know ye not?
But a sickness I feel that holds me full hot:
My belly fares not well, for it is out of estate.
3rd SHEPHERD (*Unsympathetically*)   Seldom lies the devil dead by
    the gate!
MAK (*Ignoring the thrust*)   Therefore,
Full sore am I and ill;
I stand stone-still,
I ate not a tittle
    This month and more.

1st SHEPHERD   How fares thy wife? By my hood, tell us true.
MAK   She lies lolling by the road, by the fire too,
And a house full of brew she drinks well too.
Ill speed other things that she will shift
    To do.
Eats as fast as she can,
And each year that comes to man
She brings forth a brat—an'
    Some years, two.

But were I yet more gracious, and richer at will,
Eaten out of house and home I would be still.

---

[1] *southern tooth* in pretending to be in the king's service, the actor playing
Mak may have affected a Southern—that is, London—accent

Yet she is a foul dear, if ye come at her close;
None there is looks worse, as none knows
> Better than I.
Now will ye see what I proffer:
To give all in my coffer
And tomorrow next, to offer
> Mass-pence, should she die.

(*The* SHEPHERDS *have begun to feel drowsy during this recital*)

2ND SHEPHERD   So weary with watching is none in this shire:
I would sleep if it cost me a part of my hire.
3RD SHEPHERD   And I am cold and naked, and would have a fire.
1ST SHEPHERD   I am weary of walking, and I have run in the mire.

(*To the* SECOND SHEPHERD)

> Keep the watch, you!
2ND SHEPHERD   Nay, I will lie down by,
For I must sleep or die.
3RD SHEPHERD   For sleep as good a man's son am I;
> It is my due.

(*They begin to lie down to sleep. But the* THIRD SHEPHERD *eyes* MAK *suspiciously*)

3RD SHEPHERD   But, Mak, come hither; between us you shall lie down.
MAK (*Unhappily*)   But I may hinder your sleep and make you frown.

(*The* SHEPHERDS *force him down and compel him to stretch out among them, in order to prevent him from robbing them*)

> Ah well, no dread I heed:
From my head to my toe,

(*Crossing himself*)

Manus tuas commendo,
Pontio Pilato.[1]
> Christ's cross me speed.

(*Before long the* THREE SHEPHERDS *are in a deep sleep, and* MAK *disentangles himself and rises*)

MAK   Now were time for a man that lacks what he would

---

[1] "Into your hands I commend myself, Pontius Pilate." The humor lies, of course, in the misquotation.

To stalk privily then into the fold
And nimbly to work, though not to be too bold,
For he might regret the bargain if it were told
            At the ending.
Now time for to work in the dell,
For he needs good counsel
That fain would fare well
            And has but little spending.

(*He begins to work a spell on the sleepers, drawing a circle around them*)

But about you a circle round as the moon,
Till I have done what I will, till that it be noon—
That ye lie stone-still, until I am done;
And now I shall say thereto of good words a rune
            Anon:
Over your heads my hand I light;
Out go your eyes, blind be your sight!
And now that it may come out right
            I must shift on.

(*He starts to leave in the direction of the sheep further down the field while the* SHEPHERDS *snore*)

Lord, but they sleep hard—that may one hear . . .
Was I never shepherd, but now I will shear;
Though the flock be scared, yet shall I nip near;
I must draw hitherward and mend our cheer
            From sorrow.

(*He spies a sheep that attracts him*)

A fat sheep, I daresay,
A good fleece, I dare lay;
Repay when I may—

(*Seizing the animal*)

But this will I *borrow.*

SCENE II

MAK'S *cottage: the exterior and the interior.*
At first MAK *stands outside and knocks at the door. Later he enters and the action transpires inside.*

MAK (*Knocking*)   How, Gill, art thou in? Get us some light.

WIFE　Who makes such din this time of the night?
　I am set for to spin: I think not I might
　Rise a penny to win—a curse on him alight.
　　　So fares she,
　A housewife, I ween,
　To be raced thus between.
　In house may no work be seen
　　　Because of such small chores that be.

MAK　Good wife, open the door. Do ye not see what I bring?
WIFE　Then let thou draw the latch.

(*As he enters*)

　　　　　　　　　　Ah! come in, my sweeting!
MAK (*Grumpily*)　Yea, and no thought for my long standing!
WIFE (*Observing the sheep*)　By the naked neck thou art like to
　get thy hanging.

MAK　Get away!
　I am worthy my meat,
　For in a pinch can I get
　More than they that swink and sweat
　　　All day.

　Thus if fell to my lot, Gill, I had such grace.
WIFE　It were a foul blot to be hanged for the case.
MAK　I have escaped oft from as narrow place.
WIFE　But so long goes the pot to the water, one says,
　　　At last
　Comes it home broken.
MAK　Well I know the token;
　But let it never be spoken!—
　　　But come and help fast.

(GILL *helps to take the sheep in*)

　I would it were slain and I sat down to eat:
　This twelvemonth was I not so fain for sheep-meat.
WIFE　Come they ere it be slain and hear the sheep bleat—
MAK　Then might I be taken; cold's the sweat I am in, my sweet—
　　　Go, make fast
　The outer door.
WIFE (*Going to the door*)　Yes, Mak,
　If they came at thy back—
MAK　Then got I from that pack
　　　The devil's own cast.

WIFE (*Coming back*)   A good jest I have spied, since thou
hast none:

(*Pointing to the cradle*)

Here shall we hide it till they be gone;
In the cradle may it abide. Let me alone,
And I shall lie beside in childbed and groan.

MAK   Well said!
And I shall say you are light
Of a man-child this night.
WIFE   How well it is, day bright,
That ever I bred.

This is a good guise and a far cast:
A woman's advice, it helps at the last.
I shall care never who spies, so go thou fast!
MAK   (*Outside, walking in the fields toward the sleeping* SHEPHERDS)
If I do not come ere they rise, a cold blast
Will blow; back to sleep
I go. Yet sleeps this company,
And I shall slip in privily
As it had never been me
That carried their sheep.

SCENE III

The moors.
MAK *slips in among the sleepers. The* SHEPHERDS *begin to stir.*

1ST SHEPHERD (*Rising*)   *Resurrex a mortruis:*[1] reach me a hand!
Judas carnas dominus! I may not well stand.
My foot sleeps, by Jesus, and I thirst—and
I thought that we laid us full near England.
2ND SHEPHERD (*Rising*)
Ah-ye!
Lord, I have slept well!
I am fresh as an eel,
As light I feel
As leaf on tree.

3RD SHEPHERD (*Awaking but dazed*)   *Ben'cite* be herein; so my
body quakes,

---

[1] *Resurrex a mortruis* The unlettered shepherd is babbling Latin words he
has picked up imperfectly and makes no particular sense.

My heart is out of my skin with the noise it makes.
Who makes all this din, so my brow aches?
To the door will I win. Hark, fellows, who wakes?
    We were four:
See ye anywhere Mak now?
1ST SHEPHERD   We were up ere thou.
2ND SHEPHERD   Man, I give God a vow
    That he went nowhere.

3RD SHEPHERD   (*Troubled*)   Methought he lay wrapped up in a wolf-skin.
1ST SHEPHERD   Many are thus wrapped now—that is, within!
2ND SHEPHERD   When we had long napped, methought with a gin[1]
A fat sheep he trapped without making a din.
3RD SHEPHERD   (*Pointing toward* Mak, *who pretends to be asleep*)
    Be still:
This dream makes thee wild,
It is but phantom, by the Holy Child! [2]
1ST SHEPHERD   Now God turn all things mild,
    If it be His will.

(*The* SHEPHERDS *rouse* MAK)

2ND SHEPHERD   Rise, Mak, for shame! Ye lie right long.
MAK (*Stirring*)   Now Christ's Holy Name, be it among
Us! What's this? By Saint James, I am not strong!
I hope I am the same—my neck has lain wrong
    All night!

(*As they help him up*)

Many thanks! Since yester-even,
I swear by Saint Steven,
I was flayed by a dream, so driven
    That my heart was not right.

Methought my Gill began to croak, full sad
To labor well nigh at first cock—a lad
To add to our flock; and I never glad
To have more to provide, more than ever I had.
    Ah, my head!

---

[1] *gin* trick
[2] *Holy Child* An anachronism characteristic of naïve folk literature, since the Holy Child has not yet been born. In the next few lines there are other anachronisms: "Christ's Holy Name," "By Saint James," and "by Saint Steven"—or Stephen.

A house full of young mouths—banes!
The devil knock out their brains!
Woe him that so many brats gains
   And so little bread.

I must go home, by your leave; to Gill, I thought.
But first look in my sleeve that I have stolen naught:
I am loth to grieve you or to take from you aught.
3RD SHEPHERD Go forth, and ill may you thrive!

(MAK *leaves*)

     Still I would we sought
 This morn
Whether we have all our store.
1ST SHEPHERD Good! I will go before.
 Let us meet.
2ND SHEPHERD Where?
3RD SHEPHERD At the crooked thorn.

SCENE IV

MAK'S *cottage.*

MAK (*At his door*) Undo this door! Who is here? How long shall
 I stand?
WIFE Who makes such a stir, to walk in the moon-waning?
MAK Ah, Gill, what cheer? It is I, Mak, your husband.
WIFE (*Grumpily*) Then see we here the devil himself in a band,
   Sir Guile!
 Lo, he comes with a noise about
 As if he were held by the snout,
 I may not do my work for that lout
   A hand-long while.

MAK Will ye hear what noise she makes for an excuse
 And does nothing but play about and stroke her toes!
WIFE Why, who wanders, who wakes, who comes, who goes?
 Who brews, who bakes—now who do you suppose?
   And more then
 That it is pity to behold—
 Now in hot, now in cold.
 Full woefull is the household
   That lacks women.

But what end have ye made with the shepherds, Mak?

MAK   The last word that they said when I turned my back,
  They would look that they had of their sheep all the pack;
  I fear they will not be well pleased when they their sheep lack,
      Pardie!
  But howso the sport goes
  I'm the thief they'll suppose
  And come with a full nose
      To cry out on me.

  But thou must do as thou planned.
WIFE   They'll find me able!
  I shall swaddle it right in my cradle.
  When I sup with the Devil I use the long ladle!
  I will lie down straightway. Come wrap me.
MAK (*Doing so*)   I will.
WIFE (*Sharply*)
      Behind!—
  If Coll and his mate come, to our sorrow,
  They will nip us full narrow.
MAK   But I may run and cry "Harrow"
      If the sheep they find.

WIFE   Listen close when they call—they will come anon.
  Come and make ready all, and sing thou alone:
  Sing "Lullay" you shall, for I must groan
  And cry out by the wall on Mary and John
      As if sore.
  Sing "Lullay" on fast
  When you hear them at last,
  And if I play a false cast
      Trust me no more!

SCENE V

The moors, as the SHEPHERDS *meet.*

3RD SHEPHERD   Ah, Coll, good morn: why sleep ye not?
1ST SHEPHERD   Alas, that ever was I born! We have a foul blot—
  A fat wether have we lost.
3RD SHEPHERD   God forbid; say it not!
2ND SHEPHERD   Who should have done that harm? That were a
  foul spot.
1ST SHEPHERD
      Some knave—beshrew!
  I have sought with my dogs

All Horbury shrogs,[1]
And of fifteen hogs[2]
    I lack one ewe.

3RD SHEPHERD   Now trust me if ye will—by Saint Thomas of Kent!,
Either Mak or Gill a hand to it lent.
1ST SHEPHERD   Peace, man, be still: I watched when he went;
You slander him ill, you ought to repent
    With speed.
2ND SHEPHERD   Yet as ever I thrive or be,
Though the good Lord slay me,
I would say it were he
    That did the same deed.

3RD SHEPHERD   Go we thither then, I say, and let us run fleet;
Till I know the truth, may I never bread eat.
1ST SHEPHERD   Nor take drink in my head till with him I meet.
2ND SHEPHERD   I will take to no bed until I him greet,
    My brother!
One promise I will plight:
Till I get him in sight
I will never sleep one night
    Where I sleep another.

SCENE VI

MAK's *cottage*.
MAK *is heard singing within, while* GILL *is heard groaning as though she
were delivering a child.*

3RD SHEPHERD   Will you hear how they hack away; our sir likes to
   croon.
1ST SHEPHERD   Heard I never none crack so clear out of tune.
   Call on him!
2ND SHEPHERD   Mak, undo your door—soon!
MAK   Who is that spoke, as if it were noon
    Aloft?
Who is that, I say?

(*He opens the door*)

3RD SHEPHERD   Good fellows you'd see, were it day.

---

[1] *Horbury shrogs* By this is meant the thickets of Horbury, about four miles
from Wakefield, where the play was given.
[2] *hogs* young sheep

MAK   As far as ye may,
        Friends, speak soft
  Over a sick woman's head that is at malease;
  I had sooner be dead than cause her dis-ease.
WIFE   Go to another place—I cannot breathe; please!
  Each foot ye tread goes through my nose with a squeeze,
        Woe is me.
1ST SHEPHERD   Tell us, Mak, if ye may:
  How fare ye, I say?
MAK   But are ye in this town today?—
        How fare *ye?*
  Ye have run in the mire and are wet a bit;
  I shall make you a fire, if ye will sit.

  (*Pointing at his* WIFE)

  A nurse I would hire; think ye on it.
  Well paid is my hire—my dream this is it,
        In season.
  I have brats if ye knew
  Many more than will do;

  (*With resignation*)

  But, then, we must drink as we brew,
        And that is but reason!

  I would ye dined ere you go; methinks that ye sweat.
2ND SHEPHERD   Nay, neither drink nor meat will mend us yet.
MAK   (*Innocently*)   Why, sirs, what ails ye?
3RD SHEPHERD   Our sheep we must get
  That was stolen. It is great loss that we met.

  (MAK *offers a drink*)

MAK   Sirs, drink!
  Had I been near,
  Someone should have bought it full dear.
1ST SHEPHERD   Marry, some men think that ye were.
        And that makes us think!

2ND SHEPHERD   Mak, some men think that it should be ye.
3RD SHEPHERD   Either you or your spouse, so say we.
MAK   Now if ye have suspicion against my Gill or me,
  Come and search our house, and then may ye see
        Who had her,
  Or if any sheep I got,

Either cow or stot.[1]
And Gill, my wife, rose not
     Here since she laid her.

If I am not true and loyal, to God I pray

(*Pointing to the cradle, where the sheep—the alleged child—is hidden*)

That *this* be the first meal I shall eat this day.

1ST SHEPHERD Mak, as I may fare well, take heed, I say!
"He learned early to steal that could not say nay."

(*The* SHEPHERDS *start to search the room, but* GILL *waves them away when they approach the cradle near her*)

WIFE I faint!
Out, thieves, from my dwelling!
Ye come to rob while I am swelling—

MAK Your hearts should melt now she's yelling
     In plaint.

WIFE Away, thieves from my child; over him don't pore.

MAK Knew ye how much she has borne, your hearts would be sore.
Ye do wrong, I warn you, thus to rummage before
A woman that has suffered—but I say no more!

WIFE (*Yelling*)
     Ah, my middle!
I pray to God so mild,
If I ever you beguiled,
That I *eat* this child
     That lies in this cradle.

MAK (*Pretending concern for her*)   Peace, woman, for God's pain,
    and cry not so:
Thou spill'st thy brain and fill'st me with woe.

2ND SHEPHERD (*To the other* TWO SHEPHERDS)   I think our
    sheep be slain; what find ye two?

3RD SHEPHERD All this is in vain: we may as well go:

(*Finding only rags of clothing as he searches*)

     Only tatters!
I can find no flesh,
Hard nor soft,
Salt nor fresh,
     But two bare platters.

---

[1] *stot* bullock

(*But as he approaches the cradle and sniffs the air, he makes a grimace*)

Yet live cattle, as I may have bliss, nor tame nor wild,
None has smelled so strong as this—this child!

WIFE (*Protesting*)   Ah no, so God bless and give me joy, this child
smells mild.

1ST SHEPHERD   We have aimed amiss: We were elsewhere beguiled.

(*He is about to leave*)

2ND SHEPHERD (*Also giving up the search*)
        Sir, we are done!
But sir—Our Lady him save!—
Is your child a lad?

MAK (*Proudly*)   Any lord might him have
        This child to his son.

When he wakens he has a grip that is a joy to see.

3RD SHEPHERD   Blessings on his hips, and happiness may he see.
But who were his godparents, will ye tell me?

MAK (*Floundering*)   Blessed be their lips!—

1ST SHEPHERD (*Aside*)   Now, what will the lie be?

MAK   So God them thank,—
Parkin and Gibbon Waller, be it said,
And gentle John Horne in good stead—
He that made the great riot spread,
        He with the big shank.

2ND SHEPHERD   (*Preparing to leave*)   Mak, friends will we be, for
we are all one.

MAK (*Pretending to have been hurt by their suspicions*)   *We?* Now
I must hold back, for amends is there none.
Farewell, all three, and very glad to see you gone!

(*The* SHEPHERDS *leave the house, and we see them outside*)

3RD SHEPHERD   "Fair words may there be, but love is there none
        This year."

1ST SHEPHERD (*To the* 2nd)   Gave ye the child anything?

2ND SHEPHERD   No, not a farthing.

3RD SHEPHERD   Fast back will I fling:
        Await ye me here.

(*He goes back to* MAK's *cottage, the others following him*)

Mak, take it to no grief if I come to thy lad.

MAK   Nay, ye have grieved me much and made me sad.

3RD SHEPHERD   The child it will not grieve, thy little day-star
     so glad;
  Mak, with your leave, let me give the child you have had
          But sixpence.
MAK   Nay, go away; he sleeps!
3RD SHEPHERD   Methinks, it peeps.[1]
MAK   When he wakens, he weeps;
          I pray you go hence.

(*The other* SHEPHERDS *enter*)

3RD SHEPHERD   (*Coming closer*)   Give me leave him to kiss and to
  lift up the clout.

(*He lifts the cover a little*)

  What the devil is this? He has a long snout!
1ST SHEPHERD   He is birth-marked amiss; let us not waste time
  hereabout.
2ND SHEPHERD   "From an ill-spun woof ever comes foul out."

(*As he looks closer*)

          Ay—so!
  He is like our sheep.
3RD SHEPHERD   How, Gib? May I peep?
1ST SHEPHERD   "Nature will still creep
     Where it may not go."
2ND SHEPHERD   This was a quaint trick and a far cast;
  It was a high fraud!
3RD SHEPHERD   Yea, sirs, I am aghast!
  Let's burn this bawd and bind her fast;
  A false scold hangs at the last—
          So shalt thou.

(*He has pulled the covers off*)

  Will ye see how they swaddle
  His four feet in the middle?
  Saw I never in a cradle
     A hornèd lad ere now.

MAK   (*Who stands behind them and does not see the sheep uncov-
     ered; still attempting to brazen it out*)

---

[1] *peeps* whimpers

Peace, bid I! And let be your fare;
I am he that him gat and yon woman him bare.[1]
1ST SHEPHERD (*Mocking him*)   What devil shall he be called, Mak?
 Lo, God! Mak's heir!
2ND SHEPHERD   An end to all jesting; now God give thee care
   I say!

(*As she is lying in bed, the* WIFE *does not see that they have completely uncovered the sheep*)

WIFE   As pretty child is he
 As sits on woman's knee;
 A dilly-down, perdie,
   To make one gay.

3RD SHEPHERD   I know my sheep by the ear-mark—this good token.
MAK   I tell you, sirs, hear me: his nose was broken,
 Since, as the priest told me, he was by witchcraft bespoken.
1ST SHEPHERD   This is false work and must be avenged; I have
 spoken:
   Get weapon!
WIFE   The child was taken by an elf—
 I saw it myself.
When the clock struck twelve,
   Was he mis-shapen.

2ND SHEPHERD   Ye two are right deft, and belong in the same bed.
3RD SHEPHERD   Since they maintain their theft, let us do them dead.

(*They seize* MAK)

MAK (*Seeing the game is up*)   If I trespass again, strike off my
 head.
 I'll let you be the judge!
3RD SHEPHERD (*To the others*)   Sirs, instead:
   For this trespass
 We need neither curse nor spite,
 Nor chide nor fight,
 But take him forthright
   And toss him in canvas.

(*They drag* MAK *outside and toss him lustily in a sheet while he yells with pain*)

———————
[1] *bare* bore

SCENE VII

The fields near Bethlehem in Judea.
We see the three SHEPHERDS *again, weary after their sport with* MAK
and tired with walking.

1ST SHEPHERD   Lord, how I am sore and like to burst in the breast!
In faith, I can stand no more, therefore will I rest.
2ND SHEPHERD   As a sheep of seven score Mak weighed in my fist;
To sleep anywhere methink I would list.
3RD SHEPHERD   Then I pray you,
Lie down on this green.
1ST SHEPHERD   (*Hesitating*)   On these thefts to think I yet mean.
3RD SHEPHERD   Whereto should ye be worried lean?
Do as I tell you.

They lie down to sleep; but they have barely done so when an Angel
appears above. He first sings the hymn "Gloria in Excelsis," then ad-
dresses the SHEPHERDS

ANGEL   Rise, herdsmen gentle, for now is He born
That shall take from the Fiend what Adam had lorn;[1]
That fiend to overthrow this night is He born;
God is made your Friend. Now at this morn.
He commands,
To Bedlem[2] you go see:
There lies that divine He
In a crib that full poorly
Betwixt two beasts stands.

(*The* ANGEL *disappears*)

1ST SHEPHERD   This was a quaint voice that ever yet I heard.
It is a marvel to relate thus to be stirred.
2ND SHEPHERD   Of God's son of heaven, he spoke from above,
All the wood was in lightning as he spoke of love:
I thought it fair.
3RD SHEPHERD   Of a child heard I tell
In Bedlem; I heard it well.

(*Pointing to a star that has begun to blaze*)

Yonder star, above the dell:
Let us follow him there.

---

1 *lorn* lost or forfeited
2 *Bedlem* Bethlehem

2ND SHEPHERD   Say, what was his song? Heard ye how he sang it?
  Three breves[1] to a long.
3RD SHEPHERD   Yes, marry, he thwacked it;
  Was no crotchet wrong, nor nothing lacked it.
1ST SHEPHERD   For to sing it again right as he trilled it.
        I can, if I may.
2ND SHEPHERD   Let me see how ye croon,
  Or do ye but bark at the moon?
3RD SHEPHERD   Hold your tongues! Have done!
1ST SHEPHERD
        Hark after me, I say!

(*They try to sing the hymn as best they can*)

2ND SHEPHERD   To Bedlem he bade that we should go;
  I am troubled that we tarry too slow.
3RD SHEPHERD   Be merry and not sad: of mirth is our song, lo!
  Everlasting glad in the rewards that will flow,
        No plaint may we make.
1ST SHEPHERD   Hie we thither, cheery,
  Though we be wet and weary;
  To that Child and that Lady
        Let us our way take.

2ND SHEPHERD   We find by the prophecy—let be your din!—
  Of David and Isaiah, and more therein,
  As prophesied by clergy, that on a virgin
  Should He light and lie, to redeem our sin
        And slake it.
  Our kind from woe
  To save—Isaiah said so.—
        "*Ecce virgo
        Concipict* a child that is naked." [2]
3RD SHEPHERD   Full glad may we be, and await that day
  That lovely day that He shall with His might sway.
  Lord, well for me for once and for aye!
  Might I but kneel on my knee some word for to say
        To that child.
  But the angel said
  In a crib is He laid,

---

[1] *breves* A *breve* is equal to two whole notes; a *long* is equal to six whole
  notes; a *crotchet* is a quarter note.
[2] "Behold, a virgin shall conceive." (Isaiah, 7:14)

He is poorly arrayed,
      So meek and mild.

1ST SHEPHERD   Patriarchs that have been, and prophets beforne,
  They desired to have seen this Child that is born;
  But *they* are gone full clean, from life forlorn—
  It is *we* shall see him, ere it be morn
      By token.
  When I see Him and feel,
  Then shall I know full well
  It is true as steel
      What prophets have spoken:

  To so poor as we are that he would appear,
  We the first to find and be his messenger!
2ND SHEPHERD   Go we now, let us fare: the place must be near.
3RD SHEPHERD   I am ready and eager: go we together
      To that Light!
  Lord! If Thy will it be,
  Though we are lowly all three,
  Grant us of Thy glee,
      To comfort Thy wight.[1]

(*They move on, following the star, to Bethlehem*)

SCENE VIII

The stable or manger in Bethlehem.
The SHEPHERDS *enter and kneel before the* VIRGIN *and* CHILD.

1ST SHEPHERD   Hail, comely and clean; hail, young child!
  Hail, Maker, as I mean, born of maiden so mild!
  Thou hast banned, I deem, the devil so wild;
  The evil beguiler now goes beguiled.

(*Pointing to the* CHILD)

      Lo, merry He is!
  Lo, he laughs, my sweeting,
  A welcome greeting!
  I have had my meeting—

(*Offering the* CHILD *some cherries*)

      Have a bob of cherries?

---

[1] *wight* creature

2ND SHEPHERD   Hail, sovereign Saviour, for Thou hast us sought!
Hail, Nursling, leaf and flower, that all things hath wrought!
Hail, full of favor, that made all of nought!

(*Offering a bird*)

Hail, I kneel and I cower.—A bird have I brought
Without mar.
Hail, little, tiny mop,
Of our creed thou art the crop;
I would drink from thy cup,
Little day-star.

3RD SHEPHERD   Hail, darling dear, full of godhead!
I pray Thee be near when that I have need.
Hail! Sweet is Thy cheer! And my heart would bleed
To see Thee sit here clothed so poor indeed,
With no pennies.
Hail! Thy hand put forth to us all—
I bring thee but a ball;
Take and play with it withall,
And go to the tennis.

THE VIRGIN MARY   The Father of heaven, God omnipotent,
That set all aright, His son has He sent.
My name He chose forth, and on me His light spent;
And I conceived Him forthwith through His might as God meant:
And now is the Child born.
May He keep you from woe!
I shall pray Him so.
Tell the glad news as ye go,
And remember this morn.

1ST SHEPHERD   Farewell, Lady, so fair to behold
With thy child on thy knee.
2ND SHEPHERD   —But he lies full cold.—
Lord, it is well with me! Now we go, ye may behold.
3RD SHEPHERD   In truth, already it seems to be told
Full oft
1ST SHEPHERD   What grace we have found.
2ND SHEPHERD   Come forth! Now are we won!
3RD SHEPHERD   To sing of it we're bound:
Let us sing aloft!

(*They leave the stable, singing*)

Explicit Pagina Pastorum
(*Here ends The Shepherds' Pageant*)

QUESTIONS

Discuss the ways in which the two halves of *The Second Shepherds' Play* parallel, contrast, and comment on each other. One point to be sure to notice is that the shepherds are nearly fooled by Gill's trick of concealing the sheep in the cradle. How do they finally discover the sheep? What do the delayed discovery and the means by which it is accomplished add to the humor and to the message of the play?

3
Hamlet *and Elizabethan Tragedy*

In many ways, *Hamlet* is similar to *Oedipus Rex*. Both were written at times when tragedy was just coming to its full maturity in their playwrights' cultures. Both were written by the most influential playwrights of their time. Both helped set the shape of tragedy for their own period's drama and for the drama of future ages.

Both plays have heroes who dominate their play, catching the audience's attention early in the play and holding their attention and their sympathy throughout. (Hamlet, in fact, can even address the audience in soliloquies and "asides" that no one on stage is meant to hear.) Princely in nature and position, both men seem born to rule. The heroes are somewhat alike in their situations, as well. Both must avenge their father's murder and thus remove a pollution from their land. To do so, however, they must first find out who the murderer is; and they must pursue their search among people who want the truth to remain hidden.

Here, however, the situations diverge. Oedipus' companions want to conceal the truth for Oedipus' own sake. Hamlet's opponent, Claudius, wants the truth to remain hidden because he is the murderer. The element of active, willed evil, which is absent from *Oedipus Rex,* is thus present in *Hamlet.* Hamlet must not only destroy his father's murderer; he must do so before the murderer destroys him.

Hamlet, as we suggested earlier, is a play derived from both Greek and medieval drama. From Greek tragedy, it has taken the tragic hero—dominant, strong-willed, determined to accomplish his desires. From Greek tragedy also it has taken a certain elevation of tone and insistence on the dignity of human beings. From medieval drama, it has taken the medieval desire for inclusiveness and the medieval love of significant detail. *Hamlet* is much longer than *Oedipus Rex*. It has more characters, a more complex plot, and a generous amount of comedy.

Let us look at each of these elements in turn. Regarding characters, we notice that Oedipus is unique, but that Hamlet sees himself reflected in two other characters: first in Fortinbras, another son of a warrior king whose father has died and whose uncle has seized the throne, leaving him practically powerless; and later in Laertes, another son determined to avenge himself on his father's murderer. The deeds of Laertes and Fortinbras contrast with and comment on the actions of Hamlet himself, thus enriching our view of Hamlet and his dilemma. At the same time, the actions of the three men intertwine to create three of the play's major themes: fathers and sons, honor, and thought versus action.

Regarding plot, we can be sure that the affairs of three families will create a more complex plot than the affairs of one family. Thus critics sometimes speak of the Fortinbras "overplot" (which is mostly concerned with war and kingship) and the Laertes "underplot" (concerned with private family relationships) while discussing how these two "sub-plots" complement the "main plot" (which deals with Hamlet's familial and princely concerns). But the English inclusiveness goes even beyond this, adding also a love story between Hamlet and Laertes' sister, Ophelia, a study of true versus false friendship in the persons of Horatio and Rosencrantz and Guildenstern, and a few comments on the contemporary theatre by a troupe of strolling players. There are also glimpses of three purely comic characters: two gravediggers and one intolerably affected courtier. Again, all these themes and characters are interwoven to illuminate Hamlet's character and dilemma. (The gravediggers, for instance, who seem at first wildly irrelevant, end by bringing Hamlet to a new understanding of mortality, an understanding that is crucial to his ability to face his own death.)

Comedy, in *Hamlet,* is not separate from tragedy. Rather, it is used as a means to create a fuller awareness of tragedy. Hamlet himself is a master of comic wordplay. His first speech turns on a pun; and puns and bitter quips mark his speech to Claudius and his courtiers throughout the play. Many of these quips are spoken under the guise of pretended madness; and here the audience shares secrets with Hamlet. We know he is not really mad. But those on stage think he is. (The exception is Claudius, who suspects that Hamlet is not mad, but who cannot reveal Hamlet's sanity without revealing his own crimes.) Pretending madness, therefore, Hamlet makes speeches which sound like nonsense to the courtiers, but which we recognize as referring to his father's murder and his recognition of treachery in those around him. We are thus let into Hamlet's secrets and feelings as no single character in the play is let into them. Hamlet's use of jesting speech thus becomes not merely a weapon in his fight against Claudius, but also a means of winning the sympathetic partnership of the audience. In comic speech and tragic soliloquy alike, Hamlet reveals himself to us. By the play's end, we know Hamlet as we know few other stage characters.

Adding to our sense of knowledge is the fact that Hamlet is a complex and changing character. In this he differs markedly from Oedipus, whose character remains firm and fixed until it changes so drastically in his final scene. The essentially fixed character is typical of Greek drama, which seems to have been more interested in the clash of character against character (or of character against fate) than it was in the changing or developing of a single character. It is far less typical of Elizabethan tragedy.

This emphasis on Hamlet's developing character is due to the influence of medieval Christian drama, with its concern for salvation and the dangers and triumphs of the soul. English drama was secular drama by Shakespeare's time, being performed regularly by professional troupes for paying audiences. Concern for the soul, however, remained one of its major concerns. When Elizabethan dramatists wrote tragedies, therefore, they tended to make the hero's inner concerns—his passions, his temptations, his spiritual triumphs or defeats—the central focus of their plays. Even the ghost in *Hamlet,* coming to call for revenge, warns Hamlet to "taint not thy mind, nor let thy soul contrive/Against thy mother aught." Hamlet must avenge his father and free Denmark from the polluting rule of Claudius; but he must do so in a manner that will imperil neither his own nor his mother's salvation.

When the play opens, Hamlet is a bitter man. So little at peace is he with himself or his surroundings that he seems to have little chance of fulfilling the ghost's demands. So close does he come to flinging away his own soul in pursuit of Claudius, in fact, that some critics have refused to believe that Hamlet's speeches in Act III, Scene 3, mean what they say. In fact, they mean exactly what they say. Hamlet in this scene is on the brink of disaster.

In the next scene, the "closet scene," the unexpected happens. Hamlet is caught in the wrong, realizes it, and begins the painful process of returning from his bitterness and hatreds to a reconciliation with himself, his mother, and humanity in general. Throughout the rest of the play, we watch Hamlet's speeches on human nature become gentler, his attitude more compassionate; we hear a new acceptance of his fate, a new trust in providence, revealed. By the play's end, when Hamlet gets his one chance at Claudius, he is fully ready for the task and its consequences.

And so the play ends in mingled triumph and loss: a loss to Denmark and to us in the death of Hamlet, a joy that Hamlet has nobly achieved his purpose.

One final word must be said about the language of *Hamlet,* which is like the language of no other play we will read in this book. Seeking some meter in English that would match the beauty and dignity of the meters in which classical tragedy had been written, the sixteenth-century dramatists had created blank verse. Blank verse does not rhyme. It usually has ten syllables to a line (though lines may be shorter or longer by a few syllables), and the second, fourth, sixth, eighth, and tenth syllables are generally accented more strongly than the rest. This meter was easily spoken. It was dignified and flexible. And it could slip neatly into prose (for comic scenes) or into rhymed couplets to mark a scene's end.

Blank verse was fairly new when Shakespeare began writing. In some of his early plays, it still sounds stiff and awkward. By the time he wrote *Hamlet,* however, Shakespeare was entering into a mastery of blank verse that no one has ever surpassed. The rhythms and imagery of Hamlet's language warn us of every change in his moods, from pretended madness to honest friendship to bitter passion. By the modulation of Hamlet's language, as well as by his actions, Shakespeare shows us the battle within Hamlet's soul.

If you can see *Hamlet*—live or on film—or if you can hear recordings of it, do so. If not, read as much of it aloud as you can. For readers unfamiliar with Shakespearean language, *Hamlet* is not an easy play to read. Nearly every word of it counts; so every word must be attended to. But the play is well worth the effort it takes, for it is truly one of the finest plays of all time.

WILLIAM SHAKESPEARE (1564–1616)

Hamlet

CHARACTERS

CLAUDIUS, *King of Denmark*
HAMLET, *son to the late, and nephew to the present, King*
POLONIUS, *Lord Chamberlain*
HORATIO, *friend to Hamlet*
LAERTES, *son to Polonius*
VOLTEMAND ⎫
CORNELIUS ⎪
ROSENCRANTZ ⎪ *courtiers*
GUILDENSTERN ⎬
OSRIC ⎪
A GENTLEMAN ⎭
A PRIEST
MARCELLUS ⎫ *officers*
BERNARDO ⎭
FRANCISCO, *a soldier*
REYNALDO, *servant to Polonius*
PLAYERS
TWO CLOWNS, *gravediggers*
FORTINBRAS, *Prince of Norway*
A NORWEGIAN CAPTAIN
ENGLISH AMBASSADORS
GERTRUDE, *Queen of Denmark, mother to Hamlet*
OPHELIA, *daughter to Polonius*
GHOST OF HAMLET'S FATHER
LORDS, LADIES, OFFICERS, SOLDIERS, SAILORS, MESSENGERS,
    ATTENDANTS

ACT I

Scene I

Elsinore Castle: a sentry-post

(*Enter* BERNARDO *and* FRANCISCO, *two sentinels*)

BERNARDO Who's there?

FRANCISCO Nay, answer me. Stand and unfold yourself.

BERNARDO Long live the king!

FRANCISCO Bernardo?

BERNARDO He.

FRANCISCO You come most carefully upon your hour.

BERNARDO 'Tis now struck twelve. Get thee to bed, Francisco.

FRANCISCO For this relief much thanks. 'Tis bitter cold,
And I am sick at heart.

BERNARDO Have you had quiet guard?

FRANCISCO   Not a mouse stirring.

BERNARDO Well, good night.
If you do meet Horatio and Marcellus,
The rivals[1] of my watch, bid them make haste.

(*Enter* HORATIO *and* MARCELLUS)

FRANCISCO I think I hear them. Stand, ho! Who is there?

HORATIO Friends to this ground.

MARCELLUS   And liegemen to the Dane.[2]

FRANCISCO Give you good night.

MARCELLUS   O, farewell, honest soldier.
Who hath relieved you?

FRANCISCO   Bernardo hath my place.
Give you good night.

(*Exit* FRANCISCO)

MARCELLUS   Holla, Bernardo!

BERNARDO   Say—
What, is Horatio there?

HORATIO   A piece of him.

BERNARDO Welcome, Horatio. Welcome, good Marcellus.

HORATIO What, has this thing appeared again to-night?

BERNARDO I have seen nothing.

MARCELLUS Horatio says 'tis but our fantasy,
And will not let belief take hold of him

---

[1] *rivals* sharers   [2] *Dane* King of Denmark

Touching this dreaded sight twice seen of us.
Therefore I have entreated him along
With us to watch the minutes of this night,
That, if again this apparition come,
He may approve[3] our eyes and speak to it.

HORATIO   Tush, tush, 'twill not appear.

BERNARDO   Sit down awhile,
And let us once again assail your ears,
That are so fortified against our story,
What we two nights have seen.

HORATIO   Well, sit we down,
And let us hear Bernardo speak of this.

BERNARDO   Last night of all,
When yond same star that's westward from the pole[4]
Had made his course t' illume that part of heaven
Where now it burns, Marcellus and myself,
The bell then beating one—

(*Enter* GHOST)

MARCELLUS   Peace, break thee off. Look where it comes again.

BERNARDO   In the same figure like the king that's dead.

MARCELLUS   Thou art a scholar; speak to it, Horatio.

BERNARDO   Looks 'a not like the king? Mark it, Horatio.

HORATIO   Most like. It harrows me with fear and wonder.

BERNARDO   It would be spoke to.

MARCELLUS   Speak to it, Horatio.

HORATIO   What art thou that usurp'st this time of night
Together with that fair and warlike form
In which the majesty of buried Denmark[5]
Did sometimes[6] march? By heaven I charge thee, speak.

MARCELLUS   It is offended.

BERNARDO   See, it stalks away.

HORATIO   Stay. Speak, speak. I charge thee, speak.

(*Exit* GHOST)

MARCELLUS   'Tis gone and will not answer.

BERNARDO   How now, Horatio? You tremble and look pale.
Is not this something more than fantasy?
What think you on't?

HORATIO   Before my God, I might not this believe

---

[3] *approve* confirm   [4] *pole* polestar   [5] *buried Denmark* the buried King of
Denmark   [6] *sometimes* formerly

Without the sensible and true avouch
Of mine own eyes.

MARCELLUS   Is it not like the king?

HORATIO   As thou art to thyself.
Such was the very armor he had on
When he th' ambitious Norway[7] combated.
So frowned he once when, in an angry parle,[8]
He smote the sledded Polacks on the ice.
'Tis strange.

MARCELLUS   Thus twice before, and jump[9] at this dead hour,
With martial stalk hath he gone by our watch.

HORATIO   In what particular thought to work I know not;
But, in the gross and scope[10] of my opinion,
This bodes some strange eruption to our state.

MARCELLUS   Good now, sit down, and tell me he that knows,
Why this same strict and most observant watch
So nightly toils the subject[11] of the land,
And why such daily cast of brazen cannon
And foreign mart[12] for implements of war,
Why such impress[13] of shipwrights, whose sore task
Does not divide the Sunday from the week.
What might be toward [14] that this sweaty haste
Doth make the night joint-laborer with the day?
Who is't that can inform me?

HORATIO   That can I.
At least the whisper goes so. Our last king,
Whose image even but now appeared to us,
Was as you know by Fortinbras of Norway,
Thereto pricked on by a most emulate[15] pride,
Dared to the combat; in which our valiant Hamlet
(For so this side of our known world esteemed him)
Did slay this Fortinbras; who, by a sealed compact
Well ratified by law and heraldry,[16]
Did forfeit, with his life, all those his lands
Which he stood seized [17] of to the conqueror;
Against the which a moiety competent[18]
Was gagèd [19] by our king, which had returned
To the inheritance of Fortinbras

---

[7] *Norway* King of Norway   [8] *parle* parley   [9] *jump* just, exactly   [10] *gross and scope* gross scope, general view   [11] *toils* makes toil; *subject* subjects   [12] *mart* trading   [13] *impress* conscription   [14] *toward* in preparation   [15] *emulate* jealously rivalling   [16] *law and heraldry* law of heralds regulating combat   [17] *seized* possessed   [18] *moiety competent* sufficient portion   [19] *gagèd* engaged, staked

Had he been vanquisher, as, by the same comart[20]
And carriage[21] of the article designed,
His fell to Hamlet. Now, sir, young Fortinbras,
Of unimprovèd [22] mettle hot and full,
Hath in the skirts of Norway here and there
Sharked [23] up a list of lawless resolutes[24]
For food and diet to some enterprise
That hath a stomach[25] in't; which is no other,
As it doth well appear unto our state,
But to recover of us by strong hand
And terms compulsatory those foresaid lands
So by his father lost; and this, I take it,
Is the main motive of our preparations,
The source of this our watch, and the chief head [26]
Of this posthaste and romage[27] in the land.
BERNARDO   I think it be no other but e'en so.
Well may it sort[28] that this portentous figure
Comes armèd through our watch so like the king
That was and is the question of these wars.
HORATIO   A mote[29] it is to trouble the mind's eye.
In the most high and palmy state of Rome,
A little ere the mightiest Julius fell,
The graves stood tenantless and the sheeted [30] dead
Did squeak and gibber in the Roman streets;
As stars with trains of fire and dews of blood,
Disasters[31] in the sun; and the moist star[32]
Upon whose influence Neptune's empire stands
Was sick almost to doomsday with eclipse.
And even the like precurse[33] of feared events,
As harbingers[34] preceding still [35] the fates
And prologue to the omen[36] coming on,
Have heaven and earth together demonstrated
Unto our climatures[37] and countrymen.

(*Enter* GHOST)

But soft, behold, lo where it comes again!

---

[20] *comart* joint bargain   [21] *carriage* purport   [22] *unimprovèd* unused
[23] *Sharked* snatched indiscriminately as the shark takes prey   [24] *resolutes*
desperadoes   [25] *stomach* show of venturesomeness   [26] *head* fountainhead,
source   [27] *romage* intense activity   [28] *sort* suit   [29] *mote* speck of dust
[30] *sheeted* in shrouds   [31] *Disasters* ominous signs   [32] *moist star* moon   [33] *pre-*
curse foreshadowing   [34] *harbingers* forerunners   [35] *still* constantly   [36] *omen*
calamity   [37] *climatures* regions

I'll cross it,[38] though it blast me.—Stay, illusion.

(*He spreads his arms*)

If thou hast any sound or use of voice,
Speak to me.
If there be any good thing to be done
That may to thee do ease and grace to me,
Speak to me.
If thou art privy to thy country's fate,
Which happily[39] foreknowing may avoid,
O, speak!
Or if thou hast uphoarded in thy life
Extorted treasure in the womb of earth,
For which, they say, you spirits oft walk in death,

(*The cock crows*)

Speak of it. Stay and speak. Stop it, Marcellus.
MARCELLUS   Shall I strike at it with my partisan? [40]
HORATIO   Do, if it will not stand.
BERNARDO   'Tis here.
HORATIO   'Tis here.

(*Exit* GHOST)

MARCELLUS   'Tis gone.
We do it wrong, being so majestical,
To offer it the show of violence,
For it is as the air invulnerable,
And our vain blows malicious mockery.
BERNARDO   It was about to speak when the cock crew.
HORATIO   And then it started, like a guilty thing
Upon a fearful summons. I have heard
The cock, that is the trumpet to the morn,
Doth with his lofty and shrill-sounding throat
Awake the god of day, and at his warning,
Whether in sea or fire, in earth or air,
Th' extravagant[41] and erring[42] spirit hies
To his confine; and of the truth herein
This present object made probation.[43]

---

[38] *cross it* cross its path   [39] *happily* haply, perchance   [40] *partisan* pike   [41] *extravagant* wandering beyond bounds   [42] *erring* wandering   [43] *probation* proof

MARCELLUS It faded on the crowing of the cock.
 Some say that ever 'gainst[44] that season comes
 Wherein our Saviour's birth is celebrated,
 This bird of dawning singeth all night long,
 And then, they say, no spirit dare stir abroad,
 The nights are wholesome, then no planets strike,[45]
 No fairy takes,[46] nor witch hath power to charm.
 So hallowed and so gracious is that time.
HORATIO So have I heard and do in part believe it.
 But look, the morn in russet mantle clad
 Walks o'er the dew of yon high eastward hill.
 Break we our watch up, and by my advice
 Let us impart what we have seen to-night
 Unto young Hamlet, for upon my life
 This spirit, dumb to us, will speak to him.
 Do you consent we shall acquaint him with it,
 As needful in our loves, fitting our duty?
MARCELLUS Let's do't, I pray, and I this morning know
 Where we shall find him most conveniently.

 (*Exeunt*)

Act I, Scene II

Elsinore Castle: a room of state

Flourish. Enter CLAUDIUS, *King of Denmark,* GERTRUDE *the Queen,* COUN-
CILLORS, POLONIUS *and his son* LAERTES, HAMLET, *cum aliis*[1] [*including*
VOLTEMAND *and* CORNELIUS]

KING Though yet of Hamlet our dear brother's death
 The memory be green, and that it us befitted
 To bear our hearts in grief, and our whole kingdom
 To be contracted in one brow of woe,
 Yet so far hath discretion fought with nature
 That we with wisest sorrow think on him
 Together with remembrance of ourselves.
 Therefore our sometime sister, now our queen,
 Th' imperial jointress[2] to this warlike state,
 Have we, as 'twere with a defeated joy,
 With an auspicious and a dropping eye,

---

[44] *'gainst* just before [45] *strike* work evil by influence [46] *takes* bewitches
[1] *cum aliis* with others [2] *jointress* a woman who has a jointure, or joint tenancy of an estate

With mirth in funeral and with dirge in marriage,
In equal scale weighing delight and dole,
Taken to wife. Nor have we herein barred [3]
Your better wisdoms, which have freely gone
With this affair along. For all, our thanks.
Now follows, that you know, young Fortinbras,
Holding a weak supposal of our worth,
Or thinking by our late dear brother's death
Our state to be disjoint and out of frame,
Colleaguèd [4] with this dream of his advantage,
He hath not failed to pester us with message
Importing the surrender of those lands
Lost by his father, with all bands of law,
To our most valiant brother. So much for him.
Now for ourself and for this time of meeting.
Thus much the business is: we have here writ
To Norway, uncle of young Fortinbras—
Who, impotent and bedrid, scarcely hears
Of this his nephew's purpose—to suppress
His further gait[5] herein, in that the levies,
The lists, and full proportions[6] are all made
Out of his subject; and we here dispatch
You, good Cornelius, and you, Voltemand,
For bearers of this greeting to old Norway,
Giving to you no further personal power
To business with the king, more than the scope
Of these delated [7] articles allow.
Farewell, and let your haste commend your duty.

CORNELIUS, VOLTEMAND   In that, and all things, will we show our
    duty.

KING   We doubt it nothing. Heartily farewell.

(*Exeunt* VOLTEMAND *and* CORNELIUS)

And now, Laertes, what's the news with you?
You told us of some suit. What is't, Laertes?
You cannot speak of reason to the Dane[8]
And lose your voice.[9] What wouldst thou beg, Laertes,
That shall not be my offer, not thy asking?
The head is not more native[10] to the heart,

---

[3] *barred* excluded   [4] *Colleaguèd* united   [5] *gait* going   [6] *proportions* amounts
of forces and supplies   [7] *delated* detailed   [8] *Dane* King of Denmark   [9] *lose
your voice* speak in vain   [10] *native* joined by nature

The hand more instrumental [11] to the mouth,
Than is the throne of Denmark to thy father.
What wouldst thou have, Laertes?

LAERTES   My dread lord,
Your leave and favor to return to France,
From whence though willingly I came to Denmark
To show my duty in your coronation,
Yet now I must confess, that duty done,
My thoughts and wishes bend again toward France
And bow them to your gracious leave and pardon.

KING   Have you your father's leave? What says Polonius?

POLONIUS   He hath, my lord, wrung from me my slow leave
By laborsome petition, and at last
Upon his will I sealed my hard consent.
I do beseech you give him leave to go.

KING   Take thy fair hour, Laertes. Time be thine,
And thy best graces spend it at thy will.
But now, my cousin[12] Hamlet, and my son—

HAMLET (*aside*)   A little more than kin,[13] and less than kind! [14]

KING   How is it that the clouds still hang on you?

HAMLET   Not so, my lord. I am too much in the sun.[15]

QUEEN   Good Hamlet, cast thy nighted color off,
And let thine eye look like a friend on Denmark.
Do not for ever with thy vailèd [16] lids
Seek for thy noble father in the dust.
Thou know'st 'tis common. All that lives must die,
Passing through nature to eternity.

HAMLET   Ay, madam, it is common.

QUEEN   If it be,
Why seems it so particular with thee?

HAMLET   Seems, madam? Nay, it is. I know not "seems."
'Tis not alone my inky cloak, good mother,
Nor customary suits of solemn black,
Nor windy suspiration of forced breath,
No, nor the fruitful [17] river in the eye,
Nor the dejected havior of the visage,
Together with all forms, moods, shapes of grief,

---

[11] *instrumental* serviceable   [12] *cousin* kinsman more distant than parent, child, brother, or sister   [13] *kin* related as nephew   [14] *kind* kindly in feeling, as by kind, or nature, a son would be to his father   [15] *sun* sunshine of the king's undesired favor (with the punning additional meaning of "place of a son")   [16] *vailèd* downcast   [17] *fruitful* copious

That can denote me truly. These indeed seem,
For they are actions that a man might play,
But I have that within which passeth show—
These but the trappings and the suits of woe.

KING   'Tis sweet and commendable in your nature, Hamlet,
To give these mourning duties to your father,
But you must know your father lost a father,
That father lost, lost his, and the survivor bound
In filial obligation for some term
To do obsequious[18] sorrow. But to persever[19]
In obstinate condolement is a course
Of impious stubbornness. 'Tis unmanly grief.
It shows a will most incorrect to heaven,
A heart unfortified, a mind impatient,
An understanding simple and unschooled.
For what we know must be and is as common
As any the most vulgar thing to sense,
Why should we in our peevish opposition
Take it to heart? Fie, 'tis a fault to heaven,
A fault against the dead, a fault to nature,
To reason most absurd, whose common theme
Is death of fathers, and who still hath cried,
From the first corse till he that died to-day,
"This must be so." We pray you throw to earth
This unprevailing woe, and think of us
As a father, for let the world take note
You are the most immediate to our throne,
And with no less nobility of love
Than that which dearest father bears his son
Do I impart toward you. For your intent
In going back to school in Wittenberg,
It is most retrograde[20] to our desire,
And we beseech you, bend you to remain
Here in the cheer and comfort of our eye,
Our chiefest courtier, cousin, and our son.

QUEEN   Let not thy mother lose her prayers, Hamlet.
I pray thee stay with us, go not to Wittenberg.

HAMLET   I shall in all my best obey you, madam.

KING   Why, 'tis a loving and a fair reply.
Be as ourself in Denmark. Madam, come.

---

18 *obsequious* proper to obsequies or funerals   19 *persever* persevere (accented on the second syllable, as always in Shakespeare)   20 *retrograde* contrary

This gentle and unforced accord of Hamlet
Sits smiling to my heart, in grace whereof
No jocund health that Denmark drinks to-day
But the great cannon to the clouds shall tell,
And the king's rouse[21] the heaven shall bruit[22] again,
Respeaking earthly thunder. Come away.

(*Flourish. Exeunt all but* HAMLET)

HAMLET   O that this too too sullied flesh would melt,
Thaw, and resolve itself into a dew,
Or that the Everlasting had not fixed
His canon[23] gainst self-slaughter. O God, God,
How weary, stale, flat, and unprofitable
Seem to me all the uses of this world!
Fie on't, ah, fie, 'tis an unweeded garden
That grows to seed. Things rank and gross in nature
Possess it merely.[24] That it should come to this,
But two months dead, nay, not so much, not two,
So excellent a king, that was to this
Hyperion[25] to a satyr, so loving to my mother
That he might not beteem[26] the winds of heaven
Visit her face too roughly. Heaven and earth,
Must I remember? Why, she would hang on him
As if increase of appetite had grown
By what it fed on, and yet within a month—
Let me not think on't; frailty, thy name is woman—
A little month, or ere those shoes were old
With which she followed my poor father's body
Like Niobe,[27] all tears, why she, even she—
O God, a beast that wants discourse[28] of reason
Would have mourned longer—married with my uncle,
My father's brother, but no more like my father
Than I to Hercules. Within a month,
Ere yet the salt of most unrighteous tears
Had left the flushing in her gallèd [29] eyes,
She married. O, most wicked speed, to post
With such dexterity to incestuous sheets!

---

[21] *rouse* toast drunk in wine   [22] *bruit* echo   [23] *canon* law   [24] *merely* completely   [25] *Hyperion* the sun god   [26] *beteem* allow   [27] *Niobe* the proud mother who boasted of having more children than Leto and was punished when they were slain by Apollo and Artemis, children of Leto; the grieving Niobe was changed by Zeus into a stone, which continually dropped tears   [28] *discourse* logical power or process   [29] *gallèd* irritated

It is not nor it cannot come to good.
But break my heart, for I must hold my tongue.

(*Enter* HORATIO, MARCELLUS, *and* BERNARDO)

HORATIO   Hail to your lordship!
HAMLET   I am glad to see you well.
Horatio—or I do forget myself.
HORATIO   The same, my lord, and your poor servant ever.
HAMLET   Sir, my good friend, I'll change[30] that name with you.
And what make[31] you from Wittenberg, Horatio?
Marcellus?
MARCELLUS   My good lord!
HAMLET   I am very glad to see you. (*to* BERNARDO) Good even, sir.
But what, in faith, make you from Wittenberg?
HORATIO   A truant disposition, good my lord.
HAMLET   I would not hear your enemy say so,
Nor shall you do my ear that violence
To make it truster of your own report
Against yourself. I know you are no truant.
But what is your affair in Elsinore?
We'll teach you to drink deep ere you depart.
HORATIO   My lord, I came to see your father's funeral.
HAMLET   I prithee do not mock me, fellow student.
I think it was to see my mother's wedding.
HORATIO   Indeed, my lord, it followed hard upon.
HAMLET   Thrift, thrift, Horatio. The funeral baked meats
Did coldly furnish forth the marriage tables.
Would I had met my dearest[32] foe in heaven
Or ever I had seen that day, Horatio!
My father—methinks I see my father.
HORATIO   Where, my lord?
HAMLET   In my mind's eye, Horatio.
HORATIO   I saw him once. 'A was a goodly king.
HAMLET   'A was a man, take him for all in all,
I shall not look upon his like again.
HORATIO   My lord, I think I saw him yesternight.
HAMLET   Saw? who?
HORATIO   My lord, the king your father.
HAMLET   The king my father?
HORATIO   Season your admiration[33] for a while

---

[30] *change* exchange   [31] *make* do   [32] *dearest* direst, bitterest   [33] *Season your admiration* control your wonder

With an attent ear till I may deliver
Upon the witness of these gentlemen
This marvel to you.
HAMLET   For God's love let me hear!
HORATIO   Two nights together had these gentlemen,
Marcellus and Bernardo, on their watch
In the dead waste and middle of the night
Been thus encountered. A figure like your father,
Armèd at point[34] exactly, cap-a-pe,[35]
Appears before them and with solemn march
Goes slow and stately by them. Thrice he walked
By their oppressed and fear-surprisèd eyes
Within his truncheon's[36] length, whilst they, distilled
Almost to jelly with the act of fear,
Stand dumb and speak not to him. This to me
In dreadful secrecy impart they did,
And I with them the third night kept the watch,
Where, as they had delivered, both in time,
Form of the thing, each word made true and good,
The apparition comes. I knew your father.
These hands are not more like.
HAMLET   But where was this?
MARCELLUS   My lord, upon the platform where we watched.
HAMLET   Did you not speak to it?
HORATIO   My lord, I did,
But answer made it none. Yet once methought
It lifted up it[37] head and did address
Itself to motion like as it would speak.
But even then the morning cock crew loud,
And at the sound it shrunk in haste away
And vanished from our sight.
HAMLET   'Tis very strange.
HORATIO   As I do live, my honored lord, 'tis true,
And we did think it writ down in our duty
To let you know of it.
HAMLET   Indeed, indeed, sirs, but this troubles me.
Hold you the watch to-night?
ALL   We do, my lord.
HAMLET   Armed, say you?
ALL   Armed, my lord.

---

[34] *at point* completely   [35] *cap-a pe* from head to foot   [36] *truncheon* military
commander's baton   [37] *it* its

HAMLET	From top to toe?
ALL	My lord, from head to foot.
HAMLET	Then saw you not his face?
HORATIO	O, yes, my lord. He wore his beaver[38] up.
HAMLET	What, looked he frowningly?
HORATIO	A countenance more in sorrow than in anger.
HAMLET	Pale or red?
HORATIO	Nay, very pale.
HAMLET	And fixed his eyes upon you?
HORATIO	Most constantly.
HAMLET	I would I had been there.
HORATIO	It would have much amazed you.
HAMLET	Very like, very like. Stayed it long?
HORATIO	While one with moderate haste might tell [39] a hundred.
BOTH	Longer, longer.
HORATIO	Not when I saw't.
HAMLET	His beard was grizzled,[40] no?
HORATIO	It was as I have seen it in his life,

A sable silvered.[41]

HAMLET	I will watch to-night.

Perchance 'twill walk again.

HORATIO	I warr'nt it will.
HAMLET	If it assume my noble father's person,

I'll speak to it though hell itself should gape
And bid me hold my peace. I pray you all,
If you have hitherto concealed this sight,
Let it be tenable[42] in your silence still,
And whatsomever else shall hap to-night,
Give it an understanding but no tongue.
I will requite your loves. So fare you well.
Upon the platform, 'twixt eleven and twelve
I'll visit you.

ALL	Our duty to your honor.
HAMLET	Your loves, as mine to you. Farewell.

(*Exeunt all but* HAMLET)

My father's spirit—in arms? All is not well.
I doubt[43] some foul play. Would the night were come!

---

[38] *beaver* visor or movable faceguard of the helmet   [39] *tell* count   [40] *grizzled*
grey   [41] *sable silvered* black mixed with white   [42] *tenable* held firmly
[43] *doubt* suspect, fear

Till then sit still, my soul. Foul deeds will rise,
Though all the earth o'erwhelm them, to men's eyes.

(*Exit*)

Act I, Scene III

Elsinore Castle: the chambers of POLONIUS

(*Enter* LAERTES *and* OPHELIA, *his sister*)

LAERTES   My necessaries are embarked. Farewell.
And, sister, as the winds give benefit
And convoy[1] is assistant, do not sleep,
But let me hear from you.

OPHELIA   Do you doubt that?

LAERTES   For Hamlet, and the trifling of his favor,
Hold it a fashion and a toy in blood,
A violet in the youth of primy[2] nature,
Forward, not permanent, sweet, not lasting,
The perfume and suppliance[3] of a minute,
No more.

OPHELIA   No more but so?

LAERTES   Think it no more.
For nature crescent[4] does not grow alone
In thews and bulk, but as this temple[5] waxes
The inward service of the mind and soul
Grows wide withal. Perhaps he loves you now,
And now no soil nor cautel [6] doth besmirch
The virtue of his will,[7] but you must fear,
His greatness weighed,[8] his will is not his own.
(For he himself is subject to his birth.)
He may not, as unvalued persons do,
Carve for himself, for on his choice depends
The safety and health of this whole state,
And therefore must his choice be circumscribed
Unto the voice and yielding[9] of that body
Whereof he is the head. Then if he says he loves you,
It fits your wisdom so far to believe it
As he in his particular act and place

---

[1] *convoy* means of transport   [2] *primy* of the springtime   [3] *perfume and suppliance* filling sweetness   [4] *crescent* growing   [5] *this temple* the body   [6] *cautel* deceit   [7] *will* desire   [8] *greatness weighed* high position considered   [9] *yielding* assent

May give his saying deed, which is no further
Than the main voice of Denmark goes withal.
Then weigh what loss your honor may sustain
If with too credent[10] ear you list his songs,
Or lose your heart, or your chaste treasure open
To his unmastered importunity.
Fear it, Ophelia, fear it, my dear sister,
And keep you in the rear of your affection,[11]
Out of the shot and danger of desire.
The chariest maid is prodigal enough
If she unmask her beauty to the moon.
Virtue itself scapes not calumnious strokes.
The canker[12] galls[13] the infants of the spring
Too oft before their buttons[14] be disclosed,
And in the morn and liquid dew of youth
Contagious blastments[15] are most imminent.
Be wary then; best safety lies in fear.
Youth to itself rebels, though none else near.

OPHELIA   I shall the effect of this good lesson keep
As watchman to my heart, but, good my brother,
Do not as some ungracious pastors do,
Show me the steep and thorny way to heaven,
Whiles like a puffed and reckless libertine
Himself the primrose path of dalliance treads
And recks[16] not his own rede.[17]

(*Enter* POLONIUS)

LAERTES   O, fear me not.
I stay too long. But here my father comes.
A double blessing is a double grace;
Occasion smiles upon a second leave.
POLONIUS   Yet here, Laertes? Aboard, aboard, for shame!
The wind sits in the shoulder of your sail,
And you are stayed for. There—my blessing with thee,
And these few precepts in thy memory
Look thou character.[18] Give thy thoughts no tongue,
Nor any unproportioned[19] thought his act.

---

[10] *credent* credulous   [11] *affection* feelings, which rashly lead forward into
dangers   [12] *canker* rose worm   [13] *galls* injures   [14] *buttons* buds   [15] *blastments* blights   [16] *recks* regards   [17]*rede* counsel   [18] *character* inscribe
[19] *unproportioned* unadjusted to what is right

Be thou familiar, but by no means vulgar.
Those friends thou hast, and their adoption tried,
Grapple them unto thy soul with hoops of steel,
But do not dull thy palm with entertainment
Of each new-hatched, unfledged courage.[20] Beware
Of entrance to a quarrel; but being in,
Bear't that th' opposèd may beware of thee.
Give every man thine ear, but few thy voice;
Take each man's censure,[21] but reserve thy judgment.
Costly thy habit as thy purse can buy,
But not expressed in fancy; rich, not gaudy,
For the apparel oft proclaims the man,
And they in France of the best rank and station
Are of a most select and generous chief [22] in that.
Neither a borrower nor a lender be,
For loan oft loses both itself and friend,
And borrowing dulleth edge of husbandry.[23]
This above all, to thine own self be true,
And it must follow as the night the day
Thou canst not then be false to any man.
Farewell. My blessing season[24] this in thee!

LAERTES   Most humbly do I take my leave, my lord.
POLONIUS   The time invites you. Go, your servants tend.[25]
LAERTES   Farewell, Ophelia, and remember well
What I have said to you.
OPHELIA   'Tis in my memory locked,
And you yourself shall keep the key of it.
LAERTES   Farewell.

(*Exit* LAERTES)

POLONIUS   What is't, Ophelia, he hath said to you?
OPHELIA   So please you, something touching the Lord Hamlet.
POLONIUS   Marry,[26] well bethought.
'Tis told me he hath very oft of late
Given private time to you, and you yourself
Have of your audience been most free and bounteous.
If it be so—as so 'tis put on me,
And that in way of caution—I must tell you

---

[20] *courage* man of spirit, young blood   [21] *censure* judgment   [22] *chief* eminence   [23] *husbandry* thriftiness   [24] *season* ripen and make fruitful   [25] *tend* wait   [26] *Marry* by Mary

You do not understand yourself so clearly
As it behooves my daughter and your honor.
What is between you? Give me up the truth.

OPHELIA   He hath, my lord, of late made many tenders[27]
Of his affection to me.

POLONIUS   Affection? Pooh! You speak like a green girl,
Unsifted [28] in such perilous circumstance.
Do you believe his tenders, as you call them?

OPHELIA   I do not know, my lord, what I should think.

POLONIUS   Marry, I will teach you. Think yourself a baby
That you have ta'en these tenders[29] for true pay
Which are not sterling. Tender yourself more dearly,
Or (not to crack the wind of [30] the poor phrase,
Running it thus) you'll tender me a fool.

OPHELIA   My lord, he hath importuned me with love
In honorable fashion.

POLONIUS   Ay, fashion you may call it. Go to, go to.[31]

OPHELIA   And hath given countenance to his speech, my lord,
With almost all the holy vows of heaven.

POLONIUS   Ay, springes[32] to catch woodcocks.[33] I do know,
When the blood burns, how prodigal the soul
Lends the tongue vows. These blazes, daughter,
Giving more light than heat, extinct in both
Even in their promise, as it is a-making,
You must not take for fire. From this time
Be something scanter of your maiden presence.
Set your entreatments[34] at a higher rate
Than a command to parley.[35] For Lord Hamlet,
Believe so much in him that he is young,
And with a larger tether may he walk
Than may be given you. In few, Ophelia,
Do not believe his vows, for they are brokers,[36]
Not of that dye which their investments[37] show,

---

[27] *tenders* offers   [28] *Unsifted* untested   [29] *tenders . . . Tender . . . tender* offers . . . hold in regard . . . present (a word play going through three meanings, the last use of the word yielding further complexity with its valid implications that she will show herself to him as a fool, will show him to the world as a fool, and may go so far as to present him with a baby, which would be a fool because "fool" was an Elizabethan term of endearment especially applicable to an infant as a "little innocent")   [30] *crack . . . of* make wheeze like a horse driven too hard   [31] *Go to* go away, go on (expressing impatience)   [32] *springes* snares   [33] *woodcocks* birds believed foolish   [34] *entreatments* military negotiations for surrender   [35] *parley* confer with a besieger   [36] *brokers* middlemen, panders   [37] *investments* clothes

But mere implorators of unholy suits,
Breathing like sanctified and pious bawds,
The better to beguile. This is for all:
I would not, in plain terms, from this time forth
Have you so slander[38] any moment[39] leisure
As to give words or talk with the Lord Hamlet.
Look to't, I charge you. Come your ways.
OPHELIA   I shall obey, my lord.

(*Exeunt*)

Act I, Scene IV

The sentry-post

(*Enter* HAMLET, HORATIO, *and* MARCELLUS)

HAMLET   The air bites shrewdly[1]; it is very cold.
HORATIO   It is a nipping and an eager[2] air.
HAMLET   What hour now?
HORATIO   I think it lacks of twelve.
MARCELLUS   No, it is struck.
HORATIO   Indeed? I heard it not. It then draws near the season
Wherein the spirit held his wont to walk.

(*A flourish of trumpets, and two pieces goes off*)

What does this mean, my lord?
HAMLET   The king doth wake to-night and takes his rouse,[3]
Keeps wassail, and the swaggering upspring[4] reels,
And as he drains his draughts of Rhenish[5] down
The kettledrum and trumpet thus bray out
The triumph[6] of his pledge.
HORATIO   Is it a custom?
HAMLET   Ay, marry, is't,
But to my mind, though I am native here
And to the manner born, it is a custom
More honored in the breach than the observance.[7]
This heavy-headed revel east and west
Makes us traduced and taxed of [8] other nations.
They clepe[9] us drunkards and with swinish phrase

---

[38] *slander* use disgracefully   [39] *moment* momentary
[1] *shrewdly* wickedly   [2] *eager* sharp   [3] *rouse* carousal   [4] *upspring* a German
dance   [5] *Rhenish* Rhine wine   [6] *triumph* achievement, feat (in downing a
cup of wine at one draught)   [7] *More . . . observance* better broken than observed   [8] *taxed of* censured by   [9] *clepe* call

Soil our addition,[10] and indeed it takes
From our achievements, though performed at height,
The pith and marrow of our attribute.[11]
So oft it chances in particular men
That (for some vicious mole[12] of nature in them,
As in their birth, wherein they are not guilty,
Since nature cannot choose his[13] origin)
By the o'ergrowth of some complexion,[14]
Oft breaking down the pales[15] and forts of reason,
Or by some habit that too much o'erleavens[16]
The form of plausive[17] manners—that (these men
Carrying, I say, the stamp of one defect,
Being nature's livery,[18] or fortune's star)[19]
Their virtues else, be they as pure as grace,
As infinite as man may undergo,
Shall in the general censure take corruption
From that particular fault. The dram of evil
Doth all the noble substance of a doubt,
To his own scandal.

(*Enter* GHOST)

HORATIO   Look, my lord, it comes.
HAMLET   Angels and ministers of grace defend us!
Be thou a spirit of health[20] or goblin[21] damned,
Bring with thee airs from heaven or blasts from hell,
Be thy intents wicked or charitable,
Thou com'st in such a questionable shape
That I will speak to thee. I'll call thee Hamlet,
King, father, royal Dane. O, answer me!
Let me not burst in ignorance, but tell
Why thy canonized [22] bones, hearsèd in death,
Have burst their cerements,[23] why the sepulchre
Wherein we saw thee quietly interred
Hath oped his ponderous and marble jaws
To cast thee up again. What may this mean

---

[10] *addition* reputation, title added as a distinction   [11] *attribute* reputation,
what is attributed   [12] *mole* blemish, flaw   [13] *his* its   [14] *complexion* part of
the make-up, combination of humors   [15] *pales* barriers, fences   [16] *o'erleavens*
works change throughout, as yeast ferments dough   [17] *plausive* pleasing
[18] *livery* characteristic equipment or provision   [19] *star* make-up as formed by
stellar influence   [20] *of health* sound, good   [21] *goblin* fiend   [22] *canonized*
buried with the established rites of the Church   [23] *cerements* waxed grave-
cloths

That thou, dead corse, again in complete steel,
Revisits thus the glimpses of the moon,
Making night hideous, and we fools of nature[24]
So horridly to shake our disposition
With thoughts beyond the reaches of our souls?
Say, why is this? wherefore? what should we do?

(GHOST *beckons*)

HORATIO   It beckons you to go away with it,
As if it some impartment did desire
To you alone.
MARCELLUS   Look with what courteous action
It waves you to a more removèd ground.
But do not go with it.
HORATIO   No, by no means.
HAMLET   It will not speak. Then will I follow it.
HORATIO   Do not, my lord.
HAMLET   Why, what should be the fear?
I do not set my life at a pin's fee,
And for my soul, what can it do to that,
Being a thing immortal as itself?
It waves me forth again. I'll follow it.
HORATIO   What if it tempt you toward the flood, my lord,
Or to the dreadful summit of the cliff
That beetles[25] o'er his base into the sea,
And there assume some other horrible form,
Which might deprive[26] your sovereignty of reason[27]
And draw you into madness? Think of it.
The very place puts toys[28] of desperation,
Without more motive, into every brain
That looks so many fathoms to the sea
And hears it roar beneath.
HAMLET   It waves me still.
Go on. I'll follow thee.
MARCELLUS   You shall not go, my lord.
HAMLET   Hold off your hands.
HORATIO   Be ruled. You shall not go.
HAMLET   My fate cries out
And makes each petty artere[29] in this body

---

[24] *fools of nature* men made conscious of natural limitations by a supernatural manifestation   [25] *beetles* juts out   [26] *deprive* take away   [27] *sovereignty of reason* state of being ruled by reason   [28] *toys* fancies   [29] *artere* artery

As hardy as the Nemean lion's [30] nerve.[31]
Still am I called. Unhand me, gentlemen.
By heaven, I'll make a ghost of him that lets[32] me!
I say, away! Go on. I'll follow thee.

(*Exit* GHOST, *and* HAMLET)

HORATIO   He waxes desperate with imagination.
MARCELLUS   Let's follow. 'Tis not fit thus to obey him.
HORATIO   Have after. To what issue will this come?
MARCELLUS   Something is rotten in the state of Denmark.
HORATIO   Heaven will direct it.
MARCELLUS   Nay, let's follow him.

(*Exeunt*)

Act I, Scene V

Another part of the fortifications

(*Enter* GHOST *and* HAMLET)

HAMLET   Whither wilt thou lead me? Speak. I'll go no further.
GHOST   Mark me.
HAMLET   I will.
GHOST   My hour is almost come,
    When I to sulph'rous and tormenting flames[1]
    Must render up myself.
HAMLET   Alas, poor ghost!
GHOST   Pity me not, but lend thy serious hearing
    To what I shall unfold.
HAMLET   Speak. I am bound to hear.
GHOST   So art thou to revenge, when thou shalt hear.
HAMLET   What?
GHOST   I am thy father's spirit,
    Doomed for a certain term to walk the night,
    And for the day confined to fast[2] in fires,
    Till the foul crimes done in my days of nature
    Are burnt and purged away. But that I am forbid
    To tell the secrets of my prison house,
    I could a tale unfold whose lightest word
    Would harrow up thy soul, freeze thy young blood,

---

[30] *Nemean lion* a lion slain by Hercules in the performance of one of his twelve labors   [31] *nerve* sinew   [32] *lets* hinders
[1] *flames* sufferings in purgatory (not hell)   [2] *fast* do penance

Make thy two eyes like stars start from their spheres,[3]
Thy knotted and combinèd locks to part,
And each particular hair to stand an[4] end
Like quills upon the fretful porpentine.[5]
But this eternal blazon[6] must not be
To ears of flesh and blood. List, list, O, list!
If thou didst ever thy dear father love—

HAMLET   O God!

GHOST   Revenge his foul and most unnatural murder.

HAMLET   Murder?

GHOST   Murder most foul, as in the best it is,
But this most foul, strange, and unnatural.

HAMLET   Haste me to know't, that I, with wings as swift
As meditation[7] or the thoughts of love,
May sweep to my revenge.

GHOST   I find thee apt,
And duller shouldst thou be than the fat weed
That roots itself in ease on Lethe[8] wharf,
Wouldst thou not stir in this. Now, Hamlet, hear.
'Tis given out that, sleeping in my orchard,
A serpent stung me. So the whole ear of Denmark
Is by a forgèd process[9] of my death
Rankly abused. But know, thou noble youth,
The serpent that did sting thy father's life
Now wears his crown.

HAMLET   O my prophetic soul!
My uncle?

GHOST   Ay, that incestuous, that adulterate[10] beast,
With witchcraft of his wit, with traitorous gifts—
O wicked wit and gifts, that have the power
So to seduce!—won to this shameful lust
The will of my most seeming-virtuous queen.
O Hamlet, what a falling-off was there,
From me, whose love was of that dignity
That it went hand in hand even with the vow
I made to her in marriage, and to decline

---

[3] *spheres* transparent revolving shells in each of which, according to the Ptolemaic astronomy, a planet or other heavenly body was placed   [4] *an* on   [5] *porpentine* porcupine   [6] *eternal blazon* revelation of eternity   [7] *meditation* thought   [8] *Lethe* the river in Hades which brings forgetfulness of past life to a spirit who drinks of it   [9] *forgèd process* falsified official report   [10] *adulterate* adulterous

Upon a wretch whose natural gifts were poor
To those of mine!
But virtue, as it never will be moved,
Though lewdness court it in a shape of heaven,[11]
So lust, though to a radiant angel linked,
Will sate itself in a celestial bed
And prey on garbage.
But soft, methinks I scent the morning air.
Brief let me be. Sleeping within my orchard,
My custom always of the afternoon,
Upon my secure[12] hour thy uncle stole
With juice of cursed hebona[13] in a vial,
And in the porches of my ears did pour
The leperous distilment, whose effect
Holds such an enmity with blood of man
That swift as quicksilver it courses through
The natural gates and alleys of the body,
And with a sudden vigor it doth posset[14]
And curd, like eager[15] droppings into milk,
The thin and wholesome blood. So did it mine,
And a most instant tetter[16] barked [17] about
Most lazar-like[18] with vile and loathsome crust
All my smooth body.
Thus was I sleeping by a brother's hand
Of life, of crown, of queen at once dispatched,
Cut off even in the blossoms of my sin,
Unhouseled,[19] disappointed,[20] unaneled,[21]
No reck'ning made, but sent to my account
With all my imperfections on my head.
O, horrible! O, horrible! most horrible!
If thou hast nature in thee, bear it not.
Let not the royal bed of Denmark be
A couch for luxury[22] and damnèd incest.
But howsomever thou pursues this act,
Taint not thy mind, nor let thy soul contrive
Against thy mother aught. Leave her to heaven
And to those thorns that in her bosom lodge

---

[11] *shape of heaven* angelic disguise   [12] *secure* carefree, unsuspecting   [13] *hebona* some poisonous plant   [14] *posset* curdle   [15] *eager* sour   [16] *tetter* eruption   [17] *barked* covered as with a bark   [18] *lazar-like* leper-like   [19] *Unhouseled* without the Sacrament   [20] *disappointed* unprepared spiritually   [21] *unaneled* without extreme unction   [22] *luxury* lust

To prick and sting her. Fare thee well at once.
The glowworm shows the matin[23] to be near
And gins to pale his uneffectual fire.
Adieu, adieu, adieu. Remember me.

(*Exit*)

HAMLET O all you host of heaven! O earth! What else?
And shall I couple hell? O fie! Hold, hold, my heart,
And you, my sinews, grow not instant old,
But bear me stiffly up. Remember thee?
Ay, thou poor ghost, while memory holds a seat
In this distracted globe.[24] Remember thee?
Yea, from the table[25] of my memory
I'll wipe away all trivial fond records,
All saws[26] of books, all forms,[27] all pressures[28] past
That youth and observation copied there,
And thy commandment all alone shall live
Within the book and volume of my brain,
Unmixed with baser matter. Yes, by heaven!
O most pernicious woman!
O villain, villain, smiling, damnèd villain!
My tables—meet it is I set it down
That one may smile, and smile, and be a villain.
At least I am sure it may be so in Denmark.

(*Writes*)

So, uncle, there you are. Now to my word:
It is "Adieu, adieu, remember me."
I have sworn't.

(*Enter* HORATIO *and* MARCELLUS)

HORATIO My lord, my lord!
MARCELLUS Lord Hamlet!
HORATIO Heavens secure him!
HAMLET So be it!
MARCELLUS Illo, ho, ho,[29] my lord!
HAMLET Hillo, ho, ho, boy! Come, bird, come.
MARCELLUS How is't, my noble lord?
HORATIO What news, my lord?

---

[23] *matin* morning [24] *globe* head [25] *table* writing tablet, record book
[26] *saws* wise sayings [27] *forms* mental images, concepts [28] *pressures* impressions [29] *Illo, ho, ho* cry of the falconer to summon his hawk

HAMLET   O, wonderful!

HORATIO   Good my lord, tell it.

HAMLET   No, you will reveal it.

HORATIO   Not I, my lord, by heaven.

MARCELLUS   Nor I, my lord.

HAMLET   How say you then? Would heart of man once think it?
But you'll be secret?

BOTH   Ay, by heaven, my lord.

HAMLET   There's never a villain dwelling in all Denmark
But he's an arrant knave.

HORATIO   There needs no ghost, my lord, come from the grave
To tell us this.

HAMLET   Why, right, you are in the right,
And so, without more circumstance[30] at all,
I hold it fit that we shake hands and part:
You, as your business and desires shall point you,
For every man hath business and desire
Such as it is, and for my own poor part,
Look you, I'll go pray.

HORATIO   These are but wild and whirling words, my lord.

HAMLET   I am sorry they offend you, heartily;
Yes, faith, heartily.

HORATIO   There's no offense, my lord.

HAMLET   Yes, by Saint Patrick, but there is, Horatio,
And much offense too. Touching this vision here,
It is an honest[31] ghost, that let me tell you.
For your desire to know what is between us,
O'ermaster't as you may. And now, good friends,
As you are friends, scholars, and soldiers,
Give me one poor request.

HORATIO   What is't, my lord? We will.

HAMLET   Never make known what you have seen to-night.

BOTH   My lord, we will not.

HAMLET   Nay, but swear't.

HORATIO   In faith,
My lord, not I.

MARCELLUS   Nor I, my lord—in faith.

HAMLET   Upon my sword.[32]

MARCELLUS   We have sworn, my lord, already.

---

[30] *circumstance* ceremony   [31] *honest* genuine (not a disguised demon)
[32] *sword* i.e. upon the cross formed by the sword hilt

HAMLET   Indeed, upon my sword, indeed.

(GHOST *cries under the stage*)

GHOST   Swear.

HAMLET   Ha, ha, boy, say'st thou so? Art thou there, truepenny? [33]
Come on. You hear this fellow in the cellarage.
Consent to swear.

HORATIO   Propose the oath, my lord.

HAMLET   Never to speak of this that you have seen,
Swear by my sword.

GHOST (*beneath*)   Swear.

HAMLET   Hic et ubique? [34] Then we'll shift our ground.
Come hither, gentlemen,
And lay your hands again upon my sword.
Swear by my sword
Never to speak of this that you have heard.

GHOST (*beneath*)   Swear by his sword.

HAMLET   Well said, old mole! Canst work i' th' earth so fast?
A worthy pioner! [35] Once more remove, good friends.

HORATIO   O day and night, but this is wondrous strange!

HAMLET   And therefore as a stranger give it welcome.
There are more things in heaven and earth, Horatio,
Than are dreamt of in your philosophy.[36]
But come:
Here as before, never, so help you mercy,
How strange or odd some'er I bear myself
(As I perchance hereafter shall think meet
To put an antic[37] disposition on),
That you, at such times seeing me, never shall,
With arms encumb'red [38] thus, or this head-shake,
Or by pronouncing of some doubtful phrase,
As "Well, well, we know," or "We could, an if [39] we would,"
Or "If we list to speak," or "There be, an if they might,"
Or such ambiguous giving out, to note
That you know aught of me—this do swear,
So grace and mercy at your most need help you.

GHOST (*beneath*)   Swear.

(*They swear*)

---

[33] *truepenny* honest old fellow   [34] *Hic et ubique* here and everywhere   [35] *pi-oner* pioneer, miner   [36] *your philosophy* this philosophy one hears about   [37] *antic* grotesque, mad   [38] *encumb'red* folded   [39] *an if* if

HAMLET   Rest, rest, perturbèd spirit! So, gentlemen,
    With all my love I do commend [40] me to you,
    And what so poor a man as Hamlet is
    May do t' express his love and friending to you,
  ⁓ God willing, shall not lack. Let us go in together,
    And still [41] your fingers on your lips, I pray.
    The time is out of joint. O cursèd spite
    That ever I was born to set it right!
    Nay, come, let's go together.

(*Exeunt*)

ACT II

Scene I

The chambers of POLONIUS

(*Enter old* POLONIUS, *with his man* [REYNALDO])

POLONIUS   Give him this money and these notes, Reynaldo.
REYNALDO   I will, my lord.
POLONIUS   You shall do marvellous wisely, good Reynaldo,
    Before you visit him, to make inquire
    Of his behavior.
REYNALDO   My lord, I did intend it.
POLONIUS   Marry, well said, very well said. Look you, sir,
    Enquire me first what Danskers[1] are in Paris,
    And how, and who, what means,[2] and where they keep,[3]
    What company, at what expense; and finding
    By this encompassment[4] and drift of question
    That they do know my son, come you more nearer
    Than your particular demands[5] will touch it.
    Take you as 'twere some distant knowledge of him,
    As thus, "I know his father and his friends,
    And in part him"—do you mark this, Reynaldo?
REYNALDO   Ay, very well, my lord.
POLONIUS   "And in part him, but," you may say, "not well,
    But if't be he I mean, he's very wild
    Addicted so and so." And there put on him
    What forgeries[6] you please; marry, none so rank

---

[40] *commend* entrust   [41] *still* always
[1] *Danskers* Danes   [2] *what means* what their wealth   [3] *keep* dwell   [4] *encompassment* circling about   [5] *particular demands* definite questions   [6] *forgeries* invented wrongdoings

As may dishonor him—take heed of that—
But, sir, such wanton, wild, and usual slips
As are companions noted and most known
To youth and liberty.

REYNALDO   As gaming, my lord.

POLONIUS   Ay, or drinking, fencing, swearing, quarrelling,
Drabbing.[7] You may go so far.

REYNALDO   My lord, that would dishonor him.

POLONIUS   Faith, no, as you may season[8] it in the charge.
You must not put another scandal on him,
That he is open to incontinency.[9]
That's not my meaning. But breathe his faults so quaintly[10]
That they may seem the taints of liberty,
The flash and outbreak of a fiery mind,
A savageness in unreclaimèd [11] blood,
Of general assault.[12]

REYNALDO   But, my good lord—

POLONIUS   Wherefore should you do this?

REYNALDO   Ay, my lord,
I would know that.

POLONIUS   Marry, sir, here's my drift,
And I believe it is a fetch of warrant.[13]
You laying these slight sullies on my son
As 'twere a thing a little soiled i' th' working,
Mark you,
Your party in converse, him you would sound,
Having ever[14] seen in the prenominate[15] crimes
The youth you breathe of guilty, be assured
He closes with you[16] in this consequence:[17]
"Good sir," or so, or "friend," or "gentleman"—
According to the phrase or the addition[18]
Of man and country—

REYNALDO   Very good, my lord.

POLONIUS   And then, sir, does 'a this—'a does—
What was I about to say? By the mass, I was about to say something! Where did I leave?

---

[7] *Drabbing* whoring   [8] *season* soften   [9] *incontinency* extreme sensuality
[10] *quaintly* expertly, gracefully   [11] *unreclaimèd* untamed   [12] *Of general assault* assailing all young men   [13] *fetch of warrant* allowable trick   [14] *Having ever* if he has ever   [15] *prenominate* aforementioned   [16] *closes with you* follows your lead to a conclusion   [17] *consequence* following way   [18] *addition* title

REYNALDO   At "closes in the consequence," at "friend or so," and
    "gentleman."

POLONIUS   At "closes in the consequence"—Ay, marry!
  He closes thus: "I know the gentleman;
  I saw him yesterday, or t' other day,
  Or then, or then, with such or such, and, as you say,
  There was 'a gaming, there o'ertook[19] in's rouse,[20]
  There falling[21] out at tennis"; or perchance,
  "I saw him enter such a house of sale,"
  Videlicet,[22] a brothel, or so forth.
  See you now—
  Your bait of falsehood takes this carp of truth,
  And thus do we of wisdom and of reach,[23]
  With windlasses[24] and with assays of bias,[25]
  By indirections find directions[26] out.
  So, by my former lecture and advice,
  Shall you my son. You have me, have you not?

REYNALDO   My lord, I have.

POLONIUS   God bye ye,[27] fare ye well.

REYNALDO   Good my lord.

POLONIUS   Observe his inclination in yourself.

REYNALDO   I shall, my lord.

POLONIUS   And let him ply his music.

REYNALDO   Well, my lord.

POLONIUS   Farewell.

  (*Exit* REYNALDO)

  (*Enter* OPHELIA)

                   How now, Ophelia, what's the matter?

OPHELIA   O my lord, my lord, I have been so affrighted!

POLONIUS   With what, i' th' name of God?

OPHELIA   My lord, as I was sewing in my closet,[28]
  Lord Hamlet, with his doublet[29] all unbraced,[30]
  No hat upon his head, his stockings fouled,
  Ungartered, and down-gyvèd [31] to his ankle,
  Pale as his shirt, his knees knocking each other,

---

[19] *o'ertook* overcome with drunkenness   [20] *rouse* carousal   [21] *falling out* quarrelling   [22] *Videlicet* namely   [23] *reach* far-reaching comprehension   [24] *windlasses* roundabout courses   [25] *assays of bias* devious attacks   [26] *directions* ways of procedure   [27] *God bye ye* God be with you, good-bye   [28] *closet* private living-room   [29] *doublet* jacket   [30] *unbraced* unlaced   [31] *down-gyvèd* fallen down like gyves or fetters on a prisoner's legs

And with a look so piteous in purport
As if he had been loosèd out of hell
To speak of horrors—he comes before me.
POLONIUS   Mad for thy love?
OPHELIA   My lord, I do not know,
But truly I do fear it.
POLONIUS   What said he?
OPHELIA   He took me by the wrist and held me hard.
Then goes he to the length of all his arm,
And with his other hand thus o'er his brow
He falls to such perusal of my face
As 'a would draw it. Long stayed he so.
At last, a little shaking of mine arm
And thrice his head thus waving up and down,
He raised a sigh so piteous and profound
As it did seem to shatter all his bulk
And end his being. That done, he lets me go,
And with his head over his shoulder turned
He seemed to find his way without his eyes,
For out o' doors he went without their helps
And to the last bended their light on me.
POLONIUS   Come, go with me. I will go seek the king.
This is the very ecstasy[32] of love,
Whose violent property[33] fordoes[34] itself
And leads the will to desperate undertakings
As oft as any passion under heaven
That does afflict our natures. I am sorry.
What, have you given him any hard words of late?
OPHELIA   No, my good lord; but as you did command
I did repel his letters and denied
His access to me.
POLONIUS   That hath made him mad.
I am sorry that with better heed and judgment
I had not quoted [35] him. I feared he did but trifle
And meant to wrack thee; but beshrew[36] my jealousy.
By heaven, it is as proper to our age
To cast beyond ourselves[37] in our opinions
As it is common for the younger sort
To lack discretion. Come, go we to the king.

---

[32] *ecstasy* madness [33] *property* quality [34] *fordoes* destroys [35] *quoted* observed [36] *beshrew* curse [37] *cast beyond ourselves* find by calculation more significance in something than we ought to

This must be known, which, being kept close,[38] might move[39]
More grief to hide than hate to utter love.[40]
Come.

(*Exeunt*)

Act II, Scene II

A chamber in the castle

(*Flourish. Enter* KING *and* QUEEN, ROSENCRANTZ, *and* GUILDENSTERN
[*with others*])

KING   Welcome, dear Rosencrantz and Guildenstern.
    Moreover that[1] we much did long to see you,
    The need we have to use you did provoke
    Our hasty sending. Something have you heard
    Of Hamlet's transformation—so call it,
    Sith[2] nor th' exterior nor the inward man
    Resembles that it was. What it should be,
    More than his father's death, that thus hath put him
    So much from th' understanding of himself,
    I cannot dream of. I entreat you both
    That, being of so young days brought up with him,
    And sith so neighbored to his youth and havior,[3]
    That you vouchsafe your rest here in our court
    Some little time, so by your companies
    To draw him on to pleasures, and to gather
    So much as from occasion you may glean,
    Whether aught to us unknown afflicts him thus,
    That opened [4] lies within our remedy.
QUEEN   Good gentlemen, he hath much talked of you,
    And sure I am two men there are not living
    To whom he more adheres.[5] If it will please you
    To show us so much gentry[6] and good will
    As to expend your time with us awhile
    For the supply and profit of our hope,
    Your visitation shall receive such thanks
    As fits a king's remembrance.

---

[38] *close* secret   [39] *move* cause   [40] *to hide . . . love* by such hiding of love than
there would be hate moved by a revelation of it (a violently condensed
putting of the case which is a triumph of special statement for Polonius)
[1] *Moreover that* besides the fact that   [2] *Sith* since   [3] *youth and havior*
youthful ways of life   [4] *opened* revealed   [5] *more adheres* is more attached
[6] *gentry* courtesy

ROSENCRANTZ   Both your majesties
　Might, by the sovereign power you have of us,
　Put your dread pleasures more into command
　Than to entreaty.
GUILDENSTERN   But we both obey,
　And here give up ourselves in the full bent[7]
　To lay our service freely at your feet,
　To be commanded.
KING   Thanks, Rosencrantz and gentle Guildenstern.
QUEEN   Thanks, Guildenstern and gentle Rosencrantz.
　And I beseech you instantly to visit
　My too much changèd son.—Go, some of you,
　And bring these gentlemen where Hamlet is.
GUILDENSTERN   Heavens make our presence and our practices
　Pleasant and helpful to him!
QUEEN   Ay, amen!

　(*Exeunt* ROSENCRANTZ *and* GUILDENSTERN [*with some* ATTENDANTS])

　(*Enter* POLONIUS)

POLONIUS   Th' ambassadors from Norway, my good lord,
　Are joyfully returned.
KING   Thou still [8] hast been the father of good news.
POLONIUS   Have I, my lord? Assure you, my good liege,
　I hold my duty as I hold my soul,
　Both to my God and to my gracious king,
　And I do think—or else this brain of mine
　Hunts not the trail of policy so sure
　As it hath used to do—that I have found
　The very cause of Hamlet's lunacy.
KING   O, speak of that! That do I long to hear.
POLONIUS   Give first admittance to th' ambassadors.
　My news shall be the fruit[9] to that great feast.
KING   Thyself do grace[10] to them and bring them in.

　(*Exit* POLONIUS)

　He tells me, my dear Gertrude, he hath found
　The head and source of all your son's distemper.
QUEEN   I doubt[11] it is no other but the main,
　His father's death and our o'erhasty marriage.

---

[7] *in the full bent* at the limit of bending (of a bow), to full capacity   [8] *still* always   [9] *fruit* dessert   [10] *grace* honor   [11] *doubt* suspect

KING   Well, we shall sift him.

(*Enter* AMBASSADORS [VOLTEMAND *and* CORNELIUS, *with* POLONIUS])

Welcome, my good friends.
Say, Voltemand, what from our brother Norway?

VOLTEMAND   Most fair return of greetings and desires.
Upon our first,[12] he sent out to suppress
His nephew's levies, which to him appeared
To be a preparation 'gainst the Polack,
But better looked into, he truly found
It was against your highness, whereat grieved,
That so his sickness, age, and impotence
Was falsely borne in hand,[13] sends out arrests
On Fortinbras; which he in brief obeys,
Receives rebuke from Norway, and in fine[14]
Makes vow before his uncle never more
To give th' assay[15] of arms against your majesty.
Whereon old Norway, overcome with joy,
Gives him threescore thousand crowns in annual fee
And his commission to employ those soldiers,
So levied as before, against the Polack,
With an entreaty, herein further shown,

(*Gives a paper*)

That it might please you to give quiet pass
Through your dominions for this enterprise,
On such regards[16] of safety and allowance
As therein are set down.

KING   It likes us well;
And at our more considered time[17] we'll read,
Answer, and think upon this business.
Meantime we thank you for your well-took labor.
Go to your rest; at night we'll feast together.
Most welcome home!

(*Exeunt* AMBASSADORS)

POLONIUS   This business is well ended.
My liege and madam, to expostulate[18]
What majesty should be, what duty is,

---

[12] *our first* our first words about the matter   [13] *borne in hand* deceived   [14] *in fine* in the end   [15] *assay* trial   [16] *regards* terms   [17] *considered time* convenient time for consideration   [18] *expostulate* discuss

Why day is day, night night, and time is time,
Were nothing but to waste night, day, and time.
Therefore, since brevity is the soul of wit,[19]
And tediousness the limbs and outward flourishes,
I will be brief. Your noble son is mad.
Mad call I it, for, to define true madness,
What is't but to be nothing else but mad?
But let that go.

QUEEN   More matter, with less art.

POLONIUS   Madam, I swear I use no art at all.
That he is mad, 'tis true: 'tis true 'tis pity,
And pity 'tis 'tis true—a foolish figure.[20]
But farewell it, for I will use no art.
Mad let us grant him then, and now remains
That we find out the cause of this effect—
Or rather say, the cause of this defect,
For this effect defective comes by cause.
Thus it remains, and the remainder thus.
Perpend.[21]
I have a daughter (have while she is mine),
Who in her duty and obedience, mark,
Hath given me this. Now gather, and surmise.

(Reads the letter)

"To the celestial, and my soul's idol, the most beautified
Ophelia,"—
That's an ill phrase, a vile phrase; "beautified" is a vile phrase.
But you shall hear. Thus:

(Reads)

"In her excellent white bosom, these, &c."

QUEEN   Came this from Hamlet to her?

POLONIUS   Good madam, stay awhile. I will be faithful.

(Reads)

        "Doubt thou the stars are fire;
            Doubt that the sun doth move;
        Doubt[22] truth to be a liar;
            But never doubt I love.
O dear Ophelia, I am ill at these numbers.[23] I have not art to

---

[19] *wit* understanding   [20] *figure* figure in rhetoric   [21] *Perpend* ponder
[22] *Doubt* suspect   [23] *numbers* verses

reckon my groans, but that I love thee best, O most best, believe it.
Adieu.

> Thine evermore, most dear lady,
> whilst this machine[24] is to[25] him, Hamlet."

This in obedience hath my daughter shown me,
And more above[26] hath his solicitings,
As they fell out by time, by means, and place,
All given to mine ear.

KING   But how hath she
Received his love?

POLONIUS   What do you think of me?

KING   As of a man faithful and honorable.

POLONIUS   I would fain prove so. But what might you think,
When I had seen this hot love on the wing
(As I perceived it, I must tell you that,
Before my daughter told me), what might you,
Or my dear majesty your queen here, think,
If I had played the desk or table book,[27]
Or given my heart a winking,[28] mute and dumb,
Or looked upon this love with idle sight?
What might you think? No, I went round [29] to work
And my young mistress thus I did bespeak:
"Lord Hamlet is a prince, out of thy star.[30]
This must not be." And then I prescripts[31] gave her,
That she should lock herself from his resort,
Admit no messengers, receive no tokens.
Which done, she took the fruits of my advice,
And he, repellèd, a short tale to make,
Fell into a sadness, then into a fast,
Thence to a watch,[32] thence into a weakness,
Thence to a lightness,[33] and, by this declension,
Into the madness wherein now he raves,
And all we mourn for.

KING   Do you think 'tis this?

QUEEN   It may be, very like.

POLONIUS   Hath there been such a time—I would fain know that—

---

[24] *machine* body   [25] *to* attached to   [26] *above* besides   [27] *desk or table book*
i.e. silent receiver   [28] *winking* closing of the eyes   [29] *round* roundly, plainly
[30] *star* condition determined by stellar influence   [31] *prescripts* instructions
[32] *watch* sleepless state   [33] *lightness* lightheadedness

That I have positively said " 'Tis so,"
When it proved otherwise?
KING   Not that I know.
POLONIUS (*pointing to his head and shoulder*)
   Take this from this, if this be otherwise.
   If circumstances lead me, I will find
   Where truth is hid, though it were hid indeed
   Within the center.[34]
KING   How may we try it further?
POLONIUS   You know sometimes he walks four hours together
   Here in the lobby.
QUEEN   So he does indeed.
POLONIUS   At such a time I'll loose my daughter to him.
   Be you and I behind an arras[35] then.
   Mark the encounter. If he love her not,
   And be not from his reason fallen thereon,[36]
   Let me be no assistant for a state
   But keep a farm and carters.
KING   We will try it.

   (*Enter* HAMLET [*reading on a book*])

QUEEN   But look where sadly the poor wretch comes reading.
POLONIUS   Away, I do beseech you both, away.

   (*Exit* KING *and* QUEEN [*with* ATTENDANTS])

   I'll board [37] him presently.[38] O, give me leave.
   How does my good Lord Hamlet?
HAMLET   Well, God-a-mercy.[39]
POLONIUS   Do you know me, my lord?
HAMLET   Excellent well. You are a fishmonger.[40]
POLONIUS   Not I, my lord.
HAMLET   Then I would you were so honest a man.
POLONIUS   Honest, my lord?
HAMLET   Ay, sir. To be honest, as this world goes, is to be one man
   picked out of ten thousand.
POLONIUS   That's very true, my lord.

---

[34] *center* center of the earth and also of the Ptolemaic universe   [35] *arras* hanging tapestry   [36] *thereon* on that account   [37] *board* accost   [38] *presently* at once   [39] *God-a-mercy* thank you (literally, "God have mercy!")   [40] *fishmonger* seller of harlots, procurer (a cant term used here with a glance at the fishing Polonius is doing when he offers Ophelia as bait)

HAMLET   For if the sun breed maggots in a dead dog, being a good kissing carrion[41]—Have you a daughter?

POLONIUS   I have, my lord.

HAMLET   Let her not walk i' th' sun. Conception is a blessing, but as your daughter may conceive, friend, look to't.

POLONIUS   (*aside*)   How say you by that? Still harping on my daughter. Yet he knew me not at first. 'A said I was a fishmonger. 'A is far gone, far gone. And truly in my youth I suffered much extremity for love, very near this. I'll speak to him again.—What do you read, my lord?

HAMLET   Words, words, words.

POLONIUS   What is the matter, my lord?

HAMLET   Between who? [42]

POLONIUS   I mean the matter that you read, my lord.

HAMLET   Slanders, sir, for the satirical rogue says here that old men have grey beards, that their faces are wrinkled, their eyes purging thick amber and plum-tree gum, and that they have a plentiful lack of wit, together with most weak hams. All which, sir, though I most powerfully and potently believe, yet I hold it not honesty to have it thus set down, for you yourself, sir, should be old as I am if, like a crab, you could go backward.

POLONIUS   (*aside*)   Though this be madness, yet there is method in't. —Will you walk out of the air, my lord?

HAMLET   Into my grave?

POLONIUS   Indeed, that's out of the air. (*aside*) How pregnant[43] sometimes his replies are! a happiness[44] that often madness hits on, which reason and sanity could not so prosperously be delivered of. I will leave him and suddenly contrive the means of meeting between him and my daughter.—My honorable lord, I will most humbly take my leave of you.

HAMLET   You cannot, sir, take from me anything that I will more willingly part withal[45]—except my life, except my life, except my life.

(*Enter* GUILDENSTERN *and* ROSENCRANTZ)

POLONIUS   Fare you well, my lord.

HAMLET   These tedious old fools!

POLONIUS   You go to seek the Lord Hamlet. There he is.

---

[41] *good kissing carrion* good bit of flesh for kissing   [42] *Between who* matter for a quarrel between what persons (Hamlet's willful misunderstanding) [43] *pregnant* full of meaning   [44] *happiness* aptness of expression   [45] *withal* with

ROSENCRANTZ (*to* POLONIUS)   God save you, sir!

(*Exit* POLONIUS)

GUILDENSTERN   My honored lord!

ROSENCRANTZ   My most dear lord!

HAMLET   My excellent good friends! How dost thou, Guildenstern? Ah, Rosencrantz! Good lads, how do ye both?

ROSENCRANTZ   As the indifferent[46] children of the earth.

GUILDENSTERN   Happy in that we are not over-happy. On Fortune's cap we are not the very button.

HAMLET   Nor the soles of her shoe?

ROSENCRANTZ   Neither, my lord.

HAMLET   Then you live about her waist, or in the middle of her favors?

GUILDENSTERN   Faith, her privates[47] we.

HAMLET   In the secret parts of Fortune? O, most true! she is a strumpet. What news?

ROSENCRANTZ   None, my lord, but that the world's grown honest.

HAMLET   Then is doomsday near. But your news is not true. (Let me question more in particular.) What have you, my good friends, deserved at the hands of Fortune that she sends you to prison hither?

GUILDENSTERN   Prison, my lord?

HAMLET   Denmark 's a prison.

ROSENCRANTZ   Then is the world one.

HAMLET   A goodly one; in which there are many confines,[48] wards,[49] and dungeons, Denmark being one o' th' worst.

ROSENCRANTZ   We think not so, my lord.

HAMLET   Why, then 'tis none to you, for there is nothing either good or bad but thinking makes it so. To me it is a prison.

ROSENCRANTZ   Why, then your ambition makes it one. 'Tis too narrow for your mind.

HAMLET   O God, I could be hounded in a nutshell and count myself a king of infinite space, were it not that I have bad dreams.

GUILDENSTERN   Which dreams indeed are ambition, for the very substance of the ambitious is merely the shadow of a dream.

HAMLET   A dream itself is but a shadow.

ROSENCRANTZ   Truly, and I hold ambition of so airy and light a quality that it is but a shadow's shadow.

---

[46] *indifferent* average   [47] *privates* ordinary men in private, not public, life (with obvious play upon the sexual term "private parts")   [48] *confines* places of imprisonment   [49] *wards* cells

HAMLET   Then are our beggars bodies,[50] and our monarchs and outstretched [51] heroes the beggars' shadows. Shall we to th' court?
for, by my fay,[52] I cannot reason.

BOTH   We'll wait upon[53] you.

HAMLET   No such matter. I will not sort you with the rest of my
servants, for, to speak to you like an honest man, I am most dreadfully attended. But in the beaten way of friendship, what make[54]
you at Elsinore?

ROSENCRANTZ   To visit you, my lord; no other occasion.

HAMLET   Beggar that I am, I am even poor in thanks, but I thank
you; and sure, dear friends, my thanks are too dear a halfpenny.[55]
Were you not sent for? Is it your own inclining? Is it a free visitation? Come, come, deal justly with me. Come, come. Nay, speak.

GUILDENSTERN   What should we say, my lord?

HAMLET   Why, anything—but to th' purpose. You were sent for,
and there is a kind of confession in your looks, which your modes-
ties have not craft enough to color. I know the good king and
queen have sent for you.

ROSENCRANTZ   To what end, my lord?

HAMLET   That you must teach me. But let me conjure you by the
rights of our fellowship, by the consonancy[56] of our youth, by the
obligation of our ever-preserved love, and by what more dear a
better proposer[57] can charge you withal,[58] be even[59] and direct
with me whether you were sent for or no.

ROSENCRANTZ (*aside to* GUILDENSTERN)   What say you?

HAMLET (*aside*)   Nay then, I have an eye of you.—If you love me,
hold not off.

GUILDENSTERN   My lord, we were sent for.

HAMLET   I will tell you why. So shall my anticipation prevent[60]
your discovery,[61] and your secrecy to the king and queen moult no
feather.[62] I have of late—but wherefore I know not—lost all my
mirth, forgone all custom of exercises; and indeed, it goes so heavily with my disposition that this goodly frame the earth seems to
me a sterile promontory; this most excellent canopy, the air, look
you, this brave o'erhanging firmament,[63] this majestical roof

---

[50] *bodies* solid substances, not shadows (because beggars lack ambition)
[51] *outstretched* elongated as shadows (with a corollary implication of far-
reaching with respect to the ambitions that make both heroes and monarchs
into shadows)   [52] *fay* faith   [53] *wait upon* attend   [54] *make* do   [55] *a halfpenny* at a halfpenny   [56] *consonancy* accord (in sameness of age)   [57] *proposer* propounder   [58] *withal* with   [59] *even* straight   [60] *prevent* forestall
[61] *discovery* disclosure   [62] *moult no feather* be left whole   [63] *firmament* sky

fretted [64] with golden fire—why, it appeareth nothing to me but a foul and pestilent congregation of vapors. What a piece of work is a man, how noble in reason, how infinite in faculties; in form and moving how express[65] and admirable, in action how like an angel, in apprehension how like a god: the beauty of the world, the paragon of animals! And yet to me what is this quintessence[66] of dust? Man delights not me—nor woman neither, though by your smiling you seem to say so.

ROSENCRANTZ   My lord, there was no such stuff in my thoughts.

HAMLET   Why did ye laugh then, when I said "Man delights not me"?

ROSENCRANTZ   To think, my lord, if you delight not in man, what lenten[67] entertainment the players shall receive from you. We coted [68] them on the way, and hither are they coming to offer you service.

HAMLET   He that plays the king shall be welcome—his majesty shall have tribute of me—, the adventurous knight shall use his foil and target,[69] the lover shall not sigh gratis, the humorous man[70] shall end his part in peace, the clown shall make those laugh whose lungs are tickle o' th' sere,[71] and the lady shall say her mind freely, or the blank verse shall halt[72] for't. What players are they?

ROSENCRANTZ   Even those you were wont to take such delight in, the tragedians of the city.

HAMLET   How chances it they travel? Their residence,[73] both in reputation and profit, was better both ways.

ROSENCRANTZ   I think their inhibition[74] comes by the means of the late innovation.[75]

HAMLET   Do they hold the same estimation they did when I was in the city? Are they so followed?

ROSENCRANTZ   No indeed, are they not.

HAMLET   How comes it? Do they grow rusty?

ROSENCRANTZ   Nay, their endeavor keeps in the wonted pace, but there is, sir, an eyrie[76] of children, little eyases,[77] that cry out on

---

[64] *fretted* decorated with fretwork   [65] *express* well framed   [66] *quintessence* fifth or last and finest essence (an alchemical term)   [67] *lenten* scanty   [68] *coted* overtook   [69] *foil and target* sword and shield   [70] *humorous man* eccentric character dominated by one of the humours   [71] *tickle o' th' sere* hair-triggered for the discharge of laughter ("sere": part of a gunlock)   [72] *halt* go lame   [73] *residence* residing at the capital   [74] *inhibition* impediment to acting in residence (formal prohibition?)   [75] *innovation* new fashion of having companies of boy actors play on the "private" stage (?), political upheaval (?)   [76] *eyrie* nest   [77] *eyases* nestling hawks

the top of question[78] and are most tyranically clapped for't. These are now the fashion, and so berattle[79] the common stages[80] (so they call them) that many wearing rapiers are afraid of goose-quills[81] and dare scarce come thither.

HAMLET   What, are they children? Who maintains 'em? How are they escoted? [82] Will they pursue the quality[83] no longer than they can sing? [84] Will they not say afterwards, if they should grow themselves to common players (as it is most like, if their means are no better), their writers do them wrong to make them exclaim against their own succession?

ROSENCRANTZ   Faith, there has been much to do on both sides, and the nation holds it no sin to tarre[85] them to controversy. There was, for a while, no money bid for argument[86] unless the poet and the player went to cuffs in the question.

HAMLET   Is't possible?

GUILDENSTERN   O, there has been much throwing about of brains.

HAMLET   Do the boys carry it away?

ROSENCRANTZ   Ay, that they do, my lord—Hercules and his load [87] too.

HAMLET   It is not very strange, for my uncle is King of Denmark, and those that would make mows[88] at him while my father lived give twenty, forty, fifty, a hundred ducats apiece for his picture in little. 'Sblood,[89] there is something in this more than natural, if philosophy could find it out.

A flourish

GUILDENSTERN   There are the players.

HAMLET   Gentlemen, you are welcome to Elsinore. Your hands, come then. Th' appurtenance of welcome is fashion and cere-mony. Let me comply with you in this garb,[90] lest my extent[91] to the players (which I tell you must show fairly outwards) should more appear like entertainment than yours. You are welcome. But my uncle-father and aunt-mother are deceived.

---

[78] *on the top of question* above others on matter of dispute   [79] *berattle* be-rate   [80] *common stages* "public" theatres of the "common" players, who were organized in companies mainly composed of adult actors (allusion being made to the "War of the Theatres" in Shakespeare's London)   [81] *goosequills* pens (of satirists who made out that the London public stage showed low taste)   [82] *escoted* supported   [83] *quality* profession of acting   [84] *sing* i.e. with unchanged voices   [85] *tarre* incite   [86] *argument* matter of a play   [87] *load* i.e. the whole word (with a topical reference to the sign of the Globe Theatre, a representation of Hercules bearing the world on his shoulders)   [88] *mows* grimaces   [89] *'Sblood* by God's blood   [90] *garb* fashion   [91] *extent* showing of welcome

GUILDENSTERN   In what, my dear lord?

HAMLET   I am but mad north-north-west. When the wind is south-erly I know a hawk from a handsaw.[92]

(*Enter* POLONIUS)

POLONIUS   Well be with you, gentlemen.

HAMLET   Hark you, Guildenstern—and you too—at each ear a hearer. That great baby you see there is not yet out of his swad-dling clouts.[93]

ROSENCRANTZ   Happily[94] he is the second time come to them, for they say an old man is twice a child.

HAMLET   I will prophesy he comes to tell me of the players. Mark it.—You say right, sir; a Monday morning, 'twas then indeed.

POLONIUS   My lord, I have news to tell you.

HAMLET   My lord, I have news to tell you. When Roscius[95] was an actor in Rome—

POLONIUS   The actors are come hither, my lord.

HAMLET   Buzz, buzz.

POLONIUS   Upon my honor—

HAMLET   Then came each actor on his ass—

POLONIUS   The best actors in the world, either for tragedy, comedy, history, pastoral, pastoral-comical, historical-pastoral, tragical-historical, tragical-comical-historical-pastoral; scene individable,[96] or poem unlimited.[97] Seneca[98] cannot be too heavy, nor Plautus[99] too light. For the law of writ[100] and the liberty,[101] these are the only men.

HAMLET   O Jephthah,[102] judge of Israel, what a treasure hadst thou!

POLONIUS   What treasure had he, my lord?

HAMLET   Why,
        "One fair daughter, and no more,
            The which he lovèd passing[103] well."

---

[92] *hawk* mattock or pickaxe (also called "hack"; here used apparently with a play on "hawk": a bird); *handsaw* carpenter's tool (apparently with a play on some corrupt form of "hernshaw"; heron, a bird often hunted with the hawk)   [93] *clout*s clothes   [94] *Happily* haply, perhaps   [95] *Roscius* the greatest of Roman comic actors   [96] *scene individable* drama observing the unities   [97] *poem unlimited* drama not observing the unities   [98] *Seneca* Roman writer of tragedies   [99] *Plautus* Roman writer of comedies   [100] *law of writ* ortho-doxy determined by critical rules of the drama   [101] *liberty* freedom from such orthodoxy   [102] *Jephthah* the compelled sacrificer of a dearly beloved daughter (Judges xi)   [103] *passing* surpassingly (verses are from a ballad on Jephthah)

POLONIUS (*aside*) Still on my daughter.

HAMLET Am I not i' th' right, old Jephthah?

POLONIUS If you call me Jephthah, my lord, I have a daughter that I love passing well.

HAMLET Nay, that follows not.

POLONIUS What follows then, my lord?

HAMLET Why,

"As by lot, God wot,"

and then, you know,

"It came to pass, as most like it was."

The first row[104] of the pious chanson[105] will show you more, for look where my abridgment[106] comes.

(*Enter the* PLAYERS)

You are welcome, masters, welcome, all.—I am glad to see thee well.—Welcome, good friends.—O, old friend, why, thy face is valanced [107] since I saw thee last. Com'st thou to beard me in Denmark?—What, my young lady[108] and mistress? By'r Lady, your ladyship is nearer to heaven than when I saw you last by the altitude of a chopine.[109] Pray God your voice, like a piece of un-current[110] gold, be not cracked within the ring.[111]—Masters, you are all welcome. We'll e'en to't like French falconers, fly at anything we see. We'll have a speech straight. Come, give us a taste of your quality. Come, a passionate speech.

PLAYER What speech, my good lord?

HAMLET I heard thee speak me a speech once, but it was never acted, or if it was, not above once, for the play, I remember, pleased not the million; 'twas caviary[112] to the general,[113] but it was (as I received it, and others, whose judgments in such matters cried in the top of [114] mine) an excellent play, well digested in the scenes, set down with as much modesty as cunning. I remember one said there were no sallets[115] in the lines to make the matter savory, nor no matter in the phrase that might indict the author of affectation, but called it an honest method, as wholesome as sweet, and by very much more handsome than fine. One speech

---

[104] *row* stanza [105] *chanson* song [106] *my abridgment* that which shortens my talk [107] *valanced* fringed (with a beard) [108] *young lady* boy who plays women's parts [109] *chopine* women's thick-soled shoe [110] *uncurrent* not legal tender [111] *within the ring* from the edge through the line circling the design on the coin (with a play on "ring": a sound) [112] *caviary* caviare [113] *general* multitude [114] *in the top of* more authoritatively than [115] *sallets* salads, highly seasoned passages

in't I chiefly loved. 'Twas Aeneas' tale to Dido, and thereabout of
it especially where he speaks of Priam's[116] slaughter. If it live in
your memory, begin at this line—let me see, let me see:
   "The rugged Pyrrhus, like th' Hyrcanian beast[117]—"
'Tis not so; it begins with Pyrrhus:
   "The rugged Pyrrhus, he whose sable[118] arms,
   Black as his purpose, did the night resemble
   When he lay couchèd in the ominous[119] horse,[120]
   Hath now this dread and black complexion smeared
   With heraldry more dismal.[121] Head to foot
   Now is he total gules,[122] horridly tricked [123]
   With blood of fathers, mothers, daughters, sons,
   Baked and impasted with the parching[124] streets,
   That lend a tyrannous and a damnèd light
   To their lord's murder. Roasted in wrath and fire,
   And thus o'ersizèd [125] with coagulate[126] gore,
   With eyes like carbuncles, the hellish Pyrrhus
   Old grandsire Priam seeks."
So, proceed you.

POLONIUS   Fore God, my lord, well spoken, with good accent and
good discretion.

PLAYER   "Anon he finds him,
   Striking too short at Greeks. His antique sword,
   Rebellious to his arms, lies where it falls,
   Repugnant to command. Unequal matched,
   Pyrrhus at Priam drives, in rage strikes wide,
   But with the whiff and wind of his fell [127] sword
   Th' unnervèd father falls. Then senseless[128] Ilium,
   Seeming to feel this blow, with flaming top
   Stoops to his[129] base, and with a hideous crash
   Takes prisoner Pyrrhus' ear. For lo! his sword,
   Which was declining on the milky head
   Of reverend Priam, seemed i' th' air to stick.
   So as a painted [130] tyrant Pyrrhus stood,

---

[116] *Priam's slaughter* i.e. at the fall of Troy (Aeneid II, 506 ff.)   [117] *Hyrcanian beast* tiger   [118] *sable* black   [119] *ominous* fateful   [120] *horse* the wooden horse by which the Greeks gained entrance to Troy   [121] *dismal* ill-omened   [122] *gules* red (heraldic term)   [123] *tricked* decorated in color (heraldic term)   [124] *parching* i.e. because Troy was burning   [125] *o'ersizèd* covered as with size, a glutinous material used for filling pores of plaster, etc.   [126] *coagulate* clotted   [127] *fell* cruel   [128] *senseless* without feeling   [129] *his* its   [130] *painted* pictured

And like a neutral to his will and matter[131]
Did nothing.
But as we often see, against[132] some storm,
A silence in the heavens, the rack[133] stand still,
The bold winds speechless, and the orb below
As hush as death, anon the dreadful thunder
Doth rend the region,[134] so after Pyrrhus' pause,
Arousèd vengeance sets him new awork,
And never did the Cyclops' [135] hammers fall
On Mars' armor, forged for proof eterne,[136]
With less remorse than Pyrrhus' bleeding sword
Now falls on Priam.
Out, out, thou strumpet Fortune! All you gods,
In general synod take away her power,
Break all the spokes and fellies[137] from her wheel,
And bowl the round nave[138] down the hill of heaven,
As low as to the fiends."

POLONIUS   This is too long.

HAMLET   It shall to the barber's, with your beard.—Prithee say on.
He's for a jig[139] or a tale of bawdry, or he sleeps. Say on; come to
Hecuba.

PLAYER   "But who (ah woe!) had seen the mobled [140] queen—"

HAMLET   "The mobled queen"?

POLONIUS   That's good. "Mobled queen" is good.

PLAYER   "Run barefoot up and down, threat'ning the flames
With bisson rheum;[141] a clout[142] upon that head
Where late the diadem stood, and for a robe,
About her lank and all o'erteemèd [143] loins,
A blanket in the alarm of fear caught up—
Who this had seen, with tongue in venom steeped
'Gainst Fortune's state[144] would treason have pronounced.
But if the gods themselves did see her then,
When she saw Pyrrhus make malicious sport
In mincing with his sword her husband's limbs,
The instant burst of clamor that she made

---

[131] *will and matter* purpose and its realization (between which he stands motionless)   [132] *against* just before   [133] *rack* clouds   [134] *region* sky   [135] *Cyclops* giant workmen who made armor in the smithy of Vulcan   [136] *proof
eterne* eternal protection   [137] *fellies* segments of the rim   [138] *nave* hub
[139] *jig* short comic piece with singing and dancing often presented after a
play   [140] *mobled* muffled   [141] *bisson rheum* blinding tears   [142] *clout* cloth
[143] *o'erteemèd* overproductive of children   [144] *state* government of worldly
events

(Unless things mortal move them not at all)
Would have made milch[145] the burning eyes[146] of heaven
And passion in the gods."

POLONIUS   Look, whe'r[147] he has not turned his color, and has tears in's eyes. Prithee no more.

HAMLET   'Tis well. I'll have thee speak out the rest of this soon.— Good my lord, will you see the players well bestowed? [148] Do you hear? Let them be well used, for they are the abstract and brief chronicles of the time. After your death you were better have a bad epitaph than their ill report while you live.

POLONIUS   My lord, I will use them according to their desert.

HAMLET   God's bodkin,[149] man, much better! Use every man after his desert, and who shall scape whipping? Use them after your own honor and dignity. The less they deserve, the more merit is in your bounty. Take them in.

POLONIUS   Come, sirs.

HAMLET   Follow him, friends. We'll hear a play tomorrow. (*aside to* PLAYER) Dost thou hear me, old friend? Can you play "The Murder of Gonzago"?

PLAYER   Ay, my lord.

HAMLET   We'll ha't to-morrow night. You could for a need study a speech of some dozen or sixteen lines which I would set down and insert in't, could you not?

PLAYER   Ay, my lord.

HAMLET   Very well. Follow that lord, and look you mock him not. —My good friends, I'll leave you till night. You are welcome to Elsinore.

(*Exeunt* POLONIUS *and* PLAYERS)

ROSENCRANTZ   Good my lord.

(*Exeunt* ROSENCRANTZ *and* GUILDENSTERN)

HAMLET   Ay, so, God bye to you.—Now I am alone.
O, what a rogue and peasant slave am I!
Is it not monstrous that this player here,
But in a fiction, in a dream of passion,
Could force his soul so to his own conceit[150]
That from her working all his visage wanned,
Tears in his eyes, distraction in his aspect.

---

[145] *milch* tearful (milk-giving)   [146] *eyes* i.e. stars   [147] *whe'r* whether   [148] *bestowed* lodged   [149] *God's bodkin* by God's little body   [150] *conceit* conception, idea

A broken voice, and his whole function[151] suiting
With forms to his conceit? And all for nothing,
For Hecuba!
What's Hecuba to him, or he to Hecuba,
That he should weep for her? What would he do
Had he the motive and the cue for passion
That I have? He would drown the stage with tears
And cleave the general ear with horrid speech,
Make mad the guilty and appal the free,
Confound the ignorant, and amaze indeed
The very faculties of eyes and ears.
Yet I,
A dull and muddy-mettled [152] rascal, peak[153]
Like John-a-dreams,[154] unpregnant[155] of my cause,
And can say nothing. No, not for a king,
Upon whose property and most dear life
A damned defeat was made. Am I a coward?
Who calls me villain? breaks my pate across?
Plucks off my beard and blows it in my face?
Tweaks me by the nose? gives me the lie i' th' throat
As deep as to the lungs? Who does me this?
Ha, 'swounds,[156] I should take it, for it cannot be
But I am pigeon-livered [157] and lack gall
To make oppression bitter, or ere this
I should ha' fatted all the region kites[158]
With this slave's offal.[159] Bloody, bawdy villain!
Remorseless, treacherous, lecherous, kindless[160] villain!
O, vengeance!
Why, what an ass am I! This is most brave,
That I, the son of a dear father murdered,
Prompted to my revenge by heaven and hell,
Must like a whore unpack my heart with words
And fall a-cursing like a very drab,
A stallion! [161] Fie upon't, foh! About, my brains.
Hum—
I have heard that guilty creatures sitting at a play
Have by the very cunning of the scene

---

151 *function* action of bodily powers   152 *muddy-mettled* dull-spirited
153 *peak* mope   154 *John-a-dreams* a sleepy dawdler   155 *unpregnant* barren
of realization   156 *'swounds* by God's wounds   157 *pigeon-livered* of dove-like
gentleness   158 *region kites* kites of the air   159 *offal* guts   160 *kindless* unnatural   161 *stallion* prostitute (male or female)

Been struck so to the soul that presently[162]
They have proclaimed their malefactions.
For murder, though it have no tongue, will speak
With most miraculous organ. I'll have these players
Play something like the murder of my father
Before mine uncle. I'll observe his looks.
I'll tent[163] him to the quick. If 'a do blench,[164]
I know my course. The spirit that I have seen
May be a devil, and the devil hath power
T' assume a pleasing shape, yea, and perhaps
Out of my weakness and my melancholy,
As he is very potent with such spirits,
Abuses[165] me to damn me. I'll have grounds
More relative[166] than this. The play 's the thing
Wherein I'll catch the conscience of the king.

(*Exit*)

ACT III

Scene I

A chamber in the castle

(*Enter* KING, QUEEN, POLONIUS, OPHELIA, ROSENCRANTZ, GUILDEN-
STERN, LORDS)

KING   And can you by no drift of conference[1]
Get from him why he puts on this confusion,
Grating so harshly all his days of quiet
With turbulent and dangerous lunacy?
ROSENCRANTZ   He does confess he feels himself distracted,
But from what cause 'a will by no means speak.
GUILDENSTERN   Nor do we find him forward to be sounded,
But with a crafty madness keeps aloof
When we would bring him on to some confession
Of his true state.
QUEEN   Did he receive you well?
ROSENCRANTZ   Most like a gentleman.
GUILDENSTERN   But with much forcing of his disposition.
ROSENCRANTZ   Niggard of question, but of our demands
Most free in his reply.

---

[162] *presently* immediately   [163] *tent* probe   [164] *blench* flinch   [165] *Abuses* de-
ludes   [166] *relative* pertinent
[1] *drift of conference* direction of conversation

QUEEN   Did you assay[2] him
　　To any pastime?
ROSENCRANTZ   Madam, it so fell out that certain players
　　We o'erraught[3] on the way. Of these we told him,
　　And there did seem in him a kind of joy
　　To hear of it. They are here about the court,
　　And, as I think, they have already order
　　This night to play before him.
POLONIUS   'Tis most true,
　　And he beseeched me to entreat your majesties
　　To hear and see the matter.
KING   With all my heart, and it doth much content me
　　To hear him so inclined.
　　Good gentlemen, give him a further edge[4]
　　And drive his purpose into these delights.
ROSENCRANTZ   We shall, my lord.

　　(*Exeunt* ROSENCRANTZ *and* GUILDENSTERN)

KING   Sweet Gertrude, leave us too,
　　For we have closely[5] sent for Hamlet hither,
　　That he, as 'twere by accident, may here
　　Affront[6] Ophelia.
　　Her father and myself (lawful espials[7])
　　Will so bestow ourselves that, seeing unseen,
　　We may of their encounter frankly judge
　　And gather by him, as he is behaved,
　　If't be th' affliction of his love or no
　　That thus he suffers for.
QUEEN   I shall obey you.—
　　And for your part, Ophelia, I do wish
　　That your good beauties be the happy cause
　　Of Hamlet's wildness. So shall I hope your virtues
　　Will bring him to his wonted way again,
　　To both your honors.
OPHELIA   Madam, I wish it may.

　　(*Exit* QUEEN)

POLONIUS   Ophelia, walk you here.—Gracious, so please you,
　　We will bestow ourselves.—

---

[2] *assay* try to win   [3] *o'erraught* overtook   [4] *edge* keenness of desire   [5] *closely* privately   [6] *Affront* come face to face with   [7] *espials* spies

(*To* OPHELIA)

Read on this book,
That show of such an exercise[8] may color[9]
Your loneliness. We are oft to blame in this,
'Tis too much proved, that with devotion's visage
And pious action we do sugar o'er
The devil himself.

KING (*aside*)   O, 'tis too true.
How smart a lash that speech doth give my conscience!
The harlot's cheek, beautied with plast'ring art,
Is not more ugly to[10] the thing that helps it
Than is my deed to my most painted word.
O heavy burthen!

POLONIUS   I hear him coming. Let's withdraw, my lord.

(*Exeunt* KING *and* POLONIUS)

(*Enter* HAMLET)

HAMLET   To be, or not to be—that is the question:
Whether 'tis nobler in the mind to suffer
The slings and arrows of outrageous fortune
Or to take arms against a sea of troubles
And by opposing end them. To die, to sleep—
No more—and by a sleep to say we end
The heartache, and the thousand natural shocks
That flesh is heir to. 'Tis a consummation
Devoutly to be wished. To die, to sleep—
To sleep—perchance to dream: ay, there's the rub,[11]
For in that sleep of death what dreams may come
When we have shuffled off [12] this mortal coil,[13]
Must give us pause. There's the respect[14]
That makes calamity of so long life.[15]
For who would bear the whips and scorns of time,
Th' oppressor's wrong, the proud man's contumely
The pangs of despised love, the law's delay,
The insolence of office, and the spurns
That patient merit of th' unworthy takes,
When he himself might his quietus[16] make

---

[8] *exercise* religious exercise (the book being obviously one of devotion)
[9] *color* give an appearance of naturalness to   [10] *to* compared to   [11] *rub* obstacle (literally, obstruction encountered by a bowler's ball)   [12] *shuffled off* cast off as an encumbrance   [13] *coil* to-do, turmoil   [14] *respect* consideration
[15] *of so long life* so long-lived   [16] *quietus* settlement (literally, release from debt)

With a bare bodkin? [17] Who would fardels[18] bear,
To grunt and sweat under a weary life,
But that the dread of something after death,
The undiscovered country, from whose bourn[19]
No traveller returns, puzzles the will,
And makes us rather bear those ills we have
Than fly to others that we know not of?
Thus conscience does make cowards of us all,
And thus the native hue of resolution
Is sicklied o'er with the pale cast of thought,
And enterprises of great pitch[20] and moment
With this regard [21] their currents turn awry
And lose the name of action.—Soft you now,
The fair Ophelia!—Nymph, in thy orisons[22]
Be all my sins remembered.

OPHELIA   Good my lord,
How does your honor for this many a day?

HAMLET   I humbly thank you, well, well, well.

OPHELIA   My lord, I have remembrances of yours
That I have longèd long to re-deliver.
I pray you, now receive them.

HAMLET   No, not I,
I never gave you aught.

OPHELIA   My honored lord, you know right well you did,
And with them words of so sweet breath composed
As made the things more rich. Their perfume lost,
Take these again, for to the noble mind
Rich gifts wax poor when givers prove unkind.
There, my lord.

HAMLET   Ha, ha! Are you honest? [23]

OPHELIA   My lord?

HAMLET   Are you fair?

OPHELIA   What means your lordship?

HAMLET   That if you be honest and fair, your honesty should admit
no discourse to your beauty.

OPHELIA   Could beauty, my lord, have better commerce[24] than
with honesty?

HAMLET   Ay, truly; for the power of beauty will sooner transform

---

[17] *bodkin* dagger   [18] *fardels* burdens   [19] *bourn* confine, region   [20] *pitch*
height (of a soaring falcon's flight)   [21] *regard* consideration   [22] *orisons*
prayers (because of the book of devotion she reads)   [23] *honest* chaste
[24] *commerce* intercourse

honesty from what it is to a bawd than the force of honesty can translate beauty into his likeness. This was sometime a paradox,[25] but now the time gives it proof. I did love you once.

OPHELIA   Indeed, my lord, you made me believe so.

HAMLET   You should not have believed me, for virtue cannot so inoculate[26] our old stock but we shall relish[27] of it. I loved you not.

OPHELIA   I was the more deceived.

HAMLET   Get thee to a nunnery. Why wouldst thou be a breeder of sinners? I am myself indifferent honest,[28] but yet I could accuse me of such things that it were better my mother had not borne me: I am very proud, revengeful, ambitious, with more offenses at my beck than I have thoughts to put them in, imagination to give them shape, or time to act them in. What should such fellows as I do crawling between earth and heaven? We are arrant knaves all; believe none of us. Go thy ways to a nunnery. Where's your father?

OPHELIA   At home, my lord.

HAMLET   Let the doors be shut upon him, that he may play the fool nowhere but in's own house. Farewell.

OPHELIA   O, help him, you sweet heavens!

HAMLET   If thou dost marry, I'll give thee this plague for thy dowry: be thou as chaste as ice, as pure as snow, thou shalt not escape calumny. Get thee to a nunnery. Go, farewell. Or if thou wilt needs marry, marry a fool, for wise men know well enough what monsters[29] you make of them. To a nunnery, go, and quickly too. Farewell.

OPHELIA   O heavenly powers, restore him!

HAMLET   I have heard of your paintings too, well enough. God hath given you one face, and you make yourselves another. You jig, you amble, and you lisp; you nickname God's creatures and make your wantonness[30] your ignorance.[31] Go to, I'll no more on't; it hath made me mad. I say we will have no more marriage. Those that are married already—all but one—shall live. The rest shall keep as they are. To a nunnery, go.

(*Exit*)

OPHELIA   O, what a noble mind is here o'erthrown!

---

[25] *paradox* idea contrary to common opinion   [26] *inoculate* graft   [27] *relish* have a flavor (because of original sin)   [28] *indifferent honest* moderately respectable   [29] *monsters* i.e. unnatural combinations of wisdom and uxorious folly   [30] *wantonness* affectation   [31] *your ignorance* a matter for which you offer the excuse that you don't know any better

The courtier's, soldier's, scholar's, eye, tongue, sword,
Th' expectancy and rose[32] of the fair state,
The glass[33] of fashion and the mould of form,
Th' observed of all observers, quite, quite down!
And I, of ladies most deject and wretched,
That sucked the honey of his music vows,
Now see that noble and most sovereign reason
Like sweet bells jangled, out of time and harsh,
That unmatched form and feature of blown youth
Blasted with ecstasy.[34] O, woe is me
T' have seen what I have seen, see what I see!

(*Enter* KING *and* POLONIUS)

KING   Love? his affections[35] do not that way tend,
Nor what he spake, though it lacked form a little,
Was not like madness. There's something in his soul
O'er which his melancholy sits on brood,
And I do doubt[36] the hatch and the disclose
Will be some danger; which for to prevent,
I have in quick determination
Thus set it down: he shall with speed to England
For the demand of our neglected tribute.
Haply the seas, and countries different,
With variable objects, shall expel
This something-settled [37] matter in his heart,
Whereon his brains still beating puts him thus
From fashion of himself. What think you on't?
POLONIUS   It shall do well. But yet do I believe
The origin and commencement of his grief
Sprung from neglected love.—How now, Ophelia?
You need not tell us what Lord Hamlet said.
We heard it all.—My lord, do as you please,
But if you hold it fit, after the play
Let his queen mother all alone entreat him
To show his grief. Let her be round [38] with him,
And I'll be placed, so please you, in the ear
Of all their conference. If she find him not,
To England send him, or confine him where
Your wisdom best shall think.

---

[32] *expectancy and rose* fair hope   [33] *glass* mirror   [34] *ecstasy* madness   [35] *affections* emotions   [36] *doubt* fear   [37] *something-settled* somewhat settled
[38] *round* plain-spoken

KING   It shall be so.
    Madness in great ones must not unwatched go.

(Exeunt)

Act III, Scene II

The hall of the castle

(Enter HAMLET *and three of the* PLAYERS*)*

HAMLET Speak the speech, I pray you, as I pronounced it to you, trippingly[1] on the tongue. But if you mouth it, as many of our players do, I had as lief the town crier spoke my lines. Nor do not saw the air too much with your hand, thus, but use all gently, for in the very torrent, tempest, and (as I may say) whirlwind of your passion, you must acquire and beget a temperance that may give it smoothness. O, it offends me to the soul to hear a robustious[2] periwig-pated[3] fellow tear a passion to tatters, to very rags, to split the ears of the groundlings,[4] who for the most part are capable of nothing but inexplicable dumb shows[5] and noise. I would have such a fellow whipped for o'erdoing Termagant.[6] It out-herods Herod.[7] Pray you avoid it.

PLAYER I warrant your honor.

HAMLET Be not too tame neither, but let your own discretion be your tutor. Suit the action to the word, the word to the action, with this special observance, that you o'erstep not the modesty of nature. For anything so overdone is from[8] the purpose of playing, whose end, both at the first and now, was and is, to hold, as 'twere, the mirror up to nature, to show virtue her own feature, scorn her own image, and the very age and body of the time his form and pressure.[9] Now this overdone, or come tardy off,[10] though it make the unskillful laugh, cannot but make the judicious grieve, the censure of the which one[11] must in your allowance o'erweigh a whole theatre of others. O, there be players that I have seen play, and heard others praise, and that highly (not to

---

[1] *trippingly* easily [2] *robustious* boisterous [3] *periwig-pated* wig-wearing (after the custom of actors) [4] *groundlings* spectators who paid least and stood on the ground in the pit or yard of the theatre [5] *dumb shows* brief actions without words, forecasting dramatic matter to follow (the play presented later in this scene giving an old-fashioned example) [6] *Termagant* a Saracen "god" in medieval romance and drama [7] *Herod* the raging tyrant of old Biblical plays [8] *from* apart from [9] *pressure* impressed or printed character [10] *come tardy off* brought off slowly and badly [11] *the censure of the which one* the judgment of even one of whom

speak it profanely), that neither having th' accent of Christians, nor the gait of Christian, pagan, nor man, have so strutted and bellowed that I have thought some of Nature's journeymen[12] had made men, and not made them well, they imitated humanity so abominably.

PLAYER   I hope we have reformed that indifferently[13] with us, sir.

HAMLET   O, reform it altogether! And let those that play your clowns speak no more than is set down for them, for there be of them[14] that will themselves laugh, to set on some quantity of barren spectators to laugh too, though in the mean time some necessary question of the play be then to be considered. That's villainous and shows a most pitiful ambition in the fool that uses it. Go make you ready.

(*Exeunt* PLAYERS)

(*Enter* POLONIUS, GUILDENSTERN, *and* ROSENCRANTZ)

How now, my lord? Will the king hear this piece of work?

POLONIUS   And the queen too, and that presently.[15]

HAMLET   Bid the players make haste.

(*Exit* POLONIUS)

Will you two help to hasten them?

ROSENCRANTZ   Ay, my lord.

(*Exeunt they two*)

HAMLET   What, ho, Horatio!

(*Enter* HORATIO)

HORATIO   Here, sweet lord, at your service.

HAMLET   Horatio, thou art e'en as just a man
As e'er my conversation coped withal.[16]

HORATIO   O, my dear lord—

HAMLET   Nay, do not think I flatter.
For what advancement may I hope from thee,
That no revenue hast but thy good spirits
To feed and clothe thee? Why should the poor be flattered?
No, let the candied tongue lick absurd pomp,
And crook the pregnant[17] hinges of the knee

---

12 *journeymen* workmen not yet masters of their trade   13 *indifferently* fairly well   14 *of them* some of them   15 *presently* at once   16 *conversation coped withal* intercourse with men encountered   17 *pregnant* quick to move

Where thrift[18] may follow fawning. Dost thou hear?
Since my dear soul was mistress of her choice
And could of men distinguish her election,
S' hath sealed [19] thee for herself, for thou hast been
As one in suff'ring all that suffers nothing,
A man that Fortune's buffets and rewards
Hast ta'en with equal thanks; and blest are those
Whose blood [20] and judgment are so well commeddled [21]
That they are not a pipe for Fortune's finger
To sound what stop she please. Give me that man
That is not passion's slave, and I will wear him
In my heart's core, ay, in my heart of heart,
As I do thee. Something too much of this—
There is a play to-night before the king.
One scene of it comes near the circumstance
Which I have told thee, of my father's death.
I prithee, when thou seest that act afoot,
Even with the very comment of thy soul [22]
Observe my uncle. If his occulted [23] guilt
Do not itself unkennel in one speech,
It is a damnèd ghost[24] that we have seen,
And my imaginations are as foul
As Vulcan's stithy.[25] Give him heedful note,
For I mine eyes will rivet to his face,
And after we will both our judgments join
In censure of [26] his seeming.
HORATIO   Well, my lord.
If 'a steal aught the while this play is playing,
And scape detecting, I will pay the theft.

(*Enter* TRUMPETS *and* KETTLEDRUMS, KING, QUEEN, POLONIUS, OPHE-
LIA, [ROSENCRANTZ, GUILDENSTERN, *and other* LORDS *attendant*])

HAMLET   They are coming to the play. I must be idle.[27]
Get you a place.
KING   How fares our cousin[28] Hamlet?
HAMLET   Excellent, i' faith, of the chameleon's dish.[29] I eat the air,
promise-crammed. You cannot feed capons so.

---

[18] *thrift* profit   [19] *sealed* marked   [20] *blood* passion   [21] *commeddled* mixed
together   [22] *the very . . . soul* thy deepest sagacity   [23] *occulted* hidden
[24] *damnèd ghost* evil spirit, devil   [25] *stithy* smithy   [26] *censure of* sentence
upon   [27] *be idle* be foolish, act the madman   [28] *cousin* nephew   [29] *chameleon's dish* i.e. air (which was believed the chameleon's food; Hamlet willfully takes *fares* in the sense of "feeds")

KING   I have nothing with this answer, Hamlet. These words are not mine.[30]

HAMLET   No, nor mine now. (*to Polonius*) My lord, you played once i' th' university, you say?

POLONIUS   That did I, my lord, and was accounted a good actor.

HAMLET   What did you enact?

POLONIUS   I did enact Julius Caesar. I was killed i' th' Capitol; Brutus killed me.

HAMLET   It was a brute part of him to kill so capital a calf there. Be the players ready?

ROSENCRANTZ   Ay, my lord. They stay upon your patience.[31]

QUEEN   Come hither, my dear Hamlet, sit by me.

HAMLET   No, good mother. Here's metal more attractive.

POLONIUS (*to the King*)   O ho! do you mark that?

HAMLET   Lady, shall I lie in your lap?

He lies at OPHELIA's *feet*

OPHELIA   No, my lord.

HAMLET   I mean, my head upon your lap?

OPHELIA   Ay, my lord.

HAMLET   Do you think I meant country matters?[32]

OPHELIA   I think nothing, my lord.

HAMLET   That's a fair thought to lie between maids' legs.

OPHELIA   What is, my lord?

HAMLET   Nothing.

OPHELIA   You are merry, my lord.

HAMLET   Who, I?

OPHELIA   Ay, my lord.

HAMLET   O God, your only jig-maker![33] What should a man do but be merry? For look you how cheerfully my mother looks, and my father died within's two hours.

OPHELIA   Nay, 'tis twice two months, my lord.

HAMLET   So long? Nay then, let the devil wear black, for I'll have a suit of sables.[34] O heavens! die two months ago, and not forgotten yet? Then there's hope a great man's memory may outlive his life half a year. But, by'r Lady, 'a must build churches then, or else shall 'a suffer not thinking on, with the hobby-

---

[30] *not mine* not for me as the asker of my question   [31] *stay upon your patience* await your indulgence   [32] *country matters* rustic goings-on, barnyard mating (with a play upon a sexual term)   [33] *jig-maker* writer of jigs   [34] *sables* black furs (luxurious garb, not for mourning)

horse,[35] whose epitaph is "For O, for O, the hobby-horse is forgot!"

The trumpets sound. Dumb show follows:
Enter a KING *and a* QUEEN [*very lovingly*], *the* QUEEN *embracing him, and he her.* [*She kneels; and makes show of protestation unto him.*] *He takes her up, and declines his head upon her neck. He lies him down upon a bank of flowers. She, seeing him asleep, leaves him. Anon come in another man: takes off his crown, kisses it, pours poison in the sleeper's ears, and leaves him. The* QUEEN *returns, finds the* KING *dead, makes passionate action. The poisoner, with some three or four, come in again, seem to condole with her. The dead body is carried away. The poisoner woos the* QUEEN *with gifts; she seems harsh awhile, but in the end accepts love.*

   (*Exeunt*)

OPHELIA   What means this, my lord?
HAMLET   Marry, this is miching mallecho;[36] it means mischief.
OPHELIA   Belike this show imports the argument of the play.

   (*Enter* PROLOGUE)

HAMLET   We shall know by this fellow. The players cannot keep counsel; they'll tell all.
OPHELIA   Will 'a tell us what this show meant?
HAMLET   Ay, or any show that you'll show him. Be not you ashamed to show, he'll not shame to tell you what it means.
OPHELIA   You are naught, you are naught.[37] I'll mark the play.
PROLOGUE   For us and for our tragedy,
         Here stooping to your clemency,
         We beg your hearing patiently.

   (*Exit*)

HAMLET   Is this a prologue, or the posy[38] of a ring? [39]
OPHELIA   'Tis brief, my lord.
HAMLET   As woman's love.

   (*Enter* [*two* PLAYERS *as*] KING *and* QUEEN)

[P.] KING   Full thirty times hath Phoebus' cart[40] gone round
         Neptune's salt wash and Tellus' [41] orbèd ground,
         And thirty dozen moons with borrowed [42] sheen

---

[35] *hobby-horse* traditional figure strapped round the waist of a performer in May games and morris dances   [36] *miching mallecho* sneaking iniquity   [37] *naught* indecent   [38] *posy* brief motto in rhyme ("poesy")   [39] *ring* finger ring   [40] *Phoebus' cart* the sun's chariot   [41] *Tellus* Roman goddess of the earth   [42] *borrowed* i.e. taken from the sun

About the world have times twelve thirties been,
Since love our hearts, and Hymen[43] did our hands,
Unite commutual [44] in most sacred bands.

[P.] QUEEN   So many journeys may the sun and moon
Make us again count o'er ere love be done!
But woe is me, you are so sick of late,
So far from cheer and from your former state,
That I distrust you.[45] Yet, though I distrust,
Discomfort you, my lord, it nothing must.
For women fear too much, even as they love,
And women's fear and love hold quantity,[46]
In neither aught, or in extremity.
Now what my love is, proof hath made you know,
And as my love is sized, my fear is so.
Where love is great, the littlest doubts are fear;
Where little fears grow great, great love grows there.

[F.] KING   Faith, I must leave thee, love, and shortly too;
My operant powers[47] their functions leave to do.
And thou shalt live in this fair world behind,
Honored, beloved, and haply one as kind
For husband shalt thou—

[P.] QUEEN   O, confound the rest!
Such love must needs be treason in my breast.
In second husband let me be accurst!
None wed the second but who killed the first.

HAMLET (*aside*)   That's wormwood.[48]

[P.] QUEEN   The instances[49] that second marriage move
Are base respects of thrift, but none of love.
A second time I kill my husband dead
When second husband kisses me in bed.

[P.] KING   I do believe you think what now you speak,
But what we do determine oft we break.
Purpose is but the slave to[50] memory,
Of violent birth, but poor validity,[51]
Which now like fruit unripe sticks on the tree,
But fall unshaken when they mellow be.
Most necessary 'tis that we forget
To pay ourselves what to ourselves is debt.

---

[43] *Hymen* Greek god of marriage   [44] *commutual* mutually   [45] *distrust you* fear for you   [46] *quantity* proportion   [47] *operant powers* active bodily forces   [48] *wormwood* a bitter herb   [49] *instances* motives   [50] *slave to* i.e. dependent upon for life   [51] *validity* strength

What to ourselves in passion we propose,
The passion ending, doth the purpose lose.
The violence of either grief or joy
Their own enactures[52] with themselves destroy.
Where joy most revels, grief doth most lament;
Grief joys, joy grieves, on slender accident.
This world is not for aye, nor 'tis not strange
That even our loves should with our fortunes change,
For 'tis a question left us yet to prove,
Whether love lead fortune, or else fortune love.
The great man down, you mark his favorite flies,
The poor advanced makes friends of enemies; ·
And hitherto doth love on fortune tend,
For who not needs shall never lack a friend,
And who in want a hollow friend doth try,
Directly seasons him[53] his enemy.
But, orderly to end where I begun,
Our wills and fates do so contrary run
That our devices still [54] are overthrown;
Our thoughts are ours, their ends none of our own.
So think thou wilt no second husband wed,
But die thy thoughts when thy first lord is dead.

[P.] QUEEN   Nor earth to me give food, nor heaven light,
Sport and repose lock from me day and night,
To desperation turn my trust and hope,
An anchor's[55] cheer in prison be my scope,
Each opposite that blanks[56] the face of joy
Meet what I would have well, and it destroy,
Both here and hence[57] pursue me lasting strife,
If, once a widow, ever I be wife!

HAMLET   If she should break it now!

[P.] KING   'Tis deeply sworn. Sweet, leave me here awhile.
My spirits grow dull, and fain I would beguile
The tedious day with sleep.

[P.] QUEEN   Sleep rock thy brain,

(*He sleeps*)

And never come mischance between us twain!

(*Exit*)

---

[52] *enactures* fulfillments   [53] *seasons him* ripens him into   [54] *still* always
[55] *anchor's* hermit's   [56] *blanks* blanches, makes pale   [57] *hence* in the next
world.

HAMLET   Madam, how like you this play?

QUEEN   The lady doth protest too much, methinks.

HAMLET   O, but she'll keep her word.

KING   Have you heard the argument?[58] Is there no offense in't?

HAMLET   No, no, they do but jest, poison in jest; no offense i' th' world.

KING   What do you call the play?

HAMLET   "The Mousetrap." Marry, how? Tropically.[59] This play is the image of a murder done in Vienna. Gonzago is the duke's name; his wife, Baptista. You shall see anon. 'Tis a knavish piece of work, but what o' that? Your majesty, and we that have free[60] souls, it touches us not. Let the galled[61] jade[62] winch;[63] our withers[64] are unwrung.

(*Enter* LUCIANUS)

This is one Lucianus, nephew to the king.

OPHELIA   You are as good as a chorus,[65] my lord.

HAMLET   I could interpret between you and your love, if I could see the puppets[66] dallying.

OPHELIA   You are keen, my lord, you are keen.

HAMLET   It would cost you a groaning to take off my edge.

OPHELIA   Still better, and worse.

HAMLET   So you must take your husbands.—Begin, murderer. Leave thy damnable faces and begin. Come, the croaking raven doth bellow for revenge.

LUCIANUS   Thoughts black, hands apt, drugs fit, and time agreeing,
Confederate season,[67] else no creature seeing,
Thou mixture rank, of midnight weeds collected,
With Hecate's[68] ban[69] thrice blasted, thrice infected,
Thy natural magic and dire property
On wholesome life usurps immediately.

(*Pours the poison in his ears*)

HAMLET   'A poisons him i' th' garden for his estate. His name's Gonzago. The story is extant, and written in very choice Italian. You shall see anon how the murderer gets the love of Gonzago's wife.

---

[58] *argument* plot summary   [59] *Tropically* in the way of a trope or figure (with a play on "trapically")   [60] *free* guiltless   [61] *galled* sore-backed   [62] *jade* horse   [63] *winch* wince   [64] *withers* shoulders   [65] *chorus* one in a play who explains the action   [66] *puppets* i.e. you and your lover as in a puppet show   [67] *Confederate season* the occasion being my ally   [68] *Hecate* goddess of witchcraft and black magic   [69] *ban* curse

OPHELIA   The king rises.

HAMLET   What, frighted with false fire? [70]

QUEEN   How fares my lord?

POLONIUS   Give o'er the play.

KING   Give me some light. Away!

POLONIUS   Lights, lights, lights!

(*Exeunt all but* HAMLET *and* HORATIO)

HAMLET   Why, let the strucken deer go weep,
     The hart ungallèd play.
   For some must watch, while some must sleep;
     Thus runs the world away.
Would not this, sir, and a forest of feathers[71]—if the rest of my
fortunes turn Turk[72] with me—with two Provincial roses[73] on my
razed [74] shoes, get me a fellowship in a cry[75] of players, sir?

HORATIO   Half a share.

HAMLET   A whole one, I.
   For thou dost know, O Damon dear,
     This realm dismantled was
   Of Jove himself; and now reigns here
     A very, very—peacock.

HORATIO   You might have rhymed.

HAMLET   O good Horatio, I'll take the ghost's word for a thousand
pound. Didst perceive?

HORATIO   Very well, my lord.

HAMLET   Upon the talk of the poisoning?

HORATIO   I did very well note him.

HAMLET   Aha! Come, some music! Come, the recorders! [76]
   For if the king like not the comedy,
     Why then, belike he likes it not, perdy.[77]
Come, some music!

(*Enter* ROSENCRANTZ *and* GUILDENSTERN)

GUILDENSTERN   Good my lord, vouchsafe me a word with you.

HAMLET   Sir, a whole history.

GUILDENSTERN   The king, sir—

HAMLET   Ay, sir, what of him?

---

[70] *false fire* a firing of a gun charged with powder but no shot, a blank-discharge   [71] *feathers* plumes for actors' costumes   [72] *turn Turk* turn renegade,
like a Christian turning Mohammedan   [73] *Provincial roses* ribbon rosettes
[74] *razed* decorated with cut patterns   [75] *cry* pack   [76] *recorders* musical instruments of the flute class   [77] *perdy* by God (*"par dieu"*)

GUILDENSTERN   Is in his retirement marvellous distempered.[78]

HAMLET   With drink, sir?

GUILDENSTERN   No, my lord, with choler.[79]

HAMLET   Your wisdom should show itself more richer to signify this to the doctor, for for me to put him to his purgation would perhaps plunge him into more choler.

GUILDENSTERN   Good my lord, put your discourse into some frame,[80] and start not so wildly from my affair.

HAMLET   I am tame, sir; pronounce.

GUILDENSTERN   The queen, your mother, in most great affliction of spirit hath sent me to you.

HAMLET   You are welcome.

GUILDENSTERN   Nay, good my lord, this courtesy is not of the right breed. If it shall please you to make me a wholesome answer, I will do your mother's commandment. If not, your pardon and my return shall be the end of my business.

HAMLET   Sir, I cannot.

ROSENCRANTZ   What, my lord?

HAMLET   Make you a wholesome answer; my wit's diseased. But, sir, such answer as I can make, you shall command, or rather, as you say, my mother. Therefore no more, but to the matter. My mother, you say—

ROSENCRANTZ   Then thus she says: your behavior hath struck her into amazement and admiration.[81]

HAMLET   O wonderful son, that can so stonish a mother! But is there no sequel at the heels of this mother's admiration? Impart.

ROSENCRANTZ   She desires to speak with you in her closet[82] ere you go to bed.

HAMLET   We shall obey, were she ten times our mother. Have you any further trade with us?

ROSENCRANTZ   My lord, you once did love me.

HAMLET   And do still, by these pickers and stealers.[83]

ROSENCRANTZ   Good my lord, what is your cause of distemper? You do surely bar the door upon your own liberty, if you deny your griefs to your friend.

HAMLET   Sir, I lack advancement.

ROSENCRANTZ   How can that be, when you have the voice of the king himself for your succession in Denmark?

---

[78] *distempered* out of temper, vexed (twisted by Hamlet into "deranged")   [79] *choler* anger (twisted by Hamlet into "biliousness")   [80] *frame* logical order   [81] *admiration* wonder   [82] *closet* private room   [83] *pickers and stealers* i.e. hands

HAMLET Ay, sir, but "while the grass grows" [84] the proverb is something musty.

(*Enter the* PLAYER *with recorders*)

O, the recorders. Let me see one. To withdraw[85] with you—why do you go about to recover the wind [86] of me, as if you would drive me into a toil? [87]

GUILDENSTERN O my lord, if my duty be too bold, my love is too unmannerly.[88]

HAMLET I do not well understand that. Will you play upon this pipe?

GUILDENSTERN My lord, I cannot.

HAMLET I pray you.

GUILDENSTERN Believe me, I cannot.

HAMLET I do beseech you.

GUILDENSTERN I know no touch of it, my lord.

HAMLET It is as easy as lying. Govern these ventages[89] with your fingers and thumb, give it breath with your mouth, and it will discourse most eloquent music. Look you, these are the stops.

GUILDENSTERN But these cannot I command to any utt'rance of harmony. I have not the skill.

HAMLET Why, look you now, how unworthy a thing you make of me! You would play upon me, you would seem to know my stops, you would pluck out the heart of my mystery, you would sound me from my lowest note to the top of my compass; and there is much music, excellent voice, in this little organ, yet cannot you make it speak. 'Sblood, do you think I am easier to be played on than a pipe? Call me what instrument you will, though you can fret[90] me, you cannot play upon me.

(*Enter* POLONIUS)

God bless you, sir!

POLONIUS My lord, the queen would speak with you, and presently.[91]

HAMLET Do you see yonder cloud that's almost in shape of a camel?

POLONIUS By th' mass and 'tis, like a camel indeed.

---

[84] *while the grass grows* (a proverb, ending: "the horse starves") [85] *withdraw* step aside [86] *recover the wind* come up to windward like a hunter [87] *toil* snare [88] *is too unmannerly* leads me beyond the restraint of good manners [89] *ventages* holes, vents [90] *fret* irritate (with a play on the fret-fingering of certain stringed musical instruments) [91] *presently* at once

HAMLET   Methinks it is like a weasel.
POLONIUS   It is backed like a weasel.
HAMLET   Or like a whale.
POLONIUS   Very like a whale.
HAMLET   Then I will come to my mother by and by.[92]   (*aside*)
They fool me to the top of my bent.—I will come by and by.
POLONIUS   I will say so.

(*Exit*)

HAMLET   "By and by" is easily said. Leave me, friends.

(*Exeunt all but* HAMLET)

'Tis now the very witching time of night,
When churchyards yawn, and hell itself breathes out
Contagion to this world. Now could I drink hot blood
And do such bitter business as the day
Would quake to look on. Soft, now to my mother.
O heart, lose not thy nature; let not ever
The soul of Nero[93] enter this firm bosom.
Let me be cruel, not unnatural;
I will speak daggers to her, but use none.
My tongue and soul in this be hypocrites:
How in my words somever she be shent,[94]
To give them seals[95] never, my soul, consent!

(*Exit*)

Act III, Scene III

A chamber in the castle

(*Enter* KING, ROSENCRANTZ, *and* GUILDENSTERN)

KING   I like him not, nor stands it safe with us
To let his madness range. Therefore prepare you.
I your commission will forthwith dispatch,
And he to England shall along with you.
The terms[1] of our estate[2] may not endure
Hazard so near's as doth hourly grow
Out of his brows.[3]

---

[92] *by and by* immediately   [93] *Nero* murderer of his mother   [94] *shent* reproved
[95] *seals* authentications in actions
[1] *terms* circumstances   [2] *estate* royal position   [3] *brows* effronteries (apparently with an implication of knitted brows)

GUILDENSTERN   We will ourselves provide.
  Most holy and religious fear it is
  To keep those many many bodies safe
  That live and feed upon your majesty.
ROSENCRANTZ   The single and peculiar[4] life is bound
  With all the strength and armor of the mind
  To keep itself from noyance,[5] but much more
  That spirit upon whose weal depends and rests
  The lives of many. The cess[6] of majesty
  Dies not alone, but like a gulf [7]doth draw
  What's near it with it; or 'tis a massy wheel
  Fixed on the summit of the highest mount,
  To whose huge spokes ten thousand lesser things
  Are mortised and adjoined, which when it falls,
  Each small annexment, petty consequence,
  Attends[8] the boist'rous ruin. Never alone
  Did the king sigh, but with a general groan.
KING   Arm[9] you, I pray you, to this speedy voyage,
  For we will fetters put upon this fear,
  Which now goes too free-footed.
ROSENCRANTZ   We will haste us.

  (*Exeunt* GENTLEMEN)

  (*Enter* POLONIUS)

POLONIUS   My lord, he's going to his mother's closet.
  Behind the arras I'll convey myself
  To hear the process.[10] I'll warrant she'll tax him home,[11]
  And, as you said, and wisely was it said,
  'Tis meet that some more audience than a mother,
  Since nature makes them partial, should o'erhear
  The speech, of vantage.[12] Fare you well, my liege.
  I'll call upon you ere you go to bed
  And tell you what I know.
KING   Thanks, dear my lord.

  (*Exit* POLONIUS)

  O, my offense is rank, it smells to heaven;
  It hath the primal eldest curse[13] upon't,

---

[4] *peculiar* individual   [5] *noyance* harm   [6] *cess* cessation, decease   [7] *gulf* whirlpool   [8] *Attends* joins in (like a royal attendant)   [9] *Arm* prepare   [10] *process* proceedings   [11] *tax him home* thrust home in reprimanding him   [13] *of vantage* from an advantageous position   [13] *primal eldest curse* that of Cain, who also murdered a brother

A brother's murder. Pray can I not,
Though inclination be as sharp as will.
My stronger guilt defeats my strong intent,
And like a man to double business bound
I stand in pause where I shall first begin,
And both neglect. What if this cursèd hand
Were thicker than itself with brother's blood,
Is there not rain enough in the sweet heavens
To wash it white as snow? Whereto serves mercy
But to confront the visage of offense? [14]
And what's in prayer but this twofold force,
To be forestallèd ere we come to fall,
Or pardoned being down? Then I'll look up.
My fault is past. But, O, what form of prayer
Can serve my turn? "Forgive me my foul murder"?
That cannot be, since I am still possessed
Of those effects[15] for which I did the murder,
My crown, mine own ambition, and my queen.
May one be pardoned and retain th' offense?
In the corrupted currents of this world
Offense's gilded [16] hand may shove by justice,
And oft 'tis seen the wicked prize itself
Buys out the law. But 'tis not so above.
There is no shuffling;[17] there the action[18] lies
In his true nature, and we ourselves compelled,
Even to the teeth and forehead [19] of our faults,
To give in evidence. What then? What rests?
Try what repentance can. What can it not?
Yet what can it when one cannot repent?
O wretched state! O bosom black as death!
O limèd [20] soul, that struggling to be free
Art more engaged! [21] Help, angels! Make assay.[22]
Bow, stubborn knees, and, heart with strings of steel,
Be soft as sinews of the new-born babe.
All may be well.

He kneels
    (*Enter* HAMLET)

---

[14] *offense* sin   [15] *effects* things acquired   [16] *gilded* gold-laden   [17] *shuffling*
sharp practice, double-dealing   [18] *action* legal proceeding (in heaven's court)
[19] *teeth and forehead* face-to-face recognition   [20] *limèd* caught in birdlime,
a gluey material spread as a bird-snare   [21] *engaged* embedded   [22] *assay* an
attempt

HAMLET   Now might I do it pat,²³ now 'a is a-praying,
　　And now I'll do't. And so 'a goes to heaven,
　　And so am I revenged. That would be scanned.
　　A villain kills my father, and for that
　　I, his sole son, do this same villain send
　　To heaven.
　　Why, this is hire and salary, not revenge.
　　'A took my father grossly,²⁴ full of bread,²⁵
　　With all his crimes broad blown,²⁶ as flush²⁷ as May;
　　And how his audit²⁸ stands, who knows save heaven?
　　But in our circumstance and course of thought,
　　'Tis heavy with him; and am I then revenged,
　　To take him in the purging of his soul,
　　When he is fit and seasoned for his passage?
　　No.
　　Up, sword, and know thou a more horrid hent.²⁹
　　When he is drunk asleep, or in his rage,
　　Or in th' incestuous pleasure of his bed,
　　At game a-swearing, or about some act
　　That has no relish³⁰ of salvation in't—
　　Then trip him, that his heels may kick at heaven,
　　And that his soul may be as damned and black
　　As hell, whereto it goes. My mother stays.
　　This physic but prolongs thy sickly days.

　　(*Exit*)

KING (*rises*)   My words fly up, my thoughts remain below.
　　Words without thoughts never to heaven go.

　　(*Exit*)

Act III, Scene IV

The private chamber of the QUEEN

　　(*Enter* [QUEEN] GERTRUDE *and* POLONIUS)

POLONIUS   'A will come straight. Look you lay¹ home to him.
　　Tell him his pranks have been too broad ² to bear with,
　　And that your grace hath screened and stood between

---

²³ *pat* opportunely   ²⁴ *grossly* in a state of gross unpreparedness   ²⁵ *bread*
i.e. worldly sense gratification   ²⁶ *broad blown* fully blossomed   ²⁷ *flush* vigorous   ²⁸ *audit* account   ²⁹ *more horrid hent* grasping by me on a more
horrid occasion   ³⁰ *relish* flavor
¹ *lay* thrust   ² *broad* unrestrained

Much heat and him. I'll silence me even here.
Pray you be round³ with him.

[HAMLET (*within*)   Mother, mother, mother!]

QUEEN   I'll warrant you; fear me not. Withdraw; I hear him
coming.

(POLONIUS *hides behind the arras*)

(*Enter* HAMLET)

HAMLET   Now, mother, what's the matter?

QUEEN   Hamlet, thou hast thy father much offended.

HAMLET   Mother, you have my father much offended.

QUEEN   Come, come, you answer with an idle⁴ tongue.

HAMLET   Go, go, you question with a wicked tongue.

QUEEN   Why, how now, Hamlet?

HAMLET   What's the matter now?

QUEEN   Have you forgot me?

HAMLET   No, by the rood,⁵ not so!
You are the queen, your husband's brother's wife,
And (would it were not so) you are my mother.

QUEEN   Nay, then I'll set those to you that can speak.

HAMLET   Come, come, and sit you down. You shall not budge.
You go not till I set you up a glass
Where you may see the inmost part of you.

QUEEN   What wilt thou do? Thou wilt not murder me?
Help, ho!

POLONIUS (*behind*)   What, ho! help!

HAMLET (*draws*)   How now? a rat? Dead for a ducat, dead!

(*Makes a pass through the arras and kills* POLONIUS)

POLONIUS (*behind*)   O, I am slain!

QUEEN   O me, what hast thou done?

HAMLET   Nay, I know not. Is it the king?

QUEEN   O, what a rash and bloody deed is this!

HAMLET   A bloody deed—almost as bad, good mother,
As kill a king, and marry with his brother.

QUEEN   As kill a king?

HAMLET   Ay, lady, it was my word.

(*Lifts up the arras and sees* POLONIUS)

Thou wretched, rash, intruding fool, farewell!

---

³ *round* plain-spoken   ⁴ *idle* foolish   ⁵ *rood* cross

I took thee for thy better. Take thy fortune.
Thou find'st to be too busy is some danger.—
Leave wringing of your hands. Peace, sit you down
And let me wring your heart, for so I shall
If it be made of penetrable stuff,
If damnèd custom[6] have not brazed [7] it so
That it is proof [8] and bulwark against sense.[9]

QUEEN   What have I done that thou dar'st wag thy tongue
In noise so rude against me?

HAMLET   Such an act
That blurs the grace and blush of modesty,
Calls virtue hypocrite, takes off the rose
From the fair forehead of an innocent love,
And sets a blister[10] there, makes marriage vows
As false as dicers' oaths. O, such a deed
As from the body of contraction[11] plucks
The very soul, and sweet religion[12] makes
A rhapsody of words! Heaven's face does glow,
And this solidity and compound mass,[13]
With heated visage, as against[14] the doom,[15]
Is thought-sick at the act.

QUEEN   Ay me, what act,
That roars so loud and thunders in the index? [16]

HAMLET   Look here upon this picture, and on this,
The counterfeit presentment[17] of two brothers.
See what a grace was seated on this brow:
Hyperion's[18] curls, the front[19] of Jove himself,
An eye like Mars, to threaten and command,
A station[20] like the herald Mercury
New lighted on a heaven-kissing hill—
A combination and a form indeed
Where every god did seem to set his seal
To give the world assurance of a man.
This was your husband. Look you now what follows.
Here is your husband, like a mildewed ear
Blasting his wholesome brother. Have you eyes?

---

[6] *custom* habit   [7] *brazed* hardened like brass   [8] *proof* armor   [9] *sense* feeling   [10] *blister* brand (of degradation)   [11] *contraction* the marriage contract   [12] *religion* i.e. sacred marriage vows   [13] *compound mass* the earth as compounded of the four elements   [14] *against* in expectation of   [15] *doom* Day of Judgment   [16] *index* table of contents preceding the body of a book   [17] *counterfeit presentment* portrayed representation   [18] *Hyperion* the sun god   [19] *front* forehead   [20] *station* attitude in standing

Could you on this fair mountain leave to feed,
And batten[21] on this moor? Ha! have you eyes?
You cannot call it love, for at your age
The heyday[22] in the blood is tame, it's humble,
And waits upon[23] the judgment, and what judgment
Would step from this to this? Sense[24] sure you have,
Else could you not have motion,[25] but sure that sense
Is apoplexed,[26] for madness would not err,
Nor sense to ecstasy[27] was ne'er so thralled
But it reserved some quantity of choice
To serve in such a difference. What devil was't
That thus hath cozened [28] you at hoodman-blind? [29]
Eyes without feeling, feeling without sight,
Ears without hands or eyes, smelling sans[30] all,
Or but a sickly part of one true sense
Could not so mope.[31]
O shame, where is thy blush? Rebellious hell, .
If thou canst mutine[32] in a matron's bones,
To flaming youth let virtue be as wax
And melt in her own fire. Proclaim no shame
When the compulsive[33] ardor gives the charge,[34]
Since frost itself as actively doth burn,
And reason panders will.[35]

QUEEN   O Hamlet, speak no more.
Thou turn'st mine eyes into my very soul,
And there I see such black and grainèd [36] spots
As will not leave their tinct.[37]

HAMLET   Nay, but to live
In the rank sweat of an enseamèd [38] bed,
Stewed in corruption, honeying and making love
Over the nasty sty—

QUEEN   O, speak to me no more.
These words like daggers enter in mine ears.
No more, sweet Hamlet.

HAMLET   A murderer and a villain,
A slave that is not twentieth part the tithe[39]

---

[21] *batten* feed greedily   [22] *heyday* excitement of passion   [23] *waits upon* yields
to   [24] *Sense* feeling   [25] *motion* desire, impulse   [26] *apoplexed* paralyzed
[27] *ecstasy* madness   [28] *cozened* cheated   [29] *hoodman-blind* blindman's buff
[30] *sans* without   [31] *mope* be stupid   [32] *mutine* mutiny   [33] *compulsive* compelling   [34] *gives the charge* delivers the attack   [35] *panders will* acts as procurer for desire   [36] *grainèd* dyed in grain   [37] *tinct* color   [38] *enseamèd*
grease-laden   [39] *tithe* tenth part

Of your precedent lord, a vice[40] of kings,
A cutpurse[41] of the empire and the rule,
That from a shelf the precious diadem stole
And put it in his pocket—
QUEEN   No more.

  (*Enter [the]* GHOST [*in his nightgown*[42]])

HAMLET   A king of shreds and patches—
  Save me and hover o'er me with your wings,
  You heavenly guards? What would your gracious figure?
QUEEN   Alas, he's mad.
HAMLET   Do you not come your tardy son to chide,
  That, lapsed in time and passion,[43] lets go by
  Th' important acting of your dread command?
  O, say!
GHOST   Do not forget. This visitation
  Is but to whet thy almost blunted purpose.
  But look, amazement on thy mother sits.
  O, step between her and her fighting soul!
  Conceit[44] in weakest bodies strongest works.
  Speak to her, Hamlet.
HAMLET   How is it with you, lady?
QUEEN   Alas, how is't with you,
  That you do bend your eye on vacancy,
  And with th' incorporal [45] air do hold discourse?
  Forth at your eyes your spirits wildly peep,
  And as the sleeping soldiers in th' alarm
  Your bedded hairs like life in excrements[46]
  Start up and stand an[47] end. O gentle son,
  Upon the heat and flame of thy distemper[48]
  Sprinkle cool patience. Whereon do you look?
HAMLET   On him, on him! Look you, how pale he glares!
  His form and cause conjoined, preaching to stones,
  Would make them capable.[49]—Do not look upon me,
  Lest with his piteous action you convert
  My stern effects.[50] Then what I have to do
  Will want true color—tears perchance for blood.

---

[40] *vice* clownish rogue (like the Vice of the morality plays)   [41] *cutpurse*
skulking thief   [42] *nightgown* dressing gown   [43] *lapsed . . . passion* having let
the moment slip and passion cool   [44] *Conceit* imagination   [45] *incorporal*
bodiless   [46] *excrements* outgrowths   [47] *an* on   [48] *distemper* mental disorder
[49] *capable* susceptible   [50] *effects* manifestations of emotion and purpose

QUEEN   To whom do you speak this?

HAMLET   Do you see nothing there?

QUEEN   Nothing at all; yet all that is I see.

HAMLET   Nor did you nothing hear?

QUEEN   No, nothing but ourselves.

HAMLET   Why, look you there! Look how it steals away!
   My father, in his habit as he lived!
   Look where he goes even now out at the portal!

(*Exit* GHOST)

QUEEN   This is the very coinage of your brain.
   This bodiless creation ecstasy[51]
   Is very cunning in.

HAMLET   Ecstasy?
   My pulse as yours doth temperately keep time
   And makes as healthful music. It is not madness
   That I have uttered. Bring me to the test,
   And I the matter will reword, which madness
   Would gambol [52] from. Mother, for love of grace,
   Lay not that flattering unction[53] to your soul,
   That not your trespass but my madness speaks.
   It will but skin and film the ulcerous place
   Whiles rank corruption, mining[54] all within,
   Infects unseen. Confess yourself to heaven,
   Repent what's past, avoid what is to come,
   And do not spread the compost[55] on the weeds
   To make them ranker. Forgive me this my virtue.
   For in the fatness[56] of these pursy[57] times
   Virtue itself of vice must pardon beg,
   Yea, curb[58] and woo for leave to do him good.

QUEEN   O Hamlet, thou hast cleft my heart in twain.

HAMLET   O, throw away the worser part of it,
   And live the purer with the other half.
   Good night—but go not to my uncle's bed.
   Assume a virtue, if you have it not.
   That monster custom, who all sense doth eat,
   Of habits devil, is angel yet in this,
   That to the use of actions fair and good

---

[51] *ecstasy* madness   [52] *gambol* shy (like a startled horse)   [53] *unction* ointment   [54] *mining* undermining   [55] *compost* fertilizing mixture   [56] *fatness*
gross slackness   [57] *pursy* corpulent   [58] *curb* bow to

He likewise gives a frock or livery[59]
That aptly is put on. Refrain to-night,
And that shall lend a kind of easiness
To the next abstinence; the next more easy;
For use[60] almost can change the stamp[61] of nature,
And either [. . .] [62] the devil, or throw him out
With wondrous potency. Once more, good night,
And when you are desirous to be blest,
I'll blessing beg of you.—For this same lord,
I do repent; but heaven hath pleased it so,
To punish me with this, and this with me,
That I must be their scourge and minister.
I will bestow[63] him and will answer well
The death I gave him. So again, good night.
I must be cruel only to be kind.
Thus bad begins, and worse remains behind.[64]
One word more, good lady.

QUEEN   What shall I do?

HAMLET   Not this, by no means, that I bid you do:
Let the bloat[65] king tempt you again to bed,
Pinch wanton on your cheek, call you his mouse,
And let him, for a pair of reechy[66] kisses,
Or paddling in your neck with his damned fingers,
Make you to ravel all this matter out,[67]
That I essentially am not in madness,
But mad in craft. 'Twere good you let him know,
For who that's but a queen, fair, sober, wise,
Would from a paddock,[68] from a bat, a gib,[69]
Such dear concernings[70] hide? Who would do so?
No, in despite of sense and secrecy,
Unpeg the basket on the house's top,
Let the birds fly, and like the famous ape,[71]
To try conclusions,[72] in the basket creep
And break your own neck down.

QUEEN   Be thou assured, if words be made of breath,
And breath of life, I have no life to breathe

---

[59] *livery* characteristic dress (accompanying the suggestion of "garb" in *habits*)   [60] *use* habit   [61] *stamp* impression, form   [62] A word is apparently omitted here   [63] *bestow* stow, hide   [64] *behind* to come   [65] *bloat* bloated with sense gratification   [66] *reechy* filthy   [67] *ravel . . . out* disentangle   [68] *paddock* toad   [69] *gib* tomcat   [70] *dear concernings* matters of great personal significance   [71] *famous ape* (one in a story now unknown)   [72] *conclusions* experiments

What thou hast said to me.
HAMLET   I must to England; you know that?
QUEEN   Alack,
    I had forgot. 'Tis so concluded on.
HAMLET   There's letters sealed, and my two schoolfellows,
    Whom I will trust as I will adders fanged,
    They bear the mandate;[73] they must sweep my way
    And marshal me to knavery. Let it work.
    For 'tis the sport to have the enginer[74]
    Hoist[75] with his own petar,[76] and 't shall go hard
    But I will delve one yard below their mines
    And blow them at the moon. O, 'tis most sweet
    When in one line two crafts directly meet.
    This man shall set me packing.[77]
    I'll lug the guts into the neighbor room.
    Mother, good night. Indeed, this counsellor
    Is now most still, most secret, and most grave,
    Who was in life a foolish prating knave.
    Come, sir, to draw toward an end with you.
    Good night, mother.

    (*Exit the* QUEEN. *Then exit* HAMLET, *tugging in* POLONIUS)

ACT IV

Scene I

A chamber in the castle

    (*Enter* KING *and* QUEEN, *with* ROSENCRANTZ *and* GUILDENSTERN)

KING   There's matter in these sighs. These profound heaves
    You must translate; 'tis fit we understand them.
    Where is your son?
QUEEN   Bestow this place on us a little while.

    (*Exeunt* ROSENCRANTZ *and* GUILDENSTERN)

    Ah, mine own lord, what have I seen to-night!
KING   What, Gertrude? How does Hamlet?

---

[73] *mandate* order   [74] *enginer* engineer, constructor of military engines or
works   [75] *Hoist* blown up   [76] *petar* petard, bomb or mine   [77] *packing* travelling in a hurry (with a play upon his "packing" or shouldering of Polonius'
body and also upon his "packing" in the sense of "plotting" or "contriving")

QUEEN   Mad as the sea and wind when both contend
 Which is the mightier. In his lawless fit,
 Behind the arras hearing something stir,
 Whips out his rapier, cries, "A rat, a rat!"
 And in this brainish apprehension[1] kills
 The unseen good old man.
KING   O heavy deed!
 It had been so with us, had we been there.
 His liberty is full of threats to all,
 To you yourself, to us, to every one.
 Alas, how shall this bloody deed be answered?
 It will be laid to us, whose providence[2]
 Should have kept short, restrained, and out of haunt[3]
 This mad young man. But so much was our love
 We would not understand what was most fit,
 But, like the owner of a foul disease,
 To keep it from divulging,[4] let it feed
 Even on the pith of life. Where is he gone?
QUEEN   To draw apart the body he hath killed;
 O'er whom his very madness, like some ore[5]
 Among a mineral [6] of metals base,
 Shows itself pure. 'A weeps for what is done.
KING   O Gertrude, come away!
 The sun no sooner shall the mountains touch
 But we will ship him hence, and this vile deed
 We must with all our majesty and skill
 Both countenance and excuse. Ho, Guildenstern!

(*Enter* ROSENCRANTZ *and* GUILDENSTERN)

Friends both, go join you with some further aid.
Hamlet in madness hath Polonius slain,
And from his mother's closet hath he dragged him.
Go seek him out; speak fair, and bring the body
Into the chapel. I pray you haste in this.

(*Exeunt* ROSENCRANTZ *and* GUILDENSTERN)

Come, Gertrude, we'll call up our wisest friends
And let them know both what we mean to do
And what's untimely done [. . .] [7]

---

[1] *brainish apprehension* headstrong conception   [2] *providence* foresight
[3] *haunt* association with others   [4] *divulging* becoming known   [5] *ore* vein of
gold   [6] *mineral* mine   [7] Incomplete line; Capell suggests "So, haply, slander"

Whose whisper o'er the world's diameter,
As level [8] as the cannon to his blank[9]
Transports his poisoned shot, may miss our name
And hit the woundless air. O, come away!
My soul is full of discord and dismay.

(*Exeunt*)

Act IV, Scene II

A passage in the castle

(*Enter* HAMLET)

HAMLET   Safely stowed.

GENTLEMEN (*within*)   Hamlet! Lord Hamlet!

HAMLET   But soft, what noise? Who calls on Hamlet? O, here they
come.

(*Enter* ROSENCRANTZ, GUILDENSTERN, *and others*)

ROSENCRANTZ   What have you done, my lord, with the dead body?

HAMLET   Compounded it with dust, whereto 'tis kin.

ROSENCRANTZ   Tell us where 'tis, that we may take it thence
And bear it to the chapel.

HAMLET   Do not believe it.

ROSENCRANTZ   Believe what?

HAMLET   That I can keep your counsel and not mine own. Besides,
to be demanded of a sponge, what replication[1] should be made
by the son of a king?

ROSENCRANTZ   Take you me for a sponge, my lord?

HAMLET   Ay, sir, that soaks up the king's countenance,[2] his rewards, his authorities. But such officers do the king best service in
the end. He keeps them, like an ape, in the corner of his jaw, first
mouthed, to be last swallowed. When he needs what you have
gleaned, it is but squeezing you and, sponge, you shall be dry
again.

ROSENCRANTZ   I understand you not, my lord.

HAMLET   I am glad of it. A knavish speech sleeps in[3] a foolish ear.

ROSENCRANTZ   My lord, you must tell us where the body is and go
with us to the king.

HAMLET   The body is with the king, but the king is not with the
body. The king is a thing—

---

8 *As level* with as direct aim   9 *blank* mark, central white spot on a target
1 *replication* reply   2 *countenance* favor   3 *sleeps in* means nothing to

GUILDENSTERN   A thing, my lord?

HAMLET   Of nothing.[4] Bring me to him. Hide fox, and all after.[5]

(*Exeunt*)

Act IV, Scene III

A chamber in the castle

(*Enter* KING, *and two or three*)

KING   I have sent to seek him and to find the body.
How dangerous is it that this man goes loose!
Yet must not we put the strong law on him;
He's loved of the distracted [1] multitude,
Who like not in their judgment, but their eyes,
And where 'tis so, th' offender's scourge[2] is weighed,
But never the offense. To bear all smooth and even,
This sudden sending him away must seem
Deliberate pause.[3] Diseases desperate grown
By desperate appliance are relieved,
Or not at all.

(*Enter* ROSENCRANTZ, GUILDENSTERN, *and all the rest*)

How now? What hath befallen?

ROSENCRANTZ   Where the dead body is bestowed, my lord,
We cannot get from him.

KING   But where is he?

ROSENCRANTZ   Without, my lord; guarded, to know your pleasure.

KING   Bring him before us.

ROSENCRANTZ   Ho! Bring in the lord.

(*They enter* [*with* HAMLET])

KING   Now, Hamlet, where's Polonius?

HAMLET   At supper.

KING   At supper? Where?

HAMLET   Not where he eats, but where 'a is eaten. A certain convocation of politic worms[4] are e'en at him. Your worm is your

---

[4] *Of nothing* (cf. Prayer Book, Psalm cxliv, 4, "Man is like a thing of naught:
his time passeth away like a shadow")   [5] *Hide ... after* (apparently well-
known words from some game of hide-and-seek)
[1] *distracted* confused   [2] *scourge* punishment   [3] *Deliberate pause* something
done with much deliberation   [4] *politic worms* political and craftily scheming
worms (such as Polonius might well attract)

only emperor for diet.[5] We fat all creatures else to fat us, and we fat ourselves for maggots. Your fat king and your lean beggar is but variable service[6]—two dishes, but to one table. That's the end.

KING   Alas, alas!

HAMLET   A man may fish with the worm that hath eat of a king, and eat of the fish that hath fed of that worm.

KING   What dost thou mean by this?

HAMLET   Nothing but to show you how a king may go a progress[7] through the guts of a beggar.

KING   Where is Polonius?

HAMLET   In heaven. Send thither to see. If your messenger find him not there, seek him i' th' other place yourself. But if indeed you find him not within this month, you shall nose him as you go up the stairs into the lobby.

KING   (*to* ATTENDANTS)   Go seek him there.

HAMLET   'A will stay till you come.

(*Exeunt* ATTENDANTS)

KING   Hamlet, this deed, for thine especial safety,
Which we do tender[8] as we dearly[9] grieve
For that which thou hast done, must send thee hence
With fiery quickness. Therefore prepare thyself.
The bark is ready and the wind at help,
Th' associates tend,[10] and everything is bent[11]
For England.

HAMLET   For England?

KING   Ay, Hamlet.

HAMLET   Good.

KING   So is it, if thou knew'st our purposes.

HAMLET   I see a cherub[12] that sees them. But come, for England! Farewell, dear mother.

KING   Thy loving father, Hamlet.

HAMLET   My mother—father and mother is man and wife, man and wife is one flesh, and so, my mother. Come, for England!

(*Exit*)

---

[5] *diet* food and drink (perhaps with a play upon a famous "convocation," the Diet of Worms opened by the Emperor Charles V on January 28, 1521, before which Luther appeared)   [6] *variable service* different servings of one food   [7] *progress* royal journey of state   [8] *tender* hold dear   [9] *dearly* intensely   [10] *tend* wait   [11] *bent* set in readiness (like a bent bow)   [12] *cherub* one of the cherubim (angels with a distinctive quality of knowledge)

KING   Follow him at foot;[13] tempt him with speed aboard.
Delay it not; I'll have him hence to-night.
Away! for everything is sealed and done
That else leans on[14] th' affair. Pray you make haste.

(*Exeunt all but the* KING)

And, England,[15] if my love thou hold'st at aught—
As my great power thereof may give thee sense,
Since yet thy cicatrice looks raw and red
After the Danish sword, and thy free awe[16]
Pays homage to us—thou mayst not coldly set[17]
Our sovereign process,[18] which imports at full
By letters congruing[19] to that effect
The present[20] death of Hamlet. Do it, England,
For like the hectic[21] in my blood he rages,
And thou must cure me. Till I know 'tis done,
Howe'er my haps,[22] my joys were ne'er begun.

(*Exit*)

Act IV, Scene IV

A coastal highway

(*Enter* FORTINBRAS *with his* ARMY *over the stage*)

FORTINBRAS   Go, captain, from me greet the Danish king.
Tell him that by his license Fortinbras
Craves the conveyance[1] of a promised march
Over his kingdom. You know the rendezvous.
If that his majesty would aught with us,
We shall express our duty in his eye;[2]
And let him know so.
CAPTAIN   I will do't, my lord.
FORTINBRAS   Go softly[3] on.

(*Exeunt all but the* CAPTAIN)

(*Enter* HAMLET, ROSENCRANTZ, GUILDENSTERN, *and others*)

HAMLET   Good sir, whose powers[4] are these?

---

[13] *at foot* at heel, close   [14] *leans on* is connected with   [15] *England* King of England   [16] *free awe* voluntary show of respect   [17] *set* esteem   [18] *process* formal command   [19] *congruing* agreeing   [20] *present* instant   [21] *hectic* a continuous fever   [22] *haps* fortunes
[1] *conveyance* escort   [2] *eye* presence   [3] *softly* slowly   [4] *powers* forces

CAPTAIN   They are of Norway, sir.

HAMLET   How purposed, sir, I pray you?

CAPTAIN   Against some part of Poland.

HAMLET   Who commands them, sir?

CAPTAIN   The nephew to old Norway, Fortinbras.

HAMLET   Goes it against the main[5] of Poland, sir,
Or for some frontier?

CAPTAIN   Truly to speak, and with no addition,[6]
We go to gain a little patch of ground
That hath in it no profit but the name.
To pay[7] five ducats, five, I would not farm it,
Nor will it yield to Norway or the Pole
A ranker[8] rate, should it be sold in fee.[9]

HAMLET   Why, then the Polack never will defend it.

CAPTAIN   Yes, it is already garrisoned.

HAMLET   Two thousand souls and twenty thousand ducats
Will not debate the question of this straw.
This is th' imposthume[10] of much wealth and peace,
That inward breaks, and shows no cause without
Why the man dies. I humbly thank you, sir.

CAPTAIN   God bye you, sir.

(*Exit*)

ROSENCRANTZ   Will't please you go, my lord?

HAMLET   I'll be with you straight. Go a little before.

(*Exeunt all but* HAMLET)

How all occasions do inform[11] against me
And spur my dull revenge! What is a man,
If his chief good and market of [12] his time
Be but to sleep and feed? A beast, no more.
Sure he that made us with such large discourse,[13]
Looking before and after, gave us not
That capability and godlike reason
To fust[14] in us unused. Now, whether it be
Bestial oblivion,[15] or some craven scruple
Of thinking too precisely on th' event—[16]

---

5 *main* main body   6 *addition* exaggeration   7 *To pay* i.e. for a yearly rental
of   8 *ranker* more abundant   9 *in fee* outright   10 *imposthume* abscess   11 *inform* take shape   12 *market of* compensation for   13 *discourse* power of
thought   14 *fust* grow mouldy   15 *oblivion* forgetfulness   16 *event* outcome

A thought which, quartered, hath but one part wisdom
And ever three parts coward—I do not know
Why yet I live to say, "This thing 's to do,"
Sith I have cause, and will, and strength, and means
To do't. Examples gross[17] as earth exhort me.
Witness this army of such mass and charge,[18]
Led by a delicate and tender prince,
Whose spirit, with divine ambition puffed,
Makes mouths[19] at the invisible event,
Exposing what is mortal and unsure
To all that fortune, death, and danger dare,
Even for an eggshell. Rightly to be great
Is not to stir without great argument,
But greatly to find quarrel in a straw[20]
When honor 's at the stake. How stand I then,
That have a father killed, a mother stained,
Excitements of my reason and my blood,
And let all sleep, while to my shame I see
The imminent death of twenty thousand men
That for a fantasy[21] and trick[22] of fame
Go to their graves like beds, fight for a plot
Whereon the numbers cannot try the cause,[23]
Which is not tomb enough and continent[24]
To hide the slain? O, from this time forth,
My thoughts be bloody, or be nothing worth!

(*Exit*)

Act IV, Scene V

A chamber in the castle

(*Enter* Horatio, [Queen] Gertrude, *and a* Gentleman)

QUEEN   I will not speak with her.
GENTLEMAN   She is importunate, indeed distract.[1]
　Her mood will needs be pitied.
QUEEN   　　　　　　　　　What would she have?
GENTLEMAN   She speaks much of her father, says she hears

---

[17] *gross* large and evident   [18] *charge* expense   [19] *Makes mouths* makes faces scornfully   [20] *greatly ... straw* to recognize the great argument even in some small matter   [21] *fantasy* fanciful image   [22] *trick* toy   [23] *try the cause* find space in which to settle the issue by battle   [24] *continent* receptacle
[1] *distract* insane

There's tricks[2] i' th' world, and hems, and beats her heart,
Spurns enviously[3] at straws,[4] speaks things in doubt
That carry but half sense. Her speech is nothing,
Yet the unshapèd use[5] of it doth move
The hearers to collection;[6] they aim[7] at it,
And botch[8] the words up fit to their own thoughts,
Which, as her winks and nods and gestures yield them,
Indeed would make one think there might be thought,
Though nothing sure, yet much unhappily.

HORATIO   'Twere good she were spoken with, for she may strew
Dangerous conjectures in ill-breeding minds.

QUEEN   Let her come in.

(*Exit* GENTLEMAN)

(*Aside*)

To my sick soul (as sin's true nature is)
Each toy[9] seems prologue to some great amiss.[10]
So full of artless[11] jealousy[12] is guilt
It spills[13] itself in fearing to be spilt.

(*Enter* OPHELIA [*distracted*])

OPHELIA   Where is the beauteous majesty of Denmark?

QUEEN   How now, Ophelia?

OPHELIA   (*She sings.*)
How should I your true-love know
    From another one?
By his cockle hat[14] and staff
    And his sandal shoon.[15]

QUEEN   Alas, sweet lady, what imports this song?

OPHELIA   Say you? Nay, pray you mark.

Song

He is dead and gone, lady,
    He is dead and gone;
At his head a grass-green turf,
    At his heels a stone.
O, ho!

---

[2] *tricks* deceits [3] *Spurns enviously* kicks spitefully, takes offense [4] *straws*
trifles [5] *unshapèd use* disordered manner [6] *collection* attempts at shaping
meaning [7] *aim* guess [8] *botch* patch [9] *toy* trifle [10] *amiss* calamity [11] *artless* unskillfully managed [12] *jealousy* suspicion [13] *spills* destroys [14] *cockle
hat* hat bearing a cockle shell, worn by a pilgrim who had been to the shrine
of St James of Compostela [15] *shoon* shoes

QUEEN   Nay, but Ophelia—
OPHELIA   Pray you mark.
  (*Sings*) White his shroud as the mountain snow—

  (*Enter* KING)

QUEEN   Alas, look here, my lord.
OPHELIA

Song

> Larded [16] all with sweet flowers;
>   Which bewept to the grave did not go
>   With true-love showers.

KING   How do you, pretty lady?
OPHELIA   Well, God dild [17] you! They say the owl [18] was a baker's daughter. Lord, we know what we are, but know not what we may be. God be at your table!
KING   Conceit [19] upon her father.
OPHELIA   Pray let's have no words of this, but when they ask you what it means, say you this:

Song

> To-morrow is Saint Valentine's day.
>   All in the morning betime,[20]
> And I a maid at your window,
>   To be your Valentine.
> Then up he rose and donned his clo'es
>   And dupped [21] the chamber door,
> Let in the maid, that out a maid
>   Never departed more.

KING   Pretty Ophelia!
OPHELIA   Indeed, la, without an oath, I'll make an end on't:
  (*Sings*)   By Gis[22] and by Saint Charity,
        Alack, and fie for shame!
      Young men will do't if they come to't.
        By Cock,[23] they are to blame.
      Quoth she, "Before you tumbled me,
        You promised me to wed."

---

[16] *Larded* garnished   [17] *dild* yield, repay   [18] *the owl* an owl into which, according to a folk-tale, a baker's daughter was transformed because of her failure to show whole-hearted generosity when Christ asked for bread in the baker's shop   [19] *Conceit* thought   [20] *betime* early   [21] *dupped* opened   [22] *Gis* Jesus   [23] *Cock* God (with a perversion of the name not uncommon in oaths)

He answers:
> "So would I 'a' done, by yonder sun,
> And thou hadst not come to my bed."

KING   How long hath she been thus?

OPHELIA   I hope all will be well. We must be patient, but I cannot choose but weep to think they would lay him i' th' cold ground. My brother shall know of it; and so I thank you for your good counsel. Come, my coach! Good night, ladies, good night. Sweet ladies, good night, good night.

(*Exit*)

KING   Follow her close; give her good watch, I pray you.

(*Exit* HORATIO)

O, this is the poison of deep grief; it springs
All from her father's death—and now behold!
O Gertrude, Gertrude,
When sorrows come, they come not single spies,
But in battalions: first, her father slain;
Next, your son gone, and he most violent author
Of his own just remove; the people muddied,[24]
Thick and unwholesome in their thoughts and whispers
For good Polonius' death, and we have done but greenly[25]
In hugger-mugger[26] to inter him; poor Ophelia
Divided from herself and her fair judgment,
Without the which we are pictures or mere beasts;
Last, and as much containing as all these,
Her brother is in secret come from France,
Feeds on his wonder, keeps himself in clouds,[27]
And wants[28] not buzzers[29] to infect his ear
With pestilent speeches of his father's death,
Wherein necessity, of matter beggared,[30]
Will nothing stick[31] our person to arraign[32]
In ear and ear. O my dear Gertrude, this,
Like to a murd'ring piece,[33] in many places
Gives me superfluous death.

A noise within

---

[24] *muddied* stirred up and confused   [25] *greenly* foolishly   [26] *hugger-mugger* secrecy and disorder   [27] *clouds* obscurity   [28] *wants* lacks   [29] *buzzers* whispering tale-bearers   [30] *of matter beggared* unprovided with facts   [31] *nothing stick* in no way hesitate   [32] *arraign* accuse   [33] *murd'ring piece* cannon loaded with shot meant to scatter

(*Enter a* MESSENGER)

QUEEN   Alack, what noise is this?

KING   Attend, where are my Switzers? [34] Let them guard the door.
   What is the matter?

MESSENGER   Save yourself, my lord.
   The ocean, overpeering of [35] his list,[36]
   Eats not the flats with more impiteous[37] haste
   Than young Laertes, in a riotous head,[38]
   O'erbears your officers. The rabble call him lord,
   And, as the world were now but to begin,
   Antiquity forgot, custom not known,
   The ratifiers and props of every word,[39]
   They cry, "Choose we! Laertes shall be king!"
   Caps, hands, and tongues applaud it to the clouds,
   "Laertes shall be king! Laertes king!"

A noise within

QUEEN   How cheerfully on the false trail they cry!
   O, this is counter,[40] you false Danish dogs!

KING   The doors are broke.

(*Enter* LAERTES *with others*)

LAERTES   Where is this king?—Sirs, stand you all without.

ALL   No, let's come in.

LAERTES   I pray you give me leave.

ALL   We will, we will.

LAERTES   I thank you. Keep the door.

(*Exeunt his* FOLLOWERS)

                       O thou vile king,
   Give me my father.

QUEEN   Calmly, good Laertes.

LAERTES   That drop of blood that's calm proclaims me bastard,
   Cries cuckold to my father, brands the harlot
   Even here between the chaste unsmirchèd brows
   Of my true mother.

KING   What is the cause, Laertes,
   That thy rebellion looks so giant-like?
   Let him go, Gertrude. Do not fear[41] our person.

---

[34] *Switzers* hired Swiss guards   [35] *overpeering of* rising to look over and pass
beyond   [36] *list* boundary   [37] *impiteous* pitiless   [38] *head* armed force   [39] *word*
promise   [40] *counter* hunting backward on the trail   [41] *fear* fear for

There's such divinity doth hedge a king
That treason can but peep to[42] what it would,
Acts little of his will. Tell me, Laertes,
Why thou art thus incensed. Let him go, Gertrude.
Speak, man.

LAERTES   Where is my father?

KING   Dead.

QUEEN   But not by him.

KING   Let him demand his fill.

LAERTES   How came he dead? I'll not be juggled with.
To hell allegiance, vows to the blackest devil,
Conscience and grace to the profoundest pit!
I dare damnation. To this point I stand,
That both the worlds[43] I give to negligence,[44]
Let come what comes, only I'll be revenged
Most throughly[45] for my father.

KING   Who shall stay you?

LAERTES   My will, not all the world's.
And for my means, I'll husband them so well
They shall go far with little.

KING   Good Laertes,
If you desire to know the certainty
Of your dear father, is't writ in your revenge
That swoopstake[46] you will draw both friend and foe,
Winner and loser?

LAERTES   None but his enemies.

KING   Will you know them then?

LAERTES   To his good friends thus wide I'll ope my arms
And like the kind life-rend'ring[47] pelican
Repast them with my blood.

KING   Why, now you speak
Like a good child and a true gentleman.
That I am guiltless of your father's death,
And am most sensibly[48] in grief for it,
It shall as level [49] to your judgment 'pear
As day does to your eye.

        A noise within: "Let her come in!"

---

[42] *peep to* i.e. through the barrier   [43] *both the worlds* whatever may result in
this world or the next   [44] *give to negligence* disregard   [45] *throughly* thoroughly   [46] *swoopstake* sweepstake, taking all stakes on the gambling table
[47] *life-rend'ring* life-yielding (because the mother pelican supposedly took
blood from her breast with her bill to feed her young)   [48] *sensibly* feelingly
[49] *level* plain

LAERTES   How now? What noise is that?

(*Enter* OPHELIA)

O heat, dry up my brains; tears seven times salt
Burn out the sense and virtue of mine eye!
By heaven, thy madness shall be paid by weight
Till our scale turn the beam.[50] O rose of May,
Dear maid, kind sister, sweet Ophelia!
O heavens, is't possible a young maid's wits
Should be as mortal as an old man's life?
Nature is fine[51] in love, and where 'tis fine,
It sends some precious instance[52] of itself
After the thing it loves.

OPHELIA

Song

    They bore him barefaced on the bier
        Hey non nony, nony, hey nony
        And in his grave rained many a tear—
    Fare you well, my dove!

LAERTES   Hadst thou thy wits, and didst persuade revenge,
It could not move thus.

OPHELIA   You must sing "A-down a-down, and you call him
a-down-a." O, how the wheel [53] becomes it! It is the false steward, that stole his master's daughter.

LAERTES   This nothing 's more than matter.[54]

OPHELIA   There's rosemary, that's for remembrance. Pray you, love,
remember. And there is pansies, that's for thoughts.

LAERTES   A document[55] in madness, thoughts and remembrance
fitted.

OPHELIA   There's fennel [56] for you, and columbines.[57] There's rue[58]
for you, and here's some for me. We may call it herb of grace o'
Sundays. O, you must wear your rue with a difference. There's
a daisy.[59] I would give you some violets,[60] but they withered all
when my father died. They say 'a made a good end.

(*Sings*)   For bonny sweet Robin is all my joy.

LAERTES   Thought and affliction, passion, hell itself,
She turns to favor[61] and to prettiness.

---

[50] *beam* bar of a balance   [51] *fine* refined to purity   [52] *instance* token   [53] *wheel*
burden, refrain   [54] *more than matter* more meaningful than sane speech
[55] *document* lesson   [56] *fennel* symbol of flattery   [57] *columbines* symbol of
thanklessness   [58] *rue* symbol of repentance   [59] *daisy* symbol of dissembling
[60] *violets* symbol of faithfulness   [61] *favor* charm

OPHELIA

Song

And will 'a not come again?
And will 'a not come again?
    No, no, he is dead;
    Go to thy deathbed;
He never will come again.
His beard was as white as snow,
All flaxen was his poll.[62]
    He is gone, he is gone,
    And we cast away moan.
God 'a' mercy on his soul!
And of [63] all Christian souls, I pray God. God bye you.

(*Exit*)

LAERTES   Do you see this, O God?
KING   Laertes, I must commune with your grief,
Or you deny me right. Go but apart,
Make choice of whom your wisest friends you will,
And they shall hear and judge 'twixt you and me.
If by direct or by collateral [64] hand
They find us touched,[65] we will our kingdom give,
Our crown, our life, and all that we call ours,
To you in satisfaction; but if not,
Be you content to lend your patience to us,
And we shall jointly labor with your soul
To give it due content.
LAERTES   Let this be so.
His means of death, his obscure funeral—
No trophy,[66] sword, nor hatchment[67] o'er his bones,
No noble rite nor formal ostentation[68]—
Cry to be heard, as 'twere from heaven to earth,
That[69] I must call't in question.
KING   So you shall;
And where th' offense is, let the great axe fall.
I pray you go with me.

(*Exeunt*)

---

[62] *poll* head   [63] *of* on   [64] *collateral* indirect   [65] *touched* i.e. with the crime
[66] *trophy* memorial   [67] *hatchment* coat of arms   [68] *ostentation* ceremony
[69] *That* so that

Act IV, Scene VI

A chamber in the castle

(*Enter* HORATIO *and others*)

HORATIO   What are they that would speak with me?
GENTLEMAN   Seafaring men, sir. They say they have letters for you.
HORATIO   Let them come in.

(*Exit* ATTENDANT)

> I do not know from what part of the world
> I should be greeted, if not from Lord Hamlet.

(*Enter* SAILORS)

SAILOR   God bless you, sir.
HORATIO   Let him bless thee too.
SAILOR   'A shall, sir, an't please him. There's a letter for you, sir—
it came from th' ambassador that was bound for England—if
your name be Horatio, as I am let to know it is.
HORATIO   (*reads the letter*)   "Horatio, when thou shalt have overlooked [1] this, give these fellows some means[2] to the king. They
have letters for him. Ere we were two days old at sea, a pirate of
very warlike appointment[3] gave us chase. Finding ourselves too
slow of sail, we put on a compelled valor, and in the grapple I
boarded them. On the instant they got clear of our ship; so I
alone became their prisoner. They have dealt with me like thieves
of mercy,[4] but they knew what they did: I am to do a good turn
for them. Let the king have the letters I have sent, and repair
thou to me with as much speed as thou wouldest fly death. I have
words to speak in thine ear will make thee dumb; yet are they
much too light for the bore[5] of the matter. These good fellows
will bring thee where I am. Rosencrantz and Guildenstern hold
their course for England. Of them I have much to tell thee.
Farewell.

> He that thou knowest thine, Hamlet."
> Come, I will give you way for these your letters,
> And do't the speedier that you may direct me
> To him from whom you brought them.

(*Exeunt*)

---

[1] *overlooked* surveyed, scanned   [2] *means* i.e. of access   [3] *appointment* equipment   [4] *thieves of mercy* merciful thieves   [5] *bore* caliber (as of a gun)

Act IV, Scene VII

A chamber in the castle

(*Enter* KING *and* LAERTES)

KING   Now must your conscience my acquittance seal,
And you must put me in your heart for friend,
Sith you have heard, and with a knowing ear,
That he which hath your noble father slain
Pursued my life.

LAERTES   It well appears. But tell me
Why you proceeded not against these feats[1]
So crimeful and so capital [2] in nature,
As by your safety, wisdom, all things else,
You mainly[3] were stirred up.

KING   O, for two special reasons,
Which may to you perhaps seem much unsinewed,
But yet to me they're strong. The queen his mother
Lives almost by his looks, and for myself—
My virtue or my plague, be it either which—
She is so conjunctive[4] to my life and soul
That, as the star moves not but in his sphere,
I could not but by her. The other motive
Why to a public count[5] I might not go
Is the great love the general gender[6] bear him,
Who, dipping all his faults in their affection,
Would, like the spring that turneth wood to stone,
Convert his gyves[7] to graces; so that my arrows,
Too slightly timbered for so loud a wind,
Would have reverted to my bow again,
And not where I had aimed them.

LAERTES   And so have I a noble father lost,
A sister driven into desp'rate terms,[8]
Whose worth, if praises may go back again,[9]
Stood challenger on mount[10] of all the age
For her perfections. But my revenge will come.

KING   Break not your sleeps for that. You must not think
That we are made of stuff so flat and dull
That we can let our beard be shook with danger,

---

[1] *feats* deeds   [2] *capital* punishable by death   [3] *mainly* powerfully   [4] *conjunctive* closely united   [5] *count* trial, accounting   [6] *general gender* common people   [7] *gyves* fetters   [8] *terms* circumstances   [9] *back again* i.e. to her better circumstances   [10] *on mount* on a height

And think it pastime. You shortly shall hear more.
I loved your father, and we love ourself,
And that, I hope, will teach you to imagine—

(*Enter a* MESSENGER *with letters*)

How now? What news?
MESSENGER   Letters, my lord, from Hamlet:
These to your majesty, this to the queen.
KING   From Hamlet? Who brought them?
MESSENGER   Sailors, my lord, they say; I saw them not.
They were given me by Claudio; he received them
Of him that brought them.
KING   Laertes, you shall hear them.—
Leave us.

(*Exit* MESSENGER)

(*Reads*) "High and mighty, you shall know I am set naked [11]
on your kingdom. To-morrow shall I beg leave to see your kingly
eyes; when I shall (first asking your pardon thereunto) recount
the occasion of my sudden and more strange return.   Hamlet."
What should this mean? Are all the rest come back?
Or is it some abuse,[12] and no such thing?
LAERTES   Know you the hand?
KING   'Tis Hamlet's character.[13] "Naked"!
And in a postscript here, he says "alone."
Can you devise[14] me?
LAERTES   I am lost in it, my lord. But let him come.
It warms the very sickness in my heart
That I shall live and tell him to his teeth,
"Thus diddest thou."
KING   If it be so, Laertes,
(As how should it be so? how otherwise?)
Will you be ruled by me?
LAERTES   Ay, my lord,
So you will not o'errule me to a peace.
KING   To thine own peace. If he be now returned,
As checking at[15] his voyage, and that he means
No more to undertake it, I will work him

---

[11] *naked* destitute   [12] *abuse* imposture   [13] *character* handwriting   [14] *devise*
explain to   [15] *checking at* turning aside from (like a falcon turning from its
quarry for other prey)

To an exploit now ripe in my device,
Under the which he shall not choose but fall;
And for his death no wind of blame shall breathe,
But even his mother shall uncharge the practice[16]
And call it accident.

LAERTES   My lord, I will be ruled;
The rather if you could devise it so
That I might be the organ.[17]

KING   It falls right.
You have been talked of since your travel much,
And that in Hamlet's hearing, for a quality
Wherein they say you shine. Your sum of parts
Did not together pluck such envy from him
As did that one, and that, in my regard,
Of the unworthiest siege.[18]

LAERTES   What part is that, my lord?

KING   A very riband [19] in the cap of youth,
Yet needful too, for youth no less becomes
The light and careless livery[20] that it wears
Than settled age his sables[21] and his weeds,[22]
Importing health[23] and graveness. Two months since
Here was a gentleman of Normandy.
I have seen myself, and served against, the French,
And they can well [24] on horseback, but this gallant
Had witchcraft in't. He grew unto his seat,
And to such wondrous doing brought his horse
As had he been incorpsed [25] and demi-natured [26]
With the brave beast. So far he topped [27] my thought[28]
That I, in forgery[29] of shapes and tricks,
Come short of what he did.

LAERTES   A Norman was't?

KING   A Norman.

LAERTES   Upon my life, Lamord.

KING   The very same.

LAERTES   I know him well. He is the brooch[30] indeed

---

16 *uncharge the practice* acquit the stratagem of being a plot   17 *organ* instrument   18 *siege* seat, rank   19 *riband* decoration   20 *livery* distinctive attire   21 *sables* dignified robes richly furred with sable   22 *weeds* distinctive garments   23 *health* welfare, prosperity   24 *can well* can perform well   25 *incorpsed* made one body   26 *demi-natured* made sharer of nature half and half (as man shares with horse in the centaur)   27 *topped* excelled   28 *thought* imagination of possibilities   29 *forgery* invention   30 *brooch* ornament

And gem of all the nation.
KING   He made confession[31] of you,
    And gave you such a masterly report
    For art and exercise in your defense,
    And for your rapier most especial,
    That he cried out 'twould be a sight indeed
    If one could match you. The scrimers[32] of their nation
    He swore had neither motion, guard, nor eye,
    If you opposed them. Sir, this report of his
    Did Hamlet so envenom with his envy
    That he could nothing do but wish and beg
    Your sudden coming o'er to play with you.
    Now, out of this—
LAERTES   What out of this, my lord?
KING   Laertes, was your father dear to you?
    Or are you like the painting of a sorrow,
    A face without a heart?
LAERTES   Why ask you this?
KING   Not that I think you did not love your father,
    But that I know love is begun by time,
    And that I see, in passages of proof,[33]
    Time qualifies[34] the spark and fire of it.
    There lives within the very flame of love
    A kind of wick or snuff [35] that will abate it,
    And nothing is at a like goodness still,[36]
    For goodness, growing to a plurisy,[37]
    Dies in his own too-much. That we would do
    We should do when we would, for this "would" changes,
    And hath abatements and delays as many
    As there are tongues, are hands, are accidents,
    And then this "should" is like a spendthrift sigh,
    That hurts[38] by easing. But to the quick[39] o' th' ulcer—
    Hamlet comes back; what would you undertake
    To show yourself your father's son in deed
    More than in words?
LAERTES   To cut his throat i' th' church!

---

[31] *made confession* admitted the rival accomplishments   [32] *scrimers* fencers
[33] *passages of proof* incidents of experience   [34] *qualifies* weakens   [35] *snuff*
unconsumed portion of the burned wick   [36] *still* always   [37] *plurisy* excess
[38] *hurts* i.e. shortens life by drawing blood from the heart (as was believed)
[39] *quick* sensitive flesh

KING   No place indeed should murder sanctuarize;[40]
    Revenge should have no bounds. But, good Laertes,
    Will you do this? Keep close within your chamber.
    Hamlet returned shall know you are come home.
    We'll put on[41] those shall praise your excellence
    And set a double varnish on the fame
    The Frenchman gave you, bring you in fine[42] together
    And wager on your heads. He, being remiss,[43]
    Most generous, and free from all contriving,
    Will not peruse[44] the foils, so that with ease,
    Or with a little shuffling, you may choose
    A sword unbated,[45] and, in a pass of practice,[46]
    Requite him for your father.
LAERTES   I will do't,
    And for that purpose I'll anoint my sword.
    I bought an unction[47] of a mountebank,[48]
    So mortal that, but dip a knife in it,
    Where it draws blood no cataplasm[49] so rare,
    Collected from all simples[50] that have virtue
    Under the moon, can save the thing from death
    That is but scratched withal.[51] I'll touch my point
    With this contagion, that, if I gall [52] him slightly,
    It may be death.
KING   Let's further think of this,
    Weigh what convenience both of time and means
    May fit us to our shape.[53] If this should fail,
    And that our drift[54] look[55] through our bad performance,
    'Twere better not assayed. Therefore this project
    Should have a back or second, that might hold
    If this did blast in proof.[56] Soft, let me see.
    We'll make a solemn wager on your cunnings—
    I ha't!
    When in your motion you are hot and dry—
    As make your bouts more violent to that end—
    And that he calls for drink, I'll have preferred [57] him
    A chalice for the nonce,[58] whereon but sipping,

---

[40] *sanctuarize* protect from punishment, give sanctuary to   [41] *put on* instigate
[42] *in fine* finally   [43] *remiss* negligent   [44] *peruse* scan   [45] *unbated* not blunted
[46] *pass of practice* thrust made effective by trickery   [47] *unction* ointment
[48] *mountebank* quack-doctor   [49] *cataplasm* poultice   [50] *simples* herbs   [51] *withal*
with it   [52] *gall* scratch   [53] *shape* plan   [54] *drift* intention   [55] *look* show
[56] *blast in proof* burst during trial (like a faulty cannon)   [57] *preferred* offered
[58] *nonce* occasion

If he by chance escape your venomed stuck,[59]
Our purpose may hold there.—But stay, what noise?

(*Enter* QUEEN)

QUEEN   One woe doth tread upon another's heel,
So fast they follow. Your sister 's drowned, Laertes.
LAERTES   Drowned! O, where?
QUEEN   There is a willow grows askant[60] the brook,
That shows his hoar[61] leaves in the glassy stream.
Therewith fantastic garlands did she make
Of crowflowers, nettles, daisies, and long purples,
That liberal [62] shepherds give a grosser name,
But our cold maids do dead men's fingers call them.
There on the pendent boughs her crownet[63] weeds
Clamb'ring to hang, an envious sliver broke,
When down her weedy trophies and herself
Fell in the weeping brook. Her clothes spread wide,
And mermaid-like awhile they bore her up,
Which time she chanted snatches of old lauds,[64]
As one incapable of [65] her own distress,
Or like a creature native and indued [66]
Unto that element. But long it could not be
Till that her garments, heavy with their drink,
Pulled the poor wretch from her melodious lay
To muddy death.
LAERTES   Alas, then she is drowned?
QUEEN   Drowned, drowned.
LAERTES   Too much of water hast thou, poor Ophelia,
And therefore I forbid my tears; but yet
It is our trick;[67] nature her custom holds,
Let shame say what it will. When these are gone,
The woman[68] will be out. Adieu, my lord.
I have a speech o' fire, that fain would blaze
But that this folly drowns it.

(*Exit*)

KING   Let's follow, Gertrude.
How much I had to do to calm his rage!

---

[59] *stuck* thrust   [60] *askant* alongside   [61] *hoar* grey   [62] *liberal* free-spoken, licentious   [63] *crownet* coronet   [64] *lauds* hymns   [65] *incapable of* insensible to   [66] *indued* endowed   [67] *trick* way (i.e. to shed tears when sorrowful)   [68] *woman* unmanly part of nature.

Now fear I this will give it start again;
Therefore let's follow.

(*Exeunt*)

ACT V

Scene I

A churchyard

(*Enter two* CLOWNS[1])

CLOWN   Is she to be buried in Christian burial [2] when she willfully seeks her own salvation?

OTHER   I tell thee she is. Therefore make her grave straight.[3] The crowner[4] hath sate on her, and finds it Christian burial.

CLOWN   How can that be, unless she drowned herself in her own defense?

OTHER   Why, 'tis found so.

CLOWN   It must be *se offendendo*;[5] it cannot be else. For here lies the point: if I drown myself wittingly, it argues an act, and an act hath three branches—it is to act, to do, and to perform. Argal,[6] she drowned herself wittingly.

OTHER   Nay, but hear you, Goodman Delver.[7]

CLOWN   Give me leave. Here lies the water—good. Here stands the man—good. If the man go to this water and drown himself, it is, will he nill he,[8] he goes, mark you that. But if the water come to him and drown him, he drowns not himself. Argal, he that is not guilty of his own death shortens not his own life.

OTHER   But is this law?

CLOWN   Ay marry, is't—crowner's quest[9] law.

OTHER   Will you ha' the truth on't? If this had not been a gentle-woman, she should have been buried out o' Christian burial.

CLOWN   Why, there thou say'st.[10] And the more pity that great folk should have count'nance[11] in this world to drown or hang them-selves more than their even-Christen.[12] Come, my spade. There

---

[1] *Clowns* rustics   [2] *in Christian burial* in consecrated ground with the pre-scribed service of the Church (a burial denied to suicides)   [3] *straight* straightway, at once   [4] *crowner* coroner   [5] *se offendendo* a clownish trans-formation of *"se defendendo,"* "in self-defense"   [6] *Argal* for *"ergo,"* "there-fore"   [7] *Delver* Digger   [8] *will he nill he* willy-nilly   [9] *quest* inquest   [10] *thou say'st* you have it right   [11] *count'nance* privilege   [12] *even-Christen* fellow Christian

is no ancient gentlemen but gard'ners, ditchers, and grave-makers. They hold up Adam's profession.

OTHER   Was he a gentleman?

CLOWN   'A was the first that ever bore arms.

OTHER   Why, he had none.[13]

CLOWN   What, art a heathen? How dost thou understand the Scripture? The Scripture says Adam digged. Could he dig without arms? I'll put another question to thee. If thou answerest me not to the purpose, confess thyself—

OTHER   Go to.

CLOWN   What is he that builds stronger than either the mason, the shipwright, or the carpenter?

OTHER   The gallows-maker, for that frame outlives a thousand tenants.

CLOWN   I like thy wit well, in good faith. The gallows does well. But how does it well? It does well to those that do ill. Now thou dost ill to say the gallows is built stronger than the church. Argal, the gallows may do well to thee. To't again, come.

OTHER   Who builds stronger than a mason, a shipwright, or a carpenter?

CLOWN   Ay, tell me that, and unyoke.[14]

OTHER   Marry, now I can tell.

CLOWN   To't.

OTHER   Mass,[15] I cannot tell.

CLOWN   Cudgel thy brains no more about it, for your dull ass will not mend his pace with beating. And when you are asked this question next, say "a grave-maker." The houses he makes last till doomsday. Go, get thee in, and fetch me a stoup[16] of liquor.

(*Exit* OTHER CLOWN)

(*Enter* HAMLET *and* HORATIO [*as* CLOWN *digs and sings*])

Song

In youth when I did love, did love,
    Methought it was very sweet
To contract—O—the time for—a—my behove,[17]
    O, methought there—a—was nothing—a—meet.

HAMLET   Has this fellow no feeling of his business, that 'a sings at grave-making?

---

[13] *had none* i.e. had no gentleman's coat of arms   [14] *unyoke* i.e. unharness your powers of thought after a good day's work   [15] *Mass* by the Mass   [16] *stoup* large mug   [17] *behove* behoof, benefit

HORATIO   Custom hath made it in him a property[18] of easiness.[19]

HAMLET   'Tis e'en so. The hand of little employment hath the daintier sense.[20]

CLOWN

Song

> But age with his stealing steps
>   Hath clawed me in his clutch,
> And hath shipped me intil[21] the land,
>   As if I had never been such.

(Throws up a skull)

HAMLET   That skull had a tongue in it, and could sing once. How the knave jowls[22] it to the ground, as if 'twere Cain's jawbone, that did the first murder! This might be the pate of a politician,[23] which this ass now o'erreaches;[24] one that would circumvent God, might it not?

HORATIO   It might, my lord.

HAMLET   Or of a courtier, which could say "Good morrow, sweet lord! How dost thou, sweet lord?" This might be my Lord Such-a-one, that praised my Lord Such-a-one's horse when 'a meant to beg it, might it not?

HORATIO   Ay, my lord.

HAMLET   Why, e'en so, and now my Lady Worm's, chapless,[25] and knocked about the mazzard[26] with a sexton's spade. Here's fine revolution, an we had the trick to see't. Did these bones cost no more the breeding but to play at loggets[27] with 'em? Mine ache to think on't.

CLOWN

Song

> A pickaxe and a spade, a spade,
>   For and[28] a shrouding sheet;
> O, a pit of clay for to be made
>   For such a guest is meet.

(Throws up another skull)

---

[18] *property* peculiarity   [19] *easiness* easy acceptability   [20] *daintier sense* more delicate feeling (because the hand is less calloused)   [21] *intil* into   [22] *jowls* hurls   [23] *politician* crafty schemer   [24] *o'erreaches* gets the better of (with a play upon the literal meaning)   [25] *chapless* lacking the lower chap or jaw   [26] *mazzard* head   [27] *loggets* small pieces of wood thrown in a game   [28] *For and* and

HAMLET   There's another. Why may not that be the skull of a lawyer? Where be his quiddities[29] now, his quillities,[30] his cases, his
tenures,[31] and his tricks? Why does he suffer this mad knave now
to knock him about the sconce[32] with a dirty shovel, and will not
tell him of his action of battery? Hum! This fellow might be in's
time a great buyer of land, with his statutes, his recognizances,[33]
his fines,[34] his double vouchers,[35] his recoveries. Is this the fine[36]
of his fines, and the recovery of his recoveries, to have his fine
pate full of fine dirt? Will his vouchers vouch him no more of his
purchases, and double ones too, than the length and breadth of
a pair of indentures? [37] The very conveyances[38] of his lands will
scarcely lie in this box, and must th' inheritor himself have no
more, ha?

HORATIO   Not a jot more, my lord.

HAMLET   Is not parchment made of sheepskins?

HORATIO   Ay, my lord, and of calveskins too.

HAMLET   They are sheep and calves which seek out assurance in
that. I will speak to this fellow. Whose grave 's this, sirrah?

CLOWN   Mine, sir.

(*Sings*)   O, a pit of clay for to be made
               For such a guest is meet.

HAMLET   I think it be thine indeed, for thou liest in't.

CLOWN   You lie out on't, sir, and therefore 'tis not yours. For my
part, I do not lie in't, yet it is mine.

HAMLET   Thou dost lie in't, to be in't and say it is thine. 'Tis for
the dead, not for the quick;[39] therefore thou liest.

CLOWN   'Tis a quick lie, sir; 'twill away again from me to you.

HAMLET   What man dost thou dig it for?

CLOWN   For no man, sir.

HAMLET   What woman then?

CLOWN   For none neither.

HAMLET   Who is to be buried in't?

CLOWN   One that was a woman, sir; but, rest her soul, she's dead.

HAMLET   How absolute[40] the knave is! We must speak by the

---

[29] *quiddities* subtleties (from scholastic *"quidditas,"* meaning the distinctive
nature of anything)   [30] *quillities* nice distinctions   [31] *tenures* holdings of
property   [32] *sconce* head   [33] *statutes, recognizances* legal documents or bonds
acknowledging debt   [34] *fines, recoveries* modes of converting estate tail into
fee simple   [35] *vouchers* persons vouched or called on to warrant a title
[36] *fine* end (introducing a word play involving four meanings of "fine")
[37] *pair of indentures* deed or legal agreement in duplicate   [38] *conveyances*
deeds   [39] *quick* living   [40] *absolute* positive

card,[41] or equivocation[42] will undo us. By the Lord, Horatio, this
three years I have taken note of it, the age is grown so picked [43]
that the toe of the peasant comes so near the heel of the courtier
he galls[44] his kibe.[45]—How long hast thou been a grave-maker?

CLOWN   Of all the days i' th' year, I came to't that day that our
last king Hamlet overcame Fortinbras.

HAMLET   How long is that since?

CLOWN   Cannot you tell that? Every fool can tell that. It was the
very day that young Hamlet was born—he that is mad, and sent
into England.

HAMLET   Ay, marry, why was he sent into England?

CLOWN   Why, because 'a was mad. 'A shall recover his wits there;
or, if 'a do not, 'tis no great matter there.

HAMLET   Why?

CLOWN   'Twill not be seen in him there. There the men are as mad
as he.

HAMLET   How came he mad?

CLOWN   Very strangely, they say.

HAMLET   How strangely?

CLOWN   Faith, e'en with losing his wits.

HAMLET   Upon what ground?

CLOWN   Why, here in Denmark. I have been sexton here, man and
boy, thirty years.

HAMLET   How long will a man lie i' th' earth ere he rot?

CLOWN   Faith, if 'a be not rotten before 'a die (as we have many
pocky[46] corses now-a-days that will scarce hold the laying in), 'a
will last you some eight year or nine year. A tanner will last you
nine year.

HAMLET   Why he more than another?

CLOWN   Why, sir, his hide is so tanned with his trade that 'a will
keep out water a great while, and your water is a sore decayer of
your whoreson dead body. Here's a skull now hath lien you i' th'
earth three-and-twenty years.

HAMLET   Whose was it?

CLOWN   A whoreson mad fellow's it was. Whose do you think it
was?

HAMLET   Nay, I know not.

---

[41] *by the card* by the card on which the points of the mariner's compass are
marked, absolutely to the point   [42] *equivocation* ambiguity   [43] *picked* refined, spruce   [44] *galls* chafes   [45] *kibe* chilblain   [46] *pocky* rotten (literally,
corrupted by pox, or syphilis)

CLOWN   A pestilence on him for a mad rogue! 'A poured a flagon of Rhenish[47] on my head once. This same skull, sir, was—sir—Yorick's skull, the king's jester.

HAMLET   This?

CLOWN   E'en that.

HAMLET   Let me see. (*Takes the skull.*) Alas, poor Yorick! I knew him, Horatio, a fellow of infinite jest, of most excellent fancy. He hath borne me on his back a thousand times. And now how abhorred in my imagination it is! My gorge rises at it. Here hung those lips that I have kissed I know not how oft. Where be your gibes now? Your gambols, your songs, your flashes of merriment that were wont to set the table on a roar? Not one now to mock your own grinning? Quite chapfall'n? [48] Now get you to my lady's chamber, and tell her, let her paint an inch thick, to this favor[49] she must come. Make her laugh at that. Prithee, Horatio, tell me one thing.

HORATIO   What's that, my lord?

HAMLET   Dost thou think Alexander looked o' this fashion i' th' earth?

HORATIO   E'en so.

HAMLET   And smelt so? Pah!

(*Puts down the skull*)

HORATIO   E'en so, my lord.

HAMLET   To what base uses we may return, Horatio! Why may not imagination trace the noble dust of Alexander till 'a find it stopping a bunghole?

HORATIO   'Twere to consider too curiously,[50] to consider so.

HAMLET   No, faith, not a jot, but to follow him thither with modesty[51] enough, and likelihood to lead it; as thus: Alexander died, Alexander was buried, Alexander returneth to dust; the dust is earth; of earth we make loam; and why of that loam whereto he was converted might they not stop a beer barrel?
Imperious[52] Caesar, dead and turned to clay,
Might stop a hole to keep the wind away.
O, that that earth which kept the world in awe
Should patch a wall t' expel the winter's flaw! [53]

---

[47] *Rhenish* Rhine wine   [48] *chapfall'n* lacking the lower chap, or jaw (with a play on the sense "down in the mouth," "dejected")   [49] *favor* countenance, aspect   [50] *curiously* minutely   [51] *modesty* moderation   [52] *Imperious* imperial   [53] *flaw* gust of wind

But soft, but soft awhile! Here comes the king—

(*Enter* KING, QUEEN, LAERTES, *and the* CORSE [*with* LORDS *attendant and a* DOCTOR OF DIVINITY *as* PRIEST])

The queen, the courtiers. Who is this they follow?
And with such maimèd rites? This doth betoken
The corse they follow did with desp'rate hand
Fordo[54] it[55] own life. 'Twas of some estate.[56]
Couch[57] we awhile, and mark.

(*Retires with* HORATIO)

LAERTES   What ceremony else?
HAMLET   That is Laertes,
A very noble youth. Mark.
LAERTES   What ceremony else?
DOCTOR   Her obsequies have been as far enlarged
As we have warranty. Her death was doubtful,
And, but that great command o'ersways the order,
She should in ground unsanctified have lodged
Till the last trumpet. For charitable prayers,
Shards,[58] flints, and pebbles should be thrown on her.
Yet here she is allowed her virgin crants,[59]
Her maiden strewments,[60] and the bringing home[61]
Of bell and burial.
LAERTES   Must there no more be done?
DOCTOR   No more be done.
We should profane the service of the dead
To sing a requiem and such rest to her
As to peace-parted souls.
LAERTES   Lay her i' th' earth,
And from her fair and unpolluted flesh
May violets spring! I tell thee, churlish priest,
A minist'ring angel shall my sister be
When thou liest howling.
HAMLET   What, the fair Ophelia?
QUEEN   Sweets to the sweet! Farewell.

(*Scatters flowers*)

I hoped thou shouldst have been my Hamlet's wife.

---

[54] *Fordo* destroy   [55] *it* its   [56] *estate* rank   [57] *Couch* hide   [58] *Shards* broken pieces of pottery   [59] *crants* garland   [60] *strewments* strewings of the grave with flowers   [61] *bringing home* laying to rest

I thought thy bride-bed to have decked, sweet maid,
And not have strewed thy grave.

LAERTES O, treble woe
Fall ten times treble on that cursèd head
Whose wicked deed thy most ingenious[62] sense
Deprived thee of! Hold off the earth awhile,
Till I have caught her once more in mine arms.

(Leaps in the grave)

Now pile your dust upon the quick and dead
Till of this flat a mountain you have made
T' o'ertop old Pelion[63] or the skyish head
Of blue Olympus.

HAMLET *(coming forward)* What is he whose grief
Bears such an emphasis? whose phrase of sorrow
Conjures[64] the wand'ring stars,[65] and makes them stand
Like wonder-wounded hearers? This is I,
Hamlet the Dane.

(Leaps in after LAERTES*)*

LAERTES The devil take thy soul!

(Grapples with him)

HAMLET Thou pray'st not well.
I prithee take thy fingers from my throat,
For, though I am not splenitive[66] and rash,
Yet have I in me something dangerous,
Which let thy wisdom fear. Hold off thy hand.

KING Pluck them asunder.

QUEEN Hamlet, Hamlet!

ALL Gentlemen!

HORATIO Good my lord, be quiet.

(ATTENDANTS part them, and they come out of the grave)

HAMLET Why, I will fight with him upon this theme
Until my eyelids will no longer wag.

QUEEN O my son, what theme?

---

62 *most ingenious* of quickest apprehension   63 *Pelion* a mountain in Thessaly,
like Olympus and also Ossa (the allusion being to the war in which the Titans
fought the gods and attempted to heap Ossa and Olympus on Pelion, or
Pelion and Ossa on Olympus, in order to scale heaven)   64 *Conjures* charms,
puts a spell upon   65 *wand'ring stars* planets   66 *splenitive* of fiery temper
(the spleen being considered the seat of anger)

HAMLET   I loved Ophelia. Forty thousand brothers
Could not with all their quantity of love
Make up my sum. What wilt thou do for her?
KING   O, he is mad, Laertes.
QUEEN   For love of God, forbear him.
HAMLET   'Swounds, show me what thou't do.
Woo't [67] weep? woo't fight? woo't fast? woo't tear thyself?
Woo't drink up esill? [68] eat a crocodile?
I'll do't. Dost thou come here to whine?
To outface me with leaping in her grave?
Be buried quick[69] with her, and so will I.
And if thou prate of mountains, let them throw
Millions of acres on us, till our ground,
Singeing his pate against the burning zone,
Make Ossa like a wart! Nay, an thou'lt mouth,
I'll rant as well as thou.
QUEEN   This is mere[70] madness;
And thus a while the fit will work on him.
Anon, as patient as the female dove
When that her golden couplets[71] are disclosed,[72]
His silence will sit drooping.
HAMLET   Hear you, sir.
What is the reason that you use me thus?
I loved you ever. But it is no matter.
Let Hercules himself do what he may,
The cat will mew, and dog will have his day.
KING   I pray thee, good Horatio, wait upon him.

(*Exit* HAMLET *and* HORATIO)

(*To* LAERTES)

Strengthen your patience in[73] our last night's speech.
We'll put the matter to the present push.[74]
Good Gertrude, set some watch over your son.—
This grave shall have a living monument.
An hour of quiet shortly shall we see;
Till then in patience our proceeding be.

(*Exeunt*)

---

[67] *Woo't* wilt (thou)   [68] *esill* vinegar   [69] *quick* alive   [70] *mere* absolute
[71] *couplets* pair of fledglings   [72] *disclosed* hatched   [73] *in* by calling to mind
[74] *present push* immediate trial

Act V, Scene II

The hall of the castle

(*Enter* HAMLET *and* HORATIO)

HAMLET   So much for this, sir; now shall you see the other.
  You do remember all the circumstance?

HORATIO   Remember it, my lord!

HAMLET   Sir, in my heart there was a kind of fighting
  That would not let me sleep. Methought I lay
  Worse than the mutines[1] in the bilboes.[2] Rashly,
  And praised be rashness for it—let us know,
  Our indiscretion sometime serves us well
  When our deep plots do pall,[3] and that should learn us
  There's a divinity that shapes our ends,
  Rough-hew[4] them how we will—

HORATIO   That is most certain.

HAMLET   Up from my cabin,
  My sea-gown scarfed about me, in the dark
  Groped I to find out them, had my desire,
  Fingered [5] their packet, and in fine[6] withdrew
  To mine own room again, making so bold,
  My fears forgetting manners, to unseal
  Their grand commission; where I found, Horatio—
  Ah, royal knavery!—an exact command,
  Larded [7] with many several sorts of reasons,
  Importing[8] Denmark's health, and England's too,
  With, ho! such bugs[9] and goblins in my life,[10]
  That on the supervise,[11] no leisure bated,[12]
  No, not to stay the grinding of the axe,
  My head should be struck off.

HORATIO   Is't possible?

HAMLET   Here's the commission; read it at more leisure.
  But wilt thou hear me how I did proceed?

HORATIO   I beseech you.

HAMLET   Being thus benetted round with villainies,
  Or[13] I could make a prologue to my brains,
  They had begun the play. I sat me down,

---

[1] *mutines* mutineers [2] *bilboes* fetters [3] *pall* fail [4] *Rough-hew* shape roughly
in trial form [5] *Fingered* filched [6] *in fine* finally [7] *Larded* enriched [8] *Importing* relating to [9] *bugs* bugbears [10] *in my life* to be encountered as dangers if I should be allowed to live [11] *supervise* perusal [12] *bated* deducted,
allowed [13] *Or* ere

Devised a new commission, wrote it fair.
I once did hold it, as our statists[14] do,
A baseness to write fair,[15] and labored much
How to forget that learning, but, sir, now
It did me yeoman's service.[16] Wilt thou know
Th' effect[17] of what I wrote?

HORATIO   Ay, good my lord.

HAMLET   An earnest conjuration from the king,
As England was his faithful tributary,
As love between them like the palm might flourish,
As peace should still her wheaten garland [18] wear
And stand a comma[19] 'tween their amities,
And many such-like as's of great charge,[20]
That on the view and knowing of these contents,
Without debatement further, more or less,
He should the bearers put to sudden death,
Not shriving time[21] allowed.

HORATIO   How was this sealed?

HAMLET   Why, even in that was heaven ordinant.[22]
I had my father's signet in my purse,
Which was the model [23] of that Danish seal,
Folded the writ up in the form of th' other,
Subscribed it, gave't th' impression,[24] placed it safely,
The changeling never known. Now, the next day
Was our sea-fight, and what to this was sequent[25]
Thou know'st already.

HORATIO   So Guildenstern and Rosencrantz go to't.

HAMLET   Why, man, they did make love to this employment.
They are not near my conscience; their defeat
Does by their own insinuation[26] grow.
'Tis dangerous when the baser nature comes
Between the pass[27] and fell [28] incensèd points
Of mighty opposites.

---

[14] *statists* statesmen   [15] *fair* with professional clarity (like a clerk or a scrivener, not like a gentleman)   [16] *yeoman's service* stout service such as yeomen
footsoldiers gave as archers   [17] *effect* purport   [18] *wheaten garland* adorn-
ment of fruitful agriculture   [19] *comma* connective (because it indicates con-
tinuity of thought in a sentence)   [20] *charge* burden (with a double meaning
to fit a play that makes *as's* into "asses"   [21] *shriving time* time for confession
and absolution   [22] *ordinant* controlling   [23] *model* counterpart   [24] *impression*
i.e. of the signet   [25] *sequent* subsequent   [26] *insinuation* intrusion   [27] *pass*
thrust   [28] *fell* fierce

HORATIO   Why, what a king is this!

HAMLET   Does it not, think thee, stand [29] me now upon—
He that hath killed my king, and whored my mother,
Popped in between th' election[30] and my hopes,
Thrown out his angle[31] for my proper[32] life,
And with such coz'nage[33]—is't not perfect conscience
To quit[34] him with this arm? And is't not to be damned
To let this canker[35] of our nature come
In further evil?

HORATIO   It must be shortly known to him from England
What is the issue of the business there.

HAMLET   It will be short; the interim is mine,
And a man's life 's no more than to say "one."
But I am very sorry, good Horatio,
That to Laertes I forgot myself,
For by the image of my cause I see
The portraiture of his. I'll court his favors.
But sure the bravery[36] of his grief did put me
Into a tow'ring passion.

HORATIO   Peace, who comes here?

(*Enter* OSRIC, *a courtier*)

OSRIC   Your lordship is right welcome back to Denmark.

HAMLET   I humbly thank you, sir. (*aside to* HORATIO) Dost know this waterfly?

HORATIO (*aside to* HAMLET)   No, my good lord.

HAMLET (*aside to* HORATIO)   Thy state is the more gracious, for 'tis a vice to know him. He hath much land, and fertile. Let a beast be lord of beasts, and his crib shall stand at the king's mess.[37] 'Tis a chough,[38] but, as I say, spacious in the possession of dirt.

OSRIC   Sweet lord, if your lordship were at leisure, I should impart a thing to you from his majesty.

HAMLET   I will receive it, sir, with all diligence of spirit. Put your bonnet to his right use. 'Tis for the head.

OSRIC   I thank your lordship, it is very hot.

HAMLET   No, believe me, 'tis very cold; the wind is northerly.

OSRIC   It is indifferent[39] cold, my lord, indeed.

---

[29] *stand* rest incumbent   [30] *election* i.e. to the kingship (the Danish kingship being elective)   [31] *angle* fishing line   [32] *proper* own   [33] *coz'nage* cozenage, trickery   [34] *quit* repay   [35] *canker* cancer, ulcer   [36] *bravery* ostentatious display   [37] *mess* table   [38] *chough* jackdaw, chatterer   [39] *indifferent* somewhat

HAMLET   But yet methinks it is very sultry and hot for my complexion.[40]

OSRIC   Exceedingly, my lord; it is very sultry, as 'twere—I cannot tell how. But, my lord, his majesty bade me signify to you that 'a has laid a great wager on your head. Sir, this is the matter—

HAMLET   I beseech you remember.[41]

(HAMLET *moves him to put on his hat*)

OSRIC   Nay, good my lord; for mine ease,[42] in good faith. Sir, here is newly come to court Laertes—believe me, an absolute gentleman, full of most excellent differences,[43] of very soft society[44] and great showing.[45] Indeed, to speak feelingly[46] of him, he is the card [47] or calendar[48] of gentry,[49] for you shall find in him the continent[50] of what part a gentleman would see.

HAMLET   Sir, his definement[51] suffers no perdition[52] in you, though, I know, to divide him inventorially would dozy[53] th' arithmetic of memory, and yet but yaw[54] neither[55] in respect of [56] his quick sail. But, in the verity of extolment, I take him to be a soul of great article,[57] and his infusion[58] of such dearth[59] and rareness as, to make true diction of him, his semblable[60] is his mirror, and who else would trace[61] him, his umbrage,[62] nothing more.

OSRIC   Your lordship speaks most infallibly of him.

HAMLET   The concernancy,[63] sir? Why do we wrap the gentleman in our more rawer[64] breath?

OSRIC   Sir?

HORATIO   Is't not possible to understand in another tongue? You will to't,[65] sir, really.

HAMLET   What imports the nomination[66] of this gentleman?

OSRIC   Of Laertes?

---

[40] *complexion* temperament   [41] *remember* i.e. remember you have done all that courtesy demands   [42] *for mine ease* i.e. I keep my hat off just for comfort (a conventional polite phrase)   [43] *differences* differentiating characteristics, special qualities   [44] *soft society* gentle manners   [45] *great showing* noble appearance   [46] *feelingly* appropriately   [47] *card* map   [48] *calendar* guide   [49] *gentry* gentlemanliness   [50] *continent* all-containing embodiment (with an implication of geographical continent to go with *card*)   [51] *definement* definition   [52] *perdition* loss   [53] *dozy* dizzy, stagger   [54] *yaw* hold to a course unsteadily like a ship that steers wild   [55] *neither* for all that   [56] *in respect of* in comparison with   [57] *article* scope, importance   [58] *infusion* essence   [59] *dearth* scarcity   [60] *semblable* likeness (i.e. only true likeness)   [61] *trace* follow   [62] *umbrage* shadow   [63] *concernancy* relevance   [64] *rawer breath* cruder speech   [65] *to't* i.e. get to an understanding   [66] *nomination* mention

HORATIO (*aside to* HAMLET) His purse is empty already. All's golden words are spent.

HAMLET Of him, sir.

OSRIC I know you are not ignorant—

HAMLET I would you did, sir; yet, in faith, if you did, it would not much approve me.[67] Well, sir?

OSRIC You are not ignorant of what excellence Laertes is—

HAMLET I dare not confess that, lest I should compare[68] with him in excellence; but to know a man well were to know himself.

OSRIC I mean, sir, for his weapon; but in the imputation laid on him by them, in his meed [69] he's unfellowed.

HAMLET What's his weapon?

OSRIC Rapier and dagger.

HAMLET That's two of his weapons—but well.

OSRIC The king, sir, hath wagered with him six Barbary horses, against the which he has impawned,[70] as I take it, six French rapiers and poniards, with their assigns,[71] as girdle, hangers,[72] and so. Three of the carriages, in faith, are very dear to fancy,[73] very responsive[74] to the hilts, most delicate carriages, and of very liberal conceit.[75]

HAMLET What call you the carriages?

HORATIO (*aside to* HAMLET) I knew you must be edified by the margent[76] ere you had done.

OSRIC The carriages, sir, are the hangers.

HAMLET The phrase would be more germane to the matter if we could carry a cannon by our sides. I would it might be hangers till then. But on! Six Barbary horses against six French swords, their assigns, and three liberal-conceited carriages—that's the French bet against the Danish. Why is this all impawned, as you call it?

OSRIC The king, sir, hath laid, sir, that in a dozen passes between yourself and him he shall not exceed you three hits; he hath laid on twelve for nine, and it would come to immediate trial if your lordship would vouchsafe the answer.

HAMLET How if I answer no?

OSRIC I mean, my lord, the opposition of your person in trial.

---

[67] *approve me* be to my credit [68] *compare* compete [69] *meed* worth [70] *impawned* staked [71] *assigns* appurtenances [72] *hangers* straps by which the sword hangs from the belt [73] *dear to fancy* finely designed [74] *responsive* corresponding closely [75] *liberal conceit* tasteful design, refined conception [76] *margent* margin (i.e. explanatory notes there printed)

HAMLET   Sir, I will walk here in the hall. If it please his majesty, it is the breathing time[77] of day with me. Let the foils be brought, the gentleman willing, and the king hold his purpose, I will win for him an[78] I can; if not, I will gain nothing but my shame and the odd hits.

OSRIC   Shall I redeliver you e'en so?

HAMLET   To this effect, sir, after what flourish your nature will.

OSRIC   I commend my duty to your lordship.

HAMLET   Your, yours. (*Exit* OSRIC) He does well to commend it himself; there are no tongues else for's turn.

HORATIO   This lapwing[79] runs away with the shell on his head.

HAMLET   'A did comply,[80] sir, with his dug[81] before 'a sucked it. Thus has he, and many more of the same bevy[82] that I know the drossy[83] age dotes on, only got the tune of the time and, out of an habit of encounter, a kind of yeasty collection, which carries them through and through the most fanned and winnowed [84] opinions; and do but blow them to their trial, the bubbles are out.

(*Enter a* LORD)

LORD   My lord, his majesty commended him to you by young Osric, who brings back to him that you attend him in the hall. He sends to know if your pleasure hold to play with Laertes, or that you will take longer time.

HAMLET   I am constant to my purposes; they follow the king's pleasure. If his fitness speaks, mine is ready; now or whensoever, provided I be so able as now.

LORD   The king and queen and all are coming down.

HAMLET   In happy time.[85]

LORD   The queen desires you to use some gentle entertainment[86] to Laertes before you fall to play.

HAMLET   She well instructs me.

(*Exit* LORD)

HORATIO   You will lose this wager, my lord.

HAMLET   I do not think so. Since he went into France I have been in continual practice. I shall win at the odds. But thou wouldst not think how ill all's here about my heart. But it is no matter.

---

[77] *breathing time* exercise hour   [78] *an* if   [79] *lapwing* a bird reputed to be so precocious as to run as soon as hatched   [80] *comply* observe formalities of courtesy   [81] *dug* mother's nipple   [82] *bevy* company   [83] *drossy* frivolous   [84] *fanned and winnowed* select and refined   [85] *In happy time* I am happy (a polite response)   [86] *entertainment* words of reception or greeting

HORATIO   Nay, good my lord—

HAMLET   It is but foolery, but it is such a kind of gaingiving[87] as would perhaps trouble a woman.

HORATIO   If your mind dislike anything, obey it. I will forestall their repair hither and say you are not fit.

HAMLET   Not a whit, we defy augury. There is special providence in the fall of a sparrow. If it be now, 'tis not to come; if it be not to come, it will be now; if it be not now, yet it will come. The readiness is all.[88] Since no man of aught he leaves knows, what is't to leave betimes? Let be.

A table prepared. Enter TRUMPETS, DRUMS, *and* OFFICERS *with cushions;* KING, QUEEN, OSRIC, *and all the* STATE, *with foils, daggers, and stoups of wine borne in; and* LAERTES

KING   Come, Hamlet, come, and take this hand from me.

(*The* KING *puts* LAERTES' *hand into* HAMLET's)

HAMLET   Give me your pardon, sir. I have done you wrong,
But pardon't, as you are a gentleman.
This presence[89] knows, and you must needs have heard,
How I am punished with a sore distraction.
What I have done
That might your nature, honor, and exception[90]
Roughly awake, I here proclaim was madness.
Was't Hamlet wronged Laertes? Never Hamlet.
If Hamlet from himself be ta'en away,
And when he's not himself does wrong Laertes,
Then Hamlet does it not, Hamlet denies it.
Who does it then? His madness. If't be so,
Hamlet is of the faction[91] that is wronged;
His madness is poor Hamlet's enemy.
Sir, in this audience,
Let my disclaiming from a purposed evil
Free me so far in your most generous thoughts
That I have shot my arrow o'er the house
And hurt my brother.

LAERTES   I am satisfied in nature,[92]
Whose motive in this case should stir me most
To my revenge. But in my terms of honor[93]

---

[87] *gaingiving* misgiving   [88] *all* all that matters   [89] *presence* assembly   [90] *exception* disapproval   [91] *faction* body of persons taking a side in a contention   [92] *nature* natural feeling as a person   [93] *terms of honor* position as a man of honor

I stand aloof, and will no reconcilement
Till by some elder masters of known honor
I have a voice[94] and precedent of peace
To keep my name ungored.[95] But till that time
I do receive your offered love like love,
And will not wrong it.

HAMLET   I embrace it freely,
And will this brother's wager frankly play.
Give us the foils. Come on.

LAERTES   Come, one for me.

HAMLET   I'll be your foil,[96] Laertes. In mine ignorance
Your skill shall, like a star i' th' darkest night,
Stick fiery off [97] indeed.

LAERTES   You mock me, sir.

HAMLET   No, by this hand.

KING   Give them the foils, young Osric. Cousin Hamlet,
You know the wager?

HAMLET   Very well, my lord.
Your grace has laid the odds o' the' weaker side.

KING   I do not fear it, I have seen you both;
But since he is bettered, we have therefore odds.

LAERTES   This is too heavy; let me see another.

HAMLET   This likes me well. These foils have all a length?

Prepare to play

OSRIC   Ay, my good lord.

KING   Set me the stoups of wine upon that table.
If Hamlet give the first or second hit,
Or quit[98] in answer of the third exchange,
Let all the battlements their ordnance fire.
The king shall drink to Hamlet's better breath,
And in the cup an union[99] shall he throw
Richer than that which four successive kings
In Denmark's crown have worn. Give me the cups,
And let the kettle[100] to the trumpet speak,
The trumpet to the cannoneer without,
The cannons to the heavens, the heaven to earth,

---

[94] *voice* authoritative statement   [95] *ungored* uninjured   [96] *foil* setting that
displays a jewel advantageously (with a play upon the meaning "weapon")
[97] *Stick fiery off* show in brilliant relief   [98] *quit* repay by a hit   [99] *union*
pearl   [100] *kettle* kettledrum

"Now the king drinks to Hamlet." Come, begin.

Trumpets the while

And you, the judges, bear a wary eye.
HAMLET   Come on, sir.
LAERTES   Come, my lord.

They play

HAMLET   One.
LAERTES   No.
HAMLET   Judgment?
OSRIC   A hit, a very palpable hit.

DRUM, TRUMPETS, *and* SHOT. *Flourish; a piece goes off*

LAERTES   Well, again.
KING   Stay, give me drink. Hamlet, this pearl is thine.
Here's to thy health. Give him the cup.
HAMLET   I'll play this bout first; set it by awhile.
Come. (*They play*) Another hit. What say you?
LAERTES   A touch, a touch; I do confess't.
KING   Our son shall win.
QUEEN   He's fat,[101] and scant of breath.
Here, Hamlet, take my napkin,[102] rub thy brows.
The queen carouses[103] to thy fortune, Hamlet.
HAMLET   Good madam!
KING   Gertrude, do not drink.
QUEEN   I will, my lord; I pray you pardon me.

Drinks

KING (*aside*)   It is the poisoned cup; it is too late.
HAMLET   I dare not drink yet, madam—by and by.
QUEEN   Come, let me wipe thy face.
LAERTES   My lord, I'll hit him now.
KING   I do not think't.
LAERTES (*aside*)   And yet it is almost against my conscience.
HAMLET   Come for the third, Laertes. You but dally.
I pray you pass with your best violence;
I am afeard you make a wanton[104] of me.

---

[101] *fat* not physically fit, out of training   [102] *napkin* handkerchief   [103] *carouses* drinks a toast   [104] *wanton* pampered child

LAERTES   Say you so? Come on.

They play

OSRIC   Nothing neither way.
LAERTES   Have at you now!

In scuffling they change rapiers, and both are wounded with the poisoned weapon

KING   Part them. They are incensed.
HAMLET   Nay, come—again!

The QUEEN *falls*

OSRIC   Look to the queen there, ho!
HORATIO   They bleed on both sides. How is it, my lord?
OSRIC   How is't, Laertes?
LAERTES   Why, as a woodcock[105] to mine own springe,[106] Osric.
   I am justly killed with mine own treachery.
HAMLET   How does the queen?
KING   She sounds[107] to see them bleed.
QUEEN   No, no, the drink, the drink! O my dear Hamlet!
   The drink, the drink! I am poisoned.

Dies

HAMLET   O villainy! Ho! let the door be locked.
   Treachery! Seek it out.

LAERTES *falls*

LAERTES   It is here, Hamlet. Hamlet, thou art slain;
   No med'cine in the world can do thee good.
   In thee there is not half an hour's life.
   The treacherous instrument is in thy hand,
   Unbated [108] and envenomed. The foul practice[109]
   Hath turned itself on me. Lo, here I lie,
   Never to rise again. Thy mother 's poisoned.
   I can no more. The king, the king 's to blame.
HAMLET   The point envenomed too?
   Then venom, to thy work.

Hurts the KING

ALL   Treason! treason!

---

[105] *woodcock* a bird reputed to be stupid and easily trapped   [106] *springe* trap
[107] *sounds* swoons   [108] *Unbated* unblunted   [109] *practice* stratagem

KING   O, yet defend me, friends. I am but hurt.

HAMLET   Here, thou incestuous, murd'rous, damnèd Dane,
Drink off this potion. Is thy union here?
Follow my mother.

KING *dies*

LAERTES   He is justly served.
It is a poison tempered [110] by himself.
Exchange forgiveness with me, noble Hamlet.
Mine and my father's death come not upon thee,
Nor thine on me!

Dies

HAMLET   Heaven make thee free of it! I follow thee.
I am dead, Horatio. Wretched queen, adieu!
You that look pale and tremble at this chance,
That are but mutes[111] or audience to this act,
Had I but time—as this fell sergeant,[112] Death,
Is strict in his arrest—O, I could tell you—
But let it be. Horatio, I am dead;
Thou livest; report me and my cause aright
To the unsatisfied.

HORATIO   Never believe it.
I am more an antique Roman than a Dane.
Here's yet some liquor left.

HAMLET   As th' art a man,
Give me the cup. Let go. By heaven, I'll ha't!
O God, Horatio, what a wounded name,
Things standing thus unknown, shall live behind me!
If thou didst ever hold me in thy heart,
Absent thee from felicity awhile,
And in this harsh world draw thy breath in pain,
To tell my story.

A march afar off

                    What warlike noise is this?

OSRIC   Young Fortinbras, with conquest come from Poland,
To the ambassadors of England gives
This warlike volley.

HAMLET   O, I die, Horatio!

---

[110] *tempered* mixed   [111] *mutes* actors in a play who speak no lines   [112] *sergeant* sheriff's officer

The potent poison quite o'ercrows[113] my spirit.
I cannot live to hear the news from England,
But I do prophesy th' election[114] lights
On Fortinbras. He has my dying voice.[115]
So tell him, with th' occurrents,[116] more and less,
Which have solicited [117]—the rest is silence.

Dies

HORATIO   Now cracks a noble heart. Good night, sweet prince,
And flights of angels sing thee to thy rest!

March within

Why does the drum come hither?

(*Enter* FORTINBRAS, *with the* AMBASSADORS [*and with his train of* DRUM, COLORS, *and* ATTENDANTS])

FORTINBRAS   Where is this sight?
HORATIO   What is it you would see?
If aught of woe or wonder, cease your search.
FORTINBRAS   This quarry[118] cries on[119] havoc.[120] O proud Death,
What feast is toward [121] in thine eternal cell
That thou so many princes at a shot
So bloodily hast struck?
AMBASSADOR   The sight is dismal;
And our affairs from England come too late.
The ears are senseless that should give us hearing
To tell him his commandment is fulfilled,
That Rosencrantz and Guildenstern are dead.
Where should we have our thanks?
HORATIO   Not from his mouth,
Had it th' ability of life to thank you.
He never gave commandment for their death.
But since, so jump[122] upon this bloody question,
You from the Polack wars, and you from England,
Are here arrived, give order that these bodies
High on a stage[123] be placèd to the view,

---

113 *o'ercrows* triumphs over (like a victor in a cockfight)   114 *election* i.e. to the throne   115 *voice* vote   116 *occurrents* occurrences   117 *solicited* incited, provoked   118 *quarry* pile of dead (literally, of dead deer gathered after the hunt)   119 *cries on* proclaims loudly   120 *havoc* indiscriminate killing and destruction such as would follow the order "havoc," or "pillage," given to an army   121 *toward* forthcoming   122 *jump* precisely   123 *stage* platform

And let me speak to th' yet unknowing world
How these things came about. So shall you hear
Of carnal, bloody, and unnatural acts,
Of accidental judgments,[124] casual [125] slaughters,
Of deaths put on[126] by cunning and forced cause,
And, in this upshot, purposes mistook
Fall'n on th' inventors' heads. All this can I
Truly deliver.

FORTINBRAS   Let us haste to hear it,
And call the noblest to the audience.
For me, with sorrow I embrace my fortune.
I have some rights of memory[127] in this kingdom,
Which now to claim my vantage[128] doth invite me.

HORATIO   Of that I shall have also cause to speak,
And from his mouth whose voice will draw on more.[129]
But let this same be presently[130] performed,
Even while men's minds are wild, lest more mischance
On[131] plots and errors happen.

FORTINBRAS   Let four captains
Bear Hamlet like a soldier to the stage,
For he was likely, had he been put on,[132]
To have proved most royal; and for his passage[133]
The soldiers' music and the rites of war
Speak loudly for him.
Take up the bodies. Such a sight as this
Becomes the field, but here shows much amiss.
Go, bid the soldiers shoot.

(*Exeunt [marching; after the which a peal of ordinance are shot off]*)

---

[124] *judgments* retributions   [125] *casual* not humanly planned (reinforcing *accidental*)   [126] *put on* instigated   [127] *of memory* traditional and kept in mind   [128] *vantage* advantageous opportunity   [129] *more* i.e. more voices, or votes, for the kingship   [130] *presently* immediately   [131] *On* on the basis of   [132] *put on* set to perform in office   [133] *passage* death

QUESTIONS

1. The climax in *Hamlet* extends over several scenes. Which ones do you think they are? Ask yourself:
2. What states does Hamlet pass through within these scenes?
3. How do his actions after the climax contrast with his actions before it?
4. What changes in Hamlet's outlook, or in your reaction to him, begin during these climactic scenes and develop during the latter part of the play?
5. Choose some topic that shows how the climax functions as a turning-point in *Hamlet* and develop it as fully as possible, making use of specific examples not only from the climactic scenes but from earlier and later scenes as well.

4 _Modern Drama_

Our study of _Hamlet_ brought us from the early, religious drama to the first great age of professional drama in England. In this chapter, with _Major Barbara_ and _Death of a Salesman,_ we enter the modern period, another age of growth and experiment. We also read our first full-length comedy.

Comedy is preeminently social drama. Tragedy looks at its heroes when they are becoming involved in dilemmas which will separate them from their fellows or from the normal concerns of society. (Thus, Oedipus dooms himself to blindness and exile, while Hamlet accepts death as the price for freeing Denmark from Claudius.) Comedy, in contrast, studies people within society. Its concerns are most often those of every-day life; its problems are the problems involved in dealing with the people and customs of contemporary society. If the typical end of tragedy is death, with its total separation from the affairs of the world, the typical ending of comedy is marriage, with its commitment to worldly affairs. No matter how hard comic characters may struggle to escape the bonds of society—no matter what unusual methods they may use to outwit other characters or to solve some particular conflict between society's dictates and their own desires—at the play's end they return to the very society they've been fighting. The conflict has been solved, the goal or the marriage won; and society promises to go on exactly as it did before.

The fact that society remains unchanged *in* comedy, however, is no sign that the playwrights wish it to remain unchanged *by* comedy. The goal of comedy, in fact, is to show its viewers their own social follies, to make them look freshly and critically at their customary actions or attitudes. Having laughed at the foolishness of the people on stage, we may resolve to be less foolish ourselves.

George Bernard Shaw throve on this notion of comedy. For him, comedy was an ideal medium for highlighting the disparities between what people said and thought about society and what actually went on. In *Major Barbara*, he turns his attention to morals and poverty. In his preface to the play he announces his theme and his viewpoint. "In the millionaire Undershaft, I have represented a man who has become intellectually and spiritually as well as practically conscious of the irresistible natural truth which we all abhor and repudiate: to wit, that the greatest of our evils, and the worst of our crimes, is poverty, and that our first duty, to which every other consideration should be sacrificed, is not to be poor." Undershaft is the only person at the play's start who sees things as they really are. The other characters are all under some sort of delusion.

Of the others, the most dangerously placed is Major Barbara. She is already awake to many of society's shortcomings, but thinks she is battling them by retreating outside society into the Salvation Army. Her belief that the Army is outside society is her delusion. Her father must show her how thoroughly tied to society the Army is in order to make her realize that any work she does is done within society. Similarly, Adolphus Cusins, Barbara's would-be husband and professor of Greek, must be moved from his pose of noninvolvement into active participation in Undershaft's work, for Cusins' intelligence and his love for the energetic Barbara have marked him as one whom the world needs.

The basic plot of *Major Barbara*, therefore, involves bringing Barbara and Cusins from ignorance to knowledge, that their fellow human beings may benefit from their gifts. The result is a magnificently comic contrast between the drawing room, the Salvation Army shelter, and the munitions plant, as the three settings serve as background for an intense and witty duel of ideas between Undershaft, Lady Britomart, Barbara, and Adolphus Cusins. All four debaters realize the importance of the debate; all respect each other personally, even as they try to demolish each other's arguments. All share a decisiveness, an energy, and a willingness to care about ideas and people alike that set them apart from the other characters. In a world needing clear thinking and resolute action, they possess vitally needed intelligence and virtues.

The mood of *Major Barbara* is basically cheerful and energetic; that of *Death of a Salesman* is just the opposite. In this play, Arthur Miller has tried to create a modern tragedy, a tragedy of the common man. In doing so, he has deliberately set aside one of Aristotle's basic rules, which says that tragic heroes must be people we can look up to. We cannot look up to Willy Loman. Hamlet and Oedipus were both seekers of truth. Willy is afraid of the truth, because if he should realize the truth, or admit it, he admits his failures as husband, father, and salesman. And failure, by Willy's standards, is as great a crime as incest is by Oedipus'.

Miller has said that "the tragic feeling is evoked in us when we are in the presence of a character who is ready to lay down his life, if need be, to secure one thing—his sense of personal dignity." In this sense, Willy is certainly tragic; and the fact that the vision of dignity for which he kills himself is seen by many to be a false one (including, within the play, Willy's son Biff, who bitterly protests his father's choice of sham dignity over true) merely makes the tragedy the more fearful. Can we be sure that our own values are truer?

In its themes, *Death of a Salesman* embodies many of the concerns we noticed in twentieth-century fiction. In particular, it seems to focus more strongly than earlier tragedies on the interaction between the individual and society. Neither Willy nor Biff is being judged, as Barbara is, for his ability to contribute to society. But society is being judged for what it has contributed to creating Willy—and, through him, Biff. Money, normally the province of fiction or comedy, is a major subject in *Death of a Salesman*. And where money is a subject, society (which determines who shall have money, and why) is always an issue.

In form, too, *Death of a Salesman* is notably a product of the twentieth century. The language is that of everyday speech. The stage setting and costumes suggest average people. Within this frame of simple realism, however, Willy's imaginings are given life. The realities of the mind are made visible, superimposed on the realities of the world; and the audience, as so often happens in twentieth-century art, is given the task of sorting the two out.

Willy is a man on the brink of madness. He hears and sees things that are not there: scenes from the past, words from an absent brother. But whenever he hears or sees them, we hear or see them as well. One minute we see Biff as a thirty-four-year-old man, the next as a high school student; for Willy can no longer keep the past and the present apart. Intolerant of a present that contains no promises of good things to come, his mind shifts between the remembered past and an imaginary future; and his viewers must shift with him.

Watching past and present, reality and fantasy intertwine, we piece together Willy's past and his values. He could not state them so clearly as his uncontrollable mind acts them out. The soul-searching that Willy's conscious mind rejects, his unconscious mind insists on. We witness the insistence and rejection both, and so are led to our understanding of the man and his tragedy.

Preface to *Major Barbara*

FIRST AID TO CRITICS

Before dealing with the deeper aspects of Major Barbara, let me, for the credit of English literature, make a protest against an unpatriotic habit into which many of my critics have fallen. Whenever my view strikes them as being at all outside the range of, say, an ordinary suburban churchwarden, they conclude that I am echoing *Schopenhauer, Nietzsche, Ibsen, Strindberg, Tolstoy*, or some other heresiarch in northern or eastern Europe.

I confess there is something flattering in this simple faith in my accomplishment as a linguist and my erudition as a philosopher. But I cannot countenance the assumption that life and literature are so poor in these islands that we must go abroad for all dramatic material that is not common and all ideas that are not superficial. I therefore venture to put my critics in possession of certain facts concerning my contact with modern ideas.

About half a century ago, an Irish novelist, Charles Lever, wrote a story entitled A Day's Ride: A Life's Romance. It was published by Charles Dickens in Household Words, and proved so strange to the public taste that Dickens pressed Lever to make short work of it. I read scraps of this novel when I was a child; and it made an enduring impression on me. The hero was a very romantic hero, trying to live bravely, chivalrously, and powerfully by dint of mere romance-fed imagination, without courage, without means, without knowledge, without skill, without anything real except his bodily appetites. Even in my childhood I found in this poor devil's unsuccessful encounters with the facts of life, a poignant quality that romantic fiction lacked. The book, in spite of its first failure, is not dead: I saw its title the other day in the catalogue of Tauchnitz.

Now why is it that when I also deal in the tragi-comic irony of the conflict between real life and the romantic imagination, critics never affiliate me to my countryman and immediate forerunner, Charles Lever, whilst they confidently derive me from a Norwegian author of whose language I do not know three words, and of whom I knew nothing until years after the Shavian *Anschauung* was already unequivocally declared in books full of what came, ten years later, to be perfunctorily labelled Ibsenism? I was not Ibsenist even at second hand; for Lever, though he may have read Henri Beyle, *alias* Stendhal, certainly never read Ibsen. Of the books that made Lever popular, such as Charles O'Malley and Harry Lorrequer, I know nothing but the names and some of the illustrations. But the story of the day's ride and life's romance of Potts (claiming alliance with Pozzo di Borgo) caught me and fascinated me as something strange and significant, though I already knew all about Alnaschar and Don Quixote and Simon Tappertit and many another romantic hero mocked by reality. From the plays of Aristophanes to the tales of Stevenson that mockery has been made familiar to all who are properly saturated with letters.

Where, then, was the novelty in Lever's tale? Partly, I think, in a new seriousness in dealing with Potts's disease. Formerly, the contrast between madness and sanity was deemed comic: Hogarth shows us how fashionable people went in parties to Bedlam to laugh at the lunatics. I myself have had a village idiot exhibited to me as something irresistibly funny. On the stage the madman was once a regular comic figure: that was how Hamlet got his opportunity before Shakespear touched him. The originality of Shakespear's version lay in his taking the lunatic sympathetically and seriously, and thereby making an advance towards the eastern consciousness of the fact that lunacy may be inspiration in disguise, since a man who has more brains than his fellows necessarily appears as mad to them as one who has less. But Shakespear did not do for Pistol and Parolles what he did for Hamlet. The particular sort of madman they represented, the romantic make-believer, lay outside the pale of sympathy in literature: he was pitilessly despised and ridiculed here as he was in the east under the name of Alnaschar, and was doomed to be, centuries later, under the name of Simon Tappertit. When Cervantes relented over Don Quixote, and Dickens relented over Pickwick, they did not become impartial: they simply changed sides, and became friends and apologists where they had formerly been mockers.

In Lever's story there is a real change of attitude. There is no relenting towards Potts: he never gains our affections like Don Quixote and Pickwick: he has not even the infatuate courage of Tappertit. But we dare not laugh at him, because, somehow, we recognize ourselves in Potts. We may, some of us, have enough nerve, enough muscle, enough luck, enough tact or skill or address or knowledge to carry things off better than he did; to impose on the people who saw through him; to fascinate Katinka (who cut Potts so ruthlessly at the end of the story); but for all that, we know that Potts plays an enormous part in ourselves and in the world, and that the social problem is not a problem of story-book heroes of the older pattern, but a problem of Pottses, and of how to make men of them. To fall back on my old phrase, we have the feeling—one that Alnaschar, Pistol, Parolles, and Tappertit never gave us—that Potts is a piece of really scientific natural history as distinguished from funny story telling. His author is not throwing a stone at a creature of another and inferior order, but making a confession, with the effect that the stone hits each of us full in the conscience and causes our self-esteem to smart very sorely. Hence the failure of Lever's book to please the readers of Household Words. That pain in the self-esteem nowadays causes critics to raise a cry of Ibsenism. I therefore assure them that the sensation first came to me from Lever and may have come to him from Beyle, or at least out of the Stendhalian atmosphere. I exclude the hypothesis of complete originality on Lever's part, because a man can no more be completely original in that sense than a tree can grow out of air.

Another mistake as to my literary ancestry is made whenever I violate the romantic convention that all women are angels when they are not devils; that they are better looking than men; that their part in courtship is entirely passive; and that the human female form is the most beautiful object in nature. Schopenhauer wrote a splenetic essay which, as it is neither polite nor profound, was probably intended to knock this nonsense violently on the head. A sentence denouncing the idolized form as ugly has been largely quoted. The English critics have read that sentence; and I must here affirm, with as much gentleness as the implication will bear, that it has yet to be proved that they have dipped any deeper. At all events, whenever an English playwright represents a young and marriageable woman as being anything but a romantic heroine, he is disposed of without further thought as an echo of Schopenhauer. My own case is a specially hard one, because, when I implore the critics who are obsessed with the Schopenhauerian formula to remember that playwrights, like sculptors, study their figures from life, and not from philosophic essays, they reply passionately that I am not a playwright and that my stage figures do not live. But even so, I may and do ask them why, if they must give the credit of my plays to a philosopher, they do not give it to an English philosopher? Long before I ever read a word by Schopenhauer, or even knew whether he was a philosopher or a chemist, the Socialist revival of the eighteen-eighties brought me into contact, both literary and personal, with Ernest Belfort Bax, an English Socialist and philosophic essayist, whose handling of modern feminism would provoke romantic protests from Schopenhauer himself, or even Strindberg. As a matter of fact I hardly noticed Schopenhauer's disparagements of women when they came under my notice later on, so thoroughly had Bax familiarized me with the homoist attitude, and forced me to recognize the extent to which public opinion, and consequently legislation and jurisprudence, is corrupted by feminist sentiment.

Belfort Bax's essays were not confined to the Feminist question. He was a ruthless critic of current morality. Other writers have gained sympathy for dramatic criminals by eliciting the alleged "soul of goodness in things evil'; but Bax would propound some quite undramatic and apparently shabby violation of our commercial law and morality, and not merely defend it with the most disconcerting ingenuity, but actually prove it to be a positive duty that nothing but the certainty of police persecution should prevent every right-minded man from at once doing on principle.

The Socialists were naturally shocked, being for the most part morbidly moral people; but at all events they were saved later on from the delusion that nobody but Nietzsche had ever challenged our mercanto-Christian morality. I first heard the name of Nietzsche from a German mathematician, Miss Borchardt, who had read my Quintessence of Ibsenism, and told me that she saw what I had been reading: namely, Nietzsche's Jenseits von Gut und Böse. Which I protest I had never seen, and could not have read with any comfort, for want of the necessary German, if I had seen it.

Nietzsche, like Schopenhauer, is the victim in England of a single much quoted sentence containing the phrase 'big blonde beast'. On the strength of this alliteration it is assumed that Nietzsche gained his European reputation by a senseless glorification of selfish bullying as the rule of life, just as it is assumed, on the strength of the single word Superman (Übermensch) borrowed by me from Nietzsche, that I look for the salvation of society to the despotism of a single Napoleonic Superman, in spite of my careful demonstration of the folly of that outworn infatuation. But even the less recklessly superficial critics seem to believe that the modern objection to Christianity as a pernicious slave-morality was first put forward by Nietzsche. It was familiar to me before I ever heard of Nietzsche. The late Captain Wilson, author of several queer pamphlets, propagandist of a metaphysical system called Comprehensionism, and inventor of the term 'Crosstianity' to distinguish the retrograde element in Christendom, was wont thirty years ago, in the discussions of the Dialectical Society, to protest earnestly against the beatitudes of the Sermon on the Mount as excuses for cowardice and servility, as destructive of our will, and consequently of our honour and manhood. Now it is true that Captain Wilson's moral criticism of Christianity was not a historical theory of it, like Nietzsche's; but this objection cannot be made to Stuart-Glennie, the successor of Buckle as a philosophic historian, who devoted his life to the elaboration and propagation of his theory that Christianity is part of an epoch (or rather an aberration, since it began as recently as 6000 B.C. and is already collapsing) produced by the necessity in which the numerically inferior white races found themselves to impose their domination on the colored races by priestcraft, making a virtue and a popular religion of drudgery and submissiveness in this world not only as a means of achieving saintliness of character but of securing a reward in heaven. Here was the slave-morality view formulated by a Scotch philosopher of my acquaintance long before we all began chattering about Nietzsche.

As Stuart-Glennie traced the evolution of society to the conflict of races, his theory made some sensation among Socialists—that is, among the only people who were seriously thinking about historical evolution at all—by its collision with the class-conflict theory of Karl Marx.

Nietzsche, as I gather, regarded the slave-morality as having been invented and imposed on the world by slaves making a virtue of necessity and a religion of their servitude. Stuart-Glennie regarded the slave-morality as an invention of the superior white race to subjugate the minds of the inferior races whom they wished to exploit, and who would have destroyed them by force of numbers if their minds had not been subjugated. As this process is in operation still, and can be studied at first hand not only in our Church schools and in the struggle between our modern proprietary classes and the proletariat, but in the part played by Christian missionaries in reconciling the black races of Africa to their subjugation by European Capitalism, we can judge for ourselves whether the initiative came from above or below. My object here is not to argue the historical point, but simply to make our theatre critics ashamed of their habit of treating Britain as an intellectual void, and assuming that every philosophical idea, every historic theory, every criticism of our moral, religious and juridical institutions, must necessarily be either a foreign import, or else a fantastic sally (in rather questionable taste) totally unrelated to the existing body of thought. I urge them to remember that this body of thought is the slowest of growths and the rarest of blossomings, and that if there be such a thing on the philosophic plane as a matter of course, it is that no individual can make more than a minute contribution to it. In fact, their conception of clever persons parthenogenetically bringing forth complete original cosmogonies by dint of sheer 'brilliancy' is part of that ignorant credulity which is the despair of the honest philosopher, and the opportunity of the religious impostor.

The Gospel of St Andrew Undershaft

It is this credulity that drives me to help my critics out with Major Barbara by telling them what to say about it. In the millionaire Undershaft I have represented a man who has become intellectually and spiritually as well as practically conscious of the irresistible natural truth which we all abhor and repudiate: to wit, that the greatest of our evils, and the worst of our crimes is poverty, and that our first duty, to which every other consideration should be sacrificed, is not to be poor. 'Poor but honest,' 'the respectable poor,' and such phrases are as intolerable and as immoral as 'drunken but amiable,' 'fraudulent but a good after-dinner speaker,' 'splendidly criminal,' or the like. Security, the chief pretence of civilization, cannot exist where the worst of dangers, the danger of poverty, hangs over everyone's head, and where the alleged protection of our persons from violence is only an accidental result of the existence of a police force whose real business is to force the poor man to see his children starve whilst idle people overfeed pet dogs with money that might feed and clothe them.

It is exceedingly difficult to make people realize that an evil is an evil. For instance, we seize a man and deliberately do him a malicious injury: say, imprison him for years. One would not suppose that it needed any exceptional clearness of wit to recognize in this an act of diabolical cruelty. But in England such a recogntion provokes a stare of surprise, followed by an explanation that the outrage is punishment or justice or something else that is all right, or perhaps by a heated attempt to argue that we should all be robbed and murdered in our beds if such stupid villainies as sentences of imprisonment were not committed daily. It is useless to argue that even if this were true, which it is not, the alternative to adding crimes of our own to the crimes from which we suffer is not helpless submission. Chickenpox is an evil; but if I were to declare that we must either submit to it or else repress it sternly by seizing everyone who suffers from it and punishing them by inoculation with smallpox, I should be laughed at; for though nobody could deny that the result would be to prevent chickenpox to some extent by making people avoid it much more carefully, and to effect a further apparent prevention by making them conceal it very anxiously, yet people would have sense enough to see that the deliberate propagation of smallpox was a creation of evil, and must therefore be ruled out in favor of purely humane and hygienic measures. Yet in the precisely parallel case of a man breaking into my house and stealing my wife's diamonds I am expected as a matter of course to steal ten years of his life, torturing him all the time. If he tries to defeat that monstrous retaliation by shooting me, my survivors hang him. The net result suggested by the police statistics is that we inflict atrocious injuries on the burglars we catch in order to make the rest take effectual precautions against detection; so that instead of saving our wives' diamonds from burglary we only greatly decrease our chances of ever getting them back, and increase our chances of being shot by the robber if we are unlucky enough to disturb him at his work.

But the thoughtless wickedness with which we scatter sentences of imprisonment, torture in the solitary cell and on the plank bed, and flogging, on moral invalids and energetic rebels, is as nothing compared to the silly levity with which we tolerate poverty as if it were either a wholesome tonic for lazy people people or else a virtue to be embraced as St Francis embraced it. If a man is indolent, let him be poor. If he is drunken, let him be poor. If he is not a gentleman. let him be poor. If he is addicted to the fine arts or to pure science instead of to trade and finance, let him be poor. If he chooses to spend his urban eighteen shillings a week or his agricultural thirteen shillings a week on his beer and his family instead of saving it up for his old age, let him be poor. Let nothing be done for 'the undeserving': let him be poor. Serve him right! Also—somewhat inconsistently—blessed are the poor!

Now what does this Let Him Be Poor mean? It means let him be weak.

Let him be ignorant. Let him become a nucleus of disease. Let him be a standing exhibition and example of ugliness and dirt. Let him have rickety children. Let him be cheap, and drag his fellows down to his own price by selling himself to do their work. Let his habitations turn our cities into poisonous congeries of slums. Let his daughters infect our young men with the diseases of the streets, and his sons revenge him by turning the nation's manhood into scrofula, cowardice, cruelty, hypocrisy, political imbecility, and all the other fruits of oppression and malnutrition. Let the undeserving become still less deserving; and let the deserving lay up for himself, not treasures in heaven, but horrors in hell upon earth. This being so, is it really wise to let him be poor? Would he not do ten times less harm as a prosperous burglar, incendiary, ravisher or murderer, to the utmost limits of humanity's comparatively negligible impulses in these directions? Suppose we were to abolish all penalties for such activities, and decide that poverty is the one thing we will not tolerate—that every adult with less than, say, £365 a year, shall be painlessly but inexorably killed, and every hungry half naked child forcibly fattened and clothed, would not that be an enormous improvement on our existing system, which has already destroyed so many civilizations, and is visibly destroying ours in the same way?

Is there any radicle of such legislation in our parliamentary system? Well, there are two measures just sprouting in the political soil, which may conceivably grow to something valuable. One is the institution of a Legal Minimum Wage. The other, Old Age Pensions. But there is a better plan than either of these. Some time ago I mentioned the subject of Universal Old Age Pensions to my fellow Socialist Cobden-Sanderson, famous as an artist-craftsman in bookbinding and printing. 'Why not Universal Pensions for Life?' said Cobden-Sanderson. In saying this, he solved the industrial problem at a stroke. At present we say callously to each citizen 'If you want money, earn it' as if his having or not having it were a matter that concerned himself alone. We do not even secure for him the opportunity of earning it: on the contrary, we allow our industry to be organized in open dependence on the maintenance of 'a reserve army of unemployed' for the sake of 'elasticity.' The sensible course would be Cobden-Sanderson's: that is, to give every man enough to live well on, so as to guarantee the community against the possibility of a case of the malignant disease of poverty, and then (necessarily) to see that he earned it.

Undershaft, the hero of Major Barbara, is simply a man who, having grasped the fact that poverty is a crime, knows that when society offered him the alternative of poverty or a lucrative trade in death and destruction, it offered him, not a choice between opulent villainy and humble virtue, but between energetic enterprise and cowardly infamy. His conduct stands the Kantian test, which Peter Shirley's does not. Peter Shirley is what we call the honest poor man. Undershaft is what we call the wicked rich one: Shirley is Lazarus, Undershaft Dives. Well, the misery of the world is due to the fact that the great mass of men act and believe as Peter Shirley acts and believes. If they acted and believed as Undershaft acts and believes, the immediate result would be a revolution of incalculable beneficence. To be wealthy, says Undershaft, is with me a point of honor for which I am prepared to kill at the risk of my own life. This preparedness is, as he says, the final test of sincerity. Like Froissart's medieval hero, who saw that 'to rob and pill was a good life' he is not the dupe of that public sentiment against killing which is propagated and endowed by people who would otherwise be killed themselves, or of the mouth-honor paid to poverty and obedience by rich and insubordinate do-nothings who want to rob the poor without courage and command them without superiority. Froissart's knight, in placing the achievement of a good life before all the other duties—which indeed are not duties at all when they conflict with it, but plain wickedness—behaved bravely, admirably, and, in the final analysis, public-spiritedly. Medieval society, on the other hand, behaved very badly indeed in organizing itself so stupidly that a good life could be achieved by robbing and pilling. If the knight's contemporaries had been all as resolute as he, robbing and pilling would have been the shortest way to the gallows, just as, if we were all as resolute and clearsighted as Undershaft, an attempt to live by means of what is called 'an independent income' would be the shortest way to the lethal chamber. But as, thanks to our political imbecility and personal cowardice (fruits of poverty, both), the best imitation of a good life now procurable is life on an independent income, all sensible people aim at securing such an income, and are, of course, careful to legalize and moralize both it and all the actions and sentiments which lead to it and support it as an institution. What else can they do? They know, of course, that they are rich because others are poor. But they cannot help that: it is for the poor to repudiate poverty when they have had enough of it. The thing can be done easily enough: the demonstrations to the contrary made by the economists, jurists, moralists and sentimentalists hired by the rich to defend them, or even doing the work gratuitously out of sheer folly and abjectness, impose only on those who want to be imposed on.

The reason why the independent income-tax payers are not solid in defence of their position is that since we are not medieval rovers through a sparsely populated country, the poverty of those we rob prevents our having the good life for which we sacrifice them. Rich men or aristocrats with a developed sense of life—men like Ruskin and William Morris and Kropotkin—have enormous social appetites and very fastidious personal ones. They are not content with handsome houses: they want handsome cities. They are not content with bediamonded wives and blooming daughters: they complain because the charwoman is badly dressed, because the laundress smells of gin, because the sempstress is anemic, because every man they meet is not a friend and every woman not a romance. They turn up their noses at their neighbor's drains, and are made ill by the architecture of their neighbor's houses. Trade patterns made to suit vulgar people do not please them (and they can get nothing else): they cannot sleep nor sit at ease upon 'slaughtered' cabinet makers' furniture. The very air is not good enough for them: there is too much factory smoke in it. They even demand abstract conditions: justice, honor, a noble moral atmosphere, a mystic nexus to replace the cash nexus. Finally they declare that though to rob and pill with your own hand on horseback and in steel coat may have been a good life, to rob and pill by the hands of the policeman, the bailiff, and the soldier, and to underpay them meanly for doing it, is not a good life, but rather fatal to all possibility of even a tolerable one. They call on the poor to revolt, and, finding the poor shocked at their ungentlemanliness, despairingly revile the proletariat for its 'damned wantlessness' (*verdammte Bedürfnislosigkeit*).

So far, however, their attack on society has lacked simplicity. The poor do not share their tastes nor understand their art-criticisms. They do not want the simple life, nor the esthetic life; on the contrary, they want very much to wallow in all the costly vulgarities from which the elect souls among the rich turn away with loathing. It is by surfeit and not by abstinence that they will be cured of their hankering after unwholesome sweets. What they do dislike and despise and are ashamed of is poverty. To ask them to fight for the difference between the Christmas number of the Illustrated London News and the Kelmscott Chaucer is silly: they prefer the News. The difference between a stock-broker's cheap and dirty starched white shirt and collar and the comparatively costly and carefully dyed blue shirt of William Morris is a difference so disgraceful to Morris in their eyes that if they fought on the subject at all, they would fight in defence of the starch. 'Cease to be slaves, in order that you may become cranks' is not a very inspiring call to arms; nor is it really improved by substituting saints for cranks. Both terms denote men of genius; and the common man does not want to live the life of a man of genius: he would much rather live the life of a pet collie if that were the only alternative. But he does want more money. Whatever else he may be vague about, he is clear about that. He may or may not prefer Major Barbara to the Drury Lane pantomime; but he always prefers five hundred pounds to five hundred shillings.

Now to deplore this preference as sordid, and teach children that it is sinful to desire money, is to strain towards the extreme possible limit of impudence in lying and corruption in hypocrisy. The universal regard for money is the one hopeful fact in our civilization, the one sound spot in our social conscience. Money is the most important thing in the world. It represents health, strength, honor, generosity and beauty as conspicuously and undeniably as the want of it represents illness, weakness, disgrace, meanness and ugliness. Not the least of its virtues is that it destroys base people as certainly as it fortifies and dignifies noble people. It is only when it is cheapened to worthlessness for some and made impossibly dear to others, that it becomes a curse. In short, it is a curse only in such foolish social conditions that life itself is a curse. For the two things are inseparable: money is the counter that enables life to be distributed socially: it *is* life as truly as sovereigns and bank notes are money. The first duty of every citizen is to insist on having money on reasonable terms; and this demand is not complied with by giving four men three shillings each for ten or twelve hours' drudgery and one man a thousand pounds for nothing. The crying need of the nation is not for better morals, cheaper bread, temperance, liberty, culture, redemption of fallen sisters and erring brothers, nor the grace, love and fellowship of the Trinity, but simply for enough money. And the evil to be attacked is not sin, suffering, greed, priestcraft, kingcraft, demagogy, monopoly, ignorance, drink, war, pestilence, nor any other of the scapegoats which reformers sacrifice, but simply poverty.

Once take your eyes from the ends of the earth and fix them on this truth just under your nose; and Andrew Undershaft's views will not perplex you in the least. Unless indeed his constant sense that he is only the instrument of a Will or Life Force which uses him for purposes wider than his own, may puzzle you. If so, that is because you are walking either in artificial Darwinian darkness, or in mere stupidity. All genuinely religious people have that consciousness. To them Undershaft the Mystic will be quite intelligible, and his perfect comprehension of his daughter the Salvationist and her lover the Euripidean republican natural and inevitable. That, however, is not new, even on the stage. What is new, as far as I know, is that article in Undershaft's religion which recognizes in Money the first need and in poverty the vilest sin of man and society.

This dramatic conception has not, of course, been attained *per saltum*. Nor has it been borrowed from Nietzsche or from any man born beyond the Channel. The late Samuel Butler, in his own department the greatest English writer of the latter half of the XIX century, steadily inculcated the necessity and morality of a conscientious Laodiceanism in religion and of an earnest and constant sense of the importance of money. It drives one almost to despair of English literature when one sees so extraordinary a study of English life as Butler's posthumous Way of All Flesh making so little impression that when, some years later, I produce plays in which Butler's extraordinarily fresh, free and future-piercing suggestions have an obvious share, I am met with nothing but vague cacklings about Ibsen and Nietzsche, and am only too thankful that they are not about Alfred de Musset and Georges Sand. Really, the English do not deserve to have great men. They allowed Butler to die practically unknown, whilst I, a comparatively insignificant Irish journalist, was leading them by the nose into an advertisement of me which has made my own life a burden. In Sicily there is a Via Samuele Butler. When an English tourist sees it, he either asks 'Who the devil was Samuele Butler?' or wonders why the Sicilians should perpetuate the memory of the author of Hudibras.

Well, it cannot be denied that the English are only too anxious to recognize a man of genius if somebody will kindly point him out to them. Having pointed myself out in this manner with some success, I now point out Samuel Butler, and trust that in consequence I shall hear a little less in future of the novelty and foreign origin of the ideas which are now making their way into the English theatre through plays written by Socialists. There are living men whose originality and power are as obvious as Butler's and when they die that fact will be discovered. Meanwhile I recommend them to insist on their own merits as an important part of their own business.

The Salvation Army

When Major Barbara was produced in London, the second act was reported in an important northern newspaper as a withering attack on the Salvation Army, and the despairing ejaculation of Barbara deplored by a London daily as a tasteless blasphemy. And they were set right, not by the professed critics of the theatre, but by religious and philosophical publicists like Sir Oliver Lodge and Dr Stanton Coit, and strenuous Nonconformist journalists like William Stead, who not only understood the act as well as the Salvationists themselves, but also saw it in its relation to the religious life of the nation, a life which seems to lie not only outside the sympathy of many of our theatre critics, but actually outside their knowledge of society. Indeed nothing could be more ironically curious than the confrontation Major Barbara effected of the theatre enthusiasts with the religious enthusiasts. On the one hand was the playgoer, always seeking pleasure, paying exorbitantly for it, suffering unbearable discomforts for it, and hardly ever getting it. On the other hand was the Salvationist, repudiating gaiety and courting effort and sacrifice, yet always in the wildest spirits, laughing, joking, singing, rejoicing, drumming, and tambourining: his life flying by in a flash of excitement, and his death arriving as a climax of triumph. And, if you please, the playgoer despising the Salvationist as a joyless person, shut out from the heaven of the theatre, self-condemned to a life of hideous gloom; and the Salvationist mourning over the playgoer as over a prodigal with vine leaves in his hair, careering outrageously to hell amid the popping of champagne corks and the ribald laughter of sirens! Could misunderstanding be more complete, or sympathy worse misplaced?

Fortunately, the Salvationists are more accessible to the religious character of the drama than the playgoers to the gay energy and artistic fertility of religion. They can see, when it is pointed out to them, that a theatre, as a place where two or three are gathered together, takes from that divine presence an inalienable sanctity of which the grossest and profanest farce can no more deprive it than a hypocritical sermon by a snobbish bishop can desecrate Westminster Abbey. But in our professional playgoers this indispensable preliminary conception of sanctity seems wanting. They talk of actors as mimes and mummers, and, I fear, think of dramatic authors as liars and pandars, whose main business is the voluptuous soothing of the tired city speculator when what he calls the serious business of the day is over. Passion, the life of drama, means nothing to them but primitive sexual excitement: such phrases as 'impassioned poetry' or 'passionate love of truth' have fallen quite out of their vocabulary and been replaced by 'passional crime' and the like. They assume, as far as I can gather, that people in whom passion has a larger scope are passionless and therefore uninteresting. Consequently they come to think of religious people as people who are not interesting and not amusing. And so, when Barbara cuts the regular Salvation Army jokes, and snatches a kiss from her lover across his drum, the devotees of the theatre think they ought to appear shocked, and conclude that the whole play is an elaborate mockery of the Army. And then either hypocritically rebuke me for mocking, or foolishly take part in the supposed mockery!

Even the handful of mentally competent critics got into difficulties over my demonstration of the economic deadlock in which the Salvation Army finds itself. Some of them thought that the Army would not have taken money from a distiller and a cannon founder: others thought it should not have taken it: all assumed more or less definitely that it reduced itself to absurdity or hypocrisy by taking it. On the first point the reply of the Army itself was prompt and conclusive. As one of its officers said, they would take money from the devil himself and be only too glad to get it out of his hands and into God's. They gratefully acknowledged that publicans not only give them money but allow them to collect it in the bar— sometimes even when there is a Salvation meeting outside preaching teetotalism. In fact, they questioned the verisimilitude of the play, not because Mrs Baines took the money, but because Barbara refused it.

On the point that the Army ought not to take such money, its justification is obvious. It must take the money because it cannot exist without money, and there is no other money to be had. Practically all the spare money in the country consists of a mass of rent, interest, and profit, every penny of which is bound up with crime, drink, prostitution, disease, and all the evil fruits of poverty, as inextricably as with enterprise, wealth, commercial probity, and national prosperity. The notion that you can earmark certain coins as tainted is an unpractical individualist superstition. None the less the fact that all our money is tainted gives a very severe shock to earnest young souls when some dramatic instance of the taint first makes them conscious of it. When an enthusiastic young clergyman of the Established Chuch first realizes that the Ecclesiastical Commissioners receive the rents of sporting public houses, brothels, and sweating dens; or that the most generous contributor at his last charity sermon was an employer trading in female labor cheapened by prostitution as unscrupulously as a hotel keeper trades in waiters' labor cheapened by tips, or commissionaires' labor cheapened by pensions; or that the only patron who can afford to rebuild his church or his schools or give his boys' brigade a gymnasium or a library is the son-in-law of a Chicago meat King, that young clergyman has, like Barbara, a very bad quarter hour. But he cannot help himself by refusing to accept money from anybody except sweet old ladies with independent incomes and gentle and lovely ways of life. He has only to follow up the income of the sweet ladies to its industrial source, and there he will find Mrs Warren's profession and the poisonous canned meat and all the rest of it. His own stipend has the same root. He must either share the world's guilt or go to another planet. He must save the world's honor if he is to save his own. This is what all the Churches find just as the Salvation Army and Barbara find it in the play. Her discovery that she is her father's accomplice; that the Salvation Army is the accomplice of the distiller and the dynamite maker; that they can no more escape one another than they can escape the air they breathe; that there is no salvation for them through personal righteousness, but only through the redemption of the whole nation from its vicious, lazy, competitive anarchy: this discovery has been made by everyone except the Pharisees and (apparently) the professional playgoers, who still wear their Tom Hood shirts and underpay their washerwoman without the slightest misgiving as to the elevation of their private characters, the purity of their private atmospheres, and their right to repudiate as foreign to themselves the coarse depravity of the garret and the slum. Not that they mean any harm: they only desire to be, in their little private way, what they call gentlemen. They do not understand Barbara's lesson because they have not, like her, learnt it by taking their part in the larger life of the nation.

Barbara's Return to the Colors

Barbara's return to the colors may yet provide a subject for the dramatic historian of the future. To get back to the Salvation Army with the knowledge that even the Salvationists themselves are not saved yet: that poverty is not blessed, but a most damnable sin; and that when General Booth chose Blood and Fire for the emblem of Salvation instead of the Cross, he was perhaps better inspired than he knew: such knowledge, for the daughter of Andrew Undershaft, will clearly lead to something hopefuller than distributing bread and treacle at the expense of Bodger.

It is a very significant thing, this instinctive choice of the military form of organization, this substitution of the drum for the organ, by the Salvation Army. Does it not suggest that the Salvationists divine that they must actually fight the devil instead of merely praying at him? At present, it is true, they have not quite ascertained his correct address. When they do, they may give a very rude shock to that sense of security which he has gained from his experience of the fact that hard words, even when uttered by eloquent essayists and lecturers, or carried unanimously at enthusiastic public meetings on the motion of eminent reformers, break no bones. It has been said that the French Revolution was the work of Voltaire, Rousseau and the Encyclopedists. It seems to me to have been the work of men who had observed that virtuous indignation, caustic criticism, conclusive argument and instructive pamphleteering, even when done by the most earnest and witty literary geniuses, were as useless as praying, things going steadily from bad to worse whilst the Social Contract and the pamplets of Voltaire were at the height of their vogue. Eventually, as we know, perfectly respectable citizens and earnest philanthropists connived at the September massacres because hard experience had convinced them that if they contented themselves with appeals to humanity and patriotism, the aristocracy, though it would read their appeals with the greatest enjoyment and appreciation, flattering and admiring the writers, would none the less continue to conspire with foreign monarchists to undo the revolution and restore the old system with every circumstance of savage vengeance and ruthless repression of popular liberties.

The nineteenth century saw the same lesson repeated in England. It had its Utilitarians, its Christian Socialists, its Fabians (still extant): it had Bentham, Mill, Dickens, Ruskin, Carlyle, Butler, Henry George, and Morris. And the end of all their efforts is the Chicago described by Mr Upton Sinclair, and the London in which the people who pay to be amused by my dramatic representation of Peter Shirley turned out to starve at forty because there are younger slaves to be had for his wages, do not take, and have not the slightest intention of taking, any effective step to organize society in such a way as to make that everyday infamy impossible. I, who have preached and pamphleteered like any Encyclopedist, have to confess that my methods are no use, and would be no use if I were Voltaire, Rousseau, Bentham, Marx, Mill, Dickens, Carlyle, Ruskin, Butler, and Morris all rolled into one, with Euripides, More, Montaigne, Molière, Beaumarchais, Swift, Goethe, Ibsen, Tolstoy, Jesus and the prophets all thrown in (as indeed in some sort I actually am, standing as I do on all their shoulders). The problem being to make heroes out of cowards, we paper apostles and artist-magicians have succeeded only in giving cowards all the sensations of heroes whilst they tolerate every abomination, accept every plunder, and submit to every oppression. Christianity, in making a merit of such submission, has marked only that depth in the abyss at which the very sense of shame is lost. The Christian

has been like Dickens' doctor in the debtor's prison, who tells the new-
comer of its ineffable peace and security: no duns; no tyrannical col-
lectors of rates, taxes, and rent; no importunate hopes nor exacting duties;
nothing but the rest and safety of having no farther to fall.

Yet in the poorest corner of this soul-destroying Christendom vitality
suddenly begins to germinate again. Joyousness, a sacred gift long de-
throned by the hellish laughter of derision and obscenity, rises like a
flood miraculously out of the fetid dust and mud of the slums; rousing
marches and impetuous dithyrambs rise to the heavens from people
among whom the depressing noise called 'sacred music' is a standing joke;
a flag with Blood and Fire on it is unfurled, not in murderous rancor, but
because fire is beautiful and blood is vital and splendid red; Fear, which
we flatter by calling Self, vanishes; and transfigured men and women
carry their gospel through a transfigured world, calling their leader General, themselves captains and brigadiers, and their whole body an Army:
praying, but praying only for refreshment, for strength to fight, and for
needful MONEY (a notable sign, that); preaching, but not preaching submission; daring ill-usage and abuse, but not putting up with more of it
than is inevitable; and practising what the world will let them practise,
including soap and water, color and music. There is danger in such
activity; and where there is danger there is hope. Our present security is
nothing, and can be nothing, but evil made irresistible.

Weaknesses of the Salvation Army

For the present, however, it is not my business to flatter the Salvation
Army. Rather must I point out to it that it has almost as many weak-
nessess as the Church of England itself. It is building up a business organization which will compel it eventually to see that its present staff of
enthusiast-commanders shall be succeeded by a bureaucracy of men of
business who will be no better than bishops, and perhaps a good deal more
unscrupulous. That has always happened sooner or later to great orders
founded by saints; and the order founded by St William Booth is not
exempt from the same danger. It is even more dependent than the Church
on rich people who would cut off supplies at once if it began to preach
that indispensable revolt against poverty which must also be a revolt
against riches. It is hampered by a heavy contingent of pious elders who
are not really Salvationists at all, but Evangelicals of the old school. It
still, as Commissioner Howard affirms, 'sticks to Moses,' which is flat
nonsense at this time of day if the Commissioner means, as I am afraid he
does, that the Book of Genesis contains a trustworthy scientific account of
the origin of species, and that the god to whom Jephthah sacrificed his
daughter is any less obviously a tribal idol than Dagon or Chemosh.

Further, there is still too much other-worldliness about the Army. Like

Frederick's grenadier, the Salvationist wants to live for ever (the most monstrous way of crying for the moon); and though it is evident to anyone who has ever heard General Booth and his best officers that they would work as hard for human salvation as they do at present if they believed that death would be the end of them individually, they and their followers have a bad habit of talking as if the Salvationists were heroically enduring a very bad time on earth as an investment which will bring them in dividends later on in the form, not of a better life to come for the whole world, but of an eternity spent by themselves personally in a sort of bliss which would bore any active person to a second death. Surely the truth is that the Salvationists are unusually happy people. And is it not the very diagnostic of true salvation that it shall overcome the fear of death? Now the man who has come to believe that there is no such thing as death, the change so called being merely the transition to an exquisitely happy and utterly careless life, has not overcome the fear of death at all: on the contrary, it has overcome him so completely that he refuses to die on any terms whatever. I do not call a Salvationist really saved until he is ready to lie down cheerfully on the scrap heap, having paid scot and lot and something over, and let his eternal life pass on to renew its youth in the battalions of the future.

Then there is the nasty lying habit called confession, which the Army encourages because it lends itself to dramatic oratory, with plenty of thrilling incident. For my part, when I hear a convert relating the violences and oaths and blasphemies he was guilty of before he was saved, making out that he was a very terrible fellow then and is the most contrite and chastened of Christians now, I believe him no more than I believe the millionaire who says he came up to London or Chicago as a boy with only three halfpence in his pocket. Salvationists have said to me that Barbara in my play would never have been taken in by so transparent a humbug as Snobby Price; and certainly I do not think Snobby could have taken in any experienced Salvationist on a point on which the Salvationist did not wish to be taken in. But on the point of conversion all Salvationists wish to be taken in; for the more obvious the sinner the more obvious the miracle of his conversion. When you advertize a converted burglar or reclaimed drunkard as one of the attractions at an experience meeting, your burglar can hardly have been too burglarious or your drunkard too drunken. As long as such attractions are relied on, you will have your Snobbies claiming to have beaten their mothers when they were as a matter of prosaic fact habitually beaten by them, and your Rummies of the tamest respectability pretending to a past of reckless and dazzling vice. Even when confessions are sincerely autobiographic we should beware of assuming that the impulse to make them was pious or that the interest of the hearers is wholesome. As well might we assume that the poor people who insist on shewing disgusting ulcers to district visitors are convinced hygienists, or that the curiosity which sometimes welcomes such exhibitions is a pleasant and creditable one. One is often tempted to suggest that those who pester our police superintendents with confessions of murder might very wisely be taken at their word and executed, except in the few cases in which a real murderer is seeking to be relieved of his guilt by confession and expiation. For though I am not, I hope, an unmerciful person, I do not think that the inexorability of the deed once done should be disguised by any ritual, whether in the confessional or on the scaffold.

And here my disagreement with the Salvation Army, and with all propagandists of the Cross (which I loathe as I loathe all gibbets) becomes deep indeed. Forgiveness, absolution, atonement, are figments: punishment is only a pretence of cancelling one crime by another; and you can no more have forgiveness without vindictivenesss than you can have a cure without a disease. You will never get a high morality from people who conceive that their misdeeds are revocable and pardonable, or in a society where absolution and expiation are officially provided for us all. The demand may be very real; but the supply is spurious. Thus Bill Walker, in my play, having assaulted the Salvation Lass, presently finds himself overwhelmed with an intolerable conviction of sin under the skilled treatment of Barbara. Straightway he begins to try to unassault the lass and deruffianize his deed, first by getting punished for it in kind, and, when that relief is denied him, by fining himself a pound to compensate the girl. He is foiled both ways. He finds the Salvation Army is inexorable as fact itself. It will not punish him: it will not take his money. It will not tolerate a redeemed ruffian: it leaves him no means of salvation except ceasing to be a ruffian. In doing this, the Salvation Army instinctively grasps the central truth of Christianity and discards its central superstition: that central truth being the vanity of revenge and punishment, and that central superstition the salvation of the world by the gibbet.

For, be it noted, Bill has assaulted an old and starving woman also; and for this worse offence he feels no remorse whatever, because she makes it clear that her malice is as great as his own. 'Let her have the law of me, as she said she would,' says Bill: 'what I done to her is no more on what you might call my conscience than sticking a pig.' This shews a perfectly natural and wholesome state of mind on his part. The old woman, like the law she threatens him with, is perfectly ready to play the game of retaliation with him: to rob him if he steals, to flog him if he strikes, to murder him if he kills. By example and precept the law and public opinion teach him to impose his will on others by anger, violence, and cruelty, and to wipe off the moral score by punishment. That is sound Crosstianity. But this Crosstianity has got entangled with something which Barbara calls Christianity, and which unexpectedly causes her to refuse to play the hangman's game of Satan casting out Satan. She refuses to prosecute a drunken ruffian; she converses on equal terms with a blackguard to whom no lady should be seen speaking in the public street: in short, she imitates Christ. Bill's conscience reacts to this just as naturally as it does to the old woman's threats. He is placed in a position of unbearable moral inferiority, and strives by every means in his power to escape from it, whilst he is still quite ready to meet the abuse of the old woman by attempting to smash a mug on her face. And that is the triumphant justification of Barbara's Christianity as against our system of judicial punishment and the vindictive villain-thrashings and 'poetic justice' of the romantic stage.

For the credit of literature it must be pointed out that the situation is only partly novel. Victor Hugo long ago gave us the epic of the convict and the bishop's candlesticks, of the Crosstian policeman annihilated by his encounter with the Christian Valjean. But Bill Walker is not, like Valjean, romantically changed from a demon into an angel. There are millions of Bill Walkers in all classes of society today; and the point which I, as a professor of natural psychology, desire to demonstrate, is that Bill, without any change in his character or circumstances whatsoever, will react one way to one sort of treatment and another way to another.

In proof I might point to the sensational object lesson provided by our commercial millionaires today. They begin as brigands: merciless, unscrupulous, dealing out ruin and death and slavery to their competitors and employees, and facing desperately the worst that their competitors can do to them. The history of the English factories, the American Trusts, the exploitation of African gold, diamonds, ivory and rubber, outdoes in villainy the worst that has ever been imagined of the buccaneers of the Spanish Main. Captain Kidd would have marooned a modern Trust magnate for conduct unworthy of a gentleman of fortune. The law every day seizes on unsuccessful scoundrels of this type and punishes them with a cruelty worse than their own, with the result that they come out of the torture house more dangerous than they went in, and renew their evil doing (nobody will employ them at anything else) until they are again seized, again tormented, and again let loose, with the same result.

But the successful scoundrel is dealt with very differently, and very Christianly. He is not only forgiven: he is idolized, respected, made much of, all but worshipped. Society returns him good for evil in the most extravagant overmeasure. And with what result? He begins to idolize himself, to respect himself, to live up to the treatment he receives. He preaches sermons; he writes books of the most edifying advice to young men, and actually persuades himself that he got on by taking his own advice; he endows educational institutions; he supports charities; he dies finally in the odor of sanctity, leaving a will which is a monument of public spirit and bounty. And all this without any change in his character. The spots of the leopard and the stripes of the tiger are as brilliant

as ever; but the conduct of the world towards him has changed; and his
conduct has changed accordingly. You have only to reverse your attitude
towards him—to lay hands on his property, revile him, assault him, and
he will be a brigand again in a moment, as ready to crush you as you are
to crush him, and quite as full of pretentious moral reasons for doing it.

In short, when Major Barbara says that there are no scoundrels, she is
right: there are no absolute scoundrels, though there are impracticable
people of whom I shall treat presently. Every reasonable man (and
woman) is a potential scoundrel and a potential good citizen. What a man
is depends on his character; but what he does and what we think of what
he does, depends on his circumstances. The characteristics that ruin a
man in one class make him eminent in another. The characters that behave differently in different circumstances behave alike in similar circumstances. Take a common English character like that of Bill Walker. We
meet Bill everywhere: on the judicial bench, on the episcopal bench, in
the Privy Council, at the War Office and Admiralty, as well as in the Old
Bailey dock or in the ranks of casual unskilled labor. And the morality of
Bill's characteristics varies with these various circumstances. The faults of
the burglar are the qualities of the financier: the manners and habits of a
duke would cost a city clerk his situation. In short, though character is
independent of circumstances, conduct is not; and our moral judgments
of character are not: both are circumstantial. Take any condition of life
in which the circumstances are for a mass of men practically alike: felony,
the House of Lords, the factory, the stables, the gipsy encampment or
where you please! In spite of diversity of character and temperament, the
conduct and morals of the individuals in each group are as predicable and
as alike in the main as if they were a flock of sheep, morals being mostly
only social habits and circumstantial necessities. Strong people know this
and count upon it. In nothing have the master-minds of the world been
distinguished from the ordinary suburban season-ticket holder more than
in their straightforward perception of the fact that mankind is practically
a single species, and not a menagerie of gentlemen and bounders, villains
and heroes, cowards and daredevils, peers and peasants, grocers and
aristocrats, artisans and laborers, washerwomen and duchesses, in which
all the grades of income and caste represent distinct animals who must
not be introduced to one another or intermarry. Napoleon constructing a
galaxy of generals and courtiers, and even of monarchs, out of his collection of social nobodies; Julius Cæsar appointing as governor of Egypt the
son of a freedman—one who but a short time before would have been
legally disqualified for the post even of a private soldier in the Roman
army; Louis XI making his barber his privy councillor: all these had in
their different ways a firm hold of the scientific fact of human equality,
expressed by Barbara in the Christian formula that all men are children
of one father. A man who believes that men are naturally divided into

upper and lower and middle classes morally is making exactly the same mistake as the man who believes that they are naturally divided in the same way socially. And just as our persistent attempts to found political institutions on a basis of social inequality have always produced long periods of destructive friction relieved from time to time by violent explosions of revolution; so the attempt—will Americans please note—to found moral institutions on a basis of moral inequality can lead to nothing but unnatural Reigns of the Saints relieved by licentious Restorations; to Americans who have made divorce a public institution turning the face of Europe into one huge sardonic smile by refusing to stay in the same hotel with a Russian man of genius who has changed wives without the sanction of South Dakota; to grotesque hypocrisy, cruel persecution, and final utter confusion of conventions and compliances with benevolence and respectability. It is quite useless to declare that all men are born free if you deny that they are born good. Guarantee a man's goodness and his liberty will take care of itself. To guarantee his freedom on condition that you approve of his moral character is formally to abolish all freedom whatsoever, as every man's liberty is at the mercy of a moral indictment which any fool can trump up against everyone who violates custom, whether as a prophet or as a rascal. This is the lesson Democracy has to learn before it can become anything but the most oppressive of all the priesthoods.

Let us now return to Bill Walker and his case of conscience against the Salvation Army. Major Barbara, not being a modern Tetzel, or the treasurer of a hospital, refuses to sell absolution to Bill for a sovereign. Unfortunately, what the Army can afford to refuse in the case of Bill Walker, it cannot refuse in the case of Bodger. Bodger is master of the situation because he holds the purse strings. 'Strive as you will,' says Bodger, in effect: 'me you cannot do without. You cannot save Bill Walker without my money.' And the Army answers, quite rightly under the circumstances, 'We will take money from the devil himself sooner than abandon the work of Salvation.' So Bodger pays his conscience-money and gets the absolution that is refused to Bill. In real life Bill would perhaps never know this. But I, the dramatist whose business it is to shew the connexion between things that seem apart and unrelated in the haphazard order of events in real life, have contrived to make it known to Bill, with the result that the Salvation Army loses its hold of him at once.

But Bill may not be lost, for all that. He is still in the grip of the facts and of his own conscience, and may find his taste for blackguardism permanently spoiled. Still, I cannot guarantee that happy ending. Walk through the poorer quarters of our cities on Sunday when the men are not working, but resting and chewing the cud of their reflections. You will find one expression common to every mature face: the expression of cynicism. The discovery made by Bill Walker about the Salvation Army has been made by everyone there. They have found that every man has his price; and they have been foolishly or corruptly taught to mistrust and despise him for that necessary and salutary condition of social existence. When they learn that General Booth, too, has his price, they do not admire him because it is a high one, and admit the need of organizing society so that he shall get it in an honorable way: they conclude that his character is unsound and that all religious men are hypocrites and allies of their sweaters and oppressors. They know that the large subscriptions which help to support the Army are endowments, not of religion, but of the wicked doctrine of docility in poverty and humility under oppression; and they are rent by the most agonizing of all the doubts of the soul, the doubt whether their true salvation must not come from their most abhorrent passions, from murder, envy, greed, stubbornness, rage, and terrorism, rather than from public spirit, reasonableness, humanity, generosity, tenderness, delicacy, pity and kindness. The confirmation of that doubt, at which our newspapers have been working so hard for years past, is the morality of militarism; and the justification of militarism is that circumstances may at any time make it the true morality of the moment. It is by producing such moments that we produce violent and sanguinary revolutions, such as the one now in progress in Russia and the one which Capitalism in England and America is daily and diligently provoking.

At such moments it becomes the duty of the Churches to evoke all the powers of destruction against the existing order. But if they do this, the existing order must forcibly suppress them. Churches are suffered to exist only on condition that they preach submission to the State as at present capitalistically organized. The Church of England itself is compelled to add to the thirtysix articles in which it formulates its religious tenets, three more in which it apologetically protests that the moment any of these articles comes in conflict with the State it is to be entirely renounced, abjured, violated, abrogated and abhorred, the policeman being a much more important person than any of the Persons of the Trinity. And this is why no tolerated Church nor Salvation Army can ever win the entire confidence of the poor. It must be on the side of the police and the military, no matter what it believes or disbelieves; and as the police and the military are the instruments by which the rich rob and oppress the poor (on legal and moral principles made for the purpose), it is not possible to be on the side of the poor and of the police at the same time. Indeed the religious bodies, as the almoners of the rich, become a sort of auxiliary police, taking off the insurrectionary edge of poverty with coals and blankets, bread and treacle, and soothing and cheering the victims with hopes of immense and inexpensive happiness in another world when the process of working them to premature death in the service of the rich is complete in this.

Christianity and Anarchism

Such is the false position from which neither the Salvation Army nor the Church of England nor any other religious organization whatever can escape except through a reconstitution of society. Nor can they merely endure the State passively, washing their hands of its sins. The State is constantly forcing the consciences of men by violence and cruelty. Not content with exacting money from us for the maintenance of its soldiers and policemen, its gaolers and executioners, it forces us to take an active personal part in its proceedings on pain of becoming ourselves the victims of its violence. As I write these lines, a sensational example is given to the world. A royal marriage has been celebrated, first by sacrament in a cathedral, and then by a bullfight having for its main amusement the spectacle of horses gored and disembowelled by the bull, after which, when the bull is so exhausted as to be no longer dangerous, he is killed by a cautious matador. But the ironic contrast between the bullfight and the sacrament of marriage does not move anyone. Another contrast—that between the splendor, the happiness, the atmosphere of kindly admiration surrounding the young couple, and the price paid for it under our abominable social arrangements in the misery, squalor and degradation of millions of other young couples—is drawn at the same moment by a novelist, Mr Upton Sinclair, who chips a corner of the veneering from the huge meat packing industries of Chicago, and shews it to us as a sample of what is going on all over the world underneath the top layer of prosperous plutocracy. One man is sufficiently moved by that contrast to pay his own life as the price of one terrible blow at the responsible parties. His poverty has left him ignorant enough to be duped by the pretence that the innocent young bride and bridegroom, put forth and crowned by plutocracy as the heads of a State in which they have less personal power than any policeman, and less influence than any Chairman of a Trust, are responsible. At them accordingly he launches his sixpennorth of fulminate, missing his mark, but scattering the bowels of as many horses as any bull in the arena, and slaying twentythree persons, besides wounding ninetynine. And of all these, the horses alone are innocent of the guilt he is avenging: had he blown all Madrid to atoms with every adult person in it, not one could have escaped the charge of being an accessory, before, at, and after the fact, to poverty and prostitution, to such wholesale massacre of infants as Herod never dreamt of, to plague, pestilence and famine, battle, murder and lingering death—perhaps not one who had not helped, through example, precept, connivance, and even clamor, to teach the dynamiter his well-learnt gospel of hatred and vengeance, by approving every day of sentences of years of imprisonment so infernal in their unnatural stupidity and panic-stricken cruelty, that their advocates can disavow neither the dagger nor the bomb without stripping the mask of justice and humanity from themselves also.

Be it noted that at this very moment there appears the biography of one of our dukes, who, being a Scot, could argue about politics, and therefore stood out as a great brain among our aristocrats. And what, if you please, was his grace's favorite historical episode, which he declared he never read without intense satisfaction? Why, the young General Bonapart's pounding of the Paris mob to pieces in 1795, called in playful approval by our respectable classes 'the whiff of grapeshot,' though Napoleon, to do him justice, took a deeper view of it, and would fain have had it forgotten. And since the Duke of Argyll was not a demon, but a man of like passions with ourselves, by no means rancorous or cruel as men go, who can doubt that all over the world proletarians of the ducal kidney are now revelling in 'the whiff of dynamite' (the flavor of the joke seems to evaporate a little, does it not?) because it was aimed at the class they hate even as our argute duke hated what he called the mob.

In such an atmosphere there can be only one sequel to the Madrid explosion. All Europe burns to emulate it. Vengeance! More blood! Tear 'the Anarchist beast' to shreds. Drag him to the scaffold. Imprison him for life. Let all civilized States band together to drive his like off the face of the earth; and if any State refuses to join, make war on it. This time the leading London newspaper, anti-Liberal and therefore anti-Russian in politics, does not say 'Serve you right' to the victims, as it did, in effect, when Bobrikoff, and De Plehve, and Grand Duke Sergius, were in the same manner unofficially fulminated into fragments. No: fulminate our rivals in Asia by all means, ye brave Russian revolutionaries; but to aim at an English princess! monstrous! hideous! hound down the wretch to his doom; and observe, please, that we are a civilized and merciful people, and, however much we may regret it, must not treat him as Ravaillac and Damiens were treated. And meanwhile, since we have not yet caught him, let us soothe our quivering nerves with the bullfight, and comment in a courtly way on the unfailing tact and good taste of the ladies of our royal houses, who, though presumably of full normal natural tenderness, have been so effectually broken in to fashionable routine that they can be taken to see the horses slaughtered as helplessly as they could no doubt be taken to a gladiator show, if that happened to be the mode just now.

Strangely enough, in the midst of this raging fire of malice, the one man who still has faith in the kindness and intelligence of human nature is the fulminator, now a hunted wretch, with nothing, apparently, to secure his triumph over all the prisons and scaffolds of infuriate Europe except the revolver in his pocket and his readiness to discharge it at a moment's notice into his own or any other head. Think of him setting out to find a gentleman and a Christian in the multitude of human wolves howling for his blood. Think also of this: that at the very first essay he finds what he seeks, a veritable grandee of Spain, a noble, high-thinking, unter-rified, malice-void soul, in the guise—of all masquerades in the world!—of a modern editor. The Anarchist wolf, flying from the wolves of pluto-cracy, throws himself on the honor of the man. The man, not being a wolf (nor a London editor), and therefore not having enough sympathy with his exploit to be made bloodthirsty by it, does not throw him back to the pursuing wolves—gives him, instead, what help he can to escape, and sends him off acquainted at last with a force that goes deeper than dynamite, though you cannot buy so much of it for sixpence. That right-eous and honorable high human deed is not wasted on Europe, let us hope, though it benefits the fugitive wolf only for a moment. The plu-tocratic wolves presently smell him out. The fugitive shoots the unlucky wolf whose nose is nearest; shoots himself; and then convinces the world, by his photograph, that he was no monstrous freak of reversion to the tiger, but a good looking young man with nothing abnormal about him except his appalling courage and resolution (that is why the terrified shriek Coward at him): one to whom murdering a happy young couple on their wedding morning would have been an unthinkably unnatural abomination under rational and kindly human circumstances.

Then comes the climax of irony and blind stupidity. The wolves, balked of their meal of fellow-wolf, turn on the man, and proceed to torture him, after their manner, by imprisonment, for refusing to fasten his teeth in the throat of the dynamiter and hold him down until they came to finish him.

Thus, you see, a man may not be a gentleman nowadays even if he wishes to. As to being a Christian, he is allowed some latitude in that matter, because, I repeat, Christianity has two faces. Popular Christianity has for its emblem a gibbet, for its chief sensation a sanguinary execution after torture, for its central mystery an insane vengeance bought off by a trumpery expiation. But there is a nobler and profounder Christianity which affirms the sacred mystery of Equality, and forbids the glaring futility and folly of vengeance, often politely called punishment or justice. The gibbet part of Christianity is tolerated. The other is criminal felony. Connoisseurs in irony are well aware of the fact that the only editor in England who denounces punishment as radically wrong, also repu-diates Christianity; calls his paper The Freethinker; and has been im-prisoned for 'bad taste' under the law against blasphemy.

Sane Conclusions

And now I must ask the excited reader not to lose his head on one side or the other, but to draw a sane moral from these grim absurdities. It is not good sense to propose that laws against crime should apply to principals only and not to accessories whose consent, counsel, or silence may secure impunity to the principal. If you institute punishment as part of the law, you must punish people for refusing to punish. If you have a police, part of its duty must be to compel everybody to assist the police. No doubt if your laws are unjust, and your policemen agents of oppression, the result will be an unbearable violation of the private consciences of citizens. But that cannot be helped: the remedy is, not to license everybody to thwart the law if they please, but to make laws that will command the public assent, and not to deal cruelly and stupidly with lawbreakers. Everybody disapproves of burglars; but the modern burglar, when caught and overpowered by a householder, usually appeals, and often, let us hope, with success, to his captor not to deliver him over to the useless horrors of penal servitude. In other cases the law-breaker escapes because those who could give him up do not consider his breach of the law a guilty action. Sometimes, even, private tribunals are formed in opposition to the official tribunals; and these private tribunals employ assassins as executioners, as was done, for example, by Mahomet before he had established his power officially, and by the Ribbon lodges of Ireland in their long struggle with the landlords. Under such circumstances, the assassin goes free although everybody in the district knows who he is and what he has done. They do not betray him, partly because they justify him exactly as the regular Government justifies its official executioner, and partly because they would themselves be assassinated if they betrayed him: another method learnt from the official government. Given a tribunal, employing a slayer who has no personal quarrel with the slain; and there is clearly no moral difference between official and unofficial killing.

In short, all men are anarchists with regard to laws which are against their consciences, either in the preamble or in the penalty. In London our worst anarchists are the magistrates, because many of them are so old and ignorant that when they are called upon to administer any law that is based on ideas or knowledge less than half a century old, they disagree with it, and being mere ordinary homebred private Englishmen without any respect for law in the abstract, naively set the example of violating it. In this instance the man lags behind the law; but when the law lags behind the man, he becomes equally an anarchist. When some huge change in social conditions, such as the industrial revolution of the eighteenth and nineteenth centuries, throws our legal and industrial institutions out of date, Anarchism becomes almost a religion. The whole force of the most energetic geniuses of the time in philosophy, economics, and art, concentrates itself on demonstrations and reminders that morality and law are only conventions, fallible and continually obsolescing. Tragedies in which the heroes are bandits, and comedies in which law-abiding and conventionally moral folk are compelled to satirize themselves by outraging the conscience of the spectators every time they do their duty, appear simultaneously with economic treatises entitled 'What is Property?'

Theft!' and with histories of 'The Conflict between Religion and Science.'

Now this is not a healthy state of things. The advantages of living in society are proportionate, not to the freedom of the individual from a code, but to the complexity and subtlety of the code he is prepared not only to accept but to uphold as a matter of such vital importance that a law-breaker at large is hardly to be tolerated on any plea. Such an attitude becomes impossible when the only men who can make themselves heard and remembered throughout the world spend all their energy in raising our gorge against current law, current morality, current respectability, and legal property. The ordinary man, uneducated in social theory even when he is schooled in Latin verse, cannot be set against all the laws of his country and yet persuaded to regard law in the abstract as vitally necessary to society. Once he is brought to repudiate the laws and institutions he knows, he will repudiate the very conception of law and the very groundwork of institutions, ridiculing human rights, extolling brainless methods as 'historical,' and tolerating nothing except pure empiricism in conduct, with dynamite as the basis of politics and vivisection as the basis of science. That is hideous; but what is to be done? Here am I, for instance, by class a respectable man, by common sense a hater of waste and disorder, by intellectual constitution legally minded to the verge of pedantry, and by temperament apprehensive and economically disposed to the limit of old-maidishness; yet I am, and have always been, and shall now always be, a revolutionary writer, because our laws make law impossible; our liberties destroy all freedom; our property is organized robbery; our morality is an impudent hypocrisy; our wisdom is administered by inexperienced or malexperienced dupes, our power wielded by cowards and weaklings, and our honor false in all its points. I am an enemy of the existing order for good reasons; but that does not make my attacks any less encouraging or helpful to people who are its enemies for bad reasons. The existing order may shriek that if I tell the truth about it, some foolish person may drive it to become still worse by trying to assassinate it. I cannot help that, even if I could see what worse it could do than it is already doing. And the disadvantage of that worst even from its own point of view is that society, with all its prisons and bayonets and whips and ostracisms and starvations, is powerless in the face of the Anarchist who is prepared to sacrifice his own life in the battle with it. Our natural safety from the cheap and devastating explosives which every Russian student can make, and every Russian grenadier has learnt to handle in Manchuria, lies in the fact that brave and resolute men, when they are rascals, will not risk their skins for the good of humanity, and, when they are not, are sympathetic enough to care for humanity, abhorring murder, and never committing it until their consciences are outraged beyond endurance. The remedy is, then, simply not to outrage their consciences.

Do not be afraid that they will not make allowances. All men make very large allowances indeed before they stake their own lives in a war to the death with society. Nobody demands or expects the millennium. But there are two things that must be set right, or we shall perish, like Rome, of soul atrophy disguised as empire.

The first is, that the daily ceremony of dividing the wealth of the country among its inhabitants shall be so conducted that no crumb shall, save as a criminal's ration, go to any able-bodied adults who are not producing by their personal exertions not only a full equivalent for what they take, but a surplus sufficient to provide for their superannuation and pay back the debt due for their nurture.

The second is that the deliberate infliction of malicious injuries which now goes on under the name of punishment be abandoned; so that the thief, the ruffian, the gambler, and the beggar, may without inhumanity be handed over to the law, and made to understand that a State which is too humane to punish will also be too thrifty to waste the life of honest men in watching or restraining dishonest ones. That is why we do not imprison dogs. We even take our chance of their first bite. But if a dog delights to bark and bite, it goes to the lethal chamber. That seems to me sensible. To allow the dog to expiate his bite by a period of torment, and then let him loose in a much more savage condition (for the chain makes a dog savage) to bite again and expiate again, having meanwhile spent a great deal of human life and happiness in the task of chaining and feeding and tormenting him, seems to me idiotic and superstitious. Yet that is what we do to men who bark and bite and steal. It would be far more sensible to put up with their vices, as we put up with their illnesses, until they give more trouble than they are worth, at which point we should, with many apologies and expressions of sympathy, and some generosity in complying with their last wishes, place them in the lethal chamber and get rid of them. Under no circumstances should they be allowed to expiate their misdeeds by a manufactured penalty, to subscribe to a charity, or to compensate the victims. If there is to be no punishment there can be no forgiveness. We shall never have real moral responsibility until everyone knows that his deeds are irrevocable, and that his life depends on his usefulness. Hitherto, alas! humanity has never dared face these hard facts. We frantically scatter conscience money and invent systems of conscience banking, with expiatory penalties, atonements, redemptions, salvations, hospital subscription lists and what not, to enable us to contract-out of the moral code. Not content with the old scapegoat and sacrificial lamb, we deify human saviors, and pray to miraculous virgin intercessors. We attribute mercy to the inexorable; soothe our consciences after committing murder by throwing ourselves on the bosom of divine love; and shrink even from our own gallows because we are forced to admit that it, at least, is irrevocable—as if one hour of imprisonment were not as irrevocable as any execution!

If a man cannot look evil in the face without illusion, he will never know what it really is, or combat it effectually. The few men who have been able (relatively) to do this have been called cynics, and have sometimes had an abnormal share of evil in themselves, corresponding to the abnormal strength of their minds; but they have never done mischief unless they intended to do it. That is why great scoundrels have been beneficent rulers whilst amiable and privately harmless monarchs have ruined their countries by trusting to the hocus-pocus of innocence and guilt, reward and punishment, virtuous indignation and pardon, instead of standing up to the facts without either malice or mercy. Major Barbara stands up to Bill Walker in that way, with the result that the ruffian who cannot get hated, has to hate himself. To relieve this agony he tries to get punished; but the Salvationist whom he tries to provoke is as merciless as Barbara, and only prays for him. Then he tries to pay, but can get nobody to take his money. His doom is the doom of Cain, who, failing to find either a savior, a policeman, or an almoner to help him to pretend that his brother's blood no longer cried from the ground, had to live and die a murderer. Cain took care not to commit another murder, unlike our railway shareholders (I am one) who kill and maim shunters by hundreds to save the cost of automatic couplings, and make atonement by annual subscriptions to deserving charities. Had Cain been allowed to pay off his score, he might possibly have killed Adam and Eve for the mere sake of a second luxurious reconciliation with God afterwards. Bodger, you many depend on it, will go on to the end of his life poisoning people with bad whisky, because he can always depend on the Salvation Army or the Church of England to negotiate a redemption for him in consideration of a trifling percentage of his profits.

There is a third condition too, which must be fulfilled before the great teachers of the world will cease to scoff at its religions. Creeds must become intellectually honest. At present there is not a single credible established religion in the world. That is perhaps the most stupendous fact in the whole world-situation. This play of mine, Major Barbara, is, I hope, both true and inspired; but whoever says that it all happened, and that faith in it and understanding of it consist in believing that it is a record of an actual occurrence, is, to speak according to Scripture, a fool and a liar, and is hereby solemnly denounced and cursed as such by me, the author, to all posterity.

London, June 1906

BERNARD SHAW (1856–1950)

Major Barbara

ACT I

It is after dinner in January 1906, in the library in LADY BRITOMART
UNDERSHAFT'S *house in Wilton Crescent. A large and comfortable settee
is in the middle of the room, upholstered in dark leather. A person sitting
on it (it is vacant at present) would have, on his right,* LADY BRITOMART'S
*writing table, with the lady herself busy at it; a smaller writing table
behind him on his left; the door behind him on* LADY BRITOMART'S *side;
and a window with a window seat directly on his left. Near the window
is an armchair.*

LADY BRITOMART *is a woman of fifty or thereabouts, well dressed and
yet careless of her dress, well bred and quite reckless of her breeding,
well mannered and yet appallingly outspoken and indifferent to the opinion of her interlocutors, amiable and yet peremptory, arbitrary, and high-
tempered to the last bearable degree, and withal a very typical managing
matron of the upper class, treated as a naughty child until she grew into
a scolding mother, and finally settling down with plenty of practical ability
and worldly experience, limited in the oddest way with domestic and class
limitations, conceiving the universe exactly as if it were a large house in
Wilton Crescent, though handling her corner of it very effectively on that
assumption, and being quite enlightened and liberal as to the books in the
library, the pictures on the walls, the music in the portfolios, and the
articles in the papers.*

Her son, STEPHEN, *comes in. He is a gravely correct young man under
25, taking himself very seriously, but still in some awe of his mother, from
childish habit and bachelor shyness rather than from any weakness of
character.*

STEPHEN Whats the matter?

LADY BRITOMART Presently, Stephen.

STEPHEN *submissively walks to the settee and sits down. He takes up a
Liberal weekly called The Speaker.*

LADY BRITOMART Dont begin to read, Stephen. I shall require all
your attention.

STEPHEN It was only while I was waiting—

LADY BRITOMART Dont make excuses, Stephen. (*He puts down The
Speaker.*) Now! (*She finishes her writing; rises; and comes to the
settee.*) I have not kept you waiting very long, I think.

STEPHEN Not at all, mother.

LADY BRITOMART Bring me my cushion. (*He takes the cushion from the chair at the desk and arranges it for her as she sits down on the settee.*) Sit down. (*He sits down and fingers his tie nervously.*) Dont fiddle with your tie, Stephen: there is nothing the matter with it.

STEPHEN I beg your pardon. (*He fiddles with his watch chain instead.*)

LADY BRITOMART Now are you attending to me, Stephen?

STEPHEN Of course, mother.

LADY BRITOMART No: it's not of course. I want something much more than your everyday matter-of-course attention. I am going to speak to you very seriously, Stephen. I wish you would let that chain alone.

STEPHEN (*hastily relinquishing the chain*) Have I done anything to annoy you, mother? If so, it was quite unintentional.

LADY BRITOMART (*astonished*) Nonsense! (*With some remorse.*) My poor boy, did you think I was angry with you?

STEPHEN What is it, then, mother? You are making me very uneasy.

LADY BRITOMART (*squaring herself at him rather aggressively*) Stephen: may I ask how soon you intend to realize that you are a grown-up man, and that I am only a woman?

STEPHEN (*amazed*) Only a—

LADY BRITOMART Dont repeat my words, please: it is a most aggravating habit. You must learn to face life seriously, Stephen. I really cannot bear the whole burden of our family affairs any longer. You must advise me: you must assume the responsibility.

STEPHEN I!

LADY BRITOMART Yes, you, of course. You were 24 last June. Youve been at Harrow and Cambridge. Youve been to India and Japan. You must know a lot of things, now; unless you have wasted your time most scandalously. Well, advise me.

STEPHEN (*much perplexed*) You know I have never interfered in the household—

LADY BRITOMART No: I should think not. I dont want you to order the dinner.

STEPHEN I mean in our family affairs.

LADY BRITOMART Well, you must interfere now for they are getting quite beyond me.

STEPHEN (*troubled*) I have thought sometimes that perhaps I ought; but really, mother, I know so little about them; and what I do know is so painful! it is so impossible to mention some things to you—(*he stops, ashamed*).

LADY BRITOMART   I suppose you mean your father.

STEPHEN (*almost inaudibly*) Yes.

LADY BRITOMART   My dear: we cant go on all our lives not mentioning him. Of course you were quite right not to open the subject until I asked you to; but you are old enough now to be taken into my confidence, and to help me to deal with him about the girls.

STEPHEN   But the girls are all right. They are engaged.

LADY BRITOMART (*complacently*) Yes: I have made a very good match for Sarah. Charles Lomax will be a millionaire at 35. But that is ten years ahead; and in the meantime his trustees cannot under the terms of his father's will allow him more than £800 a year.

STEPHEN   But the will says also that if he increases his income by his own exertions, they may double the increase.

LADY BRITOMART   Charles Lomax's exertions are much more likely to decrease his income than to increase it. Sarah will have to find at least another £800 a year for the next ten years; and even then they will be as poor as church mice. And what about Barbara? I thought Barbara was going to make the most brilliant career of all of you. And what does she do? Joins the Salvation Army; discharges her maid; lives on a pound a week and walks in one evening with a professor of Greek whom she has picked up in the street, and who pretends to be a Salvationist, and actually plays the big drum for her in public because he has fallen head over ears in love with her.

STEPHEN   I was certainly rather taken aback when I heard they were engaged. Cusins is a very nice fellow, certainly: nobody would ever guess that he was born in Australia; but—

LADY BRITOMART   Oh, Adolphus Cusins will make a very good husband. After all, nobody can say a word against Greek: it stamps a man at once as an educated gentleman. And my family, thank Heaven, is not a pig-headed Tory one. We are Whigs, and believe in liberty. Let snobbish people say what they please: Barbara shall marry, not the man they like, but the man *I* like.

STEPHEN   Of course I was thinking only of his income. However, he is not likely to be extravagant.

LADY BRITOMART   Dont be too sure of that, Stephen. I know your quiet, simple, refined, poetic people like Adolphus: quite content with the best of everything! They cost more than your extravagant people, who are always as mean as they are second rate. No: Barbara will need at least £2000 a year. You see it means two additional households. Besides, my dear, you must marry soon. I dont approve of the present fashion of philandering bachelors and late marriages; and I am trying to arrange something for you.

STEPHEN It's very good of you, mother; but perhaps I had better arrange that for myself.

LADY BRITOMART Nonsense! you are much too young to begin matchmaking: you would be taken in by some pretty little nobody. Of course I dont mean that you are not to be consulted: you know that as well as I do. (STEPHEN *closes his lips and is silent.*) Now dont sulk, Stephen.

STEPHEN I am not sulking, mother. What has all this got to do with—with—with my father?

LADY BRITOMART My dear Stephen: where is the money to come from? It is easy enough for you and the other children to live on my income as long as we are in the same house; but I cant keep four families in four separate houses. You know how poor my father is: he has barely seven thousand a year now; and really, if he were not the Earl of Stevenage, he would have to give up society. He can do nothing for us. He says, naturally enough, that it is absurd that he should be asked to provide for the children of a man who is rolling in money. You see, Stephen, your father must be fabulously wealthy, because there is always a war going on somewhere.

STEPHEN You need not remind me of that, mother. I have hardly ever opened a newspaper in my life without seeing our name in it. The Undershaft torpedo! The Undershaft quick firers! The Undershaft ten inch! the Undershaft disappearing rampart gun! the Undershaft submarine! and now the Undershaft aerial battleship! At Harrow they called me the Woolwich Infant. At Cambridge it was the same. A little brute at King's who was always trying to get up revivals, spoilt my Bible—your first birthday present to me—by writing under my name, "Son and heir to Undershaft and Lazarus, Death and Destruction Dealers: address Christendom and Judea." But that was not so bad as the way I was kowtowed to everywhere because my father was making millions by selling cannons.

LADY BRITOMART It is not only the cannons, but the war loans that Lazarus arranges under cover of giving credit for the cannons. You know, Stephen, it's perfectly scandalous. Those two men, Andrew Undershaft and Lazarus, positively have Europe under their thumbs. That is why your father is able to behave as he does. He is above the law. Do you think Bismarck or Gladstone or Disraeli could have openly defied every social and moral obligation all their lives as your father has? They simply wouldnt have dared. I asked Gladstone to take it up. I asked The Times to take it up. I asked the Lord Chamberlain to take it up. But it was just like asking them to declare war on the Sultan. They wouldnt. They said they couldnt touch him. I believe they were afraid.

STEPHEN   What could they do? He does not actually break the law.

LADY BRITOMART   Not break the law! He is always breaking the law. He broke the law when he was born: his parents were not married.

STEPHEN   Mother! Is that true?

LADY BRITOMART   Of course it's true: that was why we separated.

STEPHEN   He married without letting you know that!

LADY BRITOMART   (*rather taken aback by this inference*)   Oh no. To do Andrew justice, that was not the sort of thing he did. Besides, you know the Undershaft motto: Unashamed. Everybody knew.

STEPHEN   But you said that was why you separated.

LADY BRITOMART   Yes, because he was not content with being a foundling himself: he wanted to disinherit you for another foundling. That was what I couldnt stand.

STEPHEN   (*ashamed*)   Do you mean for—for—for—

LADY BRITOMART   Dont stammer, Stephen. Speak distinctly.

STEPHEN   But this is so frightful to me, mother. To have to speak to you about such things!

LADY BRITOMART   It's not pleasant for me, either, especially if you are still so childish that you must make it worse by a display of embarrassment. It is only in the middle classes, Stephen, that people get into a state of dumb helpless horror when they find that there are wicked people in the world. In our class, we have to decide what is to be done with wicked people; and nothing should disturb our self-possession. Now ask your question properly.

STEPHEN   Mother: have you no consideration for me? For Heaven's sake either treat me as a child, as you always do, and tell me nothing at all or tell me everything and let me take it as best I can.

LADY BRITOMART   Treat you as a child! What do you mean? It is most unkind and ungrateful of you to say such a thing. You know I have never treated any of you as children. I have always made you my companions and friends, and allowed you perfect freedom to do and say whatever you like, so long as you liked what I could approve of.

STEPHEN   (*desperately*)   I daresay we have been the very imperfect children of a very perfect mother; but I do beg you to let me

alone for once, and tell me about this horrible business of my
father wanting to set me aside for another son.

LADY BRITOMART (*amazed*)   Another son! I never said anything of
the kind. I never dreamt of such a thing. This is what comes of
interrupting me.

STEPHEN   But you said—

LADY BRITOMART (*cutting him short*)   Now be a good boy, Stephen,
and listen to me patiently. The Undershafts are descended from
a foundling in the parish of St Andrew Undershaft in the city.
That was long ago, in the reign of James the First. Well, this
foundling was adopted by an armorer and gun-maker. In the
course of time the foundling succeeded to the business; and from
some notion of gratitude, or some vow or something, he adopted
another foundling, and left the business to him. And that foundling did the same. Ever since that, the cannon business has always been left to an adopted foundling named Andrew Undershaft.

STEPHEN   But did they never marry? Were there no legitimate
sons?

LADY BRITOMART   Oh yes: they married just as your father did;
and they were rich enough to buy land for their own children
and leave them well provided for. But they always adopted and
trained some foundling to succeed them in the business; and of
course they always quarrelled with their wives furiously over it.
Your father was adopted in that way and he pretends to consider
himself bound to keep up the tradition and adopt somebody to
leave the business to. Of course I was not going to stand that.
There may have been some reason for it when the Undershafts
could only marry women in their own class, whose sons were not
fit to govern great estates. But there could be no excuse for passing over my son.

STEPHEN (*dubiously*)   I am afraid I should make a poor hand of
managing a cannon foundry.

LADY BRITOMART   Nonsense! you could easily get a manager and
pay him a salary.

STEPHEN   My father evidently had no great opinion of my capacity.

LADY BRITOMART   Stuff, child! you were only a baby: it had nothing to do with your capacity. Andrew did it on principle, just as
he did every perverse and wicked thing on principle. When my
father remonstrated, Andrew actually told him to his face that
history tells us of only two successful institutions: one the Undershaft firm, and the other the Roman Empire under the Antonines.

That was because the Antonine emperors all adopted their successors. Such rubbish! The Stevenages are as good as the Antonines, I hope: and you are a Stevenage. But that was Andrew all over. There you have the man! Always clever and unanswerable when he was defending nonsense and wickedness: always awkward and sullen when he had to behave sensibly and decently!

STEPHEN   Then it was on my account that your home life was broken up, mother. I am sorry.

LADY BRITOMART   Well, dear, there were other differences. I really cannot bear an immoral man. I am not a Pharisee, I hope; and I should not have minded his merely doing wrong things: we are none of us perfect. But your father didnt exactly do wrong things: he said them and thought them: that was what was so dreadful. He really had a sort of religion of wrongness. Just as one doesnt mind men practising immorality so long as they own that they are in the wrong by preaching morality; so I couldnt forgive Andrew for preaching immorality while he practised morality. You would all have grown up without principles, without any knowledge of right and wrong, if he had been in the house. You know, my dear, your father was a very attractive man in some ways. Children did not dislike him; and he took advantage of it to put the wickedest ideas into their heads, and make them quite unmanageable. I did not dislike him myself: very far from it; but nothing can bridge over moral disagreement.

STEPHEN   All this simply bewilders me, mother. People may differ about matters of opinion, or even about religion; but how can they differ about right and wrong? Right is right; and wrong is wrong; and if a man cannot distinguish them properly, he is either a fool or a rascal: thats all.

LADY BRITOMART (*touched*)   Thats my own boy (*she pats his cheek*)! Your father never could answer that: he used to laugh and get out of it under cover of some affectionate nonsense. And now that you understand the situation, what do you advise me to do?

STEPHEN   Well, what can you do?

LADY BRITOMART   I must get the money somehow.

STEPHEN   We cannot take money from him. I had rather go and live in some cheap place like Bedford Square or even Hampstead than take a farthing of his money.

LADY BRITOMART   But after all, Stephen, our present income comes from Andrew.

STEPHEN (*shocked*)   I never knew that.

LADY BRITOMART   Well, you surely didnt suppose your grandfather had anything to give me. The Stevenages could not do everything for you. We gave you social position. Andrew had to contribute something. He had a very good bargain, I think.

STEPHEN (*bitterly*) We are utterly dependent on him and his cannons, then?

LADY BRITOMART Certainly not: the money is settled. But he provided it. So you see it is not a question of taking money from him or not: it is simply a question of how much. I dont want any more for myself.

STEPHEN Nor do I.

LADY BRITOMART But Sarah does; and Barbara does. That is, Charles Lomax and Adolphus Cusins will cost them more. So I must put my pride in my pocket and ask for it, I suppose. That is your advice, Stephen, is it not?

STEPHEN No.

LADY BRITOMART (*sharply*) Stephen!

STEPHEN Of course if you are determined—

LADY BRITOMART I am not determined: I ask your advice; and I am waiting for it. I will not have all the responsibility thrown on my shoulders.

STEPHEN (*obstinately*) I would die sooner than ask him for another penny.

LADY BRITOMART (*resignedly*) You mean that *I* must ask him. Very well, Stephen: it shall be as you wish. You will be glad to know that your grandfather concurs. But he thinks I ought to ask Andrew to come here and see the girls. After all, he must have some natural affection for them.

STEPHEN Ask him here!!!

LADY BRITOMART Do not repeat my words, Stephen. Where else can I ask him?

STEPHEN I never expected you to ask him at all.

LADY BRITOMART Now dont tease, Stephen. Come! you see that it is necessary that he should pay us a visit, dont you?

STEPHEN (*reluctantly*) I suppose so, if the girls cannot do without his money.

LADY BRITOMART Thank you, Stephen: I knew you would give me the right advice when it was properly explained to you. I have asked your father to come this evening. (STEPHEN *bounds from his seat*.) Dont jump, Stephen: it fidgets me.

STEPHEN (*in utter consternation*) Do you mean to say that my father is coming here tonight—that he may be here at any moment?

LADY BRITOMART (*looking at her watch*) I said nine. (*He gasps. She rises.*) Ring the bell, please. (STEPHEN *goes to the smaller writing table; presses a button on it; and sits at it with his elbows on the table and his head in his hands, outwitted and over-whelmed.)* It is ten minutes to nine yet; and I have to prepare the girls. I asked Charles Lomax and Adolphus to dinner on purpose that they might be here. Andrew had better see them in case he should cherish any delusion as to their being capable of supporting their wives. *(The butler enters:* LADY BRITOMART *goes behind the settee to speak to him.)* Morrison: go up to the drawing room and tell everybody to come down here at once. *(*MORRISON *withdraws.* LADY BRITOMART *turns to* STEPHEN.*)* Now remember, Stephen: I shall need all your countenance and authority. *(He rises and tries to recover some vestige of these attributes.)* Give me a chair, dear. *(He pushes a chair forward from the wall to where she stands, near the smaller writing table. She sits down; and he goes to the armchair, into which he throws himself.)* I dont know how Barbara will take it. Ever since they made her a major in the Salvation Army she has developed a propensity to have her own way and order people about which quite cows me sometimes. It's not ladylike: I'm sure I dont know where she picked it up. Anyhow, Barbara shant bully me but still it's just as well that your father should be here before she has time to refuse to meet him or make a fuss. Dont look nervous, Stephen: it will only encourage Barbara to make difficulties. *I* am nervous enough, goodness knows; but I dont shew it.

SARAH *and* BARBARA *come in with their respective young men,* CHARLES LOMAX *and* ADOLPHUS CUSINS. SARAH *is slender, bored, and mundane.* BARBARA *is robuster, jollier, much more energetic.* SARAH *is fashionably dressed:* BARBARA *is in Salvation Army uniform.* LOMAX, *a young man about town, is like many other young men about town. He is afflicted with a frivolous sense of humor which plunges him at the most inopportune moments into paroxysms of imperfectly suppressed laughter.* CUSINS *is a spectacled student, slight, thin haired, and sweet voiced, with a more complex form of* LOMAX's *complaint. His sense of humor is intellectual and subtle, and is complicated by an appalling temper. The lifelong struggle of a benevolent temperament and a high conscience against impulses of inhuman ridicule and fierce impatience has set up a chronic strain which has visibly wrecked his constitution. He is a most implacable, determined, tenacious, intolerant person who by mere force of character presents himself as—and indeed actually is—considerate, gentle, explanatory, even mild and apologetic, capable possibly of murder, but not of cruelty or coarseness. By the operation of some instinct which is not merciful enough to blind him with the illusions of love, he is obstinately bent on marrying* BARBARA. LOMAX *likes* SARAH *and thinks it will be rather a lark to marry her. Consequently he has not attempted to resist* LADY BRITOMART's *arrangements to that end.*

All four look as if they had been having a good deal of fun in the drawing room. The girls enter first, leaving the swains outside. SARAH *comes to the settee.* BARBARA *comes in after her and stops at the door.*

BARBARA   Are Cholly and Dolly to come in?

LADY BRITOMART (*forcibly*)   Barbara: I will not have Charles called Cholly: the vulgarity of it positively makes me ill.

BARBARA   It's all right, mother: Cholly is quite correct nowadays. Are they to come in?

LADY BRITOMART   Yes, if they will behave themselves.

BARBARA (*through the door*)   Come in, Dolly; and behave yourself.

BARBARA *comes to her mother's writing table.* CUSINS *enters smiling, and wanders towards* LADY BRITOMART.

SARAH (*calling*)   Come in, Cholly. (LOMAX *enters, controlling his features very imperfectly, and places himself vaguely between* SARAH *and* BARBARA.)

LADY BRITOMART (*peremptorily*)   Sit down, all of you. (*They sit.* CUSINS *crosses to the window and seats himself there.* LOMAX *takes a chair.* BARBARA *sits at the writing table and* SARAH *on the settee.*) I dont in the least know what you are laughing at, Adolphus. I am surprised at you, though I expected nothing better from Charles Lomax.

CUSINS (*in a remarkably gentle voice*)   Barbara has been trying to teach me the West Ham Salvation March.

LADY BRITOMART   I see nothing to laugh at in that; nor should you if you are really converted.

CUSINS (*sweetly*)   You were not present. It was really funny, I believe.

LOMAX   Ripping.

LADY BRITOMART   Be quiet, Charles. Now listen to me, children. Your father is coming here this evening.

General stupefaction. LOMAX, SARAH, *and* BARBARA *rise:* SARAH *scared, and* BARBARA *amused and expectant.*

LOMAX (*remonstrating*)   Oh I say!

LADY BRITOMART   You are not called on to say anything, Charles.

SARAH   Are you serious, mother?

LADY BRITOMART   Of course I am serious. It is on your account, Sarah, and also on Charles's. (*Silence,* SARAH *sits, with a shrug.* CHARLES *looks painfully unworthy.*) I hope you are not going to object, Barbara.

BARBARA   I! why should I? My father has a soul to be saved like everybody else. He's quite welcome as far as I am concerned. (*She sits on the table, and softly whistles "Onward, Christian Soldiers".*)

LOMAX (*still remonstrant*)   But really, dont you know! Oh I say!

LADY BRITOMART (*frigidly*)   What do you wish to convey, Charles?

LOMAX   Well, you must admit that this is a bit thick.

LADY BRITOMART (*turning with ominous suavity to* CUSINS).   Adolphus: you are a professor of Greek. Can you translate Charles Lomax's remarks into reputable English for us?

CUSINS (*cautiously*)   If I may say so, Lady Brit, I think Charles has rather happily expressed what we feel. Homer, speaking of Autolycus, uses the same phrase. πυκινὸν δόμον ἐλθεῖν means a bit thick.

LOMAX (*handsomely*)   Not that I mind, you know, if Sarah dont. (*He sits.*)

LADY BRITOMART (*crushingly*)   Thank you. Have I your permission, Adolphus, to invite my own husband to my own house?

CUSINS (*gallantly*)   You have my unhesitating support in everything you do.

LADY BRITOMART   Tush! Sarah: have you nothing to say?

SARAH   Do you mean that he is coming regularly to live here?

LADY BRITOMART   Certainly not. The spare room is ready for him if he likes to stay for a day or two and see a little more of you; but there are limits.

SARAH   Well, he cant eat us, I suppose. *I* dont mind.

LOMAX (*chuckling*)   I wonder how the old man will take it.

LADY BRITOMART   Much as the old woman will, no doubt, Charles.

LOMAX (*abashed*)   I didnt mean—at least—

LADY BRITOMART   You didnt think, Charles. You never do; and the result is, you never mean anything. And now please attend to me, children. Your father will be quite a stranger to us.

LOMAX   I suppose he hasnt seen Sarah since she was a little kid.

LADY BRITOMART   Not since she was a little kid, Charles, as you express it with that elegance of diction and refinement of thought that seem never to desert you. Accordingly—er—(*impatiently*) Now I have forgotten what I was going to say. That comes of your provoking me to be sarcastic, Charles. Adolphus: will you kindly tell me where I was.

CUSINS (*sweetly*)   You were saying that as Mr Undershaft has not seen his children since they were babies, he will form his opinion of the way you have brought them up from their behavior tonight, and that therefore you wish us all to be particularly careful to conduct ourselves well, especially Charles.

LADY BRITOMART (*with emphatic approval*)   Precisely.

LOMAX   Look here, Dolly: Lady Brit didnt say that.

LADY BRITOMART (*vehemently*) I did, Charles. Adolphus's recollection is perfectly correct. It is most important that you should be good; and I do beg you for once not to pair off into opposite corners and giggle and whisper while I am speaking to your father.

BARBARA All right, mother. We'll do you credit. (*She comes off the table, and sits in her chair with ladylike elegance.*)

LADY BRITOMART Remember, Charles, that Sarah will want to feel proud of you instead of ashamed of you.

LOMAX Oh I say! theres nothing to be exactly proud of, dont you know.

LADY BRITOMART Well, try and look as if there was.

MORRISON, *pale and dismayed, breaks into the room in unconcealed disorder.*

MORRISON Might I speak a word to you, my lady?

LADY BRITOMART Nonsense! Shew him up.

MORRISON Yes, my lady. (*He goes.*)

LOMAX Does Morrison know who it is?

LADY BRITOMART Of course. Morrison has always been with us.

LOMAX It must be a regular corker for him, dont you know.

LADY BRITOMART Is this a moment to get on my nerves, Charles, with your outrageous expressions?

LOMAX But this is something out of the ordinary, really—

MORRISON (*at the door*) The—er—Mr Undershaft. (*He retreats in confusion.*)

ANDREW UNDERSHAFT *comes in. All rise.* LADY BRITOMART *meets him in the middle of the room behind the settee.*

ANDREW *is, on the surface, a stoutish, easygoing elderly man, with kindly patient manners, and an engaging simplicity of character. But he has a watchful, deliberate, waiting, listening face, and formidable reserves of power, both bodily and mental, in his capacious chest and long head. His gentleness is partly that of a strong man who has learnt by experience that his natural grip hurts ordinary people unless he handles them very carefully, and partly the mellowness of age and success. He is also a little shy in his present very delicate situation.*

LADY BRITOMART Good evening, Andrew.

UNDERSHAFT How d'ye do, my dear.

LADY BRITOMART You look a good deal older.

UNDERSHAFT (*apologetically*) I am somewhat older. (*Taking her hand with a touch of courtship.*) Time has stood still with you.

LADY BRITOMART (*throwing away his hand*) Rubbish! This is your family.

UNDERSHAFT (*surprised*) Is it so large? I am sorry to say my memory is failing very badly in some things. (*He offers his hand with paternal kindness to* LOMAX.)

LOMAX (*jerkily shaking his hand*)   Ahdedoo.

UNDERSHAFT   I can see you are my eldest. I am very glad to meet you again, my boy.

LOMAX (*remonstrating*)   No, but look here dont you know— (*Overcome.*) Oh I say!

LADY BRITOMART (*recovering from momentary speechlessness*)   Andrew: do you mean to say that you dont remember how many children you have?

UNDERSHAFT   Well, I am afraid I—. They have grown so much— er. Am I making any ridiculous mistake? I may as well confess: I recollect only one son. But so many things have happened since, of course—er—

LADY BRITOMART (*decisively*)   Andrew: you are talking nonsense. Of course you have only one son.

UNDERSHAFT   Perhaps you will be good enough to introduce me, my dear.

LADY BRITOMART   That is Charles Lomax, who is engaged to Sarah.

UNDERSHAFT   My dear sir, I beg your pardon.

LOMAX   Notatall. Delighted, I assure you.

LADY BRITOMART   This is Stephen.

UNDERSHAFT (*bowing*)   Happy to make your acquaintance, Mr Stephen. Then (*going to* CUSINS) you must be my son. (*Taking* CUSINS' *hands in his.*) How are you, my young friend? (*To* LADY BRITOMART.) He is very like you, my love.

CUSINS   You flatter me, Mr Undershaft. My name is Cusins: engaged to Barbara. (*Very explicitly.*) That is Major Barbara Undershaft, of the Salvation Army. This is Sarah, your second daughter. This is Stephen Undershaft, your son.

UNDERSHAFT   My dear Stephen, I beg your pardon.

STEPHEN   Not at all.

UNDERSHAFT   Mr. Cusins: I am much indebted to you for explaining so precisely. (*Turning to* SARAH.) Barbara, my dear—

SARAH (*prompting him*)   Sarah.

UNDERSHAFT   Sarah, of course. (*They shake hands. He goes over to* BARBARA.) Barbara—I am right this time, I hope?

BARBARA   Quite right. (*They shake hands.*)

LADY BRITOMART (*resuming command*)   Sit down, all of you. Sit down, Andrew. (*She comes forward and sits on the settee.* CUSINS *also brings his chair forward on her left.* BARBARA *and* STEPHEN *resume their seats.* LOMAX *gives his chair to* SARAH *and goes for another.*)

UNDERSHAFT   Thank you, my love.

LOMAX (*conversationally, as he brings a chair forward between the writing table and the settee, and offers it to* UNDERSHAFT) Takes you some time to find out exactly where you are, dont it?

UNDERSHAFT (*accepting the chair, but remaining standing*) That is not what embarrasses me, Mr Lomax. My difficulty is that if I play the part of a father, I shall produce the effect of an intrusive stranger; and if I play the part of a discreet stranger, I may appear a callous father.

LADY BRITOMART There is no need for you to play any part at all, Andrew. You had much better be sincere and natural.

UNDERSHAFT (*submissively*) Yes, my dear: I daresay that will be best. (*He sits down comfortably.*) Well, here I am. Now what can I do for you all?

LADY BRITOMART You need not do anything, Andrew. You are one of the family. You can sit with us and enjoy yourself.

A painfully conscious pause. BARBARA *makes a face at* LOMAX, *whose too long suppressed mirth immediately explodes in agonized neighings.*

LADY BRITOMART (*outraged*) Charles Lomax: if you can behave yourself, behave yourself. If not, leave the room.

LOMAX I'm awfully sorry, Lady Brit; but really you know, upon my soul! (*He sits on the settee between* LADY BRITOMART *and* UNDERSHAFT, *quite overcome.*)

BARBARA Why dont you laugh if you want to, Cholly? It's good for your inside.

LADY BRITOMART Barbara: you have had the education of a lady. Please let your father see that; and dont talk like a street girl.

UNDERSHAFT Never mind me, my dear. As you know, I am not a gentleman; and I was never educated.

LOMAX (*encouragingly*) Nobody'd know it, I assure you. You look all right, you know.

CUSINS Let me advise you to study Greek, Mr Undershaft. Greek scholars are privileged men. Few of them know Greek; and none of them know anything else; but their position is unchallengeable. Other languages are the qualifications of waiters and commercial travelers: Greek is to a man of position what the hallmark is to silver.

BARBARA Dolly: dont be insincere. Cholly: fetch your concertina and play something for us.

LOMAX (*jumps up eagerly, but checks himself to remark doubtfully to* UNDERSHAFT) Perhaps that sort of thing isnt in your line, eh?

UNDERSHAFT I am particularly fond of music.

LOMAX (*delighted*) Are you? Then I'll get it. (*He goes upstairs for the instrument.*)

UNDERSHAFT   Do you play, Barbara?

BARBARA   Only the tambourine. But Cholly's teaching me the concertina.

UNDERSHAFT   Is Cholly also a member of the Salvation Army?

BARBARA   No: he says it's bad form to be a dissenter. But I dont despair of Cholly. I made him come yesterday to a meeting at the dock gates, and take the collection in his hat.

UNDERSHAFT   (*looks whimsically at his wife*)!!

LADY BRITOMART   It is not my doing, Andrew. Barbara is old enough to take her own way. She has no father to advise her.

BARBARA   Oh yes she has. There are no orphans in the Salvation Army.

UNDERSHAFT   Your father there has a great many children and plenty of experience, eh?

BARBARA   (*looking at him with quick interest and nodding*)   Just so. How did you come to understand that? (LOMAX *is heard at the door trying the concertina.*)

LADY BRITOMART   Come in, Charles. Play us something at once.

LOMAX   Righto! (*He sits down in his former place, and preludes.*)

UNDERSHAFT   One moment, Mr Lomax. I am rather interested in the Salvation Army. Its motto might be my own: Blood and Fire.

LOMAX   (*shocked*)   But not your sort of blood and fire, you know.

UNDERSHAFT   My sort of blood cleanses: my sort of fire purifies.

BARBARA   So do ours. Come down tomorrow to my shelter—the West Ham shelter—and see what we're doing. We're going to march to a great meeting in the Assembly Hall at Mile End. Come and see the shelter and then march with us: it will do you a lot of good. Can you play anything?

UNDERSHAFT   In my youth I earned pennies, and even shillings occasionally, in the streets and in public house parlors by my natural talent for stepdancing. Later on, I became a member of the Undershaft orchestral society, and performed passably on the tenor trombone.

LOMAX   (*scandalized—putting down the concertina*)   Oh I say!

BARBARA   Many a sinner has played himself into heaven on the trombone, thanks to the Army.

LOMAX   (*to* BARBARA, *still rather shocked*)   Yes, but what about the cannon business, dont you know? (*To* UNDERSHAFT.) Getting into heaven is not exactly in your line, is it?

LADY BRITOMART   Charles!!!

LOMAX   Well; but it stands to reason, dont it? The cannon business may be necessary and all that: we cant get on without cannons; but it isnt right, you know. On the other hand, there may be a certain amount of tosh about the Salvation Army—I belong to the Established Church myself—but still you cant deny that it's religion; and you cant go against religion, can you? At least unless youre downright immoral, dont you know.

UNDERSHAFT You hardly appreciate my position, Mr Lomax—

LOMAX *(hastily)* I'm not saying anything against you personally—

UNDERSHAFT Quite so, quite so. But consider for a moment. Here I am, a profiteer in mutilation and murder. I find myself in a specially amiable humor just now because, this morning, down at the foundry, we blew twenty-seven dummy soldiers into fragments with a gun which formerly destroyed only thirteen.

LOMAX *(leniently)* Well, the more destructive war becomes, the sooner it will be abolished, eh?

UNDERSHAFT Not at all. The more destructive war becomes the more fascinating we find it. No, Mr Lomax: I am obliged to you for making the usual excuse for my trade; but I am not ashamed of it. I am not one of those men who keep their morals and their business in watertight compartments. All the spare money my trade rivals spend on hospitals, cathedrals, and other receptacles for conscience money, I devote to experiments and researches in improved methods of destroying life and property. I have always done so; and I always shall. Therefore your Christmas card moralities of peace on earth and goodwill among men are of no use to me. Your Christianity, which enjoins you to resist not evil, and to turn the other cheek, would make me a bankrupt. My morality—my religion—must have a place for cannons and torpedoes in it.

STEPHEN *(coldly—almost sullenly)* You speak as if there were half a dozen moralities and religions to choose from, instead of one true morality and one true religion.

UNDERSHAFT For me there is only one true morality; but it might not fit you, as you do not manufacture aerial battleships. There is only one true morality for every man; but every man has not the same true morality.

LOMAX *(overtaxed)* Would you mind saying that again? I didnt quite follow it.

CUSINS It's quite simple. As Euripides says, one man's meat is another man's poison morally as well as physically.

UNDERSHAFT Precisely.

LOMAX Oh, that! Yes, yes, yes. True. True.

STEPHEN In other words, some men are honest and some are scoundrels.

BARBARA Bosh! There are no scoundrels.

UNDERSHAFT Indeed? Are there any good men?

BARBARA   No. Not one. There are neither good men nor scoundrels: there are just children of one Father; and the sooner they stop calling one another names the better. You neednt talk to me: I know them. Ive had scores of them through my hands: scoundrels, criminals, infidels, philanthropists, missionaries, county councillors, all sorts. Theyre all just the same sort of sinner; and theres the same salvation ready for them all.

UNDERSHAFT   May I ask have you ever saved a maker of cannons?

BARBARA   No. Will you let me try?

UNDERSHAFT   Well, I will make a bargain with you. If I go to see you tomorrow in your Salvation Shelter, will you come the day after to see me in my cannon works?

BARBARA   Take care. It may end in your giving up the cannons for the sake of the Salvation Army.

UNDERSHAFT   Are you sure it will not end in your giving up the Salvation Army for the sake of the cannons?

BARBARA   I will take my chance of that.

UNDERSHAFT   And I will take my chance of the other. (*They shake hands on it.*) Where is your shelter?

BARBARA   In West Ham. At the sign of the cross. Ask anybody in Canning Town. Where are your works?

UNDERSHAFT   In Perivale St Andrews. At the sign of the sword. Ask anybody in Europe.

LOMAX   Hadnt I better play something?

BARBARA   Yes. Give us Onward, Christian Soldiers.

LOMAX   Well, thats rather a strong order to begin with, dont you know. Suppose I sing Thourt passing hence, my brother. It's much the same tune.

BARBARA   It's too melancholy. You get saved, Cholly; and youll pass hence, my brother, without making such a fuss about it.

LADY BRITOMART   Really, Barbara, you go on as if religion were a pleasant subject. Do have some sense of propriety.

UNDERSHAFT   I do not find it an unpleasant subject, my dear. It is the only one that capable people really care for.

LADY BRITOMART   (*looking at her watch*)   Well, if you are determined to have it, I insist on having it in a proper and respectable way. Charles: ring for prayers.

General amazement. STEPHEN *rises in dismay.*

LOMAX   (*rising*)   Oh I say!

UNDERSHAFT   (*rising*)   I am afraid I must be going.

LADY BRITOMART   You cannot go now, Andrew: it would be most improper. Sit down. What will the servants think?

UNDERSHAFT   My dear: I have conscientious scruples. May I suggest a compromise? If Barbara will conduct a little service in the drawing room, with Mr Lomax as organist, I will attend it willingly. I will even take part, if a trombone can be procured.

LADY BRITOMART   Dont mock, Andrew.

UNDERSHAFT   (*shocked—to* BARBARA)   You dont think I am mocking, my love, I hope.

BARBARA   No, of course not; and it wouldnt matter if you were: half the Army came to their first meeting for a lark. (*Rising.*) Come along. (*She throws her arm round her father and sweeps him out, calling to the others from the threshold.*) Come, Dolly. Come, Cholly.

LADY BRITOMART   I will not be disobeyed by everybody. Adolphus: sit down. (*He does not.*) Charles: you may go. You are not fit for prayers: you cannot keep your countenance.

LOMAX   Oh I say! (*He goes out.*)

LADY BRITOMART   (*continuing*)   But you, Adolphus, can behave yourself if you choose to. I insist on your staying.

CUSINS   My dear Lady Brit: there are things in the family prayer book that I couldnt bear to hear you say.

LADY BRITOMART   What things, pray?

CUSINS   Well, you would have to say before all the servants that we have done things we ought not to have done, and left undone things we ought to have done, and that there is no health in us. I cannot bear to hear you doing yourself such an injustice, and Barbara such an injustice. As for myself, I flatly deny it: I have done my best. I shouldnt dare to marry Barbara—I couldnt look you in the face—if it were true. So I must go to the drawing room.

LADY BRITOMART   (*offended*)   Well, go. (*He starts for the door.*) And remember this, Adolphus (*he turns to listen*): I have a very strong suspicion that you went to the Salvation Army to worship Barbara and nothing else. And I quite appreciate the very clever way in which you systematically humbug me. I have found you out. Take care Barbara doesnt. Thats all.

CUSINS   (*with unruffled sweetness*)   Dont tell on me. (*He steals out.*)

LADY BRITOMART   Sarah: if you want to go, go. Anything's better than to sit there as if you wished you were a thousand miles away.

SARAH   (*languidly*)   Very well, mamma. (*She goes.*)

LADY BRITOMART, *with a sudden flounce, gives way to a little gust of tears.*

STEPHEN   (*going to her*)   Mother: whats the matter?

LADY BRITOMART   (*swishing away her tears with her handkerchief*)

Nothing. Foolishness. You can go with him, too, if you like, and leave me with the servants.

STEPHEN   Oh, you mustnt think that, mother. I—I dont like him.

LADY BRITOMART   The others do. That is the injustice of a woman's lot. A woman has to bring up her children; and that means to restrain them, to deny them things they want, to set them tasks, to punish them when they do wrong, to do all the unpleasant things. And then the father, who has nothing to do but pet them and spoil them, comes in when all her work is done and steals their affection from her.

STEPHEN   He has not stolen our affection from you. It is only curiosity.

LADY BRITOMART   (*violently*)   I wont be consoled, Stephen. There is nothing the matter with me. (*She rises and goes towards the door.*)

STEPHEN   Where are you going, mother?

LADY BRITOMART   To the drawing room, of course. (*She goes out. Onward, Christian Soldiers, on the concertina, with tambourine accompaniment, is heard when the door opens.*) Are you coming, Stephen?

STEPHEN   No. Certainly not. (*She goes. He sits down on the settee, with compressed lips and an expression of strong dislike.*)

ACT II

The yard of the West Ham shelter of the Salvation Army is a cold place on a January morning. The building itself, an old warehouse, is newly whitewashed. Its gabled end projects into the yard in the middle, with a door on the ground floor, and another in the loft above it without any balcony or ladder, but with a pulley rigged over it for hoisting sacks. Those who come from this central gable end into the yard have the gateway leading to the street on their left, with a stone horse-trough just beyond it, and, on the right, a penthouse shielding a table from the weather. There are forms at the table; and on them are seated a man and a woman, both much down on their luck, finishing a meal of bread (one thick slice each, with margarine and golden syrup) and diluted milk.

The man, a workman out of employment, is young, agile, a talker, a poser, sharp enough to be capable of anything in reason except honesty or altruistic considerations of any kind. The woman is a commonplace old bundle of poverty and hard-worn humanity. She looks sixty and probably is forty-five. If they were rich people, gloved and muffed and well wrapped up in furs and overcoats, they would be numbed and miserable; for it is a grindingly cold raw January day; and a glance at the background of grimy warehouses and leaden sky visible over the whitewashed walls of the yard would drive any idle rich person straight to the Mediterranean. But these two, being no more troubled with visions of the Mediterranean than of the moon, and being compelled to keep more of their clothes in the pawnshop, and less on their persons, in winter than in summer, are not depressed by the cold: rather are they stung into vivacity, to which their meal has just now given an almost jolly turn. The man takes a pull at his mug, and then gets up and moves about the yard with his hands deep in his pockets, occasionally breaking into a stepdance.

THE WOMAN   Feel better arter your meal, sir?

THE MAN   No. Call that a meal! Good enough for you, praps, but wot is it to me, an intelligent workin man.

THE WOMAN   Workin man! Wot are you?

THE MAN   Painter.

THE WOMAN (*sceptically*)   Yus, I dessay.

THE MAN   Yus, you dessay! I know. Every loafer that cant do nothink calls isself a painter. Well, I'm a real painter: grainer, finisher, thirty-eight bob a week when I can get it.

THE WOMAN   Then why dont you go and get it?

THE MAN   I'll tell you why. Fust: I'm intelligent—fffff! it's rotten cold here (*he dances a step or two*)—yes: intelligent beyond the station o life into which it has pleased the capitalists to call me; and they dont like a man that sees through em. Second, an intelligent bein needs a doo share of appiness; so I drink somethink cruel when I get the chawnce. Third, I stand by my class and do as little as I can so's to leave arf the job for me fellow workers. Fourth, I'm fly enough to know wots inside the law and wots outside it; and inside it I do as the capitalists do: pinch wot I can lay me ands on. In a proper state of society I am sober, industrious and honest: in Rome, so to speak, I do as the Romans do. Wots the consequence? When trade is bad—and it's rotten bad just now—and the employers az to sack arf their men, they generally start on me.

THE WOMAN   Whats your name?

THE MAN   Price. Bronterre O'Brien Price. Usually called Snobby Price, for short.

THE WOMAN   Snobby's a carpenter, aint it? You said you was a painter.

PRICE   Not that kind of snob, but the genteel sort. I'm too uppish, owing to my intelligence, and my father being a Chartist and a reading, thinking man: a stationer, too. I'm none of your common hewers of wood and drawers of water; and dont you forget it. (*He returns to his seat at the table, and takes up his mug.*) Wots your name?

THE WOMAN   Rummy Mitchens, sir.

PRICE (*quaffing the remains of his milk to her*)   Your elth, Miss Mitchens.

RUMMY (*correcting him*)   Missis Mitchens.

PRICE   Wot! Oh Rummy, Rummy! Respectable married woman, Rummy, gittin rescued by the Salvation Army by pretendin to be a bad un. Same old game!

RUMMY   What am I to do? I cant starve. Them Salvation lasses is dear good girls; but the better you are, the worse they likes to think you were before they rescued you. Why shouldnt they av a bit o credit, poor loves? theyre worn to rags by their work. And where would they get the money to rescue us if we was to let on we're no worse than other people? You know what ladies and gentlemen are.

PRICE   Thievin swine! Wish I ad their job, Rummy, all the same. Wot does Rummy stand for? Pet name praps?

RUMMY   Short for Romola.

PRICE   For wot!?

RUMMY   Romola. It was out of a new book. Somebody me mother wanted me to grow up like.

PRICE   We're companions in misfortune, Rummy. Both on us got names that nobody cawnt pronounce. Consequently I'm Snobby and youre Rummy because Bill and Sally wasnt good enough for our parents. Such is life!

RUMMY   Who saved you, Mr Price? Was it Major Barbara?

PRICE   No: I come here on my own. I'm going to be Bronterre O'Brien Price, the converted painter. I know wot they like. I'll tell em how I blasphemed and gambled and wopped my poor old mother—

RUMMY (*shocked*)   Used you to beat your mother?

PRICE   Not likely. She used to beat me. No matter: you come and listen to the converted painter, and youll hear how she was a pious woman that taught me me prayers at er knee, an how I used to come home drunk and drag her out o bed be er snow white airs, an lam into er with the poker.

RUMMY   Thats whats so unfair to us women. Your confessions is just as big lies as ours: you dont tell what you really done no more than us; but you men can tell your lies right out at the meetins and be made much of for it, while the sort o confessions we az to make az to be whispered to one lady at a time. It aint right, spite of all their piety.

PRICE   Right! Do you spose the Army'd be allowed if it went and did right? Not much. It combs our air and makes us good little blokes to be robbed and put upon. But I'll play the game as good as any of em. I'll see somebody struck by lightnin, or hear a voice sayin "Snobby Price: where will you spend eternity?" I'll av a time of it, I tell you.

RUMMY You wont be let drink, though.

PRICE I'll take it out in gorspellin, then. I dont want to drink if I can get fun enough any other way.

JENNY HILL, *a pale, overwrought, pretty Salvation lass of 18, comes in through the yard gate, leading* PETER SHIRLEY, *a half hardened, half worn-out elderly man, weak with hunger.*

JENNY (*supporting him*) Come! pluck up. I'll get you something to eat. Youll be all right then.

PRICE (*rising and hurrying officiously to take the old man off* JENNY's *hands*) Poor old man! Cheer up, brother: youll find rest and peace and appiness ere. Hurry up with the food, miss: e's fair done. (*Jenny hurries into the shelter.*) Ere, buck up, daddy! she's fetchin y'a thick slice of breadn treacle, an a mug o skyblue. (*He seats him at the corner of the table.*)

RUMMY (*gaily*) Keep up your old art! Never say die!

SHIRLEY I'm not an old man. I'm only 46. I'm as good as ever I was. The grey patch come in my hair before I was thirty. All it wants is three pennorth o hair dye: am I to be turned on the streets to starve for it? Holy God! I've worked ten to twelve hours a day since I was thirteen, and paid my way all through; and now am I to be thrown into the gutter and my job given to a young man that can do it no better than me because Ive black hair that goes white at the first change?

PRICE (*cheerfully*) No good jawrin about it. Youre ony a jumped-up, jerked-off, orspittle-turned-out incurable of an ole workin man: who cares about you? Eh? Make the thievin swine give you a meal: theyve stole many a one from you. Get a bit o your own back. (JENNY *returns with the usual meal.*) There you are, brother. Awsk a blessin an tuck that into you.

SHIRLEY (*looking at it ravenously but not touching it, and crying like a child*) I never took anything before.

JENNY (*petting him*) Come, come! the Lord sends it to you: he wasn't above taking bread from his friends; and why should you be? Besides, when we find you a job you can pay us for it if you like.

SHIRLEY (*eagerly*) Yes, yes: thats true. I can pay you back: it's only a loan. (*Shivering.*) Oh Lord! oh Lord! (*He turns to the table and attacks the meal ravenously.*)

JENNY Well, Rummy, are you more comfortable now?

RUMMY God bless you, lovey! youve fed my body and saved my

soul, havent you? (JENNY, *touched, kisses her.*) Sit down and rest
a bit: you must be ready to drop.

JENNY   Ive been going hard since morning. But theres more work
than we can do. I mustnt stop.

RUMMY   Try a prayer for just two minutes. Youll work all the
better after.

JENNY (*her eyes lighting up*)   Oh isnt it wonderful how a few minutes prayer revives you! I was quite lightheaded at twelve o'clock,
I was so tired; but Major Barbara just sent me to pray for five
minutes; and I was able to go on as if I had only just begun.
(*To* PRICE.) Did you have a piece of bread?

PRICE (*with unction*)   Yes, miss; but Ive got the piece that I value
more; and thats the peace that passeth hall hannerstennin.

RUMMY (*fervently*)   Glory Hallelujah!

BILL WALKER, *a rough customer of about 25, appears at the yard gate
and looks malevolently at* JENNY.

JENNY   That makes me so happy. When you say that, I feel wicked
for loitering here. I must get to work again.

*She is hurrying to the shelter, when the new-comer moves quickly up to
the door and intercepts her. His manner is so threatening that she retreats
as he comes at her truculently, driving her down the yard.*

BILL   Aw knaow you. Youre the one that took awy maw girl. Youre
the one that set er agen me. Well, I'm gowin to ev er aht. Not
that Aw care a carse for er or you: see? Bat Aw'll let er knaow;
and Aw'll let you knaow. Aw'm gowing to give her a doin thatll
teach er to cat awy from me. Nah in wiv you and tell er to cam
aht afore Aw cam in and kick er aht. Tell er Bill Walker wants
er. She'll knaow wot thet means; and if she keeps me witin itll be
worse. You stop to jawr beck at me: and Aw'll stawt on you:
d'ye eah? Theres your wy. In you gow. (*He takes her by the arm
and slings her towards the door of the shelter. She falls on her
hand and knee.* RUMMY *helps her up again.*)

PRICE (*rising, and venturing irresolutely towards* BILL)   Easy there,
mate. She aint doin you no arm.

BILL   Oo are you callin mite? (*Standing over him threateningly.*)
Youre gowin to stend ap for er, aw yer? Put ap your ends.

RUMMY (*running indignantly to him to scold him*)   Oh, you great
brute—(*He instantly swings his left hand back against her face.
She screams and reels back to the trough, where she sits down,
covering her bruised face with her hands and rocking herself and
moaning with pain.*)

JENNY (*going to her*)   Oh, God forgive you! How could you strike an old woman like that?

BILL (*seizing her by the hair so violently that she also screams, and tearing her away from the old woman*)   You Gawd forgimme again an Aw'll Gawd forgive you one on the jawr thetll stop you pryin for a week. (*Holding her and turning fiercely on* PRICE.) Ev you ennything to sy agen it?

PRICE (*intimidated*)   No, matey: she aint anything to do with me.

BILL   Good job for you! Aw'd pat two meals into you and fawt you with one finger arter, you stawved cur. (*To* JENNY.) Nah are you gowin to fetch aht Mog Ebbijem; or em Aw to knock your fice off you and fetch her meself?

JENNY (*writhing in his grasp*)   Oh please someone go in and tell Major Barbara—(*she screams again as he wrenches her head down; and* PRICE *and* RUMMY *flee into the shelter*).

BILL   You want to gow in and tell your Mijor of me, do you?

JENNY   Oh please dont drag my hair. Let me go.

BILL   Do you or downt you? (*She stifles a scream.*) Yus or nao?

JENNY   God give me strength—

BILL (*striking her with his fist in the face*)   Gow an shaow her thet, and tell her if she wants one lawk it to cam and interfere with me. (JENNY, *crying with pain, goes into the shed. He goes to the form and addresses the old man.*) Eah: finish your mess; an git aht o mah wy.

SHIRLEY (*springing up and facing him fiercely, with the mug in his hand*)   You take a liberty with me, and I'll smash you over the face with the mug and cut your eye out. Aint you satisfied— young whelps like you—with takin the bread out o the mouths of your elders that have brought you up and slaved for you, but you must come shovin and cheekin and bullyin in here, where the bread o charity is sickenin in our stummicks?

BILL (*contemptuously, but backing a little*)   Wot good are you, you aold palsy mag? Wot good are you?

SHIRLEY   As good as you and better. I'll do a day's work agen you or any fat young soaker of your age. Go and take my job at Horrockses, where I worked for ten year. They want young men there: they cant afford to keep men over forty-five. They're very sorry—give you a character and happy to help you to get anything suited to your years—sure a steady man wont be long out of a job. Well, let em try you. Theyll find the differ. What do you know? Not as much as how to beeyave yourself—layin your dirty fist across the mouth of a respectable woman!

BILL   Downt provowk me to ly it acrost yours: d'ye eah?

SHIRLEY (*with blighting contempt*)   Yes: you like an old man to hit, dont you, when youve finished with the women. I ain't seen you hit a young one yet.

BILL (*stung*) You loy, you aold soupkitchener, you. There was a yang menn eah. Did Aw offer to itt him or did Aw not?

SHIRLEY Was he starvin or was he not? Was he a man or only a crossed-eyed thief an a loafer? Would you hit my son-in-law's brother?

BILL Oo's ee?

SHIRLEY Todger Fairmile o Balls Pond. Him that won £20 off the Japanese wrastler at the music hall by standin out 17 minutes 4 seconds agen him.

BILL (*sullenly*) Aw'm nao music awl wrastler. Ken he box?

SHIRLEY Yes: an you cant.

BILL Wot! Aw cawnt, cawnt Aw? Wots thet you sy (*threatening him*)?

SHIRLEY (*not budging an inch*) Will you box Todger Fairmile if I put him on to you? Say the word.

BILL (*subsiding with a slouch*) Aw'll stend ap to enny menn alawv, if he was ten Todger Fairmawls. But Aw dont set ap to be a perfeshnal.

SHIRLEY (*looking down on him with unfathomable disdain*) You box! Slap an old woman with the back o your hand! You hadnt even the sense to hit her where the magistrate couldnt see the mark of it, you silly young lump of conceit and ignorance. Hit a girl in the jaw and ony make her cry! If Todger Fairmile's done it, she wouldnt a got up inside o ten minutes, no more than you would if he got on to you. Yah! I'd set about you myself if I had a week's feedin in me instead o two months' starvation. (*He turns his back on him and sits down moodily at the table.*)

BILL (*following him and stooping over him to drive the taunt in*) You loy! youve the bread and treacle in you that you cam eah to beg.

SHIRLEY (*bursting into tears*) Oh God! it's true: I'm only an old pauper on the scrap heap. (*Furiously.*) But youll come to it yourself; and then youll know. Youll come to it sooner than a teetotaller like me, fillin yourself with gin at this hour o the mornin!

BILL Aw'm nao gin drinker, you oald lawr; but wen Aw want to give my girl a bloomin good awdin Aw lawk to ev a bit o devil in me: see? An eah Aw emm, talkin to a rotten aold blawter like you sted o givin her wot for. (*Working himself into a rage.*) Aw'm gowin in there to fetch her aht. (*He makes vengefully for the shelter door.*)

SHIRLEY Youre goin to the station on a stretcher, more likely; and theyll take the gin and the devil out of you there when they get you inside. You mind what youre about: the major here is the Earl o Stevenage's granddaughter.

BILL (*checked*)   Garn!

SHIRLEY   Youll see.

BILL (*his resolution oozing*)   Well, Aw aint dan nathin to er.

SHIRLEY   Spose she said you did! who'd believe you?

BILL (*very uneasy, skulking back to the corner of the penthouse*) Gawd! theres no jastice in this cantry. To think wot them people can do! Aw'm as good as er.

SHIRLEY   Tell her so. It's just what a fool like you would do.

BARBARA, *brisk and businesslike, comes from the shelter with a note book, and addresses herself to* SHIRLEY. BILL, *cowed, sits down in the corner on a form, and turns his back on them.*

BARBARA   Good morning.

SHIRLEY (*standing up and taking off his hat*)   Good morning, miss.

BARBARA   Sit down: make yourself at home. (*He hesitates; but she puts a friendly hand on his shoulder and makes him obey.*) Now then! since youve made friends with us, we want to know all about you. Names and addresses and trades.

SHIRLEY   Peter Shirley. Fitter. Chucked out two months ago because I was too old.

BARBARA (*not at all surprised*)   Youd pass still. Why didnt you dye your hair?

SHIRLEY   I did. Me age come out at a coroner's inquest on me daughter.

BARBARA   Steady?

SHIRLEY   Teetotaller. Never out of a job before. Good worker. And sent to the knackers like an old horse!

BARBARA   No matter: if you did your part God will do his.

SHIRLEY (*suddenly stubborn*)   My religion's no concern of anybody but myself.

BARBARA (*guessing*)   I know. Secularist?

SHIRLEY (*hotly*)   Did I offer to deny it?

BARBARA   Why should you? My own father's a Secularist, I think. Our Father—yours and mine—fulfils himself in many ways; and I daresay he knew what he was about when he made a Secularist of you. So buck up, Peter! we can always find a job for a steady man like you. (SHIRLEY, *disarmed and a little bewildered, touches his hat. She turns from him to* BILL.) Whats your name?

BILL (*insolently*)   Wots thet to you?

BARBARA (*calmly making a note*)   Afraid to give his name. Any trade?

BILL   Oo's afride to give is nime? (*Doggedly, with a sense of heroically defying the House of Lords in the person of Lord Stevenage.*) If you want to bring a chawge agen me, bring it. (*She waits, unruffled.*) Moy nime's Bill Walker.

BARBARA (*as if the name were familiar: trying to remember how*) Bill Walker? (*Recollecting.*) Oh, I know: youre the man that Jenny Hill was praying for inside just now. (*She enters his name in her note book.*)

BILL   Oo's Jenny Ill? And wot call as she to pry for me?

BARBARA   I dont know. Perhaps it was you that cut her lip.

BILL (*defiantly*)   Yus, it was me that cat her lip. Aw aint afride o you.

BARBARA   How could you be, since youre not afraid of God? Youre a brave man, Mr Walker. It takes some pluck to do our work here; but none of us dare lift our hand against a girl like that, for fear of her father in heaven.

BILL (*sullenly*)   I want nan o your kentin jawr. I spowse you think Aw cam eah to beg from you, like this demmiged lot eah. Not me. Aw downt want your bread and scripe and ketlep. Aw dont belive in your Gawd, no more than you do yourself.

BARBARA (*sunnily apologetic and ladylike, as on a new footing with him*). Oh, I beg your pardon for putting your name down, Mr Walker. I didn't understand. I'll strike it out.

BILL (*taking this as a slight, and deeply wounded by it*)   Eah! you let maw nime alown. Aint it good enaff to be in your book?

BARBARA (*considering*)   Well, you see, theres no use putting down your name unless I can do something for you, is there? Whats your trade?

BILL (*still smarting*)   Thets nao concern o yours.

BARBARA   Just so. (*Very businesslike.*) I'll put you down as (*writing*) the man who—struck—poor little Jenny Hill—in the mouth.

BILL (*rising threateningly*)   See eah. Awve ed enaff o this.

BARBARA (*quite sunny and fearless*)   What did you come to us for?

BILL   Aw cam for maw gel, see? Aw cam to tike her aht o this and to brike er jawr for er.

BARBARA (*complacently*)   You see I was right about your trade. (BILL, *on the point of retorting furiously, finds himself, to his great shame and terror, in danger of crying instead. He sits down again suddenly.*)   Whats her name?

BILL (*dogged*)   Er nime's Mog Ebbijem: thets wot her nime is.

BARBARA   Mog Habbijam! Oh, she's gone to Canning Town, to our barracks there.

BILL (*fortified by his resentment of* MOG'S *perfidy*)   Is she? (*Vindictively*). Then Aw'm gowin to Kennintahn arter her. (*He*

crosses to the gate; hesitates; finally comes back at BARBARA.) Are
you loyin to me to git shat o me?

BARBARA   I dont want to get shut of you. I want to keep you here
and save your soul. Youd better stay: youre going to have a bad
time today, Bill.

BILL   Oo's gowin to give it to me? You, preps?

BARBARA   Someone you dont believe in. But youll be glad afterwards.

BILL   (*slinking off*)   Aw'll gow to Kennintahn to be aht o reach o
your tangue. (*Suddenly turning on her with intense malice.*) And
if Aw downt fawnd Mog there, Aw'll cam beck and do two years
for you, selp me Gawd if Aw downt!

BARBARA   (*a shade kindlier, if possible*)   It's no use, Bill. She's got
another bloke.

BILL   Wot!

BARBARA   One of her own converts. He fell in love with her when
he saw her with her soul saved, and her face clean, and her hair
washed.

BILL   (*surprised*)   Wottud she wash it for, the carroty slat? It's red.

BARBARA   It's quite lovely now, because she wears a new look in her
eyes with it. It's a pity youre too late. The new bloke has put
your nose out of joint, Bill.

BILL   Aw'll put his nowse aht o joint for him. Not that Aw care a
carse for er, mawnd thet. But Aw'll teach her to drop me as if
Aw was dirt. And Aw'll teach him to meddle with maw Judy.
Wots iz bleedin nime?

BARBARA   Sergeant Todger Fairmile.

SHIRLEY   (*rising with grim joy*)   I'll go with him, miss. I want to
see them two meet. I'll take him to the infirmary when it's over.

BILL   (*to* SHIRLEY, *with undissembled misgiving*)   Is thet im you
was speakin on?

SHIRLEY   Thats him.

BILL   Im that wrastled in the music awl?

SHIRLEY   The competitions at the National Sportin Club was
worth nigh a hundred a year to him. He's gev em up now for
religion; so he's a bit fresh for want of the exercise he was accustomed to. He'll be glad to see you. Come along.

BILL   Wots is wight?

SHIRLEY   Thirteen four. (BILL'*s last hope expires.*)

BARBARA   Go and talk to him, Bill. He'll convert you.

SHIRLEY   He'll convert your head into a mashed potato.

BILL   (*sullenly*)   Aw aint afride of im. Aw aint afride of ennybody.
Bat e can lick me. She's dan me. (*He sits down moodily on the
edge of the horse trough.*)

SHIRLEY   You aint going. I thought not. (*He resumes his seat.*)

BARBARA   (*calling*)   Jenny!

JENNY   (*appearing at the shelter door with a plaster on the corner of her mouth*)   Yes, Major.

BARBARA   Send Rummy Mitchens out to clear away here.

JENNY   I think she's afraid.

BARBARA   (*her resemblance to her mother flashing out for a moment*)   Nonsense! she must do as she's told.

JENNY   (*calling into the shelter*)   Rummy: the Major says you must come.

JENNY *comes to* BARBARA, *purposely keeping on the side next* BILL, *lest he should suppose that she shrank from him or bore malice.*

BARBARA   Poor little Jenny! Are you tired? (*Looking at the wounded cheek.*) Does it hurt?

JENNY   No: it's all right now. It was nothing.

BARBARA   (*critically*)   It was as hard as he could hit, I expect. Poor Bill! You dont feel angry with him, do you?

JENNY   Oh no, no, no: indeed I dont, Major, bless his poor heart! (BARBARA *kisses her; and she runs away merrily into the shelter.* BILL *writhes with an agonizing return of his new and alarming symptoms, but says nothing.* RUMMY MITCHENS *comes from the shelter.*)

BARBARA   (*going to meet* RUMMY)   Now Rummy, bustle. Take in those mugs and plates to be washed; and throw the crumbs about for the birds.

RUMMY *takes the three plates and mugs; but* SHIRLEY *takes back his mug from her, as there is still some milk left in it.*

RUMMY   There aint any crumbs. This aint a time to waste good bread on birds.

PRICE   (*appearing at the shelter door*)   Gentleman come to see the shelter, Major. Says he's your father.

BARBARA   All right. Coming. (SNOBBY *goes back into the shelter, followed by* BARBARA.)

RUMMY   (*stealing across to* BILL *and addressing him in a subdued voice, but with intense conviction*)   I'd av the lor of you, you flat eared pignosed potwalloper, if she'd let me. Youre no gentleman, to hit a lady in the face. (BILL, *with greater things moving in him, takes no notice.*)

SHIRLEY   (*following her*)   Here! in with you and dont get yourself into more trouble by talking.

RUMMY (*with hauteur*)   I aint ad the pleasure o being hintroduced to you, as I can remember. (*She goes into the shelter with the plates.*)

SHIRLEY   Thats the—

BILL (*savagely*)   Downt you talk to me, d'ye eah? You lea me alown, or Aw'll do you a mischief. Aw'm not dirt under your feet, ennywy.

SHIRLEY (*calmly*)   Dont you be afeerd. You aint such prime company that you need expect to be sought after. (*He is about to go into the shelter when* BARBARA *comes out, with* UNDERSHAFT *on her right.*)

BARBARA   Oh, there you are, Mr Shirley! (*Between them.*) This is my father: I told you he was a Secularist, didn't I? Perhaps youll be able to comfort one another.

UNDERSHAFT (*startled*)   A Secularist! Not the least in the world: on the contrary, a confirmed mystic.

BARBARA   Sorry, I'm sure. By the way, papa, what is your religion? in case I have to introduce you again.

UNDERSHAFT   My religion? Well, my dear, I am a Millionaire. That is my religion.

BARBARA   Then I'm afraid you and Mr Shirley wont be able to comfort one another after all. Youre not a Millionaire, are you, Peter?

SHIRLEY   No; and proud of it.

UNDERSHAFT (*gravely*)   Poverty, my friend, is not a thing to be proud of.

SHIRLEY (*angrily*)   Who made your millions for you? Me and my like. Whats kep us poor? Keepin you rich. I wouldnt have your conscience, not for all your income.

UNDERSHAFT   I wouldnt have your income, not for all your conscience, Mr Shirley. (*He goes to the penthouse and sits down on a form.*)

BARBARA (*stopping* SHIRLEY *adroitly as he is about to retort*)   You wouldnt think he was my father, would you, Peter? Will you go into the shelter and lend the lasses a hand for a while: we're worked off our feet.

SHIRLEY (*bitterly*)   Yes: I'm in their debt for a meal, aint I?

BARBARA   Oh, not because youre in their debt, but for love of them, Peter, for love of them. (*He cannot understand, and is rather scandalized.*) There! dont stare at me. In with you; and give that conscience of yours a holiday (*bustling him into the shelter*).

SHIRLEY (*as he goes in*)   Ah! it's a pity you never was trained to use your reason, miss. Youd have been a very taking lecturer on Secularism.

BARBARA *turns to her father.*

UNDERSHAFT   Never mind me, my dear. Go about your work; and let me watch it for a while.

BARBARA   All right.

UNDERSHAFT   For instance, whats the matter with that outpatient over there?

BARBARA   (*looking at* BILL, *whose attitude has never changed, and whose expression of brooding wrath has deepened*)   Oh, we shall cure him in no time. Just watch. (*She goes over to* BILL *and waits. He glances up at her and casts his eyes down again, uneasy, but grimmer than ever.*) It would be nice to just stamp on Mog Habbijam's face, wouldnt it, Bill?

BILL   (*starting up from the trough in consternation*)   It's a loy: Aw never said so. (*She shakes her head.*) Oo taold you wot was in moy mawnd?

BARBARA   Only your new friend.

BILL   Wot new friend?

BARBARA   The devil, Bill. When he gets round people they get miserable, just like you.

BILL   (*with a heartbreaking attempt at devil-may-care cheerfulness*)   Aw aint miserable. (*He sits down again, and stretches his legs in an attempt to seem indifferent.*)

BARBARA   Well, if youre happy, why dont you look happy, as we do?

BILL   (*his legs curling back in spite of him*)   Aw'm eppy enaff, Aw tell you. Woy cawnt you lea me alown? Wot ev I dan to you? Aw aint smashed your fice, ev Aw?

BARBARA   (*softly: wooing his soul*)   It's not me thats getting at you, Bill.

BILL   Oo else is it?

BARBARA   Somebody that doesnt intend you to smash women's faces, I suppose. Somebody or something that wants to make a man of you.

BILL   (*blustering*)   Mike a menn o me! Aint Aw a menn? eh? Oo sez Aw'm not a menn?

BARBARA   Theres a man in you somewhere, I suppose. But why did he let you hit poor little Jenny Hill? That wasnt very manly of him, was it?

BILL   (*tormented*)   Ev dan wiv it, Aw tell you. Chack it. Aw'm sick o your Jenny Ill and er silly little fice.

BARBARA   Then why do you keep thinking about it? Why does it keep coming up against you in your mind? Youre not getting converted, are you?

BILL (*with conviction*)   Not ME. Not lawkly.

BARBARA   Thats right, Bill. Hold out against it. Put out your strength. Dont lets get you cheap. Todger Fairmile said he wrestled for three nights against his salvation harder than he ever wrestled with the Jap at the music hall. He gave in to the Jap when his arm was going to break. But he didnt give in to his salvation until his heart was going to break. Perhaps youll escape that. You havnt any heart, have you?

BILL   Wot d'ye mean? Woy aint Aw got a awt the sime as ennybody else?

BARBARA   A man with a heart wouldnt have bashed poor little Jenny's face, would he?

BILL (*almost crying*)   Ow, will you lea me alown? Ev Aw ever offered to meddle with you, that you cam neggin and provowkin me lawk this? (*He writhes convulsively from his eyes to his toes.*)

BARBARA (*with a steady soothing hand on his arm and a gentle voice that never lets him go*)   It's your soul thats hurting you, Bill, and not me. Weve been through it all ourselves. Come with us, Bill. (*He looks wildly round.*) To brave manhood on earth and eternal glory in heaven. (*He is on the point of breaking down.*) Come. (*A drum is heard in the shelter; and* BILL, *with a gasp, escapes from the spell as* BARBARA *turns quickly.* ADOLPHUS *enters from the shelter with a big drum.*) Oh! there you are, Dolly. Let me introduce a new friend of mine, Mr Bill Walker. This is my bloke, Bill: Mr Cusins. (CUSINS *salutes with his drumstick.*)

BILL   Gowin to merry im?

BARBARA   Yes.

BILL (*fervently*)   Gawd elp im! Gaw-aw-aw-awd elp im!

BARBARA   Why? Do you think he wont be happy with me?

BILL   Awve aony ed to stend it for a mawnin: e'll ev to stend it for a lawftawm.

CUSINS   That is a frightful reflection, Mr Walker. But I cant tear myself away from her.

BILL   Well, Aw ken. (*To* BARBARA.) Eah do you knaow where Aw'm gowin to, and wot Aw'm gowin to do?

BARBARA   Yes: youre going to heaven; and youre coming back here before the week's out to tell me so.

BILL   You loy. Aw'm gowin to Kennintahn, to spit in Todger Fairmawl's eye. Aw beshed Jenny Ill's fice; an nar Aw'll git me aown fice beshed and cam bec and shaow it to er. Ee'll itt me ardern Aw itt her. Thatll mike us square. (*To* ADOLPHUS.) Is thet fair or is it not? Youre a genlmn: you oughter knaow.

BARBARA   Two black eyes wont make one white one, Bill.

BILL   Aw didnt awst you. Cawnt you never keep your mahth shat?
Oy awst the genlmn.

CUSINS   (*reflectively*)   Yes: I think youre right, Mr Walker. Yes:
I should do it. It's curious: it's exactly what an ancient Greek
would have done.

BARBARA   But what good will it do?

CUSINS   Well, it will give Mr Fairmile some exercise; and it will
satisfy Mr Walker's soul.

BILL   Rot! there aint nao sach a thing as a saoul. Ah kin you tell
wevver Awve a saoul or not? You never seen it.

BARBARA   Ive seen it hurting you when you went against it.

BILL   (*with compressed aggravation*)   If you was maw gel and took
the word awt o me mahth lawk thet, Aw'd give you sathink youd
feel urtin, Aw would. (*To* ADOLPHUS.) You tike maw tip, mite.
Stop er jawr or youll doy afoah your tawm (*With intense expression.*) Wore aht: thets wot youll be: wore aht. (*He goes away
through the gate.*)

CUSINS   (*looking after him*)   I wonder!

BARBARA   Dolly! (*indignant, in her mother's manner*).

CUSINS   Yes, my dear, it's very wearing to be in love with you. If
it lasts, I quite think I shall die young.

BARBARA   Should you mind?

CUSINS   Not at all. (*He is suddenly softened, and kisses her over
the drum, evidently not for the first time, as people cannot kiss
over a big drum without practice.* UNDERSHAFT *coughs.*)

BARBARA   It's all right, papa, weve not forgotten you. Dolly: explain the place to papa: I havnt time. (*She goes busily into the
shelter.*)

UNDERSHAFT *and* ADOLPHUS *now have the yard to themselves.* UNDER-
SHAFT, *seated on a form, and still keenly attentive, looks hard at* ADOL-
PHUS. ADOLPHUS *looks hard at him.*

UNDERSHAFT   I fancy you guess something of what is in my mind,
Mr Cusins. (CUSINS *flourishes his drumsticks as if in the act of
beating a lively rataplan, but makes no sound.*) Exactly so. But
suppose Barbara finds you out!

CUSINS   You know, I do not admit that I am imposing on Barbara.
I am quite genuinely interested in the views of the Salvation
Army. The fact is, I am a sort of collector of religions; and the
curious thing is that I find I can believe them all. By the way, have
you any religion?

UNDERSHAFT   Yes.

CUSINS   Anything out of the common?

UNDERSHAFT   Only that there are two things necessary to Salvation.

CUSINS (*disappointed, but polite*)   Ah, the Church Catechism. Charles Lomax also belongs to the Established Church.

UNDERSHAFT   The two things are—

CUSINS   Baptism and—

UNDERSHAFT   No. Money and gunpowder.

CUSINS (*surprised, but interested*)   That is the general opinion of our governing classes. The novelty is in hearing any man confess it.

UNDERSHAFT   Just so.

CUSINS   Excuse me: is there any place in your religion for honor, justice, truth, love, mercy and so forth?

UNDERSHAFT   Yes: they are the graces and luxuries of a rich, strong, and safe life.

CUSINS   Suppose one is forced to choose between them and money or gunpowder?

UNDERSHAFT   Choose money and gunpowder; for without enough of both you cannot afford the others.

CUSINS   That is your religion?

UNDERSHAFT   Yes.

The cadence of this reply makes a full close in the conversation. CUSINS *twists his face dubiously and contemplates* UNDERSHAFT. UNDERSHAFT *contemplates him.*

CUSINS   Barbara wont stand that. You will have to choose between your religion and Barbara.

UNDERSHAFT   So will you, my friend. She will find out that that drum of yours is hollow.

CUSINS   Father Undershaft: you are mistaken: I am a sincere Salvationist. You do not understand the Salvation Army. It is the army of joy, of love, of courage: it has banished the fear and remorse and despair of the old hell-ridden evangelical sects: it marches to fight the devil with trumpet and drum, with music and dancing, with banner and palm, as becomes a sally from heaven by its happy garrison. It picks the waster out of the public house and makes a man of him: it finds a worm wriggling in a back kitchen, and lo! a woman! Men and woman of rank too, sons and daughters of the Highest. It takes the poor professor of Greek, the most artificial and self-suppressed of human creatures, from his meal of roots, and lets loose the rhapsodist in him; reveals the true worship of Dionysos to him; sends him down the public street drumming dithyrambs (*he plays a thundering flourish on the drum*).

UNDERSHAFT   You will alarm the shelter.

CUSINS   Oh, they are accustomed to these sudden ecstasies. However, if the drum worries you—(*he pockets the drumsticks; un-
hooks the drum and stands it on the ground opposite the gateway*).

UNDERSHAFT   Thank you.

CUSINS   You remember what Euripides says about your money and
gunpowder?

UNDERSHAFT   No.

CUSINS (*declaiming*)

>   One and another
> In money and guns may outpass his brother;
> And men in their millions float and flow
> And seethe with a million hopes as leaven;
> And they win their will; or they miss their will;
> And their hopes are dead or are pined for still;
>   But who'er can know
>   As the long days go
> That to live is happy, has found his heaven.

My translation: what do you think of it?

UNDERSHAFT   I think, my friend, that if you wish to know, as the
long days go, that to live is happy, you must first acquire money
enough for a decent life, and power enough to be your own master.

CUSINS   You are damnably discouraging. (*He resumes his declama-
tion.*)

>   Is it so hard a thing to see
>   That the spirit of God—whate'er it be—
> The law that abides and changes not, ages long,
> The Eternal and Nature-born: these things be strong?
> What else is Wisdom? What of Man's endeavor,
> Of God's high grace so lovely and so great?
> To stand from fear set free? to breathe and wait?
> To hold a hand uplifted over Fate?
> And shall not Barbara be loved for ever?

UNDERSHAFT   Euripides mentions Barbara, does he?

CUSINS   It is a fair translation. The word means Loveliness.

UNDERSHAFT   May I ask—as Barbara's father—how much a year
she is to be loved for ever on?

CUSINS   As for Barbara's father, that is more your affair than mine.
I can feed her by teaching Greek: that is about all.

UNDERSHAFT   Do you consider it a good match for her?

CUSINS (*with polite obstinacy*)   Mr Undershaft: I am in many ways a weak, timid, ineffectual person; and my health is far from satisfactory. But whenever I feel that I must have anything, I get it, sooner or later. I feel that way about Barbara. I dont like marriage: I feel intensely afraid of it; and I dont know what I shall do with Barbara or what she will do with me. But I feel that I and nobody else must marry her. Please regard that as settled.— Not that I wish to be arbitrary; but why should I waste your time in discussing what is inevitable?

UNDERSHAFT You mean that you will stick at nothing: not even the conversion of the Salvation Army to the worship of Dionysos.

CUSINS The business of the Salvation Army is to save, not to wrangle about the name of the pathfinder. Dionysos or another: what does it matter?

UNDERSHAFT (*rising and approaching him*) Professor Cusins: you are a young man after my own heart.

CUSINS Mr Undershaft: you are, as far as I am able to gather, a most infernal old rascal; but you appeal very strongly to my sense of ironic humor.

UNDERSHAFT *mutely offers his hand. They shake.*

UNDERSHAFT (*suddenly concentrating himself*) And now to business.

CUSINS Pardon me. We are discussing religion. Why go back to such an uninteresting and unimportant subject as business?

UNDERSHAFT Religion is our business at present, because it is through religion alone that we can win Barbara.

CUSINS Have you, too, fallen in love with Barbara?

UNDERSHAFT Yes, with a father's love.

CUSINS A father's love for a grown-up daughter is the most dangerous of all infatuations. I apologize for mentioning my own pale, coy, mistrustful fancy in the same breath with it.

UNDERSHAFT Keep to the point. We have to win her; and we are neither of us Methodists.

CUSINS That doesnt matter. The power Barbara wields here—the power that wields Barbara herself—is not Calvinism, not Presbyterianism, not Methodism—

UNDERSHAFT Not Greek Paganism either, eh?

CUSINS I admit that. Barbara is quite original in her religion.

UNDERSHAFT (*triumphantly*) Aha! Barbara Undershaft would be. Her inspiration comes from within herself.

CUSINS How do you suppose it got there?

UNDERSHAFT (*in towering excitement*) It is the Undershaft inheritance. I shall hand on my torch to my daughter. She shall make my converts and preach my gospel—

CUSINS What! Money and gunpowder!

UNDERSHAFT   Yes, money and gunpowder. Freedom and power. Command of life and command of death.

CUSINS   (*urbanely: trying to bring him down to earth*)   This is extremely interesting, Mr Undershaft. Of course you know that you are mad.

UNDERSHAFT   (*with redoubled force*)   And you?

CUSINS   Oh, mad as a hatter. You are welcome to my secret since I have discovered yours. But I am astonished. Can a madman make cannons?

UNDERSHAFT   Would anyone else than a madman make them? And now (*with surging energy*) question for question. Can a sane man translate Euripides?

CUSINS   No.

UNDERSHAFT   (*seizing him by the shoulder*)   Can a sane woman make a man of a waster or a woman of a worm?

CUSINS   (*reeling before the storm*)   Father Colossus—Mammoth Millionaire—

UNDERSHAFT   (*pressing him*)   Are there two mad people or three in this Salvation shelter today?

CUSINS   You mean Barbara is as mad as we are?

UNDERSHAFT   (*pushing him lightly off and resuming his equanimity suddenly and completely*)   Pooh, Professor! let us call things by their proper names. I am a millionaire; you are a poet: Barbara is a savior of souls. What have we three to do with the common mob of slaves and idolators? (*He sits down again with a shrug of contempt for the mob.*)

CUSINS   Take care! Barbara is in love with the common people. So am I. Have you never felt the romance of that love?

UNDERSHAFT   (*cold and sardonic*)   Have you ever been in love with Poverty, like St Francis? Have you ever been in love with Dirt, like St Simeon! Have you ever been in love with disease and suffering, like our nurses and philanthropists? Such passions are not virtues, but the most unnatural of all the vices. This love of the common people may please an earl's granddaughter and a university professor; but I have been a common man and a poor man; and it has no romance for me. Leave it to the poor to pretend that poverty is a blessing: leave it to the coward to make a religion of his cowardice by preaching humility: we know better than that. We three must stand together above the common people: how else can we help their children to climb up beside us? Barbara must belong to us, not to the Salvation Army.

CUSINS   Well, I can only say that if you think you will get her away from the Salvation Army by talking to her as you have been talking to me, you dont know Barbara.

UNDERSHAFT   My friend: I never ask for what I can buy.

CUSINS (*in a white fury*)   Do I understand you to imply that you can buy Barbara?

UNDERSHAFT   No; but I can buy the Salvation Army.

CUSINS   Quite impossible.

UNDERSHAFT   You shall see. All religious organizations exist by selling themselves to the rich.

CUSINS   Not the Army. That is the Church of the poor.

UNDERSHAFT   All the more reason for buying it.

CUSINS   I dont think you quite know what the Army does for the poor.

UNDERSHAFT   Oh yes I do. It draws their teeth: that is enough for me as a man of business.

CUSINS   Nonsense! It makes them sober—

UNDERSHAFT   I prefer sober workmen. The profits are larger.

CUSINS   —honest—

UNDERSHAFT   Honest workmen are the most economical.

CUSINS—attached to their homes—

UNDERSHAFT   So much the better: they will put up with anything sooner than change their shop.

CUSINS   —happy—

UNDERSHAFT   An invaluable safeguard against revolution.

CUSINS   —unselfish—

UNDERSHAFT   Indifferent to their own interests, which suits me exactly.

CUSINS   —with their thoughts on heavenly things—

UNDERSHAFT (*rising*)   And not on Trade Unionism nor Socialism. Excellent.

CUSINS (*revolted*)   You really are an infernal old rascal.

UNDERSHAFT (*indicating* PETER SHIRLEY, *who has just come from the shelter and strolled dejectedly down the yard between them*) And this is an honest man!

SHIRLEY   Yes; and what av I got by it? (*He passes on bitterly and sits on the form, in the corner of the penthouse.*)

SNOBBY PRICE, *beaming sanctimoniously, and* JENNY HILL, *with a tambourine full of coppers, come from the shelter and go to the drum, on which* JENNY *begins to count the money.*

UNDERSHAFT (*replying to* SHIRLEY)   Oh, your employers must have got a good deal by it from first to last. (*He sits on the table, with one foot on the side form,* CUSINS, *overwhelmed, sits down on the same form nearer the shelter.* BARBARA *comes from the shelter to the middle of the yard. She is excited and a little overwrought.*)

BARBARA Weve just had a splendid experience meeting at the other gate in Cripps's lane. Ive hardly ever seen them so much moved as they were by your confession, Mr Price.

PRICE I could almost be glad of my past wickedness if I could believe that it would elp to keep hathers stright.

BARBARA So it will, Snobby. How much, Jenny?

JENNY Four and tenpence, Major.

BARBARA Oh Snobby, if you had given your poor mother just one more kick, we should have got the whole five shillings!

PRICE If she heard you say that, miss, she'd be sorry I didnt. But I'm glad. Oh what a joy it will be to her when she hears I'm saved!

UNDERSHAFT Shall I contribute the odd twopence, Barbara? The millionaire's mite, eh? (*He takes a couple of pennies from his pocket.*)

BARBARA How did you make that twopence?

UNDERSHAFT As usual. By selling cannons, torpedoes, submarines, and my new patent Grand Duke hand grenade.

BARBARA Put it back in your pocket. You cant buy your salvation here for twopence: you must work it out.

UNDERSHAFT Is twopence not enough? I can afford a little more, if you press me.

BARBARA Two million millions would not be enough. There is bad blood on your hands; and nothing but good blood can cleanse them. Money is no use. Take it away. (*She turns to* CUSINS.) Dolly: you must write another letter for me to the papers. (*He makes a wry face.*) Yes: I know you dont like it; but it must be done. The starvation this winter is beating us: everybody is unemployed. The General says we must close this shelter if we cant get more money. I force the collections at the meetings until I am ashamed: dont I, Snobby?

PRICE It's a fair treat to see you work it, miss. The way you got them up from three-and-six to four-and-ten with that hymn, penny by penny and verse by verse, was a caution. Not a Cheap Jack on Mile End Waste could touch you at it.

BARBARA Yes; but I wish we could do without it. I am getting at last to think more of the collection than of the people's souls. And what are those hatfuls of pence and halfpence? We want thousands! tens of thousands! hundreds of thousands! I want to convert people, not to be always begging for the Army in a way I'd die sooner than beg for myself.

UNDERSHAFT (*in profound irony*) Genuine unselfishness is capable of anything, my dear.

BARBARA (*unsuspectingly, as she turns away to take the money from the drum and put it in a cash bag she carries*) Yes, isnt it? (UNDERSHAFT *looks sardonically at* CUSINS.)

CUSINS (*aside to* UNDERSHAFT) Mephistopheles! Machiavelli!

BARBARA (*tears coming into her eyes as she ties the bag and pockets it*) How are we to feed them? I cant talk religion to a man with bodily hunger in his eyes. (*Almost breaking down.*) It's frightful.

JENNY (*running to her*) Major, dear—

BARBARA (*rebounding*) No: dont comfort me. It will be all right. We shall get the money.

UNDERSHAFT How?

JENNY By praying for it, of course. Mrs Baines says she prayed for it last night; and she has never prayed for it in vain: never once. (*She goes to the gate and looks out into the street.*)

BARBARA (*who has dried her eyes and regained her composure*) By the way, dad, Mrs Baines has come to march with us to our big meeting this afternoon and she is very anxious to meet you, for some reason or other. Perhaps she'll convert you.

UNDERSHAFT I shall be delighted, my dear.

JENNY (*at the gate: excitedly*) Major! Major! here's that man back again.

BARBARA What man?

JENNY The man that hit me. Oh, I hope he's coming back to join us.

BILL WALKER, *with frost on his jacket, comes through the gate, his hands deep in his pockets and his chin sunk between his shoulders, like a cleaned-out gambler. He halts between* BARBARA *and the drum.*

BARBARA Hullo, Bill! Back already!

BILL (*nagging at her*) Bin talkin ever sence, ev you?

BARBARA Pretty nearly. Well, has Todger paid you out for poor Jenny's jaw?

BILL Nao e aint.

BARBARA I thought your jacket looked a bit snowy.

BILL Sao it is snaowy. You want to knaow where the snaow cam from, downt you?

BARBARA Yes.

BILL Well, it cam from orf the grahnd in Pawkinses Corner in Kennintahn. It got rabbed orf be maw shaoulders: see?

BARBARA Pity you didnt rub some off with your knees, Bill! That would have done you a lot of good.

BILL (*with sour mirthless humor*) Aw was sivin anather menn's knees at the tawm. E was kneelin on moy ed, e was.

JENNY Who was kneeling on your head?

BILL   Todger was. E was pryin for me: pryin camfortable wiv me
as a cawpet. Sow was Mog. Sao was the aol bloomin meeting.
Mog she sez "Ow Lawd brike is stabborn sperrit; bat downt urt is
dear art." Thet was wot she said. "Downt urt is dear art"! An er
blowk—thirteen stun four!—kneelin wiv all is wight on me.
Fanny, aint it?

JENNY   Oh no. We're so sorry, Mr Walker.

BARBARA   (*enjoying it frankly*)   Nonsense! of course it's funny.
Served you right, Bill! You must have done something to him
first.

BILL   (*doggedly*)   Aw did wot Aw said Aw'd do. Aw spit in is eye.
E looks ap at the skoy and sez, "Ow that Aw should be fahnd
worthy to be spit upon for the gospel's sike!" e sez; an Mog sez
"Glaory Allelloolier!"; and then e called me Braddher, an dahned
me as if Aw was a kid and he was me mather worshin me a
Setterda nawt. Aw ednt jast nao shaow wiv im at all. Arf the
street pryed; an the tather arf larfed fit to split theirselves. (*To*
BARBARA.) There are you settisfawd nah?

BARBARA   (*her eyes dancing*)   Wish I'd been there, Bill.

BILL   Yus: youd a got in a hextra bit o talk on me, wouldnt you?

JENNY   I'm so sorry, Mr Walker.

BILL   (*fiercely*)   Downt you gow being sorry for me: youve no call.
Listen eah. Aw browk your jawr.

JENNY   No, it didnt hurt me: indeed it didnt, except for a
moment. It was only that I was frightened.

BILL   Aw downt want to be forgive be you, or be ennybody. Wot
Aw did Aw'll py for. Aw trawd to gat me aown jawr browk to
settisfaw you—

JENNY   (*distressed*)   Oh no—

BILL   (*impatiently*)   Tell y' Aw did: cawnt you listen to wots being
taold you? All Aw got be it was being mide a sawt of in the pab-
lic street for me pines. Well, if Aw cawnt settisfaw you one wy,
Aw ken anather. Listen eah! Aw ed two quid sived agen the
frost; an Awve a pahnd of it left. A mite o mawn last week ed
words with the judy e's gowing to merry. E give er wot-for; an
e's bin fawned fifteen bob. E ed a rawt to itt er cause they was
gowin to be merrid; but Aw ednt nao rawt to itt you; sao put
anather fawv bob on an call it a pahnd's worth. (*He produces a
sovereign.*) Eahs the manney. Tike it, and lets ev no more o
your forgivin an prying and your Mijor jawrin me. Let wot Aw
dan be dan an pide for; and let there be a end of it.

JENNY   Oh, I couldn't take it, Mr Walker. But if you would give
a shilling or two to poor Rummy Mitchens! you really did hurt
her; and she's old.

BILL (*contemptuously*) Not lawkly. Aw'd give her anather as soon as look at er. Let her ev the lawr o me as she threatened! She aint forgiven me: not mach. Wot Aw dan to er is not on me mawnd—wot she (*indicating* BARBARA) mawt call on me conscience—no more than stickin a pig. It's this Christian gime o yours that Aw wownt ev plyed agen me: this bloomin forgivin an neggin an jawrin that mikes a menn thet sore that iz lawf's a burdn to im. Aw wownt ev it, Aw tell you; sao tike your manney and stop thraowin your silly beshed fice hap agen me.

JENNY Major: may I take a little of it for the Army?

BARBARA No: the Army is not to be bought. We want your soul, Bill; and we'll take nothing less.

BILL (*bitterly*) Aw knaow. Me an maw few shillins is not good enaff for you. Youre a earl's grendorter, you are. Nathink less than a andered pahnd for you.

UNDERSHAFT Come, Barbara! you could do a great deal of good with a hundred pounds. If you will set this gentleman's mind at ease by taking his pound, I will give the other ninety-nine.

BILL, *dazed by such opulence, instinctively touches his cap.*

BARBARA Oh, youre too extravagant, papa. Bill offers twenty pieces of silver. All you need offer is the other ten. That will make the standard price to buy anybody who's for sale. I'm not; and the Army's not. (*To* BILL.) Youll never have another quiet moment, Bill, until you come around to us. You cant stand out against your salvation.

BILL (*sullenly*) Aw cawnt stend aht agen music awl wrastlers and awtful tangued women. Awve offered to py. Aw can do no more. Tike it or leave it. There it is. (*He throws the sovereign on the drum, and sits down on the horse trough. The coin fascinates* SNOBBY PRICE, *who takes an early opportunity of dropping his cap on it.*)

MRS BAINES *comes from the shelter. She is dressed as a Salvation Army Commissioner. She is an earnest looking woman of about 40, with a caressing, urgent voice, and an appealing manner.*

BARBARA This is my father, Mrs Baines. (UNDERSHAFT *comes from the table, taking his hat off with marked civility.*) Try what you can do with him. He wont listen to me, because he remembers what a fool I was when I was a baby. (*She leaves them together and chats with* JENNY.)

MRS BAINES Have you been shewn over the shelter, Mr Undershaft? You know the work we're doing, of course.

UNDERSHAFT (*very civilly*) The whole nation knows it, Mrs Baines.

MRS BAINES   No, sir: the whole nation does not know it, or we should not be crippled as we are for want of money to carry our work through the length and breadth of the land. Let me tell you that there would have been rioting this winter in London but for us.

UNDERSHAFT   You really think so?

MRS BAINES   I know it. I remember 1886, when you rich gentlemen hardened your hearts against the cry of the poor. They broke the windows of your clubs in Pall Mall.

UNDERSHAFT   (*gleaming with approval of their method*)   And the Mansion House Fund went up next day from thirty thousand pounds to seventy-nine thousand! I remember quite well.

MRS BAINES   Well, wont you help me to get at the people? They wont break windows then. Come here, Price. Let me shew you to this gentleman (PRICE *comes to be inspected*). Do you remember the window breaking?

PRICE   My ole father thought it was the revolution, maam.

MRS BAINES   Would you break windows now?

PRICE   Oh no, maam. The windows of eaven av bin opened to me. I know now that the rich man is a sinner like myself.

RUMMY   (*appearing above at the loft door*)   Snobby Price!

SNOBBY   Wot is it?

RUMMY   Your mother's askin for you at the other gate in Cripps's Lane. She's heard about your confession (PRICE *turns pale.*)

MRS BAINES   Go, Mr Price; and pray with her.

JENNY   You can go through the shelter, Snobby.

PRICE   (*to* MRS BAINES)   I couldnt face her now, maam, with all the weight of my sins fresh on me. Tell her she'll find her son at ome, waitin for her in prayer. (*He skulks off through the gate, incidentally stealing the sovereign on his way out by picking up his cap from the drum.*)

MRS BAINES   (*with swimming eyes*)   You see how we take the anger and the bitterness against you out of their hearts, Mr Undershaft.

UNDERSHAFT   It is certainly most convenient and gratifying to all large employers of labor, Mrs Baines.

MRS BAINES   Barbara: Jenny: I have good news: most wonderful news. (JENNY *runs to her.*) My prayers have been answered. I told you they would, Jenny, didnt I?

JENNY   Yes, yes.

BARBARA   (*moving nearer to the drum*)   Have we got money enough to keep the shelter open?

MRS BAINES   I hope we shall have enough to keep all the shelters open. Lord Saxmundham has promised us five thousand pounds—

BARBARA   Hooray!

JENNY   Glory!

MRS BAINES —if—

BARBARA "If!" If what?

MRS BAINES —if five other gentlemen will give a thousand each to make it up to ten thousand.

BARBARA Who is Lord Saxmundham? I never heard of him.

UNDERSHAFT (*who has pricked up his ears at the peer's name, and is now watching* BARBARA *curiously*) A new creation, my dear. You have heard of Sir Horace Bodger?

BARBARA Bodger! Do you mean the distiller? Bodger's whisky!

UNDERSHAFT That is the man. He is one of the greatest of our public benefactors. He restored the cathedral at Hakington. They made him a baronet for that. He gave half a million to the funds of his party: they made him a baron for that.

SHIRLEY What will they give him for the five thousand?

UNDERSHAFT There is nothing left to give him. So the five thousand, I should think, is to save his soul.

MRS BAINES Heaven grant it may! Oh Mr Undershaft, you have some very rich friends. Cant you help us towards the other five thousand? We are going to hold a great meeting this afternoon at the Assembly Hall in the Mile End Road. If I could only announce that one gentleman had come forward to support Lord Saxmundham, others would follow. Dont you know somebody? couldnt you? wouldnt you? (*her eyes fill with tears*) oh, think of those poor people, Mr Undershaft: think of how much it means to them, and how little to a great man like you.

UNDERSHAFT (*sardonically gallant*) Mrs Baines: you are irresistible. I cant disappoint you; and I cant deny myself the satisfaction of making Bodger pay up. You shall have your five thousand pounds.

MRS BAINES Thank God!

UNDERSHAFT You dont thank me?

MRS BAINES Oh sir, dont try to be cynical: dont be ashamed of being a good man. The Lord will bless you abundantly; and our prayers will be like a strong fortification round you all the days of your life. (*With a touch of caution.*) You will let me have the cheque to shew at the meeting, wont you? Jenny: go in and fetch a pen and ink. (JENNY *runs to the shelter door.*)

UNDERSHAFT Do not disturb Miss Hill: I have a fountain pen. (JENNY *halts. He sits at the table and writes the cheque.* CUSINS *rises to make room for him. They all watch him silently.*)

BILL (*cynically, aside to* BARBARA, *his voice and accent horribly debased*) Wot prawce selvytion nah?

BARBARA Stop. (UNDERSHAFT *stops writing: they all turn to her in surprise.*) Mrs Baines: are you really going to take this money?

MRS BAINES (*astonished*) Why not, dear?

BARBARA   Why not! Do you know what my father is? Have you forgotten that Lord Saxmundham is Bodger the whisky man? Do
you remember how we implored the County Council to stop him
from writing Bodger's Whisky in letters of fire against the sky; so
that the poor drink-ruined creatures on the Embankment could
not wake up from their snatches of sleep without being reminded
of their deadly thirst by that wicked sky sign? Do you know that
the worst thing I have had to fight here is not the devil, but
Bodger, Bodger, Bodger, with his whisky, his distilleries, and his
tied houses? Are you going to make our shelter another tied house
for him, and ask me to keep it?

BILL   Rotten dranken whisky it is too.

MRS BAINES   Dear Barbara: Lord Saxmundham has a soul to be
saved like any of us. If heaven had found the way to make a good
use of his money, are we to set ourselves up against the answer
to our prayers?

BARBARA   I know he has a soul to be saved. Let him come down
here; and I'll do my best to help him to his salvation. But he
wants to send his cheque down to buy us, and go on being as
wicked as ever.

UNDERSHAFT   (*with a reasonableness which* CUSINS *alone perceives
to be ironical*)   My dear Barbara: alcohol is a very necessary
article. It heals the sick—

BARBARA   It does nothing of the sort.

UNDERSHAFT   Well, it assists the doctor: that is perhaps a less questionable way of putting it. It makes life bearable to millions of
people who could not endure their existence if they were quite
sober. It enables Parliament to do things at eleven at night that
no sane person would do at eleven in the morning. Is it Bodger's
fault that this inestimable gift is deplorably abused by less than
one per cent of the poor? (*He turns again to the table; signs the
cheque; and crosses it.*)

MRS BAINES   Barbara: will there be less drinking or more if all
those poor souls we are saving come tomorrow and find the doors
of our shelters shut in their faces? Lord Saxmundham gives us
the money to stop drinking—to take his own business from him.

CUSINS   (*impishly*)   Pure self-sacrifice on Bodger's part, clearly!
Bless dear Bodger! (BARBARA *almost breaks down as* ADOLPHUS,
too, fails her.)

UNDERSHAFT   (*tearing out the cheque and pocketing the book as he
rises and goes past* CUSINS *to* MRS BAINES)   I also, Mrs Baines,
may claim a little disinterestedness. Think of my business! think
of the widows and orphans! the men and lads torn to pieces with
shrapnel and poisoned with lyddite! (MRS BAINES *shrinks; but
he goes on remorselessly*) the oceans of blood, not one drop of

which is shed in a really just cause! the ravaged crops! the peaceful peasants forced, women and men, to till their fields under the fire of opposing armies on pain of starvation! the bad blood of the fierce little cowards at home who egg on others to fight for the gratification of their national vanity! All this makes money for me: I am never richer, never busier than when the papers are full of it. Well, it is your work to preach peace on earth and good will to men. (MRS BAINES'S *face lights up again.*) Every convert you make is a vote against war. (*Her lips move in prayer.*) Yet I give you this money to help you to hasten my own commercial ruin. (*He gives her the cheque.*)

CUSINS (*mounting the form in an ecstasy of mischief*)   The millennium will be inaugurated by the unselfishness of Undershaft and Bodger. Oh be joyful! (*He takes the drumsticks from his pocket and flourishes them.*)

MRS BAINES (*taking the cheque*)   The longer I live the more proof I see that there is an Infinite Goodness that turns everything to the work of salvation sooner or later. Who would have thought that any good could have come out of war and drink? And yet their profits are brought today to the feet of salvation to do its blessed work. (*She is affected to tears.*)

JENNY (*running to* MRS BAINES *and throwing her arms round her*)   Oh dear! how blessed, how glorious it all is!

CUSINS (*in a convulsion of irony*)   Let us seize this unspeakable moment. Let us march to the great meeting at once. Excuse me just an instant. (*He rushes into the shelter.* JENNY *takes her tambourine from the drum head.*)

MRS BAINES   Mr Undershaft: have you ever seen a thousand people fall on their knees with one impulse and pray? Come with us to the meeting. Barbara shall tell them that the Army is saved, and saved through you.

CUSINS (*returning impetuously from the shelter with a flag and a trombone, and coming between* MRS BAINES *and* UNDERSHAFT)   You shall carry the flag down the first street, Mrs Baines (*he gives her the flag*). Mr Undershaft is a gifted trombonist: he shall intone an Olympian diapason to the West Ham Salvation March. (*Aside to* UNDERSHAFT, *as he forces the trombone on him.*) Blow, Machiavelli, blow.

UNDERSHAFT (*aside to him, as he takes the trombone*)   The Trumpet in Zion! (CUSINS *rushes to the drum, which he takes up and puts on.* UNDERSHAFT *continues, aloud.*) I will do my best. I could vamp a bass if I knew the tune.

CUSINS   It is a wedding chorus from one of Donizetti's operas; but we have converted it. We convert everything to good here, includ-

ing Bodger. You remember the chorus. 'For thee immense rejoicing—immenso giubilo—immenso giubilo.' (*With drum obbligato.*)
Rum tum ti tum tum, tum tum ti ta—

BARBARA   Dolly: you are breaking my heart.

CUSINS   What is a broken heart more or less here? Dionysos Undershaft has descended. I am possessed.

MRS BAINES   Come, Barbara: I must have my dear Major to carry
the flag with me.

JENNY   Yes, yes, Major darling.

CUSINS   (*snatches the tambourine out of* JENNY's *hand and mutely
offers it to* BARBARA.)

BARBARA (*coming forward a little as she puts the offer behind her
with a shudder, whilst* CUSINS *recklessly tosses the tambourine
back to* JENNY *and goes to the gate*)   I cant come.

JENNY   Not come!

MRS BAINES (*with tears in her eyes*)   Barbara: do you think I am
wrong to take the money?

BARBARA (*impulsively going to her and kissing her*)   No, no: God
help you, dear, you must: you are saving the Army. Go; and may
you have a great meeting!

JENNY   But arnt you coming?

BARBARA   No. (*She begins taking off the silver S brooch from her
collar.*)

MRS BAINES   Barbara: what are you doing?

JENNY   Why are you taking your badge off? You cant be going
to leave us, Major.

BARBARA (*quietly*)   Father: come here.

UNDERSHAFT (*coming to her*)   My dear! (*Seeing that she is going
to pin the badge on his collar, he retreats to the penthouse in
some alarm.*)

BARBARA (*following him*)   Don't be frightened. (*She pins the badge
on and steps back towards the table, shewing him to the others.*)
There! It's not much for £5000, is it?

MRS BAINES   Barbara: if you wont come and pray with us, promise
me you will pray for us.

BARBARA   I cant pray now. Perhaps I shall never pray again.

MRS BAINES   Barbara!

JENNY   Major!

BARBARA (*almost delirious*)   I cant bear any more. Quick march!

CUSINS (*calling to the procession in the street outside*)   Off we go.
Play up, there! Immenso giubilo. (*He gives the time with his
drum; and the band strikes up the march, which rapidly becomes
more distant as the procession moves briskly away.*)

MRS BAINES   I must go, dear. Youre overworked: you will be all right tomorrow. We'll never lose you. Now Jenny: step out with the old flag. Blood and Fire! (*She marches out through the gate with her flag.*)

JENNY   Glory Hallelujah! (*Flourishing her tambourine and marching.*)

UNDERSHAFT (*to* CUSINS, *as he marches out past him easing the slide of his trombone*)   "My ducats and my daughter"!

CUSINS (*following him out*)   Money and gunpowder!

BARBARA   Drunkenness and Murder! My God: why hast thou forsaken me?

She sinks on the form with her face buried in her hands. The march passes away into silence. BILL WALKER *steals across to her.*

BILL (*taunting*)   Wot prawce selvytion nah?

SHIRLEY   Don't you hit her when she's down.

BILL   She it me wen aw wiz dahn. Waw shouldnt Aw git a bit o me aown beck?

BARBARA (*raising her head*)   I didnt take your money, Bill. (*She crosses the yard to the gate and turns her back on the two men to hide her face from them.*)

BILL (*sneering after her*)   Naow, it warnt enaff for you. (*Turning to the drum, he misses the money.*)   Ellow! If you aint took it sammun else ez. Weres it gorn? Bly me if Jenny Ill didnt tike it arter all!

RUMMY (*screaming at him from the loft*)   You lie, you dirty blackguard! Snobby Price pinched it off the drum when he took up his cap. I was up here all the time an see im do it.

BILL   Wot! Stowl may manney! Waw didnt you call thief on him, you silly aold macker you?

RUMMY   To serve you aht for ittin me acrost the fice. It's cost y'pahnd, that az. (*Raising a pæn of squalid triumph.*)   I done you. I'm even with you. Uve ad it aht o y—(BILL *snatches up* SHIRLEY's *mug and hurls it at her. She slams the loft door and vanishes. The mug smashes against the door and falls in fragments.*)

BILL (*beginning to chuckle*)   Tell us, aol menn, wot o'clock this mawnin was it wen im as they call Snobby Prawce was sived?

BARBARA (*turning to him more composedly, and with unspoiled sweetness*)   About half past twelve, Bill. And he pinched your pound at a quarter to two. *I* know. Well, you cant afford to lose it. I'll send it to you.

BILL (*his voice and accent suddenly improving*)   Not if Aw wiz to stawve for it. Aw aint to be bought.

SHIRLEY   Aint you? Youd sell yourself to the devil for a pint o beer; only there aint no devil to make the offer.

BILL (*unashamed*)   Sao Aw would, mite, and often ev, cheerful. But she cawnt baw me. (*Approaching* BARBARA.) You wanted maw soul, did you? Well, you aint got it.

BARBARA   I nearly got it, Bill. But weve sold it back to you for ten thousand pounds.

SHIRLEY   And dear at the money!

BARBARA   No, Peter: it was worth more than money.

BILL (*salvationproof*)   It's nao good: you cawnt get rahnd me nah. Aw downt blieve in it; and Awve seen tody that Aw was rawt. (*Going.*) Sao long, aol soupkitchener! Ta, ta, Mijor Earl's Grendorter! (*Turning at the gate.*) Wot prawce selvytion nah? Snobby Prawce! Ha! ha!

BARBARA (*offering her hand*)   Goodbye, Bill.

BILL (*taken aback, half plucks his cap off; then shoves it on again defiantly*)   Get aht. (BARBARA *drops her hand, discouraged. He has a twinge of remorse.*) But thets aw rawt, you knaow. Nathink pasnl. Naow mellice. Sao long, Judy. (*He goes.*)

BARBARA   No malice. So long, Bill.

SHIRLEY (*shaking his head*)   You make too much of him, miss, in your innocence.

BARBARA (*going to him*)   Peter: I'm like you now. Cleaned out, and lost my job.

SHIRLEY   Youve youth an hope. Thats two better than me.

BARBARA   I'll get you a job, Peter. Thats hope for you: the youth will have to be enough for me. (*She counts her money.*) I have just enough left for two teas at Lockharts, a Rowton doss for you, and my tram and bus home. (*He frowns and rises with offended pride. She takes his arm.*) Dont be proud, Peter: it's sharing between friends. And promise me youll talk to me and not let me cry. (*She draws him towards the gate.*)

SHIRLEY   Well, I'm not accustomed to talk to the like of you—

BARBARA (*urgently*)   Yes, yes: you must talk to me. Tell me about Tom Paine's books and Bradlaugh's lectures. Come along.

SHIRLEY   Ah, if you would only read Tom Paine in the proper spirit, miss! (*They go out through the gate together.*)

ACT III

Next day after lunch LADY BRITOMART *is writing in the library in Wilton Crescent.* SARAH *is reading in the armchair near the window.* BARBARA, *in ordinary fashionable dress, pale and brooding, is on the settee.* CHARLES

LOMAX *enters. He starts on seeing* BARBARA *fashionably attired and in low spirits.*

LOMAX   Youve left off your uniform!

BARBARA *says nothing; but an expression of pain passes over her face.*

LADY BRITOMART (*warning him in low tones to be careful*)   Charles!

LOMAX (*much concerned, coming behind the settee and bending sympathetically over* BARBARA)   I'm awfully sorry, Barbara. You know I helped you all I could with the concertina and so forth. (*Momentously.*) Still, I have never shut my eyes to the fact that there is a certain amount of tosh about the Salvation Army. Now the claims of the Church of England—

LADY BRITOMART   Thats enough, Charles. Speak of something suited to your mental capacity.

LOMAX   But surely the Church of England is suited to all our capacities.

BARBARA (*pressing his hand*)   Thank you for your sympathy, Cholly. Now go and spoon with Sarah.

LOMAX (*dragging a chair from the writing table and seating himself affectionately by* SARAH's *side*)   How is my ownest today?

SARAH   I wish you wouldnt tell Cholly to do things, Barbara. He always comes straight and does them. Cholly: we're going to the works this afternoon.

LOMAX   What works?

SARAH   The cannon works.

LOMAX   What? your governor's shop!

SARAH   Yes.

LOMAX   Oh I say!

CUSINS *enters in poor condition. He also starts visibly when he sees* BARBARA *without her uniform.*

BARBARA   I expected you this morning, Dolly. Didnt you guess that?

CUSINS (*sitting down beside her*)   I'm sorry. I have only just breakfasted.

SARAH   But weve just finished lunch.

BARBARA   Have you had one of your bad nights?

CUSINS   No: I had rather a good night: in fact, one of the most remarkable nights I have ever passed.

BARBARA   The meeting?

CUSINS   No: after the meeting.

LADY BRITOMART   You should have gone to bed after the meeting. What were you doing?

CUSINS   Drinking.

LADY BRITOMART ⎤ Adolphus!
SARAH   ⎥ Dolly!
BARBARA   ⎰ Dolly!
LOMAX   ⎦ Oh I say!

LADY BRITOMART   What were you drinking, may I ask?

CUSINS   A most devilish kind of Spanish burgundy, warranted free from added alcohol: a Temperance burgundy in fact. Its richness in natural alcohol made any addition superfluous.

BARBARA   Are you joking, Dolly?

CUSINS (*patiently*)   No. I have been making a night of it with the nominal head of this household: that is all.

LADY BRITOMART   Andrew made you drunk!

CUSINS   No: he only provided the wine. I think it was Dionysos who made me drunk. (*To* BARBARA.) I told you I was possessed.

LADY BRITOMART   Youre not sober yet. Go home to bed at once.

CUSINS   I have never before ventured to reproach you, Lady Brit; but how could you marry the Prince of Darkness?

LADY BRITOMART   It was much more excusable to marry him than to get drunk with him. That is a new accomplishment of Andrew's, by the way. He usent to drink.

CUSINS   He doesnt now. He only sat there and completed the wreck of my moral basis, the rout of my convictions, the purchase of my soul. He cares for you, Barbara. That is what makes him so dangerous to me.

BARBARA   That has nothing to do with it, Dolly. There are larger loves and diviner dreams than the fireside ones. You know that, dont you?

CUSINS   Yes: that is our understanding. I know it. I hold to it. Unless he can win me on that holier ground he may amuse me for a while; but he can get no deeper hold, strong as he is.

BARBARA   Keep to that; and the end will be right. Now tell me what happened at the meeting?

CUSINS   It was an amazing meeting. Mrs Baines almost died of emotion. Jenny Hill simply gibbered with hysteria. The Prince of Darkness played his trombone like a madman: its brazen roarings were like the laughter of the damned. 117 conversions took place then and there. They prayed with the most touching sincerity and gratitude for Bodger, and for the anonymous donor of the £5000. Your father would not let his name be given.

LOMAX   That was rather fine of the old man, you know. Most chaps would have wanted the advertisement.

CUSINS   He said all the charitable institutions would be down on him like kites on a battle-field if he gave his name.

LADY BRITOMART   Thats Andrew all over. He never does a proper thing without giving an improper reason for it.

CUSINS   He convinced me that I have all my life been doing improper things for proper reasons.

LADY BRITOMART   Adolphus: now that Barbara has left the Salvation Army, you had better leave it too. I will not have you playing that drum in the streets.

CUSINS   Your orders are already obeyed, Lady Brit.

BARBARA   Dolly: were you ever really in earnest about it? Would you have joined if you had never seen me?

CUSINS   (*disingenuously*)   Well—er—well, possibly, as a collector of religions—

LOMAX   (*cunningly*)   Not as a drummer, though, you know. You are a very clearheaded brainy chap, Dolly; and it must have been apparent to you that there is a certain amount of tosh about—

LADY BRITOMART   Charles: if you must drivel, drivel like a grown-up man and not like a schoolboy.

LOMAX   (*out of countenance*)   Well, drivel is drivel, dont you know, whatever a man's age.

LADY BRITOMART   In good society in England, Charles, men drivel at all ages by repeating silly formulas with an air of wisdom. Schoolboys make their own formulas out of slang, like you. When they reach your age, and get political private secretaryships and things of that sort, they drop slang and get their formulas out of the Spectator or The Times. You had better confine yourself to The Times. You will find that there is a certain amount of tosh about The Times; but at least its language is reputable.

LOMAX   (*overwhelmed*)   You are so awfully strong-minded, Lady Brit—

LADY BRITOMART   Rubbish! (MORRISON *comes in.*) What is it?

MORRISON   If you please, my lady, Mr Undershaft has just drove up to the door.

LADY BRITOMART   Well, let him in (MORRISON *hesitates.*) Whats the matter with you?

MORRISON   Shall I announce him, my lady; or is he at home here, so to speak, my lady?

LADY BRITOMART   Announce him.

MORRISON   Thank you, my lady. You wont mind my asking, I hope. The occasion is in a manner of speaking new to me.

LADY BRITOMART   Quite right. Go and let him in.

MORRISON   Thank you, my lady. (*He withdraws.*)

LADY BRITOMART   Children: go and get ready. (SARAH *and* BARBARA *go upstairs for their out-of-door wraps.*) Charles: go and tell Stephen to come down here in five minutes: you will find him in the drawing room. (CHARLES *goes.*) Adolphus: tell them to send round the carriage in about fifteen minutes. (ADOLPHUS *goes.*)

MORRISON (*at the door*)   Mr Undershaft.

UNDERSHAFT *comes in.* MORRISON *goes out.*

UNDERSHAFT   Alone! How fortunate!

LADY BRITOMART (*rising*)   Dont be sentimental, Andrew. Sit down. (*She sits on the settee: he sits beside her, on her left. She comes to the point before he has time to breath.*) Sarah must have £800 a year until Charles Lomax comes into his property. Barbara will need more, and need it permanently, because Adolphus hasnt any property.

UNDERSHAFT (*resignedly*)   Yes, my dear: I will see to it. Anything else? for yourself, for instance?

LADY BRITOMART   I want to talk to you about Stephen.

UNDERSHAFT (*rather wearily*)   Dont, my dear. Stephen doesnt interest me.

LADY BRITOMART   He does interest me. He is our son.

UNDERSHAFT   Do you really think so? He has induced us to bring him into the world; but he chose his parents very incongruously, I think. I see nothing of myself in him, and less of you.

LADY BRITOMART   Andrew: Stephen is an excellent son, and a most steady, capable, highminded young man. You are simply trying to find an excuse for disinheriting him.

UNDERSHAFT   My dear Biddy: the Undershaft tradition disinherits him. It would be dishonest of me to leave the cannon foundry to my son.

LADY BRITOMART   It would be most unnatural and improper of you to leave it to anyone else, Andrew. Do you suppose this wicked and immoral tradition can be kept up for ever? Do you pretend that Stephen could not carry on the foundry just as well as all the other sons of the big business houses?

UNDERSHAFT   Yes: he could learn the office routine without understanding the business, like all the other sons; and the firm would go by its own momentum until the real Undershaft—probably an Italian or a German—would invent a new method and cut him out.

LADY BRITOMART   There is nothing that any Italian or German could do that Stephen could not do. And Stephen at least has breeding.

UNDERSHAFT   The son of a foundling! Nonsense!

LADY BRITOMART   My son, Andrew! And even you may have good blood in your veins for all you know.

UNDERSHAFT   True. Probably I have. That is another argument in favour of a foundling.

LADY BRITOMART   Andrew: dont be aggravating. And dont be wicked. At present you are both.

UNDERSHAFT   This conversation is part of the Undershaft tradition, Biddy. Every Undershaft's wife has treated him to it ever since the house was founded. It is mere waste of breath. If the tradition be ever broken it will be for an abler man than Stephen.

LADY BRITOMART (*pouting*)   Then go away.

UNDERSHAFT (*deprecatory*)   Go away!

LADY BRITOMART   Yes: go away. If you will do nothing for Stephen, you are not wanted here. Go to your foundling, whoever he is; and look after him.

UNDERSHAFT   The fact is, Biddy—

LADY BRITOMART   Dont call me Biddy. I dont call you Andy.

UNDERSHAFT   I will not call my wife Britomart: it is not good sense. Seriously, my love, the Undershaft tradition has landed me in a difficulty. I am getting on in years; and my partner Lazarus has at last made a stand and insisted that the succession must be settled one way or the other; and of course he is quite right. You see, I havent found a fit successor yet.

LADY BRITOMART (*obstinately*)   There is Stephen.

UNDERSHAFT   Thats just it: all the foundlings I can find are exactly like Stephen.

LADY BRITOMART   Andrew!!

UNDERSHAFT   I want a man with no relations and no schooling: that is, a man who would be out of the running altogether if he were not a strong man. And I cant find him. Every blessed foundling nowadays is snapped up in his infancy by Barnardo homes, or School Board officers, or Boards of Guardians; and if he shews the least ability he is fastened on by schoolmasters; trained to win scholarships like a racehorse; crammed with secondhand ideas; drilled and disciplined in docility and what they call good taste; and lamed for life so that he is fit for nothing but teaching. If you want to keep the foundry in the family, you had better find an eligible foundling and marry him to Barbara.

LADY BRITOMART   Ah! Barbara! Your Pet! You would sacrifice Stephen to Barbara.

UNDERSHAFT   Cheerfully. And you, my dear, would boil Barbara to make soup for Stephen.

LADY BRITOMART   Andrew: this is not a question of our likings and dislikings: it is a question of duty. It is your duty to make Stephen your successor.

UNDERSHAFT   Just as much as it is your duty to submit to your husband. Come, Biddy! these tricks of the governing class are of no use with me. I am one of the governing class myself; and it is waste of time giving tracts to a missionary. I have the power in this matter; and I am not to be hum-bugged into using it for your purposes.

LADY BRITOMART   Andrew: you can talk my head off; but you cant change wrong into right. And your tie is all on one side. Put it straight.

UNDERSHAFT (*disconcerted*)   It won't stay unless it's pinned (*he fumbles at it with childish grimaces*)—

STEPHEN *comes in.*

STEPHEN (*at the door*)   I beg your pardon (*about to retire*).

LADY BRITOMART   No: come in, Stephen. (*Stephen comes forward to his mother's writing table.*)

UNDERSHAFT (*not very cordially*)   Good afternoon.

STEPHEN (*Coldly*)   Good afternoon.

UNDERSHAFT (*to* LADY BRITOMART)   He knows all about the tradition, I suppose?

LADY BRITOMART   Yes. (*To* STEPHEN.)   It is what I told you last night, Stephen.

UNDERSHAFT (*sulkily*)   I understand you want to come into the cannon business.

STEPHEN   *I* go into trade! Certainly not.

UNDERSHAFT (*opening his eyes, greatly eased in mind and manner*)   Oh! in that case—

LADY BRITOMART   Cannons are not trade, Stephen. They are enterprise.

STEPHEN   I have no intention of becoming a man of business in any sense. I have no capacity for business and no taste for it. I intend to devote myself to politics.

UNDERSHAFT (*rising*)   My dear boy: this is an immense relief to me. And I trust it may prove an equally good thing for the country. I was afraid you would consider yourself disparaged and slighted. (*He moves towards* STEPHEN *as if to shake hands with him.*)

LADY BRITOMART (*rising and interposing*)   Stephen: I cannot allow you to throw away an enormous property like this.

STEPHEN (*stiffly*)   Mother: there must be an end of treating me as a child, if you please. (LADY BRITOMART *recoils, deeply wounded by his tone.*) Until last night I did not take your attitude seriously, because I did not think you meant it seriously. But I find now that you left me in the dark as to matters which you should have explained to me years ago. I am extremely hurt and offended. Any further discussion of my intentions had better take place with my father, as between one man and another.

LADY BRITOMART   Stephen! (*She sits down again, her eyes filling with tears.*)

UNDERSHAFT (*with grave compassion*)   You see, my dear, it is only the big men who can be treated as children.

STEPHEN   I am sorry, mother, that you have forced me—

UNDERSHAFT (*stopping him*)   Yes, yes, yes, yes: thats all right, Stephen. She wont interfere with you any more: your independence is achieved: you have won your latchkey. Dont rub it in; and above all, dont apologize. (*He resumes his seat.*) Now what about your future, as between one man and another—I beg your pardon, Biddy: as between two men and a woman.

LADY BRITOMART (*who has pulled herself together strongly*)   I quite understand, Stephen. By all means go your own way if you feel strong enough. (STEPHEN *sits down magisterially in the chair at the writing table with an air of affirming his majority.*)

UNDERSHAFT   It is settled that you do not ask for the succession to the cannon business.

STEPHEN   I hope it is settled that I repudiate the cannon business.

UNDERSHAFT   Come, come! dont be so devilishly sulky: it's boyish. Freedom should be generous. Besides, I owe you a fair start in life in exchange for disinheriting you. You cant become prime minister all at once. Havent you a turn for something? What about literature, art, and so forth?

STEPHEN   I have nothing of the artist about me, either in faculty or character, thank Heaven!

UNDERSHAFT   A philosopher, perhaps? Eh?

STEPHEN   I make no such ridiculous pretension.

UNDERSHAFT   Just so. Well, there is the army, the navy, the Church, the Bar. The Bar requires some ability. What about the Bar?

STEPHEN   I have not studied law. And I am afraid I have not the necessary push—I believe that is the name barristers give to their vulgarity—for success in pleading.

UNDERSHAFT   Rather a difficult case, Stephen. Hardly anything left but the stage, is there? (STEPHEN *makes an impatient movement.*) Well, come! is there anything you know or care for?

STEPHEN (*rising and looking at him steadily*)   I know the difference between right and wrong.

UNDERSHAFT (*hugely tickled*)   You dont say so! What! no capacity for business, no knowledge of law, no sympathy with art, no pretension to philosophy; only a simple knowledge of the secret that has puzzled all the philosophers, baffled all the lawyers, muddled all the men of business, and ruined most of the artists: the secret of right and wrong. Why, man, youre a genius, a master of masters, a god! At twenty-four, too!

STEPHEN (*keeping his temper with difficulty*)   You are pleased to be facetious. I pretend to nothing more than any honorable English gentleman claims as his birthright (*he sits down angrily*).

UNDERSHAFT   Oh, thats everybody's birthright. Look at poor little Jenny Hill, the Salvation lassie! she would think you were laughing at her if you asked her to stand up in the street and teach grammar or geography or mathematics or even drawing room dancing; but it never occurs to her to doubt that she can teach morals and religion. You are all alike, you respectable people. You cant tell me the bursting strain of a ten-inch gun, which is a very simple matter; but you all think you can tell me the bursting strain of a man under temptation. You darent handle high explosives; but youre all ready to handle honesty and truth and justice and the whole duty of man, and kill one another at that game. What a country! What a world!

LADY BRITOMART (*uneasily*)   What do you think he had better do, Andrew?

UNDERSHAFT   Oh, just what he wants to do. He knows nothing and he thinks he knows everything. That points clearly to a political career. Get him a private secretaryship to someone who can get him an Under Secretaryship; and then leave him alone. He will find his natural and proper place in the end on the Treasury Bench.

STEPHEN (*springing up again*)   I am sorry, sir, that you force me to forget the respect due to you as my father. I am an Englishman and I will not hear the Government of my country insulted. (*He thrusts his hands in his pockets, and walks angrily across to the window.*)

UNDERSHAFT (*with a touch of brutality*)   The government of your country! *I* am the government of your country: I, and Lazarus. Do you suppose that you and half a dozen amateurs like you, sitting in a row in that foolish gabble shop, can govern Undershaft and Lazarus? No, my friend: you will do what pays us. You will make war when it suits us, and keep peace when it doesnt. You will find out that trade requires certain measures when we have decided on those measures. When I want anything to keep my dividends up, you will discover that my want is a national need. When other people want something to keep my dividends down, you will call out the police and military. And in return you shall have the support and applause of my newspapers, and the delight of imagining that you are a great statesman. Government of your country! Be off with you, my boy, and play with your caucuses and leading articles and historic parties and great leaders and burning questions and the rest of your toys. *I* am going back to my counting-house to pay the piper and call the tune.

STEPHEN (*actually smiling, and putting his hand on his father's shoulder with indulgent patronage*) Really, my dear father, it is impossible to be angry with you. You dont know how absurd all this sounds to me. You are very properly proud of having been industrious enough to make money; and it is greatly to your credit that you have made so much of it. But it has kept you in circles where you are valued for your money and deferred to for it, instead of in the doubtless very old-fashioned and behind-the-times public school and university where I formed my habits of mind. It is natural for you to think that money governs England; but you must allow me to think I know better.

UNDERSHAFT   And what does govern England, pray?

STEPHEN   Character, father, character.

UNDERSHAFT   Whose character? Yours or mine?

STEPHEN   Neither yours nor mine, father, but the best elements in the English national character.

UNDERSHAFT   Stephen: Ive found your profession for you. Youre a born journalist. I'll start you with a high-toned weekly review. There!

Before STEPHEN *can reply* SARAH, BARBARA, LOMAX, *and* CUSINS *come in ready for walking.* BARBARA *crosses the room to the window and looks out.* CUSINS *drifts amiably to the armchair.* LOMAX *remains near the door, whilst* SARAH *comes to her mother.*

STEPHEN *goes to the smaller writing table and busies himself with his letters.*

SARAH   Go and get ready, mamma: the carriage is waiting. (LADY BRITOMART *leaves the room.*)

UNDERSHAFT (*to* SARAH)   Good day, my dear. Good afternoon, Mr Lomax.

LOMAX (*vaguely*)   Ahdedoo.

UNDERSHAFT (*to* CUSINS)   Quite well after last night, Euripides, eh?

CUSINS   As well as can be expected.

UNDERSHAFT   Thats right. (*To* BARBARA.)   So you are coming to see my death and devastation factory, Barbara?

BARBARA (*at the window*)   You came yesterday to see my salvation factory. I promised you a return visit.

LOMAX (*coming forward between* SARAH *and* UNDERSHAFT)   Youll find it awfully interesting. Ive been through the Woolwich Arsenal and it gives you a ripping feeling of security, you know, to think of the lot of beggars we could kill if it came to fighting. (*To* UNDERSHAFT, *with sudden solemnity.*) Still, it must be rather an awful reflection for you, from the religious point of view as it were. Youre getting on, you know, and all that.

SARAH   You dont mind Cholly's imbecility, papa, do you?

LOMAX (*much taken aback*)   Oh I say!

UNDERSHAFT   Mr Lomax looks at the matter in a very proper spirit, my dear.

LOMAX   Just so. Thats all I meant, I assure you.

SARAH   Are you coming, Stephen?

STEPHEN   Well, I am rather busy—er—(*Magnanimously.*)   Oh well, yes: I'll come. That is, if there is room for me.

UNDERSHAFT   I can take two with me in a little motor I am experimenting with for field use. You wont mind its being rather unfashionable. It's not painted yet; but it's bullet proof.

LOMAX (*appalled at the prospect of confronting Wilton Crescent in an unpainted motor*)   Oh I say!

SARAH   The carriage for me, thank you. Barbara doesnt mind what she's seen in.

LOMAX   I say, Dolly, old chap: do you really mind the car being a guy? Because of course if you do I'll go in it. Still—

CUSINS   I prefer it.

LOMAX   Thanks awfully, old man. Come, my ownest. (*He hurries out to secure his seat in the carriage.* SARAH *follows him.*)

CUSINS (*moodily walking across to* LADY BRITOMART's *writing table*)   Why are we two coming to this Works Department of Hell? that is what I ask myself.

BARBARA   I have always thought of it as a sort of pit where lost creatures with blackened faces stirred up smoky fires and were driven and tormented by my father. Is it like that, dad?

UNDERSHAFT (*scandalized*)   My dear! It is a spotlessly clean and beautiful hillside town.

CUSINS   With a Methodist chapel? Oh do say theres a Methodist chapel.

UNDERSHAFT   There are two: a Primitive one and a sophisticated one. There is even an Ethical Society; but it is not much patronized, as my men are all strongly religious. In the High Explosives Sheds they object to the presence of Agnostics as unsafe.

CUSINS   And yet they dont object to you!

BARBARA   Do they obey all your orders?

UNDERSHAFT   I never give them any orders. When I speak to one of them it is "Well, Jones, is the baby doing well? and has Mrs

Jones made a good recovery?" "Nicely, thank you, sir." And thats all.

CUSINS But Jones has to be kept in order. How do you maintain discipline among your men?

UNDERSHAFT I dont. They do. You see, the one thing Jones wont stand is any rebellion from the man under him, or any assertion of social equality between the wife of the man with 4 shillings a week less than himself, and Mrs Jones! Of course they all rebel against me, theoretically. Practically, every man of them keeps the man just below him in his place. I never meddle with them. I never bully them. I dont even bully Lazarus. I say that certain things are to be done; but I dont order anybody to do them. I dont say, mind you, that there is no ordering about and snubbing and even bullying. The men snub the boys and order them about; the carmen snub the sweepers; the artisans snub the unskilled laborers; the foremen drive and bully both the laborers and artisans; the assistant engineers find fault with the foremen; the chief engineers drop on the assistants; the departmental managers worry the chiefs; and the clerks have tall hats and hymnbooks and keep up the social tone by refusing to associate on equal terms with anybody. The result is a colossal profit, which comes to me.

CUSINS (*revolted*) You really are a—well, what I was saying yesterday.

BARBARA What was he saying yesterday?

UNDERSHAFT Never mind, my dear. He thinks I have made you unhappy. Have I?

BARBARA Do you think I can be happy in this vulgar silly dress? I! who have worn the uniform. Do you understand what you have done to me? Yesterday I had a man's soul in my hand. I set him in the way of life with his face to salvation. But when we took your money he turned back to drunkenness and derision. (*With intense conviction.*) I will never forgive you that. If I had a child, and you destroyed its body with your explosives—if you murdered Dolly with your horrible guns—I could forgive you if my forgiveness would open the gates of heaven to you. But to take a human soul from me, and turn it into the soul of a wolf! that is worse than any murder.

UNDERSHAFT Does my daughter despair so easily? Can you strike a man to the heart and leave no mark on him?

BARBARA (*her face lighting up*) Oh, you are right: he can never be lost now: where was my faith?

CUSINS Oh, clever clever devil!

BARBARA You may be a devil; but God speaks through you sometimes. (*She takes her father's hands and kisses them.*) You have given me back my happiness: I feel it deep down now, though my spirit is troubled.

UNDERSHAFT You have learnt something. That always feels at first as if you had lost something.

BARBARA Well, take me to the factory of death; and let me learn something more. There must be some truth or other behind all this frightful irony. Come, Dolly. (*She goes out.*)

CUSINS My guardian angel! (*To* UNDERSHAFT.) Avaunt! (*He follows* BARBARA.)

STEPHEN (*quietly, at the writing table*) You must not mind Cusins, father. He is a very amiable good fellow; but he is a Greek scholar and naturally a little eccentric.

UNDERSHAFT Ah, quite so. Thank you, Stephen. Thank you. (*He goes out.*)

STEPHEN *smiles patronizingly; buttons his coat responsibly; and crosses the room to the door.* LADY BRITOMART, *dressed for out-of-doors, opens it before he reaches it. She looks round for the others; looks at* STEPHEN *and turns to go without a word.*

STEPHEN (*embarrassed*) Mother—

LADY BRITOMART Dont be apologetic, Stephen. And dont forget that you have outgrown your mother. (*She goes out.*)

Perivale St Andrews lies between two Middlesex hills, half climbing the northern one. It is an almost smokeless town of white walls, roofs of narrow green slates or red tiles, tall trees, domes, campaniles, and slender chimney shafts, beautifully situated and beautiful in itself. The best view of it is obtained from the crest of a slope about half a mile to the east, where the high explosives are dealt with. The foundry lies hidden in the depths between, the tops of its chimneys sprouting like huge skittles into the middle distance. Across the crest runs an emplacement of concrete, with a firestep, and a parapet which suggests a fortification, because there is a huge cannon of the obsolete Woolwich Infant pattern peering across it at the town. The cannon is mounted on an experimental gun carriage: possibly the original model of the UNDERSHAFT *disappearing rampart gun alluded to by* STEPHEN. *The firestep, being a convenient place to sit, is furnished here and there with straw disc cushions; and at one place there is the additional luxury of a fur rug.*

BARBARA *is standing on the firestep, looking over the parapet towards the town. On her right is the cannon; on her left the end of a shed raised on piles, with a ladder of three or four steps up to the door, which opens outwards and has a little wooden landing at the threshold, with a fire bucket in the corner of the landing. Several dummy soldiers more or less mutilated, with straw protruding from their gashes, have been shoved out of the way under the landing. A few others are nearly upright against the shed; and one has fallen forward and lies, like a grotesque corpse, on the emplacement. The parapet stops short of the shed, leaving a gap which is the beginning of the path down the hill through the foundry to the town. The rug is on the firestep near this gap. Down on the emplacement behind the cannon is a trolley carrying a huge conical bombshell with a red band painted on it. Further to the right is the door of an office, which, like the sheds, is of the lightest possible construction.*

    CUSINS *arrives by the path from the town.*

BARBARA Well?

CUSINS Not a ray of hope. Everything perfect! wonderful! real! It only needs a cathedral to be a heavenly city instead of a hellish one.

BARBARA Have you found out whether they have done anything for old Peter Shirley?

CUSINS They have found him a job as gatekeeper and timekeeper. He's frightfully miserable. He calls the time-keeping brainwork, and says he isnt used to it; and his gate lodge is so splendid that he's ashamed to use the rooms, and skulks in the scullery.

BARBARA Poor Peter!

STEPHEN *arrives from the town. He carries a fieldglass.*

STEPHEN (*enthusiastically*) Have you two seen the place? Why did you leave us?

CUSINS I wanted to see everything I was not intended to see; and Barbara wanted to make the men talk.

STEPHEN Have you found anything discreditable?

CUSINS No. They call him Dandy Andy and are proud of his being a cunning old rascal; but it's all horribly, frightfully, immorally, unanswerably perfect.

SARAH *arrives.*

SARAH Heavens! what a place! (*She crosses to the trolley.*) Did you see the nursing home? (*She sits down on the shell.*)

STEPHEN Did you see the libraries and schools?

SARAH Did you see the ball room and the banqueting chamber in the Town Hall!?

STEPHEN Have you gone into the insurance fund, the pension fund, the building society, the various applications of cooperation!?

UNDERSHAFT *comes from the office, with a sheaf of telegrams in his hand.*

UNDERSHAFT Well, have you seen everything? I'm sorry I was called away. (*Indicating the telegrams.*) Good news from Manchuria.

STEPHEN   Another Japanese victory?

UNDERSHAFT   Oh, I dont know. Which side wins does not concern us here. No: the good news is that the aerial battleship is a tremendous success. At the first trial it has wiped out a fort with three hundred soldiers in it.

CUSINS (*from the platform*)   Dummy soldiers?

UNDERSHAFT (*striding across to* STEPHEN *and kicking the prostrate dummy brutally out of his way*)   No: the real thing.

CUSINS *and* BARBARA *exchange glances. Then* CUSINS *sits on the step and buries his face in his hands.* BARBARA *gravely lays her hand on his shoulder. He looks up at her in whimsical desperation.*

UNDERSHAFT   Well, Stephen, what do you think of the place?

STEPHEN   Oh, magnificent. A perfect triumph of modern industry. Frankly, my dear father, I have been a fool: I had no idea of what it all meant: of the wonderful forethought, the power of organization, the administrative capacity, the financial genius, the colossal capital it represents. I have been repeating to myself as I came through your streets "Peace hath her victories no less renowned than War." I have only one misgiving about it all.

UNDERSHAFT   Out with it.

STEPHEN   Well, I cannot help thinking that all this provision for every want of your workmen may sap their independence and weaken their sense of responsibility. And greatly as we enjoyed our tea at that splendid restaurant—how they gave us all that luxury and cake and jam and cream for threepence I really cannot imagine!—still you must remember that restaurants break up home life. Look at the continent, for instance! Are you sure so much pampering is really good for the men's characters?

UNDERSHAFT   Well you see, my dear boy, when you are organizing civilization you have to make up your mind whether trouble and anxiety are good things or not. If you decide that they are, then, I take it, you simply dont organize civilization; and there you are, with trouble and anxiety enough to make us all angels! But if you decide the other way, you may as well go through with it. However, Stephen, our characters are safe here. A sufficient dose of anxiety is always provided by the fact that we may be blown to smithereens at any moment.

SARAH   By the way, papa, where do you make the explosives?

UNDERSHAFT   In separate little sheds like that one. When one of them blows up, it costs very little, and only the people quite close to it are killed.

STEPHEN, *who is quite close to it, looks at it rather scaredly, and moves away quickly to the cannon. At the same moment the door of the shed is thrown abruptly open; and a foreman in overalls and list slippers comes out on the little landing and holds the door for* LOMAX, *who appears in the doorway.*

LOMAX (*with studied coolness*)   My good fellow: you neednt get into a state of nerves. Nothing's going to happen to you; and I suppose it wouldnt be the end of the world if anything did. A little bit of British pluck is what you want, old chap. (*He descends and strolls across to* SARAH.)

UNDERSHAFT (*to the foreman*)   Anything wrong, Bilton?

BILTON (*with ironic calm*)   Gentleman walked into the high explosives shed and lit a cigaret, sir: thats all.

UNDERSHAFT   Ah, quite so. (*Going over to* LOMAX.) Do you happen to remember what you did with the match?

LOMAX   Oh come! I'm not a fool. I took jolly good care to blow it out before I chucked it away.

BILTON   The top of it was red hot inside, sir.

LOMAX   Well, suppose it was! I didnt chuck it into any of your messes.

UNDERSHAFT   Think no more of it, Mr. Lomax. By the way, would you mind lending me your matches.

LOMAX (*offering his box*)   Certainly.

UNDERSHAFT   Thanks. (*He pockets the matches.*)

LOMAX (*lecturing to the company generally*)   You know, these high explosives dont go off like gunpowder, except when theyre in a gun. When theyre spread loose, you can put a match to them without the least risk: they just burn quietly like a bit of paper. (*Warming to the scientific interest of the subject.*) Did you know that, Undershaft? Have you ever tried?

UNDERSHAFT   Not on a large scale, Mr Lomax. Bilton will give you a sample of guncotton when you are leaving if you ask him. You can experiment with it at home. (BILTON *looks puzzled.*)

SARAH   Bilton will do nothing of the sort, papa. I suppose it's your business to blow up the Russians and Japs; but you might really stop short of blowing up poor Cholly. (BILTON *gives it up and retires into the shed.*)

LOMAX   My ownest, there is no danger. (*He sits beside her on the shell.*)

LADY BRITOMART *arrives from the town with a bouquet.*

LADY BRITOMART (*impetuously*)   Andrew: you shouldnt have let me see this place.

UNDERSHAFT   Why, my dear?

LADY BRITOMART   Never mind why: you shouldnt have: thats all. To think of all that (*indicating the town*) being yours! and that you have kept it to yourself all these years!

UNDERSHAFT   It does not belong to me. I belong to it. It is the Undershaft inheritance.

LADY BRITOMART   It is not. Your ridiculous cannons and that noisy banking foundry may be the Undershaft inheritance; but all that plate and linen, all that furniture and those houses and orchards and gardens belong to us. They belong to me: they are not a man's business. I wont give them up. You must be out of your senses to throw them all away; and if you persist in such folly, I will call in a doctor.

UNDERSHAFT   (*stooping to smell the bouquet*)   Where did you get the flowers, my dear?

LADY BRITOMART   Your men presented them to me in your William Morris Labor Church.

CUSINS   Oh! It needed only that. A Labor Church! (*He mounts the firestep distractedly, and leans with his elbows on the parapet, turning his back to them.*)

LADY BRITOMART   Yes, with Morris's words in mosaic letters ten feet high around the dome. NO MAN IS GOOD ENOUGH TO BE ANOTHER MAN'S MASTER. The cynicism of it!

UNDERSHAFT   It shocked the men at first, I am afraid. But now they take no more notice of it than of the ten commandments in church.

LADY BRITOMART   Andrew: you are trying to put me off the subject of the inheritance by profane jokes. Well, you shant. I dont ask it any longer for Stephen: he has inherited far too much of your perversity to be fit for it. But Barbara has rights as well as Stephen. Why should not Adolphus succeed to the inheritance? I could manage the town for him and he can look after the cannons, if they are really necessary.

UNDERSHAFT   I should ask nothing better if Adophus were a foundling. He is exactly the sort of new blood that is wanted in English business. But he's not a foundling; and theres an end of it. (*He makes for the office door.*)

CUSINS   (*turning to them*)   Not quite. (*They all turn and stare at him.*) I think—Mind! I am not committing myself in any way as to my future course—but I think the foundling difficulty can be got over. (*He jumps down to the emplacement.*)

UNDERSHAFT   (*coming back to him*)   What do you mean?

CUSINS   Well, I have something to say which is in the nature of a confession.

SARAH
LADY BRITOMART
BARBARA } Confession!
STEPHEN

LOMAX Oh I say!

CUSINS Yes, a confession. Listen, all. Until I met Barbara I thought myself in the main an honorable, truthful man, because I wanted the approval of my conscience more than I wanted anything else. But the moment I saw Barbara, I wanted her far more than the approval of my conscience.

LADY BRITOMART Adolphus!

CUSINS It is true. You accused me yourself, Lady Brit, of joining the Army to worship Barbara; and so I did. She bought my soul like a flower at a street corner; but she bought it for herself.

UNDERSHAFT What! Not for Dionysos or another?

CUSINS Dionysos and all the others are in herself. I adored what was divine in her, and was therefore a true worshipper. But I was romantic about her too. I thought she was a woman of the people, and that a marriage with a professor of Greek would be far beyond the wildest social ambitions of her rank.

LADY BRITOMART Adolphus!!

LOMAX Oh I say!!!

CUSINS When I learnt the horrible truth—

LADY BRITOMART What do you mean by the horrible truth, pray?

CUSINS That she was enormously rich; that her grandfather was an earl; that her father was the Prince of Darkness—

UNDERSHAFT Chut!

CUSINS —and that I was only an adventurer trying to catch a rich wife, then I stooped to deceive her about my birth.

BARBARA *(rising)* Dolly!

LADY BRITOMART Your birth! Now Adolphus, dont dare to make up a wicked story for the sake of these wretched cannons. Remember: I have seen photographs of your parents; and the Agent General for South Western Australia knows them personally and has assured me that they are most respectable married people.

CUSINS So they are in Australia; but here they are outcasts. Their marriage is legal in Australia, but not in England. My mother is my father's deceased wife's sister; and in this island I am consequently a foundling. *(Sensation.)*

BARBARA Silly! *(She climbs to the cannon, and leans, listening, in the angle it makes with the parapet.)*

CUSINS Is the subterfuge good enough, Machiavelli?

UNDERSHAFT *(thoughtfully)* Biddy: this may be a way out of the difficulty.

LADY BRITOMART   Stuff! A man cant make cannons any the better for being his own cousin instead of his proper self (*she sits down on the rug with a bounce that expresses her downright contempt for their casuistry*).

UNDERSHAFT (*to* CUSINS)   You are an educated man. That is against the tradition.

CUSINS   Once in ten thousand times it happens that the schoolboy is a born master of what they try to teach him. Greek has not destroyed my mind: it has nourished it. Besides, I did not learn it at an English public school.

UNDERSHAFT   Hm! Well, I cannot afford to be too particular: you have cornered the foundling market. Let it pass. You are eligible, Euripides: you are eligible.

BARBARA   Dolly: yesterday morning, when Stephen told us all about the tradition, you became very silent, and you have been strange and excited ever since. Were you thinking of your birth then?

CUSINS   When the finger of Destiny suddenly points at a man in the middle of his breakfast, it makes him thoughtful.

UNDERSHAFT   Aha! You have had your eye on the business, my young friend, have you?

CUSINS   Take care! There is an abyss of moral horror between me and your accursed aerial battleships.

UNDERSHAFT   Never mind the abyss for the present. Let us settle the practical details and leave your final decision open. You know that you will have to change your name. Do you object to that?

CUSINS   Would any man named Adolphus—any man called Dolly! —object to be called something else?

UNDERSHAFT   Good. Now, as to money! I propose to treat you handsomely from the beginning. You shall start at a thousand a year.

CUSINS (*with sudden heat, his spectacles twinkling with mischief*) A thousand! You dare offer a miserable thousand to the son-in-law of a millionaire! No, by Heavens, Machiavelli! you shall not cheat me. You cannot do without me; and I can do without you. I must have two thousand five hundred a year for two years. At the end of that time, if I am a failure, I go. But if I am a success, and stay on, you must give me the other five thousand.

UNDERSHAFT   What other five thousand?

CUSINS   To make the two years up to five thousand a year. The two thousand five hundred is only half pay in case I should turn out a failure. The third year I must have ten per cent on the profits.

UNDERSHAFT (*taken aback*)   Ten per cent! Why, man, do you know what my profits are?

CUSINS   Enormous, I hope: otherwise I shall require twenty-five per cent.

UNDERSHAFT   But, Mr Cusins, this is a serious matter of business. You are not bringing any capital into the concern.

CUSINS   What! no capital! Is my mastery of Greek no capital? Is my access to the subtlest thought, the loftiest poetry yet attained by humanity, no capital? My character! my intellect! my life! my career! what Barbara calls my soul! are these no capital? Say another word; and I double my salary.

UNDERSHAFT   Be reasonable—

CUSINS   (*peremptorily*)   Mr Undershaft: you have my terms. Take them or leave them.

UNDERSHAFT   (*recovering himself*)   Very well, I note your terms; and I offer you half.

CUSINS   (*disgusted*)   Half!

UNDERSHAFT   (*firmly*)   Half.

CUSINS   You call yourself a gentleman; and you offer me half!!

UNDERSHAFT   I do not call myself a gentleman; but I offer you half.

CUSINS   This to your future partner! your successor! your son-in-law!

BARBARA   You are selling your own soul, Dolly, not mine. Leave me out of the bargain, please.

UNDERSHAFT   Come! I will go a step further for Barbara's sake. I will give you three fifths; but that is my last word.

CUSINS   Done!

LOMAX   Done in the eye! Why, *I* get only eight hundred, you know.

CUSINS   By the way, Mac, I am a classical scholar not an arithmetical one. Is three fifths more than half or less?

UNDERSHAFT   More, of course.

CUSINS   I would have taken two hundred and fifty. How you can succeed in business when you are willing to pay all that money to a University don who is obviously not worth a junior clerk's wages!—well! What will Lazarus say?

UNDERSHAFT   Lazarus is a gentle romantic Jew who cares for nothing but string quartets and stalls at fashionable theatres. He will be blamed for your rapacity in money matters, poor fellow! as he has hitherto been blamed for mine. You are a shark of the first order, Euripides. So much the better for the firm!

BARBARA   Is the bargain closed, Dolly? Does your soul belong to him now?

CUSINS   No: the price is settled: that is all. The real tug of war is still to come. What about the moral question?

LADY BRITOMART   There is no moral question in the matter at all, Adolphus. You must simply sell cannons and weapons to people whose cause is right and just, and refuse them to foreigners and criminals.

UNDERSHAFT (*determinedly*)   No: none of that. You must keep the true faith of an Armorer, or you dont come in here.

CUSINS   What on earth is the true faith of an Armorer?

UNDERSHAFT   To give arms to all men who offer an honest price for them, without respect of persons or principles: to aristocrat and republican, to Nihilist and Tsar, to Capitalist and Socialist, to Protestant and Catholic, to burglar and policeman, to black man, white man and yellow man, to all sorts and conditions, all nationalities, all faiths, all follies, all causes and all crimes. The first Undershaft wrote up in his shop IF GOD GAVE THE HAND, LET NOT MAN WITHHOLD THE SWORD. The second wrote up ALL HAVE THE RIGHT TO FIGHT: NONE HAVE THE RIGHT TO JUDGE. The third wrote up TO MAN THE WEAPON: TO HEAVEN THE VICTORY. The fourth had no literary turn; so he did not write up anything; but he sold cannons to Napoleon under the nose of George the Third. The fifth wrote up PEACE SHALL NOT PREVAIL SAVE WITH A SWORD IN HER HAND. The sixth, my master, was the best of all. He wrote up NOTHING IS EVER DONE IN THIS WORLD UNTIL MEN ARE PREPARED TO KILL ONE ANOTHER IF IT IS NOT DONE. After that, there was nothing left for the seventh to say. So he wrote up, simply, UNASHAMED.

CUSINS   My good Machiavelli. I shall certainly write something up on the wall; only, as I shall write it in Greek, you wont be able to read it. But as to your Armorer's faith, if I take my neck out of the noose of my own morality I am not going to put it into the noose of yours. I shall sell cannons to whom I please and refuse them to whom I please. So there!

UNDERSHAFT   From the moment when you become Andrew Undershaft, you will never do as you please again. Dont come here lusting for power, young man.

CUSINS   If power were my aim I should not come here for it. You have no power.

UNDERSHAFT   None of my own, certainly.

CUSINS   I have more power than you, more will. You do not drive this place: it drives you. And what drives the place?

UNDERSHAFT (*enigmatically*)   A will of which I am a part.

BARBARA (*startled*)   Father! Do you know what you are saying; or are you laying a snare for my soul?

CUSINS   Dont listen to his metaphysics, Barbara. The place is driven by the most rascally part of society, the money hunters, the pleasure hunters, the military promotion hunters; and he is their slave.

UNDERSHAFT   Not necessarily. Remember the Armorer's Faith. I will take an order from a good man as cheerfully as from a bad one. If you good people prefer preaching and shirking to buying my weapons and fighting the rascals, dont blame me. I can make cannons: I cannot make courage and conviction. Bah! you tire me, Euripides, with your morality mongering. Ask Barbara: she understands. (*He suddenly reaches up and takes* BARBARA's *hands, looking powerfully into her eyes.*) Tell him, my love, what power really means.

BARBARA   (*hypnotized*)   Before I joined the Salvation Army, I was in my own power and the consequence was that I never knew what to do with myself. When I joined it, I had not time enough for all the things I had to do.

UNDERSHAFT   (*approvingly*)   Just so. And why was that, do you suppose?

BARBARA   Yesterday I should have said, because I was in the power of God. (*She resumes her self-possession, withdrawing her hands from his with a power equal to his own.*) But you came and shewed me that I was in the power of Bodger and Undershaft. Today I feel—oh! how can I put it into words? Sarah: do you remember the earthquake at Cannes, when we were little children?—how little the surprise of the first shock mattered compared to the dread and horror of waiting for the second? That is how I feel in this place today. I stood on the rock I thought eternal; and without a word of warning it reeled and crumbled under me. I was safe with an infinite wisdom watching me, an army marching to Salvation with me; and in a moment, at a stroke of your pen in a cheque book, I stood alone; and the heavens were empty. That was the first shock of the earthquake: I am waiting for the second.

UNDERSHAFT   Come, come, my daughter! dont make too much of your little tinpot tragedy. What do we do here when we spend years of work and thought and thousands of pounds of solid cash on a new gun or an aerial battleship that turns out just a hairsbreadth wrong after all? Scrap it. Scrap it without wasting another hour or another pound on it. Well, you have made for yourself something that you call a morality or a religion or what not. It doesnt fit the facts. Well, scrap it. Scrap it and get one that does fit. That is what is wrong with the world at present. It scraps its obsolete steam engines and dynamos; but it wont scrap its old prejudices and its old moralities and its old religions and its old political constitutions. Whats the result? In machinery it does very well; but in morals and religion and politics it is working at a loss that brings it nearer bankruptcy every year. Dont persist in that folly. If your old religion broke down yesterday, get a newer and a better one for tomorrow.

BARBARA Oh how gladly I would take a better one to my soul! But you offer me a worse one. (*Turning on him with sudden vehemence.*) Justify yourself: shew me some light through the darkness of this dreadful place, with its beautifully clean workshops, and respectable workmen, and model homes.

UNDERSHAFT Cleanliness and respectability do not need justification, Barbara: they justify themselves. I see no darkness here, no dreadfulness. In your Salvation shelter I saw poverty, misery, cold and hunger. You gave them bread and treacle and dreams of heaven. I give from thirty shillings a week to twelve thousand a year. They find their own dreams but I look after the drainage.

BARBARA And their souls?

UNDERSHAFT I save their souls just as I saved yours.

BARBARA (*revolted*) You saved my soul! What do you mean?

UNDERSHAFT I fed you and clothed you and housed you. I took care that you should have money enough to live handsomely— more than enough; so that you could be wasteful, careless, generous. That saved your soul from the seven deadly sins.

BARBARA (*bewildered*) The seven deadly sins!

UNDERSHAFT Yes, the deadly seven. (*Counting on his fingers.*) Food, clothing, firing, rent, taxes, respectability and children. Nothing can lift those seven millstones from Man's neck but money and the spirit cannot soar until the millstones are lifted. I lifted them from your spirit. I enabled Barbara to become Major Barbara; and I saved her from the crime of poverty.

CUSINS Do you call poverty a crime?

UNDERSHAFT The worst of crimes. All the other crimes are virtues beside it: all the other dishonors are chivalry itself by comparison. Poverty blights whole cities; spreads horrible pestilences; strikes dead the very souls of all who come within sight, sound, or smell of it. What you call crime is nothing: a murder here and a theft there, a blow now and a curse then: what do they matter? they are only the accidents and illnesses of life: there are not fifty genuine professional criminals in London. But there are millions of poor people, abject people, dirty people, ill fed, ill clothed people. They poison us morally and physically: they kill the happiness of society: they force us to do away with our own liberties and to organize unnatural cruelties for fear they should rise against us and drag us down into their abyss. Only fools fear crime: we all fear poverty. Pah! (*turning on* BARBARA) you talk of your half-saved ruffian in West Ham: you accuse me of dragging his soul back to perdition. Well, bring him to me here; and

I will drag his soul back again to salvation for you. Not by words and dreams; but by thirty-eight shillings a week, a sound house in a handsome street and a permanent job. In three weeks he will have a fancy waistcoat; in three months a tall hat and a chapel sitting; before the end of the year he will shake hands with a duchess at a Primrose League meeting, and join the Conservative Party.

BARBARA   And will he be the better for that?

UNDERSHAFT   You know he will. Dont be a hypocrite, Barbara. He will be better fed, better housed, better clothed, better behaved; and his children will be pounds heavier and bigger. That will be better than an American cloth mattress in a shelter, chopping firewood, eating bread and treacle, and being forced to kneel down from time to time to thank heaven for it: knee drill, I think you call it. It is cheap work converting starving men with a Bible in one hand and a slice of bread in the other. I will undertake to convert West Ham to Mahometanism on the same terms. Try your hand on my men: their souls are hungry because their bodies are full.

BARBARA   And leave the east end to starve?

UNDERSHAFT   (*his energetic tone dropping into one of bitter and brooding remembrance*)   *I* was an east ender. I moralized and starved until one day I swore that I would be a full-fed free man at all costs; that nothing should stop me except a bullet, neither reason nor morals nor the lives of other men. I said "Thou shalt starve ere I starve"; and with that word I became free and great. I was a dangerous man until I had my will: now I am a useful, beneficent, kindly person. That is the history of most self-made millionaires, I fancy. When it is the history of every Englishman we shall have an England worth living in.

LADY BRITOMART   Stop making speeches, Andrew. This is not the place for them.

UNDERSHAFT   (*punctured*)   My dear: I have no other means of conveying my ideas.

LADY BRITOMART   Your ideas are nonsense. You got on because you were selfish and unscrupulous.

UNDERSHAFT   Not at all. I had the strongest scruples about poverty and starvation. Your moralists are quite unscrupulous about both: they make virtues of them. I had rather be a thief than a pauper. I had rather be a murderer than a slave. I dont want to be either; but if you force the alternative on me, then, by Heaven, I'll choose the braver and more moral one. I hate poverty and slavery worse than any other crimes whatsoever. And let me tell you this.

Poverty and slavery have stood up for centuries to your sermons and leading articles: they will not stand up to my machine guns. Dont preach at them: dont reason with them. Kill them.

BARBARA   Killing. Is that your remedy for everything?

UNDERSHAFT   It is the final test of conviction, the only lever strong enough to overturn a social system, the only way of saying Must. Let six hundred and seventy fools loose in the streets; and three policemen can scatter them. But huddle them together in a certain house in Westminster; and let them go through certain ceremonies and call themselves certain names until at last they get the courage to kill; and your six hundred and seventy fools become a government. Your pious mob fills up ballot papers and imagines it is governing its masters; but the ballot paper that really governs is the paper that has a bullet wrapped up in it.

CUSINS   That is perhaps why, like most intelligent people, I never vote.

UNDERSHAFT   Vote! Bah! When you vote, you only change the names of the cabinet. When you shoot, you pull down governments, inaugurate new epochs, abolish old orders and set up new. Is that historically true. Mr Learned Man, or is it not?

CUSINS   It is historically true. I loathe having to admit it. I repudiate your sentiments. I abhor your nature. I defy you in every possible way. Still, it is true. But it ought not to be true.

UNDERSHAFT   Ought! ought! ought! ought! ought! Are you going to spend your life saying ought, like the rest of our moralists? Turn your oughts into shalls, man. Come and make explosives with me. Whatever can blow men up can blow society up. The history of the world is the history of those who had courage enough to embrace this truth. Have you the courage to embrace it, Barbara?

LADY BRITOMART   Barbara: I positively forbid you to listen to your father's abominable wickedness. And you, Adolphus, ought to know better than to go about saying that wrong things are true. What does it matter whether they are true if they are wrong?

UNDERSHAFT   What does it matter whether they are wrong if they are true?

LADY BRITOMART   (*rising*)   Children: come home instantly. Andrew: I am exceedingly sorry I allowed you to call on us. You are wickeder than ever. Come at once.

BARBARA   (*shaking her head*)   It's no use running away from wicked people, mamma.

LADY BRITOMART   It is every use. It shews your disapprobation of them.

BARBARA It does not save them.

LADY BRITOMART I can see that you are going to disobey me. Sarah: are you coming home or are you not?

SARAH I daresay it's very wicked of papa to make cannons; but I dont think I shall cut him on that account.

LOMAX (*pouring oil on the troubled waters*) The fact is, you know, there is a certain amount of tosh about this notion of wickedness. It doesnt work. You must look at facts. Not that I would say a word in favor of anything wrong; but then, you see, all sorts of chaps are always doing all sorts of things; and we have to fit them in somehow, dont you know. What I mean is that you cant go cutting everybody; and thats about what it comes to. (*Their rapt attention to his eloquence makes him nervous.*) Perhaps I dont make myself clear.

LADY BRITOMART You are lucidity itself, Charles. Because Andrew is successful and has plenty of money to give to Sarah, you will flatter him and encourage him in his wickedness.

LOMAX (*unruffled*) Well, where the carcase is, there will the eagles be gathered, dont you know. (*To* UNDERSHAFT.) Eh? What?

UNDERSHAFT Precisely. By the way, may I call you Charles?

LOMAX Delighted. Cholly is the usual ticket.

UNDERSHAFT (*to* LADY BRITOMART) Biddy—

LADY BRITOMART (*violently*) Dont dare call me Biddy. Charles Lomax: you are a fool. Adolphus Cusins: you are a Jesuit. Stephen: you are a prig. Barbara: you are a lunatic. Andrew: you are a vulgar tradesman. Now you all know my opinion; and my conscience is clear, at all events (*she sits down with a vehemence that the rug fortunately softens*).

UNDERSHAFT My dear: you are the incarnation of morality. (*She snorts.*) Your conscience is clear and your duty done when you have called everybody names. Come, Euripides! it is getting late; and we all want to get home. Make up your mind.

CUSINS Understand this, you old demon—

LADY BRITOMART Adolphus!

UNDERSHAFT Let him alone, Biddy. Proceed, Euripides.

CUSINS You have me in a horrible dilemma. I want Barbara.

UNDERSHAFT Like all young men, you greatly exaggerate the difference between one young woman and another.

BARBARA Quite true, Dolly.

CUSINS I also want to avoid being a rascal.

UNDERSHAFT (*with biting contempt*) You lust for personal righteousness, for self-approval, for what you call a good conscience, for what Barbara calls salvation, for what I call patronizing people who are not so lucky as yourself.

CUSINS   I do not: all the poet in me recoils from being a good man. But there are things in me that I must reckon with. Pity—

UNDERSHAFT   Pity! The scavenger of misery.

CUSINS   Well, love.

UNDERSHAFT   I know. You love the needy and the outcast: you love the oppressed races, the negro, the Indian ryot, the underdog everywhere. Do you love the Japanese? Do you love the French? Do you love the English?

CUSINS   No. Every true Englishman detests the English. We are the wickedest nation on earth; and our success is a moral horror.

UNDERSHAFT   That is what comes of your gospel of love, is it?

CUSINS   May I not love even my father-in-law?

UNDERSHAFT   Who wants your love, man? By what right do you take the liberty of offering it to me? I will have your due heed and respect, or I will kill you. But your love! Damn your impertinence!

CUSINS   (*grinning*)   I may not be able to control my affections, Mac.

UNDERSHAFT   You are fencing, Euripides. You are weakening: your grip is slipping. Come! try your last weapon. Pity and love have broken in your hand: forgiveness is still left.

CUSINS   No: forgiveness is a beggar's refuge. I am with you there: we must pay our debts.

UNDERSHAFT   Well said. Come! you will suit me. Remember the words of Plato.

CUSINS   (*starting*)   Plato! You dare quote Plato to me!

UNDERSHAFT   Plato says, my friend, that society cannot be saved until either the Professors of Greek take to making gunpowder, or else the makers of gunpowder become Professors of Greek.

CUSINS   Oh, tempter, cunning tempter!

UNDERSHAFT   Come! choose, man, choose.

CUSINS   But perhaps Barbara will not marry me if I make the wrong choice.

BARBARA   Perhaps not.

CUSINS   (*desperately perplexed*)   You hear!

BARBARA   Father: do you love nobody?

UNDERSHAFT   I love my best friend.

LADY BRITOMART   And who is that, pray?

UNDERSHAFT   My bravest enemy. That is the man who keeps me up to the mark.

CUSINS   You know, the creature is really a sort of poet in his way. Suppose he is a great man, after all!

UNDERSHAFT   Suppose you stop talking and make up your mind, my young friend.

CUSINS But you are driving me against my nature. I hate war.

UNDERSHAFT Hatred is the coward's revenge for being intimidated. Dare you make war on war? Here are the means: my friend Mr Lomax is sitting on them.

LOMAX (*springing up*) Oh I say! You dont mean that this thing is loaded, do you? My ownest: come off it.

SARAH (*sitting placidly on the shell*) If I am to be blown up, the more thoroughly it is done the better. Dont fuss, Cholly.

LOMAX (*to* UNDERSHAFT, *strongly remonstrant*) Your own daughter, you know!

UNDERSHAFT So I see. (*To* CUSINS.) Well, my friend, may we expect you here at six tomorrow morning?

CUSINS (*firmly*) Not on any account. I will see the whole establishment blown up with its own dynamite before I will get up at five. My hours are healthy, rational hours: eleven to five.

UNDERSHAFT Come when you please: before a week you will come at six and stay until I turn you out for the sake of your health. (*Calling.*) Bilton! (*He turns to* LADY BRITOMART, *who rises.*) My dear: let us leave these two young people to themselves for a moment. (BILTON *comes from the shed.*) I am going to take you through the guncotton shed.

BILTON (*barring the way*) You cant take anything explosive in here, sir.

LADY BRITOMART What do you mean? Are you alluding to me?

BILTON (*unmoved*) No, maam. Mr Undershaft has the other gentleman's matches in his pocket.

LADY BRITOMART (*abruptly*) Oh! I beg your pardon! (*She goes into the shed.*)

UNDERSHAFT Quite right, Bilton, quite right: here you are. (*He gives* BILTON *the box of matches.*) Come, Stephen. Come, Charles. Bring Sarah. (*He passes into the shed.*)

BILTON *opens the box and deliberately drops the matches into the firebucket.*

LOMAX Oh! I say. (BILTON *stolidly hands him the empty box.*) Infernal nonsense! Pure scientific ignorance! (*He goes in.*)

SARAH Am I all right, Bilton?

BILTON Youll have to put on list slippers, miss: thats all. Weve got em inside. (*She goes in.*)

STEPHEN (*very seriously to* CUSINS) Dolly, old fellow, think. Think before you decide. Do you feel that you are a sufficiently practical man? It is a huge undertaking, an enormous responsibility. All this mass of business will be Greek to you.

CUSINS Oh, I think it will be much less difficult than Greek.

STEPHEN   Well, I just want to say this before I leave you to yourselves. Dont let anything I have said about right and wrong prejudice you against this great chance in life. I have satisfied myself that the business is one of the highest character and a credit to our country. (*Emotionally.*) I am very proud of my father. I— (*Unable to proceed, he presses* CUSINS' *hand and goes hastily into the shed, followed by* BILTON.)

BARBARA *and* CUSINS, *left alone together, look at one another silently.*

CUSINS   Barbara: I am going to accept this offer.

BARBARA   I thought you would.

CUSINS   You understand, dont you, that I had to decide without consulting you. If I had thrown the burden of the choice on you, you would sooner or later have despised me for it.

BARBARA   Yes: I did not want you to sell your soul for me any more than for this inheritance.

CUSINS   It is not the sale of my soul that troubles me: I have sold it too often to care about that. I have sold it for a professorship. I have sold it for an income. I have sold it to escape being imprisoned for refusing to pay taxes for hangmen's ropes and unjust wars and things that I abhor. What is all human conduct but the daily and hourly sale of our souls for trifles? What I am now selling it for is neither money nor position nor comfort, but for reality and for power.

BARBARA   You know that you will have no power, and that he has none.

CUSINS   I know. It is not for myself alone. I want to make power for the world.

BARBARA   I want to make power for the world too; but it must be spiritual power.

CUSINS   I think all power is spiritual: these cannons will not go off by themselves. I have tried to make spiritual power by teaching Greek. But the world can never be really touched by a dead language and a dead civilization. The people must have power; and the people cannot have Greek. Now the power that is made here can be wielded by all men.

BARBARA   Power to burn women's houses down and kill their sons and tear their husbands to pieces.

CUSINS   You cannot have power for good without having power for evil too. Even mother's milk nourishes murderers as well as heroes. This power which only tears men's bodies to pieces has never been so horribly abused as the intellectual power, the imaginative power, the poetic, religious power that can enslave men's souls. As a teacher of Greek I gave the intellectual man weapons against the common man. I now want to give the common man weapons against the intellectual man. I love the common people. I want to arm them against the lawyers, the doctors, the priests, the literary men, the professors, the artists, and the politicians, who, once in authority, are more disastrous and tyrannical than all the fools, rascals, and impostors. I want a power simple enough for common men to use, yet strong enough to force the intellectual oligarchy to use its genius for the general good.

BARBARA Is there no higher power than that (*pointing to the shell*)?

CUSINS Yes; but that power can destroy the higher powers just as a tiger can destroy a man: therefore Man must master that power first. I admitted this when the Turks and Greeks were last at war. My best pupil went out to fight for Hellas. My parting gift to him was not a copy of Plato's Republic, but a revolver and a hundred Undershaft cartridges. The blood of every Turk he shot—if he shot any—is on my head as well as on Undershaft's. That act committed me to this place for ever. Your father's challenge has beaten me. Dare I make war on war? I must. I will. And now, is it all over between us?

BARBARA (*touched by his evident dread of her answer*) Silly baby Dolly! How could it be!

CUSINS (*overjoyed*) Then you—you—you—Oh for my drum! (*He flourishes imaginary drumsticks.*)

BARBARA (*angered by his levity*) Take care, Dolly, take care. Oh, if only I could get away from you and from father and from it all! if I could have the wings of a dove and fly away to heaven!

CUSINS And leave me!

BARBARA Yes, you, and all the other naughty mischievous children of men. But I cant. I was happy in the Salvation Army for a moment. I escaped from the world into a paradise of enthusiasm and prayer and soul saving; but the moment our money ran short, it all came back to Bodger: it was he who saved our people: he, and the Prince of Darkness, my papa. Undershaft and Bodger: their hands stretch everywhere: when we feed a starving fellow creature, it is with their bread, because there is no other bread; when we tend the sick, it is in the hospitals they endow; if we turn from the churches they build, we must kneel on the stones of the streets they pave. As long as that lasts, there is no getting away from them. Turning our backs on Bodger and Undershaft is turning our backs on life.

CUSINS I thought you were determined to turn your back on the wicked side of life.

BARBARA There is no wicked side: life is all one. And I never

wanted to shirk my share in whatever evil must be endured,
whether it be sin or suffering. I wish I could cure you of middle-
class ideas, Dolly.

CUSINS (*gasping*)   Middle cl—! A snub! A social snub to me from
the daughter of a foundling!

BARBARA   That is why I have no class, Dolly: I come straight out
of the heart of the whole people. If I were middle-class I should
turn my back on my father's business; and we should both live in
an artistic drawing room, with you reading the reviews in one
corner, and I in the other at the piano, playing Schumann: both
very superior persons, and neither of us a bit of use. Sooner than
that, I would sweep out the guncotton shed, or be one of Bodger's
barmaids. Do you know what would have happened if you had
refused papa's offer?

CUSINS   I wonder!

BARBARA   I should have given you up and married the man who
accepted it. After all, my dear old mother has more sense than
any of you. I felt like her when I saw this place—felt that I must
have it—that never, never, never could I let it go; only she
thought it was the houses and the kitchen ranges and the linen
and china, when it was really all the human souls to be saved:
not weak souls in starved bodies, sobbing with gratitude for a
scrap of bread and treacle, but fullfed, quarrelsome, snobbish, uppish creatures, all standing on their little rights and dignities, and
thinking that my father ought to be greatly obliged to them for
making so much money for him—and so he ought. That is where
salvation is really wanted. My father shall never throw it in my
teeth again that my converts were bribed with bread. (*She is
transfigured.*) I have got rid of the bribe of bread. I have got rid
of the bribe of heaven. Let God's work be done for its own sake:
the work he had to create us to do because it cannot be done
except by living men and women. When I die, let him be in my
debt, not I in his; and let me forgive him as becomes a woman of
my rank.

CUSINS   Then the way of life lies through the factory of death?

BARBARA   Yes, through the raising of hell to heaven and of man to
God, through the unveiling of an eternal light in the Valley of
The Shadow. (*Seizing him with both hands.*) Oh, did you think
my courage would never come back? did you believe that I was a
deserter? that I, who have stood in the streets, and taken my
people to my heart, and talked of the holiest and greatest things
with them, could ever turn back and chatter foolishly to fashionable people about nothing in a drawing room? Never, never,
never, never: Major Barbara will die with the colors. Oh! and

I have my dear little Dolly boy still; and he has found me my place and my work. Glory Hallelujah! (*She kisses him.*)

CUSINS   My dearest: consider my delicate health. I cannot stand as much happiness as you can.

BARBARA   Yes: it is not easy work being in love with me, is it? But it's good for you. (*She runs to the shed, and calls, childlike.*) Mamma! Mamma! (BILTON *comes out of the shed, followed by* UNDERSHAFT.) I want Mamma.

UNDERSHAFT   She is taking off her list slippers, dear. (*He passes on to* CUSINS.) Well? What does she say?

CUSINS   She has gone right up into the skies.

LADY BRITOMART   (*coming from the shed and stopping on the steps, obstructing* SARAH, *who follows with* LOMAX. BARBARA *clutches like a baby at her mother's skirt*)   Barbara: when will you learn to be independent and to act and think for yourself? I know, as well as possible what that cry of "Mamma, Mamma," means. Always running to me!

SARAH   (*touching* LADY BRITOMART's *ribs with her finger tips and imitating a bicycle horn*)   Pip! pip!

LADY BRITOMART   (*highly indignant*)   How dare you say Pip! pip! to me, Sarah? You are both very naughty children. What do you want, Barbara?

BARBARA   I want a house in the village to live in with Dolly. (*Dragging at the skirt.*) Come and tell me which one to take.

UNDERSHAFT   (*to* CUSINS)   Six o'clock tomorrow morning, Euripides.

QUESTIONS

In *Major Barbara,* Shaw has come near to creating a *psychomachia,* a battle between opposing forces for Barbara's soul. Traditionally (as in "Young Goodman Brown," for instance), the battling forces would be those of good and evil, heaven and hell. What has Shaw done to this tradition in *Major Barbara?* How is he using—and altering—it to bring home the message of his play?

ARTHUR MILLER (1915–   )

Death of a Salesman

Certain Private Conversations in Two Acts and a Requiem

C H A R A C T E R S

WILLY LOMAN
LINDA
BIFF
HAPPY
BERNARD
THE WOMAN
CHARLEY
UNCLE BEN
HOWARD WAGNER
JENNY
STANLEY
MISS FORSYTHE
LETTA

The action takes place in WILLY LOMAN'S *house and yard and in various places he visits in the New York and Boston of today.*

Throughout the play, in the stage directions, left and right mean stage left and stage right.

ACT ONE

An Overture

A melody is heard, played upon a flute. It is small and fine, telling of grass and trees and the horizon. The curtain rises.

Before us is the Salesman's house. We are aware of towering, angular shapes behind it, surrounding it on all sides. Only the blue light of the sky falls upon the house and forestage; the surrounding area shows an angry glow of orange. As more light appears, we see a solid vault of apartment houses around the small, fragile-seeming home. An air of the dream clings to the place, a dream rising out of reality. The kitchen at center seems actual enough, for there is a kitchen table with three chairs, and a refrig-

erator. *But no other fixtures are seen. At the back of the kitchen there is a draped entrance, which leads to the living room. To the right of the kitchen, on a level raised two feet, is a bedroom furnished only with a brass bedstead and a straight chair. On a shelf over the bed a silver athletic trophy stands. A window opens onto the apartment house at the side.*

Behind the kitchen, on a level raised six and a half feet, is the boys' bedroom, at present barely visible. Two beds are dimly seen, and at the back of the room a dormer window. (This bedroom is above the unseen living room.) At the left a stairway curves up to it from the kitchen.

The entire setting is wholly or, in some places, partially transparent. The roof-line of the house is one-dimensional; under and over it we see the apartment buildings. Before the house lies an apron, curving beyond the forestage into the orchestra. This forward area serves as the back yard as well as the locale of all WILLY'S *imaginings and of his city scenes. Whenever the action is in the present the actors observe the imaginary wall-lines, entering the house only through its door at the left. But in the scenes of the past these boundaries are broken, and characters enter or leave a room by stepping "through" a wall onto the forestage.*

From the right, WILLY LOMAN, *the Salesman, enters, carrying two large sample cases. The flute plays on. He hears but is not aware of it. He is past sixty years of age, dressed quietly. Even as he crosses the stage to the doorway of the house, his exhaustion is apparent. He unlocks the door, comes into the kitchen, and thankfully lets his burden down, feeling the soreness of his palms. A word-sigh escapes his lips—it might be "Oh, boy, oh, boy." He closes the door, then carries his cases out into the living room, through the draped kitchen doorway.*

LINDA, *his wife, has stirred in her bed at the right. She gets out and puts on a robe, listening. Most often jovial, she has developed an iron repression of her exceptions to* WILLY'S *behavior—she more than loves him, she admires him, as though his mercurial nature, his temper, his massive dreams and little cruelties, served her only as sharp reminders of the turbulent longings within him, longings which she shares but lacks the temperament to utter and follow to their end.*

LINDA (*hearing* WILLY *outside the bedroom, calls with some trepidation*) Willy!

WILLY It's all right. I came back.

LINDA Why? What happened? (*Slight pause*) Did something happen, Willy?

WILLY No, nothing happened.

LINDA You didn't smash the car, did you?

WILLY (*with casual irritation*) I said nothing happened. Didn't you hear me?

LINDA Don't you feel well?

WILLY I'm tired to the death. (*The flute has faded away. He sits on the bed beside her, a little numb*) I couldn't make it. I just couldn't make it, Linda.

LINDA (*very carefully, delicately*)   Where were you all day? You look terrible.

WILLY   I got as far as a little above Yonkers. I stopped for a cup of coffee. Maybe it was the coffee.

LINDA   What?

WILLY (*after a pause*)   I suddenly couldn't drive any more. The car kept going off onto the shoulder, y'know?

LINDA (*helpfully*)   Oh. Maybe it was the steering again. I don't think Angelo knows the Studebaker.

WILLY   No, it's me, it's me. Suddenly I realize I'm goin' sixty miles an hour and I don't remember the last five minutes. I'm—I can't seem to—keep my mind to it.

LINDA   Maybe it's your glasses. You never went for your new glasses.

WILLY   No, I see everything. I came back ten miles an hour. It took me nearly four hours from Yonkers.

LINDA (*resigned*)   Well, you'll just have to take a rest, Willy, you can't continue this way.

WILLY   I just got back from Florida.

LINDA   But you didn't rest your mind. Your mind is overactive, and the mind is what counts, dear.

WILLY   I'll start out in the morning. Maybe I'll feel better in the morning. (*She is taking off his shoes*) These goddam arch supports are killing me.

LINDA   Take an aspirin. Should I get you an aspirin? It'll soothe you.

WILLY (*with wonder*)   I was driving along, you understand? And I was fine. I was even observing the scenery. You can imagine, me looking at scenery, on the road every week of my life. But it's so beautiful up there, Linda, the trees are so thick, and the sun is warm. I opened the windshield and just let the warm air bathe over me. And then all of a sudden I'm goin' off the road! I'm tellin' ya, I absolutely forgot I was driving. If I'd've gone the other way over the white line I might've killed somebody. So I went on again—and five minutes later I'm dreamin' again, and I nearly—(*He presses two fingers against his eyes*) I have such thoughts, I have such strange thoughts.

LINDA   Willy, dear. Talk to them again. There's no reason why you can't work in New York.

WILLY   They don't need me in New York. I'm the New England man. I'm vital in New England.

LINDA   But you're sixty years old. They can't expect you to keep traveling every week.

WILLY   I'll have to send a wire to Portland. I'm supposed to see

Brown and Morrison tomorrow morning at ten o'clock to show the line. Goddammit, I could sell them! (*He starts putting on his jacket*)

LINDA (*taking the jacket from him*)   Why don't you go down to the place tomorrow and tell Howard you've simply got to work in New York? You're too accommodating, dear.

WILLY   If old man Wagner was alive I'd a been in charge of New York now! That man was a prince, he was a masterful man. But that boy of his, that Howard, he don't appreciate. When I went north the first time, the Wagner Company didn't know where New England was!

LINDA   Why don't you tell those things to Howard, dear?

WILLY (*encouraged*)   I will, I definitely will. Is there any cheese?

LINDA   I'll make you a sandwich.

WILLY   No, go to sleep. I'll take some milk. I'll be up right away. The boys in?

LINDA   They're sleeping. Happy took Biff on a date tonight.

WILLY (*interested*)   That so?

LINDA   It was so nice to see them shaving together, one behind the other, in the bathroom. And going out together. You notice? The whole house smells of shaving lotion.

WILLY   Figure it out. Work a lifetime to pay off a house. You finally own it, and there's nobody to live in it.

LINDA   Well, dear, life is a casting off. It's always that way.

WILLY   No, no, some people—some people accomplish something. Did Biff say anything after I went this morning?

LINDA   You shouldn't have criticized him, Willy, especially after he just got off the train. You mustn't lose your temper with him.

WILLY   When the hell did I lose my temper? I simply asked him if he was making any money. Is that a criticism?

LINDA   But, dear, how could he make any money?

WILLY (*worried and angered*)   There's such an undercurrent in him. He became a moody man. Did he apologize when I left this morning?

LINDA   He was crestfallen, Willy. You know how he admires you. I think if he finds himself, then you'll both be happier and not fight any more.

WILLY   How can he find himself on a farm? Is that a life? A farm-hand? In the beginning, when he was young, I thought, well, a young man, it's good for him to tramp around, take a lot of different jobs. But it's more than ten years now and he has yet to make thirty-five dollars a week!

LINDA   He's finding himself, Willy.

WILLY   Not finding yourself at the age of thirty-four is a disgrace!

LINDA   Shh!

WILLY   The trouble is he's lazy, goddammit!

LINDA   Willy, please!

WILLY   Biff is a lazy bum!

LINDA   They're sleeping. Get something to eat. Go on down.

WILLY   Why did he come home? I would like to know what brought him home.

LINDA   I don't know. I think he's still lost, Willy. I think he's very lost.

WILLY   Biff Loman is lost. In the greatest country in the world a young man with such—personal attractiveness, gets lost. And such a hard worker. There's one thing about Biff—he's not lazy.

LINDA   Never.

WILLY   (*with pity and resolve*)   I'll see him in the morning; I'll have a nice talk with him. I'll get him a job selling. He could be big in no time. My God! Remember how they used to follow him around in high school? When he smiled at one of them their faces lit up. When he walked down the street . . . (*He loses himself in reminiscences*)

LINDA   (*trying to bring him out of it*)   Willy, dear, I got a new kind of American-type cheese today. It's whipped.

WILLY   Why do you get American when I like Swiss?

LINDA   I just thought you'd like a change—

WILLY   I don't want a change! I want Swiss cheese. Why am I always being contradicted?

LINDA   (*with a covering laugh*)   I thought it would be a surprise.

WILLY   Why don't you open a window in here, for God's sake?

LINDA   (*with infinite patience*)   They're all open, dear.

WILLY   The way they boxed us in here. Bricks and windows, windows and bricks.

LINDA   We should've bought the land next door.

WILLY   The street is lined with cars. There's not a breath of fresh air in the neighborhood. The grass don't grow any more, you can't raise a carrot in the back yard. They should've had a law against apartment houses. Remember those two beautiful elm trees out there? When I and Biff hung the swing between them?

LINDA   Yeah, like being a million miles from the city.

WILLY   They should've arrested the builder for cutting those down. They massacred the neighborhood. (*Lost*) More and more I think of those days, Linda. This time of year it was lilac and wisteria. And then the peonies would come out, and the daffodils. What fragrance in this room!

LINDA   Well, after all, people had to move somewhere.

WILLY   No, there's more people now.

LINDA   I don't think there's more people. I think—

WILLY   There's more people! That's what's ruining this country!
Population is getting out of control. The competition is madden-
ing! Smell the stink from that apartment house! And another one
on the other side . . . How can they whip cheese?

On WILLY's *last line,* BIFF *and* HAPPY *raise themselves up in their beds,
listening.*

LINDA   Go down, try it. And be quiet.

WILLY   (*turning to* LINDA, *guiltily*)   You're not worried about me,
are you, sweetheart?

BIFF   What's the matter?

HAPPY   Listen!

LINDA   You've got too much on the ball to worry about.

WILLY   You're my foundation and my support, Linda.

LINDA   Just try to relax, dear. You make mountains out of mole-
hills.

WILLY   I won't fight with him any more. If he wants to go back
to Texas, let him go.

LINDA   He'll find his way.

WILLY   Sure. Certain men just don't get started till later in life.
Like Thomas Edison, I think. Or B. F. Goodrich. One of them
was deaf. (*He starts for the bedroom doorway*) I'll put my
money on Biff.

LINDA   And Willy—if it's warm Sunday we'll drive in the country.
And we'll open the windshield, and take lunch.

WILLY   No, the windshields don't open on the new cars.

LINDA   But you opened it today.

WILLY   Me? I didn't. (*He stops*) Now isn't that peculiar! Isn't
that a remarkable—(*He breaks off in amazement and fright as
the flute is heard distantly*)

LINDA   What, darling?

WILLY   That is the most remarkable thing.

LINDA   What, dear?

WILLY   I was thinking of the Chevvy. (*Slight pause*) Nineteen
twenty-eight . . . when I had that red Chevvy—(*Breaks off*) That
funny? I coulda sworn I was driving that Chevvy today.

LINDA   Well, that's nothing. Something must've reminded you.

WILLY   Remarkable. Ts. Remember those days? The way Biff used
to simonize that car? The dealer refused to believe there was
eighty thousand miles on it. (*He shakes his head*) Heh! (*To*
LINDA) Close your eyes, I'll be right up. (*He walks out of the
bedroom*)

HAPPY   (*to* BIFF)   Jesus, maybe he smashed up the car again!

LINDA (*calling after* WILLY)   Be careful on the stairs, dear! The cheese is on the middle shelf! (*She turns, goes over to the bed, takes his jacket, and goes out of the bedroom*)

Light has risen on the boys' room. Unseen, WILLY *is heard talking to himself, "Eighty thousand miles," and a little laugh.* BIFF *gets out of bed, comes downstage a bit, and stands attentively.* BIFF *is two years older than his brother* HAPPY, *well built, but in these days bears a worn air and seems less self-assured. He has succeeded less, and his dreams are stronger and less acceptable than* HAPPY's. HAPPY *is tall, powerfully made. Sexuality is like a visible color on him, or a scent that many women have discovered. He, like his brother, is lost, but in a different way, for he has never allowed himself to turn his face toward defeat and is thus more confused and hard-skinned, although seemingly more content.*

HAPPY (*getting out of bed*)   He's going to get his license taken away if he keeps that up. I'm getting nervous about him, y'know, Biff?

BIFF   His eyes are going.

HAPPY   No, I've driven with him. He sees all right. He just doesn't keep his mind on it. I drove into the city with him last week. He stops at a green light and then it turns red and he goes. (*He laughs*)

BIFF   Maybe he's color-blind.

HAPPY   Pop? Why he's got the finest eye for color in the business. You know that.

BIFF (*sitting down on his bed*)   I'm going to sleep.

HAPPY   You're not still sour on Dad, are you, Biff?

BIFF   He's all right, I guess.

WILLY (*underneath them, in the living-room*)   Yes, sir, eighty thousand miles—eighty-two thousand!

BIFF   You smoking?

HAPPY (*holding out a pack of cigarettes*)   Want one?

BIFF (*taking a cigarette*)   I can never sleep when I smell it.

WILLY   What a simonizing job, heh!

HAPPY (*with deep sentiment*)   Funny, Biff, y'now? Us sleeping in here again? The old beds. (*He pats his bed affectionately*) All the talk that went across those two beds, huh? Our whole lives.

BIFF   Yeah. Lotta dreams and plans.

HAPPY (*with a deep and masculine laugh*)   About five hundred women would like to know what was said in this room.

They share a soft laugh.

BIFF   Remember that big Betsy something—what the hell was her name—over on Bushwick Avenue?

HAPPY (*combing his hair*)   With the collie dog!

BIFF That's the one. I got you in there, remember?

HAPPY Yeah, that was my first time—I think. Boy, there was a pig! (*They laugh, almost crudely*) You taught me everything I know about women. Don't forget that.

BIFF I bet you forgot how bashful you used to be. Especially with girls.

HAPPY Oh, I still am, Biff.

BIFF Oh, go on.

HAPPY I just control it, that's all. I think I got less bashful and you got more so. What happened, Biff? Where's the old humor, the old confidence? (*He shakes* BIFF's *knee.* BIFF *gets up and moves restlessly about the room*) What's the matter?

BIFF Why does Dad mock me all the time?

HAPPY He's not mocking you, he—

BIFF Everything I say there's a twist of mockery on his face. I can't get near him.

HAPPY He just wants you to make good, that's all. I wanted to talk to you about Dad for a long time, Biff. Something's—happening to him. He—talks to himself.

BIFF I noticed that this morning. But he always mumbled.

HAPPY But not so noticeable. It got so embarrassing I sent him to Florida. And you know something? Most of the time he's talking to you.

BIFF What's he say about me?

HAPPY I can't make it out.

BIFF What's he say about me?

HAPPY I think the fact that you're not settled, that you're still kind of up in the air . . .

BIFF There's one or two other things depressing him, Happy.

HAPPY What do you mean?

BIFF Never mind. Just don't lay it all to me.

HAPPY But I think if you just got started—I mean—is there any future for you out there?

BIFF I tell ya, Hap, I don't know what the future is. I don't know —what I'm supposed to want.

HAPPY What do you mean?

BIFF Well, I spent six or seven years after high school trying to work myself up. Shipping clerk, salesman, business of one kind or another. And it's a measly manner of existence. To get on that subway on the hot mornings in summer. To devote your whole life to keeping stock, or making phone calls, or selling or buying. To suffer fifty weeks of the year for the sake of a two-week vacation, when all you really desire is to be outdoors, with your shirt

off. And always to have to get ahead of the next fella. And still—
that's how you build a future.

HAPPY   Well, you really enjoy it on a farm? Are you content out
there?

BIFF (*with rising agitation*)   Hap, I've had twenty or thirty different kinds of jobs since I left home before the war, and it always
turns out the same. I just realized it lately. In Nebraska when I
herded cattle, and the Dakotas, and Arizona, and now in Texas.
It's why I came home now, I guess, because I realized it. This
farm I work on, it's spring there now, see? And they've got about
fifteen new colts. There's nothing more inspiring or—beautiful
than the sight of a mare and a new colt. And it's cool there now,
see? Texas is cool now, and it's spring. And whenever spring
comes to where I am, I suddenly get the feeling, my God, I'm
not gettin' anywhere! What the hell am I doing, playing around
with horses, twenty-eight dollars a week! I'm thirty-four years old,
I oughta be makin' my future. That's when I come running home.
And now, I get here, and I don't know what to do with myself.
(*After a pause*) I've always made a point of not wasting my life,
and everytime I come back here I know that all I've done is to
waste my life.

HAPPY   You're a poet, you know that, Biff? You're a—you're an
idealist!

BIFF   No, I'm mixed up very bad. Maybe I oughta get married.
Maybe I oughta get stuck into something. Maybe that's my trouble. I'm like a boy. I'm not married, I'm not in business, I just
—I'm like a boy. Are you content, Hap? You're a success, aren't
you? Are you content?

HAPPY   Hell, no!

BIFF   Why? You're making money, aren't you?

HAPPY (*moving about with energy, expressiveness*)   All I can do
now is wait for the merchandise manager to die. And suppose I
get to be merchandise manager? He's a good friend of mine, and
he just built a terrific estate on Long Island. And he lived there
about two months and sold it, and now he's building another
one. He can't enjoy it once it's finished. And I know that's just
what I would do. I don't know what the hell I'm workin' for.
Sometimes I sit in my apartment—all alone. And I think of the
rent I'm paying. And it's crazy. But then, it's what I always
wanted. My own apartment, a car, and plenty of women. And
still, goddammit, I'm lonely.

BIFF (*with enthusiasm*)   Listen, why don't you come out West with
me?

HAPPY   You and I, heh?

BIFF   Sure, maybe we could buy a ranch. Raise cattle, use our muscles. Men built like we are should be working out in the open.

HAPPY (*avidly*) The Loman Brothers, heh?

BIFF (*with vast affection*) Sure, we'd be known all over the counties!

HAPPY (*enthralled*) That's what I dream about, Biff. Sometimes I want to just rip my clothes off in the middle of the store and outbox that goddam merchandise manager. I mean I can outbox, outrun, and outlift anybody in that store, and I have to take orders from those common, petty sons-of-bitches till I can't stand it any more.

BIFF   I'm tellin' you, kid, if you were with me I'd be happy out there.

HAPPY (*enthused*) See, Biff, everybody around me is so false that I'm constantly lowering my ideals . . .

BIFF   Baby, together we'd stand up for one another, we'd have someone to trust.

HAPPY   If I were around you—

BIFF   Hap, the trouble is we weren't brought up to grub for money. I don't know how to do it.

HAPPY   Neither can I!

BIFF   Then let's go!

HAPPY   The only thing is—what can you make out there?

BIFF   But look at your friend. Builds an estate and then hasn't the peace of mind to live in it.

HAPPY   Yeah, but when he walks into the store the waves part in front of him. That's fifty-two thousand dollars a year coming through the revolving door, and I got more in my pinky finger than he's got in his head.

BIFF   Yeah, but you just said—

HAPPY   I gotta show some of those pompous, self-important executives over there that Hap Loman can make the grade. I want to walk into the store the way he walks in. Then I'll go with you, Biff. We'll be together yet, I swear. But take those two we had tonight. Now weren't they gorgeous creatures?

BIFF   Yeah, yeah, most gorgeous I've had in years.

HAPPY   I get that any time I want, Biff. Whenever I feel disgusted. The only trouble is, it gets like bowling or something. I just keep knockin' them over and it doesn't mean anything. You still run around a lot?

BIFF   Naa. I'd like to find a girl—steady, somebody with substance.

HAPPY   That's what I long for.

BIFF   Go on! You'd never come home.

HAPPY   I would! Somebody with character, with resistance! Like Mom, y'know? You're gonna call me a bastard when I tell you this. That girl Charlotte I was with tonight is engaged to be married in five weeks. (*He tries on his new hat*)

BIFF   No kiddin'!

HAPPY   Sure, the guy's in line for the vice-presidency of the store. I don't know what gets into me, maybe I just have an over-developed sense of competition or something, but I went and ruined her, and furthermore I can't get rid of her. And he's the third executive I've done that to. Isn't that a crummy characteristic? And to top it all, I go to their weddings! (*Indignantly, but laughing*) Like I'm not supposed to take bribes. Manufacturers offer me a hundred-dollar bill now and then to throw an order their way. You know how honest I am, but it's like this girl, see. I hate myself for it. Because I don't want the girl, and, still, I take it and—I love it!

BIFF   Let's go to sleep.

HAPPY   I guess we didn't settle anything, heh?

BIFF   I just got one idea that I think I'm going to try.

HAPPY   What's that?

BIFF   Remember Bill Oliver?

HAPPY   Sure, Oliver is very big now. You want to work for him again?

BIFF   No, but when I quit he said something to me. He put his arm on my shoulder, and he said, "Biff, if you ever need anything, come to me."

HAPPY   I remember that. That sounds good.

BIFF   I think I'll go to see him. If I could get ten thousand or even seven or eight thousand dollars I could buy a beautiful ranch.

HAPPY   I bet he'd back you. 'Cause he thought highly of you, Biff. I mean, they all do. You're well liked, Biff. That's why I say to come back here, and we both have the apartment. And I'm tellin' you, Biff, any babe you want . . .

BIFF   No, with a ranch I could do the work I like and still be something. I just wonder though. I wonder if Oliver still thinks I stole that carton of basketballs.

HAPPY   Oh, he probably forgot that long ago. It's almost ten years. You're too sensitive. Anyway, he didn't really fire you.

BIFF   Well, I think he was going to. I think that's why I quit. I was never sure whether he knew or not. I know he thought the world of me, though. I was the only one he'd let lock up the place.

WILLY (*below*)   You gonna wash the engine, Biff?
HAPPY   Shh!

BIFF *looks at* HAPPY, *who is gazing down, listening.* WILLY *is mumbling in the parlor.*

HAPPY   You hear that?

They listen. WILLY *laughs warmly.*

BIFF (*growing angry*)   Doesn't he know Mom can hear that?
WILLY   Don't get your sweater dirty, Biff!

A look of pain crosses BIFF's *face.*

HAPPY   Isn't that terrible? Don't leave again, will you? You'll find a job here. You gotta stick around. I don't know what to do about him, it's getting embarrassing.
WILLY   What a simonizing job!
BIFF   Mom's hearing that!
WILLY   No kiddin', Biff, you got a date? Wonderful!
HAPPY   Go on to sleep. But talk to him in the morning, will you?
BIFF (*reluctantly getting into bed*)   With her in the house. Brother!
HAPPY (*getting into bed*)   I wish you'd have a good talk with him.

The light on their room begins to fade.

BIFF (*to himself in bed*)   That selfish, stupid . . .
HAPPY   Sh . . . Sleep, Biff.

Their light is out. Well before they have finished speaking, WILLY's *form is dimly seen below in the darkened kitchen. He opens the refrigerator, searches in there, and takes out a bottle of milk. The apartment houses are fading out, and the entire house and surroundings become covered with leaves. Music insinuates itself as the leaves appear.*

WILLY   Just wanna be careful with those girls, Biff, that's all. Don't make any promises. No promises of any kind. Because a girl, y'know, they always believe what you tell 'em, and you're very young, Biff, you're too young to be talking seriously to girls.

Light rises on the kitchen. WILLY, *talking, shuts the refrigerator door and comes downstage to the kitchen table. He pours milk into a glass. He is totally immersed in himself, smiling faintly.*

WILLY   Too young entirely, Biff. You want to watch your schooling first. Then when you're all set, there'll be plenty of girls for a boy like you. (*He smiles broadly at a kitchen chair*) That so? The girls pay for you? (*He laughs*) Boy, you must really be makin' a hit.

WILLY *is gradually addressing—physically—a point offstage, speaking
through the wall of the kitchen, and his voice has been rising in volume
to that of a normal conversation.*

WILLY I been wondering why you polish the car so careful. Ha!
Don't leave the hubcabs, boys. Get the chamois to the hubcaps.
Happy, use newspaper on the windows, it's the easiest thing.
Show him how to do it, Biff! You see, Happy? Pad it up, use it
like a pad. That's it, that's it, good work. You're doin' all right,
Hap. (*He pauses, then nods in approbation for a few seconds,
then looks upward*) Biff, first thing we gotta do when we get time
is clip that big branch over the house. Afraid it's gonna fall in a
storm and hit the roof. Tell you what. We get a rope and sling
her around, and then we climb up there with a couple of saws
and take her down. Soon as you finish the car, boys, I wanna see
ya. I got a surprise for you, boys.
BIFF (*offstage*) Whatta ya got, Dad?
WILLY No, you finish first. Never leave a job till you're finished—
remember that. (*Looking toward the "big trees"*) Biff, up in Albany I saw a beautiful hammock. I think I'll buy it next trip,
and we'll hang it right between those two elms. Wouldn't that
be something? Just swingin' there under those branches. Boy, that
would be . . .

Young BIFF *and Young* HAPPY *appear from the direction* WILLY *was addressing.* HAPPY *carries rags and a pail of water.* BIFF, *wearing a sweater
with a block "S," carries a football.*

BIFF (*pointing in the direction of the car offstage*) How's that,
Pop, professional?
WILLY Terrific. Terrific job, boys. Good work, Biff.
HAPPY Where's the surprise, Pop?
WILLY In the back seat of the car.
HAPPY Boy! (*He runs off*)
BIFF What is it, Dad? Tell me, what'd you buy?
WILLY (*laughing, cuffs him*) Never mind, something I want you
to have.
BIFF (*turns and starts off*) What is it, Hap?
HAPPY (*offstage*) It's a punching bag!
BIFF Oh, Pop!
WILLY It's got Gene Tunney's signature on it!

HAPPY *runs onstage with a punching bag.*

BIFF Gee, how'd you know we wanted a punching bag?
WILLY Well, it's the finest thing for the timing.

HAPPY (*lies down on his back and pedals with his feet*)   I'm losing weight, you notice, Pop?

WILLY (*to* HAPPY)   Jumping rope is good too.

BIFF   Did you see the new football I got?

WILLY (*examining the ball*)   Where'd you get a new ball?

BIFF   The coach told me to practice my passing.

WILLY   That so? And he gave you the ball, heh?

BIFF   Well, I borrowed it from the locker room. (*He laughs confidentially*)

WILLY (*laughing with him at the theft*)   I want you to return that.

HAPPY   I told you he wouldn't like it!

BIFF (*angrily*)   Well, I'm bringing it back!

WILLY (*stopping the incipient argument, to* HAPPY)   Sure, he's gotta practice with a regulation ball, doesn't he? (*To* BIFF) Coach'll probably congratulate you on your initiative!

BIFF   Oh, he keeps congratulating my initiative all the time, Pop.

WILLY   That's because he likes you. If somebody else took that ball there'd be an uproar. So what's the report, boys, what's the report?

BIFF   Where'd you go this time, Dad? Gee we were lonesome for you.

WILLY (*pleased, puts an arm around each boy and they come down to the apron*)   Lonesome, heh?

BIFF   Missed you every minute.

WILLY   Don't say? Tell you a secret, boys. Don't breathe it to a soul. Someday I'll have my own business, and I'll never have to leave home any more.

HAPPY   Like Uncle Charley, heh?

WILLY   Bigger than Uncle Charley! Because Charley is not—liked. He's liked, but he's not—well liked.

BIFF   Where'd you go this time, Dad?

WILLY   Well, I got on the road, and I went north to Providence. Met the Mayor.

BIFF   The Mayor of Providence!

WILLY   He was sitting in the hotel lobby.

BIFF   What'd he say?

WILLY   He said, "Morning!" And I said, "You got a fine city here, Mayor." And then he had coffee with me. And then I went to Waterbury. Waterbury is a fine city. Big clock city, the famous Waterbury clock. Sold a nice bill there. And then Boston—Boston is the cradle of the Revolution. A fine city. And a couple of other towns in Mass., and on to Portland and Bangor and straight home!

BIFF   Gee, I'd love to go with you sometime, Dad.

WILLY   Soon as summer comes.

HAPPY   Promise?

WILLY   You and Hap and I, and I'll show you all the towns. America is full of beautiful towns and fine, upstanding people. And they know me, boys, they know me up and down New England. The finest people. And when I bring you fellas up, there'll be open sesame for all of us, 'cause one thing, boys: I have friends. I can park my car in any street in New England, and the cops protect it like their own. This summer, heh?

BIFF and HAPPY *(together)*   Yeah! You bet!

WILLY   We'll take our bathing suits.

HAPPY   We'll carry your bags, Pop!

WILLY   Oh, won't that be something! Me comin' into the Boston stores with you boys carryin' my bags. What a sensation!

BIFF *is prancing around, practicing passing the ball.*

WILLY   You nervous, Biff, about the game?

BIFF   Not if you're gonna be there.

WILLY   What do they say about you in school, now that they made you captain?

HAPPY   There's a crowd of girls behind him everytime the classes change.

BIFF *(taking* WILLY's *hand)*   This Saturday, Pop, this Saturday—just for you, I'm going to break through for a touchdown.

HAPPY   You're supposed to pass.

BIFF   I'm takin' one play for Pop. You watch me, Pop, and when I take off my helmet, that means I'm breakin' out. Then you watch me crash through that line!

WILLY *(kisses* BIFF)   Oh, wait'll I tell this in Boston!

BERNARD *enters in knickers. He is younger than* BIFF, *earnest and loyal, a worried boy.*

BERNARD   Biff, where are you? You're supposed to study with me today.

WILLY   Hey, looka Bernard. What're you lookin' so anemic about, Bernard?

BERNARD   He's gotta study, Uncle Willy. He's got Regents next week.

HAPPY *(tauntingly, spinning* BERNARD *around)*   Let's box, Bernard!

BERNARD   Biff! *(He gets away from* HAPPY)   Listen, Biff, I heard Mr. Birnbaum say that if you don't start studyin' math he's gonna flunk you, and you won't graduate. I heard him!

WILLY   You better study with him, Biff. Go ahead now.

BERNARD I heard him!

BIFF Oh, Pop, you didn't see my sneakers! (*He holds up a foot for* WILLY *to look at*)

WILLY Hey, that's a beautiful job of printing!

BERNARD (*wiping his glasses*) Just because he printed University of Virginia on his sneakers doesn't mean they've got to graduate him, Uncle Willy!

WILLY (*angrily*) What're you talking about? With scholarships to three universities they're gonna flunk him?

BERNARD But I heard Mr. Birnbaum say—

WILLY Don't be a pest, Bernard! (*To his boys*) What an anemic!

BERNARD Okay, I'm waiting for you in my house, Biff.

BERNARD *goes off. The* LOMANS *laugh.*

WILLY Bernard is not well liked, is he?

BIFF He's liked, but he's not well liked.

HAPPY That's right, Pop.

WILLY That's just what I mean. Bernard can get the best marks in school, y'understand, but when he gets out in the business world, y'understand, you are going to be five times ahead of him. That's why I thank Almighty God you're both built like Adonises. Because the man who makes an appearance in the business world, the man who creates personal interest, is the man who gets ahead. Be liked and you will never want. You take me, for instance. I never have to wait in line to see a buyer. "Willy Loman is here!" That's all they have to know, and I go right through.

BIFF Did you knock them dead, Pop?

WILLY Knocked 'em cold in Providence, slaughtered 'em in Boston.

HAPPY (*on his back, pedaling again*) I'm losing weight, you notice, Pop?

LINDA *enters, as of old, a ribbon in her hair, carrying a basket of washing.*

LINDA (*with youthful energy*) Hello, dear!

WILLY Sweetheart!

LINDA How'd the Chevvy run?

WILLY Chevrolet, Linda, is the greatest car ever built. (*To the boys*) Since when do you let your mother carry wash up the stairs?

BIFF Grab hold there, boy!

HAPPY Where to, Mom?

LINDA Hang them up on the line. And you better go down to your friends, Biff. The cellar is full of boys. They don't know what to do with themselves.

BIFF   Ah, when Pop comes home they can wait!

WILLY   (*laughs appreciatively*)   You better go down and tell them what to do, Biff.

BIFF   I think I'll have them sweep out the furnace room.

WILLY   Good work, Biff.

BIFF   (*goes through wall-line of kitchen to doorway at back and calls down*)   Fellas! Everybody sweep out the furnace room! I'll be right down!

VOICES   All right! Okay, Biff.

BIFF   George and Sam and Frank, come out back! We're hangin' up the wash! Come on, Hap, on the double! (*He and* HAPPY *carry out the basket*)

LINDA   The way they obey him!

WILLY   Well, that's training, the training. I'm tellin' you, I was sellin' thousands and thousands, but I had to come home.

LINDA   Oh, the whole block'll be at that game. Did you sell anything?

WILLY   I did five hundred gross in Providence and seven hundred gross in Boston.

LINDA   No! Wait a minute, I've got a pencil. (*She pulls pencil and paper out of her apron pocket*)   That makes your commission . . . Two hundred—my God! Two hundred and twelve dollars!

WILLY   Well, I didn't figure it yet, but . . .

LINDA   How much did you do?

WILLY   Well, I—I did—about a hundred and eighty gross in Providence. Well, no—it came to—roughly two hundred gross on the whole trip.

LINDA   (*without hesitation*)   Two hundred gross. That's . . . (*She figures*)

WILLY   The trouble was that three of the stores were half closed for inventory in Boston. Otherwise I woulda broke records.

LINDA   Well, it makes seventy dollars and some pennies. That's very good.

WILLY   What do we owe?

LINDA   Well, on the first there's sixteen dollars on the refrigerator—

WILLY   Why sixteen?

LINDA   Well, the fan belt broke, so it was a dollar eighty.

WILLY   But it's brand new.

LINDA   Well, the man said that's the way it is. Till they work themselves in, y'know.

They move through the wall-line into the kitchen.

WILLY   I hope we didn't get stuck on that machine.

LINDA   They got the biggest ads of any of them!

WILLY   I know, it's a fine machine. What else?

LINDA   Well, there's nine-sixty for the washing machine. And for the vacuum cleaner there's three and a half due on the fifteenth. Then the roof, you got twenty-one dollars remaining.

WILLY   It don't leak, does it?

LINDA   No, they did a wonderful job. Then you owe Frank for the carburetor.

WILLY   I'm not going to pay that man! That goddam Chevrolet, they ought to prohibit the manufacture of that car!

LINDA   Well, you owe him three and a half. And odds and ends, comes to around a hundred and twenty dollars by the fifteenth.

WILLY   A hundred and twenty dollars! My God, if business don't pick up I don't know what I'm gonna do!

LINDA   Well, next week you'll do better.

WILLY   Oh, I'll knock 'em dead next week. I'll go to Hartford. I'm very well liked in Hartford. You know, the trouble is, Linda, people don't seem to take to me.

They move onto the forestage.

LINDA   Oh, don't be foolish.

WILLY   I know it when I walk in. They seem to laugh at me.

LINDA   Why? Why would they laugh at you? Don't talk that way, Willy.

WILLY *moves to the edge of the stage.* LINDA *goes into the kitchen and starts to darn stockings.*

WILLY   I don't know the reason for it, but they just pass me by. I'm not noticed.

LINDA   But you're doing wonderful, dear. You're making seventy to a hundred dollars a week.

WILLY   But I gotta be at it ten, twelve hours a day. Other men— I don't know—they do it easier. I don't know why—I can't stop myself—I talk too much. A man oughta come in with a few words. One thing about Charley. He's a man of few words, and they respect him.

LINDA   You don't talk too much, you're just lively.

WILLY *(smiling)*   Well, I figure, what the hell, life is short, a couple of jokes. *(To himself)* I joke too much! *(The smile goes)*

LINDA   Why? You're—

WILLY   I'm fat. I'm very—foolish to look at, Linda. I didn't tell you, but Christmas time I happened to be calling on F. H. Stewarts, and a salesman I know, as I was going in to see the buyer I heard him say something about—walrus. And I—I cracked him

right across the face. I won't take that. I simply will not take that.
But they do laugh at me. I know that.

LINDA   Darling . . .

WILLY   I gotta overcome it. I know I gotta overcome it. I'm not
dressing to advantage, maybe.

LINDA   Willy, darling, you're the handsomest man in the world—

WILLY   Oh, no, Linda.

LINDA   To me you are. (*Slight pause*) The handsomest.

From the darkness is heard the laughter of a woman. WILLY *doesn't turn
to it, but it continues through* LINDA's *lines.*

LINDA   And the boys, Willy. Few men are idolized by their children the way you are.

Music is heard as behind a scrim, to the left of the house. THE WOMAN,
dimly seen, is dressing.

WILLY   (*with great feeling*)   You're the best there is, Linda, you're
a pal, you know that? On the road—on the road I want to grab
you sometimes and just kiss the life outa you.

*The laughter is loud now, and he moves into a brightening area at the
left, where* THE WOMAN *has come from behind the scrim and is standing,
putting on her hat, looking into a "mirror" and laughing.*

WILLY   'Cause I get so lonely—especially when business is bad and
there's nobody to talk to. I get the feeling that I'll never sell
anything again, that I won't make a living for you, or a business,
a business for the boys. (*He talks through* THE WOMAN's *subsiding laughter;* THE WOMAN *primps at the "mirror."*) There's so
much I want to make for—

THE WOMAN   Me? You didn't make me, Willy. I picked you.

WILLY   (*pleased*)   You picked me?

THE WOMAN   (*who is quite proper-looking,* WILLY's *age*)   I did. I've
been sitting at that desk watching all the salesmen go by, day in,
day out. But you've got such a sense of humor, and we do have
such a good time together, don't we?

WILLY   Sure, sure. (*He takes her in his arms*) Why do you have
to go now?

THE WOMAN   It's two o'clock . . .

WILLY   No, come on in! (*He pulls her*)

THE WOMAN   . . . my sisters'll be scandalized. When'll you be back?

WILLY   Oh, two weeks about. Will you come up again?

THE WOMAN   Sure thing. You do make me laugh. It's good for me.
(*She squeezes his arm, kisses him*) And I think you're a wonderful man.

WILLY   You picked me, heh?

THE WOMAN   Sure. Because you're so sweet. And such a kidder.

WILLY   Well, I'll see you next time I'm in Boston.

THE WOMAN   I'll put you right through to the buyers.

WILLY (*slapping her bottom*)   Right. Well, bottoms up!

THE WOMAN (*slaps him gently and laughs*)   You just kill me, Willy. (*He suddenly grabs her and kisses her roughly*) You kill me. And thanks for the stockings. I love a lot of stockings. Well, good night.

WILLY   Good night. And keep your pores open!

THE WOMAN   Oh, Willy!

THE WOMAN *bursts out laughing, and* LINDA's *laughter blends in.* THE WOMAN *disappears into the dark. Now the area at the kitchen table brightens.* LINDA *is sitting where she was at the kitchen table, but now is mending a pair of her silk stockings.*

LINDA   You are, Willy. The handsomest man. You've got no reason to feel that—

WILLY (*coming out of* THE WOMAN's *dimming area and going over to* LINDA)   I'll make it all up to you, Linda, I'll—

LINDA   There's nothing to make up, dear. You're doing fine, better than—

WILLY (*noticing her mending*)   What's that?

LINDA   Just mending my stockings. They're so expensive—

WILLY (*angrily, taking them from her*)   I won't have you mending stockings in this house! Now throw them out!

LINDA *puts the stockings in her pocket.*

BERNARD (*entering on the run*)   Where is he? If he doesn't study!

WILLY (*moving to the forestage, with great agitation*)   You'll give him the answers!

BERNARD   I do, but I can't on a Regents! That's a state exam! They're liable to arrest me!

WILLY   Where is he? I'll whip him, I'll whip him!

LINDA   And he'd better give back that football, Willy, it's not nice.

WILLY   Biff! Where is he? Why is he taking everything?

LINDA   He's too rough with the girls, Willy. All the mothers are afraid of him!

WILLY   I'll whip him!

BERNARD   He's driving the car without a license!

THE WOMAN's *laugh is heard.*

WILLY   Shut up!

LINDA   All the mothers—

WILLY   Shut up!

BERNARD (*backing quietly away and out*)   Mr. Birnbaum says he's
stuck up.

WILLY   Get outa here!

BERNARD   If he doesn't buckle down he'll flunk math! (*He goes
off*)

LINDA   He's right, Willy, you've gotta—

WILLY   (*exploding at her*)   There's nothing the matter with him!
You want him to be a worm like Bernard? He's got spirit, personality . . .

As he speaks, LINDA, *almost in tears, exits into the living room.* WILLY *is
alone in the kitchen, wilting and staring. The leaves are gone. It is night
again, and the apartment houses look down from behind.*

WILLY   Loaded with it. Loaded! What is he stealing? He's giving
it back, isn't he? Why is he stealing? What did I tell him? I
never in my life told him anything but decent things.

HAPPY *in pajamas has come down the stairs;* WILLY *suddenly becomes
aware of* HAPPY's *presence.*

HAPPY   Let's go now, come on.

WILLY   (*sitting down at the kitchen table*)   Huh! Why did she
have to wax the floors herself? Everytime she waxes the floors she
keels over. She knows that!

HAPPY   Shh! Take it easy. What brought you back tonight?

WILLY   I got an awful scare. Nearly hit a kid in Yonkers. God!
Why didn't I go to Alaska with my brother Ben that time! Ben!
That man was a genius, that man was success incarnate! What
a mistake! He begged me to go.

HAPPY   Well, there's no use in—

WILLY   You guys! There was a man started with the clothes on his
back and ended up with diamond mines!

HAPPY   Boy, someday I'd like to know how he did it.

WILLY   What's the mystery? The man knew what he wanted and
went out and got it! Walked into a jungle, and comes out, the
age of twenty-one, and he's rich! The world is an oyster, but you
don't crack it open on a mattress!

HAPPY   Pop, I told you I'm gonna retire you for life.

WILLY   You'll retire me for life on seventy goddam dollars a week?
And your women and your car and your apartment, and you'll
retire me for life! Christ's sake, I couldn't get past Yonkers today! Where are you guys, where are you? The woods are burning!
I can't drive a car!

CHARLEY *has appeared in the doorway. He is a large man, slow of speech,
laconic, immovable. In all he says, despite what he says, there is pity, and,*

*now, trepidation. He has a robe over pajamas, slippers on his feet. He
enters the kitchen.*

CHARLEY Everything all right?

HAPPY Yeah, Charley, everything's . . .

WILLY What's the matter?

CHARLEY I heard some noise. I thought something happened. Can't
we do something about the walls? You sneeze in here, and in my
house hats blow off.

HAPPY Let's go to bed, Dad. Come on.

CHARLEY *signals to* HAPPY *to go.*

WILLY You go ahead, I'm not tired at the moment.

HAPPY (*to* WILLY) Take it easy, huh? (*He exits*)

WILLY What're you doin' up?

CHARLEY (*sitting down at the kitchen table opposite* WILLY)
Couldn't sleep good. I had a heartburn.

WILLY Well, you don't know how to eat.

CHARLEY I eat with my mouth.

WILLY No, you're ignorant. You gotta know about vitamins and
things like that.

CHARLEY Come on, let's shoot. Tire you out a little.

WILLY (*hesitantly*) All right. You got cards?

CHARLEY (*taking a deck from his pocket*) Yeah, I got them. Someplace. What is it with those vitamins?

WILLY (*dealing*) They build up your bones. Chemistry.

CHARLEY Yeah, but there's no bones in a heartburn.

WILLY What are you talkin' about? Do you know the first thing
about it?

CHARLEY Don't get insulted.

WILLY Don't talk about something you don't know anything about.

They are playing. Pause.

CHARLEY What're you doin' home?

WILLY A little trouble with the car.

CHARLEY Oh. (*Pause*) I'd like to take a trip to California.

WILLY Don't say.

CHARLEY You want a job?

WILLY I got a job, I told you that. (*After a slight pause*) What
the hell are you offering me a job for?

CHARLEY Don't get insulted.

WILLY Don't insult me.

CHARLEY I don't see no sense in it. You don't have to go on this
way.

WILLY   I got a good job. (*Slight pause*) What do you keep comin'
in here for?

CHARLEY   You want me to go?

WILLY   (*after a pause, withering*) I can't understand it. He's going
back to Texas again. What the hell is that?

CHARLEY   Let him go.

WILLY   I got nothin' to give him, Charley. I'm clean, I'm clean.

CHARLEY   He won't starve. None a them starve. Forget about him.

WILLY   Then what have I got to remember?

CHARLEY   You take it too hard. To hell with it. When a deposit
bottle is broken you don't get your nickel back.

WILLY   That's easy enough for you to say.

CHARLEY   That ain't easy for me to say.

WILLY   Did you see the ceiling I put up in the living-room?

CHARLEY   Yeah, that's a piece of work. To put up a ceiling is a
mystery to me. How do you do it?

WILLY   What's the difference?

CHARLEY   Well, talk about it.

WILLY   You gonna put up a ceiling?

CHARLEY   How could I put up a ceiling?

WILLY   Then what the hell are you bothering me for?

CHARLEY   You're insulted again.

WILLY   A man who can't handle tools is not a man. You're disgusting.

CHARLEY   Don't call me disgusting, Willy.

UNCLE BEN, *carrying a valise and an umbrella, enters the forestage from
around the right corner of the house. He is a stolid man, in his sixties,
with a mustache and an authoritative air. He is utterly certain of his destiny, and there is an aura of far places about him. He enters exactly as
WILLY speaks.*

WILLY   I'm getting awfully tired, Ben.

BEN'S *music is heard.* BEN *looks around at everything.*

CHARLEY   Good, keep playing; you'll sleep better. Did you call me
Ben?

BEN *looks at his watch.*

WILLY   That's funny. For a second there you reminded me of my
brother Ben.

BEN   I only have a few minutes. (*He strolls, inspecting the place.*
WILLY *and* CHARLEY *continue playing*)

CHARLEY   You never heard from him again, heh? Since that time?

WILLY   Didn't Linda tell you? Couple of weeks ago we got a letter
from his wife in Africa. He died.

CHARLEY   That so.

BEN (*chuckling*)   So this is Brooklyn, eh?

CHARLEY   Maybe you're in for some of his money.

WILLY   Naa, he had seven sons. There's just one opportunity I had with that man . . .

BEN   I must make a train, William. There are several properties I'm looking at in Alaska.

WILLY   Sure, sure! If I'd gone with him to Alaska that time, everything would've been totally different.

CHARLEY   Go on, you'd froze to death up there.

WILLY   What're you talking about?

BEN   Opportunity is tremendous in Alaska, William. Surprised you're not up there.

WILLY   Sure, tremendous.

CHARLEY   Heh?

WILLY   There was the only man I ever met who knew the answers.

CHARLEY   Who?

BEN   How are you all?

WILLY (*taking a pot, smiling*)   Fine, fine.

CHARLEY   Pretty sharp tonight.

BEN   Is Mother living with you?

WILLY   No, she died a long time ago.

CHARLEY   Who?

BEN   That's too bad. Fine specimen of a lady, Mother.

WILLY (*to* CHARLEY)   Heh?

BEN   I'd hoped to see the old girl.

CHARLEY   Who died?

BEN   Heard anything from Father, have you?

WILLY (*unnerved*)   What do you mean, who died?

CHARLEY (*taking a pot*)   What're you talkin' about?

BEN (*looking at his watch*)   William, it's half-past eight!

WILLY (*as though to dispel his confusion he angrily stops* CHARLEY's *hand*)   That's my build!

CHARLEY   I put the ace—

WILLY   If you don't know how to play the game I'm not gonna throw my money away on you!

CHARLEY (*rising*)   It was my ace, for God's sake!

WILLY   I'm through, I'm through!

BEN   When did Mother die?

WILLY   Long ago. Since the beginning you never knew how to play cards.

CHARLEY (*picks up the cards and goes to the door*)   All right! Next time I'll bring a deck with five aces.

WILLY   I don't play that kind of game!

CHARLEY   (*turning to him*)   You ought to be ashamed of yourself!

WILLY   Yeah?

CHARLEY   Yeah! (*He goes out*)

WILLY   (*slamming the door after him*)   Ignoramus!

BEN   (*as* WILLY *comes toward him through the wall-line of the kitchen*)   So you're William.

WILLY   (*shaking* BEN's *hand*)   Ben! I've been waiting for you so long! What's the answer? How did you do it?

BEN   Oh, there's a story in that.

LINDA *enters the forestage, as of old, carrying the wash basket.*

LINDA   Is this Ben?

BEN   (*gallantly*)   How do you do, my dear.

LINDA   Where've you been all these years? Willy's always wondered why you—

WILLY   (*pulling* BEN *away from her impatiently*)   Where is Dad? Didn't you follow him? How did you get started?

BEN   Well, I don't know how much you remember.

WILLY   Well, I was just a baby, of course, only three or four years old—

BEN   Three years and eleven months.

WILLY   What a memory, Ben!

BEN   I have many enterprises, William, and I have never kept books.

WILLY   I remember I was sitting under the wagon in—was it Nebraska?

BEN   It was South Dakota, and I gave you a bunch of wild flowers.

WILLY   I remember you walking away down some open road.

BEN   (*laughing*)   I was going to find Father in Alaska.

WILLY   Where is he?

BEN   At that age I had a very faulty view of geography, William. I discovered after a few days that I was heading due south, so instead of Alaska, I ended up in Africa.

LINDA   Africa!

WILLY   The Gold Coast!

BEN   Principally diamond mines.

LINDA   Diamond mines!

BEN   Yes, my dear. But I've only a few minutes—

WILLY   No! Boys! Boys! (*Young* BIFF *and* HAPPY *appear*)   Listen to this. This is your Uncle Ben, a great man! Tell my boys, Ben!

BEN   Why, boys, when I was seventeen I walked into the jungle, and when I was twenty-one I walked out. (*He laughs*)   And by God I was rich.

WILLY (*to the boys*) You see what I been talking about? The greatest things can happen!

BEN (*glancing at his watch*) I have an appointment in Ketchikan Tuesday week.

WILLY No, Ben! Please tell about Dad. I want my boys to hear. I want them to know the kind of stock they spring from. All I remember is a man with a big beard, and I was in Mamma's lap, sitting around a fire, and some kind of high music.

BEN His flute. He played the flute.

WILLY Sure, the flute, that's right!

New music is heard, a high, rollicking tune.

BEN Father was a very great and a very wild-hearted man. We would start in Boston, and he'd toss the whole family into the wagon, and then he'd drive the team right across the country; through Ohio, and Indiana, Michigan, Illinois, and all the Western states. And we'd stop in the towns and sell the flutes that he'd made on the way. Great inventor, Father. With one gadget he made more in a week than a man like you could make in a lifetime.

WILLY That's just the way I'm bringing them up, Ben—rugged, well liked, all-around.

BEN Yeah? (*To* BIFF) Hit that, boy—hard as you can. (*He pounds his stomach*)

BIFF Oh, no, sir!

BEN (*taking boxing stance*) Come on, get to me! (*He laughs*)

WILLY Go to it, Biff! Go ahead, show him!

BIFF Okay! (*He cocks his fists and starts in*)

LINDA (*to* WILLY) Why must he fight, dear?

BEN (*sparring with* BIFF) Good boy! Good boy!

WILLY How's that, Ben, heh?

HAPPY Give him the left, Biff!

LINDA Why are you fighting?

BEN Good boy! (*Suddenly comes in, trips* BIFF, *and stands over him, the point of his umbrella poised over* BIFF's *eye*)

LINDA Look out, Biff!

BIFF Gee!

BEN (*patting* BIFF's *knee*) Never fight fair with a stranger, boy. You'll never get out of the jungle that way. (*Taking* LINDA's *hand and bowing*) It was an honor and a pleasure to meet you, Linda.

LINDA (*withdrawing her hand coldly, frightened*) Have a nice— trip.

BEN (*to* WILLY) And good luck with your—what do you do?

WILLY   Selling.

BEN   Yes. Well... (*He raises his hand in farewell to all*)

WILLY   No, Ben, I don't want you to think... (*He takes* BEN's *arm to show him*) It's Brooklyn, I know, but we hunt too.

BEN   Really, now.

WILLY   Oh, sure, there's snakes and rabbits and—that's why I moved out here. Why, Biff can fell any one of these trees in no time! Boys! Go right over to where they're building the apartment house and get some sand. We're gonna rebuild the entire front stoop right now! Watch this, Ben!

BIFF   Yes, sir! On the double, Hap!

HAPPY   (*as he and* BIFF *run off*)   I lost weight, Pop, you notice?

CHARLEY *enters in knickers, even before the boys are gone.*

CHARLEY   Listen, if they steal any more from that building the watchman'll put the cops on them!

LINDA   (*to* WILLY)   Don't let Biff...

BEN *laughs lustily.*

WILLY   You shoulda seen the lumber they brought home last week. At least a dozen six-by-tens worth all kinds a money.

CHARLEY   Listen, if that watchman—

WILLY   I gave them hell, understand. But I got a couple of fearless characters there.

CHARLEY   Willy, the jails are full of fearless characters.

BEN   (*clapping* WILLY *on the back, with a laugh at* CHARLEY)   And the stock exchange, friend!

WILLY   (*joining in* BEN's *laughter*)   Where are the rest of your pants?

CHARLEY   My wife bought them.

WILLY   Now all you need is a golf club and you can go upstairs and go to sleep. (*To* BEN) Great athlete! Between him and his son Bernard they can't hammer a nail!

BERNARD   (*rushing in*)   The watchman's chasing Biff!

WILLY   (*angrily*)   Shut up! He's not stealing anything!

LINDA   (*alarmed, hurrying off left*)   Where is he? Biff, dear! (*She exits*)

WILLY   (*moving toward the left, away from* BEN)   There's nothing wrong. What's the matter with you?

BEN   Nervy boy. Good!

WILLY   (*laughing*)   Oh, nerves of iron, that Biff!

CHARLEY   Don't know what it is. My New England man comes back and he's bleedin', they murdered him up there.

WILLY   It's contacts, Charley, I got important contacts!

CHARLEY (*sarcastically*) Glad to hear it, Willy. Come in later, we'll shoot a little casino. I'll take some of your Portland money. (*He laughs at* WILLY *and exits*)

WILLY (*turning to* BEN) Business is bad, it's murderous. But not for me, of course.

BEN I'll stop by on my way back to Africa.

WILLY (*longingly*) Can't you stay a few days? You're just what I need, Ben, because I—I have a fine position here, but I—well, Dad left when I was such a baby and I never had a chance to talk to him and I still feel—kind of temporary about myself.

BEN I'll be late for my train.

They are at opposite ends of the stage.

WILLY Ben, my boys—can't we talk? They'd go into the jaws of hell for me, see, but I—

BEN William, you're being first-rate with your boys. Outstanding, manly chaps!

WILLY (*hanging on to his words*) Oh, Ben, that's good to hear! Because sometimes I'm afraid that I'm not teaching them the right kind of— Ben, how should I teach them?

BEN (*giving great weight to each word, and with a certain vicious audacity*) William, when I walked into the jungle, I was seventeen. When I walked out I was twenty-one. And, by God, I was rich! (*He goes off into darkness around the right corner of the house*)

WILLY ... was rich! That's just the spirit I want to imbue them with! To walk into a jungle! I was right! I was right! I was right!

BEN *is gone, but* WILLY *is still speaking to him as* LINDA, *in nightgown and robe, enters the kitchen, glances around for* WILLY, *then goes to the door of the house, looks out and sees him. Comes down to his left. He looks at her.*

LINDA Willy, dear? Willy?

WILLY I was right!

LINDA Did you have some cheese? (*He can't answer*) It's very late, darling. Come to bed, heh?

WILLY (*looking straight up*) Gotta break your neck to see a star in this yard.

LINDA You coming in?

WILLY Whatever happened to that diamond watch fob? Remember? When Ben came from Africa that time? Didn't he give me a watch fob with a diamond in it?

LINDA   You pawned it, dear. Twelve, thirteen years ago. For Biff's radio correspondence course.

WILLY   Gee, that was a beautiful thing. I'll take a walk.

LINDA   But you're in your slippers.

WILLY   (*starting to go around the house at the left*)   I was right! I was! (*Half to* LINDA, *as he goes, shaking his head*)   What a man! There was a man worth talking to I was right!

LINDA   (*calling after* WILLY)   But in your slippers, Willy!

WILLY *is almost gone when* BIFF, *in his pajamas, comes down the stairs and enters the kitchen.*

BIFF   What is he doing out there?

LINDA   Sh!

BIFF   God Almighty, Mom, how long has he been doing this?

LINDA   Don't, he'll hear you.

BIFF   What the hell is the matter with him?

LINDA   It'll pass by morning.

BIFF   Shouldn't we do anything?

LINDA   Oh, my dear, you should do a lot of things, but there's nothing to do, so go to sleep.

HAPPY *comes down the stairs and sits on the steps.*

HAPPY   I never heard him so loud, Mom.

LINDA   Well, come around more often; you'll hear him. (*She sits down at the table and mends the lining of* WILLY's *jacket*)

BIFF   Why didn't you ever write me about this, Mom?

LINDA   How would I write to you? For over three months you had no address.

BIFF   I was on the move. But you know I thought of you all the time. You know that, don't you, pal?

LINDA   I know, dear, I know. But he likes to have a letter. Just to know that there's still a possibility for better things.

BIFF   He's not like this all the time, is he?

LINDA   It's when you come home he's always the worst.

BIFF   When I come home?

LINDA   When you write you're coming, he's all smiles, and talks about the future, and—he's just wonderful. And then the closer you seem to come, the more shaky he gets, and then, by the time you get here, he's arguing, and he seems angry at you. I think it's just that maybe he can't bring himself to—to open up to you. Why are you so hateful to each other? Why is that?

BIFF   (*evasively*)   I'm not hateful, Mom.

LINDA   But you no sooner come in the door than you're fighting!

BIFF   I don't know why. I mean to change. I'm tryin', Mom, you understand?

LINDA   Are you home to stay now?

BIFF   I don't know. I want to look around, see what's doin'.

LINDA   Biff, you can't look around all your life, can you?

BIFF   I just can't take hold, Mom. I can't take hold of some kind of a life.

LINDA   Biff, a man is not a bird, to come and go with the springtime.

BIFF   Your hair . . . (*He touches her hair*) Your hair got so gray.

LINDA   Oh, it's been gray since you were in high school. I just stopped dyeing it, that's all.

BIFF   Dye it again, will ya? I don't want my pal looking old. (*He smiles*)

LINDA   You're such a boy! You think you can go away for a year and . . . You've got to get it into your head now that one day you'll knock on this door and there'll be strange people here—

BIFF   What are you talking about? You're not even sixty, Mom.

LINDA   But what about your father?

BIFF   (*lamely*)   Well, I meant him too.

HAPPY   He admires Pop.

LINDA   Biff, dear, if you don't have any feeling for him, then you can't have any feeling for me.

BIFF   Sure I can, Mom.

LINDA   No. You can't just come to see me, because I love him. (*With a threat, but only a threat, of tears*) He's the dearest man in the world to me, and I won't have anyone making him feel unwanted and low and blue. You've got to make up your mind now, darling, there's no leeway any more. Either he's your father and you pay him that respect, or else you're not to come here. I know he's not easy to get along with—nobody knows that better than me—but . . .

WILLY   (*from the left, with a laugh*)   Hey, hey, Biffo!

BIFF   (*starting to go out after* WILLY)   What the hell is the matter with him? (HAPPY *stops him*)

LINDA   Don't—don't go near him!

BIFF   Stop making excuses for him! He always, always wiped the floor with you. Never had an ounce of respect for you.

HAPPY   He's always had respect for—

BIFF   What the hell do you know about it?

HAPPY   (*surlily*)   Just don't call him crazy!

BIFF   He's got no character—Charley wouldn't do this. Not in his own house—spewing out that vomit from his mind.

HAPPY   Charley never had to cope with what he's got to.

BIFF   People are worse off than Willy Loman. Believe me, I've seen them!

LINDA   Then make Charley your father, Biff. You can't do that, can you? I don't say he's a great man. Willy Loman never made a lot of money. His name was never in the paper. He's not the finest character that ever lived. But he's a human being, and a terrible thing is happening to him. So attention must be paid. He's not to be allowed to fall into his grave like an old dog. Attention, attention must be finally paid to such a person. You called him crazy—

BIFF   I didn't mean—

LINDA   No, a lot of people think he's lost his—balance. But you don't have to be very smart to know what his trouble is. The man is exhausted.

HAPPY   Sure!

LINDA   A small man can be just as exhausted as a great man. He works for a company thirty-six years this March, opens up unheard-of territories to their trademark, and now in his old age they take his salary away.

HAPPY   (*indignantly*)   I didn't know that, Mom.

LINDA   You never asked, my dear! Now that you get your spending money someplace else you don't trouble your mind with him.

HAPPY   But I gave you money last—

LINDA   Christmas time, fifty dollars! To fix the hot water it cost ninety-seven fifty! For five weeks he's been on straight commission, like a beginner, an unknown!

BIFF   Those ungrateful bastards!

LINDA   Are they any worse than his sons? When he brought them business, when he was young, they were glad to see him. But now his old friends, the old buyers that loved him so and always found some order to hand him in a pinch—they're all dead, retired. He used to be able to make six, seven calls a day in Boston. Now he takes his valises out of the car and puts them back and takes them out again and he's exhausted. Instead of walking he talks now. He drives seven hundred miles, and when he gets there no one knows him any more, no one welcomes him. And what goes through a man's mind, driving seven hundred miles home without having earned a cent? Why shouldn't he talk to himself? Why? When he has to go to Charley and borrow fifty dollars a week and pretend to me that it's his pay? How long can that go on? How long? You see what I'm sitting here and waiting for? And you tell me he has no character? The man who never worked a day but for your benefit? When does he get the medal for that? Is this his reward—to turn around at the age of sixty-

three and find his sons, who he loved better than his life, one a
philandering bum—

HAPPY   Mom!

LINDA   That's all you are, my baby! (*To* BIFF) And you! What
happened to the love you had for him? You were such pals! How
you used to talk to him on the phone every night! How lonely he
was till he could come home to you!

BIFF   All right, Mom. I'll live here in my room, and I'll get a job.
I'll keep away from him, that's all.

LINDA   No, Biff. You can't stay here and fight all the time.

BIFF   He threw me out of this house, remember that.

LINDA   Why did he do that? I never knew why.

BIFF   Because I know he's a fake and he doesn't like anybody
around who knows!

LINDA   Why a fake? In what way? What do you mean?

BIFF   Just don't lay it all at my feet. It's between me and him—
that's all I have to say. I'll chip in from now on. He'll settle for
half my pay check. He'll be all right. I'm going to bed. (*He starts
for the stairs*)

LINDA   He won't be all right.

BIFF   (*turning on the stairs, furiously*)   I hate this city and I'll stay
here. Now what do you want?

LINDA   He's dying, Biff.

HAPPY *turns quickly to her, shocked.*

BIFF   (*after a pause*)   Why is he dying?

LINDA   He's been trying to kill himself.

BIFF   (*with great horror*)   How?

LINDA   I live from day to day.

BIFF   What're you talking about?

LINDA   Remember I wrote you that he smashed up the car again?
In February?

BIFF   Well?

LINDA   The insurance inspector came. He said that they have evidence. That all these accidents in the last year—weren't—weren't
—accidents.

HAPPY   How can they tell that? That's a lie.

LINDA   It seems there's a woman . . . (*She takes a breath as . . .*)

⎰BIFF   (*sharply but contained*)   What woman?
⎱LINDA   (*simultaneously*)   . . . and this woman . . .

LINDA   What?

BIFF   Nothing. Go ahead.

LINDA   What did you say?

BIFF   Nothing. I just said what woman?

HAPPY   What about her?

LINDA   Well, it seems she was walking down the road and saw his car. She says that he wasn't driving fast at all, and that he didn't skid. She says he came to that little bridge, and then deliberately smashed into the railing, and it was only the shallowness of the water that saved him.

BIFF   Oh, no, he probably just fell asleep again.

LINDA   I don't think he fell asleep.

BIFF   Why not?

LINDA   Last month . . . (*With great difficulty*) Oh, boys, it's so hard to say a thing like this! He's just a big stupid man to you, but I tell you there's more good in him than in many other people. (*She chokes, wipes her eyes*) I was looking for a fuse. The lights blew out, and I went down the cellar. And behind the fuse box —it happened to fall out—was length of rubber pipe—just short.

HAPPY   No kidding?

LINDA   There's a little attachment on the end of it. I knew right away. And sure enough, on the bottom of the water heater there's a new little nipple on the gas pipe.

HAPPY   (*angrily*)   That—jerk.

BIFF   Did you have it taken off?

LINDA   I'm—I'm ashamed to. How can I mention it to him? Every day I go down and take away that little rubber pipe. But, when he comes home, I put it back where it was. How can I insult him that way? I don't know what to do. I live from day to day, boys. I tell you, I know every thought in his mind. It sounds so old-fashioned and silly, but I tell you he put his whole life into you and you've turned your backs on him. (*She is bent over in the chair, weeping, her face in her hands*) Biff, I swear to God! Biff, his life is in your hands!

HAPPY   (*to* BIFF)   How do you like that damned fool!

BIFF   (*kissing her*)   All right, pal, all right. It's all settled now. I've been remiss. I know that, Mom. But now I'll stay, and I swear to you, I'll apply myself. (*Kneeling in front of her, in a fever of self-reproach*) It's just—you see, Mom, I don't fit in business. Not that I won't try. I'll try, and I'll make good.

HAPPY   Sure you will. The trouble with you in business was you never tried to please people.

BIFF   I know, I—

HAPPY   Like when you worked for Harrison's. Bob Harrison said you were tops, and then you go and do some damn fool thing like whistling whole songs in the elevator like a comedian.

BIFF (*against* HAPPY)   So what? I like to whistle sometimes.

HAPPY   You don't raise a guy to a responsible job who whistles in the elevator!

LINDA   Well, don't argue about it now.

HAPPY   Like when you'd go off and swim in the middle of the day instead of taking the line around.

BIFF (*his resentment rising*)   Well, don't you run off? You take off sometimes, don't you? On a nice summer day?

HAPPY   Yeah, but I cover myself!

LINDA   Boys!

HAPPY   If I'm going to take a fade the boss can call any number where I'm supposed to be and they'll swear to him that I just left. I'll tell you something that I hate to say, Biff, but in the business world some of them think you're crazy.

BIFF (*angered*)   Screw the business world!

HAPPY   All right, screw it! Great, but cover yourself!

LINDA   Hap, Hap!

BIFF   I don't care what they think! They've laughed at Dad for years, and you know why? Because we don't belong in this nuthouse of a city! We should be mixing cement on some open plain, or—or carpenters. A carpenter is allowed to whistle!

WILLY *walks in from the entrance of the house, at left.*

WILLY   Even your grandfather was better than a carpenter. (*Pause. They watch him*) You never grew up. Bernard does not whistle in the elevator, I assure you.

BIFF (*as though to laugh* WILLY *out of it*)   Yeah, but you do, Pop.

WILLY   I never in my life whistled in an elevator! And who in the business world thinks I'm crazy?

BIFF   I didn't mean it like that, Pop. Now don't make a whole thing out of it, will ya?

WILLY   Go back to the West! Be a carpenter, a cowboy, enjoy yourself!

LINDA   Willy, he was just saying—

WILLY   I heard what he said!

HAPPY (*trying to quiet* WILLY)   Hey, Pop, come on now ...

WILLY (*continuing over* HAPPY's *line*)   They laugh at me, heh? Go to Filene's, go to the Hub, go to Slattery's, Boston. Call out the name Willy Loman and see what happens! Big shot!

BIFF   All right, Pop.

WILLY   Big!

BIFF   All right!

WILLY   Why do you always insult me?

BIFF   I didn't say a word. (*To* LINDA) Did I say a word?

LINDA   He didn't say anything, Willy.

WILLY   (*going to the doorway of the living-room*)   All right, good night, good night.

LINDA   Willy, dear, he just decided . . .

WILLY   (*to* BIFF)   If you get tired hanging around tomorrow, paint the ceiling I put up in the living-room.

BIFF   I'm leaving early tomorrow.

HAPPY   He's going to see Bill Oliver, Pop.

WILLY   (*interestedly*)   Oliver? For what?

BIFF   (*with reserve, but trying, trying*)   He always said he'd stake me. I'd like to go into business, so maybe I can take him up on it.

LINDA   Isn't that wonderful?

WILLY   Don't interrupt. What's wonderful about it? There's fifty men in the City of New York who'd stake him. (*To* BIFF) Sporting goods?

BIFF   I guess so. I know something about it and—

WILLY   He knows something about it! You know sporting goods better than Spalding, for God's sake! How much is he giving you?

BIFF   I don't know, I didn't even see him yet, but—

WILLY   Then what're you talkin' about?

BIFF   (*getting angry*)   Well, all I said was I'm gonna see him, that's all!

WILLY   (*turning away*)   Ah, you're counting your chickens again.

BIFF   (*starting left for the stairs*)   Oh, Jesus, I'm going to sleep!

WILLY   (*calling after him*)   Don't curse in this house!

BIFF   (*turning*)   Since when did you get so clean?

HAPPY   (*trying to stop them*)   Wait a . . .

WILLY   Don't use that language to me! I won't have it!

HAPPY   (*grabbing* BIFF, *shouts*)   Wait a minute! I got an idea. I got a feasible idea. Come here, Biff, let's talk this over now, let's talk some sense here. When I was down in Florida last time, I thought of a great idea to sell sporting goods. It just came back to me. You and I, Biff—we have a line, the Loman Line. We train a couple of weeks, and put on a couple of exhibitions, see?

WILLY   That's an idea!

HAPPY   Wait! We form two basketball teams, see? Two water-polo teams. We play each other. It's a million dollars' worth of publicity. Two brothers, see? The Loman Brothers. Displays in the Royal Palms—all the hotels. And banners over the ring and the basketball court: "Loman Brothers." Baby, we could sell sporting goods!

WILLY   That is a one-million-dollar idea!

LINDA   Marvelous!

BIFF   I'm in great shape as far as that's concerned.

HAPPY   And the beauty of it is, Biff, it wouldn't be like a business. We'd be out playin' ball again . . .

BIFF (*enthused*)   Yeah, that's . . .

WILLY   Million-dollar . . .

HAPPY   And you wouldn't get fed up with it, Biff. It'd be the family again. There'd be the old honor, and comradeship, and if you wanted to go off for a swim or somethin'—well, you'd do it! Without some smart cooky gettin' up ahead of you!

WILLY   Lick the world! You guys together could absolutely lick the civilized world.

BIFF   I'll see Oliver tomorrow. Hap, if we could work that out . . .

LINDA   Maybe things are beginning to—

WILLY (*wildly enthused, to* LINDA)   Stop interrupting! (*To* BIFF) But don't wear sport jacket and slacks when you see Oliver.

BIFF   No, I'll—

WILLY   A business suit, and talk as little as possible, and don't crack any jokes.

BIFF   He did like me. Always liked me.

LINDA   He loved you!

WILLY (*to* LINDA)   Will you stop! (*To* BIFF) Walk in very serious. You are not applying for a boy's job. Money is to pass. Be quiet, fine, and serious. Everybody likes a kidder, but nobody lends him money.

HAPPY   I'll try to get some myself, Biff. I'm sure I can.

WILLY   I see great things for you kids, I think your troubles are over. But remember, start big and you'll end big. Ask for fifteen. How much you gonna ask for?

BIFF   Gee, I don't know—

WILLY   And don't say "Gee." "Gee" is a boy's word. A man walking in for fifteen thousand dollars does not say "Gee!"

BIFF   Ten, I think, would be top though.

WILLY   Don't be so modest. You always started too low. Walk in with a big laugh. Don't look worried. Start off with a couple of your good stories to lighten things up. It's not what you say, it's how you say it—because personality always wins the day.

LINDA   Oliver always thought the highest of him—

WILLY   Will you let me talk?

BIFF   Don't yell at her, Pop, will ya?

WILLY (*angrily*)   I was talking, wasn't I?

BIFF   I don't like you yelling at her all the time, and I'm tellin' you, that's all.

WILLY   What're you, takin' over this house?

LINDA   Willy—

WILLY (*turning on her*)   Don't take his side all the time, goddammit!

BIFF (*furiously*)   Stop yelling at her!

WILLY (*suddenly pulling on his cheek, beaten down, guilt ridden*) Give my best to Bill Oliver—he may remember me. (*He exits through the living-room doorway*)

LINDA (*her voice subdued*)   What'd you have to start that for? (BIFF *turns away*) You see how sweet he was as soon as you talked hopefully? (*She goes over to* BIFF) Come up and say good night to him. Don't let him go to bed that way.

HAPPY   Come on, Biff, let's buck him up.

LINDA   Please, dear. Just say good night. It takes so little to make him happy. Come. (*She goes through the living-room doorway, calling upstairs from within the living-room*) Your pajamas are hanging in the bathroom, Willy!

HAPPY (*looking toward where* LINDA *went out*)   What a woman! They broke the mold when they made her. You know that, Biff?

BIFF   He's off salary. My God, working on commission!

HAPPY   Well, let's face it: he's no hot-shot selling man. Except that sometimes, you have to admit, he's a sweet personality.

BIFF (*deciding*)   Lend me ten bucks, will ya? I want to buy some new ties.

HAPPY   I'll take you to a place I know. Beautiful stuff. Wear one of my striped shirts tomorrow.

BIFF   She got gray. Mom got awful old. Gee, I'm gonna go in to Oliver tomorrow and knock him for a—

HAPPY   Come on up. Tell that to Dad. Let's give him a whirl. Come on.

BIFF (*steamed up*)   You know, with ten thousand bucks, boy!

HAPPY (*as they go into the living-room*)   That's the talk, Biff, that's the first time I've heard the old confidence out of you! (*From within the living-room, fading off*) You're gonna live with me, kid, and any babe you want just say the word . . .

The last lines are hardly heard. They are mounting the stairs to their parents' bedroom.

LINDA (*entering her bedroom and addressing* WILLY, *who is in the bathroom. She is straightening the bed for him*)   Can you do anything about the shower? It drips.

WILLY (*from the bathroom*)   All of a sudden everything falls to pieces! Goddam plumbing, oughta be sued, those people. I hardly finished putting it in and the thing . . . (*His words rumble off*)

LINDA   I'm just wondering if Oliver will remember him. You think he might?

WILLY (*coming out of the bathroom in his pajamas*) Remember him? What's the matter with you, you crazy? If he'd've stayed with Oliver he'd be on top by now! Wait'll Oliver gets a look at him. You don't know the average caliber any more. The average young man today—(*he is getting into bed*)—is got a caliber of zero. Greatest thing in the world for him was to bum around.

BIFF *and* HAPPY *enter the bedroom. Slight pause.*

WILLY (*stops short, looking at* BIFF) Glad to hear it, boy.

HAPPY He wanted to say good night to you, sport.

WILLY (*to* BIFF) Yeah. Knock him dead, boy. What'd you want to tell me?

BIFF Just take it easy, Pop. Good night. (*He turns to go*)

WILLY (*unable to resist*) And if anything falls off the desk while you're talking to him—like a package or something—don't you pick it up. They have office boys for that.

LINDA I'll make a big breakfast—

WILLY Will you let me finish? (*To* BIFF) Tell him you were in the business in the West. Not farm work.

BIFF All right, Dad.

LINDA I think everything—

WILLY (*going right through her speech*) And don't undersell yourself. No less than fifteen thousand dollars.

BIFF (*unable to bear him*) Okay. Good night, Mom. (*He starts moving*)

WILLY Because you got a greatness in you, Biff, remember that. You got all kinds a greatness... (*He lies back, exhausted.* BIFF *walks out*)

LINDA (*calling after* BIFF) Sleep well, darling!

HAPPY I'm gonna get married, Mom. I wanted to tell you.

LINDA Go to sleep, dear.

HAPPY (*going*) I just wanted to tell you.

WILLY Keep up the good work. (HAPPY *exits*) God ... remember that Ebbets Field game? The championship of the city?

LINDA Just rest. Should I sing to you?

WILLY Yeah. Sing to me. (LINDA *hums a soft lullaby*) When that team came out—he was the tallest, remember?

LINDA Oh, yes. And in gold.

BIFF *enters the darkened kitchen, takes a cigarette, and leaves the house. He comes downstage into a golden pool of light. He smokes, staring at the night.*

WILLY Like a young god. Hercules—something like that. And the sun, the sun all around him. Remember how he waved to me?

Right up from the field, with the representatives of three colleges standing by? And the buyers I brought, and the cheers when he came out—Loman, Loman, Loman! God almighty, he'll be great yet. A star like that, magnificent, can never really fade away!

The light on WILLY *is fading. The gas heater begins to glow through the kitchen wall, near the stairs, a blue flame beneath red coils.*

LINDA (*timidly*)   Willy dear, what has he got against you?
WILLY   I'm so tired. Don't talk any more.

BIFF *slowly returns to the kitchen. He stops, stares toward the heater.*

LINDA   Will you ask Howard to let you work in New York?
WILLY   First thing in the morning. Everything'll be all right.

BIFF *reaches behind the heater and draws out a length of rubber tubing. He is horrified and turns his head toward* WILLY'S *room, still dimly lit, from which the strains of* LINDA'S *desperate but monotonous humming rise.*

WILLY (*staring through the window into the moonlight*)   Gee, look at the moon moving between the buildings!

BIFF *wraps the tubing around his hand and quickly goes up the stairs.*

Curtain

ACT TWO

Music is heard, gay and bright. The curtain rises as the music fades away. WILLY, *in shirt sleeves, is sitting at the kitchen table, sipping coffee, his hat in his lap.* LINDA *is filling his cup when she can.*

WILLY   Wonderful coffee. Meal in itself.
LINDA   Can I make you some eggs?
WILLY   No. Take a breath.
LINDA   You look so rested, dear.
WILLY   I slept like a dead one. First time in months. Imagine, sleeping till ten on a Tuesday morning. Boys left nice and early, heh?
LINDA   They were out of here by eight o'clock.
WILLY   Good work!
LINDA   It was so thrilling to see them leaving together. I can't get over the shaving lotion in this house!
WILLY (*smiling*)   Mmm—
LINDA   Biff was very changed this morning. His whole attitude seemed to be hopeful. He couldn't wait to get downtown to see Oliver.

WILLY   He's heading for a change. There's no question, there simply are certain men that take longer to get—solidified. How did he dress?

LINDA   His blue suit. He's so handsome in that suit. He could be a—anything in that suit!

WILLY *gets up from the table.* LINDA *holds his jacket for him.*

WILLY   There's no question, no question at all. Gee, on the way home tonight I'd like to buy some seeds.

LINDA (*laughing*)   That'd be wonderful. But not enough sun gets back there. Nothing'll grow any more.

WILLY   You wait, kid, before it's all over we're gonna get a little place out in the country, and I'll raise some vegetables, a couple of chickens . . .

LINDA   You'll do it yet, dear.

WILLY *walks out of his jacket.* LINDA *follows him.*

WILLY   And they'll get married, and come for a weekend. I'd build a little guest house. 'Cause I got so many fine tools, all I'd need would be a little lumber and some peace of mind.

LINDA (*joyfully*)   I sewed the lining . . .

WILLY   I could build two guest houses, so they'd both come. Did he decide how much he's going to ask Oliver for?

LINDA (*getting him into the jacket*)   He didn't mention it, but I imagine ten or fifteen thousand. You going to talk to Howard today?

WILLY   Yeah. I'll put it to him straight and simple. He'll just have to take me off the road.

LINDA   And Willy, don't forget to ask for a little advance, because we've got the insurance premium. It's the grace period now.

WILLY   That's a hundred . . . ?

LINDA   A hundred and eight, sixty-eight. Because we're a little short again.

WILLY   Why are we short?

LINDA   Well, you had the motor job on the car . . .

WILLY   That goddam Studebaker!

LINDA   And you got one more payment on the refrigerator . . .

WILLY   But it just broke again!

LINDA   Well, it's old, dear.

WILLY   I told you we should've bought a well-advertised machine. Charley bought a General Electric and it's twenty years old and it's still good, that son-of-a-bitch.

LINDA   But, Willy—

WILLY   Whoever heard of a Hastings refrigerator? Once in my life I would like to own something outright before it's broken! I'm always in a race with the junkyard! I just finished paying for the car and it's on its last legs. The refrigerator consumes belts like a goddam maniac. They time those things. They time them so when you finally paid for them, they're used up.

LINDA   (*buttoning up his jacket as he unbuttons it*)   All told, about two hundred dollars would carry us, dear. But that includes the last payment on the mortgage. After this payment, Willy, the house belongs to us.

WILLY   It's twenty-five years!

LINDA   Biff was nine years old when we bought it.

WILLY   Well, that's a great thing. To weather a twenty-five year mortgage is—

LINDA   It's an accomplishment.

WILLY   All the cement, the lumber, the reconstruction I put in this house! There ain't a crack to be found in it any more.

LINDA   Well, it served its purpose.

WILLY   What purpose? Some stranger'll come along, move in, and that's that. If only Biff would take this house, and raise a family . . . (*He starts to go*) Good-by, I'm late.

LINDA   (*suddenly remembering*)   Oh, I forgot! You're supposed to meet them for dinner.

WILLY   Me?

LINDA   At Frank's Chop House on Forty-eighth near Sixth Avenue.

WILLY   Is that so! How about you?

LINDA   No, just the three of you. They're gonna blow you to a big meal!

WILLY   Don't say! Who thought of that?

LINDA   Biff came to me this morning, Willy, and he said, "Tell Dad, we want to blow him to a big meal." Be there six o'clock. You and your two boys are going to have dinner.

WILLY   Gee whiz! That's really somethin'. I'm gonna knock Howard for a loop, kid. I'll get an advance, and I'll come home with a New York job. Goddammit, now I'm gonna do it!

LINDA   Oh, that's the spirit, Willy!

WILLY   I will never get behind a wheel the rest of my life!

LINDA   It's changing, Willy, I can feel it changing!

WILLY   Beyond a question. G'by, I'm late. (*He starts to go again*)

LINDA   (*calling after him as she runs to the kitchen table for a handkerchief*)   You got your glasses?

WILLY   (*feels for them, then comes back in*)   Yeah, yeah, got my glasses.

LINDA (*giving him the handkerchief*)   And a handkerchief.

WILLY   Yeah, handkerchief.

LINDA   And your saccharine?

WILLY   Yeah, my saccharine.

LINDA   Be careful on the subway stairs.

She kisses him, and a silk stocking is seen hanging from her hand. WILLY *notices it.*

WILLY   Will you stop mending stockings? At least while I'm in the house. It gets me nervous. I can't tell you. Please.

LINDA *hides the stocking in her hand as she follows* WILLY *across the forestage in front of the house.*

LINDA   Remember, Frank's Chop House.

WILLY (*passing the apron*)   Maybe beets would grow out there.

LINDA (*laughing*)   But you tried so many times.

WILLY   Yeah. Well, don't work hard today. (*He disappears around the right corner of the house*)

LINDA   Be careful!

As WILLY *vanishes,* LINDA *waves to him. Suddenly the phone rings. She runs across the stage and into the kitchen and lifts it.*

LINDA   Hello? Oh, Biff! I'm so glad you called, I just . . . Yes, sure, I just told him. Yes, he'll be there for dinner at six o'clock, I didn't forget. Listen, I was just dying to tell you. You know that little rubber pipe I told you about? That he connected to the gas heater? I finally decided to go down the cellar this morning and take it away and destroy it. But it's gone! Imagine? He took it away himself, it isn't there! (*She listens*) When? Oh, then you took it. Oh—nothing, it's just that I'd hoped he'd taken it away himself. Oh, I'm not worried, darling, because this morning he left in such high spirits, it was like the old days! I'm not afraid any more. Did Mr. Oliver see you? . . . Well, you wait there then. And make a nice impression on him, darling. Just don't perspire too much before you see him. And have a nice time with Dad. He may have big news too! . . . That's right, a New York job. And be sweet to him tonight, dear. Be loving to him. Because he's only a little boat looking for a harbor. (*She is trembling with sorrow and joy*) Oh, that's wonderful, Biff, you'll save his life. Thanks, darling. Just put your arm around him when he comes into the restaurant. Give him a smile. That's the boy . . . Good-by, dear. . . . You got your comb? . . . That's fine. Good-by, Biff dear.

In the middle of her speech, HOWARD WAGNER, *thirty-six, wheels on a small typewriter table on which is a wire-recording machine and proceeds to plug it in. This is on the left forestage. Light slowly fades on* LINDA *as it rises on* HOWARD. HOWARD *is intent on threading the machine and only glances over his shoulder as* WILLY *appears.*

WILLY   Pst! Pst!

HOWARD   Hello, Willy, come in.

WILLY   Like to have a little talk with you, Howard.

HOWARD   Sorry to keep you waiting. I'll be with you in a minute.

WILLY   What's that, Howard?

HOWARD   Didn't you ever see one of these? Wire recorder.

WILLY   Oh. Can we talk a minute?

HOWARD   Records things. Just got delivery yesterday. Been driving me crazy, the most terrific machine I ever saw in my life. I was up all night with it.

WILLY   What do you do with it?

HOWARD   I bought it for dictation, but you can do anything with it. Listen to this. I had it home last night. Listen to what I picked up. The first one is my daughter. Get this. (*He flicks the switch and "Roll out the Barrel" is heard being whistled*) Listen to that kid whistle.

WILLY   That is lifelike, isn't it?

HOWARD   Seven years old. Get that tone.

WILLY   Ts, ts. Like to ask a little favor if you . . .

The whistling breaks off, and the voice of HOWARD's *daughter is heard.*

HIS DAUGHTER   "Now you, Daddy."

HOWARD   She's crazy for me! (*Again the same song is whistled*) That's me! Ha! (*He winks*)

WILLY   You're very good!

The whistling breaks off again. The machine runs silent for a moment.

HOWARD   Sh! Get this now, this is my son.

HIS SON   "The capital of Alabama is Montgomery; the capital of Arizona is Phoenix; the capital of Arkansas is Little Rock; the capital of California is Sacramento . . ." (*and on, and on*)

HOWARD   (*holding up five fingers*)   Five years old, Willy!

WILLY   He'll make an announcer some day!

HIS SON   (*continuing*)   "The capital . . ."

HOWARD   Get that—alphabetical order! (*The machine breaks off suddenly*) Wait a minute. The maid kicked the plug out.

WILLY   It certainly is a—

HOWARD   Sh, for God's sake!

HIS SON   "It's nine o'clock, Bulova watch time. So I have to go to sleep."

WILLY   That really is—

HOWARD   Wait a minute! The next is my wife.

They wait.

HOWARD'S VOICE   "Go on, say something." (*Pause*) "Well, you gonna talk?"

HIS WIFE   "I can't think of anything."

HOWARD'S VOICE   "Well, talk—it's turning."

HIS WIFE (*shyly, beaten*)   "Hello." (*Silence*) "Oh, Howard, I can't talk into this . . ."

HOWARD (*snapping the machine off*)   That was my wife.

WILLY   That is a wonderful machine. Can we—

HOWARD   I tell you, Willy, I'm gonna take my camera, and my bandsaw, and all my hobbies, and out they go. This is the most fascinating relaxation I ever found.

WILLY   I think I'll get one myself.

HOWARD   Sure, they're only a hundred and a half. You can't do without it. Supposing you wanna hear Jack Benny, see? But you can't be at home at that hour. So you tell the maid to turn the radio on when Jack Benny comes on, and this automatically goes on with the radio . . .

WILLY   And when you come home you . . .

HOWARD   You can come home twelve o'clock, one o'clock, any time you like, and you get yourself a Coke and sit yourself down, throw the switch, and there's Jack Benny's program in the middle of the night!

WILLY   I'm definitely going to get one. Because lots of time I'm on the road, and I think to myself, what I must be missing on the radio!

HOWARD   Don't you have a radio in the car?

WILLY   Well, yeah, but who ever thinks of turning it on?

HOWARD   Say, aren't you supposed to be in Boston?

WILLY   That's what I want to talk to you about, Howard. You got a minute? (*He draws a chair in from the wing*)

HOWARD   What happened? What're you doing here?

WILLY   Well . . .

HOWARD   You didn't crack up again, did you?

WILLY   Oh, no. No . . .

HOWARD   Geez, you had me worried there for a minute. What's the trouble?

WILLY   Well, tell you the truth, Howard. I've come to the decision that I'd rather not travel any more.

HOWARD   Not travel! Well, what'll you do?

WILLY   Remember, Christmas time, when you had the party here? You said you'd try to think of some spot for me here in town.

HOWARD   With us?

WILLY   Well, sure.

HOWARD   Oh, yeah, yeah. I remember. Well, I couldn't think of anything for you, Willy.

WILLY   I tell ya, Howard. The kids are all grown up, y'know. I don't need much any more. If I could take home—well, sixty-five dollars a week, I could swing it.

HOWARD   Yeah, but Willy, see I—

WILLY   I tell ya why, Howard. Speaking frankly and between the two of us, y'know—I'm just a little tired.

HOWARD   Oh, I could understand that, Willy. But you're a road man, Willy, and we do a road business. We've only got a half-dozen salesmen on the floor here.

WILLY   God knows, Howard, I never asked a favor of any man. But I was with the firm when your father used to carry you in here in his arms.

HOWARD   I know that, Willy, but—

WILLY   Your father came to me the day you were born and asked me what I thought of the name of Howard, may he rest in peace.

HOWARD   I appreciate that, Willy, but there just is no spot here for you. If I had a spot I'd slam you right in, but I just don't have a single solitary spot.

He looks for his lighter. WILLY *has picked it up and gives it to him. Pause.*

WILLY   (*with increasing anger*)   Howard, all I need to set my table is fifty dollars a week.

HOWARD   But where am I going to put you, kid?

WILLY   Look, it isn't a question of whether I can sell merchandise, is it?

HOWARD   No, but it's a business, kid, and everybody's gotta pull his own weight.

WILLY   (*desperately*)   Just let me tell you a story, Howard—

HOWARD   'Cause you gotta admit, business is business.

WILLY   (*angrily*)   Business is definitely business, but just listen for a minute. You don't understand this. When I was a boy—eighteen, nineteen—I was already on the road. And there was a question in my mind as to whether selling had a future for me. Because in those days I had a yearning to go to Alaska. See, there were three gold strikes in one month in Alaska, and I felt like going out. Just for the ride, you might say.

HOWARD   (*barely interested*)   Don't say.

WILLY Oh, yeah, my father lived many years in Alaska. He was an adventurous man. We've got quite a little streak of self-reliance in our family. I thought I'd go out with my older brother and try to locate him, and maybe settle in the North with the old man. And I was almost decided to go, when I met a salesman in the Parker House. His name was Dave Singleman. And he was eighty-four years old, and he'd drummed merchandise in thirty-one states. And old Dave, he'd go up to his room, y'understand, put on his green velvet slippers—I'll never forget—and pick up his phone and call the buyers, and without ever leaving his room, at the age of eighty-four, he made his living. And when I saw that, I realized that selling was the greatest career a man could want. 'Cause what could be more satisfying than to be able to go, at the age of eighty-four, into twenty or thirty different cities, and pick up a phone, and be remembered and loved and helped by so many different people? Do you know? when he died—and by the way he died the death of a salesman, in his green velvet slippers in the smoker of the New York, New Haven and Hartford, going into Boston—when he died, hundreds of salesmen and buyers were at his funeral. Things were sad on a lotta trains for months after that. (*He stands up.* HOWARD *has not looked at him*) In those days there was personality in it, Howard. There was respect, and comradeship, and gratitude in it. Today, it's all cut and dried, and there's no chance for bringing friendship to bear—or personality. You see what I mean? They don't know me any more.

HOWARD (*moving away, to the right*) That's just the thing, Willy.

WILLY If I had forty dollars a week—that's all I'd need. Forty dollars, Howard.

HOWARD Kid, I can't take blood from a stone, I—

WILLY (*desperation is on him now*) Howard, the year Al Smith was nominated, your father came to me and—

HOWARD (*starting to go off*) I've got to see some people, kid.

WILLY (*stopping him*) I'm talking about your father! There were promises made across this desk! You mustn't tell me you've got people to see—I put thirty-four years into this firm, Howard, and now I can't pay my insurance! You can't eat the orange and throw the peel away—a man is not a piece of fruit! (*After a pause*) Now pay attention. Your father—in 1928 I had a big year. I averaged a hundred and seventy dollars a week in commissions.

HOWARD (*impatiently*) Now, Willy, you never averaged—

WILLY (*banging his hand on the desk*) I averaged a hundred and seventy dollars a week in the year of 1928! And your father came to me—or rather, I was in the office here—it was right over this desk—and he put his hand on my shoulder—

HOWARD (*getting up*)   You'll have to excuse me, Willy, I gotta see some people. Pull yourself together. (*Going out*) I'll be back in a little while.

On HOWARD's *exit, the light on his chair grows very bright and strange.*

WILLY   Pull myself together! What the hell did I say to him? My God, I was yelling at him! How could I! (WILLY *breaks off, staring at the light, which occupies the chair, animating it. He approaches this chair, standing across the desk from it*) Frank, Frank, don't you remember what you told me that time? How you put your hand on my shoulder, and Frank . . .

He leans on the desk and as he speaks the dead man's name he accidentally switches on the recorder, and instantly

HOWARD'S SON   ". . . of New York is Albany. The capital of Ohio is Cincinnati, the capital of Rhode Island is . . ." (*The recitation continues*)

WILLY (*leaping away with fright, shouting*)   Ha! Howard! Howard! Howard!

HOWARD (*rushing in*)   What happened?

WILLY (*pointing at the machine, which continues nasally, childishly, with the capital cities*)   Shut it off! Shut it off!

HOWARD (*pulling the plug out*)   Look, Willy . . .

WILLY (*pressing his hands to his eyes*)   I gotta get myself some coffee. I'll get some coffee . . .

WILLY *starts to walk out.* HOWARD *stops him.*

HOWARD (*rolling up the cord*)   Willy, look . . .

WILLY   I'll go to Boston.

HOWARD   Willy, you can't go to Boston for us.

WILLY   Why can't I go?

HOWARD   I don't want you to represent us. I've been meaning to tell you for a long time now.

WILLY   Howard, are you firing me?

HOWARD   I think you need a good long rest, Willy.

WILLY   Howard—

HOWARD   And when you feel better, come back, and we'll see if we can work something out.

WILLY   But I gotta earn money, Howard. I'm in no position to—

HOWARD   Where are your sons? Why don't your sons give you a hand?

WILLY   They're working on a very big deal.

HOWARD This is no time for false pride, Willy. You go to your
ˈsons and you tell them that you're tired. You've got two great
boys, haven't you?

WILLY Oh, no question, no question, but in the meantime...

HOWARD Then that's that, heh?

WILLY All right, I'll go to Boston tomorrow.

HOWARD No, no.

WILLY I can't throw myself on my sons. I'm not a cripple!

HOWARD Look, kid, I'm busy this morning.

WILLY (*grasping* HOWARD's *arm*) Howard, you've got to let me
go to Boston!

HOWARD (*hard, keeping himself under control*) I've got a line of
people to see this morning. Sit down, take five minutes, and pull
yourself together, and then go home, will ya? I need the office,
Willy. (*He starts to go, turns, remembering the recorder, starts
to push off the table holding the recorder*) Oh, yeah. Whenever
you can this week, stop by and drop off the samples. You'll feel
better, Willy, and then come back and we'll talk. Pull yourself
together, kid, there's people outside.

HOWARD *exits, pushing the table off left.* WILLY *stares into space, exhausted. Now the music is heard—*BEN's *music—first distantly, then closer,
closer. As* WILLY *speaks,* BEN *enters from the right. He carries valise and
umbrella.*

WILLY Oh, Ben, how did you do it? What is the answer? Did you
wind up the Alaska deal already?

BEN Doesn't take much time if you know what you're doing. Just
a short business trip. Boarding ship in an hour. Wanted to say
good-by.

WILLY Ben, I've got to talk to you.

BEN (*glancing at his watch*) Haven't the time, William.

WILLY (*crossing the apron to* BEN) Ben, nothing's working out.
I don't know what to do.

BEN Now, look here, William. I've bought timberland in Alaska
and I need a man to look after things for me.

WILLY God, timberland! Me and my boys in those grand outdoors!

BEN You've a new continent at your doorstep, William. Get out
of these cities, they're full of talk and time payments and courts
of law. Screw on your fists and you can fight for a fortune up
there.

WILLY Yes, yes! Linda, Linda!

LINDA *enters as of old, with the wash.*

LINDA Oh, you're back?

BEN I haven't much time.

WILLY No, wait! Linda, he's got a proposition for me in Alaska.

LINDA But you've got—(*To* BEN) He's got a beautiful job here.

WILLY But in Alaska, kid, I could—

LINDA You're doing well enough, Willy!

BEN (*to* LINDA) Enough for what, my dear?

LINDA (*frightened of* BEN *and angry at him*) Don't say those things to him! Enough to be happy right here, right now. (*To* WILLY, *while* BEN *laughs*) Why must everybody conquer the world? You're well liked, and the boys love you, and someday— (*to* BEN)—why, old man Wagner told him just the other day that if he keeps it up he'll be a member of the firm, didn't he, Willy?

WILLY Sure, sure. I am building something with this firm, Ben, and if a man is building something he must be on the right track, mustn't he?

BEN What are you building? Lay your hand on it. Where is it?

WILLY (*hesitantly*) That's true, Linda, there's nothing.

LINDA Why? (*To* BEN) There's a man eighty-four years old—

WILLY That's right, Ben, that's right. When I look at that man I say, what is there to worry about?

BEN Bah!

WILLY It's true, Ben. All he has to do is go into any city, pick up the phone, and he's making his living and you know why?

BEN (*picking up his valise*) I've got to go.

WILLY (*holding* BEN *back*) Look at this boy!

BIFF, *in his high school sweater, enters carrying suitcase.* HAPPY *carries* BIFF's *shoulder guards, gold helmet, and football pants.*

WILLY Without a penny to his name, three great universities are begging for him, and from there the sky's the limit, because it's not what you do, Ben. It's who you know and the smile on your face! It's contacts, Ben, contacts! The whole wealth of Alaska passes over the lunch table at the Commodore Hotel, and that's the wonder, the wonder of this country, that a man can end with diamonds here on the basis of being liked! (*He turns to* BIFF) And that's why when you get out on that field today it's important. Because thousands of people will be rooting for you and loving you. (*To* BEN, *who has again begun to leave*) And Ben! when he walks into a business office his name will sound out like a bell and all the doors will open to him! I've seen it, Ben, I've seen it a thousand times! You can't feel it with your hand like timber, but it's there!

BEN Good-by, William.

WILLY   Ben, am I right? Don't you think I'm right? I value your advice.

BEN   There's a new continent at your doorstep, William. You could walk out rich. Rich! (*He is gone*)

WILLY   We'll do it here, Ben! You hear me? We're gonna do it here!

Young BERNARD *rushes in. The gay music of the Boys is heard.*

BERNARD   Oh, gee, I was afraid you left already!

WILLY   Why? What time is it?

BERNARD   It's half-past one!

WILLY   Well, come on, everybody! Ebbets Field next stop! Where's the pennants? (*He rushes through the wall-line of the kitchen and out into the living-room*)

LINDA (*to* BIFF)   Did you pack fresh underwear?

BIFF (*who has been limbering up*)   I want to go!

BERNARD   Biff, I'm carrying your helmet, ain't I?

HAPPY   No, I'm carrying the helmet.

BERNARD   Oh, Biff, you promised me.

HAPPY   I'm carrying the helmet.

BERNARD   How am I going to get in the locker room?

LINDA   Let him carry the shoulder guards. (*She puts her coat and hat on in the kitchen*)

BERNARD   Can I, Biff? 'Cause I told everybody I'm going to be in the locker room.

HAPPY   In Ebbets Field it's the clubhouse.

BERNARD   I meant the clubhouse. Biff!

HAPPY   Biff!

BIFF (*grandly, after a slight pause*)   Let him carry the shoulder guards.

HAPPY (*as he gives* BERNARD *the shoulder guards*)   Stay close to us now.

WILLY *rushes in with the pennants.*

WILLY (*handing them out*)   Everybody wave when Biff comes out on the field. (HAPPY *and* BERNARD *run off*) You set now, boy?

The music has died away.

BIFF   Ready to go, Pop. Every muscle is ready.

WILLY (*at the edge of the apron*)   You realize what this means?

BIFF   That's right, Pop.

WILLY (*feeling* BIFF'S *muscles*)   You're comin' home this afternoon captain of the All-Scholastic Championship Team of the City of New York.

BIFF   I got it, Pop. And remember, pal, when I take off my helmet, that touchdown is for you.

WILLY   Let's go! (*He is starting out, with his arm around* BIFF, *when* CHARLEY *enters, as of old, in knickers*) I got no room for you, Charley.

CHARLEY   Room? For what?

WILLY   In the car.

CHARLEY   You goin' for a ride? I wanted to shoot some casino.

WILLY   (*furiously*) Casino! (*Incredulously*) Don't you realize what today is?

LINDA   Oh, he knows, Willy. He's just kidding you.

WILLY   That's nothing to kid about!

CHARLEY   No, Linda, what's goin' on?

LINDA   He's playing in Ebbets Field.

CHARLEY   Baseball in this weather?

WILLY   Don't talk to him. Come on, come on! (*He is pushing them out*)

CHARLEY   Wait a minute, didn't you hear the news?

WILLY   What?

CHARLEY   Don't you listen to the radio? Ebbets Field just blew up.

WILLY   You go to hell! (CHARLEY *laughs*) (*Pushing them out*) Come on, come on! We're late.

CHARLEY   (*as they go*)   Knock a homer, Biff, knock a homer!

WILLY   (*the last to leave, turning to* CHARLEY)   I don't think that was funny, Charley. This is the greatest day of his life.

CHARLEY   Willy, when are you going to grow up?

WILLY   Yeah, heh? When this game is over, Charley, you'll be laughing out of the other side of your face. They'll be calling him another Red Grange. Twenty-five thousand a year.

CHARLEY   (*kidding*)   Is that so?

WILLY   Yeah, that's so.

CHARLEY   Well, then, I'm sorry. Willy. But tell me something.

WILLY   What?

CHARLEY   Who is Red Grange?

WILLY   Put up your hands. Goddam you, put up your hands!

CHARLEY, *chuckling, shakes his head and walks away, around the left corner of the stage.* WILLY *follows him. The music rises to a mocking frenzy.*

WILLY   Who the hell do you think you are, better than everybody else? You don't know everything, you big, ignorant, stupid . . . Put up your hands!

Light rises, on the right side of the forestage, on a small table in the reception room of CHARLEY's *office. Traffic sounds are heard.* BERNARD, *now mature, sits whistling to himself. A pair of tennis rackets and an overnight bag are on the floor beside him.*

WILLY (*offstage*)   What are you walking away for? Don't walk away! If you're going to say something say it to my face! I know you laugh at me behind my back. You'll laugh out of the other side of your goddam face after this game. Touchdown! Touchdown! Eighty thousand people! Touchdown! Right between the goal posts.

BERNARD *is a quiet, earnest, but self-assured young man.* WILLY's *voice is coming from right upstage now.* BERNARD *lowers his feet off the table and listens.* JENNY, *his father's secretary, enters.*

JENNY (*distressed*)   Say, Bernard, will you go out in the hall?
BERNARD   What is that noise? Who is it?
JENNY   Mr. Loman. He just got off the elevator.
BERNARD (*getting up*)   Who's he arguing with?
JENNY   Nobody. There's nobody with him. I can't deal with him any more, and your father gets all upset everytime he comes. I've got a lot of typing to do, and your father's waiting to sign it. Will you see him?
WILLY (*entering*)   Touchdown! Touch—(*He sees* JENNY) Jenny, Jenny, good to see you. How're ya? Working'? Or still honest?
JENNY   Fine. How've you been feeling?
WILLY   Not much any more, Jenny. Ha, ha! (*He is surprised to see the rackets*)
BERNARD   Hello, Uncle Willy.
WILLY (*almost shocked*)   Bernard! Well, look who's here! (*He comes quickly, guiltily, to* BERNARD *and warmly shakes his hand*)
BERNARD   How are you? Good to see you.
WILLY   What are you doing here?
BERNARD   Oh, just stopped by to see Pop. Get off my feet till my train leaves. I'm going to Washington in a few minutes.
WILLY   Is he in?
BERNARD   Yes, he's in his office with the accountant. Sit down.
WILLY (*sitting down*)   What're you going to do in Washington?
BERNARD   Oh, just a case I've got there, Willy.
WILLY   That so? (*Indicating the rackets*) You going to play tennis there?
BERNARD   I'm staying with a friend who's got a court.
WILLY   Don't say. His own tennis court. Must be fine people, I bet.
BERNARD   They are, very nice. Dad tells me Biff's in town.
WILLY (*with a big smile*)   Yeah, Biff's in. Working on a very big deal, Bernard.

BERNARD   What's Biff doing?

WILLY   Well, he's been doing very big things in the West. But he decided to establish himself here. Very big. We've having dinner. Did I hear your wife had a boy?

BERNARD   That's right. Our second.

WILLY   Two boys! What do you know!

BERNARD   What kind of a deal has Biff got?

WILLY   Well, Bill Oliver—very big sporting-goods man—he wants Biff very badly. Called him in from the West. Long distance, carte blanche, special deliveries. Your friends have their own private tennis court?

BERNARD   You still with the old firm, Willy?

WILLY   (*after a pause*)   I'm—I'm overjoyed to see how you made the grade, Bernard, overjoyed. It's an encouraging thing to see a young man really—really— Looks very good for Biff—very— (*He breaks off, then*) Bernard—(*He is so full of emotion, he breaks off again*)

BERNARD   What is it, Willy?

WILLY   (*small and alone*)   What—what's the secret?

BERNARD   What secret?

WILLY   How—how did you? Why didn't he ever catch on?

BERNARD   I wouldn't know that, Willy.

WILLY   (*confidentially, desperately*)   You were his friend, his boyhood friend. There's something I don't understand about it. His life ended after that Ebbets Field game. From the age of seventeen nothing good ever happened to him.

BERNARD   He never trained himself for anything.

WILLY   But he did, he did. After high school he took so many correspondence courses. Radio mechanics; television; God knows what, and never made the slightest mark.

BERNARD   (*taking off his glasses*)   Willy, do you want to talk candidly?

WILLY   (*rising, faces* BERNARD)   I regard you as a very brilliant man, Bernard. I value your advice.

BERNARD   Oh, the hell with the advice, Willy. I couldn't advise you. There's just one thing I've always wanted to ask you. When he was supposed to graduate, and the math teacher flunked him—

WILLY   Oh, that son-of-a-bitch ruined his life.

BERNARD   Yeah, but, Willy, all he had to do was go to summer school and make up that subject.

WILLY   That's right, that's right.

BERNARD   Did you tell him not to go to summer school?

WILLY   Me? I begged him to go. I ordered him to go!

BERNARD   Then why wouldn't he go?

WILLY   Why? Why! Bernard, that question has been trailing me like a ghost for the last fifteen years. He flunked the subject, and laid down and died like a hammer hit him!

BERNARD   Take it easy, kid.

WILLY   Let me talk to you—I got nobody to talk to. Bernard, Bernard, was it my fault? Y'see? It keeps going around in my mind, maybe I did something to him. I got nothing to give him.

BERNARD   Don't take it so hard.

WILLY   Why did he lay down? What is the story there? You were his friend!

BERNARD   Willy, I remember, it was June, and our grades came out. And he'd flunked math.

WILLY   That son-of-a-bitch!

BERNARD   No, it wasn't right then. Biff just got very angry, I remember, and he was ready to enroll in summer school.

WILLY   (*surprised*)   He was?

BERNARD   He wasn't beaten by it at all. But then, Willy, he disappeared from the block for almost a month. And I got the idea that he'd gone up to New England to see you. Did he have a talk with you then?

WILLY *stares in silence.*

BERNARD   Willy?

WILLY   (*with a strong edge of resentment in his voice*)   Yeah, he came to Boston. What about it?

BERNARD   Well, just that when he came back—I'll never forget this, it always mystifies me. Because I'd thought so well of Biff, even though he'd always taken advantage of me. I loved him, Willy, y'know? And he came back after that month and took his sneakers—remember those sneakers with "University of Virginia" printed on them? He was so proud of those, wore them every day. And he took them down in the cellar, and burned them up in the furnace. We had a fist fight. It lasted at least half an hour. Just the two of us, punching each other down the cellar, and crying right through it. I've often thought of how strange it was that I knew he'd given up his life. What happened in Boston, Willy?

WILLY *looks at him as at an intruder.*

BERNARD   I just bring it up because you asked me.

WILLY   (*angrily*)   Nothing. What do you mean, "What happened?" What's that got to do with anything?

BERNARD   Well, don't get sore.

WILLY   What are you trying to do, blame it on me? If a boy lays down is that my fault?

BERNARD   Now, Willy, don't get—

WILLY   Well, don't—don't talk to me that way! What does that mean, "What happened?"

CHARLEY *enters. He is in his vest, and he carries a bottle of bourbon.*

CHARLEY   Hey, you're going to miss that train. (*He waves the bottle*)

BERNARD   Yeah, I'm going. (*He takes the bottle*) Thanks, Pop. (*He picks up his rackets and bag*) Good-by, Willy, and don't worry about it. You know, "If at first you don't succeed . . ."

WILLY   Yes, I believe in that.

BERNARD   But sometimes, Willy, it's better for a man just to walk away.

WILLY   Walk away?

BERNARD   That's right.

WILLY   But if you can't walk away?

BERNARD   (*after a slight pause*)   I guess that's when it's tough. (*Extending his hand*) Good-by, Willy.

WILLY   (*shaking* BERNARD'S *hand*)   Good-by, boy.

CHARLEY   (*an arm on* BERNARD'S *shoulder*)   How do you like this kid? Gonna argue a case in front of the Supreme Court.

BERNARD   (*protesting*)   Pop!

WILLY   (*genuinely shocked, pained, and happy*)   No! The Supreme Court!

BERNARD   I gotta run. 'By, Dad!

CHARLEY   Knock 'em dead, Bernard!

BERNARD *goes off.*

WILLY   (*as* CHARLEY *takes out his wallet*)   The Supreme Court! And he didn't even mention it!

CHARLEY   (*counting out money on the desk*)   He don't have to— he's gonna do it.

WILLY   And you never told him what to do, did you? You never took any interest in him.

CHARLEY   My salvation is that I never took any interest in anything. There's some money—fifty dollars. I got an accountant inside.

WILLY   Charley, look . . . (*With difficulty*) I got my insurance to pay. If you can manage it—I need a hundred and ten dollars.

CHARLEY *doesn't reply for a moment; merely stops moving.*

WILLY I'd draw it from my bank but Linda would know, and
    I . . .
CHARLEY Sit down, Willy.
WILLY (*moving toward the chair*) I'm keeping an account of
    everything, remember. I'll pay every penny back. (*He sits*)
CHARLEY Now listen to me, Willy.
WILLY I want you to know I appreciate . . .
CHARLEY (*sitting down on the table*) Willy, what're you doin'?
    What the hell is goin' on in your head?
WILLY Why? I'm simply . . .
CHARLEY I offered you a job. You can make fifty dollars a week.
    And I won't send you on the road.
WILLY I've got a job.
CHARLEY Without pay? What kind of a job is a job without pay?
    (*He rises*) Now, look, kid, enough is enough. I'm no genius but
    I know when I'm being insulted.
WILLY Insulted!
CHARLEY Why don't you want to work for me?
WILLY What's the matter with you? I've got a job.
CHARLEY Then what're you walkin' in here every week for?
WILLY (*getting up*) Well, if you don't want me to walk in here—
CHARLEY I am offering you a job.
WILLY I don't want your goddam job!
CHARLEY When the hell are you going to grow up?
WILLY (*furiously*) You big ignoramus, if you say that to me again
    I'll rap you one! I don't care how big you are! (*He's ready to
    fight*)

Pause.

CHARLEY (*kindly, going to him*) How much do you need, Willy?
WILLY Charley, I'm strapped. I'm strapped. I don't know what to
    do. I was just fired.
CHARLEY Howard fired you?
WILLY That snotnose. Imagine that? I named him. I named him
    Howard.
CHARLEY Willy, when're you gonna realize that them things don't
    mean anything? You named him Howard, but you can't sell that.
    The only thing you got in this world is what you can sell. And
    the funny thing is that you're a salesman, and you don't know
    that.
WILLY I've always tried to think otherwise, I guess. I always felt
    that if a man was impressive, and well liked, that nothing—
CHARLEY Why must everybody like you? Who liked J. P. Morgan?

Was he impressive? In a Turkish bath he'd look like a butcher. But with his pockets on he was very well liked. Now listen, Willy, I know you don't like me, and nobody can say I'm in love with you, but I'll give you a job because—just for the hell of it, put it that way. Now what do you say?

WILLY   I—I just can't work for you, Charley.

CHARLEY   What're you, jealous of me?

WILLY   I can't work for you, that's all, don't ask me why.

CHARLEY (*angered, takes out more bills*)   You been jealous of me all your life, you damned fool! Here, pay your insurance. (*He puts the money in* WILLY's *hand*)

WILLY   I'm keeping strict accounts.

CHARLEY   I've got some work to do. Take care of yourself. And pay your insurance.

WILLY (*moving to the right*)   Funny, y'know? After all the highways, and the trains, and the appointments, and the years, you end up worth more dead than alive.

CHARLEY   Willy, nobody's worth nothin' dead. (*After a slight pause*) Did you hear what I said?

WILLY *stands still, dreaming.*

CHARLEY   Willy!

WILLY   Apologize to Bernard for me when you see him. I didn't mean to argue with him. He's a fine boy. They're all fine boys, and they'll end up big—all of them. Someday they'll all play tennis together. Wish me luck, Charley. He saw Bill Oliver today.

CHARLEY   Good luck.

WILLY (*on the verge of tears*)   Charley, you're the only friend I got. Isn't that a remarkable thing? (*He goes out*)

CHARLEY   Jesus!

CHARLEY *stares after him a moment and follows. All light blacks out. Suddenly raucous music is heard, and a red glow rises behind the screen at right.* STANLEY, *a young waiter, appears, carrying a table, followed by* HAPPY, *who is carrying two chairs.*

STANLEY (*putting the table down*)   That's all right, Mr. Loman, I can handle it myself. (*He turns and takes the chairs from* HAPPY *and places them at the table*)

HAPPY (*glancing around*)   Oh, this is better.

STANLEY   Sure, in the front there you're in the middle of all kinds a noise. Whenever you got a party, Mr. Loman, you just tell me and I'll put you back here. Y'know, there's a lotta people they don't like it private, because when they go out they like to see a lotta action around them because they're sick and tired to stay in the house by theirself. But I know you, you ain't from Hackensack. You know what I mean?

HAPPY (*sitting down*)   So how's it coming, Stanley?

STANLEY   Ah, it's a dog's life. I only wish during the war they'd a took me in the Army. I coulda been dead by now.

HAPPY   My brother's back, Stanley.

STANLEY   Oh, he come back, heh? From the Far West.

HAPPY   Yeah, big cattle man, my brother, so treat him right. And my father's coming too.

STANLEY   Oh, your father too!

HAPPY   You got a couple of nice lobsters?

STANLEY   Hundred per cent, big.

HAPPY   I want them with the claws.

STANLEY   Don't worry, I don't give you no mice. (HAPPY *laughs*) How about some wine? It'll put a head on the meal.

HAPPY   No. You remember, Stanley, that recipe I brought you from overseas? With the champagne in it?

STANLEY   Oh, yeah, sure. I still got it tacked up yet in the kitchen. But that'll have to cost a buck apiece anyways.

HAPPY   That's all right.

STANLEY   What'd you, hit a number or somethin'?

HAPPY   No, it's a little celebration. My brother is—I think he pulled off a big deal today. I think we're going into business together.

STANLEY   Great! That's the best for you. Because a family business, you know what I mean?—that's the best.

HAPPY   That's what I think.

STANLEY   'Cause what's the difference? Somebody steals? It's in the family. Know what I mean? (*Sotto voce*) Like this bartender here. The boss is goin' crazy what kinda leak he's got in the cash register. You put it in but it don't come out.

HAPPY (*raising his head*)   Sh!

STANLEY   What?

HAPPY   You notice I wasn't lookin' right or left, was I?

STANLEY   No.

HAPPY   And my eyes are closed.

STANLEY   So what's the—?

HAPPY   Strudel's comin'.

STANLEY (*catching on, looks around*)   Ah, no, there's no—

He breaks off as a furred, lavishly dressed girl enters and sits at the next table. Both follow her with their eyes.

STANLEY   Geez, how'd ya know?

HAPPY   I got radar or something. (*Staring directly at her profile*) Oooooooo . . . Stanley.

STANLEY   I think that's for you, Mr. Loman.

HAPPY   Look at that mouth. Oh, God. And the binoculars.

STANLEY   Geez, you got a life, Mr. Loman.

HAPPY   Wait on her.

STANLEY (*going to the* GIRL's *table*)   Would you like a menu, ma'am?

GIRL   I'm expecting someone, but I'd like a—

HAPPY   Why don't you bring her—excuse me, miss, do you mind? I sell champagne, and I'd like you to try my brand. Bring her a champagne, Stanley.

GIRL   That's awfully nice of you.

HAPPY   Don't mention it. It's all company money. (*He laughs*)

GIRL   That's a charming product to be selling, isn't it?

HAPPY   Oh, gets to be like everything else. Selling is selling, y'know.

GIRL   I suppose.

HAPPY   You don't happen to sell, do you?

GIRL   No, I don't sell.

HAPPY   Would you object to a compliment from a stranger? You ought to be on a magazine cover.

GIRL (*looking at him a little archly*)   I have been.

STANLEY *comes in with a glass of champagne.*

HAPPY   What'd I say before, Stanley? You see? She's a cover girl.

STANLEY   Oh, I could see, I could see.

HAPPY (*to the* GIRL)   What magazine?

GIRL   Oh, a lot of them. (*She takes the drink*) Thank you.

HAPPY   You know what they say in France, don't you? "Champagne is the drink of the complexion"—Hya, Biff!

BIFF *has entered and sits with* HAPPY.

BIFF   Hello, kid. Sorry I'm late.

HAPPY   I just got here. Uh, Miss—?

GIRL   Forsythe.

HAPPY   Miss Forsythe, this is my brother.

BIFF   Is Dad here?

HAPPY   His name is Biff. You might've heard of him. Great football player.

GIRL   Really? What team?

HAPPY   Are you familiar with football?

GIRL   No, I'm afraid I'm not.

HAPPY Biff is quarterback with the New York Giants.

GIRL Well, that is nice, isn't it? (*She drinks*)

HAPPY Good health.

GIRL I'm happy to meet you.

HAPPY That's my name. Hap. It's really Harold, but at West Point they called me Happy.

GIRL (*now really impressed*) Oh, I see. How do you do? (*She turns her profile*)

BIFF Isn't Dad coming?

HAPPY You want her?

BIFF Oh, I could never make that.

HAPPY I remember the time that idea would never come into your head. Where's the old confidence, Biff?

BIFF I just saw Oliver—

HAPPY Wait a minute. I've got to see that old confidence again. Do you want her? She's on call.

BIFF Oh, no. (*He turns to look at the* GIRL)

HAPPY I'm telling you. Watch this. (*Turning to the* GIRL) Honey? (*She turns to him*) Are you busy?

GIRL Well, I am . . . but I could make a phone call.

HAPPY Do that, will you, honey? And see if you can get a friend. We'll be here for a while. Biff is one of the greatest football players in the country.

GIRL (*standing up*) Well, I'm certainly happy to meet you.

HAPPY Come back soon.

GIRL I'll try.

HAPPY Don't try, honey, try hard.

The GIRL *exits.* STANLEY *follows, shaking his head in bewildered admiration.*

HAPPY Isn't that a shame now? A beautiful girl like that? That's why I can't get married. There's not a good woman in a thousand. New York is loaded with them, kid!

BIFF Hap, look—

HAPPY I told you she was on call!

BIFF (*strangely unnerved*) Cut it out, will ya? I want to say something to you.

HAPPY Did you see Oliver?

BIFF I saw him all right. Now look, I want to tell Dad a couple of things and I want you to help me.

HAPPY What? Is he going to back you?

BIFF Are you crazy? You're out of your goddam head, you know that?

HAPPY   Why? What happened?

BIFF (*breathlessly*)   I did a terrible thing today, Hap. It's been the strangest day I ever went through. I'm all numb, I swear.

HAPPY   You mean he wouldn't see you?

BIFF   Well, I waited six hours for him, see? All day. Kept sending my name in. Even tried to date his secretary so she'd get me to him, but no soap.

HAPPY   Because you're not showin' the old confidence, Biff. He remembered you, didn't he?

BIFF (*stopping* HAPPY *with a gesture*)   Finally, about five o'clock, he comes out. Didn't remember who I was or anything. I felt like such an idiot, Hap.

HAPPY   Did you tell him my Florida idea?

BIFF   He walked away. I saw him for one minute. I got so mad I could've torn the walls down! How the hell did I ever get the idea I was a salesman there? I even believed myself that I'd been a salesman for him! And then he gave me one look and— I realized what a ridiculous lie my whole life has been! We've been talking in a dream of fifteen years. I was a shipping clerk.

HAPPY   What'd you do?

BIFF (*with great tension and wonder*)   Well, he left, see. And the secretary went out. I was all alone in the waiting-room. I don't know what came over me, Hap. The next thing I know I'm in his office—paneled walls, everything. I can't explain it. I—Hap, I took his fountain pen.

HAPPY   Geez, did he catch you?

BIFF   I ran out. I ran down all eleven flights. I ran and ran and ran.

HAPPY   That was an awful dumb—what'd you do that for?

BIFF (*agonized*)   I don't know, I just—wanted to take something, I don't know. You gotta help me, Hap. I'm gonna tell Pop.

HAPPY   You crazy? What for?

BIFF   Hap, he's got to understand that I'm not the man somebody lends that kind of money to. He thinks I've been spiting him all these years and it's eating him up.

HAPPY   That's just it. You tell him something nice.

BIFF   I can't.

HAPPY   Say you got a lunch date with Oliver tomorrow.

BIFF   So what do I do tomorrow?

HAPPY   You leave the house tomorrow and come back at night and say Oliver is thinking it over. And he thinks it over for a couple of weeks, and gradually it fades away and nobody's the worse.

BIFF   But it'll go on forever!

HAPPY   Dad is never so happy as when he's looking forward to something!

WILLY *enters.*

HAPPY   Hello, scout!

WILLY   Gee, I haven't been here in years!

STANLEY *has followed* WILLY *in and sets a chair for him.* STANLEY *starts off but* HAPPY *stops him.*

HAPPY   Stanley!

STANLEY *stands by, waiting for an order.*

BIFF   (*going to* WILLY *with guilt, as to an invalid*)   Sit down, Pop. You want a drink?

WILLY   Sure, I don't mind.

BIFF   Let's get a load on.

WILLY   You look worried.

BIFF   N-no. (*To* STANLEY)   Scotch all around. Make it doubles.

STANLEY   Doubles, right. (*He goes*)

WILLY   You had a couple already, didn't you?

BIFF   Just a couple, yeah.

WILLY   Well, what happened, boy? (*Nodding affirmatively, with a smile*) Everything go all right?

BIFF   (*takes a breath, then reaches out and grasps* WILLY's *hand*) Pal . . . (*He is smiling bravely, and* WILLY *is smiling too*) I had an experience today.

HAPPY   Terrific, Pop.

WILLY   That so? What happened?

BIFF   (*high, slightly alcoholic, above the earth*)   I'm going to tell you everything from first to last. It's been a strange day. (*Silence. He looks around, composes himself as best he can, but his breath keeps breaking the rhythm of his voice*) I had to wait quite a while for him, and—

WILLY   Oliver?

BIFF   Yeah, Oliver. All day, as a matter of cold fact. And a lot of —instances—facts, Pop, facts about my life came back to me. Who was it, Pop? Who ever said I was a salesman with Oliver?

WILLY   Well, you were.

BIFF   No, Dad, I was a shipping clerk.

WILLY   But you were practically—

BIFF   (*with determination*)   Dad, I don't know who said it first, but I was never a salesman for Bill Oliver.

WILLY   What're you talking about?

BIFF   Let's hold on to the facts tonight, Pop. We're not going to get anywhere bullin' around. I was a shipping clerk.

WILLY (*angrily*)   All right, now listen to me—

BIFF   Why don't you let me finish?

WILLY   I'm not interested in stories about the past or any crap of that kind because the woods are burning, boys, you understand? There's a big blaze going on all around. I was fired today.

BIFF (*shocked*)   How could you be?

WILLY   I was fired, and I'm looking for a little good news to tell your mother, because the woman has waited and the woman has suffered. The gift of it is that I haven't got a story left in my head, Biff. So don't give me a lecture about facts and aspects. I am not interested. Now what've you got to say to me?

STANLEY *enters with three drinks. They wait until he leaves.*

WILLY   Did you see Oliver?

BIFF   Jesus, Dad!

WILLY   You mean you didn't go up there?

HAPPY   Sure he went up there.

BIFF   I did. I—saw him. How could they fire you?

WILLY (*on the edge of his chair*)   What kind of a welcome did he give you?

BIFF   He won't even let you work on commission?

WILLY   I'm out! (*Driving*)   So tell me, he gave you a warm welcome?

HAPPY   Sure, Pop, sure!

BIFF (*driven*)   Well, it was kind of—

WILLY   I was wondering if he'd remember you. (*To* HAPPY) Imagine, man doesn't see him for ten, twelve years and gives him that kind of a welcome!

HAPPY   Damn right!

BIFF (*trying to return to the offensive*)   Pop, look—

WILLY   You know why he remembered you, don't you? Because you impressed him in those days.

BIFF   Let's talk quietly and get this down to the facts, huh?

WILLY (*as though* BIFF *had been interrupting*)   Well, what happened? It's great news, Biff. Did he take you into his office or'd you talk in the waiting-room?

BIFF   Well, he came in, see, and—

WILLY (*with a big smile*)   What'd he say? Betcha he threw his arm around you.

BIFF   Well, he kinda—

WILLY   He's a fine man. (*To* HAPPY) Very hard man to see, y'know.

HAPPY (*agreeing*)   Oh, I know.

WILLY (*to* BIFF)   Is that where you had the drinks?

BIFF   Yeah, he gave me a couple of—no, no!

HAPPY (*cutting in*)   He told him my Florida idea.

WILLY   Don't interrupt. (*To* BIFF) How'd he react to the Florida idea?

BIFF   Dad, will you give me a minute to explain?

WILLY   I've been waiting for you to explain since I sat down here! What happened? He took you into his office and what?

BIFF   Well—I talked. And—and he listened, see.

WILLY   Famous for the way he listens, y'know. What was his answer?

BIFF   His answer was—(*He breaks off, suddenly angry*) Dad, you're not letting me tell you what I want to tell you!

WILLY (*accusing, angered*)   You didn't see him, did you?

BIFF   I did see him!

WILLY   What'd you insult him or something? You insulted him, didn't you?

BIFF   Listen, will you let me out of it, will you just let me out of it!

HAPPY   What the hell!

WILLY   Tell me what happened!

BIFF (*to* HAPPY)   I can't talk to him!

A single trumpet note jars the ear. The light of green leaves stains the house, which holds the air of night and a dream. Young BERNARD *enters and knocks on the door of the house.*

YOUNG BERNARD (*frantically*)   Mrs. Loman, Mrs. Loman!

HAPPY   Tell him what happened!

BIFF (*to* HAPPY)   Shut up and leave me alone!

WILLY   No, no! You had to go and flunk math!

BIFF   What math? What're you talking about?

YOUNG BERNARD   Mrs. Loman, Mrs. Loman!

LINDA *appears in the house, as of old.*

WILLY (*wildly*)   Math, math, math!

BIFF   Take it easy, Pop!

YOUNG BERNARD   Mrs. Loman!

WILLY (*furiously*)   If you hadn't flunked you'd've been set by now!

BIFF   Now, look, I'm gonna tell you what happened, and you're going to listen to me.

YOUNG BERNARD   Mrs. Loman!

BIFF   I waited six hours—

HAPPY What the hell are you saying?

BIFF I kept sending in my name but he wouldn't see me. So finally he ... (*He continues unheard as light fades low on the restaurant*)

YOUNG BERNARD Biff flunked math!

LINDA No!

YOUNG BERNARD Birnbaum flunked him! They won't graduate him!

LINDA But they have to. He's gotta go to the university. Where is he? Biff! Biff!

YOUNG BERNARD No, he left. He went to Grand Central.

LINDA Grand— You mean he went to Boston!

YOUNG BERNARD Is Uncle Willy in Boston?

LINDA Oh, maybe Willy can talk to the teacher. Oh, the poor, poor boy!

Light on house area snaps out.

BIFF (*at the table, now audible, holding up a gold fountain pen*) ... so I'm washed up with Oliver, you understand? Are you listening to me?

WILLY (*at a loss*) Yeah, sure. If you hadn't flunked—

BIFF Flunked what? What're you talking about?

WILLY Don't blame everything on me! I didn't flunk math—you did! What pen?

HAPPY That was awful dumb, Biff, a pen like that is worth—

WILLY (*seeing the pen for the first time*) You took Oliver's pen?

BIFF (*weakening*) Dad, I just explained it to you.

WILLY You stole Bill Oliver's fountain pen!

BIFF I didn't exactly steal it! That's just what I've been explaining to you!

HAPPY He had it in his hand and just then Oliver walked in, so he got nervous and stuck it in his pocket!

WILLY My God, Biff!

BIFF I never intended to do it, Dad!

OPERATOR'S VOICE Standish Arms, good evening!

WILLY (*shouting*) I'm not in my room!

BIFF (*frightened*) Dad, what's the matter? (*He and* HAPPY *stand up*)

OPERATOR Ringing Mr. Loman for you!

WILLY I'm not there, stop it!

BIFF (*horrified, gets down on one knee before* WILLY) Dad, I'll make good, I'll make good. (WILLY *tries to get to his feet.* BIFF *holds him down*) Sit down now.

WILLY   No, you're no good, you're no good for anything.

BIFF   I am, Dad, I'll find something else, you understand? Now don't worry about anything. (*He holds up* WILLY's *face*) Talk to me, Dad.

OPERATOR   Mr. Loman does not answer. Shall I page him?

WILLY   (*attempting to stand, as though to rush and silence the Operator*)   No, no, no!

HAPPY   He'll strike something, Pop.

WILLY   No, no . . .

BIFF   (*desperately, standing over* WILLY)   Pop, listen! Listen to me! I'm telling you something good. Oliver talked to his partner about the Florida idea. You listening? He—he talked to his partner, and he came to me . . . I'm going to be all right, you hear? Dad, listen to me, he said it was just a question of the amount!

WILLY   Then you . . . got it?

HAPPY   He's gonna be terrific, Pop!

WILLY   (*trying to stand*)   Then you got it, haven't you? You got it! You got it!

BIFF   (*agonized, holds* WILLY *down*)   No, no. Look, Pop. I'm supposed to have lunch with them tomorrow. I'm just telling you this so you'll know that I can still make an impression, Pop. And I'll make good somewhere, but I can't go tomorrow, see?

WILLY   Why not? You simply—

BIFF   But the pen, Pop!

WILLY   You give it to him and tell him it was an oversight!

HAPPY   Sure, have lunch tomorrow!

BIFF   I can't say that—

WILLY   You were doing a crossword puzzle and accidentally used his pen!

BIFF   Listen, kid, I took those balls years ago, now I walk in with his fountain pen? That clinches it, don't you see? I can't face him like that! I'll try elsewhere.

PAGE'S VOICE   Paging Mr. Loman!

WILLY   Don't you want to be anything?

BIFF   Pop, how can I go back?

WILLY   You don't want to be anything, is that what's behind it?

BIFF   (*now angry at* WILLY *for not crediting his sympathy*)   Don't take it that way! You think it was easy walking into that office after what I'd done to him? A team of horses couldn't have dragged me back to Bill Oliver!

WILLY   Then why'd you go?

BIFF   Why did I go? Why did I go! Look at you! Look at what's become of you!

Off left, THE WOMAN *laughs.*

WILLY   Biff, you're going to go to that lunch tomorrow, or—
BIFF   I can't go. I've got no appointment!
HAPPY   Biff, for ...!
WILLY   Are you spiting me?
BIFF   Don't take it that way! Goddammit!
WILLY   (*strikes* BIFF *and falters away from the table*)   You rotten little louse! Are you spiting me?
THE WOMAN   Someone's at the door, Willy!
BIFF   I'm no good, can't you see what I am?
HAPPY   (*separating them*)   Hey, you're in a restaurant! Now cut it out, both of you! (*The girls enter*)   Hello, girls, sit down.

THE WOMAN *laughs, off left.*

MISS FORSYTHE   I guess we might as well. This is Letta.
THE WOMAN   Willy, are you going to wake up?
BIFF   (*ignoring* WILLY)   How're ya, miss, sit down. What do you drink?
MISS FORSYTHE   Letta might not be able to stay long.
LETTA   I gotta get up very early tomorrow. I got jury duty. I'm so excited! Were you fellows ever on a jury?
BIFF   No, but I been in front of them! (*The girls laugh*)   This is my father.
LETTA   Isn't he cute? Sit down with us, Pop.
HAPPY   Sit him down, Biff!
BIFF   (*going to him*)   Come on, slugger, drink us under the table. To hell with it! Come on, sit down, pal.

On BIFF'*s last insistence,* WILLY *is about to sit.*

THE WOMAN   (*now urgently*)   Willy, are you going to answer the door!

THE WOMAN'*s call pulls* WILLY *back. He starts right, befuddled.*

BIFF   Hey, where are you going?
WILLY   Open the door.
BIFF   The door?
WILLY   The washroom ... the door ... where's the door?
BIFF   (*leading* WILLY *to the left*)   Just go straight down.

WILLY *moves left.*

THE WOMAN   Willy, Willy, are you going to get up, get up, get up, get up?

WILLY *exits left.*

LETTA   I think it's sweet you bring your daddy along.

MISS FORSYTHE   Oh, he isn't really your father!

BIFF (*at left, turning to her resentfully*)   Miss Forsythe, you've just seen a prince walk by. A fine, troubled prince. A hard-working, unappreciated prince. A pal, you understand? A good companion. Always for his boys.

LETTA   That's so sweet.

HAPPY   Well, girls, what's the program? We're wasting time. Come on, Biff. Gather round. Where would you like to go?

BIFF   Why don't you do something for him?

HAPPY   Me!

BIFF   Don't you give a damn for him, Hap?

HAPPY   What're you talking about? I'm the one who—

BIFF   I sense it, you don't give a good goddam about him. (*He takes the rolled-up hose from his pocket and puts it on the table in front of* HAPPY) Look what I found in the cellar, for Christ's sake. How can you bear to let it go on?

HAPPY   Me? Who goes away? Who runs off and—

BIFF   Yeah, but he doesn't mean anything to you. You could help him—I can't! Don't you understand what I'm talking about? He's going to kill himself, don't you know that?

HAPPY   Don't I know it! Me!

BIFF   Hap, help him! Jesus . . . help him . . . Help me, help me, I can't bear to look at his face! (*Ready to weep, he hurries out, up right*)

HAPPY (*starting after him*)   Where are you going?

MISS FORSYTHE   What's he so mad about?

HAPPY   Come on, girls, we'll catch up with him.

MISS FORSYTHE (*as* HAPPY *pushes her out*)   Say, I don't like that temper of his!

HAPPY   He's just a little overstrung, he'll be all right!

WILLY (*off left, as* THE WOMAN *laughs*)   Don't answer! Don't answer!

LETTA   Don't you want to tell your father—

HAPPY   No, that's not my father. He's just a guy. Come on, we'll catch Biff, and, honey, we're going to paint this town! Stanley, where's the check! Hey, Stanley!

They exit. STANLEY *looks toward left.*

STANLEY (*calling to* HAPPY *indignantly*)   Mr. Loman! Mr. Loman!

STANLEY *picks up a chair and follows them off. Knocking is heard off left.*

The Woman *enters, laughing.* Willy *follows her. She is in a black slip; he is buttoning his shirt. Raw, sensuous music accompanies their speech.*

willy   Will you stop laughing? Will you stop?

the woman   Aren't you going to answer the door? He'll wake the whole hotel.

willy   I'm not expecting anybody.

the woman   Whyn't you have another drink, honey, and stop being so damn self-centered?

willy   I'm so lonely.

the woman   You know you ruined me, Willy? From now on, whenever you come to the office, I'll see that you go right through to the buyers. No waiting at my desk any more, Willy. You ruined me.

willy   That's nice of you to say that.

the woman   Gee, you are self-centered! Why so sad? You are the saddest, self-centeredest soul I ever did see-saw. (*She laughs. He kisses her*) Come on inside, drummer boy. It's silly to be dressing in the middle of the night. (*As knocking is heard*) Aren't you going to answer the door?

willy   They're knocking on the wrong door.

the woman   But I felt the knocking. And he heard us talking in here. Maybe the hotel's on fire!

willy (*his terror rising*)   It's a mistake.

the woman   Then tell him to go away!

willy   There's nobody there.

the woman   It's getting on my nerves, Willy. There's somebody standing out there and it's getting on my nerves!

willy (*pushing her away from him*)   All right, stay in the bathroom here, and don't come out. I think there's a law in Massachusetts about it, so don't come out. It may be that new room clerk. He looked very mean. So don't come out. It's a mistake, there no fire.

The knocking is heard again. He takes a few steps away from her, and she vanishes into the wing. The light follows him, and now he is facing Young Biff, *who carries a suitcase.* Biff *steps toward him. The music is gone.*

biff   Why didn't you answer?

willy   Biff! What are you doing in Boston?

biff   Why didn't you answer? I've been knocking for five minutes, I called you on the phone—

willy   I just heard you. I was in the bathroom and had the door shut. Did anything happen home?

BIFF   Dad—I let you down.

WILLY   What do you mean?

BIFF   Dad . . .

WILLY   Biffo, what's this about? (*Putting his arm around* BIFF) Come on, let's go downstairs and get you a malted.

BIFF   Dad, I flunked math.

WILLY   Not for the term?

BIFF   The term. I haven't got enough credits to graduate.

WILLY   You mean to say Bernard wouldn't give you the answers?

BIFF   He did, he tried, but I only got a sixty-one.

WILLY   And they wouldn't give you four points?

BIFF   Birnbaum refused absolutely. I begged him, Pop, but he won't give me those points. You gotta talk to him before they close the school. Because if he saw the kind of man you are, and you just talked to him in your way, I'm sure he'd come through for me. The class came right before practice, see, and I didn't go enough. Would you talk to him? He'd like you, Pop. You know the way you could talk.

WILLY   You're on. We'll drive right back.

BIFF   Oh, Dad, good work! I'm sure he'll change it for you!

WILLY   Go downstairs and tell the clerk I'm checkin' out. Go right down.

BIFF   Yes, sir! See, the reason he hates me, Pop—one day he was late for class so I got up at the blackboard and imitated him. I crossed my eyes and talked with a lithp.

WILLY   (*laughing*)   You did? The kids like it?

BIFF   They nearly died laughing!

WILLY   Yeah? What'd you do?

BIFF   The thquare root of thixthy twee is . . . (WILLY *bursts out laughing;* BIFF *joins him*) And in the middle of it he walked in!

WILLY *laughs and* THE WOMAN *joins in offstage.*

WILLY   (*without hesitation*)   Hurry downstairs and—

BIFF   Somebody in there?

WILLY   No, that was next door.

THE WOMAN *laughs offstage.*

BIFF   Somebody got in your bathroom!

WILLY   No, it's the next room, there's a party—

THE WOMAN   (*enters, laughing. She lisps this*)   Can I come in? There's something in the bathtub, Willy, and it's moving!

WILLY *looks at* BIFF, *who is staring open-mouthed and horrified at* THE WOMAN.

WILLY   Ah—you better go back to your room. They must be finished painting by now. They're painting her room so I let her
take a shower here. Go back, go back ... (*He pushes her*)

THE WOMAN (*resisting*)   But I've got to get dressed, Willy, I
can't—

WILLY   Get out of here! Go back, go back ... (*Suddenly striving
for the ordinary*) This is Miss Francis, Biff, she's a buyer. They're
painting her room. Go back, Miss Francis, go back ...

THE WOMAN   But my clothes, I can't go out naked in the hall!

WILLY (*pushing her offstage*)   Get outa here! Go back, go back!

BIFF *slowly sits down on his suitcase as the argument continues offstage.*

THE WOMAN   Where's my stockings? You promised me stockings,
Willy!

WILLY   I have no stockings here!

THE WOMAN   You had two boxes of size nine sheers for me, and I
want them!

WILLY   Here, for God's sake, will you get outa here!

THE WOMAN (*enters holding a box of stockings*)   I just hope there's
nobody in the hall. That's all I hope. (*To* BIFF) Are you football
or baseball?

BIFF   Football.

THE WOMAN (*angry, humiliated*)   That's me too. G'night. (*She
snatches her clothes from* WILLY, *and walks out*)

WILLY (*after a pause*)   Well, better get going. I want to get to the
school first thing in the morning. Get my suits out of the closet.
I'll get my valise. (BIFF *doesn't move*) What's the matter? (BIFF
remains motionless, tears falling) She's a buyer. Buys for J. H.
Simmons. She lives down the hall—they're painting. You don't
imagine—(*He breaks off. After a pause*) Now listen, pal, she's
just a buyer. She sees merchandise in her room and they have to
keep it looking just so ... (*Pause. Assuming command*) All right,
get my suits. (BIFF *doesn't move*) Now stop crying and do as I
say. I gave you an order. Biff, I gave you an order! Is that what
you do when I give you an order? How dare you cry! (*Putting
his arm around* BIFF) Now look, Biff, when you grow up you'll
understand about these things. You mustn't—you mustn't over-
emphasize a thing like this. I'll see Birnbaum first thing in the
morning.

BIFF   Never mind.

WILLY (*getting down beside* BIFF)   Never mind! He's going to give
you those points. I'll see to it.

BIFF   He wouldn't listen to you.

WILLY He certainly will listen to me. You need those points for the U. of Virginia.

BIFF I'm not going there.

WILLY Heh? If I can't get him to change that mark you'll make it up in summer school. You've got all summer to—

BIFF (*his weeping breaking from him*) Dad ...

WILLY (*infected by it*) Oh, my boy ...

BIFF Dad ...

WILLY She's nothing to me, Biff. I was lonely, I was terribly lonely.

BIFF You—you gave her Mama's stockings! (*His tears break through and he rises to go*)

WILLY (*grabbing for* BIFF) I gave you an order!

BIFF Don't touch me, you—liar!

WILLY Apologize for that!

BIFF You fake! You phony little fake! You fake! (*Overcome, he turns quickly and weeping fully goes out with his suitcase.* WILLY *is left on the floor on his knees*)

WILLY I gave you an order! Biff, come back here or I'll beat you! Come back here! I'll whip you!

STANLEY *comes quickly in from the right and stands in front of* WILLY.

WILLY (*shouts at* STANLEY) I gave you an order ...

STANLEY Hey, let's pick it up, pick it up, Mr. Loman. (*He helps* WILLY *to his feet*) Your boys left with the chippies. They said they'll see you home.

A second WAITER *watches some distance away.*

WILLY But we were supposed to have dinner together.

Music is heard, WILLY's *theme.*

STANLEY Can you make it?

WILLY I'll—sure, I can make it. (*Suddenly concerned about his clothes*) Do I—I look all right?

STANLEY Sure, you look all right. (*He flicks a speck off* WILLY's *lapel*)

WILLY Here—here's a dollar.

STANLEY Oh, your son paid me. It's all right.

WILLY (*putting it in* STANLEY's *hand*) No, take it. You're a good boy.

STANLEY Oh, no, you don't have to ...

WILLY Here—here's some more, I don't need it any more. (*After a slight pause*) Tell me—is there a seed store in the neighborhood?

STANLEY   Seeds? You mean like to plant?

As WILLY *turns,* STANLEY *slips the money back into his jacket pocket.*

WILLY   Yes. Carrots, peas . . .

STANLEY   Well, there's hardware stores on Sixth Avenue, but it may be too late now.

WILLY (*anxiously*)   Oh, I'd better hurry. I've got to get some seeds. (*He starts off to the right*) I've got to get some seeds, right away. Nothing's planted. I don't have a thing in the ground.

WILLY *hurries out as the light goes down.* STANLEY *moves over to the right after him, watches him off. The other* WAITER *has been staring at* WILLY.

STANLEY (*to the* WAITER)   Well, whatta you looking at?

The WAITER *picks up the chairs and moves off right.* STANLEY *takes the table and follows him. The light fades on this area. There is a long pause, the sound of the flute coming over. The light gradually rises on the kitchen, which is empty.* HAPPY *appears at the door of the house, followed by* BIFF. HAPPY *is carrying a large bunch of long-stemmed roses. He enters the kitchen, looks around for* LINDA. *Not seeing her, he turns to* BIFF, *who is just outside the house door, and makes a gesture with his hands, indicating "Not here, I guess." He looks into the living-room and freezes. Inside,* LINDA, *unseen, is seated,* WILLY's *coat on her lap. She rises ominously and quietly and moves toward* HAPPY, *who backs up into the kitchen, afraid.*

HAPPY   Hey, what're you doing up? (LINDA *says nothing but moves toward him implacably*) Where's Pop? (*He keeps backing to the right, and now* LINDA *is in full view in the doorway to the living-room*) Is he sleeping?

LINDA   Where were you?

HAPPY (*trying to laugh it off*)   We met two girls, Mom, very fine types. Here, we brought you some flowers. (*Offering them to her*) Put them in your room, Ma.

She knocks them to the floor at BIFF's *feet. He has now come inside and closed the door behind him. She stares at* BIFF, *silent.*

HAPPY   Now what'd you do that for? Mom, I want you to have some flowers—

LINDA (*cutting* HAPPY *off, violently to* BIFF)   Don't you care whether he lives or dies?

HAPPY (*going to the stairs*)   Come upstairs, Biff.

BIFF (*with a flare of disgust, to* HAPPY)   Go away from me! (*To* LINDA)   What do you mean, lives or dies? Nobody's dying around here, pal.

LINDA   Get out of my sight! Get out of here!

BIFF   I wanna see the boss.

LINDA   You're not going near him!

BIFF   Where is he? (*He moves into the living-room and* LINDA *follows*)

LINDA   (*shouting after* BIFF)   You invite him for dinner. He looks forward to it all day—(BIFF *appears in his parents' bedroom, looks around, and exits*)—and then you desert him there. There's no stranger you'd do that to!

HAPPY   Why? He had a swell time with us. Listen, when I— (LINDA *comes back into the kitchen*)—desert him I hope I don't outlive the day!

LINDA   Get out of here!

HAPPY   Now look, Mom . . .

LINDA   Did you have to go to women tonight? You and your lousy rotten whores!

BIFF *re-enters the kitchen.*

HAPPY   Mom, all we did was follow Biff around trying to cheer him up! (*To* BIFF) Boy, what a night you gave me!

LINDA   Get out of here, both of you, and don't come back! I don't want you tormenting him any more. Go on now, get your things together! (*To* BIFF) You can sleep in his apartment. (*She starts to pick up the flowers and stops herself*) Pick up this stuff, I'm not your maid any more. Pick it up, you bum, you!

HAPPY *turns his back to her in refusal.* BIFF *slowly moves over and gets down on his knees, picking up the flowers.*

LINDA   You're a pair of animals! Not one, not another living soul would have had the cruelty to walk out on that man in a restaurant!

BIFF   (*not looking at her*)   Is that what he said?

LINDA   He didn't have to say anything. He was so humiliated he nearly limped when he came in.

HAPPY   But, Mom, he had a great time with us—

BIFF   (*cutting him off violently*)   Shut up!

Without another word, HAPPY *goes upstairs.*

LINDA   You! You didn't even go in to see if he was all right!

BIFF   (*still on the floor in front of* LINDA, *the flowers in his hand; with self-loathing*)   No. Didn't. Didn't do a damned thing. How do you like that, heh? Left him babbling in a toilet.

LINDA   You louse. You . . .

BIFF   Now you hit it on the nose! (*He gets up, throws the flowers in the wastebasket*) The scum of the earth, and you're looking at him!

LINDA   Get out of here!

BIFF   I gotta talk to the boss, Mom. Where is he?

LINDA   You're not going near him. Get out of this house!

BIFF   (*with absolute assurance, determination*)   No. We're gonna have an abrupt conversation, him and me.

LINDA   You're not talking to him!

Hammering is heard from outside the house, off right. BIFF *turns toward the noise.*

LINDA   (*suddenly pleading*)   Will you please leave him alone?

BIFF   What's he doing out there?

LINDA   He's planting the garden!

BIFF   (*quietly*)   Now? Oh, my God!

BIFF *moves outside,* LINDA *following. The light dies down on them and comes up on the center of the apron as* WILLY *walks into it. He is carrying a flashlight, a hoe, and a handful of seed packets. He raps the top of the hoe sharply to fix it firmly, and then moves to the left, measuring off the distance with his foot. He holds the flashlight to look at the seed packets, reading off the instructions. He is in the blue of night.*

WILLY   Carrots . . . quarter-inch apart. Rows . . . one-foot rows. (*He measures it off*) One foot. (*He puts down a package and measures off*) Beets. (*He puts down another package and measures again*) Lettuce. (*He reads the package, puts it down*) One foot— (*He breaks off as* BEN *appears at the right and moves slowly down to him*) What a proposition, ts, ts. Terrific, terrific. 'Cause she's suffered, Ben, the woman has suffered. You understand me? A man can't go out the way he came in, Ben, a man has got to add up to something. You can't, you can't—(BEN *moves toward him as though to interrupt*) You gotta consider, now. Don't answer so quick. Remember, it's a guaranteed twenty-thousand-dollar proposition. Now look, Ben, I want you to go through the ins and outs of this thing with me. I've got nobody to talk to, Ben, and the woman has suffered, you hear me?

BEN   (*standing still, considering*)   What's the proposition?

WILLY   It's twenty thousand dollars on the barrelhead. Guaranteed, gilt-edged, you understand?

BEN   You don't want to make a fool of yourself. They might not honor the policy.

WILLY   How can they dare refuse? Didn't I work like a coolie to meet every premium on the nose? And now they don't pay off? Impossible!

BEN It's called a cowardly thing, William.

WILLY Why? Does it take more guts to stand here the rest of my life ringing up a zero?

BEN (*yielding*) That's a point, William. (*He moves, thinking, turns*) And twenty thousand—that *is* something one can feel with the hand, it is there.

WILLY (*now assured, with rising power*) Oh, Ben, that's the whole beauty of it! I see it like a diamond, shining in the dark, hard and rough, that I can pick up and touch in my hand. Not like— like an appointment! This would not be another damned-fool appointment, Ben, and it changes all the aspects. Because he thinks I'm nothing, see, and so he spites me. But the funeral— (*Straightening up*) Ben, that funeral will be massive! They'll come from Maine, Massachusetts, Vermont, New Hampshire! All the old-timers with the strange license plates—that boy will be thunderstruck, Ben, because he never realized—I am known! Rhode Island, New York, New Jersey—I am known, Ben, and he'll see it with his eyes once and for all. He'll see what I am, Ben! He's in for a shock, that boy!

BEN (*coming down to the edge of the garden*) He'll call you a coward.

WILLY (*suddenly fearful*) No, that would be terrible.

BEN Yes. And a damned fool.

WILLY No, no, he mustn't, I won't have that! (*He is broken and desperate*)

BEN He'll hate you, William.

The gay music of the Boys is heard.

WILLY Oh, Ben, how do we get back to all the great times? Used to be so full of light, and comradeship, the sleigh-riding in winter, and the ruddiness on his cheeks. And always some kind of good news coming up, always something nice coming up ahead. And never even let me carry the valises in the house, and simonizing, simonizing that little red car! Why, why can't I give him something and not have him hate me?

BEN Let me think about it. (*He glances at his watch*) I still have a little time. Remarkable proposition, but you've got to be sure you're not making a fool of yourself.

BEN *drifts off upstage and goes out of sight.* BIFF *comes down from the left.*

WILLY (*suddenly conscious of* BIFF, *turns and looks up at him, then begins picking up the packages of seeds in confusion*)   Where the hell is that seed? (*Indignantly*) You can't see nothing out here! They boxed in the whole goddam neighborhood!

BIFF   There are people all around here. Don't you realize that?

WILLY   I'm busy. Don't bother me.

BIFF   (*taking the hoe from* WILLY)   I'm saying good-by to you, Pop. (WILLY *looks at him, silent, unable to move*) I'm not coming back any more.

WILLY   You're not going to see Oliver tomorrow?

BIFF   I've got no appointment, Dad.

WILLY   He put his arm around you, and you've got no appointment?

BIFF   Pop, get this now, will you? Everytime I've left it's been a fight that sent me out of here. Today I realized something about myself and I tried to explain it to you and I—I think I'm just not smart enough to make any sense out of it for you. To hell with whose fault it is or anything like that. (*He takes* WILLY's *arm*) Let's just wrap it up, heh? Come on in, we'll tell Mom. (*He gently tries to pull* WILLY *to left*)

WILLY   (*frozen, immobile, with guilt in his voice*)   No, I don't want to see her.

BIFF   Come on! (*He pulls again, and* WILLY *tries to pull away*)

WILLY   (*highly nervous*)   No, no, I don't want to see her.

BIFF   (*tries to look into* WILLY's *face, as if to find the answer there*) Why don't you want to see her?

WILLY   (*more harshly now*)   Don't bother me, will you?

BIFF   What do you mean, you don't want to see her? You don't want them calling you yellow, do you? This isn't your fault; it's me, I'm a bum. Now come inside! (WILLY *strains to get away*) Did you hear what I said to you?

WILLY *pulls away and quickly goes by himself into the house.* BIFF *follows.*

LINDA   (*to* WILLY)   Did you plant, dear?

BIFF   (*at the door, to* LINDA)   All right, we had it out. I'm going and I'm not writing any more.

LINDA   (*going to* WILLY *in the kitchen*)   I think that's the best way, dear. 'Cause there's no use drawing it out, you'll just never get along.

WILLY *doesn't respond.*

BIFF   People ask where I am and what I'm doing, you don't know, and you don't care. That way it'll be off your mind and you can start brightening up again. All right? That clears it, doesn't it?

(WILLY *is silent, and* BIFF *goes to him*) You gonna wish me luck, scout? (*He extends his hand*) What do you say?

LINDA   Shake his hand, Willy.

WILLY   (*turning to her, seething with hurt*)   There's no necessity to mention the pen at all, y'know.

BIFF   (*gently*)   I've got no appointment, Dad.

WILLY   (*erupting fiercely*)   He put his arm around . . . ?

BIFF   Dad, you're never going to see what I am, so what's the use of arguing? If I strike oil I'll send you a check. Meantime forget I'm alive.

WILLY   (*to* LINDA)   Spite, see?

BIFF   Shake hands, Dad.

WILLY   Not my hand.

BIFF   I was hoping not to go this way.

WILLY   Well, this is the way you're going. Good-by.

BIFF *looks at him a moment, then turns sharply and goes to the stairs.*

WILLY   (*stops him with*)   May you rot in hell if you leave this house!

BIFF   (*turning*)   Exactly what is it that you want from me?

WILLY   I want you to know, on the train, in the mountains, in the valleys, wherever you go, that you cut down your life for spite!

BIFF   No, no.

WILLY   Spite, spite, is the word of your undoing! And when you're down and out, remember what did it. When you're rotting somewhere beside the railroad tracks, remember, and don't you dare blame it on me!

BIFF   I'm not blaming it on you!

WILLY   I won't take the rap for this, you hear?

HAPPY *comes down the stairs and stands on the bottom step, watching.*

BIFF   That's just what I'm telling you!

WILLY   (*sinking into a chair at the table, with full accusation*)   You're trying to put a knife in me—don't think I don't know what you're doing!

BIFF   All right, phony! Then let's lay it on the line. (*He whips the rubber tube out of his pocket and puts it on the table*)

HAPPY   You crazy—

LINDA   Biff! (*She moves to grab the hose, but* BIFF *holds it down with his hand*)

BIFF   Leave it there! Don't move it!

WILLY   (*not looking at it*)   What is that?

BIFF   You know goddam well what that is.

WILLY   (*caged, wanting to escape*)   I never saw that.

BIFF   You saw it. The mice didn't bring it into the cellar! What is this supposed to do, make a hero out of you? This supposed to make me sorry for you?

WILLY   Never heard of it.

BIFF   There'll be no pity for you, you hear it? No pity!

WILLY   (*to* LINDA)   You hear the spite!

BIFF   No, you're going to hear the truth—what you are and what I am!

LINDA   Stop it!

WILLY   Spite!

HAPPY   (*coming down toward* BIFF)   You cut it now!

BIFF   (*to* HAPPY)   The man don't know who we are! The man is gonna know! (*To* WILLY) We never told the truth for ten minutes in this house!

HAPPY   We always told the truth!

BIFF   (*turning on him*)   You big blow, are you the assistant buyer? You're one of the two assistants to the assistant, aren't you?

HAPPY   Well, I'm practically—

BIFF   You're practically full of it! We all are! And I'm through with it. (*To* WILLY) Now hear this, Willy, this is me.

WILLY   I know you!

BIFF   You know why I had no address for three months? I stole a suit in Kansas City and I was in jail. (*To* LINDA, *who is sobbing*) Stop crying. I'm through with it.

LINDA *turns away from them, her hands covering her face.*

WILLY   I suppose that's my fault!

BIFF   I stole myself out of every good job since high school!

WILLY   And whose fault is that?

BIFF   And I never got anywhere because you blew me so full of hot air I could never stand taking orders from anybody! That's whose fault it is!

WILLY   I hear that!

LINDA   Don't, Biff!

BIFF   It's goddam time you heard that! I had to be boss big shot in two weeks, and I'm through with it!

WILLY   Then hang yourself! For spite, hang yourself!

BIFF   No! Nobody's hanging himself, Willy! I ran down eleven flights with a pen in my hand today. And suddenly I stopped, you hear me? And in the middle of that office building, do you hear this? I stopped in the middle of that building and I saw—the sky. I saw the things that I love in this world. The work and the food and time to sit and smoke. And I looked at the pen and said to myself, what the hell am I grabbing this for? Why am I trying to become what I don't want to be? What am I doing in an office, making a contemptuous, begging fool of myself, when all I want is out there, waiting for me the minute I say I know who I am! Why can't I say that, Willy? (*He tries to make* WILLY *face him, but* WILLY *pulls away and moves to the left*)

WILLY (*with hatred, threateningly*)   The door of your life is wide open!

BIFF   Pop! I'm a dime a dozen, and so are you!

WILLY (*turning on him now in an uncontrolled outburst*)   I am not a dime a dozen! I am Willy Loman, and you are Biff Loman!

BIFF *starts for* WILLY, *but is blocked by* HAPPY. *In his fury,* BIFF *seems on the verge of attacking his* FATHER.

BIFF   I am not a leader of men, Willy, and neither are you. You were never anything but a hard-working drummer who landed in the ash can like all the rest of them! I'm one dollar an hour, Willy! I tried seven states and couldn't raise it. A buck an hour! Do you gather my meaning? I'm not bringing home any prizes any more, and you're going to stop waiting for me to bring them home!

WILLY (*directly to* BIFF)   You vengeful, spiteful mut!

BIFF *breaks from* HAPPY. WILLY, *in fright, starts up the stairs.* BIFF *grabs him.*

BIFF (*at the peak of his fury*)   Pop, I'm nothing! I'm nothing, Pop. Can't you understand that? There's no spite in it any more. I'm just what I am, that's all.

BIFF'S *fury has spent itself, and he breaks down, sobbing, holding on to* WILLY, *who dumbly fumbles for* BIFF'S *face.*

WILLY (*astonished*)   What're you doing? What're you doing? (*To* LINDA) Why is he crying?

BIFF (*crying, broken*)   Will you let me go, for Christ's sake? Will you take that phony dream and burn it before something happens? (*Struggling to contain himself, he pulls away and moves to the stairs*) I'll go in the morning. Put him—put him to bed. (*Exhausted,* BIFF *moves up the stairs to his room*)

WILLY (*after a long pause, astonished, elevated*)   Isn't that—isn't that remarkable? Biff—he likes me!

LINDA   He loves you, Willy!

HAPPY (*deeply moved*)   Always did, Pop.

WILLY   Oh, Biff! (*Staring wildly*) He cried! Cried to me. (*He is choking with his love, and now cries out his promise*) That boy —that boy is going to be magnificent!

BEN *appears in the light just outside the kitchen.*

BEN   Yes, outstanding, with twenty thousand behind him.

LINDA (*sensing the racing of his mind, fearfully, carefully*)   Now come to bed, Willy. It's all settled now.

WILLY (*finding it difficult not to rush out of the house*)   Yes, we'll sleep. Come on. Go to sleep, Hap.

BEN   And it does take a great kind of a man to crack the jungle.

In accents of dread, BEN's *idyllic music starts up.*

HAPPY (*his arm around* LINDA)   I'm getting married, Pop, don't forget it. I'm changing everything. I'm gonna run that department before the year is up. You'll see, Mom. (*He kisses her*)

BEN   The jungle is dark but full of diamonds, Willy.

WILLY *turns, moves, listening to* BEN.

LINDA   Be good. You're both good boys, just act that way, that's all.

HAPPY   'Night, Pop. (*He goes upstairs*)

LINDA (*to* WILLY)   Come, dear.

BEN (*with greater force*)   One must go in to fetch a diamond out.

WILLY (*to* LINDA, *as he moves slowly along the edge of the kitchen, toward the door*)   I just want to get settled down, Linda. Let me sit alone for a little.

LINDA (*almost uttering her fear*)   I want you upstairs.

WILLY (*taking her in his arms*)   In a few minutes, Linda. I couldn't sleep right now. Go on, you look awful tired. (*He kisses her*)

BEN   Not like an appointment at all. A diamond is rough and hard to the touch.

WILLY   Go on now. I'll be right up.

LINDA   I think this is the only way, Willy.

WILLY   Sure, it's the best thing.

BEN   Best thing!

WILLY   The only way. Everything is gonna be—go on, kid, get to bed. You look so tired.

LINDA   Come right up.

WILLY   Two minutes.

LINDA *goes into the living-room, then reappears in her bedroom.* WILLY *moves just outside the kitchen door.*

WILLY   Loves me. (*Wonderingly*) Always loved me. Isn't that a remarkable thing? Ben, he'll worship me for it!

BEN (*with promise*)   It's dark there, but full of diamonds.

WILLY   Can you imagine that magnificence with twenty thousand dollars in his pocket?

LINDA (*calling from her room*)   Willy! Come up!

WILLY (*calling into the kitchen*)   Yes! Yes. Coming! It's very smart, you realize that, don't you, sweetheart? Even Ben sees it. I gotta go, baby. 'By! 'By! (*Going over to* BEN, *almost dancing*) Imagine? When the mail comes he'll be ahead of Bernard again!

BEN   A perfect proposition all around.

WILLY   Did you see how he cried to me? Oh, if I could kiss him, Ben!

BEN   Time, William, time!

WILLY   Oh, Ben, I always knew one way or another we were gonna make it, Biff and I!

BEN (*looking at his watch*)   The boat. We'll be late. (*He moves slowly off into the darkness*)

WILLY (*elegiacally, turning to the house*)   Now when you kick off, boy, I want a seventy-yard boot, and get right down the field under the ball, and when you hit, hit low and hit hard, because it's important, boy. (*He swings around and faces the audience*) There's all kinds of important people in the stands, and the first thing you know ... (*Suddenly realizing he is alone*) Ben! Ben, where do I ... ? (*He makes a sudden movement of search*) Ben, how do I ... ?

LINDA (*calling*)   Willy, you coming up?

WILLY (*uttering a gasp of fear, whirling about as if to quiet her*) Sh! (*He turns around as if to find his way; sounds, faces, voices, seem to be swarming in upon him and he flicks at them, crying*) Sh! Sh! (*Suddenly music, faint and high, stops him. It rises in intensity, almost to an unbearable scream. He goes up and down on his toes, and rushes off around the house*) Shhh!

LINDA   Willy?

*There is no answer. * LINDA *waits. * BIFF *gets up off his bed. He is still in his clothes. * HAPPY *sits up. * BIFF *stands listening.*

LINDA (*with real fear*)   Willy, answer me! Willy!

There is the sound of a car starting and moving away at full speed.

LINDA   No!

BIFF (*rushing down the stairs*)   Pop!

*As the car speeds off, the music crashes down in a frenzy of sound, which becomes the soft pulsation of a single cello string. * BIFF *slowly returns to his bedroom. He and * HAPPY *gravely don their jackets. * LINDA *slowly walks out of her room. The music has developed into a dead march. The leaves of day are appearing over everything. * CHARLEY *and * BERNARD, *somberly* *dressed, appear and knock on the kitchen door.* BIFF *and* HAPPY *slowly descend the stairs to the kitchen as* CHARLEY *and* BERNARD *enter. All stop a moment when* LINDA, *in clothes of mourning, bearing a little bunch of roses, comes through the draped doorway into the kitchen. She goes to* CHARLEY *and takes his arm. Now all move toward the audience, through the wall-line of the kitchen. At the limit of the apron,* LINDA *lays down the flowers, kneels, and sits back on her heels. All stare down at the grave.*

REQUIEM

CHARLEY   It's getting dark, Linda.

LINDA *doesn't react. She stares at the grave.*

BIFF   How about it, Mom? Better get some rest, heh? They'll be closing the gate soon.

LINDA *makes no move. Pause.*

HAPPY (*deeply angered*)   He had no right to do that. There was no necessity for it. We would've helped him.

CHARLEY (*grunting*)   Hmmm.

BIFF   Come along, Mom.

LINDA   Why didn't anybody come?

CHARLEY   It was a very nice funeral.

LINDA   But where are all the people he knew? Maybe they blame him.

CHARLEY   Naa. It's a rough world, Linda. They wouldn't blame him.

LINDA   I can't understand it. At this time especially. First time in thirty-five years we were just about free and clear. He only needed a little salary. He was even finished with the dentist.

CHARLEY   No man only needs a little salary.

LINDA   I can't understand it.

BIFF   There were a lot of nice days. When he'd come home from a trip; or on Sundays, making the stoop; finishing the cellar; putting on the new porch; when he built the extra bathroom; and put up the garage. You know something, Charley, there's more of him in that front stoop than in all the sales he ever made.

CHARLEY   Yeah. He was a happy man with a batch of cement.

LINDA   He was so wonderful with his hands.

BIFF   He had the wrong dreams. All, all, wrong.

HAPPY (*almost ready to fight* BIFF)   Don't say that!

BIFF   He never knew who he was.

CHARLEY (*stopping* HAPPY's *movement and reply. To* BIFF)   Nobody dast blame this man. You don't understand: Willy was a salesman. And for a salesman, there is no rock bottom to the life. He don't put a bolt to a nut, he don't tell you the law or give you medicine. He's a man way out there in the blue, riding on a smile and a shoeshine. And when they start not smiling back—that's an earthquake. And then you get yourself a couple of spots on your hat, and you're finished. Nobody dast blame this man. A salesman is got to dream, boy. It comes with the territory.

BIFF Charley, the man didn't know who he was.

HAPPY (*infuriated*) Don't say that!

BIFF Why don't you come with me, Happy?

HAPPY I'm not licked that easily. I'm staying right in this city, and I'm gonna beat this racket! (*He looks at* BIFF, *his chin set*) The Loman Brothers!

BIFF I know who I am, kid.

HAPPY All right, boy. I'm gonna show you and everybody else that Willy Loman did not die in vain. He had a good dream. It's the only dream you can have—to come out number-one man. He fought it out here, and this is where I'm gonna win it for him.

BIFF (*with a hopeless glance at* HAPPY, *bends toward his mother*) Let's go, Mom.

LINDA I'll be with you in a minute. Go on, Charley. (*He hesitates*) I want to, just for a minute. I never had a chance to say good-by.

CHARLEY *moves away, followed by* HAPPY. BIFF *remains a slight distance up and left of* LINDA. *She sits there, summoning herself. The flute begins, not far away, playing behind her speech.*

LINDA Forgive me, dear. I can't cry. I don't know what it is, but I can't cry. I don't understand it. Why did you ever do that? Help me, Willy, I can't cry. It seems to me that you're just on another trip. I keep expecting you. Willy, dear, I can't cry. Why did you do it? I search and search and I search, and I can't understand it, Willy. I made the last payment on the house today. Today, dear. And there'll be nobody home. (*A sob rises in her throat*) We're free and clear. (*Sobbing more fully, released*) We're free. (BIFF *comes slowly toward her*) We're free . . . We're free . . .

BIFF *lifts her to her feet and moves out up right with her in his arms.* LINDA *sobs quietly.* BERNARD *and* CHARLEY *come together and follow them, followed by* HAPPY. *Only the music of the flute is left on the darkening stage as over the house the hard towers of the apartment buildings rise into sharp focus, and*

The Curtain Falls

QUESTIONS

1. How well do you think Miller has succeeded in making a tragic hero out of Willy Loman? Discuss. Consider the rest of the questions in forming your answer.
2. How does your response to Willy compare or differ from your response to Oedipus and/or Hamlet?
3. How does Miller's dramatization of Willy's hallucinations function?
4. What is the effect of teaming this unrealistic penetration into Willy's mind with the highly realistic language and plot?
5. How are social comment and family tensions interwoven within the play?

POETRY

1 Reading Poetry

Poetry may well be the oldest of all literary forms. Certainly, a great deal of the oldest literature of which we have written records is in verse. Yet today poetry is often regarded as the most sophisticated or difficult of literary forms. What has happened to cause the change? Why should something which seems so difficult to us today have seemed so natural to our ancestors? There are, I suspect, two answers to these questions. The first deals with music; the second with memory.

Poetry is musical, or at least rhythmic, speech. It is also usually a harmonious speech, employing words whose sounds echo each other or blend well. It may even be set to music, to be chanted or sung rather than simply spoken.

Because of its musical nature, poetry is easily remembered. Everyone knows how much easier it is to memorize the words to a song than to memorize even a few paragraphs from a newspaper or textbook. Poetry can thus serve as an aid to memory. If you must remember something, and have no written notes to help you, you can make a song of what you need to remember, and your chances of keeping it in your head will improve.

In almost any society, the desire to keep records, remember events, or tell stories, precedes the invention of writing. Poetry, being pleasant and memorable, is then the natural first form for histories and tales. Once the art of writing develops, however, poetry is no longer essential. But it is still pleasing, and has by now a tradition of use behind it. Prose takes over for record-keeping and transmitting technical information, but poetry keeps its hold on certain important affairs. Songs are still written to celebrate victories and loves, to mourn deaths, and to worship.

The printing of books, which gave so many people access to written words, has been one factor in the promotion of prose in our society. The invention of radio and television—whose announcers universally speak in the blandest, least musical cadences possible—has been another factor. After the age of nursery rhymes, most of us live in a world where the cadences of poetry are no longer part of our everyday life. Moreover, we live in a society where so many written and spoken words bombard us that we learn to skim through them quickly for whatever information they carry. We take no time to look for beauty of words or rhythm—which very likely isn't there anyway.

Poetry, however, cannot be read rapidly. Newspapers can be, and, in fact, are meant to be. Fiction can be. And, again, some of it is meant for the quick, careless reader, though most good fiction improves with slow, thoughtful reading. Drama, in general, must be read more slowly, to catch the sound of the individual speeches. But poetry must be read most slowly of all. It requires not only that we read it silently at the same pace that we would read it aloud, but also that we pause after we read it, to think about it for a few moments at least, to savor the mood the poem has created before we go on to something else.

It is no wonder, then, that poetry sometimes seems strange or difficult. Almost every other influence in our environment is telling us, "Hurry up! Grab the central fact or idea I'm selling and run!" Poetry is saying, "Slow down! Enjoy the music; let yourself become part of the emotion. I have many suggestions to make. Take time to let them unfold for you." In today's rush of prepackaged ideas, the stubborn individualism and refusal to be hurried which poetry represents is indeed unusual.

But anything which lets us think for ourselves, which offers us a chance to find our own feelings, ideas, and emotions, is worth pursuing. And poetry certainly encourages this kind of thinking and reflection. Moreover, once we agree to slow down enough to savor a poem completely, we discover that poetry is very similar to the literature we've been enjoying all along. Like fiction and drama, poetry tells us of people, of what it means to them and to us to be human. And, like the other forms of literature, it relays this information through the sound of human voices.

So closely related are poetry, fiction, and drama, in fact, that it is sometimes hard to tell which is which. Some poetic dramas seem better suited for reading than for performance. Should they be classed as poetry or as plays? Similarly, there are narratives that tell a complete story in verse. Should they be considered fiction as well as poetry? Or shall we simply ignore the classifications and enjoy each work for what we like best in it, whether that be a supposedly "poetic" quality, such as rhythm, or a supposedly "fictional" or "dramatic" one, such as plot, characterization, or dramatic irony?

We must, then, read poetry with the same close attention we give to all our readings in this course. Poetry, too, demands these basic questions:

1. Who is speaking?
2. What kind of person is he or she? In what mood? Thinking what thoughts? Feeling what emotions?
3. Of whom or what is he or she speaking?
4. How is this person or object being described?
5. What attitudes are being projected?
6. Are we led to share the attitudes and emotions in sympathy, or to rebel against them with feelings of anger or irony?

But, since poetry is both the most structured and the most subjective of literary forms, we may also ask questions about its forms and its sounds, to learn how they contribute to the poem's effect on us. In doing this, we may get some sense of what qualities we want to consider poetic.

Because poetry is a genre of great variety, it cannot be easily defined. Only by reading a variety of poems can we create our knowledge of poetry, enhance our enjoyment of it, and gain a sense of what it has to offer us.

Let us begin, therefore, by reading some traditional ballads. Ballads are tales told in song. Traditional ballads (or folk ballads) are songs that have been passed from one singer to another, not by being writtten down but by being sung, heard, and re-sung.* Ballads are thus very like folk tales in their mode of creation and in their sense of the audience. So we may expect that the voices within the ballads will be like the voices of those archetypal storytellers we first met when reading fiction. And yet ballads are sung. Their creators are singers, not speakers. How, then, will these tales sung in verse differ from tales told in prose? How will their stories be told? What will we hear that we have not heard before?

Read the ballads, and then decide what you think are the characteristics of ballads and how you think they differ from tales told in prose. To clarify your thinking, you may want to consider how the tales sung by these ballads would be told if they were written as stories, or how some story would be changed if it were turned into a ballad. You might even try your hand at writing a ballad yourself.

---

* This oral tradition accounts for the number of variations ballads possess. A singer may repeat a ballad just as he or she first heard it; or he or she may change the ballad slightly, either on purpose or accidentally. A third singer then learns this new version, and either preserves or changes it. Thus a ballad of any great age may exist in many versions, each being sung by a different group of singers.

ANONYMOUS

Get Up and Bar the Door

It fell about the Martinmas[1] time,
    And a gay time it was then,
When our good wife got puddings[2] to make,
    And she's boild them in the pan.

5 The wind sae cauld blew south and north,
    And blew into the floor;
Quoth our goodman to our goodwife,
    "Gae out and bar the door."

"My hands is in my hussyfskap,[3]
10   Goodman, as ye may see;
An it shoud nae be barrd this hundred year,
    It's no be barrd for me."

They made a paction tween them twa,
    They made it firm and sure,
15 That the first word whaeer shoud speak,
    Shoud rise and bar the door.

Then by there came two gentlemen,
    At twelve oclock at night,
And they could neither see house nor hall,
20   Nor coal nor candle-light.

"Now whether is this a rich man's house,
    Or whether is it a poor?"
But neer a word wad ane o them speak,
    For barring of the door.

25 And first they ate the white puddings,
    And then they ate the black;
Tho muckle[4] thought the goodwife to hersel,
    Yet neer a word she spake.

Then said the one unto the other,
30   "Here, man, tak ye my knife;

---

[1] November 11.
[2] Sausages.
[3] Household chores.
[4] Much.

Do ye tak aff the auld man's beard,
    And I'll kiss the goodwife."

"But there's nae water in the house,
    And what shall we do than?"
35 "What ails ye at the pudding-broo,
    That boils into the pan?"

O up then started our goodman,
    An angry man was he:
"Will ye kiss my wife before my een,
40   And scad me wi pudding-bree?"

Then up and started our goodwife,
    Gied three skips on the floor:
"Goodman, you've spoken the foremost word,
    Get up and bar the door."

Lord Randal

"O where ha you been, Lord Randal, my son?
And where ha you been, my handsome young man?"
"I ha been at the greenwood; mother, mak my bed soon,
For I'm wearied wi hunting, and fain wad lie down."

5 "An wha met ye there, Lord Randal, my son?
An wha met you there, my handsome young man?"
"O I met wi my true-love; mother, mak my bed soon,
For I'm wearied wi hunting, and fain wad lie down."

"And what did she give you, Lord Randal, my son?
10 And what did she give you, my handsome young man?"
"Eels fried in a pan; mother, mak my bed soon,
For I'm wearied wi huntin, and fain wad lie down."

"And wha gat your leavins, Lord Randal, my son?
And wha gat your leavins, my handsome young man?"
15 "My hawks and my hounds; mother, mak my bed soon,
For I'm wearied wi hunting, and fain wad lie down."

"And what becam of them, Lord Randal, my son?
And what becam of them, my handsome young man?"
"They stretched their legs out and died; mother, mak my bed soon,
20 For I'm wearied wi huntin, and fain wad lie down."

"O I fear you are poisoned, Lord Randal, my son!
I fear you are poisoned, my handsome young man!"
"O yes, I am poisoned: mother, mak my bed soon,
For I'm sick at the heart, and I fain wad lie down."

25 "What d'ye leave to your mother, Lord Randal, my son?
What d'ye leave to your mother, my handsome young man?"
"Four and twenty milk kye;[1] mother, mak my bed soon,
For I'm sick at the heart, and I fain wad lie down."

"What d'ye leave to your sister, Lord Randal, my son?
30 What d'ye leave to your sister, my handsome young man?"
"My gold and my silver; mother, mak my bed soon,
For I'm sick at the heart, an I fain wad lie down."

"What d'ye leave to your brother, Lord Randal, my son?
What d'ye leave to your brother, my handsome young man?"
35 "My houses and my lands; mother, mak my bed soon,
For I'm sick at the heart, and I fain wad lie down."

"What d'ye leave to your true-love, Lord Randal, my son?
What d'ye leave to your true-love, my handsome young man?"
"I leave her hell and fire; mother, mak my bed soon,
40 For I'm sick at the heart, and I fain wad lie down."

The Cherry-Tree Carol

Joseph was an old man,
    and an old man was he,
When he wedded Mary,
    in the land of Galilee.

5 Joseph and Mary walked
    through an orchard good,
Where was cherries and berries,
    so red as any blood.

Joseph and Mary walked
10   through an orchard green,
Where was berries and cherries,
    as thick as might be seen.

---

[1] Kine = cows.

O then bespoke Mary,
    so meek and so mild:
15 "Pluck me one cherry, Joseph,
    for I am with child."

O then bespoke Joseph:
    with words most unkind:
"Let him pluck thee a cherry
20   that brought thee with child."

O then bespoke the babe,
    within his mother's womb:
"Bow down then the tallest tree,
    for my mother to have some."

25 Then bowed down the highest tree
    unto his mother's hand;
Then she cried, "See, Joseph,
    I have cherries at command."

O then bespoke Joseph:
30   "I have done Mary wrong;
But cheer up, my dearest,
    and be not cast down."

Then Mary plucked a cherry,
    as red as the blood,
35 Then Mary went home
    with her heavy load.

Then Mary took her babe,
    and sat him on her knee,
Saying, "My dear son, tell me
40   what this world will be."

"O I shall be as dead, mother,
    as the stones in the wall;
O the stones in the streets, mother,
    shall mourn for me all.

45 "Upon Easter-day, mother,
    my uprising shall be;
O the sun and the moon, mother,
    shall both rise with me."

ELEMENTS OF POETRY

2 *Repetition and Rhythm*

Two elements prominent in ballads are **repetition** and **rhythm.** Sometimes single words or phrases are repeated for emphasis, as in "Lord Randal": "O where ha you been. . . . And where ha you been." Sometimes one or more lines appear in every verse as a refrain: "Mother, mak my bed soon,/For I'm wearied wi hunting, and fain wad lie down." In each case, the repetition emphasizes both the content and the rhythm of the ballad, calling our attention to the meter (that is, to the rhythmic pattern of each line) or to the grouping of lines into stanzas.

Of the three ballads printed in the previous chapter, "Lord Randal" is easily the most repetitive. In fact, it is built on a technique known as *incremental repetition.* At least half of each line is repeated from stanza to stanza, and the pattern of question and answer never varies. Yet the changes that occur reveal and develop the dying lord's story.

Repetition is important not only in ballads, but in lyric poetry in general. It is most pronounced in songs, as in the next example. But it appears frequently (and often quite subtly) in spoken lyrics as well. Let us look at some poems in which repetition plays an important role, and let us see what effects are being gained by it.

ANONYMOUS ELIZABETHAN LYRIC

Back and Side Go Bare

Back and side go bare, go bare,
 Both foot and hand go cold;
But, belly, God send thee good ale enough,
 Whether it be new or old.

5 I cannot eat but little meat,
 My stomach is not good;
But sure I think that I can drink
 With him that wears a hood.
Though I go bare, take ye no care,
10 I am nothing a-cold;
I stuff my skin so full within
 Of jolly good ale and old.
   Back and side go bare, go bare, &c.

I love no roast but a nutbrown toast,
15 And a crab[1] laid in the fire;
A little bread shall do me stead,
 Much bread I not desire.
No frost nor snow, no wind, I trow,
 Can hurt me if I would,
20 I am so wrapt, and throughly lapt
 Of jolly good ale and old.
   Back and side go bare, go bare, &c.

And Tib my wife, that as her life
 Loveth well good ale to seek,
25 Full oft drinks she, till ye may see
 The tears run down her cheek.
Then doth she troll to me the bowl,
 Even as a maltworm should;
And saith, "Sweetheart, I took my part
30 Of this jolly good ale and old."
   Back and side go bare, go bare, &c.

Now let them drink, till they nod and wink,
 Even as good fellows should do;
They shall not miss to have the bliss
35 Good ale doth bring men to.

---

[1] Crabapple.

And all poor souls that have scourèd bowls,
   Or have them lustily trolled,
God save the lives of them and their wives,
   Whether they be young or old.
40   Back and side go bare, go bare,
       Both foot and hand go cold;
      But, belly, God send thee good ale enough,
       Whether it be new or old.

QUESTIONS

1. How would you characterize this song? What is its mood?
2. How does the refrain help set the mood of the song? What is gained by having the refrain sung before the first verse?
3. What other repetitions of sounds do you find in the poem? What do they contribute? (Note: Two important categories here are rhyme—the use of words that end with the same sound, like *cold* and *old*—and alliteration, the use of words that begin with the same sound, like *back* and *bare*.)
4. Discuss the progression of thought and feeling from the first stanza's, "I cannot eat . . ." to the final stanza's, "God save the lives . . . ." What sense of completeness does the progression give to the song?

THOMAS HARDY (1840–1928)

The Ruined Maid

"O 'Melia, my dear, this does everything crown!
Who could have supposed I should meet you in Town?
And whence such fair garments, such prosperi-ty?"—
"O didn't you know I'd been ruined?" said she.

5 —"You left us in tatters, without shoes or socks,
Tired of digging potatoes, and spudding up docks;[1]
And now you've gay bracelets and bright feathers three!"—
"Yes: that's how we dress when we're ruined," said she.

  —"At home in the barton[2] you said 'thee' and 'thou,'
10 And 'thik oon,' and 'theäs oon,' and 't'other'; but now
Your talking quite fits 'ee for high compa-ny!"—
"Some polish is gained with one's ruin," said she.

---

[1] Digging up weeds.
[2] Farmyard.

—"Your hands were like paws then, your face blue and bleak
But now I'm bewitched by your delicate cheek,
15 And your little gloves fit as on any la-dy!"—
"We never do work when we're ruined," said she.

—"You used to call home-life a hag-ridden dream,
And you'd sigh, and you'd sock; but at present you seem
To know not of megrims[3] or melancho-ly!"—
20 "True. One's pretty lively when ruined," said she.

—"I wish I had feathers, a fine sweeping gown,
And a delicate face, and could strut about Town!"—
"My dear—a raw country girl, such as you be,
Cannot quite expect that. You ain't ruined," said she.

QUESTIONS

1. How does Hardy use question and answer to characterize the two women?
2. What balance exists here between the two sides of the dialogue? What is the effect of the repetitions in the final line of each stanza?
3. What sort of tone or consciousness would you expect to find in a poem about a "ruined maid" that is absent from this poem? What effect does this have on the tone of the poem and the characterization of the speakers? On the poet's apparent attitude toward them?

ANONYMOUS MIDDLE ENGLISH LYRIC

All Night by the Rose

All night by the rose, rose—
    All night by the rose I lay;
Dared I not the rose steal,
    And yet I bore the flower away.

QUESTIONS

This medieval lyric uses repetition with a difference. What is the rose of which this singer sings? What is the point of the shift from "rose" to "flower" in the final line? How would you explain the riddle suggested by the last two lines? In short, what has the singer gained by his repetition of "rose" and "flower" that a simple recital of events would miss?

---

[3] Low spirits.

WILLIAM BLAKE (1757–1827)

From **Songs of Innocence**

The Lamb

Little Lamb, who made thee?
Dost thou know who made thee?
Gave thee life & bid thee feed,
By the stream & o'er the mead;
5   Gave thee clothing of delight,
Softest clothing wooly bright;
Gave thee such a tender voice,
Making all the vales rejoice!
Little Lamb who made thee?
10   Dost thou know who made thee?

Little Lamb I'll tell thee,
Little Lamb I'll tell thee!
He is callèd by thy name,
For he calls himself a Lamb:
15   He is meek & he is mild,
He became a little child:
I a child & thou a lamb,
We are callèd by his name.
Little Lamb God bless thee.
20   Little Lamb God bless thee.

From **Songs of Experience**

The Tyger

Tyger! Tyger! burning bright
In the forests of the night,
What immortal hand or eye
Could frame thy fearful symmetry?

5   In what distant deeps or skies
Burnt the fire of thine eyes?
On what wings dare he aspire?
What the hand, dare seize the fire?

And what shoulder, & what art,
10   Could twist the sinews of thy heart?
And when thy heart began to beat,
What dread hand? & what dread feet?

What the hammer? what the chain?
In what furnace was thy brain?
15 What the anvil? what dread grasp
Dare its deadly terrors clasp?

When the stars threw down their spears,
And water'd heaven with their tears,
Did he smile his work to see?
20 Did he who made the Lamb make thee?

Tyger! Tyger! burning bright
In the forests of the night,
What immortal hand or eye
Dare frame thy fearful symmetry?

QUESTIONS

If you were to write an essay on "The Lamb" and "The Tyger," you might start with the following question:

1. Both "The Lamb" and "The Tyger" are essentially religious poems. Yet they seem to describe two different aspects of religious feeling. How would you characterize each aspect? How does the first fit the conception of "innocence," the second of "experience"? How are the animals, and the feelings they represent, characterized within the poem?

To develop the answer, you could then look at the following aspects of each poem:

2. "The Lamb" and "The Tyger" have almost the same rhythm, being based on a seven-syllable line with the odd-numbered syllables accented: Ty-ger! Ty-ger! burn-ing bright. But "The Lamb" varies this meter in places, while "The Tyger" holds to it firmly throughout. Look at the rhythm and repetitions carefully in each poem, and then explain how they reinforce each other. Why is the effect so different for each poem?

3. "The Lamb" and "The Tyger" both make use of repeated questions. How does their use in "The Lamb" differ from their use in "The Tyger"? How do these differences help create the contrasting tones of the two poems?

4. What images are connected with the lamb? with the tiger? How are they related? how contrasted?

5. What attitude does the speaker seem to have toward each animal? With what evidence would you support your answer to this question?

E. E. CUMMINGS (1894–1963)

All in green went my love riding

All in green went my love riding
on a great horse of gold
into the silver dawn.

four lean hounds crouched low and smiling
5 the merry deer ran before.

Fleeter be they than dappled dreams
the swift sweet deer
the red rare deer.

Four red roebuck at a white water
10 the cruel bugle sang before.

Horn at hip went my love riding
riding the echo down
into the silver dawn.

four lean hounds crouched low and smiling
15 the level meadows ran before.

Softer be they than slippered sleep
the lean lithe deer
the fleet flown deer.

Four fleet does at a gold valley
20 the famished arrow sang before.

Bow at belt went my love riding
riding the mountain down
into the silver dawn.

four lean hounds crouched low and smiling
25 the sheer peaks ran before.

Paler be they than daunting death
the sleek slim deer
the tall tense deer.

Four tall stags at a green mountain
30 the lucky hunter sang before.

All in green went my love riding
on a great horse of gold
into the silver dawn.

four lean hounds crouched low and smiling
35 my heart fell dead before.

QUESTIONS

1. Incremental repetition is used in this modern poem for an almost ballad-like effect. But how would you describe the way stanzas are linked in this poem?
2. What effects would you say the poem achieves? How would you distinguish between its effects and those of traditional ballads?

3

Compression and Verse Forms

To write a short story based on the tale told in "Lord Randal" or "Get Up and Bar the Door" would require at least one thousand words. (That would be roughly the length of "If Not Higher"—quite a short story, as stories go.) These two ballads, however, have less than five hundred words each, including refrains and repetitions. And even though the ballads are much shorter than a very short story, they seem long and loosely constructed when they are compared with such tightly written lyrics as "The Tyger."

Verse, then, is a highly compressed form. Eliminating inessentials—the name of Lord Randal's sweetheart, the reason she killed him—it takes us directly to the heart of a situation, to the one or two moments most highly charged with emotion. In the case of "Lord Randal," this technique reduces the ballad to a single moment, that in which mother and son discover that the son has been poisoned. In the case of "Get Up and Bar the Door," it produces a ballad centering on two episodes: the one that begins the quarrel and the one that ends it.

Time becomes flexible in these ballads, as one memorable moment is juxtaposed with the next, ignoring all that may have gone between: "Then by there came two gentlemen,/At twelve oclock at night." We can imagine that the lateness of the hour would have made the silent house seem even stranger than it was to the "gentlemen," and we may also suspect that quite a few hours must have passed since the feuding

couple made their pact. But all the singer gives us is the crucial hour—
"twelve"—and the number of intruders. The time between incidents is not
important. The conflict between the couple is.

Similarly, "The Cherry-Tree Carol" moves with almost no consciousness of elapsed time from the wedding of Joseph and Mary to the scene
in the orchard to a final scene between Mary and her infant son. In each
case, a simple "then" defines the sequence, whether the incidents follow
each other instantly, as in "then bespoke the babe," "then bowed down
the highest tree," and "O then bespoke Joseph," or whether a gap of
several months is indicated: "Then Mary took her babe." The passage of
time, which happens to everyone, is of no concern to the singer. The
unique situation of parents confronted with their child's divinity engrosses
all the attention, linking together the unusual circumstances of Joseph's
marriage, the miracle in the orchard, and Christ's prophecy of his death
and resurrection. "The Cherry-Tree Carol" assumes that its hearers are
all familiar with the story of Christ's birth and death; it therefore feels
free to concentrate on those aspects of the legend that bear on its central
theme, leaving us to place·them in chronological time if we wish.

Every literary form is somewhat selective in its choice of times and
episodes, and in the amount of attention it gives to each. "If Not Higher,"
for example, tells its tale of a conflict between two types of religion by
focusing on two men and spending half of its narration following the two
through a single hour of a morning. Similarly, *Oedipus Rex*'s tale of the
fall of a king focuses on the last day of his reign, a day of crisis and
steadily mounting emotion. But neither drama nor fiction can match the
intense selectivity, the rigorous paring-down, of poetry.

Poetic form demands compression. A line of eight or ten syllables, a
stanza of two, four, or six lines will not allow any wasted words. The poet
must pare away all the needless background and inessential details in
order to fit the essential ones into those brief stanzas.

Yet this strictness of form also helps the hearer to accept the compression it produces. We would not accept so few details as "Lord Randal"
gives us in a prose account of his death. Nor could the information given
in "The Lamb" or "The Tyger" stand alone as prose. Ballad and lyric
alike need the cadence of their verse—the rhyme, the rhythm, the rounded-
off pattern formed by the stanzas—to give our ear and mind the sense of
completeness and satisfaction that allows us to enjoy the brief, tightly
focused statements their poetry makes.

Compression, then, is another technique that allows the material presented and the form of its presentation to reinforce each other, providing
for the reader not only a satisfying unity, but also one that seems notably
poetic. Let us now examine that technique in action by looking at a few
types of poetry which have compression as their most notable feature,
beginning with the oldest of these forms, the **epigram.**

Epigrams may be serious or humorous, flattering or insulting. But they are usually descriptive of a person, animal, or object; and they are invariably brief. Probably the most popular type today is the *satiric epigram,* a form that can be described as a description with a sting. Here is an example:

COUNTEE CULLEN (1903–1946)

For a Lady I Know

She even thinks that up in heaven
Her class lies late and snores,
While poor black cherubs rise at seven
To do celestial chores.

QUESTIONS

1. What single fact do the four lines of this poem tell us about the "Lady" who is their subject?
2. What further facts do they suggest about her?
3. How do words like "her class" and "poor black cherubs" characterize the lady and the attitudes which the poet suggests she holds?
4. What do words like "snores" and "celestial chores" do for the poem? What do they suggest about the poet's attitude?

Not all brief poems with a punch are epigrams, however. The following poem has a sting of its own and is as highly compressed in technique as any poem you will see. Yet its structure is not that of the epigram. How would you define it?

GWENDOLYN BROOKS (1915–   )

We Real Cool

The Pool Players.
Seven at the Golden Shovel.

We real cool. We
Left school. We

5   Lurk late. We
Strike straight. We

Sing sin. We
Thin gin. We

Jazz June. We
10 Die soon.

QUESTIONS

1. What does the subtitle tell us about the speakers of the poem?
2. How do the speakers characterize themselves?
3. Discuss the use of repetition in the poem.
4. Note also the breaks in the pattern. Why has Brooks placed the word "We" at the end of each line rather than letting it come at the beginning as it does in the first line? Is the word "We" stressed more heavily, less heavily, or just as heavily at the end of the line as it would be at the beginning? What happens to the verbs? Does placing them at the beginning of the line give them any extra stress? What happens to the length of the last line? What effect does it produce?
5. What does Brooks seem to be saying in this poem about the "Seven" or about people like them? How does the form of her poem express or emphasize her feelings?

Another extremely brief form, which was introduced to English and American poetry in the twentieth century, is the **imagist** poem. Imagist poetry grew out of an interest in Oriental poetry, especially in the brief, seventeen-syllable form known as *haiku*. (The poems by Pound that follow are sometimes called haiku.) As the word *imagist* implies, this poetry focuses on a single sensory image—a sight, sound, or feeling—and presents it in as brief and vivid a form as the writer can manage. Read the following three poems, and then ask what image each poem starts from and what further images it uses to reinforce the first one. How are the images combined? How would you contrast the form and effect of these poems with the form and effect of the epigrams you have just read, or with the effect and form of Blake's lyrics?

EZRA POUND (1885–1972)

In a Station of the Metro

The apparition of these faces in the crowd;
Petals on a wet, black bough.

DENISE LEVERTOV (1923–   )

Six Variations (part iii)

Shlup, shlup, the dog
as it laps up
water
makes intelligent
5   music, resting
now and then to take breath in irregular
measure.

H. D. (HILDA DOOLITTLE) (1886–1961)

Heat

O wind, rend open the heat,
cut apart the heat,
rend it to tatters.

Fruit cannot drop
5   through this thick air—
fruit cannot fall into heat
that presses up and blunts
the points of pears
and rounds the grapes.

10 Cut the heat—
plough through it,
turning it on either side
of your path.

Here is one more poem by Pound, who was one of the founders of
imagist poetry. What does this poem do with imagist techniques? How
does it differ from the preceding poems?

L'Art 1910

Green arsenic smeared on an egg-white cloth,
Crushed strawberries! Come, let us feast our eyes.

Finally, we should look at some poems by Emily Dickinson. No study of
compression in poetry would be complete without looking at the work of

this American poet, who was far ahead of her time in the concentration and spareness of her verse. Notice, in the following two poems, how images of light and motion bridge the gap between the physical and spiritual worlds and between our own physical and spiritual responses to these worlds.

EMILY DICKINSON (1830–1886)

There's a Certain Slant of Light (#258)

There's a certain Slant of light,
Winter Afternoons—
That oppresses, like the Heft
Of Cathedral Tunes—

5 Heavenly Hurt, it gives us—
We can find no scar,
But internal difference,
Where the Meanings, are—

None may teach it—Any—
10 'Tis the Seal Despair—
An imperial affliction
Sent us of the Air—

When it comes, the Landscape listens—
Shadows—hold their breath—
15 When it goes, 'tis like the Distance
On the look of Death—

Tell All the Truth but Tell It Slant (#1129)

Tell all the Truth but tell it slant—
Success in Circuit lies
Too bright for our infirm Delight
The Truth's superb surprise
5 As Lightning to the Children eased
With explanation kind
The Truth must dazzle gradually
Or every man be blind—

QUESTIONS

1. Give examples of images of light and motion in these poems. How are the two types of images connected?

2. Give examples of lines or phrases that you think are particularly good examples of compression. How is Dickinson creating this effect? For what purpose is she using it?

3. What does being human seem to mean in these poems? What aspects of our nature are being emphasized? (Note that we as readers are definitely included in these descriptions of what being human entails. How are we brought into them?)

4

Word Choice: Meanings and Suggestions

Common Phrases and New Meanings

Our study of ballads gave us insight into the use of repetition and selectivity in poetry, and thus into poetry's balance of narrative and rhythmic patterns. We saw that poetry is based on the combination of satisfying sounds and sharply focused content. And we saw how the pattern of sounds and words created by the skillful use of rhythm, repetition, and word-sound can be used to heighten the effect of compression or to set a mood.

But ballads could not tell us a great deal about word choice in poetry. For ballads, like other oral poetry, tend to rely on a shared vocabulary of predictable phrases and stock epithets. Hearing ballads, we recognize in them traditional terms, pairings, and comparisons: "my true-love," "my hawks and my hounds," "the sun and the moon," "as red as the blood," and "as dead as the stones." We are not meant to linger on any of them, or on any particular line. Rather, we let each recognized phrase add its bit to mood or situation, while we reserve our main attention for the pattern made by the story as it unfolds.

In written poetry, on the other hand, word choice is all-important. The play on words by which the medieval lyricist turns a pun on "rose" and "flower" into a song of triumphant love, the indelicate verb "snores" with which Cullen mocks his "lady's" pretensions to gentility, and even the archaic spelling of "tyger," which gives Blake's beast its first hint of strangeness and mystery, all testify to the power of the well-chosen word. The words themselves are not unusual ones; but they surprise us when they appear, nonetheless. They call on us to pay attention and reward us for our attention by bringing their overtones of meaning and suggestion into the poem, enriching our enjoyment and understanding.

The language of poetry, then, is not necessarily composed of strange, unusual, or uniquely "poetic" words. More often, poetry gains its effects through unexpected juxtapositions of common words, bringing new meaning into the ordinary. Look, for instance, at this poem by Emily Dickinson, and see how significance may be given to the simplest language.

The Bustle in a House (#1078)

The Bustle in a House
The Morning after Death
Is solemnest of industries
Enacted upon Earth—

5 The Sweeping up the Heart
And putting Love away
We shall not want to use again
Until Eternity.

The language of the first stanza is almost like prose. A few extra words, and it would be a simple prose statement: The bustle that takes place in a house, the day after someone who lived there has died, represents one of the most solemn tasks on earth. (The word "industries" may seem a bit strange in this context. At the time when this poem was written, however, it was used to denote any sort of labor, just as the word "industrious" does today.)

In the second stanza, however, we notice a change. Here the poet is amplifying her first statement. She is explaining that the "bustle" is caused by the housecleaning that takes place between a death and the funeral, and that it is "solemn" because the workers must reconcile themselves to the loss of a loved one. In fact, the workers are coming to grips with their emotions even as they do the chores.

She does not, however, resort to wordy explanations. Rather, she combines housework and emotions in a tightly compressed pair of images. The verbs of the second stanza speak of housecleaning matters, the nouns of love. It is not dust which is swept up, but "the heart"; not blankets to be put away, but "love." The combination conveys the sense of loss. "The sweeping up the heart," in particular, suggests that the heart is broken, is in pieces; and the thought of a broken heart, in turn, suggests grief.

But the poet also says that the grief and loss are not permanent. "Love" is not thrown away, but rather "put away" to be used again on a future occasion. "Until eternity": the phrase suggests a fearfully long wait, but insists, nonetheless, that the waiting will end. "Eternity" thus balances "earth," tempering the present sense of loss with faith in restoration. And in that balance the poem ends and rests.

Suggestion and Interpretation

The language of Blake's "The Tyger" is stranger and more complex than Dickinson's. The description of the tiger as "Burning bright/In the forests of the night" links notions of burning passion, glowing cat-eyes, dark trees, and forests of stars to create, from words that literally are near nonsense, a beast half earthly and half unearthly, combining in his "fearful symmetry" brutal ferocity and supernatural beauty.

"The Tyger" again brings us to realize that word choice in poetry often means choosing words that can carry many meanings at once and then combining those words for the greatest power of suggestion. As the medieval lover's rose was more than a flower, so Blake's tiger is more than mere animal. But it was a great deal easier to decide what the rose signified than it is to interpret the tiger. The striking images and the strong sense of awe that pervade the poem insist that the tiger stands for something special in its questioner's eyes. But they will not tell us specifically what that something is. In this the language of the poem is poetic—it moves always toward greater suggestiveness, never toward a narrowing of meaning. As a result, the tiger symbolizes many things for many people, with all readers bringing their own experiences to this "Song of Experience" and coming away with their own visions of what the tiger can mean for them.

Sound, sense, and suggestion all blend in poetry. Words gain new relevance, new connections. They carry several meanings, suggest several more, and join with other words to suggest yet further meanings. Word choice, the craft of selecting and joining words to enrich their power to communicate, is one of the basic skills of the poet's craft.

Since the rhythms of the following two poems are smoother than those of "The Bustle in the House," and their rhymes are more satisfyingly matched, they have a more traditional sound. Yet their use of language resembles that in Dickinson's poem in that their words and syntax, basically simple and straightforward, are highlighted by a few unexpected words or images. Discuss what you think the highlights in these poems are, and how you think they function.

WILLIAM WORDSWORTH (1770–1850)

She Dwelt Among the Untrodden Ways

She dwelt among the untrodden ways
   Beside the springs of Dove.
A Maid whom there were none to praise
   And very few to love;

5 A violet by a mossy stone
   Half hidden from the eye!
—Fair as a star, when only one
   Is shining in the sky.

She lived unknown, and few could know
10   When Lucy ceased to be;
But she is in her grave, and, oh,
   The difference to me!

ROBERT HERRICK (1591–1674)

Upon Julia's Clothes

Whenas in silks my Julia goes,
Then, then, methinks, how sweetly flows
The liquefaction of her clothes.

Next, when I cast mine eyes and see
5 The brave vibration each way free,
O how that glittering taketh me!

Again, the following poem presents a straightforward statement. But here the language is slightly richer, the play on words is more pronounced, and the words take on more resonance of meaning. Discuss the poem and its language. How does the choice of words give the poem more impact than its main statement, "Many friends of mine have died," would have?

A. E. HOUSMAN (1859–1936)

With Rue My Heart Is Laden

With rue my heart is laden
   For golden friends I had,
For many a rose-lipt maiden
   And many a lightfoot lad.

5 By brooks too broad for leaping
  The lightfoot boys are laid;
  The rose-lipt girls are sleeping
  In fields where roses fade.

QUESTIONS

1. What repetitions do you find in the poem? How does the second stanza develop the images begun in the first stanza?
2. How does the word "golden" in line 2 fit into the mood and imagery?
3. Note the heavy use of "r" and "l" sounds. What effect does the alliteration of these sounds produce? What other examples of alliteration can you find in the poem? How would you summarize your view of Housman's choice of words for sound and sense?

The next two poems are written in free verse, a verse form invented in the early twentieth century. Free verse is marked by uneven line lengths and often by the absence of rhyme, as well. Note how these poems mix repetition and compression to create their very different effects.

CARL SANDBURG (1878–1967)

Cool Tombs

When Abraham Lincoln was shoveled into the tombs, he forgot the
  copperheads and the assassin . . . in the dust, in the cool tombs.
And Ulysses Grant lost all thought of con men and Wall Street, cash
  and collateral turned ashes . . . in the dust, in the cool tombs.
5 Pocahontas' body, lovely as a poplar, sweet as a red haw in November
  or a pawpaw in May, did she wonder? does she remember? . . . in
  the dust, in the cool tombs?
Take any streetful of people buying clothes and groceries, cheering a
  hero or throwing confetti and blowing tin horns . . . tell me if the
10 lovers are losers . . . tell me if any get more than the lovers . . . in
  the dust . . . in the cool tombs.

QUESTIONS

1. What images are associated with each person? Why have they been chosen? What do they suggest?
2. Is there a message to the poem? If so, what is it? How does the poem travel from its opening statements to its final suggestions?
3. How would you describe the sound of this poem? the rhythm? How do sound and rhythm fit the meaning of the poem? How do they create its mood?

EZRA POUND (1885–1972)

These Fought in Any Case[1]

These fought in any case,
and some believing,
> pro domo,[2] in any case . . .

Some quick to arm,
5 some for adventure,
some from fear of weakness,
some from fear of censure,
some for love of slaughter, in imagination,
learning later . . .
10 some in fear, learning love of slaughter;

Died some, pro patria,
> non "dulce" non "et decor"[3] . . .
walked eye-deep in hell
believing in old men's lies, then unbelieving
15 came home, home to a lie,
home to many deceits,
home to old lies and new infamy;
usury age-old and age-thick
and liars in public places.

20 Daring as never before, wastage as never before.
Young blood and high blood,
fair cheeks, and fine bodies;

fortitude as never before

frankness as never before,
25 disillusions as never told in the old days,
hysterias, trench confessions,
laughter out of dead bellies.

QUESTIONS

1. How would you describe the tone of voice in this poem? What do the repe-

---

[1] Section IV from "E. P. Ode pour L'Election de Son Sépulcre" ("E. P. Ode on the Selection of His Tomb").

[2] "For homeland."

[3] An ironic allusion to the famous line of Horace: "Dulce et decorum est pro patria mori" ("It is sweet and fitting to die for one's country").

titions contribute to it? The word choice? (Be sure you give examples to prove your assertions.)
2. What attitude does the poem suggest towards the soldiers of which it speaks? Is the attitude simple or complex? How is it suggested?
3. What of the poem's attitude to war in general?
4. An **ode** is a poem of irregular form. How does Pound use irregularity of form to reinforce the suggestions his poem makes?
5. Although "Cool Tombs" and "These Fought in Any Case" are both written in free verse, and make heavy use of repetition, the **tone** and **pace** of the two poems are completely different. Why?

The words in this next poem deserve special notice. Their underlying tone and syntax is more casual and friendly than anything we have met so far. And yet Cummings has taken enormous liberties with words and syntax alike, even to the point of inventing new words and positioning each word individually on the page. To what new responses does the resulting poem seem to invite you?

E. E. CUMMINGS (1894–1963)

in Just-   spring

in Just-
spring   when the world is mud-
luscious the little
lame balloonman

5 whistles   far   and wee

and eddieandbill come
running from marbles and
piracies and it's
spring

10 when the world is puddle-wonderful

the queer
old balloonman whistles
far   and   wee
and bettyandisbel come dancing

15 from hop-scotch and jump-rope and

it's
spring

                    and
                         the
20   goat-footed

          balloonMan   whistles
          far
          and
          wee

QUESTIONS

1. In analyzing this poem, we may begin with its wordplay. How do compound
   words such as "mud-luscious" and "puddle-wonderful" affect the sound and
   meaning of the lines in which they occur? How many meanings does the
   word "wee" have, and what is the effect of using it? The balloon-man is described through incremental repetition, beginning as "lame" and ending as
   "goat-footed." Why goat-footed?
2. We may then note two unusual rhythmic devices, the breaking of lines in the
   middle of words or phrases, and the spacing out or running together of words.
   And we may ask how these affect the sound and mood of the poem, and our
   sense of the scene it describes.
3. Then we may put this play with words and rhythms together with the poem's
   use of names and detail, and ask how Cummings creates and enhances his
   description. What does the intent of the poem seem to be? What message
   does it seem to carry? How do the sound and word choices create the tone
   and the message?

THE SPEAKER IN THE POEM

5

The Speaker's Voice

We have said that ballads, being traditional, oral poetry, rely on common words and images rather than on the unique images of written poetry. We may now make one final distinction by remarking that this stylization of ballads leaves these songs lacking uniquely memorable voices. A deserted lover in one ballad, for instance, sounds much like a deserted lover in any other ballad. They will speak at least some of the same words in the same tones and rhythms. This is not the case in written poetry, where we would take the appearance of a lover who sounds like any other lover as the sign of a second-rate poem. If we read twenty lyrics about love—or even twenty lyrics about lost love—we expect to hear twenty different voices.

This reflection brings us to one of the basic paradoxes of poetry. Because of its use of rhythm and sound patterns, the language of poetry may be the farthest of all literary languages from everyday speech. Yet the voices within poems are the most intimate of literary voices, speaking to us most vividly and directly and conveying to us most openly the speaker's deepest and most immediate emotions. No other form of literature demands so much care and craft in its writing as poetry; yet no other form can seem to present the spontaneous flow of emotion as convincingly as poetry can.

Because poetry can so thoroughly convince us that in responding to it we are sharing a genuine, strongly felt emotion, it can attract our strongest response. Subjectively, this is good; it represents poetry doing what it should do. Objectively, however, poetry's seeming frankness raises the critical danger that we may mistake the voice within the poem for the voice of the poet. The further danger then arises that we may generalize from a single poem, slipping from the critically acceptable statement, "Blake's 'Tyger' presents the tiger as a beautiful but terrifying creature" to the unacceptable, "As 'The Tyger' shows, Blake was afraid of tigers."

We cannot fall into this error so easily in drama or fiction, where the number of characters and the abundance of circumstantial detail continually warn us of the distance between author and work. Poetry, however, often has but one voice in a poem. The voice often speaks in the first person: "All night by the rose I lay." And the intensity of emotion that is felt only in the climactic scenes of fiction and drama may illuminate an entire lyric. This combination of single voice, first person, and unflagging intensity of emotion often obliterates the distance between the poet and speaker. If the speaker then gives us the slightest hint that he or she may represent the poet, we become all too willing to make the identification.

But we must not make the identification so simply. We can speak of a poet's voice—can compare Blake's voice to Dickinson's, for example. But when we do this we must compare all the voices from at least a dozen of Blake's poems to all the voices from an equal number of Dickinson's. We can then speak either of a range of voices that seems typical of each poet or of some specific characteristics that remain constant through all their individual voices. Moreover, we may equally well make comparisons between voices belonging to a single poet—comparing the voices of Blake's early poems to those of his later poems, for instance—which we could not do if the voice in each poem were the poet's only voice.

To further emphasize this distance between speaker and poet, we may look again at poems such as "We Real Cool" and "All Night by the Rose." They seem to speak to us as directly and to be as immediately felt as any other poems, but we know no author for "All Night by the Rose" and are sure that Gwendolyn Brooks is not seven adolescents in a pool hall.

The poem is the poet's vision, nothing more. Its speakers may be inside the action (as in "All Night by the Rose") or outside it (as in "The Cherry-Tree Carol"). They may have elements of the poet's own situation or emotions in them, or they may not. But they are speakers and not writers; they are the poet's creations and not the poet's self.

For discussing speakers who do seem to mirror their poets, we have the useful critical term **persona.** The speakers of "The Lamb" and "The Tyger," of "There's a Certain Slant of Light," and of "All Night by the Rose" may be called their poets' personae. Personae represent one aspect of their poet's personality or experience, isolated from the rest of the poet's life, dramatized, and re-created through art. Poets—like all human beings—are complex and changeable. Personae are simpler: fixed, changeless, and slightly exaggerated. Unlike their makers, who must respond to the many demands of the everyday world in which they live, personae exist only within their poems and respond only to the thoughts and sensations that gave the poems birth.

Here, for the further study of speakers in poetry, are three groups of poems. The first two groups employ speakers who might well be spoken of as personae; the third has speakers who cannot. Be aware, as you read these poems, of sound and language and total effect. But pay most attention to the characterization of the speakers and to the varying voices with which they speak.

THEODORE ROETHKE (1908–1963)

My Papa's Waltz

The whiskey on your breath
Could make a small boy dizzy;
But I hung on like death:
Such waltzing was not easy.

5 We romped until the pans
Slid from the kitchen shelf;
My mother's countenance
Could not unfrown itself.

The hand that held my wrist
10 Was battered on one knuckle;
At every step you missed
My right ear scraped a buckle.

You beat time on my head
With a palm caked hard by dirt,
15 Then waltzed me off to bed
Still clinging to your shirt.

I Knew a Woman

I knew a woman, lovely in her bones,
When small birds sighed, she would sigh back at them;
Ah, when she moved, she moved more ways than one:
The shapes a bright container can contain!
5 Of her choice virtues only gods should speak,
Or English poets who grew up on Greek
(I'd have them sing in chorus, cheek to cheek).

How well her wishes went! She stroked my chin,
She taught me Turn, and Counter-turn, and Stand;
10 She taught me Touch, that undulant white skin;
I nibbled meekly from her proffered hand;
She was the sickle; I, poor I, the rake,
Coming behind her for her pretty sake
(But what prodigious mowing we did make).

15 Love likes a gander, and adores a goose:
Her full lips pursed, the errant note to seize;
She played it quick, she played it light and loose;
My eyes, they dazzled at her flowing knees;
Her several parts could keep a pure repose,
20 Or one hip quiver with a mobile nose
(She moved in circles, and those circles moved).

Let seed be grass, and grass turn into hay:
I'm martyr to a motion not my own;
What's freedom for? To know eternity.
25 I swear she cast a shadow white as stone.
But who would count eternity in days?
These old bones live to learn her wanton ways:
(I measure time by how a body sways).

QUESTIONS

1. What is the subject of each of these poems? What is the emotional state of
   the speaker?
2. How does the language of the two poems compare? What sort of images does
   each use? How does the language match the subject and mood in each?
3. How would you characterize the speaker of each poem? What would you have
   to say to move from a characterization of the speakers to a characterization
   of the poets?

ANONYMOUS—MIDDLE ENGLISH LYRIC

Western Wind

Western wind, when will thou blow,
    The small rain down can rain?
Christ, if my love were in my arms
    And I in my bed again.

SIR JOHN SUCKLING (1609–1642)

The Constant Lover

Out upon it! I have loved
    Three whole days together;
And am like to love three more,
    If it prove fair weather!

5 Time shall moult away his wings,
    Ere he shall discover
In the whole wide world again
    Such a constant lover.

But the spite on't is, no praise
10   Is due at all to me:
Love with me had made no stays,
    Had it any been but she.

Had it any been but she,
    And that very face,
15 There had been at least ere this
    A dozen dozen in her place!

SIR THOMAS WYATT (1503–1542)

They Flee from Me

They flee from me that sometime did me seek
With naked foot stalking in my chamber.
I have seen them gentle, tame, and meek
That now are wild and do not remember
5 That sometime they put themselves in danger
To take bread at my hand; and now they range
Busily seeking with a continual change.

Thankèd be Fortune, it hath been otherwise
Twenty times better; but once in special,
10 In thin array after a pleasant guise,
When her loose gown from her shoulders did fall,
And she me caught in her arms long and small;
And therewithall sweetly did me kiss,
And softly said, "Dear heart, how like you this?"

15 It was no dream; I lay broad waking.
   But all is turned thorough my gentleness
   Into a strange fashion of forsaking;
   And I have leave to go of her goodness,
   And she also to use newfangleness.
20 But since that I so kindely am served,
   I fain would know what she hath deserved.

QUESTIONS

1. "They Flee from Me" starts with a very general statement: "They flee from me." It ends with a very specific question, "what she hath deserved." Moreover, it starts and ends in the present tense; but the second stanza is almost entirely in the past tense. How do these two movements—from the general to the specific and from present to past to present—give you a feel for the movement of the speaker's mind? (Notice especially the part played by the second stanza. How does its content contrast with that of the other two stanzas? What happens to the language and tone of voice? Why does the speaker then insist that "It was no dream; I lay broad waking"; and what does that string of bald monosyllables do for your sense of him and his state of mind?)

2. Having noticed how the language, mood, and tone of voice of the second stanza of "They Flee from Me" differ from those of the first stanza, you must now consider what changes take place in the third stanza. Notice the terms "strange fashion" and "newfangleness," and the irony employed in "goodness" and "kindely." What tone of voice is entering the poem here? What sort of turn does the change from statement to question in the last two lines give to the end of the poem? Does it involve you in any way, or make you feel any closer to the speaker?

3. In all, how many tones of voice do you find in "They Flee from Me"? How do they combine to give you your final characterization of the speaker?

4. What themes do all three of the preceding poems have in common?

5. How would you characterize the speaker or speakers, the language, and the tone of voice in each poem? How do they differ from each other?

THOMAS HARDY (1840–1928)

The Man He Killed

"Had he and I but met
   By some old ancient inn,
We should have sat us down to wet
   Right many a nipperkin![1]

---

[1] About a half-pint.

5   "But ranged as infantry,
     And staring face to face,
  I shot at him as he at me,
     And killed him in his place.

     "I shot him dead because—
10   Because he was my foe,
  Just so: my foe of course he was;
     That's clear enough; although

     "He thought he'd 'list, perhaps,
     Off-hand like—just as I—
15 Was out of work—had sold his traps—
     No other reason why.

     "Yes; quaint and curious war is!
     You shoot a fellow down
  You'd treat if met where any bar is,
20   Or help to half-a-crown."

WILLIAM BUTLER YEATS (1865–1939)

An Irish Airman Foresees His Death[1]

I know that I shall meet my fate
Somewhere among the clouds above;
Those that I fight I do not hate,
Those that I guard I do not love;
5 My country is Kiltartan Cross,[2]
My countrymen Kiltartan's poor,
No likely end could bring them loss
Or leave them happier than before.
Nor law, nor duty bade me fight,
10 Nor public men, nor cheering crowds,
A lonely impulse of delight
Drove to this tumult in the clouds;
I balanced all, brought all to mind,
The years to come seemed waste of breath,
15 A waste of breath the years behind
In balance with this life, this death.

---

[1] Major Robert Gregory, son of Yeats's friend and patroness Lady Augusta Gregory, was killed in action in 1918.

[2] Kiltartan is an Irish village near Coole Park, the estate of the Gregorys.

QUESTIONS

1. What theme is common to these two poems?
2. How would you compare the two speakers?
3. How would you characterize the tone of each poem? the language? (Note the use of repetition. What effect does it produce in Hardy's poem? In Yeats's? How does it help characterize each speaker?)
4. How does the difference in character and mood of the two speakers contribute to the difference in overall effect of the two poems? (What reaction does each poet seem to want from you? What message—if any—does his poem seem to carry?)

6

The Speaker's Vision

Like other writers, poets find their visions in three basic sources: the world around them, their own experiences, and their inner vision of what is or might be. The speakers of their poems, who are charged with communicating these visions, may therefore be either observers, recording scenes and experiences for our mutual pleasure and insight; or they may be visionaries, recasting real or imagined scenes to produce a new vision for our sharing. We can see the distinction clearly enough in poems we have already read. The speakers in "Get Up and Bar the Door," "The Cherry-Tree Carol," and "All Night by the Rose" are reporters. They simply tell us what occurred and let us draw our own conclusions about it. The speakers of "We Real Cool" and "For a Lady I Know" are also reporters, but less obviously because we sense that the poets are not as objective as their speakers. The speakers provide no interpretation, show no emotion. But the poets' attitudes come through, nonetheless. Indeed, much of the effectiveness of these poems comes from the disparity between the speakers' objectivity and the poets' concern, a disparity felt by the reader as irony. But that is a subject we will speak of more thoroughly in the next chapter.

We can also recall poems in which the speaker was primarily a visionary. Dickinson's poems come to mind here, and Blake's. "The Lamb" and "The Tyger" are far more concerned with the religious visions the animals arouse in Blake's speakers than they are with the animals themselves;

and "Tell All the Truth" is pure vision, having no objective scene or experience whatever as its starting point. Another visionary is the speaker of Pound's "These Fought in Any Case," who draws on visions of so many real or imagined soldiers that we soon lose all sense of individuals in the more compelling vision of the war itself.

These, then, are poems that mark the two extremes of the speaker's stance, the objective extreme and the visionary extreme. Between them come those poems (probably typical of the majority of poems) in which the speaker is reporter and interpreter both. These poems balance what is seen and what is felt, allowing neither to overwhelm the other. Their speakers report on what is happening while explaining or suggesting its implications. Thus, "There's a Certain Slant of Light" conveys its atmospheric sensation most vividly by interpreting its spiritual overtones. And poems such as "in Just- spring," "My Papa's Waltz," and "I Knew a Lady" blend recollection and response so perfectly that it's hard to say where one stops and the other begins. Through the speaker's emotional response, the vision is made real for us; reporter, responder, and interpreter are one.

The poems we shall look at in this chapter blend objective and visionary stances, observation and interpretation. Take careful note of the speaker's character and stance within each poem. Before you answer any of the questions, make sure you know what sort of person is speaking, to what the speaker is responding, and how much of the speaker's response is to things outside himself or herself and how much to inner visions or emotions.

The common factor in the first two poems is memory. Read each poem, and then discuss:

1. The details by which the memories are presented.
2. The comparisons and contrasts created between the memories and the speaker's present circumstances or emotional state.
3. Any sense of movement through time the poem may create, and the way in which it creates it.
4. What we are told in the poem's concluding stanza, and what sense of the speaker's feelings or attitudes the conclusion gives us.

DANTE GABRIEL ROSSETTI (1828–1882)

The Woodspurge

The wind flapped loose, the wind was still,
Shaken out dead from tree and hill:
I had walked on at the wind's will,—
I sat now, for the wind was still.

5 Between my knees my forehead was,—
My lips, drawn in, said not Alas!
My hair was over in the grass,
My naked ears heard the day pass.

My eyes, wide open, had the run
10 Of some ten weeds to fix upon;
Among those few, out of the sun,
The woodspurge flowered, three cups in one.

From perfect grief there need not be
Wisdom or even memory:
15 One thing then learnt remains to me,—
The woodspurge has a cup of three.

D. H. LAWRENCE (1885–1930)

Piano

Softly, in the dusk, a woman is singing to me;
Taking me back down the vista of years, till I see
A child sitting under the piano, in the boom of the tingling strings
And pressing the small, poised feet of a mother who smiles as she
    sings.

5 In spite of myself, the insidious mastery of song
Betrays me back, till the heart of me weeps to belong
To the old Sunday evenings at home, with winter outside
And hymns in the cozy parlor, the tinkling piano our guide.

So now it is vain for the singer to burst into clamor
10 With the great black piano appassionato. The glamour
Of childish days is upon me, my manhood is cast
Down in the flood of remembrance, I weep like a child for the past.

The next four poems all concern the relationship between people and nature. In the first two, the relationship is simply that between the speaker and some aspect of nature. In the third, however, the speaker is more concerned with the responses of "a young child" than he is with his own. And the final poem concerns not only the speaker's response to and sense of his relationship with nature, but also the relationship of other men and the corresponding relationship of nature to men. How would you compare the responses of the speakers in these four poems? How is nature (or that part of nature which is in question) treated in each poem? How is the speaker's own vision highlighted?

SIR PHILIP SIDNEY (1554–1586)

From **Astrophil and Stella**

Sonnet 31

With how sad steps, O moon, thou climb'st the skies!
  How silently, and with how wan a face!
  What! may it be that even in heavenly place
  That busy archer his sharp arrows tries?
5 Sure, if that long-with-love-acquainted eyes
  Can judge of love, thou feel'st a lover's case;
  I read it in thy looks—thy languished grace
  To me, that feel the like, thy state descries.
Then, even of fellowship, O moon, tell me,
10 Is constant love deemed there but want of wit?
  Are beauties there as proud as here they be?
Do they above love to be loved, and yet
  Those lovers scorn whom that love doth possess?
  Do they call virtue there ungratefulness?

QUESTIONS

1. The technique of having the speaker seem to address someone or something within a poem is called **apostrophe**. What use is Sidney making of apostrophe in this poem?
2. What features of the moon's appearance does the speaker note? What interpretation does he put on them? Why?
3. Who is "that busy archer"? What overtones does his mention lend to the poem?
4. Why does the speaker claim "fellowship" with the moon? What do his questions to her tell you of his own state?
5. How would you describe the tone of the poem? How seriously does the speaker seem to take his interpretation of the moon's condition? What seems to be his attitude toward his own state?

JOHN KEATS (1795–1821)

When I Have Fears

When I have fears that I may cease to be
  Before my pen has gleaned my teeming brain,
Before high-piled books, in charactery,[1]
  Hold like rich garners the full ripened grain;

5 When I behold, upon the night's starred face,
   Huge cloudy symbols of a high romance,
And think that I may never live to trace
   Their shadows, with the magic hand of chance;
And when I feel, fair creature of an hour,
10   That I shall never look upon thee more,
Never have relish in the faery power
   Of unreflecting love;—then on the shore
Of the wide world I stand alone, and think
Till love and fame to nothingness do sink.

QUESTIONS

1. Since the whole poem is one sentence, its syntax gets a bit complicated. Let's
   start, therefore, by examining it clause by clause, beginning with the three
   "when" clauses that make up the first eleven-and-a-half lines of the poem:
   What are the first four lines concerned with? the second four? the third?
   How are the three tied together? (Who is the "fair creature of an hour"?
   Why might the speaker call her this at this point in this poem?)
2. What overtones do words like "rich," "romance," "magic," and "faery" give
   to the poem? What contrast do they suggest between the poet's wishes and
   his sense of reality?
3. Then look at the final clause of the sentence—the last two-and-a-half lines.
   What action does it show the speaker taking? How explicit are his feelings
   made? What are you left to fill in?

GERARD MANLEY HOPKINS (1844–1889)

Spring and Fall

To a young child

Márgarét, are you gríeving
Over Goldengrove unleaving?
Leáves, líke the things of man, you
With your fresh thoughts care for, can you?
5 Áh; ás the heart grows older
It will come to such sights colder
By and by, nor spare a sigh
Though worlds of wanwood leafmeal lie;
And yet you wíll weep and know why.
10 Now no matter, child, the name:
Sórrow's spríngs áre the same.

---

[1] Characters, writing.

Nor mouth had, no nor mind, expressed
What heart heard of, ghost guessed:
It is the blight man was born for,
15 It is Margaret you mourn for.

QUESTIONS

1. First, let us make sure we understand what is happening in the poem, by asking such questions as:
   a. What is the opening situation? What sort of person does the speaker seem to be? What sort of person is Margaret?
   b. With what situation does the poem end?
2. Then let us look more closely at the language of the poem:
   a. List the words you think Hopkins has invented. Of what words do they remind you? What suggestions do they carry? To judge by their context, what do you think they mean?
   b. Notice that Hopkins has marked certain words to be accented, even though they might not be accented in normal speech. What do these accents do to emphasize the sound of the words in the lines in which they occur? What do they do to the pace and rhythm of the lines?
3. Then we can return to the sense of the poem, to look more closely at the progression of thought it contains and thus more fully characterize our sense of the poem and the speaker.
   a. How would you characterize the speaker's questions to Margaret in the first four lines? What does the speaker's attitude toward Margaret seem to be? (How does the word "Goldengrove" help set the tone and attitude?)
   b. What shift takes place in the speaker's thoughts in the next five lines? In what situation is he seeing Margaret? Where is he getting his insight into what will happen to her?
   c. Note the shift back to the present in line ten. What is the tone of this line? What feelings does it seem to convey?
   d. What insight into Margaret's current situation is contained in the last four lines? (What is "the blight man was born for"?) Why does the speaker think Margaret is weeping? What is the difference between his perception of her tears and her own?
   e. The final couplet is still addressed directly to Margaret. But does it suggest any generalization? What in the speaker's ideas and tone would make such generalization possible?

RALPH WALDO EMERSON (1803–1882)

Hamatreya[1]

Bulkeley, Hunt, Willard, Hosmer, Meriam, Flint,[2]
Possessed the land which rendered to their toil
Hay, corn, roots, hemp, flax, apples, wool and wood.

---

[1] A variant of Maitreya, a Hindu god.
[2] Early settlers of Concord.

Each of these landlords walked amidst his farm,
5 Saying, "'Tis mine, my children's and my name's.
How sweet the west wind sounds in my own trees!
How graceful climb those shadows on my hill!
I fancy these pure waters and the flags
Know me, as does my dog: we sympathize;
10 And, I affirm, my actions smack of the soil."

Where are these men? Asleep beneath their grounds:
And strangers, fond as they, their furrows plough.
Earth laughs in flowers, to see her boastful boys
Earth-proud, proud of the earth which is not theirs;
15 Who steer the plough, but cannot steer their feet
Clear of the grave.
They added ridge to valley, brook to pond,
And sighed for all that bounded their domain;
"This suits me for a pasture; that's my park;
20 We must have clay, lime, gravel, granite-ledge,
And misty lowland, where to go for peat.
The land is well,—lies fairly to the south.
'Tis good, when you have crossed the sea and back,
To find the sitfast acres where you left them."
25 Ah! the hot owner sees not Death, who adds
Him to his land, a lump of mould the more.
Hear what the Earth says:—

EARTH SONG

"Mine and yours;
Mine, not yours.
30 Earth endures;
Stars abide—
Shine down in the old sea;
Old are the shores;
But where are old men?
35 I who have seen much,
Such have I never seen.

"The lawyer's deed
Ran sure,
In tail,[3]
40 To them, and to their heirs

---

[3] Entailed.

Who shall succeed,
Without fail,
Forevermore.

"Here is the land,
45   Shaggy with wood,
With its old valley,
Mound and flood.
But the heritors?—
Fled like the flood's foam.
50   The lawyer, and the laws,
And the kingdom,
Clean swept herefrom.

"They called me theirs,
Who so controlled me;
55   Yet every one
Wished to stay, and is gone,
How am I theirs,
If they cannot hold me,
But I hold them?"

60   When I heard the Earth-song
I was no longer brave;
My avarice cooled
Like lust in the chill of the grave.

QUESTIONS

Despite the complexity of voices in this poem, the progression of thought and feeling is fairly straightforward. Make up your own questions, therefore, and discuss what you feel to be the outstanding features of the poem.

7

Beyond the Speaker:
The Double Vision of Irony

Irony exists whenever we say one thing and mean the opposite. "An exam? What fun!" is an ironic statement. More generally, irony exists whenever we feel a disparity between what someone says or thinks and what we know to be the truth. Irony can be intentional or unintentional, depending on whether the speaker means the statement to be ironic or not. When Oedipus swears vengeance on Laïos' killer, and we know he is ignorantly condemning himself, we feel the irony of the situation. This is an unintentional irony on Oedipus' part. We feel the disparity between what Oedipus intends to happen and what we know will happen; and we feel it precisely because Oedipus does not.

In contrast, when Hamlet, in the graveyard scene, is made so intensely aware of the disparity between the spiritual ideals and bodily weakness, we share his sense of conscious irony.

> Imperious Caesar, dead and turned to clay,
> Might stop a hole to keep the wind away.
> O, that that earth which held the world in awe
> Should patch a wall t'expel the winter's flaw!

The contrast between "earth" and "world" is ironic, the more so since both words point to a truth. Caesar was a hero who held men's awe and admiration; Caesar is dead and dust. Two disparate truths about man are thus revealed in these four lines, together with Hamlet's sorrow that the disparity between the truths should be as great as it is, that the realities of the graveyard should so mock the ambitions of the spirit. By his rhyming wordplay, Hamlet thus expresses the irony he feels, brings it home to us in heightened form, and allows us to see him—and ourselves—as beings deeply moved by our sense of people's ironic limitations.

The emotions of irony thus arise from our perceptions of a conflict between intent or ideal and reality. The technique of irony consists of creating a parallel disparity in words, by creating an opposition between the apparent meaning of the words and their ironic significance. Always there is some hint of pain in irony, some overtone of pity or anger. And always the emotion is a shared one: shared between reader and speaker if the irony is intentional, shared between reader and writer if it is not.

In responding to irony, then, we are aligning ourselves with someone whose perceptions we share, having been invited—as one right-thinking person by another—to share both the ironist's view of the subject and the emotions of scorn or pity or rage that go with it. Always, therefore, there will be some hint of argument (implicit or explicit) in an ironic poem. And always, the use of irony will produce some distancing of effect, as we stand back and judge the presented disparity.

Beyond these basic facts, however, we will see that irony is a technique that allows many variations of meaning, tone, and effect. As with most definitions, when we have defined a poem as ironic, we have only begun to talk about its construction, its meaning, and its power to touch us.

As you read the poems that follow, decide:

1. What disparity is being highlighted?
2. What ideals or beliefs that you hold are being appealed to? Is the appeal explicit or implicit?
3. Is the speaker conscious or unconscious of the irony of his or her speech?
4. If there is more than one voice in the poem, how are they contrasted? What part does the contrast play in your sense of the poem's irony?
5. What range of feelings does the poem suggest?

Then discuss each poem more fully, making whatever points you think are most helpful in deciding what role the irony plays in your appreciation of the poem as a whole.

ADRIENNE RICH (1929–   )

Aunt Jennifer's Tigers

Aunt Jennifer's tigers prance across a screen,
Bright topaz denizens of a world of green.
They do no not fear the men beneath the tree;
They pace in sleek chivalric certainty.

5 Aunt Jennifer's fingers fluttering through her wool
  Find even the ivory needle hard to pull.
  The massive weight of Uncle's wedding band
  Sits heavily upon Aunt Jennifer's hand.

  When Aunt is dead, her terrified hands will lie
10 Still ringed with ordeals she was mastered by.
  The tigers in the panel that she made
  Will go on prancing, proud and unafraid.

GEORGE MEREDITH (1828–1909)

From **Modern Love**

Sonnet 17

At dinner, she is hostess, I am host.
Went the feast ever cheerfuller? She keeps
The Topic over intellectual deeps
In buoyancy afloat. They see no ghost.
5 With sparkling surface-eyes we ply the ball;
It is in truth a most contagious game:
HIDING THE SKELETON shall be its name.
Such play as this the devils might appal!
But here's the greater wonder; in that we,
10 Enamored of an acting naught can tire,
Each other, like true hypocrites, admire;
Warm-lighted looks, Love's ephemeridae,[1]
Shoot gayly o'er the dishes and the wine.
We waken envy of our happy lot.
15 Fast, sweet, and golden, shows the marriage-knot.
Dear guests, you now have seen Love's corpse-light shine.

A. E. HOUSMAN (1859–1936)

From **A Shropshire Lad**

When I Was One-and-Twenty

When I was one-and-twenty
  I heard a wise man say,
"Give crowns and pounds and guineas
  But not your heart away;

---

[1] Short-lived May flies.

5 Give pearls away and rubies
      But keep your fancy free."
   But I was one-and-twenty,
      No use to talk to me.

   When I was one-and-twenty
10   I heard him say again,
      "The heart out of the bosom
         Was never given in vain;
      'Tis paid with sighs a plenty
         And sold for endless rue."
15 And I am two-and-twenty,
      And oh, 'tis true, 'tis true.

WILLIAM BUTLER YEATS (1865–1939)

The Folly of Being Comforted

One that is ever kind said yesterday:
"Your well-belovèd's hair has threads of gray,
And little shadows come about her eyes;
Time can but make it easier to be wise
5 Though now it seem impossible, and so
All that you need is patience."

                              Heart cries, "No,
I have not a crumb of comfort, not a grain.
Time can but make her beauty over again:
Because of that great nobleness of hers
10 The fire that stirs about her, when she stirs,
Burns but more clearly. O she had not these ways
When all the wild summer was in her gaze."

O heart! O heart! if she'd but turn her head,
You'd know the folly of being comforted.

PERCY BYSSHE SHELLEY (1792–1822)

Ozymandias

I met a traveler from an antique land
Who said: Two vast and trunkless legs of stone
Stand in the desert . . . Near them, on the sand,
Half sunk, a shattered visage lies, whose frown,
5 And wrinkled lip, and sneer of cold command,

Tell that its sculptor well those passions read
Which yet survive, stamped on these lifeless things,
The hand that mocked them, and the heart that fed:
And on the pedestal these words appear:
10 "My name is Ozymandias, king of kings:
Look on my works, ye Mighty, and despair!"
Nothing beside remains. Round the decay
Of that colossal wreck, boundless and bare
The lone and level sands stretch far away.

W. H. AUDEN (1907–1973)

The Unknown Citizen

(To JS/07/M/378
This Marble Monument
Is Erected by the State)

He was found by the Bureau of Statistics to be
One against whom there was no official complaint,
And all the reports on his conduct agree
That, in the modern sense of an old-fashioned word, he was a saint,
5 For in everything he did he served the Greater Community.
Except for the War till the day he retired
He worked in a factory and never got fired,
But satisfied his employers, Fudge Motors Inc.
Yet he wasn't a scab or odd in his views,
10 For his Union reports that he paid his dues,
(Our report on his Union shows it was sound)
And our Social Psychology workers found
That he was popular with his mates and liked a drink.
The Press are convinced that he bought a paper every day
15 And that his reactions to advertisements were normal in every way.
Policies taken out in his name prove that he was fully insured,
And his Health-card shows he was once in hospital but left it cured.
Both Producers Research and High-Grade Living declare
He was fully sensible to the advantages of the Instalment Plan
20 And had everything necessary to the Modern Man,
A phonograph, a radio, a car, and a frigidaire.
Our researchers into Public Opinion are content
That he held the proper opinions for the time of year;
When there was peace, he was for peace; when there was war, he
        went.
25 He was married and added five children to the population,

Which our Eugenist says was the right number for a parent of his
        generation,
And our teachers report that he never interfered with their education.
Was he free? Was he happy? The question is absurd:
Had anything been wrong, we should certainly have heard.

HENRY REED (1914–   )

From **Lessons of the War**
To Alan Mitchell

Vixi duellis nuper idoneus
Et militavi non sine gloria[1]

Naming of Parts

Today we have naming of parts. Yesterday,
We had daily cleaning. And tomorrow morning,
We shall have what to do after firing. But today,
Today we have naming of parts. Japonica
5 Glistens like coral in all of the neighboring gardens,
        And today we have naming of parts.

This is the lower sling swivel. And this
Is the upper sling swivel, whose use you will see,
When you are given your slings. And this is the piling swivel,
10 Which in your case you have not got. The branches
Hold in the gardens their silent, eloquent gestures,
        Which in our case we have not got.

This is the safety-catch, which is always released
With an easy flick of the thumb. And please do not let me
15 See anyone using his finger. You can do it quite easy
If you have any strength in your thumb. The blossoms
Are fragile and motionless, never letting anyone see
        Any of them using their finger.

And this you can see is the bolt. The purpose of this
20 Is to open the breech, as you see. We can slide it
Rapidly backwards and forwards: we call this

---

[1] From a poem of Horace, with the word "puellis" (girls) altered to "duellis"
(battles). "Of late I have lived capably amongst battles and I have served not
without glory."

Easing the spring. And rapidly backwards and forwards
The early bees are assaulting and fumbling the flowers:
    They call it easing the Spring.

25 They call it easing the Spring: it is perfectly easy
If you have any strength in your thumb: like the bolt,
And the breech, and the cocking-piece, and the point of balance,
Which in our case we have not got; and the almond-blossom
Silent in all of the gardens and the bees going backwards and for-
    wards,
30   For today we have naming of parts.

IMAGERY

8

Similes, Metaphors, and Personification

The three basic elements of any poem are the vision it embodies, the speaker who gives voice to the vision, and the language that creates voice and vision alike. (By stretching the terminology a bit, we could call them the three V's: voice, vision, and vocabulary.) In our last chapters, we examined the ways in which the language of a poem—its vocabulary, its connotations, its sounds—created and characterized the poem's speaker. Now it is time to look at the ways in which the language creates the vision.

Vision in literature always implies a shared vision. Originating in the writer's mind, the vision is first translated into words and then recreated in our minds, to be felt by us as it was felt by its writer. When we come to the end of a poem, therefore, the feeling we experience is likely to be a blend of recognition and surprise. We will have seen something familiar—perhaps even something of ourselves—as we had never seen it before.

There are two ways in which poets can go about creating this feeling. The first is to word their vision so precisely that we feel we are seeing things with a new closeness and clearness. This is the method chosen by Levertov in "Six Variations (part iii)," Rossetti in "The Woodspurge," and Lawrence in "Piano."

The second method relies on figures of speech or on unexpected comparisons to lead us into making connections we may not have made before. This is Pound's method in "In a Station of the Metro," where human "faces in the crowd" are seen as "petals on a wet black bough," beauty and impersonality mingling. It is Dickinson's method, too, when she describes her "certain slant of light" as being one which "oppresses, like the weight/ Of cathedral tunes."

This trick of mingling appeals to different senses in a single image—of describing a sound in terms of color, or a sight in terms of sound or feel— is called *synaesthesia*. Rather than trying to define a type of light in terms of its appearance, Dickinson compares it to a sound. But she speaks of both in terms of weight that presses down physically or spiritually. The word "cathedral," meanwhile, not only defines the solemn, religious music that parallels the "slant of light," but also prepares us for the image of "heavenly hurt" introduced in the next line. Thus the poem weaves its pattern of imagery.

We have, then, already met poems that make use of both the literal and the figurative styles of imagery. To make sure the contrast is clear, however, let's look at two poems on one subject, and see how the language works in each.

WALT WHITMAN (1819–1892)

The Dalliance of the Eagles

Skirting the river road, (my forenoon walk, my rest,)
Skyward in air a sudden muffled sound, the dalliance of the eagles,
The rushing amorous contact high in space together,
The clinching interlocking claws, a living, fierce, gyrating wheel,
5 Four beating wings, two beaks, a swirling mass tight grappling,
In tumbling turning clustering loops, straight downward falling,
Till o'er the river pois'd, the twain yet one, a moment's lull,
A motionless still balance in the air, then parting, talons loosing,
Upward again on slow-firm pinions slanting, their separate diverse
    flight,
10 She hers, he his, pursuing.

ALFRED, LORD TENNYSON (1809–1892)

The Eagle

He clasps the crag with crooked hands;
Close to the sun in lonely lands,
Ringed with the azure world, he stands.

The wrinkled sea beneath him crawls;
5 He watches from his mountain walls,
And like a thunderbolt he falls.

Obviously, these are very dissimilar poems. One, talking of a single eagle who remains unmoving throughout most of the poem, creates an atmosphere of space and solitude. The other, speaking of two eagles, seems a constant rush of motion. In part, it is the sound of the words the poets have chosen which create these different atmospheres. Tennyson's words, lines, and sentences are all short, and the stop at the end of each line is strongly marked. Whitman uses longer lines, with less pronounced breaks between them; and his sentences are so involved and complex that they keep the reader's mind and voice in almost constant motion as dizzying as that of the eagles themselves. Yet the basic difference in the way these eagles are shown to us lies not in their motion or motionlessness, but rather in the imagery in which they are described.

If we go through each poem, noting carefully each descriptive term used, we will discover a marked contrast. Whitman relies heavily on adjectives, particularly on participles (adjectives formed from verbs). *Clinching, interlocking, living, gyrating, beating, swirling, grappling, tumbling, turning, clustering, falling*—from these comes the poem's sense of action, as well as much of its power of description. The poet's stance is primarily that of the observer. Taking a walk, he has been startled first by the "sudden muffled sound" and then by the sight of the eagles; and he describes sight and sound alike as carefully and vividly as he can:

> The clinching interlocking claws, a living, fierce, gyrating
>   wheel,
> Four beating wings, two beaks, a swirling mass tight
>   grappling,
> In tumbling turning clustering loops, straight downward
>   falling.

Tennyson's fragment, too, is pure description. But its phrasing and its imagery come as much from the poet's imagination as from his powers of observation. Where Whitman uses no words that could not, in sober prose, be applied to an eagle, Tennyson uses almost none which could. His eagle is presented largely in terms which compare it to other things: an old man, grown crooked with age; an explorer in "lonely lands"; a thunderbolt. By calling our attention to these other things, he draws on our feelings about them (respect, for instance, or awe) and uses those feelings to influence our feelings about the eagle itself. Thus, instead of a bird's "clinching . . . claws," Tennyson's eagle has "crooked hands." He "stands"—which, to some readers, may sound more human than birdlike—and "watches," as men and birds both do. Later, he "falls"—an ambiguous verb. The landscape in which he is pictured is similarly humanized. The lands are "lonely," the sea is "wrinkled" and "crawls." There is exaggeration (or **hyperbole**) as well. The eagle's perch is "close to the sun"; the sky against which he is seen is an entire "azure world"; the eagle falls "like a thunderbolt." High and remote, yet somehow in his very remoteness human, Tennyson's eagle presents a striking image of a being in lofty isolation.

By linking disparate things, by forcing us to think of one thing in terms of another, poets make us see those things in new ways, creating new images, calling forth unexpected emotions, fostering new insights. With homely and familiar images, they bring strange things closer to us, while with exotic images they cast new light on everyday things. Abstract ideas are given vivid life by concrete images, while more abstract imagery suggests new significance for particular items or experiences. Poets can speak of their subjects in the most precise, closely fitting words they can find; or they can seek out unexpected, startling terms which will call our own imaginations and creative impulses into play. Since it is so largely this choice of how language will be handled in any given poem which determines our sense of that poem, our first or final reaction to it—the totally different feelings which Whitman's torrent of precisely denotative adjectives and Tennyson's careful balance of connotations of humanity, space, and isolation provoke—it will be worth our while to examine some of the techniques which poets use in the creation of imagery. Let us look, therefore, at some of the commoner forms of imagery found in poetry. Since comparisons are often the result of figurative speech, we will start with figures that are forms of comparison: the explicit comparisons, the simile and the metaphor; and the implicit ones, implied metaphor and personification.

Simile

A **simile** is a comparison, and is always stated as such. You will always find *like, as, so,* or some such word of comparison within it. Usually, the things it compares resemble each other in only one or two ways, differing in all other respects. An eagle and a thunderbolt are not really much alike; yet the fact that both go from the sky to the ground can allow Tennyson to declare that "like a thunderbolt he falls." In the differences between the two lies the simile's power. The fact that a thunderbolt is so much swifter, so much more powerful and dangerous than the eagle, lends a sense of speed and power and danger to the eagle's fall. A simile may be as brief as the traditional "red as blood," or it may be considerably more complicated, as in this example from "Tell All the Truth":

> As Lightning to the Children eased
> With explanation kind
> The Truth must dazzle gradually
> Or every man be blind—

Notice the use of similes in the following poem.

LANGSTON HUGHES (1902–1967)

Harlem

What happens to a dream deferred?

Does it dry up
like a raisin in the sun?
Or fester like a sore—
5 And then run?
Does it stink like rotten meat?
Or crust and sugar over—
like a syrupy sweet?

Maybe it just sags
10 like a heavy load.

Or does it explode?

QUESTIONS

1. What relationship do the various similes have to each other and to the subject of the poem, as defined by the title and first line?
2. What has been done with the last simile? Why?

Metaphor and Implied Metaphor

Like similes, **metaphors** are direct comparisons of one object with another. In metaphors, however, the fusion between the two objects is more complete, for metaphor uses no "as" or "like" to separate the two things being compared. Instead, a metaphor simply declares that *A* "is" *B;* one element of the comparison becomes, for the moment at least, the other.

Some metaphors go even farther and omit the "is." They simply talk about *A* as if it were *B*, using terms appropriate to *B*. They may not even name *B* at all, but let us guess what it is from the words being used. In this case, the metaphor becomes an **implied metaphor**.

Since a simile merely says that A is "like" B, it needs to find only one point or moment of similarity between two otherwise dissimilar objects in order to achieve its effect. (For example, the cherry that is "red as the blood" resembles blood in no other way.) Metaphors, in contrast, tend to make more detailed claims for closer likenesses between the subjects of their comparisons. Notice, for instance, how many points of similarity are suggested by the metaphors in the next two poems. Ask yourself, in each case, what points of comparison the metaphor makes openly or explicitly, and what further points of comparison it suggests to you.

JOHN KEATS (1795–1821)

On First Looking into Chapman's Homer

Much have I travelled in the realms of gold,
   And many goodly states and kingdoms seen;
   Round many western islands have I been
Which bards in fealty to Apollo hold.

5 Oft of one wide expanse had I been told
   That deep-browed Homer ruled as his demesne;
   Yet did I never breathe its pure serene
Till I heard Chapman speak out loud and bold:
Then felt I like some watcher into his ken;
10 When a new planet swims of the skies
   Or like stout Cortez when with eagle eyes
   He stared at the Pacific—and all his men
Looked at each other with a wild surmise—
   Silent, upon a peak in Darien.

QUESTIONS

1. The vocabulary in the first eight lines of this poem is taken mostly from the Middle Ages and its system of feudalism: "realms" for kingdoms, for example; "bards" for poets; "fealty" for the system under which a nobleman would rule part of a country, being himself ruled by a king or a greater nobleman; and "demesne" for the nobleman's domain, the part of the country he ruled. ("Oft" for "often," "serene" for "air," and "ken" for "knowledge" are also old words which are no longer in daily use.) Apollo, on the other hand, comes from classical mythology, and is the god of poets. (He's also the god of the sun, but that doesn't particularly enter into this poem.) Homer is an ancient Greek poet and Chapman a sixteenth-century English poet who translated Homer's *Iliad* into English verse. The question therefore arises, "Why should Keats use the language of the Middle Ages and the metaphor of travelling to talk about his joy in reading poetry and the great delight he felt when his discovery of Chapman's translation let him feel that he was really hearing Homer for the first time?"
2. When Keats does discover Chapman's translation, two new similes occur to him that support the traveller metaphor. What is the first (ll. 9–10)? What sort of progression has been made: how does the new identity the poet feels resemble his earlier identity as traveller? how is it different? what sort of feelings go with each identity? (Note the phrase "a new planet"; why *new?*)
3. In lines 11–14, the second simile is set out. Whom does Keats feel like now? What kind of feelings go with this third identity? How do they form a climax for the poem? (It was really Balboa, and not Cortez, who was the first European to see the Pacific Ocean. Does this make any difference to your enjoyment of the poem?)

CARL SANDBURG (1878–1967)

Fog

The fog comes
on little cat feet.
It sits looking
over harbor and city
5 on silent haunches
and then moves on.

Personification

Implied metaphors, being more compact and requiring the reader to share in their creation slightly more than regular metaphors do, are frequent in poetry. But one type appears so frequently that it has a name of its own. This is **personification,** the trick of talking about some non-human thing as if it were human. We saw personification used in Blake's "When the stars threw down their spears," in the "Earth Song" of Emerson's "Hamatreya," and in the "crooked hands" of Tennyson's "Eagle."

The poems in the rest of this chapter are notable for their figures of speech. They can thus serve both as exercises in identifying metaphors, similes, and implied metaphors, and as poems illustrating how these figures of speech can help create tone and meaning in poetry. Read each of the poems through at least once. Then go through the poem and note the figures of speech you find in it. Identify each one: is it a simile, a metaphor, an implied metaphor, a personification? Decide what elements make up the comparison: what is being compared to what? And jot down your ideas on why the poet might have wanted his or her readers to think about that comparison.

When you have done this, read the poem through once more. Then look again at the figures of speech you have found. Decide how each relates to the subject of the poem, and how each contributes to your sense of the speaker's feelings toward that subject. Decide, too, how many subjects of comparison there are. Is each subject compared to one other thing, or is one subject compared to several things?

If one subject is compared to one other thing, is that comparison developed at any length? If it is, what does its development lend your sense of the poem and its progression?

If one subject is compared to more than one other thing, or if several subjects of comparison exist, how are the different images fitted together? Are unrelated images juxtaposed for you to fit into some total picture; or does the speaker suggest some relationship of similarity or contrast between them? How does the pattern thus created of related or juxtaposed images help create your sense of the speaker's vision, of the poem's meaning or movement?

Finally, read the poem through once again to see whether you are satisfied with the conclusions you have come to, or whether you think there are other things which should be said about the poem or its imagery. (Note: This may sound like a very complicated procedure. But the method of reading through, looking closely, and reading through again is the best method I know for paying attention to details of technique without losing your grip on the poem as a whole. When dealing with relatively simple poems, it's a handy practice. When dealing with more complex poetry, it's essential.)

BEN JONSON (1572–1637)

From **A Pindaric Ode**

It is not growing like a tree
    In bulk, doth make man better be;
Or, standing long an oak, three hundred year,
To fall a log at last, dry, bald, and sear:
5   A lily of a day
        Is fairer far, in May,
    Although it fall and die that night;
    It was the plant and flower of light.
In small proportions we just beauties see,
10 And in short measures life may perfect be.

DENISE LEVERTOV (1923–   )

Losing Track

Long after you have swung back
away from me
I think you are still with me:

you come in close to the shore
5 on the tide
and nudge me awake the way

a boat adrift nudges the pier:
am I a pier
half-in half-out of the water?

10 and in the pleasure of that communion
I lose track,
the moon I watch goes down, the

tide swings you away before
I know I'm
15 alone again long since,

mud sucking at gray and black
timbers of me,
a light growth of green dreams drying.

WILLIAM WORDSWORTH (1770–1850)

Composed upon Westminster Bridge, September 3, 1802

Earth has not anything to show more fair:
Dull would he be of soul who could pass by
A sight so touching in its majesty;
This City now doth, like a garment, wear
5 The beauty of the morning; silent, bare,
Ships, towers, domes, theaters, and temples lie
Open unto the fields, and to the sky;
All bright and glittering in the smokeless air.
Never did sun more beautifully steep
10 In his first splendor, valley, rock, or hill;
Ne'er saw I, never felt, a calm so deep!
The river glideth at his own sweet will:
Dear God! the very houses seem asleep;
And all that mighty heart is lying still!

SYLVIA PLATH (1932–1963)

Morning Song

Love set you going like a fat gold watch.
The midwife slapped your footsoles, and your bald cry
Took its place among the elements.

Our voices echo, magnifying your arrival. New statue.
5 In a drafty museum, your nakedness
Shadows our safety. We stand round blankly as walls.

I'm no more your mother
Than the cloud that distils a mirror to reflect its own slow
Effacement at the wind's hand.

10 All night your moth-breath
   Flickers among the flat pink roses. I wake to listen:
   A far sea moves in my ear.

   One cry, and I stumble from bed, cow-heavy and floral
   In my Victorian nightgown.
15 Your mouth opens clean as a cat's. The window square

   Whitens and swallows its dull stars. And now you try
   Your handful of notes;
   The clear vowels rise like balloons.

Most metaphors and similes have a certain timelessness to them. Wordsworth's vision of London asleep, Hughes's picture of energy turning angry in Harlem, are both visions of something real and, therefore, enduring. In the following poem, however, the metaphorical vision is transitory and illusory. Nonetheless, it illuminates the speaker's view of the world. Note the movement of the imagery from metaphorical to literal within the poem. Consider how it expresses and develops the statement made by the poem's title. (Note particularly the "difficult balance" in the last line. What meanings does that phrase have here at the end of the poem?) Then discuss how the metaphor's statement and development creates both the specific picture of the waking man and the wider vision that fills the speaker's mind.

RICHARD WILBUR (1921–   )

Love Calls Us to the Things of This World

   The eyes open to a cry of pulleys,
   And spirited from sleep, the astounded soul
   Hangs for a moment bodiless and simple
   As false dawn.
5   Outside the open window
   The morning air is all awash with angels.

   Some are in bed-sheets, some are in blouses,
   Some are in smocks: but truly there they are.
   Now they are rising together in calm swells
10 Of halcyon feeling, filling whatever they wear
   With the deep joy of their impersonal breathing;

   Now they are flying in place, conveying
   The terrible speed of their omnipresence, moving

And staying like white water; and now of a sudden
15 They swoon down into so rapt a quiet
That nobody seems to be there.
                              The soul shrinks

    From all that it is about to remember,
From the punctual rape of every blessèd day,
20 And cries,
              "Oh, let there be nothing on earth but laundry,
Nothing but rosy hands in the rising steam
And clear dances done in the sight of heaven."

    Yet, as the sun acknowledges
25 With a warm look the world's hunks and colors,
The soul descends once more in bitter love
To accept the waking body, saying now
In a changed voice as the man yawns and rises,

    "Bring them down from their ruddy gallows;
30 Let there be clean linen for the backs of thieves;
Let lovers go fresh and sweet to be undone,
And the heaviest nuns walk in a pure floating
Of dark habits,
                  keeping their difficult balance."

9 *Symbol and Allegory*

Similes and metaphors make their comparisons quickly and explicitly. They occupy a line or two; and then they are set, ready for further development, but equally ready to be superseded by another simile or metaphor. How the poet uses them, or how many are used within a poem, is up to the poet. The range of possibilities is wide.

Symbol and allegory, however, tend to dominate the poems in which they are used. Moreover, they usually stand alone: one symbol or allegory is usually the most any given poem can support.

Similes and metaphors are used to make us look more attentively at the poem's subject: at the beauty of an evening or early morning scene, at laundry on a clothesline, at a new-born child. They appeal directly to our senses: "cow-heavy," "clean as a cat's," "the clear vowels rise like balloons." Often, they illuminate some larger question: Which is better, a long life or a perfect one? "What happens to a dream deferred?" What are some of the feelings a new mother might have toward her child and her own motherhood? But they illuminate the larger question by keeping our attention on the things they describe: lilies and rotten meat and early-morning cries.

Symbols and allegories, on the other hand, urge us to look beyond the literal significance of the poem's statements or action. "All Night by the Rose," for instance, asks us to go beyond its descriptions of a man and a flower and imagine what they might mean in terms of a man and a woman. "The Tyger" does not call our attention to tigers so much as it calls it to the awesome qualities suggested by the tiger's fierce beauty and the godlike powers involved in the beast's creation. If we wish, in fact, "The Tyger" can take us even further, to the question of the existence of evil, as symbolized by the tiger's murderous nature. How far we wish to pursue the questionings begun by the poem is up to us.

When we meet with imagery that seems to be calling to us to look beyond the immediate event and its emotional ramifications, we may suspect we are dealing with symbol or allegory. But how are we to distinguish which we are dealing with?

An **allegory** always tells of an action. The events of that action should make sense literally (a man can sleep next to a rose bush, if he wishes); but they make more profound sense through a second, allegorical, interpretation. Usually, that second interpretation will have a spiritual or a psychological significance; for allegories are particularly good at using physical actions to describe the workings of the human mind and spirit. "Young Goodman Brown," we recall, was an allegory of this type. On the literal level, it described a young man's encounter with witchcraft (or his dream of witchcraft). On the allegorical level, it described the process by which a person (who can be anyone, male or female) loses faith in human goodness.

In allegory, then, we are given a story which presents a one-to-one correspondence between some physical action (most often an encounter of some kind) and some second action (usually psychological or spiritual), with each step in the literal tale corresponding to a parallel step on the allegorical level. **Symbolism** may likewise present us with a tale or an action. But it may equally well present us with a description of some unchanging being or object. And it is more likely to suggest several possible interpretations than it is to insist on a single one.

In "Ozymandias," for instance, the whole tale of the power and fall of the king is symbolic. But the most striking symbol within it is the broken statue with its vainly boastful inscription. (For many of us, it's the sight of that statue that leaps to mind when anyone says "Ozymandias." The full tale tends to come as an afterthought.)

And how do we explain the tale's symbolism? Does the king's fall symbolize the fall of the proud (which would give the poem a moral interpretation), the fall of tyranny (which would give it a political one), or merely the inevitable destruction by time of human lives and civilizations? May we not, in fact, read overtones of all three types of meaning into the traveller's tale? Certainly the tyrant, with his "sneer of cold command" seems unpleasant enough for us to rejoice in his overthrow. But the sculptor, he with "the hand that mocked" the sneer, is dead as well; and even his longer-enduring work is half destroyed. How do we feel about that? The picture the sonnet paints is straightforward enough; its tone and message are somewhat more complicated.

Some symbols are conventional; and these will suggest a single interpretation. "The Lamb," relying on the traditional association of the lamb as Christ, is an example of conventional symbolism in poetry. Alternatively, the poet may invent a symbol and provide its interpretation as well. In general, however, symbols in poetry ask the reader to interpret them. The interaction between poet and reader thus admits the greatest possible freedom of suggestion and response.

As you read the following poems, decide whether you think them better interpreted symbolically or allegorically. How would you discuss the poem's language, imagery, and progression to support your interpretation?

GEORGE HERBERT (1593–1633)

Love (III)

Love bade me welcome; yet my soul drew back,
    Guilty of dust and sin.
But quick-eyed Love, observing me grow slack
    From my first entrance in,
5 Drew nearer to me, sweetly questioning
    If I lacked anything.

"A guest," I answered, "worthy to be here."
    Love said, "You shall be he."
"I, the unkind, ungrateful? Ah my dear,
10   I cannot look on Thee."
Love took my hand, and smiling, did reply,
    "Who made the eyes but I?"

"Truth, Lord, but I have marred them; let my shame
    Go where it doth deserve."
15 "And know you not," says Love, "who bore the blame?"
    "My dear, then I will serve."
"You must sit down," says Love, "and taste my meat."
    So I did sit and eat.

WILLIAM BLAKE (1757–1827)

From Songs of Experience

The Sick Rose

O Rose, thou art sick.
The invisible worm
That flies in the night
In the howling storm

5 Has found out thy bed
  Of crimson joy,
  And his dark secret love
  Does thy life destroy.

RALPH WALDO EMERSON (1803–1882)

Days

Daughters of Time, the hypocritic Days,
Muffled and dumb like barefoot dervishes,
And marching single in an endless file,
Bring diadems and fagots in their hands.
5 To each they offer gifts after his will,
Bread, kingdoms, stars, and sky that holds them all.
I, in my pleached garden, watched the pomp,
Forgot my morning wishes, hastily
Took a few herbs and apples, and the Day
10 Turned and departed silent. I, too late,
Under her solemn fillet saw the scorn.

ROBERT FROST (1874–1963)

The Road Not Taken

Two roads diverged in a yellow wood,
And sorry I could not travel both
And be one traveler, long I stood
And looked down one as far as I could
5 To where it bent in the undergrowth;

Then took the other, as just as fair,
And having perhaps the better claim,
Because it was grassy and wanted wear;
Though as for that, the passing there
10 Had worn them really about the same,

And both that morning equally lay
In leaves no step had trodden black.
Oh, I kept the first for another day!
Yet knowing how way leads on to way,
15 I doubted if I should ever come back.

I shall be telling this with a sigh
Somewhere ages and ages hence:
Two roads diverged in a wood, and I—
I took the one less traveled by,
20 And that has made all the difference.

ALLEN GINSBERG (1926–   )

In back of the real

railroad yard in San Jose
   I wandered desolate
in front of a tank factory
   and sat on a bench
5 near the switchman's shack.

A flower lay on the hay on
   the asphalt highway
—the dread hay flower
I thought—It had a
10 brittle black stem and
   corolla of yellowish dirty
spikes like Jesus' inchlong
   crown, and a soiled
dry center cotton tuft
15   like a used shaving brush
that's been lying under
   the garage for a year.

Yellow, yellow flower, and
   flower of industry,
20 tough spikey ugly flower,
   flower nonetheless,
with the form of the great yellow
   Rose in your brain!
This is the flower of the World.

JOHN KEATS (1795–1821)

Ode on a Grecian Urn

I

Thou still unravished bride of quietness,
   Thou foster-child of silence and slow time,
Sylvan historian, who canst thus express

A flowery tale more sweetly than our rhyme:
5 What leaf-fringed legend haunts about thy shape
    Of deities or mortals, or of both,
       In Tempe or the dales of Arcady?[1]
    What men or gods are these? What maidens loath?
What mad pursuit? What struggle to escape?
10   What pipes and timbrels? What wild ecstasy?

      2

Heard melodies are sweet, but those unheard
    Are sweeter; therefore, ye soft pipes, play on;
Not to the sensual ear, but, more endeared,
    Pipe to the spirit ditties of no tone:
15 Fair youth, beneath the trees, thou canst not leave
    Thy song, nor ever can those trees be bare;
      Bold Lover, never, never canst thou kiss,
Though winning near the goal—yet, do not grieve;
      She cannot fade, though thou hast not thy bliss,
20   Forever wilt thou love, and she be fair!

      3

Ah, happy, happy boughs! that cannot shed
    Your leaves, nor ever bid the Spring adieu;
And, happy melodist, unwearièd,
    Forever piping songs forever new;
25 More happy love! more happy, happy love!
    Forever warm and still to be enjoyed,
      Forever panting, and forever young;
All breathing human passion far above,
    That leaves a heart high-sorrowful and cloyed,
30   A burning forehead, and a parching tongue.

      4

Who are these coming to the sacrifice?
    To what green altar, O mysterious priest,
Lead'st thou that heifer lowing at the skies,
    And all her silken flanks with garlands dressed?
35 What little town by river or sea shore,

---

[1] The vale of Tempe and Arcady (Arcadia) in Greece are symbolic of pastoral
beauty.

Or mountain-built with peaceful citadel,
    Is emptied of this folk, this pious morn?
And, little town, thy streets for evermore
    Will silent be; and not a soul to tell
40   Why thou art desolate, can e'er return.

       5

O Attic[2] shape! Fair attitude! with brede[3]
    Of marble men and maidens overwrought,
With forest branches and the trodden weed;
    Thou, silent form, dost tease us out of thought
45 As doth eternity: Cold Pastoral!
    When old age shall this generation waste,
       Thou shalt remain, in midst of other woe
    Than ours, a friend to man, to whom thou say'st,
"Beauty is truth, truth beauty,—that is all
50   Ye know on earth, and all ye need to know."

---

[2] Grecian, especially Athenian.
[3] Embroidery.

10

Conceits and Allusions

Metaphors and similes, because of their instant appeal, are usually the first types of figurative speech to catch our attention. Symbols and allegories, which develop as their poems progress, require more preparation from us if we are to enjoy them fully. They offer themselves only to those who are willing not only to read closely and well, but also to go beyond the poem's literal meaning into a realm of wider suggestion. Conceits and allusions may be momentary or poem-wide in scope; but they are the most demanding figures of all, requiring extreme alertness and some outside knowledge in order to unravel them.

Conceits

A **conceit** could be defined as an outrageous metaphor, but a more traditional definition is a comparison between two highly dissimilar objects. Conceits are often developed at some length, revealing and weighing point after point of comparison or contrast between their two objects. In love poetry, they often grow out of Renaissance traditions that depict the man as a warrior and the woman as a walled town; he attacks, she defends herself or surrenders. Or the man might be a hunter and the woman a wild animal. Or she might be the warrior, wounding him with sharp looks or sharper words. Or, if she were kinder, she might be a treasure mine, or a goddess of love. (The list could go on and on.) Some

Renaissance poets take the conceits seriously; others play with them, making use of the surprise that can come from turning an expected cliche upside down.

With the metaphysical poets of the seventeenth century, the unexpected becomes a key ingredient in the conceit. The metaphysical poets used conceits not only in love poetry, but in religious poetry as well, thereby creating for both types of poetry conceits of unparalleled complexity and ingenuity. Physics, astronomy, navigation—any science, any intellectual endeavor might yield a conceit which viewed the soul's progress and passions as parallels to the workings of the universe it inhabited. The resulting poetry tends to be remarkably tough intellectually (you read this poetry *very* slowly the first few times), but also remarkably free, self-assured, and optimistic in its visions.

Here is an example of conceits in metaphysical poetry. Note that there are two main clusters of imagery in the poem. The first turns on maps and voyages, the second on the image of Christ as "the second Adam." And note also that the two are connected by the concept of the soul's journey to salvation as an annihilation of time and space and by the physical image of the sick man, flat on his back in bed and sweating heavily with fever.

JOHN DONNE (1572–1631)

Hymn to God My God, in My Sickness

Since I am coming to that holy room,
  Where, with thy choir of Saints for evermore,
I shall be made thy music; as I come
  I tune the instrument here at the door,
5 And what I must do then, think now before.

Whilst my physicians by their love are grown
  Cosmographers, and I their map, who lie
Flat on this bed, that by them may be shown
  That this is my Southwest discovery
10 *Per fretum febris,*[1] by these straits to die,

I joy, that in these straits, I see my west;[2]
  For, though their currents yield return to none,
What shall my west hurt me? As west and east
  In all flat maps (and I am one) are one,
15 So death doth touch the Resurrection.

---

[1] Through the straits of fever.
[2] My death.

Is the Pacific Sea my home? Or are
   The eastern riches? Is Jerusalem?
Anyan,[3] and Magellan, and Gibraltàr,
   All straits, and none but straits, are ways to them,
20   Whether where Japhet dwelt, or Cham, or Shem.[4]

We think that Paradise and Calvary,
   Christ's Cross, and Adam's tree, stood in one place;
Look Lord, and find both Adams met in me;
   As the first Adam's sweat surrounds my face,
25   May the last Adam's blood my soul embrace.

So, in his purple wrapped receive me, Lord,
   By these thorns give me his other crown;
And as to others' souls I preached thy word,
   Be this my text, my sermon to mine own,
30   Therefore that he may raise, the Lord throws down.

Allusions

Conceits ask that we bring some knowledge to our reading if we are to understand their implications. For example, we must understand the distortions of space involved in making a flat map represent a round world if we are to understand Donne's hymn. An **allusion** likewise asks us to bring some knowledge to our reading. For an allusion may be defined as a reference to some work of art or literature, or to some well-known person, event, or story. If we do not catch the reference, then we will miss the point of the allusion. Read, for example, the following poem. Can you spot the allusion it contains?

HENRY REED (1914–   )

From **Lessons of the War**

Unarmed Combat

In due course of course you will all be issued with
Your proper issue; but until tomorrow,
You can hardly be said to need it; and until that time,
We shall have unarmed combat. I shall teach you

---

[3] Modern Annam, then thought of as a strait between Asia and America.
[4] Sons of Noah, said to have settled Europe, Asia, and Africa after the flood.

5 The various holds and rolls and throws and breakfalls
    Which you may sometimes meet.

And the various holds and rolls and throws and breakfalls
Do not depend on any sort of weapon,
But only on what I might coin a phrase and call
10 The ever-important question of human balance,
And the ever-important need to be in a strong
    Position at the start.

There are many kinds of weakness about the body
Where you would least expect, like the ball of the foot.
15 But the various holds and rolls and throws and breakfalls
Will always come in useful. And never be frightened
To tackle from behind: it may not be clean to do so,
    But this is global war.

So give them all you have, and always give them
20 As good as you get; it will always get you somewhere.
(You may not know it, but you can tie a Jerry
Up without rope; it is one of the things I shall teach you.)
Nothing will matter if only you are ready for him.
    The readiness is all.

25 *The readiness is all.* How can I help but feel
I have been here before? But somehow then,
I was the tied-up one. How to get out
Was always then my problem. And even if I had
A piece of rope I was always the sort of person
30   Who threw the rope aside.

And in my time I have given them all I had,
Which was never as good as I got, and it got me nowhere.
And the various holds and rolls and throws and breakfalls
Somehow or other I always seemed to put
35 In the wrong place. And as for war, my wars
    Were global from the start.

Perhaps I was never in a strong position,
Or the ball of my foot got hurt, or I had some weakness
Where I had least expected. But I think I see your point.
40 While awaiting a proper issue, we must learn the lesson
Of the ever-important question of human balance.
    It is courage that counts.

Things may be the same again; and we must fight
Not in the hope of winning but rather of keeping
45   Something alive: so that when we meet our end,
It may be said that we tackled wherever we could,
That battle-fit we lived, and though defeated,
        Not without glory fought.

Now compare this poem with "Naming of Parts," printed on p. 832.
Note that "Naming of Parts" keeps to one lightly ironic tone throughout,
while "Unarmed Combat" turns openly serious as soon as the instructor's
word "ready" in line 23 brings Hamlet's words, "The readiness is all," to
mind. (If you want to check the context of the line as it appears in
Hamlet, you'll find it on p. 575.) What thoughts (half suggested by the
instructor's previous words, half by the new train of thought arising from
the quotation) fill out and finish the poem? How do they fill out your
view of the speaker? And what part does the quotation itself play in
allowing this shift of tone, both by its presence and by the echoes it
raises in your mind of Hamlet and his views on living and dying?

In a more light-hearted vein, here's a poem that's virtually all allusion—
but first, since you may not have met it before, is the poem it alludes to.
Notice that the second poem makes no direct reference to the first, but
that its whole effectiveness lies in its irreverent echoes of the earlier poem.
What picture do we get of this poem's speaker?

ANONYMOUS—MIDDLE ENGLISH LYRIC

Sumer Is Icumen In [1]

Sumer is icumen in,
    Lhude sing cuccu!
Groweth sed and bloweth med
    And springth the wude nu.
5   Sing cuccu!

----

[1] *Translation:*

Spring has come in,
    Loudly sing cuckoo!
Grows seed and blooms mead
    And springs the wood now.
        Sing cuckoo!

Ewe bleats after lamb,
    Lows after calf the cow,

Bullock starts, buck farts;
    Merrily sing cuckoo!
        Cuckoo! cuckoo!
Well sing thou cuckoo.
Cease thou never now!

Sing cuckoo now etc.

Awe bleteth after lomb,
   Lhouth after calve cu,
Bulluc sterteth, bucke verteth;
   Murie sing cuccu!
10   Cuccu! cuccu!
Wel sings thu cuccu.
Ne swik thu naver nu!

Sing cuccu nu, Sing cuccu!
Sing cuccu, Sing cuccu nu!

EZRA POUND (1885–1972)

Ancient Music

Winter is icumen in,
Lhude sing Goddamm,
Raineth drop and staineth slop,
And how the wind doth ramm!
5   Sing : Goddamm.
Skiddeth bus and sloppeth us,
An ague hath my ham.
Freezeth river, turneth liver,
      Damn you, sing : Goddamm.
10 Goddamm, Goddamm, 'tis why I am, Goddamm,
      So 'gainst the winter's balm.
Sing goddamm, damm, sing Goddamm,
Sing goddamm, sing goddam, DAMM.

Discuss how the speakers of the following three poems use conceits or allusions to praise the women they love and enlarge on the benefits of love. (You will want to concentrate on the poem's imagery; but note also the use of apostrophe, or direct address, and the different tones and logical progressions within each poem. Use the questions that follow each poem to help you.)

EDMUND SPENSER (1552?–1599)

From **Amoretti**

Sonnet 15

Ye tradefull Merchants, that with weary toyle,
Do seeke most pretious things to make your gain,
And both the Indias of their treasure spoile,

What needeth you to seeke so farre in vaine?
5 For loe, my Love doth in her selfe containe
All this worlds riches that may farre be found:
If saphyres, loe her eies be saphyres plaine;
If rubies, loe hir lips be rubies sound;
If pearles, hir teeth be pearles both pure and round;
10 If yvorie, her forhead yvory weene;
If gold, her locks are finest gold on ground;
If silver, her faire hands are silver sheene:
But that which fairest is but few behold:—
Her mind, adornd with vertues manifold.

QUESTIONS

1. To whom is the poet speaking in the opening four lines (and, by implication, in the rest of the poem as well)? Why should he select this audience? How do the merchants differ from the poet? What do the words "weary" and "in vain" suggest about them or their activities?
2. What similarities do you find among the string of metaphors which occupy lines 7–12?
3. How does the conclusion continue the theme of treasure? How does it alter it? (Note especially the phrase "adorned with virtues manifold.") What new questions does the conclusion raise about the usefulness of the merchants' search for precious things?

WILLIAM SHAKESPEARE (1564–1616)

Sonnet 18

Shall I compare thee to a summer's day?
Thou art more lovely and more temperate:
Rough winds do shake the darling buds of May,
And summer's lease hath all too short a date:
5 Sometime too hot the eye of heaven shines,
And often is his gold complexion dimmed;
And every fair from fair sometime declines,
By chance or nature's changing course untrimmed:
But thy eternal summer shall not fade
10 Nor lose possession of that fair thou ow'st,[1]
Nor shall Death brag thou wand'rest in his shade,
When in eternal lines to time thou grow'st.
So long as men can breathe or eyes can see,
So long lives this, and this gives life to thee.

---

[1] Ownest.

QUESTIONS

This sonnet, too, starts with a question relating to physical qualities—beauty and temperature—and ends up dealing with intangible ones. By what contrasts and what train of logic does it achieve this progression? (Note in particular the "summer's day" of line 1, "the eye of heaven" in line 5, and "eternal summer" in line 9. These phrases mark the starting points of three stages in the argument, with the last two lines marking the final stage. And be warned that "fair" has three meanings. It's a noun meaning "a lovely thing," an adjective meaning "lovely", and a noun meaning "beauty.")

JOHN DONNE (1572–1631)

The Sun Rising

Busy old fool, unruly sun,
    Why dost thou thus
Through windows and through curtains call on us?
Must to thy motions lovers' seasons run?
5   Saucy, pedantic wretch, go chide
      Late schoolboys and sour 'prentices,
  Go tell court huntsmen that the king will ride,
  Call country ants to harvest offices.
Love, all alike, no season knows nor clime,
10 Nor hours, days, months, which are the rags of time.

      Thy beams, so reverend and strong
        Why shouldst thou think?
I could eclipse and cloud them with a wink,
But that I would not lose her sight so long.
15   If her eyes have not blinded thine,
      Look, and tomorrow late tell me
  Whether both th' Indias of spice and mine
  Be where thou left'st them, or lie here with me;
Ask for those kings whom thou saw'st yesterday,
20 And thou shalt hear: All here in one bed lay.

      She's all states, and all princes I;
        Nothing else is.
Princes do but play us; compared to this,
All honor's mimic, all wealth alchemy.
25   Thou, sun, art half as happy as we,
      In that the world's contracted thus;
  Thine age asks ease, and since thy duties be
To warm the world, that's done in warming us.
Shine here to us, and thou art everywhere;
30 This bed thy center is, these walls thy sphere.

QUESTIONS

1. This poem falls into the category of *aubades,* or "dawn songs." What dramatic value does this placement in time give it?
2. Note that here again earthly riches are first equated with the woman's beauty and then devalued by it, and that time is forced to yield to timelessness. How does Donne's treatment of these conceits differ from those of Shakespeare and Spenser?
3. In general, how would you compare this love poem with those two earlier ones?

The next three poems are spoken by discontented lovers. What could you say about the ways in which they use conceits or allusions to describe their predicaments or convince themselves or their hearers that some change should be made?

SIR PHILIP SIDNEY (1554–1586)

From **Astrophil and Stella**

Leave Me, O Love

Leave me, O Love, which reachest but to dust,
And thou, my mind, aspire to higher things.
Grow rich in that which never taketh rust.
Whatever fades but fading pleasure brings.

5 Draw in thy beams and humble all thy might
To that sweet yoke where lasting freedoms be,
Which breaks the clouds and opens forth the light
That doth both shine and give us sight to see.

O take fast hold; let that light be thy guide
10 In this small course which birth draws out to death,
And think how evil becometh him to slide
Who seeketh heaven and comes of heavenly breath.
    Then farewell, world! Thy uttermost I see!
    Eternal Love, maintain thy life in me.

ANDREW MARVELL (1621–1678)

To His Coy Mistress

Had we but world enough, and time,
This coyness, lady, were no crime.
We would sit down, and think which way

To walk, and pass our long love's day.
5   Thou by the Indian Ganges' side
Shouldst rubies find; I by the tide
Of Humber would complain. I would
Love you ten years before the Flood,
And you should, if you please, refuse
10 Till the conversion of the Jews.
My vegetable love should grow
Vaster than empires, and more slow;
An hundred years should go to praise
Thine eyes and on thy forehead gaze,
15 Two hundred to adore each breast,
But thirty thousand to the rest:
An age at least to every part,
And the last age should show your heart.
For, lady, you deserve this state,
20 Nor would I love at lower rate.
      But at my back I always hear
Time's wingèd chariot hurrying near;
And yonder all before us lie
Deserts of vast eternity.
25 Thy beauty shall no more be found,
Nor in thy marble vault shall sound
My echoing song; then worms shall try
That long preserved virginity,
And your quaint honor turn to dust,
30 And into ashes all my lust.
The grave's a fine and private place,
But none, I think, do there embrace.
      Now, therefore, while the youthful hue
Sits on thy skin like morning dew,
35 And while thy willing soul transpires
At every pore with instant fires,
Now let us sport us while we may,
And now, like amorous birds of prey,
Rather at once our time devour
40 Than languish in his slow-chapped power.
Let us roll all our strength and all
Our sweetness up into one ball,
And tear our pleasures with rough strife
Thorough the iron gates of life.
45 Thus, though we cannot make our sun
Stand still, yet we will make him run.

ROBERT GRAVES (1895–   )

Down, Wanton, Down!

Down, wanton, down! Have you no shame
That at the whisper of Love's name,
Or Beauty's, presto! up you raise
Your angry head and stand at gaze?

5 Poor bombard-captain, sworn to reach
The ravelin and effect a breach—
Indifferent what you storm or why,
So be that in the breach you die!

Love may be blind, but Love at least
10 Knows what is man and what mere beast;
Or Beauty wayward, but requires
More delicacy from her squires.

Tell me, my witless, whose one boast
Could be your staunchness at the post,
15 When were you made a man of parts
To think fine and profess the arts?

Will many-gifted Beauty come
Bowing to your bald rule of thumb,
Or Love swear loyalty to your crown?
20 Be gone, have done! Down, wanton, down!

11 *Patterns of Imagery*

So far, we have spoken of different figures of speech in isolation. In practice, however, the various figures are almost always found in combination with each other. "Days," for instance, is an allegory. But the various gifts the Days carry are symbolic; and the phrase "morning wishes" is metaphorical. Moreover, just as form and meaning reinforce each other, so a poem's figures of speech reinforce each other to create the poem's overall patterns of meaning and imagery. When we discuss a poem, we may start by discussing some particularly striking aspect; and that may mean a particular use of imagery. But eventually we will want to talk of the complete poem; and that will mean talking of the patterns it contains.

The poems in the last chapter were heavily patterned. The Renaissance poems tended to be static, stating a position and then elaborating on it. The metaphysical poems showed more movement, following the speaker's mind through the ramifications of an idea or situation. The poems in this chapter will also display carefully worked-out patterns of imagery. And, as most of them are somewhat longer poems, the patterns will be even more complex. But these poems will also show a freer and more passionate movement, for they come either from the Romantic poetry of the nineteenth century or from twentieth-century poets who were influenced by that movement. In the more melodious rhythms and harmonies of these poems, we find a vivid sense of immediacy, of unfolding memories or emotions, of minds and spirits caught up in vision and experience. Flowing sound and richly suggestive imagery create the sense of intense experience which was a trademark of the Romantic movement, and which still provides some overtones of meaning to the common use of the word "romantic."

As you read the following poems, be prepared for shifts of emotion as much as for shifts of thought. Note how these more modern poets create scenes, moods, and speakers through sound and imagery.

PERCY BYSSHE SHELLEY (1792–1822)

Ode to the West Wind

1

O wild West Wind, thou breath of Autumn's being,
Thou, from whose unseen presence the leaves dead
Are driven, like ghosts from an enchanter fleeing,

Yellow, and black, and pale, and hectic red,
5 Pestilence-stricken multitudes: O thou,
Who chariotest to their dark wintry bed

The wingèd seeds, where they lie cold and low,
Each like a corpse within its grave, until
Thine azure sister of the Spring shall blow

10 Her clarion o'er the dreaming earth, and fill
(Driving sweet buds like flocks to feed in air)
With living hues and odors plain and hill:

Wild Spirit, which art moving everywhere;
Destroyer and preserver; hear, oh, hear!

2

15 Thou on whose stream, mid the steep sky's commotion,
Loose clouds like earth's decaying leaves are shed,
Shook from the tangled boughs of Heaven and Ocean,

Angels of rain and lightning: there are spread
On the blue surface of thine aery surge,
20 Like the bright hair uplifted from the head

Of some fierce Maenad, even from the dim verge
Of the horizon to the zenith's height,
The locks of the approaching storm. Thou dirge

Of the dying year, to which this closing night
25 Will be the dome of a vast sepulcher,
Vaulted with all thy congregated might

Of vapors, from whose solid atmosphere
Black rain, and fire, and hail will burst: oh, hear!

3

Thou who didst waken from his summer dreams
30 The blue Mediterranean, where he lay,
Lulled by the coil of his crystàlline streams,

Beside a pumice isle in Baiae's bay,
And saw in sleep old palaces and towers
Quivering within the wave's intenser day,

35 All overgrown with azure moss and flowers
So sweet, the sense faints picturing them! Thou
For whose path the Atlantic's level powers

Cleave themselves into chasms, while far below
The sea-blooms and the oozy woods which wear
40 The sapless foliage of the ocean, know

Thy voice, and suddenly grow gray with fear,
And tremble and despoil themselves: oh, hear!

4

If I were a dead leaf thou mightest bear;
If I were a swift cloud to fly with thee;
45 A wave to pant beneath thy power, and share

The impulse of thy strength, only less free
Than thou, O uncontrollable! If even
I were as in my boyhood, and could be

The comrade of thy wanderings over Heaven,
50 As then, when to outstrip thy skiey speed
Scarce seemed a vision; I would ne'er have striven

As thus with thee in prayer in my sore need.
Oh, lift me as a wave, a leaf, a cloud!
I fall upon the thorns of life! I bleed!

55 A heavy weight of hours has chained and bowed
One too like thee: tameless, and swift, and proud.

5

Make me thy lyre, even as the forest is:
What if my leaves are falling like its own!
The tumult of thy mighty harmonies

60 Will take from both a deep, autumnal tone,
Sweet though in sadness. Be thou, Spirit fierce,
My spirit! Be thou me, impetuous one!

Drive my dead thoughts over the universe
Like withered leaves to quicken a new birth!
65 And, by the incantation of this verse,

Scatter, as from an unextinguished hearth
Ashes and sparks, my words among mankind!
Be through my lips to unawakened earth

The trumpet of a prophecy! O Wind,
70 If Winter comes, can Spring be far behind?

JOHN KEATS (1795–1821)

Ode to a Nightingale

I

My heart aches, and a drowsy numbness pains
    My sense, as though of hemlock I had drunk,
Or emptied some dull opiate to the drains
    One minute past, and Lethe-wards[1] had sunk:
5 'Tis not through envy of thy happy lot,
    But being too happy in thine happiness—
        That thou, light-wingèd Dryad of the trees,
            In some melodious plot
    Of beechen green, and shadows numberless,
10   Singest of summer in full-throated ease.

---

[1] Towards the river Lethe, in the underworld.

2

O, for a draught of vintage! that hath been
   Cooled a long age in the deep-delvèd earth,
Tasting of Flora[2] and the country green,
   Dance, and Provençal song, and sunburnt mirth!
15 O for a beaker full of the warm South,
    Full of the true, the blushful Hippocrene,[3]
      With beaded bubbles winking at the brim,
        And purple-stainèd mouth;
    That I might drink, and leave the world unseen,
20   And with thee fade away into the forest dim:

3

Fade far away, dissolve, and quite forget
   What thou among the leaves hast never known,
The weariness, the fever, and the fret
   Here, where men sit and hear each other groan;
25 Where palsy shakes a few, sad, last gray hairs,
    Where youth grows pale, and spectre-thin, and dies,
      Where but to think is to be full of sorrow
        And leaden-eyed despairs,
    Where Beauty cannot keep her lustrous eyes,
30   Or new Love pine at them beyond tomorrow.

4

Away! away! for I will fly to thee,
   Not charioted by Bacchus and his pards,[4]
But on the viewless wings of Poesy,
   Though the dull brain perplexes and retards:
35 Already with thee! tender is the night,
    And haply the Queen-Moon is on her throne,
      Clustered around by all her starry Fays;
        But here there is no light,
    Save what from heaven is with the breezes blown
40   Through verdurous glooms and winding mossy ways.

5

I cannot see what flowers are at my feet,
   Nor what soft incense hangs upon the boughs,

---

[2] Goddess of flowers.
[3] Fountain of the Muses on Mt. Helicon.
[4] Leopards drawing the chariot of Bacchus, god of wine.

But, in embalmèd darkness, guess each sweet
  Wherewith the seasonable month endows
45 The grass, the thicket, and the fruit-tree wild;
    White hawthorn, and the pastoral eglantine;
      Fast fading violets covered up in leaves;
        And mid-May's eldest child,
  The coming musk-rose, full of dewy wine,
50   The murmurous haunt of flies on summer eves.

                    6

Darkling[5] I listen; and for many a time
  I have been half in love with easeful Death,
Called him soft names in many a musèd rhyme,
  To take into the air my quiet breath;
55 Now more than ever seems it rich to die,
    To cease upon the midnight with no pain,
      While thou art pouring forth thy soul abroad
        In such an ecstasy!
  Still wouldst thou sing, and I have ears in vain—
60   To thy high requiem become a sod.

                    7

Thou wast not born for death, immortal Bird!
  No hungry generations tread thee down;
The voice I hear this passing night was heard
  In ancient days by emperor and clown:
65 Perhaps the selfsame song that found a path
    Through the sad heart of Ruth, when, sick for home,
      She stood in tears amid the alien corn:
        The same that oft-times hath
  Charmed magic casements, opening on the foam
70   Of perilous seas, in faery lands forlorn.

                    8

Forlorn! the very word is like a bell
  To toll me back from thee to my sole self!
Adieu! the fancy cannot cheat so well
  As she is famed to do, deceiving elf.

---

[5] In the darkness.

75 Adieu! adieu! thy plaintive anthem fades
    Past the near meadows, over the still stream,
      Up the hill side; and now 'tis buried deep
        In the next valley-glades:
    Was it a vision, or a waking dream?
    Fled is that music:—Do I wake or sleep?

MATTHEW ARNOLD (1822–1888)

Dover Beach

The sea is calm tonight.
The tide is full, the moon lies fair
Upon the straits;—on the French coast the light
Gleams and is gone; the cliffs of England stand,
5 Glimmering and vast, out in the tranquil bay.
Come to the window, sweet is the night-air!
Only, from the long line of spray
Where the sea meets the moon-blanched land,
Listen! you hear the grating roar
10 Of pebbles which the waves draw back, and fling,
At their return, up the high strand,
Begin, and cease, and then again begin,
With tremulous cadence slow, and bring
The eternal note of sadness in.

15 Sophocles long ago
Heard it on the Aegean, and it brought
Into his mind the turbid ebb and flow
Of human misery; we
Find also in the sound a thought,
20 Hearing it by this distant northern sea.

The Sea of Faith
Was once, too, at the full, and round earth's shore
Lay like the folds of a bright girdle furled.
But now I only hear
25 Its melancholy, long, withdrawing roar,
Retreating, to the breath
Of the night-wind, down the vast edges drear
And naked shingles of the world.

Ah, love, let us be true
30 To one another! for the world, which seems

To lie before us like a land of dreams,
So various, so beautiful, so new,
Hath really neither joy, nor love, nor light,
Nor certitude, nor peace, nor help for pain;
35 And we are here as on a darkling plain
Swept with confused alarms of struggle and flight,
Where ignorant armies clash by night.

WILLIAM BUTLER YEATS (1865–1939)

Sailing to Byzantium

I

That is no country for old men. The young
In one another's arms, birds in the trees
—Those dying generations—at their song,
The salmon-falls, the mackerel-crowded seas,
5 Fish, flesh, or fowl, commend all summer long
Whatever is begotten, born, and dies.
Caught in that sensual music all neglect
Monuments of unageing intellect.

2

An aged man is but a paltry thing,
10 A tattered coat upon a stick, unless
Soul clap its hands and sing, and louder sing
For every tatter in its mortal dress,
Nor is there singing school but studying
Monuments of its own magnificence;
15 And therefore I have sailed the seas and come
To the holy city of Byzantium.

3

O sages standing in God's holy fire
As in the gold mosaic of a wall,
Come from the holy fire, perne in a gyre,
20 And be the singing-masters of my soul.
Consume my heart away; sick with desire
And fastened to a dying animal
It knows not what it is; and gather me
Into the artifice of eternity.

4

25 Once out of nature I shall never take
   My bodily form from any natural thing,
   But such a form as Grecian goldsmiths make
   Of hammered gold and gold enamelling
   To keep a drowsy Emperor awake;
30 Or set upon a golden bough to sing
   To lords and ladies of Byzantium
   Of what is past, or passing, or to come.

DYLAN THOMAS (1914–1953)

Fern Hill

Now as I was young and easy under the apple boughs
About the lilting house and happy as the grass was green,
      The night above the dingle starry,
         Time let me hail and climb
5   Golden in the heydays of his eyes,
And honored among wagons I was prince of the apple towns
And once below a time I lordly had the trees and leaves
         Trail with daisies and barley
      Down the rivers of the windfall light.

10 And as I was green and carefree, famous among the barns
About the happy yard and singing as the farm was home,
      In the sun that is young once only,
         Time let me play and be
      Golden in the mercy of his means,
15 And green and golden I was huntsman and herdsman, the calves
Sang to my horn, the foxes on the hills barked clear and cold,
         And the sabbath rang slowly
      In the pebbles of the holy streams.

All the sun long it was running, it was lovely, the hay
20 Fields high as the house, the tunes from the chimneys, it was air
         And playing, lovely and watery
            And fire green as grass.
         And nightly under the simple stars
As I rode to sleep the owls were bearing the farm away,
25 All the moon long I heard, blessed among stables, the night-jars
         Flying with the ricks, and the horses
            Flashing into the dark.

And then to awake, and the farm, like a wanderer white
With the dew, come back, the cock on his shoulder: it was all
30   Shining, it was Adam and maiden,
                The sky gathered again
            And the sun grew round that very day.
So it must have been after the birth of the simple light
In the first, spinning place, the spellbound horses walking warm
35   Out of the whinnying green stable
                On to the fields of praise.

And honored among foxes and pheasants by the gay house
Under the new made clouds and happy as the heart was long,
            In the sun born over and over,
40   I ran my heedless ways,
                My wishes raced through the house high hay
And nothing I cared, at my sky blue trades, that time allows
In all his tuneful turning so few and such morning songs
            Before the children green and golden
45   Follow him out of grace,

Nothing I cared, in the lamb white days, that time would take me
Up to the swallow thronged loft by the shadow of my hand,
            In the moon that is always rising,
                Nor that riding to sleep
50   I should hear him fly with the high fields
And wake to the farm forever fled from the childless land.
Oh as I was young and easy in the mercy of his means,
                Time held me green and dying
            Though I sang in my chains like the sea.

SOUND

12 *Meter and Its Variations*

Sound in poetry is a function of two elements: the rhythm of a poem's lines, and the sounds of its words. Throughout our study of poetry, we have been aware of the important part sound and rhythm play in establishing our sense of a poem. But we have been more concerned with recognizing how the sounds of a given poem reinforce its ideas or emotions than with classifying the sounds themselves; and so we have not paused to build up a vocabulary of technical terms for meter and versification. Now it is time to learn that vocabulary, so that we may supplement our discussions of character and language in poetry with more detailed comments on the techniques of sound that reinforce them. Since rhythm is perhaps the most basic element of sound in a poem, and meter the most basic element of rhythm, we will start with meter.

Meter is the term used to describe the underlying rhythm of a poem, based on the number and the placement of stressed syllables in each line. In most poetry, these **stresses** will fall into a pattern and the pattern will have a particular name: *iambic pentameter,* for instance, to name one of the most common. When we learn to **scan** a poem, therefore, to find out the rhythm or meter in which it is written, these stresses and their patterns are what we will be looking at.

What do we mean by a *stress,* or a *stressed syllable?* We mean that the word or syllable involved is one to which our voice will give greater emphasis than to its neighbors. Every word of more than one syllable in English has one accented, or stressed, syllable and one or more unaccented or unstressed ones. Thus, in the word *human* we stress the first syllable: *hú - man;* while in the word *humane* we stress the second: *hu - máne.* When we speak a sentence, these natural accents, or stresses, will be heard. Usually they will be joined by a second type of stress, one used for emphasis. If I say, "Is she coming?," for instance, and leave the strongest stress on the first syllable of *coming* ("Is she *coming?*"), there will be nothing startling in the sentence. If, however, I move the accent to the word *is* ("*Is* she coming?"), I sound doubtful or surprised that she'd come; while if I accent the word *she* (" Is *she* coming?") the stressed word suggests that "she" is the last person I would have expected (or perhaps wanted) to come. The emphasis may fall in an expected or an unexpected place. But it is sure to fall somewhere, for English is a heavily accented language; it sounds neither normal nor natural without the contrast of its stressed and unstressed syllables.

The number of stresses in a line of poetry, therefore, is the number of syllables on which our voice naturally tends to put a stronger emphasis. The emphasis must be natural; it must come either from the sound of the words themselves or from the meaning and emphasis of the lines. Thus, we must be able to find the meter by reading naturally; we should not distort either the sense or the natural rhythm of the lines to make them fit some preconceived meter.

So basic is this matter of stresses, in fact, that line lengths receive their names according to the number of stressed syllables they contain. One simply counts up the stressed syllables, translates the resulting number into Greek, and adds the word "meter" to finish out the term, as follows:

1. **Dimeter:** two stresses per line

   "Díe soón"

2. **Trimeter:** three stresses

   Dóst thou knów who máde thee?

3. **Tetrameter:** four stresses

   "Tell all the truth but tell it slánt"

4. **Pentameter:** five stresses:

   "Leáve me, O Loóve, which reáches bút to dust,"

5. **Hexameter:** six stresses (also known as an *alexandrine*)

   Which, like a wóunded snake, drags its slow length alóng."

By counting the number of stresses per line, we thus discover the skeleton of a poem's rhythm. The question then becomes how those stresses are linked. In **accentual poetry,** they are linked by *alliteration* or *assonance.* There will be (usually) four stressed syllables per line; and two or three of them will start with the same sound or contain the same vowel. Here is an example, from a poem you will meet again at the chapter's end:

> Bitter breast-cares have I abided,
> Known on my keel many a care's hold,
> And dire sea-surge, and there I oft spent
> Narrow nightwatch nigh the ship's head
> While she tossed close to cliffs. Coldly afflicted,
> My feet were by frost benumbed.

The first line is marked by the alliteration of "bitter" and "breast" and the assonance of "I" and "abided." The second is similarly linked by the alliteration of the "k" sound in "keel" and "care" and the assonance of the "o" sound in "known" and "hold." But the other lines are all marked by the alliteration of one sound each: "s" in the third line, "n" in the fourth, "c" in the fifth, and "f" in the sixth. This is the patterning of Old English poetry, a patterning used for several hundred years before the Norman Conquest brought French influences and rhymed verse to England. Since that time, accentual poetry has been relatively rare. One nineteenth-century poet, Gerard Manley Hopkins, however, worked out an accentual style of his own, which he called **sprung rhythm.** His style reflects the Old English influence in its irregular placement of stresses and its marked use of alliteration and assonance.

Most English and American verse is **accentual syllabic.** This means that its rhythm depends not only on the number of stressed syllables, but also on the total number of syllables per line, and on the placement of the stresses within that totality. Tetrameter lines, for instance, vary in length from the four stressed syllables of "We real cool. We," to the eight syllables, half of them stressed, of "Tell all the truth but tell it slant," to the eleven or twelve syllables (every third syllable stressed) of "You left us in tatters, without shoes or socks,/Tired of digging potatoes and spudding up docks."

To define its various combinations of stressed and unstressed syllables, therefore, accentual-syllabic meters divide each line of poetry into **feet,** a **foot** consisting of one stressed syllable with its attendant unstressed syllables. Each type of foot—that is, each pattern of syllables—is given a name. An unstressed syllable followed by a stressed one, for instance (*the word*) is an **iamb;** two unstressed syllables followed by a stressed one (*that she heard*) make an **anapest.** The meter of the poem thus consists of the *name of the foot* most frequently found in the poem joined to the basic *line length.* "There's a certain slant of light" thus becomes **iambic trimeter,** despite the fact that not all its feet are iambs and not all its lines have three feet.

With this background in mind, let us chart the types of feet most commonly found in English poetry. One of the most common **duple meters** is the **iambic,** which has two syllables, the second stressed.

> Tell áll | the trúth | but téll | it slańt

The **trochaic** has two syllables, the first stressed.

> Dóst thou | knów who | máde thee?

One of the two most common **triple meters** is the **anapestic:** with three syllables, the last stressed.

> And thére | was my Ró- | land to béar | the whole weíght

The **dactylic** has three syllables, the first stressed.

> Táking me | báck down the | vísta of | yéars, till I | sée

One should also know the **spondee,** a two-syllable foot with both syllables accented. The spondee is used only to lend particular emphasis or variety to poetry written in other meters; there is no "spondaic meter." The **amphibrach** is a three-syllable foot with the accent on the middle syllable. Unlike the spondee, the amphibrach can be used as a sustained meter; but it's not an easy meter to work with and isn't often used for an entire poem. The **monosyllabic foot** has one syllable, accented; Gwendolyn Brooks' "We Real Cool" is an example of this foot in action. The **paeon** is a four-syllable foot. It may be called *first paeon, second paeon, third paeon,* or *fourth paeon,* depending on whether the accented syllable comes first, second, third, or fourth. There may also be a secondary accent within the foot. Traditional ballads are often written in paeonic meters.

Meter, then, will create the basic rhythm of a poem, setting up a pattern to be repeated or varied with each line. Seldom does the pattern remain perfectly regular, for to hold too closely to a meter in spoken verse is to risk monotony and boredom.

How does a poet avoid monotony? By shifting stresses, so that a poem written in iambic meter will have some feet which are trochees and some which are spondees. By adding syllables, so that an iambic line will contain an occasional dactyl or anapest. By dropping syllables, substituting a pause for the expected sound, or laying greater stress on the remaining syllables, as when a spondee is substituted for an anapest.

More importantly, poets vary their meters by making the sense of the poem, and the cadence of the speaker's voice, move in counterpoint to the rhythm.

> The sea is calm tonight.
> The tide is full, the moon lies fair
> Upon the straits;—on the French coast the light
> Gleams and is gone; the cliffs of England stand,
> Glimmering and vast, out in the tranquil bay.

The first statement fits the first line perfectly. But the next overlaps the second line, so that your voice cannot stop on "fair," but must continue with "Upon the straits." A pause, then, and the thought continues through that line and half of the next; then pauses more briefly, finishes the line with a slight pause, and comes to rest at the end of the fifth line. Because your voice stops at the end of them, the first and fifth lines are called *end-stopped* lines. Because the movement of thought and phrase forces your voice to continue past their ends, the second, third, and fourth lines are called *run-on* lines. Both end-stopped and run-on lines may contain internal pauses. We find one such pause after "full" in the second line, one after "straits" in the third," one after "gone" in the fourth, and one after "vast" in the fifth. These pauses are called **cesuras;** and their use and placement are vital in breaking the rhythms of poetry to create the sound of a speaking voice.

In contrast to "Dover Beach" (which you might want to reread in its entirety, to notice how flexible the lines are throughout), recall Blake's poems, "The Lamb" and "The Tyger." Notice how many of their lines are end-stopped, and how the regularity of the rhythm, with its procession of end-stopped lines and repeated questions, gives these poems almost the sound of incantations, sounds far removed from the wistful accents of Arnold's speaker. But notice, too, that even here, although each phrase is strongly separated from its fellows and heavily accented, the length of the phrases still varies, and cesuras and occasional run-on lines are still found:

> What the hammer? what the chain?
> In what furnace was thy brain?
> What the anvil? what dread grasp
> Dare its deadly terrors clasp?

We may notice, too, that Blake restricts himself to seven-syllable lines in "The Tyger," and to a patterned alternation between trimeter and tetrameter lines in "The Lamb," while Arnold varies his line lengths in "Dover Beach," the lines growing longer as the speaker warms to his topic. And, finally, we notice that all the lines quoted from Blake and Arnold end with stressed syllables. Your voice rises slightly to the stress at the end of these lines, and they are therefore said to have a **rising rhythm.** In contrast, lines which end on unstressed syllables—"O wild West Wind, thou breath of Autumn's being"—are said to have a **falling rhythm.** It's a small thing, but it can create subtle variations in tone.

These, then, are the basic meters of accentual-syllabic verse and the most common devices used to lend them variety. You will no doubt find many other devices at work as you continue your study of poetry. And you will also find that in much modern verse, such as that of Whitman and Cummings, the rules of accentual-syllabic verse have been replaced

by the uncharted techniques and devices of **free verse.** Pauses and phras-
ings in free verse tend to be visual devices as well as rhythmic ones; line
lengths and stress placement vary at the poet's will. Sounds are still being
shaped with care, but the writers of free verse are being equally careful
to avoid setting up rules to which critics can then bind them. In free verse,
as in all verse, ultimately the total effect is the sole criterion.

Here are a modern translation of an Old English poem and a brief example of Hopkins' sprung rhythm. How would you compare and contrast
the two types of verse?

ANONYMOUS (Eighth Century)

The Seafarer (Modern version by Ezra Pound)

May I for my own self song's truth reckon,
Journey's jargon, how I in harsh days
Hardship endured oft.
Bitter breast-cares have I abided,
5 Known on my keel many a care's hold,
And dire sea-surge, and there I oft spent
Narrow nightwatch nigh the ship's head
While she tossed close to cliffs. Coldly afflicted,
My feet were by frost benumbed.
10 Chill its chains are; chafing signs
Hew my heart round and hunger begot.
Mere-weary mood. Lest man know not
That he on dry land loveliest liveth,
List how I, care-wretched, on ice-cold sea,
15 Weathered the winter, wretched outcast
Deprived of my kinsmen;
Hung with hard ice-flakes, where hail-scur flew,
There I heard naught save the harsh sea
And ice-cold wave, at whiles the swan cries,
20 Did for my games the gannet's clamor,
Sea-fowls' loudness was for me laughter,
The mews' singing all my mead-drink.
Storms, on the stone-cliffs beaten, fell on the stern
In icy feathers; full oft the eagle screamed
25 With spray on his pinion.
                          Not any protector
May make merry man faring needy.
This he little believes, who aye in winsome life
Abides 'mid burghers some heavy business,
Wealthy and wine-flushed, how I weary oft

30 Must bide above brine.
    Neareth nightshade, snoweth from north,
    Frost froze the land, hail fell on earth then,
    Corn of the coldest. Nathless there knocketh now
    The heart's thought that I on high streams
35 The salt-wavy tumult traverse alone.
    Moaneth alway my mind's lust
    That I fare forth, that I afar hence
    Seek out a foreign fastness.
    For this there's no mood-lofty man over earth's midst,
40 Not though he be given his good, but will have in his youth greed;
    Nor his deed to the daring, nor his king to the faithful
    But shall have his sorrow for sea-fare
    Whatever his lord will.
    He hath not heart for harping, nor in ring-having
45 Nor winsomeness to wife, nor world's delight
    Nor any whit else save the wave's slash,
    Yet longing comes upon him to fare forth on the water.
    Bosque taketh blossom, cometh beauty of berries,
    Fields to fairness, land fares brisker,
50 All this admonisheth man eager of mood,
    The heart turns to travel so that he then thinks
    On flood-ways to be far departing.
    Cuckoo calleth with gloomy crying,
    He singeth summerward, bodeth sorrow,
55 The bitter heart's blood. Burgher knows not—
    He the prosperous man—what some perform
    Where wandering them widest draweth.
    So that but now my heart burst from my breastlock,
    My mood 'mid the mere-flood,
60 Over the whale's acre, would wander wide.
    On earth's shelter cometh oft to me,
    Eager and ready, the crying lone-flyer,
    Whets for the whale-path the heart irresistibly,
    O'er tracks of ocean; seeing that anyhow
65 My lord deems to me this dead life
    On loan and on land, I believe not
    That any earth-weal eternal standeth
    Save there be somewhat calamitous
    That, ere a man's tide go, turn it to twain.
70 Disease or oldness or sword-hate
    Beats out the breath from doom-gripped body.
    And for this, every earl whatever, for those speaking after—
    Laud of the living, boasteth some last word,

That he will work ere he pass onward,
75 Frame on the fair earth 'gainst foes his malice,
Daring ado, . . .
So that all men shall honor him after
And his laud beyond them remain 'mid the English,
Aye, for ever a lasting life's-blast,
80 Delight 'mid the doughty.
                              Days little durable,
And all arrogance of earthen riches,
There come now no kings nor Caesars
Nor gold-giving lords like those gone.
Howe'er in mirth most magnified,
85 Whoe'er lived in life most lordliest,
Drear all this excellence, delights undurable!
Waneth the watch, but the world holdeth.
Tomb hideth trouble. The blade is layed low.
Earthly glory ageth and seareth.
90 No man at all going the earth's gait,
But age fares against him, his face paleth,
Grey-haired he groaneth, knows gone companions,
Lordly men, are to earth o'ergiven,
Nor may he then the flesh-cover, whose life ceaseth,
95 Nor eat the sweet nor feel the sorry,
Nor stir hand nor think in mid heart,
And though he strew the grave with gold,
His born brothers, their buried bodies
Be an unlikely treasure hoard.

QUESTIONS

Notice the movement of the speaker's mood and thought. How does he characterize himself? What response does he seek from his audience?

GERARD MANLEY HOPKINS (1844–1889)

Pied Beauty

Glory be to God for dappled things—
    For skies of couple-colour as a brindled cow;
        For rose-moles all in stipple upon trout that swim;
Fresh-firecoal chestnut-falls; finches wings;
5   Landscape plotted and pieced—fold, fallow, and plough;
        And áll trádes, their gear and tackle and trim.

All things, counter, original, spare, strange;
    Whatever is fickle, freckled (who knows how?)
        With swift, slow; sweet, sour; adazzle, dim;
10 He fathers-forth whose beauty is past change:
                Praise him.

QUESTIONS

1. How do the examples of dappled things given in lines 2–4 differ from those in lines 5 and 6? How do those in the first stanza (lines 2–6) differ from those in the second stanza (lines 7–9)? What has Hopkins expanded the notion of "dappled things" to include?
2. What holds all these examples and images together? Is there any unity to them; anything single or unchanging behind them? If so, what is it? How and where in the poem is it expressed? How important is it to the speaker's vision of "pied beauty"?

Now read these two examples of accentual-syllabic verse. Note the metrical techniques which make the first sound like a song. The second is like the voice of a man arguing with himself.

ALFRED, LORD TENNYSON (1809–1892)

The Splendor Falls on Castle Walls

The splendor falls on castle walls
    And snowy summits old in story:
The long light shakes across the lakes,
    And the wild cataract leaps in glory.
5 Blow, bugle, blow, set the wild echoes flying,
Blow, bugle; answer, echoes, dying, dying, dying.

O hark, O hear! how thin and clear,
    And thinner, clearer, farther going!
O sweet and far from cliff and scar
10   The horns of Elfland faintly blowing!
Blow, let us hear the purple glens replying:
Blow, bugle; answer, echoes, dying, dying, dying.

O love, they die in yon rich sky,
    They faint on hill or field or river;
15 Our echoes roll from soul to soul,
    And grow for ever and for ever.
Blow, bugle, blow, set the wild echoes flying,
And answer, echoes, answer, dying, dying, dying.

QUESTIONS

1. What is the meter of the main part of the poem? What is the meter of the refrain? What has been achieved by combining the two?
2. What does Tennyson mean by the phrase "our echoes" (line 15)? How do these echoes differ from the other "echoes" of which the poem speaks?
3. Fairyland and fairy things are usually pictured in literature as being immortal and unchanging, in contrast to the mortality of people and human things. Why does Tennyson reverse that contrast in this poem?
4. How do sound and imagery combine in this poem to reinforce the speaker's message?

GEORGE HERBERT (1593–1633)

The Collar[1]

<blockquote>

I struck the board[2] and cried, "No more!
    I will abroad!
What, shall I ever sigh and pine?
My lines and life are free: free as the road,
5 Loose as the wind, as large as store.
    Shall I be still in suit?[3]
Have I no harvest but a thorn
To let me blood, and not restore
What I have lost with cordial[4] fruit?
10   Sure there was wine
Before my sighs did dry it; there was corn
    Before my tears did drown it.
  Is the year only lost to me?
    Have I no bays[5] to crown it,
15 No flowers, no garlands gay? all blasted?
      All wasted?
Not so, my heart; but there is fruit,
    And thou hast hands.
Recover all thy sigh-blown age
20 On double pleasures. Leave thy cold dispute
Of what is fit and not. Forsake thy cage,
      Thy rope of sands,

</blockquote>

---

[1] The iron band encircling the neck of a prisoner or slave; also perhaps a pun on "choler" as "rebellious anger."
[2] Dining table.
[3] Always petitioning.
[4] Restorative.
[5] Laurels.

Which petty thoughts have made and made to thee
　　Good cable, to enforce and draw,
25　　　　And be thy law,
While thou didst wink and wouldst not see.
　　　　Away! take heed!
　　　　I will abroad!
Call in thy death's-head there! Tie up thy fears!
30　　　　He that forbears
　　To suit and serve his need,
　　　　Deserves his load."
But as I raved, and grew more fierce and wild
　　　　At every word,
35　Methought I heard one calling, "Child!"
　　And I replied, "My Lord."

QUESTIONS

Discuss how the movement of sound in "The Collar" helps create the sound of the speaker arguing with himself. (Note the addition of a second voice near the end of the poem. How do the speech of this second voice and the speaker's response to it bring the poem to its resolution?)

Look back at the poems you have read in this book. Select several which you like particularly well. Analyze their meters and the techniques by which they are varied. Then discuss how these metrical techniques enhance your enjoyment of the poems.

13 *Rhyme Schemes and Verse Forms*

Although rhyme is not found in all poetry written in English, it has been so important in the history of English and American verse that we often first divide poetry into two categories—rhymed and unrhymed—and then divide further from there. Accepting that categorization for the moment, we will note that unrhymed poems tend to fall into one of three major divisions: accentual verse, which has existed from Old English times and which we met in "The Seafarer" and "Pied Beauty"; blank verse (unrhymed iambic pentameter), a sixteenth-century invention of which Hamlet's soliloquies are classic examples; or free verse, sometimes called by the French name *vers libre,* a modern (and not always unrhymed) form which we met in the works of such diverse poets as Whitman, Cummings, Pound, and Levertov.

Rhymed Verse

Rhymed verse is harder to classify. There are so many ways of combining rhymed lines! Still, one can distinguish between those forms of rhymed verse which have a fixed total length (such as the **limerick,** with five lines; the **sonnet,** with fourteen; and the **villanelle,** with nineteen) and those which do not. Rhymed verse with no fixed length is usually composed of **stanzas.** Each stanza usually has a fixed length; but the number of stanzas, and hence the length of the poem as a whole, remain variable.

Underlying both types of rhymed verse, however, stand the basic combinations of rhyme. These embrace two-, three-, and four-line patterns, called the couplet, triplet, terza rima, and the quatrain. The **couplet** has two consecutive lines that rhyme:

> So long as men can breathe or eyes can see,
> So long lives this, and this gives life to thee.

The **tercet** or **triplet** has three lines that rhyme:

> He clasps the crag with crooked hands;
> Close to the sun in lonely lands,
> Ringed with the azure world, he stands.

The **terza rima** also has three lines, but only the first and last rhyme. When terza rima stanzas are linked together, the middle line of one stanza rhymes with the first and third lines of the stanza which follows.

> O wild West Wind, thou breath of Autumn's being,
> Thou, from whose unseen presence the leaves dead
> Are driven, like ghosts from an enchanter fleeing,
>
> Yellow, and black, and pale, and hectic red,
> Pestilence-stricken multitudes: O thou
> Who chariotest to their dark wintry bed

The **quatrain** has four lines joined by any one of the following rhyme schemes:

1. Second and fourth lines rhyming (*abcb*):

> When I was one-and-twenty
>   I heard a wise man say,
> "Give crowns and pounds and guineas
>   But not your heart away;

2. First and third, second and fourth lines rhyming (*abab*):

> She even thinks that up in heaven
> Her class lies late and snores,
> While poor black cherubs rise at seven
> To do celestial chores.

3. First and fourth, second and third lines rhyming (*abba*):

> Earth hath not anything to show more fair!
> Dull would he be of soul who could pass by
> A sight so touching in its majesty.
> The city now doth, like a garment, wear

4. First and second, third and fourth lines rhyming (*aabb*):

"O 'Melia, my dear, this does everything crown!
Who could have supposed I should meet you in Town?
And whence such fair garments, such prosperi-ty?"—
"O didn't you know I'd been ruined?" said she.

Any of these patterns can stand alone as a stanza. Or they may be combined or added to to produce more complicated stanzas, such as the **rime royal** in which Wyatt's "They Flee from Me" is written. Turn back to that poem (p. 815) now. What is its rhyme scheme?

Odes, Sonnets, Limericks, and Villanelles

Let us now look at some rhymed forms of fixed length: the villanelle, the limerick, the sonnet, and the ode. Of these, the **ode** is unique in being a form in which both the length of individual lines and stanzas and the rhyme scheme are left to the poet's discretion. In Keats' "Ode On a Grecian Urn" and "Ode to a Nightingale" and in Shelley's "Ode to the West Wind," we saw three patterns. And in Wordsworth's "Ode: Intimations of Immortality from Recollections of Early Childhood," printed at the end of this chapter, we will see another. (Keats' and Shelley's odes are sometimes called *Horatian odes,* because the form of their stanzas is constant. Wordsworth's is an *irregular ode,* because the stanzas themselves vary. All, however, share the elevated tone which is the chief characteristic of the ode in English poetry.)

The limerick and villanelle, in contrast, are narrowly defined. A **limerick** must have five lines. The first, second, and fifth are rhyming trimeter lines; the third and fourth are rhyming dimeter lines. Limericks are almost always humorous, often obscene, and so seldom considered as serious poetry that their writers sometimes strive for ear-torturing badness in rhyme and rhythm.

The **villanelle** is a serious form, but also a tightly controlled one. Entire lines, as well as rhymes, are repeated within this form to make up its prescribed pattern. Here is one of the finest twentieth-century villanelles. Analyze its form and discuss what the poet has done with it.

DYLAN THOMAS (1914–1953)

Do Not Go Gentle into That Good Night

Do not go gentle into that good night,
Old age should burn and rave at close of day;
Rage, rage against the dying of the light.

Though wise men at their end know dark is right,
5 Because their words had forked no lightning they
Do not go gentle into that good night.

Good men, the last wave by, crying how bright
Their frail deeds might have danced in a green bay,
Rage, rage against the dying of the light.

10 Wild men who caught and sang the sun in flight,
And learn, too late, they grieved it on its way,
Do not go gentle into that good night.

Grave men, near death, who see with blinding sight
Blind eyes could blaze like meteors and be gay,
15 Rage, rage against the dying of the light.

And you, my father, there on the sad height,
Curse, bless, me now with your fierce tears, I pray.
Do not go gentle into that good night.
Rage, rage against the dying of the light.

The most popular of the defined forms, however, is the **sonnet.** Sonnets are always fourteen lines long. Traditionally, they are divided into two main forms. The **Petrarchan sonnet** consists of an octet, rhymed *abba abba,* and a sestet, rhymed either *cdcdcd* or *cdecde;* and the **Shakespearean sonnet,** with three quatrains, usually rhymes *abab cdcd efef,* and a couplet at the end, *gg.*

Of these two sonnet forms, the Shakespearean usually seems the more emphatic. Because no sound needs to be used more than twice, it is also slightly easier to write. It was the favored form during the Renaissance. The Petrarchan sonnet, on the other hand, tends to have a somewhat smoother flow and often seems more graceful. It was therefore preferred by the Romantic poets of the nineteenth century.

The sonnet came into English as a love poem: we have read love sonnets by Shakespeare, Sidney, and Spenser. But it has proved capable of handling almost any subject and of expressing many moods and tones. Look back, for example, at "Ozymandias" (p. 830) and "Composed upon Westminister Bridge" (p. 842). And look, too, at the following examples of what can be done with the sonnet form.

WILLIAM SHAKESPEARE (1564–1616)

Sonnet 116

Let me not to the marriage of true minds
Admit impediments. Love is not love
Which alters when it alteration finds,

Or bends with the remover to remove.
5 O no! it is an ever-fixèd mark
That looks on tempests and is never shaken;
It is the star to every wand'ring bark,
Whose worth's unknown, although his height be taken.
Love's not Time's fool, though rosy lips and cheeks
10 Within his bending sickle's compass come.
Love alters not with his brief hours and weeks,
But bears it out even to the edge of doom.
    If this be error, and upon me proved,
    I never writ, nor no man ever loved.

JOHN DONNE (1572–1631)

Sonnet 10

Death, be not proud, though some have callèd thee
Mighty and dreadful, for thou art not so;
For those whom thou think'st thou dost overthrow
Die not, poor Death, nor yet canst thou kill me.
5 From rest and sleep, which but thy pictures be,
Much pleasure; then from thee much more must flow;
And soonest our best men with thee do go,
Rest of their bones and souls' delivery.
Thou'rt slave to fate, chance, kings, and desperate men,
10 And dost with poison, war, and sickness dwell;
And poppy or charms can make us sleep as well
And better than thy stroke. Why swell'st thou then?
One short sleep past, we wake eternally,
And Death shall be no more: Death, thou shalt die.

JOHN MILTON (1608–1674)

On His Blindness

When I consider how my light is spent,
Ere half my days, in this dark world and wide,
And that one talent which is death to hide
Lodged with me useless, though my soul more bent
5 To serve therewith my Maker, and present
My true account, lest he returning chide,
"Doth God exact day labor, light denied?"
I fondly ask; but Patience, to prevent
That murmur, soon replies: "God doth not need

10 Either man's work or his own gifts; who best
   Bear his mild yoke, they serve him best. His state
   Is kingly: thousands at his bidding speed
   And post o'er land and ocean without rest.
   They also serve who only stand and wait."

GERARD MANLEY HOPKINS (1844–1899)

(Carrion Comfort[1])

Not, I'll not, carrion comfort, Despair, not feast on thee;
Not untwist—slack they may be—these last strands of man
In me ór, most weary, cry *I can no more.* I can;
Can something, hope, wish day come, not choose not to be.

5 But ah, but O thou terrible, why wouldst thou rude on me
   Thy wring-world right foot rock? lay a lionlimb against me? scan
   With darksome devouring eyes my bruisèd bones? and fan,
   O in turns of tempest, me heaped there; me frantic to avoid thee and
      flee?

Why? That my chaff might fly; my grain lie, sheer and clear.
10 Nay in all that toil, that coil, since (seems) I kissed the rod,
   Hand rather, my heart lo! lapped strength, stole joy, would laugh,
      chéer.
   Cheer whom though? the hero whose heaven-handling flung me, fóot
      tród
   Me? or me that fought him? O which one? is it each one? That
      night, that year
   Of now done darkness I wretch lay wrestling with (my God!) my
      God.

LOUIS MacNEICE (1907–1963)

Sunday Morning

Down the road someone is practicing scales,
The notes like little fishes vanish with a wink of tails,
Man's heart expands to tinker with his car
For this is Sunday morning, Fate's great bazaar;
5 Regard these means as ends, concentrate on this Now,

---

[1] The title was added by Robert Bridges.

And you may grow to music or drive beyond Hindhead anyhow,
Take corners on two wheels until you go so fast
That you can clutch a fringe or two of the windy past,
That you can abstract this day and make it to the week of time
10 A small eternity, a sonnet self-contained in rhyme.
But listen, up the road, something gulps, the church spire
Opens its eight bells out, skulls' mouths which will not tire
To tell how there is no music or movement which secures
Escape from the weekday time. Which deadens and endures.

ROBERT FROST (1874–1963)

Design

I found a dimpled spider, fat and white,
On a white heal-all, holding up a moth
Like a white piece of rigid satin cloth—
Assorted characters of death and blight
5 Mixed ready to begin the morning right,
Like the ingredients of a witches' broth—
A snow-drop spider, a flower like a froth,
And dead wings carried like a paper kite.

What had that flower to do with being white,
10 The wayside blue and innocent heal-all?
What brought the kindred spider to that height,
Then steered the white moth thither in the night?
What but design of darkness to appall?—
If design govern in a thing so small.

The following ode by the early Romantic poet, William Wordsworth, makes skillful use of rhyme and rhythm both. Yet, for all its careful contrivance, it maintains a remarkable freshness of tone, in keeping with its subject of early joys and maturer delights. In form, the poem is an **irregular ode.** Therefore, its stanzas vary among themselves, changing shape to follow the motions of the poet's mind. The basic meter remains iambic throughout, but line lengths and rhyme schemes shift constantly. The result is an unusual blend of patterning and fluidity that sometimes mutes its tone to a thoughtful expression of philosophy, sometimes rises to a hymn of joyful praise.

The ode deals with the relations between the human soul, nature, and immortality. In it, Wordsworth suggests not only that we know immortality after death, but that we know it before birth as well: "trailing clouds of glory do we come, / From God, who is our home." The ode thus celebrates the heaven-like joy the young child sees in the natural world; and it laments the dulling of that joy that occurs when the child, responding to the novelty of his mundane existence, turns his mind more fully upon earthly things. Yet the final tone is not sorrow, but a greater joy, as Wordsworth passes beyond mourning this early loss into celebrating the fully human joys and loves which are the gift of the mature soul.

As you read the ode, pay careful attention to the way Wordsworth develops this train of thought, and notice how the sound and shape of the stanzas convey the changing emotions the speaker feels.

WILLIAM WORDSWORTH (1770–1850)

Ode

Intimations of Immortality from Recollections
of Early Childhood

The Child is father of the Man;
And I could wish my days to be
Bound each to each by natural piety.

I

There was a time when meadow, grove, and stream,
The earth, and every common sight,
    To me did seem
    Apparelled in celestial light,
5 The glory and the freshness of a dream.
It is not now as it hath been of yore;—
    Turn wheresoe'er I may,
      By night or day,
The things which I have seen I now can see no more.

2

10   The Rainbow comes and goes,
    And lovely is the Rose,
    The Moon doth with delight
Look round her when the heavens are bare;
    Waters on a starry night
15   Are beautiful and fair;
    The sunshine is a glorious birth;
    But yet I know, where'er I go,
That there hath past away a glory from the earth.

3

Now, while the birds thus sing a joyous song,
20   And while the young lambs bound
        As to the tabor's sound,
To me alone there came a thought of grief:
A timely utterance gave that thought relief,
        And I again am strong:
25 The cataracts blow their trumpets from the steep;
No more shall grief of mine the season wrong;
I hear the Echoes through the mountains throng,
The Winds come to me from the fields of sleep,
        And all the earth is gay;
30   Land and sea
        Give themselves up to jollity,
        And with the heart of May
        Doth every Beast keep holiday;—
        Thou Child of Joy,
35 Shout round me, let me hear thy shouts, thou happy Shepherd-boy!

4

Ye blessèd Creatures, I have heard the call
        Ye to each other make; I see
The heavens laugh with you in your jubilee;
        My heart is at your festival,
40   My head hath its coronal,
The fulness of your bliss, I feel—I feel it all.
            Oh evil day! if I were sullen
            While Earth herself is adorning,
                This sweet May-morning,
45   And the Children are culling
                On every side,
        In a thousand valleys far and wide,
        Fresh flowers; while the sun shines warm,
And the Babe leaps up on his Mother's arm:—
50   I hear, I hear, with joy I hear!
        —But there's a Tree, of many, one,
A single Field which I have looked upon,
Both of them speak of something that is gone:
        The Pansy at my feet
55   Doth the same tale repeat:
Whither is fled the visionary gleam?
Where is it now, the glory and the dream?

5

Our birth is but a sleep and a forgetting:
The Soul that rises with us, our life's Star,
60   Hath had elsewhere its setting,
          And cometh from afar:
       Not in entire forgetfulness,
       And not in utter nakedness,
But trailing clouds of glory do we come
65   From God, who is our home:
Heaven lies about us in our infancy!
Shares of the prison-house begin to close
          Upon the growing Boy,
             But He
70 Beholds the light, and whence it flows,
          He sees it in his joy;
The Youth, who daily farther from the east
          Must travel, still is Nature's Priest,
          And by the vision splendid
75   Is on his way attended;
At length the Man perceives it die away,
And fade into the light of common day.

6

Earth fills her lap with pleasures of her own;
Yearnings she hath in her own natural kind,
80 And, even with something of a Mother's mind,
          And no unworthy aim,
       The homely Nurse doth all she can
To make her Foster-child, her Inmate Man,
          Forget the glories he hath known,
85 And that imperial palace whence he came.

7

Behold the Child among his new-born blisses,
A six years' Darling of a pigmy size!
See, where 'mid work of his own hand he lies,
Fretted by sallies of his mother's kisses,
90 With light upon him from his father's eyes!
See, at his feet, some little plan or chart,
Some fragment from his dream of human life,
Shaped by himself with newly-learnèd art;

A wedding or a festival,
95   A mourning or a funeral;
            And this hath now his heart,
            And unto this he frames his song:
                Then will he fit his tongue
        To dialogues of business, love, or strife;
100   But it will not be long
            Ere this be thrown aside,
            And with new joy and pride
        The little Actor cons another part;
        Filling from time to time his "humorous stage"
105   With all the Persons, down to palsied Age,
        That Life brings with her in her equipage;
                As if his whole vocation
                Were endless imitation.

                    8

        Thou, whose exterior semblance doth belie
110   Thy Soul's immensity;
        Thou best Philosopher, who yet dost keep
        Thy heritage, thou Eye among the blind,
        That, deaf and silent, read'st the eternal deep,
        Haunted for ever by the eternal mind,—
115   Mighty Prophet! Seer blest!
                On whom those truths do rest,
        Which we are toiling all our lives to find,
        In darkness lost, the darkness of the grave;
        Thou, over whom thy Immortality
120   Broods like the Day, a Master o'er a Slave,
        A Presence which is not to be put by;
        Thou little Child, yet glorious in the might
        Of heaven-born freedom on thy being's height,
        Why with such earnest pains dost thou provoke
125   The years to bring the inevitable yoke,
        Thus blindly with thy blessedness at strife?
        Full soon thy Soul shall have her earthly freight,
        And custom lie upon thee with a weight,
        Heavy as frost, and deep almost as life!

                    9

130   O joy! that in our embers
            Is something that doth live,
            That nature yet remembers

What was so fugitive!
The thought of our past years in me doth breed
135 Perpetual benediction: not indeed
For that which is most worthy to be blest;
Delight and liberty, the simple creed
Of Childhood, whether busy or at rest,
With new-fledged hope still fluttering in his breast:—
140   Not for these I raise
      The song of thanks and praise;
   But for those obstinate questionings
   Of sense and outward things,
   Falling from us, vanishings;
145   Blank misgivings of a Creature
Moving about in worlds not realised,
High instincts before which our mortal Nature
Did tremble like a guilty Thing surprised:
    But for those first affections,
150   Those shadowy recollections,
    Which, be they what they may,
Are yet the fountain-light of all our day,
Are yet a master-light of all our seeing;
   Uphold us, cherish, and have power to make
155 Our noisy years seem moments in the being
Of the eternal Silence: truths that wake,
     To perish never:
Which neither listlessness, nor mad endeavor,
    Nor Man nor Boy,
160 Nor all that is at enmity with joy,
Can utterly abolish or destroy!
   Hence in a season of calm weather
    Though inland far we be,
Our Souls have sight of that immortal sea
165   Which brought us hither,
    Can in a moment travel thither,
And see the Children sport upon the shore,
And hear the mighty waters rolling evermore.

        10

   Then sing, ye Birds, sing, sing a joyous song!
170   And let the young Lambs bound
     As to the tabor's sound!
We in thought will join your throng,
   Ye that pipe and ye that play,
   Ye that through your hearts to-day

175 Feel the gladness of the May!
What though the radiance which was once so bright
Be now for ever taken from my sight,
 Though nothing can bring back the hour
Of splendor in the grass, of glory in the flower;
180 We will grieve not, rather find
  Strength in what remains behind;
  In the primal sympathy
  Which having been must ever be;
  In the soothing thoughts that spring
185 Out of human suffering;
  In the faith that looks through death,
In years that bring the philosophic mind.

   I I

And O, ye Fountains, Meadows, Hills, and Groves,
Forebode not any severing of our loves!
190 Yet in my heart of hearts I feel your might;
I only have relinquished one delight
To live beneath your more habitual sway.
I love the Brooks which down their channels fret,
Even more than when I tripped lightly as they;
195 The innocent brightness of a new-born Day
   Is lovely yet;
The Clouds that gather round the setting sun
Do take a sober coloring from an eye
That hath kept watch o'er man's mortality;
200 Another race hath been, and other palms are won.
Thanks to the human heart by which we live,
Thanks to its tenderness, its joys, and fears,
To me the meanest flower that blows can give
Thoughts that do often lie too deep for tears.

AN ANTHOLOGY OF POEMS

COUNTRY AND CITY SCENES

CHRISTOPHER MARLOWE (1564–1593)

The Passionate Shepherd to His Love

Come live with me, and be my love,
And we will all the pleasures prove
That hills and valleys, dales and fields,
And all the craggy mountains yields.

5 And we will sit upon the rocks,
Seeing the shepherds feed their flocks,
By shallow rivers, to whose falls
Melodious birds sings madrigals.

And I will make thee beds of roses
10 And a thousand fragrant posies.
A cap of flowers, and a kirtle
Embroidered all with leaves of myrtle;

A gown made of the finest wool,
Which from our pretty lambs we pull,
15 Fair linèd slippers, for the cold,
With buckles of the purest gold;

A belt of straw and ivy-buds
With coral clasps and amber studs.
And if these pleasures may thee move,
20 Come live with me, and be my love.

The shepherds' swains shall dance and sing
For thy delight each May morning.
If these delights thy mind may move,
Then live with me, and be my love.

SIR WALTER RALEGH (1552?–1618)

The Nymph's Reply to the Shepherd

If all the world and love were young,
And truth in every shepherd's tongue,
These pretty pleasures might me move
To live with thee and be thy love.

5 Time drives the flocks from field to fold
When rivers rage and rocks grow cold,
And Philomel becometh dumb;
The rest complains of cares to come.

The flowers do fade, and wanton fields
10 To wayward winter reckoning yields;
A honey tongue, a heart of gall,
Is fancy's spring, but sorrow's fall.

Thy gowns, thy shoes, thy beds of roses,
Thy cap, thy kirtle, and thy posies
15 Soon break, soon wither, soon forgotten—
In folly ripe, in reason rotten.

Thy belt of straw and ivy buds,
Thy coral clasps and amber studs,
All these in me no means can move
20 To come to thee and be thy love.

But could youth last and love still breed,
Had joys no date nor age no need,
Then these delights my mind might move
To live with thee and be thy love.

ROBERT BROWNING (1812–1889)

Home-Thoughts, from Abroad

I

Oh, to be in England
Now that April's there,
And whoever wakes in England
Sees, some morning, unaware,

5 That the lowest boughs and the brushwood sheaf
   Round the elm-tree bole are in tiny leaf,
   While the chaffinch sings on the orchard bough
   In England—now!

2

And after April, when May follows,
10 And the whitethroat builds, and all the swallows!
   Hark, where my blossomed pear-tree in the hedge
   Leans to the field and scatters on the clover
   Blossoms and dewdrops—at the bent spray's edge—
   That's the wise thrush; he sings each song twice over,
15 Lest you should think he never could recapture
   The first fine careless rapture!
   And though the fields look rough with hoary dew,
   All will be gay when noontide wakes anew
   The buttercups, the little children's dower
20 —Far brighter than this gaudy melon-flower!

WILLIAM BLAKE (1757–1827)

London

I wander thro' each charter'd street,
Near where the charter'd Thames does flow,
And mark in every face I meet
Marks of weakness, marks of woe.

5 In every cry of every Man,
   In every Infant's cry of fear,
   In every voice, in every ban,
   The mind-forg'd manacles I hear.

How the Chimney-sweeper's cry
10 Every blackning Church appalls;
   And the hapless Soldier's sigh
   Runs in blood down Palace walls.

But most thro' midnight streets I hear
How the youthful Harlot's curse
15 Blasts the new-born Infant's tear,
   And blights with plagues the Marriage hearse.

---

¹ Complain.

T. S. ELIOT (1888–1965)

The Love Song of J. Alfred Prufrock

S'io credesse che mia risposta fosse
A persona che mai tornasse al mondo,
Questa fiamma staria senza piu scosse.
Ma perciocche giammai di questo fondo
Non torno vivo alcun, s'i'odo il vero,
Senza tema d'infamia ti rispondo.[1]

Let us go then, you and I,
When the evening is spread out against the sky
Like a patient etherized upon a table;
Let us go, through certain half-deserted streets,
5 The muttering retreats
Of restless nights in one-night cheap hotels
And sawdust restaurants with oyster-shells:
Streets that follow like a tedious argument
Of insidious intent
10 To lead you to an overwhelming question . . .

Oh, do not ask, "What is it?"
Let us go and make our visit.

In the room the women come and go
Talking of Michelangelo.

15 The yellow fog that rubs its back upon the window-panes
The yellow smoke that rubs its muzzle on the window-panes
Licked its tongue into the corners of the evening,
Lingered upon the pools that stand in drains,
Let fall upon its back the soot that falls from chimneys,
20 Slipped by the terrace, made a sudden leap,
And seeing that it was a soft October night,
Curled once about the house, and fell asleep.

And indeed there will be time
For the yellow smoke that slides along the street,
25 Rubbing its back upon the window-panes;

---

[1] "If I thought that my response were given to one who would ever return to the world, this flame would move no more. But since never from this depth has man returned alive, if what I hear is true, without fear of infamy I answer thee." In Dante's *Inferno* these words are addressed to the poet by the spirit of Guido da Montefeltro.

There will be time, there will be time
To prepare a face to meet the faces that you meet;
There will be time to murder and create,
And time for all the works and days of hands
30 That lift and drop a question on your plate;
Time for you and time for me,
And time yet for a hundred indecisions,
And for a hundred visions and revisions,
Before the taking of a toast and tea.

35 In the room the women come and go
Talking of Michelangelo.

And indeed there will be time
To wonder, "Do I dare?" and, "Do I dare?"
Time to turn back and descend the stair,
40 With a bald spot in the middle of my hair—
[They will say: "How his hair is growing thin!"]
My morning coat, my collar mounting firmly to the chin,
My necktie rich and modest, but asserted by a simple pin—
[They will say: "But how his arms and legs are thin!"]
45 Do I dare
Disturb the universe?
In a minute there is time
For decisions and revisions which a minute will reverse.

For I have known them all already, known them all:
50 Have known the evenings, mornings, afternoons,
I have measured out my life with coffee spoons;
I know the voices dying with a dying fall
Beneath the music from a farther room.
    So how should I presume?

55 And I have known the eyes already, known them all—
The eyes that fix you in a formulated phrase,
And when I am formulated, sprawling on a pin,
When I am pinned and wriggling on the wall,
Then how should I begin
60 To spit out all the butt-ends of my days and ways?
    And how should I presume?

And I have known the arms already, known them all—
Arms that are braceleted and white and bare
[But in the lamplight, downed with light brown hair!]

65 Is it perfume from a dress
   That makes me so digress?
   Arms that lie along a table, or wrap about a shawl.
       And should I then presume?
       And how should I begin?

                    . . . . .

70 Shall I say, I have gone at dusk through narrow streets
   And watched the smoke that rises from the pipes
   Of lonely men in shirt-sleeves, leaning out of windows? . . .

   I should have been a pair of ragged claws
   Scuttling across the floors of silent seas.

                    . . . . .

75 And the afternoon, the evening, sleeps so peacefully!
   Smoothed by long fingers,
   Asleep . . . tired . . . or it malingers,
   Stretched on the floor, here beside you and me.
   Should I, after tea and cakes and ices,
80 Have the strength to force the moment to its crisis?
   But though I have wept and fasted, wept and prayed,
   Though I have seen my head [grown slightly bald] brought in upon a
       platter,
   I am no prophet—and here's no great matter;
   I have seen the moment of my greatness flicker,
85 And I have seen the eternal Footman hold my coat, and snicker,
   And in short, I was afraid.

   And would it have been worth it, after all,
   After the cups, the marmalade, the tea,
   Among the porcelain, among some talk of you and me,
90 Would it have been worth while,
   To have bitten off the matter with a smile,
   To have squeezed the universe into a ball
   To roll it toward some overwhelming question,

   To say: "I am Lazarus, come from the dead,
95 Come back to tell you all, I shall tell you all"—
   If one, settling a pillow by her head,
       Should say: "That is not what I meant at all.
       That is not it, at all."

   And would it have been worth it, after all,
100 Would it have been worth while,
   After the sunsets and the dooryards and the sprinkled streets,
   After the novels, after the teacups, after the skirts that trail along the
       floor—

And this, and so much more?—
It is impossible to say just what I mean!
105 But as if a magic lantern threw the nerves in patterns on a screen:
Would it have been worth while
If one, settling a pillow or throwing off a shawl,
And turning toward the window, should say:
    "That is not it at all,
110   That is not what I meant, at all."

                    .   .   .   .   .

No! I am not Prince Hamlet, nor was meant to be;
Am an attendant lord, one that will do
To swell a progress, start a scene or two,
Advise the prince; no doubt, an easy tool,
115 Deferential, glad to be of use,
    Politic, cautious, and meticulous;
    Full of high sentence, but a bit obtuse;
    At times, indeed, almost ridiculous—
    Almost, at times, the Fool.

120 I grow old . . . I grow old . . .
I shall wear the bottoms of my trousers rolled.

Shall I part my hair behind? Do I dare to eat a peach?
I shall wear white flannel trousers, and walk upon the beach.
I have heard the mermaids singing, each to each.

125 I do not think that they will sing to me.

I have seen them riding seaward on the waves
Combing the white hair of the waves blown back
When the wind blows the water white and black.

We have lingered in the chambers of the sea
130 By sea-girls wreathed with seaweed red and brown
Till human voices wake us, and we drown.

RICHARD WILBUR (1921–   )

Place Pigalle

Now homing tradesmen scatter through the streets
Toward suppers, thinking on improved conditions,
While evening, with a million simple fissions,
Takes up its warehouse watches, storefront beats,
5 By nursery windows its assigned positions.

Now at the corners of the Place Pigalle
Bright bars explode against the dark's embraces;
The soldiers come, the boys with ancient faces.
Seeking their ancient friends, who stroll and loll
10 Amid the glares and glass: electric graces.

The puppies are asleep, and snore the hounds;
But here wry hares, the soldier and the whore,
Mark off their refuge with a gaudy door,
Brazen at bay, and boldly out of bounds:
15 The puppies dream, the hounds superbly snore.

Ionized innocence: this pair reclines,
She on the table, he in a tilting chair,
With Arden ease; her eyes as pale as air
Travel his priestgoat face; his hand's thick tines
20 Touch the gold whorls of her Corinthian hair.

"Girl, if I love thee not, then let me die;
Do I not scorn to change my state with kings?
Your muchtouched flesh, incalculable, which wrings
Me so, now shall I gently seize in my
25 Desperate soldier's hands which kill all things."

ROBERT LOWELL (1917–1977)

For the Union Dead

"Relinquunt Omnia Servare Rem Publican."[1]

The old South Boston Aquarium stands
in a Sahara of snow now. Its broken windows are boarded.
The bronze weathervane cod has lost half its scales.
The airy tanks are dry.

5 Once my nose crawled like a snail on the glass;
my hand tingled
to burst the bubbles
drifting from the noses of the cowed, compliant fish.

My hand draws back. I often sigh still
10 for the dark downward and vegetating kingdom
of the fish and reptile. One morning last March,
I pressed against the new barbed and galvanized

---

[1] "They gave up all to serve the republic."

fence on the Boston Common. Behind their cage,
yellow dinosaur steamshovels were grunting
15 as they cropped up tons of mush and grass
to gouge their underworld garage.

Parking spaces luxuriate like civic
sandpiles in the heart of Boston.
A girdle of orange, Puritan-pumpkin colored girders
20 braces the tingling Statehouse,

shaking over the excavations, as it faces Colonel Shaw
and his bell-cheeked Negro infantry
on St. Gaudens' shaking Civil War relief,
propped by a plank splint against the garage's earthquake.

25 Two months after marching through Boston,
half the regiment was dead;
at the dedication,
William James could almost hear the bronze Negroes breathe.

Their monument sticks like a fishbone
30 in the city's throat.
Its Colonel is as lean
as a compass-needle.

He has an angry wrenlike vigilance,
a greyhound's gentle tautness;
35 he seems to wince at pleasure,
and suffocate for privacy.

He is out of bounds now. He rejoices in man's lovely,
peculiar power to choose life and die—
when he leads his black soldiers to death,
40 he cannot bend his back.

On a thousand small town New England greens,
the old white churches hold their air
of sparse, sincere rebellion; frayed flags
quilt the graveyards of the Grand Army of the Republic.

45 The stone statues of the abstract Union Soldier
grow slimmer and younger each year—
wasp-waisted, they doze over muskets
and muse through their sideburns . . .

Shaw's father wanted no monument
50 except the ditch,
where his son's body was thrown
and lost with his "niggers."

The ditch is nearer.
There are no statues for the last war here;
55 on Boylston Street, a commercial photograph
shows Hiroshima boiling

over a Mosler Safe, the "Rock of Ages"
that survived the blast. Space is nearer.
When I crouch to my television set,
60 the drained faces of Negro school-children rise like balloons.

Colonel Shaw
is riding on his bubble,
he waits
for the blessèd break.

65 The Aquarium is gone. Everywhere,
giant finned cars nose forward like fish;
a savage servility
slides by on grease.

LAWRENCE FERLINGHETTI (1919–   )

The pennycandystore beyond the El

The pennycandystore beyond the El
is where I first
                        fell in love
                                    with unreality
5 Jellybeans glowed in the semi-gloom
of that september afternoon
A cat upon the counter moved among
                                    the licorice sticks
                        and tootsie rolls
10   and Oh Boy Gum

Outside the leaves were falling as they died

A wind had blown away the sun

A girl ran in
Her hair was rainy
15 Her breasts were breathless in the little room

Outside the leaves were falling
                    and they cried
                              Too soon! too soon!

ALLEN GINSBERG (1926–   )

A Supermarket in California

What thoughts I have of you tonight, Walt Whitman, for I
walked down the sidestreets under the trees with a headache self-
conscious looking at the full moon.

In my hungry fatigue, and shopping for images, I went into the
neon fruit supermarket, dreaming of your enumerations!

What peaches and what penumbras! Whole families shopping at
night! Aisles full of husbands! Wives in the avocados, babies in the
tomatoes!—and you, Garcia Lorca,[1] what were you doing down by
the watermelons?

I saw you, Walt Whitman, childless, lonely old grubber, poking
among the meats in the refrigerator and eyeing the grocery boys.

5   I heard you asking questions of each: Who killed the pork chops?
What price bananas? Are you my Angel?

I wandered in and out of the brilliant stacks of cans following
you, and followed in my imagination by the store detective.

We strode down the open corridors together in our solitary fancy
tasting artichokes, possessing every frozen delicacy, and never passing
the cashier.

Where are we going, Walt Whitman? The doors close in an
hour. Which way does your beard point tonight?

(I touch your book and dream of our odyssey in the supermarket
and feel absurd.)

10   Will we walk all night through solitary streets? The trees add
shade to shade, lights out in the houses, we'll both be lonely.

Will we stroll dreaming of the lost America of love past blue
automobiles in driveways, home to our silent cottage?

---

[1] Federigo García Lorca (1899–1936), Spanish poet and playwright. He was murdered at the start of the Spanish Civil War; his works were suppressed by the
Franco government.

Ah, dear father, graybeard, lonely old courage-teacher, what
America did you have when Charon quit poling his ferry and you
got out on a smoking bank and stood watching the boat disappear
on the black waters of Lethe? [2]

AMIRI BARAKA (LeROI JONES) (1934–   )

W.W.

Back home the black women are all beautiful,
and the white ones fall back, cutoff from 1000
years stacked booty, and Charles of the Ritz
where jooshladies turn into billy burke in blueglass
5 kicks. With wings, and jingly bew-teeful things.
The black women in Newark are fine. Even with all that grease
in their heads. I mean even the ones where the wigs
slide around, and they coming at you 75 degrees off course.
I could talk to them. Bring them around. To something.
10 Some kind of quick course, on the sidewalk, like Hey baby
why don't you take that thing off yo' haid. You look like
Miss Muffet in a runaway ugly machine. I mean. Like that.

---

[2] Charon, in Greek myth, ferried the shades of the dead to Hades across Lethe,
River of Forgetfulness.

PORTRAITS

WILLIAM COWPER (1731–1800)

The Castaway

Obscurest night involved the sky,
 Th' Atlantic billows roared,
When such a destined wretch as I,
 Washed headlong from on board,
5 Of friends, of hope, of all bereft,
His floating home forever left.

No braver chief could Albion boast
 Then he with whom he went,
Nor ever ship left Albion's coast,
10 With warmer wishes sent.
He loved them both, but both in vain,
Nor him beheld, nor her again.

Not long beneath the whelming brine,
 Expert to swim, he lay;
15 Nor soon he felt his strength decline,
 Or courage die away;
But waged with death a lasting strife,
Supported by despair of life.

He shouted; nor his friends had failed
20 To check the vessel's course,
But so the furious blast prevailed,
 That, pitiless perforce,
They left their outcast mate behind,
And scudded still before the wind.

25 Some succor yet they could afford;
 And, such as storms allow,

The cask, the coop, the floated cord,
    Delayed not to bestow.
But he (they knew) nor ship, nor shore,
30 Whate're they gave, should visit more.

Nor, cruel as it seemed, could he
    Their haste himself condemn,
Aware that flight, in such a sea,
    Alone could rescue them;
35 Yet bitter felt it still to die
Deserted, and his friends so nigh.

He long survives, who lives an hour
    In ocean, self-upheld;
And so long he, with unspent power,
40   His destiny repelled;
And ever, as the minutes flew,
Entreated help, or cried, "Adieu!"

At length, his transient respite past,
    His comrades, who before
45 Had heard his voice in every blast,
    Could catch the sound no more.
For then, by toil subdued, he drank
The stifling wave, and then he sank.

No poet wept him: but the page
50   Of narrative sincere,
That tells his name, his worth, his age,
    Is wet with Anson's tear.
And tears by bards or heroes shed
Alike immortalize the dead.

55 I therefore purpose not, or dream,
    Descanting on his fate,
To give the melancholy theme
    A more enduring date:
But misery still delights to trace
60 Its semblance in another's case.

No voice divine the storm allayed,
    No light propitious shone;
When, snatched from all effectual aid,
    We perished, each alone:
65 But I beneath a rougher sea,
And whelmed in deeper gulfs than he.

ALFRED, LORD TENNYSON (1809–1892)

Ulysses

It little profits than an idle king,
By this still hearth, among these barren crags,
Matched with an aged wife, I mete and dole
Unequal laws unto a savage race,
5 That hoard, and sleep, and feed, and know not me.
I cannot rest from travel; I will drink
Life to the lees. All times I have enjoyed
Greatly, have suffered greatly, both with those
That loved me, and alone; on shore, and when
10 Through scudding drifts the rainy Hyades[1]
Vexed the dim sea: I am become a name;
For always roaming with a hungry heart
Much have I seen and known—cities of men
And manners, climates, councils, governments,
15 Myself not least, but honored of them all;
And drunk delight of battle with my peers,
Far on the ringing plains of windy Troy.
I am a part of all that I have met;
Yet all experience is an arch wherethrough
20 Gleams that untraveled world whose margin fades
For ever and for ever when I move.
How dull it is to pause, to make an end,
To rust unburnished, not to shine in use!
As though to breathe were life! Life piled on life
25 Were all too little, and of one to me
Little remains; but every hour is saved
From that eternal silence, something more,
A bringer of new things; and vile it were
For some three suns to store and hoard myself,
30 And this gray spirit yearning in desire
To follow knowledge like a sinking star,
Beyond the utmost bound of human thought.

    This is my son, mine own Telemachus,
To whom I leave the scepter and the isle—
35 Well-loved of me, discerning to fulfil
This labor, by slow prudence to make mild
A rugged people, and through soft degrees

---

[1] A group of stars in the constellation Taurus, whose rise with the sun heralded the spring rains.

Subdue them to the useful and the good.
Most blameless is he, centered in the sphere
40 Of common duties, decent not to fail
In offices of tenderness, and pay
Meet adoration to my household gods,
When I am gone. He works his work, I mine.

There lies the port; the vessel puffs her sail;
45 There gloom the dark, broad seas. My mariners,
Souls that have toiled, and wrought, and thought with me—
That ever with a frolic welcome took
The thunder and the sunshine, and opposed
Free hearts, free foreheads—you and I are old;
50 Old age hath yet his honor and his toil.
Death closes all; but something ere the end,
Some work of noble note, may yet be done,
Not unbecoming men that strove with Gods.
The lights begin to twinkle from the rocks:
55 The long day wanes: the slow moon climbs: the deep
Moans round with many voices. Come, my friends,
'Tis not too late to seek a newer world.
Push off, and sitting well in order smite
The sounding furrows; for my purpose holds
60 To sail beyond the sunset, and the baths
Of all the western stars, until I die.
It may be that the gulfs will wash us down;
It may be we shall touch the Happy Isles,
And see the great Achilles, whom we knew.
65 Though much is taken, much abides; and though
We are not now that strength which in old days
Moved earth and heaven, that which we are, we are;
One equal temper of heroic hearts,
Made weak by time and fate, but strong in will
70 To strive, to seek, to find, and not to yield.

ROBERT BROWNING (1812–1889)

The Bishop Orders His Tomb at Saint Praxed's Church

Rome, 15—

Vanity, saith the preacher, vanity!
Draw round my bed: is Anselm keeping back?
Nephews[1]—sons mine . . . ah God, I know not! Well—

She, men would have to be your mother once,
5 Old Gandolf envied me, so fair she was!
What's done is done, and she is dead beside,
Dead long ago, and I am Bishop since,
And as she died so must we die ourselves,
And thence ye may perceive the world's a dream.
10 Life, how and what is it? As here I lie
In this state-chamber, dying by degrees,
Hours and long hours in the dead night, I ask
"Do I live, am I dead?" Peace, peace seems all.
Saint Praxed's ever was the church for peace;
15 And so, about this tomb of mine. I fought
With tooth and nail to save my niche, ye know:
—Old Gandolf cozened me, despite my care;
Shrewd was that snatch from out the corner South
He graced his carrion with, God curse the same!
20 Yet still my niche is not so cramped but thence
One sees the pulpit o' the epistle side,[2]
And somewhat of the choir, those silent seats,
And up into the aery dome where live
The angels, and a sunbeam's sure to lurk:
25 And I shall fill my slab of basalt there,
And 'neath my tabernacle take my rest,
With those nine columns round me, two and two,
The odd one at my feet where Anselm stands:
Peach-blossom marble all, the rare, the ripe
30 As fresh-poured red wine of a mighty pulse.
—Old Gandolf with his paltry onion-stone,
Put me where I may look at him! True peach,
Rosy and flawless: how I earned the prize!
Draw close: that conflagration of my church
35 —What then? So much was saved if aught were missed!
My sons, ye would not be my death? Go dig
The white-grape vineyard where the oil-press stood,
Drop water gently till the surface sink,
And if ye find . . . Ah God, I know not, I! . . .
40 Bedded in store of rotten fig-leaves soft,
And corded up in a tight olive-frail,
Some lump, ah God, of *lapis lazuli*,
Big as a Jew's head cut off at the nape,
Blue as a vein o'er the Madonna's breast . . .

---

[1] Euphemism for illegitimate sons.
[2] The right-hand side, as one faces the altar.

45 Sons, all have I bequeathed you, villas, all,
    That brave Frascati villa with its bath,
    So, let the blue lump poise between my knees,
    Like God the Father's globe on both his hands
    Ye worship in the Jesu Church so gay,
50 For Gandolf shall not choose but see and burst!
    Swift as a weaver's shuttle fleet our years:
    Man goeth to the grave, and where is he?
    Did I say basalt for my slab, sons? Black—
    'Twas ever antique-black I meant! How else
55 Shall ye contrast my frieze to come beneath?
    The bas-relief in bronze ye promised me,
    Those Pans and Nymphs ye wot of, and perchance
    Some tripod,³ thyrsus,⁴ with a vase or so,
    The Saviour at his sermon on the mount,
60 Saint Praxed in a glory, and one Pan
    Ready to twitch the Nymph's last garment off,
    And Moses with the tables . . . but I know
    Ye mark me not! What do they whisper thee,
    Child of my bowels, Anselm? Ah, ye hope
65 To revel down my villas while I gasp
    Bricked o'er with beggar's moldy travertine
    Which Gandolf from his tomb-top chuckles at!
    Nay, boys, ye love me—all of jasper, then!
    'Tis jasper ye stand pledged to, lest I grieve
70 My bath must needs be left behind, alas!
    One block, pure green as a pistachio nut,
    There's plenty jasper somewhere in the world—
    And have I not Saint Praxed's ear to pray
    Horses for ye, and brown Greek manuscripts,
75 And mistresses with great smooth marbly limbs?
    —That's if ye carve my epitaph aright,
    Choice Latin, picked phrase, Tully's⁵ every word,
    No gaudy ware like Gandolf's second line—
    Tully, my masters? Ulpian⁶ serves his need!
80 And then how I shall lie through centuries,
    And hear the blessed mutter of the mass,
    And see God made and eaten all day long,

---

³ Three-legged stool used by the oracle at Delphi.
⁴ Staff carried by Dionysus and his followers.
⁵ Marcus Tullius Cicero, master of Latin prose style.
⁶ Domitius Ulpianus, third century Roman jurist, noted for bad prose.

And feel the steady candle-flame, and taste
Good strong thick stupefying incense-smoke!
85 For as I lie here, hours of the dead night,
Dying in state and by such slow degrees,
I fold my arms as if they clasped a crook,
And stretch my feet forth straight as stone can point,
And let the bedclothes, for a mortcloth, drop
90 Into great laps and folds of sculptor's-work:
And as yon tapers dwindle, and strange thoughts
Grow, with a certain humming in my ears,
About the life before I lived this life,
And this life too, popes, cardinals, and priests,
95 Saint Praxed at his sermon on the mount,[7]
Your tall pale mother with her talking eyes,
And new-found agate urns as fresh as day,
And marble's language, Latin pure, discreet
—Aha, ELUCESCEBAT[8] quoth our friend?
100 No Tully, said I, Ulpian at the best!
Evil and brief hath been my pilgrimage.
All *lapis*, all, sons! Else I give the Pope
My villas! Will ye ever eat my heart?
Ever your eyes were as a lizard's quick,
105 They glitter like your mother's for my soul,
Or ye would heighten my impoverished frieze,
Piece out its starved design, and fill my vase
With grapes, and add a vizor and a Term,[9]
And to the tripod you would tie a lynx
110 That in his struggle throws the thyrsus down,
To comfort me on my entablature
Whereon I am to lie till I must ask
"Do I live, am I dead?" There, leave me, there!
For ye have stabbed me with ingratitude
115 To death—ye wish it—God, ye wish it! Stone—
Gritstone, a-crumble! Clammy squares which sweat
As if the corpse they keep were oozing through—
And no more *lapis* to delight the world!
Well go! I bless ye. Fewer tapers there,
120 But in a row: and, going, turn your backs
—Aye, like departing altar-ministrants,
And leave me in my church, the church for peace,

---

[7] The bishop's failing mind attributes the Sermon on the Mount to Saint Praxed
(a woman) instead of Christ.
[8] "He was illustrious," an example of Ulpian Latin.
[9] A mask and bust on a pedestal.

That I may watch at leisure if he leers—
Old Gandolf, at me, from his onion-stone,
125 As still he envied me, so fair she was!

WALLACE STEVENS (1879–1955)

The World as Meditation

J'ai passé trop de temps à travailler mon violon, à voyager.
Mais l'exercice essentiel du compositeur—la méditation—
rien ne l'a jamais suspendu en moi . . . Je vis un rêve
permanent, qui ne s'arrête ni nuit ni jour. GEORGES ENESCO[1]

Is it Ulysses that approaches from the east,[2]
The interminable adventurer? The trees are mended.
That winter is washed away. Someone is moving

On the horizon and lifting himself up above it.
5 A form of fire approaches the cretonnes of Penelope,
Whose mere savage presence awakens the world in which she dwells.

She has composed, so long, a self with which to welcome him,
Companion to his self for her, which she imagined,
Two in a deep-founded sheltering, friend and dear friend.

10 The trees had been mended, as an essential exercise
In an inhuman meditation, larger than her own.
No winds like dogs watched over her at night.

She wanted nothing he could not bring her by coming alone.
She wanted no fetchings. His arms would be her necklace
15 And her belt, the final fortune of their desire.

But was it Ulysses? Or was it only the warmth of the sun
On her pillow? The thought kept beating in her like her heart.
The two kept beating together. It was only day.

---

1 "I have spent too much time working at my violin and traveling. But the essential
exercise of the composer—meditation—nothing has ever kept me from that . . . I
live a continuous dream that ceases neither night nor day." Georges Enesco
(1881–1955), Romanian musician.

2 Ulysses, during the Trojan war and thereafter, was away from Ithaca for twenty
years. His wife, Penelope, remained at home awaiting his return.

It was Ulysses and it was not. Yet they had met,
20 Friend and dear friend and a planet's encouragement.
The barbarous strength within her would never fail.

She would talk a little to herself as she combed her hair,
Repeating his name with its patient syllables,
Never forgetting him that kept coming constantly so near.

T. S. ELIOT (1888–1965)

Journey of the Magi

"A cold coming we had of it,
Just the worst time of the year
For a journey, and such a long journey:
The ways deep and the weather sharp,
5 The very dead of winter."[1]
And the camels galled, sore-footed, refractory,
Lying down in the melting snow.
There were times we regretted
The summer palaces on slopes, the terraces,
10 And the silken girls bringing sherbet.
Then the camel men cursing and grumbling
And running away, and wanting their liquor and women,
And the night-fires going out, and the lack of shelters,
And the cities hostile and the towns unfriendly
15 And the villages dirty and charging high prices:
A hard time we had of it.
At the end we preferred to travel all night,
Sleeping in snatches,
With the voices singing in our ears, saying
20 That this was all folly.

Then at dawn we came down to a temperate valley,
Wet, below the snow line, smelling of vegetation;
With a running stream and a water-mill beating the darkness,
And three trees on the low sky,
25 And an old white horse galloped away in the meadow.
Then we came to a tavern with vine-leaves over the lintel,
Six hands at an open door dicing for pieces of silver,
And feet kicking the empty wine-skins.
But there was no information, and so we continued

---

[1] Adapted from a 17th-century sermon of Lancelot Andrewes.

30 And arrived at evening, not a moment too soon
Finding the place; it was (you may say) satisfactory.

All this was a long time ago, I remember,
And I would do it again, but set down
This set down
35 This: were we led all that way for
Birth or Death? There was a Birth, certainly,
We had evidence and no doubt. I had seen birth and death,
But had thought they were different; this Birth was
Hard and bitter agony for us, like Death, our death.
40 We returned to our places, these Kingdoms,
But no longer at ease here, in the old dispensation,
With an alien people clutching their gods.
I should be glad of another death.

E. E. CUMMINGS (1894–1963)

the Cambridge ladies who live in furnished souls

the Cambridge ladies who live in furnished souls
are unbeautiful and have comfortable minds
(also, with the church's protestant blessings,
daughters, unscented shapeless spirited)
5 they believe in Christ and Longfellow, both dead,
are invariably interested in so many things—
at the present writing one still finds
delighted fingers knitting for the is it Poles?
perhaps. While permanent faces coyly bandy
10 scandal of Mrs. N and Professor D
. . . . the Cambridge ladies do not care, above
Cambridge if sometimes in its box of
sky lavender and cornerless, the
moon rattles like a fragment of angry candy

JOHN CROWE RANSOM (1888–1974)

Bells for John Whiteside's Daughter

There was such speed in her little body,
And such lightness in her footfall,
It is no wonder her brown study
Astonishes us all.

5 Her wars were bruited in our high window.
We looked among orchard trees and beyond
Where she took arms against her shadow,
Or harried unto the pond

The lazy geese, like a snow cloud
10 Dripping their snow on the green grass,
Tricking and stopping, sleepy and proud,
Who cried in goose, Alas,

For the tireless heart within the little
Lady with rod that made them rise
15 From their noon apple-dreams and scuttle
Goose-fashion under the skies!

But now go the bells, and we are ready,
In one house we are sternly stopped
To say we are vexed at her brown study,
20 Lying so primly propped.

GWENDOLYN BROOKS (1917–   )

The Bean Eaters

They eat beans mostly, this old yellow pair .
Dinner is a casual affair.
Plain chipware on a plain and creaking wood,
Tin flatware.

5 Two who are Mostly Good.
Two who have lived their day,
But keep on putting on their clothes
And putting things away.

And remembering . . .
10 Remembering, with twinklings and twinges,
As they lean over the beans in their rented back room that is full of
beads and receipts and dolls and clothes, tobacco crumbs, vases
and fringes.

ANNE SEXTON (1928–1974)

Her Kind

I have gone out, a possessed witch,
haunting the black air, braver at night;
dreaming evil, I have done my hitch
over the plain houses, light by light:
5 lonely thing, twelve-fingered, out of mind.
A woman like that is not a woman, quite.
I have been her kind.
I have found the warm caves in the woods,
filled them with skillets, carvings, shelves,
10 closets, silks, innumerable goods;
fixed the suppers for the worms and the elves:
whining, rearranging the disaligned.
A woman like that is misunderstood.
I have been her kind.

15 I have ridden in your cart, driver,
waved my nude arms at villages going by,
learning the last bright routes, survivor
where your flames still bite my thigh
and my ribs crack where your wheels wind.
20 A woman like that is not ashamed to die.
I have been her kind.

POETS ON POETRY

ROBERT HERRICK (1591–1674)

From **Hesperides**

The Argument[1] of His Book

I sing of brooks, of blossoms, birds, and bowers:
Of April, May, or June, and July flowers.
I sing of May-poles, hock-carts, wassails, wakes,
Of bridegrooms, brides, and of their bridal cakes.
5 I write of youth, of love, and have access
By these, to sing of cleanly wantonness.
I sing of dews, of rains, and piece by piece
Of balm, of oil, of spice, and ambergris.
I sing of times trans-shifting; and I write
10 How roses first came red, and lilies white.
I write of groves, of twilights, and I sing
The court of Mab, and of the Fairy King.
I write of hell; I sing (and ever shall)
Of heaven, and hope to have it after all.

WILLIAM SHAKESPEARE (1564–1616)

Sonnet 55

Not marble nor the gilded monuments
Of princes shall outlive this powerful rime;
But you shall shine more bright in these contents
Than unswept stone, besmeared with sluttish time.
5 When wasteful war shall statues overturn,

---

[1] "Argument" is the term formerly used for a brief summary of the contents of a book.

And broils root out the work of masonry,
Nor Mars his sword nor war's quick fire shall burn
The living record of your memory.
'Gainst death and all oblivious enmity
10 Shall you pace forth; your praise shall still find room
Even in the eyes of all posterity
That wear this world out to the ending doom.
　So, till the Judgment that yourself arise,
　　You live in this, and dwell in lovers' eyes.

EMILY DICKINSON (1830–1886)

The Poets Light but Lamps (#883)

The Poets light but Lamps—
Themselves—go out—
The Wicks they stimulate—
If vital Light

5 Inhere as do the Suns—
Each Age a Lens
Disseminating their
Circumference—

WALT WHITMAN (1819–1892)

Out of the Cradle Endlessly Rocking

Out of the cradle endlessly rocking,
Out of the mocking-bird's throat, the musical shuttle,
Out of the Ninth-month midnight,
Over the sterile sands and the fields beyond, where the child leaving
　　his bed wander'd alone, bareheaded, barefoot,
5 Down from the shower'd halo,
Up from the mystic play of shadows twining and twisting as if they
　　were alive,
Out from the patches of briers and blackberries,
From the memories of the bird that chanted to me,
From your memories sad brother, from the fitful risings and fallings
　　I heard,
10 From under that yellow half-moon late-risen and swollen as if with
　　tears,
From those beginning notes of yearning and love there in the mist,
From the thousand responses of my heart never to cease,

From the myriad thence-arous'd words,
From the word stronger and more delicious than any,
15 From such as now they start the scene revisiting,
As a flock, twittering, rising, or overhead passing,
Borne hither, ere all eludes me, hurriedly,
A man, yet by these tears a little boy again,
Throwing myself on the sand, confronting the waves,
20 I, chanter of pains and joys, uniter of here and hereafter,
Taking all hints to use them, but swiftly leaping beyond them,
A reminiscence sing.

One Paumanok,[1]
When the lilac-scent was in the air and Fifth-month grass was grow-
ing,
25 Up this seashore in some briers,
Two feather'd guests from Alabama, two together,
And their nest, and four light-green eggs spotted with brown,
And every day the he-bird to and fro near at hand,
And every day the she-bird crouch'd on her nest, silent, with bright
eyes,
30 And every day I, a curious boy, never too close, never disturbing
them,
Cautiously peering, absorbing, translating.

Shine! shine! shine!
Pour down your warmth, great sun!
While we bask, we two together.

35 *Two together!*
Winds blow south, or winds blow north,
Day come white, or night come black,
Home, or rivers and mountains from home,
Singing all time, minding no time,
40 *While we two keep together.*

Till of a sudden,
May-be kill'd unknown to her mate,
One forenoon, the she-bird crouch'd not on the nest,
Nor return'd that afternoon, nor the next,
45 Nor ever appear'd again.

---

[1] The Indian name for Long Island.

And thenceforward all summer in the sound of the sea,
And at night under the full of the moon in calmer weather,
Over the hoarse surging of the sea,
Or flitting from brier to brier by day,
50 I saw, I heard at intervals the remaining one, the he-bird,
The solitary guest from Alabama.

Blow! blow! blow!
Blow up sea-winds along Paumanok's shore;
I wait and I wait till you blow my mate to me.

55 Yes, when the stars glisten'd,
All night long on the prong of a moss-scallop'd stake,
Down almost amid the slapping waves,
Sat the lone singer wonderful causing tears.

He call'd on his mate,
60 He pour'd forth the meanings which I of all men know.

Yes my brother I know,
The rest might not, but I have treasur'd every note,
For more than once dimly down to the beach gliding,
Silent, avoiding the moonbeams, blending myself with the shadows,
65 Recalling now the obscure shapes, the echoes, the sounds and sights
     after their sorts,
The white arms out in the breakers tirelessly tossing,
I, with bare feet, a child, the wind wafting my hair,
Listen'd long and long.

Listen'd to keep, to sing, now translating the notes,
70 Following you my brother.

Soothe! soothe! soothe!
Close on its wave soothes the wave behind,
And again another behind embracing and lapping, every one close,
But my love soothes not me, not me.

75 *Low hangs the moon, it rose late,*
It is lagging—O I think it is heavy with love, with love.

O madly the sea pushes upon the land,
With love, with love.

O night! do I not see my love fluttering out among the breakers?
80 *What is that little black thing I see there in the white?*

Loud! loud! loud!
Loud I call to you, my love!
High and clear I shoot my voice over the waves,
Surely you must know who is here, is here,
85 *You must know who I am, my love.*

Low-hanging moon!
What is that dusky spot in your brown yellow?
O it is the shape, the shape of my mate!
O moon do not keep her from me any longer.

90 *Land! land! O land!*
Whichever way I turn, O I think you could give me my mate back
again if you only would,
For I am almost sure I see her dimly whichever way I look.

O rising stars!
Perhaps the one I want so much will rise, will rise with some of you.

95 *O throat! O trembling throat!*
Sound clearer through the atmosphere!
Pierce the woods, the earth,
Somewhere listening to catch you must be the one I want.

Shake out carols!
100 *Solitary here, the night's carols!*
Carols of lonesome love! death's carols!
Carols under that lagging, yellow, waning moon!
O under that moon where she droops almost down into the sea!
O reckless despairing carols.

105 *But soft! sink low!*
Soft! let me just murmur,
And do you wait a moment you husky-nois'd sea,
For somewhere I believe I heard my mate responding to me,
So faint, I must be still, be still to listen,
110 *But not altogether still, for then she might not come immediately*
to me.

Hither my love!
Here I am! here!
With this just-sustain'd note I announce myself to you,
This gentle call is for you my love, for you.

115 *Do not be decoy'd elsewhere,*
     That is the whistle of the wind, it is not my voice,
     That is the fluttering, the fluttering of the spray,
     Those are the shadows of leaves.

     O darkness! O in vain!
120 *O I am very sick and sorrowful.*

     O brown halo in the sky near the moon, drooping upon the sea!
     O troubled reflection in the sea!
     O throat! O throbbing heart!
     And I singing uselessly, uselessly all the night.

125 *O past! O happy life! O songs of joy!*
     In the air, in the woods, over fields,
     Loved! loved! loved! loved! loved!
     But my mate no more, no more with me!
     We two together no more.

130 The aria sinking,
     All else continuing, the stars shining,
     The winds blowing, the notes of the bird continuous echoing,
     With angry moans the fierce old mother incessantly moaning,
     On the sands of Paumanok's shore gray and rustling,
135 The yellow half-moon enlarged, sagging down, drooping, the face of
       the sea almost touching,
     The boy ecstatic, with his bare feet the waves, with his hair the
       atmosphere dallying,
     The love in the heart long pent, now loose, now at last tumultuously
       bursting,
     The aria's meaning, the ears, the soul, swiftly depositing,
     The strange tears down the cheeks coursing,
140 The colloquy there, the trio, each uttering,
     The undertone, the savage old mother incessantly crying,
     To the boy's soul's questions sullenly timing, some drown'd secret
       hissing,
     To the outsetting bard.

     Demon or bird! (said the boy's soul,)
145 Is it indeed toward your mate you sing? or is it really to me?
     For I, that was a child, my tongue's use sleeping, now I have heard
       you,
     Now in a moment I know what I am for, I awake,
     And already a thousand singers, a thousand songs, clearer, louder

and more sorrowful than yours,
A thousand warbling echoes have started to life within me, never
    to die.

150 O you singer solitary, singing by yourself, projecting me,
O solitary me listening, never more shall I cease perpetuating you,
Never more shall I escape, never more the reverberations,
Never more the cries of unsatisfied love be absent from me,
Never again leave me to be the peaceful child I was before what
    there in the night,
155 By the sea under the yellow and sagging moon,
The messenger there arous'd, the fire, the sweet hell within,
The unknown want, the destiny of me.

O give me the clew! (it lurks in the night here somewhere,)
O if I am to have so much, let me have more!

160 A word then, (for I will conquer it,)
The word final, superior to all,
Subtle, sent up—what is it?—I listen;
Are you whispering it, and have been all the time, you sea-waves?
Is that it from your liquid rims and wet sands?

165 Whereto answering, the sea,
Delaying not, hurrying not,
Whisper'd me through the night, and very plainly before daybreak,
Lisp'd to me the low and delicious word death,
And again death, death, death, death,
170 Hissing melodious, neither like the bird nor like my arous'd child's
    heart,
But edging near as privately for me rustling at my feet,
Creeping thence steadily up to my ears and leaving me softly all over,
Death, death, death, death, death.

Which I do not forget,
175 But fuse the song of my dusky demon and brother,
That he sang to me in the moonlight on Paumanok's gray beach,
With the thousand responsive songs at random,
My own songs awaked from that hour,
And with them the key, the word up from the waves,
180 The word of the sweetest song and all songs,
That strong and delicious word which, creeping to my feet,
(Or like some old crone rocking the cradle, swathed in sweet gar-
    ments, bending aside,)
The sea whisper'd me.

JAMES WELDON JOHNSON (1871–1938)

O Black and Unknown Bards

O black and unknown bards of long ago,
How came your lips to touch the sacred fire?
How, in your darkness, did you come to know
The power and beauty of the minstrel's lyre?
5 Who first from midst his bonds lifted his eyes?
Who first from out the still watch, lone and long,
Feeling the ancient faith of prophets rise
Within his dark-kept soul, burst into song?

Heart of what slave poured out such melody
10 As "Steal away to Jesus"? On its strains
His spirit must have nightly floated free,
Though still about his hands he felt his chains.
Who heard great "Jordan roll"? Whose starward eye
Saw chariot "swing low"? And who was he
15 That breathed that comforting, melodic sigh,
"Nobody knows de trouble I see"?

What merely living clod, what captive thing,
Could up toward God through all its darkness grope,
And find within its deadened heart to sing
20 These songs of sorrow, love and faith, and hope?
How did it catch that subtle undertone,
That note in music heard not with the ears?
How sound the elusive reed so seldom blown,
Which stirs the soul or melts the heart to tears?

25 Not that great German master[1] in his dream
Of harmonies that thundered amongst the stars
At the creation, ever heard a theme
Nobler than "Go down, Moses." Mark its bars,
How like a mighty trumpet-call they stir
30 The blood. Such are the notes that men have sung
Going to valorous deeds; such tones there were
That helped make history when Time was young.

There is a wide, wide wonder in it all,
That from degraded rest and servile toil
35 The fiery spirit of the seer should call
These simple children of the sun and soil.

---

[1] Beethoven.

O black slave singers, gone, forgot, unfamed,
You—you alone, of all the long, long line
Of those who've sung untaught, unknown, unnamed,
40 Have stretched out upward, seeking the divine.

You sang not deeds of heroes or of kings;
No chant of bloody war, no exulting paean
Of arms-won triumphs; but your humble strings
You touched in chord with music empyrean.
45 You sang far better than you knew; the songs
That for your listeners' hungry hearts sufficed
Still live—but more than this to you belongs:
You sang a race from wood and stone to Christ.

A. E. HOUSMAN (1859–1936)

"Terence, This Is Stupid Stuff . . ."

"Terence, this is stupid stuff:
You eat your victuals fast enough;
There can't be much amiss, 'tis clear,
To see the rate you drink your beer.
5 But oh, good Lord, the verse you make,
It gives a chap the belly-ache.
The cow, the old cow, she is dead;
It sleeps well, the hornèd head:
We poor lads, 'tis our turn now
10 To hear such tunes as killed the cow.
Pretty friendship 'tis to rhyme
Your friends to death before their time
Moping melancholy mad:
Come, pipe a tune to dance to, lad."

15   Why, if 'tis dancing you would be,
There's brisker pipes than poetry.
Say, for what were hop-yards meant,
Or why was Burton built on Trent?[1]
Oh many a peer of England brews
20 Livelier liquor than the Muse,
And malt does more than Milton can
To justify God's ways to man.

---

[1] A town noted for its breweries.

Ale, man, ale's the stuff to drink
For fellows whom it hurts to think:
25 Look into the pewter pot
To see the world as the world's not.
And faith, 'tis pleasant till 'tis past:
The mischief is that 'twill not last.
Oh I have been to Ludlow fair
30 And left my necktie God knows where,
And carried half-way home, or near,
Pints and quarts of Ludlow beer:
Then the world seemed none so bad,
And I myself a sterling lad;
35 And down in lovely muck I've lain,
Happy till I woke again.
Then I saw the morning sky:
Heigho, the tale was all a lie;
The world, it was the old world yet,
40 I was I, my things were wet,
And nothing now remained to do
But begin the game anew.

Therefore, since the world has still
Much good, but much less good than ill,
45 And while the sun and moon endure
Luck's a chance, but trouble's sure,
I'd face it as a wise man would,
And train for ill and not for good.
'Tis true, the stuff I bring for sale
50 Is not so brisk a brew as ale:
Out of a stem that scored the hand
I wrung it in a weary land.
But take it: if the smack is sour,
The better for the embittered hour;
55 It should do good to heart and head
When your soul is in my soul's stead;
And I will friend you, if I may,
In the dark and cloudy day.

There was a king reigned in the East:
60 There, when kings will sit to feast,
They get their fill before they think
With poisoned meat and poisoned drink.
He gathered all that springs to birth
From the many-venomed earth;

65 First a little, thence to more,
He sampled all her killing store;
And easy, smiling, seasoned sound,
Sate the king when healths went round.
They put arsenic in his meat
70 And stared aghast to watch him eat;
They poured strychnine in his cup
And shook to see him drink it up:
They shook, they stared as white's their shirt:
Them it was their poison hurt.
75 —I tell the tale that I heard told.
Mithridates,[2] he died old.

ROBINSON JEFFERS (1887–1962)

Love the Wild Swan

"I hate my verses, every line, every word.
Oh pale and brittle pencils ever to try
One grass-blade's curve, or the throat of one bird
That clings to twig, ruffled against white sky.
5 Oh cracked and twilight mirrors ever to catch
One color, one glinting flash, of the splendor of things.
Unlucky hunter, Oh bullets of wax,
The lion beauty, the wild-swan wings, the storm of the wings."
—This wild swan of a world is no hunter's game.
10 Better bullets than yours would miss the white breast,
Better mirrors than yours would crack in the flame.
Does it matter whether you hate your . . . self? At least
Love your eyes that can see, your mind that can
Hear the music, the thunder of the wings. Love the wild swan.

Cassandra[1]

The mad girl with the staring eyes and long white fingers
Hooked in the stones of the wall,
The storm-wrack hair and the screeching mouth: does it matter, Cassandra,
Whether the people believe

---

[2] King of Pontus in the first century B.C., who made himself immune to certain poisons by taking them frequently in small doses.
[1] Princess of Troy, gifted with the power of prophecy but doomed never to be believed.

5 Your bitter fountain? Truly men hate the truth; they'd liefer
  Meet a tiger on the road.
  Therefore the poets honey their truth with lying; but religion-
  Venders and political men
  Pour from the barrel, new lies on the old, and are praised for kindly
10 Wisdom. Poor bitch, be wise.
  No: you'll still mumble in a corner a crust of truth, to men
  And gods disgusting.—You and I, Cassandra.

DYLAN THOMAS (1914–1953)

In My Craft or Sullen Art

In my craft or sullen art
Exercised in the still night
When only the moon rages
And the lovers lie abed
5 With all their griefs in their arms,
I labor by singing light
Not for ambition or bread
Or the strut and trade of charms
On the ivory stages
10 But for the common wages
Of their most secret heart.

Not for the proud man apart
From the raging moon I write
On these spindrift pages
15 Nor for the towering dead
With their nightingales and psalms
But for the lovers, their arms
Round the griefs of the ages,
Who pay no praise or wages
20 Nor heed my craft or art.

MARIANNE MOORE (1887–1972)

Poetry

I, too, dislike it: there are things that are important beyond all this
      fiddle.
  Reading it, however, with a perfect contempt for it, one discovers
      in

it after all, a place for the genuine.
     Hands that can grasp, eyes
5   that can dilate, hair that can rise
               if it must, there things are important not because a

high-sounding interpretation can be put upon them but because they are
     useful. When they become so derivative as to become unintelligble,
     the same thing may be said for all of us, that we
10   do not admire what
          we cannot understand: the bat
               holding on upside down or in quest of something to

eat, elephants pushing, a wild horse taking a roll, a tireless wolf under
     a tree, the immovable critic twitching his skin like a horse that
          feels a flea, the base-
15   ball fan, the statistician—
          nor is it valid
               to discriminate against "business documents and

school-books";[1] all these phenomena are important. One must make
     a distinction
     however: when dragged into prominence by half poets, the result
          is not poetry,
20   nor till the poets among us can be
          "literalists of
          the imagination" [2]—above
               insolence and triviality and can present

for inspection, "imaginary gardens with real toads in them," shall we
     have
25   it. In the meantime, if you demand on the one hand,
          the raw material of poetry in
          all its rawness and
          that which is on the other hand
               genuine, you are interested in poetry.

---

[1] Moore's note cites the Diary of Tolstoy: "poetry is everything with the exception of business documents and school books."
[2] From Yeats, *Ideas of Good and Evil.*

ARCHIBALD MACLEISH (1892–   )

Ars Poetica

A poem should be palpable and mute
As a globed fruit,

Dumb
As old medallions to the thumb,

5 Silent as the sleeve-worn stone
Of casement ledges where the moss has grown—

A poem should be wordless
As the flight of birds.

A poem should be motionless in time
10 As the moon climbs,

Leaving, as the moon releases
Twig by twig the night-entangled trees,

Leaving, as the moon behind the winter leaves
Memory by memory the mind—

15 A poem should be motionless in time
As the moon climbs.

A poem should be equal to:
Not true.

For all the history of grief
20 An empty doorway and a maple leaf.

For love
The leaning grasses and two lights above the sea—

A poem should not mean
But be.

Index of Terms

Accentual poetry, 824, 875
Accentual syllabic verse, 875, 877, 881
Action, 4. *See also* Plot
  and allegory, 845, 846
  Aristotle on, 377
  concentration on, 30
  consistency in, 378
  in drama, 382
  and emotion, 5
  in fiction, 157
  giving meaning to, 17
  in *Hamlet,* 460
  in longer tales, 130
  in modern tales, 17
  in narrative, 17, 21, 22
  patterns of, 7, 381, 382
  and settings, 58, 159
  symbolic import of, 32
  in "Young Goodman Brown," 46
Actors, 381
  in Greek drama, 385
  in medieval drama, 384
  and performance, 379–380
Allegory, 46
  in fiction, 158
  in poetry, 845–847
  symbols in, 846, 847, 863
Alliteration, 790, 807, 875
Allusions, 854
Amphibrach, 876
Anapest, 875
Anapestic meter, 876
Apostrophe, 822, 857
"Asides"
  of *Hamlet,* 459
Assonance, 875
Atmosphere, 45. *See also* Mood
Aubades, 860
Audience
  in drama, 379
  Hamlet's, 459, 461
  and first-person narration, 81, 82
  and Greek drama, 386–387
  in medieval drama, 384, 385

Ballads, 788, 796
  meter of, 876

  vs. poems, 803
  vs. tales, 783
  traditional, 783
Blank verse,
  in *Hamlet,* 884
  in Renaissance drama, 462

Cadence, 876
Cesura, 877
Character, 4, 7, 30, 31, 32
  Aristotle on, 377–378
  comic, 583
  consistency of, 378
  in drama, 378–382
  in fiction, 157, 158
  first-person narrator as, 82, 83
  fixed vs. developing, 461
  in Greek drama, 461
  Hamlet vs. *Oedipus,* 459, 460, 461
  in medieval drama, 387
  in modern drama, 583, 584, 585
  in modern tales, 17
  and setting, 58
  and society, 157–159
Characterization
  in drama, 382
  in "The Lottery", 30, 31, 32
  patterns of, 7, 381, 382
  in poetry, 812–813
Character study, 157–217
Chorus, in Greek drama, 385
Christmas plays, 384
City scenes, 899–910
Climax, 80
Coherence, 5
Comedy
  ending in, 387, 583
  in Greek drama, 385, 387
  in *Hamlet,* 460
  in medieval drama, 387, 388
  as social drama, 583
  vs. tragedy, 583
Comic speech, 460, 461
Common phrases, in poetry, 803
Compression
  technique, 796, 797, 804
  and word-sound, 803

Conceits, 852–853
Conflict, 80
    in comedy, 583–584
    in drama, 381
    in fiction, 381
    in Greek tragedy, 461
Consistency, as Aristotelian standard,
    378
Corpus Christi plays, 384, 387
Counterpoint, 876
Country scenes, in poetry, 899–910
Couplets, 462, 885
"Cycle plays," medieval, 384, 386,
    386n., 387, 388

Dactylic meter, 876
Denouement, 80
Dialogue, in Greek drama, 385
Diction, 377
Didactic school of literature, 6
Dilemma, 460
Dimeter, 874
Drama
    American, 388
    Aristotle on, 377
    elements of, 377–378
    English, 379, 383–388
    European, 388
    vs. fiction, 379–380
    Greek, 377–378, 385–386, 387, 460
    language for, 381
    Latin, 384
    medieval, 383–385, 387, 460–461
    modern, 583, 585
    reading, 377–382, 782
    Roman, 386
    social, 583

Easter plays, 384
Effect, and irony, 828
Elizabethan tragedy, 459–462
Emotions
    and action, 5
    in narration, 33
    poetry and, 811, 864
End-stopped lines, 877
English drama, 379, 383–388
Epigram, 797–798
    satiric, 798

Episodes, 385
Epithets, 803
Experience, in poetry, 819
Exposition, 80, 158

Fact, questions of, 6
Fairy tales, 158
Falling rhythm, 877
Fantasy, 157, 158
Fate, 378, 461
Feeling, in narration, 32, 33. *See also*
    Emotions
Feet, 875
Festivals
    and Greek drama, 385, 386
    and medieval drama, 384, 386
Fiction, 377, 782
    conflict in, 381
    vs. drama, 377–378
    elements of, 378
    flexibility of, 157–158
    as narrative, 17–156
    origins of, 378
    and society, 158–159
    themes, 585
    time in, 157
    voice in, 378, 379
Figures of speech, 834, 840, 863
    allusions, 854
    conceits, 852–853
    metaphors, 838
    similes, 837
First-person narrator, 81, 380–381
Folk ballads, 783. *See also* Ballads
Folk tales, 17
    and ballads, 783
    style of, 158, 159
Foot, 875
    monosyllabic, 876
Forms
    in Greek vs. medieval drama, 387
    and meaning, 863
    verse 796, 797, 884–887. *See also*
        Verse forms
"Frame story," 156
Free verse, 807, 884

Greek drama, 385–386, 387
    Aristotle on, 377–378

character in, 461
Hamlet derived from, 450–460
Greek tragedy, 386, 460

Haiku, 799
Hamlet
   blank verse in, 884
   comedy in, 460
   irony in, 827
Hero
   of comedy, 387
   Elizabethan, 459, 461
   Hamlet vs. Oedipus, 450, 460
   tragic, 386, 387, 460, 583, 584–585
Hexameter, 874
"High seriousness," 6
Horatian ode, 886
Hyperbole, 836

Iamb, 875
Iambic meter, 876
Iambic pentameter, 873, 884
Iambic trimeter, 875
Imagery
   of Hamlet's language, 462
   patterns of, 7, 381, 863–864
   style of, 835, 843
Images, common vs. unique, 803
Imagist poetry, 799
Implied metaphor, 837, 838
Incremental repetition, 788, 795
Interpretation, 3
   limits to, 7, 8
   in poetry, 805
   questions of, 6
Inevitability, Aristotelian concept of, 378n.
Irony, 82
   double vision of, 827–828
   in poetry, 819
Irregular ode, 886, 890

Judgment, 10–14

Language, 5
   in *Death of a Salesman,* 585
   in drama, 381–382
   in *Hamlet,* 460–461, 462

of medieval drama, 384
patterns of, 7, 381, 382
in poetry, 803–805, 834
Shakespearean, 462
Latin drama, 384
Limerick, 884, 886
Lines. *See also* Meter
   end-stopped, 877
   run-on, 877
Literature. *See also* Drama; Fiction
   analytic response to, 10–14
   writing about, 9–14
Lyrics, repetition in, 788, 791

Meaning, 6
   and action, 17
   and imagery, 863
   and irony, 828
   metaphorical, 46
   new, 803
   in poetry, 840
   word choice and, 803
Medieval cycle plays, 384, 386, 386n., 387, 388
Medieval drama, 383–385, 387, 460–461
Message, 6
Metaphor, 837, 838, 843, 845
   conceit as, 852
   implied, 837, 838
   music as, 196
   patterns of, 7
   physical setting as, 159
Metaphysical poetry, 853
Meter, 788, 793, 873–878
   in drama, 462
   duple, 876
   paeonic, 876
   triple, 876
Modern drama, 583, 585
Monosyllabic foot, 876
Mood, 864
   Major Barbara vs. *Death of a Salesman,* 584–585
   in poetry, 803
Movement, Aristotelian concept of, 378n.
Music, 377, 383, 384, 386
"Mystery plays," 384

Narration
  art of, 17
  in longer tales, 130
Narrative
  fiction as, 17–156
  in poetry, 803
Narrator, 20, 21, 32, 130, 157, 378
  blocking of, 130
  first-person, 81–156, 380
  objective, 34–80, 81, 82
  omniscient, 34–80, 81, 82
  patterns in, 82
  role of, 31, 32
  voice of 17, 21, 22, 31, 34, 157, 159, 378
  in "Young Goodman Brown," 46
Nativity plays, 387, 388
Newspapers, reading of, 782

Objective narrator, 34–80
Odes, 885, 886, 890
Oedipus Rex, 386–388
Omniscient narrator, 34, 59, 81, 82
"Overplot," 460

Pace, 809
Paeon, 876
Pageants, 384
Parody, 385
Pattern, 6, 7
  of action, 7, 381, 382
  in characterization, 381
  in drama, 381, 382
  in first-person narrative, 82
  of imagery, 863–864
  narrative, 803
  of rhythm, 803, 811
  rounded-off, 797
  sound, 811
Pentameter, 874
Pentameter, iambic, 873
Perceptions, changing, 8
Persona, 812
Personification, 837, 840
Petrarchan sonnet, 887
Plays
  composition of, 377
  cycle, 387–388
  medieval, 383–384

satyr, 387
shepherd, 388
text of, 380
Plot, 4
  Aristotle on, 378
  in Elizabethan tragedy, 460
  of *Major Barbara,* 584
Poetic speech, 386
Poetry
  accentual, 875
  characterization in, 812–813
  in drama, 381
  elements of, 834
  haiku, 799
  imagist, 799
  interpretation in, 805
  irony in, 827–828
  metaphor in, 837, 838
  metaphysical, 853
  meter in, 873–878
  Old English, 875
  oral, 803
  patterns of imagery in, 863–864
  personification in, 837, 840
  poets on, 923–936
  portraits in, 911–922
  reading, 781–783
  Renaissance, 863
  Romantic, 863, 864
  rhyme schemes in, 884
  simile in, 837
  sound in, 873
  speaker in, 819–820
  suggestion in, 805
  symbols in, 846, 863
  voice in, 811–813
  word choice in, 803
Poets on poetry, 923–936
Portraits, in poetry, 911–922
Prose, blank verse and, 462
Protagonist, 386
Psychomachia, 46, 693
Puns, 460
  in *Hamlet,* 460
  in poetry, 803

Quatrain, 885
Questions
  of fact, 6

of interpretation, 6
as poetic device, 793
Quips, in *Hamlet,* 460

Realism, 157, 158
of *Death of a Salesman,* 585
in fiction, 157
in "The Lottery," 32
Refrain, in ballads, 788
Religious ritual, and drama, 383, 384, 385
Renaissance poetry, 863
Repetition
in ballads, 788
incremental, 788, 795
in medieval lyric, 791
Resolution, 80
Reviewers, role of, 11–12
Rhyme
in drama, 381
in poetry, 790, 797, 881, 884–887
Rhymed couplets, and drama, 462
Rhythm
in ballads, 788
falling, 877
in *Hamlet*'s language, 462
in poetry, 788, 793, 797, 803, 810
rising, 877
in sound patterns, 811
in speech, 381
sprung, 875, 877
Rime royal, 885
Rising rhythm, 877
Roman drama, 386
Romantic poetry, 863, 864
Run-on lines, 877

Satiric epigram, 798
Satyr play, 385, 387
Scan, 873
Scenery, 377
Scenes, in poetry, 864
Second actor, 385
Sense, in poetry, 805
Settings
and action, 159
meaning in, 58
physical, 159
social, 159

Shakespearean sonnet, 887
Shepherds' plays, 386–388
Simile, 837, 843, 845
Social comment, 157–217
Society
and fiction, 158–159
and modern drama, 583, 584, 585
Soliloquies, 459, 461
Song, 386
in Greek tragedy, 385, 386
in medieval drama, 383–384
Sonnet, 884, 886, 887
Sound, in poetry, 805, 873
See also Voice
Speaker, in poetry, 819–820, 864
Speech
comic, 461
in drama, 381
patterns of, 381
poetic, 386
Spectacle, 377
Spondee, 876
Sprung rhythm, 875, 878
Staging
of *Death of a Salesman,* 585
of medieval drama, 384, 385, 386, 388
of Greek plays, 377, 385, 386
Stanza, 884
Stories
enjoyment of, 9
structure of, 80
Storyteller, 17, 378. *See also* Narrator; Voice
Stream of consciousness, 378–379
Stress, in poetry, 873–877
Stresses, shifting, 876
Style, 11
accentual, 875
in fiction, 158
of imagery, 835
"Subplot," 460
Suggestion
in poetry, 803, 804, 805
word choice and, 803
Syllable, stressed, 873–874
Symbolism, 21
and allegory, 845–847
in poetry, 846, 863

Synaesthesia, 835
Syntax, 805, 809, 823

Tales, 17, 20
    vs. ballads, 783
    folk tales, 17, 158, 159
Tercet, 885
Terza rima, 885
Tetrameter, 374
Theme, 6, 7
    of contemporary literature, 159, 585
    in Hamlet, 460
    of *Major Barbara,* 584
Third actor, 385
Thought
    Aristotelian category, 377
    patterns of, 381
Time
    in fiction, 157
    and verse forms, 796, 797
Tone, 22, 130
    in *Hamlet,* 460
    and irony, 828
    of narration, 22
    in poetry, 809, 840
    in sound patterns, 811
    and voice, 379
Tragedy
    vs. comedy, 583
    Elizabethan, 459–462
    ending in, 386, 583
    essentials of, 386–387
    Greek, 385–386, 460
    heroes in, 583
    modern, 584–585
Trimeter, 874

Trimeter, iambic, 875
Triplet, 885
Trochaic meter, 876

"Underplot," 460
Unity, 5
    in verse form, 797

Values
    of authors, 32, 33
    in fiction, 157
    of literature, 14
    in narration, 33
Verse forms, 796
    accentual, 884
    accentual-syllabic, 875, 877, 881
    blank, 884
    free, 807, 878, 884
    rhymed, 381, 881, 884
    unrhymed, 462, 884
Vers libre, 884
Villanelle, 884, 886
Vision
    double, 827
    in poetry, 812, 819, 834
    speaker's, 819–820
Voice, 378, 379. *See also* Speech
    and narration, 21, 22, 31, 34, 159
    in poetry, 811–814, 834

Word choice, in poetry, 803, 804
Wordplay
    in *Hamlet,* 460
    in poetry, 810
Writing assignments, 11–12

Index of Authors and Titles

All in green went my love riding, 793
All Night by the Rose, 791
Ancient Music, 857
ANONYMOUS, 857
   All Night by the Rose, 791
   Back and Side Go Bare, 789
   Cherry-Tree Carol, The, 786
   Get Up and Bar the Door, 784
   Lord Randal, 785
   Seafarer, The, 878
   Second Shepherd's Play, The, 433
   Sumer Is Icumen In, 856
   Western Wind, 814
Argument of His Book, The, 923
ARNOLD, MATTHEW, 869
Ars Poetica, 936
AUDEN, W. H., 831
Aunt Jennifer's Tigers, 828

Back and Side Go Bare, 789
BALDWIN, JAMES, 169
Balloon, The, 370
BARAKA, AMIRI, 910
BARTH, JOHN, 350
BARTHELME, DONALD, 370
Bartleby the Scrivener, 84
Bean Eaters, The, 921
Bells for John Whiteside's Daughter, 920
Bishop Orders His Tomb at Saint Praxed's Church, The, 914
BLAKE, WILLIAM, 792, 847, 901
BORGES, JORGE LUIS, 344
Bright and Morning Star, 291
BROOKS, GWENDOLYN, 798, 921
BROWNING, ROBERT, 900, 914
Bucket-Rider, The, 246
Bustle in a House, The, 804
BYRON, GEORGE GORDON, LORD, 4

Cambridge ladies who live in furnished souls, the, 920
CAMUS, ALBERT, 47
(Carrion Comfort), 889
Cassandra, 933
Castaway, The, 911
Cherry-Tree Carol, The, 786

Chrysanthemums, The, 281
Collar, The, 882
Composed upon Westminster Bridge, September 3, 1802, 842
CONRAD, JOSEPH, 131
Constant Lover, The, 815
Cool Tombs, 807
Counterparts, 237
COWPER, WILLIAM, 911
CRANE, STEPHEN, 60
CULLEN, COUNTEE, 798
CUMMINGS, E. E., 793, 809, 920

Dalliance of the Eagles, The, 835
Days, 848
Death of a Salesman, 694
Design, 890
DICKINSON, EMILY, 801, 804, 924
DONNE, JOHN, 853, 859, 888
Do Not Go Gentle into That Good Night, 886
DOOLITTLE, HILDA, 800
Dover Beach, 869
Down, Wanton, Down!, 862

Eagle, The, 835
ELIOT, T. S., 902, 919
EMERSON, RALPH WALDO, 824, 848

Fall of the House of Usher, The, 221
FAULKNER, WILLIAM, 160
FERLINGHETTI, LAWRENCE, 908
Fern Hill, 871
Fog, 840
Folly of Being Comforted, The, 830
For a Lady I Know, 798
For the Union Dead, 906
FROST, ROBERT, 848, 890

Get Up and Bar the Door, 784
GILMAN, CHARLOTTE PERKINS, 116
GINSBERG, ALLEN, 849, 909
GLASSNER, JOHN, 433
Good Man Is Hard to Find, A, 330
GRAVES, ROBERT, 862
Guest, The, 47

Hamatreya, 824
Hamlet, 463
HARDY, THOMAS, 248, 790, 816
Harlem, 838
HAWTHORNE, NATHANIEL, 35
H. D., 800
Heat, 800
Help Her to Believe, 197
HEMINGWAY, ERNEST, 261
HERBERT, GEORGE, 847, 882
Her Kind, 922
HERRICK, ROBERT, 806, 923
Home-Thoughts, from Abroad, 900
HOPKINS, GERARD MANLEY, 823, 880, 889
HOUSMAN, A. E., 806, 829, 931
How I Contemplated the World from the Detroit House of Correction and Began My Life Over Again, 204
How I Finally Lost My Heart, 320
HUGHES, LANGSTON, 838
Hymn to God My God, in My Sickness, 853

If Not Higher, 18
I Knew a Woman, 813
In a Station of the Metro, 799
In back of the real, 849
In Just- spring, 809
In My Craft or Sullen Art, 934
Irish Airman Foresees His Death, An, 817

JACKSON, SHIRLEY, 23
JEFFERS, ROBINSON, 933
JOHNSON, JAMES WELDON, 930
JONES, LE ROI, 910
JONSON, BEN, 841
Journey of the Magi, 919
JOYCE, JAMES, 237

KAFKA, FRANZ, 246
KEATS, JOHN, 4, 822, 839, 849, 866

Lamb, The, 792
L'Art 1910, 800
LAWRENCE, D. H., 248, 821

Leave Me, O Love, 860
LESSING, DORIS, 320
LEVERTOV, DENISE, 800, 841
London, 901
Lord Randal, 785
Losing Track, 841
Lost in the Funhouse, 350
Lottery, The, 23
Love (III), 847
Love Calls Us to the Things of This World, 843
Love Song of J. Alfred Prufrock, The, 902
Love the Wild Swan, 933
LOWELL, ROBERT, 906

MAC LEISH, ARCHIBALD, 936
MAC NEICE, LOUIS, 889
Major Barbara, 614
Major Barbara, preface to, 586
Man He Killed, The, 816
MARLOWE, CHRISTOPHER, 899
MARVELL, ANDREW, 860
MELVILLE, HERMAN, 84
MEREDITH, GEORGE, 829
MILLER, ARTHUR, 694
MILTON, JOHN, 888
MOORE, MARIANNE, 934
Morning Song, 842
My Papa's Waltz, 813

Naming of Parts, 832
Nymph's Reply to the Shepherd, The, 900

OATES, JOYCE CAROL, 204
O Black and Unknown Bards, 930
O'CONNOR, FLANNERY, 330
Ode: Intimations of Immortality from Recollections of Early Childhood, 891
Ode on a Grecian Urn, 849
Ode to a Nightingale, 866
Ode to the West Wind, 864
Oedipus Rex, 389
OLSEN, TILLIE, 197
On First Looking into Chapman's Homer, 839

On His Blindness, 888
Open Boat, The, 60
Out of the Cradle Endlessly Rocking, 924
Ozymandias, 830

Passionate Shepherd to His Love, The, 899
pennycandystore beyond the El, The, 908
PERETZ, I. L., 18
Piano, 821
Pied Beauty, 880
Pindaric Ode, A, 841
Place Pigalle, 905
PLATH, SYLVIA, 842
POE, EDGAR ALLAN, 221
Poetry, 934
Poets Light but Lamps, The, 924
POUND, EZRA, 799, 800, 808, 857
Preface to *Major Barbara*, 586

RALEGH, SIR WALTER, 900
RANSOM, JOHN CROWE, 920
REED, HENRY, 832, 854
RICH, ADRIENNE, 828
Road Not Taken, The, 848
Rocking-Horse Winner, The, 248
ROETHKE, TREODORE, 813
Rose for Emily, A, 160
ROSSETTI, DANTE GABRIEL, 820
Ruined Maid, The, 790

Sailing to Byzantium, 870
SANDBURG, CARL, 807, 840
Seafarer, The, 878
Second Shepherd's Play, The, 433
SEXTON, ANNE, 922
SHAKESPEARE, WILLIAM, 463, 858, 887, 923
SHAW, BERNARD, 586, 614
She Dwelt Among the Untrodden Ways, 806
SHELLEY, PERCY BYSSHE, 830, 864
Sick Rose, The, 847
SIDNEY, SIR PHILIP, 822, 860
Six Variations (part iii), 800
Snows of Kilimanjaro, The, 261

Sonnet 10 (Donne), 888
Sonnet 17 (Meredith), 829
Sonnet 18 (Shakespeare), 858
Sonnet 55 (Shakespeare), 923
Sonnet 116 (Shakespeare), 887
Sonnet 31 (Sidney), 822
Sonnet 15 (Spenser), 857
Sonny's Blues, 169
SOPHOCLES, 389
South, The, 344
So We'll Go No More A-Roving, 4
SPENSER, EDMUND, 857
Splendor Falls on Castle Walls, The, 881
Spring and Fall, 823
STEINBECK, JOHN, 281
STEVENS, WALLACE, 918
SUCKLING, SIR JOHN, 815
Sumer Is Icumen In, 856
Sunday Morning, 889
Sun Rising, The, 859
Supermarket in California, A, 909

Tell All the Truth but Tell It Slant, 801
TENNYSON, ALFRED, LORD, 835, 881, 913
"Terence, This Is Stupid Stuff . . .", 931
There's a Certain Slant of Light, 801
These Fought in Any Case, 808
They Flee from Me, 815
THOMAS, DYLAN, 871, 886, 934
To His Coy Mistress, 860
Tyger, The, 792

Ulysses, 913
Unarmed Combat, 854
Unknown Citizen, The, 831
Upon Julia's Clothes, 806

We Real Cool, 798
Western Wind, 814
When I Have Fears, 822
When I Was One-and-Twenty, 829
WHITMAN, WALT, 835, 924
WILBUR, RICHARD, 843, 905
With Rue My Heart Is Laden, 806

Woodspurge, The, 820
WORDSWORTH, WILLIAM, 806, 842, 891
World as Meditation, The, 918
WRIGHT, RICHARD, 291
w. w., 910
WYATT, SIR THOMAS, 815

YEATS, WILLIAM BUTLER, 817, 830, 870
Yellow Wall-Paper, The, 116
Young Goodman Brown, 35
Youth, 131

Index of First Lines

"A cold coming we had of it, 919
All in green went my love riding, 793
All night by the rose, rose– 791
A poem should be palpable and mute, 936
At dinner, she is hostess, I am host. 829
Aunt Jennifer's tigers prance across a screen, 828

Back and side go bare, go bare, 789
Back home the black women are all beautiful, 910
Bulkeley, Hunt, Willard, Hosmer, Meriam, Flint, 824
Busy old fool, unruly sun, 859

Come live with me, and be my love, 899

Daughters of Time, the hypocritic Days, 848
Death, be not proud, though some have called thee, 888
Do not go gentle into that good night, 886
Down the road someone is practicing scales, 889
Down, wanton, down! Have you no shame, 862

Earth has not anything to show more fair: 842

Glory be to God for dappled things— 880
Green arsenic smeared on an egg-white cloth, 800

"Had he and I but met, 816
Had we but world enough, and time, 860
He clasps the crag with crooked hands; 835
He was found by the Bureau of Statistics to be, 831

If all the world and love were young, 900
I found a dimpled spider, fat and white, 890
"I hate my verses, every line, every word. 933
I have gone out, a possessed witch, 922
I knew a woman, lovely in her bones, 813
I know that I shall meet my fate, 817
I met a traveller from an antique land, 830
In due course of course you will all be issued with, 854
In Just— 809
In my craft or sullen art, 934
I sing of brooks, of blossoms, birds, and bowers: 923
Is it Ulysses that approaches from the east, 918
I struck the board and cried, "No more! 882
It fell about the Martinmas time, 784
It is not growing like a tree, 841
It little profits than an idle king, 913
I, too, dislike it: there are things that are important beyond all this fiddle. 934

I wander thro' each charter'd street, 901

Joseph was an old man, 786

Leave me, O Love, which reachest but to dust, 860
Let me not to the marriage of true minds, 887
Let us go then, you and I, 902
Little Lamb, who made thee? 792
Long after you have swung back, 841
Love bade me welcome; yet my soul drew back, 847
Love set you going like a fat gold watch. 842

Márgarét, are you gríeving, 823
May I for my own self song's truth reckon, 878
Much have I travelled in the realms of gold, 839
My heart aches, and a drowsy numbness pains, 866

Not, I'll not, carrion comfort, Despair, not feast on thee; 889
Not marble nor the gilded monuments, 923
Now as I was young and easy under the apple boughs, 871
Now homing tradesmen scatter through the streets, 905

O black and unknown bards of long ago, 930
Obscurest night involved the sky, 911
Oh, to be in England, 900
"O 'Melia, my dear, this does everything crown! 790
One that is ever kind said yesterday: 830
O Rose, thou art sick. 847
Out of the cradle endlessly rocking, 924
Out upon it! I have loved, 815
"O where ha you been, Lord Randal, my son? 785
O wild West Wind, thou breath of Autumn's being, 864
O wind, rend open the heat, 801

railroad yard in San Jose, 849

Shall I compare thee to a summer's day? 858
She dwelt among the untrodden ways, 806
She even thinks that up in heaven, 798
Shlup, shlup, the dog, 800
Since I am coming to that holy room, 853
Skirting the river road, (my forenoon walk, my rest,), 835
Softly, in the dusk, a woman is singing to me; 821
So we'll go no more a-roving, 4
Sumer is icumen in, 856

Tell all the Truth but tell it slant— 801
"Terence, this is stupid stuff: 931
That is no country for old men. The young, 870

The apparition of these faces in the crowd; 799
The Bustle in a House, 804
the Cambridge ladies who live in furnished souls, 920
The eyes open to a cry of pulleys, 843
The fog comes, 840
The mad girl with the staring eyes and long white fingers, 933
The old South Boston Aquarium stands, 906
The pennycandystore beyond the El, 908
The Poets light but Lamps— 924
There was a time when meadow, grove, and stream, 891
There was such speed in her little body, 920
There's a certain Slant of light, 801
The Sea is calm tonight. 869
These fought in any case, 808
The splendor falls on castle walls, 881
The whiskey on your breath, 813
The wind flapped loose, the wind was still, 820
They eat beans mostly, this old yellow pair. 921
They flee from me that sometime did me seek, 815
Thou still unravished bride of quietness, 849
Today we have naming of parts. Yesterday, 832
Two roads diverged in a yellow wood, 848
Tyger! Tyger! burning bright, 792

Vanity, saith the preacher, vanity! 914

We real cool. We, 798
Western wind, when will thou blow, 814
What happens to a dream deferred? 838
What thoughts I have of you tonight, Walt Whitman, 909
When Abraham Lincoln was shoveled into the tombs, he forgot the, 807
Whenas in silks my Julia goes, 806
When I consider how my light is spent, 888
When I have fears that I may cease to be, 822
When I was one-and-twenty, 829
Winter is icumen in, 857
With how sad steps, O moon, thou climb'st the skies! 822
With rue my heart is laden, 806

Ye tradefull Merchants, that with weary toyle, 857